"No other guide has as much to offer . . . these books are a pleasure to read." Gene Shalit on the *Today Show*

". . . Excellently organized for the casual traveler who is looking for a mix of recreation and cultural insight."
Washington Post

★★★★★ (5-star rating) "Crisply written and remarkably personable. Cleverly organized so you can pluck out the minutest fact in a moment. Satisfyingly thorough."
Réalités

"The information they offer is up-to-date, crisply presented but far from exhaustive, the judgments knowledgeable but not opinionated." *New York Times*

"The individual volumes are compact, the prose succinct, and the coverage up-to-date and knowledgeable . . . The format is portable and the index admirably detailed."
John Barkham Syndicate

". . . An abundance of excellent directions, diversions, and facts, including perspectives and getting-ready-to-go advice — succinct, detailed, and well organized in an easy-to-follow style." *Los Angeles Times*

"They contain an amount of information that is truly staggering, besides being surprisingly current."
Detroit News

"These guides address themselves to the needs of the modern traveler demanding precise, qualitative information . . . Upbeat, slick, and well put together."
Dallas Morning News

". . . Attractive to look at, refreshingly easy to read, and generously packed with information." *Miami Herald*

"These guides are as good as any published, and much better than most." *Louisville* (Kentucky) *Times*

Stephen Birnbaum Travel Guides

Acapulco
Bahamas, Turks & Caicos
Barcelona
Bermuda
Boston
Canada
Cancun, Cozumel, and Isla Mujeres
Caribbean
Chicago
Disneyland
Eastern Europe
Europe
Europe for Business Travelers
Florence
France
Great Britain
Hawaii
Ireland
Italy
Ixtapa & Zihuatanejo
London
Los Angeles
Mexico
Miami & Ft. Lauderdale
New York
Paris
Portugal
Rome
San Francisco
South America
Spain
United States
USA for Business Travelers
Venice
Walt Disney World
Western Europe

CONTRIBUTING EDITORS

Burton Anderson
Maria Grazia Asselle
Janet Bennett
Frederick H. Brengelman
Kevin Causey
Stephanie Curtis
Marcia Feltheimer
Alan Friedman
Dwight V. Gast
Sari Gilbert
Marilyn Green
Judith Harris
Barbara Hults
Anthony Iannacci
Arlene Inge
Bruce Johnston
Catherine Lauge
Theordora Lurie
Diane Melville
Michael Mewshaw
John Meyer
Wendy Owen
Linda Parseghian
Clare Pedrick
Susan Pierres
Peter Rosenwald
Taryn Schneider
Patricia Schultz
Janet Stobart
Phoebe Tait
Robert Tine
David Wickers
Anne Marshall Zwack

MAPS **B. Andrew Mudryk**
SYMBOLS **Gloria McKeown**

A Stephen Birnbaum Travel Guide

Birnbaum's ITALY 1992

Stephen Birnbaum
Alexandra Mayes Birnbaum
EDITORS

Lois Spritzer
EXECUTIVE EDITOR

Laura L. Brengelman
Managing Editor

Mary Callahan
Ann-Rebecca Laschever
Beth Schlau
Dana Margaret Schwartz
Associate Editors

Gene Gold
Assistant Editor

HarperPerennial
A Division of HarperCollins*Publishers*

For Giovanna and Luca Salvadore who are responsible for so many of our most memorable moments in Italy.

 For information address HarperCollins*Publishers,* 10 East 53rd Street, New York, NY 10022.

FIRST EDITION

ISSN: 0749-2561 (Stephen Birnbaum Travel Guides)
ISSN: 0890-1139 (Italy)
ISBN: 0-06-278015-8 (pbk.)

92 93 94 95 96 CC/WP 10 9 8 7 6 5 4 3 2 1

Contents

GETTING READY TO GO

A compendium of all the practical travel data you need to plan your vacation down to the final detail.

When and How to Go

Preparing

On the Road

Sources and Resources

PERSPECTIVES

A cultural and historical survey of Italy's past and present, its people, politics, and heritage.

THE CITIES

Thorough, qualitative guides to each of the 13 cities most often visited by vacationers and businesspeople. Each section, a comprehensive report of the city's most appealing attractions and amenities, is designed to be used on the spot. Directions and recommendations are immediately accessible because each guide is presented in a consistent form.

DIVERSIONS

A selective guide to more than 20 active and cerebral vacations, including the places to pursue them where your quality of experience is likely to be highest.

For the Experience

For the Body

For the Mind

DIRECTIONS

The most spectacular routes and roads, most arresting natural wonders, and most magnificent palazzos, villas, and gardens — all organized into 20 specific driving tours.

A Word from the Editor

In the course of our roamings around Italy to collect data for this guide, it became increasingly obvious that "Italians" are a rare species. Oh, we found lots of folks who were enthusiastic about describing themselves as Venetian, Milanese, Roman, or Neapolitan, but almost no one who would characterize himself or herself as an Italian. This is hardly inexplicable in a nation that became unified only as recently as 1870, and where regional distinctions are such a source of local pride and delight.

Our guidebook contradicts the fiction that Italy is any sort of homogeneous country, a nation with a single face and similar sensitivities stretching from Sicily to the Swiss border. As anyone who has traveled widely in Italy soon discovers, nothing could be farther from the truth. The atmosphere and ambience that thrive across the length of the Italian peninsula are spectacularly varied, and in trying to provide an accurate guide to each distinct region, the travel editor often feels as though at least a dozen distinct countries are demanding attention — not entirely incomprehensible, since about that number of sovereign city-states once occupied the boundaries of what modern maps now cavalierly call Italy.

It isn't easy blending these diverse districts into a coherent whole. Making some sense of the relationship between the high-powered citizens of Milanese commerce and their somnolent siblings down on the *fattoria* in Calabria takes some doing. No less trying is the task of relating raucous Romans to the more dour and dignified denizens of Venice's canals.

In very practical terms, it's these very broad differences — which have existed throughout the spectrum of Italian history — that provide the most compelling reason for the creation of this detailed guide to Italian life and landscape. Where travelers once routinely visited only Rome — and said they'd seen Italy — there's a far broader recognition nowadays that Rome is no more an accurate mirror of Italy than New York is an accurate image of the many faces of the United States. This guide to Italy continues our own recognition of the increasing need to treat the world's most popular travel destinations in considerably greater depth.

Such treatment only mirrors an increasingly pervasive trend among travelers — the frequent return to treasured foreign travel spots. Once upon a time, even the most dedicated traveler would visit distant parts of the world no more than once in a lifetime — usually as part of that fabled Grand Tour. But greater numbers of would-be sojourners are now availing themselves of the easy opportunity to visit favored parts of the world over and over again.

So where once it was routine to say you'd "seen" a particular country after a very superficial, once-over-lightly encounter, the more perceptive travelers of today recognize that it's entirely possible to have only skimmed the surface of a specific travel destination even after having visited that place more than a dozen times. Similarly, repeated visits to a single site permit true exploration of special interests, whether they be sporting, artistic, or intellectual.

For those of us who spent several years working out the special system under which we present information in this series, the luxury of being able to devote nearly as much space as we'd like to just a single country is as close to paradise as guide writers and editors ever get. But clearly this is not the first guide to the glories of Italy — one suspects that guides of one sort or another have existed at least since Caesar's legions began their expansionist exercises. Guides to Italy have existed literally for centuries, so a traveler might logically ask why another one is necessary.

Our answer is that the nature of travel to Italy — and even of the travelers who now routinely make the trip — has changed dramatically of late. For the past 2,000 years or so, travel to and through Italy was an extremely elaborate undertaking, one that required extensive advance planning. Even as recently as the 1950s, a person who had actually been to Rome, Venice, Florence, or Milan could dine out on his or her experiences for years, since such adventures were quite extraordinary and usually the province of the privileged alone.

With the advent of jet air travel in the late 1950s, however, and of increased-capacity, wide-body aircraft during the 1960s, travel to and around these once distant lands became extremely common. In fact, in more than 2 decades of nearly unending inflation, airfares may be the only commodity in the world that have actually gone down in price.

Attitudes as well as costs have also changed significantly in the last couple of decades. Beginning with the so-called flower children of the 1960s, international travel lost much of its aura of mystery. Whereas their parents might have been happy with just a superficial sampling of Florence or Venice, these young people simply picked up and settled in various parts of Europe for an indefinite stay. While living as inexpensively as possible, they adapted to the local lifestyle, and generally immersed themselves in things European.

Thus began an explosion of travel to and through Italy. And over the years, the development of inexpensive charter flights and packages fueled and sharpened the new American interest in and appetite for more extensive exploration.

Now, in the 1990s, those same flower children who were in the forefront of the modern travel revolution have undeniably aged. While it may be impolite to point out that they are probably well into their untrustworthy thirties and forties, their original zeal for travel remains undiminished. For them it's hardly news that the way to get from Milan to the Adriatic is to head south, make a left, and then wait for the uncrowded beachfronts to appear. Such experienced and knowledgeable travelers have decided precisely where they want to go and are more often searching for ideas and insights to expand their already sophisticated travel consciousness.

Obviously, any guidebook to Italy must keep pace with and answer the real needs of today's travelers. That's why we've tried to create a guide that's specifically organized, written, and edited for this more demanding modern audience, travelers for whom qualitative information is infinitely more desirable than mere quantities of unappraised data. We think that this book and the other guides in our series represent a new generation of guides, one that is especially responsive to modern needs and interests.

For years, dating back as far as Herr Baedeker, travel guides have tended to be encyclopedic, seemingly much more concerned with demonstrating expertise in geography and history than with a real analysis of the sorts of things that actually concern a typical modern tourist. But today, when it is hardly necessary to tell a traveler where Rome is, (in many cases, the traveler has been there nearly as often as the guidebook editors), it becomes the responsibility of those editors to provide new perspectives and to suggest new directions in order to make the guide genuinely valuable.

That's exactly what we've tried to do in this series. I think you'll notice a different, more contemporary tone to the text, as well as an organization and focus that are distinctive and more functional. And even a random reading of what follows will demonstrate a substantial departure from the standard guidebook orientation, for we've not only attempted to provide information of a more compelling sort, but we also have tried to present the data in a format that makes it particularly accessible.

Needless to say, it's difficult to decide precisely what to include in a guidebook of this size — and what to omit. Early on, we realized that giving up the encyclopedic approach precluded our listing every single route and restaurant, a realization that helped define our overall editorial focus. Similarly, when we discussed the possibility of presenting certain information in other than strict geographic order, we found that the new format enabled us to arrange data in a way we feel best answers the questions travelers typically ask.

Large numbers of specific questions have provided the real editorial skeleton for this book. The volume of mail I regularly receive emphasizes that modern travelers want very precise information, so we've tried to organize our material in the most responsive way possible. Readers who want to know the best restaurants around Bologna or the best places to find inexpensive couture in Milan will have no trouble extracting that data from this guide.

Travel guides are, understandably, reflections of personal taste, and putting one's name on a title page obviously puts one's preferences on the line. But I think I ought to amplify just what "personal" means. I don't believe in the sort of personal guidebook that's a palpable misrepresentation on its face. It is, for example, hardly possible for any single travel writer to visit thousands of restaurants (and nearly as many hotels) in any given year and provide accurate appraisals of each. And even if it were physically possible for one human being to survive such an itinerary, it would of necessity have to be done at a dead sprint and the perceptions derived therefrom would probably be less valid than those of any other intelligent individual visiting the same establishments. It is, therefore, impossible (especially in a large, annually revised guidebook *series* such as we offer) to have only one person provide all the data on the entire world.

I also happen to think that such individual orientation is of substantially less value to readers. Visiting a single hotel for just one night or eating one hasty meal in a random restaurant hardly equips anyone to provide appraisals that are of more than passing interest. No amount of doggedly alliterative or oppressively onomatopoeic text can camouflage a technique that is essentially specious. We have, therefore, chosen what I like to describe as the "thee and me" approach to restaurant and hotel evaluation and, to a somewhat more limited degree, to the sites and sights we have included in the other sections of our text. What this really reflects is a personal sampling tempered by intelligent counsel from informed local sources, and these additional friends-of-the-editors are almost always residents of the city and or area about which they are consulted.

Despite the presence of several editors, a considerable number of writers, researchers, and local correspondents, very precise editing and tailoring keep our text fiercely subjective. So what follows is purposely designed to be the gospel according to the Birnbaums, and represents as much of our own taste and preferences as we can manage. It is probable, therefore, that if you like your cities stylish and your mountainsides uncrowded, prefer small hotels with personality to huge high-rise anonymities, and can't tolerate pasta or fresh fish that's been relentlessly overcooked, we're likely to have a long and meaningful relationship. Readers with dissimilar tastes may be less enraptured.

I also should point out something about the person to whom this guidebook is directed. Above all, he or she is a "visitor." This means that such elements as restaurants have been specifically picked to provide the visitor with a representative, enlightening, stimulating, and above all, pleasant experience. Since so many extraneous considerations can affect the reception and service accorded a regular restaurant patron, our choices can in no way be construed as an exhaustive guide to resident dining. We think we've listed all the best places, in various price ranges, but they were chosen with a visitor's enjoyment in mind.

Other evidence of how we've tried to tailor our text to reflect changing travel habits is most apparent in the section we call DIVERSIONS. Where once it was common for travelers to spend a foreign visit nailed to a single spot, the emphasis today is more on pursuing some athletic enterprise or special interest while seeing the surrounding countryside. So we've organized every activity we could reasonably evaluate and organized the material in a way that is especially accessible to activists of either an athletic or cerebral bent. It is no longer necessary, therefore, to wade through a pound or two of superfluous prose just to find the very best crafts shop or the quaintest country inn within a reasonable distance of your destination.

If there is a single thing that best characterizes the revolution in and evolution of current travel habits, it is that most travelers now consider travel a right rather than a privilege. No longer is a trip to the far corners of the country — or to Europe or the Orient — necessarily a once-in-a-lifetime thing; nor is the idea of visiting exotic, foreign places in the least worrisome. Travel today translates as the enthusiastic desire to sample all of the world's opportunities, to find that elusive quality of experience that is not only enriching but comfortable. For that reason, we've tried to make what follows not only helpful and enlightening but the sort of welcome companion of which every traveler dreams.

Finally, I also should point out that every good travel guide is a living enterprise; that is, no part of this text is carved in stone. In our annual revisions, we refine, expand, and further hone all our material to serve your travel needs better. To this end, no contribution is of greater value to us than your personal reaction to what we have written, as well as information reflecting your own experiences while using the book. We earnestly and enthusiastically solicit your comments about this guide *and* your opinions and perceptions about places you have recently visited. In this way, we will be able to provide the most current information — including the actual experiences of recent travelers — and to make those experiences more readily available to others. Please write to us at 60 E. 42nd St., New York, NY 10165.

We sincerely hope to hear from you.

STEPHEN BIRNBAUM

How to Use This Guide

? A great deal of care has gone into the organization of this guidebook, and we believe that it represents a real breakthrough in the presentation of travel material. Our aim is to create a new, more modern generation of travel books, and to make this guide the most useful and practical travel tool available today.

Our text is divided into five basic sections in order to present information in the best way on every possible aspect of an Italian vacation. This organization itself should alert you to the vast and varied opportunities available, as well as indicate all the specific data necessary to plan a successful trip. You won't find much of the conventional "quaint villages and beautiful scenery" text here; we've chosen instead to deliver more useful and practical information. Prospective itineraries tend to speak for themselves, and with so many diverse travel opportunities, we feel our main job is to highlight what's where and to provide basic information — how, when, where, how much, and what's best — to assist you in making the most intelligent choices possible.

Here is a brief summary of the basic five sections and what you can expect to find in each. We believe that you will find both your travel planning and en-route enjoyment enhanced by having this book at your side.

GETTING READY TO GO

This mini-encyclopedia of practical travel facts is a sort of know-it-all companion with all the precise information necessary to create a successful trip to and through Italy. There are entries on more than 2 dozen separate topics, including how to get where you're going, what preparations to make before leaving, what to expect in the different regions of Italy, what your trip is likely to cost, and how to avoid prospective problems. The individual entries are specific, realistic, and where appropriate, cost-oriented.

We expect you to use this section most in the course of planning your trip, for its ideas and suggestions are intended to simplify this often confusing period. Entries are intentionally concise, in an effort to get to the meat of the matter with the least extraneous prose. These entries are augmented by extensive lists of specific sources from which to obtain even more specialized data, plus some suggestions for obtaining travel information on your own.

PERSPECTIVES

Any visit to an unfamiliar destination is enhanced and enriched by understanding the cultural and historical heritage of that area. We have, therefore, provided just such an introduction to Italy, its past and present, politics, literature, dining, music, art, and architecture.

THE CITIES

Individual reports are presented on the 13 Italian cities most visited by travelers, prepared with the aid of researchers, contributors, professional journalists, and other experts on the spot. Although useful at the planning stage, THE CITIES is really designed to be taken along and used on the spot. Each report offers a short-stay guide within a consistent format: An essay introduces the city as a contemporary place to live and visit; *At-a-Glance* material is actually a site-by-site survey of the most important, interesting, and sometimes most eclectic sights to see and things to do; *Sources and Resources* is a concise listing of pertinent tourism information, meant to answer a broad range of potentially pressing questions as they arise — from simple things such as the address of the local tourist office, how to get around, which sightseeing tours to take, when special events occur, to something more difficult like where to find the best nightspot or hail a taxi, which are the chic places to shop, and where the best skiing, golf, tennis, fishing, and swimming are to be found. *Best in Town* lists our collection of cost-and-quality choices of the best places to eat and sleep on a variety of budgets.

DIVERSIONS

This section is designed to help travelers find the very best places in which to pursue a wide range of physical and cerebral activities, without having to wade through endless pages of unrelated text. This very selective guide lists the broadest possible range of vacation activities, including where to pursue them.

We start with a list of possibilities that offer various places to stay and eat, and move to those that require some perspiration — sports preferences and other rigorous pursuits — and go on to report on a number of more intellectual and spiritual vacation opportunities. In every case, our suggestion of a particular location — and often our recommendation of a specific resort — is intended to guide you to that special place where the quality of experience is likely to be highest. Whether you seek golf courses or tennis courts, want to go fishing or bicycling, or are searching for Italy's most chic hotels or most esoteric museums, tours of spectacular resorts or epic shopping excursions, each category is the equivalent of a comprehensive checklist of the absolute best in Italy.

DIRECTIONS

Here are 20 itineraries that range all across Italy, along the most beautiful routes and roads, past the most spectacular natural wonders, through its most historic cities and countryside. DIRECTIONS is the only section of the book that is organized geographically, and its itineraries cover the touring highlights of Italy in short, independent journeys of 5 to 7 days' duration. Itineraries can be connected for longer trips, or used individually for short, intensive explorations.

Each entry includes a guide to sightseeing highlights; a qualitative guide to accommodations and food along the road (small inns, castle-hotels, country hotels); and suggestions for activities.

Although each of this book's sections has a distinct format and a special function, they have all been designed to be used together to provide a complete inventory of travel information. To use this book to full advantage, take a few minutes to read the table of contents and random entries in each section to get a firsthand feel of how it all fits together.

Pick and choose needed information. Assume, for example, that you have always wanted to take that typically Italian vacation, an eating tour of the country's temples of gastronomy, but you never really knew how to organize it or where to go. Turn first to the chapter entitled *Dining in Italy* in the PERSPECTIVES section, where you will find a discussion of the food specialties and wines of the various regions, advice on Italian menus, manners, and methods, plus a glossary of the different kinds of pasta. Next, choose specific restaurants from the selections offered in each city chapter in THE CITIES, in each tour route in DIRECTIONS, and in the roundup of the best in the country called *Buon Appetito: The Best Restaurants of Italy* in the DIVERSIONS section. Then, refer to *Useful Words and Phrases,* GETTING READY TO GO, to help you with everything from making reservations to deciphering the menu. We also discuss special food and wine tours to Italy.

In other words, the sections of this book are building blocks designed to help you put together the best possible trip. Use them selectively as a tool, a source of ideas, a reference work for accurate facts, and a guide to the best buys, the most exciting sights, the most pleasant accommodations, the tastiest food — *the best travel experience* that you can have in Italy.

SWITZERLAND
Alps
Bolzano
Dolomites
Adige River
Brenta River
Trento
Udine
Lake Como
Aosta
Lake Maggiore
L. Lugano
L. Iseo
FRANCE
Bergamo
Milan
Brescia
Verona
Padua
Venice
Lake Garda
Turin
Po River
Po River
Gulf of Venice
Parma
Ferrara
Alps
Genoa
Bologna
Ravenna
Riviera
Gulf of Genoa
Apennines
MONACO
Pisa
Florence
SAN MARINO
Arno River
Ligurian Sea
Siena
Arezzo
Tiber River
Perugia
Elba
Tuscan Archipelago
CORSICA
VATICAN CITY
Rome
Mediterranean
Costa Smeralda
Olbia
Pontine Is.
SARDINIA
Tyrrhenian Sea
Cagliari
Egadi Islands
Palermo
TUNISIA
Pantelleria

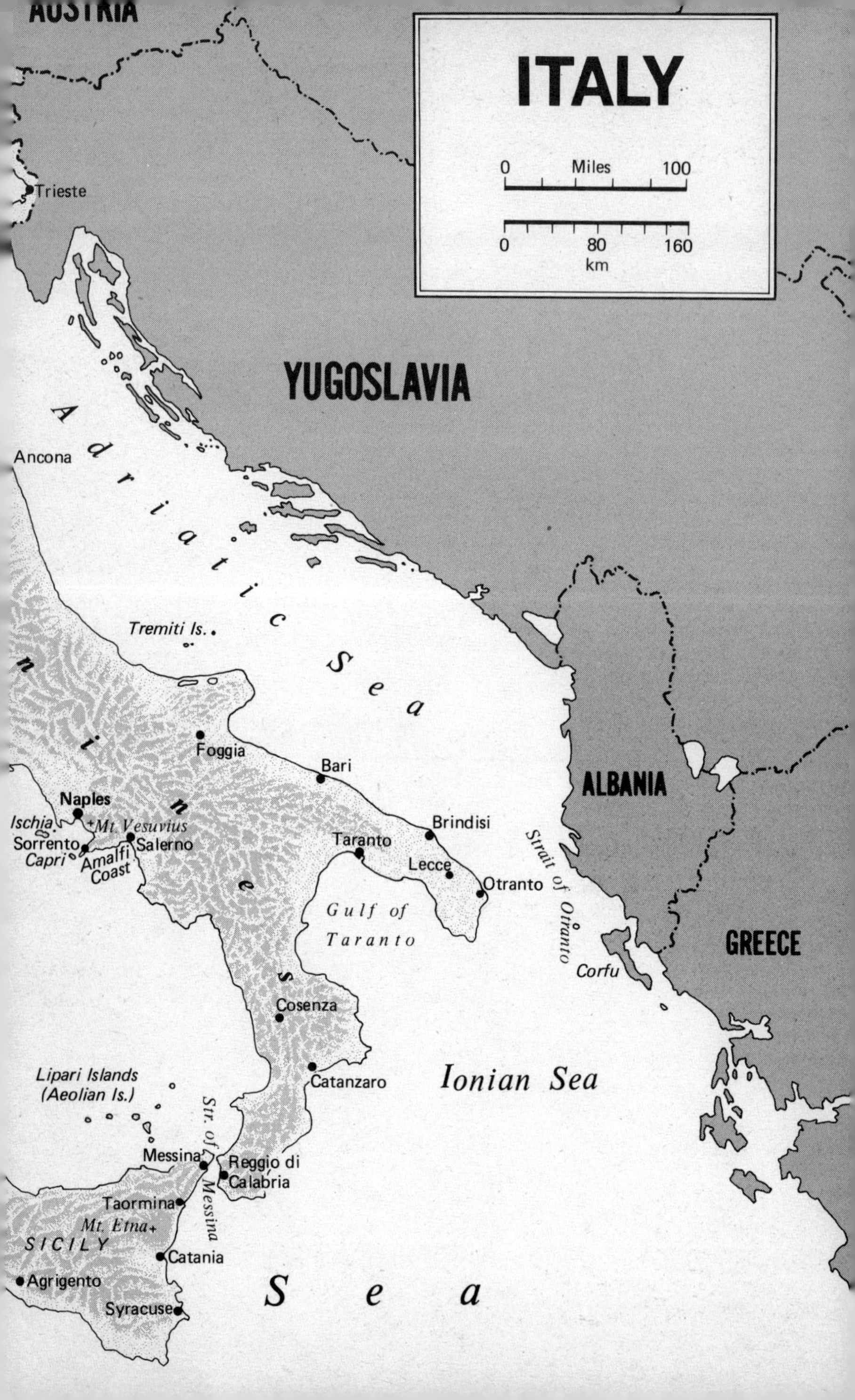

AUSTRIA
ITALY
0 Miles 100
0 80 160
km
YUGOSLAVIA
Trieste
Ancona
Adriatic Sea
Tremiti Is.
Foggia
Bari
Naples
Ischia
Mt. Vesuvius
Sorrento
Capri
Salerno
Amalfi Coast
Brindisi
Taranto
Lecce
Otranto
Strait of Otranto
Gulf of Taranto
ALBANIA
GREECE
Corfu
Cosenza
Catanzaro
Ionian Sea
Lipari Islands (Aeolian Is.)
Str. of Messina
Messina
Reggio di Calabria
Taormina
Mt. Etna
SICILY
Catania
Agrigento
Syracuse
Sea

GETTING READY TO GO

When and How to Go

When to Go

There really isn't a "best" time to visit Italy. For North Americans, as well as Europeans, the period from mid-May to mid-September has long been — and remains — the peak travel period, traditionally the most popular vacation time.

It is important to emphasize that Italy is hardly a single-season destination; more and more travelers who have a choice are enjoying the substantial advantages of off-season travel. Though some of the lesser tourist attractions may have shorter hours or may closing during the off-season — roughly November through *Easter* — the major ones remain open and tend to be less crowded, as are some cities, as well as other parts of the country. During the off-season people relax and Italian life proceeds at a more leisurely pace, and a lively social and cultural calendar flourishes. What's more, travel generally is less expensive.

If Italy is the destination, there are other reasons to depart somewhat from tradition. Travelers who prefer to see Italian cities when they're filled with Italians rather than foreign visitors should avoid the month of August (when all Italians who can manage it are out of town); those who prefer not to risk the possibility of a heat wave should avoid both July and August. Furthermore, the traditional high-season travel period does not provide much sense of the reality of travel in Italy, since the crowds increase notably just before *Easter* in many parts of the country. In other parts of the country — particularly the south — the weather generally cooperates to make the season endure through October. Thus, while May, June, and September are ideal times for a visit, April and October are almost as desirable. These months immediately before and after the peak summer months — what the travel industry refers to as the shoulder season — often are sought out because they offer fair weather and somewhat smaller crowds. But be aware that very near high-season prices can prevail, notably in certain popular resort areas.

For some, the most convincing argument in favor of off-season travel is the economic one. Getting there and staying there is more affordable during less popular travel periods, as airfares, hotel rooms, and car rental rates go down and less expensive package tours become available; the independent traveler can go farther on less, too. Europe is not like the Caribbean, where high season and low season are precisely defined and rates drop automatically on a particular date. But many Italian hotels reduce rates during the off-season, and on the Italian Riviera, and at other seaside resorts, savings can be as much as 30%. Although smaller guesthouses, inns, and other establishments in some areas may close during the off-season in response to reduced demand, there still are plenty of alternatives, and, in cities, cut-rate "mini-break" packages — for stays of more than 1 night, especially over a weekend (when business travelers traditionally go home) — are more common.

A definite bonus to visiting during the off-season is that even the most basic services are performed more efficiently. In theory, off-season service is identical to that offered during high season, but the fact is that the absence of demanding crowds inevitably begets much more thoughtful and personal attention. The very same staff that barely can manage to get fresh towels onto the racks during the height of summer at coastal resort areas has the time to chat pleasantly in the spring or fall. And it is not only hotel service that benefits from the absence of the high-season mobs.

There are some notable exceptions to this rule. The general tourism off-season is high season for skiers in the Dolomites, meaning higher prices and crowds everywhere there is snow. Most major cities in Italy hold at least one international business or industrial show each year (the annual fall and spring fashion shows in Milan, for example). Particularly in the larger cities, such major trade shows or conferences held at the time of your visit are sure to affect the availability not only of discounts, but even of a place to stay. *Carnevale* in Venice also occurs during the off-season, but it's hardly a time hoteliers need to drum up business. In addition, during harvest festivals, off-season discounts also may not exist.

In short, like many other popular places, Italy's vacation appeal has become multi-seasonal. But the noted exceptions notwithstanding, most travel destinations are decidedly less trafficked and less expensive during the winter.

CLIMATE: Even though the northern Italian cities of Bolzano and Milan are at approximately the same latitude as Canada's Quebec and Montreal, respectively, and Palermo in Sicily is only a bit farther north than Richmond or San Francisco, the tendency is to think of Italy as a sunny southern country. True, a Mediterranean climate blesses most of the land with summers that are dry and warm to hot and winters mild enough that precipitation is rain rather than snow. But there is more to the climate than that, given the country's long, narrow boot-like shape, the length of its coastline, and the fact that roughly three-quarters is covered with hills and mountains.

The great barrier of the Alps, which top the boot much like a turned-over, fur-lined cuff, and the Apennines, which run the entire length of the peninsula, are a prime cause of climatic diversity. Alpine winters are long and severe, but at the same time the Alps shield the Lombardy Lakes region from the worst rigors of the northern European winter. Both the Alps and the Apennines protect the narrow coastal strip of Liguria from cold north winds and reinforce the influence of its Mediterranean exposure, producing winter temperatures much like those of Naples or Sicily and nurturing winter flowers that are shipped all over Europe. The rest of the north, however, is not similarly favored. Across the Apennines, the vast plain of the Po River has a climate of the continental type, running to extremes. Winters can be damp, foggy, and penetratingly cold; summers are hot, without the pleasant coolness of the Alps and only partly moderated by proximity to the sea.

The peninsula proper conforms to the Mediterranean type. In general, the farther south one goes, the milder winter temperatures become, although summer temperatures rise only to a limited extent. Summers do become progressively drier; fall and winter, progressively wetter. Snow is a rare and fleeting phenomenon, except in the higher reaches of the Apennines. Instead there is rain, heavier in most areas in October, November, and December than at any other time of the year. Some familiar winds embellish the weather pattern: Cold is colder when the *tramontana,* a cold, dry wind from the north, is blowing; hot is suffocating when the scirocco sweeps across the Mediterranean from Africa, heavy with dust and accumulated moisture.

But it bears repeating that the weather in any given spot depends on its position vis-à-vis the mountains and water. At any latitude, winters can be raw in the Apennines and mild along the shore. The coastlines of Naples and Salerno, with steep, rocky promontories at their back, are subtropical sweeps of oranges and lemons, characterized by a mean annual temperature of 62F or above and by at least 5 months a year with mean temperatures of 68F or above. Such readings are more typical of the island of Sicily, which is only 90 miles from North Africa at its closest point and thus comes by its subtropical climate naturally. Both Sicily and Sardinia have long, hot, and dry summers and warm winters. Taormina, with an average winter temperature of 55F, has been attracting refugees from the cold since the beginning of the century. (*Please note that although temperatures usually are recorded on the Cel-*

sius scale in Italy, for purposes of clarity we use the more familiar Fahrenheit scale.)

Venice can reach a muggy 90F in July and August, rendering the aroma from its canals less than agreeable. Although there rarely is extreme cold in winter, precipitation ranges from fine mist to torrential downpour, and when the *bora* blows in from the northeast Adriatic, the effect can be more chilling than Alpine snow. Woolens and sweaters under wind- and raingear are needed, and if the *acqua alta* (high water) comes up over the canal banks, high rubber boots are handy for slogging around.

In Milan, temperatures generally are moderate, although the city sometimes suffers extremes. Summer can be hot and airless, with temperatures as high as the mid-80s; winter can be cold, wet, and foggy, accompanied by below-freezing temperatures and occasional snow.

The weather in Florence, much farther south but set in a bowlful of hills, tends to be more severe. Temperatures range from the 60s to the 90s from mid-June to mid-September, and summer can be stifling. In winter, the temperature rarely drops below freezing, ranging from the low 30s to the 50s from December through mid-March, but the cold is damp and often gripping.

In Rome, average July and August temperatures hover around the low to mid-80s, but a heavy scirocco can push the maximum above 100F. A refreshing breeze often provides relief on summer evenings. Winters are moderate, with temperatures averaging in the high 40s from December through February. The temperature seldom drops below freezing, and snow is very rare, but the *tramontana* can be chilly (definitely overcoat weather) and winter rains are heavy.

Summer in Naples is hot, with average highs in the mid-80s. Winter, though milder than in more northern parts of Italy, is rainy.

The following chart lists seasonal temperature ranges in major cities to help in planning.

AVERAGE TEMPERATURES (in °F)

City	*January*	*April*	*July*	*October*
Bari	43–54	52–64	70–84	59–70
Bergamo	29–42	46–64	63–83	49–63
Bologna	30–41	50–64	68–86	54–68
Bolzano	23–41	45–66	61–82	45–66
Cagliari	45–57	52–66	70–86	59–73
Cosenza	39–52	45–66	64–90	54–72
Florence	36–48	46–66	64–86	52–68
Genoa	41–52	52–63	70–81	59–68
Milan	32–41	50–64	68–84	52–63
Naples	39–54	48–64	64–84	54–72
Olbia	45–59	50–66	66–84	57–73
Palermo	46–61	52–68	70–86	61–77
Rome	41–52	50–66	68–86	55–72
San Marino	36–45	46–61	64–82	52–64
San Remo	45–55	52–66	68–82	59–72
Siena	37–45	46–61	64–82	54–59
Stromboli	50–59	54–66	70–88	63–77
Taormina	46–57	54–66	72–88	61–73
Taranto	43–54	52–64	72–86	61–72
Trieste	37–45	50–63	68–82	55–64
Turin	28–39	46–64	66–84	48–63
Udine	32–43	46–63	63–82	50–66
Venice	34–43	50–63	66–81	52–66
Verona	32–43	48–64	63–84	50–64

Travelers can get current readings and 3-day Accu-Weather forecasts through *American Express Travel Related Services*' Worldwide Weather Report number. By dialing 900-WEATHER and punching in either the area code for most major cities in the US or an access code for numerous travel destinations worldwide, an up-to-date recording will provide current temperature, sky conditions, wind speed and direction, heat index, relative humidity, local time, highway reports, and beach and boating reports or ski conditions (where appropriate). For locations in Italy, punch in the first three letters of the city (service includes Como, Florence, Genoa, Milan, Naples, Palermo, Rome, Turin, and Venice). For instance, by entering ROM you will hear the weather report for Rome. This 24-hour service can be accessed from any touch-tone phone in the US or Canada and costs 95¢ per minute. The charge will show up on your phone bill. For a free list of the areas covered, send a self-addressed, stamped envelope to *1-900-WEATHER,* 261 Central Ave., Farmingdale, NY 11735.

SPECIAL EVENTS: Many travelers want to schedule a trip to Italy to coincide with a special event. The highlight of a sports lover's trip may be attending the Italian championship of a favorite game. For a music lover, a concert in a great cathedral or in a splendid natural setting may be an especially thrilling experience, and much more memorable than seeing the same place on an ordinary sightseeing itinerary. Theatergoers may find a classical drama performed in an ancient amphitheater powerfully evocative — even if they don't understand the language. For history buffs, not to mention dedicated photographers, there are numerous folkloric happenings whose participants look as though they had stepped out of the Middle Ages or the Renaissance.

Italy's special events tend to fall into three categories. Festivals of the performing arts usually are presentations of music, especially opera, although there also are festivals of dance, drama, and film. Religious ceremonies and processions are tied to the liturgical calendar or result from the accumulation of centuries of tradition around a historical fact — often they continue to fulfill a vow of thanksgiving for deliverance from some natural disaster. These occur in towns of all sizes throughout Italy, but they are especially common in the south and in Sicily and Sardinia, where they are among the few remaining occasions to see islanders gloriously turned out in traditional regional costumes.

Historical reenactments or displays of historical pageantry are another type of event, particularly common in central Italy. The focus of the event usually is a medieval or Renaissance game, contest, or mock combat, generally preceded or followed by a parade of citizens in historical costume and by exhibitions of flag throwing, the baton twirling of days long gone. These wondrously photogenic occasions are the delight of visitors, but it's a mistake to think they are put on simply to stimulate tourism. In most cases, the games actually *were* played by the ancestors of the modern Italians, pitting halves, quarters, and smaller sections of a community against each other. Some games are said to commemorate a specific event and, therefore, can be traced to a particular date, although their origins usually are lost in time. Florence's *Calcio in Costume,* for instance, commemorates a "soccer" match played in defiance of the invading imperial troops of Charles V and dates from 1530; when the time came for the Florentines to show their mettle, they already knew what and how to play.

Thus Italy has *giostre* (jousts), *tornei* (tournaments), *balestrieri* (crossbowmen), and the *Palio* (strictly speaking, a banner awarded to the winner of a competition; more broadly, the competition itself, possibly translated as "stakes"). In some cases, they are indeed reenactments; in others, there has been hardly any lapse between the modern revival and the historical counterpart. Of the numerous *Palio* contests in Italy, the most famous, that of Siena, has been documented as far back as 1310, and has been a part of Sienese life almost uninterruptedly for centuries. No one who's seen it doubts that for the Sienese, the two midsummer incarnations are their counterparts of the *World Series* and the *Super Bowl,* contested in turn.

The events noted on the following pages are the major ones, but they are only a sampling. Among the many not mentioned are numerous music festivals that proliferate as spring progresses into summer and numerous festivities for the feast day of the patron saint of a town or city, a day that generally also is a local holiday. A further cause for celebration not exhausted by the list below is the harvesting of the grape. Almost every district that makes wine also makes merry about it. If you see colored lights being strung around a piazza in September or October and a bandstand and booths going up, it's likely that a *sagra dell'uva* (feast, or consecration, of the grape) is about to begin, and you'll be in for some festive tasting.

The calendar of special events in Italy is a busy one from *Easter* through September, but if you're visiting at another time of the year, don't despair. In any city, the regular cultural season is under way from late fall through spring and a great deal is happening. *Christmas,* too, is a nice time to visit. The first sign of the season is the arrivals in towns of the *zampognari,* shepherds who roam the streets playing the *zampogna,* a strange bagpipe-like instrument that makes a haunting sound. *Christmas* decorations are not as ubiquitous or as showy as they are in the US; on the other hand, the tradition of the *presepe* (manger scene) still is strong. Italians always make time to go from church to church comparing the scenes, especially in Naples, where the making of *presepi* reached a state of high art in the 18th century. The season lasts through *Epiphany* (January 6), when good Italian children receive a second round of gifts from an old witch known as the *Befana* (bad children, should any exist, receive lumps of coal). *New Year's* celebrations range from spirited to downright dangerous, especially in Rome and in the south. Firecrackers begin to explode in the afternoon and increase as the evening advances, making it imperative for partygoers to be off the streets and at their destinations early. (The next day, newspapers report the number of fingers and eyes lost to this practice, and in recent years, it seems, a good number of gunshots have been added to the traditional fireworks.) At the stroke of midnight, Romans throw open their windows and throw out the old — plates, bottles, furniture — to make room for the new, and they do it with a vengeance.

The events noted below are listed according to the months in which they usually occur. We have indicated specific dates where possible, however, as there can be some variation from year to year, check with the Italian Government Travel Office for the exact dates of anything that may be of interest and for current schedules of fairs, festivals, and other events. For more information on major events, see *Italy's Most Colorful Festas* in DIVERSIONS and *Special Events* in the individual city reports of THE CITIES.

January/February

Almond Blossom Festival: Folk festival of song, dance, costumes, and fireworks. Held in the first half of February. Agrigento.

Carnevale: Pre-*Lenten* festivities reviving and rivaling those of the last days of the Venetian Republic. Masked and costumed merrymakers prowl the city; balls, parties, and other gala happenings take place indoors and out. Begins 10 days before *Ash Wednesday* (February 24 this year). Venice.

Carnevale: Pre-*Lenten* festivities known for parades (usually four) of colorful, humorous floats featuring larger-than-life caricatures. Begins 10 days before *Ash Wednesday* (February 24). Viareggio.

Festival of San Remo: Three days of competition for the best new Italian pop song — "Volare" was a winner during the late 1950s. February. San Remo.

March/April

Sa Sartiglia: Pre-*Lenten* festivities with 17th-century origins. The highlight is a race of horsemen in masquerade jousting at stars. Sunday and Tuesday before *Ash Wednesday* (March 1–4 this year). Oristano.

Investiture of the Captains Regent: Twice-yearly ceremony inaugurating this tiny republic's new rulers, who serve 6-month terms. Held in the presence of foreign diplomats and uniformed armed forces. April 1 and October 1. San Marino.

Holy Week Processions: Activities include a pilgrimage by hooded penitents and a procession of the mysteries, when eight groups of statues depicting the Passion of Christ — the *misteri* — are carried about town. *Holy Thursday* and *Good Friday* (April 16 and 17 this year). Taranto.

Procession of the Mysteries: Twenty groups of statues are carried on the shoulders of townsfolk for a grueling 24 hours in this descendant of a medieval Passion play. *Good Friday* (April 17). Trapani.

Easter Services: Byzantine-rite celebration featuring colorful traditional costume in a town founded by Albanians in the 15th century. *Easter Sunday* (April 19 this year). Piana degli Albanesi, province of Palermo, Sicily.

Scoppio del Carro: Traditional explosion of a cartful of fireworks, at the Duomo. Noon, *Easter Sunday* (April 19). Florence.

Urbi et Orbi: Papal blessing of the faithful in St. Peter's Square. Noon, *Easter Sunday* (April 19). Rome.

Fiera Internazionale di Milano: Italy's biggest international trade fair, held since 1920. April. Milan.

May

Sagra di Sant'Efisio: Four-day-long religious procession to and from the shrine of the saint 18 miles away. Cortege of traditionally costumed islanders is most colorful for the departure and the return. May 1 to 4. Cagliari.

Miracle of San Gennaro: Twice-yearly gathering of Neapolitans at the Duomo for the recurrence of the miracle — the liquefying of the saint's blood — that keeps their city safe. Saturday preceding the first Sunday in May (May 2 this year) and September 19. Naples.

Corsa dei Ceri (Race of the Candles): Traditional folkloric event, dating from the 12th century or earlier. Three massive wooden shrines are paraded through town and then raced to their year-round resting place near the top of a mountain. May 15. Gubbio.

Columbus Festivities From May 15 through August 15, Genoa — the city from which Columbus departed on the voyage that resulted in the discovery of America — will be hosting a number of events celebrating the 500th anniversary of that occasion. The theme is "Christopher Columbus: The Ship and the Sea." (For details see *Genoa* in THE CITIES.)

Palio San Secondo: A procession in 13th-century costume, accompanied by flag throwing. May 20. Asti.

Cavalcata Sarda (Sardinian Cavalcade): Folk festival drawing men and women from all over the island in spectacular traditional costumes. Next to last Sunday in May (May 24 this year). Sassari.

Festa del Grillo (Cricket Day): A day in the park for the Florentines, who buy crickets in cages and set them free. *Ascension Thursday* (May 28 this year). Florence.

Palio dei Balestrieri: Match in medieval costume between the crossbowmen of Gubbio and Sansepolcro, with flag throwing and a historical procession. Last Sunday in May (May 31 this year). Gubbio. (Also held in September in Sansepolcro.)

Maggio Musicale Fiorentino: One of Italy's most important music festivals, with artists of international renown. Festival continues into June. Florence.

June

Infiorata: This 200-year-old festival includes a procession through a street carpeted with paintings entirely of flowers. A Sunday in mid-June. Genzano di Roma.

Regatta of the Four Ancient Maritime Republics: Colorful, choreographed parade of boats and a race pitting the four old rivals. Rotates annually among Genoa, Amalfi, Pisa, and Venice. It is Venice's turn this year, however, due to the 500th anniversary celebration of Columbus's discovery of America, there also will be a regatta in Genoa.

Gioco del Calcio (Calcio in Costume): Rough and tumble soccer match in 16th-century costume. Three games are played, one usually June 24, the *Feast of St. John the Baptist.* Florence.

Festa del Giglio (Lily Festival): Three-hour procession of eight huge allegorical towers, each with a band playing at its base and each shouldered by 40 men. June 28. Nola.

Palio Marinaro dei Rioni: A rowing race with the participants sporting traditional costumes. June 29. Genoa.

Festival of Two Worlds: Gian Carlo Menotti's creation, a celebration of music, dance, theater, painting, and sculpture, in an Umbrian hill town. Late June to mid-July. Spoleto.

Esposizione Internazionale d'Arte Moderna: Commonly known as the *Venice Biennale,* this international exhibition of modern art, begun in the 1890s, is held this year and in other even-numbered years, June through October. Venice.

July

Palio: The most famous and most popular of Italy's traditional events includes a parade in full 15th-century dress, flag throwing, and a wild bareback horse race around the town square. July 2 and August 16. Siena.

Festa di Santa Rosalia: Processions, bands, fireworks, and decorated Sicilian carts honor the city's patron saint. Culminates July 15 with a street procession in which a statue of the saint is carried reverently through the city. The second part of this festival is held in early September. July 10 to 15. Palermo.

Umbria Jazz Festival: Italy's most important jazz get-together. A week of daily concerts outdoors and nightly jam sessions in the clubs. Perugia, Terni, and other locations in the region.

International Ballet Festival: More than 3 weeks of nightly performances by visiting companies. Nervi.

Festa del Redentore (Feast of the Redeemer): Fireworks, all-night picnics afloat, and a cross-canal procession over a bridge of boats to give thanks for the lifting of a 16th-century plague. Third Saturday night and Sunday in July (July 18 to 19 this year). Venice.

Gioco del Ponte (Battle of the Bridge): Parade in medieval costume followed by a pitched battle from north and south of the Arno for possession of the middle of the bridge. Last Sunday in July (July 26 this year). Pisa.

Verona Opera Festival: Three or four operas, a ballet, and concerts outdoors in a 20,000-seat Roman amphitheater. Each night's performance begins with the lighting of 20,000 candles. Early July through August. Verona.

Baths of Caracalla Opera Season: Two months of open-air opera staged in the ruins of 3rd-century Roman baths and noted for elephantine productions of *Aïda.* Early July through August. Rome.

Arena Sferisterio Opera Season: Mostly opera, but also ballet outdoors in a 19th-century arena. Mid-July to mid-August. Macerata.

Taormina Festival: An international film competition in conjunction with theater, music, and dance performances, some in an ancient Greco-Roman amphitheater. Mid-July through August. Taormina.

August

Torneo della Quintana: Historical pageantry, including jousting and a parade in 15th-century costume. First Sunday in August (August 2 this year). Ascoli Piceno.

Palio del Golfo: A 2,000-meter rowing contest, held the second Sunday in August (August 9). La Spezia.

La Candelora (Festival of the Candlesticks): Folkloric happening with secular and religious roots. Representatives of medieval guilds parade huge candlesticks through the Old Town to commemorate the ending of the plague in 1652. August 14. Sassari.

Ferragosto (Assumption Day): Italians celebrate the joyous assumption of Mary into heaven with fireworks. (And many of those who have not already left on vacation join a nationwide exodus.) August 15.

Palio: Started in 1310, in honor of the Madonna di Provenzano, this is the second of such festivities (the first in July), and includes a rousing bareback horse race around the town square. August 16. Siena.

Puccini Opera Season: The composer's operas performed in the open air in the place where he lived and wrote. Torre del Lago.

Sagra del Redentore: Two-part celebration: a religious pilgrimage and a folk festival of Sardinian songs and dances with a parade of thousands in regional costume. August 29 (the procession) and another day that varies from year to year. Nuoro.

Rossini Opera Festival: A mid-August to mid-September bel canto salute to the composer, in the city of his birth. Pesaro.

International Film Festival: Two weeks of screenings, with the international film crowd and plenty of homegrown paparazzi livening the Lido scene. Late August to early September. Venice.

Stresa Musical Weeks: Three or four weeks of symphony, chamber music, and recitals by world-famous soloists and young winners of international competitions. Late August to late September. Stresa.

September

Palio della Balestra: Held in a field called the Cava dei Balestrieri, this crossbowmen's contest and parade in Renaissance costume celebrates the foundation of the world's smallest republic and honors its patron saint. September 3. San Marino.

Festa di Santa Rosalia: The second part of a festival begun in July, a statue of the saint is carried in procession to a sanctuary on nearby Monte Pellegrino. Held in early September. Palermo.

Living Chess Game: Played with people costumed as chess pieces and the town square as chessboard. Held in even-numbered years; first Sunday in September and the immediately preceding Saturday (September 6 and 5 this year). Marostica.

Giostra del Saraceno: Reenactment of a medieval joust. Knights in armor representing the town's four quarters attack an effigy of a Saracen and vie for the golden lance. First Sunday in September (September 6 this year). Arezzo.

Regata Storica (Historical Regatta): Parade of decorated boats, 15th-century style, and a gondola race on the Grand Canal. First Sunday in September (September 6 this year). Venice.

Palio dei Balestrieri: Return match between costumed crossbowmen of Gubbio and Sansepolcro. (Also held in Gubbio on May 31.) Second Sunday in September (September 13 this year). Sansepolcro.

Giostra della Quintana: Historical pageantry, including a day of jousting and a parade in 17th-century costume the night before. Second Sunday in September (September 13 this year). Foligno.

Miracle of San Gennaro: Feast day in honor of the city's patron saint and second-yearly occurrence of the miracle (the first is May 2). September 19. Naples.

Palio: As with Siena's *Palio,* this ancient festival features costumed participants, a bareback horse race, and flag throwing. Third Sunday in September (September 20 this year). Asti.

Festival delle Sagre–Festa del Vino Douja d'Or: A day-long cookout of local food specialties during a week-long wine festival. Asti.

October

Investiture of the Captains Regent: Second of the twice-yearly ceremonies inaugurating the republic's new rulers (the first is held April 1). October 1. San Marino.

Fiera del Tartufo (Truffle Fair): Harvest festival celebrating food, wine, the famous local white truffle, and the skill of the truffle dog. Alba.

November

Marionette Festival: Sicilian *pupi* take center stage, but guest puppets from elsewhere in Europe perform, too. These 2-weeks of puppetry are held at the *Museo Internazionale delle Marionette* in Palermo.

Festa della Madonna della Salute: Another cross-canal pilgrimage on a bridge of boats constructed between Santa Maria del Giglio and the Chiesa di Santa Maria della Salute to give thanks for the lifting of a plague — this time a 17th-century one (see also July). November 21. Venice.

December

Opening Night at La Scala: Beginning of the season at the world's most celebrated opera house. Traditionally held on December 7, *Feast Day of Sant'Ambrogio,* patron saint of the city. Milan.

Traveling by Plane

Flying is the most efficient way to get to Italy, and it is the quickest, most convenient means of travel between different parts of the country once you are there. (Cruise ships that call at Italian ports generally function as hotels for passengers cruising European waters, rather than as especially efficient transportation to a single country or between individual destinations.)

The air space between North America and Europe is the most heavily trafficked in the world. It is served by dozens of airlines, almost all of which sell seats at a variety of prices, under a vast spectrun of requirements and restrictions. Since you probably will spend more for your airfare than for any other single item in your travel budget, try to take advantage of the lowest fares offered by either scheduled airlines or charter companies. You should know what kinds of flights are available, the rules under which air travel operates, and all the special package options.

SCHEDULED FLIGHTS: Among the dozens of airlines serving Europe from the United States, those currently offering regularly scheduled direct and connecting flights to Italy, many on a daily basis, are *Air France, Alitalia, American, Austrian Airlines,*

British Airways, Delta, Iberia, Icelandair, KLM, Lufthansa, Sabena, SAS, SwissAir, TAP Air Portugal, and *TWA.*

Gateways – At present, nonstop and direct flights (meaning, usually, that there is no change of flight number between the originating and terminating cities, though there may be one or more stops en route and perhaps a change of plane) depart from Atlanta, Boston, Chicago, Los Angeles, Miami, and New York. Nonstop or direct, nearly all of these flights land at Milan's Malpensa Airport or Rome's Leonardo da Vinci Airport (also known as Fiumicino). In summer, *Alitalia* operates a direct flight from New York via Rome to Palermo's Punta Raisi Airport. *Alitalia* also has a direct flight from New York to Venice's Marco Polo Airport, with a change of plane in Milan.

Tickets – When traveling on one of the many regularly scheduled flights, a full-fare ticket provides maximum travel flexibility (although at considerable expense), because there are no advance booking requirements. A prospective passenger can buy a ticket for a flight right up to the minute of takeoff — if a seat is available. If your ticket is for a round trip, you can make the return reservation whenever you wish — months before you leave or the day before you return. Assuming foreign immigration requirements are met, you can stay at your destination for as long as you like. (Tickets generally are good for a year and can be renewed if not used.) You also can cancel your flight at any time without penalty. However, while it is true that this category of ticket can be purchased at the last minute, it is advisable to reserve well in advance during popular vacation periods and around holiday times.

Fares – Airfares continue to change so rapidly that even experts find it difficult to keep up with them. This ever-changing situation is due to a number of factors, including airline deregulation, volatile labor relations, increasing fuel costs, and vastly increased competition.

Perhaps the most common misconception about fares on scheduled airlines is that the cost of the ticket determines how much service will be provided on the flight. This is true only to a certain extent. A far more realistic rule of thumb is that the less you pay for your ticket, the more restrictions and qualifications are likely to come into play before you board the plane (as well as after you get off). These qualifying aspects relate to the months (and the days of the week) during which you must travel, how far in advance you must purchase your ticket, the minimum and maximum amount of time you may or must remain away, your willingness to decide on a return date at the time of booking — and your ability to stick to that decision. It is not uncommon for passengers sitting side by side on the same wide-body jet to have paid fares varying by hundreds of dollars, and all too often the traveler paying more would have been equally willing (and able) to accept the terms of the far less expensive ticket.

In general, the great variety of fares between the US and Italy can be reduced to four basic categories, including first class, coach (also called economy or tourist class), and excursion or discount fares. A fourth category, called business class, has been added by many airlines in recent years. In addition, Advance Purchase Excursion (APEX) fares offer savings under certain conditions.

In a class by itself is the *Concorde,* the supersonic jet developed jointly by France and Great Britain that cruises at speeds of 1,350 miles an hour (twice the speed of sound) and makes transatlantic crossings in half the time (3½ hours from New York to Paris) of conventional, subsonic jets. *Air France* offers *Concorde* service between New York and Paris; *British Airways* flies from Miami, Washington, DC, and New York to London. Service is "single" class (with champagne and caviar all the way), and the fare is expensive, about 20% more than a first class ticket on a subsonic aircraft. Some discounts have been offered, but time is the real gift of the *Concorde.* For travelers to Italy, this "gift" may be more or less valuable as compared to the time of a direct flight when taking connections from Paris or London into account.

A **first class** ticket is your admission to the special section of the aircraft — larger seats, more legroom, sleeperette seating on some wide-body aircraft, better (or more elaborately served) food, free drinks and headsets for movies and music channels, and above all, personal attention. First class fares are about twice those of full-fare economy, although both first class passengers and those paying full-fare ecomony fares are entitled to reserve seats and are sold tickets on an open reservation system. An additional advantage of a first class ticket is that if you're planning to visit several cities within Italy or elsewhere in Europe, you may include any number of stops en route to or from your most distant destination, provided that certain set restrictions regarding maximum mileage limits and flight routes are respected.

Not too long ago, there were only two classes of air travel, first class and all the rest, usually called economy or tourist. Then **business class** came into being — one of the most successful of recent airline innovations. At first, business class passengers were merely curtained off from the other economy passengers. Now a separate cabin or cabins — usually toward the front of the plane — is the norm. While standards of comfort and service are not as high as in first class, they represent a considerable improvement over conditions in the rear of the plane, with roomier seats, more leg and shoulder space between passengers, and fewer seats abreast. Free liquor and headsets, a choice of meal entrées, and a separate counter for speedier check-in are other inducements. As in first class, a business class passenger may travel on any scheduled flight he or she wishes, may buy a one-way or round-trip ticket, and have the ticket remain valid for a year. There are no minimum or maximum stay requirements, no advance booking requirements, and no cancellation penalties, and the fare allows the same free stopover privileges as first class. Airlines often have their own names for their business class service — such as Prima Business Class on *Alitalia* and Ambassador Class on *TWA*.

The terms of the **coach** or **economy** fare may vary slightly from airline to airline, and in fact from time to time airlines may be selling more than one type of economy fare. Coach or economy passengers sit more snugly, as many as 10 in a single row on a wide-body jet, behind the first class and business class sections. Normally, alcoholic drinks are not free, nor are the headsets (except on *British Airways,* which does offer these free of charge). If there are two economy fares on the books, one (often called "regular economy") still may include a number of free stopovers. The other, less expensive fare (often called "special economy") may limit stopovers to one or two, with a charge (typically $25) for each one. Like first class passengers, however, passengers paying the full coach fare are subject to none of the restrictions that usually are attached to less expensive excursion and discount fares. There are no advance booking requirements, no minimum stay requirements, and no cancellation penalties. Tickets are sold on an open reservation system: They can be bought for a flight right up to the minute of takeoff (if seats are available), and if the ticket is round-trip, the return reservation can be made anytime you wish. Both first class and coach tickets generally are good for a year, after which they can be renewed if not used, and if you ultimately decide not to fly at all, your money will be refunded. The cost of economy and business class tickets does not vary much in the course of the year between the US and Italy, though on some transatlantic routes they vary from a basic (low-season) price in effect most of the year to a peak (high-season) price during the summer.

Excursion and other **discount** fares are the airlines' equivalent of a special sale and usually apply to round-trip bookings only. These fares generally differ according to the season and the number of travel days permitted. They are only a bit less flexible than full-fare economy tickets and are, therefore, often useful for both business and holiday travelers. Most round-trip excursion tickets include strict minimum and maximum stay requirements and can be changed only within the specified time limits. So don't count on extending a ticket beyond the prescribed time of return or staying less time than required. Different airlines may have different regulations concerning the number of stopovers permitted, and sometimes excursion fares are less expensive during midweek. The availability of these reduced-rate seats is most limited at busy times such as holidays. Discount or excursion fare ticket holders sit with the coach passengers, and, for all intents and purposes, are indistinguishable from them. They receive all the same basic services, even though they may have paid anywhere between 30% and 55% less for the trip. Obviously, it's wise to make plans early enough to qualify for this less expensive transportation if possible.

These discount or excursion fares may masquerade under a variety of names, they may vary from city to city (from the East Coast to the West Coast, especially), but they invariably have strings attached. A common requirement is that the ticket be purchased a certain number of days — usually no fewer than 7 or 14 days — in advance of departure, though it may be booked weeks or months in advance (it has to be "ticketed," or paid for, shortly after booking, however). The return reservation usually has to be made at the time of the original ticketing and cannot be changed later than a certain number of days (again, usually 7 or 14 days) before the return flight. If events force a passenger to change the return reservation after the date allowed, the difference between the round-trip excursion rate and the round-trip coach rate probably will have to be paid, though most airlines allow passengers to use their discounted fares by standing by for an empty seat, even if they don't otherwise have standby fares. Another common condition is a minimum and maximum stay requirement; for example, 1 to 6 days or 6 to 14 days (but including at least a Saturday night). Last, cancellation penalties of up to 50% of the full price of the ticket have been assessed — check the specific penalty in effect when you purchase your discount/excursion ticket — so careful planning is imperative.

Of even greater risk — and bearing the lowest price of all the current discount fares — is the ticket where no change at all in departure and/or return flights is permitted, and where the ticket price is totally nonrefundable. If you do buy a nonrefundable ticket, you should be aware of a new policy followed by many airlines that may make it easier to change your plans if necessary. For a fee — set by each airline and payable at the airport when checking in — you *may* be able to change the time or date of a return flight on a nonrefundable ticket. However, if the nonrefundable ticket price for the replacement flight is higher than that of the original (as often is the case when trading in a weekday for a weekend flight), you will have to pay the difference. Any such change must be made a certain number of days in advance — in some cases as little as 2 days — of either the original or the replacement flight, whichever is earlier; restrictions are set by the individual carrier. (Travelers holding a nonrefundable or other restricted ticket who must change their plans due to a family emergency should know that some carriers may make special allowances in such situations; for further information, see *Medical and Legal Aid and Consular Services,* in this section.)

In the past, some excursion fares offered for travel to Europe came unencumbered by advance booking requirements and cancellation penalties, permitted one stopover (but not a free one) in each direction, and had "open jaws," meaning that you could fly to one city and depart from another, arranging and paying for your own transportation between the two. Although, for the most part, excursion fares of this type are no longer offered on flights between the US and the majority of European destinations, they still do exist on flights between the US and Italy, where they cost about a third less than economy. The ticket currently is good for a minimum of 6 days and a maximum of 6 months abroad.

There also is a newer, often less expensive, type of excursion, the **APEX**, or **Advance Purchase Excursion**, fare. As with traditional excursion fares, passengers paying an APEX fare sit with and receive the same basic services as any other coach or economy passenger, even though they may have paid up to 50% less for their seats. In return, they are subject to certain restrictions. In the case of most flights to Europe, the ticket usually is good for a minimum of 7 days abroad and a maximum, currently, of 2 to

6 months (depending on the airline and the destination); as its name implies, it must be "ticketed" or paid for in its entirety a certain period of time before departure — usually 21 days.

The drawback to an APEX fare is that it penalizes travelers who change their minds — and travel plans. The return reservation must be made at the time of the original ticketing, and if for some reason you change your schedule while abroad, you will have to pay a penalty of $100 or 10% of the ticket value, whichever is greater, as long as you travel within the validity period of your ticket. But, if you change your return to a date less than the minimum stay or more than the maximum stay, the difference between the round-trip APEX fare and the full round-trip coach rate will have to be paid. There also is a penalty of anywhere from $75 to $125 or more for canceling or changing a reservation *before* travel begins — check the specific penalty in effect when you purchase your ticket. No stopovers are allowed on an APEX ticket, but it is possible to create an "open-jaw" effect by buying an APEX on a split-ticket basis; for example, flying to Rome and returning from Milan. The total price would be half the price of an APEX to Rome plus half the price of an APEX to Milan. APEX tickets to Italy are sold at basic and peak rates (peak season is around May through September) and may include surcharges for weekend flights.

There also is a Winter or Super APEX fare, which may go under different names for different carriers (for instance, some airlines call it "Eurosaver"). Similar to the regular APEX fare, it costs slightly less but is more restrictive. Depending on the airline and destination, it usually is available only for off-peak winter travel and is limited to a stay of between 7 and 21 days. Advance purchase still is required (currently, 30 days prior to travel), and ticketing must be completed within 48 hours of reservation. The fare is nonrefundable, except in cases of hospitalization or death.

Another type of fare that sometimes is available is the **youth** fare. At present, most airlines flying to Italy are using a form of APEX fare as a youth fare for those through age 25. The maximum stay is extended to a year, and the return booking must be left open. Seats can be reserved no more than 3 days before departure, and tickets must be purchased when the reservation is made. The return is booked from Italy in the same manner, no more than 3 days before flight time. On most airlines, there is no cancellation penalty, but the fare is subject to availability, so it may be difficult to book a return during peak travel periods and, as with the regular APEX fare, it may not even be available for travel to or from Italy during high season or may be offered only on selected routes. Note that *Alitalia* and other carriers offer youth fares to both Milan and Rome.

Standby fares, at one time the rock-bottom price at which a traveler could fly to Europe, have become elusive. At the time of this writing, most major scheduled airlines did not regularly offer standby fares on direct flights to Italy. Because airline fares and their conditions constantly change, bargain hunters should not hesitate to ask if such a fare exists at the time they plan to travel. Travelers to Italy also should inquire about the possibility of connecting flights through other European countries that may be offered on a standby basis.

While the definition of standby varies somewhat from airline to airline, it generally means that you make yourself available to buy a ticket for a flight (usually no sooner than the day of departure), then literally stand by on the chance that a seat will be empty. Once aboard, however, a standby passenger has the same meal service and frills (or lack of them) enjoyed by others in the economy class compartment.

Something else to check is the possibility of qualifying for a **GIT** (Group Inclusive Travel) fare, which requires that a specified dollar amount of ground arrangements be purchased, in advance, along with the ticket. The requirements vary as to the number of travel days and stopovers permitted, and the minimum number of passengers required for a group. The actual fares also vary, but the cost will be spelled out in brochures distributed by the tour operators handling the ground arrangements. In the past, GIT fares were among the least expensive available from the established carriers, but the prevalence of discount fares has caused group fares to all but disappear from some air routes. Travelers reading brochures on group package tours to Italy will find that, in almost all cases, the applicable airfare given as a sample (to be added to the price of the land package to obtain the total tour price) is an APEX fare, the same discount fare available to the independent traveler.

The major airlines serving Italy from the US also may offer individual excursion fare rates similar to GIT fares, which are sold in conjunction with ground accommodation packages. Previously called ITX, and sometimes referred to as individual tour-basing fares, these fares generally are offered as part of "air/hotel/car/transfer packages," and can reduce the cost of an economy fare by more than a third. The packages are booked for a specific amount of time, with return dates specified; rescheduling and cancellation restrictions and penalties vary from carrier to carrier. At the time of this writing, this type of fare was offered to Italy by *Alitalia* and *TWA,* and although their offerings did not represent substantial savings over the standard economy fare, it is worth checking at the time you plan to travel. (For further information on package options, see *Package Tours,* in this section.)

Travelers looking for the least expensive possible airfares should, finally, scan the pages of their hometown newspapers (especially the Sunday travel sections) for announcements of special promotional fares. Most airlines offer their most attractive special fares to encourage travel during slow seasons, and to inaugurate and publicize new routes. Even if none of these factors applies, prospective passengers can be fairly sure that the number of discount seats per flight at the lowest price is strictly limited, or that the fare offering includes a set expiration date — which means it's absolutely necessary to move fast to enjoy the lowest possible price.

Among other special airline promotional deals for which you should be on the lookout are discount or upgrade coupons, sometimes offered by the major carriers and found in mail order merchandise catalogues. For instance, airlines sometimes issue coupons that typically cost around $25 each and are good for a percentage discount or an upgrade on an international airline ticket — including flights to Italy. The only requirement beyond the fee generally is that a coupon purchaser must buy at least one item from the catalogue. There usually are some minimum airfare restrictions before the coupon is redeemable, but in general these are worthwhile offers. Restrictions often include certain blackout days (when the coupon cannot be used at all), usually imposed during peak travel periods. These coupons are particularly valuable to business travelers who tend to buy full-fare tickets, and while the coupons are issued in the buyer's name, they can be used by others who are traveling on the same itinerary.

It's always wise to ask about discount or promotional fares and about any conditions that might restrict booking, payment, cancellation, and changes in plans. Check the prices from neighboring cities. A special rate may be offered in a nearby city but not in yours, and it may be enough of a bargain to warrant your leaving from that city. Ask if there is a difference in price for midweek versus weekend travel, or if there is a further discount for traveling early in the morning or late at night. Also be sure to investigate package deals, which are offered by virtually every airline. These may include a car rental, accommodations, and dining and/or sightseeing features, in addition to the basic airfare, and the combined cost of packaged elements usually is considerably less than the cost of the exact same elements when purchased separately.

If in the course of your research you come across a deal that seems too good to be true, keep in mind that logic may not be a component of deeply discounted airfares — there's not always any sane relationship between miles to be flown and the price to get there. More often than not, the level of competition on a given route dictates the degree of discount, and don't be dissuaded from accepting an offer that sounds irresistible just because it also sounds illogical. Better to buy that inexpensive fare while it's being offered and worry about the sense — or absence thereof — while you're flying to your desired destination.

When you're satisfied that you've found the lowest possible price for which you can conveniently qualify (you may have to call the airline more than once, because different airline reservations clerks have been known to quote different prices), make your booking. Then, to protect yourself against fare increases, purchase and pay for your ticket as soon as possible after you've received a confirmed reservation. Airlines generally will honor their tickets, even if the operative price at the time of your flight is higher than the price you paid; if fares go up between the time you *reserve* a flight and the time you *pay* for it, you likely will be out of luck. Finally, with excursion or discount fares, it is important to remember that when a reservations clerk says that you must purchase a ticket by a specific date, this is an absolute deadline. Miss the deadline and the airline may automatically cancel your reservation without telling you.

■ **Note:** Another wrinkle in the airfare scene is that if the fares go *down* after you purchase your ticket, you *may* be entitled to a refund of the difference. However, this is posssible only in certain situations — availability and advance purchase restrictions pertaining to the lower rate are set by the airline. If you suspect that you may be able to qualify for such a refund, check with your travel agent or the airline.

Frequent Flyers – Among the leading carriers serving Italy, *American, British Airways, Delta,* and *TWA* offer a bonus system to frequent travelers. After the first 10,000 miles, for example, a passenger might be eligible for a first class seat for the coach fare; after another 10,000 miles, he or she might receive a discount on his or her next ticket purchase. The value of the bonuses continues to increase as more miles are logged. Once you are signed up for such a program, if flying to Europe on *Air France, SAS, SwissAir,* or another European-based airline, ask if the miles to be flown may be applied toward your collective bonus mileage account with a US carrier. For example, miles flown on *Alitalia* can be applied to *Continental, United,* and *USAir* frequent flyer mileage programs.

Bonus miles also may be earned by patronizing affiliated car rental companies or hotel chains, or by using one of the credit cards that now offers this reward. In deciding whether to accept such a credit card from one of the issuing organizations that tempt you with frequent flyer mileage bonuses on a specific airline, first determine whether the interest rate charged on the unpaid balance is the same as (or less than) possible alternate credit cards, and whether the annual "membership" fee also is equal or lower. If these charges are slightly higher than those of competing cards, weigh the difference against the potential value in airfare savings. Also ask about any bonus miles awarded just for signing up — 1,000 is common, 5,000 generally the maximum.

For the most up-to-date information on frequent flyer bonus options, you may want to send for the monthly newsletter *Frequent.* Issued by Frequent Publications, it provides current information about frequent flyer plans in general, as well as specific data about promotions, awards, and combination deals to help you keep track of the profusion — and confusion — of current and upcoming availabilities. For a year's subscription, send $33 to Frequent Publications, 4715-C Town Center Dr., Colorado Springs, CO 80916 (phone: 800-333-5937).

There also is a monthly magazine called *Frequent Flyer,* but unlike the newsletter mentioned above, its focus is primarily on newsy articles of interest to business travelers and other frequent flyers. Published by Official Airline Guides (PO Box 58543, Boulder, CO 80322-8543; phone: 800-323-3537), *Frequent Flyer* is available for $24 for a 1-year subscription.

Low-Fare Airlines – Increasingly, in today's economic climate, the stimulus for special fares is the appearance of new airlines associated with bargain rates. On these airlines, all seats on any given flight generally sell for the same price, which is somewhat below the lowest discount fare offered by the larger, more established airlines. It is important to note that tickets offered by the smaller airlines specializing in low-cost travel frequently are not subject to the same restrictions as the lowest-priced ticket offered by the more established carriers. They may not require advance purchase or mimimum and maximum stays, may involve no cancellation penalties, and may be available one way or round trip. A disadvantage to low-fare airlines, however, is that when something goes wrong, such as delayed baggage or a flight cancellation due to equipment breakdown, their smaller fleets and fewer flights mean that passengers may have to wait longer for a solution than they would on one of the equipment-rich major carriers.

One airline offering a consistently low fare to Europe is *Virgin Atlantic* (phone: 800-862-8621 or 212-242-1330), which flies daily from New York (Newark Airport) to London (Gatwick Airport). The airline sells tickets in several categories, including business or "upper" class, economy, APEX, and nonrefundable variations on standby. Fares from New York to London include Late Saver fares — which must be purchased not less than 7 days prior to travel — and Late Late Saver fares — which are purchased no later than 1 day prior to travel. Travelers to Italy will have to take a second flight from London, but still may save money. To determine the potential savings, add the cost of the transatlantic fare and the cost of connecting flights to come up with the total ticket price. Remember, too, that since Italy is such a popular holiday destination with the British, low-priced package programs frequently are available from British-based tour operators and bucket shops.

In a class by itself is *Icelandair,* a scheduled airline long known as a good source of low-cost flights to Europe. *Icelandair* flies from Baltimore/Washington, DC, New York, and Orlando, via Reykjavik (Iceland), to Copenhagen (Denmark), Glasgow and London (Great Britain), Gothenburg (Sweden), Helsinki (Finland), Luxembourg (in the country of the same name), and Oslo (Norway). In addition, the airline increases the options for its passengers by offering "thru-fares" on connecting flights from Luxembourg to a variety of European cities, including Rome. (The price of the intra-European flight — aboard Luxembourg's *Luxair* — is included in the price *Icelandair* quotes for the transatlantic portion of the travel to these additional destinations.)

Icelandair sells tickets in a variety of categories, from unrestricted economy fares to a sort of standby "3-days-before" fare (which functions just like the youth fares described above but has no age requirement). Travelers should be aware, however, that most *Icelandair* flights stop in Reykjavik for 45 minutes en route to and from Luxembourg — a minor delay for most, but one that further prolongs the trip for passengers who will wait again in Luxembourg to board connecting flights to their ultimate destinations. For reservations and tickets, contact a travel agent or *Icelandair* (phone: 800-223-5500 or 212-967-8888).

Intra-European Fares – The cost of the round trip across the Atlantic is not the only expense to be considered. Flights between European cities, when booked in Europe, can be quite expensive.

Recent Common Market moves toward airline deregulation are expected to lead gradually to a greater variety of budget fares. In the meantime, however, the high cost of fares between most European cities can be avoided by careful use of stopover rights on the higher-priced transatlantic tickets — first class, business class, and full-fare economy. If your ticket doesn't allow stopovers, ask about PEX, Super PEX, APEX, and other excursion fares. If you are able to comply with applicable restrictions and can use them, you may save as much as 35% to 50% off full-fare economy. Note that these fares, which once could be bought only after arrival in Europe, now are sold in the US and can be bought before departure.

It is not easy to inform yourself about stopover possibilities by talking to most airline reservations clerks. More than likely, an inquiry concerning any projected trip will prompt the reply that a particular route is nonstop aboard the carrier in question, thereby precluding stopovers completely, or that the carrier does not fly to all the places you want to visit. It may take additional inquiries, perhaps with the aid of a travel agent, to determine the full range of options regarding stopover privileges.

Travelers might be able to squeeze in visits to London, Paris, or Madrid on a first class ticket to Rome, for instance; and Rome might be only the first of many free European stopovers possible on a one-way or round-trip ticket to a city in Eastern Europe or points beyond. The airline that flies you on the first leg of your trip across the Atlantic issues the ticket, though you may have to use several different airlines in order to complete your journey. First class tickets are valid for a full year, so there's no rush.

Domestic service within Italy is provided by *Alitalia* and its subsidiaries *ATI (Aero Trasporti Italiani), Alisarda* (which has flights between cities on the mainland and Sardinia), and *Avianova,* (which connects many of the smaller cities with Florence, Milan, and Rome). Full economy fares prevail on their flights; among the few reductions are youth fares, children's fares, infants' fares, weekend promotional fares, and night fares. These reductions generally are available only if the ticket is bought in Italy and may provide a discount of between 30% and 50%. Discounted transatlantic and intra-European airfare packages may be offered by other carriers in other countries, but, in the case of travel to and within Italy, these options currently are limited, if available at all. Still, it pays to ask a travel agent or the airline if any special intra-European fares apply at the time you plan to travel.

Taxes and Other Fees – Travelers who have shopped for the best possible flight at the lowest possible price should be warned that a number of extras will be added to that price and collected by the airline or travel agent who issues the ticket. These taxes *usually* (but not always) are included in the prices quoted by airline reservations clerks.

The $6 International Air Transportation Tax is a departure tax paid by all passengers flying from the US to a foreign destination. A $10 US Federal Inspection Fee is levied on all air and cruise passengers who arrive in the US from outside North America (those arriving from Canada, Mexico, the Caribbean, and US territories are exempt). Still another fee is charged by some airlines to cover more stringent security procedures, prompted by recent terrorist incidents. The 8% federal US Transportation Tax applies to travel within the US or US territories, as well as to passengers flying between US cities en route to a foreign destination if the trip includes a stopover of more than 12 hours at a US point. Someone flying from Los Angeles to New York and stopping in New York for more than 12 hours before boarding a flight to Rome, for instance, would pay the 8% tax on the domestic portion of the trip.

Reservations – For those who don't have the time or patience to investigate personally all possible air departures and connections for a proposed trip, a travel agent can be of inestimable help. A good agent should have all the information on which flights go where and when, and which categories of tickets are available on each. Most have computerized reservation links with the major carriers, so that a seat can be reserved and confirmed in minutes. An increasing number of agents also possess fare-comparison computer programs, so they often are very reliable sources of detailed competitive price data. (For more information, see *How to Use a Travel Agent,* in this section.)

When making reservations through a travel agent, ask the agent to give the airline your home phone number, as well as your daytime business phone number. All too often the agent uses the agency number as the official contact for changes in flight plans. Especially during the winter, weather conditions hundreds or even thousands of miles away can wreak havoc with flight schedules. Aircraft are constantly in use, and a plane delayed in the Orient or on the West Coast can miss its scheduled flight from the East Coast the next morning. The airlines are fairly reliable about getting this sort of information to passengers if they can reach them; diligence does little good at 10 PM if the airline has only the agency's or an office number.

Reconfirmation is strongly recommended for all international flights (though it is not usually required on US domestic flights) and, in the case of flights to Italy, it is a good idea to confirm your round-trip reservations — especially the return leg — as well as any point-to-point flights within Europe. Some (though increasingly fewer) reservations to and from international destinations are automatically canceled after a required reconfirmation period (typically 72 hours) has passed — even if you have a confirmed, fully paid ticket in hand. It always is wise to call ahead to make sure that the airline did not slip up in entering your original reservation, or in registering any changes you may have made since, and that it has your seat reservation and/or special meal request in the computer. If you look at the printed information on the ticket, you'll see the airline's reconfirmation policy stated explicitly. Don't be lulled into a false sense of security by the "OK" on your ticket next to the number and time of the flight. This only means that a reservation has been entered; a reconfirmation still may be necessary. If in doubt — call.

If you plan not to take a flight on which you hold a confirmed reservation, by all means inform the airline. Because the problem of no-shows is a constant expense for airlines, they are allowed to overbook flights, a practice that often contributes to the threat of denied boarding for a certain number of passengers (see "Getting Bumped," below).

Seating – For most types of tickets, airline seats usually are assigned on a first-come, first-served basis at check-in, although some airlines make it possible to reserve a seat at the time of ticket purchase. Always check in early for your flight, even with advance seat assignments. A good rule of thumb for international flights is to arrive at the airport *at least* 2 hours before the scheduled departure to give yourself plenty of time in case there are long lines.

Most airlines furnish seating charts, which make choosing a seat much easier, but there are a few basics to consider. You must decide whether you prefer a window, aisle, or middle seat. On flights where smoking is permitted, you also should specify if you prefer the smoking or nonsmoking section.

The amount of legroom provided (as well as chest room, especially when the seat in front of you is in a reclining position) is determined by pitch, a measure of the distance between the back of the seat in front of you and the front of the back of your seat. The amount of pitch is a matter of airline policy, not the type of plane you fly. First class and business class seats have the greatest pitch, a fact that figures prominently in airline advertising. In economy class or coach, the standard pitch ranges from 33 to as little as 31 inches — downright cramped.

The number of seats abreast, another factor determining comfort, depends on a combination of airline policy and airplane dimensions. First class and business class have the fewest seats per row. Economy generally has 9 seats per row on a DC-10 or an L-1011, making either one slightly more comfortable than a 747, on which there normally are 10 seats per row. Charter flights on DC-10s and L-1011s, however, often have 10 seats per row and can be noticeably more cramped than 747 charters, on which the seating normally remains at 10 per row.

Airline representatives claim that most aircraft are more stable toward the front and midsection, while seats farthest from the engines are quietest. Passengers who have long legs and are traveling on a wide-body aircraft might request a seat directly behind a door or emergency exit, since these seats often have greater than average pitch, or a seat in the first row of a given section, which offers extra legroom — although these seats are increasingly being reserved for passengers who are willing (and able) to perform certain tasks in the event of emergency evacuation. It often is impossible, however, to see the movie from these seats, which are directly behind the plane's exits. Be aware that the first row of the economy section (called a "bulkhead" seat) on a conventional aircraft (not a widebody) does *not* offer extra legroom, since the fixed partition will not permit passengers to slide their feet under it, and that watching a movie from this first row seat can be difficult and uncomfortable. These bulkhead seats do, however, provide ample room to use a bassinet or safety seat and often are reserved for families traveling with children.

A window seat protects you from aisle traffic and clumsy serving carts and also provides a view, while an aisle seat enables you to get up and stretch your legs without disturbing anyone. Middle seats are the least desirable, and seats in the last row are the worst of all, since they seldom recline fully. If you wish to avoid children on your flight or if you find that you are sitting in an especially noisy section, you usually are free to move to any unoccupied seat — if there is one.

If you are overweight, you may face the prospect of a long flight with special trepidation. Center seats in the alignments of wide-body 747s, L-1011s, and DC-10s are about 1½ inches wider than those on either side, so larger travelers tend to be more comfortable there.

Despite all these rules of thumb, finding out which specific rows are near emergency exits or at the front of a wide-body cabin can be difficult because seating arrangements on two otherwise identical planes vary from airline to airline. There is, however, a quarterly publication called *Airline Seating Guide* that publishes seating charts for most major US airlines and many foreign carriers as well. Your travel agent should have a copy, or you can buy the US edition for $39.95 per year and the international edition for $44.95. Order from Carlson Publishing Co., Box 888, Los Alamitos, CA 90720 (phone: 800-728-4877 or 213-493-4877).

Simply reserving an airline seat in advance, however, actually may guarantee very little. Most airlines require that passengers arrive at the departure gate at least 45 minutes (sometimes more) ahead of time to hold a seat reservation. *Alitalia,* for example, may cancel seat assignments and may not honor reservations of passengers not checked in some period of time — usually around 45 minutes to 1 hour, depending on the airport — before scheduled departure time, and they *ask* travelers to check in at least 2 hours before international flights. It pays to read the fine print on your ticket carefully and plan ahead.

A far better strategy is to visit an airline ticket office (or one of a select group of travel agents) to secure an actual boarding pass for your specific flight. Once this has been issued, airline computers show you as checked in, and you effectively own the seat you have selected (although some carriers may not honor boarding passes of passengers arriving at the gate less than 10 minutes before departure). This also is good — but not foolproof — insurance against getting bumped from an overbooked flight and is, therefore, an especially valuable tactic at peak travel times.

Smoking – One decision regarding choosing a seat has been taken out of the hands of many travelers who smoke. Effective February 25, 1990, the US government imposed a ban that prohibits smoking on all flights scheduled for 6 hours or less within the US and its territories. The new regulation applies to both domestic and international carriers serving these routes.

In the case of flights to Italy, these rules do not apply to nonstop flights from the US, or those with a *continuous* flight time of over 6 hours between stops in the US or its territories. Smoking is not permitted on segments of international flights where the time between US landings is under 6 hours — for instance, flights that include a stopover (even with no change of plane) or connecting flights. To further complicate the situation, several individual carriers are banning smoking altogether on certain routes. (As we went to press, this ban had not yet extended to carriers flying between the US and Italy — for instance, *Alitalia* allows smoking on all transatlantic flights.)

On those flights that do permit smoking, the US Department of Transportation has determined that nonsmoking sections must be enlarged to accommodate all passengers who wish to sit in one. The airline does not, however, have to shift seating to accommodate nonsmokers who arrive late for a flight or travelers flying standby, and in general not all airlines can guarantee a seat in the nonsmoking section on international flights. Cigar and pipe smoking are prohibited on all flights, even in the smoking sections.

For a wallet-size guide, which notes in detail the rights of nonsmokers according to these regulations, send a self-addressed, stamped envelope to *ASH (Action on Smoking and Health),* Airline Card, 2013 H St. NW, Washington, DC 20006 (phone: 202-659-4310).

Meals – If you have specific dietary requirements, be sure to let the airline know well before departure time. The available meals include vegetarian, seafood, kosher, Muslim, Hindu, high-protein, low-calorie, low-cholesterol, low-fat, low-sodium, diabetic, bland, and children's menus. There is no extra charge for this option. It usually is necessary to request special meals when you make your reservations — check-in time is too late. It's also wise to reconfirm that your request for a special meal has made its way into the airline's computer — the time to do this is 24 hours before departure. (Note that special meals generally are not available on intra-European flights on small local carriers. If this poses a problem, try to eat before you board, or bring a snack with you.)

Baggage – Travelers from the US face two different kinds of rules. When you fly on a US airline or on a major international carrier, US baggage regulations will be in effect. Though airline baggage allowances vary slightly, in general all passengers are allowed to carry on board, without charge, one piece of luggage that will fit easily under a seat of the plane or in an overhead bin, and whose combined dimensions (length, width, and depth) do not exceed 45 inches. A reasonable amount of reading material, camera equipment, and a handbag also are allowed. In addition, all passengers are allowed to check two bags in the cargo hold: one usually not to exceed 62 inches when length, width, and depth are combined, the other not to exceed 55 inches in combined dimensions. Generally no single bag may weigh more than 70 pounds. This weight restriction, however, may vary on transatlantic flights on some European airlines, ranging from as much as 88 pounds permitted for first class passengers to as little as 50 pounds for economy class — so check with the specific carrier in advance.

On many intra-European flights, including domestic service within Italy, baggage allowances may be subject to the old weight determination, under which each economy or discount passenger is allowed only a total of 44 pounds of luggage without additional charge. First class or business class passengers are allowed a total of 66 pounds. (If you are flying from the US to Europe and connecting to a domestic flight, you generally will be allowed the same amount of baggage as on the international flight. If you break your trip and then take a domestic flight, the local carrier's weight restrictions apply.)

Charges for additional, oversize, or overweight bags usually are made at a flat rate; the actual dollar amount varies from carrier to carrier. If you plan to travel with any special equipment or sporting gear, be sure to check with the airline beforehand. Most have specific procedures for handling such baggage, and you may have to pay for transport regardless of how much other baggage you have checked. Golf clubs and skis may be checked through as luggage (most airlines are accustomed to handling them), but tennis rackets should be carried onto the plane. Some airlines require that bicycles be partially dismantled and packaged (see *Camping and Caravanning, Hiking and Biking,* in this section).

Airline policies regarding baggage allowances for children vary and usually are based on the percentage of full adult fare paid. Although on many US carriers children who are ticket holders are entitled to the same baggage allowance as a full-fare passenger, some carriers allow only one bag per child, which sometimes must be smaller than an adult's bag (around 39 to 45 inches in combined dimensions). Often there is no luggage allowance for a child traveling on an adult's lap or in a bassinet. Particularly for international carriers, it's always wise to check ahead. (For more information, see *Hints for Traveling with Children,* in this section.)

To reduce the chances of your luggage going astray, remove all airline tags from previous trips, label each bag inside and out — with your business address rather than your home address on the outside, to prevent thieves from knowing whose house might be unguarded. Lock everything and double-check the tag that the airline attaches to make sure that it is correctly coded for your destination: MXP for Malpensa Airport in Milan, or FCO for Leonardo da Vinci Airport (better known as Fiumicino) in Rome, for instance.

If your bags are not in the baggage claim area after your flight, or if they're damaged, report the problem to airline personnel immediately. Keep in mind that policies regarding the specific time limit within which you have to make your claim vary from carrier to carrier. Fill out a report form on your lost or damaged luggage and keep a copy of it and your original baggage claim check. If you must surrender the check to claim a damaged bag, get a receipt for it to prove that you did, indeed, check your baggage on the flight. If luggage is missing, be sure to give the airline your destination and/or a telephone number where you can be reached. Also take the name and number of the person in charge of recovering lost luggage.

Most airlines have emergency funds for passengers stranded away from home without their luggage, but if it turns out your bags are truly lost and not simply delayed, do not then and there sign any paper indicating you'll accept an offered settlement. Since the airline is responsible for the value of your bags within certain statutory limits ($1,250 per passenger for lost baggage on a US domestic flight; $9.07 per pound or $20 per kilo for checked baggage and up to $400 per passenger for unchecked baggage on an international flight), you should take some time to assess the extent of your loss (see *Insurance,* in this section). It's a good idea to keep records indicating the value of the contents of your luggage. A wise alternative is to take a Polaroid picture of the most valuable of your packed items just after putting them in your suitcase.

Considering the increased incidence of damage to baggage, it's now more than ever a good idea to keep the sales slips that confirm how much you paid for your bags. These are invaluable in establishing the value of damaged luggage and eliminate any arguments. A better way to protect your precious gear from the luggage-eating conveyors is to try to carry it on board whenever possible.

Be aware that airport security increasingly is an issue all over Europe, and the Italians take it very seriously. Heavily armed police patrol the airports, and unattended luggage of any description may be confiscated and quickly destroyed. Passengers checking in at a European airport may undergo at least two separate inspections of their tickets, passports, and luggage by courteous but serious airline personnel — who ask passengers if their baggage has been out of their possession between packing and the airport or if they have been given gifts or other items to transport — before checked items are accepted.

Airline Clubs – US carriers often have clubs for travelers who pay for membership. These are not solely for first class passengers, although a first class ticket *may* entitle a passenger to lounge privileges. Membership (which, by law, requires a fee) entitles the traveler to use the private lounges at airports along their route, to refreshments served in these lounges, and to check-cashing privileges at most of their counters. Extras include special telephone numbers for individual reservations, embossed luggage tags, and a membership card for identification. Airlines serving Italy that offer membership in such clubs include the following:

American: The *Admirals Club.* Single yearly membership $125 (plus a onetime $50 initiation fee); spouse an additional $70 per year.
British Airways: The *Executive Club.* Single yearly membership is £125 (about $200 at press time). Note that there is no discounted rate for a spouse.
Delta: The Crown Club. Single yearly membership $150; spouse an additional $50 per year.
TWA: The *Ambassador Club.* Single yearly membership $150, spouse an additional $25; lifetime memberships also available.

Note that such companies do not have club facilities in all airports. Other airlines also offer a variety of special services in many airports.

Getting Bumped – A special air travel problem is the possibility that an airline will accept more reservations (and sell more tickets) than there are seats on a given flight. This is entirely legal and is done to make up for "no-shows," passengers who don't show up for a flight for which they have made reservations and bought tickets. If the airline has oversold the flight and everyone does show up, there simply aren't enough seats. When this happens, the airline is subject to stringent rules designed to protect travelers.

In such cases, the airline first seeks ticket holders willing to give up their seats voluntarily in return for a negotiable sum of money, or some other inducement, such as an offer of upgraded seating on the next flight or a voucher for a free trip at some other time. If there are not enough volunteers, the airline may bump passengers against their wishes.

Anyone inconvenienced in this way, however, is entitled to an explanation of the criteria used to determine who does and does not get on the flight, as well as compensation if the resulting delay exceeds certain limits. If the airline can put the bumped passengers on an alternate flight that is *scheduled to arrive* at their original destination within 1 hour of their originally scheduled arrival time, no compensation is owed. If the delay is more than 1 hour but less than 2 hours on a domestic US flight, they must be paid denied-boarding compensation equivalent to the one-way fare to their destination (but not more than $200). If the delay is more than 2 hours after the original arrival time on a domestic flight or more than 4 hours on an international flight, the compensation must be doubled (not more than $400). The airline also may offer bumped travelers a voucher for a free flight instead of the denied-boarding compensation. The passenger may be given the choice of either the money or the voucher, the dollar value of which may be no less than the monetary compensation to which the passenger would be entitled. The voucher is not a substitute for the bumped passenger's original ticket; the airline continues to honor that as well.

Keep in mind that these regulations and policies are only for flights leaving the US, and do *not* apply to charters or to inbound flights originating abroad, even on US carriers. Airlines carrying passengers between foreign destinations are free to determine what compensation they will pay to passengers who are bumped because of overbooking. They generally spell out their policies on airline tickets. Some foreign airline policies are similar to the US policy; however, don't assume all carriers will be as generous.

To protect yourself as best you can against getting bumped, arrive at the airport early, allowing plenty of time to check in and get to the gate. If the flight is oversold, ask immediately for the written statement explaining the airline's policy on denied-boarding compensation and its boarding priorities. If the airline refuses to give you this information, or if you feel it has not handled the situation properly, file a complaint with both the airline and the appropriate government agency (see "Consumer Protection," below).

Delays and Cancellations – The above compensation rules also do not apply if the flight is canceled or delayed, or if a smaller aircraft is substituted because of mechanical problems. Each airline has its own policy for assisting passengers whose flights are delayed or canceled or who must wait for another flight because their original one was overbooked. Most airline personnel will make new travel arrangements if necessary. If the delay is longer than 4 hours, the airline may pay for a phone call or telegram, a meal, and, in some cases, a hotel room and transportation to it.

■ **Caution:** If you are bumped or miss a flight, be sure to ask the airline to notify other airlines on which you have reservations or connecting flights. When your name is taken off the passenger list of your initial flight, the computer usually cancels all of your reservations automatically, unless *you* take steps to preserve them.

CHARTER FLIGHTS: By booking a block of seats on a specially arranged flight, charter operators offer travelers air transportation, for a substantial reduction over the full coach or economy fare. These operators may offer air-only charters (selling transportation alone) or charter packages (the flight plus a combination of land arrangements such as accommodations, meals, tours, or car rentals). Charters are especially attractive to people living in smaller cities or out-of-the-way places, because they frequently leave from nearby airports, saving travelers the inconvenience and expense of getting to a major gateway.

From the consumer's standpoint, charters differ from scheduled airlines in two main respects: You generally need to book and pay in advance, and you can't change the itinerary or the departure and return dates once you've booked the flight. In practice, however, these restrictions don't always apply. Today, although most charter flights still require advance reservations, some permit last-minute bookings (when there are unsold seats available), and some even offer seats on a standby basis.

Though charters almost always are round trip, and it is unlikely that you would be sold a one-way seat on a round-trip flight, on rare occasions, one-way tickets on charters are offered. Although it may be possible to book a one-way charter in the US, giving you more flexibility in scheduling your return, note that US regulations pertaining to charters may be more permissive than the charter laws of other countries. For example, if you want to book a one-way foreign charter back to the US, you may find advance booking rules in force.

Some things to keep in mind about the charter game:

1. It cannot be repeated often enough that if you are forced to cancel your trip, you can lose much (and possibly all) of your money unless you have cancellation insurance, which is a *must* (see *Insurance,* in this section). Frequently, if the cancellation occurs far enough in advance (often 6 weeks or more), you may forfeit only a $25 or $50 penalty. If you cancel only 2 or 3 weeks before the flight, there may be no refund at all unless you or the operator can provide a substitute passenger.
2. Charter flights may be canceled by the operator up to 10 days before departure for any reason, usually underbooking. Your money is returned in this event, but there may be too little time for you to make new arrangements.
3. Most charters have little of the flexibility of regularly scheduled flights regarding refunds and the changing of flight dates; if you book a return flight, you must be on it or lose your money.
4. Charter operators are permitted to assess a surcharge, if fuel or other costs warrant it, of up to 10% of the airfare up to 10 days before departure.

5. Because of the economics of charter flights, your plane almost always will be full, so you will be crowded, though not necessarily uncomfortable. There is, however, a new movement among charter airlines to provide flight accommodations that are comfort-oriented. For instance, US-based *Tower Air* provides the equivalent of a business class section on its charter flights from the US to Rome.

To avoid problems, *always* choose charter flights with care. When you consider a charter, ask your travel agent who runs it and carefully check the company. The Better Business Bureau in the company's home city can report on how many complaints, if any, have been lodged against it in the past. Protect yourself with trip cancellation and interruption insurance, which can help safeguard your investment if you or a traveling companion is unable to make the trip and must cancel too late to receive a full refund from the company providing your travel services. (This is advisable whether you're buying a charter flight alone or a tour package for which the airfare is provided by charter or scheduled flight.)

Bookings – If you do fly on a charter, read the contract's fine print carefully and pay particular attention to the following:

Instructions concerning the payment of the deposit and its balance and to whom the check is to be made payable. Ordinarily, checks are made out to an escrow account, which means the charter company can't spend your money until your flight has safely returned. This provides some protection for you. To ensure the safe handling of your money, make out your check to the escrow account, the number of which must appear by law on the brochure, though all too often it is on the back in fine print. Write the details of the charter, including the destination and dates, on the face of the check; on the back, print "For Deposit Only." Your travel agent may prefer that you make out your check to the agency, saying that it will then pay the tour operator the fee minus commission. It is perfectly legal to write the check as we suggest, however, and if your agent objects too vociferously (he or she should trust the tour operator to send the proper commission), consider taking your business elsewhere. If you don't make your check out to the escrow account, you lose the protection of that escrow should the trip be canceled. Furthermore, recent bankruptcies in the travel industry have served to point out that even the protection of escrow may not be enough to safeguard a traveler's investment. More and more, insurance is becoming a necessity. The charter company should be bonded (usually by an insurance company), and if you want to file a claim against it, the claim should be sent to the bonding agent. The contract will set a time limit within which a claim must be filed.

Specific stipulations and penalties for cancellations. Most charters allow you to cancel up to 45 days in advance without major penalty, but some cancellation dates are 50 to 60 days before departure.

Stipulations regarding cancellation and major changes made by the charterer. US rules say that charter flights may not be canceled within 10 days of departure except when circumstances — such as natural disasters or political upheavals — make it impossible to fly. Charterers may make "major changes," however, such as in the date or place of departure or return, but you are entitled to cancel and receive a full refund if you don't accept these changes. A price increase of more than 10% at any time up to 10 days before departure is considered a major change; no price increase is allowed during the 10 days immediately before departure.

Among the charter operators flying between the US and Italy are the following:

Air Europa (136 E. 57th St., Suite 1602, New York, NY 10022; phone: 212-888-7010)

American Trans Air (PO Box 51609, Indianapolis, IN 46251; phone: 317-243-4150).

Council Charter (205 E. 42nd St., New York, NY 10017; phone: 800-223-7402 or 212-661-0311).

Tower Air (Hangar 8, JFK International Airport, Jamaica, NY 11430; phone: 718-917-4306).

Unitravel (1177 N. Warson Rd., St. Louis, MO 63132; phone: 800-325-2222 or 314-569-2501).

For the full range of possibilities at the time you plan to travel, you may want to subscribe to the travel newsletter *Jax Fax,* which regularly features a list of charter companies and packagers offering seats on charter flights and may be a source for other charter flights to Italy. For a year's subscription send a check or money order for $12 to *Jax Fax,* 397 Post Rd., Darien, CT 06820 (phone: 203-655-8746).

DISCOUNTS ON SCHEDULED FLIGHTS: Promotional fares often are called discount fares because they cost less than what used to be the standard airline fare — full-fare economy. Nevertheless, they cost the traveler the same whether they are bought through a travel agent or directly from the airline. Tickets that cost less if bought from some outlet other than the airline do exist, however. While it is likely that the vast majority of travelers flying to Italy in the near future will be doing so on a promotional fare or charter rather than on a "discount" air ticket of this sort, it still is a good idea for cost-conscious consumers to be aware of the latest developments in the budget airfare scene. Note that the following discussion makes clear-cut distinctions among the types of discounts available based on how they reach the consumer; in actual practice, the distinctions are not nearly so precise.

Courier Travel – There was a time when traveling as a courier was a sort of underground way to save money and visit otherwise unaffordable destinations, but more and more, this once exotic idea is becoming a very "establishment" exercise. "Courier" means no more than a traveler who accompanies freight of one sort or another, and typically that freight replaces what otherwise would be the traveler's checked baggage. Be prepared, therefore, to carry all your own personal travel gear in a carry-on bag. In addition, the so-called courier usually pays only a portion of the total airfare — the freight company pays the remainder — and the courier also may be assessed a small registration fee. Note that many courier flights can be booked in advance (sometimes as much as 3 months) and that flights usually are round trip.

There are dozens of courier companies operating actively around the globe, and several publications provide information on courier opportunities:

A Simple Guide to Courier Travel, by Jesse L. Riddle, is a particularly good reference guide to courier travel. Published by the Carriage Group (PO Box 2394, Lake Oswego, OR 97035; phone: 800-344-9375), it's available for $14.95, including postage and handling.

Travel Secrets (PO Box 2325, New York, NY 10108; phone: 212-245-8703). Provides information useful to those considering traveling as a courier and often lists specific US and Canadian courier companies. Monthly; a year's subscription costs $33.

Travel Unlimited (PO Box 1058, Allston, MA 02134-1058; no phone). Lists courier companies and agents worldwide. Monthly; for a year's subscription send $25.

World Courier News (PO Box 77471, San Francisco, CA 94107; no phone). Provides information on courier opportunities, as well as useful tips. Each issue highlights a different destination. Monthly; for a year's subscription send $20.

Among the companies that regularly send couriers to Italy are the following:

Courier Travel Service (530 Central Ave., Cedarhurst, NY 11516; phone: 800-922-2FLY or 516-374-2299).

Discount Travel International (152 W. 72nd St., Suite 223, New York, NY 10023; phone: 212-655-5151).

Excaliber International Courier (c/o *Way to Go Travel,* 3317 Barham Blvd., Hollywood, CA 90068; phone: 213-851-2572).
World Courier (13742 Guy Brewer Blvd., Jamaica, NY 11434; phone: 718-978-9552).

In addition, *Now Voyager* (74 Varick St., Suite 307, New York, NY 10013; phone: 212-431-1616) is a referral agency that matches would-be couriers up with courier companies.

Net Fare Sources – The newest notion for reducing the costs of travel services comes from travel agents who offer individual travelers "net" fares. Defined simply, a net fare is the bare minimum amount at which an airline or tour operator will carry a prospective traveler. It doesn't include the amount that normally would be paid to the travel agent as a commission. Traditionally, such commissions amount to about 10% on domestic fares and from 10% to 20% on international fares — not counting significant additions to these commission levels that are paid retroactively when agents sell more than a specific volume of tickets or trips for a single supplier. At press time, at least one travel agency in the US was offering travelers the opportunity to purchase tickets and/or tours for a net price. Instead of earning income from individual commissions, this agency assesses a fixed fee that may or may not provide a bargain for travelers; it requires a little arithmetic to determine whether to use the services of a net travel agent or those of one who accepts conventional commissions. One of the potential drawbacks of buying from agencies selling travel services at net fares is that some airlines refuse to do business with them, thus possibly limiting your flight options.

Travel Avenue is a fee-based agency that rebates its ordinary agency commission to the customer. For domestic flights, they will find the lowest retail fare, then rebate 7% to 10% (depending on the airline selected) of that price minus a $10 ticket-writing charge. The rebate percentage for international flights varies from 5% to 16% (again depending on the airline), and the ticket-writing fee is $25. The ticket-writing charge is imposed per ticket; if the ticket includes more than eight separate flights, an additional $10 or $25 fee is charged. Customers using free flight coupons pay the ticket-writing charge, plus an additional $5 coupon-processing fee.

Travel Avenue will rebate on all tickets including heavily discounted fares and senior citizen passes. Available 7 days a week, reservations should be made far enough in advance to allow the tickets to be sent by first class mail, since extra charges accrue for special handling. It's possible to economize further by making your own airline reservation, then asking *Travel Avenue* only to write/issue your ticket. For travelers outside the Chicago area, business may be transacted by phone and purchases charged to a credit card. For further information, contact *Travel Avenue* at 641 W. Lake St., Suite 201, Chicago, IL 60606-1012 (phone: 312-876-1116 in Illinois; 800-333-3335 elsewhere in the US).

Consolidators and Bucket Shops – Other vendors of travel services can afford to sell tickets to their customers at an even greater discount because the airline has sold the tickets to them at a substantial discount (usually accomplished by sharply increasing commissions to that vendor), a practice in which many airlines indulge, albeit discreetly, preferring that the general public not know they are undercutting their own "list" prices. Airlines anticipating a slow period on a particular route sometimes sell off a certain portion of their capacity at a very great discount to a wholesaler, or consolidator. The wholesaler sometimes is a charter operator who resells the seats to the public as though they were charter seats, which is why prospective travelers perusing the brochures of charter operators with large programs frequently see a number of flights designated as "scheduled service." As often as not, however, the consolidator, in turn, sells the seats to a travel agency specializing in discounting.

Airlines also can sell seats directly to such an agency, which thus acts as its own consolidator. The airline offers the seats either at a net wholesale price, but without the volume-purchase requirement that would be difficult for a modest retail travel agency to fulfill, or at the standard price, but with a commission override large enough (as high as 50%) to allow both a profit and a price reduction to the public.

Travel agencies specializing in discounting sometimes are called "bucket shops," a term fraught with connotations of unreliability in this country. But in today's highly competitive travel marketplace, more and more conventional travel agencies are selling consolidator-supplied tickets, and the old bucket shops' image is becoming respectable. Agencies that specialize in discounted tickets exist in most large cities, and usually can be found by studying the smaller ads in the travel sections of Sunday newspapers.

Before buying a discounted ticket, whether from a bucket shop or a conventional, full-service travel agency, keep the following considerations in mind: To be in a position to judge the amount of money you'll be saving, first find out the "list" prices of tickets to your destination. Then, do some comparison shopping among agencies. Also bear in mind that a ticket that may not differ much in price from one available directly from the airline may, however, allow the circumvention of such things as the advance purchase requirement. If your plans are less than final, be sure to find out about any other restrictions, such as penalties for canceling a flight or changing a reservation. Most discount tickets are non-endorsable, meaning they can be used only on the airline that issued them, and they usually are marked "nonrefundable" to prevent their being cashed in for a list price refund.

A great many bucket shops are small businesses operating on a thin margin, so it's a good idea to check the local Better Business Bureau for any complaints registered against the one with which you're dealing before parting with any money. If you still do not feel reassured, consider buying discounted tickets only through a conventional travel agency, which can be expected to have found its own reliable source of consolidator tickets — some of the largest consolidators, in fact, sell only to travel agencies.

A few bucket shops require payment in cash or by certified check or money order, but if credit cards are accepted, use that option. Note, however, if buying from a charter operator selling both scheduled and charter flights, that the scheduled seats are not protected by the regulations — including the use of escrow accounts — governing the charter seats. Well-established charter operators, nevertheless, may extend the same protections to their scheduled flights, and when this is the case, consumers should be sure that the payment option selected directs their money into the escrow account.

Among the numerous consolidators offering discount fares to Italy (and Europe in general) are the following:

Bargain Air (655 Deep Valley Dr., Suite 355, Rolling Hills, CA 90274; phone: 800-347-2345 or 213-377-2919).

Council Charter (205 E. 42nd St., New York, NY 10017; phone: 800-223-7402 or 212-661-0311).

Euro Asia Express (475 El Camino Real, Millbrae, CA 94030; phone: 800-782-9624 or 415-692-9966 in California; 800-782-9625 elsewhere in the US).

Maharaja/Consumer Wholesale (393 Fifth Ave., 2nd Floor, New York, NY 10016; phone: 212-213-2020 in New York State; 800-223-6862 elsewhere in the US).

TFI Tours International (34 W. 37th St., 12th Floor, New York, NY 10001; phone: 212-736-1140).

Travac Tours and Charters (989 Sixth Ave., New York, NY 10018; phone: 212-563-3303).

25 West Tours (2490 Coral Way, Miami, FL 33145; phone: 305-856-0810; 800-423-6954 in Florida; 800-252-5052 elsewhere in the US).

Unitravel (1177 N. Warson Rd., St. Louis, MO 63132; phone: 314-569-0900 in Missouri; 800-325-2222 elsewhere in the US).

■ **Note:** Although rebating and discounting are becoming increasingly common, there is some legal ambiguity concerning them. Strictly speaking, it is legal to discount domestic tickets, but not international tickets. On the other hand, the law that prohibits discounting, the Federal Aviation Act of 1958, is consistently ignored these days, in part because consumers benefit from the practice and in part because many illegal arrangements are indistinguishable from legal ones. Since the line separating the two is so fine that even the authorities can't always tell the difference, it is unlikely that most consumers would be able to do so, and in fact it is not illegal to *buy* a discounted ticket. If the issue of legality bothers you, ask the agency whether any ticket you're about to buy would be permissible under the above-mentioned act.

OTHER DISCOUNT TRAVEL SOURCES: An excellent source of information on economical travel opportunities is the *Consumer Reports Travel Letter,* published monthly by Consumers Union. It keeps abreast of the scene on a wide variety of fronts, including package tours, rental cars, insurance, and more, but it is especially helpful for its comprehensive coverage of airfares, offering guidance on all the options from scheduled flights on major or low-fare airlines to charters and discount sources. For a year's subscription, send $37 ($57 for 2 years) to *Consumer Reports Travel Letter* (PO Box 53629, Boulder, CO 80322-3629; phone: 800-999-7959). For information on other travel newsletters, see *Books, Newspapers, Magazines, and Newsletters,* in this section.

Last-Minute Travel Clubs – Still another way to take advantage of bargain airfares is open to those who have a flexible schedule. A number of organizations, usually set up as last-minute travel clubs and functioning on a membership basis, routinely keep in touch with travel suppliers to help them dispose of unsold inventory at discounts of between 15% and 60%. A great deal of the inventory consists of complete package tours and cruises, but some clubs offer air-only charter seats and, occasionally, seats on scheduled flights.

Members pay an annual fee and receive a toll-free hotline telephone number to call for information on imminent trips. In some cases, they also receive periodic mailings with information on bargain travel opportunities for which there is more advance notice. Despite the suggestive names of the clubs providing these services, last-minute travel does not necessarily mean that you cannot make plans until literally the last minute. Trips can be announced as little as a few days or as much as 2 months before departure, but the average is from 1 to 4 weeks' notice.

Among the organizations regularly offering such discounted travel opportunities to Italy are the following:

Discount Club of America (61-33 Woodhaven Blvd., Rego Park, NY 11374; phone: 800-321-9587 or 718-335-9612). Annual fee: $39 per family.

Discount Travel International (Ives Building, 114 Forrest Ave., Suite 205, Narberth, PA 19072; phone: 800-334-9294 or 215-668-7184). Annual fee: $45 per household.

Encore Short Notice (4501 Forbes Blvd., Lanham, MD 20706; phone: 301-459-8020; 800-638-0930 for customer service). Annual fee: $48 per family.

Last Minute Travel (1249 Boylston St., Boston, MA 02215; phone: 800-LAST-MIN or 617-267-9800). No fee.

Moment's Notice (425 Madison Ave., New York, NY 10017; phone: 212-486-0503). Annual fee: $19.95 per family.

Spur-of-the-Moment Tours and Cruises (10780 Jefferson Blvd., Culver City, CA

90230; phone: 213-839-2418 in California; 800-343-1991 elsewhere in the US). No fee.

Traveler's Advantage (3033 S. Parker Rd., Suite 1000, Aurora, CO 80014; phone: 800-548-1116). Annual fee: $49 per family.

Vacations to Go (2411 Fountain View, Suite 201, Houston, TX 77057; phone: 800-338-4962). Annual fee: $19.95 per family.

Worldwide Discount Travel Club (1674 Meridian Ave., Miami Beach, FL 33139; phone: 305-534-2082). Annual fee: $40 per person; $50 per family.

Generic Air Travel – Organizations that apply the same flexible-schedule idea to air travel only and sell tickets at literally the last minute also exist. The service they provide sometimes is known as "generic" air travel, and it operates somewhat like an ordinary airline standby service, except that the organizations running it offer seats on not one but several scheduled and charter airlines.

One pioneer of generic flights is *Airhitch* (2790 Broadway, Suite 100, New York, NY 10025; phone: 212-864-2000), which arranges flights to Italy from various US gateways. Prospective travelers register by paying a fee (applicable toward the fare) and stipulate a range of acceptable departure dates and their desired destination, along with alternate choices. The week before the date range begins, they are notified of at least two flights that will be available during the time period, agree on one, and remit the balance of the fare to the company. If they do not accept any of the suggested flights, they lose their deposit; if, through no fault of their own, they do not ultimately get on any agreed-on flight, all of their money is refunded. Return flights are arranged the same way.

Bartered Travel – Suppose a hotel buys advertising space in a newspaper. As payment, the hotel gives the publishing company the use of a number of hotel rooms in lieu of cash. This is barter, a common means of exchange among hotels, airlines, car rental companies, cruise lines, tour operators, restaurants, and other travel service companies. When a bartering company finds itself with empty airline seats (or excess hotel rooms, or cruise ship cabin space, and so on) and offers them to the public, considerable savings can be enjoyed.

Bartered-travel clubs often offer discounts of up to 50% to members, who pay an annual fee (approximately $50 at press time) which entitles them to select the flights, cruises, hotel rooms, or other travel services that the club obtained by barter. Members usually present a voucher, club credit card, or scrip (a dollar-denomination voucher negotiable only for the bartered product) to the hotel, which in turn subtracts the dollar amount from the bartering company's account.

Selling bartered travel is a perfectly legitimate means of retailing. One advantage to club members is that they don't have to wait until the last minute to obtain flight or room reservations.

Among the companies specializing in bartered travel, several that frequently offer members travel services to and in Italy include the following:

IGT (In Good Taste) Services (1111 Lincoln Rd., 4th Floor, Miami Beach, FL 33139; phone: 800-444-8872 or 305-534-7900). Annual fee: $48 per family.

Travel Guild (18210 Redmond Way, Redmond, WA 98052; phone: 206-861-1900). Annual fee: $48 per family.

Travel World Leisure Club (225 W. 34th St., Suite 2203, New York, NY 10122; phone: 800-444-TWLC or 212-239-4855). Annual fee: $50 per family.

CONSUMER PROTECTION: Consumers who feel that they have not been dealt with fairly by an airline should make their complaints known. Begin with the customer service representative at the airport where the problem occurs. If he or she cannot resolve your complaint to your satisfaction, write to the airline's consumer office. In a businesslike, typed letter, explain what reservations you held, what happened, the names of the employees involved, and what you expect the airline to do to remedy the situation. Send copies (never the originals) of the tickets, receipts, and other documents that back your claims. Ideally, all correspondence should be sent via certified mail, return receipt requested. This provides proof that your complaint was received.

Passengers with consumer complaints — lost baggage, compensation for getting bumped, violations of smoking and nonsmoking rules, deceptive practices by an airline, charter regulations — who are not satisfied with the airline's response should contact the US Department of Transportation (DOT), Consumer Affairs Division (400 Seventh St. SW, Room 10405, Washington, DC 20590; phone: 202-366-2220). DOT personnel stress, however, that consumers initially should direct their complaints to the airline that provoked them.

Travelers with an unresolved complaint involving a foreign carrier also can contact the US Department of Transportation. DOT personnel will do what they can to help resolve all such complaints, although their influence may be limited.

Consumers with complaints against specific Italian airlines or other travel-related services can write to the local tourist board (the Azienda Provinciale di Turismo) in the city where the problem occurred — the national tourist office (see *Tourist Information Offices,* in this section) should be able to provide this information. Outline the specifics in Italian in as much detail as possible. (Keep in mind that, if a translator is required, this correspondence could get expensive.) The tourist board will try to resolve the complaint or, if it is out of their jurisdiction, will refer the matter to the proper authorities, and will notify you in writing (in Italian) of the result of their inquiries and/or any action taken.

Remember, too, that the federal Fair Credit Billing Act permits purchasers to refuse payment for credit card charges where services have not been delivered, so the onus of dealing with the receiver for a bankrupt airline falls on the credit card company. Do not rely on another airline to honor the ticket you're holding, since the days when virtually all major carriers subscribed to a default protection program that bound them to do so are long gone. Some airlines may voluntarily step forward to accommodate the stranded passengers of a fellow carrier, but this is now an entirely altruistic act.

The deregulation of US airlines has meant that a traveler must find out for himself or herself what he or she is entitled to receive. The US Department of Transportation's informative consumer booklet, *Fly Rights,* is a good place to start. To receive a copy, send $1 to the Superintendent of Documents (US Government Printing Office, Washington, DC 20402-9325; phone: 202-783-3238). Specify its stock number, 050-000-00513-5, and allow 3 to 4 weeks for delivery.

■ **Note:** Those who tend to experience discomfort due to the change in air pressure while flying may be interested in the free pamphlet *Ears, Altitude and Airplane Travel;* for a copy send a self-addressed, stamped, business-size envelope to the *American Academy of Otolaryngology* (One Prince St., Alexandria, VA 22314; phone: 703-836-4444). And for when you land, *Overcoming Jet Lag* offers some helpful tips on minimizing post-flight stress; it is available from Berkeley Publishing Group (PO Box 506, Mail Order Dept., East Rutherford, NJ 07073; phone: 800-631-8571) for $6.95, plus shipping and handling.

Traveling by Ship

There was a time when traveling by ship was extraordinarily expensive, time consuming, utterly elegant, and was utilized almost exclusively for getting from one point to another. Alas, the days when steamships reigned as the primary means of transatlantic transportation are gone, days when Italy,

France, Sweden, Germany, Norway, the Netherlands, and England — and the US — had fleets of passenger liners that offered week-plus trips across the North Atlantic. Only one ship (*Cunard*'s *Queen Elizabeth 2*) continues to offer this kind of service between the US and Europe with any degree of regularity; others make "positioning" cruises a few times a year at most. At the same time, the possibility of booking passage to Europe on a cargo ship is becoming less practical. Fewer and fewer travelers, therefore, first set foot on Italian soil with sea legs developed during an ocean voyage.

Although fewer travelers to Europe are choosing sea travel as a means of transport to a specific destination, more and more people are cruising *around* Europe. No longer primarily pure transportation, cruising currently is riding a wave of popularity as a leisure activity in its own right, and the host of new ships (and dozens of rebuilt old ones) testifies dramatically to the attraction of vacationing on the high seas. And due to the growing popularity of travel along coastal and inland waterways, more and more travelers — particularly repeat travelers — are climbing aboard some kind of waterborne conveyance once they've arrived in Europe, and are seeing Italy as part of a Mediterranean cruise, from the banks of a canal or river, or taking a ferry to one of the Italian islands.

Many modern-day cruise ships seem much more like motels-at-sea than the classic liners of a couple of generations ago, but they are consistently comfortable and passengers often are pampered. Cruise prices are quite reasonable, and since the single cruise price covers all the major items in a typical vacation — transportation, accommodations, all meals, and entertainment, and a full range of social activities, sports, and recreation — a traveler need not fear any unexpected assaults on the family travel budget.

When selecting a cruise, your basic criteria should be where you want to go, the time you have available, how much you want to spend, and the kind of environment that best suits your style and taste (in which case price is an important determinant). Rely on the suggestions of a travel agent — preferably one specializing in cruises (see "A final note on picking a cruise," below) — but be honest with the agent (and with yourself) in describing the type of atmosphere you're seeking. Ask for suggestions from friends who have been on cruises; if you trust their judgment, they should be able to suggest a ship on which you'll feel comfortable.

There are a number of moments in the cruise-planning process when discounts are available from the major cruise lines, so it may be possible to enjoy some diminution of the list price almost anytime you book passage on a cruise ship. For those willing to commit early — say 4 to 6 months before sailing — most of the major cruise lines routinely offer a 10% reduction off posted prices, in addition to the widest selection of cabins. For those who decide to sail rather late in the game — say, 4 to 6 weeks before departure — savings often are even greater — an average of 20% — as steamship lines try to fill up their ships. The only negative aspect is that the choice of cabins tends to be limited, although it is possible that a fare upgrade will be offered to make this limited cabin selection more palatable. In addition, there's the option of buying from a discount travel club or a travel agency that specializes in last-minute bargains; these discounters and other discount travel sources are discussed at the end of *Traveling by Plane,* above.

Most of the time, the inclusion of air transportation in the cruise package costs significantly less than if you were to buy the cruise separately and arrange your own air transportation to the port. If you do decide on one of these economical air/sea packages, be forewarned that it is not unusual for the pre-arranged flight arrangements to be less than convenient. The problems often arrive with the receipt of your cruise ticket, which also includes the airline ticket for the flight to get you to and from the ship dock. This is normally the first time you see the flights on which you have been booked and can appraise the convenience of the departure and arrival times. The cruise ship lines generally are not very forthcoming about altering flight schedules, and your own travel agent also may have difficulty in rearranging flight times or carriers. That means that the only remaining alternative is to ask the line to forget about making your flight arrangements and to pay for them separately by yourself. This may be more costly, but it's more likely to give you an arrival and departure schedule that will best conform to the sailing and docking times of the ship on which you will be cruising.

Cruise lines promote sailings to and around Europe as "get away from it all" vacations. But prospective cruise ship passengers will find that the variety of cruises is tremendous, and the quality, while generally high, varies depending on shipboard services, the tone of shipboard life, the cost of the cruise, and operative itineraries. Although there are less expensive ways to see Europe, the romance and enjoyment of a sea voyage remain irresistible for many, so a few points should be considered by such sojourners before they sign on for a seagoing vacation (after all, it's hard to get off in mid-ocean). Herewith, a rundown on what to expect from a cruise, a few suggestions on what to look for and arrange when purchasing passage on one, and some representative sailings to and around Italy.

CABINS: The most important factor in determining the price of a cruise is the cabin. Cabin prices are set according to size and location. The size can vary considerably on older ships, less so on newer or more recently modernized ones, and may be entirely uniform on the very newest vessels.

Shipboard accommodations utilize the same pricing pattern as hotels. Suites, which consist of a sitting room–bedroom combination and occasionally a private small deck that could be compared to a patio, cost the most. Prices for other cabins (interchangeably called staterooms) usually are more expensive on the upper passenger decks, less expensive on lower decks; if a cabin has a bathtub instead of a shower, the price probably will be higher. The outside cabins with portholes cost more than inside cabins without views and generally are preferred — although many experienced cruise passengers eschew the more expensive accommodations for they know they will spend very few waking hours in their cabins. As in all forms of travel, accommodations are more expensive for single travelers. If you are traveling on your own but want to share a double cabin to reduce the cost, some ship lines will attempt to find someone of the same sex willing to share quarters (see *Hints for Single Travelers,* in this section).

FACILITIES AND ACTIVITIES: You may not use your cabin very much — organized shipboard activities are geared to keep you busy. A standard schedule might consist of swimming, sunbathing, and numerous other outdoor recreations. Evenings are devoted to leisurely dining, lounge shows or movies, bingo and other organized games, gambling, dancing, and a midnight buffet. Your cruise fare includes all of these activities — except the cost of drinks.

Most cruise ships have at least one major social lounge, a main dining room, several bars, an entertainment room that may double as a discotheque for late dancing, an exercise room, indoor games facilities, at least one pool, and shopping facilities, which can range from a single boutique to an arcade. Still others have gambling casinos and/or slot machines, card rooms, libraries, children's recreation centers, indoor pools (as well as one or more on open decks), separate movie theaters, and private meeting rooms. Open deck space should be ample, because this is where most passengers spend their days at sea.

Usually there is a social director and staff to organize and coordinate activities. Evening entertainment is provided by professionals. Movies are mostly first-run and drinks are moderate in price (or should be) because a ship is exempt from local taxes when at sea.

■ **Note:** To be prepared for possible illnesses at sea, travelers should get a prescription from their doctor for medicine to counteract motion sickness. All ships with more than 12 passengers have a doctor on board, plus facilities for handling sickness or medical emergencies.

Shore Excursions – These side trips almost always are optional and available at extra cost. Before you leave, do a little basic research about the Italian ports you'll be visiting and decide what sights will interest you. If several of the most compelling of these are some distance from the pier where your ship docks, chances are that paying for a shore excursion will be worth the money.

Shore excursions usually can be booked through your travel agent at the same time you make your cruise booking, but this is worthwhile only if you can get complete details on the nature of each excursion being offered. If you can't get these details, better opt to purchase your shore arrangements after you're on board. Your enthusiasm for an excursion may be higher once you are on board because you will have met other passengers with whom to share the excitement of "shore leave." And depending on your time in port, you may decide to eschew the guided tour and venture out on your own.

Meals – All meals on board almost always are included in the basic price of a cruise, and the food generally is abundant and quite palatable. Evening meals are taken in the main dining room, where tables are assigned according to the passengers' preferences. Tables usually accommodate from 2 to 10; specify your preference when you book your cruise. If there are two sittings, you also can specify which one you want at the time you book or, at the latest, when you board the ship. Later sittings usually are more leisurely. Breakfast frequently is available in your cabin, as well as in the main dining room. For lunch, many passengers prefer the buffet offered on deck, usually at or near the pool, but again, the main dining room is available.

DRESS: Most people pack too much for a cruise on the assumption that their daily attire should be chic and every night is a big event. Comfort is a more realistic criterion. Daytime wear on most ships is decidedly casual. Evening wear for most cruises is dressy-casual. Formal attire probably is not necessary for 1-week cruises, optional for longer ones. (For information on choosing and packing a basic wardrobe, see *How to Pack,* in this section.)

TIPS: Tips are a strictly personal expense, and you *are* expected to tip — in particular, your cabin and dining room stewards. The general rule of thumb (or palm) is to expect to pay from 10% to 20% of your total cruise budget for gratuities — the actual amount within this range is based on the length of the cruise and the extent of personalized services provided. Allow $2 to $5 a day for each cabin and dining room steward (more if you wish), and additional sums for very good service. (*Note:* Tips should be paid by and for each individual in a cabin, whether there are one, two, or more.) Others who may merit tips are the deck steward who sets up your chair at the pool or elsewhere, the wine steward in the dining room, porters who handle your luggage (tip them individually at the time they assist you), and any others who provide personal service. On some ships you can charge your bar tab to your cabin; throw in the tip when you pay it at the end of the cruise. Smart travelers tip twice during the trip: about midway through the cruise and at the end; even wiser travelers tip a bit at the start of the trip to ensure better service throughout.

Although some cruise lines do have a no-tipping policy and you are not penalized by the crew for not tipping, naturally, you aren't penalized for tipping, either. If you can restrain yourself, it is better not to tip on those few ships that discourage it. However, never make the mistake of not tipping on the majority of ships, where it is a common, expected practice. (For further information on calculating gratuities, see *Tipping,* in this section.)

SHIP SANITATION: The US Public Health Service (PHS) currently inspects all passenger vessels calling at US ports, so very precise information is available on which ships meet its requirements and which do not. The further requirement that ships immediately report any illness that occurs on board adds to the available data.

The problem for a prospective cruise passenger is to determine whether the ship on which he or she plans to sail has met the official sanitary standard. US regulations require the PHS to publish actual grades for the ships inspected (rather than the old pass or fail designation), so it's now easy to determine any cruise ship's status. Nearly 4,000 travel agents, public health organizations, and doctors receive a copy of each monthly ship sanitation summary, but be aware that not all travel agents fully understand what this ship inspection program is all about. The best advice is to deal with a travel agent who specializes in cruise bookings, for he or she is most likely to have the latest information on the sanitary conditions of all cruise ships (see "A final note on picking a cruise," below). To receive a copy of the most recent summary or a particular inspection report, contact Chief, Vessel Sanitation Program, Center for Environmental Health and Injury Control, 1015 N. America Way, Room 107, Miami, FL 33132 (phone: 305-536-4307).

TRANSATLANTIC CROSSINGS: There are several cruise lines that sail between the US and Europe. Some include Italian ports as part of their European itinerary, while on others passengers may disembark at ports elsewhere in the Mediterranean and sail, fly, or drive to Italy.

For seagoing enthusiasts, *Cunard*'s *Queen Elizabeth 2* is one of the largest and most comfortable vessels afloat and each year the *QE2* schedules approximately a dozen round-trip transatlantic crossings between June and, usually, December. The *QE2* normally sets its course from New York to Southampton, England (a 5-day trip), and then sails directly back to the US, although on a few of the crossings it proceeds from Southampton to Cherbourg, France, or to other European ports before turning back across the Atlantic. (Similarly, on some crossings, the ship calls at various East Coast US ports in addition to New York, thus giving passengers a choice of where to embark or disembark.)

For travelers on crossings *not* scheduled to call at their desired destination, travelers can take an intra-European flight from Southampton to Italy, and then take a transatlantic flight home. Another alternative is to take one of the ferries departing from Southampton — such as the *Sealink* ferry from Southampton to Le Havre, France — and make connections onward to Italy.

For those sailing to Europe on the *QE2* and flying home, another option for travel in Italy is based on the validity period of the return ticket. Following the transatlantic crossing, passengers have a specified time — up to 40 days for first class passengers and 15 days for the less expensive fares — during which they can tour Italy. Usually the included transatlantic flight must be to selected US gateways served by *British Airways,* but passengers may return to other gateways by paying a supplement. Those who want to splurge can apply the air allowance included in such air/sea packages toward a ticket aboard *British Airways*' supersonic *Concorde,* although the difference between the basic allowance and the *Concorde* fare is substantial. There are no maximum stay restrictions for passengers who upgrade to a return flight on the *Concorde.*

Cunard also offers various European tour packages applicable to the basic air/sea offer. Among the packages offered is an Alpine Splendor package, featuring a stop in the Italian Dolomites, and a Best of Europe package, including a trip on the famed *Venice Simplon–Orient Express* train. (For further information on this luxury train, see *Traveling by Train,* in this section.) For further information, check with your travel agent, call *British Airways* (phone: 800-AIRWAYS), or contact *Cunard* (555 Fifth Ave., New York, NY 10017; phone: 800-872-4770 or 800-5-CUNARD).

Positioning Cruises – Another interesting possibility for those who have the time is what the industry calls a positioning cruise. This is the sailing of a US- or Caribbean-based vessel from its winter berth to the city in Europe from which it will be offering summer cruise programs. Eastbound positioning cruises take place in the spring; westbound cruises return in the fall. Since ships do not make the return trip until they need to position themselves for the next cruise season, most lines offering positioning cruises have some air/sea arrangement that allows passengers to fly home economically — though the cruises themselves are not an inexpensive way to travel.

Typically, the ships set sail from Florida or from San Juan, Puerto Rico, and cross the Atlantic to any one of a number of European ports where the trip may be broken — including Italian ports such as Genoa and Venice — before proceeding to cruise European waters (for example, the Mediterranean, the Baltic Sea, the Black Sea, the Norwegian fjords). Passengers can elect to stay aboard for the basic transatlantic segment alone or for both the crossing and the subsequent European cruise. Ports of call on such crossings and subsequent itineraries may vary substantially from year to year. For the most current information on operative itineraries, ask your travel agent or contact the cruise line directly.

Among the ships that offer positioning cruises to Italy are the following:

Royal Cruise Line (One Maritime Plaza, Suite 1400, San Francisco, CA 94111; phone: 800-227-5628 or 415-956-7200). Offers a 19-day transatlantic positioning cruise aboard the *Golden Odyssey* from Aruba (in the Caribbean) to Venice. This year, *Royal Cruise Line*'s *Crown Odyssey* also will make a 21-day trip from San Juan (Puerto Rico) to Athens, with a stop in Rome.

Royal Viking Line (95 Merrick Way, Coral Gables, FL 33134; phone: 800-422-8000). The *Royal Viking Sun* makes a 20-day westbound positioning cruise between Rome and Ft. Lauderdale.

Sun Line (1 Rockefeller Plaza, Suite 315, New York, NY 10020; phone: 800-445-6400 or 212-397-6400). The *Stella Solaris* makes a 21-day cruise from Ft. Lauderdale to Piraeus (Greece) that includes a stop in Livorno, Messina, and Rome.

INTRA-EUROPEAN CRUISES: The Mediterranean Sea is one of the world's most popular and picturesque cruising grounds, busy with ships offering sailings of varying lengths from spring through fall. But while many Mediterranean cruises include at least one stop in Italy and many begin or end in an Italian port, few regularly devote a significant portion of the itinerary to exploring Italian territory. Those interested in including a cruise to other European waters before, during, or after their trip to Italy will, however, find that a number of European cruises depart from Italian ports — primarily Genoa and Venice. (Also see *Sailing the Seas of Italy,* DIVERSIONS.)

Among the intra-European cruises calling at Italian ports are the following:

Club Med (3 E. 54th St., New York, NY 10022; phone: 800-CLUB-MED). The 617-foot *Club Med I* vessel makes 7-day round-trip sailings from Toulon (France) that stop in Portofino and Portovenere.

Costa Cruises (World Trade Center, 80 SW 8th St., Miami, FL 33130-3097; phone: 800-447-6877). The *Costa Marina* makes 7-day round-trip cruises from Genoa that stop in Palermo and Naples. The *Danae* makes 11-day cruises between Venice and Athens (Greece) that stop in Taormina. The *Eugenio Costa* makes 10-day round-trip cruises from Genoa that stop in Naples. The *Enrico Costa* makes 7-day round-trip cruises from Venice.

Crystal Cruises (2121 Ave. of the Stars, Los Angeles, CA 90067; phone 800-446-6645). Offers 12-day cruises aboard the *Crystal Harmony* between Rome and Lisbon (Portugal) that stop in Livorno and Naples. This ship also makes 13-day cruises between Rome and Piraeus (Greece) that stop in Naples and Venice, as well as 13-day round-trip cruises from Rome that also call at these ports.

Cunard (555 Fifth Ave., New York, NY 10017; phone: 800-872-4770 or 800-5-CUNARD). The *QE2* makes 10-day round-trip intra-European sailings from Southampton that call at Naples. The luxurious *Sea Goddess I* and *Sea Goddess II* both offer 7- and 10-night cruises aboard these ships that feature stops in

Capri, Portofino, Rome, Sorrento, and Taormina. The *Princess* makes 14-day cruises between Venice and Athens (Greece), as well as 7-day round-trip voyages from Venice, stopping in Catania on Sicily.

Epirotiki Lines (551 Fifth Ave., New York, NY 10176; phone: 800-221-2470 or 212-599-1750). Their 14-night cruises, aboard the *Odysseus,* sail between Venice and Genoa and call at Messina.

Ocean Cruise Lines (1510 SE 17th St., Ft. Lauderdale, FL 33316; phone: 800-556-8850 or 305-764-3500). The *Ocean Princess* makes 7-day cruises between Venice and Nice (France) that stop at Elba, Sorrento, and the Lipari Islands.

Paquet French Cruises (240 S. Country Rd., Palm Beach, FL 33480; phone: 800-999-0555). Their 18-day Music Festival round-trip cruise from Toulon aboard the *Mermoz* includes a visit in Livorno, Naples, and Sicily.

P&O Cruises (c/o *Express Travel Services,* Empire State Building, Suite 7718, 350 Fifth Ave., New York, NY 10118; phone: 800-223-5799 or 212-629-3630). Offers a number of 2-week cruises that begin and end in Southampton (England). Among Italian ports visited aboard the *Canberra* are Cagliari, Genoa, Naples, Livorno, and Trieste. The *Sea Princess* calls at Alghero, Civitavecchia, Elba, Golfo Aranci, Livorno, Naples, and Santa Margherita.

Princess Cruises (10100 Santa Monica Blvd., Los Angeles, CA 90067; phone: 800-421-0522). Offers a 12-day cruise aboard the *Royal Princess* between Venice and Barcelona (Spain); ports of call include Livorno, Messina, and Rome. This ship also sails between Barcelona and London, calling at Livorno and Rome.

Raymond & Whitcomb (400 Madison Ave., New York, NY 10017; phone: 212-759-3960). Offers a 12-night voyage aboard the *Argonaut* that sails between Genoa and Lisbon (Portugal); this ship also makes 15-day sailings between Genoa and Venice. Both cruises call at Calabria, Palermo, Pisa, Ravello, and Ravenna.

Royal Cruise Line (One Maritime Plaza, Suite 1400, San Francisco, CA 94111; phone: 800-227-5628 or 415-956-7200). The *Crown Odyssey* makes a 12-day Great Capitals of Europe that starts in London and ends in Venice; ports of call include Portofino and Rome. Other sailings aboard the *Crown Odyssey* include two 12-day cruises that depart from Lisbon (Portugal); the first stops Florence and Rome, the second in Rome and Taormina. The *Golden Odyssey* makes 12-day Best of Italy, France, and the Greek Isles cruise that stops in Capri, Portofino, and Ravenna.

Royal Viking Line (95 Merrick, Coral Gables, FL 33134; phone: 800-634-8000 or 305-422-8000). The *Royal Viking Queen* makes 12-day cruises between Seville (Spain) to Venice that stop in Sicily en route. This ship also sails on week-long cruises from Venice to Athens. The *Royal Viking Sun* makes 7-day cruises between Monte Carlo and Genoa and 10-day cruises between Athens and Venice.

Sea Bourn Cruise Lines (55 Francisco St., San Francisco, CA 94133; phone: 800-351-9595). The luxurious *Sea Bourn Pride* and the *Sea Bourn Spirit* both offer a variety of intra-European cruises each year, including a 7-day Mediterranean cruise departing from Venice that also calls at Civitavecchia (the port for Rome). Although you can contact *Sea Bourn Cruise Lines* for a brochure, for additional information and reservations, contact a travel agent.

Sun Lines (1 Rockefeller Plaza, Suite 315, New York, NY 10020; phone: 800-445-6400 or 212-397-6400). The *Stella Maris* makes a 7-day round-trip cruise between Venice and Nice (France); ports of call including Capri, Elba, Messina, Portofino, and Sorrento.

Swan Hellenic Cruises (c/o *Esplanade Tours,* 581 Boylston St., Boston, MA

02116; phone: 800-426-5492 or 617-266-7465). Offers a variety of 17-day Mediterranean cruises departing from Venice; Genoa, Naples, and Sicily are among the Italian ports of call.

Wind Star Cruises (300 Elliot Ave. W., Seattle, WA 98119; phone: 800-258-7245). The *Wind Star* makes 7-day round-trip cruises from Nice that stop in Portofino and Portovenere.

FREIGHTERS: An alternative to cruise ships is travel by freighter. These are cargo ships that also take a limited number of passengers (usually about 12) in reasonably comfortable accommodations. The idea of traveling by freighter has long appealed to romantic souls, but there are a number of drawbacks to keep in mind before casting off. Once upon a time, a major advantage of freighter travel was its low cost, but this is no longer the case. Though freighters usually are less expensive than cruise ships, the difference is not as great as it once was. Accommodations and recreational facilities vary, but freighters were not designed to amuse passengers, so it is important to appreciate the idea of freighter travel itself. Schedules are erratic, and the traveler must fit his or her timetable to that of the ship. Passengers have found themselves waiting as long as a month for a promised sailing, and because freighters follow their cargo commitments, it is possible that a scheduled port could be omitted at the last minute or a new one added.

Anyone contemplating taking a freighter from a US port across the Atlantic should be aware that at press time, only two freighter lines were carrying passengers on such crossings:

Lykes Lines (Lykes Center, 300 Poydras St., New Orleans, LA 70130; phone: 504-523-6611 in Louisiana; 800-535-1861 elsewhere). This line sails every 14 days from Galveston, Texas (via the East Coast, where Port Newark is the final port of embarkation) to the western and eastern Mediterranean, stopping first at Livorno (Italy), then in Turkey, Israel, and Egypt, again at Livorno, and then at Naples (Italy), before turning back across the Atlantic. This lines also sails from New Orleans and Norfolk (Virginia) to Antwerp (Belgium), Bremerhaven (Germany), Felixstowe (England), Le Havre (France), and Rotterdam (the Netherlands).

Yugoslav Great Lakes Lines (c/o *Freighter World Cruises;* see listing below). Offers freighter service from Montreal (Canada) to Italian ports. There generally are two departures each month and depending on the cargo, the usual route is a first port of call in Yugoslavia, followed by Genoa, Livorno, Naples or Salerno, and Trieste.

The following specialists deal only (or largely) in freighter travel. They provide information, schedules, and, when you're ready to sail, booking services.

Freighter World Cruises, Inc. (180 S. Lake Ave., Suite 335, Pasadena, CA 91101; phone: 818-449-3106). A freighter travel agency that acts as general agent for several freighter lines. Publishes the twice-monthly *Freighter Space Advisory,* listing space available on sailings worldwide. A subscription costs $27 a year, $25 of which can be credited toward the cost of a cruise.

Pearl's Travel Tips (9903 Oaks Lane, Seminole, FL 34642; phone: 813-393-2919). Run by Ilse Hoffman, who finds sailings for her customers and sends them off with all kinds of valuable information and advice.

TravLtips Cruise and Freighter Travel Association (PO Box 188, Flushing, NY 11358; phone: 800-872-8584 or 718-939-2400). A freighter travel agency and club ($15 per year or $25 for 2 years) whose members receive the bimonthly *TravLtips* magazine of cruise and freighter travel.

Those interested in freighter travel also may want to subscribe to *Freighter Travel News,* a publication of the *Freighter Travel Club of America.* A year's subscription to this monthly newsletter costs $18. To subscribe, write to the club at 3524 Harts Lake Rd., Roy, WA 98580.

Another monthly newsletter that may be of interest to those planning to cruise European waters is *Ocean and Cruise News,* which offers comprehensive coverage of the latest on the cruise ship scene. A year's subscription costs $24. Contact *Ocean and Cruise News,* PO Box 92, Stamford, CT 06904 (phone: 203-329-2787).

■ **A final note on picking a cruise:** A "cruise-only" travel agency can best help you choose a cruise ship and itinerary. Cruise-only agents are best equipped to tell you about a particular ship's "personality," the kind of person with whom you'll likely be traveling on a particular ship, what dress is acceptable (it varies from ship to ship), and much more. Travel agencies that specialize in booking cruises usually are members of the *National Association of Cruise Only Agencies (NACOA).* For a listing of the agencies in your area (requests are limited to three states), send a self-addressed, stamped envelope to *NACOA,* PO Box 7209, Freeport, NY 11520, or call 516-378-8006.

FERRIES: Numerous ferries link the Italian mainland with Sicily and Sardinia, with the many smaller Italian islands, and with other Mediterranean countries. Nearly all of them carry both passengers and cars — you simply drive on and drive off in most cases — and most routes are in service year-round. Some operators offer reduced rates for round-trip excursions, midweek travel, or off-season travel. Space for cars should be booked as early as possible, especially for July and August crossings, even though most lines schedule more frequent departures during the summer. Note that long journeys, of 8 to 10 hours or more, tend to be scheduled overnight.

Italy's largest shipping line, *Tirrenia,* operates most of the car- and passenger-carrying services from the mainland to Sicily and Sardinia and between the two islands, including daily service between Naples and Palermo on Sicily (a 10-hour ride), between Genoa and Porto Torres on Sardinia (12½ hours), between Civitavecchia (the port for Rome) and Olbia on Sardinia (7 hours), and between Civitavecchia and Cagliari on Sardinia (13 hours). Other *Tirrenia* services, varying from once a week to three or four times weekly, include connections from Genoa to Palermo (a 23-hour ride, the longest route), from Naples to Catania on Sicily, from Genoa to Cagliari and Olbia, from Naples and Livorno to Cagliari, and from Livorno to Porto Torres. In addition, service is offered once or twice weekly between Palermo and Cagliari and between Cagliari and Trapani on Sicily.

All of these services are overnight, and the least expensive ticket, deck class (*posto ponte*), does not necessarily buy a seat. A reserved armchair (*poltrona*) indoors that reclines airline-style costs a bit more; second and first class cabins cost still more. In Italy, reservations can be made and tickets purchased at *Tirrenia* offices in the cities served and through travel agents. Reservations and tickets for cars and first and second class cabins (but not *poltrone*) also are available from *Tirrenia*'s representative in the US, *Extra Value Travel* (683 S. Collier Blvd., Marco Island, FL 33937; phone: 813-394-3384). Allow plenty of time to make the arrangements — at least 3 weeks before your trip off-season and 2 to 3 months in advance for summer crossings.

Other companies provide additional service between the mainland and Italy's two largest islands. Among these are *Trans Tirreno Express* and *Italian State Railways (Ferrovie Italiane dello Stato),* whose car and passenger ferries connect Civitavecchia with Golfo Aranci, Sardinia, and Villa San Giovanni and Reggio Calabria with Messina, Sicily. Sicily also is connected to the mainland by *Aliscafi SNAV* hydrofoils, which make the crossing from Naples to Palermo (summer only, via the island of Ustica) in only 5 hours (compared with 10 hours by ferry) and shorten the crossing from Reggio Calabria to Messina to only 20 minutes. For the addresses of the *Italian State Railways,* see *Traveling by Train,* in this section; for information on *Trans Tirreno Express* service, ask at local tourist offices in Italy.

Ferries operated by *Siremar* (in Palermo; phone: 91-582-688), *Caremar* (in Naples; phone: 81-551-5384) and *Toremar* (in Livorno; phone: 586-896-372) make connections with the smaller Italian islands. *Siremar* car and passenger ferries leave from Naples and Milazzo, Sicily, for the main islands of the Aeolian, or Lipari, group (Lipari, Stromboli, Panarea, Vulcano, Salina, Filicudi, Alicudi) lying north of Sicily. Hydrofoil service from the mainland and Sicily to and between various of the same islands is provided by *Siremar* and *Aliscafi SNAV* (in Naples; phone: 81-761-2348). The island of Ustica, north of Palermo, is reached by *Siremar* ferries and hydrofoils from Palermo, as well as by *Aliscafi SNAV* hydrofoils (summer only) from Naples. The Egadi Islands (Favignana, Levanzo, Marettimo), just off the west coast of Sicily, also are served by *Siremar* ferries and hydrofoils departing from Trapani; and the island of Pantelleria, closer to Tunisia than to Sicily, and the faraway Pelagie Islands (Lampedusa and Linosa) are reached by *Siremar* ferries only, the former from Trapani and the latter two from Porto Empedocle, Sicily.

Caremar ferries make numerous runs daily year-round from Naples and Sorrento to Capri. Equally frequent hydrofoil services to Capri are provided by *Caremar, Aliscafi SNAV,* and *Alilauro* (phone: 81-681041). Capri, furthermore, can be reached by the ferries of other lines, and in summer ferries and hydrofoils operate to and from points along the Amalfi Coast and to and from Ischia.

The islands of the Tuscan archipelago (Elba, Capraia, Giglio, and others) are served mainly by *Toremar* ferries and hydrofoils. The most direct service to Elba, the largest island in the group (in fact, the third-largest Italian island, after Sicily and Sardinia), leaves from Piombino and arrives in Portoferraio many times daily year-round, taking 1 hour by car and passenger ferry and 30 minutes by hydrofoil. The Livorno to Portoferraio route, also operated daily year-round, takes approximately 3 hours if direct, more with a stop at Capraia. Additional ferries and hydrofoils from Piombino and Portoferraio serve other ports on Elba, while the island of Giglio, farther south, is reached by ferries from Porto Santo Stefano.

An island group in the Adriatic Sea, the Tremiti Islands, off the coast of the Puglia region, is served by *Adriatica,* the major Italian shipping line operating in the Adriatic. *Adriatica* also operates car ferries to Yugoslavia, with departures from Trieste, Venice, Ancona, Pescara, and Bari, Split, and Dubrovnik, and is the operator of the major car-ferry service to Greece. The sailings are overnight, departing from Brindisi at approximately 10:30 PM and calling at Corfu and Igoumenítsa the next day, prior to an early evening arrival at Patras. Supplementary summer sailings leave Brindisi earlier and go directly to Patras, arriving at approximately 1 PM the next day. Additional service is offered from Venice to Piraeus, the island of Crete, and Alexandria. For information or reservations, contact *Adriatica*'s US representative, *Extra Value Travel* (683 S. Collier Blvd., Marco Island, FL 33937; phone: 813-394-3384). Reservations are especially advisable for high-season sailings from mid-July to mid-August.

Other ferry lines, *Fragline* and *Hellenic Mediterranean Lines,* for example, have similar service from Brindisi to Corfu, Igoumenítsa, and Patras, and then to Athens by bus. In addition, *Jadrolinija* ferries sail from Ancona to Patras and from Patras to Venice twice a week. They also depart from Ancona to make various stops along the Yugoslav coast. *Minoan Lines* has departures five times a week from Ancona to Patras, with stops in Corfu and Igoumenítsa. The *Jadrolinija* and *Minoan* lines are represented in the US by *International Cruise Center* (250 Old Country Road, Mineola, NY 11501;

phone: 800-221-3254 or 516-747-8880). For information about *Fragline* ferries, contact the *International Cruise Center* or *Time and Tide, Inc.* (1416 Second Ave., New York, NY 10021; phone: 800-472-8999 or 212-861-2500).

Italy also has ferry links with other countries in and around the Mediterranean. *Adriatica* sails from Venice via Piraeus and Iraklion (Heraklion) to Alexandria, Egypt. *Tirrenia* sails from Naples, Catania, and Syracuse to Malta, and from Genoa, Trapani, and Cagliari to Tunis. There are numerous links to Bastia, Corsica, from La Spezia, Livorno, and Piombino, by *Corsica Line* and *Navarma* ferries. *Navarma* (phone: 565-918664 in Portoferraio) also serves Sardinia from Livorno.

Traveling by Train

Perhaps the most economical, and often the most satisfying, way to see a lot of a foreign country in a relatively short time is by rail. It certainly is the quickest way to travel between two cities up to 300 miles apart (beyond that, a flight normally would be quicker, even counting the time it takes to get to and from the airport). But time isn't always the only consideration. Traveling by train is a way to keep moving and to keep seeing at the same time. The fares usually are reasonable, and with the special discounts available to visitors, it can be an almost irresistible bargain. You only need to get to a station on time; after that, put your watch in your pocket and relax. You may not get to your destination exactly at the appointed hour, but you'll have a marvelous time looking out the window and enjoying the ride.

TRAINS: While North Americans have been raised to depend on their cars, Europeans have long been able to depend on public transportation. The government-owned and -operated *Ferrovie Italiane dello Stato (FS)* — known to the English-speaking world as *Italian State Railways* — runs a dense network of trains over nearly 10,000 miles of track extending from the tunnels and passes of the Alps to the heel of the boot in Puglia and the toe in Calabria. Nor do the trains stop there, even though the tracks do; the train ferry carries the cars across the water from Villa San Giovanni, Calabria, to Messina, Sicily, where the rails resume, one main line branching south along the coast to Syracuse and the other west along the coast to Palermo. Sicily has only a few secondary lines, and Sardinia's main line, running from Olbia to Sassari, Oristano, and Cagliari, is not much more than a secondary line, but at least on the Italian mainland there are few places of interest to a visitor that cannot be reached by rail.

The Italian rolling stock ranges from ultramodern, in which passengers speed along between principal cities in quiet, air conditioned comfort, to antiquated, in which they clack from stop to local stop on upholstered wooden seats. The trains don't all run on time, even though older Italians are fond of recalling Mussolini's efforts to achieve punctuality, and they frequently are stopped completely by strikes. But kilometer for kilometer they are among the least expensive in Europe. Consequently, they are crowded, especially on weekends and during the summer, and ticket lines can be long.

From most to least direct, trains in Italy are classified as follows:

EuroCity (EC): Fast international trains that connect major European cities and provide a high level of service.

InterCity (IC): Similar to *EC* trains, these trains operate only within Italian borders. This category includes the high-speed *Pendolino,* which runs at 288 kmh (180 mph), and makes the nonstop Rome–Milan trip in only 4 hours; reservations are compulsory. All *IC* trains have both first and second class available, with the exception of the *Pendolino,* which only offers first class.

Rapido: Somewhat faster express trains that also link major Italian cities.

Espresso: Long-distance express trains that stop at main stations.
Diretto: Semi-express trains trains that stop at many stations.
Locale: Local trains that stop at all stations.

Except for the *locali,* many of which are second class *(seconda classe)* only, and the *Pendolino,* which is first class only, all trains have both first class and second class cars.

Gone are the *Trans-Europe Express (TEE)* trains that came into being in the 1950s to provide the continent with efficient, luxurious, all first class service. Because of the expense to operate them, *TEE*s have been all but phased out in Europe and none remain in Italy; in fact, many *EuroCity* and *InterCity* trains are former *TEE*s to which second class has been added.

Some large cities have two or more stations, with service to different parts of the country leaving from different stations, so make sure you know the name of the station for your train.

ACCOMMODATIONS, FARES, SERVICES: Fares on Italian trains are based on a combination of the distance traveled and the quality of accommodations chosen. A ticket in first class costs approximately 30% to 40% more than a ticket in second class. Because of this, first class usually is less crowded. Those electing to travel second class, however — as most Italians do — probably will find it perfectly satisfactory, provided the train is not full and they find a seat. If they don't, and seats are available in first class, they are permitted to upgrade their tickets aboard the train, paying the conductor the difference in classes. Traditionally, seating is arranged in compartments, with three or four passengers on one side facing a like number on the other side, but increasingly, in the newer cars, compartments have been replaced by a central-aisle design.

Tickets can be purchased at train stations, at offices of the *Italian State Railways'* own travel agency, *Compagnia Italiana Turismo (CIT),* at other travel agencies displaying the *FS* sign, and, if necessary, on the train, though they cost more that way. They also can be bought at *CIT* offices in the US (addresses are given in "Further Information," below) where, given fluctuations in the rate of exchange, they may cost more or less than they would if bought in Italy.

As a rule, a round-trip ticket (*biglietto di andata e ritorno*) costs simply double the price of a one-way (*andata* or *corsa semplice*) ticket. An exception is a round-trip ticket between stations a maximum of 250 kilometers (156 miles) from each other, for which there is a reduction of 15% — provided the ticket is bought in Italy and not the US.

Other discounts that allow both Italians and foreign visitors to economize on train travel tend to be available only to selected groups of people. For instance, children under 4 travel free on Italian trains as long as they do not occupy a seat, and children ages 4 through 11 travel at half price. In addition, the *Family Card (Carta Famiglia)* provides a discount for families of at least four members traveling together and the *Silver Card (Carta d'Argento)* qualifies senior citizens for reduced rail fares; both of these special tickets can be purchased only in Italy. Those who plan to do a lot of train travel may find that a rail pass (see "Passes," later in this section) is an equally good bargain.

Some *EuroCity* and *InterCity* trains require payment of a supplement for all departures. The supplement includes the price of a reserved seat when seat reservations are obligatory *(a prenotazione obbligatoria),* as they are on some *InterCity* trains; when seat reservations are optional *(a prenotazione facoltativa),* the reservation fee is in addition to, not included in, the supplement. (On some *EuroCity* trains, seat reservations are optional and free to those in possession of a national pass, and the supplement is included.)

Both first and second class seats on most trains can be reserved in advance for a flat fee per seat. Reservations reduce flexibility, but they are advisable during the summer on popular routes — particularly long-distance routes. They also are advisable at holiday times (but note that no reservations except the obligatory ones are accepted for trains departing a few days before *Christmas* and *Easter*) and at any time of the year if it is imperative that you be on a particular train.

Reservations for first class and sometimes second class seats can be made before you leave home; in high season it's suggested you do this as early as 6 weeks and no later than 4 weeks before your intended train ride. Once in Italy, seats can be reserved as much as 2 months in advance, with the reservation period closing usually 3 to 6 hours before the departure of the train.

There is a price to pay for making reservations in the US: Whereas the fee per seat is only $3 at present (about 3,800 lire), communications charges for reservations made from this side of the Atlantic ($10 for the initial reservation, $5 for each subsequent one) do add up. So consider buying tickets here and making reservations, even those that are obligatory, after your arrival in Italy.

Sleeping accommodations are found on overnight trains going long distances, such as between Milan and Rome, Naples, Bari, and Brindisi; Rome or Naples and Sicily; Rome and Venice, Turin, and Genoa; and between Italy and other European countries. Two types of arrangements are possible: "couchettes" *(cuccette)* and "wagon-lits," or sleepers *(vetture-letti)*.

Couchettes, available in both first and second class versions, basically are the coach seats of a compartment converted to sleeping berths, with pillows, sheets, and blankets. First class couchettes contain four berths per compartment (an upper and a lower on each side of the aisle); second class couchettes have six (an upper, middle, and lower on each side). Since couchettes cost only a standard supplement per person ($15 to $20 per person if bought in the US) above the first or second class fare, they are a relatively inexpensive way to get a night's rest aboard the train. However, they provide privacy only for those traveling with a family or other group that can use the whole compartment; individual travelers are mixed with strangers of either sex.

Sleepers are actual bedroom compartments providing one to three beds with a mattress, pillow, sheets, and blanket, plus a washbasin with hot and cold water. Several kinds of compartments are available, though not always on every train. Singles, specials, and doubles are all first class accommodations. The single and special are individual compartments, with the special being slightly smaller and less expensive; the double is for two people who have booked it together. Tourist compartments (*T2*s and *T3*s) are second class compartments for two and three people traveling together or for strangers, though unlike couchette accommodations, strangers of the opposite sex are segregated. Sleeper accommodations, in Italy require payment of the basic first class or second class fare (based on the distance to be traveled) plus a supplement that varies with the type of compartment. From least to most expensive, sleeping car arrangements can cost anywhere from double the price of a couchette to ten times more.

Dining facilities on the trains vary. Long-distance trains have a dining car *(vettura-ristorante);* reservations can be made after boarding. Other trains have self-service or *trattoria* cars, where cafeteria-style tray meals are eaten at tables. An even greater number of trains have "mini-bar" service: An ambulatory vendor dispenses sandwiches and beverages from a cart. If you're sure that you'll want to eat en route, it's a good idea to inquire beforehand exactly what meal service is offered on the train you'll be taking. If none is offered, remember that box lunches are for sale at many stations and that when trains pull into larger stations, sandwiches, wine, and other drinks can be purchased from vendors with carts on the platform. Purchases are made quickly, money and food passing through the windows.

Passengers are allowed to carry 20 kilos (44 pounds) of baggage free, but since luggage in your possession is not weighed, you could conceivably carry more. Some trains are equipped with a place to put luggage just inside the doors, but otherwise you will have to hoist your suitcase onto an overhead rack. If you have too much luggage to handle yourself, it can be sent as registered baggage (the cost of this service depends on weight and distance), but it does not always travel on the same train as you do. Most major stations have a baggage checkroom *(deposito bagagli)* where you can temporarily free yourself of surplus bags. (Due to recent bomb scares, luggage lockers are increasingly less common in railroad stations in most European countries — Italy included.) It always is a good idea to travel as light as possible: Porters are in short supply at most stations, and self-service luggage carts frequently are scarce as well.

Special Services and Connections – Trains that carry cars *(Trasporto a Bagaglio di Auto al Seguito del Viaggiatore)* operate on international routes or on long-distance national routes — from northern cities such as Bologna, Bolzano, Genoa, Milan, and Turin, to southern cities such as Bari, Brindisi, Naples, Rome (connecting with car ferries for Greece), Piombino (for car ferries to Elba), and Villa San Giovanni in Calabria (connecting with car ferries for Sicily) — and allow those traveling by car to take to the rails while their vehicle travels with them on the same train. Book well in advance, especially in summer (the reservation period opens 2 months in advance of travel and closes 2 weeks and 24 hours in advance for international routes and national routes respectively).

Those planning to drive also should be aware that cars can be rented at a number of railroad stations from major international and national Italian car rental companies. Passengers may be able to reserve a car before boarding the train and find it waiting for them at their destination. (For information on a combination rail pass and rental car program, see "Passes," below.)

Ferries and buses also are part of the *FS* network. In addition to the ferry that carries passengers aboard the train across the Strait of Messina to Sicily, *Italian State Railways* operates conventional car and passenger ferries between the mainland and Sardinia. It also cooperates with the railroad systems of other European countries in running *Europabus,* which offers all-inclusive escorted sightseeing tours geared to the foreign visitor. Itineraries can cover one or more European countries and range anywhere from a few days to 2 weeks.

Some helpful hints regarding traveling by train in Italy are as follows:

- You can charge tickets to your *Carte Blanche, Diner's Club, MasterCard,* or *Visa* credit card at the larger Italian train stations, and if you're buying your ticket on the train you can even pay in foreign currency provided you're traveling on one of the main lines.
- The *orario ferroviario* (train timetable) on display in stations shows *arrivi* (arrivals) and *partenze* (departures); the *binario* is the track. If the train you're considering taking operates on *giorni festivi,* it operates on Sundays and public holidays only; the other days, including Saturdays, are *giorni feriali.*
- A standardized pictorial code has been fashioned to indicate the many amenities offered at train stations — including restaurants, post and telegraph offices, exchange bureaus, and diaper-changing facilities. Large train stations such as those in Milan and Rome have an *albergo diurno* (day hotel) where you can take a bath or shower, have your hair done, get a shave, or even rent a room by the hour to sleep.
- Before standing in line for information, look around for *FS* train schedules posted near the tracks in most stations; you may very well be able to get all the information you need from these — without the wait.

OTHER RAILROADS: Some trains in Italy have nothing to do with *FS,* although the average first-time visitor is unlikely to encounter them. An exception is the narrow-gauge *Circumvesuviana Railway,* which travels back and forth between Naples and Sorrento and is a handy way to visit Pompeii.

The *Orient Express* also passes through Italy. The legendary *Orient Express* of old, the luxury hotel on wheels that carried tourists and tycoons, kings and conspirators, from London and Paris via Eastern Europe to Istanbul made its final run in 1977 but has since been revived as the *Venice Simplon–Orient Express.* Twice-weekly year-round, this train runs between Venice and London, giving passengers a nostalgic taste of the golden age of rail travel aboard sumptuously restored carriages of the 1920s. For information, contact *Venice Simplon–Orient Express,* 1155 Ave. of the Americas, 30th Floor, New York, NY 10036 (phone: 800-524-2420).

PASSES: Rail passes are offered by most European railroad companies. They allow unlimited train travel within a set time period, frequently include connecting service via other forms of transportation, and can save the traveler a considerable amount of money, as well as time. The only requirement is validation of the pass by an information clerk on the day of your first rail trip; thereafter, there is no need to stand in line — and lines can be very long during peak travel periods — to buy individual tickets for subsequent trips. Designed primarily for foreign visitors, these passes generally must be bought in the US (or some other foreign location) prior to arrival in Europe. Although these passes can be among the best bargains around, be sure to look into the comparable cost of individual train tickets which — depending on the number of days you plan to travel — may work out to be less expensive.

The Eurailpass, the first and best known of all rail passes, is valid for travel in Italy, as well as in 16 other countries — Austria, Belgium, Denmark, Finland, France, Germany, Greece, Holland, Hungary, Ireland, Luxembourg, Norway, Portugal, Spain, Sweden, and Switzerland. It entitles holders to 15 or 21 days or 1, 2, or 3 months of unlimited first class travel, plus many extras, including free travel or substantial reductions on some ferry crossings (such as the Italy-Greece services of certain shipping lines), river trips, lake steamers, and transportation by bus and private railroads, as well as scheduled *Europabus* services, and airport to city center rail connections. Since the Eurailpass is a first class pass, Eurail travelers can ride just about any European train they wish, including special express trains, without paying additional supplements. The only extras are the nominal reservation fee and sleeper and couchette costs.

A Eurailpass for children under 12 is half the adult price (children under 4 travel free) but includes the same features. The Eurail Youthpass, for travelers under 26 years of age, is slightly different, in that it is valid for travel in second class only.

The Eurail Saverpass resembles the basic Eurailpass, except that it provides 15 days of unlimited first class travel for three people traveling together during peak season; two people traveling together qualify if travel takes place entirely between October 1 and March 31. It provides savings of approximately $100 per ticket as compared to the price of a 15-day Eurailpass.

Another option is the Eurail Flexipass, which can be used for first class travel on any 5 days within a 15-day period, 9 days within a 21-day period, or 14 days within a 30-day period. All of these passes must be bought before you go, either from a travel agent, a US office of *CIT* (see below) or the French, German, or Swiss railway companies. A *Eurail Aid* office in Europe will replace lost passes when proper documentation is provided; a reissuance fee is charged. (A list of *Eurail Aid* offices throughout Europe is provided when you buy a Eurailpass; you also can ask at any *FS* or *CIT* office in Italy for the nearest location.)

Also note that both the 7-day Eurailpass and the 9-day Eurail Flexipass can be combined with 3 to 8 days of car rental through *Hertz.* The program, marketed under the name *Hertz* EurailDrive Escape, includes a car rental with unlimited mileage, basic insurance, and taxes, as well as some drop-off options within most of the countries of rental. Reservations must be made in the US at least 7 days in advance by calling *Hertz* at 800-654-3001.

The Eurailpass is a bargain for those who will be traveling widely throughout Europe, but for those who will be traveling strictly within Italy, the less expensive Italian Tourist Ticket *(BTLC* or *Biglietto Turistico di Libera Circolazione),* Italy's own unlimited-mileage pass, is the better alternative. It is issued for either first class or second class travel for periods of 8, 15, 21, or 30 days, with children under 12 entitled to their own passes at half the adult price. Holders of the pass are exempt from paying all fast-train supplements. The *Italian Tourist Ticket* is meant for non-residents of Italy only and can be bought either before going abroad through *CIT* offices or travel agents or in Italy at main train stations, *CIT* offices, and other travel agencies displaying the *FS* sign.

Another type of ticket, the Italian Kilometric Ticket *(Biglietto Chilometrico)* is not truly a rail pass, but it does allow unlimited mileage up to a point. The purchaser is entitled to travel a total distance of 3,000 kilometers (1,875 miles) in as many as 20 trips within a period of 2 months. This is a generous allowance and one that the average traveler might not exhaust during the course of the typical vacation, but the advantage of the ticket is that it may be used by up to five people, who do not have to be members of the same family. When used by more than one person, the total distance of any trip is multiplied by the number of adults taking the trip (children under 12 are charged for half the distance traveled). The Italian Kilometric Ticket is sold in either first class or second class versions, but unlike the Eurailpass or the *BTLC* it does not exempt holders from paying supplements. The ticket is further unlike a rail pass in that it must be validated before each use rather than before the first use only. It can be bought from *CIT* offices (addresses below) or travel agents in the US or at main train stations, *CIT* offices, and travel agencies in Italy.

FURTHER INFORMATION: In addition to its many offices in Europe, the *Italian State Railways*' own travel agency, *CIT,* has two offices in the US that make reservations, sell tickets and rail passes, and provide information on all *FS* services:

California: 6033 W. Century Blvd., Suite 980, Los Angeles, CA 90045 (phone: 213-338-8620 or 800-CIT-RAIL in California).

New York State: 594 Broadway, Suite 307, New York, NY 10012 (phone: 212-274-0590).

Canada: 1450 City Councillors, Montreal, Quebec H3A 2E6, Canada (phone: 514-845-9101); 111 Avenue Rd., Suite 808, Toronto, Ontario M5R 3J8, Canada (phone: 416-927-7712).

When contacting these offices for information, be sure to ask for their free flyer, which gives the prices of the various rail passes valid in Italy along with sample first class and second class fares for point-to-point travel between a number of Italian cities and between the main cities in Italy and the rest of Europe. These prices are useful in calculating whether a rail pass would be worth your while. Distances in kilometers also are given between the sample Italian cities, a help in judging the usefulness of the kilometric ticket.

The official timetable of the *Italian State Railways, Il Treno,* a bulky tome sold in stations and at newsstands in Italy, contains more than anyone except a railroad clerk needs to know. *CIT* offices in the US also occasionally make available *Treni Principali,* a small booklet that is widely distributed throughout Italy. It contains timetables of the main rail services between towns and cities of any size in Italy, and although it is written in Italian, most of the writing is confined to footnotes and the essential schedule information can be extracted without too much difficulty.

Rail Europe is the North American representative of a number of European railway companies. The following offices provide helpful information for travelers in Italy, sell Eurailpasses, and make reservations and sell tickets for both *Italian State Railways* and connecting service to and through other European countries:

California: 360 Post St., San Francisco, CA 94108 (phone: 415-982-1993).

Florida: 800 Corporate Dr., Suite 108, Ft. Lauderdale, FL 33334 (phone: 305-776-2729).

Illinois: 11 E. Adams St., Suite 906, Chicago, IL 60603 (phone: 312-427-8691).
New York State: 226-230 Westchester Ave., White Plains, NY 10604 (phone: 914-682-5172).
Texas: 6060 N. Central Ave., Suite 220, Dallas, TX 75206 (phone: 214-691-5573).
Canada: 2087 Dundas East, Suite 204, Mississauga, Ontario L4X 1M2, Canada (phone: 416-602-4195); 643 Notre Dame Ouest, Suite 200, Montreal, Quebec HC3 1H8 Canada (phone: 514-392-1311); 409 Granville St., Suite 452, Vancouver, British Columbia B6C 1T2, Canada (phone: 604-688-6707).

Particularly if Italy is only a part of a more extensive trip through Europe or even farther afield, you may want to consult broader sources before finalizing plans. Both the *Eurail Traveler's Guide* (which contains a railroad map) and the *Eurail Timetable* are free from Eurailpass (Box 10383, Stamford, CT 06904-2383), as well as from the Eurail Distribution Centre (Box 300, Succursale R, Montreal, Quebec H2S 3K9 Canada). The *Eurail Guide,* by Kathryn Turpin and Marvin Saltzman, is available in most travel bookstores; it also can be ordered from Eurail Guide Annuals (27540 Pacific Coast Hwy., Malibu, CA 90265; phone: 213-457-7286) for $14.95, plus shipping and handling. *Europe by Eurail,* by George Wright Ferguson, is available from Globe Pequot Press (PO Box Q, Chester, CT 06412; phone: 203-526-9571) for $14.95, plus shipping and handling. The latter two guides discuss train travel in general, contain information on Italy and other countries included in the Eurail network (the Saltzman book also discusses Eastern Europe and the rest of the world), and suggest numerous sightseeing excursions by rail from various base cities.

You also may want to buy the *Thomas Cook European Timetable,* a weighty and detailed compendium of European international and national rail services that constitutes the most revered and accurate railway reference in existence. The *Timetable* comes out monthly, but because most European countries — including Italy — switch to summer schedules at the end of May (and back to winter schedules at the end of September), the June edition offers the first complete summer schedule (and October the first complete winter schedule). The February through May editions, however, contain increasingly more definitive supplements on upcoming summer schedules that can be used to plan a trip. The *Thomas Cook European Timetable* is available in some travel bookstores or can be ordered from the *Forsyth Travel Library* (PO Box 2975, Shawnee Mission, KS 66201-1375; phone: 800-367-7984 or 913-384-0496) for $21.95, plus shipping and handling; credit card orders also are accepted by phone.

Finally, although any travel agent can assist you in making arrangements to tour Italy by rail, you may want to consult a train travel specialist, such as *Accent on Travel,* 1030 Curtis St., Suite 201, Menlo Park, CA 94025 (phone: 415-326-7330 in California; 800-347-0645 elsewhere in the US).

Traveling by Car

Driving certainly is the most flexible way to explore out-of-the way regions of Italy. The privacy, comfort, and convenience of touring by car can't be matched by any other form of transport. Trains often whiz much too fast past too many enticing landscapes, tunnel through or pass between hills and mountains rather than climb up and around them for a better view, and frequently deposit passengers in an unappealing part of town. Buses have greater range, but they still don't permit many spur-of-the-moment stops and starts. In a car you go where you want when you want, and can stop along the way as often as you like for a meal, a photograph, or a particularly appealing view.

If you plan to visit only large cities, a car is *not* a good idea because historic centers usually are full of *zone pedonali* (pedestrian zones) and are so threaded with one-way streets that they drive even the natives wild. Nor will a car always get you inside the walls and to the tops of all those quaint hill towns where the center is a maze of narrow streets better negotiated by man or beast than motorcar. Such towns usually allow residents to park at their doors, if that's possible, but have a parking lot or two midway up where visitors can leave their cars while they proceed on foot.

For the rest, however, Italy is ideally suited for driving tours. Distances between points of interest usually are reasonable, and the historical and cultural density is such that the flexibility of a car can be used to maximum advantage. A traveler can cover large amounts of territory visiting major sites or spend the same amount of time motoring from one small village to another while exploring the countryside. (See DIRECTIONS for our choices of the most interesting driving routes.)

Travelers who wish to cover the country from the tip of its snow-capped peaks to the toe of its boot can count on a good system of superhighways to help them make time, including the well-known Autostrada del Sole (Highway of the Sun), which connects Milan and Bologna, Florence, Rome, Naples, Salerno, and, finally, Reggio Calabria. (Superhighways usually are not the scenic way to go, but the Autostrada del Sole, as it cuts across the Apennines between Bologna and Florence, is an emphatic exception.) Travelers choosing to explore only one region will find that the secondary and even lesser roads are well surfaced and generally in good condition; even farther off the beaten track, this usually is the case. Either way, there is plenty of satisfying scenery en route.

But driving isn't an inexpensive way to travel. Gas prices are far higher in Europe than in North America — and Italy's are among the very highest — and car rentals seldom are available at bargain rates. Keep in mind, however, that driving becomes more economical with more passengers. Because the price of getting wheels abroad will be more than an incidental expense, it is important to investigate every alternative before making a final choice. Many travelers find this expense amply justified when considering that rather than just the means to an end, a well-planned driving route can be an important part of the adventure.

Before setting out, make certain that everything you need is in order. If at all possible, discuss your intended trip with someone who already has driven the route to find out about road conditions and available services. If you can't speak to someone personally, try to read about others' experiences. Automobile clubs (see below) and the Italian Government Travel Office in the US can be good sources of travel information, although when requesting brochures and maps, be sure to specify the areas you are planning to visit. (Also see "Roads and Maps," below.)

Driving – According to Italian regulations, a US citizen is required to have an International Driving Permit (IDP) — essentially a translation of the driver's US license into 9 languages — to drive a car in Italy. The IDP must be accompanied by your US license to be valid. Italian regulations are not always enforced, and foreign drivers are known to have driven in Italy without incident using only their regular license. Nevertheless, it is strongly recommended that American drivers obtain an International Driving Permit before driving *any* car in Italy.

You can obtain your IDP before you leave from most branches of the *American Automobile Association (AAA).* Applicants must be at least 18 years old, and the application must be accompanied by two passport-size photos (some *AAA* branches have a photo machine available), a valid US driver's license, and a fee of $10. The IDP is good for 1 year.

Proof of liability insurance also is required and is a standard part of any car rental contract. (To be sure of having the appropriate coverage, let the rental staff know in advance about the national borders you plan to cross.) If buying a car and using it abroad, the driver must carry an International Insurance Certificate, known as a Green Card *(Carta Verde).* Your insurance agent or carrier can arrange for a special policy to cover you in Europe, and will automatically issue your Green Card.

Contrary to first impressions, Italians tend to be skillful, if not disciplined, drivers. Also contrary to first impressions, rules of the road do exist. Driving is on the right side of the road, as in most of Europe; passing is on the left. Unless otherwise indicated, those coming from the right at intersections have the right of way, but streetcars have priority over other vehicles, and pedestrians, provided they are on the diagonal stripes at "zebra" crossings, have priority over all vehicles. On mountain passes, traffic going up has priority over traffic coming down.

Keep in mind, when touring along Europe's scenic roadways, that it is all too easy to inch up over the speed limit. And use alcohol sparingly prior to getting behind the wheel. Although the Italians do not have specific laws pertaining to drinking and driving, as in other European countries, they are most zealous in prosecuting those who commit infractions under the influence. Police also have the power to levy on-the-spot fines for other infractions such as speeding, failure to stop at a red light, and failure to wear seat belts. The use of seat belts is compulsory, and motorcycle drivers are required to wear helmets. High-beam lights should not be used in cities and towns and use the horn sparingly — only in emergencies and when approaching blind curves on country roads. In many Italian towns and cities, honking is discouraged during the day and forbidden at night; flash your headlights instead. And watch out for bicycles and motor scooters — they are everywhere.

Pictorial direction signs are standardized under the International Roadsign System and their meanings are indicated by their shapes — triangular signs indicate danger; circular signs give instructions; and rectangular signs are informative. Driving in Italian and other European cities can be a tricky proposition, since many of them do not have street signs at convenient corners, but instead identify their byways with plaques attached to the walls of corner buildings. These often are difficult to spot until you've passed them, and since most streets don't run parallel to one another, taking the next turn can lead you astray. Fortunately, most European cities and towns post numerous signs pointing the way to the center of the city, and plotting a course to your destination from there may be far easier (unless you are facing rush hour traffic). In Italy, look for the signs that read CENTRO CITTA..

Also note highway signs showing distance from point to point are in kilometers rather than miles (1 mile equals approximately 1.6 kilometers; 1 kilometer equals approximately .62 mile). And speed limits are in kilometers per hour, so think twice before hitting the gas when you see a speed limit of 100. That means 62 miles per hour. In most towns, the speed limit is 50 kph (31 mph). On secondary roads outside towns, the speed limit is generally 90 kph (56 mph). On superhighways *(autostrade)* the speed limit is higher: 130 kph (81 mph). It is lower — 110 kph (69 mph) — on weekends and during certain holiday periods.

■ **Note:** Pay particular attention to parking signs in large cities throughout Italy, especially those indicating "control zones," where an unattended parked car presents a serious security risk. If you park in a restricted zone, unlike in the US (where you chance only getting a ticket or being towed), you may return to find that the trunk and doors have been blown off by overly cautious security forces.

Roads and Maps – Italy's network of highways is as well maintained as any in North America, with a system comparable to the American highway system: expressways, first class roads, and well-surfaced secondary roads.

Traffic congestion is at its worst on main roads — particularly those radiating from major cities — on the days before and after public holidays and on the last days of July and the first days of August. In fact, since most Italians take their vacations in August, traffic on roads leading to beaches or mountains is so bad on these latter days that authorities monitoring road conditions have come to refer to them as the annual *grande esodo* (great exodus) and, via the media, begin counseling the nation's drivers well ahead of time as to the best days, hours, and routes for departure. Bottlenecks also occur on the days surrounding August 15 (*Ferragosto* or *Assumption Day*), the date by which every Italian family that has not already done so will plan to set out on vacation. Weekends at the end of August and the beginning of September tend to be tied up with the traffic of the *grande rientro* (great re-entry). Look for signs pointing out detours or alternative routes to popular holiday destinations. Service stations, information points, and tourist offices distribute free maps of the alternate routes, which may be the long way around but probably will get you to your destination faster in the end by bypassing the bottlenecks.

Italy's *autostrade* are designated by the letter A, with A1, A2, and A3, from Milan to Reggio Calabria, making up the Autostrada del Sole. Except for free stretches in the vicinity of cities, most *autostrade* are toll roads, and they are fairly expensive. They save time, gas, and wear and tear on the car, but they are not the roads to take if you want to browse and linger along the way. Other roads are the *strade statali* (state, or national, roads), designated by SS and a number and sometimes better known by their ancient names, such as Via Aurelia, Via Flaminia, and Via Cassia; the unnumbered *strade provinciali* (provincial roads); and the *strade comunali* (local roads). Most of these are much more picturesque than the superhighways.

Excellent road maps of Italy are published by the *Italian Touring Club,* or *Automobile Club d'Italia (ACI).* Several series are available, but the *Carta Automobilistica d'Italia,* which covers the whole country in two maps on a scale of 1:800,000 (1 centimeter equals 8 kilometers), should be sufficient for the needs of most motorists. The *Grande Carta Stradale d'Italia* series of 15 regional maps (1:200,000; 1 centimeter equals 2 kilometers) is useful for those traveling extensively in one region. A road atlas, *Atlante Stradale d'Italia,* uses the latter scale to map the country in three volumes (northern, central, and southern Italy). Besides all the other information that they contain, *ACI* maps highlight especially scenic stretches in green, making it easy for motorists to pick out the most desirable travel routes. Another source of good road maps of Italy is the *Istituto Geografico De Agostini (IGDA),* which publishes several series in a variety of scales, including a series of regional maps on a scale of 1:250,000.

Both the *ACI* and the *IGDA* maps are available throughout Italy and at certain map stores and travel bookstores in the US, but if they prove difficult to find, *Michelin*'s red map No. 988, published by the French tire company, may suit your purposes equally well. On a scale of 1:1,000,000 (1 centimeter equals 10 kilometers), it covers the entire country in considerable detail, and it, too, uses a contrasting color to highlight choice travel routes. Michelin maps are readily available in bookstores and map shops throughout the US, and also can be ordered from the company's US headquarters, Michelin Guides and Maps (PO Box 3305, Spartanburg, SC 29304-3305; phone: 803-599-0850 in South Carolina; 800-423-0485 elsewhere in the US). A new edition of each map appears every year; if you're not buying directly from the publisher, make sure that the edition you buy is no more than 2 years old by opening one fold and checking the publication date, given just under the black circle with the map number.

Other good sources of current information on European road destinations and Italian routes are the atlases, maps, and guides published by Rand McNally. Rand McNally publications are available in most bookstores or can be bought directly from the following Rand McNally retail stores: 444 N. Michigan Ave., Chicago, IL 60611 (phone: 312-321-1751); 150 S. Wacker Dr., Chicago, IL 60606 (phone: 312-332-2009); 150 E. 52nd St., New York, NY 10022 (phone: 212-758-7488); 595 Market St., San Francisco, CA 94105-2803 (phone: 415-777-3131).

Freytag & Berndt's excellent series of 28 road maps ($8.95 each) covers most major destinations throughout Europe and includes 5 general maps of Italy and 5 city maps (Cortina, Florence, Meran, Milan, and Venice). The US distributor of these maps and a good source of just about any other map available is *Map Link* (25 E. Mason St., Suite 201, Santa Barbara, CA 93101; phone: 805-965-4402). Among their hundreds of maps of Italy are the following: the *De Agostini* series (including 17 regional maps; $10.95 each), *FMB* series (including 50 city plans, regional, and provincial maps; $6.95 to $9.95), *Kummerly & Frey* series (including 14 regional maps; $8.95 each), *LAC* series (including 17 regional maps and 85 maps of Italian provinces at $5.95 each), and *RV* series (including 7 regional maps; $11.95 each). They also carry a selection of country-wide maps of Italy. If they don't have the map you want in stock, they will order it for you. You may want to order their comprehensive guide to maps worldwide, *The World Map Directory* ($29.95).

The *American Automobile Association (AAA)* also provides several useful reference sources, including a map of Italy and the Balkan Peninsula, an overall Europe planning map, the 600-page *Travel Guide to Europe* (the price varies from branch to branch), and the 64-page *Motoring Europe* ($7.25). These are available from most local *AAA* offices (see below). Another invaluable guide, *Euroad: The Complete Guide to Motoring in Europe,* is available for $8.80, including postage and handling, from *VLE Limited,* PO Box 444, Tenafly, NJ 07670; phone: 201-585-5080 or 212-580-8030).

Automobile Clubs and Roadside Assistance – Most European automobile clubs offer emergency service to any breakdown victim, whether a club member or not; however, only members of these clubs or affiliated clubs may have access to certain information services and receive discounted or free towing and repair services.

Members of the *American Automobile Association (AAA)* often are automatically entitled to a number of services from foreign clubs. With over 31 million members in chapters throughout the US and Canada, the *AAA* is the largest automobile club in North America. *AAA* affiliates throughout the US provide a variety of travel services to members, including a travel agency, trip planning, fee-free traveler's checks, and reimbursement for foreign roadside assistance. They will help plan an itinerary, send a map with clear routing directions, and even make hotel reservations. These services apply to travel in both the US and Europe. Although *AAA* members receive maps and brochures for no charge or at a discount, non-members also can order from an extensive selection of highway and topographical maps at most *AAA* branches. You can join the *AAA* through local chapters (listed in the telephone book under *AAA*) or contact the national office at 1000 AAA Dr., Heathrow, FL 32746-5063 (phone: 407-444-8544).

Italy's main automobile club, the *Automobile Club d'Italia* (*ACI;* 261 Via Cristoforo Colombo, Rome 00185; phone: 6-5106; or 8 Via Marsala, Rome 00185; phone: 6-49981), provides emergency service on *autostrade* and other roads throughout the country. Though it isn't necessary to belong to *ACI* to qualify for emergency assistance, service is cheaper, and sometimes free, if you are a member. By reciprocal arrangement, *ACI* automatically extends to *American Automobile Association* members the same courtesies and assistance it extends to its own members.

If you break down on the road, immediate emergency procedure is to get the car off the road. If the road has a narrow shoulder, try to get all the way off, even if you have to hang off the shoulder a bit. Better yet, try to make it to an area where the shoulder is wider — if you are crawling along well below the speed limit, use your emergency flashers to warn other drivers. Although the universal signal for help is raising the hood, and tying a white handkerchief or rag to the door handle or radio antenna, in Italy, a portable triangular reflector *(triangolo)* must be placed as a warning to other drivers behind any car that is stalled or blocking the road for any other reason. This piece of necessary equipment is provided with rental cars; otherwise, it can be rented from *ACI* offices. Don't leave the car unattended, and don't try any major repairs on the road.

For breakdown assistance, call 116 or, on *autostrade,* use the special SOS call boxes.

ACI also has a 24-hour telephone assistance center with English-speaking operators to provide information on road and weather conditions, hotels, and other tourist questions (phone: 6-4212).

Aside from these options, a driver in distress will have to contact the nearest service center by pay phone. And, although English is spoken in Italy, if language is a barrier in explaining your dilemma, by dialing 15, you should be able to reach an international operator who can stay on the line as an interpreter. (For further information on calling for help, see *Mail, Telephone, and Electricity* and *Medical and Legal Aid and Consular Services,* both in this section.) Car rental companies also make provisions for breakdowns, emergency service, and assistance; ask for a number to call when you pick up the vehicle.

Gasoline – Called *benzina* in Italy, gasoline is sold by the liter (which is slightly more than 1 quart; approximately 3.8 liters equal 1 US gallon). Regular or leaded gas (also called *benzina*) is sold in two grades: *normale* and *super.* Diesel is widely available (diesel fuel pumps normally carry a sign for *gasolio*), but unleaded fuel (called *benzina verde* or *benzina senza piombo*) is only now being introduced in Europe and may be difficult (or even impossible) to find in Italy.

Gas prices everywhere rise and fall depending on the world supply of oil, and an American traveling overseas is further affected by the prevailing rate of exchange, so it is difficult to say exactly how much fuel will cost when you travel. It is not difficult to predict, however, that gas prices will be substantially higher than you are accustomed to paying in the US. And note: Gas prices in Italy are among the highest in Europe.

Travelers driving in Italy have at least one advantage over native drivers, namely the price they pay for fuel. Tourists can purchase discount coupons that can be redeemed later at gas stations around Italy. These coupons are available upon entry at major airports — including Rome's Fiumicino and Milan's Malpensa — as well as at the border; the total number of coupons purchasable may vary from place to place, but whatever the number of coupons offered for sale, the face amount can be used at gas stations throughout the country to pay for approximately 15% to 20% more gas. Coupons must be purchased in foreign currency, and may be used by foreigners driving either their own or rental cars. The whole idea is to promote auto touring in Italy by visitors — that is, to get them out of the major urban centers and into the surrounding countryside — and the savings on gas makes auto touring a bit less pricey.

Particularly when traveling in rural areas, fill up whenever you come to a gas station. It may be a long way to the next open station. (Even in more populated areas, it may be difficult to find an open station on Sundays or holidays.) You don't want to get stranded on an isolated stretch — so it is a good idea to bring along an extra few gallons in a steel container. (Plastic containers tend to break when a car is bouncing over rocky roads. This, in turn, creates the danger of fire should the gasoline ignite from a static electricity spark. Plastic containers also may burst at high altitudes.)

Considering the cost of gas in Italy relative to US prices, gas economy is of particular concern. The prudent traveler should plan an itinerary and make as many reservations as possible in advance in order not to waste gas figuring out where to go, stay, or eat. Drive early in the day, when there is less traffic. Then leave your car at the hotel and use local transportation whenever possible after you arrive at your destination.

Although it may be as dangerous to drive at a speed much below the posted limit as it is to drive above it — particularly on toll *autostrade,* superhighways where the speed limit may be as high as 130 kph (81 mph) — at 88 kph (55 mph) a car gets 25% better mileage than at 112 kph (70 mph). The number of miles per liter or gallon also is increased by driving smoothly.

RENTING A CAR: Although there are other options, such as leasing or outright purchase, most travelers who want to drive in Europe simply rent a car. Travelers to Italy can rent a car through a travel agent or international rental firm before leaving home, or from a local company once they are in Europe. Another possibility, also arranged before departure, is to rent the car as part of a larger travel package (see "Fly/Drive Packages," below, as well as *Package Tours,* in this section).

Renting a car in Italy is not inexpensive, but it is possible to economize by determining your own needs and then shopping around among the car rental companies until you find the best deal. As you comparison shop, keep in mind that rates vary considerably, not only from city to city, but also from location to location within the same city. For instance, it might be less expensive to rent a car in the center of a city than at the airport. Ask about special rates or promotional deals, such as weekend or weekly rates, bonus coupons for airline tickets, or 24-hour rates that include gas and unlimited mileage.

Rental car companies operating in Europe can be divided into three basic categories: large international companies; national or regional companies; and smaller local companies. Because of aggressive local competition, the cost of renting a car can be less expensive once a traveler arrives in Italy compared to the prices quoted in advance in the US. Local companies usually are less expensive than the international giants.

Given this situation, it's tempting to wait until arriving to scout out the lowest-priced rental from the company located the farthest from the airport high-rent district and offering no pick-up services. But if your arrival coincides with a holiday or a peak travel period, you may be disappointed to find that even the most expensive car in town was spoken for months ago. Whenever possible, it is best to reserve in advance, anywhere from a few days in slack periods to a month or more during the busier seasons.

Renting from the US – Travel agents can arrange foreign rentals for clients, but it is just as easy to call and rent a car yourself. Listed below are some of the major international rental companies represented in Italy that have information and reservations numbers that can be dialed toll-free from the US:

Avis (phone: 800-331-1084). Has 196 locations in Italy.
Budget (phone: 800-527-0700). Has over 30 locations in Italy.
Dollar Rent-a-Car (known in Europe as *Eurodollar;* phone: 800-800-6000). Has over 65 locations in Italy.
Hertz (phone: 800-654-3001). Has over 75 locations in Italy.
National (known in Europe as *Europcar;* phone: 800-CAR-EUROPE). Has over 125 locations in Italy.

Note that *Avis* also offers two helpful free services for customers traveling in Italy, as well as in other European countries: the "Know Before You Go" US hotline (phone: 212-876-AVIS); and an "On Call Service" for customers calling once in Europe. Both provide travelers with tourist information on Belgium, France, Germany, Great Britain, Holland, Italy, and Switzerland. Topics may range from questions about driving (distances, gasoline prices, and license requirements) to queries about currency, customs, tipping, and weather. (Callers to the US number then receive a personal letter confirming the information discussed.) For the European service, there is a different toll-free number in each country; the numbers are given to you when you rent from *Avis* (personnel at these number speak English).

Another special service is *Avis*'s Europe Message Center, which operates like any answering service in that it will take phone messages any time day or night for *Avis* customers. *Avis* renters are given a telephone number in Europe that they can leave with anyone who wants to contact them while they are touring; if your rental car comes with a car phone, *Avis* will give this number to callers (with your permission). The tourers themselves can call a toll-free number to pick up messages or leave word for family, friends, or business colleagues. To utilize the service, a renter picks up his or her car at an *Avis* outlet in Europe, and then simply calls the Message Center and registers with the rental agreement number. It's even possible to leave an itinerary — which can be altered later if necessary — making messages easy to leave and/or pick up.

It also is possible to rent a car before you go by contacting any of a number of smaller or less well known US companies that do not operate worldwide. These organizations specialize in European auto travel, including leasing and car purchase in addition to car rental, or actually are tour operators with a well-established European car rental program. These firms, whose names and addresses are listed below, act as agents for a variety of European suppliers, offer unlimited mileage almost exclusively, and frequently manage to undersell their larger competitors by a significant margin.

There are legitimate bargains in car rentals provided you shop for them. Call all the familiar car rental names whose toll-free numbers are given above (don't forget to ask about their special discount plans), and then call the smaller companies listed below. In the recent past, the latter have tended to offer significantly lower rates, but it always pays to compare. Begin your comparison shopping early, because the best deals may be booked to capacity quickly and may require payment 14 to 21 days or more before picking up the car.

Auto Europe (PO Box 1097, Camden, ME 04843; phone: 207-236-8235; 800-223-5555 throughout the US; 800-458-9503 in Canada). Offers rentals at almost 200 locations in Italy.

Europe by Car (One Rockefeller Plaza, New York, NY 10020; phone: 212-581-3040 in New York State; 800-223-1516 elsewhere in the US; and 9000 Sunset Blvd., Los Angeles, CA 90069; phone: 800-252-9401 or 213-272-0424). Offers rentals in Alghero, Bari, Catania, Florence, Genoa, Milan, Naples, Palermo, Pisa, Rome, Turin, and Venice.

Foremost Euro-Car (5430 Van Nuys Blvd., Suite 306, Van Nuys, CA 91401; phone: 800-272-3299 or 818-786-1960). Offers rentals at over 30 locations in Italy.

Kemwel Group (106 Calvert St., Harrison, NY 10528; phone: 800-678-0678 or 914-835-5555). Offers rentals at over 20 locations in Italy.

Maiellano Tours (441 Lexington Ave., Suite 1002, New York, NY 10017; phone: 800-223-1616 or 212-687-7725). A tour operator specializing in Italy, this company also offers car rentals at 135 locations throughout Italy.

Meier's World Travel (6033 W. Century Blvd., Suite 1080, Los Angeles, CA 90045; phone: 800-937-0700). In conjunction with a number of major car rental companies (such as *Hertz*), they can arrange economical rentals throughout Italy.

And for travelers for whom driving is more than just a means of getting from here to there, *European Car Reservations* (349 W. Commercial St., Suite 2950, East Rochester, NY 14445; phone: 800-535-3303) rents top-of-the-line Alfa Romeos and Mercedes at over 55 locations in Italy. Prices are hardly inexpensive, but many feel the pleasure of being behind the wheel of an Alpha Romeo 164 is worth the cost. (For those looking for a tamer experience, however, this company also rents more sedate models.)

One of the ways to keep the cost of car rentals down is to deal with a car rental consolidator, such as *Connex International* (23 N. Division St., Peekskill, NY 10566; phone: 800-333-3949 or 914-739-0066). *Connex*'s main business is negotiating with virtually all of the major car rental agencies for the lowest possible prices for its customers. This company arranges rentals throughout Europe, including over 200 locations in cities and towns throughout Italy.

CIT (Compagnia Italiana Turismo) also has a car rental program similar to those offered by some of the companies listed above. For information, contact *CIT Tours* in the US (594 Broadway, Suite 307, New York, NY 10012; phone: 212-274-0596 or 800-223-7987).

Local Rentals – It long has been common wisdom that the least expensive way to rent a car is to make arrangements in Europe. This is less true today than it used to be. Many medium to large European car rental companies have become the overseas suppliers of stateside companies such as those mentioned previously, and often the stateside agency, by dint of sheer volume, has been able to negotiate more favorable rates for its US customers than the European firm offers its own. Still, lower rates may be found by searching out small, strictly local rental companies overseas, whether at less than prime addresses in major cities or in more remote areas. But to find them you must be willing to invest a sufficient amount of vacation time comparing prices on the scene. You also must be prepared to return the car to the location that rented it; drop-off possibilities are likely to be limited.

The brochures of some of the smaller car rental companies, often available from tourist board offices in the US, can serve as a useful basis for comparison. Once overseas, local tourist authorities may be able to supply the names of local rental companies, and the local phone book is another good place to begin. (For further information on local rental companies, see the individual city reports in THE CITIES.) Also bear in mind that a rail-and-drive pass offered by *Hertz,* EurailDrive Escape, is valid in Italy and all the other countries of the Eurail network. (For further information, see *Traveling by Train,* in this section.)

Requirements – Whether you decide to rent a car in advance from a large international rental company with European branches or wait to rent from a local company, you should know that renting a car is rarely as simple as signing on the dotted line and roaring off into the night. If you are renting for personal use, you must have a valid driver's license, as well as an International Driving Permit (see "Driving," above), and will have to convince the renting agency that (1) you are personally creditworthy, and (2) you will bring the car back at the stated time. This will be easy if you have a major credit card; most rental companies accept credit cards in lieu of a cash deposit, as well as for payment of your final bill. If you prefer to pay in cash, leave your credit card imprint as a "deposit," then pay your bill in cash when you return the car.

If you are planning to rent a car once in Europe, *Avis, Budget, Hertz,* and other US rental companies usually *will* rent to travelers paying in cash and leaving either a credit card imprint or a substantial amount of cash as a deposit. This is not necessarily standard policy, however, as other international chains, and a number of local and regional European companies will *not* rent to an individual who doesn't have a valid credit card. In this case, you may have to call around to find a company that accepts cash.

Also keep in mind that although the minimum age to drive a car in Italy is 18 years, the minimum age to rent a car is set by the rental company. (Restrictions vary from company to company, as well as at different locations.) Many firms have a minimum age requirement of 21 years, some raise that to 23 or 25 years, and for some models of cars it rises to 30 years. The upper age limit at many companies is between 69 and 75; others have no upper limit or may make drivers above a certain age subject to special conditions.

Costs – Finding the most economical car rental will require some telephone shopping on your part. As a *general* rule, expect to hear lower prices quoted by the smaller, strictly local companies than by the well-known international names, with those of the national Italian companies falling somewhere between the two.

Comparison shopping always is advisable, however, because the company that has the least expensive rentals in one country may not have the least expensive in another, and even the international giants offer discount plans whose conditions are easy for most travelers to fulfill. For instance, *Budget* and *National* offer discounts of anywhere from 10% to 30% off their usual rates (according to the size of the car and the duration of the rental), provided that the car is reserved a certain number of days before departure (usually 7 to 14 days, but it can be less), is rented for a minimum period (5 days or, more often, a week), is paid for at the time of booking, and, in most cases, is returned to the same location that supplied it or to another in the same country. Similar discount plans include *Hertz*'s Affordable Europe and *Avis*'s Supervalue Rates Europe.

If driving short distances for only a day or two, the best deal may be a per-day, per-mile (or per-kilometer) rate: You pay a flat fee for each day you keep the car, plus a per-mile (or per-kilometer) charge. An increasingly common alternative is to be granted a certain number of free miles or kilometers each day and then be charged on a per-mile or per-kilometer basis over that number.

A better alternative for touring the countryside may be a flat per-day rate with unlimited free mileage; this certainly is the most economical rate if you plan to drive over 100 miles (160 km). Make sure that the low, flat daily rate that catches your eye, however, is indeed a per-day rate: Often the lowest price advertised by a company turns out to be available only with a minimum 3-day rental — fine if you want the car that long, but not the bargain it appears if you really intend to use it no more than 24 hours for in-city driving. Flat weekly rates also are available, as are some flat monthly rates that represent a further saving over the daily rate. (Note: When renting a car in Italy, the term "mileage" may refer either to miles or kilometers.)

Other factors influencing cost naturally include the type of car you rent. Rentals are based on a tiered price system, with different sizes of cars — variations of budget, economy, regular, and luxury — often listed as A (the smallest and least expensive) through F, G, or H, and sometimes even higher. Charges may increase by only a few dollars a day through several categories of subcompact and compact cars — where most of the competition is — then increase by great leaps through the remaining classes of full-size and luxury cars and passenger vans. The larger the car, the more it costs to rent and the more gas it consumes, but for some people the greater comfort and extra luggage space of a larger car (in which bags and sporting gear can be safely locked out of sight) may make it worth the additional expense. Be warned, too, that relatively few European cars have automatic transmissions, and those that do are more likely to be in the F group than the A group. Similarly, cars with air conditioning are likely to be found in the more expensive categories only. Most expensive are sleek sports cars, but, again, for some people the thrill of driving such a car — for a week or a day — may be worth it.

Electing to pay for collision damage waiver (CDW) protection will add considerably to the cost of renting a car. You may be responsible for the *full value* of the vehicle being rented, but you can dispense with the possible obligation by buying the offered waiver at a cost of about $11 to $13 a day. Before making any decisions about optional collision damage waivers, check with your own insurance agent and determine whether your personal automobile insurance policy covers rented vehicles; if it does, you probably won't need to pay for the waiver. Be aware, too, that increasing numbers of credit cards automatically provide CDW coverage if the car rental is charged to the appropriate credit card. However, the specific terms of such coverage differ sharply among individual credit card companies, so check with the credit card company for information on the nature and amount of coverage provided. Business travelers also should be aware that, at the time of this writing, *American Express* had withdrawn its automatic CDW coverage from some corporate *Green* card accounts — watch for similar cutbacks by other credit card companies.

Overseas, the amount renters may be liable for should damage occur has not risen to the heights it has in the US. In addition, some European car rental agreements include collision damage waiver coverage. In this case, the CDW supplement frees the renter from liability for the *deductible* amount — as opposed to the standard CDW coverage, described above, which releases the driver from liability for the full value of the car. In Italy, this deductible typically ranges anywhere from $1,500 to $2,500 at present, but can be much higher for some luxury car groups. As with the full collision damage waiver, the cost of waiving this liability — which can be as high as $25 a day —

is far from negligible, however. Drivers who rent cars in the US often are able to decline the CDW because many personal automobile insurance policies (subject to their own deductibles) extend to rental cars; unfortunately, such coverage usually does not extend to cars rented for use outside the US and Canada. Similarly, CDW coverage provided by some credit cards if the rental is charged to the card may be limited to cars rented in the US or Canada.

When inquiring about CDW coverage and costs, you should be aware that a number of the major international car rental companies now are automatically including the cost of this waiver in their quoted prices. This does not mean that they are absorbing this cost and you are receiving free coverage — total rental prices have increased to include the former CDW charge. The disadvantage of this inclusion is that you probably will not have the option to refuse this coverage, and will end up paying the added charge — even if you already are adequately covered by your own insurance policy or through a credit card company.

Additional costs to be added to the price tag include drop-off charges or one-way service fees. The lowest price quoted by any given company may apply only to a car that is returned to the same location from which it was rented. A slightly higher rate may be charged if the car is to be returned to a different location (even within the same city), and a considerably higher rate may prevail if the rental begins in one country and ends in another.

A further consideration: Don't forget that all car rentals are subject to Value Added Tax (VAT). This tax rarely is included in the rental price that's advertised or quoted, but it always must be paid — whether you pay in advance in the US or pay it when you drop off the car. In Italy, the VAT rate on car rentals currently is 19%.

There is a wide variation in this tax from country to country. One-way rentals bridging two countries used to be exempt from tax, but this is no longer the case. In general, the tax on one-way rentals is determined by the country in which the car has been rented, so even if you intend to visit only Italy, you still might consider a nearby country as the pick-up point — the tax rate in Belgium is 25% (no great bargain), but in Germany it is 14%; in Spain and Luxembourg, 12%; and in Switzerland, no tax is charged. For a tourer planning to explore the northern regions of Italy, therefore, there's a strong financial incentive to pick up his or her rental car in Switzerland and then drive across the nearby Italian border (at a 19% car rental cost saving!).

Some rental agencies that do not maintain their own fleets use a contractor, whose country of registration determines the rate of taxation. An example is *Kemwel Group,* whose one-way rentals from all countries except Germany, Holland, Italy, Portugal, and Sweden are taxed at the Danish rate of 22%. *Kemwel*'s special programs offer savings to the client planning to tour throughout Europe (particularly through countries where the tax rate is higher). Their UltraSaver tariffs are offered throughout Europe, including the following locations in Italy: Bologna, Brindisi, Catania, Florence, Genoa, Messina, Mestre, Milan, Naples, Palermo, Pisa, Rome, Taormina, Turin, and Venice. These programs offer full insurance coverage (with a $100 deductible) and all European VAT, plus unlimited mileage. If part of a fly/drive package (see below) booked through *Kemwel,* rates may be even lower. Bookings must be reserved and paid for at least 7 days before delivery of the car, and the vehicle must be returned to the *Kemwel* garage from which it was originally rented. For further information, contact *Kemwel Group,* 106 Calvert St., Harrison, NY 10528 (phone: 800-678-0678 or 914-835-5555).

Also, don't forget to factor in the price of gas. Rental cars usually are delivered with a full tank of gas. (This is not always the case, however, so check the gas gauge when picking up the car, and have the amount of gas noted on your rental agreement if the tank is not full.) Remember to fill the tank before you return the car or you will have to pay to refill it, and gasoline at the car rental company's pump always is much more expensive than at a service station. This policy may vary for smaller local and regional companies; ask when picking up the vehicle. Before you leave the lot, also check that the rental car has a spare tire and jack in the trunk.

Finally, currency fluctuation is another factor to consider. Most brochures quote rental prices in US dollars, but these dollar amounts frequently are only guides; that is, they represent the prevailing rate of exchange at the time the brochure was printed. The rate may be very different when you call to make a reservation, and different again when the time comes to pay the bill (when the amount owed may be paid in cash in foreign currency or as a charge to a credit card, which is recalculated at a still later date's rate of exchange). Some companies guarantee rates in dollars (often for a slight surcharge), but this is an advantage only when the value of the dollar is steadily declining overseas. If the dollar is growing stronger overseas, you may be better off with rates guaranteed in Italian lire.

Fly/Drive Packages – Airlines, charter companies, car rental companies, and tour operators have been offering fly/drive packages for years, and even though the basic components of the packages have changed somewhat — return airfare, a car waiting at the airport, and perhaps a night's lodging all for one inclusive price used to be the rule — the idea remains the same. You rent a car *here* for use *there* by booking it along with other arrangements for the trip. These days, the very minimum arrangement possible is the result of a tie-in between a car rental company and an airline, which entitles customers to a rental car for less than the company's usual rates, provided they show proof of having booked a flight on that airline.

Slightly more elaborate fly/drive packages can be found listed under various names (go-as-you-please, self-drive, or, simply, car tours) in the independent vacations sections of tour catalogues. Their most common ingredients are the rental car plus some sort of hotel voucher plan, with the applicable airfare listed separately. You set off on your trip with a block of prepaid accommodations vouchers, a list of hotels that accept them (usually members of a hotel chain or association), and a reservation for the first night's stay, after which the staff of each hotel books the next one for you or you make your own reservations. Naturally, the greater the number of establishments participating in the scheme, the more freedom you have to range at will during the day's driving and still be near a place to stay for the night.

The cost of these combination packages generally varies according to the size of the car and the quality of the hotels; there usually is an additional drop-off charge if the car is picked up in one city and returned in another. Most packages are offered at several different price levels, ranging from a standard plan covering stays in hotels to a budget plan using accommodations such as small inns, farmhouses, or family-run *pensioni.* Airlines also have special rental car rates available when you book their flights, often with a flexible hotel voucher program. Less flexible car tours provide a rental car, a hotel plan, and a set itinerary that permits no deviation because the hotels all are reserved in advance. For information on packagers of car tours, see *Package Tours,* in this section.

LEASING: Anyone planning to be in Europe for 3 weeks or more should compare the cost of renting a car with the cost of leasing one for the same period. While the money saved by leasing — rather than renting for a 23-day (the minimum) or 30-day period — may not be great, what is saved over the course of a long-term lease — 45, 60, 90 days, or more — amounts to hundreds, even thousands, of dollars. Part of the savings is due to the fact that leased cars are exempt from the stiff taxes applicable to rented cars. In addition, leasing plans provide for collision insurance with no deductible amount, so there is no need to add the daily cost of collision damage waiver protection (an option offered by rental companies — see above). A further advantage of a car lease — actually a financed purchase/repurchase plan — is that you reserve your car by specific make and model rather than by group only, and it is delivered to you fresh from the factory.

Unfortunately, leasing as described above is offered only in Belgium and France, and the savings it permits can be realized to the fullest only if the cars are picked up and returned in those countries. While leased cars can be delivered to other countries — including Italy — the charge for this service can be very high, and on top of this must be added an identical return charge. If you don't intend to keep the car very long, the two charges can nullify the amount saved by leasing rather than renting, so you will have to do some arithmetic. It is possible to lease a car in countries other than Belgium and France, but most of the plans offered are best described as long-term rentals at preferential rates. They differ from true leasing in that you will pay tax and collision damage waiver protection (though it may be included in the quoted price), and the cars usually are late-model used cars rather than brand-new.

One of the major car leasing companies is *Renault,* offering leases of new cars for 23 days to 6 months. The cars are exempt from tax, all insurance is included, and there is no mileage charge. There is no pick-up or drop-off charge for some locations in France; charges for other locations throughout Europe (including Milan) vary substantially. For further information and reservations, ask your travel agent or contact *Renault USA,* 650 First Ave., New York, NY 10016 (phone: 212-532-1221 in New York State; 800-221-1052 elsewhere in the US).

Peugeot also offers a similar leasing arrangement, called the "Peugeot Vacation Plan." In accordance with the standard type of financed purchase/repurchase plan, travelers pick up the car in France, paying at the time of pick-up to use the car for a specified period of time (anywhere between 22 and 175 days), and at the end of this pre-arranged period return it to *Peugeot.* The tax-free temporary "purchase" includes unlimited mileage, factory warranty, full collision damage waiver coverage (no deductible), and 24-hour towing and roadside assistance. Pick-up and drop-off locations and charges are similar to *Renault*'s. *Peugeot*'s "European Delivery" program is a full-purchase program, including shipment of the car to the US, as discussed below. For further information, contact *Peugeot Motors of America* (1 Peugeot Plaza, Lyndhurst, NJ 07071; phone: 201-935-8400). Some of the car rental firms listed above — *Auto Europe, Europe by Car, Foremost Euro-Car,* and *Kemwel* — also arrange European car leases.

BUYING A CAR: If your plans include both buying a new car of European make and a driving tour of Europe, it's possible to combine the two ventures and save some money on each. By buying the car abroad and using it during your vacation, you pay quite a bit less for it than the US dealer would charge and at the same time avoid the expense of renting a car during your holiday. There are two basic ways to achieve this desired end, but one, factory delivery, is far simpler than the other, direct import.

Factory delivery means that you place an order for a car in the US and then pick it up in Europe, often literally at the factory gate. It also means that your new car is built to American specifications, complying with all US emission and safety standards. Because of this, only cars made by manufacturers who have established a formal program for such sales to American customers may be bought at the factory. At present, the list includes Audi, BMW, Jaguar, Mercedes-Benz, Peugeot, Porsche, Saab, Volkswagen, and Volvo, among others (whose manufacturers generally restrict their offerings to those models they ordinarily export to the US). The factory delivery price, in US dollars, usually runs about 5% to 15% below the sticker price of the same model at a US dealership and includes US Customs duty, but the cost of the incidentals and the insurance necessary for driving the car around Europe are extra, except in BMW's plan.

One of the few disadvantages of factory delivery is that car manufacturers make only a limited number of models available each year, and for certain popular models you may have to get in line early in the season. Another is that you must take your trip when the car is ready, not when you are, although you usually will have 8 to 10 weeks' notice. The actual place of delivery can vary; it is more economical to pick up the car at the factory, but arrangements sometimes — but not always — can be made to have it delivered elsewhere for an extra charge. For example, Jaguars (although the company is now owned by Ford) must be ordered through a US dealer and picked up at the factory in Coventry, England, however, they also can be dropped off for shipment home in any number of European cities. For information, write to *Jaguar Cars,* 555 MacArthur Blvd., Mahwah, NJ 07430 (phone: 201-818-8500).

Cars for factory delivery usually can be ordered either through one of the manufacturer's authorized dealers in the US or through companies — among them *Europe by Car, Foremost Euro-Car,* and *Kemwel* (see above for contact information) — that specialize in such transactions. (Note that *Foremost Euro-Car* services all of the US for rentals and leasing, but they arrange *sales* only for California residents.) Another company arranging car sales abroad is *Ship Side Tax Free World on Wheels BV,* 600B Lake St., Suite A, Ramsey, NJ 07446 (phone: 201-818-0400).

Occasionally an auto manufacturer offers free or discounted airfare in connection with a European delivery program. This year, Mercedes-Benz has a program including discounted round-trip airfare ($500 for two economy fare seats or one business class seat) from any US gateway served by *Delta, Lufthansa,* or *SwissAir,* to Stuttgart (where the buyer picks up the car), plus a 2-night stay at the local *Hilton* or *Ramada* hotel, and 15 days' free comprehensive road insurance. For details, contact *Mercedes-Benz of North America,* 1 Mercedes Dr., Montvale, NJ 07645 (phone: 800-458-8202).

The other way to buy a car abroad **direct import**, sometimes is referred to as "gray market" buying. It is perfectly legal, but not totally hassle-free. Direct import means that you buy abroad a car that was meant for use abroad, not one built according to US specifications. It can be new or used, and may even include — if made for use in Great Britain or Ireland — a steering wheel on the right side. The main drawback to direct import is that the process of modification to bring the car into compliance with US standards is expensive and time consuming; it typically costs from $5,000 to $7,000 in parts and labor and takes from 2 to 6 months. In addition, the same shipping, insurance, and miscellaneous expenses (another $2,000 to $5,000, according to estimates) that would be included in the factory delivery price must be added to the purchase price of the car, and the considerable burden of shepherding it on its journey from showroom to home garage usually is borne by the purchaser. Direct-import dealers do exist (they are not the same as your local, factory-authorized foreign car dealer, with whom you are now in competition), but even if you use one, you still need to do a great deal of paperwork yourself.

Once upon a time, the main advantage of the direct-import method — besides the fact that it can be used for makes and models not available on factory delivery programs — was that much more money could be saved importing an expensive car. Given today's exchange rates, however, the method's potential greater gain is harder to realize and must be weighed against its greater difficulties. Still, if direct importing interests you, you can obtain a list of those makes and models approved for conversion in this country, and of the converters licensed to bring them up to US specifications, by contacting the Environmental Protection Agency, Manufacturers' Operations Division, EN-340-F, Investigations/Imports Section, 401 M St. SW, Washington, DC 20460 (phone: 202-382-2479).

If you have special problems getting your car into the US, you might consider contacting a specialist in vehicle importation, such as Daniel Kokal, an independent regulatory consultant. His address is 15014 Kamputa Dr., Centerville, VA 22020 (phone: 703-818-9009).

Package Tours

If the mere thought of buying a package for travel to and through Italy conjures up visions of a race through ten cities in as many days in lockstep with a horde of frazzled fellow travelers, remember that packages have come a long way. For one thing, not all packages necessarily are escorted tours, and the one you buy does not have to include any organized touring at all — nor will it necessarily include traveling companions. If it does, however, you'll find that people of all sorts — many just like yourself — are taking advantage of packages today because they are economical and convenient, save you an immense amount of planning time, and exist in such variety that it's virtually impossible not to find one that fits at least the majority of your travel preferences. Given the high cost of travel these days, packages have emerged as a particularly wise buy.

In essence, a package is an amalgam of travel services that can be purchased in a single transaction. A package (tour or otherwise) to and through Italy may include any or all of the following: round-trip transatlantic transportation, local transportation (and/or car rentals), accommodations, some or all meals, sightseeing, entertainment, transfers to and from the hotel at each destination, taxes, tips, escort service, and a variety of incidental features that might be offered as options at additional cost. In other words, a package can be any combination of travel elements, from a fully escorted tour offered at an all-inclusive price to a simple fly/drive booking allowing you to move about totally on your own. Its principal advantage is that it saves money: The cost of the combined arrangements invariably is well below the price of all of the same elements if bought separately, and particularly if transportation is provided by charter or discount flight, the whole package could cost less than just a round-trip economy airline ticket on a regularly scheduled flight. A package provides more than economy and convenience: It releases the traveler from having to make individual arrangements for each separate element of a trip.

Tour programs generally can be divided into two categories — "escorted" (or locally hosted) and "independent." An escorted tour means that a guide will accompany the group from the beginning of the tour through to the return flight; a locally hosted tour means that the group will be met upon arrival at each location by a different local host. On independent tours, there generally is a choice of hotels, meal plans, and sightseeing trips in each city, as well as a variety of special excursions. The independent plan is for travelers who do not want a totally set itinerary but who do prefer confirmed hotel reservations. Whether choosing an escorted or independent tour, always bring along complete contact information for your tour operator in case a problem arises, although US tour operators often have European affiliates who can give additional assistance or make other arrangements on the spot.

To determine whether a package — or, more specifically, *which* package — fits your travel plans, start by evaluating your interests and needs, deciding how much and what you want to spend, see, and do. Gather whatever package tour information is available for your schedule. Be sure that you take the time to read the brochure *carefully* to determine precisely what is included. Keep in mind that travel brochures are written to entice you into signing up for a package tour. Often the language is deceptive and devious. For example, a brochure may quote the lowest prices for a package tour based on facilities that are unavailable during the off-season, undesirable at any season, or just plain nonexistent. Information such as "breakfast included" (as it often is in packages to Italy) or "plus tax" (which can add up) should be taken into account. Note, too, that the prices quoted in brochures almost always are based on double occupancy: The rate listed is for each of two people sharing a double room, and if you travel alone, the supplement for single accommodations can raise the price considerably (see *Hints for Single Travelers,* in this section).

In this age of erratic airfares, the brochure most often will *not* include the price of an airline ticket in the price of the package, though sample fares from various gateway cities usually will be listed separately, to be added to the price of the ground arrangements. Before figuring your actual cost, check the latest fares with the airlines, because the samples invariably are out of date by the time you read them. If the brochure gives more than one category of sample fares per gateway city — such as an individual tour-basing fare, a group fare, an excursion, APEX, or other discount ticket — your travel agent or airline tour desk will be able to tell you which one applies to the package you choose, depending on when you travel, how far in advance you book, and other factors. (An individual tour-basing fare is a fare computed as part of a package that includes land arrangements, thereby entitling a carrier to reduce the air portion almost to the absolute minimum. Though it always represents a saving over full-fare coach or economy, lately the individual tour-basing fare has not been as inexpensive as the excursion and other discount fares that also are available to individuals. The group fare usually is the least expensive fare, and it is the tour operator, not you, who makes up the group.) When the brochure does include round-trip transportation in the package price, don't forget to add the cost of round-trip transportation from your home to the departure city to come up with the total cost of the package.

Finally, read the general information regarding terms and conditions and the responsibility clause (usually in fine print at the end of the descriptive literature) to determine the precise elements for which the tour operator is — and is not — liable. Here the tour operator frequently expresses the right to change services or schedules as long as equivalent arrangements are offered. This clause also absolves the operator of responsibility for circumstances beyond human control, such as floods, or injury to you or your property. In reading, ask the following questions:

1. Does the tour include airfare or other transportation, sightseeing, meals, transfers, taxes, baggage handling, tips, or any other services? Do you want all these services?
2. If the brochure indicates that "some meals" are included, does this mean a welcoming and farewell dinner, two breakfasts, or every evening meal?
3. What classes of hotels are offered? If you will be traveling alone, what is the single supplement?
4. Does the tour itinerary or price vary according to the season?
5. Are the prices guaranteed; that is, if costs increase between the time you book and the time you depart, can surcharges unilaterally be added?
6. Do you get a full refund if you cancel? If not, be sure to obtain cancellation insurance.
7. Can the operator cancel if too few people join? At what point?

One of the consumer's biggest problems is finding enough information to judge the reliability of a tour packager, since individual travelers seldom have direct contact with the firm putting the package together. Usually, a retail travel agent is interposed between customer and tour operator, and much depends on his or her candor and cooperation. So ask a number of questions about the tour you are considering. For example:

- Has the travel agent ever used a package provided by this tour operator?
- How long has the tour operator been in business? Check the Better Business Bureau in the area where the tour operator is based to see if any complaints have been filed against it.
- Is the tour operator a member of the *United States Tour Operators Association*

(USTOA; 211 E. 51st St., Suite 12B, New York, NY 10022; phone: 212-944-5727)? The *USTOA* will provide a list of its members on request; it also offers a useful brochure, *How to Select a Package Tour.*

- How many and which companies are involved in the package?
- If air travel is by charter flight, is there an escrow account in which deposits will be held; if so, what is the name of the bank?

This last question is very important. US law requires that tour operators place every charter passenger's deposit and subsequent payment in a proper escrow account. Money paid into such an account cannot legally be used except to pay for the costs of a particular package or as a refund if the trip is canceled. To ensure the safe handling of your money, make your check payable to the escrow account — by law, the name of the depository bank must appear in the operator-participant contract, and usually is found in that mass of minuscule type on the back of the brochure. Write the details of the charter, including the destination and dates, on the face of the check; on the back, print "For Deposit Only." Your travel agent may prefer that you make your check out to the agency, saying that it will then pay the tour operator the fee minus commission. But it is perfectly legal to write your check as we suggest, and if your agent objects too strongly (the agent should have sufficient faith in the tour operator to trust him or her to send the proper commission), consider taking your business elsewhere. If you don't make your check out to the escrow account, you lose the protection of that escrow should the trip be canceled or the tour operator or travel agent fail. Furthermore, recent bankruptcies in the travel industry have served to point out that even the protection of escrow may not be enough to safeguard your investment. Increasingly, insurance is becoming a necessity (see *Insurance,* in this section), and payment by credit card has become popular since it offers some additional safeguards if the tour operator defaults.

■ **A word of advice:** Purchasers of vacation packages who feel they're not getting their money's worth are more likely to get a refund if they complain in writing to the operator — and bail out of the whole package immediately. Alert the tour operator or resort manager to the fact that you are dissatisfied, that you will be leaving for home as soon as transportation can be arranged, and that you expect a refund. They may have forms to fill out detailing your complaint; otherwise, state your case in a letter. Even if the availability of transportation home detains you, your dated, written complaint should help in procuring a refund from the operator.

SAMPLE PACKAGES TO ITALY: There are so many packages available to Italy today that it's probably safe to say that just about any arrangement anyone might want is available for as long as it is wanted, whether it's to hit the country's highlights, to explore a selected region in depth, or to visit only Rome. The keynote is flexibility.

Escorted Tours – Those seeking the maximum in structure will find that the classic sightseeing tour by motorcoach, fully escorted and all-inclusive (or nearly), has withstood the test of time and still is well represented among the programs of the major tour operators. Typically, these itineraries begin in a major city and last anywhere from 1 to 3 weeks, or more.

At their briefest, such tours may begin in Milan, move east to Venice, and then travel down the backbone of Italy to Florence and Rome, often with a detour to the Naples area to see Pompeii, Capri, and the Amalfi Drive before returning to Rome for departure. With more time, they may begin and end in Milan or Rome and trace a long, narrow loop around the country, adding a variety of secondary sights to the itinerary. Tours concentrating on the north of Italy or on the south, including the island of Sicily, also are easy to find, although tours exploring a single region in depth are not common. The notable exception is Sicily, which often is packaged on its own.

Hotel accommodations in these packages usually are characterized as first class or better, with private baths or showers accompanying all rooms, although more than a few tour packagers offer less expensive alternatives by providing more modest lodgings. These packages tend to be all-inclusive, although the number of included meals may vary considerably and (even in Italy) wine is included only when the tour literature clearly states so. Among such packages are the following:

Abercrombie & Kent (1520 Kensington Rd., Suite 212, Oak Brook, IL 60521; phone: 708-954-2944 in Illinois; 800-323-7308 elsewhere in the US). Offers all-inclusive Great Italy Express tours that take care of just about everything — right down to a traveling bellhop to handle your baggage. These 11-day structured tours visit over a dozen different Italian cities; travel to each city is by rail and within the area by motorcoach. As this tour operator is a wholesaler, bookings must be made through a travel agent.

Amelia Tours (280 Old Country Road, Hicksville, NY 11801; phone: 800-742-4591 or 516-433-0696). Their 5-, 7-, and 13-day escorted packages tour Sicily by motorcoach. The 13-day package provides a special focus on local culture and folklore.

American Express Travel Related Services (offices throughout the US; phone: 800-241-1700 for information and local branches). Their escorted motorcoach tours of Italy, include a 13-day Romantic Italy package, a 10- to 18-day Best of Italy package, a 14-day Italian Masters package, and a 17-day Italian Renaissance tour. This tour operator prefers that bookings be made through travel agents.

Donna Franca Tours (470 Commonwealth Ave., Boston, MA 02215; phone: 617-227-3111 in Massachusetts; 800-225-6290 elsewhere in the US). Offers four different escorted motorcoach tours of Italy: a 10- to 21-day Italian Fever package visiting northern Italy, a 7-day Sicily Only tour, a 14-day Sicily Fever tour that also visits other parts of Italy, and a 14-day Best of Italy tour that visits major cities. This tour operator prefers that bookings be made through travel agents.

Esplanade Tours (581 Boylston St., Boston, MA 02116; phone: 800-426-5492 or 617-266-7465). Offers five different escorted motorcoach tours: a 12-day Villas and Gardens of Italy package, a 12-day Italian Marches package, a 14-day Hilltowns of Italy tour, a 15-day tour of Sicily, and 16-day Renaissance Italy package.

Globus-Gateway and Cosmos (95-25 Queens Blvd., Rego Park, NY 11374; phone: 800-221-0090; or 150 S. Los Robles Ave., Pasadena, CA 91101; phone: 818-449-2019 or 800-556-5454). These affiliated agencies offer numerous tours of Italy, including a 9-day Italy's Great Cities package that visits Florence, Rome, and Venice, a 13-day Italian Mosaic package, and a 15-day Italy to Sicily tour. Note that bookings must be made through a travel agent.

Insight International Tours (745 Atlantic Ave., Suite 720, Boston, MA 02111; phone: 800-582-8380 or 617-426-6666). Offers a 16-day Grand Italy escorted motorcoach tour. As this tour operator is a wholesaler, bookings must be made through a travel agent.

Maupintour (PO Box 807, Lawrence, KA 66044; phone: 800-255-4266). Offers three escorted motorcoach tours of Italy: a 12-day Italy's Famous Places package, a 12-day Sicily and Calabria tour, and a 19-day Grand and Leisurely package.

Olson Travel World (1334 Parkview Ave., Suite 210, Manhattan Beach, CA 90266; phone: 800-421-5785 or 213-546-8400). Their escorted, highly structured packages include a 14-day, all-inclusive Italian Interlude tour that visit major cities.

Perillo Tours (577 Chestnut Ridge Rd., Woodcliff Lake, NJ 07675; phone: 800-431-1515). Offers five escorted motorcoach tours of Italy: a 13-day Italy South package, a 14-day Italian North package, a 13-day tour of Florence, Rome, and Venice, a 10-day tour of the same cities during the quieter off-season, and a 10-day tour that also visits Sorrento.

Trafalgar Tours (11 E. 26th St., New York, NY 10010; phone: 212-689-8977 in New York City; 800-854-0103 elsewhere in the US). Offers a 14-day Splendors of Italy escorted motorcoach tour. Bookings are made through travel agents, but you can contact *Trafalgar Tours* directly for information.

Travcoa (PO Box 2630, Newport Beach, CA 92658; phone: 800-992-2004 or 714-476-2800 in California; 800-992-2003 elsewhere in the US). Offers a lineup of all-inclusive, escorted motorcoach tours, including a 17-day Hilltowns of Southern Italy tour, a 16-day Classic Italy package, and 22- to 26-day multi-country Carnival in Europe package that visit Rome and Venice.

Travel Time (17 N. State St., Chicago, IL 60602 (phone: 800-621-4725). Offers a leisurely 25-day Autumn in Italy motorcoach tour for those interested in touring the Italian countryside in the less hectic fall months.

TWA Getaway Tours (phone: 800-GETAWAY). Offers a wide variety of motorcoach tours throughout Europe, including four escorted tours of Italy: an 8-day Roman Holiday package, a 9-day Best of Italy tour of northern Italy, a 15-day Allegro tour, and a 12-day Italy by Train package.

In addition, *CIT Tours* (part of *CIT,* the US representative of *Italian State Railways.* offers a number of escorted motorcoach tours of Italy, including 8-day Heart of Italy and Sicilian Carousel tours, an 11-day Pleasures of Italy package, and a 19-day Italy Fantastica package. Semi-escorted tours also are offered. Bookings can be made through a travel agent or one of the North American offices of *CIT* (see "Further Information" in *Traveling by Train,* in this section, for addresses).

Independent Tours – Less restrictive arrangements for travelers who prefer more independence than that found on escorted tours are listed in the semi-escorted and hosted sections of tour catalogues. These may combine some aspects of an escorted tour, such as moving from place to place by motorcoach, with longer stays in one spot, where participants are at liberty but a host or hostess — that is, a representative of the tour company — is available at a local office or even in the hotel to answer questions and assist in arranging activities and optional excursions.

Another equally common type of package available to Italy is the car tour or fly/drive arrangement, often described in brochures as a self-drive or go-as-you-please tour. These are independent vacations, geared to travelers who want to cover as much ground as they might on an escorted group sightseeing tour but who prefer to do it on their own. The most flexible plans include no more than a map, a rental car, and a block of as many prepaid hotel vouchers as are needed for the length of the stay (the packages typically are 4 or 7 days long, extendable by individual extra days or additional package segments), along with a list of participating hotels at which the vouchers are accepted. In most cases, only the first night's accommodation is reserved; from then on, travelers book their rooms one stop ahead as they drive from place to place, creating their own itinerary as they go. When the hotels are members of a chain or association — which they usually are — the staff of the last hotel will reserve the next one for you. In other cases, there may be a choice of reserving all accommodations before departure —

usually for a fee. Operators offering these packages usually sell vouchers in more than one price category: Travelers may have the option of upgrading hotel accommodations by paying a supplement directly to more expensive hostelries or can economize by chosing to stay in simple *pensioni* or modest inns. Another type of fly/drive arrangement is slightly more restrictive in that the tour packager supplies an itinerary that must be followed day by day, with a specific hotel to be reached each night. Often these plans are more deluxe as well.

Fly/drive packages to and around Italy include the following:

Abercrombie & Kent International (1520 Kensington Rd., Suite 212, Oak Brook, IL 60521; phone: 708-954-2944 in Illinois; 800-323-7308 elsewhere in the US). Their customized self-drive or chauffeured tours of Italy include stays in hotels that are converted manor houses, castles, and other stately homes.

AutoVenture (425 Pike St., Suite 502, Seattle, WA 98101; phone: 206-624-6033 in Washington State; 800-426-7502 elsewhere in the US). This company's deluxe car tours last anywhere from 6 to 14 days and are available in either a self-drive or chauffeured version. Their 8-day Renaissance Road itinerary features overnight stays in hotels that are elegant converted villas or otherwise noteworthy.

David B. Mitchell & Company (200 Madison Ave., New York, NY 10016; phone: 800-372-1323 or 212-889-4822). Also offers luxurious self-drive or chauffeured tours, which include stays in elegant *Relais & Châteaux* member establishments (see our discussion of accommodations, in *On the Road,* in this section). Among their offerings are a 10-day La Dolce Vita tour of Tuscany and the Italian Riviera (with an optional 3-day extension to Italy's Lake Country) and a 14-day La Terra Cotta package that visits Florence, Rome, Siena, and Venice. Also arranges customized tours for 7-days or longer.

Extra Value Travel (683 S. Collier Blvd., Marco Island, FL 33937; phone: 800-255-2847). In conjunction with international car rental companies, offers week-long fly/drive bookings throughout Italy.

Stay-Put City and Resort Packages – A further possibility for independent travelers is a "stay-put" package in Italy. These appeal to travelers who want to be on their own and remain in one place for the duration of their vacation, although it is not unusual for travelers to buy more than one package at a time.

Rome, Florence, and Venice are the most frequent destinations for this type of package. Basically, a city package — no matter what the city — includes round-trip transfers between airport and hotel, a choice of hotel accommodations (usually including continental breakfast) in several price ranges, plus any number of other features that you may not need or want but would lose valuable time arranging if you did. Common package features are 1 or 2 half-day guided tours of the city; passes for unlimited travel by underground (subway) or bus; discount cards for shops, museums, and restaurants; temporary membership in and admission to clubs, casinos, discotheques, or other nightspots; and car rental for some or all of your stay. Other features may be anything from a souvenir travel bag to a tasting of local wines or dinner and a show.

These packages usually are a week long — although 4-day and 14-day packages also are available, and most packages can be extended by extra days — and often are hosted; that is, a representative of the tour company may be available at a local office or even in the hotel to answer questions, handle problems, and assist in arranging activities and optional excursions. A similar stay-put resort package generally omits the sightseeing tour and may offer some sort of daily meal plan if accommodations are in hotels; accommodations in apartment hotels with kitchenettes are another common alternative.

Among the stay-put packages offered in Italy are the following:

American Express Travel Related Services (offices throughout the US; phone: 800-241-1700 for information and local branches). Offers city packages to Florence, Milan, Rome, and Venice. Although there is a 2-day minimum, packages can be arranged for as long as you like.

British Airways Holidays (phone: 800-AIRWAYS). Offers a Four City Classic package that includes 3 days in London and 3 days each in Florence, Rome, and Venice. Transportation between the cities is by air and rail; extended-stay options are available for all packages.

Jet Vacations (1775 Broadway, New York, NY 10019; phone: 800-JET-0999 or 212-247-0999). Offers city packages in Florence, Milan, Rome, and Venice, with no specified length-of-stay requirements.

Marsans International (19 W. 34th St., Suite 302, New York, NY 10001; phone: 212-239-3880 in New York State; 800-223-6114 elsewhere in the US). Offers 5-day city packages in Rome and customized city packages throughout Italy. Note that their specialty is arranging packages for Spanish-speaking clients.

Meier's World Travel, Inc. (6033 W. Century Blvd., Suite 1080, Los Angeles, CA 90045; phone: 800-937-0700). Arranges 3-night customized city packages throughout Italy.

Petrabax Tours (97-45 Queens Blvd., Suite 505, Rego Park, NY 11374; phone: 718-897-7272 in New York State; 800-367-6611 elsewhere). Offers 4-day or longer city tours in Florence, Milan, Rome, and Venice. Also caters to Spanish-speaking clientele.

TWA Getaway Tours (phone: 800-GETAWAY). Offers numerous city packages throughout Europe, including an 8-day Rome city package.

World of Oz (211 E. 43rd St., New York, NY 10017; phone: 800-248-0234 or 212-661-0580). Offers customized city tours throughout Italy for a minimum of 3 nights.

Special-Interest Packages – Special-interest tours are a growing sector of the travel industry. These are similar to the packages discussed above, with the exception that the package — whether it be of the all-inclusive motorcoach, fly/drive, or stay-put variety — is designed with a particular focus in mind, such as cultural events, history, or Italy's fine food and wines.

Programs focusing on food and wine are prominent among such packages put together for visitors to Italy. Note, though, that they tend to be quite structured arrangements rather than independent ones, and they rarely are created with the budget traveler in mind. Also note that inclusive as they may be, few food and wine tours include *all* meals in the package price. This is not necessarily a cost-cutting technique on the part of the packager; rather, because of the lavishness of some of the meals, others may be left to the discretion of the participants, not only to allow time for leisure, but also to allow for differing rates of metabolism. Similarly, even on wine tours that spend entire days in practically full-time tasting, unlimited table wine at meals may not be included in the package price. The brochures usually are clear about what comes with the package and when.

For groups of 10 or more travelers, *Travel Concepts* (62 Commonwealth Ave., Suite 3, Boston, MA 02116; phone: 617-266-8450) offers a variety of custom-designed food and wine tours throughout Europe. Although there is no pre-planned itinerary in Italy, they can design one for individuals or groups.

There also are special-interest packages catering to travelers particularly interested in the arts and/or cultural studies. Among these are the packages for classical music and opera lovers offered by *Dailey-Thorp* (315 W. 57th St., New York, NY 10019; phone: 212-307-1555). Their roster is always changing, but the company regularly sends a group to opening night at *La Scala* in December. At other times, the tours visit various Italian music festivals such as Florence's *Maggio Musicale,* the *Rossini Festival* at Pesaro, Stresa's *Musical Weeks,* and the outdoor opera at the *Arena of Verona* and take in performances at Venice's *Teatro La Fenice,* Turin's *Teatro Regio,* Florence's *Teatro Comunale,* and Rome's *Teatro dell'Opera,* in addition to Milan's *La Scala.* Itineraries also include music-related activities such as visits to sites associated with the composers or their works.

For art enthusiasts, *Prospect Art Tours* (454-458 Chiswick High Rd., London W45TT, England; phone: 81-995-2151 or 81-995-2163) offers 5- to 15-day packages visiting key museums, private galleries, and art collections in major cities throughout Italy. Their Italian tours each emphasize a different artistic theme — such as the work of a particular artist or the art or architecture of a particular region or period.

Since Italy is a land of pilgrimage, it is also the destination of tours geared to Roman Catholic travelers. One company specializing in such tours is *Catholic Travel* (10018 Cedar La., Kensington, MD 20895; phone: 301-564-1904). The company plans about 10 Italy tours each year in high season, led by a spiritual director and visiting about 10 cities on a 15-day itinerary. A papal audience is included. For Jewish travelers, the *American Jewish Congress* (15 E. 84th St., New York, NY 10028; phone: 212-879-4588 in New York State; 800-221-4694 elsewhere in the US) regularly arranges tours to Europe in addition to its tours to Israel. Recent itineraries included a 16-day Grand Tour trip that included 8 days in Italy (Rome, Florence, and Venice), with an overnight train ride to Paris on the *Venice Simplon–Orient Express.*

And for those who want to tour Italy from on high, the *Bombard Society* (6727 Curran St., McLean, VA 22101; phone: 800-862-8537 or 703-448-9407) offers a 5-day ballooning package exploring Tuscany — from on high and with feet on the ground. The packages include daily flights via hot-air balloon (flown by pilots, not tour participants), sightseeing, hotel accommodations, and meals, many of which are candlelit buffets served after the day's flight. Their 7-day tour also includes 3 days in Siena during the *Palio* festival.

Sports Packages – Ski packages are foremost among the sports-related packages to Italy. The foundation of the package usually is a week or two of hotel or condominium accommodations at a ski resort (Bormio, Cervinia, Cortina d'Ampezzo, Courmayeur, Madonna di Campiglio, Selva di Val Gardena, and Sestriere are the common destinations), and for those choosing the hotel rather than the apartment, the price often includes a meal plan of breakfast and dinner daily. The other features of a ski vacation — round-trip bus, train, or rental car transportation between the airport and the resort, ski passes, baggage handling, taxes, and tips — are included in varying combinations according to the packager. If transatlantic transportation is by charter flight (not unusual on ski packages), airfare, too, will be included in the price. If not, the applicable "group ski" or other fare will be listed separately.

Among the numerous packagers offering ski packages to Italy are the following:

Adventures on Skis (815 North Rd., Westfield, MA 01085; phone: 413-568-2855 or 800-447-1144 in Massachusetts; 800-628-9655 elsewhere in the US). Offers 7-night ski packages to Alta Badia, Cortina, and Selva di Val Gardena.

Alpine Skiing and Travel (534 New State Hwy., Raynham, MA 02767; phone: 508-823-7707; 800-551-8822 in Massachusetts; 800-343-9676 elsewhere in the US). Offers 7-day (or longer) ski packages Cortina and Selva di Val Gardena.

Central Holiday Tours (206 Central Ave., Jersey City, NJ 07307; phone: 800-526-6045). Their ski package in the Italian Alps are offered in conjunction with *Alitalia* and booked through travel agents. Although there is a minimum stay for some departures, most of the packages are 1 week long; discounts of 30% on group ski lessons are possible at all the resorts.

Club Med (40 W. 57th St., New York, NY 10019; phone: 800-CLUB-MED). Vacation packages at the *Club Med* ski resort in Sestriere include lessons at the *Club*'s private ski school and all lift passes.

Steve Lohr's Skiworld and Travel (206 Central Ave., Jersey City, NJ, 07307; phone: 201-798-3900 in New Jersey; 800-223-1306 elsewhere in the US). Offers week-long ski packages to Bormio, Cervinia, and Cortina.

Special-interest tours for practitioners and spectators of other sports include many biking and hiking tours of varying difficulty. For the names and addresses of their organizers, see *Camping and Caravanning, Hiking and Biking,* in this section.

Among sport packages popular throughout Europe — including Italy — are golf packages. Customized golf packages to Italy are offered by *Golfing Holidays* (231 E. Millbrae Ave., Millbrae, CA 94030; phone: 415-697-0230) and *ITC Golf Tours* (4439 Atlantic Ave., Suite 205, Long Beach, CA 90807; phone: 800-257-4981 or 213-595-6905).

Other packages include those focused on — and guaranteeing entrance in — marathons. *Marathon Tours* (108 Main St., Charlestown, MA 02129; phone: 617-242-7845) sends runners off to participate in an annual marathon race in Venice.

Horseback riding holidays are the province of *FITS Equestrian* (2011 Alamo Pintado Rd., Solvang, CA 93463; phone: 805-688-9494). The choices — not for beginners — include 1 week of riding in Sardinia and Tuscany. *Equitour* (P.O. Box 807, Dubois, WY; phone: 307-455-3363 in Wyoming; 800-545-0019 elsewhere in the US) offers 8-day riding packages near Florence and Rome.

Sports-oriented special-interest packages also include many bicycle and hiking tours of varying levels of difficulty. For the names and addresses of their organizers, see *Camping and Caravanning, Hiking and Biking,* below.

And for those seeking a relaxing vacation focusing on physical health and beautification, spa packages cover arrangements at Italy's thermal resorts. These usually are 1 week long and provide accommodations, some or all meals, and one or two treatments daily (classic spa treatments such as manual or hydromassage, mud baths, and so on), often with the option of a beauty program rather than the basic spa regimen. *Health and Fitness Vacations* (2911 Grand Ave., Suite 3A, Mayfair in the Grove, Miami, FL 33133; phone: 305-445-3876), a specialist in spa vacations throughout Europe, has packages to Abano Terme near Venice, to Montecatini Terme, the well-known spa about 30 miles (48 km) northwest of Florence, and to the island of Ischia.

Camping and Caravanning, Hiking and Biking

CAMPING: Italy welcomes campers, whether they come alone or with a group, with tents or in recreational vehicles — generally known in Europe as "caravans" (a term that technically refers to towable campers as opposed to fully motorized vehicles as opposed to the fully motorized vehicles known as "minibuses" or "minivans"). Camping probably is the best way to enjoy the Italian countryside. And, fortunately, campgrounds in Italy are plentiful. Italy has thousands of campgrounds, or *campeggi,* the majority located on the northern lakes and on the coasts of the Adriatic, Tyrrhenian, and Ligurian seas. They are used by millions of people a year, many of them foreigners.

Where to Camp – Caravanning is extremely popular with European vacationers, and many parks cater more to the caravanner than to the tent dweller. Italian campgrounds are graded by stars: Degree of organization, quality of accommodations, and rates increase according to the number of stars. Some campgrounds have minimal facilities, and others are quite elaborate, with a variety of amenities on the premises. Most sites are open from about *Easter* through October.

Language barrier aside, directors of campgrounds often have a great deal of information about their region, and some even will arrange local tours or recommend sports facilities or attractions in the immediate area. Campgrounds also provide the atmosphere and opportunity to meet other travelers and exchange useful information. Too much so, sometimes — the popularity of European campgrounds causes them to be quite crowded during the summer, and campsites can be so close together that any attempt at privacy or getting away from it all is sabotaged. As campgrounds fill quickly throughout the season, and, the more isolated sites always go first, it's a good idea to arrive early in the day and reserve your chosen spot — which leaves you free to explore the area for the rest of the day. (Whenever possible, try to call ahead and arrange a "pitch" in advance. At the height of the season, if you do not have advance reservations, you may be lucky to get even a less desirable site.)

Fees for camping in Italy frequently are not inclusive; the operator of a site should furnish you with information about billing when you check in. At the end of your stay you will be given a "fiscal receipt" or an "invoice" that will itemize tax and surcharges. The rates usually are reasonble; there also may be a surcharge for tents and vehicles.

In some communities it is possible to camp free on public grounds. Ask the city police or local tourist information office about regulations. To camp on private property you first must obtain the permission of the landowner or tenant — and assume the responsibility of leaving the land exactly as you found it in return for the hospitality.

Italian campgrounds generally are well marked. Still, it's best to have a map or check the information available in one of the numerous comprehensive guides to sites across the Continent and/or the sources listed below. It also may be difficult to find camping facilities open before June or after September, so a guide that gives this information comes in particularly handy off-season.

In the US, camping maps, brochures, and lists of sites across the Continent are distributed by the European tourist offices, and a variety of useful publications also are available from American and European automobile clubs and other associations. The *Automobile Club d'Italia (ACI)* publishes a paperback book, *Campeggi in Italia,* a succinct and specific outline of facilities at sites, organized by localities. To obtain the book or make reservations, before you go contact *Federcampeggio* (Via Vittorio Emanuele, Casella Postale 11, Calenzano 23-50041, Florence, Italy; phone: 55-882391). Allow plenty of time to receive the guide, which comes with a booking form, and to then make your reservations. *Federcampeggio* also publishes a camping map available free from that organization or from the Italian Government Travel Office. To make reservations after you're in Italy (this is a chancy venture), contact *Federcampeggio*'s international reservation headquarters at the address above.

The *American Automobile Association (AAA)* also offers a number of useful resources, including its 600-page *Travel Guide to Europe* and the 64-page *Motoring Europe,* as well as a variety of useful maps; contact the nearest branch of *AAA* or the national office (see *Traveling by Car,* in this section). In addition, the *Automobile Association of Great Britain (AA)* publishes a comprehensive guide, *Camping and Caravanning in Europe* ($12.95), which lists over 4,000 sites throughout Europe, as well as other information of interest to campers in Italy. It is available from *AA* Publishing (Fanum House, Basingstoke, Hampshire RG21 2EA, England; phone: 256-20123), from the *British Travel Bookshop* (40 W. 57th St., New York, NY 10019; phone: 212-765-0898), and in other travel bookstores.

The French international camping organization *Fédération Internationale de Camping et Caravaning* issues a pass, called a *carnet,* that entitles the bearer to a modest discount on camping fees throughout Europe, and is actually required at some Italian campgrounds. It is available in the US from the *National Campers and Hikers Association* (4804 Transit Rd., Bldg. 2, Depew, NY 14043; phone: 716-668-6242) for a fee of $30, which includes membership in the association, as well as camping information. In Italy, it also is available from *Federcampeggio* (address above) or the *Automobile Club d'Italia* (261 Via Cristoforo Colombo, Rome 00185; phone: 6-5106; or 8 Via Marsala, Rome 00185; phone: 6-49981). Additionally, local tourist offices in Italy may provide brochures about camping in the area, although these probably will not be available in English.

Most experienced campers prefer to bring their own tried and true equipment, but camping equipment is available for sale or rent throughout Italy. For information on outfitters, consult the above-mentioned guides to camping and caravanning or contact the national tourist offices in the US which may be able to refer you to reliable Italian dealers.

Keep in mind that accessible food will lure scavenging wildlife, which may invade tents and vehicles. Also, even if you are assured that the campground where you are staying provides potable water, it is safer to use bottled, purified, or boiled water for drinking. To purify tap water, either use a water purification kit (available at most camping supply stores) or bring the water to a full, *rolling* boil over a campstove. It also is inadvisable to use water from streams, rivers, or lakes — even purified.

Organized Camping Trips – A packaged camping tour abroad is a good way to have your cake and eat it, too. The problems of advance planning and day-to-day organizing are left to someone else, yet you still reap the benefits that shoestring travel affords and can enjoy the insights of experienced guides and the company of other campers. Be aware, however, that these packages usually are geared to the young, with ages 18 and 35 as common limits. Transfer from place to place is by bus or van (as on other sightseeing tours), overnights are in tents, and meal arrangements vary. Often there is a kitty that covers meals in restaurants or in the camps; sometimes there is a chef, and sometimes the cooking is done by the participants themselves. When considering a packaged camping tour, be sure to find out if equipment is included and what individual participants are required to bring.

The *Specialty Travel Index* (305 San Anselmo Ave., Suite 313, San Anselmo, CA 94960; phone: 415-459-4900) is a directory to special-interest travel and an invaluable resource. Listings include tour operators specializing in camping, as well as myriad other interests that combine nicely with a camping trip, such as biking, motorcycling, horseback riding, ballooning, and boating. The index costs $6 per copy, $10 for a year's subscription of two issues.

Among such packages are the camping tours of Italy offered by the following:

Autotours (20 Craven Ter., London W2, England; phone: 44-71-258-0272). Their camping trips depart from London and range from 3 to 10 weeks. A variety of Italian itineraries is available.

Himalayan Travel (PO Box 481, Greenwich, CT 06836; phone: 800-225-2380). Offers a variety of camping trips throughout Europe, including a multi-country tour that includes camping in Italy.

World Tracks Limited (12 Abingdon Rd., London W8 6AF, England; phone: 71-937-3028). Offers a number of motorcoach camping trips that traverse Europe, including Italy, and last anywhere from 21 to 49 days in length.

Also note that a number of packagers listed below under "Hiking" and "Biking" may offer these pursuits in combination with camping — it pays to call and ask when planning your trip.

Recreational Vehicles – Known in Europe as caravans, recreational vehicles (RVs) will appeal most to the kind of person who prefers the flexibility of accommodation —

there are countless campgrounds throughout Europe and many of them provide RV hookups — and enjoys camping with a little extra comfort.

An RV undoubtedly saves a traveler a great deal of money on accommodations; in-camp cooking saves money on food as well. However, it is important to remember that renting an RV is a major expense; also, any kind of RV increases gas consumption considerably.

Although the term "recreational vehicle" is applied to all manner of camping vehicles, whether towed or self-propelled, generally the models available for rent in Italy and nearby countries are either towable campers (caravans) or motorized RVs. The motorized models usually are either minivans or minibuses — vans customized in various ways for camping, often including elevated roofs — or larger, coach-type, fully equipped homes on wheels, requiring electrical hookups at night to run the TV set, air conditioning, and kitchen appliances. Although most models are equipped with standard shift, occasionally automatic shift vehicles may be available for an additional charge.

Towed vehicles can be hired overseas, but usually are not offered by US or international companies. Motorized models are available from international and regional car rental companies in the major cities (see *Traveling by Car,* earlier in this section), although you probably will have to do some calling around to find one.

If you are planning to caravan all over Europe, make sure that the appliances in the vehicle you choose are equipped to deal with the electrical and gas standards of all countries on your itinerary. There are differences, for instance, between the bottled stove gas supplied in various countries. You should have either a sufficient supply of the gas your camper requires or equipment that can use more than one type. When towing a camper, note that something towed is not automatically covered by the liability insurance of the primary vehicle, so the driver's Green Card (called a *Carta Verde* in Italy) must carry a specific endorsement that covers the towed vehicle.

Whether driving a camper or towing, it is essential to have some idea of the terrain you'll be encountering en route. Only experienced drivers should drive campers, especially in northern Italy where the terrain is quite steep. In fact, grades often are too steep for certain vehicles to negotiate and some roads are off limits to towed caravans. Also be aware that mountain passes and tunnels crossing the borders into France, Switzerland, Austria, and Yugoslavia sometimes are closed in winter, depending on altitude, road grade, and severity of the weather. The *AAA* and other guides noted above provide detailed information on principal passes and tunnels. Your best source of information on specific weather and road conditions is the *Automobile Club d'Italia*'s phone assistance center (phone: 6-4212; operators speak English). Local tourist offices are another good source of road information.

Among the companies offering RV rentals in Italy or in other European countries (which can be driven into Italy) are the following:

Auto Europe (PO Box 1907, Camden, ME 04843; phone: 207-236-8235 in Maine; 800-223-5555 elsewhere in the US). Offers minibus rentals in France, Germany, and Great Britain.

Avis Car Away (6- Rue de Caen, Paris 92400; phone: 1-43-34-15-81). Affiliated with *Avis* car rentals, this company rents fully-equipped motor homes in France.

Avis Rent-A-Car (6128 E. 38th St., Tulsa, OK 74135 (phone: 800-331-1084, ext. 7719). This division of *Avis* offers minibus rentals at numerous locations throughout Italy, as well as in France, the Netherlands, and Switzerland.

Connex International (23 N. Division St., Peekskill, NY 10566; phone: 800-333-3949 or 914-739-0066). Rents minibuses in Spain and motorized RVs in Germany, Great Britain, and the Netherlands.

Europe by Car (One Rockefeller Plaza, New York, NY 10020; phone: 212-581-3040 in New York State; 800-223-1516 elsewhere in the US; and 9000 Sunset Blvd., Los Angeles, CA 90069; phone: 800-252-9401 or 213-272-0424). Rents minibuses in Italy, as well as Austria, Belgium, Denmark, France, Germany, Greece, Hungary, Ireland, Luxembourg, the Netherlands, and Switzerland, as well as RVs in Germany.

FCI Location (Zone Industrielle de Sant-Brendan, Quentin 22800, France; phone: 33-96-74-08-36). Rents motorized RVs in France.

Foremost Euro-Car (5430 Van Nuys Blvd., Suite 306, Van Nuys, CA 91401; phone: 800-272-3299 or 818-786-1960). Rents motorized RVs in Germany and Great Britain.

Kemwel Group (106 Calvert St., Harrison, NY 10528; phone: 800-678-0678 or 914-835-5555). Rents minibuses throughout Europe, including Italy.

Trois Soleils (Maison Trois Soleils, 2 Rte. de Paris, Ittenheim 67117, France; phone: 33-88-69-17-17). Rents motorized RVs, as well as some basic campers in France.

The general policy with the above agencies is to make reservations far enough in advance to receive a voucher required to pick up the vehicle at the designated location in Europe. RV rentals also may be arranged on arrival from a number of other European companies. For additional rental sources, ask at local car rental companies and national tourist board offices. Whether arranging the rental before leaving the US or once in Europe, make reservations as early as possible as the supply of RVs is limited and the demand great.

Useful information on RVs is available from the following sources:

Living on Wheels, by Richard A. Wolters. Provides useful information on how to choose and operate a recreational vehicle. As it's currently out of print, check your library.

Recreational Vehicle Industry Association (*RVIA;* PO Box 2999, Reston, VA 22090-2999). Issues a useful complimentary package of information on RVs, as well as a 24-page magazine-size guide, *Set Free in an RV* ($3), and a free catalogue of RV sources and consumer information. Write to the association for these and other publications.

Recreational Vehicle Rental Association (*RVRA;* 3251 Old Lee Hwy., Suite 500, Fairfax, VA 22030; phone: 800-336-0355 or 703-591-7130). This RV dealers group publishes an annual rental directory, *Who's Who in RV Rentals* ($7.50).

TL Enterprises (29901 Agoura Rd., Agoura, CA 91301; phone: 818-991-4980) publishes two monthly magazines for RV enthusiasts: *Motorhome* and *Trailer Life.* A year's subscription to either costs $22; a combined subscription to both costs $44. Members of the *TL Enterprises' Good Sam Club* can subscribe for half price and also receive discounts on a variety of other RV services; membership costs $19 per year.

Trailblazer (1000 124th Ave. NE, Bellevue, WA 98005; phone: 206-455-8585). A recreational-vehicle and motorhome magazine. A year's subscription costs $24.

HIKING: If you would rather eliminate all the gear and planning and take to the outdoors unencumbered, park the car and go for a day's hike. By all means, cover as much area as you can by foot; you'll see everything in far more detail than you would from the window of any conveyance. Walking is a good way to explore any country, and Italy is no exception. Trails abound in Italy, as does specific information on how to find them. Tourist authorities distribute information sheets on walking and mountaineering, and there are numerous other sources for those intent on getting about on their own.

The possibilities range from an easy day's jaunt to the popular and difficult Tour du Mont-Blanc, a 100-mile route around the mountain massif taking in Italy, as well as France and Switzerland. The best hiking trails are in northern Italy, in the Lombardy Lakes district and in the Dolomites. The terrain there is hilly to mountainous. If you are physically fit — that is, if you can walk a strenuous 5 to 10 miles a day — you will truly enjoy hiking this scenic Alpine region. Serious hiking — with backpack and compass — in southern Italy, however, can be less than rewarding. Especially during peak season — from May to October — the weather is hot and the traffic along footpaths, which generally run parallel to roadways, is heavy. For information on suggested hikes through Italy's national parks, see *Walking* in DIVERSIONS.

Among the few hiking guidebooks specifically about Italy are *Backpacking and Walking in Italy* by Stefano Ardito (Bradt Publishers; $15.95) and *Dolomites of Italy: A Travel Guide* by James and Ann Goldsmith (Hunter Publishing; $17.95); both are available from the *Tattered Cover* (2955 East First Ave., Denver, CO 80206; phone: 800-833-9327 or 303-322-7727). Two good general books on Europe that include Italian trails are *Tramping in Europe* by J. Sydney Jones (out of print; check your library) and *100 Hikes in the Alps* by Ira Spring and Harvey Edwards (The Mountaineers, 1985; $10.95). The latter is particularly informative, containing 16 suggested hikes along the French, Swiss, and Austrian borders.

Another guidebook is the Rome volume of the *Walking Through* series, which is available from *VLE Limited* (PO Box 444, Ft. Lee, NJ 07024; phone: 201-585-5080 or 212-580-8030) for $3. And be sure to see our own new *Birnbaum's Florence 1992, Birnbaum's Rome 1992,* and *Birnbaum's Venice 1992* ($10 each), edited by Stephen Birnbaum and Alexandra Mayes Birnbaum, which include walks to and through these cities' most spectacular sites and little-known corners. Available in most bookstores, these guides also can be ordered from HarperCollins Publishers (Order Dept., Keystone Park, Scranton, PA 18512; phone: 800-242-7737).

Freytag & Berndt, the Austrian map company, also publishes a series of eight excellent topographical maps designed for hikers. They are available for $5.95 from *Map Link* (25 E. Mason St., Santa Barbara, CA 93101; phone: 805-965-4402), which stocks a wealth of other maps useful for hikers.

Italian touring, hiking, and mountaineering organizations are a particularly good source of trail information suitable for the average hiker. The *Club Alpino Italiano* (3 Via Ugo Foscolo, Milan 20121; phone: 2-72-023085) owns about 600 huts in the mountain districts and annually publishes a book including a map and information on access, equipment, and tariffs for each site. The club also has highly qualified instructors and guides who assist travelers with itineraries, excursions, and arrangements for any specialized mountain sport.

The *Touring Club Italiano* (10 Corso Italia, Milan 20122; phone: 2-852-6225) also publish detailed maps, guides, and other information useful to hikers. Additional *Touring Club Italiano* offices are in Bari and Rome. For long visits, membership in one of these local clubs is suggested.

■ **A word of warning:** It is particularly important to wear socks, long pants, and long-sleeve shirts when hiking in heavily wooded areas due to the danger of Neuro Borreliosis, which is spread through the bite of the deer tick and other ticks. First diagnosed years ago in Europe, this disease recently has become familiar to Americans as Lyme Borreliosis (also known as "Lyme Tick Disease"). A strong insect repellent designed to repel ticks also may be helpful. The initial symptoms of this disease often are a swelling and/or a rash, generally accompanied by flu-like symptoms — such as fever and aching muscles. Readily curable in the early stages through antibiotics, if left untreated it can lead to serious complications. For information on areas of contagion, precautions, and treatment, contact the *Lyme*

Borreliosis Foundation (PO Box 462, Tolland, CT 06084; phone: 203-871-2900). A number of helpful hints also is provided in *Ticks and What You Can Do About Them,* which is available from Wilderness Press (2440 Bancroft Way, Berkeley, CA 94704; phone: 800-443-7227 or 510-843-8080).

Organized Hiking Trips – Those who prefer to travel as part of an organized group should contact the following organizations:

Alternative Travel Groups (69-71 Banbury, Oxford, England 0X2 6PE; phone: 800-527-5997). The motto of this company is "The best way to see a country is on foot." Among its numerous itineraries worldwide, they offer several walking tours of Italy: an 18-day Path to Rome tour, an 11-day tour of southern Tuscany, a 9-day Verona and the Dolomites tour, a 9-day Way to Assisi tour, and a 9-day tour of Sicily.

American Youth Hostels (PO Box 37613, Washington, DC 20013-7613; phone: 202-783-6161). Although as we went to press they were not offering a specific Italian excursion, their itineraries vary from year to year, so check at the time you plan to travel.

Butterfield & Robinson (70 Bond St., Suite 300, Toronto, Ontario M5B 1X3, Canada; phone: 800-387-1147 or 416-864-1354). Their numerous Italian hiking tours emphasize easy exercise and the finest in dining and accommodations — definitely not "roughing it."

Country Cycling Tours (140 W. 83rd St., New York, NY 10024; phone: 212-874-5151). Offers 7- to 8-day walking tours in Tuscany.

Distant Journeys (PO Box 1211, Camden, ME 04843; phone: 207-799-5507 from June 1 to October 15; 207-236-9788 during the rest of the year). Offers a 12-day hiking tour that begins and ends in France but includes hiking in the Italian Alps.

Forum Travel International (91 Gregory, #21, Pleasant Hill, CA 94523; phone: 510-671-2900). Offers a number of enticing itineraries in Italy, in four grades of difficulty — the most energetic grade covering as many as 20 miles a day, and geared to those already accustomed to hard mountain walking.

Genet Expeditions (PO Box 230861, Anchorage, AK 99523 (phone: 800-33-GENET or 907-561-2123). Offers a hiking/climbing tour that includes the Italian side of Mont Blanc in the Alps.

Himalayan Travel (PO Box 481, Greenwich, CT 06836; phone: 800-225-2380). Offers inn-to-inn hiking trips in Italy in Tuscany and Cinque Terre. Their multi-country hiking/camping package also visits Italy.

Mountain Travel-Sobek (6420 Fairmount Ave., El Cerrito, CA 94530; phone: 415-527-8100 in California; 800-227-2384 elsewhere in the US). This adventure-trip specialist offers a variety of hiking tours throughout Europe, including a 13-day hike in Piemonte, part of which included a 10-day hike rated "moderate" — meaning that participants need not carry heavy packs while hiking 3 to 6 hours a day in the foothills. Horses transport the equipment, and accommodations are in small mountain inns or refuges. More challenging itineraries take on the Alps, including the famous Tour du Mont-Blanc.

Sierra Club (Outing Department, 730 Polk St., San Francisco, CA 94109; phone: 415-776-2211). Offers a selection of trips each year, usually about 2 weeks in length. Recent itineraries included a hike through the Italian Dolomites; other tours in Italy combined hiking with biking or canoeing. Some are backpacking trips, moving to a new camp each day; others make day hikes from a base camp.

Wilderness Travel (801 Allston Way, Berkeley, CA 94710; phone: 800-247-6700 or 510-548-0420). Their 12-day tour of Italy's medieval hill towns takes in

Volterra, San Gimignano, and Siena, following country paths through Tuscany. Accommodations are in small country inns, and participants get to sample local food and wines (the fall departure coincides with the grape harvest). Another itinerary is a 12-day trip along the Italian Riviera.

An alternative to dealing directly with the above companies is to contact *All Adventure Travel,* a specialist in hiking and biking trips worldwide. This company, which acts as a representative for numerous special tour packagers offering such outdoor adventures, can provide a wealth of detailed information about each packager and programs offered. They also will help you design and arrange all aspects of a personalized itinerary. This company operates much like a travel agency, collecting commissions from the packagers. Therefore, there is no additional charge for these services. For information, contact *All Adventure Travel,* PO Box 4307, Boulder, CO 80306 (phone: 800-537-4025 or 303-499-1981).

BIKING: Italians are such cycling enthusiasts that they even have a patron saint for the sport — the Madonna del Ghisallo, whose statue adorns the town of Bellagio on Lake Como! And for young and/or fit travelers, the bicycle does offer a marvelous tool for exploring Italy. Throughout the country, secondary roads thread through picturesque stretches of the countryside. Biking does have its drawbacks: Little baggage can be carried, travel is slow, and cyclists are exposed to the elements. However, should a cyclist need rest or refuge from the weather, there always is a welcoming bar or comfortable *pensione* around the next bend.

The best biking is in the north, which, except for the Alps, tends to be flatter than the rest of this mountainous country. A popular region is the northern lakes area; grades are steep, but the scenery is worth the effort. Farther south the secondary roads may be in poor condition and clogged with traffic; it's a good idea to travel with a biking tour group for which the best routes have been worked out in advance.

Besides being a viable way to tour Italy — and to burn calories to make room for larger portions of Italian food — biking is a great way to meet people. Remember, however, that although many residents of Italy do speak some English, this is not likely to be the case in rural areas, so pack a copy of an Italian-English phrase book if your command of Italian is not up to par. (For a list of helpful terms and basic expressions, see *Useful Words and Phrases,* in this section.)

A good book to help you plan a trip is *Bicycle Touring in Europe* by Karen and Gary Hawkins available for $11.95 from Pantheon Books (201 E. 50th St., New York, NY 10022; phone: 800-726-0600). It offers information on buying and equipping a touring bike, useful clothing and supplies, and helpful techniques for the long-distance biker. Another good general book is *Europe by Bike,* by Karen and Terry Whitehall ($10.95; Mountaineers Books, 1011 SW Klickitat Way, Suite 107, Seattle, WA 98134; phone: 800-553-4453).

Detailed maps will infinitely improve a biking tour, and are available from a number of sources. In addition to those offered by the *Touring Club Italiano* (see "Hiking" above), the excellent Michelin maps (on a scale of 1:200,000) provide detailed and clear road references. They are available from Michelin Guides and Maps (PO Box 3305, Spartanburg, SC 29304-3305; phone: 803-599-0850 in South Carolina; 800-423-0485 elsewhere in the US). A number of other maps, not distributed in the US, can be purchased en route in Italy.

One of the best sources for detailed topographical maps and just about any other type of map (of just about anywhere in the world) is *Map Link* (25 E. Mason St., Santa Barbara, CA 93101; phone: 805-965-4402). Their comprehensive guide *The World Map Directory* ($29.95) includes a wealth of sources, and if they don't stock a map of the area in which you are interested (or the type of map best suited to your outdoor exploration), they will order it for you. But it is likely that they'll have something to meet your needs — they stock hundreds of maps of Italy, including a wide range of topographical maps.

Choosing, Renting, and Buying a Bike – Although many bicycling enthusiasts choose to take along their own bikes, bicycles can be rented throughout Italy. Long and short rentals are available; however, particularly in rural areas, it may pay to check ahead. Also note that some Italian train stations offer "rent it here, leave it there" programs that allow you to rent a bike and return it at another station.

As an alternative to renting, you might consider buying a bicycle in Italy. Bicycle shops in Italy that rent bikes also usually sell them and buying a used bike might be even less expensive than a long-term rental. For information on bicycle rental shops in Italian cities, see *Sources and Resources* in the individual city reports of THE CITIES.

If you do buy a bike and plan on taking it home, remember that it will be subject to an import duty by US Customs if its price (or the total of purchases made abroad) exceeds $400. When evaluating this cost, take into account additional charges for shipping. A European bicycle purchased in the US should have proof-of-purchase papers to avoid potential customs problems. Even the smallest towns usually have a bike shop, so it's not difficult to replace or add to gear; however, because tires and tubes are sized to metric dimensions in Italy, when riding your own bike, bring extras from home.

Airlines going from the US (or elsewhere) to Europe generally allow bicycles to be checked as baggage and require that the pedals be removed, handlebars be turned sideways, and the bike be in a shipping carton (which some airlines provide, subject to availability — call ahead to make sure). If buying a shipping carton from a bicycle shop, check the airline's specifications and also ask about storing the carton at the destination airport so you can use it again for the return flight. Although some airlines charge only a nominal fee, if the traveler already has checked two pieces of baggage, there may be an excess baggage charge of $70 to $80 for the bicycle. As regulations vary from carrier to carrier, be sure to call well before departure to find out your airline's specific regulations. As with other baggage, make sure that the bike is thoroughly labeled with your name, a business address and phone number, and the correct airport destination code. Also note that most Italian trains have facilities for bicycle transport.

Biking Tours – A number of organizations offer bike tours in Italy. Linking up with a bike tour is more expensive than traveling alone, but with experienced leaders, an organized tour often becomes an educational, as well as a very social, experience.

One of the attractions of a bike tour is that the shipment of equipment — the bike — is handled by organizers, and the shipping fee is included in the total tour package. Travelers simply deliver the bike to the airport, already disassembled and boxed; shipping cartons can be obtained from most bicycle shops with little difficulty. Bicyclists not with a tour must make their own arrangements with the airline, and there are no standard procedures for this (see above). Although some tour organizers will rent bikes, most prefer that participants bring a bike with which they are already familiar. Another attraction of *some* tours is the existence of a "sag wagon" to carry extra luggage, fatigued cyclists, and their bikes, too, when pedaling another mile is impossible.

Most bike tours are scheduled from May to October, last 1 or 2 weeks, are limited to 20 to 25 people, and provide lodging in inns or hotels, though some use hostels or even tents. Tours vary considerably in style and ambience, so request brochures from several operators in order to make the best decision. When contacting groups, be sure to ask about the maximum number of people on the trip, the maximum number of miles to be traveled each day, and the degree of difficulty of the biking; these details should determine which tour you join and can greatly affect your enjoyment of the experience. Planning ahead is essential because trips often fill up 6 months or more in advance.

Among the companies offering biking tours in Italy are the following:

Backroads Bicycle Touring (1516 Fifth St., Berkeley, CA 94710-1713; phone: 800-245-3874 or 510-527-1555). Offers superior food and accommodations on its tours, which are geared to beginning and intermediate riders. Among their itineraries is an 8-day biking tour of Tuscany.

Baumeler Tours (10 Grand Ave., Rockville Centre, NY 11570-9861; phone: 516-766-6160, collect, in New York State; 800-6-ABROAD elsewhere in the US). Specializing in bicycling tours, both individual and escorted, this company offers a number of itineraries in Europe, including 8-day biking tours of Tuscany.

Butterfield & Robinson (70 Bond St., Suite 300, Toronto, Ontario M5B 1X3, Canada; phone: 800-387-1147 or 416-864-1354). Offers a number of first class biking tours, many quite sophisticated in focus and including luxurious accommodations and fine dining en route. Trips are geared to various age groups and are rated at four levels of difficulty. Offers 7-day tours in northern Italy and 8-day tours of Puglia, Tuscany, and Umbria.

Country Cycling Tours (140 W. 83rd St., New York, NY 10024; phone: 800-284-8954 or 212-874-5151). Offers an 8-day biking tour of Tuscany.

Earth Ventures (2625 N. Meridien St., Suige 612, Indianapolis, IN 46208-7705; phone: 317-926-0453). Itineraries include 11- to 42-day biking trips that tour the Italian Riviera, Rome, Tuscany, and Umbria, as well as various regions in northern and southern Italy.

Eurobike (PO Box 40, DeKalb, IL 60115; phone: 800-252-1990 or 815-758-8851). Offers a 17-day biking tour that visits Milan, Montecatini, Pisa, Rome, and Venice.

Progressive Travel Ltd. (1932 First Ave., Suite 1100, Seattle, WA 98101; phone: 800-245-2229 or 206-443-4225). Offers 8-day inn-to-inn biking itineraries from Venice to Milan.

Rocky Mountain Cycling Tours (PO Box 1978, Canmore, Alberta T0L 0M0, Canada; phone: 800-661-2453 or 403-678-6770). Organizes an 8-day biking tour of Tuscany and Umbria.

Travent International (PO Box 305, Waterbury Center, VT 05677-0305; phone: 800-325-3009 or 802-244-5153). Offers an 8-day biking tour centered around Venice. Also offers custom biking trips throughout Italy.

Other useful sources of information on bicycling in Italy include the following:

American Youth Hostels (PO Box 37613, Washington, DC 20013-7613; phone: 202-783-6161). A number of biking tours are sponsored annually by this non-profit organization and its local chapters. Membership is open to all ages and departures are geared to various age groups and levels of skill and frequently feature accommodations in hostels — along with hotels for adults and campgrounds for younger participants.

Cyclists' Touring Club (*CTC;* Cotterell House, 69 Meadrow, Godalming, Surrey GU7 3HS, England; phone: 483-41-7217). Britain's largest cycling association, this group organizes tours of numerous countries, including Italy. *CTC* has a number of planned routes available in pamphlet form for bikers on their own and helps members plan their own tours. The club also publishes a yearly handbook, as well as magazines.

International Bicycle Touring Society (*IBTS;* PO Box 6979, San Diego, CA 92106-0979; phone: 619-226-TOUR). This nonprofit organization regularly sponsors low-cost bicycle tours led by member volunteers. Participants must be over 21. For information, send $2 plus a self-addressed, stamped envelope.

League of American Wheelmen (190 W. Ostend St., Suite 120, Baltimore, MD 21230; phone: 301-539-3399). This organziation publishes *Tourfinder,* a list of organizations that sponsor bicycle tours worldwide. The list is free with membership ($25 individual, $30 family) and can be obtained by non-members who send $5. The *League* also can put you in touch with biking groups in your area.

Preparing

Calculating Costs

$ A realistic appraisal of your travel expenses is the most crucial bit of planning you will undertake before any trip. It also is, unfortunately, one for which it is most difficult to give precise, practical advice.

After several years of living relatively high on the hog, travel from North America to Europe dropped off precipitously in 1987 in response, among other considerations, to the relative weakness of the US dollar on the Continent. Many Americans who had enjoyed bargain prices while touring through Europe only a couple of years before, found that disadvantageous exchange rates really put a crimp in their travel planning. But even though the halcyon days of dollar domination seem over for the present, discount fares and the availability of charter flights can greatly reduce the cost of a European vacation. Package tours can even further reduce costs, as European providers of travel services try to win back their American clients in the 1990s.

While Italy never has been one of Europe's least expensive destinations, it always has been popular with both the first-time and the seasoned traveler, and it is certainly one where the competition for American visitors works to inspire surprisingly affordable travel opportunities. Nevertheless, most travelers still have to plan carefully and manage their travel funds prudently.

In Italy, estimating travel expenses depends on the mode of transportation you choose, the part or parts of the country you plan to visit, how long you will stay, and in some cases, what time of year you plan to travel. In addition to the basics of transportation, hotels, meals, and sightseeing, you have to take into account seasonal price changes that apply on certain air routings and at popular vacation destinations, as well as the vagaries of currency exchange.

In general, it's usually also a good idea to organize your trip so that you pay for as much of it as you can in Italy, using lire purchased from Italian banks (which, barring interim variations, generally offer a more advantageous rate of exchange than US sources). That means minimizing the amount of advance deposits paid in US greenbacks and deferring as many bills as possible until you arrive in Europe, although the economies possible through prepaid package tours and other special deals may offset the savings in currency exchange. (For further information on managing money abroad, see *Credit and Currency,* in this section.)

DETERMINING A BUDGET: When calculating costs, start with the basics, the major expenses being transportation, accommodations, and food. However, don't forget such extras as local transportation, shopping, and such miscellaneous items as laundry and tips. The reasonable cost of these items usually is a positive surprise to your budget. Ask about special discount passes that provide unlimited travel by the day or the week on regular city transportation. Entries in the individual city reports in THE CITIES give helpful information on local transportation options.

Other expenses, such as the cost of local sightseeing tours, will vary from city to city. Tourist information offices are plentiful throughout Italy, and most of the better hotels will have someone at the front desk to provide a rundown on the costs of local tours and full-day excursions in and out of the city. Travel agents or railway booking offices (see *Traveling by Train,* in this section) can provide information on rail tours. The local tourist authority, also can provide information on current discount offerings (for offices in the US, see *Tourist Information Offices.*

Budget-minded families can take advantage of some of the more economical accommodations options to be found in Italy (see our discussion of accommodations in *On the Road,* in this section). Campgrounds are particularly inexpensive, and they are located throughout the country (see *Camping and Caravanning, Hiking and Biking,* in this section). Picnicking is another excellent way to cut costs, and Italy abounds with well-groomed parks (known as *giardini*) and idyllic pastoral settings. A stop at a local market can provide a feast of regional specialties at a surprisingly economical price compared to the cost of a restaurant lunch.

In planning any travel budget, it also is wise to allow a realistic amount for both entertainment and recreation. Are you planning to spend time sightseeing and visiting local museums? Do you intend to spend your days skiing at a popular resort? Is daily golf or tennis a part of your plan? Will your children be disappointed if they don't take a gondola ride in Venice? Finally, don't forget that if haunting clubs, discotheques, or other nightspots is an essential part of your vacation, or you feel that one performance at *La Scala* in Milan may not be enough, allow for the extra cost of nightlife.

If at any point in the planning process it appears impossible to estimate expenses, consider this suggestion: The easiest way to put a ceiling on the price of all these elements is to buy a package tour. A totally planned and escorted one, with almost all transportation, rooms, meals, sightseeing, local travel, tips, and a dinner show or two included and prepaid, provides a pretty exact total of what the trip will cost beforehand, and the only surprise will be the one you spring on yourself by succumbing to some irresistible, expensive souvenir. And keep in mind, particularly when calculating the major expenses, that costs vary according to fluctuations in the exchange rate — that is, how much of a given foreign currency a dollar will buy.

■ **Note:** The volatility of exchange rates means that between the time you originally make your hotel reservations and the day you arrive, the price in US dollars may vary substantially from the price originally quoted. To avoid paying more than you expected, it's wise to confirm rates by writing directly to hotels or by calling their representatives in the US.

Planning a Trip

Travelers fall into two categories: those who make lists and those who do not. Some people prefer to plot the course of their trip to the finest detail, with contingency plans and alternatives at the ready. For others, the joy of a voyage is its spontaneity; exhaustive planning only lessens the thrill of anticipation and the sense of freedom.

For most travelers, however, any week-plus trip to Italy can be too expensive for an "I'll take my chances" type of attitude. Even perennial gypsies and anarchistic wanderers have to take into account the time-consuming logistics of getting around, and even with minimal baggage, they need to think about packing. Hence, at least some planning is crucial.

This is not to suggest that you work out your itinerary in minute detail before you go, but it's still wise to decide certain basics at the very start: where to go, what to do, and how much to spend. These decisions require a certain amount of consideration. So before rigorously planning specific details, you might want to establish your general travel objectives:

1. How much time will you have for the entire trip, and how much of it are you willing to spend getting where you're going?
2. What interests and/or activities do you want to pursue while on vacation? Do you want to visit one, a few, or several different places?
3. At what time of year do you want to go?
4. What kind of geography or climate would you prefer?
5. Do you want peace and privacy or lots of activity and company?
6. How much money can you afford to spend for the entire vacation?

You now can make almost all of your own travel arrangements if you have time to follow through with hotels, airlines, tour operators, and so on. But you'll probably save considerable time and energy if you have a travel agent make arrangements for you. The agent also should be able to advise you of alternate arrangements of which you may not be aware. Only rarely will a travel agent's services cost a traveler any money, and they may even save you some (see *How to Use a Travel Agent,* below).

If it applies to your schedule and destination, pay particular attention to the dates when off-season rates go into effect. In major tourism areas, accommodations may cost less during the off-season (and the weather often is perfectly acceptable at this time). Off-season rates frequently are lower for car rentals and other facilities, too. In general, it is a good idea to be aware of holiday weeks, as rates at hotels generally are higher during these periods and rooms normally are heavily booked.

Make plans early. During the summer season and other holiday periods, make hotel reservations at least a month in advance in all major cities. If you are flying at peak times and want to benefit from the savings of discount fares or charter programs, purchase tickets as far ahead as possible. Many Italian hotels require deposits before they will guarantee reservations, and this most often is the case during peak travel periods. (Be sure you have a receipt for any deposit or use a credit card.) Religious and national holidays also are times requiring reservations well in advance in Italy.

Before your departure, find out what the weather is likely to be at your destination. Consult *When to Go,* in this section, for information on climatic variations and a chart of average temperatures. See *How to Pack,* in this section, for some suggestions on how to decide what clothes to take. Also see THE CITIES for information on special events that may occur during your stay. The city chapters also provide essential information on local transportation and other services and resources.

Make a list of any valuable items you are carrying with you, including credit card numbers and the serial numbers of your traveler's checks. Put copies in your purse or pocket, and leave other copies at home. Put a label with your name and home address on the inside of your luggage for identification in case of loss. Put your name and business address — *never your home address* — on a label on the outside of your luggage. (Those who run businesses from home should use the office address of a friend or relative.)

Review your travel documents. If you are traveling by air, check that your ticket has been filled in correctly. The left side of the ticket should have a list of each stop you will make (even if you are only stopping to change planes), beginning with your departure point. Be sure that the list is correct, and count the number of copies to see that you have one for each plane you will take. If you have confirmed reservations, be sure that the column marked "status" says "OK" beside each flight. Have in hand vouchers or proof of payment for any reservation for which you've paid in advance; this includes hotels, transfers to and from the airport, sightseeing tours, car rentals, and tickets to special events.

Although policies vary from carrier to carrier, it's still smart to reconfirm your flight

48 to 72 hours before departure, both going and returning. Reconfirmation is particularly recommended for point-to-point flights within Europe. If you will be driving while in Italy, bring your driver's license, International Driver's Permit, and any other necessary documentation — such as proof of insurance. In addition, all drivers are required by law to carry a portable emergency reflector (called a *triangolo*).

Finally, you always should bear in mind that despite the most careful plans, things do not always occur on schedule. If you maintain a flexible attitude and try to accept minor disruptions as less than cataclysmic, you will enjoy yourself a lot more.

How to Use a Travel Agent

A reliable travel agent remains the best source of service and information for planning a trip abroad, whether you have a specific itinerary and require an agent only to make reservations or you need extensive help in sorting through the maze of airfares, tour offerings, hotel packages, and the scores of other arrangements that may be involved in a trip to Italy.

Know what you want from a travel agent so that you can evaluate what you are getting. It is perfectly reasonable to expect your agent to be a thoroughly knowledgeable travel specialist, with information about your destination and, even more crucial, a command of current airfares, ground arrangements, and other wrinkles in the travel scene.

Most travel agents work through computer reservations systems (CRS). These are used to assess the availability and cost of flights, hotels, and car rentals, and through them they can book reservations. Despite reports of "computer bias," in which a computer may favor one airline over another, the CRS should provide agents with the entire spectrum of flights available to a given destination and the complete range of fares in considerably less time than it takes to telephone the airlines individually — and at no extra cost to the client.

Make the most intelligent use of a travel agent's time and expertise; understand the economics of the industry. As a client, traditionally you pay nothing for the agent's services; with few exceptions, it's all free, from hotel bookings to advice on package tours. Any money the travel agent makes on the time spent arranging your itinerary — booking hotels or flights, or suggesting activities — comes from commissions paid by the suppliers of these services — the airlines, hotels, and so on. These commissions generally run from 10% to 15% of the total cost of the service, although suppliers often reward agencies that sell their services in volume with an increased commission, called an override. In most instances, you'll find that travel agents make their time and experience available to you at no cost, and you do not pay more for an airline ticket, package tour, or other product bought from a travel agent than you would for the same product bought directly from the supplier.

Exceptions to the general rule of free service by a travel agent are the agencies beginning to practice net pricing. In essence, such agencies return their commissions and overrides to their customers and make their income by charging a flat fee per transaction instead (thus adding a charge after a reduction for the commissions has been made).Net fares and fees are a growing practice, though hardly widespread.

Even a conventional travel agent sometimes may charge a fee for special services. These chargeable items may include long-distance telephone or cable costs incurred in making a booking, reserving a room in a place that does not pay a commission (such as a small, out-of-the-way hotel), or special attention such as planning a highly personalized itinerary. A fee also may be assessed in instances of deeply discounted airfares.

Choose a travel agent with the same care with which you would choose a doctor or lawyer. You will be spending a good deal of money on the basis of the agent's judgment, so you have a right to expect that judgment to be mature, informed, and interested. At the moment, unfortunately, there aren't many standards within the travel agent industry to help you gauge competence, and the quality of individual agents varies enormously.

At present, only nine states have registration, licensing, or other forms of travel agent–related legislation on their books. Rhode Island licenses travel agents; Florida, Hawaii, Iowa, and Ohio register them; and California, Illinois, Oregon, and Washington have laws governing the sale of transportation or related services. While state licensing of agents cannot absolutely guarantee competence, it can at least ensure that an agent has met some minimum requirements.

Perhaps the best-prepared agents are those who have completed the CTC Travel Management program offered by the *Institute of Certified Travel Agents* and carry the initials CTC (Certified Travel Counselor) after their names. This indicates a relatively high level of expertise. For a free list of CTCs in your area, send a self-addressed, stamped, #10 envelope to *ICTA,* 148 Linden St., Box 82-56, Wellesley, MA 02181 (phone: 617-237-0280 in Massachusetts; 800-542-4282 elsewhere in the US).

An agent's membership in the *American Society of Travel Agents (ASTA)* can be a useful guideline in making a selection. But keep in mind that *ASTA* is an industry organization, requiring only that its members be licensed in those states where required; be accredited to represent the suppliers whose products they sell, including airline and cruise tickets; and adhere to its Principles of Professional Conduct and Ethics code. *ASTA* does not guarantee the competence, ethics, or financial soundness of its members, but it does offer some recourse if you feel you have been dealt with unfairly. Complaints may be registered with *ASTA* (Consumer Affairs Dept., PO Box 23992, Washington, DC 20026-3992; phone: 703-739-2782). First try to resolve the complaint directly with the supplier. For a list of *ASTA* members in your area, send a self-addressed, stamped, #10 envelope to *ASTA,* Public Relations Dept., at the address above.

There also is the *Association of Retail Travel Agents (ARTA),* a smaller but highly respected trade organization similar to *ASTA.* Its member agencies and agents similarly agree to abide by a code of ethics, and complaints about a member can be made to *ARTA*'s Grievance Committee, 1745 Jeff Davis Hwy., Arlington, VA 22202-3402 (phone: 800-969-6069 or 703-553-7777).

Perhaps the best way to find a travel agent is by word of mouth. If the agent (or agency) has done a good job for your friends over a period of time, it probably indicates a certain level of commitment and competence. Always ask not only for the name of the company but for the name of the specific agent with whom your friends dealt, for it is that individual who will serve you, and quality can vary widely within a single agency. There are some superb travel agents in the business, and they can facilitate vacation or business arrangements.

Entry Requirements and Documents

A valid US passport is the only document a US citizen needs to enter Italy, and that same passport also is needed to reenter the US. As a general rule, a US passport entitles the bearer to remain in Italy for up to 90 days as a tourist. Those wishing to stay longer can apply at any police station *(questura)* for individual extensions of 90 days each (up to a total visit of 6 months per stay — if your applications are accepted), which is readily granted provided the applicant can prove that he or she is a bona fide tourist with an independent means of support and no intention to work or study in Italy. Resident aliens of the US should inquire at the nearest Italian consulate to find out what documents they need to enter Italy; similarly, US citizens intending to work, study, or reside in Italy should address themselves to the consulate.

Few tourists are aware that they are required to register with the police within 3 days of their arrival in Italy. If you are staying in a hotel, the staff takes care of this formality for you, using particulars gleaned from your passport. If you are staying in a private home, you are supposed to do it yourself, but since the authorities rely on you to come to them, enforcement is not customary. If, having registered, you then move to another private home in a different town, you are supposed to register again.

Vaccination certificates are required only if the traveler is entering from an area of contagion as defined by the World Health Organization and, as the US is considered an area "free from contagion," an international vaccination certificate no longer is required for entering Italy for a short period of time. Because smallpox is considered eradicated from the world, only a few countries continue to require visitors to have a smallpox vaccination certificate. You certainly will not need one to travel to Italy or return to the US.

VISAS: Visas are required for study, residency, or work, and US citizens should address themselves to the Italian embassy or consulate well in advance of a proposed trip. Visas of this type are available for stays in Italy of up to 1 year. Note that although visas for study often are issued, it is much more difficult to get a visa permitting you to work in the country. The ready processing of a visa application also may be based on the duration of the visa you are requesting — visas for studying in Italy for several months are likely to be processed more quickly than year-long residency visas. Proof of substantial means of independent financial support during the stay also is pertinent to the acceptance of any long-term–stay application.

At least two items are necessary to apply for a visa: a valid passport and a completed visa form. (These forms may be obtained by sending a self-addressed, stamped envelope to any Italian consulate with a written request.) Depending on the type of visa you are requesting, additional documentation may be required. There are no processing fees for visas. Application must be made at the Italian consulate within your jurisdiction (see *The Italian Embassy and Consulates in the US,* in this section, for addresses). Visas normally are issued on the spot; however, if there is a backlog, you may have to return to pick it up a few days later. To avoid frustration and wasted time, it is a good idea to call ahead to check during what hours and days visa requests are accepted.

PASSPORTS: While traveling in Italy, carry your passport with you at all times (for an exception to this rule, see our note "When Checking In," below). If you lose your passport while abroad, immediately report the loss to the nearest US consulate or embassy (see *Medical and Legal Aid and Consular Services,* in this section, for locations in Italy). You can get a 3-month temporary passport directly from the consulate, but you must fill out a "loss of passport" form and follow the same application procedure — and pay the same fees — as you did for the original (see below). It's likely to speed things up if you have a record of your passport number and the place and date of its issue (a photocopy of the first page of your passport is perfect). Keep this information separate from your passport — you might want to give it to a traveling companion to hold or put it in the bottom of your suitcase.

US passports are now valid for 10 years from the date of issue (5 years for those under age 18). The expired passport itself is not renewable but must be turned in along with your application for a new and valid one (you will get it back, voided, when you receive the new one). Normal passports contain 24 pages, but frequent travelers can request a 48-page passport at no extra cost. Every individual, regardless of age, must have his or her own passport. Family passports no longer are issued. Passports can be renewed by mail with forms obtained at designated locations only if the expired passport was issued no more than 12 years before the date of application for renewal and it was not issued before the applicant's 16th birthday. The rules regarding teens under 18 and younger applicants may vary depending on age and when their previous passport was issued. Those who are eligible to apply by mail must send the completed form with the expired passport, two photos (see description below), and $55 (no execution fee required) to the nearest passport agency office. Delivery can take as little as 2 weeks or as long as 6 weeks during the busiest season — from approximately mid-March to mid-September.

Adults applying for the first time and younger applicants who must apply for a passport in person (as well as those who cannot wait for mail application turnaround) can do so at one of the following places:

1. The State Department passport agencies in Boston, Chicago, Honolulu, Houston, Los Angeles, Miami, New Orleans, New York City, Philadelphia, San Francisco, Seattle, Stamford, CT, and Washington, DC.
2. A federal or state courthouse.
3. Any of the 1,000 post offices across the country with designated acceptance facilities.

Application blanks are available at all these offices and must be presented with the following:

1. Proof of US citizenship. This can be a previous passport or one in which you were included. If you are applying for your first passport and were born in the United States, an original or certified birth certificate is the required proof. If you were born abroad, a Certificate of Naturalization, a Certificate of Citizenship, a Report of Birth Abroad of a Citizen of the United States, or a Certification of Birth is necessary.
2. Two 2-by-2-inch, front-view photographs in color or black and white, with a light, plain background, taken within the previous 6 months. These must be taken by a photographer rather than a machine.
3. A $65 passport fee ($40 for travelers under 18), which includes a $10 execution fee. *Note:* Your best bet is to bring the exact amount in cash (no change is given) or a separate check or money order for each passport (although families can combine several passport fees on one check or money order).
4. Proof of identity. Again, this can be a previous passport, a Certificate of Naturalization or of Citizenship, a driver's license, or a government ID card with a physical description or a photograph. Failing any of these, you should be accompanied by a blood relative or a friend of at least 2 years' standing who will testify to your identity. Credit cards or social security cards do not suffice as proof of identity — but note that since 1988, US citizens *must* supply their social security numbers.

As getting a passport — or international visa — through the mail can mean waiting as much as 6 weeks or more, a new mini-industry has cropped up in those cities where there is a US passport office. The yellow pages currently list quite a few organizations willing to wait on line to expedite obtaining a visa or passport renewal; there's even one alternative for those who live nowhere near the cities mentioned above. In the nation's capital there's an organization called the *Washington Passport and Visa Service.* It may be the answer for folks in need of special rapid action, since this organization can get a passport application or renewal turned around in a single day. What's more, their proximity to an embassy or consulate of every foreign country represented in the US helps to speed the processing of visa applications as well. The fee for a 5- to 7-day turnaround is $30; for next-day service the charge is $50; and for same-day service they charge $90. For information, application forms, and other prices, contact *Washington Passport and Visa Service,* 2318 18th St. NW, Washington, DC 20009 (phone: 800-272-7776).

If you need an emergency passport, it also is possible to be issued a passport in a matter of hours by going directly to your nearest passport office (there is no way, however, to avoid waiting in line). Explain the nature of the emergency, usually as serious as a death in the family; a ticket in hand for a flight the following day also will suffice. Should the emergency occur outside of business hours, all is not lost. There's a 24-hour telephone number in Washington, DC (phone: 202-634-3600) that can put you in touch with a State Department duty officer who may be able to expedite your application.

- **When Checking In:** Some Italian hotels may ask you to surrender your passport for 24 hours. While we all get a little nervous when we're parted from our passports, the US State Department's passport division advises that it's a perfectly acceptable procedure. The purpose usually is a local requirement to check the validity of the passport and ascertain whether the passport holder is a fugitive or has a police record. Many hotels merely will ask that you enter your passport number on your registration card. If a hotel does take your passport, make sure it's returned to you the next day.

DUTY AND CUSTOMS: As a general rule, the requirements for bringing the majority of items into Italy is that they must be in quantities small enough not to imply commercial import.

Among the items that may be taken into Italy duty-free are 400 cigarettes and 1.1 pounds (500 grams) of cigars or pipe tobacco, 2 bottles of wine and 1 bottle of hard liquor, 2 still cameras and 10 rolls of film for each camera, 1 movie camera or camcorder and 10 film reels or cartridges for either, and personal effects and sports equipment appropriate to a pleasure trip.

If you are bringing along a computer, camera, or any other electronic equipment for your own use that you will be taking back to the US, you should register the item with the US Customs Service in order to avoid paying duty both entering and returning from Italy. (Also see *Customs and Returning to the US,* in this section.) For information on this procedure, as well as for a variety of pamphlets on US customs regulations, contact the local office of the US Customs Service or the central office, PO Box 7407, Washington, DC 20044 (phone: 202-566-8195).Additional information regarding customs regulations is available from the Italian Government Travel Office. See *Tourist Information Offices,* in this section, for addresses in the US.

- **One rule to follow:** When passing through customs, it is illegal not to declare dutiable items; penalties range from stiff fines and seizure of the goods to prison terms. So don't try to sneak anything through — it just isn't worth it.

Insurance

It is unfortunate that most decisions to buy travel insurance are impulsive and usually are made without any real consideration of the traveler's existing policies. Therefore, the first person with whom you should discuss travel insurance is your own insurance broker, not a travel agent or the clerk behind the airport insurance counter. You may discover that the insurance you already carry — homeowner's policies and/or accident, health, and life insurance — protects you adequately while you travel and that your real needs are in the more mundane areas of excess value insurance for baggage or trip cancellation insurance.

TYPES OF INSURANCE: To make insurance decisions intelligently, you first should understand the basic categories of travel insurance and what they cover. Then you can decide what you should have in the broader context of your personal insurance needs, and you can choose the most economical way of getting the desired protection: through riders on existing policies; with onetime short-term policies; through a special program put together for the frequent traveler; through coverage that's part of a travel club's benefits; or with a combination policy sold by insurance companies through brokers, automobile clubs, tour operators, and travel agents.

There are seven basic categories of travel insurance:

1. Baggage and personal effects insurance
2. Personal accident and sickness insurance
3. Trip cancellation and interruption insurance
4. Default and/or bankruptcy insurance
5. Flight insurance (to cover injury or death)
6. Automobile insurance (for driving your own or a rented car)
7. Combination policies

Baggage and Personal Effects Insurance – Ask your insurance agent if baggage and personal effects are included in your current homeowner's policy, or if you will need a special floater to cover you for the duration of a trip. The object is to protect your bags and their contents in case of damage or theft anytime during your travels, not just while you're in flight and covered by the airline's policy. Furthermore, only limited protection is provided by the airline. Baggage liability varies from carrier to carrier, but generally speaking, on domestic flights, luggage usually is insured to $1,250 — that's per passenger, not per bag. For most international flights, including domestic portions of international flights, the airline's liability limit is approximately $9.07 per pound or $20 per kilo (which comes to about $360 per 40-pound suitcase) for checked baggage and up to $400 per passenger for unchecked baggage. These limits should be specified on your airline ticket, but to be awarded any amount, you'll have to provide an itemized list of lost property, and if you're including new and/or expensive items, be prepared for a request that you back up your claim with sales receipts or other proofs of purchase.

If you are carrying goods worth more than the maximum protection offered by the airline, bus, or train company, consider excess value insurance. Additional coverage is available from the airlines at an average, currently, of $1 to $2 per $100's worth of coverage, up to a maximum of $5,000. This insurance can be purchased at the airline counter when you check in, though you should arrive early to fill out the necessary forms and to avoid holding up other passengers.

Major credit card companies also provide coverage for lost or delayed baggage — and this coverage often also is over and above what the airline will pay. The basic coverage usually is automatic for all cardholders who use the credit card to purchase tickets, but to qualify for additional coverage, cardholders generally must enroll.

American Express: Provides $500 coverage for checked baggage; $1,250 for carry-on baggage; and $250 for valuables, such as cameras and jewelry.

Carte Blanche and Diners Club: Provide $1,250 free insurance for checked or carry-on baggage that's lost or damaged.

Discover Card: Offers $500 insurance for checked baggage and $1,250 for carry-on baggage — but to qualify for this coverage cardholders first must purchase additional flight insurance (see "Flight Insurance," below).

MasterCard and Visa: Baggage insurance coverage set by the issuing institution.

Additional baggage and personal effects insurance also is included in certain of the combination travel insurance policies discussed below.

■ **A note of warning:** Be sure to read the fine print of any excess value insurance policy; there often are specific exclusions, such as cash, tickets, furs, gold and silver objects, art, and antiques. And remember that insurance companies ordinarily will pay only the depreciated value of the goods rather than their replacement value. The best way to protect the items you're carrying in your luggage is to take photos of your valuables and keep a record of the serial numbers of such items as cameras, typewriters, laptop computers, radios, and so on. This will establish that you do, indeed, own the objects. If your luggage disappears en route or is damaged, deal with the situation immediately. If an airline loses your luggage, you will be asked to fill out a Property Irregularity Report before you leave the airport. If your property disappears at other transportation centers, tell the local company, but also report it to the police (since the insurance company will check with the police when processing the claim). When traveling by train, if you are sending excess luggage as registered baggage, remember that some trains may not have provisions for extra cargo; if your baggage does not arrive when you do, it may not be lost, just on the next train!

Personal Accident and Sickness Insurance – This covers you in case of illness during your trip or death in an accident. Most policies insure you for hospital and doctor's expenses, lost income, and so on. In most cases, it is a standard part of existing health insurance policies, though you should check with your broker to be sure that your policy will pay for any medical expenses incurred abroad. If not, take out a separate vacation accident policy or an entire vacation insurance policy that includes health and life coverage.

Two examples of such comprehensive health and life insurance coverage are the travel insurance packages offered by *Wallach & Co:*

HealthCare Global: This insurance package, which can be purchased for periods of 10 to 180 days, is offered for two age groups: Men and women up to age 75 receive $25,000 medical insurance and $50,000 accidental injury or death benefit; those from ages 76 to 84 are eligible for $12,500 medical insurance and $25,000 injury or death benefit. For either policy, the cost for a 10-day period is $25.

HealthCare Abroad: This program is available to individuals up to age 75. For $3 per day (minimum 10 days, maximum 90 days), policy holders receive $100,000 medical insurance and $25,000 accidental injury or death benefit.

Both of these basic programs also may be bought in combination with trip cancellation and baggage insurance at extra cost. For further information, write to *Wallach & Co.,* 243 Church St. NW, Suite 100-D, Vienna, VA 22180 (phone: 703-281-9500 in Virginia; 800-237-6615 elsewhere in the US).

Trip Cancellation and Interruption Insurance – Most charter and package tour passengers pay for their travel well before departure. The disappointment of having to miss a vacation because of illness or any other reason pales before the awful prospect that not all (and sometimes none) of the money paid in advance might be returned. So cancellation insurance for any package tour is a must.

Although cancellation penalties vary (they are listed in the fine print of every tour brochure, and before you purchase a package tour you should know exactly what they are), rarely will a passenger get more than 50% of this money back if forced to cancel within a few weeks of scheduled departure. Therefore, if you book a package tour or charter flight, you should have trip cancellation insurance to guarantee full reimbursement or refund should you, a traveling companion, or a member of your immediate family get sick, forcing you to cancel your trip or *to return home early.*

The key here is *not* to buy just enough insurance to guarantee full reimbursement for the cost of the package or charter in case of cancellation. The proper amount of coverage should be sufficient to reimburse you for the cost of having to catch up with a tour after its departure or having to travel home at the full economy airfare if you have to forgo the return flight of your charter. There usually is quite a discrepancy between a charter fare and the amount charged to travel the same distance on a regularly scheduled flight at full economy fare.

Trip cancellation insurance is available from travel agents and tour operators in two forms: as part of a short-term, all-purpose travel insurance package (sold by the travel agent); or as specific cancellation insurance designed by the tour operator for a specific charter tour. Generally, tour operators' policies are less expensive, but also less inclusive. Cancellation insurance also is available directly from insurance companies or their agents as part of a short-term, all-inclusive travel insurance policy.

Before you decide on a policy, read each one carefully. (Either type can be purchased from a travel agent when you book the charter or package tour.) Be certain that your policy includes enough coverage to pay your fare from the farthest destination on your itinerary should you have to miss the charter flight. Also, be sure to check the fine print for stipulations concerning "family members" and "pre-existing medical conditions," as well as allowances for living expenses if you must delay your return due to bodily injury or illness.

Default and/or Bankruptcy Insurance – Although trip cancellation insurance usually protects you if *you* are unable to complete — or begin — your trip, a fairly recent innovation is coverage in the event of default and/or bankruptcy on the part of the tour operator, airline, or other travel supplier. In some travel insurance packages, this contingency is included in the trip cancellation portion of the coverage; in others, it is a separate feature. Either way, it is becoming increasingly important. Whereas sophisticated travelers have long known to beware of the possibility of default or bankruptcy when buying a charter flight or tour package, in recent years more than a few respected scheduled airlines have unexpectedly revealed their shaky financial condition, sometimes leaving hordes of stranded ticket holders in their wake. Moreover, the value of escrow protection of a charter passenger's funds lately has been unreliable. While default/bankruptcy insurance will not ordinarily result in reimbursement in time to pay for new arrangements, it can ensure that you will get your money back, and even independent travelers buying no more than an airplane ticket may want to consider it.

Flight Insurance – Airlines have carefully established limits of liability for injury to or the death of passengers on international flights. For all international flights to, from, or with a stopover in the US, all carriers are liable for up to $75,000 per passenger. For all other international flights, the liability is based on where you purchase the ticket: If booked in advance in the US, the maximum liability is $75,000; if arrangements are made abroad, the liability is $10,000. But remember, these liabilities are not the same thing as insurance policies; every penny that an airline eventually pays in the case of injury or death may be subject to a legal battle.

But before you buy last-minute flight insurance from an airport vending machine, consider the purchase in light of your total existing insurance coverage. A careful review of your current policies may reveal that you already are amply covered for accidental death, sometimes up to three times the amount provided for by the flight insurance you're buying in the airport.

Be aware that airport insurance, the kind typically bought at a counter or from a vending machine, is among the most expensive forms of life insurance coverage, and that even within a single airport, rates for approximately the same coverage vary widely. Often policies sold in vending machines are more expensive than those sold over the counter, even when they are with the same national company.

If you buy your plane ticket with a major credit card, you generally receive automatic insurance coverage at no extra cost. Additional coverage usually can be obtained at extremely reasonable prices, but a cardholder must sign up for it in advance. (Note that rates vary slightly for residents of some states.) As we went to press, the travel accident and life insurance policies of the major credit cards were as follows:

American Express: Automatically provides $100,000 in insurance to its *Green, Gold,* and *Optima* cardholders, and $500,000 to *Platinum* cardholders. With *American Express,* $4 per ticket buys an additional $250,000 worth of flight insurance; $6.50 buys $500,000 worth; and $13 provides an added $1 million worth of coverage.

Carte Blanche: Automatically provides $150,000 flight insurance. An additional $250,000 worth of insurance is available for $4; $500,000 costs $6.50.

Diners Club: Provides $350,000 free flight insurance. An additional $250,000 worth of insurance is available for $4; $500,000 costs $6.50.

Discover Card: Provides $500,000 free flight insurance. An additional $250,000 worth of insurance is available for $4; $500,000 costs $6.50.

MasterCard and Visa: Insurance coverage set by the issuing institution.

Automobile Insurance – Public liability and property damage (third-party) insurance is compulsory in Europe, and whether you drive your own car or a rental you must carry insurance. Car rentals in Italy usually include public liability, property damage, fire, and theft coverage and, sometimes (depending on the car rental company), collision damage coverage with a deductible.

In your car rental contract, you'll see that for about $11 to $13 a day, you may buy optional collision damage waiver (CDW) protection. (If partial coverage with a deductible is included in the rental contract, the CDW will cover the deductible in the event of an accident, and can cost as much as $25 per day.) If you do not accept the CDW coverage, you may be liable for as much as the full retail cost of the rental car, and by paying for the CDW you are relieved of all responsibility for any damage to the car. Before agreeing to this coverage, however, check with your own broker about your existing personal automobile insurance policy. It very well may cover your entire liability exposure without any additional cost, or you automatically may be covered by the credit card company to which you are charging the cost of your rental. To find out the amount of rental car insurance provided by major credit cards contact the issuing institutions.

You also should know that an increasing number of the major international car rental companies automatically are including the cost of the CDW in their basic rates. Car rental prices have increased to include this coverage, although rental company ad campaigns may promote this as a new, improved rental package "benefit." The disadvantage of this inclusion is that you may not have the option to turn down the CDW — even if you already are adequately covered by your own insurance policy or through a credit card company.

Your rental contract (with the appropriate insurance box checked off), as well as proof of your personal insurance policy, if applicable, are required as proof of insurance. If you will be driving your own car in Italy, you must carry an International Insurance Certificate or Green Card *(Carta Verde),* available through insurance brokers in the US.

Combination Policies – Short-term insurance policies, which may include a combination of any or all of the types of insurance discussed above, are available through retail insurance agencies, automobile clubs, and many travel agents. These combination policies are designed to cover you for the duration of a single trip.

Policies of this type include the following:

Access America International: A subsidiary of the Blue Cross/Blue Shield plans of New York and Washington, DC, now available nationwide. Contact *Access*

America, 600 Third Ave., PO Box 807, New York, NY 10163 (phone: 800-284-8300 or 212-490-5345).

Carefree: Underwritten by The Hartford. Contact *Carefree Travel Insurance,* Arm Coverage, PO Box 310, Mineola, NY 11501 (phone: 800-645-2424 or 516-294-0220).

NEAR Services: In addition to a full range of travel services, this organization offers a comprehensive travel insurance package. An added feature is coverage for lost or stolen airline tickets. Contact *NEAR Services,* 450 Prairie Ave., Suite 101, Calumet City, IL 60409 (phone: 708-868-6700 in the Chicago area; 800-654-6700 elsewhere in the US and Canada).

Tele-Trip: Underwritten by the Mutual of Omaha Companies. Contact *Tele-Trip Co.,* PO Box 31685, 3201 Farnam St., Omaha, NE 68131 (phone: 402-345-2400 in Nebraska; 800-228-9792 elsewhere in the US).

Travel Assistance International: Provided by Europ Assistance Worldwide Services, and underwritten by Transamerica Occidental Life Insurance. Contact *Travel Assistance International,* 1333 15th St. NW, Suite 400, Washington, DC 20005 (phone: 202-331-1609 in Washington, DC; 800-821-2828 elsewhere in the US).

Travel Guard International: Underwritten by the Insurance Company of North America, it is available through authorized travel agents, or contact *Travel Guard International,* 1145 Clark St., Stevens Point, WI 54481 (phone: 715-345-0505 in Wisconsin; 800-826-1300 elsewhere in the US).

Travel Insurance PAK: Underwritten by The Travelers. Contact *The Travelers Companies,* Ticket and Travel Plans, One Tower Sq., Hartford, CT 06183-5040 (phone: 203-277-2319 in Connecticut; 800-243-3174 elsewhere in the US).

WorldCare Travel Assistance Association: This organization offers insurance packages underwritten by Transamerica Occidental Life Insurance Company and Transamerica Premier Insurance Company. Contact *WorldCare Travel Assistance Association,* 605 Market St., Suite 1300, San Francisco, CA 94105 (phone: 800-666-4993 or 415-541-4991).

How to Pack

No one can provide a completely foolproof list of precisely what to pack, so it's best to let common sense, space, and comfort guide you. Keep one maxim in mind: Less is more. You simply won't need as much clothing as you think, and you are far more likely to need a forgotten accessory — or a needle and thread or scissors — than a particular piece of clothing.

As with almost anything relating to travel, a little planning can go a long way.

1. Where are you going — city, country, or both?
2. How many total days will you be gone?
3. What's the average temperature likely to be during your stay?

The goal is to remain perfectly comfortable, neat, clean, and adequately fashionable, but to pack as little as possible. Learn to travel light by following two firm packing principles:

1. Organize your travel wardrobe around a single color — blue or brown, for example — that allows you to mix, match, and layer clothes. Holding firm to one color scheme will make it easy to eliminate items of clothing that don't harmonize.
2. Never overpack to ensure a supply of fresh clothing — shirts, blouses, under-

wear — for each day of a long trip. Use hotel laundries to wash and clean clothes. If these are too expensive, there are self-service laundries (called *lavanderie* or *lavanderie automatiche*) in most towns of any size.

CLIMATE AND CLOTHES: Exactly what you pack for your trip will be a function of where you are going and when and the kinds of things you intend to do. A few degrees can make all the difference between being comfortably attired and very real suffering, so your intial step should be to find out what the general weather conditions are likely to be in the areas you will visit.

Although Rome (sitting astride latitude 41°53′) is about even with Providence, Rhode Island, the weather in Italy is milder than at similar latitudes in North America. Residents of the US will find that the same wardrobe they would wear in the Middle Atlantic United States will, with a few adjustments, also be appropriate for most parts of Italy in the same season.

Anyone going to Italy from the late fall through the early spring, however, should take into account that while central heating is prevalent, interiors often are not heated to the same degree they would be in the US. Thus, although there is no need to prepare for subzero winters, most people probably will feel more comfortable wearing heavier clothing indoors than they might at home — for instance, sweaters rather than lightweight shirts and blouses.

In Italy, warm clothes — even some kind of topcoat — are needed in winter in addition to lighter clothing. Even in the south of Italy, old stone *palazzi* can be chilly and damp inside when the sun is blazing outside. During the winter months in north and central Italy, the temperature can drop below freezing, while in the south a milder mean temperature of around 55 F is the norm. Depending on where you're traveling, summer temperatures range anywhere from the 60s to the upper 90s. Rain gear is advisable in the late fall and early winter. A raincoat with a zip-out lining — and a hood or rain hat — is a versatile choice. If you decide to take an umbrella, a compact telescoping model is best.

More information about the climate in Italy, along with a chart of average low and high temperatures for specific cities, is given in *When to Go,* in this section.

Keeping temperature and climate in mind, consider the problem of luggage. Plan on one suitcase per person (and in a pinch, remember it's always easier to carry two small suitcases than to schlepp one that is roughly the size of downtown Detroit). Standard 26- or 28-inch suitcases can be made to work for 1 week or 1 month, and unless you are going for only a weekend, never cram wardrobes for two people into one suitcase. Hanging bags are best for dresses, suits and jackets.

FASHION: On the whole, Italy is no more formal than North America, but the celebrated Italian sense of style — a subject apart from the question of formality versus informality — is a genuine thing. Since this knack for knowing almost intuitively what is fashionable is acquired slowly rather than on the eve of a trip, the best rule to follow in choosing a travel wardrobe is to be guided by your own taste. And although Italians do enjoy dressing up, formal attire is necessary only for the most elegant occasions — such as opening night at Milan's *La Scala* opera house (though European students have been attending the opera in blue jeans for years).

The dress code in Italy, however, is not quite as informal as many tourists think it is. Less revealing clothing is particularly recommended for visiting churches. Women are no longer required to cover their heads and wear long sleeves, but in some churches (such as St. Peter's in Rome), some sort of sleeve is required. Tank tops on men and short shorts on either sex also are inappropriate for churches.

Layering is the key to comfort — particularly when touring in parts of the countryside where mornings and evenings can be chilly even when the days are mild. No matter where you are traveling in Italy, however, layering is a good way to prepare for atypical temperatures or changes in the weather and even in a heat wave, an extra layer will be welcome for exploring the catacombs in Rome. Recommended basics are a lightweight wool or heavy cotton turtleneck, which can be worn under a shirt and perhaps a third layer, such as a pullover sweater, jacket, or windbreaker. In warmer weather, substitute T-shirts and lightweight cotton shirts or sweaters for the turtleneck and wool layers. As the weather changes, you can add or remove clothes as required.

And finally — since the best touring of Italy's ruins, churches, and countryside is done on foot — it is essential to bring comfortable shoes (often this means an old pair, already worn in). Even in the evening, when you anticipate walking no farther than to the nearest restaurant, women should avoid spike heels. Cobblestones are ubiquitous, and chunkier heels have a better chance of not getting caught — and ruined.

Your carry-on luggage should contain a survival kit with the basic things you will need in case your luggage gets lost or stolen: a toothbrush, toothpaste, all medications, a sweater, nightclothes, and a change of underwear. With these essential items at hand, you will be prepared for any unexpected occurrence that separates you from your suitcase. If you have many 1- or 2-night stops, you can live out of your survival case without having to unpack completely at each hotel.

Sundries – If you are traveling in the heat of summer and will be spending a lot of time outdoors, pack special items so you won't spend your entire vacation horizontal in a hotel room (or hospital) because of sunburn. Be sure to take a sun hat (to protect hair as well as skin), sunscreen, and tanning lotion. Also, if you are heading for a vacation on skis, do not underestimate the effect of the sun's glare off snowy slopes, especially in higher altitudes — your face and neck are particularly susceptible to a burning.

Other items you might consider packing are a pocket-size flashlight with extra batteries, a small sewing and first-aid kit (see *Staying Healthy,* in this section, for recommended components), binoculars, and a camera or camcorder (see *Cameras and Equipment,* in this section).

■ **Note:** For those on the go, *Travel Mini Pack* offers numerous products — from toilet articles to wrinkle remover spray — in handy travel sizes, as well as travel accessories such as money pouches, foreign currency calculators, and even a combination hair dryer/iron. For a catalogue, contact *Travel Mini Pack,* PO Box 571, Stony Point, NY 10980 (phone: 914-429-8281).

PACKING: The basic idea of packing is to get everything into the suitcase and out again with as few wrinkles as possible. Simple, casual clothes — shirts, jeans and slacks, permanent press skirts — can be rolled into neat, tight sausages that keep other packed items in place and leave the clothes themselves amazingly unwrinkled. However, for items that are too bulky or delicate for even careful rolling, a suitcase should be packed with the heaviest items on the bottom, toward the hinges, so that they will not wrinkle more perishable clothes. Candidates for the bottom layer include shoes (stuff them with small items to save space), a toilet kit, handbags (stuff them to help keep their shape), and an alarm clock. Fill out this layer with things that will not wrinkle or will not matter if they do, such as sweaters, socks, a bathing suit, gloves, and underwear.

If you get this first, heavy layer as smooth as possible with the fill-ins, you will have a shelf for the next layer — the most easily wrinkled items, like slacks, jackets, shirts, dresses, and skirts. These should be buttoned and zipped and laid along the whole length of the suitcase with as little folding as possible. When you do need to make a fold, do it on a crease (as with pants), along a seam in the fabric, or where it will not show (such as shirttails). Alternate each piece of clothing, using one side of the suitcase, then the other, to make the layers as flat as possible. Make the layers even and the total contents of your bag as full and firm as possible to keep things from shifting around during transit. On the top layer put the things you will want at once: nightclothes, a bathing suit, an umbrella or raincoat, a sweater.

With men's two-suiter suitcases, follow the same procedure. Then place jackets on hangers, straighten them out, and leave them unbuttoned. If they are too wide for the suitcase, fold them lengthwise down the middle, straighten the shoulders, and fold the sleeves in along the seams.

While packing, it is a good idea to separate each layer of clothes with plastic cleaning bags, which will help preserve pressed clothes while they are in the suitcase. Unpack your bags as soon as you get to your hotel. Nothing so thoroughly destroys freshly cleaned and pressed clothes as sitting for days in a suitcase. Finally, if something is badly wrinkled and can't be professionally pressed before you must wear it, hang it for several hours in a bathroom where the bathtub has been filled with very hot water; keep the bathroom door closed so the room becomes something of a steamroom. It really works miracles.

SOME FINAL PACKING HINTS: Apart from the items you pack as carry-on lugagge (see above), always keep all necessary medicine, valuable jewelry (best left at home due to the high level of street crime), and travel or business documents in your purse, briefcase, or carry-on bag — *not in the luggage you will check.* Tuck a bathing suit into your handbag or briefcase, too; in the event of lost baggage, it's frustrating to be without one. And whether in your overnight bag or checked luggage, cosmetics and any liquids should be packed in plastic bottles or at least wrapped in plastic bags and tied.

Golf clubs and skis may be checked through as luggage (most airlines are accustomed to handling them), but tennis rackets should be carried onto the plane. Some airlines require that bicycles be partially dismantled and packaged (see *Camping and Caravanning, Hiking and Biking,* in this section). Check with the airline before departure to see if there is a specific regulation concerning any special equipment or sporting gear you plan to take.

Hints for Handicapped Travelers

From 40 to 50 million people in the US alone have some sort of disability, and over half this number are physically handicapped. Like everyone else today, they — and the uncounted disabled millions around the world — are on the move. More than ever before, they are demanding facilities they can use comfortably, and they are being heard.

Unfortunately, Italy, a country of many hills and steps, has been comparatively slow in developing access for the handicapped. In recent years, however, efforts have been made to correct this situation. A number of Italian cities have published accessibility guides, and there are several organizations offering assistance programs in Italy (see below). Still, in some areas, only a few of the best hotels and restaurants are easily accessible to a person in a wheelchair, and unless you are on a special tour for the handicapped, you will need to rely mostly on taxis for transportation. However, with ingenuity and the help of an able-bodied traveling companion, you can get around this fascinating country well enough to thoroughly enjoy its varied delights. What the Italians lack in facilities for the handicapped they more than make up for in willingness to help when necessary.

PLANNING: Collect as much information as you can about your specific disability and facilities for the disabled in Italy. Make your travel arrangements well in advance and specify to all services involved the exact nature of your condition or restricted mobility, as your trip will be much more comfortable if you know that there are accommodations and facilities to suit your needs. The best way to find out if your intended destination can accommodate a handicapped traveler is to write or call the local tourist authority or hotel and ask specific questions. If you require a corridor of a certain width to maneuver a wheelchair or if you need handles on the bathroom walls for support, ask the hotel manager. A travel agent or the local chapter or national office of the organization that deals with your particular disability — for example, the *American Foundation for the Blind* or the *American Heart Association* — will supply the most up-to-date information on the subject. The following organizations offer general information on access:

ACCENT on Living (PO Box 700, Bloomington, IL 61702; phone: 309-378-2961). This information service for persons with disabilities provides a free list of travel agencies specializing in arranging trips for the disabled; for a copy send a self-addressed, stamped envelope. Also offers a wide range of publications, including a quarterly magazine ($8 per year; $14 for 2 years) for persons with disabilities.

Information Center for Individuals with Disabilities (Fort Point Pl., 1st Floor, 27-43 Wormwood St., Boston, MA 02210; phone: 800-462-5015 in Massachusetts; 617-727-5540/1 elsewhere in the US; both numbers provide voice and TDD — telecommunications device for the deaf). The center offers information and referral services on disability-related issues, publishes fact sheets on travel agents, tour operators, and other travel resources, and can help you research your trip.

Mobility International USA (*MIUSA;* PO Box 3551, Eugene, OR 97403; phone: 503-343-1284; both voice and TDD). This US branch of *Mobility International* (the main office is at 228 Borough High St., London SE1 1JX, England; phone: 71-403-5688; the Italian affiliate is *Associazone per L'Assistenza,* 29 Via San Barnaba, Milano I-20122, Italy; phone: 25-512009), a nonprofit British organization with affiliates worldwide, offers members advice and assistance — including information on accommodations and other travel services, and publications applicable to the traveler's disability. It also offers a quarterly newsletter and a comprehensive sourcebook, *A World of Options for the 90s: A Guide to International Education Exchange, Community Service and Travel for Persons with Disabilities* ($14 for members; $16 for non-members). Membership includes the newsletter and is $20 a year; subscription to the newsletter alone is $10 annually.

National Rehabilitation Information Center (8455 Colesville Rd., Suite 935, Silver Spring, MD 20910; phone: 301-588-9284). A general information, resource, research, and referral service.

Paralyzed Veterans of America (*PVA;* PVA/ATTS Program, 801 18th St. NW, Washington, DC 20006; phone: 202-416-7708 in Washington, DC; 800-424-8200 elsewhere in the US). The members of this national service organization all are veterans who have suffered spinal cord injuries, but it offers advocacy services and information to all persons with a disability. *PVA* also sponsors *Access to the Skies,* a program that coordinates the efforts of the national and international air travel industry in providing airport and airplane access for the disabled. Members receive several helpful publications, as well as regular notification of conferences on subjects of interest to the disabled traveler.

Royal Association for Disability and Rehabilitation (*RADAR;* 25 Mortimer St., London W1N 8AB, England; phone: 44-71-637-5400). Offers a number of publications for the handicapped, including *Holidays and Travel Abroad 1991/92 — A Guide for Disabled People,* a comprehensive guidebook focusing on international travel. This publications can be ordered by sending payment in British pounds to *RADAR.* As we went to press, it cost just over £6; call for current pricing before ordering.

Society for the Advancement of Travel for the Handicapped (*SATH;* 26 Court St., Penthouse, Brooklyn, NY 11242; phone: 718-858-5483). To keep abreast of developments in travel for the handicapped as they occur, you may want to join *SATH,* a nonprofit organization whose members include consumers, as well as travel service professionals who have experience (or an interest) in travel for the handicapped. For an annual fee of $45 ($25 for students and travelers who are 65 and older) members receive a quarterly newsletter and have access to extensive information and referral services. *SATH* also offers two useful publications: *Travel Tips for the Handicapped* (a series of informative fact sheets) and *The United States Welcomes Handicapped Visitors* (a 48-page guide covering domestic transportation and accommodations that includes useful hints for travelers with disabilities abroad); to order, send a self-addressed, #10 envelope and $1 per title for postage.

Travel Information Service (Moss Rehabilitation Hospital, 1200 W. Tabor Rd., Philadelphia, PA 19141-3099; phone: 215-456-9600 for voice; 215-456-9602 for TDD). This service assists physically handicapped people in planning trips and supplies detailed information on accessibility for a nominal fee.

Blind travelers should contact the *American Foundation for the Blind* (15 W. 16th St., New York, NY 10011; phone: 212-620-2147 in New York State; 800-232-5463 elsewhere in the US) and *The Seeing Eye* (Box 375, Morristown, NJ 07963-0375; phone: 201-539-4425); both provide useful information on resources for the visually impaired. *Note:* Any dog brought into Italy, including Seeing Eye dogs, must have a certificate guaranteeing that the animal is rabies-free. The animal must be vaccinated against rabies not less than 20 days or more than 11 months before departure. This certificate, which can be obtained at the Italian Government Travel Office (for addresses, see *Tourist Information Offices,* in this section), must be signed by the veterinarian administering the vaccination and certified and stamped by a veterinarian who is designated as an inspector by the US Department of Agriculture (USDA). For the location of the nearest regional USDA-certified office providing this service, as well as for other useful information, contact the US Department of Agriculture, APHIS, VS, 2568A Riva Rd., Room 207, Annapolis, MD 21401. *The American Society for the Prevention of Cruelty to Animals* (*ASPCA,* Education Dept., 441 E. 92 St., New York, NY 10128; phone: 212-876-7700) offers a useful booklet, *Traveling With Your Pet,* which lists inoculation and other requirements by country. It is available for $5 (including postage and handling).

In addition, there are a number of publications — from travel guides to magazines — of interest to handicapped travelers. Among these are the following:

Access to the World, by Louise Weiss, offers sound tips for the disabled traveler. Published by Facts on File (460 Park Ave. S., New York, NY 10016; phone: 212-683-2244 in New York State; 800-322-8755 elsewhere in the US; 800-443-8323 in Canada), it costs $16.95. Check with your local bookstore; it also can be ordered by phone with a credit card.

The Diabetic Traveler (PO Box 8223 RW, Stamford, CT 06905; phone: 203-327-5832) is a useful quarterly newsletter. Each issue highlights a single destination or type of travel and includes information on general resources and hints for diabetics. A 1-year subscription costs $15. When subscribing, ask for the free fact sheet including an index of special articles; back issues are available for $4 each.

Guide to Traveling with Arthritis, a free brochure available by writing to the Upjohn Company (PO Box 307-B, Coventry, CT 06238), provides lots of good, commonsense tips on planning your trip and how to be as comfortable as possible when traveling by car, bus, train, cruise ship, or plane.

Handicapped Travel Newsletter is regarded as one of the best sources of information for the disabled traveler. It is edited by wheelchair-bound Vietnam veteran Michael Quigley, who has traveled to 93 countries around the world. Issued every 2 months (plus special issues), a subscription is $10 per year. Write to *Handicapped Travel Newsletter,* PO Box 269, Athens, TX 75751 (phone: 214-677-1260).

Handi-Travel: A Resource Book for Disabled and Elderly Travellers, by Cinnie Noble, is a comprehensive travel guide full of practical tips for those with disabilities affecting mobility, hearing, or sight. To order this book, send $12.95, plus shipping and handling, to the *Canadian Rehabilitation Council for the Disabled,* 45 Sheppard Ave. E., Suite 801, Toronto, Ontario M2N 5W9, Canada (phone: 416-250-7490; both voice and TDD).

The Itinerary (PO Box 2012, Bayonne, NJ 07002-2012; phone: 201-858-3400). This bimonthly travel magazine for people with disabilities includes information on accessibility, listings of tours, news of adaptive devices, travel aids, and special services, as well as numerous general travel hints. A subscription costs $10 a year.

The Physically Disabled Traveler's Guide, by Rod W. Durgin and Norene Lindsay, rates accessibility of a number of travel services and includes a list of organizations specializing in travel for the disabled. It is available for $9.95, plus shipping and handling, from Resource Directories, 3361 Executive Pkwy., Suite 302, Toledo, OH 43606 (phone: 419-536-5353 in the Toledo area; 800-274-8515 elsewhere in the US).

Ticket to Safe Travel offers useful information for travelers with diabetes. A reprint of this article is available free from local chapters of the *American Diabetes Association.* For the nearest branch, contact the central office at 505 Eighth Ave., 21st Floor, New York, NY 10018 (phone: 212-947-9707 in New York State; 800-232-3472 elsewhere in the US).

Travel for the Patient with Chronic Obstructive Pulmonary Disease, a publication of the George Washington University Medical Center, provides some sound practical suggestions for those with emphysema, chronic bronchitis, asthma, or other lung ailments. To order, send $2 to Dr. Harold Silver, 1601 18th St. NW, Washington, DC 20009 (phone: 202-667-0134).

Traveling Like Everybody Else: A Practical Guide for Disabled Travelers, by Jacqueline Freedman and Susan Gersten, offers the disabled tips on traveling by car, cruise ship, and plane, as well as lists of accessible accommodations, tour operators specializing in tours for disabled travelers, and other resources. It is available for $11.95, plus postage and handling, from Modan Publishing, PO Box 1202, Bellmore, NY 11710 (phone: 516-679-1380).

Travel Tips for Hearing-Impaired People, a free pamphlet for deaf and hearing-impaired travelers, is available from the *American Academy of Otolaryngology* (One Prince St., Alexandria, VA 22314; phone: 703-836-4444). For a copy, send a self-addressed, stamped, business-size envelope to the academy.

Travel Tips for People with Arthritis, a free 31-page booklet published by the *Arthritis Foundation,* provides helpful information regarding travel by car, bus, train, cruise ship, or plane, planning your trip, medical considerations, and ways to conserve your energy while traveling. It also includes listings of helpful resources, such as associations and travel agencies that operate tours for disabled travelers. For a copy, contact your local *Arthritis Foundation* chapter, or write to the national office, PO Box 19000, Atlanta, GA 30326 (phone: 404-872-7100).

A few more basic resources to look for are *Travel for the Disabled,* by Helen Hecker ($9.95), and by the same author, *Directory of Travel Agencies for the Disabled* ($19.95). *Wheelchair Vagabond,* by John G. Nelson, is another useful guide for travelers confined to a wheelchair (hardcover, $14.95; paperback, $9.95). All three are published by Twin Peaks Press, PO Box 129, Vancouver, WA 98666 (phone: 800-637-CALM or 206-694-2462).

Other good sources of information include branches of the Italian Government Travel Office, both in the US and Italy (see *Tourist Information Offices,* in this section).

In recent years, the following Italian cities have published accessibility guides, entitled *Guide di Accessibilità,* covering hotels, *pensioni,* museums, and other facilities: Bergamo, Bologna, Caserta, Legnano, Milan, Padua, Piacenza, Reggio Emilia, Syracuse, Turin, Udine, Varese, Venice, Verona, and Vicenza. These publications may be available at local tourist offices in these areas.

For accessibility information and referral services while in Italy, contact one of the three following organizations:

Italian Spastic Society (4/H Via Sipro, Rome 00136, Italy; phone: 6-389604).
ANMIC (2 Via Crescenzio, Rome 00110, Italy; phone: 6-8077831).
Harvey Club (38 Via Luosi, Milan 20131, Italy).

For accommodations designed for the disabled traveler, visitors should try the *Golden Tulip,* an accessible European chain, which has 12 locations in Italy — four in Rome, three in Venice, three in Florence, and two in Milan. For information and reservations, contact *Golden Tulip,* a division of *KLM Royal Dutch Airlines,* 437 Madison Ave., New York, NY 10022 (phone: 800-333-1212).

Two organizations based in Great Britain offer information for handicapped persons traveling throughout Europe. *Tripscope* (63 Esmond Rd., London W4 1JE, England; phone: 44-81-994-9294) is a telephone-based information and referral service (not a booking agent) that can help with transportation options for journeys throughout Europe. It may, for instance, be able to recommend outlets leasing small family vehicles adapted to accommodate wheelchairs. *Tripscope* also provides information on cassettes for blind or visually impaired travelers, and accepts written requests for information from those with speech impediments. And for general information, there's *Holiday Care Service* (2 Old Bank Chambers, Station Rd., Horley, Surrey RH6 9HW, England; phone: 44-293-774535), a first-rate, free advisory service on accommodations, transportation, and holiday packages throughout Europe for disabled visitors.

Regularly revised hotel and restaurant guides use the symbol of access (person in a wheelchair; see the symbol at the beginning of this section) to point out accommodations suitable for wheelchair-bound guests. Among such publications are the red *Michelin Guide to Italy* ($19.95; Michelin Guides and Maps, PO Box 3305, Spartanburg, SC 29304-3305; phone: 803-599-0850 in South Carolina; 800-423-0485 elsewhere in the US), both found in general and travel bookstores.

PLANE: The US Department of Transportation (DOT) has ruled that US airlines must accept all passengers with disabilities. As a matter of course, US airlines were pretty good about accommodating handicapped passengers even before the ruling, although each airline has somewhat different procedures. Foreign airlines also are generally good about accommodating the disabled traveler, but again, policies vary from carrier to carrier. Ask for specifics when you book your flight.

Disabled passengers should always make reservations well in advance, and should provide the airline with all relevant details of their condition. These details include information on mobility and equipment that you will need the airline to supply — such as a wheelchair for boarding or portable oxygen for in-flight use. Be sure that the person to whom you speak fully understands the degree of your disability — the more details provided, the more effective help the airline can give you.

On the day before the flight, call back to make sure that all arrangements have been prepared, and arrive early on the day of the flight so that you can board before the rest of the passengers. It's a good idea to bring a medical certificate with you, stating your specific disability or the need to carry particular medicine.

Because most airports have jetways (corridors connecting the terminal with the door of the plane), a disabled passenger usually can be taken as far as the plane, and sometimes right onto it, in a wheelchair. If not, a narrow boarding chair may be used to take you to your seat. Your own wheelchair, which will be folded and put in the baggage compartment, should be tagged as escort luggage to assure that it's available at planeside upon landing rather than in the baggage claim area. Travel is not quite as simple if your wheelchair is battery-operated: Unless it has non-spillable batteries, it might not be accepted on board, and you will have to check with the airline ahead of time to find out how the batteries and the chair should be packaged for the flight. Usually people in wheelchairs are asked to wait until other passengers have disembarked. If you are making a tight connection, be sure to tell the attendant.

Passengers who use oxygen may not use their personal supply in the cabin, though it may be carried on the plane as cargo when properly packed and labeled. If you will need oxygen during the flight, the airline will supply it to you (there is a charge) provided you have given advance notice — 24 hours to a few days, depending on the carrier.

Useful information on every stage of air travel, from planning to arrival, is provided in the booklet *Incapacitated Passengers Air Travel Guide.* To receive a free copy, write to the *International Air Transport Association* (Publications Sales Department, 2000 Peel St., Montreal, Quebec H3A 2R4, Canada; phone: 514-844-6311). Another helpful publication is *Air Transportation of Handicapped Persons,* which explains the general guidelines that govern air carrier policies. For a copy of this free booklet, write to the US Department of Transportation (Distribution Unit, Publications Section, M-443-2, Washington, DC 20590) and ask for "Free Advisory Circular #AC-120-32." *Access Travel: A Guide to the Accessibility of Airport Terminals,* a free publication of the *Airport Operators Council International,* provides information on more than 500 airports worldwide — including major airports throughout Europe — and offers ratings of 70 features, such as accessibility to bathrooms, corridor width, and parking spaces. For a copy, contact the Consumer Information Center (Dept. 563W, Pueblo, CO 81009; phone: 719-948-3334).

Among the major US carriers serving Italy, the following airlines have TDD toll-free lines in the US for the hearing-impaired:

American Airlines: 800-582-1573 in Ohio; 800-543-1573 elsewhere in the US.
Delta: 800-831-4488.
TWA: 800-252-0622 in California; 800-421-8480 elsewhere in the US.

SHIP: Among the ships calling at ports in Italy, *Cunard*'s *Queen Elizabeth 2, Crystal Cruises' Crystal Harmony,* and *Royal Cruise Line*'s *Crown Odyssey* are considered the best-equipped vessels for the physically disabled. Handicapped travelers are advised to book reservations at least 90 days in advance to reserve specialized cabins.

For those in wheelchairs or with limited mobility, one of the best sources for evaluating a ship's accessibility is the free chart issued by the *Cruise Lines International Association* (500 Fifth Ave., Suite 1407, New York, NY 10110; phone: 212-921-0066). The chart lists accessible ships and indicates whether they accommodate standard-size or only narrow wheelchairs, have ramps, wide doors, low or no doorsills, handrails in the rooms, and so on. (For information on ships cruising around Italy, see *Traveling by Ship,* in this section.)

GROUND TRANSPORTATION: Perhaps the simplest solution to getting around is to travel with an able-bodied companion who can drive. Another alternative in Italy is to hire a driver/translator with a car — be sure to get a recommendation from a reputable source. The organizations listed above may be able to help you make arrangements — another source is your hotel concierge.

If you are accustomed to driving your own hand-controlled car and are determined to rent one, you may have to do some extensive research, as in Italy it is difficult to find rental cars fitted with hand controls. If agencies do provide hand-controlled cars, they are apt to be offered only on a limited basis in major metropolitan areas and usually are in high demand. The best course is to contact the major car rental agencies listed in *Traveling by Car,* in this section, well before your departure; but be forewarned: You still may be out of luck. Other sources for information on vehicles adapted for the handicapped are the organizations discussed above.

The *American Automobile Association (AAA)* publishes a useful booklet, *The Handicapped Driver's Mobility Guide.* Contact the central office of your local *AAA* club for availability and pricing, which may vary at different branch offices.

Although taxis and public transportation also are available in Italy, accessibility for the disabled varies and may be limited in rural areas, as well as in some cities. Check with a travel agent or tourist authorities for information.

TRAIN: Trains in Europe generally are not well adapted to wheelchairs, but timetables often specify which departures are accessible. And on trains that cannot accommodate wheelchairs, depending on the type of train, special arrangements sometimes may be made in advance through the station manager — for instance, wheelchair-bound travelers may be able to travel in the guard's car. For further information on Italian trains, contact the *Italian State Railways*' representatives in the US (addresses are listed in *Traveling by Train,* in this section) or ask for information at regional rail offices in Italy.

BUS: In general, bus travel is not recommended for travelers who are totally wheelchair-bound unless they have someone along who can lift them on and off or they are members of a group tour designed for the handicapped and are using a specially outfitted bus. If you have some mobility, however, you'll find local personnel usually quite happy to help you board and exit.

TOURS: Programs designed for the physically impaired are run by specialists who have researched hotels, restaurants, and sites to be sure they present no insurmountable obstacles. The following travel agencies and tour operators specialize in making group and individual arrangements for travelers with physical or other disabilities.

Access: The Foundation for Accessibility by the Disabled (PO Box 356, Malverne, NY 11565; phone: 516-887-5798). A travelers' referral service that acts as an intermediary with tour operators and agents worldwide, and provides information on accessibility at various locations.

Accessible Tours/Directions Unlimited (720 N. Bedford Rd., Bedford Hills, NY 10507; phone: 914-241-1700 in New York State; 800-533-5343 elsewhere in the continental US). Arranges group or individual tours for disabled persons traveling in the company of able-bodied friends or family members. Accepts the unaccompanied traveler if completely self-sufficient.

Dialysis at Sea Cruises (611 Barry Place, Indian Rocks Beach, FL 34635; phone: 813-596-7604 or 800-544-7604). Offers cruises that include the medical services of a nephrologist (a specialist in kidney disease) and a staff of dialysis nurses. Family, friends, and companions are welcome to travel on these cruises, but the number of dialysis patients usually is limited to roughly ten travelers per trip.

Evergreen Travel Service (4114 198th St. SW, Suite 13, Lynnwood, WA 98036-6742; phone: 206-776-1184 or 800-435-2288 throughout the continental US and Canada). Offers worldwide tours and cruises for the disabled (Wings on Wheels Tours), sight-impaired/blind (White Cane Tours), and hearing-impaired/deaf (Flying Fingers Tours). Most programs are first class or deluxe, and include a trained escort.

Flying Wheels Travel (143 W. Bridge St., Box 382, Owatonna, MN 55060; phone: 507-451-5005 or 800-535-6790). Handles both tours and individual arrangements.

Handi-Travel (First National Travel Ltd., Thornhill Sq., 300 John St., Suite 405, Thornhill, Ontario L3T 5W4, Canada; phone: 416-731-4714). Handles tours and individual arrangements.

USTS Travel Horizons (11 E. 44th St., New York, NY 10017; phone: 800-487-8787 or 212-687-5121). Travel agent and registered nurse Mary Ann Hamm designs trips for individual travelers requiring all types of kidney dialysis and handles arrangements for the dialysis.

Whole Person Tours (PO Box 1084, Bayonne, NJ 07002-1084; phone: 201-858-3400). Handicapped owner Bob Zywicki travels the world with his wheelchair and offers a lineup of escorted tours (many conducted by him) for the disabled. *Whole Person Tours* also publishes *The Itinerary,* a bimonthly newsletter for disabled travelers (see the publication source list above).

Travelers who would benefit from being accompanied by a nurse or physical therapist also can hire a companion through *Traveling Nurses' Network,* a service provided by Twin Peaks Press (PO Box 129, Vancouver, WA 98666; phone: 800-637-CALM or 206-694-2462). For a $10 fee, clients receive the names of three nurses, whom they can then contact directly; for a $125 fee, the agency will make all the hiring arrangements for the client. Travel arrangements also may be made in some cases — the fee for this further service is determined on an individual basis.

A similar service is offered by *MedEscort International* (ABE International Airport, PO Box 8766, Allentown, PA 18105; phone: 800-255-7182 in the continental US; elsewhere, call 215-791-3111). Clients can arrange to be accompanied by a nurse, paramedic, respiratory therapist, or physician through *MedEscort.* The fees are based on the disabled traveler's needs. *MedEscort* also can assist in making travel arrangements.

Hints for Single Travelers

Just about the last trip in human history on which the participants were neatly paired was the voyage of Noah's Ark. Ever since, passenger lists and tour groups have reflected the same kind of asymmetry that occurs in real life, as countless individuals set forth to see the world unaccompanied (or unencumbered, depending on your outlook) by spouse, lover, friend, or relative.

The truth is that the travel industry is not very fair to people who vacation by themselves. People traveling alone almost invariably end up paying more than individuals traveling in pairs. Most travel bargains, including package tours, accommodations, resort packages, and cruises, are based on *double-occupancy* rates. This means that the per-person price is offered on the basis of two people traveling together and sharing a double room (which means they each will spend a good deal more on meals and extras). The single traveler will have to pay a surcharge, called a single supplement, for exactly the same package. In extreme cases, this can add as much as 30% to 55% to the basic per-person rate.

Don't despair, however. Throughout Italy, there are scores of smaller hotels, *pensioni,* and other hostelries where, in addition to a cozier atmosphere, prices still are quite reasonable for the single traveler. Some cruise lines have begun to offer special cruises for singles, and some resorts cater to the single traveler.

The obvious, most effective alternative is to find a traveling companion. Even special "singles' tours" that promise no supplements usually are based on people sharing double rooms. Perhaps the most recent innovation along these lines is the creation of organizations that "introduce" the single traveler to other single travelers, somewhat like a dating service. Some charge fees, others are free, but the basic service offered is the same: to match an unattached person with a compatible travel mate, often as part of the company's own package tours. Among such organizations are the following:

Jane's International (2603 Bath Ave., Brooklyn, NY 11214; phone: 718-266-2045). This service puts potential traveling companions in touch with one another. No age limit, no fee.

Odyssey Network (118 Cedar St., Wellesley, MA 02181; phone: 617-237-2400). Originally founded to match single women travelers, this company now includes men in its enrollment. *Odyssey* offers a quarterly newsletter for members who are seeking a travel companion, and occasionally organizes small group tours. A newsletter subscription is $50.

Partners-in-Travel (PO Box 491145, Los Angeles, CA 90049; phone: 213-476-4869). Members receive a list of singles seeking traveling companions; prospective companions make contact through the agency. The membership fee is $40 per year and includes a chatty newsletter (6 issues per year).

Travel Companion Exchange (PO Box 833, Amityville, NY 11701; phone: 516-454-0880). This group publishes a newsletter for singles and a directory of individuals looking for travel companions. On joining, members fill out a lengthy questionnaire and write a small listing (much like an ad in a personal column). Based on these listings, members can request copies of profiles and contact prospective traveling companions. It is wise to join well in advance of your planned vacation so that there's enough time to determine compatibility and plan a joint trip. Membership fees, including the newsletter, are $36 for 6 months or $60 a year for a single-sex listing; $66 and $120, respectively, for a complete listing. Subscription to the newsletter alone costs $24 for 6 months or $36 per year.

Also note that certain cruise lines offer guaranteed share rates for single travelers, whereby cabin mates are selected on request. For instance, two cruise lines that provide guaranteed share rates are *Cunard* (phone: 800-221-4770) and *Royal Cruise Line* (phone: 415-956-7200 or 800-622-0538 in California; 800-227-4534 elsewhere in the US).

In addition, a number of tour packagers cater to single travelers. These companies offer packages designed for individuals interested in vacationing with a group of single travelers or in being matched with a traveling companion. Among the better established of these agencies are the following:

Contiki Holidays (1432 E. Katella Ave., Anaheim, CA 92805; phone: 714-937-0611; 800-624-0611 in California; 800-626-0611 elsewhere in the continental US). Specializes in vacations for 18- to 35-year-olds. Packages to Italy frequently are offered. As this packager is a wholesaler, reservations must be booked through a travel agent.

Cosmos This tour operator offers budget motorcoach tours of Europe — including Italy — with a guaranteed-share plan whereby singles who wish to share rooms (and avoid paying the single supplement) are matched by the tour escort with individuals of the same sex and charged the basic double-occupancy tour price. Contact the firm at one of its three North American branches: 95-25 Queens Blvd., Rego Park, NY 11374 (phone: 800-221-0090 from the eastern US); 150 S. Los Robles Ave., Pasadena, CA 91101 (phone 818-449-0919 or 800-556-5454 from the western US); 1801 Eglinton Ave. W., Suite 104, Toronto, Ontario M6E 2H8, Canada (phone: 416-787-1281).

Gallivanting (515 East 79 St., Suite 20F, New York, NY 10021; phone: 800-933-9699 or 212-988-0617). Caters to singles from 25 to 55 and offers a trip to Italy featuring the history, archeology, architecture and art of Assisi, Florence,

Rome, and Pompeii; also arranges custom tours. Single-share guarantee when bookings are paid for 75 days in advance.

Insight International Tours (745 Atlantic Ave., Boston MA 02111; phone: 800-582-8380 or 617-482-2000). Offers a matching service for single travelers. Several tours are geared for travelers in the 18 to 35 age group.

Saga International Holidays (120 Boylston St., Boston MA 02116; phone: 617-451-6808 or 800-343-0273). A subsidiary of a British company specializing in older travelers, many of them single, *Saga* offers a broad selection of packages for people age 60 and over or those 50 to 59 traveling with someone 60 or older. Although anyone can book a *Saga* trip, a $15 club membership includes a subscription to their newsletter, as well as other publications and travel services — such as a matching service for single travelers.

Singles in Motion (545 W. 236th St., Suite 1D, Riverdale, NY 10463; phone: 212-884-4464). Offers a number of packages for single travelers, including tours, cruises, and excursions focusing on outdoor activities such as hiking and biking.

Singleworld (401 Theodore Fremd Ave., Rye, NY 10580; phone: 914-967-3334 or 800-223-6490 in the continental US). This club books members on its tours and cruises, and arranges shared accommodations, allowing individual travelers to avoid the single supplement charge. Departures for all tours are categorized by age group — for those 35 or younger; for all ages. Members also receive a quarterly newsletter; the yearly membership fee is $25.

Solo Flights (127 S. Compo Rd., Westport, CT 06880; phone: 203-226-9993). Represents a number of packagers and cruise lines and books singles on individual and group tours.

STI (8619 Reseda Blvd., Suite 103, Northridge, CA 91324; phone: 800-525-0525). Specializes in travel for 18- to 30-year-olds. Offers multi-country escorted tours ranging from 2 weeks to 2 months, including itineraries in Italy.

Travel in Two's (239 N. Broadway, Suite 3, N. Tarrytown, NY 10591; phone: 914-631-8409). This company books solo travelers on packages offered by a number of companies (at no extra cost to clients), offers its own tours, and matches singles with traveling companions. Many offerings are listed in their quarterly *Singles Vacation Newsletter,* which costs $7.50 per issue or $20 per year.

A good book for single travelers is *Traveling On Your Own* by Eleanor Berman, which offers tips on traveling solo and includes information on trips for singles, ranging from outdoor adventures to educational programs. Available in bookstores, it also can be ordered by sending $12.95, plus postage and handling, to Random House, Order Dept., 400 Hahn Rd., Westminster, MD 21157 (phone: 800-733-3000).

Single travelers also may want to subscribe to *Going Solo,* a newsletter that offers helpful information on going on your own. Issued eight times a year, a subscription costs $36. Contact Doerfer Communications, PO Box 1035, Cambridge, MA 02238 (phone: 617-876-2764).

An attractive alternative for the single traveler who is particularly interested in meeting Italians is *Club Med,* which operates scores of resorts in more than 37 countries worldwide and caters to the single traveler, as well as couples and families. Though the clientele often is under 30, there is a considerable age mix: the average age is 37 and the majority of these guests are European. *Club Med* has 4 Italian resorts: Three summer resorts — *Donoratico* (Livorno), *Metaponto* (Brindisi), and *Otranto* (Otranto) — and one ski resort — *Sestrieres* (Sestriere). *Club Med* offers single travelers package-rate vacations including airfare, food, wine, lodging, entertainment, and athletic facilities. The atmosphere is relaxed, the dress informal, and the price reasonable. For information, contact *Club Med,* 3 E. 54th St., New York, NY 10022 (phone: 800-CLUB-MED).

For other possibilities that include an opportunity to visit with Italians and accommodations alternatives suitable for single travelers, see our discussion of accommodations in *On the Road,* in this section.

WOMEN AND STUDENTS: Two specific groups of single travelers deserve special mention: women and students. Countless women travel by themselves in Italy, and such an adventure need not be feared.

A single woman need not worry about her personal safety any *more* than anywhere else, but be forewarned that Italian men like to show their appreciation of women and sometimes their attentions can be a bit disconcerting. Some women love this direct approach; others find it enraging. So be prepared to deal with men of the Mediterranean temperament. Remember that any reply you make to an overture will be regarded, in Italian culture, as encouragement. The best defense (if you feel a defense is needed) always is to be with other people when you are in public places, especially off the beaten track. An obvious solution is to travel with a group.

One lingering inhibition many female travelers still harbor is that of eating alone in public places. The trick is to relax and enjoy your meal and surroundings; while you may run across the occasional unenlightened waiter, dining solo is no longer uncommon.

■ **Note:** Be aware that jewelry and purse snatching has reached epidemic proportions in major Italian cities. Wise travelers should leave all that glitters at home.

Studying Abroad – A large number of single travelers are students. Travel *is* education. Travel broadens a person's knowledge and deepens his or her perception of the world in a way no media or "armchair" experience ever could. In addition, to study a country's language, art, culture, or history in one of its own schools is to enjoy the most productive method of learning.

By "student" we do not necessarily mean a person who wishes to matriculate at a foreign university to earn an academic degree. Nor do we necessarily mean a younger person. A student is anyone who wishes to include some sort of educational program in a trip to Italy.

There are many benefits for students abroad, and the way to begin to discover them is to consult the *Council on International Educational Exchange (CIEE).* This organization, which runs a variety of well-known work, study, and travel programs for students, is the US sponsor of the International Student Identity Card (ISIC). Reductions on airfare, other transportation, and entry fees to most museums and other exhibitions are only some of the advantages of the card. To apply for it, write to *CIEE* at one of the following addresses: 205 E. 42nd St., New York, NY 10017 (phone: 212-661-1414); 312 Sutter St., Suite 407, San Francisco, CA 94108 (phone: 415-421-3473); and 919 Irving St., Suite 102, San Francisco, CA 94122 (phone: 415-566-6222). Mark the letter "Attn. Student ID." Application requires a $14 fee, a passport-size photograph, and proof that you are a matriculating student (this means either a transcript or a letter or bill from your school registrar with the school's official seal; high school and junior high school students can use their report cards). There is no maximum age limit, but participants must be at least 12 years old. The *ID Discount Guide,* which gives details of the discounts country by country, is free with membership. Another free publication of *CIEE* is the informative, annual, 64-page *Student Travel Catalog,* which covers all aspects of youth-travel abroad for vacation trips, jobs, or study programs, and also includes a list of other helpful publications. You can order the catalogue from the Information and Student Services Department at the New York address given above.

There also is a *CIEE* office in Rome (233 Via della Lungara, Rome 00165 Italy; phone: 6-683-2109). A student travel office in Italy that also may be of assistance is *Centro Turistico Studentesco e Giovanile* (66 Via Nazionale, Rome 00184; phone: 6-479931).

Another card of value in Europe, and also available through *CIEE,* is the Federation of International Youth Travel Organizations (FIYTO) card, which provides many of the benefits of the ISIC card. In this case, cardholders need not be students, but merely under age 26. To apply, send $14 with a passport-size photo and proof of birthdate to *CIEE* at one of the addresses above.

CIEE also sponsors charter flights in the spring and summer to Italy that are open to students and non-students of any age. Flights between New York and Milan or Rome (with budget-priced add-ons available from Seattle, San Francisco, Los Angeles, Boston, Miami, and Washington, D.C.) leave at least twice weekly in high season, less frequently at other times. Youth fares also may be offered by some scheduled airlines offering transatlantic service to Italy. To find out about current discounts and restrictions, contact the individual carriers. (Also see *Traveling by Plane,* in this section.)

For extensive travel throughout Europe, there is a version of the Eurailpass restricted to travelers (including non-students) under 26 years of age. The Eurail Youthpass entitles the bearer to either 1 or 2 months of unlimited second class rail travel in 17 countries, including Italy. In addition, it is honored on many European steamers and ferries and on railroad connections between the airport and the center of town in various cities. The pass also entitles the bearer to reduced rates on some bus lines in several countries. The Eurail Youthpass can be purchased only by those living outside Europe or North Africa, and it must be purchased before departure. Eurailpasses can be bought from a US travel agent or from the US representatives of the *Italian State Railways* and other European railways (for further information, see *Traveling by Train,* in this section).

Students and singles in general should keep in mind that youth hostels exist in many cities throughout Italy. They always are inexpensive, generally clean and well situated, and they are a sure place to meet other people traveling alone. Hundreds of hostels are run by the *Italian Youth Hostels Association,* called *Associazione Italiana Alberghi per la Gioventù (AIG),* one of the hosteling associations of 68 countries that make up the *International Youth Hostel Federation (IYHF);* membership in one of the national associations affords access to the hostels of the rest. To join the American affiliate, *American Youth Hostels (AYH),* contact the national office (PO Box 37613, Washington, DC 20013-7613; phone: 202-783-6161), or the local *AYH* council nearest you. As we went to press, the following membership rates were in effect: $25 for adults (between 18 and 54), $10 for youths (17 and under), $15 for seniors (55 and up), and $35 for family membership. *Hostelling North America,* which lists hostels in the US and Canada, comes with your *AYH* card (non-members can purchase the handbook for $5, plus postage and handling); the *Guide to Budget Accommodation, Volume 1,* covers hostels in Europe (*Volume 2* covers the rest of the world) and must be purchased ($10.95, plus postage and handling).

Those who go abroad without an *AYH* card may purchase a youth hostel International Guest Card (for the equivalent of about $18), and obtain information on local youth hostels by contacting one of the national youth hostel associations in Italy (*AIG* headquarters in Italy are at 44 Via Cavour, Rome 00184; phone: 6-4746755).

And there's always camping. Virtually any area of the countryside in Italy has a place to pitch a tent and enjoy the scenery. (For more information, see *Camping and Caravanning, Hiking and Biking,* in this section.)

Opportunities for study range from summer or academic-year courses in the language and civilization of Italy designed specifically for foreigners (including those whose school days are well behind them) to long-term university attendance by those intending to take a degree.

The study programs listed below are but a few of the popular and diverse courses available in Italy. For a complete listing of programs administered by Italian institutions, contact the *Italian Cultural Institute (Instituto Italiano di Cultura),* which has five locations in the US: 500 N. Michigan Ave., Suite 530, Chicago, IL 60611 (phone: 312-822-9545); 12400 Wilshire Blvd., Suite 310, Los Angeles, CA 90025 (phone: 213-207-4737); 686 Park Ave., New York, NY 10021 (phone: 212-879-4242); 425 Bush St., Suite 305, San Francisco, CA 94108 (phone: 415-788-7142); and 1601 Fuller St. NW, Washington, DC 20009 (phone: 202-328-5500).

Several foreign study programs in Italy include the following:

Eurocentre (9 Piazza Santo Spirito, Florence 50125, Italy; phone: 55-213030). Part of an international foundation with headquarters in Zurich and schools of language and civilization in several other European countries, the *Eurocentre* branch in Italy is in a Renaissance palazzo in the heart of Florence. In addition to providing excellent Italian language instruction, the center emphasizes teaching its students about Italian art and architecture, some of the finest examples of which can be seen from the school's windows.

Società Dante Alighieri (27 Piazza Firenze, Rome 00186, Italy; phone: 6-687-3722). The *Dante* is a worldwide organization for the diffusion of Italian culture, with 400 branches teaching Italian to more than 50,000 students a year. The Rome branch offers courses in art, music, theater, furniture, and interior decoration; it sponsors films, concerts, lecture series, and assorted excursions. There are four 2-month terms from October to May plus a 2-month summer term in June and July. Fees are quite low and instruction first-rate.

Università Italiana per Stranieri (Palazzo Gallenga, 4 Piazza Fortebraccio, Perugia 06100, Italy; phone: 75-64344). Founded in 1925 by the Italian government, the "University for Foreigners" is housed in the 18th-century Palazzo Gallenga of Perugia. Well run, with a diverse student body and nominally priced courses in subjects as varied as elementary Italian and Etruscology, it puts much of the country's regular university system to shame. Courses of varying lengths — from 4 weeks to 9 months — are offered throughout the year.

Complete details on more than 3,000 available courses abroad (including universities in Italy) and suggestions on how to apply are contained in two books published by the *Institute of International Education* (IIE Books, Publications Office, 809 UN Plaza, New York, NY 10017; phone: 212-984-5412): *Vacation Study Abroad* ($26.95, plus shipping and handling) and *Academic Year Abroad* ($31.95, plus shipping and handling). A third book, *Teaching Abroad,* costs $21.95, plus shipping and handling. IIE Books also offers a free pamphlet called *Basic Facts on Study Abroad.*

The *National Registration Center for Study Abroad* (*NRCSA,* PO Box 1393, Milwaukee, WI 53201; phone: 414-278-0631) also offers a publication called the *Worldwide Classroom: Study Abroad and Learning Vacations in 40 Countries: 1991-1992,* available for $5, plus $3 shipping and handling, which includes information on over 160 schools and cultural centers that offer courses for Americans with the primary focus on foreign language and culture.

Those who are interested in a "learning vacation" abroad also may be interested in *Travel and Learn* by Evelyn Kaye. This guide to educational travel discusses a wide range of opportunities — everything from archaeology to whale watching — and provides information on organizations that offer programs in these areas of interest. The book is available in bookstores for $23.95; or you can send $26 (which includes shipping charges) to Blue Penguin Publications (147 Sylvan Ave., Leonia, NJ 07605; phone: 800-800-8147 or 201-461-6918). *Learning Vacations* by Gerson G. Eisenberg also provides extensive information on seminars, workshops, courses, and so on — in a wide variety of subjects. Available in bookstores, it also can be ordered from Peterson's Guides (PO Box 2123, Princeton, NJ 08543-2123; phone: 800-338-3282 or 609-243-9111) for $11.95, plus shipping and handling.

Work, Study, Travel Abroad: The Whole World Handbook, issued by the *Council on International Educational Exchange (CIEE),* is an informative, chatty guide on study programs, work opportunities, and travel hints, with a particularly good section on Italy. It is available for $10.95, plus shipping and handling, from *CIEE* (address above).

AFS Intercultural Programs (313 E. 43rd St., New York, NY 10017; phone 800-AFS-INFO or 212-949-4242) sets up exchanges between US and foreign high school students on an individual basis for a semester or a whole academic year.

National Association of Secondary School Principals (*NASSP,* 1904 Association Dr., Reston, VA 22091; phone: 703-860-0200), an association of administrators, teachers, and state education officials, sponsors *School Partnership International,* a program in which secondary schools in the US are linked with partner schools abroad for an annual short-term exchange of students and faculty.

If you are interested in a home-stay travel program, in which you learn about European culture by living with a family, contact the *Experiment in International Living* (PO Box 676, Brattleboro, VT 05302-0676; phone: 802-257-7751 in Vermont; 800-345-2929 elsewhere in the continental US), which sponsors home-stay educational travel in more than 40 countries, including locations throughout Italy. The organization aims its programs at high school or college students.

Another organization specializing in travel as an educational experience is the *American Institute for Foreign Study (AIFS)* (102 Greenwich Ave., Greenwich, CT 06830; phone: 800-727-AIFS, 203-869-9090, or 203-863-6087). Students can enroll for the full academic year or for any number of semesters. *AIFS* caters primarily to bona fide high school or college students, but its non-credit international learning programs are open to independent travelers of all ages (approximately 20% of *AIFS* students are over 25).

Hints for Older Travelers

Special discounts and more free time are just two factors that have given Americans over age 65 a chance to see the world at affordable prices. Senior citizens make up an ever-growing segment of the travel population, and the trend among them is to travel more frequently and for longer periods of time.

PLANNING: When planning a vacation, prepare your itinerary with one eye on your own physical condition and the other on a topographical map. Keep in mind variations in climate, terrain, and altitudes, which may pose some danger for anyone with heart or breathing problems.

Older travelers may find the following publications of interest:

The Discount Guide for Travelers Over 55, by Caroline and Walter Weintz, is an excellent book for budget-conscious older travelers. It is available by sending $7.95, plus shipping and handling, to Penguin USA (Att. Cash Sales, 120 Woodbine St., Bergenfield, NJ 07621); when ordering, specify the ISBN number: 0-525-48358-6.

Going Abroad: 101 Tips for the Mature Traveler offers tips on preparing for your trip, commonsense precautions en route, and some basic travel terminology. This concise, free booklet is available from *Grand Circle Travel,* 347 Congress St., Boston, MA 02210 (phone: 800-221-2610 or 617-350-7500).

The International Health Guide for Senior Citizen Travelers, by Dr. W. Robert

Lange, covers such topics as trip preparations, food and water precautions, adjusting to weather and climate conditions, finding a doctor, motion sickness, jet lag, and so on. Also includes a list of resource organizations that provide medical assistance for travelers. It is available for $4.95 postpaid from Pilot Books, 103 Cooper St., Babylon, NY 11702 (phone: 516-422-2225).

The Mature Traveler is a monthly newsletter that provides information on travel discounts, places of interest, useful tips, and other topics of interest for travelers 49 and up. To subscribe, send $21.95 to GEM Publishing Group, PO Box 50820, Reno, NV 89513 (phone: 702-786-7419).

Travel Easy: The Practical Guide for People Over 50, by Rosalind Massow, discusses a wide range of subjects — from trip planning, transportation options, and preparing for departure to avoiding and handling medical problems en route. It's available for $6.50 to members of the *American Association of Retired Persons (AARP),* and for $8.95 to non-members; call about current charges for postage and handling. Order from *AARP* Books, c/o Customer Service, Scott, Foresman & Company, 1900 E. Lake Ave., Glenview, IL 60025 (phone: 708-729-3000).

Travel Tips for Older Americans is a useful booklet that provides good, basic advice. This US State Department publication (stock number: 044-000-02270-2) can be ordered by sending a check or money order for $1 to the Superintendent of Documents (US Government Printing Office, Washington, DC 20402) or by calling 202-783-3238 and charging the order to a credit card.

Unbelievably Good Deals & Great Adventures That You Absolutely Can't Get Unless You're Over 50, by Joan Rattner Heilman, offers travel tips for older travelers, including discounts on accommodations and transportation, as well as a list of organizations for seniors. It is available for $7.95, plus shipping and handling, from Contemporary Books, 180 N. Michigan Ave., Chicago, IL 60601 (phone: 312-782-9181).

HEALTH: Health facilities in Italy generally are excellent; however, an inability to speak the language can pose a serious problem, not in receiving treatment at large hospitals, where many doctors and other staff members will speak English, but in getting help elsewhere or in getting to the place where help is available. A number of organizations exist to help travelers avoid or deal with a medical emergency overseas. For information on these services, see *Medical and Legal Aid and Consular Services,* in this section.

Pre-trip medical and dental checkups are strongly recommended. In addition, be sure to take along any prescription medication you need, enough to last *without a new prescription* for the duration of your trip; pack all medications with a note from your doctor for the benefit of airport authorities. If you have specific medical problems, bring prescriptions and a "medical file" composed of the following:

1. A summary of medical history, current diagnosis.
2. A list of drugs to which you are allergic.
3. Your most recent electrocardiogram, if you have heart problems.
4. Your doctor's name, address, and telephone number.

DISCOUNTS AND PACKAGES: Since guidelines change from place to place, it is a good idea to inquire in advance about discounts for transportation, hotels, concerts, movies, museums, and other activities. The Italian Government Travel Offices in the US and the local tourist information offices in Italy can give the most up-to-date information about discounts and programs for older travelers (for addresses see *Tourist Information Offices,* in this section, as well as the individual city reports in THE CITIES).

Many hotel chains, airlines, cruise lines, bus companies, car rental companies, and other travel suppliers offer discounts to older travelers. For instance, senior citizens who are members of *United*'s Silver Wings Club are eligible for 10% discounts on *Alitalia* flights between the US and Italy. US airlines such as *American, TWA,* and *United* offer those age 62 and over (and one traveling companion per qualifying senior citizen) discounts on flights from the US to Italy. Other airlines also offer discounts for passengers age 60 (or 62) and over, which also may apply to one traveling companion. For information on current prices and applicable restrictions, contact the individual carriers.

In addition, the *Carta d'Argento* (Silver Card) entitles men and women over 60 to a 30% discount on rail fares in Italy. The card can be bought in Italy at rail stations, *CIT* offices (see *Traveling by Train,* in this section), and certain other travel agencies on presentation of a passport. The cost is about $5 and the card is good for a year. Other discounts exist in Italy, but it's not easy for short-term visitors to take advantage of them. Still, wherever you go and whatever you do, it can't hurt to ask if there are special rates for senior citizens.

Some discounts, however, are extended only to bona fide members of certain senior citizens organizations. Because the same organizations frequently offer package tours to both domestic and international destinations, the benefits of membership are twofold: Those who join can take advantage of discounts as individual travelers and also reap the savings that group travel affords. In addition, because the age requirements for some of these organizations are quite low (or nonexistent), the benefits can begin to accrue early.

In order to take advantage of these discounts, you should carry proof of your age (or eligibility). A driver's license, membership card in a recognized senior citizen's organization, or a Medicare card should be adequate. Among the organizations dedicated to helping older travelers see the world are the following:

American Association of Retired Persons (*AARP;* 1909 K St. NW, Washington, DC 20049; phone: 202-872-4700). The largest and best known of these organizations. Membership is open to anyone 50 or over, whether retired or not; dues are $5 a year, $12.50 for 3 years, or $35 for 10 years, and include spouse. The *AARP* Travel Experience Worldwide program, available through *American Express Travel Related Services* offers members tours, cruises, and other travel programs worldwide designed exclusively for older travelers. Members can book these services by calling *American Express* at 800-927-0111 for land and air travel, or 800-745-4567 for cruises.

Mature Outlook (Customer Service Center, 6001 N. Clark St., Chicago, IL 60660; phone: 800-336-6330). Through its *Travel Alert,* tours, cruises, and other vacation packages are available to members at special savings. Hotel and car rental discounts and travel accident insurance also are available. Membership is open to anyone 50 years of age or older, costs $9.95 a year, and includes a bimonthly newsletter and magazine, as well as information on package tours.

National Council of Senior Citizens (1331 F St., Washington, DC 20005; phone: 202-347-8800). Here, too, the emphasis is on keeping costs low. This nonprofit organization offers members a different roster of package tours each year, as well as individual arrangements through its affiliated travel agency *(Vantage Travel Service).* Although most members are over 50, membership is open to anyone (regardless of age) for an annual fee of $12 per person or couple. Lifetime membership costs $150.

Certain travel agencies and tour operators offer special trips geared to older travelers. Among them are the following:

Evergreen Travel Service (4114 198th St. SW, Suite 13, Lynnwood, WA 98036-6742; phone: 206-776-1184 or 800-435-2288 throughout the continental US and Canada). This specialist in trips for persons with disabilities recently introduced Lazybones Tours, a program offering leisurely tours for older travelers. Most programs are first class or deluxe, and include an escort.

Grandtravel (6900 Wisconsin Ave., Suite 706, Chevy Chase, MD 20815; phone: 301-986-0790 in Maryland; 800-247-7651 elsewhere in the US). An agency that specializes in trips for grandparents and their grandchildren (aunts and uncles are welcome, too), bringing the generations together through travel. Several itineraries coincide with school vacations and emphasize historic and natural sites. Transportation, accommodations, and activities are thoughtfully arranged to meet the needs of the young and the young-at-heart.

Insight International Tours (745 Atlantic Ave., Boston, MA 02111; phone: 800-582-8380 or 617-482-2000). Offers a matching service for single travelers. Several tours are geared for mature travelers.

OmniTours (1 Northfield Plaza, Northfield, IL 60093; phone: 800-962-0060 or 708-441-5250). Offers combination air and rail group tours designed for travelers 50 years and older.

Saga International Holidays (120 Boylston St., Boston MA 02116; phone: 617-451-6808 or 800-343-0273). A subsidiary of a British company catering to older travelers, *Saga* offers a broad selection of packages for people age 60 and over or those 50 to 59 traveling with someone 60 or older. Although anyone can book a *Saga* trip, a $15 club membership includes a subscription to their newsletter, as well as other publications and travel services.

Many travel agencies, particularly the larger ones, are delighted to make presentations to help a group of senior citizens select destinations. A local chamber of commerce should be able to provide the names of such agencies. Once a time and place are determined, an organization member or travel agent can obtain group quotations for transportation, accommodations, meal plans, and sightseeing. Larger groups usually get the best breaks.

Another choice open to older travelers is a trip that includes an educational element. *Elderhostel,* a nonprofit organization, offers programs at educational institutions worldwide, including the universities of Padua and Verona in Italy. The foreign programs generally last about 2 weeks, and include double-occupancy accommodations in hotels or student residence halls and all meals. Travel to the programs usually is by designated scheduled flights, and participants can arrange to extend their stay at the end of the program. Elderhostelers must be at least 60 years old (younger if a spouse or companion qualifies), in good health, and not in need of special diets. For a free catalogue describing the program and current offerings, write to *Elderhostel* (75 Federal St., Boston, MA 02110; phone: 617-426-7788). Those interested in the program also can borrow slides at no charge or purchase an informational videotape for $5.

Interhostel, a program sponsored by the Division of Continuing Education of the University of New Hampshire, sends travelers back to school at cooperating institutions in 25 countries on 4 continents. Participants attend lectures on the history, economy, politics, and cultural life of the country they are visiting, go on field trips to pertinent points of interest, and take part in activities meant to introduce them to their foreign contemporaries. In Italy, there are programs in Florence. Trips are for 2 weeks; accommodations are on campus in university residence halls or off campus in modest hotels (double occupancy). Groups are limited to 35 to 40 participants who are at least 50 years old (or at least 40 if a participating spouse is at least 50), physically active, and not in need of special diets. For further information or to receive the three free seasonal catalogues, contact *Interhostel,* UNH Division of Continuing Education, 6 Garrison Ave., Durham, NH 03824 (phone: 800-733-9753 or 603-862-1147).

Hints for Traveling with Children

What better way to encounter the world's variety than in the company of the wide-eyed *bambini* of your family? Italians love children and will bend over backward to accommodate them. Their presence does not have to be a burden or an excessive expense. The current generation of discounts for children and family package deals can make a trip together quite reasonable.

A family trip will be an investment in your children's future, making Italian geography and history come alive to them, and leaving a sure memory that will be among the fondest you will share with them someday. Their insights will be refreshing to you; their impulses may take you to unexpected places with unexpected dividends. The experience will be invaluable to them at any age.

PLANNING: Here are several hints for making a trip with children easy and fun.

1. Children, like everyone else, will derive more pleasure from a trip if they know something about the country before they arrive. Begin their education about a month before you leave. Using maps, travel magazines, and books, give children a clear idea of where you are going and how far away it is.
2. Children should help to plan the itinerary, and where you go and what you do should reflect some of their ideas. If they know something about the sites they'll visit, they will have the excitement of recognition when they arrive.
3. Children also will enjoy learning some Italian phrases — a few basics like "*mi scusi*" ("excuse me"), "*grazie*" ("thank you"), "*buon giorno*" ("good morning" or "good day"), "*arrivederci*" ("good-bye"), and the casual "*ciao*" ("so long").
4. Familiarize the children with lire. Give them an allowance for the trip, and be sure they understand just how far it will or won't go.
5. Give children specific responsibilities: The job of carrying their own flight bags and looking after their personal things, along with some other light travel chores, will give them a stake in the journey.
6. Give each child a travel diary or scrapbook to take along.

Children's books about Italy provide an excellent introduction to the country and its culture. Some particularly good titles include the following:

Art For Children is a delightful series by Ernest Raboff (HarperCollins; $11.95 hardcover; $5.95 paperback) designed to introduce children ages 5 to 12 to famous artists and their works. There are 16 books in the series, each one concentrating on a different artist. *Michelangelo* ($7.95, paperback) and *Raphael* ($5.95, paperback) are good introductions to the magnificent paintings of these masters that you may see in Italy.

Castle, by David Macaulay (Houghton Mifflin; $14.95 hardcover; $6.95 paperback). Using text and drawings, this books shows how castles were built in the 13th century, and is particularly suited to helping children from kindergarten to grade 5 learn about the castles they may see in Italy.

Cathedral: The Story of Its Construction, by the same author (Houghton Mifflin; $14.95 hardcover; $6.95 paperback). Another interesting and informative book — a must for those visiting St. Peter's in the Vatican and other great cathedrals in Italy.

Great Painters (G. P. Putnam & Sons; $20.95). This beautifully illustrated book, by Pierro Ventura, is an excellent introduction to painting for older children (ages 12 and up). It discusses Italian Old Masters.

Living in Ancient Rome, by Odile Bombard (Young Discovery Library; $4.95) offers children a historical perspective of Italy.

This Is Rome and This Is Venice, two books in Miroslav Sasek's travel series for children in grades 3 to 6, are wonderful introductions to these popular destinations. This series is out of print, but may be available at your local library.

Welcome to Ancient Rome, by Ann Millard (Passport Books, National Textbook Company; $4.95), is a tiny but information-packed book for children in grade four and up.

These and other children's books can be found at many general bookstores and libraries. Bookstores specializing in children's books include the following:

Books of Wonder (132 7th Ave., New York, NY 10011; phone: 212-989-3270; or 464 Hudson St., New York, NY 10014; phone: 212-645-8006). Carries both new and used books for children.

Cheshire Cat (5512 Connecticut Ave. NW, Washington, DC 20015; phone: 202-244-3956). Specializes in books for children of all ages.

Eeyore's Books for Children (2212 Broadway, New York, NY 10024; phone: 212-362-0634; or 25 E. 83rd St., New York, NY 10028; phone: 212-988-3404). Carries an extensive selection of children's books; features a special travel section.

Reading Reptile, Books and Toys for Young Mammals (4120 Pennsylvania, Kansas City, MO 64111; phone: 816-753-0441). Carries books for children and teens to age 15.

Red Balloon (891 Grand Ave., St. Paul, MN 55105; phone: 612-224-8320). Carries both new and used books for children.

White Rabbit Children's Books (7755 Girard Ave., La Jolla, CA 92037; phone: 619-454-3518). Carries books and music for children (and parents).

Another source of children's books perfect to take on the road is *The Family Travel Guides Catalogue.* This detailed booklet contains informative and amusing titles focusing on numerous countries, including Italy. For instance, the *Travel Papers,* a series of short articles full of useful facts for families, covers Italy. The *Travel Papers* and the catalogue are available from Carousel Press (PO Box 6061, Albany, CA 94706; phone: 415-527-5849), which also is the mail-order supplier of all titles listed in the catalogue.

And for parents, *Travel With Your Children* (*TWYCH;* 80 Eighth Ave., New York, NY 10011; phone: 212-206-0688) publishes a newsletter, *Family Travel Times,* that focuses on families with young travelers and offers helpful hints. An annual subscription (10 issues) is $35 and includes a copy of the "Airline Guide" issue (updated every other year), which focuses on the subject of flying with children. This special issue is available separately for $10.

Another newsletter devoted to family travel is *Getaways.* This quarterly publication provides reviews of family-oriented literature, activities, and useful travel tips. To subscribe, send $25 to *Getaways,* Att. Ms. Brooke Kane, PO Box 11511, Washington, DC 20008 (phone: 703-534-8747).

Also of interest to parents traveling with their children is *How to Take Great Trips With Your Kids,* by psychologist Sanford Portnoy and his wife, Joan Flynn Portnoy. The book includes helpful tips from fellow family travelers, tips on economical accommodations and touring by car, recreational vehicle, and train, as well as over 50 games to play with your children en route. It is available for $8.95, plus shipping and handling, from Harvard Common Press, 535 Albany St., Boston, MA 02118 (phone: 617-423-5803). Another title worth looking for is *Great Vacations with Your Kids,* by Dorothy Jordan (Dutton; $12.95).

Another book on family travel, *Travel with Children* by Maureen Wheeler, offers a wide range of practical tips on traveling with children, and includes accounts of the author's family travel experiences. It is available for $10.95, plus shipping and handling, from Lonely Planet Publications, Embarcadero West, 112 Linden St., Oakland, CA 94607 (phone: 510-893-8555).

Finally, parents arranging a trip with their children may want to deal with an agency specializing in family travel such as *Let's Take the Kids* (1268 Devon Ave., Los Angeles, CA 90024; phone: 800-726-4349 or 213-274-7088). In addition to arranging and booking trips for individual families, this group occasionally organizes trips for single-parent families traveling together. They also offer a parent travel network, whereby parents who have been to a particular destination can evaluate it for others.

GETTING THERE AND GETTING AROUND: Begin early to investigate all available family discount and charter flights, as well as any package deals and special rates offered by the major airlines.

PLANE: When you make your reservations, tell the airline that you are traveling with a child. Children ages 2 through 12 generally travel at about a half to two-thirds of the regular full fare adult ticket prices on most international flights. This children's fare, however, usually is much higher than the excursion fare, which is applicable to any traveler regardless of age. On many international flights, children under 2 travel at about 10% of the adult fare if they sit on an adult's lap. A second infant without a second adult would pay the fare applicable to children ages 2 through 11.

Although some airlines will, on request, supply bassinets for infants, most carriers encourage parents to bring their own safety seat on board, which then is strapped into the airline seat with a regular seat belt. This is much safer — and certainly more comfortable — than holding the child in your lap. If you do not purchase a seat for your baby, you have the option of bringing the infant restraint along on the off-chance that there might be an empty seat next to yours — in which case some airlines will let you use that seat at no charge for your baby and infant seat. However, if there is no empty seat available, the infant seat no doubt will have to be checked as baggage (and you may have to pay an additional charge), since it generally does not fit under the seat or in the overhead racks.

The safest bet is to pay for a seat — this usually will be the same as fares applicable to children ages 2 through 11. It usually is cheaper to pay for an adult excursion rate than the discounted children's fare.

Be forewarned: Some safety seats designed primarily for use in cars do not fit into plane seats properly. Although nearly all seats manufactured since 1985 carry labels indicating whether they meet federal standards for use aboard planes, actual seat sizes may vary from carrier to carrier. At the time of this writing, the FAA was in the process of reviewing and revising the federal regulations regarding infant travel and safety devices — it was still to be determined if children should be *required* to sit in safety seats and whether the airlines will have to provide them.

If using one of these infant restraints, you should try to get bulkhead seats which will provide extra room to care for your child during the flight. You also should request a bulkhead seat when using a bassinet — again, this is not as safe as strapping the child in. On some planes bassinets hook into a bulkhead wall; on others it is placed on the floor in front of you. (Note that bulkhead seats often are reserved for families traveling with children.) As a general rule, babies should be held during takeoff and landing.

Request seats on the aisle if you have a toddler or if you think you will need to use the bathroom frequently. Carry onto the plane all you will need to care for and occupy your children during the flight — formula, diapers, a sweater, books, favorite stuffed animals, and so on. Dress your baby simply, with a minimum of buttons and snaps, because the only place you may have to change a diaper is at your seat or in a small lavatory. The flight attendant can warm a bottle for you.

On most US carriers, you also can ask for a hot dog or hamburger instead of the airline's regular dinner if you give at least 24 hours' notice. Some, but not all, airlines have baby food aboard. While you should bring along toys from home, also ask about children's diversions. Some carriers have terrific free packages of games, coloring books, and puzzles.

When the plane takes off and lands, make sure your baby is nursing or has a bottle, pacifier, or thumb in its mouth. This sucking will make the child swallow and help to clear stopped ears. A piece of hard candy will do the same thing for an older child.

Parents traveling by plane with toddlers, children, or teenagers may want to consult *When Kids Fly,* a free booklet published by Massport (Public Affairs Department, 10 Park Plaza, Boston, MA 02116-3971; phone: 617-973-5600), which includes helpful information on airfares for children, infant seats, what to do in the event of overbooked or cancelled flights, and so on.

■ **Note:** Newborn babies, whose lungs may not be able to adjust to the altitude, should not be taken aboard an airplane. And some airlines may refuse to allow a pregnant woman in her 8th or 9th month to fly. Check with the airline ahead of time, and carry a letter from your doctor stating that you are fit to travel — and indicating the estimated date of birth.

SHIP, TRAIN, AND BUS: Some shipping lines offer cruises that feature special activities for children, particularly during periods that coincide with major school holidays like *Christmas, Easter,* and the summer months. On such cruises, children may be charged special cut-rate fares, and there are youth counselors to organize activities. Occasionally, a shipping line even offers free passage during the summer months for children under age 16 occupying a stateroom with two (full-fare) adult passengers. Your travel agent should know which cruise lines offer such programs.

If you plan to travel by train when abroad, note that on *Italian State Railways,* children under 4 (accompanied by an adult) travel free, provided they do not occupy a seat; children under 4 occupying a seat and from ages 4 through 11 also often travel at a lower fare. Depending on how much rail traveling your family will be doing in Italy, you might consider buying the discounted Family Card *(Carta Famiglia).* The Eurailpass, which is good for unlimited train travel throughout Europe, including Italy, is half price for children ages 4 through 12. For further information, see *Traveling by Ship* and *Traveling by Train,* as well as the individual city reports in THE CITIES.

CAR: Traveling by car allows greater flexibility in traveling and packing. You may want to stock the car with a variety of favorite snacks, and if you bring along an ice chest and a grill you can stop for picnics. Games and simple toys, such as magnetic checkerboards or drawing pencils and pads, also provide a welcome diversion. Frequent stops so that children can run around make car travel much easier.

ACCOMMODATIONS AND MEALS: Often a cot for a child will be placed in a hotel room at little or no extra charge. If you wish to sleep in separate rooms, special rates sometimes are available for families; some places do not charge for children under a certain age. In many of the larger chain hotels, the staffs are more used to children. These hotels also are likely to have swimming pools or gamerooms — both popular with most youngsters. Many large resorts also have recreation centers for children. Cabins, bungalows, condominiums, and other rental options offer families privacy, flexibility, some kitchen facilities, and often lower costs.

You might want to look into accommodations along the way that will add to the color of your trip. For instance, reconverted country villas, farmhouses, and well-run *pensioni* throughout Italy provide a delightful experience for the whole family and permit a view of Italian life different from that gained in a conventional hotel.

Among the least expensive options is a camping facility; many are situated in beautiful, out-of-the-way spots, and generally are good, well equipped, and less expensive than any hotel. For further information on accommodations options for the whole family, see our discussions in *On the Road,* and for information on camping facilities, see *Camping and Caravanning, Hiking and Biking,* both in this section.

Better hotels in Italy may be able to arrange for a sitter for the times you will want to be without the children — for an evening's entertainment or a particularly rigorous stint of sightseeing. Whether the sitter is hired directly or through an agency, ask for and check references.

At mealtime, don't deny yourself or your children the delights of a new style of cooking. Your children probably already love pizza and pasta, but they need to know, too, that Italians eat many other equally delicious foods that they will want to try: risotto (rice), polenta (cornmeal porridge), minestrone (vegetable soup), gelato (ice cream). Before leaving on vacation, you might sample a few standard Italian dishes in a good restaurant. Encourage your children to try new things. And don't forget about picnics. Note that although milk is pasteurized and water is potable in large cities, it's wise to stick to bottled water for small children and for those with sensitive stomachs.

Knowledge of the probable locations of restrooms is a necessity when you travel with children. In Italy, ask for *il gabinetto.* You will find restrooms in hotels and restaurants, museums, theaters, and other public places you visit, as well as near all the major sites, especially in Rome. All airport and railway stations have them. The *Albergo Diurno,* a day-hotel in Rome's Stazione Termini, has baths and showers, as well as toilet facilities.

Things to Remember

1. If you are spending your vacation touring many places, pace the days with children in mind. Break the trip into half-day segments, with running around or "doing" time built in. Keep travel time on the road to a maximum of 4 to 5 hours a day.
2. Don't forget that a child's attention span is far shorter than an adult's. Children don't have to see every sight or all of any sight to learn something from their trip; watching, playing with, and talking to other children can be equally enlightening.
3. Let your children lead the way sometimes; their perspective is different from yours, and they may lead you to things you would never have noticed on your own.
4. Remember the places that children love to visit: aquariums, zoos, amusement parks, beaches, nature trails, and so on. Among the activities that may pique their interest are bicycling, snorkeling, boat trips, horseback riding, visiting children's museums, and viewing natural habitat exhibits.

Staying Healthy

The surest way to return home in good health is to be prepared for medical problems that might occur on vacation. Below, we've outlined some things you need to think about before you go.

Older travelers or anyone suffering from a chronic medical condition, such as diabetes, high blood pressure, cardiopulmonary disease, asthma, or ear, eye, or sinus trouble, should consult a physician before leaving home. Those with conditions requiring special consideration when traveling should consider seeing, in addition to their regular physician, a specialist in travel medicine. For a referral in a particular community, contact the nearest medical school or ask a local doctor to recommend such a specialist. Dr. Leonard Marcus, a member of the *American Committee on Clinical Tropical Medicine and Travelers' Health,* provides a directory of more than 100 travel doctors across the country. For a copy, send a 9-by-12-inch self-addressed, stamped envelope, plus postage, to Dr. Marcus at 148 Highland Ave., Newton, MA 02165 (phone: 617-527-4003).

FIRST AID: Put together a compact, personal medical kit including Band-Aids, first-aid cream, antiseptic, nose drops, insect repellent, aspirin, an extra pair of prescription glasses or contact lenses (and a copy of your prescription for glasses or contact lenses), sunglasses, over-the-counter remedies for diarrhea, indigestion, and motion sickness, a thermometer, and a supply of those prescription medicines you take regularly.

In a corner of your kit, keep a list of all the drugs you have brought and their purpose, as well as duplicate copies of your doctor's prescriptions (or a note from your doctor). As brand names may vary in different countries, it's a good idea to ask your doctor for the generic name of any drugs you use so that you can ask for their equivalent should you need a refill.

It also is a good idea to ask your doctor to prepare a medical identification card that includes such information as your blood type, your social security number, any allergies or chronic health problems you have, and your medical insurance information. Considering the essential contents of your kit, keep it with you, rather than in your checked luggage.

SUNBURN: The burning power of the sun can quickly cause severe sunburn or sunstroke. To protect yourself against these ills, wear sunglasses, take along a broad-brimmed hat and cover-up, and use a sunscreen lotion.

WATER SAFETY: Italy's seas, especially the Mediterranean, can be treacherous. A few precautions are necessary. Beware of the undertow, that current of water running back down the beach after a wave has washed ashore; it can knock you off your feet and into the surf. Even more dangerous is the riptide, a strong current of water running against the tide, which can pull you out to sea. If you get caught offshore, don't panic or try to fight the current, because it only will exhaust you; instead, ride it out while waiting for it to subside, which usually happens not too far from shore, or try swimming away parallel to the beach.

Sharks are sometimes sighted, but they usually don't come in close to shore, and they are well fed on fish. Should you meet up with one, just swim away as quietly and smoothly as you can, without shouting or splashing. Although not aggressive, eels can be dangerous when threatened. If snorkeling or diving in coastal waters or freshwater lakes or streams, beware of crevices where these creatures may be lurking. The tentacled Portuguese man-of-war and other jellyfish also may drift in quiet salt waters for food and often wash up onto the beach; the long tentacles of these creatures sting whatever they touch — a paste made of household vinegar and unseasoned meat tenderizer is the recommended treatment.

If complications, allergic reactions (such as breathlessness, fever, or cramps), or signs of serious infection result from any of the above circumstances, *see a doctor.*

INSECTS AND OTHER PESTS: Flies and mosquitoes can be troublesome, so it is a good idea to use some form of topical insect repellent — those containing DEET (N,N-diethyl-m-toluamide) are among the most common and effective. The US Environmental Protection Agency (EPA) stresses that you should not use any pesticide that has not been approved by the EPA (check the label) and that all such preparations should be used in moderation. If picnicking or camping, burn mosquito coils or candles containing allethrin, pyrethrin, or citronella, or use a pyrethrum-containing flying-insect spray. For further information about active ingredients in repellents, call the *National Pesticide Telecommunications Network*'s 24-hour hotline number: 800-858-7378.

If you do get bitten — by mosquitoes, horse or black flies, or other bugs — the itching can be relieved with baking soda, topical first-aid cream, or antihistamine tablets. Should a bite become infected, treat it with a disinfectant or antibiotic cream.

Though rarer, bites from snakes or spiders can be serious. If possible, always try to catch the villain for identification purposes. If bitten by these creatures or *any* wild animal, the best course of action may be to head directly to the nearest emergency ward or outpatient clinic of a hospital. Cockroaches, waterbugs, and termites thrive in warm climates, but pose no serious health threat.

If you are bitten and you develop a rash and flu-type symptom, you may have been bitten by a tick carrying what is known as Lyme Borreliosis disease (known as "Lyme Tick Disease") and you should consult a physician. Many Americans believe that this disease is unique to the US; however, it was first diagnosed in Europe — where it is called Neuro Borreliosis — and has been a problem there for years. Caution should be taken in all wooded areas. For further information on this rapidly spreading problem, see *Camping and Caravanning, Hiking and Biking,* in this section.

FOOD AND WATER: Tap water generally is clean and potable throughout most of Italy. You may want to drink bottled water, as do the Italians, at least at the beginning of the trip. This is not because there is something wrong with the water, as far as the residents are concerned, but new microbes in the digestive tract to which you have not become accustomed may cause mild stomach or intestinal upsets. Particularly in rural areas, the water supply may not be thoroughly purified, and local residents either have developed immunities to the natural bacteria or boil it for drinking. You also should avoid drinking water from freshwater streams, rivers, or pools. In campgrounds water usually is indicated as drinkable or for washing only — again, if you're not sure, ask.

Milk is pasteurized throughout Italy, and dairy products are safe to eat, as are fruit, vegetables, meat, poultry, and fish. Because of Mediterranean pollution, however, fish and shellfish should be eaten cooked, and make sure it is *fresh,* particularly in the heat of summer, when inadequate refrigeration is an additional concern.

Following all these precautions will not guarantee an illness-free trip, but it should minimize the risk. As a final hedge against economic if not physical problems, make sure your health insurance will cover all eventualities while you are away. If not, there are policies designed specifically for travel. Many are worth investigating. As with all insurance, they seem like a waste of money until you need them. For further information, see *Insurance* and *Medical and Legal Aid and Consular Services,* both in this section.

HELPFUL PUBLICATIONS: Practically every phase of health care — before, during, and after a trip — is covered in *The New Traveler's Health Guide,* by Drs. Patrick J. Doyle and James E. Banta. It is available for $4.95, plus postage and handling, from Acropolis Books Ltd., 13950 Park Center Rd., Herndon, VA 22071 (phone: 800-451-7771 or 703-709-0006).

The *Traveling Healthy Newsletter,* which is published six times a year, also is brimming with health-related travel tips. For a year's subscription, which costs $24, contact Dr. Karl Neumann (108-48 70th Rd., Forest Hills, NY 11375; phone: 718-268-7290). Dr. Neumann also is the editor of the useful free booklet, *Traveling Healthy,* which is available by writing to the *Travel Healthy Program* (PO Box 10208, New Brunswick, NJ 08906-9910; phone: 215-732-4100).

For more information regarding preventive health care for travelers, contact the *International Association for Medical Assistance to Travelers* (*IAMAT;* 417 Center St., Lewiston, NY 14092; phone: 716-754-4883). The Centers for Disease Control also publishes an interesting booklet, *Health Information for International Travel.* To order send a check or money order for $5 to the Superintendent of Documents (US Government Printing Office, Washington, DC 20402), or charge it to your credit card by calling 202-783-3238. For information on vaccination requirements, disease outbreaks, and other health information pertaining to traveling abroad, you also can call the Centers for Disease Control's 24-hour International Health Requirements and Recommendations Information Hotline: 404-332-4559.

On the Road

Credit and Currency

It may seem hard to believe, but one of the greatest (and least understood) costs of travel is money itself. Your one single objective in relation to the care and retention of travel funds is to make them stretch as far as possible. When you do spend money, it should be on things that expand and enhance your travel experience, with no buying power lost due to carelessness or lack of knowledge. This requires more than merely ferreting out the best airfare or the most charming budget hotel. It means being canny about the management of money itself. Herewith, a primer on making money go as far as possible overseas.

CURRENCY: The basic unit of currency in Italy is the Italian **lira** (the plural is **lire**). But because the value of the single lira is so low, it is non-negotiable as an individual unit, and there is no 1-lira coin or bill. (It is common in Italy to pay 1,500 lire for a cup of coffee and tens of thousands for a single meal.) Lire are distributed in coin denominations of 10, 20, 50, 100, 200, and 500, and in bill denominations of 1,000, 2,000, 5,000, 10,000, 20,000, 50,000, and 100,000. The value of Italian currency in relation to the US dollar fluctuates daily, affected by a wide variety of phenomena.

Although US dollars may be accepted in Italy (particularly at points of entry), you certainly will lose a percentage of your dollar's buying power if you do not take the time to convert it into lire. By paying for goods and services in the local currency, you save money by not negotiating invariably unfavorable exchange rates for every small purchase, and avoid difficulty where US currency is not readily — or happily — accepted. *Throughout this book, unless specifically stated otherwise, prices are given in US dollars.*

If bringing any large sum (over $15,000) into Italy — in cash and/or traveler's checks — it's advisable to fill out the V-2 customs form that will be provided on request on board your flight to Italy, on which you can declare all money you are bringing into the country. US law requires that anyone taking more than $10,000 into or out of the US must report this fact on customs form No. 4790, which is available from US Customs. If taking over $10,000 out of the US, you must report this *before* leaving the US; if returning with such an amount, you should include this information on your customs declaration. Although travelers usually are not questioned by customs officials about currency when entering or leaving, the sensible course is to observe all regulations just to be on the safe side.

FOREIGN EXCHANGE: Because of the volatility of exchange rates, be sure to check the current value of the Italian lira before finalizing any travel budget. And before you actually depart on your trip, be aware of the most advantageous exchange rates offered by various financial institutions — US banks, currency exchange firms, or Italian banks.

For the best sense of current trends, follow the rates posted in the financial section of your local newspaper or in such international newspapers as the *International Herald Tribune.* You can check with your own bank or with *Thomas Cook Foreign Exchange* (for the nearest location, call 800-972-2192 in Illinois; 800-621-0666 elsewhere in the US). *Harold Reuter and Company,* a currency exchange service in New York City (200 Park Ave., Suite 332 E., New York, NY 10166; phone: 212-661-0826) also is particularly helpful in determining current trends in exchange rates. *Ruesch International* also offers up-to-date foreign currency information and currency-related services (such as converting Italian lire VAT refund checks into US dollars; see *Duty Free Shopping and Value Added Tax,* in this section). *Ruesch* also offers a pocket-size *Foreign Currency Guide* (good for estimating general equivalents while planning) and a helpful brochure, *6 Foreign Exchange Tips for the Traveler.* Contact *Ruesch International* at one of the following addresses: 3 First National Plaza, Suite 2020, Chicago, IL 60602 (phone: 312-332-5900); 1925 Century Park E., Suite 240, Los Angeles, CA 90067 (phone: 213-277-7800); 608 Fifth Ave., "Swiss Center," New York, NY 10020 (phone: 212-977-2700); or 1350 Eye St. NW, 10th Floor and street level, Washington, DC 20005 (phone: 800-424-2923 or 202-408-1200).

In Italy, you will find the official rate of exchange posted in banks, airports, money exchange houses, hotels, and some shops. As a general rule, expect to get more local currency for your US dollar at banks than at any other commercial establishment. Exchange rates may change from day to day, and most banks offer the same (or very similar) exchange rates. In a pinch, the convenience of exchanging money in your hotel — sometimes on a 24-hour basis — *may* make up for the difference in the exchange rate. Don't try to bargain in banks or hotels — no one will alter the rates for you.

A money exchange house *(cambio)* is a financial institution that charges a fee for the service of exchanging dollars for local currency. When considering alternatives, be aware that although the rate again varies among these establishments, the rates of exchange offered are bound to be slightly less favorable than the terms offered at nearby banks — again, don't be surprised if you get fewer lire for your dollar than the rate published in the papers.

That said, however, the following rules of thumb are worth remembering.

Rule number one: Never (repeat: *never*) exchange dollars for foreign currency at hotels, restaurants, or retail shops. If you do, you are sure to lose a significant amount of your US dollar's buying power. If you do come across a storefront exchange counter offering what appears to be an incredible bargain, there's too much counterfeit specie in circulation to take the chance (see Rule number three, below).

Rule number two: Estimate your needs carefully; if you overbuy, you lose twice — buying and selling back. Every time you exchange money, someone is making a profit, and rest assured it isn't you. Use up foreign notes before leaving, saving just enough for last-minute incidentals and tips.

Rule number three: Don't buy money on the black market. The exchange rate may be better, but it is a common practice to pass off counterfeit bills to unsuspecting foreigners who aren't familiar with the local currency. It's usually a sucker's game, and you almost always are the sucker; it also can land you in jail.

Rule number four: Learn the local currency quickly and keep abreast of daily fluctuations in the exchange rate. These are listed in the English-language *International Herald Tribune* daily for the preceding day, as well as in every major newspaper in Europe. Rates change to some degree every day. For rough calculations, it is quick and safe to use round figures, but for purchases and actual currency exchanges, carry a small pocket calculator to help you compute the exact rate. Inexpensive calculators specifically designed to convert currency amounts for travelers are widely available.

When changing money, don't be afraid to ask how much commission you're being charged, and the exact amount of the prevailing exchange rate. In fact, in any exchange of money for goods or services, you should work out the rate before making any payment.

TIP PACKS: It's not a bad idea to buy a *small* amount of Italian coins and banknotes before your departure. But note the emphasis on "small," because, for the most part, you are better off carrying the bulk of your travel funds to Italy in US dollar traveler's checks (see below). Still, the advantages of tip packs are threefold:

1. You become familiar with the currency (really the only way to guard against making mistakes or being cheated during your first few hours in a new country).
2. You are guaranteed some money should you arrive when a bank or exchange counter isn't open or available. You don't have to depend on hotel desks, porters, or taxi drivers to change your money.

A "tip pack" is the only foreign currency you should buy before you leave. If you do run short upon arrival, US dollars often are accepted at points of entry. In other areas, they either *may* be accepted, or someone may accommodate you by changing a small amount — though invariably at a less than advantageous rate.

TRAVELER'S CHECKS: It's wise to carry traveler's checks while on the road instead of (or in addition to) cash, since it's possible to replace them if they are stolen or lost; you usually can receive partial or full replacement funds the same day if you have your purchase receipt and proper identification. Issued in various denominations and available in both US dollars and lire, with adequate proof of identification (credit cards, driver's license, passport) traveler's checks are as good as cash in most hotels, restaurants, stores, and banks.

Don't assume, however, that restaurants, small shops, and other establishments are going to be able to change checks of large denominations. Worldwide, more and more establishments are beginning to restrict the amount of traveler's checks they will accept or cash, so it is wise to purchase at least some of your checks in small denominations — say, $10 and $20. Also, don't expect to change them into US dollars except at banks and international airports.

Although traveler's checks are available in foreign currencies such as lire, the exchange rates offered by the issuing companies in the US generally are far less favorable than those available from banks both in the US and abroad. Therefore, it usually is better to carry the bulk of your travel funds abroad in US dollar–denomination traveler's checks.

Every type of traveler's check is legal tender in banks around the world and each company guarantees full replacement if checks are lost or stolen. After that the similarity ends. Some charge a fee for purchase, others are free; you can buy traveler's checks at almost any bank, and some are available by mail. Most important, each traveler's check issuer differs slightly in its refund policy — the amount refunded immediately, the accessibility of refund locations, the availability of a 24-hour refund service, and the time it will take for you to receive replacement checks. For instance, *American Express* guarantees replacement of lost or stolen traveler's checks in under 3 hours at any *American Express* office — other companies may not be as prompt. (Note that *American Express*'s 3-hour policy is based on the traveler's being able to provide the serial numbers of the lost checks. Without these numbers, refunds can take much longer.)

We cannot overemphasize the importance of knowing how to replace lost or stolen checks. All of the traveler's check companies have agents around the world, both in their own name and at associated agencies (usually, but not necessarily, banks), where refunds can be obtained during business hours. Most of them also have 24-hour toll-free telephone lines, and some even will provide emergency funds to tide you over on a Sunday.

Be sure to make a photocopy of the refund instructions that will be given to you by the issuing institution at the time of purchase. To avoid complications should you need to redeem lost checks (and to speed up the replacement process), keep the purchase receipt and an accurate list, by serial number, of the checks that have been spent or cashed. You may want to incorporate this information in an "emergency packet," also including your passport number and date of issue, the numbers of the credit cards you are carrying, and any other bits of information you shouldn't be without. Always keep these records separate from the checks and the original records themselves (you may want to give them to a traveling companion to hold).

Although most people understand the desirability of carrying funds in the form of traveler's checks as protection against loss or theft, an equally good reason is that US dollar traveler's checks invariably get a better rate of exchange than cash does — usually by at least 1% (although the discrepancy has been known to be substantially higher). The reasons for this are technical, but potential savings exist and it is a fact of travel life that should not be ignored.

That 1% won't do you much good, however, if you already have spent it buying your traveler's checks. Several of the major traveler's check companies charge 1% for the acquisition of their checks. To receive fee-free traveler's checks you may have to meet certain qualifications — for instance, *Thomas Cook* checks issued in US currency are free if you make your travel arrangements through its travel agency. *American Express* traveler's checks are available without charge to members of the *American Automobile Association.* Holders of some credit cards (such as the *American Express Platinum* card) also may be entitled to free traveler's checks. The issuing institution (e.g., the particular bank at which you purchase them) may itself charge a fee. If you purchase traveler's checks at a bank in which you or your company maintains significant accounts (especially commercial accounts of some size), the bank may absorb the 1% fee as a courtesy.

American Express, Bank of America, Citicorp, Thomas Cook, MasterCard, and *Visa* all offer traveler's checks. Here is a list of the major companies issuing traveler's checks and the numbers to call in the event that loss or theft makes replacement necessary:

American Express: To report lost or stolen checks in the US, call 800-221-7282. In Italy, *American Express* advises travelers to call 1-6-787-2000 toll-free or 44-273571-600 (in Brighton, England), collect. You also can call 801-968-8300 (in the US), collect, or contact the nearest *American Express* office.

Bank of America: To report lost or stolen checks in the US, call 800-227-3460. In Italy, call 1-6-787-4010; elsewhere worldwide, call 415-624-5400 or 415-622-3800, collect.

Citicorp: To report lost or stolen checks in the US, call 800-645-6556. In Italy and elsewhere worldwide, call 813-623-1709 or 813-626-4444, collect.

MasterCard: To report lost or stolen checks in the US, call 800-223-9920. In Italy, call the New York office at 212-974-5696, collect.

Thomas Cook MasterCard: To report lost or stolen checks in the US, call 800-223-9920. In Italy, call 609-987-7300 (in the US) or 44-733-502995 (in Peterborough, England), collect, and they will direct you to the nearest branch of *Thomas Cook* or *Wagons-Lits,* their European agent.

Visa: To report lost or stolen checks in the continental US, call 800-227-6811. In Italy, call 415-574-7111 (in the US) or 44-71-937-8091 (in London), collect.

CREDIT CARDS: Some establishments you encounter during the course of your travels may not honor any credit cards and some may not honor all cards, so there is a practical reason to carry more than one. Most US credit cards, including the principal bank cards, are honored in Italy; however, keep in mind that some cards may be issued under different names in Europe. For example, *MasterCard* may go under the name *Access* or *Eurocard,* and *Visa* often is called *Carte Bleue* — wherever these equivalents are accepted, *MasterCard* and *Visa* may be used. The following is a list of credit cards that enjoy wide domestic and international acceptance:

American Express: Cardholders can cash personal checks for traveler's checks and cash at *American Express* or its representatives' offices in the US up to the following limits (within any 21-day period): $1,000 for *Green* and *Optima* cardholders; $5,000 for *Gold* cardholders; and $10,000 for *Platinum* cardholders. Check cashing also is available to cardholders who are guests at participating hotels (up to $250) and for holders of airline tickets at participating airlines (up to $50). Free travel accident, baggage, and car rental insurance if ticket or rental is charged to card; additional insurance also is available for additional cost. For further information or to report a lost or stolen *American Express* card, call 800-528-4800 throughout the continental US; in Italy, contact a local *American Express* office or call 212-477-5700, collect.

Carte Blanche: Free travel accident, baggage, and car rental insurance if ticket or rental is charged to card; additional insurance also is available at additional cost. For medical, legal and travel assistance worldwide, call 800-356-3448 throughout the US; in Italy, call 214-680-6480, collect. For further information or to report a lost or stolen *Carte Blanche* card, call 800-525-9135 throughout the US; in Italy, call 303-790-2433, collect.

Diners Club: Emergency personal check cashing for cardholders staying at participating hotels and motels (up to $250 per stay). Free travel accident, baggage, and car rental insurance if ticket or rental is charged to card; additional insurance also is available for an additional fee. For medical, legal, and travel assistance worldwide, call 800-356-3448 throughout the US; in Italy, call 214-680-6480, collect. For further information or to report a lost or stolen *Diners Club* card, call 800-525-9135 throughout the US; in Italy, call 303-790-2433, collect.

Discover Card: Offered by a subsidiary of Sears, Roebuck & Co., it provides cardholders with cash advances at numerous automatic teller machines and *Sears* stores throughout the US. For further information and to report a lost or stolen *Discover* card, call 800-DISCOVER throughout the US; in Italy, call 302-323-7652, collect.

MasterCard: Cash advances are available at participating banks worldwide. Check with your issuing bank for information. *MasterCard* also offers a 24-hour emergency lost card service; call 800-826-2181 throughout the US; 314-275-6690, collect, from abroad.

Visa: Cash advances are available at participating banks worldwide. Check with your issuing bank for information. *Visa* also offers a 24-hour emergency lost card service; call 800-336-8472 throughout the US. In Italy, call 415-574-7700, collect.

One of the thorniest problems relating to the use of credit cards abroad concerns the rate of exchange at which a purchase is charged. Be aware that the exchange rate in effect on the date that you make a foreign purchase or pay for a foreign service has nothing at all to do with the rate of exchange at which your purchase is billed to you when you get the invoice (sometimes months later) in the US. The amount which the credit card company charges is either a function of the exchange rate at which the establishment's bank processed it or the rate in effect on the day your charge is received at the credit card center. (There is a 1-year limit on the time a shop or hotel can take to forward its charge slips.)

The principle at work in this credit card–exchange rate roulette is simple, but very hard to predict. You make a purchase at a particular dollar versus local currency exchange rate. If the dollar gets stronger in the time between purchase and billing, your purchase actually costs you less than you anticipated. If the dollar drops in value during the interim, you pay more than you thought you would. There isn't much you can do about these vagaries except to follow one very broad, very clumsy rule of thumb: If the dollar is doing well at the time of purchase, its value increasing against the local currency, use your credit card on the assumption it still will be doing well when billing takes place. If the dollar is doing badly, assume it will continue to do badly and pay with traveler's checks or cash. If you get too badly stuck, the best recourse is to complain, loudly. Be aware, too, that most credit card companies charge an unannounced, un-itemized 1% fee for converting foreign currency charges to US dollars.

SENDING MONEY ABROAD: If you have used up your traveler's checks, cashed as many emergency personal checks as your credit card allows, drawn on your cash advance line to the fullest extent, and still need money, have it sent abroad via one of the following services:

American Express (phone: 800-543-4080). Offers a service called "Moneygram," completing money transfers in anywhere from 10 minutes to 2 days. The sender can go to any *American Express* office in the US and can transfer money by presenting cash, a personal check, money order, or credit card — *Discover, Mastercard, Visa,* or *American Express Optima Card* (no other *American Express* or other credit cards are accepted). *American Express Optima* cardholders also can arrange for this transfer over the phone. The minimum transfer charge is $25, which rises with the amount of the transaction; the sender can forward funds of up to $10,000 per transaction (credit card users are limited to the amount of pre-established credit line). To collect at the other end, the receiver must show identification (passport, driver's license, or other picture ID) at an *American Express* office in Florence, Milan, Rome, or Venice. For further information on this service, call 800-543-4080.

Western Union Telegraph Company (phone: 800-325-4176 throughout the US). A friend or relative can go, cash in hand, to any *Western Union* office in the US, where, for a *minimum* charge of $13 (it rises with the amount of the transaction), the funds will be transferred to *Western Union*'s Italian correspondent bank, *Credito Italiano,* which has branches in major Italian cities. When the money arrives in Italy, you will not be notified — you must go to the bank to inquire. Although transfers generally take anywhere from 2 to 5 business days, at the time of this writing transfers to Italy generally were ranging from 6 to 9 business days (because all transfers of money first must go through the *Bank of Milan*). However, *Western Union* has recently opened a branch office in Rome to which money can be transferred in an hour or less. The funds will be turned over in lire, based on the rate of exchange in effect on the day of receipt. For a higher fee, the US party to this transaction may call *Western Union* with a *MasterCard* or *Visa* number to send up to $2,000, although larger transfers will be sent to a predesignated location.

If you are literally down to your last few lire, the nearest US consulate (see *Medical and Legal Aid and Consular Services,* in this section) will let you call home to set these matters in motion.

CASH MACHINES: Automatic teller machines (ATMs) are increasingly common worldwide. If your bank participates in one of the international ATM networks (most do), the bank will issue you a "cash card" along with a personal identification code or number (also called a PIC or PIN). You can use this card at any ATM in the same electronic network to check your account balances, transfer monies between checking and savings accounts, and — most important for a traveler — withdraw cash instantly. Network ATMs generally are located in banks, commercial and transportation centers, and near major tourist attractions.

Some financial institutions offer exclusive automatic teller machines for their own customers only at bank branches. At the time of this writing, ATMs which *are* connected generally belong to one of two international networks, *Cirrus* (phone: 800-4-

CIRRUS) or *Plus System* (phone: 800-THE-PLUS). At the time of this writing, however, only *Cirrus* had ATM locations in Italy. There was an agreement pending between these two companies to join their networks, which, when finalized, will allow users of either system to withdraw funds from any *Cirrus* or *Plus System* ATM.

Accommodations

From elegant, centuries-old palazzi to modern, functional high-rises and modest, inexpensive hostelries carved out of people's city flats or reconverted country villas, it's easy to be comfortable and well cared for on almost any budget in Italy. Admittedly, Italy is full of deluxe establishments providing expensive services to people with money to burn, but more affordable alternatives always have been available, particularly in the countryside.

On the whole, deluxe and first class accommodations in Italy, especially in the large metropolitan centers (Milan and Rome, for instance), are considerably more expensive than the same types of accommodations in the US. When the dollar is strong, such top-of-the-line establishments are within the range of a great number of travelers who otherwise are not able to afford them. But lately, the generally unfavorable rate of exchange in Italy and elsewhere on the Continent has rendered princely accommodations very pricey. And the cost of deluxe accommodations in Italy can be stratospherically high.

If you're watching your budget, however, you will be pleased to find in Italy even a larger selection and a greater variety of accommodations within your range than is the case at home. And at the lower end of the price scale, you will not always have to forgo charm. While a fair number of inexpensive establishments are simply no-frills, "generic" places to spend the night, even the sparest room may have the cachet of having once been the nightly retreat of a monk or a nun. And some of the most delightful places to stay are the smaller, less expensive, often family-run *pensioni,* a type of accommodation peculiar to Italy and no longer what it once was, but still in existence.

Once upon a time, such things as the superiority of New World plumbing made many of the numerous less expensive accommodations alternatives unacceptable for North Americans. Today, the gap has closed considerably, and in Italy the majority of the hostelries catering to the tourist trade are likely to be adequate in their basic facilities.

HOTELS AND PENSIONI: Hotels may be large or small, part of a chain or independent, new and of the "international standard" type or well established and traditional. There are built-for-the-purposes premises and converted stately homes and villas, resort hotels offering plenty of opportunities for recreation, and smaller tourist hotels offering virtually none.

One way to help you select the type of hotel that fits your finances and personal needs is to become familiar with the official hotel grading system used in Italy. Not too long ago, Italian hotels *(alberghi)* were officially classified according to their quality of service and level of amenities as deluxe, first class, second class, third class, and fourth class. Now they are classified in terms of stars, with five stars or five stars plus "L" corresponding to the former deluxe, the highest rating; four stars corresponding to first class; three stars to second class; two stars to third class; and one star to fourth class.

Hotels are placed in categories by the provincial or local tourist boards and then are assigned a range of rates they may charge for different types of rooms (single or double, with or without bath or a view). By law, they are not permitted to charge more than the maximum in their category, and if you are in doubt, a rate card should be available at the reception desk. The maximum rate that may be charged for a particular room also is posted inside the room, usually on the back of the door.

Keep in mind, however, that behind these grades may be found anything from a luxurious villa, redolent of Italian history to a large, modern, and functional high-rise or a simple, family-run hostelry. While the results of the assessments may not tally with your own judgment, by knowing the rating in advance you'll have a reasonable idea of the type of accommodations to expect — and their price.

The Italian Government Travel Office (ENIT) offers lists of hotels in Italy's main cities, giving the class of each, its address, and a few other details (such as the existence of a restaurant, air conditioning, parking facilities, and so on), but no telephone numbers. One-star, or fourth class, hotels are not listed, and price ranges for individual hotels are not given, but a general range of prices for each of the four hotel categories is included. (Note that each of these lists covers one Italian city.)

In addition, ENIT distributes hotel guides published by Italy's regional, provincial, and local tourist boards that list hotels in all categories. In most cases, the listing for each hotel includes its address and telephone number, category, number of rooms, amenities, accessibility for the disabled, and minimum and maximum prices. Though the latter are unavoidably out of date by the time of publication, they include service charges and value added tax and can be considered indicative.

Italy's *pensioni* (the anglicized spelling is pensions) used to be somewhat like our boarding houses. Not as large as hotels, with fewer services and a homier atmosphere, they tended to cater to those staying awhile and usually required guests to take one or both of their main meals in the house. Sophisticated travelers prized them because they often offered a good deal more character and intimacy than a hotel in a comparable price range. Whatever may be sacrificed in the way of front desk and other services at regular hotels usually is compensated for at *pensioni* by an element of charm.

Pensioni, too, were rated under the previous classification system, with a first class *pensione* the equivalent of a second class hotel, a second class *pensione* the equivalent of a third class hotel, and a third class *pensione* the equivalent of a fourth class hotel. For some time, however, *pensioni* have been changing. Most no longer discourage 1-night stays, many have dispensed with meal requirements, and some have eliminated full meal service, turning the dining room into a more informal breakfast room. In fact, there no longer is an official distinction between hotels and *pensioni,* and most accommodations brochures no longer list them separately. You still will find them among the three-star, two-star, and one-star listings in newer hotel brochures using the star system, but unless an establishment has retained the word in its name, there is no way to tell that it was once a *pensione.*

The simplest hotels in Italy are the *locande.* Roughly translated as "inns," these are modest lodgings indeed, and whether brochures use the star system or class system to list establishments, they will be among the least expensive entries. Quite often, they are found in small towns and rural areas, and it is not uncommon for them actually to be restaurants with no more than a few rooms to rent.

The rates posted in Italian hotel rooms include service charges and value added tax (VAT — 19% in five-star hotels, 9% in others), so receiving the bill at the end of a stay rarely is a cause for shock. If the locality imposes a visitor's tax (a minimal amount, called the *imposta di soggiorno*), that, too, usually is included in the posted price. No surcharge may be made for central heating, but a surcharge (often per person) for air conditioning is allowed.

In addition, some Italian hotels actually display minimum and maximum prices on the front door, where they are easily legible from the street. The posted prices generally include service and, except in a few cases, all taxes. (The prices posted usually are for double rooms.) The price of breakfast often is quoted and itemized separately from the room price. Note that breakfast almost always is a continental one of coffee or tea, bread or rolls, butter, and jam, and, particularly in the more modest establishments, there is an increasing tendency for these items to be cellophane- or foil-wrapped — you may save money and enjoy breakfast more by taking it at the nearest café (known as a "bar" in Italy).

Many localities have official high- and low-season rates and thus post two sets of prices per room. This is especially true of resort areas, where, at the height of the season, it may be difficult to get a room in either a hotel or a *pensione* unless you stay a certain number of nights and agree to take some meals, on a half-board *(mezza pensione)* — that is, breakfast and one other meal per day — or full-board *(pensione completa)* basis. (If you are staying at a resort hotel with a private beach, be sure to clarify at the outset whether there is an extra charge for use of the beach facilities — don't assume that it's all free.)

In Italy, a single room is a *camera singola;* a double room is a *camera doppia.* If you request a single and are given a double, it may not cost more than the maximum price for a single room. If you specify a double, you may be asked whether you prefer a *camera a due letti* (twin-bedded room) or a *camera matrimoniale* (with a double bed). A single room to which an extra bed has been added may not cost more than a double room, and a double room to which an extra bed has been added may not increase in price by more than 35%. And the price of a double usually holds whether it's occupied by one or two people.

If you are traveling on a shoestring, you will be interested to know that a great many rooms that do not have a private bath or shower (*bagno privato* or *doccia privata*) do have a sink with hot and cold running water (occasionally cold water only) and often a bidet. Sometimes there even is a toilet. Thus you can save money by denying yourself the luxury of a private bathroom and still not be totally without convenience. Some places have showers or baths down the hall that guests may use — often for free or for a nominal fee.

As in other countries, a number of well-known international hotel chains or associations have properties in Italy, particularly in major cities. Among these are the following (with toll-free reservations numbers to call in the US):

Best Western (phone: 800-528-1234). Has over 85 properties in Italy.

Forte Hotels International (formerly *Trusthouse Forte;* phone: 800-225-5843). Has 1 property each in Fuiggi, Milan, and Rome.

Hilton International (phone: 800-445-8667). Owned by the Ladbroke's gambling group of Great Britain, there is no proprietary connection with the US *Hilton* chain. Has 2 properties in Italy: 1 in Milan and 1 in Rome.

Holiday Inn (phone: 800-465-4329). Has 3 properties in Rome.

Ibis and Novotel (c/o *Resinter Reservations,* 2 Overhill Rd., Scarsdale, NY 10583; phone: 800-221-4542). Together, these two chains have 1 property in Bologna and 4 in Milan.

Inter-Continental (phone: 800-327-0200). Has 1 property in Rome and 1 in Sorrento.

Minotels Europe (phone: 800-336-4668). Has 28 properties in Italy.

Ramada (phone: 800-272-6232). Has 1 property each in Taormina and Venice.

Sheraton (phone: 800-325-3535). Has 1 property each in Bari, Catania, Florence, Padua, and Rome.

Among the larger Italian chains — whose names may be less familiar but many of whom nevertheless have a US office that will provide information and take reservations — are the following:

CIGA Hotels (745 5th Ave., Suite 1201, New York, NY 10151; phone: 800-221-2340 or 212-935-9540). A group of 22 luxury hotels (16 on the mainland, and 6 on the island of Sardinia). A brochure describing these properties is available.

Jolly Hotels (22 E. 38th St., New York, NY 10016; phone: 212-213-1468; 800-247-1277 in New York State; 800-221-2626 elsewhere in the US). Has 35 hotels largely in the four-star category. A brochure describing these properties is available.

MotelAgip (1 Via Aurelia, Rome 00163; phone: 6-637-9001). Italy's largest motel chain with numerous properties throughout the country. A booklet providing details and locations of each Italian property is available.

Another European hotel chain is the *Pullman International* group of deluxe and first class *Pullman* hotels in the following cities: 1 each in Florence, Rome, Venice, and the island of Sardinia, and 2 in Bologna. For information and reservations, contact *Pullman International* (1500 Broadway, New York, NY 10036; phone: 800-223-9862 or 212-719-9363). Another group *Utell International* (810 N. 96th St., Omaha, NE 68114-2594; phone: 800-44-UTELL) represents 67 properties in Italy.

RELAIS & CHÂTEAUX: Most members of this association are in France, but the group has grown to include dozens of establishments in many other countries, including approximately 24 in Italy.

These establishments are of particular interest to travelers who wish lodgings reflecting the ambience, style, and, frequently, the history of the places they are visiting. Some properties actually are palaces or ancient castles (several dating back to the 13th century), which have been converted into hotels. Others — the *relais* — are old inns, manor houses, even converted mills, convents, and monasteries. A few well-known city and resort establishments are included, such as the *Regency* in Florence and the *Lord Byron* in Rome, but most are in quiet country surroundings, and frequently are graced with parklands, ponds, and flowering gardens.

Members of the *Relais & Châteaux* group often are expensive, though no more than you would pay for deluxe, authentically elegant accommodations and service anywhere in the world (and many are not all that costly). Accommodations and service from one *relais* or château to another can range from simple but comfortable to elegantly deluxe, but they all maintain very high standards (the kitchens are equal to the accommodations) in order to retain their memberships, as they are appraised annually.

Another group of members, *Relais Gourmands,* is composed of exceptionally fine restaurants. These establishments also may have rooms for rent, but the establishments are *not* rated on the basis of their accommodations, so they may not match (or even come close to) the standards of room quality maintained by the others. At the time of this writing, there were four *Gourmands* members in Italy — in Bologna, Florence, Milan, and Rome.

An illustrated catalogue of all the *Relais & Châteaux* properties is published annually and is available for $5 from *Relais & Châteaux* (2400 Lazy Hollow, Suite 152D, Houston, TX 77063) or from *David B. Mitchell & Company* (200 Madison Ave., New York, NY 10016; phone: 800-372-1323 or 212-696-1323). The association also can provide information on member properties. Reservations can be made directly with the establishments, through *David B. Mitchell & Company,* or through a travel agency.

BED AND BREAKFAST ESTABLISHMENTS AND OTHER ACCOMMODATIONS: Bed and breakfast establishments (commonly known as B&Bs) are a staple of the lower-cost lodging scene in many parts of Europe, and are found wherever there are extra rooms to let in a private home and a host or hostess willing to attend to the details of hospitality. In Italy, and elsewhere on the Continent, they are increasingly common, and not only in rural areas.

Bed and breakfast establishments provide exactly what the name implies. It is unusual for a bed and breakfast establishment to offer the extra services found in conventional hostelries, so the bed and breakfast route often is the least expensive way to go.

Beyond the obvious fundamentals, nothing else is predictable about bed and breakfast establishments. The bed may be in an extra room in a family home, in an apartment with a separate entrance, or in a free-standing cottage elsewhere on the host's property. Some homes have only one room to let, wherease others may be large enough to have another party or two in residence at the same time. In European B&Bs, private baths are the exception rather than the rule. The breakfast most often will be a version of the standard, light, continental breakfast: fruit plus juice; toast, roll, or homemade bread, with jam or marmalade; and coffee or tea. Although the exception rather than the rule in Italy, in rural areas, the breakfast may be a heartier one, and as often as not (any language barrier aside) served along with some family history to add to the local lore. If you're in a studio with a kitchenette, you may be furnished with the makings and have to prepare it for yourself. Despite their name, some B&Bs offer an evening meal as well — by prior arrangement and at extra cost.

Some hosts enjoy helping guests with tips on what to see and do and even serve as informal tour guides, while in other places your privacy won't be disturbed. Whichever the case, the beauty of bed and breakfast establishments is that you'll always have a warm reception and the opportunity to meet many more inhabitants of the region than you otherwise would, which means that you'll experience their hospitality in a special fashion.

Bed and breakfast establishments range from private homes and lovely mansions to small inns and guesthouses Although some hosts may be contacted directly, as in the US, others prefer that arrangements be made through a reservations service. The general procedure for making reservations through bed and breakfast services is that you contact them with your requirements and they help find the right place, then confirm your reservations upon receipt of a deposit. Any further information needed will be provided either by the service or the owner of the bed and breakfast establishment.

To avoid disappointment, find out as much as you can before you book. A useful source of information on bed and breakfast reservation services and establishments overseas is the *Bed & Breakfast Reservations Services Worldwide,,* a trade association of B&B reservations services, which provides a list of its members for $3. To order the most recent edition, contact them at PO Box 39000, Washington, DC 20016 (phone: 800-842-1486).

Farmhouses – In the country, city people rediscover the sounds of songbirds and the smell of grass. Suburbanites get the chance to poke around an area where the nearest neighbor lives miles away. Parents can say to their children, "No, milk does not originate in a cardboard carton," and prove it. Youngsters can meet people who live differently, think differently, and have different values. But even if there were no lessons to be learned, a stay at a farm would be a decidedly pleasant way to pass a couple of weeks, so it's no wonder that throughout Italy there are numerous farms welcoming guests.

If the idea of staying in the country, especially the idea of spending time on a working farm, appeals to you, you should know something about *Agriturist.* Founded in 1965, this organization promotes country vacations as a means to several worthy ends, among them bridging the cultural gap between the city and the country, familiarizing urban dwellers with the production of typical local foods and handicrafts, safeguarding the landscape by finding new uses for abandoned rural buildings, and providing farmers in hill and mountain areas with alternative sources of income.

The organization is made up of farm families throughout Italy who have some sort of accommodations to let, and although there are many variations, there are three basic possibilities: You rent a furnished room, frequently without private bath, in the family's own living quarters or in an independent structure, on a half- or full-board basis; you rent a furnished apartment, house, or other lodging complete with kitchen and bath; or you camp, on a fully equipped campsite or with acccess to essential services only. Depending on the situation, you may be alone with your hosts or there may be several parties occupying rooms and apartments on the same premises; you may be right on a farm or isolated some distance from it.

There are a wide range of choices: You can rent an apartment in the mountains of the Valle d'Aosta; stay with a family that grows olives, grapes, and grain in Umbria; or opt to be within striking distance of the sea on land belonging to a fruit farmer in Sicily. Opportunities for swimming, fishing, horseback riding, and other outdoor activities abound. *Agriturist* rates the accommodations as basic, comfortable, or superior but makes no guarantee that the price charged at any particular place corresponds to its rating. For the most part, however, prices are quite inexpensive.

The major drawback to arranging an *Agriturist* vacation is the lack of information in English. The *Guida dell'Ospitalità Rurale* (Guide to Rural Hospitality), lists members in all regions, with descriptions of facilities offered by each and an indication of any languages spoken besides Italian, is largely in Italian. It contains approximately 1,600 farm listings. The guide can be consulted at the Italian Government Travel Office (ENIT) offices; otherwise, contact *Agriturist* (101 Corso Vittorio Emanuele, Rome 00186, Italy; phone: 6-651-2342). There is a charge of about $11 for each of the guides. Regional *Agriturist* offices have their own listings, and if you plan to visit just one or two regions, it's probably more efficient to deal with the regional offices directly. ENIT can provide their addresses and phone numbers. Arrangements are made directly with the proprietors of the properties listed, and in most cases a knowledge of Italian helps.

Rental Options – An attractive alternative for the visitor content to stay in one spot for a week or more is to rent one of the numerous properties available throughout Italy. These offer a wide range of luxury and convenience, depending on the price you want to pay. One of the advantages to staying in a house, apartment (usually called a "flat" overseas), or other rented vacation home is that you will feel much more like a visitor than a tourist.

Known to Europeans as a "holiday let" or a "self-catering holiday," a vacation in a furnished rental has both the advantages and disadvantages of living "at home" abroad. It can be less expensive than staying in a first class hotel, although very luxurious and expensive rentals are available, too. It has the comforts of home, including a kitchen, which means potential savings on food. Furthermore, it gives a sense of the country that a large hotel often cannot. On the other hand, a certain amount of housework is involved because if you don't eat out, you have to cook, and though some rentals (especially the luxury ones) include a cleaning person, most don't. (If the rental doesn't include daily cleaning, arrangements often can be made with a maid service.)

For a family, two or more couples, or a group of friends, the per-person cost — even for a luxurious rental — can be quite reasonable. Weekly and monthly rates are available to reduce costs still more. But best of all is the amount of space that no conventional hotel room can equal. As with hotels, the rates for properties in some areas are seasonal, rising during the peak travel season, while for others they remain the same year-round. To have your pick of the properties available, you should begin to make arrangements for a rental at least 6 months in advance.

There are several ways of finding a suitable rental property. Most provincial and local tourist boards in Italy have information on companies arranging rentals in their areas. US branches of the Italian Government Travel Office have lists of agents who specialize in villa and apartment rentals, and a number of local tourist boards issue region-by-region guides to cottages, castles, houses, bungalows, chalets, villas, and flats for rent that meet some range of minimum standards.

Many tour operators regularly include a few rental packages among their offerings; these generally are available through a travel agent. In addition, a number of companies specialize in rental vacations. Their plans typically include rental of the property (or several properties, but usually for a minimum stay per location), a rental car, and airfare.

The companies listed below rent a wide range of properties in Italy. They handle the booking and confirmation paperwork and can be expected to provide more information about the properties than that which might ordinarily be gleaned from a short listing in an accommodations guide.

At Home Abroad (405 E. 56th St., Apt. 6H, New York, NY 10022; phone: 212-421-9165). Handles apartments to villas and exceptionally stately homes, especially at the sea and in the countryside, in Tuscany and Umbria. Photographs of properties and a newsletter are available for a $50 registration fee.

Blake's Vacations (4918 Dempster St., Skokie, IL 60077; phone: 800-628-8118). Rents country houses in Tuscany.

Castles, Cottages and Flats (7 Faneuil Hall Marketplace, Boston, MA 02109; phone: 617-742-6030). Handles a variety of properties in Italy. Small charge ($5) for receipt of main catalogue, refundable upon booking.

Eastone Overseas Accommodations (198 Southampton Dr., Jupiter, FL 33458; phone: 407-575-6991). Handles apartments, cottages, houses, castles, and villas in major cities throughout Italy, in Tuscany, and on the Italian Riviera.

Europa-Let (PO Box 3537, Ashland, OR 97520; phone: 800-462-4486 or 503-482-5806). Offers apartments, cottages, and villas in Rome, Tuscany, and Umbria.

Grandluxe International (165 Chestnut St., Allendale, NJ 07401; phone: 201-327-2333). Rents apartments, castles, villas, country homes, and farmhouses throughout Italy.

Hideaways International (15 Goldsmith St., PO Box 1270, Littleton, MA 01460; phone: 800-843-4433 or 508-486-8955). Rents apartments, private homes, and villas in Florence, Siena, and Tuscany, as well as on the Amalfi Coast and the Italian Riviera.

Hometours International (1170 Broadway, Suite 614, New York, 10001; phone: 800-367-4668 or 212-689-0851). Handles apartments and country houses in Sorrento and Tuscany, and on Capri and the Italian Riviera.

International Lodging Corp. (300 1st Ave., Suite 7C, New York, NY 10009; phone: 212-228-5900). Rents flats and some country homes in Perugia, Rome, Tuscany, and Umbria.

Livingstone Holidays (1720 E. Garry Ave., Suite 236, Santa Ana, CA 92705; phone: 714-476-2823). Handles cottages in Florence, Naples, Tuscany, and Umbria. Small charge ($2 to $3) for larger brochures.

Rent a Vacation Everywhere (*RAVE;* 328 Main St. E., Suite 526, Rochester, NY 14604; phone: 716-454-6440). Rentals include moderate to luxurious apartments in Rome and Florence plus a few in Milan; villas on the Italian Riviera and around Lake Como; and properties in Tuscany ranging from rustic farmhouses to the elegant estates of the landed gentry.

Vacanze in Italia (PO Box 297, Falls Village, CT 06031; phone: 800-533-5405). This organization specializes in apartments and houses in the Tuscan and Umbrian countryside, especially in the chianti classico area near Siena, but it also has a few properties in the Puglia region and some small apartments in Florence, Rome, and Venice.

VHR Worldwide (235 Kensington Ave., Norwood, NJ 07648; phone: 201-767-9393, locally; 800-NEED-A-VILLA). Rents apartments, country homes, and villas in Arezzo, Florence, Frascati, Rome, Sicily, and Siena.

Villas International Ltd. (605 Market St. Suite 510, San Francisco, CA 94105; phone: 800-221-2260 or 415-281-0910). Apartments in cities — Rome, Florence, and Venice — are a specialty. Elsewhere there are apartments, villas, and chalets in the northern lake district, villas and apartments on the Amalfi Coast, the Italian Riviera, Sardinia, and Sicily, and anything from a cottage to a restored farmhouse or a modern villa in Tuscany and Umbria.

In addition, Suzanne T. Pidduck, an individual agent, arranges rentals of apartments, houses, and villas, primarily in Tuscany and Umbria, with some listings in Puglia, Calabria, Sicily, around Lake Garda (in Lombardy), and north of Rome. For further information, contact her at 1742 Calle Corva, Camarillo, CA 93010; phone: 800-726-6702 or 805-987-5278).

And for further information, including a general discussion of all forms of vacation rentals, evaluating costs, and information on rental opportunities in Italy, see *A Traveler's Guide to Vacation Rentals in Europe.* Available in general bookstores, it also can be ordered from Penguin USA (120 Woodbine St., Bergenfield, NJ 07621; phone: 800-526-0275 and ask for cash sales) for $11.95, plus postage and handling.

In addition, a useful publication, the *Worldwide Home Rental Guide,* lists properties throughout Europe, as well as the managing agencies. Issued twice annually, single copies may be available at larger newsstands for $10 an issue. For a year's subscription, send $18 to *Worldwide Home Rental Guide,* PO Box 2842, Sante Fe, NM 87504 (phone: 505-988-5188).

When considering a particular vacation rental property, look for answers to the following questions:

- How do you get from the airport to the property?
- If the property is on the shore, how far is the nearest beach? Is it sandy or rocky and is it safe for swimming?
- What size and number of beds are provided?
- How far is the property from whatever else is important to you, such as a golf course or nightlife?
- How far is the nearest market?
- Are baby-sitters, cribs, bicycles, or anything else you may need for your children available?
- Is maid service provided daily?
- Are air conditioning and a phone provided?
- Is a car rental part of the package? Is a car necessary?

Before deciding which rental is for you, make sure you have satisfactory answers to all your questions. Ask your travel agent to find out or call the company involved directly.

HOME EXCHANGES: Still another alternative for travelers who are content to stay in one place during their vacation is a home exchange: The Smith family from Chicago moves into the home of the Rossi family in Rome, while the Rossis enjoy a stay in the Smiths' home. The home exchange is an exceptionally inexpensive way to ensure comfortable, reasonable living quarters with amenities that no hotel possibly could offer; often the trade includes a car. Moreover, it allows you to live in a new community in a way that few tourists ever do: For a little while, at least, you will become something of a resident.

Several companies publish directories of individuals and families willing to trade homes with others for a specific period of time. In some cases, you must be willing to list your own home in the directory; in others, you can subscribe without appearing in it. Most listings are for straight exchanges only, but each directory also has a number of listings placed by people interested in either exchanging or renting (for instance, if they own a second home). Other arrangements include exchanges of hospitality while owners are in residence or youth exchanges, where your teenager is put up as a guest in return for your putting up their teenager at a later date. A few house-sitting opportunities also are available. In most cases, arrangements for the actual exchange take place directly between you and the foreign host. There is no guarantee that you will find a listing in the area in which you are interested, but each of the organizations given below includes Italian homes among its hundreds or even thousands of foreign listings.

Home Base Holidays (7 Park Ave., London N13 5PG, England; phone: 81-886-8752). For $48 a year, subscribers receive four listings, with an option to list in all four.

Intervac US/International Home Exchange Service (Box 190070, San Francisco, CA 94119; phone: 415-435-3497). Some 8,000 listings. For $45 (plus postage), subscribers receive copies of the three directories published yearly, and are entitled to list their home in one of them; a black-and-white photo may be included with the listing for an additional $11. A $5 discount is given to travelers over age 62.

Loan-A-Home (2 Park La., Apt. 6E, Mt. Vernon, NY 10552; phone: 914-664-7640). Specializes in long-term (4 months or more — excluding July and August) housing arrangements worldwide for students, professors, businesspeople, and retirees, although its two annual directories (with supplements) carry a small list of short-term rentals and/or exchanges. $35 for a copy of one directory and one supplement; $45 for two directories and two supplements.

Vacation Exchange Club (PO Box 820, Haleiwa, HI 96712; phone: 800-638-3841). Some 10,000 listings. For $50, the subscriber receives two directories — one in late winter, one in the spring — and is listed in one.

World Wide Exchange (1344 Pacific Ave., Suite 103, Santa Cruz, CA 95060; phone: 408-476-4206). The $45 annual membership fee includes one listing (for house, yacht, or motorhome) and three guides.

Worldwide Home Exchange Club (13 Knightsbridge Green, London SW1X 7QL, England; phone: 71-589-6055; or 806 Brantford Ave., Silver Spring, MD 20904; no phone). Handles over 1,500 listings a year worldwide. For $25 a year, you will receive two listings, as well as supplements.

Better Homes and Travel (formerly *Home Exchange International*), with an office in New York, and representatives in Los Angeles, London, Paris, and Milan, functions differently in that it publishes no directory and shepherds the exchange process most of the way. Interested parties supply the firm with photographs of themselves and their homes, information on the type of home they want and where, and a registration fee of $50. The company then works with its other offices to propose a few possibilities, and only when a match is made do the parties exchange names, addresses, and phone numbers. For this service, *Better Homes and Travel* charges a closing fee, which ranges from $150 to $500 for switches from 2 weeks to 3 months in duration, and from $300 to $600 for longer switches. Contact *Better Homes and Travel* at 30 E. 33rd St., New York, NY 10016 (phone: 212-689-6608).

HOME STAYS: If the idea of actually staying in a private home as the guest of an Italian family appeals to you, check with the *United States Servas Committee,* which maintains a list of hosts throughout the world (at present, there are about 750 listings in Italy) willing to throw open their doors to foreigners, entirely free of charge.

The aim of this nonprofit cultural program is to promote international understanding and peace, and every effort is made to discourage freeloaders. *Servas* will send you an application form and the name of the nearest of some 200 interviewers around the US for you to contact. After the interview, if you're approved, you'll receive documentation certifying you as a *Servas* traveler. There is a membership fee of $45 per person, as well as a deposit of $15 to receive the host list, refunded on its return. The list gives the name, address, age, occupation, and other particulars of each host, including languages spoken. From then on, it is up to you to write to prospective hosts directly, and *Servas* makes no guarantee that you will be accommodated.

Servas stresses that you should choose only people you really want to meet, and that during your stay (which normally lasts between 2 nights and 2 weeks) you should be interested mainly in your hosts, not in sightseeing. It also suggests that one way to show your appreciation once you've returned home is to become a host yourself. The minimum age of a *Servas* traveler is 18 (however, children under 18 may accompany their parents), and though quite a few are young people who've just finished college, there are travelers (and hosts) in all age ranges and occupations. Contact *Servas* at 11 John St., Room 407, New York, NY 10038 (phone: 212-267-0252).

You also might be interested in a publication called *International Meet-the-People Directory,* published by the *International Visitor Information Service.* It lists several agencies in a number of foreign countries (37 worldwide, 18 in Europe, including Italy) that arrange home visits for Americans, either for dinner or overnight stays. To order a copy, send $5.95 to the *International Visitor Information Service* (733 15th St. NW, Suite 300, Washington, DC 20005; phone: 202-783-6540). For other local organizations and services offering home exchanges, contact the local tourist authority.

Convents, Monasteries, and Seminaries – More than a few travelers to Italy elect to stay in convents, monasteries, seminaries, and other religious institutions that provide room and board to paying guests. You need not be a pilgrim to take advantage of this economical solution to the problem of where to stay abroad; in fact, a number of such institutions are officially rated in the Italian hotel system, generally as one-star or fourth class hotels, formerly *pensioni.* Staying in a religious institution is not exactly like staying in a hotel, however. Some are for men only and some for women only, although most accept couples. A great many also observe a curfew, doors closing promptly at 10 or 11 PM. The Italian Government Travel Office can supply a list of institutions offering accommodations in some cities, but if nothing is available for the cities you want to visit, write directly to the archdiocese of each city or town in question. (Address the envelope simply to the Arcidiocesi di Milano, Milano, Italia, for example.)

Time Zones, Business Hours, and Public Holidays

TIME ZONES: The countries of Europe fall into three time zones. Greenwich Mean Time — the time in Greenwich, England, at longitude 0°0′ — is the base from which all other time zones are measured. Areas in zones west of Greenwich have earlier times and are called Greenwich Minus; those to the east have later times and are called Greenwich Plus. For example, New York City — which falls into the Greenwich Minus 5 time zone — is 5 hours earlier than Greenwich, England. When it is noon in Greenwich, it is 7 AM in New York and Washington, DC. Italy falls into the Greenwich plus 1 time zone, which means that the time is 1 hour later than in Greenwich, and when it is noon in Rome, it is 6 AM in New York and Washington, DC.

Like most western European nations, Italy moves its clocks ahead an hour in the spring and back an hour in the fall, corresponding to Daylight Saving Time, although the date of the change tends to be earlier in both cases by a couple of weeks than the date we have adopted in the US. For several weeks in the spring, then, the time difference between the US and Italy is 1 hour greater than usual; for a short period in the fall, there is a 1 hour less differential.

Italian and other European timetables use a 24-hour clock to denote arrival and departure times, which means that hours are expressed sequentially from 1 AM. By this method, 9 AM is recorded as 0900, noon as 1200, 1 PM as 1300, 6 PM as 1800, midnight as 2400, and so on. For example, the departure of a train at 7 AM will be announced as "0700"; one leaving at 7 PM will be noted as "1900."

BUSINESS HOURS: Travelers who are used to the American workday may be surprised to find that the Italians, like many other Europeans, follow a more eccentric schedule. Banks usually are open Mondays through Fridays from 8:35 AM to 1:30 PM and from 3:00 to 4:00 PM; they are closed Saturdays, Sundays, and national holidays.

As a *general* rule, businesses (smaller shops and offices) are open from 9 AM to 7 or 8 PM with a generous siesta break of 2 to 2½ hours, starting at 12:30 or 1 PM. The overall trend is moving toward shorter 1-hour breaks, and among the current examples of this change are the many offices in the north of Italy that work straight through the day and close earlier in the evening; shops, too, may take a shorter lunch break and close earlier. Still, in the south, including Rome, only bars, newsstands, and the most energetic entrepreneurs operate during the midday break. Large department stores and other large emporia, however, may stagger employees' lunch breaks and remain open straight through from 9 or 10 AM to anywhere between 6 and 8 PM..

Another variation on the theme: Shops may be open all day Saturday or Saturday mornings only, depending on the kind of shop (retailer, dry cleaner, grocery, and so on), the season (summer, the rest of the year), and the city, and those that stay open on Saturday afternoons then may close on Monday mornings. The moral to this story is that if you're having some alterations done on a last-minute purchase and are planning to pick up the item on a Saturday afternoon or Monday morning just before taking a cab to the airport, make sure the store will be *open.* Almost all shops are closed on Sundays. Public buildings and museums have relatively short hours and are closed 1 day a week, usually Mondays. Restaurants have a *riposo settimanale* ("weekly repose"), which entitles them to be closed 1 day each week; the day varies from restaurant to restaurant. Hours in general tend to be a bit later in summer, and they vary from city to city; check local listings in THE CITIES and DIRECTIONS.

PUBLIC HOLIDAYS: Italy shuts down more thoroughly on public holidays than does the US. Banks and offices are closed tight, and so are shops — holidays are not considered occasions for clearance sales. Public buildings and museums usually close as well.

Italian public holidays this year are as follows:

New Year's Day (January 1)
Epiphany (January 6)
Easter Monday (April 20)
Liberation Day (April 25)
Labor Day (May 1)
Ferragosto or the Assumption of the Virgin (August 15)
All Saints' Day (November 1)
Immaculate Conception (December 8)
Christmas Day (December 25)

Also note that the day after *Christmas* (December 26), the feast day of St. Stephen, is a public holiday in Italy. Prior to 1977, several more days were considered holidays, but they were abolished in an effort to discourage Italians from constructing *ponti* (bridges) and taking off extra days when a holiday fell close to a weekend. One of the holidays suppressed, *Epiphany* (the day children receive gifts from a witchlike old woman, the *Befana*) was reinstated by popular demand.

The feast day of a city's patron saint is a local public holiday. Among these are the feast day of St. Mark, celebrated on April 25 in Venice; of St. John the Baptist, June 24 in Florence; of Sts. Peter and Paul, June 29 in Rome; St. Januarius (San Gennaro), September 19 in Naples; and St. Ambrose, December 7 in Milan. *Easter* also can be a 4-day event — *Good Friday* through *Easter Monday.*

San Marino celebrates most of the Italian public holidays, except Italy's *Liberation Day.* San Marino also has a few of its own public holidays (although most business stay open on these days):

Feast of St. Agatha (February 5)
Investiture of the Captains Regent (April 1 and October 1)
San Marino's Day (September 3)

Mail, Telephone, and Electricity

MAIL: The Italian Postal Service maintains over 10,000 post offices throughout Italy, including small outlets such as those in train stations and airports. Most are open from 8:30 AM to 2 PM Mondays through Fridays and until noon on Saturdays and the last day of the month. In larger cities, counters at main post offices may be open as late as 7:30 or 8 PM, although not necessarily for all services. In international airports, they are open 24 hours a day for registered mail and telegram services. Mail rates change frequently, following the upward trend of everything else; stamps are bought at the post office and at authorized tobacconists — ask for *francobolli.* Letters can be mailed in the red letter boxes found on the street, but it is better to mail them (and certainly packages) directly from post offices.

Be advised that delivery from Italy can be slow (especially if you send something any distance by surface mail) and erratic (postcards, even air mail ones, seem to be given no priority at all, so don't use them for important messages). Send mail *posta aerea* (air mail) if it's going any distance, and to ensure or further speed delivery of an important letter, send it as *raccomandata* (registered mail) or *espresso* (express or special delivery). Many travelers prefer not to use the Italian post office at all and hold their mail for international delivery until they leave Italy. Others, at least in Rome (and this includes travelers and natives alike), consider the Vatican post office, just to the side of St. Peter's, much more reliable. (If you're going to use the Vatican post office, don't buy *Italian* stamps — the Vatican has its own.)

If your correspondence is important, you may want to send it via one of the special courier services: *Federal Express, DHL,* and other international services are available in Italy. The cost is considerably higher than sending something via the postal services — but the assurance of its timely arrival is worth it.

If you're mailing to an address within Italy, another way to ensure or speed delivery is to use the five-digit postal code. It breaks the country down into regions, provinces, towns or cities, and even into districts within cities, and since many small towns in Italy have very similar names, the postal code always should be specified — delivery of a letter may depend on it. Put it on the envelope immediately after the name of the town or city and on the same line. If you do not have the correct postal code, an Italian consulate in the US (see *The Italian Embassy and Consulates in the US,* in this section, for addresses) may be able to look it up for you. Alternatively, you could call the addressee directly — if you have the telephone number — and although this will be costly, it may be worth it to ensure delivery of your correspondence.

There are several places that will receive and hold mail for travelers in Italy. Mail sent to you at a hotel and clearly marked *fermo in posta* (literally "hold mail") is one safe approach. Post offices also will extend this service to you if the mail is addressed to the equivalent of US general delivery, called *Posta Restante* in Italy. This probably is the best way for travelers to have mail sent if they do not have a definite address. Have your correspondent print your last name in big block letters on the envelope (lest there be any doubt as to which is your last name). As there often are several post office locations in major cities, it is important that the address and/or specific name of the office be indicated (not just the name of the city). Be sure to call at the correct office when inquiring after mail. Also, don't forget to take your passport with you when you go to collect it. Most Italian post offices require formal identification before they will release anything; there also may be a small charge for picking up your mail.

If you are an *American Express* customer (a cardholder, a carrier of *American Express* traveler's checks, or traveling on an *American Express Travel Related Services* tour) you can have mail sent to its offices in cities along your route (there are four offices in Italy: 1 each in Florence, Milan, Naples, and Rome). Letters are held free of charge — registered mail and packages are not accepted. You must be able to show an *American Express* card, traveler's checks, or a voucher proving you are on one of the company's tours to avoid paying for mail privileges. Those who aren't clients must pay a nominal charge each time they inquire if they have received mail, whether or not they actually have a letter. There also is a forwarding fee, for clients and non-clients alike. Mail should be addressed to you, care of *American Express,* and should be marked "Client Mail Service." Additional information on its mail service and addresses of *American Express* offices in Italy are listed in the pamphlet *Services and Offices,* available from any US branch of *American Express.*

While US embassies and consulates abroad will not under ordinary circumstances accept mail for tourists, they may hold mail for US citizens in an emergency situation, especially if the papers sent are important. It is best to inform them either by separate letter or cable, or by phone (particularly if you are in the country already), that you will be using their address for this purpose.

TELEPHONE: The Italian telephone system is not too different from the US system. The number of digits in an Italian phone number, however, may vary considerably, and to confuse matters, a city code may be included in the digits quoted as the "local" number. If you dial a number directly and your call does not go through, either the circuits are busy, or you may need to add or delete one or several digits. If you have tried several times and are sure that you have the correct number, have an international operator place the call — however, this will be more expensive than dialing directly. (To reach an international operator in the US, dial "0" for a local operator and ask him or her to connect you.)

The procedure for calling anywhere in Italy from the US is as follows: dial 011 (the international access code) + 39 (the country code) + the city code + the local number. For example, to place a call from anywhere in the US to Rome, dial 011 + 39 + 6 (the city code for Rome) + the local number.

The procedure for calling the US from Italy is as follows: dial 00 (the international access code) + 1 (the US country code) + the area code + the local number. For instance, to call New York from anywhere in Italy, dial 00 + 1 + 212 + the local number. For calling from one Italian city to another simply dial 0 + the city code + the local number; and for calls within the same city code coverage area, simply dial the local number.

If you don't know the city code, check the front of a telephone book or ask an international operator. Note that Italian telephone directories and other sources may include the 0 (used for dialing within Italy) as part of the area code; when dialing from the US, follow the procedure described above, *leaving off the 0.*

Italcable, Italy's major international phone company, introduced a new feature, Country Direct Service, in 1989. By dialing 172-1011 from any telephone in Florence, Milan, Naples, or Rome, you can phone the US direct, either by calling collect or by using your credit card. An American operator will answer. (Note that as we went to press, *Italcable* was in the process of extending this service to include other cities throughout Italy.)

To reach a local operator (who probably won't speak much — if any — English) dial 0. If you need an English-speaking operator to help you, dial 170 to make a call to the US, or dial 15 to reach an English-speaking operator for a call within Europe.

For emergency service throughout Italy: Dial 113 — the public emergency assistance number of the state police — or 112 — the immediate action service number of the *carabinieri* (much as you would dial 911 in the US). An alternative would be to dial 15 for an international operator or 187 for international directory assistance operator, either of whom should be able to connect you to emergency services. For further information on what to do in the event of an emergency, see *Medical and Legal Aid and Consular Services,* in this section.

Pay telephones in Italy can be found in cafés and restaurants (look for the sign outside — a yellow disk with the outline of a telephone or a receiver in black) and, less commonly, in booths on the street. (All too often, however, these are out of order — if you're lucky, a *guasto* sign will warn you.) There are two kinds of pay phones: The old-fashioned kind works with a *gettone* (token) only, which can be bought for 200 lire from a bar or restaurant cashier and at newsstands; newer phones function with *gettoni,* 200 lire, or two 100 lire coins. To use a *gettone,* place it in the slot at the top of the phone. When your party answers — and *not* before — push the button at the top of the phone, causing the token to drop (otherwise the answering party will not be able to hear you). If your party doesn't answer, hang up and simply lift the unused *gettone* out of the slot. In newer phones using either *gettoni* or coins, the coins or *gettoni* drop automatically when you put them in, as in US phones; if your party doesn't answer, you have to press the return button (sometimes repeatedly) to get them back.

Long-distance *(interurbano)* calls, including international ones, also can be made from pay phones. You will need anywhere from several to a fistful of *gettoni* or coins, or magnetic cards (available in 5,000 or 10,000 lire values at *SIP* offices — see below). If you have trouble or if you cannot raise a sufficient amount of change, remember that long-distance and international calls also can be made from the *Posto Telefonico Pubblico* (PTP) — literally the "public telephone place." In fact, this is perhaps the simplest way to place such a call. In a small town, the PTP may be no more than a booth in the corner of a bar. In larger cities, it will be either the local *SIP (Società Italiana per l'Esercizio Telefonico)* or *ASST (Azienda di Stato per i Servizi Telefonici)* office. Go to the telephone counter and explain what kind of call you want to make and to where. (A collect call is a *comunicazione "R"* or *con pagamento a destinazione;* a person-to-person call is a *comunicazione personale* or *con preavviso;* a station-to-station call is a *comunicazione posto a posto.*) You may be assigned a *cabina* (booth) from which to direct-dial the call yourself, or the clerk may put the call through for you, telling you which *cabina* to go to when he or she is about to connect the call. In either case, after you have hung up, return to the counter and pay the clerk for the call. Using the PTP allows you to avoid stiff hotel switchboard surcharges and to dispense with the hassle of pay telephones. The only drawback to their use is that in a city of any size there usually is a line of people waiting for an empty booth.

Although the majority of Italian pay phones still take tokens or coins, phones that take specially designated phone cards are increasingly common, particularly in metropolitan areas and at major tourist destinations. These telephone cards have been instigated to cut down on vandalism, as well as to free callers from the necessity of carrying around a pocketful of change, and are sold in various lire denominations. The units per card, like message units in US phone parlance, are a combination of time and distance. To use such a card, you insert it into a slot in the phone and dial the number you wish to reach. A display gradually will count down the value that remains on your card. When you run out of units on the card, you can insert another. In Italy, these phone cards are available from any SIP telephone center.

Although you can use a telephone company credit card number on any phone, pay phones that take major credit cards are increasingly common worldwide, particularly in transportation and tourism centers. Also now available is the "affinity card," a combined telephone calling card/bank credit card that can be used for domestic and international calls. Cards of this type include the following:

AT&T/Universal (phone: 800-662-7759). Cardholders can charge calls to the US from overseas.

Executive Telecard International (phone: 800-950-3800). Cardholders can charge calls to the US from overseas, as well as between most European countries.

Sprint Visa (phone: 800-446-7625). Cardholders can charge calls to the US from overseas.

Similarly, *MCI VisaPhone* (phone: 800-866-0099) can add phone card privileges to the services available through your existing *Visa* card. This service allows you to use your *Visa* account number, plus an additional code, to charge calls on any touch-tone phone in the US and Europe.

Hotel Surcharges – A lot of digits may be involved once a caller starts dialing beyond national borders, but avoiding operator-assisted calls can cut costs considerably and bring rates into a somewhat more reasonable range — except for calls made through hotel switchboards. One of the most unpleasant surprises travelers encounter in many foreign countries is the amount they find tacked on to their hotel bill for telephone calls, because foreign hotels routinely add on astronomical surcharges. (It's not at all uncommon to find 300% or 400% added to the actual telephone charges.)

Until recently, the only recourse against this unconscionable overcharging was to call collect when phoning from abroad or to use a telephone credit card — available through a simple procedure from any local US phone company. (Note, however, that even if you use a telephone credit card, some hotels still may charge a fee for line usage.) Now *American Telephone and Telegraph (AT&T)* offers *USA Direct,* a service that connects users, via a toll-free number, with an *AT&T* operator in the US, who will then put the call through at the standard international rate. Another new feature of this service is that travelers abroad can reach US toll-free (800) numbers by calling a *USA Direct* operator, who will connect them. Charges for all calls made through *USA Direct* appear on the caller's regular US phone bill. To reach this service in Italy, dial 172-1011. For a brochure and wallet card listing the toll-free number for other European countries, contact International Information Service, *AT&T Communications,* 635 Grant St., Pittsburgh, PA 15219 (phone: 800-874-4000).

AT&T also has put together *Teleplan,* an agreement among certain hoteliers that sets a limit on surcharges for calls made by guests from their rooms. As we went to press, *Teleplan* was in effect only in selected hotels in Rome. *Teleplan* agreements stipulate a flat, low rate for credit card or collect calls, and a flat percentage on calls paid for at the hotel. For further information, contact *AT&T*'s International Information Service (address above).

Until these services become universal, it's wise to ask the surcharge rate *before* calling from a hotel. If the rate is high, it's best to use a telephone credit card, make a collect call, or place the call and ask the party to call right back. If none of these choices is possible, to avoid surcharges make international calls from the local post office or one of the special telephone centers located throughout Italy (see above). Another way to keep down the cost of telephoning from Italy is to leave a copy of your itinerary and telephone numbers with people in the US so that they can call you instead.

A particularly useful service for travelers to Italy is *AT&T*'s Language Line Service. By calling 800-628-8486, you will be connected with an interpreter in any one of 143 languages and dialects (including Italian), who will provide on-line interpretative services for $3.50 a minute. From the US, this service is particularly useful for booking travel services in Europe where English is not spoken — or not fluently spoken — such as Italy. Once in Europe, this number can be reached by using the *USA Direct* toll-free (800) number connection feature described above. For further information, contact *AT&T* at the address above or call 800-752-6096.

Other Resources – Particularly useful for planning a trip is *AT&T*'s *Toll-Free 800*

Directory, which lists thousands of companies with 800 numbers, both alphabetically (white pages) and by category (yellow pages), including a wide range of travel services — from travel agents to transportation and accommodations. Issued in a consumer edition for $9.95 and a business edition for $14.95, both are available from *AT&T Phone Centers* or by calling 800-426-8686. Other useful directories for use before you leave and on the road include the *Toll-Free Travel & Vacation Information Directory* ($4.95 postpaid from Pilot Books, 103 Cooper St., Babylon, NY 11702; phone: 516-422-2225) and *The Phone Booklet* (send $2 to *Scott American Corporation,* Box 88, West Redding, CT 06896).

ELECTRICITY: The US runs on 110-volt, 60-cycle alternating current; most of Italy runs on 220-volt, 50-cycle alternating current, although 125-volt current still exists in some areas. (The voltage rarely is indicated on the outlet or anywhere else in hotel rooms, so it's always best to ask each time you change addresses.) The difference between US and European voltage means that, without a converter, the motor of a US appliance used overseas at 220 volts would run at twice the speed at which it's meant to operate and would quickly burn out. (US appliances may be run on 125 volts — but, again, this is not recommended, as they still may burn out.)

Travelers can solve the problem by buying a lightweight converter to transform foreign voltage into the US kind (there are several types of converters, depending on the wattage of the appliance) or by buying dual-voltage appliances, which convert from one to the other at the flick of a switch (hair dryers of this sort are common). The difference between the 50-cycle and 60-cycle currents will cause no problem — the American appliance simply will run more slowly — but it still will be necessary to deal with differing socket configurations before plugging in. To be fully prepared, bring along an extension cord (in older or rural establishments the electrical outlet may be farther from the sink than the cord on your razor or hair dryer can reach), and a wall socket adapter with a full set of plugs to ensure that you'll be able to plug in anywhere.

One good source for sets of plugs and adapters for use worldwide is the *Franzus Company* (PO Box 142, Beacon Falls, CT 06403; phone: 203-723-6664). *Franzus* also publishes a useful brochure, *Foreign Electricity Is No Deep Dark Secret,* which provides information about converters and adapter plugs for electric appliances to be used abroad but manufactured for use in the US. To obtain a free copy, send a self-addressed, stamped envelope to *Franzus* at the above address; a catalogue of other travel accessories is available on request.

Medical and Legal Aid and Consular Services

MEDICAL AID IN ITALY: Nothing ruins a vacation or business trip more effectively than sudden injury or illness. You will discover, in the event of an emergency, that most tourist facilities — transportation companies, hotels, and resorts — are equipped to handle the situation quickly and efficiently. Most Italian towns and cities of any size have a public hospital, and even the tiniest village has a medical clinic or private physician nearby. All hospitals are prepared for emergency cases, and many hospitals also have walk-in clinics designed to serve people who do not really need emergency service, but who have no place to go for immediate medical attention.

The general level of medical care available in Italy is not as consistent as it is in some other European countries, but the Italian health care system does encompass the same basic specialties and services that are available in the US. Although Italian medicine has been nationalized, its administration is carried out on the local level, and private practice continues to flourish. Also, the training and licensing of doctors *(medici)* and health care workers is not strictly regulated. For these reasons, the qualifications of health care professionals vary widely from region to region and from hospital to hospital. You can get excellent care — up-to-date and efficiently rendered — in full-service, government-run teaching hospitals associated with universities in major northern cities, as far south as Rome.

Before you go, be sure to check with your insurance company about the applicability of your hospitalization and major medical policies while you're abroad; many policies do not apply, and others are not accepted in Italy. Older travelers should know that Medicare does not make payments outside the US. Although hospitalization is less expensive in Italy than it is in the US, if your medical policy does not protect you while you're traveling, there are comprehensive combination policies specifically designed to fill the gap. (For a discussion of medical insurance and a list of inclusive combination policies, see *Insurance,* in this section.)

If a bona fide emergency occurs, an inability to speak Italian can pose a serious problem, not in receiving treatment at a large teaching hospital — where many doctors are likely to speak English — but in getting help elsewhere or in getting to the place where help is available. The fastest way to receive attention may be to go directly to the emergency room of the nearest hospital. Driving routes are usually marked with the international sign — the white "H" on a blue background (even though the Italian word for hospital is *ospedale*).

If you need immediate help, such as to call an ambulance, call the public emergency assistance number of the state police — 113 — or the immediate action service number of the *carabinieri* — 112. (The latter is the approximate equivalent of calling 911 in the US). State immediately that you are a foreign tourist and then the nature of your problem and your location. It is best to explain your problem (or have it explained) in Italian, as police, ambulance dispatchers, and other emergency personnel probably will not be bilingual, and they may be unable to determine the nature of the emergency, what equipment will be needed, or even where to send the ambulance. If you do not speak Italian and cannot find someone to translate for you, ask if there is anyone at the emergency center that speaks English ("*C'è qualcuno che parla inglese?*"), or dial 15 for an international operator who can make the call to the local emergency service and stay on the line as interpreter. (You also can dial 187 for international information to reach an English-speaking operator.)

Italian law specifies that seriously injured, ill, or unconscious persons be taken directly to one of the public hospitals. (After treatment in the emergency room, *pronto soccorso,* a patient in stable condition may transfer to the hospital of his or her choice.) The efficiency and speed of the service will be variable. If you require an ambulance, be aware that, in some cases, it may provide only transportation to the nearest public hospital. At the time of this writing, advanced EMS technology (similar to that provided in the US) was only just being added in Italy.

There are two types of hospitals in Italy — public and private. The non-public ones are called *case di cura* (houses of care or cure), villas, or clinics — to distinguish them from public hospitals. In addition, although these local services are the preferred option, in cases of extreme medical emergency, US military hospitals on bases in Livorno, Naples, Sigonella (Sicily), and Vicenza may treat travelers (of any nationality) who are seriously ill or injured until their conditions are stabilized — assuming that the US hospital has the facilities for the treatment required — and then transfer them to another hospital.

If a doctor is needed for something less than an emergency, there are several ways to find one. If you are staying in a hotel or resort, ask for help in reaching a doctor or other emergency services, or for the house physician, who may visit you in your room or ask you to visit an office. Travelers staying at a hotel of any size probably will find that the doctor on call speaks at least a modicum of English — if not, request one who does. When you register at a hotel, it's not a bad idea to include your home address and telephone number: this will facilitate the process of notifying friends, relatives, or your own doctor in case of an emergency.

Dialing one of the national emergency numbers (112 or 113) also may be of help (again, if you can speak Italian). It also usually is possible to obtain a referral through a US consulate (see addresses and phone numbers below) or directly through a hospital, especially if it is an emergency. If you are already at the hospital, you may see the specialist there, or you may make an appointment to be seen at his or her office.

Italian drugstores, *farmacie,* mainly sell medications. Toiletries and cosmetics are sold in *profumerie* (perfume shops) or in stores such as the *Standa* and *Upim* chains. *Farmacie* are identified by a red cross or a caduceus in front, and there is one open 24 hours a day in every city. Night duty rotates and each *farmacia* has a schedule posted on its door or front window identifying the evening's on-call pharmacist. After regular hours, you must ring the night bell. Local newspapers also often provide a listing of 24-hour drugstores. In small towns, where none may be officially open or on call after normal business hours, you may be able to have one open in an emergency situation — such as a diabetic needing insulin — although you may be charged a fee for this off-hour service.

Bring along a copy of any prescription you may have from your doctor in case you should need a refill. In the case of minor complaints, Italian pharmacists (who are identified by a gold badge on the lapel) *may* fill a foreign prescription; however, do not count on this. In most cases, you will need a local doctor to rewrite the prescription. Even in an emergency, a traveler will more than likely be given only enough of a drug to last until a local prescription can be obtained.

Americans also will notice that some drugs sold only by prescription in the US are sold over the counter in Italy (and vice versa). Though this can be very handy, be aware that common cold medicines and aspirin that contain codeine or other controlled substances will not be allowed back into the US.

Emergency assistance also is available from the various medical programs designed for travelers who have chronic ailments or whose illness requires them to return home:

International Association of Medical Assistance to Travelers (*IAMAT;* 417 Center St., Lewiston, NY 14092; phone: 716-754-4883). Entitles members to the services of participating doctors around the world, as well as clinics and hospitals in various locations. Participating physicians agree to adhere to a basic charge of around $40 to see a patient referred by *IAMAT.* To join, simply write to *IAMAT;* in about 3 weeks you will receive a membership card, the booklet of members, and an inoculation chart. A nonprofit organization, *IAMAT* appreciates donations; with a donation of $25 or more, you will receive a set of worldwide climate charts detailing weather and sanitary conditions. (Delivery can take up to 5 weeks, so plan ahead.)

International SOS Assistance (PO Box 11568, Philadelphia, PA 19116; phone: 800-523-8930 or 215-244-1500). Subscribers are provided with telephone access — 24 hours a day, 365 days a year — to a worldwide, monitored, multilingual network of medical centers. A phone call brings assistance ranging from a telephone consultation to transportation home by ambulance or aircraft, or, in some cases, transportation of a family member to wherever you are hospitalized. Individual rates are $35 for 2 weeks of coverage ($3.50 for each additional day), $70 for 1 month, or $240 for 1 year; couple and family rates also are available.

Medic Alert Foundation (2323 N. Colorado, Turlock, CA 95380; phone: 800-ID-ALERT or 209-668-3333). If you have a health condition that may not be readily perceptible to the casual observer — one that might result in a tragic error in an emergency situation — this organization offers identification emblems specifying such conditions. The foundation also maintains a computerized central file from which your complete medical history is available 24 hours a day by phone (the telephone number is clearly inscribed on the emblem). The onetime membership fee (between $25 and $45) is based on the type of metal from which the emblem is made — the choices range from stainless steel to 10K gold-filled.

TravMed (PO Box 10623, Baltimore, MD 21204; phone: 800-732-5309 or 301-296-5225). For $3 per day, subscribers receive comprehensive medical assistance while abroad. Major medical expenses are covered up to $100,000, and special transportation home or of a family member to wherever you are hospitalized is provided at no additional cost.

■ **Note:** Those who are unable to take a reserved flight due to personal illness or who must fly home unexpectedly due to a family emergency should be aware that airlines may offer a discounted airfare (or arrange a partial refund) if the traveler can demonstrate that his or her situation is indeed a legitimate emergency. Your inability to fly or the illness or death of an immediate family member usually must be substantiated by a doctor's note or the name, relationship, and funeral home from which the deceased will be buried. In such cases, airlines often will waive certain advance purchase restrictions or you may receive a refund check or voucher for future travel at a later date. Be aware, however, that this bereavement fare may not necessarily be the least expensive fare available and, if possible, it is best to have a travel agent check all possible flights through a computer reservations system (CRS).

LEGAL AID AND CONSULAR SERVICES: There is one crucial place to keep in mind when outside the US, namely, the American Services section of the US Consulate. If you are injured or become seriously ill, the consulate will direct you to medical assistance and notify your relatives. If, while abroad, you become involved in a dispute that could lead to legal action, the consulate, once again, is the place to turn.

It usually is far more alarming to be arrested abroad than at home. Not only are you alone among strangers, but the punishment can be worse. Granted, the US Consulate can advise you of your rights and provide a list of lawyers, but it cannot interfere with local legal process. Except for minor infractions of the local traffic code, there is no reason for any law-abiding traveler to run afoul of immigration, customs, or any other law enforcement authority.

The best advice is to be honest and law-abiding. If you get a traffic ticket, pay it. If you are approached by drug hawkers, ignore them. The penalties for possession of marijuana, cocaine, and other narcotics are even more severe abroad than in the US. (If you are picked up for any drug-related offense, do not expect US foreign service officials to be sympathetic. Chances are they will notify a lawyer and your family and that's about all. See "Drugs," below.)

In the case of minor traffic accidents (such as a fender bender), it often is most expedient to settle the matter before the police get involved. If, however, you are involved in a serious accident, where an injury or fatality results, the first step is to contact the nearest US consulate (for addresses, see below) and ask the consul to locate a lawyer to assist you. If you have a traveling companion, ask him or her to call the consulate (unless either of you has a local contact who can help you quickly). Competent English-speaking lawyers practice throughout Europe, and it is possible to obtain good legal counsel on short notice.

The US Department of State in Washington, DC, insists that any US citizen who is arrested abroad has the right to contact the US embassy or consulate "immediately," but it may be a while before you are given permission to use a phone. Do not labor under the illusion, however, that in a scrape with foreign officialdom the consulate can act as an arbitrator or ombudsman on a US citizen's behalf. Nothing could be farther from the truth. Consuls have no power, authorized or otherwise, to subvert, alter, or contravene the legal processes, however unfair, of the foreign country in which they serve. Nor can a consul oil the machinery of a foreign bureaucracy or provide legal advice. The consul's responsibilities do encompass "welfare duties," including providing a list of lawyers and information on local sources of legal aid, informing relatives in the US, and organizing and administrating any defense monies sent from home. If a case is tried unfairly or the punishment seems unusually severe, the consul can make a formal complaint to the authorities. For questions about US citizens arrested abroad, how to get money to them, and other useful information, call the *Citizens' Emergency Center* of the Office of Special Consular Services in Washington, DC, at 202-647-5225. (For further information about this invaluable hotline, see below.)

Other welfare duties, not involving legal hassles, cover cases of both illness and destitution. If you should get sick, the US consul can provide names of doctors and dentists, as well as the names of all local hospitals and clinics; the consul also will contact family members in the US and help arrange special ambulance service for a flight home. In a situation involving "legitimate and proven poverty" of an US citizen stranded abroad without funds, the consul will contact sources of money (such as family or friends in the US), apply for aid to agencies in foreign countries, and in a last resort — which is *rarely* — arrange for repatriation at government expense, although this is a loan that must be repaid. And in case of natural disasters or civil unrest, consulates around the world handle the evacuation of US citizens if it becomes necessary.

The consulate is not occupied solely with emergencies and is certainly not there to aid in trivial situations, such as canceled reservations or lost baggage, no matter how important these matters may seem to the victimized tourist. The main duties of any consulate are administrating statutory services, such as the issuance of passports and visas; providing notarial services; distributing VA, social security, and civil service benefits to US citizens; taking depositions; handling extradition cases; and reporting to Washington the births, deaths, and marriages of US citizens living within the consulate's domain.

We hope that none of the information in this section will be necessary during your stay in Italy. If you can avoid legal hassles altogether, you will have a much more pleasant trip. If you become involved in an imbroglio, the local authorities may spare you legal complications if you make clear your tourist status. And if you run into a confrontation that might lead to legal complications developing with a citizen or with local authorities, the best tactic is to apologize and try to leave as gracefully as possible. Do not get into fights with residents, no matter how belligerent or provocative they are in a given situation.

The US Embassy in Italy is at 121 Via Veneto, Rome 00187 (phone: 6-46741). Following is a list of US consulates in Italy. Note that mailing addresses may be different — so call before sending anything to these offices.

Florence: US Consulate, 38 Lungarno Amerigo Vespucci, Florence 50123 (phone: 55-239-8276).

Genoa: US Consulate, Banca d'America e d'Italia Bldg., 6 Piazza Portello, Genoa 16124 (phone: 10-282741 through 5).
Milan: US Consulate, 210 Via Principe Amedeo, Milan 20121 (phone: 2-900-4559).
Naples: US Consulate, Piazza della Repubblica, Naples 80122 (phone: 81-761-4303).
Palermo: US Consulate, 1 Via Vaccarini, Palermo 90143 (phone: 91-343532).
Turin: US Consulate, 23 Via Pomba, Turin 10123 (phone: 11-517-437).

You can obtain a booklet with addresses of most US embassies and consulates around the world by writing to the Superintendent of Documents (US Government Printing Office, Washington, DC 20402), and asking for publication #78-77, *Key Offices of Foreign Service Posts.*

As mentioned above, the US State Department operates a *Citizens' Emergency Center,* which offers a number of services to American travelers abroad and their families at home. In addition to giving callers up-to-date information on trouble spots, the center will contact authorities abroad in an attempt to locate a traveler or deliver an urgent message. In case of illness, death, arrest, destitution, or repatriation of a US citizen on foreign soil, it will relay information to relatives at home if the consulate is unable to do so. Travel advisory information is available 24 hours a day to people with touch-tone phones (phone: 202-647-5225). Callers with rotary phones can get travel advisory information at this number from 8:15 AM to 10 PM (Eastern Standard Time) on weekdays; 9 AM to 3 PM on Saturdays. In the event of an emergency, this number also may be called during these hours. For emergency calls only, at all other times, call 202-634-3600 and ask for the Duty Officer.

Drinking and Drugs

DRINKING: The Italians are well known for their production and enjoyment of fine wines, aperitifs, and liqueurs, and many would not contemplate a dinner — or even lunch — unaccompanied by a glass of wine. Even children drink wine diluted with water at mealtime. Aperitifs such as Campari and Martini Dry (dry vermouth) are typical before-meal drinks, and *digestivi* (digestives) or liqueurs are the finishing touches to a good dinner. In general, local wine and other liquor are the best buys, so take this opportunity to savor them at the source.

As in the US, national taxes on alcohol affect the prices of liquor in Italy, not — as used to be the case — the fact that they are manufactured in other countries. For instance, gin is as cheap in Italy as in Great Britain. As a general rule, mixed drinks (which are less common in Italy) and some types of liquor are more expensive than at home. If you like a drop before dinner, a good way to save money is to buy a bottle of your favorite brand at the airport before leaving the US and enjoy it in your hotel before setting forth.

Wine and beer are viewed more casually in Italy than in the US and can be bought at wine shops, supermarkets, and bars (where they are sold only by the bottle and are more expensive than in the stores). There are few restrictions on the sale of wine and liquor in Italy: Although the legal drinking age for purchasing or ordering alcohol is 18, it is not strictly enforced, and it can be sold 7 days a week, 365 days a year. However, on holidays you may have some trouble finding a store open for business.

Bars, as cafés in Italy are called, serve wine, beer, aperitifs, liqueurs, and liquor, as well as coffee, soft drinks, and light fare, such as *panini* (small sandwiches) and *crostini* (canapes). They generally are open in the morning, sometimes as early as 5 or 6 AM, and close at around 11 PM or midnight. Nightclubs and discos close later.

Visitors to Italy may bring in 2 liters of wine and 1 liter of liquor per person. If you are buying any quantity of alcohol (such as a case of wine) in Italy and traveling through other European countries on your route back to the US, you will have to pass through customs and pay duty at each border crossing, so you might want to arrange to have it shipped home. Whether bringing it with you or shipping, you will have to pay US import duties on any quantity over the allowed 1 liter (see *Customs and Returning to the US,* in this section).

DRUGS: Illegal narcotics are as prevalent in Italy as in the US, but the moderate legal penalties and vague social acceptance that marijuana has gained in the US have no equivalents in Italy. Due to the international war on drugs, enforcement of drug laws is becoming increasingly strict throughout the world. Local European narcotics officers and customs officials are renowned for their absence of understanding and lack of a sense of humor — especially where foreigners are concerned.

Opiates and barbiturates, and other increasingly popular drugs — "white powder" substances like heroin and cocaine, and "crack" (the cocaine derivative) — continue to be of major concern to narcotics officials. Most European countries — including Italy — have toughened laws regarding illegal drugs and narcotics, and it is important to bear in mind that the type or quantity of drugs involved is of minor importance. The maximum penalties may be imposed for possessing even *traces* of illegal drugs. There is a high conviction rate in these cases, and bail for foreigners is rare. Persons arrested are subject to the laws of the country they are visiting, and there isn't much that the US consulate can do for drug offenders beyond providing a list of lawyers. The best advice we can offer is this: Don't carry, use, buy, or sell illegal drugs.

Those who carry medicines that contain a controlled drug should be sure to have a current doctor's prescription with them. Ironically, travelers can get into almost as much trouble coming through US customs with over-the-counter drugs picked up abroad that contain substances that are controlled in the US. Cold medicines, pain relievers, and the like often have codeine or codeine derivatives that are illegal, except by prescription, in the US. Throw them out before leaving for home.

- **Be forewarned:** US narcotics agents warn travelers of the increasingly common ploy of drug dealers asking travelers to transport a "gift" or other package back to the US. Don't be fooled into thinking that the protection of US law applies abroad — accused of illegal drug trafficking, you will be considered guilty until you prove your innocence. In other words, do not, under any circumstances, agree to take anything across the border for a stranger.

Tipping

Throughout Italy (and most of the rest of Europe) you will find the custom of including some kind of service charge — generally 12% to 15% — in the bill for a meal or accommodations more common than in the US. This can confuse Americans not familiar with the custom. On the one hand, many a traveler, unaware of this policy, has left many a superfluous *mancia* (tip). On the other hand, travelers aware of this policy may make the mistake of assuming that it takes care of everything. It doesn't. While "service included" in theory eliminates any question of how much and whom to tip, in practice there still are occasions when on-the-spot tips are appropriate. Among these are tips to show appreciation for special services, as well as tips meant to say "thank you" for services rendered. So keep a pocketful of 1,000-lire notes and hand these out like dollar bills.

In Italian restaurants, the service charge (called *servizio complesso*) may appear in one of two ways: It either already is calculated in the prices listed or will be added to *il conto* (the final bill). For the most part, if you see a notation at the bottom of the menu — such as *compreso* or *incluso* — without a percentage figure, the charge should be included in the prices; if a percentage figure is indicated, the service charge has not yet been added. To further confuse the issue, not every restaurant notes if its policy is to include service and at what point the charge is added. If you are at all unsure, you should feel no embarrassment about asking a waiter.

Servizio complesso generally ranges from 12% to 15%. In the rare instance where it isn't added, a 15% tip — just as in the US — usually is a safe figure, although one should never hesitate to penalize poor service or reward excellent and efficient attention by leaving less or more. If the tip has been added, no further gratuity is expected — though it's a common practice in Italy for diners to leave an extra 5% for the waiter (leave a lower percentage for larger tabs).

Although it's not necessary to tip the maître d' of most restaurants — unless he has been especially helpful in arranging a special party or providing a table (slipping him something in a crowded restaurant *may* get you seated sooner or procure a preferred table) — when tipping is desirable or appropriate, the least amount should be around the current equivalent of $5. In the finest restaurants, where a multiplicity of servers are present, plan to tip 5% to the captain. In Italy, the sommelier (wine waiter) usually is not tipped for simply serving the wine, although if he has selected the wine for you, it is customary to leave him 10% of the price of the bottle.

When eating or drinking standing up at a café counter, the procedure is to pay at the cash register first and then take the small receipt *(scontrino)* over to the counter, where you leave it with a few coins, depending on what you're having — coffee, drinks with sandwiches, pastries, and so on — as you order from the bar attendant. If you're sitting at a café table, service may or may not be included, and a good rule of thumb is to leave 5% to 10% (depending on your inclination) in either case. The more elegant the establishment, the more likely that service is included, but 5% to 10% extra still is customary; at a corner bar in an ordinary neighborhood, service probably isn't included, but no more than 5% to 10% would be expected.

In allocating gratuities at a restaurant, pay particular attention to what has become the standard credit card charge form, which now includes separate places for gratuities for waiters and/or captains. If these separate boxes are not on the charge slip, simply ask the waiter or captain how these separate tips should be indicated. Be aware, too, of the increasingly common, devious practice of placing the amount of an entire restaurant bill (in which service already has been included) in the top box of a charge slip, leaving the "tip" and "total" boxes ominously empty. Don't be intimidated: Leave the "tip" box blank and just repeat the total amount next to "total" before signing. In some establishments, tips indicated on credit card receipts may not be given to the help, so you may want to leave tips in cash.

As in restaurants, visitors usually will find a service charge of 12% to 15% included in their final bill at most Italian hotels. No additional gratuities are required — or expected — beyond this billed service charge. It is unlikely, however, that a service charge will be added to bills in small guesthouses or other modest establishments. In these cases, guests should let their instincts be their guide; no tipping is expected by members of the family who own the establishment, but it is a nice gesture to leave something for others — such as a dining room waiter or a maid — who may have been helpful. A gratuity of around $1 per night is adequate in most cases.

If a hotel does not automatically add a service charge, it is perfectly proper for guests to ask to have an extra 10% to 15% added to their bill, to be distributed among those who served them. This may be an especially convenient solution in a large hotel, where it's difficult to determine just who out of a horde of attendants actually performed particular services.

For those who prefer to distribute tips themselves, a chambermaid generally is tipped at the rate of around $1 per day. Tip the concierge or hall porter for specific services only, with the amount of such gratuities dependent on the level of service provided. For any special service you receive in a hotel, a tip is expected — the current equivalent of $1 being the minimum for a small service.

Bellhops, doormen, and porters at hotels and transportation centers generally are tipped at the rate of around $1 per piece of luggage, along with a small additional amount if a doorman helps with a cab or car. Once upon a time, taxi drivers in Europe would give you a rather odd look if presented with a tip for a fare, but times have changed, and 10% to 15% of the amount on the meter is now a standard gratuity.

Miscellaneous tips: Tipping ushers in a movie house, theater, or concert hall used to be the rule, but is becoming less common — the best policy is to check what other patrons are doing and follow suit. Often the program is not free and in lieu of a tip it is common practice to purchase a program from the person who seats you. Sightseeing tour guides also should be tipped. If you are traveling in a group, decide together what you want to give the guide and present it from the group at the end of the tour ($1 per person is a reasonable tip). If you have been individually escorted, the amount paid should depend on the degree of your satisfaction, but it should not be less than 10% of the total tour price. Museum and monument guides also are usually tipped, and it is a nice touch to tip a caretaker who unlocks a small church or turns on the lights in a chapel for you in some out-of-the-way town.

In barbershops and beauty salons, tip as you would at home, keeping in mind that the percentages vary according to the type of establishment — 10% in the most expensive salons; 15% to 20% in less expensive establishments. (As a general rule, the person who washes your hair should get an additional small tip.) The washroom attendants in these places, or wherever you see one, should get a small tip — they usually set out a little plate with a coin already on it indicating the suggested denomination. Don't forget service station attendants, for whom about $1 for cleaning the windshield or other attention is not unusual.

Duty-Free Shopping and Value Added Tax

DUTY-FREE SHOPS: Note that at the time of this writing, because of the newly integrated European economy, there were some questions as to the fate and number of duty-free shops that would be maintained in international airports in European Economic Community (EEC) member countries. It appears, however, that those traveling between EEC countries and any country *not* a member of the Common Market will still be entitled to buy duty-free items. Since the United States is not a Common Market member, duty-free purchases by US travelers will, presumably, remain as is even after the end of 1992.

If common sense says that it always is less expensive to buy goods in an airport duty-free shop than to buy them at home or in the streets of a foreign city, travelers should be aware of some basic facts. Duty-free, first of all, does not mean that the goods travelers buy will be free of duty when they return to the US. Rather, it means that the shop has paid no import tax acquiring goods of foreign make because the goods are not to be used in the country where the shop is located. This is why duty-free goods are available only in the restricted, passengers-only area of international airports or are delivered to departing passengers on the plane. In a duty-free store, travelers save money only on goods of foreign make because they are the only items on which an import tax would be charged in any other store. There usually is no saving on locally made items, but in countries such as Italy that impose Value Added Taxes (see below) that are refundable to foreigners, the prices in airport duty-free shops also are minus this tax, sparing travelers the often cumbersome procedures they otherwise have to follow to obtain a VAT refund.

Beyond this, there is little reason to delay buying locally made merchandise and/or souvenirs until reaching the airport (for information on local specialties, see the individual city chapters in THE CITIES and *Shopping in Italy,* in DIVERSIONS). In fact, because airport duty-free shops usually pay high rents, the locally made goods sold in them may well be more expensive than they would be in downtown stores. The real bargains are foreign goods, but — let the buyer beware — not all foreign goods are automatically less expensive in an airport duty-free shop. You can get a good deal on even small amounts of perfume, costing less than the usually required minimum purchase, tax-free. Other fairly standard bargains include spirits, smoking materials, cameras, clothing, watches, chocolates, and other food and luxury items — but first be sure to know what these items cost elsewhere. Terrific savings do exist (they are the reason for such shops, after all), but so do overpriced items that an unwary shopper might find equally tempting. In addition, if you wait to do your shopping at airport duty-free shops, you will be taking the chance that the desired item is out of stock or unavailable.

Duty-free shops are located in most major international airports throughout Europe. Rome's Leonardo da Vinci Airport at Fiumicino has a number of duty-free and tax-free shops selling everything from liquor and perfumes to clothing, gifts, jewelry, cameras, toys, and food specialties. But its range of style choices and sizes does not approach that of downtown shops, so it's not recommended that you wait to begin your spree at the airport unless you are willing to choose from comparatively slim pickings. Milan's Malpensa Airport also has a small duty-free shop.

- **Buyer Beware:** You may come across shops *not* at airports that call themselves duty-free shops. These require shoppers to show a foreign passport but are subject to the same rules as other stores, including paying import duty on foreign items. What "tax-free" means in the case of these establishments is something of an advertising strategy: They are announcing loud and clear that they do, indeed, offer the VAT refund service — sometimes on the spot (minus a fee for higher overhead). Prices may be no better at these stores and could be even higher due to the addition of this service.

VALUE ADDED TAX: Commonly abbreviated as VAT, this is a tax levied by various European countries, including Italy, and added to the purchase price of most goods and services. In Italy, it is known as the *imposta sul valore aggiunto* (IVA), and it ranges from 18% to 38%.

The tax is meant to apply only to residents of Italy (and is already included in the price tag), but visitors are required to pay it, too, unless they have purchases shipped directly to an address abroad by the store — not a recommended procedure for most Italian purchases. If visitors pay the tax and take purchases with them, however, they are usually entitled to a refund under retail export schemes that have been in operation throughout Italy for several years.

In Italy, although a VAT-refund scheme exists, it is not as inclusive or streamlined as in some other European countries, and there are several points to keep in mind. First, a refund is granted only if the price of an item (or the total of purchases made at one store) is 605,000 lire (about $550) or more, and multiple purchases in a single shop may *not* be grouped to reach the minimum as is frequently allowed in other countries. Second, the store must agree to participate in the tax-refund procedure — paperwork is involved and although stores are obliged to offer the refund when asked, many find a way to circumvent it. Quite often, if you have spent a large amount of money in one shop, the shopkeeper will offer you a discount rather than bother with the forms. On the other hand, if you have already been given a discount, it may disappear if you insist on a tax refund.

Before making any major purchase, first determine if you are entitled to and will be able to receive a refund. As the tax can add substantially to the purchase price, if you will not be reimbursed you may want to consider shopping elsewhere.

To claim the refund, shoppers must ask the store clerk for a refund form (an original plus two copies) filled out with your full name, address, passport number, and a description of the purchase. At departure time, this same document must be presented with the merchandise (do not pack it in the bottom of your suitcase) to Italian customs officials, who will stamp the original and return it and the copies to you. The stamped original should be sent back to the store by registered mail (from any country other than Italy) within 3 months of the date of purchase. Stores have 15 days from receipt of the stamped invoice to send out the refund, but since the Italian post office is not known for the speed of its deliveries, there may be a considerable wait.

Also note that at Malpensa Airport in Milan and Leonardo da Vinci Airport (better known as Fiumicino) in Rome you may be able to receive an on-the-spot cash VAT refund at desks near customs and passport control (an Italian customs official can direct you). There will be a small charge for this service, deducted from the refund.

A VAT refund by dollar check or credited to a credit card account is relatively hassle-free, but should you receive a check in lire, you'll probably find that your US bank will assess a fee, as much as $15 or more, for converting it into US dollars. Far less costly is sending the foreign currency check (after endorsing it) to *Ruesch International,* which will convert it to a check in US dollars for a $2 fee (deducted from the dollar check). Other services include commission-free traveler's checks and foreign currency which can be ordered by mail. Contact *Ruesch International* at one of the following addresses: 191 Peachtree St., Atlanta, GA 30303 (phone: 404-222-9300); 3 First National Plaza, Suite 2020, Chicago, IL 60602 (phone: 312-332-5900); 1925 Century Park E., Suite 240, Los Angeles, CA 90067 (phone: 213-277-7800); 608 Fifth Ave., "Swiss Center," New York, NY 10020 (phone: 212-977-2700); and 1350 Eye St. NW, 10th Floor and street level, Washington, DC 20005 (phone: 800-424-2923 or 202-408-1200).

Two other methods of reimbursement are possible if the purchases in Italy are made by credit card. The preferable one is that the store will agree to make two credit card charges, one for the price of the goods, the other for the amount of the tax. Then, when the stamped copy of the form arrives from customs, the store simply tears up the charge slip for the sales tax and the amount never appears on your account. The other possibility is that, upon receipt of the stamped form, the store requests the international billing center to credit your account with the amount of the sales tax.

Religion on the Road

Italy is predominantly Catholic and every town, right down to the most isolated village, has its own church. And in larger, more heavily populated areas, some amount of religious variety is reflected in the churches of other denominations, synagogues, and an occasional mosque or temple.

The surest source of information on English-language religious services in an unfamiliar country is the desk clerk of the hotel or guesthouse in which you are staying; the local tourist information office, a US consul, or a church of another religious affiliation also may be able to provide this information. If you aren't in an area with

The allotment for individual "unsolicited" gifts mailed from abroad (no more than one per day per recipient) is $50 retail value per gift. These gifts do not have to be declared and are not included in your duty-free exemption (see below). Although you should include a receipt for purchases with each package, the examiner is empowered to impose a duty based on his or her assessment of the value of the goods. The duty owed is collected by the US Postal Service when the package is delivered (also see below). More information on mailing packages home from abroad is contained in the US Customs Service pamphlet *Buyer Beware, International Mail Imports* (see below for where to write for this and other useful brochures).

CLEARING CUSTOMS: This is a simple procedure. Forms are distributed by airline or ship personnel before arrival. (Note that a $5-per-person service charge — called a user fee — is collected by airlines and cruise lines to help cover the cost of customs checks, but this is included in the ticket price.) If your purchases total no more than the $400 duty-free limit, you need only fill out the identification part of the form and make an oral declaration to the customs inspector. If entering with more than $400 worth of goods, you must submit a written declaration.

Customs agents are businesslike, efficient, and not unkind. During the peak season, clearance can take time, but this generally is because of the strain imposed by a number of jumbo jets simultaneously discharging their passengers, not because of unwarranted zealousness on the part of the customs people.

Efforts to streamline procedures used to include the so-called Citizens' Bypass Program, which allowed US citizens whose purchases were within their duty-free allowance to go to the "green line," where they simply showed their passports to the customs inspector. Although at the time of this writing this procedure still is being followed at some international airports in the US, most airports have returned to an earlier system. US citizens arriving from overseas now have to go through a passport check by the Immigration & Naturalization Service (INS) prior to recovering their baggage and proceeding to customs. (US citizens will not be on the same line as foreign visitors, but this additional wait does delay clearance on re-entry into the US.) Although all passengers have to go through this passport inspection, those entering with purchases within the duty-free limit may be spared a thorough customs inspection; however, inspectors still retain the right to search any luggage they choose — so don't do anything foolish.

It is illegal not to declare dutiable items; not to do so, in fact, constitutes smuggling, and the penalty can be anything from stiff fines and seizure of the goods to prison sentences. It simply isn't worth doing. Nor should you go along with the suggestions of foreign merchants who offer to help you secure a bargain by deceiving customs officials in any way. Such transactions frequently are a setup, using the foreign merchant as an agent of US customs. Another agent of US customs is TECS, the Treasury Enforcement Communications System, a computer that stores all kinds of pertinent information on returning citizens. There is a basic rule to buying goods abroad, and it should never be broken: *If you can't afford the duty on something, don't buy it.* Your list or verbal declaration should include all items purchased abroad, as well as gifts received abroad, purchases made at the behest of others, the value of repairs, and anything brought in for resale in the US.

Do not include in the list items that do not accompany you, i.e., purchases that you have mailed or had shipped home. As mentioned above, these are dutiable in any case, even if for your own use and even if the items that accompany your return from the same trip do not exhaust your duty-free exemption. It is a good idea, if you have accumulated too much while abroad, to mail home any personal effects (made and bought in the US) that you no longer need rather than your foreign purchases. These personal effects pass through US Customs as "American goods returned" and are not subject to duty.

If you cannot avoid shipping home your foreign purchases, however, the US Customs Service suggests that the package be clearly marked "Not for Sale," and that a copy of the bill of sale be included. The US Customs examiner usually will accept this as indicative of the article's fair retail value, but if he or she believes it to be falsified or feels the goods have been seriously undervalued, a higher retail value may be assigned.

FORBIDDEN ITEMS: Narcotics, plants, and many types of food are not allowed into the US. Drugs are totally illegal, with the exception of medication prescribed by a physician. It's a good idea not to travel with too large a quantity of any given prescription drug (although, in the event that a pharmacy is not open when you need it, bring along several extra doses) and to have the prescription on hand in case any question arises either abroad or when reentering the US.

Any sculpture that is part of an architectural structure, any authentic archaeological find or other artifacts considered by the Italian government to be a "national treasure" may not be exported from Italy. If you do not obtain prior permission of the proper regulatory agencies, such items will be confiscated at the Italian border, and you will run the risk of being fined or imprisoned. People interested in purchasing anything that might qualify as such an item should check in advance with the *Istituto delle Belle Arti* (or the nearest US consulate if further assistance is required).

Tourists have long been forbidden to bring into the US foreign-made US trademarked articles purchased abroad (if the trademark is recorded with customs) without written permission. It's now permissible to enter with one such item in your possession as long as it's for personal use.

The US Customs Service implements the rigorous Department of Agriculture regulations concerning the importation of vegetable matter, seeds, bulbs, and the like. Living vegetable matter may not be imported without a permit, and everything must be inspected, permit or not. Approved items (which do not require a permit) include dried bamboo and woven items made of straw; beads made of most seeds (but not jequirity beans — the poisonous scarlet and black seed of the rosary pea); cones of pine and other trees; roasted coffee beans; most flower bulbs; flowers (without roots); dried or canned fruits, jellies, or jams; polished rice; dried beans and teas; herb plants (not witchweed); nuts (but not acorns, chestnuts, or any nuts with outer husks); dried lichens, mushrooms, truffles, shamrocks, and seaweed; and most dried spices.

Other processed foods and baked goods usually are okay. Regulations on meat products generally depend on the country of origin and manner of processing. As a rule, commercially canned meat, hermetically sealed and cooked in the can so that it can be stored without refrigeration, is permitted, but not all canned meat fulfills this requirement. Be careful when buying European-made pâté, for instance. Goose liver pâté in itself is acceptable, but the pork fat that often is part of it, either as an ingredient or a rind, may not be. Even canned pâtés may not be admitted for this reason. (The imported ones you see in US stores have been prepared and packaged according to US regulations.) Also, do not attempt to bring any cheese, sausages, or salamis back from Italy because they will not be allowed into the country, and the inevitable confiscation of a Parma ham would be a terrible loss, given its cost. So before stocking up on a newfound favorite, it pays to check in advance — otherwise you might have to leave it behind.

The US Customs Service also enforces federal laws that prohibit the entry of articles made from the furs or hides of animals on the endangered species list. Beware of shoes, bags, and belts made of crocodile and certain kinds of lizard, and anything made of tortoiseshell; this also applies to preserved crocodiles, lizards, and turtles sometimes sold in gift shops. And if you're shopping for big-ticket items, beware of fur coats made from the skins of spotted cats. They are sold in Europe, but they will be confiscated upon your return to the US, and there will be no refund. For information about other animals on the endangered species list, contact the Department of the Interior, US Fish and Wildlife Service (Publications Unit, 4401 N. Fairfax Dr., Room 130, Arlington,

VA 22203; phone: 703-358-1711), and ask for the free publication *Facts About Federal Wildlife Laws.*

Also note that some foreign governments prohibit the export of items made from certain species of wildlife, and the US honors any such restrictions. Before you go shopping in any foreign country, check with the US Department of Agriculture (G110 Federal Bldg., Hyattsville, MD 20782; phone: 301-436-8413) and find out what items are prohibited from the country you will be visiting.

The US Customs Service publishes a series of free pamphlets with customs information. It includes *Know Before You Go,* a basic discussion of customs requirements pertaining to all travelers; *Buyers Beware, International Mail Imports; Travelers' Tips on Bringing Food, Plant, and Animal Products into the United States; Importing a Car; GSP and the Traveler; Pocket Hints; Currency Reporting; Pets, Wildlife, US Customs; Customs Hints for Visitors (Nonresidents);* and *Trademark Information for Travelers.* For the entire series or individual pamphlets, write to the US Customs Service (PO Box 7407, Washington, DC 20044) or contact any of the seven regional offices, in Boston, Chicago, Houston, Long Beach (California), Miami, New Orleans, and New York. The US Customs Service has a tape-recorded message whereby callers using touch-tone phones can get more information on various topics; the number is 202-566-8195. These pamphlets provide great briefing material, but if you still have questions when you're in Europe, contact the nearest US consulate.

Sources and Resources

Tourist Information Offices

The Italian Government Travel Offices in North America generally are the best sources of travel information, and most of their publications are free for the asking. When requesting brochures and maps, state the areas you plan to visit, as well as your particular interests: accommodations, restaurants, special events, tourist attractions, guided tours, and facilities for specific sports and other activities. There is no need to send a self-addressed, stamped envelope with your request, unless specified.

The best places for tourist information in each Italian city are listed in the *Sources and Resources* section of the individual city reports in THE CITIES. Following is a list of the Italian Government Tourist Offices in the US.

Italian Government Travel Office (Ente Nazionale Italiano di Turismo, ENIT)

Chicago: 500 N. Michigan Ave., Chicago, IL 60611 (phone: 312-644-0990).

New York: 630 Fifth Ave., Suite 1565, New York, NY 10111 (phone: 212-245-4822).

San Francisco: 360 Post St., Suite 801, San Francisco, CA 94108 (phone: 415-392-6206).

Note that there is no official San Marino government tourist office in the US, but the San Marino consulates listed below (see *The Italian Embassy and Consulates in the US*) handle requests for travel information.

If your query cannot be answered by ENIT, you may want to write directly to the appropriate tourist authorities in Italy. A comprehensive list of tourist boards in principal cities (including a number of smaller cities not covered in the THE CITIES chapters in this guide), as well as a wealth of other useful miscellany is provided in the Italian Government Travel Office's free booklet, *General Information for Traveler's to Italy.*

In Italy, regions are broken down into provinces, and most cities and larger towns have a Provincial Tourist Board (Ente Provinciale per il Turismo, EPT), which supplies information about both the city and the surrounding province. Furthermore, all towns with an interest in serving tourists have a Local Tourist Board (Azienda Autonoma di Soggiorno e Turismo, AAST). Thus, for any given town, the correct office to write for information may be either the EPT or the AAST (in the case of a large city or town) or the AAST (in the case of a small one). There are far too many of these — more than 100 EPT offices and still more AAST offices — to list here, but the Italian Government Travel Office should be able to supply any address you need. You also can request information about any major city in Italy from the tourist office cited (with address and phone number) in *Sources and Resources* in the relevant CITIES chapter.

The Italian Embassy and Consulates in the US

The Italian government maintains an embassy and a number of consulates in the US. One of their primary functions is to provide visas for certain resident aliens (depending on their country of origin) and for Americans planning to visit longer than 6 months, or to study, reside, or work in Italy. Consulates also are empowered to sign official documents and to notarize copies or translations of US documents, which may be necessary for those papers to be considered legal in Italy.

The Italian Embassy is located at 1601 Fuller St. NW, Washington, DC 20009 (phone: 202-328-5500). Listed below are the Italian consulates in the US. In general, these offices are open 9 AM to 1 PM, Mondays through Fridays — call ahead to be sure.

Italian Consulates in the US

Boston: Italian Consulate-General, 100 Boylston St., Suite 900, Boston, MA 02116 (phone: 617-542-0483).

Chicago: Italian Consulate-General, 500 N. Michigan Ave., Chicago, IL 60611 (phone: 312-467-1550).

Detroit: Italian Consulate, Buhl Bldg., 535 Griswold, Suite 1840, Detroit, MI 48226 (phone: 313-963-8560).

Houston: Italian Consulate, 1300 Post Oak Rd., Suite 660, Houston, TX 77056 (phone: 713-850-7520).

Los Angeles: Italian Consulate-General, 12400 Wilshire Blvd., Suite 300, Los Angeles, CA 90025 (phone: 213-820-0622).

New Orleans: Italian Consulate, 630 Camp St., New Orleans, LA 70130 (phone: 504-524-2271).

New York: Italian Consulate, 690 Park Ave., New York, NY 10021 (phone: 212-737-9100).

Philadelphia: Italian Consulate-General, 421 Chestnut St., Philadelphia, PA 19106 (phone: 215-592-7329).

San Francisco: Italian Consulate-General, 2590 Webster St., San Francisco, CA 94115 (phone: 415-931-4924).

Following is a list of San Marino consulates, which are a source of travel information about the republic of San Marino. Note that there are no border formalities between Italy and San Marino, and your US passport is the only document required for a visit of 3 months or less.

San Marino Consulates in the US

New York: San Marino Consulate-General, 186 Leher Ave., Elmont, NY 11003 (phone: 516-437-4699).

Troy, MI: San Marino Consulate, 1685 E. Big Beaver Rd., Troy, MI 48083 (phone: 313-528-1190, Wednesdays and Saturdays only).

Washington, DC: San Marino Consulate-General, 1899 L St. NW, Suite 500, Washington, DC 20036 (phone: 202-223-3517).

The *Italian Cultural Institute (Istituto Italiano di Cultura)* is the Italian Embassy's cultural arm abroad. It serves as a liaison between the American and Italian people and is an especially good source of information. There are five branches in the US:

Chicago: 500 N. Michigan Ave., Suite 530, Chicago, IL 60611 (phone: 312-822-9545).

Los Angeles: 12400 Wilshire Blvd., Suite 310, Los Angeles, CA 90025 (phone: 213-207-4737).

New York City: 686 Park Ave., New York, NY 10021 (phone: 212-879-4242).

San Francisco: 425 Bush St., Suite 305, San Francisco, CA 94108 (phone: 415-788-7142).

Washington, DC: 1601 Fuller St. NW, Washington, DC 20009 (phone: 202-328-5500).

The New York branch maintains a library of books, periodicals, and newspapers that is open to the public; San Francisco, too, has a small library, open to the public by appointment. A free booklet published three times a year lists cultural events in Italy — theater, folklore, cinema, and exhibitions. Copies are available on request from any of the offices listed above.

Theater and Special Event Tickets

In more than one section of this book you will read about events that spark your interest — everything from music festivals and special theater seasons to sporting championships — along with telephone numbers and addresses to which to write for descriptive brochures, reservations, or tickets. The Italian Government Travel Office can supply information on these and other special events and festivals that take place in Italy, though they cannot in all cases provide the actual program or detailed information on ticket prices.

Since many of these occasions often are fully booked well in advance, you should think about having your booking in hand before you go. In some cases, tickets may be reserved over the phone and charged to a credit card, or you can send an international money order or foreign draft. If you do write, remember that any request from the US should be accompanied by an International Reply Coupon to ensure a response (send two of them for an airmail response). These international coupons, money orders, and drafts are available at US post offices.

For further information, write for the *European Travel Commission*'s extensive list of events scheduled for the entire year for its 24 member countries (including Italy). For a free copy, send a self-addressed, stamped, business-size (4 x 9½) envelope to "European Events," *European Travel Commission,* PO Box 1754, New York, NY 10185.

Books, Newspapers, Magazines, and Newsletters

Throughout GETTING READY TO GO, numerous books and brochures have been recommended as good sources of further information on a variety of topics.

Suggested Reading – The list below comprises books we have read and think worthwhile; it is by no means complete — but meant merely to start you on your way. These titles include some informative guides to special interests, solid historical accounts, and books that call your attention to things you might not otherwise notice, as well as a smattering of fiction to get you into the Italian spirit. (For a detailed discussion of Italy's literary heritage, see *Literature* in PERSPECTIVES.)

Travel

Birnbaum's Florence 1992, edited by Stephen Birnbaum and Alexandra Mayes Birnbaum (HarperCollins; $10).
Birnbaum's Rome 1992, edited by Stephen Birnbaum and Alexandra Mayes Birnbaum (HarperCollins; $10).
Birnbaum's Venice 1992, edited by Stephen Birnbaum and Alexandra Mayes Birnbaum (HarperCollins; $10).
Florence Explored, by Rupert Scott (New Amsterdam Books; $14.95).
Italian Country Inns and Villas, by Karen Brain (Warner Books; $12.95).
Italian Days, by Barbara Grizutti Harrison (Houghton Mifflin; $12.95).
Italian Gardens, by Alex Ramsey and Helena Attlee (Seven Hills Books; $19.95).
Italy: The Places in Between, by Kate Simon (HarperCollins; $12.95, paperback).
Playing Away, by Michael Mewshaw (Holt; $9.95).
Sicilian Carousel, by Lawrence Durrell (Viking; $14.95).
The Stones of Florence, by Mary McCarthy (Harcourt Brace Jovanovich; $7.95).
Venice Observed, by Mary McCarthy (Harcourt Brace Jovanovich; $4.95).
When in Rome: The Humorists' Guide to Italy, edited by Rober Wechsler (Catbird Press; $9.95).
The World of Venice, by James Morris (Harcourt Brace Jovanovich; $8.95, paperback).

History, Biography, and Culture

The Agony and the Ecstasy, by Irving Stone (Doubleday hardcover, $19.95; NAL paperback, $5.95).
The Architecture of the Italian Renaissance, by Peter Murray (Schocken; $10.95).
The Art of the Renaissance, by Linda and Peter Murray (World of Art Series, Thames and Hudson; $11.95).
Autobiography, by Benvenuto Cellini (Penguin Classics; $5.95).
The Book of the Courtier, by Baldassare Castiglione (Doubleday; $8.95).
Christopher Columbus, by Gianni Granzotto (University of Oklahoma Press; $11.95).
The Civilization of the Renaissance in Italy, by Jacob Burckhardt (HarperCollins; Vol. 1: $6.95; Vol. 2: $7.95).
A Concise Encyclopedia of the Italian Renaissance, edited by J. R. Hale (World of Art Series, Thames and Hudson; $11.95).
The Decline and Fall of the Roman Empire, by Edward Gibbon (Penguin; $6.95).
The Diary of the First Voyage of Christopher Columbus, edited by Oliver Dunn and James E. Kelly, Jr. (University of Oklahoma Press; $65 hardcover, $24.95 paperback).
Four Voyages of Christopher Columbus, by Cecil Jane (Dover Publications; $12.-95).
The High Renaissance and Mannerism, by Linda Murray (World of Art Series, Thames and Hudson; $11.95).
History of Italian Renaissance Art: Painting, Sculpture, Architecture, by Frederick Hartt (Abrams; $55).
The Italians, by Luigi Barzini (Atheneum; $9.95).
The Last Italian Portrait of a People, by William Murray (Prentice Hall Press; $21.95).
Lives of the Artists, by Giorgio Vasari (Penguin Classics; published in two volumes, $5.95 each).
Love and War in the Apennines, by Eric Newby (Penguin; $8.95).
The Prince, by Niccolò Machiavelli (Prometheus Books; $3.95).
The Romans, by R. H. Barrow (Penguin; $5.95).

Roman Art and Architecture, by Mortimer Wheeler (World of Art Series, Thames and Hudson; $11.95).
The Story of Art, by E. H. Gombrich (Prentice Hall; $36.67).
War in Val d'Orcia, by Iris Origo (Godine; $12.95).

Literature

The Assisi Murders, by Timothy Holme (Walker & Co.; $16.95).
Crown of Columbus, by Michael Dorris and Louise Erdrich (HarperCollins; $22).
The Evening of the Holiday, by Shirley Hazzard (Penguin; $6.95).
The Marshall and the Madwomen, by Magdalen Nabb (Penguin; $3.95).
The Name of the Rose, by Umberto Eco (Warner Books; $5.95).
A Room with A View, by E.M. Forster (Penguin; $4.50).
Summer's Lease, by John Mortimer (Penguin; $7.95).

Food, Wine, and Shopping

Celebrating Italy, by Carol Field (William Morrow; $24.95).
The Classic Italian Cook Book and More Classic Italian Cooking, by Marcella Hazan (Knopf hardcover, $25; Ballantine paperback; $5.95).
Eating In Italy: A Traveler's Guide to the Gastronomic Pleasures of Northern Italy, by Faith Heller Willinger (Morrow; $12.45).
The Food of Italy, by Waverley Root (Vintage; $10.95).
Honey from a Weed, by Patience Gray (North Point Press; $15.95).
Italian Wine, by Victor Hazan (Knopf; $18.95).
Italy the Beautiful Cookbook, by Lorenza de Medici (Knapp Press; $39.95).
Made in Italy: A Shopper's Guide to Rome, Florence, Venice, and Milan, by Annie Brody and Patricia Schultz (Workman Publishers; $14.95).
Marling Menu-Master for Italy, by Clare F. and William E. Marling (Altarinda Books; $5.95).
Pasta Classica, by Julia Della Croce (Penguin; $25).
Simon & Schuster's Guide to Italian Wines (Simon & Schuster; $8.95, paperback).
A Table in Tuscany, by Leslie Forbes (Penguin; $14.95).
The Wine Atlas of Italy, by Burton Anderson (Simon & Schuster; $40).
Vino, by Burton Anderson's (Little, Brown; $29.95).
Wines of Italy, by David Gleave (Price Stearn; $12.95).

In addition, *Culturgrams* is a handy series of pamphlets that provides a good sampling of information on the people, cultures, sights, and bargains to be found in over 90 countries around the world. Each four-page, newsletter-size leaflet covers one country, and Italy is included in the series. The topics included range from customs and courtesies to lifestyles and demographics. These fact-filled pamphlets are published by the David M. Kennedy Center for International Studies at Brigham Young University; for an order form contact the group c/o Publication Services (280 HRCB, Provo, UT 84602; phone: 801-378-6528). When ordering from 1 to 5 *Culturgrams,* the price is $1 each; 6 to 49 pamphlets cost 50¢ each; and for larger quantities, the price per copy goes down proportionately.

Another source of cultural information is *Do's and Taboos Around the World,* compiled by the Parker Pen Company and edited by Roger E. Axtell. It focuses on protocol, customs, etiquette, hand gestures and body language, gift giving, the dangers of using US jargon, and so on, and can be fun to read even if you're not going anyplace. It's available for $10.95 in bookstores or through John Wiley & Sons, 1 Wiley Dr., Somerset, NJ 08875 (phone: 908-469-4400).

Sources – The books listed above may be ordered directly from the publishers or found in the travel section of any good general bookstore or any sizable public library. If you still can't find something, the following stores and/or mail-order houses also specialize in travel literature. They offer books on the US along with guides to the rest of the world, and in some cases, even an old Baedeker or two.

Book Passage (51 Tamal Vista Blvd., Corte Madera, CA 94925; phone: 415-927-0960 in California; 800-321-9785 elsewhere in the US). Travel guides and maps to all areas of the world. A free catalogue is available.

The Complete Traveller (199 Madison Ave., New York, NY 10016; phone: 212-685-9007). Travel guides and maps. A catalogue is available for $2.

Forsyth Travel Library (PO Box 2975, Shawnee Mission, KS 66201-1375; phone: 800-367-7984 or 913-384-3440). Travel guides and maps, old and new, to all parts of the world, including Italy. Ask for the "Worldwide Travel Books and Maps" catalogue.

Gourmet Guides (2801 Leavenworth Ave., San Francisco, CA 94133; phone: 415-771-3671). Travel guides and maps, along with cookbooks. Mail-order lists available on request.

Phileas Fogg's Books and Maps (87 *Stanford Shopping Center,* Palo Alto, CA 94304; phone: 800-533-FOGG or 415-327-1754). Travel guides, maps, and language aids.

Tattered Cover (2955 E. First Ave., Denver, CO 80206; phone: 800-833-9327 or 303-322-7727). The travel department alone of this enormous bookstore carries over 7,000 books, as well as maps and atlases. No catalogue is offered (the list is too extensive), but a newsletter, issued three times a year, is available on request.

Thomas Brothers Maps & Travel Books (603 W. Seventh St., Los Angeles, CA 90017; phone: 213-627-4018). Maps (including road atlases, street guides, and wall maps), guidebooks, and travel accessories.

Traveller's Bookstore (22 W. 52nd St., New York, NY 10019; phone: 212-664-0995). Travel guides, maps, literature, and accessories. A catalogue is available for $2.

In addition, *Rizzoli Editore,* the Italian publishing company, has several bookstores in the US. The stores carry a vast array of books of all publishers, a great selection of art and architecture books, and numerous travel guides to various countries, particularly English- and Italian-language guides to Italy. They also carry newspapers, magazines, and records from Italy and publications of the *Italian Touring Club* (in Italian). The largest store is *Rizzoli International Bookstore & Gallery* (31 W. 57th St., New York, NY 10019; phone: 212-759-2424). Other locations are as follows:

Boston: Copley Place, 100 Huntington Ave., Boston, MA 02116 (phone: 617-437-0700).

Chicago: Water Tower Place, 835 N. Michigan Ave., Chicago, IL 60611 (phone: 312-642-3500).

Costa Mesa, CA: South Coast Plaza, 3333 Bristol, Costa Mesa, CA 92626 (phone: 714-957-3331).

New York City: 454 West Broadway, New York, NY 10012 (phone: 212-674-1616); 3 World Financial Center, Winter Garden, New York, NY 10281 (phone: 212-385-1400); and in *Bloomingdale's,* 59th St. and Lexington Ave., New York, NY 10022 (212-705-2156).

Williamsburg, VA: Merchant's Square, Williamsburg, VA 23187 (phone: 804-229-9821).

NEWSPAPERS AND MAGAZINES: A subscription to the *International Herald Tribune* also is a good idea for dedicated travelers. This English-language newspaper is written and edited mostly in Paris, and is *the* newspaper read most regularly and avidly by Americans abroad to keep up with world news, US news, sports, the stock market (US and foreign), fluctuations in the exchange rate, and an assortment of help-wanted ads, real estate listings, and personals, global in scope. Published 6 days a week (Saturday and Sunday are combined in one edition), it is available at newsstands throughout the US and in cities worldwide. In addition to being available on newsstands in Italy (particularly in major cities such as Rome), larger hotels may have copies in the lobby for guests — if you don't see a copy, ask the hotel concierge if it is available. A 1-year's subscription in the US costs $349. To subscribe, write or call the Subscription Manager, *International Herald Tribune,* 850 Third Ave., 10th Floor, New York, NY 10022 (phone: 800-882-2884 or 212-752-3890).

Among the major US publications that can be bought in Italy (generally a day or two after distribution in the US) in many of larger cities and resort areas, at hotels, airports, and newsstands, are the *The New York Times, USA Today,* and the *Wall Street Journal.* As with other imports, expect these and other US publications to cost more in Italy than in the US.

Before or after your trip, you may want to subscribe to a publication that specializes in information about Italy. A very interesting magazine for Italophiles is *Italy Italy,* which comes out 6 times a year, full of beautifully illustrated travel articles bound to whet your appetite for a visit or to provoke nostalgia for a return. Subscriptions are available for $30 a year from *Speedimpex,* 45-45 39th St., Long Island City, NY 11104 (phone: 718-392-7477).

Italians are well known for their fine food, and sampling the regional fare is likely to be one of the highlights of any visit. You will find reading about local edibles worthwhile before you go or after you return. *Gourmet,* a magazine specializing in food, frequently features mouth-watering articles on Italian *cucina,* although its scope is much broader. It is available at newsstands throughout the US for $2.50 an issue or for $18 a year from *Gourmet* (PO Box 53780, Boulder, CO 80322; phone: 800-365-2454). There are numerous additional magazines for every special interest available; check at your library information desk for a directory of such publications, or look over the selection offered by a well-stocked newsstand.

NEWSLETTERS: Throughout GETTING READY TO GO we have mentioned specific newsletters which our readers may be interested in consulting for further information. One of the very best sources of detailed travel information is *Consumer Reports Travel Letter.* Published monthly by Consumers Union (PO Box 53629, Boulder, CO 80322-3629; phone: 800-999-7959), it offers comprehensive coverage of the travel scene on a wide variety of fronts. A year's subscription costs $37; 2 years, $57.

The following travel newsletters also provide useful up-to-date information on travel services and bargains:

Entree (PO Box 5148, Santa Barbara, CA 93150; phone: 805-969-5848). This newsletter caters to a sophisticated, discriminating traveler with the means to explore the places mentioned. Subscribers have access to a 24-hour hotline providing information on restaurants and accommodations around the world. Monthly; a year's subscription costs $59.

The Hideaway Report (Harper Associates, PO Box 50, Sun Valley, ID 83353; phone: 208-622-3193). This monthly source highlights retreats — including Italian idylls — for sophisticated travelers. A year's subscription costs $90.

Romantic Hideaways (217 E. 86th St., Suite 258, New York, NY 10028; phone: 212-969-8682). This monthly newsletter leans toward those special places made for those traveling in twos. A year's subscription costs $65.

Travel Smart (Communications House, 40 Beechdale Rd., Dobbs Ferry, NY 10522; phone: 914-693-8300 in New York; 800-327-3633 elsewhere in the US).

This monthly covers a wide variety of trips and travel discounts. A year's subscription costs $44.

■ **Computer Services:** Anyone who owns a personal computer and a modem can subscribe to a database service providing everything from airline schedules and fares to restaurant listings. Two such services of particular use to travelers are *CompuServe* (5000 Arlington Center Blvd., Columbus, OH 43220; phone: 800-848-8199 or 614-457-8600; $39.95 to join, plus usage fees of $6 to $12.50 per hour) and *Prodigy Services* (445 Hamilton Ave., White Plains, NY 10601; phone: 800-822-6922 or 914-993-8000; $12.95 per month's subscription, plus variable usage fees). Before using any computer bulletin-board services, be sure to take precautions to prevent downloading of a computer "virus." First install one of the programs designed to screen out such nuisances.

Genealogy Hunts

Unfortunately for modern-day pretenders to the throne, only a privileged few will find their ancestral roots reverently inscribed in the exclusive *Libro d'Oro della Nobiltà Italiana* (Golden Book of the Italian Nobility), published by the *Istituto Araldico Romano* (Via Santa Maria dell'Anima, Rome 00186; phone: 6-1395) and available in most genealogical libraries. This is just as well. The monarchy was outlawed in Italy in 1946, and having to check if you're listed in the *Libro d'Oro* is like wanting to know the price of a Lamborghini — if you have to ask, it's not for you. Also, be forewarned that there are no proven extant lines of descent extending back to the ancient Etruscans, Greeks, or Romans, despite many impassioned claims to the contrary. (However, if behavior is any indication of kinship, these claims may have some basis. The ancient Romans were so eager to prove that they had descended from the city's founding fathers that they had their *sacra gentilica* — family tree, Roman style — painted on the walls of their homes, and fake ancestor portraits and spurious pedigrees were not unknown even then. Rather than dusty canvases, though, these parvenus proudly displayed phony portrait busts, and Aeneas replaced the *Mayflower* as the preferred point of ancestral departure.)

Happily for contemporary ancestor worshipers, Italians have kept meticulous records, beginning as far back as the 13th century, and legitimate evidence of Italian forebears — no matter how humble their origins — usually is yours for the searching. With a little digging around, there's a good change that you'll be able to visit the church where your Great Uncle Sal married your Great Aunt Rosa before leaving for America, or the port where your grandfather waved good-bye to the Old Country, or the cemetery where your mother's family has been resting quietly for centuries.

Constructing a family tree is a backward process: You need to start with your parents' dates and places of birth, their parents' dates and birthplaces, and so on — as far back as your search will take you. It should be a considerable stretch since it's quite possible to trace Italian families to about 1500, when it became obligatory for baptisms to be registered in parish churches. To obtain the relevant documents, make sure you have the exact names of each ancestor (remember, many Italian surnames were irrevocably, if unwittingly, changed through clerical misspellings at Ellis Island and other ports of entry), as well as the names of any family members closely related to the ancestor you are researching. You can request many different types of documents that contain information about a previous generation: for example, birth and death certificates, marriage licenses, emigration and immigration records, and baptism and christening records.

PRELIMINARY RESEARCH: Try to gather as much information as possible before your trip. For example, check with your local library and state offices for local published records, regional archives, and local history. The US Library of Congress (Local History and Genealogy Room, Jefferson Building, Washington, DC 20540; phone: 202-707-5537) and the New York Public Library (Division of United States History, Local History, and Genealogy, Room 315N, 42nd St. & 5th Ave., New York, NY 10018; phone: 212-930-0828) both have extensive facilities for in-person research, but you may want to call these institutions in advance to find out if they do have material relevant to your search.

The *Family History Library of the Church of Jesus Christ of Latter-Day Saints* has more than 32,000 reels of Italian genealogical records on microfilm, available for consultation in person at its headquarters (35 North West Temple St., Salt Lake City, UT 84150; phone: 801-240-2331) or through any of its branch libraries. Using the Mormons' index reels, you can, for a small fee, borrow from Salt Lake City microfilm records of any Italian town. Film should arrive at the branch library in about 6 weeks, and loans are renewable for 2-week periods up to 6 months. There is no charge for reviewing a film at the headquarters in Salt Lake City.

The *Italian Cultural Institute* (for addresses see *Tourist Information Offices,* above) publishes an information sheet on how to go about researching your Italian ancestry. Look in your library for T. Beard and D. Demong's *How to Find Your Family Roots* (McGraw-Hill, 1977), which contains an excellent list of genealogical resources available in both Italian and English.

An indispensable resource found in most libaries is the scholarly reference guide, *The World of Learning* (Europa Publications), which lists libraries and archives throughout Italy. Also look in your library for T. Beard's and D. Demong's comprehensive *How to Find Your Family Roots* (McGraw-Hill, 1977), which contains an excellent list of available genealogical resources. *In Search of Your European Roots* by Angus Baxter (Geneological Publishing Co., 1985) contains an excellent chapter on Italy.

Several other books worth consulting include the *International Vital Records Handbook* ($24.95), by Thomas Jay Kemp, and *Do's and Don't's for Ancestor-Hunters* ($10.95) by Angus Baxter. Both are available from the Genealogical Publishing Company (1001 N. Calvert St., Baltimore, MD 21202-3897; phone: 301-837-8271).

Further tips can be provided by *Omnibus,* a publication of the Augustan Society (PO Box P, Torrance, CA 90508; phone: 213-320-7766). This magazine, which comes out once or twice a year, includes information on genealogy for those researching their family history in any of several European countries, including Italy. A 4 years' subscription costs $40. You also may want to subscribe to the *Ancestry Newsletter,* edited by Robb Barr and published bimonthly by Ancestry Incorporated (PO Box 476, Salt Lake City, UT 84110; phone: 800-531-1790). It contains practical information on how to research your ancestry. A 1 year's subscription costs $12.

REQUESTING RECORDS: Before 1865, personal records — baptism, confirmation, marriage, and death — were kept, as a rule, only by parish churches. Thus, to obtain information on your family prior to 1865, you should begin by writing either to the parish priest or to the bishop holding territorial jurisdiction. Since 1865, birth, marriage, death, and citizenship records have been kept by the *comuni* (municipalities), so you must write to the *comune* from which your ancestors came. Address your request to the *Ufficio di Stato Civile* in the town where the birth, death, or marriage took place. While many of the offices have English-speaking personnel, making a request in Italian usually will facilitate matters considerably. The form letter given below will be of great use in your research (send a separate letter for each ancestor).

In Italy, the Ministry of Foreign Affairs (Ministero degli Affari Esteri, 1 Piazzale Farnesina, Rome 00194; phone: 6-63691) has an Office for Research and Studies of Emigration (Ufficio Ricerche e Studi dell'Emigrazione), which may be of assistance.

DIGGING DEEPER: Once you've done your basic research, you might want to turn to some older records or even use them as duplicates to verify information you've already accumulated. The following are some of the records most readily available by mail or in person.

Certificates of Family Genealogy – Write to the General Records Office (Ufficio Anagrafe) in the town where your family member lived to obtain a certificate of your family genealogy *(certificato di stato di famiglia)* giving names, relationships, birthdates, and birthplaces of all living family members at the time of recording. These certificates usually date from about the turn of the century and can go back as far as 1869.

Emigration Records – Write to the prefecture of the province of the emigrant's birthplace or port of departure to obtain documentation of an ancestor's emigration from about 1869 to the present. Addresses of provincial prefectures are available from *Unione delle Province d'Italia,* 4 Piazza Cardelli, Rome 00186 (phone: 6-687-3672).

Draft Records – For draft records dating from 1869 to the present, write to the military district in charge of an ancestor's town of residence (*Distretto Militare,* name of town), giving birthdates and birthplaces. Some conscription records go back to the Napoleonic era (as early as 1792).

Clerical Surveys – To obtain Catholic parish records *(status animarum),* contact the Central Office for Italian Emigration (UCEI, 3 Via Chiavari, Rome 00186; phone: 6-686-1200) for addresses of local parishes. Records of birthdates, marriage dates, and other biographical information exist, irregularly, from the beginning of the 18th century.

Protestant Parish Registers – Write to the *Genealogical Society* in Salt Lake City (address above) for the addresses of 16 Waldensian parishes in the Piedmont district. The parish records include information similar to Catholic clerical surveys and date from 1685.

Roman Catholic Parish Records – Write to the vicar-general of the diocese involved (you can get the address from the Central Office for Italian Emigration, above) for permission to consult the records, which usually are written in Latin. Baptism and christening records, as well as marriage records, date from 1545 (1493 in the town of Fiesole) to the present. Death and burial records go back to the beginning of the 17th century.

Tax Assessment or Census Registers – Write to the *Istituto Centrale di Statistica* (16 Via Cesare Balbo, Rome 00184; phone: 6-46731) to locate the old census data *(catasti),* also called *libri di fuochi* in southern Italy and *libri degli estimi* in the north. Often dating from the 14th century, these contain so-called real estate records (actually tax records — census takers were no fools even then) of heads of households, subtenants, or taxpayers and their residences along with the amount of tax assessed. Most of the records are located in the *Archivio Segreto del Vaticano* in Rome, the *Archivio di Stato* in Florence, and the archives of the Kingdom of the Two Sicilies in Naples.

Ecclesiastical Records – For clerical records from the 13th to the 19th century, write to the *Archivio Segreto,* Città del Vaticano Rome 00185 (phone: 6-6982).

Notarial Records – Contact the Ispettore Generale of the *Archivio Notarile* (89 Via Padre Semeria, Rome 00154; phone: 6-512-6951) for records concerning wills, donations, settlements, and land sales dating from about 1340. For similar records from Waldensian Protestant archives beginning in 1610, contact the Ispettore Generale of the *Archivio di Stato di Torino,* 165 Piazza Castello, Turin 10122 (phone: 11-540382).

Other Archives – *Archivio Centrale dello Stato,* the Italian national archives, are located in a central office (Piazzale degli Archivi, Rome 00144; phone: 6-592-6204); more complete records are kept in the various former independent states that existed before the unification of Italy. There are substantial archival centers in Bologna, Florence, Genoa, Lucca, Mantua, Milan, Modena, Naples, Palermo, Parma, Siena, and Venice.

RESEARCH SERVICES: For those who would rather leave the digging to others, reputable genealogical societies in Italy will do it for you for a fee. Among them are the following:

Istituto Araldico Coccia (Count Ildebrando Coccia Urbani, director; 6 Borgo Santa Croce, Palazzo Antinori, Casella Postale 458, Florence 50122; phone: 55-242914). Write for their "international ready reckoner," which lists six programs for heraldic and genealogical research.

Istituto Araldico Genealogico Italiano (Count Guelfo Guelfi Camaiani, director; 27 Via Santo Spirito, Florence 50125; phone: 55-213090).

Istituto Storico Araldico Genealogico Internazionale (Count Luciano Pelliccioni di Poli, director; 5 Via Pio VIII, Rome 00165; no phone).

Ufficio di Consulenza Tecnica (Presso Collegio Araldico, 16 Via Santa Maria dell'Anima, Rome 00185; phone: 6-1395).

With the above information and a little *pazienza* (patience), you should have a firm grasp for a lengthy climb up your Italian family tree.

The following letter states that you wish to know the history of your family and therefore are requesting the document or documents specified regarding the person indicated by name, place of birth, and date of birth; it thanks the addressee in advance for his or her kind attention to your request.

Ufficio dei Registri di Stato Civile
Comune di (Name of municipality)
Provincia di (Name of province)
Italy

Gentilissimi Signori:

Desiderando conoscere la storia della mia famiglia, chiedo se cortesemente potreste inviarmi i seguenti certificati:

(*Check the documents desired.*)

_____ certificato di nascita (*birth certificate*)
_____ certificato di matrimonio (*marriage certificate*)
_____ certificato di morte (*death certificate*)

riguardante la persona seguente:

(*Fill in the appropriate information for your ancestor.*)

(*for a man*) Il Signor: _____ (*name of man*) _____
(*for a woman*) La Signora: _____ (*name of woman*) _____
nato/a a: _____ (*place of birth*) _____
il: _____ (*date of birth*) _____

Ringraziando Vi anticipatamente per la Vostra cortese attenzione, spero di ricevere al più presto notizie.

Distinti saluti,
(*sender's signature*)
(*name of sender*)

Weights and Measures

When traveling in Italy, you'll find that just about every quantity, whether it is distance, length, weight, or capacity, will be expressed in unfamiliar terms. In fact, this is true for travel almost everywhere in the world, since the US is one of the last countries to make its way to the metric system. Your trip to Italy will serve to familiarize you with what one day may be the weights and measures at your grocery store.

There are some specific things to keep in mind during your trip. Fruits and vegetables at a market are recorded in kilos (kilograms), as is your luggage at the airport and your body weight. (This latter is particularly pleasing to people of significant size, who instead of weighing 220 pounds hit the scales at a mere 100 kilos.) A kilo equals 2.2 pounds and 1 pound is .45 kilo. Body temperature is measured in degrees centigrade or Celsius rather than on the Fahrenheit scale, so that a normal body temperature is 37C, not 98.6F, and freezing is 0 degrees C rather than 32F.

Gasoline is sold by the liter (approximately 3.8 liters to 1 gallon). Tire pressure gauges and other equipment measure in kilograms per square centimeter rather than pounds per square inch. Highway signs are written in kilometers rather than miles (1 mile equals 1.6 kilometers; 1 kilometer equals .62 mile). And speed limits are in kilometers per hour, so think twice before hitting the gas when you see a speed limit of 100. That means 62 miles per hour.

The tables and conversion factors listed below should give you all the information you will need to understand any transaction, road sign, or map you encounter during your travels.

APPROXIMATE EQUIVALENTS

Metric Unit	Abbreviation	US Equivalent
LENGTH		
meter	m	39.37 inches
kilometer	km	.62 mile
millimeter	mm	.04 inch
CAPACITY		
liter	l	1.057 quarts
WEIGHT		
gram	g	.035 ounce
kilogram	kg	2.2 pounds
metric ton	MT	1.1 tons
ENERGY		
kilowatt	kw	1.34 horsepower

CONVERSION TABLES
METRIC TO US MEASUREMENTS

Multiply:	by:	to convert to:
LENGTH		
millimeters	.04	inches
meters	3.3	feet
meters	1.1	yards
kilometers	.6	miles
CAPACITY		
liters	2.11	pints (liquid)
liters	1.06	quarts (liquid)
liters	.26	gallons (liquid)
WEIGHT		
grams	.04	ounces (avoir.)
kilograms	2.2	pounds (avoir.)
US TO METRIC MEASUREMENTS		
LENGTH		
inches	25.0	millimeters
feet	.3	meters
yards	.9	meters
miles	1.6	kilometers
CAPACITY		
pints	.47	liters
quarts	.95	liters
gallons	3.8	liters
WEIGHT		
ounces	28.0	grams
pounds	.45	kilograms

TEMPERATURE

°F = (°C × 9/5) + 32   °C = (°F − 32) × 5/9

Cameras and Equipment

Vacations are everybody's favorite time for taking pictures and home movies. After all, most of us want to remember the places we visit — and show them off to others. Here are a few suggestions to help you get the best results from your travel photography or videography.

BEFORE THE TRIP

If you're taking your camera or camcorder out after a long period in mothballs, or have just bought a new one, check it thoroughly before you leave to prevent unexpected breakdowns or disappointing pictures.

1. Still cameras should be cleaned carefully and thoroughly, inside and out. If using a camcorder, run a head cleaner through it. You also may want to have your camcorder professionally serviced (opening the casing yourself will violate the manufacturer's warranty). Always use filters to protect your lens while traveling.
2. Check the batteries for your camera's light meter and flash, and take along extras just in case yours wear out during the trip. For camcorders, bring along extra Nickel-Cadmium (Ni-Cad) batteries; if you use rechargeable batteries, a recharger will cut down on the extras.
3. Using all the settings and features, shoot at least one test roll of film or one videocassette, using the type you plan to take along with you.

EQUIPMENT TO TAKE ALONG

Keep your gear light and compact. Items that are too heavy or bulky to be carried comfortably on a full-day excursion will likely remain in your hotel room.

1. Invest in a broad camera or camcorder strap if you now have a thin one. It will make carrying the camera much more comfortable.
2. A sturdy canvas, vinyl, or leather camera or camcorder bag, preferably with padded pockets (not an airline bag), will keep your equipment organized and easy to find. If you will be doing much shooting around the water, a waterproof case is best.
3. For cleaning, bring along a camel's hair brush that retracts into a rubber squeeze bulb. Also take plenty of lens tissue, soft cloths, and plastic bags to protect equipment from dust and moisture.

■ **Note:** If you are planning on using your camcorder in Europe, note that most European countries (including Italy) operate on a different electrical current than the US, so you should make sure that the battery charger that comes with your camcorder is compatible with the current in the countries you're visiting. You'll also need a plug adapter kit to cope with the variations in plug configurations found in Europe. And don't expect to be able to play back your tape through a European TV set or VCR. The US and Canada use a different television standard than most European countries; these systems are incompatible with each other and multiple-standard TV sets are rare.

FILM AND TAPES: If you are concerned about airport security X-rays damaging undeveloped film (X-rays do not affect processed film) or tapes, store them in one of the lead-lined bags sold in camera shops. In the US and Canada, incidents of X-ray damage to unprocessed film (exposed or unexposed) are few because low-dosage X-ray equipment is used virtually everywhere. However, when crossing international borders, travelers should know that foreign X-ray equipment used for carry-on baggage may deliver higher levels of radiation and that even more powerful X-ray equipment may be used for checked luggage, so it's best to carry your film on board. If you're traveling without a protective bag, you may want to ask to have your photo equipment inspected by hand. In the US, Federal Aviation Administration regulations require that if you request a hand inspection, you get it, but overseas the response may depend on the humor of the inspector.

One type of film that should never be subjected to X-rays is the very high speed ASA

1000; there are lead-lined bags made especially for it — and, in the event that you are refused a hand inspection, this is the only way to save your film. The walk-through metal detector devices at airports do not affect film, though the film cartridges may set them off. Because cassettes have been favorite carriers for terrorist explosives over the years, airport officials probably will insist that you put these through the X-ray machine as well. If you don't have a choice, put them through and hope for the best.

You should have no problem finding film or tapes throughout Europe. When buying film, tapes, or photo accessories the best rule of thumb is to stick to name brands with which you are familiar. Different countries have their own ways of labeling camcorder tapes, and although the variations in recording and playback standards won't affect your ability to use the tape, they will affect how quickly you record and how much time you actually have to record on the tape. The availability of film processing labs and equipment repair shops will vary from area to area.

■ **A note about courtesy and caution:** When photographing individuals in Italy (and anywhere else in the world), ask first. It's common courtesy. Furthermore, some governments have security regulations regarding the use of cameras and will not permit the photographing of certain subjects, such as particular government and military installations. When in doubt, ask.

Useful Words and Phrases

Unlike the French, who have a reputation for being snobbish and brusque if you don't speak their language perfectly, the Italians do not expect you to speak Italian — but are very flattered when you try. In many circumstances, you won't have to, because staffs at most hotels and tourist attractions, as well as at a fair number of restaurants, speak serviceable English, or at least a modicum of it, which they usually are eager to improve — and that means practicing on you. If you find yourself in a situation where your limited Italian is the only means of communication, take the plunge. Don't be afraid of misplaced accents or misconjugated verbs. (Italians themselves often lapse into the all-purpose infinitive form of the verb when speaking with a novice.) In most cases you will be understood and then will be advised on the menu, or pointed in the right direction. The list on the following pages is a selection of commonly used words and phrases to speed you on your way.

Note that in Italian, nouns are either masculine or feminine, as well as singular or plural, and the adjectives that modify them must correspond. Most nouns ending in *o* are masculine; the *o* becomes an *i* in the plural. The masculine articles are *un* (indefinite), *il* (definite singular), and *i* (definite plural), except before words beginning with the *s* sound (however spelled) and with *i* + vowel, where they are *uno, lo,* and *gli.* Most nouns ending in *a* are feminine; the *a* becomes *e* in the plural. The feminine articles are *una* (indefinite), *la* (definite singular), and *le* (definite plural). Final vowels or articles usually are contracted to an apostrophe (') before words beginning with vowels, as in *l'acqua* (the water). Singular nouns ending in *e* can be either masculine or feminine; *e* becomes *i* in the plural. Adjectives follow the nouns they modify.

Italy has several markedly different regional dialects, each with its own vocabulary and pronunciation rules. There is, however, a relatively generally accepted standard used on national radio and television and understood, if not used, by almost everybody. Traditional spelling reflects standard pronunciation fairly well. These suggestions should help you pronounce most words intelligibly.

i is pronounced as in *machine.*
e is pronounced with a sound somewhere between the vowels of *let* and *late.* It is never diphthongized, as in *lay.* Final *e* is never silent.

a is pronounced as in *father.*
o is pronounced with a sound somewhere between the vowels of *ought* and *boat.* It is never diphthongized, as in *know.*
u is pronounced as in *rude.*

In vowel letter sequences, both vowels are pronounced; *i* and *u* before vowels usually are pronounced *y* and *w,* respectively.

Italian consonants are pronounced as in English with these exceptions:

Consonants spelled double are pronounced double. Compare the *k* sounds of blacker (single consonant) and black cur (double consonant), and the *d* sounds of the Italian *cade* (he falls) and *cadde* (he fell).
p and *t* are unaspirated; that is, they are pronounced as in *spit* and *stop,* not as in *pit* and *top.*
t and *d* are dental; the tongue tip touches the upper teeth, not the gums.
s before a vowel or between a vowel and a voiced consonant *(b, d, g, v, m, n, l, r)* is pronounced *z.*
ci stands for *ch* (as in English *chip*), as does *c* before *e* or *i: ciao!* is pronounced *chow.*
gh always stands for *g,* as in English *ghost.*
gi stands for *j,* as does *g* before *e* or *i: buon giorno* is pronounced *bwon jorno.*
gn stands for the medial consonant of English *canyon: bagno* (bath) is pronounced *banyo.*
gl stands for the medial consonant of English *billion: gli* (pronoun and article) is pronounced *lyee.*
h is never pronounced.
q is pronounced as *k; qu* is pronounced *kw: cinque* (five) is pronounced *chinkweh.*
r is "rolled," as it is in Spanish or Scots.
z is pronounced *dz* word initially; within words it is pronounced either *dz* or *ts,* depending on the word.

More often than not, the vowel preceding the last consonant in the word is accented. Final vowels marked with an accent are stressed.

These are only the most basic rules, and even they may seem daunting at first, but they shouldn't remain so for long. Nevertheless, if you can't get your mouth to speak Italian, try your hands at it: With a little observation, you'll pick it up quickly and be surprised at how often your message will get across.

Greetings and Everyday Expressions

Good morning! (also, Good day!)	*Buon giorno!*
Good evening!	*Buona sera!*
Hello!	
(familiar)	*Ciao!*
(on the telephone)	*Pronto!*
How are you?	*Come sta?*
Pleased to meet you!	*Piacere!* or *Molto lieto/a!*
Good-bye!	*Arrivederci!*
(final)	*Addio!*
So long! (familiar)	*Ciao!*
Good night!	*Buona notte!*
Yes!	*Sì!*
No!	*No!*
Please!	*Per favore* or *per piacere!*

Thank you!	*Grazie!*
You're welcome!	*Prego!*
Excuse me!	
(I beg your pardon.)	*Mi scusi!*
(May I get by?; on a bus or in a crowd)	*Permesso!*
I don't speak Italian.	*Non parlo italiano.*
Do you speak English?	*Parla inglese?*
Is there someone there who speaks English?	*C'è qualcuno che parla inglese?*
I don't understand.	*Non capisco.*
Do you understand?	*Capisce?*
My name is . . .	*Mi chiamo . . .*
What is your name?	*Come si chiama?*
miss	*signorina*
madame	*signora*
mister	*signor(e)*
open	*aperto*
closed	*chiuso*
. . .for annual vacation	*chiuso per ferie*
. . .for weekly day of rest	*chiuso per riposo settimanale*
. . .for restoration	*chiuso per restauro*
Is there a strike?	*C'è uno sciopero?*
Until when?	*Fino a quando?*
entrance	*entrata*
exit	*uscita*
push	*spingere*
pull	*tirare*
today	*oggi*
tomorrow	*domani*
yesterday	*ieri*

Checking In

I would like. . .	*Vorrei. . .*
I have reserved. . .	*Ho prenotato. . .*
a single room	*una camera singola*
a double room	*una camera doppia*
a quiet room	*una camera tranquilla*
with private bath	*con bagno privato*
with private shower	*con doccia privata*
with a sea view	*con vista sul mare*
with air conditioning	*con aria condizionata*
with balcony	*con balcone/terrazza*
for one night	*per una notte*
for a few days	*per qualche giorno*
for a week	*per una settimana*
with full board	*con pensione completa*
with half board	*con mezza pensione*

Does the price include. . .	*Il prezzo comprende. . .*
breakfast	*la prima colazione*
service charge	*servizio*
taxes	*tasse*
What time is breakfast served?	*A che ora si serve la prima colazione?*
It doesn't work.	*Non funziona.*
May I pay with traveler's checks?	*Posso pagare con traveler's checks?*
Do you accept this credit card?	*Accettate questa carta di credito?*

Eating Out

ashtray	*un portacenere*
bottle	*una bottiglia*
chair	*una sedia*
cup	*una tazza*
fork	*una forchetta*
knife	*un coltello*
napkin	*un tovagliolo*
plate	*un piatto*
spoon	*un cucchiaio*
table	*una tavola*
beer	*una birra*
cocoa	*una cioccolata*
coffee	*un caffè* or *un espresso*
coffee with milk (served in a bar with steamed milk)	*un cappuccino*
(usually served at breakfast or at a bar, with warm milk — more than is in a cappuccino)	*un caffè latte*
fruit juice	*un succo di frutta*
lemonade	*una limonata*
mineral water	*acqua minerale*
carbonated	*gassata*
not carbonated	*non gassata*
orangeade	*un'aranciata*
tea	*un tè*
water	*acqua*
red wine	*vino rosso*
rosé wine	*vino rosato*
white wine	*vino bianco*
cold	*freddo/a*
hot	*caldo/a*
sweet	*dolce*
(very) dry	*(molto) secco*

bacon	*la pancetta*
bread/rolls	*il pane/i panini*
butter	*il burro*
eggs	*le uova*
hard-boiled	*un uovo sodo*
poached	*uova affogate/in camicia*
soft-boiled	*uova à la coque*
scrambled	*uova strapazzate*
sunny-side up	*uova fritte all'occhio di bue*
honey	*il miele*
jam/marmalade	*la confettura/la marmellata*
omelette	*la frittata*
orange juice	*la spremuta d'arancia*
pepper	*il pepe*
salt	*il sale*
sugar	*lo zucchero*

Waiter!	*Cameriere!*

I would like. . .	*Vorrei. . .*
a glass of	*un bicchiere di*
a bottle of	*una bottiglia di*
a half bottle of	*una mezza bottiglia di*
a carafe of	*una caraffa di*
a liter of	*un litro di*
a half liter of	*un mezzo litro di*
a quarter liter of	*un quarto di*

The check, please.	*Il conto, per favore.*
Is the service charge included?	*Il servizio è incluso?*

Shopping

bakery	*il panificio*
bookstore	*la libreria*
butcher shop	*la macelleria*
camera shop	*il negozio d'apparecchi fotografici*
delicatessen	*la salumeria/la pizzicheria*
department store	*il grande magazzino*
drugstore (for medicine)	*la farmacia*
grocery	*la drogheria/la pizzicheria*
jewelry store	*la gioielleria*
newsstand	*l'edicola/il giornalaio*
pastry shop	*la pasticceria*
perfume (and cosmetics) store	*la profumeria*
shoestore	*il negozio di scarpe*
supermarket	*il supermercato*
tobacconist	*il tabaccaio*

cheap	*a buon mercato*
expensive	*caro/a*
large	*grande*

larger	*più grande*
too large	*troppo grande*
small	*piccolo/a*
smaller	*più piccolo*
too small	*troppo piccolo*
long	*lungo/a*
short	*corto/a*
antique	*antico/a*
old	*vecchio/a*
new	*nuovo/a*
used	*usato/a*
handmade	*fatto/a a mano*
washable	*lavabile*
How much does it cost?	*Quanto costa?*
What is it made of?	*Di che cosa è fatto/a?*
camel's hair	*pelo di cammello*
cotton	*cotone*
corduroy	*velluto a coste*
lace	*pizzo*
leather	*pelle/cuoio*
linen	*lino*
silk	*seta*
suede	*pelle scamosciata*
synthetic material	*materiale sintetico*
wool	*lana*
brass	*ottone*
bronze	*bronzo*
copper	*rame*
gold	*oro*
gold plate	*placcato d'oro*
silver	*argento*
silver plate	*placcato d'argento*
stainless steel	*acciaio inossidabile*
wood	*legno*

Colors

beige	*beige*
black	*nero/a*
blue	*celeste* or *azzurro/a*
(navy)	*blu*
brown	*marrone*
gray	*grigio/a*
green	*verde*
orange	*arancio*
pink	*rosa*
purple	*viola*
red	*rosso/a*
white	*bianco/a*
yellow	*giallo/a*
dark	*scuro/a*
light	*chiaro/a*

Getting Around

north	*nord*
south	*sud*
east	*est*
west	*ovest*
right	*destra*
left	*sinistra*
straight ahead	*sempre diritto*
far	*lontano/a*
near	*vicino/a*
gas station	*la stazione di rifornimento/stazione per benzina*
train station	*la stazione ferroviaria*
bus stop	*la fermata dell'autobus*
subway	*la metropolitana*
airport	*l'aeroporto*
travel agency	*l'agenzia di viaggio*
map	*una carta geografica*
one-way ticket	*un biglietto di sola andata*
round-trip ticket	*un biglietto di andata e ritorno*
track	*il binario*
first class	*prima classe*
second class	*seconda classe*
no smoking	*non fumare/divieto di fumare*
tires	*le gomme/i pneumatici*
oil	*l'olio*
gasoline	
generic reference or regular (leaded) gas	*la benzina*
unleaded gas	*benzina verde* or *benzina senza piombo*
diesel gas	*diesel* or *gasolio*
Fill it up, please.	*Faccia il pieno, per favore.*
Where is . . . ?	*Dov'è . . . ?*
Where are . . . ?	*Dove sono . . . ?*
How many kilometers are we from . . . ?	*Quanti chilometri siamo da . . . ?*
Does this bus go to . . . ?	*Quest'autobus va a . . . ?*
What time does it leave?	*A che ora parte?*
Danger	*Pericolo*
Dead End	*Strada Senza Uscita*
Detour	*Deviazione*
Do Not Enter	*Vietato l'Accesso*
Falling Rocks	*Caduta Massi*
Men Working	*Lavori in Corso*
No Parking	*Divieto di Sosta*
No Passing	*Divieto di Sorpasso*
One Way	*Senso Unico*
Pay Toll	*Pagamento Pedaggio*
Pedestrian Zone	*Zona Pedonale*

Reduce Speed	*Rallentare*
Ring Road	*Raccordo Anulare*
Stop	*Alt*
Use Headlights in Tunnel	*Accendere i Fari in Galleria*
Yield	*Dare la Precedenza*

Personal Items and Services

aspirin	*l'aspirina*
Band-Aids	*i cerotti*
barbershop	*il barbiere*
beauty shop	*l'istituto di bellezza*
condom	*il profilattico/il preservativo*
dry cleaner	*la tintoria*
hairdresser	*il parucchiere per donna*
laundromat	*la lavanderia automatica*
laundry	*la lavanderia*
post office	*l'ufficio postale*
sanitary napkins	*gli assorbenti igienici*
shampoo	*lo shampoo*
shaving cream	*la crema da barba*
shoemaker	*il calzolaio*
soap	*il sapone*
soap powder	*il sapone in polvere*
stamps	*i francobolli*
tampons	*i tamponi*
tissues	*i fazzoletti di carta*
toilet	*il gabinetto/la toletta/il bagno*
toilet paper	*la carta igienica*
toothbrush	*lo spazzolino da denti*
toothpaste	*il dentifricio*
Where is the men's/ladies' room?	*Dov'è la toletta?*
The door will say:	
for men	*Uomini* or *Signori*
for women	*Donne* or *Signore*
Is it occupied/free?	*E occupato/libero?*

Days of the Week

Monday	*lunedì*
Tuesday	*martedì*
Wednesday	*mercoledì*
Thursday	*giovedì*
Friday	*venerdì*
Saturday	*sabato*
Sunday	*domenica*

Months

January	*gennaio*
February	*febbraio*
March	*marzo*
April	*aprile*
May	*maggio*
June	*giugno*

July	*luglio*
August	*agosto*
September	*settembre*
October	*ottobre*
November	*novembre*
December	*dicembre*

Numbers

zero	*zero*
one	*uno*
two	*due*
three	*tre*
four	*quattro*
five	*cinque*
six	*sei*
seven	*sette*
eight	*otto*
nine	*nove*
ten	*dieci*
eleven	*undici*
twelve	*dodici*
thirteen	*tredici*
fourteen	*quattordici*
fifteen	*quindici*
sixteen	*sedici*
seventeen	*diciassette*
eighteen	*diciotto*
nineteen	*diciannove*
twenty	*venti*
thirty	*trenta*
forty	*quaranta*
fifty	*cinquanta*
sixty	*sessanta*
seventy	*settanta*
eighty	*ottanta*
ninety	*novanta*
one hundred	*cento*

PERSPECTIVES

History

The 19th-century statesman Count Metternich dismissed Italy as no more than a "geographical expression." Although he was politically motivated to say this, as he pressed for Austria's interests in Venetia and Lombardy, his point was not without some merit. For Italy lagged far behind its European neighbors in developing a distinct *national* identity. It was not until 1870 — when its 20 regions were finally brought under one central government — that Italy became a unified political entity. Even into this century, the country has been divided geographically on certain governmental issues. Nevertheless, the Italian *cultural* identity has been in existence since antiquity. In fact, the name *Italy* has been used for more than 3,000 years to define this peninsula, a 1,500-mile-long landspit that stretches from the Alps into the Mediterranean.

Geography is the key to much of Italian history. In ancient times, the country's position in the Mediterranean, much like a bridge joining East and West, made it a logical way station for Greek civilization and later an effective "launching pad" for Roman conquest. On the other hand, Italy's more than 3,000 miles of coastline on the Adriatic, Ionian, and Tyrrhenian seas — as well as its 1,058-mile land frontier with France, Switzerland, and Austria — have made it an almost certain prey for foreign invaders and have contributed to the ethnic diversity of the population. At the same time, the peninsula's geographical structure, divided by the Apennine Mountains, has made possible sharply defined internal regions that developed — linguistically, artistically, politically, economically, and culturally — along noticeably distinct and separate lines. Even until fairly recent times, patriotism in Italy most often connoted loyalty and allegiance to one's home region rather than to the nation as a whole. From a historical point of view, however, Italy has always been a precise entity.

ORIGINS

The earliest known inhabitants of the Italian peninsula and islands were Latin and other Italic tribes who had settled there by 2000 BC. For the most part, these groups had only local influence and appear to have been unable to resist the sway of the Etruscans, whose origins remain controversial but who appeared in Italy about 1200 BC and who dominated vast areas of central Italy until the rise of Latin Rome.

By the 2nd millennium BC, Greek ships and traders had come with their goods, their crafts, and their culture. By the 8th century BC, the first Greek colonies were established in the Italian south, particularly in Calabria and Puglia. Sicily, and to a lesser degree Sardinia, became a battleground for rivalry between the Greeks and the Carthaginians, inhabitants of the Phoenician colony in North Africa that was allied with the Etruscans.

THE ROMANS

Rome was founded in 753 BC, when Latin and other villagers are believed to have settled on the Palatine hill. The ruler they chose was Romulus, said to be a descendant of Aeneas, Prince of Troy. Romulus was followed by three Sabine kings and by three Etruscans who left their mark in the identification they fostered between church and state.

In 509 BC, the city-state's great landowners ended the first monarchy and founded the Roman Republic. For centuries thereafter, Rome was the scene of struggle between the founding patricians and the plebeians, mostly urban artisans, who had been left out of the new power arrangements. The life of the Republic was increasingly disrupted by civil strife and social unrest, which culminated in the civil wars of the 1st century BC, the rise of Julius Caesar as emperor, his assassination by a group of angry senators in 44 BC, and the eventual establishment, in 27 BC, of the imperial monarchy under Caesar's nephew, the emperor Augustus.

Although the Roman Republic had been troubled by social problems, corruption, and power feuds among members of the ruling oligarchy, this period of Roman history witnessed the first successes of Roman military and political expansion. Paradoxically, it was probably an invasion by the Gauls into central Italy that led to the defeat and destruction of many Etruscan towns early in the 4th century BC and laid the groundwork for future Roman success.

The defeat of the Etruscans made Roman expansion northward easier in later years, and the Gallic threat also convinced many of the semi-independent Latin city-states to form alliances with Rome. For example, the ruling nobles of Capua, then the capital of the Campania region, enlisted the Romans to help against the marauding Samnite tribes of the Apennine Mountains. The eventual Roman victory, symbolized by the construction of the Appian Way from Rome to Capua, was only the first step in a series of conquests that extended Rome's power throughout the peninsula. The Republic's growing influence eventually led to conflict with some of the Greek colonies in Italy. With the defeat of Tarantum in the south in 272 BC and of the last Etruscan city, Volsinii, in 265 BC, the Romans became masters of the Italian mainland.

However, these conquests made war with Carthage inevitable. From Carthaginian bases in Spain, the great general Hannibal led his army overland through France and the Alps to Italy. He was stopped only by dissension at home. Then, in 202 BC, Carthage was defeated and destroyed by the Roman general Scipio Africanus. This victory also led to Roman rule of Spain and then Greece. The overseas empire had begun.

During the 1st century BC, Caesar conquered and colonized Gaul, a move designed as much to win him the loyalty of the Roman soldiers as to extend Rome's power further throughout Europe. When Augustus defeated Mark

Antony and the Egyptian Queen Cleopatra in 31 BC at Actium, Roman supremacy took another step forward.

Augustus's victory over Antony reestablished the Western orientation of the Roman Empire, stretching its frontiers from the Rhine and the Danube in the west to the Syrian Desert in the east. But continuing problems inside Rome threatened the stability of the regime, whose powers remained divided between the Senate and its oligarchs and the emperor. The reigns of Tiberius, Caligula, Claudius, and Nero were fraught with palace intrigues, the only major positive achievement being the conquest of Britain, begun by Claudius in AD 43.

During the 2nd century AD, under such emperors as Trajan, Hadrian, and Marcus Aurelius, periods of peace were interspersed with further territorial expansion. But by the end of Marcus Aurelius's reign, invasions by barbarians from the north had begun, and an outbreak of plague signaled the onset of a new period of chaos. With the death of Commodus, Marcus Aurelius's son, in AD 198, a series of new pretenders made their claims to the throne, and it was not until the accession of Diocletian in AD 284 that order, prosperity, and peace were at least temporarily restored. Diocletian saw that the Empire had become too big and divided its administration among himself and four other leaders. His successor, Constantine, moved the capital eastward, away from the invaders, and established Constantinople, making the split of the Empire into East and West inevitable.

With the sack of Rome in AD 410 by the Visigoths, the death knell of the Empire had inexorably sounded. Marauding German tribes gradually established kingdoms throughout the peninsula, and constant warfare brought influence increasingly into the hands of the army, while the emperors were weak and easily dethroned. The last Roman emperor in the West, Romulus Augustulus, was dethroned by a general of barbarian origin, Odoacer, in 476.

THE MIDDLE AGES

From 488 to 526, Theodoric, King of the Ostrogoths, ruled Italy from Ravenna, where he built beautiful monuments. Subsequently, the Byzantine Emperor Justinian defeated the Goths, only to open the way to new invasions by the Lombards, who set up their own dynasty. Meanwhile, the Roman papacy had become more influential, and in 754 Pope Stephen II asked Pepin, King of the Franks, to expel the Lombards. Pepin restored the city and its immediate territory to the papacy, thus establishing the basis of the future Papal States of Italy. A few decades later, Pope Leo II reestablished the form of the Western Roman Empire when he offered an imperial crown to Charlemagne, King of the Franks. However, in the north of Italy and in Rome itself, the authority of the Holy Roman Empire was often nominal, while in the south, there were repeated Saracen incursions, followed by later Norman invasions.

Beginning in the 11th century, under the formal authority of the German emperors — who were crowned in Rome but generally resided on the other side of the Alps — the towns and communities of northern and central Italy began a spurt of intense economic development and experimentation with self-rule. The major characteristics of life in these city-states, or "communes," as they were called, were government by constitution and by an elected official known variously as a *podestà* or *console* and the emergence of a merchant bourgeoisie and of a skilled urban artisan class. This situation contrasted markedly with that in the south, where the Norman King Roger II ruled Sicily and the southern mainland, and the feudal system became so firmly entrenched that its effects endured even into the 20th century, accounting for much of the difference between northern Italy and the *mezzogiorno* (south) today.

Thus, in northern and central Italy, civilization continued to mature. Venice was an independent state of international renown, and the cities of Lombardy, Umbria, and Tuscany, as well as others in Venetia, had growing cultural and trading ties with the rest of Europe. The constant conflict between pope and emperor was an unsettling factor at the time, however, reaching a high point when Frederick Barbarossa arrived with a 3,000-man invading force in 1154, seeking — unsuccessfully in the end — to unite Italy under his own authority. During the 12th and 13th centuries, most of Italy's city-states were forced to choose sides, becoming either Guelph (supporters of the papacy) or Ghibelline (allies of the emperor). Nevertheless, they prospered, even though by the middle of the 13th century a number of them were no longer democratically governed. They were now under the sway of important local families, or *signorie,* such as the Visconti of Milan (and later the Sforza), the Gonzaga of Mantua, the Malatesta of Rimini, the Este of Ferrara, and, eventually, the Medici of Florence.

Despite war, plague, and famine, the wealth and military strength of these families grew, increasing the power of the city-states they governed. There is no doubt that, as the Renaissance gathered momentum, two city-states in particular, Florence and Milan, were major players on the chessboard of Italian politics, along with the Papal States (which had recouped losses suffered during the 14th-century Babylonian captivity and the Great Schism), the still independent maritime republic of Venice, and Naples. Naples had fallen under the influence of the popes, who supported the unpopular Anjou princes, and, until the 15th century, helped fend off the Aragonese, who already were in control of Sicily.

The city-states were fully autonomous, and the courts of their ruling families often equaled or surpassed those of the great national royal families of Europe. Their courts also sponsored the most skilled and important Italian artists, writers, and scholars of the time. In this respect, none was as eminent as the city-state of Florence, ruled by the financially and politically skilled Cosimo de' Medici and later by his grandson, Lorenzo the Magnificent; these two were mostly responsible for the Tuscan city's power and prestige. Florence was, in fact, the linchpin in a formal alliance (called the Italian League) of the most powerful Italian states formed in the mid-15th century, largely at the pope's urgings, to protect Italy from foreign intervention. It was successful until the death of Lorenzo, in 1492, prompted events that led to its demise.

FOREIGN DOMINATIONS

As the alliance among the Italian states disintegrated, the French were encouraged to put forward their long-standing claims to Milan and Naples. In a series of army invasions toward the end of the 15th and beginning of the 16th centuries, the French succeeded in taking Milan twice and Naples once, but were routed after Charles V, the Hapsburg King of Spain, became Holy Roman Emperor and forged a defensive European alliance to contain the French.

For the next 200 years, the Spanish Hapsburgs were the major dominating force in Italy, with Milan, Naples, and Sicily given to King Philip II. Except for Venice and the duchy of Savoy-Piedmont, the other Italian states gradually came under Spanish domination. From an artistic and cultural point of view, the level of Italian civilization remained very high.

The War of the Spanish Succession (1701–13) ended with Austria's emergence as the dominant foreign power in Italy. The duchy of Tuscany gradually gained a reputation as one of the most liberal states in Europe, enforcing policies of free trade and suppressing ecclesiastical tribunals. Joseph II's reign in Milan was also influenced by the Enlightenment, and Naples became a major European intellectual center. However, the new sea routes to America and India led to the economic decline of most of Italy's coastal republics, although Venice's commercial downturn was to an extent hidden by its brilliance as a cultural center.

From the start, the French Revolution won support only from the liberal aristocracy and some segments of the middle class. Opposition was widespread and gradually solidified. Nevertheless, by 1806 Napoleon had annexed large portions of Italy, including Rome, Piedmont, and the Venetian possessions in Dalmatia. He abandoned the 1,200-year-old Venetian Republic to Austria and established the kingdom of Italy in central and northern Italy under his own control. In hindsight, the Napoleonic period was of great importance to Italy's future development as a modern state: The hegemony of Austria was shattered definitively; French laws and institutions left a decisive influence; trade and industry received a substantial impetus; and the invasion, combined with the intellectual influence of the Enlightenment, stimulated feelings of nationalism.

THE RISORGIMENTO

The Napoleonic period was brought to a close by the Congress of Vienna (1815) and the subsequent restoration of Europe's absolutist monarchies. Shortly thereafter, however, the influence of French ideas took hold in Italy, with the first liberal revolts in Naples (1820) and Turin (1821). The revolts were put down, and there was a general attack, particularly in Lombardy-Venetia, on the Carbonari and other "subversive" secret societies.

The French Revolution of 1830 stimulated another wave of rebellion in Italy, but at this point the nationalist movement gradually came under control of the Young Italy movement, headed by Giuseppe Mazzini, a Republican ideologue from Genoa. From exile in London, Mazzini conducted a campaign for independence that sought to involve an ever greater part of the population.

The 1848 Revolution in Paris sent another shock wave throughout Italy that more or less coincided with the Piedmont King Charles-Albert's decision to take advantage of Austrian political unrest to invade Lombardy, where the population had already risen during the Five Days of Milan, expelling the Austrians from the city. There were other revolts in Rome, where Mazzini established a short-lived republic, as well as in Palermo and Naples. Once again, however, the forces of change were to be defeated. Despite the aid of thousands of volunteers from Tuscany, Modena, Parma, and Lombardy, the Piedmontese troops were unable to defeat the Austrians.

In Rome, French troops intervened to protect the pope, and in Venice the Republicans were forced to surrender to the Austrian army in August 1849, after months of constant bombardment, famine, and plague. However, one bright spot was to have incalculable consequences for the future. Under the pressure of events and the influence of modern ideas, a liberal constitution had been promulgated in Piedmont that transformed that state into a limited monarchy with a strong parliamentary government. The only Italian state with a respectable military establishment of its own and a history of independence, Piedmont emerged as the only political entity capable of providing concrete leadership for the Risorgimento.

Mazzini's influence was as a political thinker. The man who actually forged Italian unity was Count Camillo Cavour, the Prime Minister of Piedmont. Cavour's first goal was to enlarge the Piedmontese state ruled by the House of Savoy, specifically by King Victor Emmanuel II, who had assumed control from his father, Charles-Albert, when the latter abdicated after the Italian defeat by the Austrians on March 23, 1849. Diplomatic accords with France meant that after the Austrian-French war of 1859, Piedmont was able to obtain Lombardy in return for ceding Nice and Savoy to France.

New annexations followed rebellions in other Italian states such as Tuscany and Emilia-Romagna. At this point, Cavour suspended unification efforts, to Mazzini's dismay. But Cavour's hand was forced by freedom fighter Giuseppe Garibaldi and his Thousand Red Shirts, who landed in Sicily in 1860 and moved up through the island and to Naples, deposing the Bourbon monarchy there and proclaiming conquest in the name of Victor Emmanuel. Fearful of international reactions to an attack on Rome, a Piedmontese army was sent to bar Garibaldi's advance. Garibaldi turned over Naples and Sicily to Piedmont, and in 1861 Cavour convened a national parliament that adopted the Piedmontese Constitution as the law of the new nation. Venetia became part of Italy after a third war with Austria in 1866, leaving only Rome outside a united Italy.

Pope Pius IX refused to consider an offer by Cavour for privileges within Italy for the Catholic church in return for a disclaimer to the papacy's temporal claim to Rome. After France's defeat by Prussia in 1870, the French garrison supporting the pope was withdrawn from Rome, and the situation shifted. Italian troops under General Cadorna entered the city at Porta Pia, and at last Italy became a fully united country. However, the dispute with the pope was to cast a pall over the first decades of national life; the pontiff rejected all attempts at reconciliation, excommunicated Italy's new king, and declared himself a prisoner in the Vatican. Catholics were forbidden to vote or take part in political life, and for the most part government was left to the country's anti-clericals.

CONSTITUTIONAL MONARCHY

The new kingdom of Italy was faced with a series of grave problems, not least of which was the integration into a single nation of a variety of regions with different cultural and linguistic traditions. There was widespread banditry in the south, particularly in Sicily, turmoil and armed skirmishing (until Rome and Venice were incorporated into the kingdom), and a huge foreign debt. Extreme poverty was endemic, especially in the south. Over the next half century, several million Italians, most of them from Calabria and Sicily, emigrated — the majority to the US. (In 1 decade alone — 1900–10 — 2 million went to New York City.)

From the start, the new Italian Parliament — an appointed Senate and an elected lower Chamber — was dominated by politicians from Piedmont. The main players in the political system were the Right, in the Cavour tradition, and the Left, which from 1876 was to hold a parliamentary majority and which sought to broaden the electorate and pass several important social reforms, such as compulsory primary school education. However, the Left was so severely split into factions that orderly party government became impossible. *Trasformismo,* a system of political brokerage leading to constantly shifting alliances, dominated the Parliament. Popular disillusionment led gradually to the growth of the Socialist party (founded in 1892), which by 1900 controlled about a quarter of the seats in Parliament. Fear of socialism, however, plus a reaction to the anarchist violence that took the life of King Umberto I in 1900, led to a rapprochement between the Liberals, led by Giovanni Giolitti, and the Catholics, who after 1904 had been allowed by Pope Pius X to return to political action.

The new nation also found itself in need of a foreign policy, especially since the other European countries were at first reluctant to recognize Italy, whose appearance on the diplomatic scene meant an inevitable reshaping of alliances. Seeking a place among the family of nations, the Italian government soon sought to join the race for overseas colonies. The Leftist Prime Minister Francesco Crispi sent troops to Africa to seize parts of Eritrea and Somalia in 1889. When Crispi's attempt to conquer Ethiopia in 1896 ended in military defeat at Adowa, with 4,000 Italians killed and 2,000 captured, he was driven from office. Colonial expansion was resumed under Giolitti in 1911 and 1912, when the Balkan war with Turkey left Italy in possession of both Libya and the Dodecanese Islands.

In Europe, Italian foreign policy rested primarily on membership in the Triple Alliance with Germany and Austria, although under Victor Emmanuel III and Giolitti closer ties were gradually forged with France and Great Britain. The outbreak of World War I caused great controversy in Italy, with public opinion sharply divided between those favoring neutrality, the government's initial position, and those claiming that Italy was duty-bound to live up to its Triple Alliance obligations and fight on the side of Germany and Austria.

In the end, reasons of national interest prevailed. The government secretly negotiated its entry into the war on the side of France and Britain in return for promises that the Italian-speaking areas of Austria — Trentino, Trieste, and Istria, as well as South Tyrol — would be returned to it along with new colonial concessions. On May 23, 1915, Italy declared war on Austria and, a year later, on Germany.

The decision to go to war proved fatal for Italian democracy. The long conflict took the lives of 600,000 Italians, and deprivation and low morale gripped the home front. Italy's aspirations were only partly satisfied at the Versailles Conference. It gained South Tyrol, Trentino, and Trieste, but Fiume and the Dalmatian coast remained in alien hands, to become the focus of a resurgent Italian nationalism. Italy's claim to share in the parceling out of colonies from the division of the defeated German and Turkish empires was ignored. As a result, embittered, disappointed Italians turned to a nationalistic strongman, Benito Mussolini.

THE FASCIST REGIME

Along with its sense of betrayal and frustration, Italy after World War I was faced with inflation, food shortages, an enormous war debt, and spreading strikes that threatened to further paralyze the economy. Socialist militancy was encouraged by the success of the Russian Revolution, and a Communist party was formed in 1921. Many factories were occupied by workers, and the government's inability to reassert control convinced the frightened middle classes that they would have to turn elsewhere for help.

Against this background rose Mussolini, a former Socialist who had broken with the party when it opposed Italian entry into World War I. A charismatic orator, Mussolini in 1919 had already organized his Blackshirt squads and later, in 1921, a small political party, the Fascists, which won 35 seats in Parliament and was included in a coalition government to help form a majority. In October 1922, Mussolini was asked by the king to form his own government, as prime minister, in a coalition with some of the major parties, including the Italian Popular party, the Popolari, Italy's first mass-based Catholic party and the forerunner of today's Christian Democratic party.

The Popolari withdrew from the coalition in 1923, but Mussolini revised the electoral law and in the 1924 general election won two-thirds of the seats in Parliament. In June 1924, his government was threatened by a wave of revulsion over the murder of Socialist politician Giacomo Matteotti by Fascist thugs. But when the king refused to support the opposition against him, Mussolini assumed dictatorial powers in January 1925 and thereafter ruled by decree through the Fascist Grand Council. A totalitarian system was quickly established, although both the economy and the Church continued to operate in relative freedom. One of Mussolini's major accomplishments was the 1929 signing of a concordat with the Holy See that ended the church-state breach that had existed for 50 years.

The Lateran Pacts created the Vatican State as an independent entity, restored the church's role in Italian education, recognized its jurisdiction in ecclesiastical matters, including marriage and divorce, and established Rome as a sacred city. The pacts became part of the Italian Republic's Constitution in 1948, although some aspects of church-state relations as laid out in the concordat were modified by a renegotiation ratified in 1985.

Along with doomed attempts to create a self-sufficient Italian economy, colonial expansionism and imperialism were also important aspects of Fascist policy. In the mid-1930s, Mussolini conquered and occupied Ethiopia. The League of Nations' attempt to impose economic sanctions only revived support for Mussolini and created a new wave of bitterness toward Great Britain and Western Europe. Mussolini signed alliances with Hitler's Germany and with Japan.

As in 1915, however, the military was not as well prepared as it looked. Italy suffered military setbacks or defeats in almost all of its World War II campaigns: France, Greece, Africa, and the Soviet Union. Consequently, when the Allies landed in Sicily in July 1943, they were greeted as liberators. Their arrival set off a palace coup by the Fascist Grand Council that forced Mussolini to resign and flee to the rump Fascist Republic of Salò in the Italian north, and power was restored to the undeserving Victor Emmanuel III. The king appointed a military officer, Marshal Pietro Badoglio, as prime minister. An armistice was quickly signed with the Allies, and war was declared on Germany. In the Italian south, which was liberated by the Allies, the Committee of National Liberation was set up by six anti-Fascist parties, ranging from the Christian Democrats and the Socialists to the Republicans and Communists; in the north, Resistance activities were carried on by several groups, particularly the Communists, with some help from the Allies. After the liberation of Rome in June 1944, a six-party government was established by veteran politician Ivanoe Bonomi. The following year, Mussolini was killed by partisans as he tried to flee to Switzerland.

THE ITALIAN REPUBLIC

The end of World War II left Italy with a whole spectrum of problems. The economy was seriously disrupted, many cities were partially destroyed, and hundreds of thousands of people were unemployed and homeless. To make matters worse, when peace negotiations were concluded, the Allies treated Italy as a defeated power rather than as a cobelligerent. The peace treaty limited the size of the Italian armed forces, established reparations payments, and deprived Italy of Istria, Zara, and islands in the Adriatic, all of which were restored to Yugoslavia. The colonial possessions in Africa and the Dodecanese Islands also had to be given up.

These disappointments were somewhat mitigated by the salvaging of Trieste and South Tyrol, and by the rejection by the other Allies of French claims to the Valle d'Aosta. Italy had few doubts about the direction of its postwar foreign policy. The first few years after the war were characterized by strong neutralist sentiment, somewhat prompted by the emerging East–West tensions that raised fears of another war and that came to a head with the battle over NATO membership in 1948–49. Italy's decision to join NATO has never wavered, and the Italian commitment to the Atlantic alliance has remained one of the strongest in Europe, evidenced by the relatively painless decision by a coalition government in 1979 to accept the installation of cruise missiles on Italian soil.

At the same time that Italy was moving toward close Atlantic relations, Count Carlo Sforza, the chief architect of postwar foreign policy, was laying the foundations for another major tenet of postwar policy: the commitment to European integration. At a very early stage, Sforza and Prime Minister Alcide De Gasperi realized that Italy's fate was inexorably tied to that of its Western European allies. Thus, Italy was a charter member of the European Coal and Steel Community, the Western European Union, and the European Economic Community (the Common Market), set up in 1956. (Italian foreign policy has never strayed from these two basic and overlapping orientations, and, indeed, during the late 1970s and early 1980s, the governments in power became even more active in cooperative foreign policy. For example, Italy was a major participant in the Multinational Peace Force sent to Lebanon in 1982.)

Following the end of the war in 1945, the House of Savoy could possibly have survived if King Victor Emmanuel, whose reputation had been irrevocably sullied by his relations with Mussolini, had abdicated in favor of his son Umberto immediately after the fall of Mussolini. But by the time a popular referendum on the monarchy was held in June 1946, there was so much bitterness toward the royal family that a majority of Italians voted in favor of a republican form of government, and Umberto II, who had become king in May when his father belatedly stepped down, was forced into exile in Portugal.

The June 1946 elections also chose a Constituent Assembly charged with writing a new Italian constitution to replace that of 1848. The voters, including women for the first time, gave 35 percent of the seats in the Assembly to the new Christian Democratic party, 20 percent to the Socialists, and 19 percent to the Communists. The rest of the seats were divided among smaller Italian parties, including a neo-Fascist group. The new constitution was approved, in December 1947, by an overwhelming majority; it called for a popularly elected two-house Parliament and a president, elected by the Parliament, who would have the power to appoint a prime minister and to dissolve Parliament in the event of an insoluble government crisis. The constitution also adopted the 1929 concordat that gave the Catholic church special privileges. The Italian Communists, following their postwar policy of cooperation, went along.

The first national elections under the new constitution took place in April 1948 and were preceded by months of sharp political debate reflecting the country's gradual polarization between the Left and the Right. When the vote was in, the elections had given Alcide De Gasperi's Christian Democrats a clear majority with 48% of the vote (and 305 of the 574 seats in the Chamber of Deputies), compared with the 31% won jointly by the Communists and Socialists. In 1947, De Gasperi had already succeeded in forcing the Marxist parties out of the joint tripartite coalitions that had followed the war, and after April 1948 this trend continued. For years, Italy was to be governed by the Christian Democrats alone, or in coalition with smaller centrist parties like the Social Democrats, the Liberals, and the Republicans. But the Christian Democrats, a highly fragmented political group that got both the credit for laying the foundations of postwar economic prosperity and a good part of the blame for the equally present corruption and inefficiency, were never again able to match their 1948 showing. Despite its frequent reliance on anti-communism in its electoral propaganda, the party saw its share of the vote decline gradually to an all-time low of 32.9% in the general election of 1983, although there was a slight improvement (to 34.3%) in 1987.

The reduced influence of the Christian Democrats, although they remain Italy's single largest party, reflected both disillusionment with what was viewed by many as unresponsive government and a general change in Italian society after the student movement of 1968, considered by many to be a watershed in recent Italian history. Since 1968, the traditional influence of both the Church and the Christian Democrats has shrunk sharply, as could be seen by the outcomes of the recent popular referendums on divorce and abortion, in which the "yes" votes of the progressive side of the political spectrum were victorious, despite an active Church campaign for rejection.

Discontentment with the Christian Democrats strengthened the Socialist party as a leading government force. In the early 1960s, they formed a coalition with the Christian Democrats and other Center-Left political parties. This was the culmination of the Italian Socialists' gradual pulling away from their postwar alliance with the Communist party. The Hungarian uprising of 1956, and the subsequent Soviet intervention, had led the Socialists to reject dogmatic Marxism and the Soviet Union, and to swing around to pro-Western positions. Although the Socialists have never surpassed 15% of the vote in national elections, the increasing weakness of the Christian Democrats, the continued exclusion of the powerful Communists from government, and a major political scandal in 1981 combined to give the Socialists a determining influence. In fact, between August 1983 and June 1986, the socialist Bettino Craxi enjoyed the longest uninterrupted term as prime minister in Italy's postwar history.

For a while, the Christian Democrats' inability to keep pace with Italian modernization also brought huge benefits to the Italian Communist party, which throughout the postwar period has been Italy's second-largest political group. The good government provided by the Communists in many of the cities and regions in their traditional strongholds, plus widespread political frustration in 1975 and 1976, led the party to make large electoral gains, bringing it within a few seats of overtaking the Christian Democrats and winning a vast amount of influence in the day-to-day decision making of the Italian Parliament. Indeed, in 1978 the Communist party came closer to government participation than at any other time since 1947, when it was forced out of the postwar tripartite alliance. To help deal with the labor and economic situation, as well as with spreading terrorism, the Christian Democrats and Italy's other parties officially asked the Communists to join the parliamentary majority that supported the coalition government, headed by Christian Democrat Prime Minister Giulio Andreotti.

Unfortunately, however, the day of this historic agreement coincided with the kidnapping of former Christian Democrat Premier Aldo Moro, who was subsequently murdered. This tragic event represented the height of terrorist tension in Italy during the period that Italians call *gli anni di piombo* (the "bullet" years).

On the one hand, the changes in Italian society and the frustrations caused by political unresponsiveness led to some sympathy with the Communists as a progressive force operating within the system. On the other, there was recognition of the negative aspects of the party as well. A surge of political radicalism increasingly found an outlet in terrorism or other forms of political violence. The appearance of the Red Brigades during the early 1970s, flanked by several other similar organizations such as Front Line and Communist Fighting Units, was paralleled on the far Right by subversive organizations such as the Armed Revolutionary Nuclei. What the two sides had in common was the goal of fomenting change through terrorism and murder, so that several hundred people died in terrorist attacks between 1974 and 1982. In recent years, however, the terrorist threat has abated somewhat. The major terrorist leaders are now almost all behind bars, and the widespread support that once enabled them to operate so freely and efficiently within Italian society has now almost disappeared, drastically isolating the small number of holdouts who have evaded arrest.

The "historic compromise," as Communist support to a government led by the Christian Democrats was called, ended in 1979 as a result of strains within the government and the Communist party because hardliners were unhappy with the degree of cooperation now accorded the country's capitalists. Nevertheless, this political alliance contributed to give the party a different image from those of Soviet and (then) Eastern European Communist parties from which it had already distanced itself.

The changes in Eastern Europe in 1989 and 1990 further caused change in the Italian Communist party. In March 1990, after an intense debate, the large majority of party members voted in favor of renaming the organization, as well as changing its symbol. Almost a year later, the party decided to call itself the Democratic Party of the Left, dissatisfying many members, who formed a new party — — Rifondazione Communista. But by changing its name and altering its image, the Italian Communist party hopes to gain wider support from environmentalists, feminists, and other progressive forces, and to create an alternative to the dominant Christian Democrats. They have seen their share of votes in political elections slip from 34% in 1976 to 26% in 1987 to 10% in 1991, and have been consistently excluded from taking part in Italian government.

However justified, this exclusion has had profound negative effects on the operation of the Italian political system. It means there is never an acceptable alternative to rule by the Christian Democrats and their allies. So government in Italy remains a permanent preserve of the same five parties — the Christian Democrats, Socialists, Social Democrats, Liberals, and Republicans — that have governed it, in one combination or another, for the past 44 years. Not only does this mean that no substantial change is possible — or likely — in key government decisions, but it also makes government downright difficult since all five parties agree on little more than Italy's democratic system, its mixed economy, and its pro-Western foreign policy. Everything else is compromise or deadlock, and as we went to press the number of post–World War II Italian governments had reached 50.

Even with such a shaky political foundation, Italy has been able to make a remarkable recovery from wartime impoverishment to its status as one of the world's ten most industrialized nations. Although the economy's record has been by no means unblemished, the "economic miracle" that occurred between 1950 and 1964 laid the basis for further expansion and industrial development. Admittedly, Italy's economic development since then has been marked by double-digit inflation that lasted through 1984 (and is still higher than elsewhere in the West), by high unemployment (still prevalent in some parts of the Italian south), and by a huge (and expanding) budget deficit. Also, high labor costs have hurt Italian industry abroad, and the need to import most important raw materials — particularly oil — puts a constant strain on the balance of payments. A poorly functioning bureaucracy and government indecision — not surprising, given the inevitable reliance on coalition governments — also have slowed social programs, particularly housing and health care, which lag behind general European levels and which have led to discontent and substantial numbers of strikes and other labor unrest.

This makes it all the more remarkable that Italy today is an economically thriving country, offering almost all its citizens a better standard of living than ever before. Efforts to privatize some of the country's industries — energy, electric, and banks — were being made at press time in order to decrease Italy's enormous debt before it becomes part of an integrated European community. In certain sectors, Italy has made an international name for itself, and companies such as Fiat and Alfa Romeo (automobiles), Olivetti (typewriters and communications), Montedison (chemicals), Agusta (helicopters), Pirelli (tires), Perugina (candy), Parmalat (dairy products), Gucci (leather goods), and Benetton (knitwear) are known throughout the world. In recent years, Italy also has become one of the world's major producers of robots, while its fashion designers have made *la moda italiana* into a household phrase. Indeed, from cars to shoes, products "Made in Italy" have won wide acclaim for their style, design, craftsmanship, and quality — all characteristics that contribute to making modern life interesting and vital in the 1990s.

Literature

Italy's culture is virtually impossible to understand from the comfort of an armchair, for the secrets of Italy's art, its music, and particularly its literature are locked in the landscape, the climate, and the life of the various corners of the peninsula where they are created. If there is one single key to Italian literature, it is its regional diversity.

From the fall of the Roman Empire to the unification under Garibaldi in 1860, Italy did not exist as a country but was made up of independent mini-states. And the novels of the Sicilian Giovanni Verga are as different from the writings of the Lombard Alessandro Manzoni as the spicy *spaghetti alla napoletana* is from the northern tortellini in cream sauce — all of which gives the person interested in Italy's literary heritage an ironclad excuse to embark on an on-site investigation. It is much easier to appreciate the poetry of Dante after wandering through the streets of Florence, where he first glimpsed his beloved Beatrice more than 6 centuries ago. Similarly, the dramatic impact of Carlo Levi's *Cristo si è fermato a Eboli* (Christ Stopped at Eboli) cannot be fully grasped unless you have visited one of the remote villages in the deep south and witnessed the poverty, the searing sunshine, and the people's deep-rooted superstitions and traditions.

During the Middle Ages, Italy, like France, had a strong courtly love tradition that provided the themes for the poems of troubadours — the idolization of woman and the capriciousness of love. The center of activity was Sicily, which had been conquered by the Normans in the 11th century, and there the tradition had its roots. But there was also a Tuscan school, one of whose most colorful exponents was Cecco Angiolieri of Siena (1260–1312), who adapted the chivalric style to produce a far more earthy and witty tone. One of his most unforgettable sonnets describes his wife in the morning before she puts on her makeup.

The works of Dante Alighieri (1265–1321) eclipsed all of his predecessors — and most of his successors. Today, he is still regarded as one of Western civilization's most important and influential poets. Although exact details of Dante's life are sketchy, he was born in the late 13th century and was brought up in Florence, the city that dominates his works and from which he was exiled for much of his life. He wrote during a time of bitter struggle between church and state in Europe, against the background of an Italy sharply divided by internal warfare between partisans of the pope and of the emperor — Guelphs and Ghibellines. His own Florence, after the expulsion of the Ghibellines, was further rent by rivalry between Black and White Guelphs, and Dante, of the latter faction, was expelled when the Blacks came to power. His writing is highly influenced by his political experiences, especially by his banishment from his birthplace.

Dante is credited with having established Tuscan as the language for all Italy, a measured, conscious decision on his part. Remarkably, it took hold and still endures. Dante's works include *La vita nuova* (The New Life), a love poem dedicated to Beatrice, who was to Dante what Laura was to Petrarch, and the political treatises *De monarchia* (On Monarchy) and *Il Convivio* (The Banquet). But his *Divina commedia* (Divine Comedy) dwarfs them all. This is Dante's vision of Hell, Purgatory, and Paradise, charting the poet's odyssey through all three regions, as well as of the political, dynastic, and military convolutions of his time. Dante himself called it simply *Commedia;* posterity supplied the adjective.

Francesco Petrarca (1304–74), known in English as Petrarch, is traditionally considered the father of the European love lyric and the man who invented the sonnet. His poems are dominated by the image of the woman he loved unrequitedly. She was Laura, whom he first saw in a church in Avignon on April 6, 1327, and who died on the same day 21 years later. One theory contends that Laura never actually existed, but it is more commonly believed that she was Laure de Noves, the wife of Hugues de Sade. Whatever her identity, she provided inspiration for the lovesick poet, whose style and sentiment are far more complex and sophisticated than those of the courtly love poets. His collection, *Rime* (Rhymes), broaches subjects previously untouched in Italian love poetry, not least of which is physical love.

Giovanni Boccaccio (1313–75) created Italian literature's first prose monuments. The setting for his major work, the *Decameron,* is only a stone's throw from Dante's Florence — an elegant villa in the Tuscan hill town of Fiesole. But the style and tone of the *Decameron* could not be more different from the somber and spiritual *Divine Comedy.* The *Decameron* is a collection of tales told by a group of lords and ladies seeking refuge in the clean air of Fiesole from the Black Death, which has carried off thousands of their compatriots. To while away their time and distract themselves from their troubles, they tell stories to one another. Some of the tales are sad, some touching, some even tragic, but many are ribald and earthy accounts of jealous husbands, unfaithful wives, and nuns and priests who are anything but celibate.

The dawning of the 15th century brought humanism to Italy, a movement that rejoiced in human dignity, artistry, and the excellence of learning, painting, sculpture, and architecture. The models were classical Greece and Rome, and artists and scholars reveled in digging up the statuary, architecture, and artwork of those periods. Writers cast off the fatalism of medieval times and set out to acquire firsthand knowledge, which they believed to be the key to a new and bright future. The period produced a flourishing literature, particularly in the fields of education, the plastic arts, criticism, philosophy, and history. It also saw the beginning of court literature, with noblemen such as the Medici clan of Florence acting as patrons and sponsors of the arts.

The latter half of the 15th century was dominated by characters who were first and foremost personalities and only secondarily writers. The two most notable were Lorenzo de' Medici (1448–92), prince of the famous banking family that ruled Florence during the Renaissance, and Girolamo Savonarola (1452–98), also in Florence, the fire-and-brimstone monk who preached of doom and destruction in a godless society. The former wrote mainly poetry, though his protégé Angelo Poliziano was far more talented than his master. Savonarola, who hated the Medicis, wrote inflammatory treatises. His major work, *Trionfo della croce* (Triumph of the Cross), was completed shortly before he was arrested by the Borgia Pope Alexander VI in 1496, to be hanged and then burned.

Niccolò Machiavelli (1469–1527) is known for a view of life that shocks some readers and appeals to others as realistic. His pro-military philosophy of expediency was born of a passionate involvement in the troubled Florentine Republic. Machiavelli served the republic as a diplomat before, like Dante, being banished into exile. His most famous work, *Il principe* (The Prince), is a modus operandi for an effective ruler. In it Machiavelli calls on the Medici family to use force to save the Italian city-states from the claims of foreign invaders. Although he preached the famous "the end justifies the means" theory, he also outlined the virtues necessary for a good ruler, including love for his subjects and just laws. Machiavelli's *Arte della guerra* (The Art of War) laid down the principles on which Italian compulsory military service is still based.

In his *Storia Fiorentina* (History of Florence), fellow Florentine and political historian Francesco Guicciardini (1482–1540) disagreed with Machiavelli on almost every point. He believed that things were not ordered, but happened by chance, and he refuted Machiavelli's claim that one could look to history for an example of what to expect in the future. Guicciardini also differed in his lack of optimism; he did not share Machiavelli's belief in a golden future for Italy.

The epic poem was a popular form in Italy throughout the 15th century, but it was Lodovico Ariosto (1474–1533) who raised it from a rattling tale spattered with blood and guts to the level of literature. This servant's son from Ferrara was attached to the court of the Este family, where he wrote his masterpiece, *Orlando Furioso,* over a period of 30 years. Ariosto's characters and their adventures through the world of magic spells and gory battles are the same as those of his predecessors, but they are far more finely drawn and sophisticated.

The next great member of the Ferrara school of epic poetry was Torquato Tasso (1544–95), who spent 20 years at the court under the patronage of Duke Alfonso d'Este. After Dante, Tasso generally is regarded as the prince of Italian poets, although his life was plagued by misfortune, including 7 years spent imprisoned in a mental hospital. His *Gerusalemme liberata* (Jerusalem Liberated) is more solemn, more sensuous, and more ornate than Ariosto's poem.

Italian theater has its roots in the medieval mystery plays that acted out the stories of the church, the martyrdom of saints, and the biblical origins of *Christmas* and *Easter.* Examples of these still survive in village processions that commemorate the lives of local saints. Like the religious paintings of the time, the theater was built on ritual, with flat, two-dimensional characters. The late 15th and early 16th centuries saw further development, as Italian writers began translating Latin comedies, but in these, too, stock characters went through stock situations. The plays were full of young men in love, helped or thwarted by wily servants, amid much changing of clothes and confusion of identities. In the 16th century, Machiavelli, Pietro Aretino (1492–1556), Angelo Beolco (1502–73), and Giangiorgio Trissino (1478–1550) all developed the theatrical technique. But it was Giambattista Giraldi (1504–73) of Ferrara who made the greatest strides. He shifted the focus away from the realm of kings and dukes to real people and introduced what was to become central to the development of modern theater — the concept of tragicomedy.

The 17th century was a period less remarkable for the quality of its literature than for the courage of certain notable intellectuals who dared to question principles based on a God-centered world. This century saw the birth of modern science, the thirst for knowledge in politics and theology, but it was also the age of the Inquisition. Among the largely southern-based writers who broke the mold of flowery poetry that slavishly followed the rules of Plato and Aristotle was Giordano Bruno (1548–1600), who dared to suggest that there were as many poetic styles as there were individual poetic inspirations. His individualism in extra-literary matters cost him his life — he was burned at the stake as a heretic in Rome in 1600. Galileo Galilei (1564–1642), who typified this age of intellectual discovery, won international fame for his invention of the telescope in 1609. But his attachment to Copernicus's claim that the earth moved around the sun, and not vice versa, condemned him to years in prison and a lonely death in 1642.

Wealthy, carefree Venice of the 18th century spawned Carlo Goldoni (1707–93), whose plays are full of lightheartedness, humor, and fast-paced action that often approaches farce. His best-known comedies, *La locandiera* (The Innkeeper) and *La bottega del caffè* (The Coffee Shop), are both still widely performed. One of the most prolific Italian playwrights, his works are full of social comment, but they contain no tragedy and little soul searching. Goldoni's world is populated by likable rogues trying to get themselves out of tight corners.

With Ugo Foscolo (1778–1827) came the first glimmerings of the romantic movement, with its themes of human despair, suicide, and the conviction that the only real truth was to be found in the beauty of nature. Foscolo's best-known work, the autobiographical novel *Le ultime lettere di Jacopo Ortis* (The Last Letters of Jacopo Ortis), is a study of unhappiness born of his own misery, when his fiancée married another man. Unable to bear the defeat of Napoleon and the return of Austrian domination to Italy, Foscolo left his homeland in 1816 to live in London, where he died in penury 11 years later.

In addition to its cult of individual sentiment and the self-indulgent outpourings of the soul, Italian romanticism was marked by a longing for political freedom. The movement developed against the background of the hated Austrian occupation. The revolutionary and liberal ideas expressed by this school of writers cost some of them their liberty. Silvio Pellico (1789–1854) spent 10 years in an Austrian jail, where he wrote *Le mie prigioni* (My Prisons).

Alessandro Manzoni (1785–1873) felt the burden of foreign rule particularly strongly since he was from the northern region of Lombardy, which was firmly under Austrian control. His poem *Cinque maggio* (The Fifth of May) poignantly laments the death of Napoleon, who had briefly ousted the northern invaders. But Manzoni is best known for his classic novel *I promessi sposi* (The Betrothed), the story of the young lovers Renzo and Lucia. Manzoni, like his contemporaries, had his moments of despair, but he also possessed a keen sense of humor, and the very human touches, such as the failings of the priest Don Abbondio, have made *I promessi sposi* one of the best-loved works in Italian literature.

Far more pessimistic is the mood of Giacomo Leopardi (1798–1837), the poet who comes closest to the romantics of French and English literature. To Leopardi, humans are an insignificant speck towered over by Nature, which is indifferent to human suffering yet always magnificent. This conviction gives rise to poetry of great lyric beauty. The poet's love-hate relationship with Recanati, the small town in the Marches region where he was born and raised, is central to his works. As a young boy, Leopardi showed a prodigious appetite for knowledge and spent much of his childhood in the library devouring works in Greek and Hebrew. He died at age 39, after a life plagued by ill health.

The traumatic experience of foreign occupation and the famed victory of Garibaldi and his Thousand, who brought Italy under one rule, produced a crop of patriot poets in the mid-19th century. Some, like Giovanni Prati and Goffredo Mameli, died fighting for freedom. Mameli's *Fratelli d'Italia* (Brothers of Italy) became the Italian national anthem after its author was killed in 1849. But the patriot poet par excellence was Giosuè Carducci (1835–1917), whose forceful poems are full of indignation and anger at Italy's humiliation under foreign domination. Carducci went on to become a professor of Italian literature at Bologna University, as well as a winner of the Nobel Prize for Literature, and his works have a strong classical and historical framework. But in spite of his respectability, Carducci never lost his youthful rebelliousness and the fierce republicanism that dominates the collection *Odi barbare* (Savage Odes), familiar to every Italian schoolchild.

With the demise of romanticism, a new school in Italian literature emerged, one more suited to the novel form than to poetry. This was realism — *verismo.* Sicilian-born Luigi Capuana (1839–1915) was one of the first exponents of the new trend, which sought to suppress the personality and presence of the author in favor of a scientific description of characters and events. Fellow Sicilian Giovanni Verga (1840–1922) developed the style, examining social conditions in the impoverished south, depicting in his novels poor and often unlikable wretches whose lives are filled with physical and spiritual suffering. In *Nedda,* the protagonist is a girl who loses her mother, then her lover, and finally her baby. In Verga's most famous novel, *I Malavoglia* (The House by the Medlar Tree), a family in a poor Sicilian fishing community suffers one misfortune after another. Another writer in the *verismo* vein was Grazia Deledda, whose naturalistic novels of peasants set against the background of her native Sardinia won her the Nobel Prize for Literature.

Light years apart from the sordid world of the realists was Gabriele D'Annunzio (1863–1938), one of the most flamboyant characters in Italian literature. His heroic exploits during World War I, his skill as a pilot, his colorful love affair with the actress Eleonora Duse, and his dramatic siege of the

Yugoslav border town of Fiume would have earned him a place in history even if he had never written a line. But he was also a prolific author, producing poems and novels that were highly sensual, often to the point of cruelty and sadism, and full of the human life force that was the stamp of the man himself. D'Annunzio's was a philosophy based on self-confidence and a belief in the ability of humans to achieve their aims. He espoused the Nietzschean cult of the Superman, a belief that went hand in hand with his love of fast cars and airplanes. A man of great talents, his best-known works are his poems, especially the Laudi collection, but he also wrote novels (notably *Il fuoco*), poetic prose (*Notturno*), and plays (*Francesca da Rimini*). His writings expressed many of the same hopes and ideas as Mussolini's fascism.

The gentle lyricism of Antonio Fogazzaro (1842–1911) could not have been more different from the bombastic style of D'Annunzio. Unlike D'Annunzio, whose raison d'être was passion, Fogazzaro's was the human quality of love. His best novel, *Piccolo mondo antico* (Little Old World), is the story of a Lombardy community under Austrian domination in the mid-19th century, but the suffering is tempered with a strong sense of comic indulgence for his characters, which makes them very human.

Meanwhile, the spirit of fascism was gaining momentum, and with it grew futurism, an avant-garde school inspired by the mechanical rhythms of modern life. This was the cult of the now, rejecting the past. Its chief proponent was F.T. Marinetti (1878–1944), who in 1909 launched the Futurist Manifesto, which was to have strong repercussions in European literature, freeing it from old naturalist forms and heralding a new, exciting experimental age in art. Futurist poets such as Marinetti and Giovanni Papini (1881–1956) scorned the traditional and praised only what was bizarre, ugly, and discordant. Rhymes were often abolished in favor of free verse, or prose poems, and sweet assonances forsaken in favor of jarring, rasping sounds.

But futurism was more important for the barriers it broke down than for the quality of the literature itself. In Italo Svevo (1861–1928) emerged an artist of real stature who used the new freedom of expression but rejected the positive, self-confident attitudes of D'Annunzio and Marinetti. His novels are characterized by purposelessness, full of unremarkable people leading humdrum lives — subjects previously considered too banal for literature. Svevo's major work, *La coscienza di Zeno* (The Confessions of Zeno), revolves around nothing more exceptional than the hero's attempt to give up smoking.

Any rules and conventions still intact by the time Luigi Pirandello (1867–1936) came on the scene were summarily dismantled by this highly successful revolutionary author. Pirandello, another Nobel Prize winner, tried most literary forms, but was most audacious in his plays. His characters frequently take control of the author, most strikingly in *Sei personaggi in cerca d'autore* (Six Characters in Search of an Author). Often there is no beginning, middle, or end to his plays, and his characters break off in the middle of a scene to talk to each other, or even to the audience. Gone, too, is the traditional plot. One of Pirandello's recurring themes is the gap that exists between the way we see ourselves and the image other people have of us. His life was deeply influenced by his unhappy marriage, arranged by his father, to a woman who was his cousin. His wife developed a persecution complex, accusing Piran-

services held in your own denomination, you might find it interesting to attend the service of another religion. You also might enjoy attending a service in Italian — even if you don't understand all the words. Some of the most beautiful cathedrals in the world are found in Italy, and few things are more inspiring than a high mass set amidst medieval arches and stained glass.

Customs and Returning to the US

Whether you return to the United States by air or sea, you must declare to the US Customs official at the point of entry everything you have bought or acquired while in Europe. The customs check can go smoothly, lasting only a few minutes, or can take hours, depending on the officer's instinct. To speed up the process, keep all your receipts handy and try to pack your purchases together in an accessible part of your suitcase. It might save you from unpacking all your belongings.

DUTY-FREE ARTICLES: In general, the duty-free allowance for US citizens returning from abroad is $400. This limit includes items used or worn while abroad, souvenirs for friends, and gifts received during the trip. A flat 10% duty based on the "fair retail value in country of acquisition" is assessed on the next $1,000 worth of merchandise brought in for personal use or gifts. Amounts over the basic allotment and the 10% dutiable amount are dutiable at a variety of rates. The average rate for typical tourist purchases is about 12%, but you can find out rates on specific items by consulting *Tariff Schedules of the United States* in a library or any US Customs Service office.

Families traveling together may make a joint declaration to customs, which permits one member to exceed his or her duty-free exemption to the extent that another falls short. Families also may pool purchases dutiable under the flat rate. A family of three, for example, would be eligible for up to a total of $3,000 at the 10% flat duty rate (after each member had used up his or her $400 duty-free exemption) rather than three separate $1,000 allowances. This grouping of purchases is extremely useful when considering the duty on a high-tariff item, such as jewelry or a fur coat.

Personal exemptions can be used once every 30 days; in order to be eligible, an individual must have been out of the country for more than 48 hours. If any portion of the exemption has been used once within any 30-day period or if your trip is less than 48 hours long, the duty-free allowance is cut to $25.

There are certain articles, however, that are duty-free only up to certain limits. The $25 allowance includes the following: 10 cigars (not Cuban), 60 cigarettes, and 4 ounces of perfume. Individuals eligible for the full $400 duty-free limit are allowed 1 carton of cigarettes (200), 100 cigars, and 1 liter of liquor or wine if the traveler is over 21. Alcohol above this allowance is liable for both duty and an Internal Revenue tax. Antiques, if they are 100 or more years old and you have proof from the seller of that fact, are duty-free, as are paintings and drawings if done entirely by hand. Note, however, that antiques and works of art cannot be exported from Italy without authorization from an *Istituto delle Belle Arti* (Institute of Fine Arts). These institutes can be found in all major cities throughout Italy; if you require assistance in obtaining approval, you also can contact the nearest US consulate.

To avoid paying duty twice, register the serial numbers of foreign-made watches and electronic equipment with the nearest US Customs bureau before departure; receipts of insurance policies also should be carried for other foreign-made items. (Also see the note at the end of *Entry Requirments and Documents,* in this section.)

Gold, gold medals, bullion, and up to $10,000 in currency or negotiable instruments may be brought into the US without being declared. Sums over $10,000 must be declared in writing.

dello of cruelty and unfaithfulness, which was not at all how the author saw himself. In his novel *Uno, nessuno e centomila* (One, No One and a Hundred Thousand), Pirandello describes a man whose wife points out to him that his nose is lopsided. The discovery sparks a chain of uncertainties in the mind of the hero, who had always imagined himself to be a person with a perfectly straight nose.

The Fascist regime took its toll on the artists of Italy, with exile, prison, and sometimes death facing those who expressed antigovernment feelings too vehemently. Some, like Cesare Pavese and the Jewish author Carlo Levi, were banished to remote Italian outposts. Levi used this experience to write his memorable portrait of peasant life in southern Italy, *Cristo si è fermato a Eboli* (Christ Stopped at Eboli). Antonio Gramsci (1891–1937), one of the founders of the Italian Communist party, was imprisoned for 10 years, which resulted in his death at the age of 46. It was only after Mussolini's death that Gramsci's work from this period, *Quaderni del carcere* (Prison Notebooks), was published, in 1948.

Nevertheless, this period spawned an abundance of writing talent. The mid-20th century literature of Italy is one of the richest in Europe. Three poets especially stand out during this time: Giuseppe Ungaretti (1888–1970), Eugenio Montale (1896–1983), and Salvatore Quasimodo (1901–68). Montale and Quasimodo were both awarded the Nobel Prize for Literature. Collectively, they are known as hermeticist poets, a term that refers to the new style they brought to poetry and that has close links with the French symbolists. They worked to concentrate ideas and distill images and associations using a minimum of verbiage. Ungaretti's poetry strongly reflects his experiences on the front line in World War I and the death of his 9-year-old son. But his sense of despair is always expressed in the sparest style, reducing words to the bare minimum to make maximum effect of their evocative powers. Montale's poetry employs a similar technique but has a marked quality of wry humor, often directed at himself. Sicilian-born Quasimodo interpreted the style in a more approachable manner, but the distillation was still strong. One of his classic poems, *Ed è subito sera* (And Suddenly It's Evening), captures in just three short lines a host of ideas and concepts about evening, death, and loneliness.

Meanwhile, the Italian prose tradition was anything but stagnant. One immediate success was Giuseppe Tomasi di Lampedusa's (1896–1957) *Il gattopardo* (The Leopard). A novel set in Sicily, it charts the decline of the old order through a portrait of a noble Sicilian family whose young hero, Tancredi, breaks with tradition by marrying into the nouveau riche family of the town's mayor. The book was published largely through the efforts of Giorgio Bassani (b. 1916), whose own novel *Il giardino dei Finzi Contini* (The Garden of the Finzi-Continis) has also become a modern classic.

Perhaps because of Italy's political traumas during the war, leading to the abolition of the monarchy and the flowering of communism, modern Italian literature and culture have tended to stay freer of intellectual snobbery than those of many other European countries. In Italy, good literature is usually also popular.

One of the best-known and best-loved of contemporary Italian novelists and story-tellers is Alberto Moravia (1907–1990), whose anecdotal style and portraits of life in Rome are unmistakable. He first made his mark in 1929 with *Gli indifferenti* (The Indifferent), which paints a picture of the emptiness of bourgeois life. From then until his death, Moravia continued to delight his huge readership with his finely drawn characters, often from the working classes and usually up to no good — waiters who plot to steal their friends' wives, servant girls who try to dupe their bosses.

Until his death in 1985, Italo Calvino (b. 1922) was another prolific novelist who obtained considerable recognition during his lifetime. A former partisan fighter during World War II, Calvino had an extraordinarily fertile imagination that produced tales of fantasy and make-believe, such as *Il barone rampante* (The Baron in the Trees), the story of an 18th-century nobleman who lives in the trees. But Calvino had an equally keen eye for contemporary life and for the plight of the ordinary working class in a bewildering world. Portraits such as that of Marcovaldo, the title character in a collection of his short stories, lost and confused in the concrete jungle of a northern Italian industrial city, endeared Calvino to a generation of readers, both in Italy and abroad.

Primo Levi (1919–1987), a Jewish chemist and Holocaust survivor, deserves a special place among Italian contemporary writers. He found his literary inspiration in his own tragic experiences (as well as those of his fellow inmates) and described them in vivid detail in *Se questo è un uomo* (Survival in Auschwitz), *La Tregua* (The Reawakening), and *Il sistema periodo* (The Periodic Table).

The runaway success of Umberto Eco's (b. 1932) first novel, *Il nome della rosa* (The Name of the Rose), is proof that Italy still occupies an important place in world literature. Eco, a professor at the University of Bologna, turned his hand to fiction with the publication (in 1980) of what has been described as a medieval whodunit. It is set in a Benedictine monastery, where a series of bizarre murders of monks leads a Franciscan friar in pursuit of the culprit. The novel became an immediate best seller and was translated into several languages, and it was also hailed by critics in Europe and the United States as a work of great literary merit, winning two major awards, the Premio Strega and the Prix Medici. In 1988, Eco published his second successful novel, *Il Pendolo di Foucault* (Foucault's Pendulum). Set in contemporary Europe, it tells the story of three editors who plot to take over the world by interpreting and manipulating a massive amount of information.

Dining in Italy

Next to losing your way in a foreign city, perhaps the most distressing aspect of traveling is trying to enjoy a meal in a restaurant where the waiters are distant and the menu unintelligible.

Relax. This time you're in Italy, land of the pizzeria, the café, the wine bar, and the ever-satisfying trattoria. The art of eating here is an open secret, told in the hiss of the espresso machine and the crackle of spit-roasted meats sizzling over an open fire; in tempting, brilliantly colored ice creams arranged like the paints on Giotto's palette; and in giant platters of antipasti, with each mushroom, olive, and anchovy curl arranged as carefully as a Venetian mosaic. When your waiter says, "*Buon appetito,*" it is as direct an invitation to the feast as the knife sticking out of the melon wedge that he brings to your table in the piazza.

It is really hard to get a bad meal in a country where nature has put a larder of Mediterranean vegetables, wine grapes and tree-ripened fruits, fresh-caught fish, carefully tended animals, and a forest carpeted with mushrooms outside the kitchen window. Centuries have taught cooks here not to "improve" the food too much. Give Italians some fruity olive oil, a fragrant lemon, a basket of ripe tomatoes, garlic, pepper, a few snips of basil, and a slab of parmesan cheese, and they can dress a pasta you'll remember as long as an afternoon in the *Uffizi.*

But let's get back to that table in the piazza. This time we'll order some wine and mineral water and study *la lista,* the Italian menu. Even though the traditional 3-hour lunch break is losing ground in the larger cities, restaurants still offer full meals at lunch as well as dinner. Since ordering is generally à la carte, it's easy to tailor the meal to suit your own schedule by choosing only the courses you want.

The first items listed are antipasti, those irresistible hors d'oeuvres of sliced salami and paper-thin raw beef (carpaccio), fresh figs wrapped in rosy ham, prosciutto, bits of stuffed zucchini, eggplant and roasted peppers, sweet-and-sour baby onions, seafood salads, and other temptations. Italians go easy on these nowadays, alas, often preferring a simple munch of *crostini,* rounds of toast touched with olive oil and garlic or spread with a purée of chicken livers, while waiting for the first plate, the *primo piatto.*

The *primo* is not just a small starter course but a full partner to the *secondo piatto.* Together these two dishes make up the Italian main course. The first part, also called the *minestra,* is served by itself, typical choices being a half-portion of pasta or a soup with pasta in it. In the north the rice-based specialty risotto or a savory cornmeal pudding (polenta) is served. During any visit in Italy, a traveler will eat pasta in dozens of widths, lengths, and squiggles matched to various sauces and preparations by culinary tradition, the cook's own estimate of the clinging power of a sauce to its pasta, and personal taste. Some common combinations are *pastini,* little stars and dots in broth, tubular factory-made macaroni and spaghetti with tomato sauces, and fresh, handmade egg noodles and fold-ups (often filled with meats and cheeses) with cream-based sauces.

Only after the first course has been cleared will the waiter bring the *secondo,* or meat (or chicken or fish) course, which explains why spaghetti with meatballs is seldom served in Italy. (If the fresh, crusty bread hasn't appeared yet — Italians don't usually eat bread with pasta — it will come to the table now, but minus butter; that's for breakfast). To say that the *secondo* is the meat course does little to convey the first taste of fork-tender milk-fed veal; spit-roasted baby lamb rubbed with rosemary; roast kid or suckling pig; game meats like boar, venison, partridge, and hare; or sea creatures such as octopus, squid, and skate — less familiar to Americans but to which Italian cooks turn as naturally as we do to fried chicken or filet of sole. *Contorni,* side dishes of steamed green vegetables — spinach, escarole, or asparagus, for instance — can be ordered *al burro* (with butter), *all'olio* (drizzled with olive oil), or *all'agro* (with lemon). Italians also deep-fry vegetables — pieces of zucchini and zucchini blossoms, artichokes, and peppers — which are listed on the menu as *fritti.*

Salads of crisp fresh lettuces and herbs come next, and some diners will end the meal here; most Italians, however, don't feel satisfied without cheese and fruit — a fresh peach or some cherries or berries from the sideboard or, in winter, perhaps a poached pear. The finale is an inch of rich, dark-roast espresso. And if you plan to linger, take some sweet dessert wine, for example, vin santo, with little dry biscuits (*biscotti*) for dunking.

And what about the espresso-and-cream-soaked *tiramisù* cake, the *zuppa inglese,* like English trifle, or the *Monte Bianco* chestnut purée creation on the cart in the corner? Go right ahead. But take note that most Italians don't eat dessert with the meal. They usually have their pastries in mid-afternoon or later in the evening at a café or *pasticceria.*

We use the word *restaurant* to mean a sit-down eating place, but in Italian a *ristorante* means formal dining with a wide selection of food, a full complement of waiters and stewards, and higher prices — the works. For informal meals, a simpler menu (but still excellent food), and a less budget-bending bill, even the chic crowd choose a trattoria. In current usage, *ristorante* and trattoria sometimes overlap capriciously. The word *osteria* is also seen all over Italy, and it can indicate anything from a neighborhood wine pub to a good trattoria. When in doubt, check the menu posted near the door. Remember that an automatic extra charge of about 15% will be added to the posted prices for service (*servizio*), and it is customary to leave an optional tip (5% to 10%) for the waiter on top of that. A charge for *pane e coperto* will most likely also appear on your check: Don't make a fuss if you didn't order this item — it translates as the bread and cover charge. Since fine *ristoranti* and trattorie have loyal followings, always call ahead for a table. That's also the way to be sure that you don't arrive on the establishment's weekly closing day — or during its summer hiatus.

Keep Italian dining hours in mind, too. Restaurants are generally open from 1 to 3 PM for lunch and from 8 to 10 or 11 PM for dinner. Some open at 7:30, but don't show up that early unless you want to be the only diner.

Not that you'll ever go hungry. There's always a hot roast meat sandwich, a salad, a small pizza, an omelette, sometimes a hamburger, too, or a sweet waiting at a nearby self-service hot table (*tavola calda*), café, or espresso bar. Even a wine bar serves sandwiches.

Having a breakfast of cappuccino and *pasta* at a stand-up espresso bar is a bracing way to start the day — the *pasta* (literally translated as "dough"), a brioche in this case or perhaps a crescent-shaped *cornetto.* Here, as in the ice cream shop (*gelateria*), pay the cashier first and then take the stamped receipt to the serving counter to collect your choices. In hotels, continental breakfast is standard, although a few offer ham and eggs — at a staggering price — for unadaptable Americans.

Throughout the day, Italians return to the bar for a quick espresso pick-me-up. If straight coffee is too strong, ask for a *lungo* (diluted with water), and if you want a drop of milk, order it *macchiato.* Spoon in the sugar yourself. Cappuccino comes with the familiar head of steamed milk, and *caffè con panna* is topped with whipped cream. Don't expect lemon peel with your espresso. That's mostly an American custom now, brought over years ago by southern Italians who had used it back home to cut the taste of chicory, which the poor drank instead of coffee. (Early owners of Neapolitan restaurants in America are also credited with introducing the debatable etiquette of twirling spaghetti against the bowl of a soup spoon and promoting the myth that all Italian cuisine is spaghetti with tomato sauce.)

A bar in Italy serves coffee and wine but not hard liquor, which is served in what is called an American bar, easier to find in hotels catering to foreign businesspeople than on the street. Italians simply don't go in for the hard stuff. They are, however, the world's biggest consumers of wine. There is no minimum drinking age, often to the delight of teenage tourists who routinely get a glass of wine set before them. For an *aperitivo,* a glass of white wine or Campari is usual, and after dinner Italians prefer a *digestivo* to help settle their stomachs, liqueurs, and sometimes grappa, the strong grape aquavit.

Until the spring of 1986, when a number of Italians died from lethal doses of methyl alcohol in ordinary table wine, travelers were advised to order local house wines, always economical, usually adequate, and sometimes wonderful. Italians who can ascertain the integrity of local wine makers can still do so, but prudent strangers should ask the waiter for bottled wines bearing the DOC designation, which ensures a high-quality product that is made under strict supervision.

Here's some good news for off-season visitors. The *gelaterie* now stay open year-round. (Italians used to think only fools would want ice cream cones in winter.) Don't fail to treat yourself to gelato, the soft, egg-rich ice cream, or *granite,* tongue-smarting coarse ices. There will be dozens of fanciful flavors, from deadly strong chocolate and coffee to intense fruits and berries. No wonder so many people walk out with triple scoops in a rainbow of flavors. Plan to get your ice cream when you're in the mood for strolling and people watching around the square.

In general, your lire will go further if you remember that stand-up food is often half the price of table service and that a café or restaurant table on

Piazza Navona in Rome or Piazza San Marco in Venice is like a front-row-center seat at a street theater performance. You can eat for far less in a place down the street, where you won't have to pay rent for the sidewalk.

Please don't leave Italy without at least one picnic — it's your passport to the fragrant world of the *salumeria,* the consummate delicatessen. The strings of sausages, the hams and salamis and cheeses, in various stages of aging, are sold by the *etto* (100 grams, about ¼ pound, enough for two sandwiches). Prices usually are marked, so just point and say *un etto* or *due etti* (100 or 200 grams). Then pick up some fruit, bread, and small bottles of wine, soda, and mineral water, also at the *salumeria.* On the autostrada without lunch, don't hesitate to stop in a cafeteria-style roadside eatery. They're much better than the US variety, but if you don't find what you want, walk out; the worst the serving women behind the counter will do is grumble.

ON THE ROAD

While driving along the back-country roads, the chances of stumbling across a serendipitous gastronomic treat rise dramatically. Every traveler comes home with his or her own story of walking into a plastic-tablecloth trattoria just when the owner's wife is pulling a hot loaf of bread out of the oven and the saucer-size *porcini* mushrooms she gathered at dawn are drizzled with olive oil, ready for the grill. How about braised rabbit with polenta? Some tiny wild strawberries with cream? Discoveries like these make travelers want to eat in Italy forever. In the rich, fertile north, dishes are sauced with cream and butter, and rice and corn dishes often replace pasta. Moving south, tomatoes and olive oil make the sauce, and pasta rules. Cheeses and sausages are different from region to region. It would take a lifetime of traveling to taste the full range of Italy's culinary ingenuity, but the highlights are accessible to even the most casual tourist. The traveler who knows what to look for has the best chance of choosing wisely and eating well.

ROME AND THE NORTHERN CULINARY CIRCUIT

Most of us get our first taste of Italy in Rome. If it's the only stop on your Italian itinerary, you can conduct all your culinary travels right there. Roman restaurants serve the best dishes from all over the country. But if Rome is simply your springboard to a far-ranging Italian tour, when in Rome eat Roman.

Drink the pale dry frascati wines and enjoy the wondrous little green vegetables such as incredibly sweet peas (*piselli*) and young, chokeless artichokes (prepared with mint, a favorite Roman herb in *carciofi alla romana*). Order tender egg noodles in butter (*fettuccine al burro*) or thick tubular pasta with tomato sauce and unsmoked bacon (*bucatini all'amatriciana*) and *spaghetti alla carbonara,* sauced with egg yolk, or *con vongole,* with tiny clams. More suggestions: peppery grilled chicken (*pollo alla diavola*) and roasted meats, baby lamb (*abbacchio*), and suckling pig (*porchetta*).

Rome's baby lamb comes from the Abruzzo region, which, with its neighbor Molise, makes up a rugged rustic area to the east and southeast of Rome.

In the country inns, it's hard to resist the spit-roasted meats, and along the narrow Adriatic coastline shared by these regions, be sure to investigate the various fish soups (*brodetti*). Abruzzo cooks have a distinctive way of cutting pasta into long thin strands for their lamb sauces and soups: they press the dough against a set of taut strings, and out comes *maccheroni alla chitarra.*

The landlocked region of Umbria, north of Rome, is the place to sample mushrooms and truffles. The precious black truffles grow so profusely hereabouts that Umbrians supply them to France. Sauces, stews, and stuffings are lavished with fresh mushrooms all summer, and in the fall with mushrooms and truffles. Two of Umbria's towns are famous for their specialties — Orvieto for its dry white wine and Perugia for luxurious chocolates. The region of the Marches, east of Umbria, best known for the city of Urbino, makes hearty oven-baked pasta specialties such as a rich meat and cheese lasagna known as *pasticcatta.* The string of fishing villages along the coast is a *brodetto* fancier's heaven.

But it is farther north, in Tuscany, that a visitor begins to understand what is meant by "the glories of Italian cooking;" indeed, many "glorious" French dishes can be traced to Catherine de' Medici, who brought her entourage of cooks from Florence when she left for France to marry the man who would become King Henry II. Tuscany is blessed with the finest olive oils and brunello, the country's king of wines. Tuscans even raise cattle (a rarity in Italy); the white Chianinas produce meat that is so lean that ranchers in the cholesterol-conscious US are starting to breed them. A grilled T-bone steak (*bistecca alla fiorentina*) will come extra rare unless you warn the waiter "*ben cotta.*" Try the succulent Florentine *arista,* roast pork rubbed with rosemary, and for the flavor of Tuscan game, *pappardelle con la lepre,* pasta in hare sauce. The bean and vegetable soup, *ribollita,* thickened with slices of peasant bread, is a favorite *minestra.* Don't miss meaty Tuscan white beans in olive oil. The chianti classico wines are tailor-made for Tuscany's hearty cooking. And be sure to treat yourself to a bottle of brunello wine from Montalcino, a fitting partner to the richest game and roasts.

North of Tuscany lies the gastronome's heaven, Emilia-Romagna. It has never been decided whether the title "dining room of Italy" should be accorded to the entire region or just to its principal city, Bologna. The difficulty of this dilemma becomes apparent with the first taste of mild, air-dried Parma ham (*prosciutto di Parma*) and fresh *parmigiano-reggiano,* the "real" parmesan cheese, moister than the aged wheels that are sent abroad.

In the town of Modena, home of the famous barrel-aged herbed balsamic vinegar, try *zampone,* boiled pig's foot stuffed with sausage. It's the star of Bologna's *bollito misto,* the assortment of boiled beef, veal, sausage, chicken, tongue, and more that is offered from a serving cart rolled to the table. Taste the Bolognese *ragù,* the classic meat-and-tomato pasta sauce, and pistachio-studded mortadella sausage. The Emilia-Romagna restaurants stuff their dainty egg noodle rings (*cappelletti* and tortellini) with inventive cheese and meat fillings and float them in broth or serve them with butter and cheese. The lambrusco wines here will be pleasant enough, but they are not the equals of the Emilia-Romagna kitchen. Try the distinctive walnut liqueur called nocino.

Separating Emilia-Romagna from the Mediterranean is another of Italy's narrow coasts, Liguria, a paradise for seafood lovers. Try the baked seafood pasta. The capital city, Genoa, lays claim to originating pesto. This fragrant uncooked sauce of fresh basil, pine nuts, olive oil, and cheese (mashed and blended with mortar and pestle) is found in pasta, gnocchi, soups, and salad.

North of Liguria is Piedmont, where the prized white truffle (*trifola d'Alba*) hides at the base of old oak trees — and nowhere else in Europe. It's necessary to be in Italy during the autumn to taste the truffles, but you don't have to be in Piedmont. In better restaurants everywhere in Italy, waiters will be shaving precious flakes of the *tartufo* onto pasta. Piedmontese will be shaving them over *fonduta,* fondue of melted fontina cheese, and they'll add a few crisp truffle slices to their *bagna cauda,* a garlicky, hot olive oil dip for raw vegetables. Even better known than the truffles are the wines of Piedmont — dry reds like barbera, barolo, and barbaresco, and asti spumante, sweetly sparkling Italian champagne. The wine-based *aperitivo* commonly known as vermouth was developed here.

Turn east toward Milan to find Italy's dairy country. This is Lombardy, where the cuisine is recognizable by the sweet taste of butter in the cooking and fork-tender veal prepared in simple ways such as scaloppine, osso buco (braised shanks with marrow), and *cotoletta alla milanese,* a breaded chop fried in butter and accompanied with lemon. Milan's signature dish, *risotto alla milanese, arborio* rice golden with saffron, is brought to almost every diner. The local *mascarpone* cheese, more like whipped cream, is the basis for moist, sweet confections, or, topped with sugar and berries, is a dessert in itself.

Heading still farther north toward the Dolomites and the Austrian border, polenta and Teutonic dumplings share the menu. Enjoy the prosciutto of nearby San Daniele alongside Austria's smoky ham, called *Speck.* The port city of Trieste, on the Yugoslav border, adds a third ethnic element, Serbo-Croatian cooking, to the Italo-Austrian mix — sauerkraut bean soup, *jota,* and goulash, for instance.

In Venice, order the famous scampi, served cold with olive oil and lemon, but don't neglect the local spider crab (*granseola*) or risotto blackened by the ink from the cuttlefish, *seppie,* and pungent with ocean flavor. *Pasta e fagioli* (bean and pasta soup) and polenta are favored in Venice in place of pasta in heavy sauces. And whether or not you think you like liver, try Venice's signature fork-tender liver and onion dish (*fegato alla veneziana*). The sturdy red lettuce, radicchio, which Italians serve grilled as a cooked vegetable as well as raw in salads, flourishes in the Veneto region. You will soon recognize its familiar bitter flavor in many Venetian favorites, including radicchio risotto.

LOOKING SOUTH FROM ROME

The Neapolitans invented pizza, and they still make it in every conceivable combination in friendly, crowded pizzerias. The thin-crusted, individual-size pizza is popular here (hungry folks sometimes eat two), and the *pizza Margherita* is the reliable classic — tomato, garlic, olive oil, and basil, with a liberal shower of mozzarella. The Neapolitan specialty, calzone, is a thick turnover made from pizza dough and filled with (instead of topped by) the traditional pizza sausages and cheeses.

Another singular local treat is mozzarella made from water buffalo milk. Have it *alla carrozza,* a fried sandwich, or in a salad of fresh tomato and basil. Here in the heart of plum tomato country, try an order of spaghetti with plain tomato sauce (*al pomodoro*). By the way, the spaghetti with the salty taste of anchovies and the spicy title *alla puttanesca* (woman of the evening) was invented in Naples.

Save room for afternoon visits to the dazzling pastry shops of Naples for flaky, custard-filled *sfogliatelle* and *pastiera,* the cream-and-ricotta-filled cake.

Head south from Naples into Puglia, the heel, or down through Basilicata to Calabria, the toe of Italy. The countryside here quickly explains why the term *la cucina povera* (the cuisine of the poor) is so often used to describe the cooking in these regions. The cooks are inventive, but they have few of the farm-raised meats, dairy foods, and delicate greens of their northern cousins. Expect to find fish, goat, sheep, and pigs (which do not require rich pastures), heat-loving vegetables like eggplants and squash, and that reliable standby, pasta with tomato-based sauces.

Except in the towns of Brindisi and Bari, where the ferries run between Italy and Greece, travelers are few, as are restaurants. But once a traveler has crossed the Strait of Messina to Sicily — island of oranges, sesame, and almonds — meals take on an exotic aspect. The conquering Saracens left Sicily a culinary legacy in the Middle Ages, and it endures today. Restaurants serve Arab couscous. A famous Sicilian sardine and pasta dish, *pasta con sarde,* combines the sweetness of white raisins and the crunch of pine nuts. Spectacular trompe l'oeil candy fruits are made from almond paste (*marzapane*), and towering *cassata* is sponge cake filled with nuts, candied fruits, and ricotta, sometimes with ice cream. Equally popular is the familiar little cannoli, ricotta-filled rolled pastries. We also have Sicily to thank for originating marsala, one of the greats among fortified wines and an essential ingredient of zabaglione, a foamy dessert of whipped egg yolks and wine.

The other big island, Sardinia, boasts at least two favorites: roast pig served on a bed of myrtle leaves, and crisp rounds of paper-thin shepherd's bread called *carta da musica* (music paper).

The catalogue of Italian culinary delights is nearly endless, and one of the authentic pleasures of any Italian visit is the opportunity to expand a personal list of gastronomic experiences. It is hard to imagine a nation with a table set with greater diversity and variety, all the more reason to enthusiastically accept the Italian invitation to dine.

For those travelers who can't wait to get to Italy, there is an English-language service, *Pronto! Call Italy for Dinner.* Simply call 11-39-777-95430 and request the recipe for your favorite Italian dish. A variety of recipes are available for pasta, meat, fish, seafood, and dessert. Vincent Buonassisi, an internationally known Italian chef, has chosen the recipes, using typical Italian ingredients, with an emphasis on freshness. The only charge for these morsels of information is the cost of the call to Italy; the service itself is free.

So if you want to know how to make the real *fettuccine all'Alfredo,* either before or after your Italian travels, call *Pronto!*

Because no menu in Italy is without its quota of pasta dishes — whether boiled, baked, stuffed, under a sauce, or in a soup — be sure to venture beyond the familiar spaghetti form. The glossary below will help you enjoy some possibly unfamiliar shapes.

agnolotti: round or semicircular ravioli
anellini: small rings used in soup
anolini: small pockets, usually stuffed
cannelloni: large stuffed tubes
capelli d'angelo: angel's hair — extra thin spaghetti
cappelletti: little hats
cavatelli: short curly noodles
conchiglie: ridged shells
crespelle: crêpes
farfalle: bows
fettuccine: flat, straight noodles
fusilli: spirals
gnocchi: potato dumplings
lasagna: very wide flat pasta, used in layers
linguine: narrow, flat spaghetti
maccheroni: general term for hollow pasta
orecchiette: little ears
orzo: barley shape; looks like rice
pappardelle: broad noodles
pasta verde: green pasta made with spinach
penne: quills
ravioli: stuffed squares
rigatoni: large grooved tubes
rotini: corkscrews
stelline: stars
tagliatelle: flat noodles
tortellini: stuffed rings
tortelloni: large stuffed rings
tubetti: little tubes
vermicelli: squiggly thin spaghetti
ziti: large grooved macaroni

Music

MUSIC IN ROMAN TIMES

Like painting, sculpture, and architecture, music came to Italy in classical times, chiefly through the absorption of Greek culture. Although some form of music had played a part in the ceremonies and rituals under Rome's seven kings, from the 3rd century BC on the adoption of Hellenic modes and theory came about through contact with Greek drama and recited poetry, which used music as accompaniment. Unfortunately, we have no way of reconstructing how this music sounded, but the historian Livy makes several references to the significant role of music in Roman society. Later, in the 1st century AD, music assumed even greater importance in the contests sponsored by the emperors Augustus and Nero. Public concerts of instrumental music were given in open-air theaters, while ensembles and soloists performed at more intimate banquets of wealthy patricians. Eventually music would free itself of its dependence on literary associations and become a self-sufficient means of expression.

RELIGIOUS MUSIC OF THE MIDDLE AGES

In early Christian times, music was taken over almost entirely by the needs of religious observance. Embellishment of the sacred word was entrusted to the most perfect instrument, the human voice. The basis for inspirational chant derived from a tradition different from the Greek classics — the Hebrew synagogue service. Its psalter and psalmody were adapted and expanded to suit the needs of the Christian faith. When Christianity became the state religion of the decaying Roman Empire in 315, the liturgy further developed to meet the expanded needs that came with this new status. Antiphonal, or responsive, singing, in which the congregation replies in unison to the invocation of the officiating priest, was a way of actively including the congregation in celebration of the mass. It was very effective. Its purported inventor, St. Ambrose, then Bishop of Milan, often felt compelled to confess what he saw as the sinful pleasure derived from music quite apart from the sacred text that it accompanied. Indeed, if music was to continue to serve religion, its role had to be more strictly controlled.

Gregorian chant is named for Pope Gregory the Great (560–604), who was the first great reformer of church music and who standardized the liturgy for the entire Catholic world. The Latin texts and music were meticulously edited and transcribed into a rudimentary notation system for codification. An all-male chorus, the *schola cantorum,* was formed to ensure the correct performance of the mass. Two centuries later, Gregory's reforms were reinforced by Charlemagne, who relied on the monastic organization to carry on the tradition. But music was not to remain monodic forever. The gradual introduction of harmony into religious music started a revolution that affected all Western music, secular as well as religious.

The first step, the movement from the austere Gregorian chant into polyphonic music, was essentially a natural one. The stark, unaccompanied melody, consisting of a reciting note with a final cadence, gradually gave way to variation. First the choir was diversified into parts. The authorized text and melody, the *cantus firmus,* remained inviolate and was performed by the highest male voice, the tenor (so called because it "held" the melody). The text and rhythm of the other parts remained unchanged, thus preserving the intelligibility of the words. But these parts provided the harmony for the *cantus firmus* at a regular interval below the higher pitch, and further experimentation eventually led to even greater divergence. Elaborate disjunctions in intervals and rhythms, and ultimately the introduction of different texts, gave greater weight to the musical play at the expense of textual clarity. Although such a development was frowned on in Italy, where papal authority was strongest, it was allowed to flourish unhindered north of the Alps, particularly in France. French polyphonic innovations were to filter back into Italy later in secular music, thus stimulating even more change. Italy, however, did make a significant contribution to music theory. A Benedictine monk, Guido of Arezzo (995–1050), devised a system of staff notation that established the exact pitches and time values of notes and provided the basis for the system of musical notation that is still in use.

THE RISE OF POLYPHONY

Secular polyphony moved into Italy in the 11th and 12th centuries. Pilgrimages and the Crusades stimulated increased mobility throughout Europe. Those passing through Italy on the long route to the Holy Land turned to singing as an important social activity — first religious singing, and then church melodies, were put to alternative secular lyrics. The rise of city-states and courts also encouraged secular music, as the troubadours from southern France, with their lutes and recorders, provided accompaniment not only for their Provençal love lyrics but for dance as well. Meanwhile, new forms of religious expression began to undermine the supremacy of liturgical plain chant. The *laude* was a particularly Italian phenomenon. A lyric in the vernacular that arose out of spontaneous popular piety, it was free of the modal and tonal restrictions of official church music. St. Francis of Assisi (1186–1226), who called himself "the Troubadour of Christ," was the author of several *laudi.*

MUSIC OF THE ITALIAN RENAISSANCE

The secularization of music advanced further in the 1300s, paralleling a similar development in the arts and letters. Just as Tuscan painters showed an unprecedented interest in the depiction of the world around them, and Dante, Petrarch, and Boccaccio elevated Italian language as a means of literary expression, in music, too, the Ars Nova — the new polyphonic art — was gaining ground. Initially taking its cue from the more elaborate French model, this new polyphony quickly assumed its own Italian characteristics. The main distinction lay in the innate Italian feeling for melody and the predominance of the uppermost vocal line, as opposed to northern practice, in which the various parts were more equitably and abstractly treated. New descriptive forms emerged: the *madrigale* (a vernacular lyric), the *ballata* (a lively dance tune), and the *caccia* (a hunting scene). Padua and Bologna initially vied for the lead, but both were superseded in the 14th century by Florence, where the chief exponent of the Ars Nova was the remarkable Francesco Landino (1325–97). Blinded by a childhood disease, Landino nevertheless mastered every instrument, from the voice to the organ. His achievements as poet and composer were recognized when he was crowned with the laurel wreath in Venice in 1346. Most of his work has survived and is an interesting document of the age.

In the 15th century, Italy fell behind the rest of Europe in musical development. Polyphony had as yet made no impression on religious music, and it survived mostly in the courts at Milan, Mantua, Ferrara, Naples, and especially Florence, which became an important center under the Medici ruler Lorenzo the Magnificent. A productive exchange of ideas between north and south finally began at mid-century, when significent numbers of Flemish choirmasters were employed at the Italian courts. Inevitably, church music adopted polyphony. The most noteworthy example is provided by Adriano Willaert (1482–1562), who in 1527 became *maestro di cappella* at St. Mark's in Venice. The availability of two organs in the same church enabled him to experiment with more intricate harmonies on a grander scale. Willaert's sojourn in Florence resulted in the founding of a local school that was dominated by Andrea Gabrieli (1510–86) and his nephew Giovanni (1557–1612). The school's chief characteristic was the rich tonal effects achieved through experimenting with the combinations of voice and other instruments. These three men set Venice on its way to becoming an important center for instrumental music.

Polyphony fared less well in Rome. Not only was the new form seen as obscuring the all-important text, it smacked of the north, where the papacy had lost so much power in the Protestant Reformation. The Council of Trent drew up strict guidelines for religious music. Had it not been for Giovanni Pierluigi da Palestrina (1525–94), papal patronage of change in music might have disappeared altogether. The greatest composer of the 16th century, Palestrina had spent most of his life as a choirmaster in one Roman church or another. In his hundred-odd masses, he outwardly emulated the a cappella Gregorian chant while in fact using an exquisitely refined choral harmony. History knows him as the "first musician of the Catholic church," and his religious works are the musical counterparts of Michelangelo's frescoes in the Sistine Chapel.

THE RISE OF OPERA

The Renaissance search for the classical past that fostered the revival of the visual arts in Italy also prompted the emergence of opera. In the last quarter of the 16th century, a group of intellectuals, theoreticians, and musicians in the circle of Count Giovanni de' Bardi sought to re-create the essence of Greek theater. The Camerata, as the group was called, believed that ancient drama had been chanted or sung rather than simply recited. But the text was still considered the more important element, and consequently complex polyphony was avoided. Instead, a new kind of supporting harmony developed that favored the individual musical instruments.

Chief theoretician of the Camerata was the lutanist Vincenzo Galileo (1533–91), father of the scientist Galileo Galilei. In his 1581 treatise *Dialogue Between Old and New Music,* Galileo devised the principles of the new form. The first concrete efforts in the form were produced by the singers Jacopo Peri (1561–1633) and Giulio Caccini (1550–1618). The earliest *dramma per musica* that still survives was Peri's *Dafne,* with a libretto by the poet Ottavio Rinuccini. Both composers set the librettist's *Euridice* to music. These early operas are largely in a declamatory style, with a bass accompaniment, and contain relatively few moments of song. Their interest is mostly historical. The first giant in the field was Claudio Monteverdi (1567–1643) from Cremona. This singer, viol player, and composer became associated with the Florentine Camerata and then developed his own ideas more fully under the patronage of Duke Vincenzo Gonzaga, the ruler of Mantua. It was for Gonzaga's court that Monteverdi produced the first authentic masterpiece in opera history, *Orfeo* (1607). In this work, Monteverdi respected the *stile recitativo* of the Camerata, but he assigned a greater role to the musical component by demonstrating its expressive potential. His work became central to the development of baroque music in Italy.

This new form of entertainment spread rapidly throughout the peninsula, and each city produced its own style. Rome became the style setter for the rest of the century with the establishment of a school headed by Stefano Landi (1590–1655) and Luigi Rossi (1598–1653). Opera became a favorite form of entertainment with the Roman nobility, and the Barberini family sponsored performances in the family palace as part of the pre-*Lenten* carnival festivities.

A religious answer to opera was the creation of the oratario. In contrast to opera's mythological subject matter, an oratorio presented a biblical event, in Latin, set to music, without the lavish scenery or costumes of its secular counterpart. Giacomo Carissimi (1605–74) became Rome's outstanding composer of these sacred works, which later reached a high point in England and Germany through the works of Handel and Bach.

In the 17th century, Venice superseded Rome as the opera capital of Italy, with Monteverdi's arrival in Venice as choirmaster of St. Mark's in 1613. In his later works for the stage, such as *Il ritorno di Ulisse in patria* (1641) and *L'incoronazione di Poppea* (1642), Monteverdi's style became more elaborate, with the orchestra playing a more significant role. He was succeeded by Francesco Cavalli (1602–76), Antonio Cesti (1623–90), and Alessandro Stradella (1645–82), all of whom were concerned with the musical element of opera, which stimulated composition and performance techniques well into the next century.

It was also in Venice that opera lost its exclusive association with the nobility. The melodrama became a commercial enterprise, and performances were increasingly spectacular. The world's first public opera house opened in Venice in 1627, and by the end of the century Venice had eight such establishments. Other cities followed.

THE EIGHTEENTH CENTURY

In the Age of Reason, conservatories were founded all over Italy to promote what was becoming a local industry. It was a chief export commodity as well, for Italian composers, singers, and soloists were in much demand in the non-Italian capitals of Europe. During this period the entire range of Italian musical terms, from *allegro* to *vivace,* gained universal acceptance. It was also a time of great experimentation, and although few true masterpieces were produced, opera proved to be the country's main concern. Italy's most illustrious theaters of the time, such as *San Carlo* in Naples (1737), *La Scala* in Milan (1778), and *La Fenice* in Venice (1792), were built to house opera.

Naples supplanted Venice as the operatic center largely through the accomplishments of Alessandro Scarlatti (1660–1725). He wrote more than 115 operas and is alone responsible for the creation of a new kind of opera that enjoyed overwhelming success throughout Europe.

Neapolitan opera reversed the basic tenets of opera's Florentine originators by making music the more important element. The *opera seria* (serious opera) still dealt with themes from ancient history, but its librettos were constructed in ways that separated dramatic and musical components. The heart and soul of Neapolitan opera was the extended piece known as the *da capo* aria, which Scarlatti devised to give freer reign to musical virtuosity. It consisted of a recitative, which related the actual plot, followed by the tripartite aria, which expressed the character's emotional state. The first segment ordinarily would have been complete in itself, but it was followed by a contrast in key, tempo, or mood. The aria closed with a repetition of the initial segment, but it allowed for elaborate improvisations by the singer. Clearly, when the plot was always being interrupted by a series of musical parentheses, dramatic continuity could not be maintained. On the other hand, the succession of beautiful arias sung with great skill was musically satisfying — good show business. For this reason, Italian opera spread across Europe, gaining the interest and support of even non-Italian composers. Its greatest genius was the German composer Handel, who established the tradition in England when he moved there in 1711.

Neapolitan opera made another contribution to the evolution of musical forms in the sprightly instrumental piece known as the overture. Scarlatti is credited with giving the overture a symmetrical structure with three movements — *allegro, adagio, allegro* — providing the basis for what became the orchestral symphony. But the most surprising offshoot of *opera seria* was the *opera buffa* (comic opera). Humorous intermezzos that were performed during the scenery changes of the *opera seria* proved to be the major work's antithesis. The plot was simple, often amusing, dealing with everyday people speaking in local dialect. The short arias were spontaneous and graceful tunes, and there was greater use of duets and closing finales. The two comic scenes were often so popular that they became detached from the *opera seria* and were presented independently as a short continuous comic work. The most famous example of this is *La serva padrona* (1733) by Giovanni Battista Pergolesi (1710–36). His successors Niccolò Piccinni (1728–1800), Giovanni Paisiello (1740–1816), and Domenico Cimarosa (1749–1801) took this Neapolitan invention as far afield as Paris, St. Petersburg, and Berlin.

Overshadowed by Naples, Venice nonetheless produced a variant of *opera seria* that was more balanced and richly orchestrated. While Lotti, Caldara, and Albinoni all wrote works for the stage, only those of Antonio Vivaldi (1675–1741) continue to enjoy a much-deserved revival. In the comic vein, Baldassare Galuppi (1706–85) produced a local brand in collaboration with Carlo Goldoni, whose librettos provided for greater character development.

Venice managed to establish a musical sphere of influence in northern Italy, which was far more receptive to the reforming influence of northern composers who revitalized opera later in the century. The most important exponent of the movement against the excesses and abuses of Neapolitan opera was Christoph Willibald Gluck (1714–87). With the help of his librettist Calzabigi, Gluck established a new balance between music and drama in his operas *Orfeo ed Euridice* (1762) and *Alceste* (1767). And while the child prodigy Mozart (1756–91) wrote typical Italian operas for Milan, his masterpieces in collaboration with the notorious Lorenzo da Ponte performed a similar service for the *opera buffa. Le nozze di Figaro, Don Giovanni,* and *Così fan tutte* remain the most enjoyable and satisfying of all operas, with their sublime music and careful blend of dramatic and comic elements.

Despite the 18th century's obsession with opera, Italy's most significant advances were made in the field of instrumental music, a fact that is inextricably linked to the new level of perfection attained in the making of the instruments themselves. The evolution of the viol family was complete, culminating in the supreme craftsmanship of the violin in the workshops of Giuseppe Antonio Guarneri (1687–1745) and Antonio Stradivari (1644–1737) in Cremona. The various keyboard instruments and their treatment underwent improvement and modification. The organ, perfected by the Antegnati family of Brescia, was consequently freed from its role as a mere support for the voice in sacred music. The harpsichord enjoyed a similar liberation, largely due to Alessandro Scarlatti's son, Domenico (1685–1757), whose 545 compositions showed the full potential of the harpsichord as a solo instrument. It was soon to be eclipsed by the pianoforte, invented by the Paduan Bartolomeo Crisofari in 1711, and its protagonist was to be Muzio Clementi (1752–1832), who provided the new percussion instrument with a series of exercises, *Gradus ad Parnassum,* that are still used today.

The most active center for instrumental music was understandably Venice, given its long-standing tradition dating from the 16th century. The champions of the age were now Vivaldi and Tommaso Albinoni (1674–1745). The Venetian gift for creativity in contrasting textures was admirably displayed in new forms and combinations, such as the *sonata a tre, concerto,* and *concerto grosso.* Of the two composers, Vivaldi's work has greater appeal. Nicknamed the Red Priest because of his rust-colored hair, he was excused from ecclesiastical duties for health reasons and devoted most of his time to music. His main achievement lies in the mastery of form through his 600 concertos. His inventive nature produced new combinations, such as adding wind instruments to a string ensemble. His ideas concerning the descriptive potential of abstract forms are expressed in his program concerto *The Four Seasons,* which remains his best-known work.

In the latter half of the century, Italy lost some of its natural resources through the emigration of its most gifted composers. Luigi Cherubini (1762–1842) went to Paris in 1788 and quickly learned to adapt his style to French taste and language. His operas showed some of the influence of Gluckian reforms, but in the greater use of the orchestra, substantial chorus, and insertion of the obligatory ballet he became the father of the French style of grand opera. Although Cherubini's operas are somewhat conventional, his overtures are exceptionally powerful, even earning him Beethoven's admiration. His works represented official taste in Napoleonic France, and for the last 20 years of his life he served as the director of the national conservatory. Gasparo Spontini (1774–1851) was active in Paris, where he won the favor of Empress Josephine, and subsequently in Berlin, where he helped forge German opera. Ultimately, however, neither Cherubini nor Spontini was to have any lasting effect on the younger generation of Italian composers.

THE NINETEENTH CENTURY

The romantic era met with an anomaly in Italy. While the rest of Europe was passionately involved with the fuller and freer development of instrumental forms, Italian interests lay elsewhere. Only in the figure of Niccolò Paganini (1782–1840) did the country produce a virtuoso performer and composer of international standing. Born of a musical family and blessed with exceptional talent, Paganini became the prototype of the romantic soloist. Early in his career he found the available repertory for the violin far too limited for his purposes and composed works of incredible technical complexity, which he performed to the astonishment of audiences all over Europe. His success made others possible, most notably that of the virtuoso pianist Franz Liszt.

Opera remained the chief musical concern in Italy, but not, however, as a mere extension of the highly stylized genre of the previous century. Librettists, drawing on the wealth of European literature, provided better texts, and the scores incorporated musical innovations. And unlike the previous century, the 19th century produced a steady flow of masterpieces by genius composers, resulting in the golden age of Italian opera.

The outstanding composer of this golden age was Gioacchino Rossini (1792–1868). Born into a musical family, he quickly mastered several instruments, and by the time he was 21 he had both tragic and comic masterpieces to his credit. His *Il barbiere di Siviglia* (1816) remains the supreme *opera buffa.* In Rossini's hands the genre evolved fully, as his highly individualized characters, capable of dishing out wit and satire, emerged from the stock figures of the form's Neapolitan origins. Musically, too, opera was considerably enhanced by Rossini's brilliant orchestration and spontaneity. His accomplishments in *opera seria,* which show an exceptional talent for vocal writing, have been a feature of the world's opera houses since his time.

Rossini's popularity took him all over the Continent to oversee the production of his operas. In 1824 he settled in Paris, where he revived earlier successes and wrote *Guillaume Tell,* a grand opera in four acts, his last work for the stage. He lived for several more decades, composing little and enjoying the intellectual life in Paris.

In Italy, the operatic tradition was carried on by Vincenzo Bellini (1801–35). Although his career was brief and he had none of Rossini's gaiety or talent for orchestration, Bellini secured a place in operatic history. A gentle strain of melancholy runs through his works, which are characterized by an extremely sensitive talent for vocal writing. In such works as *Norma* and *La sonnambula* (a subject better suited to comic opera), Bellini attained new depths of feeling in the perfect blend of vocal line and text. It is little wonder that Chopin was to fall under Bellini's spell in his elegiac compositions for the piano.

Gaetano Donizetti (1797–1848) brought Italian opera to mid-century. His first popular success was a sentimental comedy, *L'elisir d'amore* (1832), but he was also capable of expressing pathos and profound sentiment. His *Lucia di Lammermoor* (1835) vies with Bellini's *Norma* as the masterpiece of bel canto, but Donizetti's work is characterized by a more extensive use of the orchestra and a more subtle fusion of recitative and aria. Success took him to Paris, where he wrote a comic opera after the French fashion, replete with spoken dialogue, called *La Fille du Régiment* (1840), as well as a grand opera, *La Favorite* (1842). A few years later, he was incapacitated by the disease that was to cause his death, but his legacy consists of some 70 works for the stage.

Giuseppe Verdi (1813–1901) was the giant who closed the century. He was as much a national as a musical hero, for many of his works during the 1840s dealt with the plight of the oppressed and became associated with the struggle for freedom from foreign domination and the instinct for Italian unity. Verdi rose to greatness against all odds. Of humble birth, he was denied conservatory training and felt deeply the effects of his initial failures; it was the faith of his friends and his second wife that sustained him. Aware of opera's shortcomings, Verdi demanded better librettos, and in his highly theatrical works based on the dramas of Schiller, Hugo, Dumas, and Shakespeare the human voice became the primary means of dramatic and musical communication.

Between 1851 and 1853, Verdi composed three masterpieces for the Italian repertory, *Rigoletto, Il trovatore,* and *La traviata.* Despite their proximity in date, each opera is distinct, largely through the skillful use of orchestral color that defines the particular setting. Verdi's fame was secure, and, like his predecessors, he responded to the call of Paris; his association with French grand opera is evident in *Un ballo in maschera* (1859) and *Don Carlos* (1867). During a brief political interlude between 1861 and 1865, he became a member of the new Italian parliament. Despite the innovative features of *Aïda* (1871), however, his style was considered anachronistic as Italy began assimilating developments from beyond the Alps, where Wagner's music dramas were creating a stir. Verdi, however, had by no means exhausted his talent, and his last stage works, *Otello* (1887) and *Falstaff* (1893), with the help of composer and librettist Arrigo Boito, saw the evolution of the closed form of the traditional opera into a sung symphonic poem.

Opera felt the impact of changing literary tastes as well. *Verismo* took its cue from the slice-of-life brutality of the real world, and its use in opera was spread through the success of Bizet's *Carmen* (1875). This modern style swept away the earlier operatic conventions, as arias became short and expressive, and the orchestra was charged with the task of creating the setting and mood.

Cavalleria rusticana (1890), based on a short story about Sicilian honor by Giovanni Verga, can be considered not only the masterpiece of the style but also that of its composer, Pietro Mascagni (1863–1945). Its only real rival is *I Pagliacci* (1892), whose plot was taken from a real incident, by Ruggiero Leoncavallo (1857–1919). Others who adapted *verismo* to historical dramas included Umberto Giordano (1867–1948), who composed *Andrea Chenier* (1896), and Francesco Cilea (1866–1950), the composer of *Adriana Lecouvreur* (1902). But for all their merits, none of these composers could compete with Giacomo Puccini's consistent gift for the theater.

Puccini (1858–1924) descended from a long line of composers of sacred music, but his interests lay solely in the stage. Despite a slow start, his fresh, impulsive music flowed steadily into operas from the time of his first triumph with *Manon Lescaut* (1893). Few composers have such a large body of their works in the standard repertory, and while *La Bohème* (1896) and *Madame Butterfly* (1904) are often criticized for their sentimentality, both works are remarkable for their balance and superb musicality. *Tosca* (1900), showing a darker side, and *La fanciulla del West* (1910), often denigrated as the first "spaghetti western," are nonetheless incredibly rich scores that give evidence of a receptiveness to progressive composers and foreign trends. With *Turandot* (1926), incomplete at Puccini's death, the golden age of Italian opera came to a close.

THE TWENTIETH CENTURY

As artistic director of *La Scala* in Milan from 1898 to 1908 and 1921 to 1929, Arturo Toscanini (1867–1957), one of the world's great conductors, was integral in presenting new operas to the Italian public. Even after World War I, opera continued to be Italy's chief musical preoccupation. As a result, the country was less responsive to the European revolution in instrumental music. Links with Berlin, Vienna, and Paris were tenuously forged by the number of Italians who studied abroad and returned with new ideas. The case of Ferruccio Busoni (1866–1924) is unfortunately typical. One of the most cultured figures of his age, the composer-pianist-conductor was little appreciated on native soil and spent the better part of his creative life in Germany.

A younger generation including Alfredo Casella (1883–1947), Idelbrando Pizzetti (1880–1968), Ottorino Respighi (1879–1936), and Francesco Malipiero (1882–1973), brought continental avant-garde works of composers such as Schoenberg and Stravinsky to the attention of the Italian public. Under fascism, nationalist sentiment encouraged new music as well as the revival of forgotten masters, most notably Monteverdi and Vivaldi. The end of World War II saw a denationalization of Italian music, and dodecaphony became the medium for the successive generation headed by Luigi Dallapiccola (1904–75) and Goffredo Petrassi (b. 1904). Of the still younger composers, Bruno Maderna (1920–73) and Luciano Berio (b. 1920), in their experiments with electronic music and other media, have brought Italian music to its present status.

Painting and Sculpture

In spite of the abundance of Italian art in museums around the world, so much art remains where it originated that Italy probably has more fine art per square inch than any other country on earth. Italians live intimately with their art — it's not just in the museums. Churches, chapels, and piazzas bring art into everyday Italian life. The devout burn candles in front of masterpieces of religious painting, children routinely splash around remarkable baroque fountains, and even the humblest citizens proudly hold forth on artworks major and minor in the most remote country villages. This enthusiasm has been shared by visitors for centuries. In 1666, the French established the Prix de Rome, a fellowship that enables young artists to continue their education in Rome. Many other countries followed suit, offering similar programs that still exist. As they have done for hundreds of years, thousands of artists, students, and visitors still come to Italy each year to observe and absorb works of art firsthand.

ANCIENT ART

Much of what we know about ancient Greek civilization is derived from its influence in Italy. The Greeks left traces of their art in Magna Graecia, the southern part of the Italian peninsula, and in Sicily, which they began colonizing around the 8th century BC. Remnants of Greek art were reverently preserved by the Etruscans, who lived to the north of Magna Graecia at about the same time and who valued Greek vases so highly that they included them in their burial chambers. The Romans collected, copied, and imitated Greek art, bringing back paintings and sculpture by the boatload and using Greek artists to glorify their own empire.

One of the arts the Greeks valued most highly was vase painting. They decorated their terra cotta vessels first with black designs on the reddish clay and later in a more naturalistic red-on-black scheme. Two of the finest such vessels were found at Etruscan sites in Italy: the *Chigi* vase, an *oenochoe,* or wine pitcher, now on display at the *Museo Nazionale di Villa Giulia* in Rome, and the *François* vase, a *krater* used for mixing water and wine, which is in Florence's *Museo Archeologico.* Like many Greek vases, these depict lively battle scenes and are considered to be among the best examples of this unique art form.

Archaeological excavations in Italy have revealed much about Greek art. Pompeii and Herculaneum, excavated in the 18th century, are the best-known sites, but even more recently other dramatic discoveries have brought to light long-forgotten aspects of Greek art.

One such find occurred in 1968 in a tomb outside Paestum, a Greek colonial town near Naples. Here the supple rendering of figures in vase painting is combined for the first time with landscape and seascape elements in a type of painting on plaster walls called fresco. This technique, like many principles of Greek art and philosophy, was revived during the Renaissance.

Another discovery took place not on land but in the Ionian Sea off Riace, a coastal town in southern Italy. In 1972, a diver casually happened on two bronze statues of Greek warriors, now called the Riace bronzes and dated to about the middle of the 5th century BC. Although Italian museums are replete with examples of Greek sculpture, the bronzes on exhibit in the *Museo Archeologico Nazionale,* in Reggio di Calabria, are among the few statues that are not just Roman copies of Greek originals.

While the Greeks were occupying the south of Italy, the Etruscans were building up a network of cities in central Italy. Although the Etruscans were not considered as inventive as their Greek contemporaries, many of their works of art nevertheless show real mastery, especially the terra cotta statues they used as tomb sculptures and temple decorations. The Etruscans were also adept at bronze casting (although much of it was done by Greek artisans) and decorated their tombs with paintings influenced by motifs from Greek vases.

The Romans, likewise, took much from Greek art, including the art itself. Greek painting, sculpture, and objets d'art, much of it intended for religious purposes, were imported for use in Roman homes as decoration. In this respect, the Romans may have been the first art collectors who didn't understand what they were collecting. The insatiable Roman taste for things Greek brought many Greek artists to Rome and created a large market for copies of ancient Greek masterpieces in both Greece and Rome.

The Romans' devotion to their ancestors, coupled with their realistic approach to life, gave rise to a highly developed form of portraiture. From the Etruscans the Romans adopted the practice of making portrait busts (to the Greeks, such sculptures would have looked like severed heads), and they also excelled in painted portraits. The excavations at Pompeii reveal Roman skill at depicting other subjects in painting (still life, landscape, and trompe l'oeil architecture) and the masterful use of mosaics as well.

Like Roman architecture, Roman sculpture was meant to glorify the state and was made on a grand scale. Typical subjects were the heroic deeds of Roman generals and emperors, often executed in appropriately colossal proportions.

EARLY CHRISTIAN AND GOTHIC ART

When Christianity effectively became the official state religion with the Edict of Milan in AD 313, artists began to turn their talents toward church subjects. In AD 330 Emperor Constantine transferred the capital of the empire to the Greek town Byzantium, renaming it Constantinople. This brought the influence of Middle Eastern art forms to the provincial Italian peninsula. Sculpture, which had been used by the Romans primarily for monumental purposes, had little place in the humble new religion and was largely replaced by painting, which could be spread out on the flat walls of the new church buildings, as the predominant art form. The Latin dictum of the time, "*Quod legentibus scriptura, hoc idiotibus pictura*" ("Painting is the illiterates' reading of the scriptures"), best explains its use to educate the masses to the ways of the new religion.

Although much early Christian wall decoration was done in the relatively perishable form of fresco, another medium inherited from the Romans proved to be much more durable: mosaics. The *tesserae,* or cubes, the Romans used for floor decoration were adapted to decorate church walls. They were even improved on since for walls they did not have to be hard stone, which limited the colors that could be used. Marble *tesserae* were replaced by colored glass stones, often backed with gold to create a floating, shimmering effect. In Italy, the Adriatic naval town of Ravenna became the capital of the Western Roman Empire in 402, and the Byzantine influence flourished there in mosaics that are the best preserved outside Istanbul and the most intact in the world. The insides of domes and the walls of churches and tombs throughout the city are lined with mosaics that depict religious scenes and naturalistic landscape details such as rocks and plants that were to influence the beginnings of modern painting.

The Romanesque movement made an even briefer appearance in Italy than in most of the rest of Europe, but it is important in the evolution of Italian art because with it came the first of many distinctive personalities in the history of Italian art, Wiligelmo da Modena. This sculptor's most important work is a series of reliefs (ca. 1099–ca. 1106) on the Cathedral of Modena, showing the creation and fall of the Garden of Eden with a sense of movement and pathos that had been disregarded during the Byzantine era. As sculpture gradually regained its prominence in the Gothic period, other masters emerged, notably Nicola (1220–84) and Giovanni (1245–1314) Pisano in Tuscany, whose works show a keen interest in classical prototypes.

At this time, painting again became important, primarily because of the increased need for large altarpieces in religious ritual. Although the works of early painters such as the Tuscan Cimabue (ca. 1240–ca. 1302) and the Roman Pietro Cavallini (ca. 1250–ca. 1330) show a familiarity with contemporary sculpture, it wasn't until the early Renaissance that painters finally began to abandon the Byzantine style, which reached its peak in Italy in the early 14th century. The first of these masters was the Sienese painter Duccio (ca. 1255–ca. 1319).

THE RENAISSANCE

The term "Renaissance" is often used to mean a rebirth of interest in classical civilizations, but since the classical influence persisted all along in Italy, in the Italian context it refers more to a rebirth of the importance of the individual. During this period the great personalities in art history began to emerge. The first painter to completely break with the Byzantine tradition was Giotto (ca. 1267–1337), whose paintings are full of ingeniously detailed characterizations. A dominant personality, he was well documented by Renaissance writers. Dante wrote of Giotto's fame in his *Purgatorio,* and according to another contemporary writer, Giovanni Villani, the artist "translated painting from Greek into Latin," that is, from Eastern into Western models. The

16th-century writer Giorgio Vasari, considered the world's first art historian, praised Giotto as "a pupil of Nature and no other," and his many fresco paintings throughout Italy have a naturalistic quality that endures brilliantly today. Considered the father of the Renaissance, Giotto dominated early-14th-century painting in Florence, where he worked extensively, and throughout Tuscany.

During the following century, the 1400s or *quattrocento,* sculpture made great strides as artists began to give a new depth to their works. The Florentine Lorenzo Ghiberti (1378–1455) designed bronze reliefs for the doorways of the Florence baptistry, about which, according to Vasari, Michelangelo is supposed to have proclaimed, "O work divine! O door worthy of heaven." Even more influential was Ghiberti's apprentice, Donatello (ca. 1386–1466), who, with his friend the architect Filippo Brunelleschi (ca. 1377–1446), made extensive studies of ancient Rome. Donatello produced sculptures of a form that had not been attempted since Roman days, notably the freestanding David in Florence and an equestrian monument to Gattamelata in Padua, which served as a model for all northern Italian sculpture. One of the most important sculptures it influenced was the equestrian statue of Colleoni in Venice, executed toward the end of the century by Andrea del Verrocchio (1435–88), who was also a painter and the teacher of Leonardo da Vinci.

At the same time, the exciting notions of the Renaissance were being expressed in experiments in painting. In Florence, Masaccio's (1401–28) frescoes in the Carmine Chapel were among the earliest to explore volume; Paolo Uccello (1397–1475) became obsessed with perspective; and in the Convent of San Marco, Fra Angelico (1387–1455) made fresh use of color and line, which attained its most poetic expression in the lyrical paintings of Sandro Botticelli (ca. 1444–1510). Outside Florence, in Arezzo, Piero della Francesca (ca. 1420–92) brought wonderful new effects of light and color to the fresco tradition. In Mantua in the north, Andrea Mantegna (1431–1506) experimented with foreshortening, and in Venice, Giovanni Bellini (ca. 1430–1516) began a long tradition of fascination with color.

The Renaissance reached its peak during the 16th century, the *cinquecento,* otherwise known as the High Renaissance. Under the patronage of the Medici family in Florence, the popes in Rome, and the Sforza family in Milan, great geniuses flowered. The best-known names in all of Italian art were the great artists of this period: Leonardo da Vinci (1452–1519), Raphael (1483–1520), and Michelangelo (1475–1564). Leonardo did his painting, with its characteristic *sfumato* (mist), mostly in Milan; Raphael and Michelangelo painted in Florence and Rome, where Michelangelo also produced his famous sculptures. At the same time, another school of painting was developing in Venice: Giorgione (ca. 1478–1511), Titian (1477–1576), Jacopo Tintoretto (1518–94), and Paolo Veronese (1528–88) — all masters of the rich coloration that characterized Venetian painting.

As Renaissance artists became increasingly sophisticated, they began to break their own rules in a deliberate attempt to demonstrate their bravura; bodies became more attenuated and set in distorted poses, scale and perspective were treated irreverently, and colors became harsh. Even in its own time, the work was considered stylized or "mannered"; hence the term Mannerism.

Many of the precepts of Mannerism were laid down by the High Renaissance artists (Raphael, Michelangelo, Tintoretto), and although certain artists achieved fame in this tradition — Giulio Romano (1499–1546), Jacopo Pontormo (1494–1557), Rosso Fiorentino (1494–1540), Francesco Parmigianino (1503–40) — it was short-lived and soon gave way to the splendor of the baroque. Just before that happened, however, decorative painting reached new heights in the unique works of the Bolognese artists Ludovico Carracci (1555–1619) and his cousins Annibale (1560–1609) and Agostino (1557–1602) Carracci.

Baroque art began in Rome as political and economic power began to centralize there under the popes. As a reaction to Mannerism, forms became simpler and more direct. Caravaggio (ca. 1565–1609), with his strong chiaroscuro, or contrasting light and shadow, was the primary exponent of Mannerism in painting, while Gianlorenzo Bernini's (1598–1680) exuberant sculpture and playful fountains were its counterparts in three-dimensional works of art. Baroque was primarily a Roman phenomenon in Italy and lasted there and in the south of the country well into the 18th century, while the decorative schemes of Giovanni Battista Tiepolo (1696–1770) dominated the salons of Venice.

THE MODERN WORLD

In 1748, Herculaneum and Pompeii were dug out of the lava of Vesuvius, which had buried them for millennia. The discoveries there revived an interest in the classical past. Combined with a gradual tiring of baroque excesses, this caused the birth of a new art movement in Rome, neo-classicism. Unlike previous classical revivals, this time there was physical contact with the relics of ancient civilizations, which were examined firsthand from the excavations, and great pains were taken to reproduce them in the most scientific way possible. Antonio Canova (1757–1822) was the greatest champion of neoclassical sculpture in Rome, where Giovanni Battista Piranesi (1720–78) also produced hundreds of etchings showing both the ancient and contemporary city. In Milan to the north, Andrea Appiani (1754–1817), Napoleon's court painter in Italy, painted extensively in this style.

During the 19th century, a group of Italians working mainly in Tuscany revolted against the prevailing academic style, much as the Impressionists were doing in France. Some of these painters produced realistic, usually outdoor scenes built up from blobs, or *macchie,* of color (hence the name *macchiaioli*). Others, paralleling Romantic movements in northern Europe, preferred indoor historical scenes that reflected the prevailing taste for patriotism, as the peninsula of Italy was gradually being united for the first time in its history.

At the beginning of the 20th century, certain Italian artists, such as Amedeo Modigliani (1884–1920), emigrated to Paris. However, independent movements started up within Italy as well, notably futurism — championed by Umberto Boccioni (1882–1916), Carlo Carrà (1881–1966), Giacomo Balla (1871–1958), and Gino Severini (1883–1966) — and metaphysical painting — Giorgio de Chirico (1888–1978) and Carlo Carrà. Subsequent 20th-century movements followed the course of international art history (realist painting during the war years, abstract painting in the postwar period, minimalist and conceptualist art more recently). In recent years, however, Italian painting has again taken a leading role with the so-called neo-expressionist painters, many of whom reside in New York, making a tremendous splash in galleries and collections throughout the world.

Architecture

For centuries, Italian architects have constructed and embellished cities and buildings in their own country and throughout the world. With their formidable skill as engineers, the ancient Romans established or expanded settlements not only on the Italian peninsula but all over Europe, the Middle East, and Africa. Almost every major architectural style since ancient times originated in Italy before exerting considerable influence outside the country, often at the direct invitation of foreign rulers who recognized the Italians' preeminence in the field. Italian genius gave birth to the Renaissance in Florence and, encouraged by the French King François I, was spread to France. Austrian architecture was influenced by the northern Italian Renaissance and, later, by the baroque, a style that originated in Rome. As far away as Russia, Ivan III employed Italian engineers in Moscow during the 15th century; 3 centuries later the son of an Italian ballerina laid out St. Petersburg in a neo-classical style inspired by Rome, while the neo-classicism of Palladio influenced architecture in England and the United States. Indeed, Italy has served as the inspiration for lovers of architectural beauty virtually since the beginning of Western civilization, and architects and students have traditionally gone to Italy to complete their studies. Even for the non-specialist, the rich architectural heritage of Italy is one of the best reasons for visiting the country.

MAGNA GRAECIA

As early as the 8th century BC, the Greeks began colonizing the southern Italian peninsula and Sicily, the area known as Magna Graecia (Greater Greece). By the 6th and 5th centuries BC, Greek civilization was at its peak in Italy. During this period, the great temples of the Doric order — the Greeks' greatest contribution to architecture — were built. The best surviving examples are at Paestum on the mainland and at Agrigento, Segesta, and Syracuse on Sicily. Here the principles of Doric architecture — harmoniously proportioned, fluted columns with a slight convexity (entasis) in the shaft, topped with a simple square capital — took shape before culminating in the Parthenon in Athens.

THE ETRUSCANS

Meanwhile, beginning in the 8th century BC, the mysterious Etruscans were gradually building up their empire in the central part of the peninsula. Very little of their architecture has survived, primarily because of the impermanence of the building materials they used — wood, rubble, and clay. What remains is made of stone or terra cotta: massive stone-block city gates in Volterra, Perugia, and Todi (the Etruscans, not the Romans, deserve credit for being the first people since Babylonian times to use the arch in monumental architecture); bits of wall near Viterbo; and burial chambers outside Cerveteri and Tarquinia, hewn into the rock in sometimes ghostly simulations of real homes. The remains of temples consist mostly of stone foundations (the buildings were made of wood), although some fragments of terra cotta entablatures have also been unearthed. The temples were built along simple Greek lines; the Etruscans, however, originated the use of certain elements in their temples — the simple, unfluted columns of the Tuscan order, the high podium, the deep porch, and the wide *cella* — many of which the Romans later appropriated.

THE ROMANS

At the height of the Roman Empire in the 1st century AD, the state policy of bread and circuses generated a building boom of new theaters, amphitheaters, and stadia. Other civic needs called for factories, roads, bridges, aqueducts, triumphal arches, temples, basilicas, and even entire towns. Living conditions ranged from squalid to squanderous — blocks of tenements, urban houses with open atria, and luxurious villas.

In his *De architectura* (Treatise on Architecture), Vitruvius, the 1st-century BC Roman architect, suggests that many early Roman architects came from Greece. Even so, the Romans used Greek principles only to suit their own grandiose purposes; the Greek orders, especially the florid Corinthian (often combined with Ionic), provided mere decoration for massive Roman walls. The Romans even developed their own large-scale order — appropriately called *colossal* — to match the grandeur of their buildings.

The Romans introduced a variety of new building types. They turned the Greek temple inside out to invent the basilica for use as a meeting hall. The basilica is considered the most basic of all Roman buildings, a functional structure with solid walls on the outside and columns on the inside. The Romans also built the first standing amphitheaters (of which the Colosseum in Rome is the largest example), developed public baths (*thermae*), and introduced the triumphal arch. They also left many well-preserved examples of domestic architecture: At the ancient port of Ostia, for example, the *insulae,* concrete-and-brick tenements, survive, and the *domus,* the middle class home, is in evidence at Herculaneum and Pompeii. Roman domestic architecture reached its height in the sprawling villa outside Tivoli that once belonged to the emperor Hadrian.

Besides their architectural achievements, the Romans were also highly skilled engineers. Although they did not invent the arch or the vault, they incorporated them throughout the empire in bridges, aqueducts, amphitheaters, and other structures. And while concrete and brick had previously been used as building materials, the Romans used them so extensively in their capital that the emperor Augustus boasted that he found a city of brick and turned it into a city of marble — only to have his successors leave it largely a city of concrete.

EARLY CHRISTIAN THROUGH GOTHIC ARCHITECTURE

Roman buildings set the style for early Christian churches. The long, narrow basilica and the centrally planned mausoleum became the churches and baptistries of a later era. Numerous examples of these 5th- and 6th-century buildings exist throughout Rome and, most prominently, in Ravenna, which also has the earliest *campanili* (bell towers), added on to the churches in the 9th century.

During the Romanesque era, which in Italy began at the end of the 9th century, the use of baptistries and bell towers was common in Italian churches (the most famous bell tower is the Leaning Tower of Pisa). Italian Romanesque used brilliant white marble on church exteriors, as can be seen in Pisa, Lucca, and Pavia; brick was used extensively in Milan and Murano. Throughout this period, the number of outside influences on Italian architecture was enormous: St. Mark's in Venice remained Byzantine; southern Italian architecture is Norman; and Sicilian structures of the period resemble Norman, Saracen, and even Arabic architecture.

Gothic cathedrals in Italy did not catch on the way they did north of the Alps for several reasons: the warmer climate called for thick walls with frescoes rather than the stained glass windows that predominated in the north, the traditional materials in Italy for churches were brick or colored marbles (not limestone), and Italy was already endowed with a centuries-old architectural tradition. Nevertheless, during the 13th and 14th centuries, Gothic cathedrals were built in Siena, Florence, Orvieto, and Milan (although Milan's Duomo — perhaps the most recognizably Gothic of all — wasn't completed until the 19th century). Among the magnificent examples of nonreligious Gothic architecture are the town halls of Perugia, Siena, and Florence and the Doge's Palace in Venice, which has been described as "the most successful non-ecclesiastical building ever achieved in the Gothic style."

THE RENAISSANCE

The rebirth of classical principles, known as the Renaissance, that took place in Florence during the early 15th century was especially evident in architecture. Unlike the case of painting, there were tangible reminders everywhere of the classical past — buildings and ruins to be studied — and the architects of the time made a conscious effort to emulate the ancients: Leone Battista Alberti's (1404–72) *De re aedificatoria* (On the Art of Building; 1452), the first architectural treatise of the Renaissance, was a deliberate nod to Vetruvius.

Like the artists of the era, Renaissance architects were major personalities with highly individual styles as well as multitalented "Renaissance men." For example, Filippo Brunelleschi (ca. 1377–1446), who is considered the first Renaissance architect, was trained as a goldsmith and sculptor, and it was not until he lost the competition to design the bronze doors for Florence's baptistry that he took up architecture full time. After studying in Rome for many years, Brunelleschi returned to his native Florence to build what is regarded as the first Renaissance building, the Spedale degli Innocenti (Foundling

Hospital). Soon afterward, he began the red tile dome of the Florence Cathedral. Rising, as Alberti described it, "above the skies, ample to cover with its shadow all the Tuscan people," the dome still dominates Florence. Brunelleschi's work, with its peaceful classical interiors of white plaster and contrasting gray stone known as *pietra serena,* set the style of Florentine architecture for centuries to come.

Alberti himself was one of the most fascinating personalities of the Renaissance, as noteworthy as Leonardo da Vinci for the variety of his talents. In addition to being a theoretician, playwright, musician, painter, mathematician, scientist, and athlete, he was also one of the most influential architects of the Renaissance. His extensive studies of the ancients strongly influenced his plans for many different types of buildings (although he never actually took part in building them). The façade of the Church of Santa Maria Novella in Florence has a central doorway based on the Pantheon and is the first Renaissance structure to use "harmonic proportions," a system of measurements based on ancient music theory, which later figured prominently in Renaissance architectural ideals. Alberti is also credited with spreading the Renaissance beyond Florence: The Tempio Malatestiano, a memorial based loosely on a Roman arch, was built in Rimini; the churches of San Sebastiano and Sant'Andrea, also classically derived, were erected in Mantua.

Milan also had its share of architectural activity during the Renaissance, introduced by the Florentine architect Michelozzo di Bartolomeo (1396–1492), with his Brunelleschi-derived Portinari Chapel in the Church of Sant'Eustorgio. Another Florentine architect, Antonio Averlino Filarete (ca. 1400–ca. 1470), worked at the court of the powerful Sforza family. Besides building the symmetrical Spedale Maggiore in Milan, Filarete was responsible for a curious architectural treatise that included plans for an ideal city called Sforzinda, the first entirely symmetrical town plan in Western history (as idealistic as it was, it included provisions for a brothel on the ground floor of a 10-story "Tower of Vice and Virtue").

The theme of symmetry was later taken up by the Sforza's most famous beneficiary, Leonardo da Vinci (1452–1519), who planned a number of symmetrical churches. Although the plans were never executed, they had a tremendous influence on Donato Bramante (1444–1514), who built many centrally planned structures in Milan before fleeing to Rome when the Sforzas lost power. The classical architecture in Rome greatly influenced Bramante's work: His small, circular Tempietto of San Pietro in Montorio (1502) is considered the first piece of High Renaissance architecture and the only one of the entire Renaissance that successfully captured the classical spirit.

The High Renaissance in Rome had a reverberating effect on northern Italian architects through its influence on Galeazzo Alessi (1512–72), Michele Sanmicheli (1484–1559), and Jacopo Sansovino (1486–1570), who were active in the city in the early part of the century. Sanmicheli carried the style to his native Verona, where he resettled after the sack of Rome in 1527; Sansovino introduced it to Venice when he fled there the same year; Alessi applied it to a number of palaces in Genoa, where he settled in 1548.

Two other figures from the High Renaissance were also active in Rome: Bramante's pupil Raphael (1483–1520) and Michelangelo (1475–1564). Raphael's position as superintendent of Roman antiquities gave him the ideal opportunity to study classical architecture, as evidenced by his Villa Madama, which contains many elements derived from the Roman *thermae.* Michelangelo's most important architectural contribution in Rome was his work on the city's renowned religious landmark, St. Peter's, which was begun by Bramante and continued by Antonio da Sangallo (ca. 1483–1546).

In Florence, Michelangelo touched off the movement known as Mannerism, so called because of its affected or "mannered" style. His Medici Chapel and Laurentian library staircase, with their deliberate distortion of classical elements, influenced a number of other Florentine architects, among them Bartolomeo Ammannati (1511–92; who supervised the building of the Laurentian library's vestibule staircase), Giorgio Vasari (1511–74; the *Uffizi*), and Bernardo Buontalenti (1536–1608; the Galleria and Tribuna rooms in the *Uffizi*). Other Mannerist architects include Giulio Romano (1499–1546), who worked in Mantua; Pirro Ligorio (1510–83), who designed the fanciful Villa d'Este in Tivoli; and Giacomo Barozzi da Vignola (1507–73), who built the Church of the Gesù in Rome and continued Michelangelo's work on St. Peter's.

Another aspect of classical architecture, the villa, had its rebirth during the Renaissance. Giuliano da Sangallo (1445–1516) built a villa for the Medici family at Poggio a Caiano near Florence, actually designing a Roman temple portico as an entrance. Michelozzo (1396–1472) also built a number of villas for the Medicis in and around Florence, but the greatest villa architect of the era was Andrea Palladio (1518–80), who worked in the region around Venice. Although his classically derived *Teatro Olimpico* in Vicenza and the Venetian churches of San Giorgio Maggiore and Il Redentore are all masterpieces of Renaissance architecture, his villas had even greater influence outside Italy. The classical symmetry of places such as Villa Rotonda outside Vicenza and Villa Foscari at Malcontenta served as the inspiration for English and American estates centuries later. And, finally, as Alberti had done at the beginning of the Renaissance, in 1570 Palladio wrote a major treatise on architecture, *Quattro libri dell'architettura,* codifying the Renaissance architectural ideals of harmonic proportions and symmetry.

BAROQUE THROUGH NEO-CLASSICAL ARCHITECTURE

The baroque movement took its name from the Portuguese word *barrôcco,* used to describe pearls of odd shape. It began in Rome in the late 16th century to meet the needs of a rapidly expanding Catholic church for an architecture full of dramatic effect. Architects of the time delighted in creating new buildings, especially churches, on a grand scale, based on curved forms that conveyed a dizzying sense of movement.

After Carlo Maderno (1556–1629) finally completed the façade and nave of Michelangelo's St. Peter's Basilica, the architects who dominated the baroque period were Pietro da Cortona (1596–1669), Gianlorenzo Bernini (1598–1680), and Francesco Borromini (1599–1667). Cortona, who was also a skilled painter, designed the Church of Saints Luke and Martina in Rome; with its rich decoration and giant columns, it is considered the first fully baroque church. Bernini, equally well known as a sculptor, is credited for architectural work throughout Rome: At the Vatican he designed the oval, colonnaded piazza in front of St. Peter's, the giant *baldacchino* under Michelangelo's dome, and a grand staircase, the Scala Regia, in the Vatican Palace. In addition to his palaces and churches, Bernini sculpted many of the fountains for which Rome is famous. Like Bernini, his rival Borromini made elaborate use of the oval, as in the churches of San Carlo and Sant'Ivo della Sapienza.

Though the baroque style did not have the same explosive effect in other Italian cities that it had in Rome, it left remarkable traces throughout the peninsula. Baldassare Longhena's (1604–82) octagonal Church of Santa Maria della Salute on the Grand Canal in Venice, although based on local Byzantine and Renaissance traditions, is baroque in its sweeping theatricality. Bartolomeo Bianco (1590–1657) built the dramatic university in Genoa; Guarino Guarini (1624–83) and Filippo Juvarra (ca. 1676–1736) both erected baroque buildings in Turin; and Giuseppe Zimbalo (1620–ca. 1691) transformed the city of Lecce with his baroque churches carved in the local golden sandstone. Finally, Luigi Vanvitelli (1700–73) designed the magnificent 1,200-room Palazzo Reale at Caserta, outside Naples; begun in 1751, it is considered the last great baroque building in Italy.

The baroque was followed by a neo-classical movement, partly in reaction to the excesses of the baroque and partly because of classical archaeological discoveries in Sicily and at Paestum. The neo-classical movement was especially strong in Venice, where Tommaso Temanza (1705–89) built the Church of the Maddalena in 1760, Antonio Selva (1751–1819) put up the *Teatro La Fenice* from 1788 to 1792, and Giuseppe Jappelli (1783–1852) built the *Caffè Pedrocchi* in nearby Padua in 1816.

NINETEENTH CENTURY THROUGH THE PRESENT

The new techniques made possible by the Industrial Revolution had their effects on Italian architecture. In 1861, mass production of iron and glass enabled Giuseppe Mengoni (1829–77) to design the prototypical shopping arcade, the *Galleria Vittorio Emanuele* in Milan. Two years later, Alessandro Antonelli (1798–1888) designed his Mole Antonelliana, the iron-supported tower in Turin.

Toward the end of the century, Art Nouveau had its exponent in Italy, Giuseppe Sommaruga (1867–1917), whose Palazzo Castiglioni (1901) in Milan is one of the best examples. The next major movement was the short-lived futurism, whose major theorist was Antonio Sant'Elia (1888–1916), who believed that architecture could influence society for the better. Sant'Elia was killed during World War I, but his idealism was carried on by Giuseppe Terragni (1904–43), who founded Gruppo 7, an avant-garde architects' cooperative, in 1926. Ironically, Terragni's best-known work, the Casa del Popolo (1936) in Como, was built in the service of the Fascists.

Other important modern architects are Pierluigi Nervi (1891–1979), who built sports stadiums in Florence (1930–32) and Rome (1957, 1959); Gio Ponti (1891–1979), whose Pirelli Building (1957) in Milan is one of the most influential skyscrapers in Europe; and Giovanni Michelucci (1891–1990), whose Le Corbusier–influenced San Giovanni Battista outside Florence, also known as the Church of the Autostrada del Sole (1961), is dedicated to those who lost their lives during the building of the superhighway.

Contemporary architects are very active in Italy; professionals from around the world watch biennial and triennial exhibitions in Venice and Milan with great interest. One example is Aldo Rossi (b. 1931), creator of the *Teatro del Mondo* (designed for the *1980 Biennial* in Venice), a 250-seat floating theater that sits on the water. In 1990, he was the first Italian to be awarded the prestigious Pritzker Architecture Prize, sponsored by the Hyatt Foundation. As it has been for centuries, Italy remains at the forefront of trends in architectural styles.

THE CITIES

BOLOGNA

Bologna, the principal city of the Emilia-Romagna region, is known to Italians by a variety of nicknames: *Bologna la Dotta* (the learned), *Bologna la Turrita* (the turreted), and *Bologna la Grassa* (the fat). The first sobriquet refers to the city's university, Europe's oldest, founded in the 11th century. It still thrives today, giving the city a lively air. The second recalls the forest of medieval towers that once gave Bologna an astonishing skyline — sadly, few remain, but those that survive are indeed spectacular. *Bologna la Grassa* attests to the city's reputation as the gastronomic center of a country in which food occupies the same prominence as family, religion, and soccer.

Looking at Bologna's turbulent history, it is hard to imagine how the Bolognese have had time to do anything besides fight outsiders — and each other. By rough count, the city has been battled over, stormed, occupied, conquered, and reconquered at least 15 times — and that total doesn't include a minor odd revolt or two here and there.

Human settlement first appeared on the site of the present city sometime in the 9th century BC, followed by the Etruscans. The Etruscans named their city Felsina, and the settlement grew rapidly until it became the Etruscan capital of the entire Po Valley. For about 200 years (600–400 BC), the city enjoyed great prosperity as a result of the fertility of the surrounding plain. In fact, the extraordinarily productive farmland of Emilia-Romagna was to prove as much a curse as a blessing, since everybody wanted it.

The first marauders were the Gauls, who swooped down on ancient Etruria. They took Felsina and, some say, renamed the city Bononia, after the name of their Gaulish tribe, the Boia. Others say that the modern name of the city originated some 2 centuries later with the arrival of the Romans, who already had a flourishing seaport not far away at Rimini. In 189 BC, the Romans evicted the Gauls from Bologna and immediately set about building a new city, which was known as Bononia from this time on and gradually became Bologna. The Romans gave the city a single, extremely important reason to be: They built the consular road that joins Milan to Rimini, the Via Emilia, directly through the middle of it — and the road still slices through the heart of the city today.

Bologna's Roman period seems to have been tranquil except for a devastating fire in AD 53. In an odd twist of history, Nero, the Roman emperor at the time, insisted that Bologna be rebuilt; not long afterward he was to burn his hometown, Rome, to the ground.

With the decline of Roman influence, Bologna began to alternate between masters, a period that was to last, with few interruptions, until World War II. In 476, the city was taken by the Goths, who held it for less than a century. Then it came under the Byzantine rule of the Eastern Roman Empire. By the beginning of the 8th century, the Lombards had taken over the city; by the end of the 8th century, Charlemagne had taken it for the Franks — and promptly gave it to the pope.

A rebellion of the Bolognese in 1116 loosened the papal grip on the city, but it wasn't long before Frederick Barbarossa swept down from the north and conquered the entire area, Bologna included. Barbarossa wasn't to enjoy the fruits of his victories for too long, however. By 1176 he had been defeated at Legnano by the Lombard League, and the Bolognese immediately began a lengthy struggle to remain independent, this time resisting one of Frederick II's sons, Enzo, King of Sardinia. They succeeded, capturing Enzo and imprisoning him (in luxury) until the day he died. The palazzo in which the unfortunate king was kept still stands in the very center of the city and now bears his name.

During the next few centuries, the turmoil that afflicted the city was primarily homegrown: Three noble families battled for control — the Viscontis, the Pepolis, and the Bentivoglios, with the last finally winning out. The Bentivoglios held Bologna until 1506, when Julius II, the Warrior Pope, wrested it from their control and set out to make it the Rome of the north. Over the next several decades, the Bentivoglios tried to reconquer the city many times, but without success. Bologna was in papal hands until 1796, when it was lost again, this time to the French, who had invaded Italy under the command of Napoleon. During the next 20 years (1796–1816), the city was passed back and forth between the French and their Austrian enemies three times.

By 1816, the Austrians had taken charge and, despite being evicted often by the Bolognese themselves, they held effective sway until 1860, when the city passed, by plebiscite, to the kingdom of Savoy and thus to the kingdom of Italy. Bologna had little role in World War I, but in World War II, as the center of German resistance in the Po Valley (which the Germans used as a breadbasket for the fatherland), it was severely damaged. It took 43 separate bombardments by the Allies to dislodge the German occupiers.

Despite all this martial to-and-fro, Bologna had time to build a city of great beauty and charm, remarkably intact, considering its warlike past. (Its *centro storico* — historic center — is considered to be one of Italy's best urban conservation projects. And as the great buildings and the arcaded streets that are Bologna's signature were going up, some magnificent meals were being served. Bolognese history — not to mention its civic pride — is inextricably bound up with its food. The fertility of the surrounding land made the city a target, and its culinary traditions marked it a worthy prize.

Ask any Italian where the best food in Italy is served and the answer is sure to be "my hometown." But that is just regional chauvinism — all Italians agree that the *second* best food in Italy comes from Bologna. Food — its preparation, presentation, and consumption — is serious business in Bologna. The city has given its name to the international classic *spaghetti alla bolognese* and, less notably, to "baloney." However, a visitor will soon learn that *spaghetti alla bolognese* is better here than anywhere else in the world and that baloney is unknown locally — in fact, a Bolognese would probably be hard pressed to find any connection between delicatessen baloney and its noble ancestor, mortadella, the spiced pork sausage that has been made hereabouts since Roman times. Once you've had the real thing, it will be very hard to settle for the pale imitation that carries Bologna's name.

In Italy, the dish for which *la cucina bolognese* is most famous is a pasta called tortellini, tiny sachets stuffed with lean pork, grated cheese, eggs, and nutmeg. The best tortellini are made by hand — a good tortellini stuffer can make 6,000 an hour — and the Bolognese are quite prepared to pay more for handmade pasta than for the inferior machine-made variety. Bologna's ancient and more recent history is filled with references to the quality of tortellini — it has been featured in plays, songs, and poems. In fact, a Bolognese poet once wrote: "If the first father of the human race was lost for an apple, what would he not have done for tortellini?" Given this kind of ardor, it is not hard to believe that, in 1909, a Bolognese mailman was sentenced to 6 months in prison for assaulting a cocky Venetian who dared criticize the local tortellini.

For reasons that the Bolognese have never quite fathomed, Bologna has never really caught on as a prime stop for foreign visitors. This is both good and bad. Good because Bologna has not suffered tourist burnout. Hotel rooms are easy to find (except during one of the frequent major trade fairs or conventions), prices are comparatively moderate, and hotel workers and waiters haven't developed the surliness that afflicts a few of their counterparts in other parts of the country. Bad because Bologna deserves to be more widely appreciated. Despite the fact that Italians visit often — high rollers from Rome and Milan have been known to zip up or down the autostrada just to have lunch in the city — foreigners are still relatively rare. However, much awaits the lucky few: beautiful buildings, fabulous shops, charming and courteous people, and, best of all, the food that made Bologna *la Grassa.*

BOLOGNA AT-A-GLANCE

SEEING THE CITY: Pisa is by no means the only city in Italy that boasts a leaning tower. In the heart of Bologna, in Piazza di Porta Ravegnana, are two leaning towers, Le Due Torri, side by side. The taller of the two, the Torre degli Asinelli, was built by the Asinelli family between 1109 and 1119. It soars 320 feet above the busy streets and leans 4 feet from the perpendicular. Steep stairs — 486 of them — lead to the top, and the vista from the viewing platform is nothing short of spectacular. On a clear day, all of Bologna is visible, and most of the surrounding province as well. It is open daily from 9 AM to 6 PM; admission charge. The shorter of the twin towers is the Torre Garisenda, which dates from about the same time as its partner. It is a mere 160 feet high, and it is not open to visitors — just as well, perhaps, since it has an alarming 10-foot list. The Garisenda is thought to have once been as tall as its neighbor but was shortened for (understandable) reasons of safety in the 14th century. Taken together, the Torre Asinelli and the Torre Garisenda provide a good sense of the historic *Bologna la Turrita* — it is thought that there were once 180 such towers in the city.

SPECIAL PLACES: The heart of Bologna, Piazza di Porta Ravegnana, is made up of two adjoining squares, the huge Piazza Maggiore and the smaller Piazza del Nettuno, which takes its name from the restored robust statue of Neptune that decorates it. Clustered around these two majestic spaces are some of the major sights of the city.

CENTER

Basilica di San Petronio (Basilica of St. Petronius) – This huge church on one side of Piazza Maggiore is dedicated to St. Petronius, an early Bishop of Bologna and the town's patron saint, who was well known both for his political interests and civic-mindedness and for his devoutness. It was begun in 1390, and although work went on for the next 3 centuries or so, it was never finished, as is immediately evident in the only partly decorated façade. The bottom third is faced in marble and graced with exceptional carvings over and around the three doorways. Particularly noteworthy is the center door, capped with a lovely Madonna and Child flanked by Saints Petronius and Ambrose, an early-15th-century work by the Sienese sculptor Jacopo della Quercia. The rest of the façade is unadorned, affording a good look at an Italian Gothic cathedral "under the skin," so to speak — this is considered a fine example of Gothic brickwork.

The first impression on entering the cathedral is one of vast, unadulterated space. The dimensions — 433 feet long, 190 feet wide, 144 feet high — while grand, shrink somewhat with the realization that the building was designed to be some *300 feet longer* and was meant to be surmounted by a dome soaring 500 feet from the floor. A depleted treasury and Bologna's unsettled history account for this more "modest" structure. (Outside, beyond the apse, is a row of columns erected as part of the unfinished plan.) The interior is notable not only for its size but also for some highly original works of art in the 22 side chapels, the most peculiar of which is the *Inferno* of Giovanni da Modena in the Chapel of the Magi. This large painting is a particularly gruesome, but finely executed, fantasy vision of hell: A black beast single-mindedly devouring the damned through two mouths (one rather unconventionally placed) dominates a very busy group of devils as they fry, puncture, and flay hordes of sinners. The picture was meant to scare the living onto the straight and narrow path — and probably succeeded. Set in the floor, and running the length of the nave at a slight angle to the main altar, is the meridian line of the astronomer Gian Domenico Cassini. Laid down in 1655, the line in effect turned the entire church into a giant timepiece. A hole in the roof admits a ray of the sun that works its way along the line, showing local time. Although adjusted several times over the centuries, it is now seriously out of whack. Open daily from 7:30 AM to 6:30 PM. Piazza Maggiore.

Palazzo del Podestà (Mayor's Palace) – Directly across Piazza Maggiore from the basilica, this older building dates from the 13th century, although it was considerably remodeled about 200 years later by Aristotle Fioravanti, who also designed the Basilica of Our Lady of the Assumption in the Kremlin in Moscow. The tower that surmounts it, called the Torre dell'Arengo, dates from the original structure and contains a massive bell that was rung in times of celebration or distress as a signal for the citizenry to gather in the piazza to hear the good or bad news proclaimed from the gallery. Nestled in the corners of the vaults of the archway are four sculpted figures representing the four patrons of the city: St. Petronius, St. Florian, St. Eligius, and St. Francis. The interior of the palazzo is open from time to time for exhibits on its upper floors (admission charge). Piazza Maggiore.

Palazzo Comunale (Communal Palace) – Also facing Piazza Maggiore is this recently restored massive edifice, actually two buildings joined together. The extreme difference in façade marks where one ends and the other begins. The Palazzo Comunale, also known as the Palazzo d'Accursio, has been the seat of the Bolognese city government since the 14th century. Over the entrance is a heavy bronze statue of Pope Gregory XIII, a native of Bologna who gave his name to the calendar still in use today. The 15th-century terra cotta statue of the Virgin and Child, to the left of the pope, is by Nicolò dell'Arca, a Pugliese artist who worked extensively in Bologna. In the courtyard of the palace is a wide and gently sloping staircase said to be by Bramante; the width of the steps and their easy grade were designed specifically so they could be climbed by men on horseback — fully armed and mounted riders were always a feature of ceremonial occasions. On the first floor of the building is the Chamber of Hercules, taking its name from the giant statue of the mythical strong man that dominates the room. There is more sculpture on the second floor, in the Sala Farnese, the room in which Pope Leo X and King Francis I of France, the two most powerful men in the world at the time, met in secret in 1515. About 15 rooms are open to the public on this upper floor of the palazzo, all lavishly decorated and displaying paintings of the Bolognese school and other works that make up the Municipal Art Collections. The large windows afford excellent views of the piazza and the city. Open daily, except Tuesdays, from 9 AM to 2 PM, Sundays to 12:30 PM. Piazza Maggiore (phone: 290526).

Fontana del Nettuno (Neptune Fountain) – Whether viewed from above, from the windows of the Palazzo Comunale, or head on at street level, the proportions and grace of this famous fountain are readily apparent, and however viewed, Neptune's pose was designed to encourage a desire to walk around him. It works! One of the best examples of a Renaissance fountain in this part of Italy, it was designed by Tomaso Lareti, but actually was constructed and sculpted (1564) by a Flemish artist. His name, however, has been Italianized: No longer Jean de Boulogne, he is now known as Giambologna. The fountain was painstakingly restored in 1934 and again in 1989. Piazza del Nettuno.

Palazzo di Re Enzo (King Enzo's Palace) – Built in 1200 and last restored in 1905, this somber building has much within it to recall Bologna's violent past. From 1249 to 1272, it was the prison of the hapless King Enzo, who died here. One assumes that while Enzo was not exactly happy in it, he did live far better than the other prisoners held in the bowels of the palazzo. In the courtyard of the building is a small church, Santa Maria dei Carcerati (St. Mary of the Prisoners), built to offer last rites to prisoners as they were taken from the palazzo to their execution in Piazza Maggiore just outside. The Carroccio, the medieval battle symbol of the warlike Bolognese, is usually kept inside the palace, although it has been removed for restoration. The Carroccio, consisting of an ox cart carrying an altar, a bell, and the sacred and secular banners of Bologna, was hauled into battle and defended to the death by an elite corps of soldiers drawn from the first families of the city. Open only when there are exhibits; admission charge. Piazza del Nettuno.

Palazzo dell'Archiginnasio – Now the town library, but originally the seat of the university, this palazzo was built in the 16th century. The courtyard, corridors, and staircases are covered with the coats of arms of early professors and students, and upstairs in a theater (which the custodian will open on request) are models of the human anatomy set on pedestals. Built in the 17th century and completely rebuilt following damage in World War II, it's paneled in wood and contains two interesting anatomical figures dating from 1735. Open daily from 7 AM to noon and 3:30 to 7 PM. 1 Piazza Galvani.

Basilica di San Domenico (Church of St. Dominic) – Both this church and the site on which it stands are rich in associations with St. Dominic, who founded a convent on the spot in 1219 and died here in 1221. In the building itself, the sacristan will show, on request, the cell where he lived. An 18th-century renovation totally ruined the medieval character of the interior, but it still contains an exceptional work of art, the Arca di San Domenico, or tomb of the saint. Many artists contributed to this masterpiece, but the one who had the greatest hand in it was Nicolò da Bari, who became so famous for this work that he was ever after known as Nicolò dell'Arca. (Note that the term *arca* is an archaic one for a chest or tomb; it does not refer to an arch over the tomb.) The kneeling angel on the right of the tomb and the figures of St. Petronius (holding a model of Bologna in his arms) and St. Proculus are some of the earliest known works of Michelangelo. Be sure also to see the inlaid wooden choir stalls, made by a monk, Damiano of Bergamo, in the 15th century. Outside the church in the piazza are two curious aboveground tombs, for Rolandino de' Passeggeri and Egidio Foscherari, jurists in Bologna in the 13th and 14th centuries who adapted ancient Roman law to the needs of the day. Piazza San Domenico.

Chiesa di Santa Maria della Vita (St. Mary of Life Church) – A wonderful terra cotta *Pietà,* another masterpiece by Nicolò dell'Arca, done after 1460, normally is kept here. As we went to press, it was in the process of being restored and not available for viewing. Also known as the "Crying Marys," the group is full of movement, especially in the figure of Mary Magdalene, who is almost frantic in her grief. 10 Via Clavature.

Chiesa di Santo Stefano (St. Stephen's Church) – The complex of churches that makes up the ancient church of Santo Stefano is one of the most interesting sights in Bologna. There is not one church here but four, and once there were seven. The four churches that remain — Trinità, San Sepolcro or Calvario, Crocifisso, and Santi Vitale e Agricola, the latter dating from the 5th century and said to be the oldest ecclesiastical building in Bologna — are united in a patchwork of adjoining cloisters and passages, making the complex an extremely quiet and restful place in a very busy city. The warren of rooms contains some odd and affecting devotional objects. San Sepolcro (Holy Sepulcher), for example, contains what the 12th-century Bolognese imagined a replica of the tomb of Christ would look like. It houses relics of St. Petronius. Beyond San Sepolcro is the Cortile di Pilato (Courtyard of Pilate). Legend has it that the deep basin in the center of this beautiful courtyard is the actual bowl in which Pontius Pilate washed his hands after the condemnation of Christ. The inscription on the rim, however, dates it only to the 8th century. Beyond the courtyard is an extremely old, rather rustic *presepio,* a nativity scene that becomes a shrine of particular importance for the children of Bologna at *Christmas.* The remaining courtyard is given over to a memorial to the Bersaglieri, the mountain troops of the Italian army, who achieved immortality in Italy by seizing Rome from the pope on behalf of the new Italian nation. Open daily from 7 AM to noon and 3:30 to 6 PM. Piazza Santo Stefano.

Pinacoteca Nazionale – Established in 1797, just after the arrival of Napoleon, this picture gallery near the university contains one of the most important collections of paintings in northern Italy. Here are first-rate examples by the immortals of Italian art (particularly Bolognese painters of the 15th–19th centuries, as well as by distinguished outsiders: Giotto, Titian, Tintoretto, El Greco. Raphael's *Santa Cecilia* is the most famous picture displayed here. The huge exhibition space is beautifully restored, the paintings expertly placed and perfectly lighted. Open Tuesdays through Fridays from 9 AM to 2 PM, Saturdays and Sundays to 1 PM. Admission charge. 56 Via delle Belle Arti (phone: 243249).

ENVIRONS

Santuario della Madonna di San Luca (Sanctuary of the Madonna of St. Luke) – On the way into Bologna is one of Bologna's most distinctive landmarks — a church perched on top of a hill and approached by what appears to be an attenuated version of the Great Wall of China. The church was built on Monte della Guardia in the 18th century, and its main point of interest is an heirloom inherited from a previous church built on the same spot, an image of the Madonna said to have been painted by St. Luke but more likely painted by a Byzantine artist in the 12th century. Visitors may not be moved to come all this way to see the Madonna (which is on view once a year in the Cattedrale di San Pietro, otherwise known as the Metropolitana, on Via dell'Indipendenza), but for those who like to climb to the tops of cupolas and bell towers, the seeming wall presents a challenge. Actually, it's a portico, the most remarkable of many such walkways in Bologna (see *Extra Special,* below) and the longest in the world. Built in the 17th and 18th centuries (it took 65 years to build), it connects one of the old gates of the city, Porta Saragozza, and the church via a series of 666 covered and connected arches that climb uphill for a total distance of more than 2 miles. The view from the church is well worth the ascent, but most people take public transportation up and save the portico for a leisurely descent. Open daily from 7 AM to 12:30 PM and 2:30 to 6 PM.

■ **EXTRA SPECIAL:** Every city has a feature particularly its own — Big Ben, the Eiffel Tower, the Empire State Building — and Bologna is no exception. Here it is the arcade, or portico. Virtually all of Bologna's central streets are lined with covered walkways, gracefully arched and vaulted passages that lead for miles, so that it is possible to walk from one end of town to the other in the rain without getting wet — except when crossing streets. All told, there are just under 30 miles of *portici,* and they have been around a long time. They were born sometime in the 11th or 12th century, when the old wooden city of the Dark Ages was being rebuilt in stone; porticoes went up in front of each building, and gradually they were joined to make the continuous complex seen today. By 1400 their existence had been codified — uniform heights and widths were established — and laws stated that new buildings had to join the arcades whether their owners wanted to or not. The *portici* have become as much a part of Bolognese life as tortellini and mortadella — they are always crowded with strollers, gossips, and students studying the manifestoes pasted on the inner walls. Not everybody has appreciated them, however. Goethe thought they were dark, ugly, and impractical. The local newspapers criticized him savagely for this heretical opinion and suggested that he might be happier elsewhere. Goethe left.

SOURCES AND RESOURCES

TOURIST INFORMATION: The Azienda di Promozione Turistica (APT; headquartered at 45 Via Marconi; phone: 237413) is open only from 9 AM to 12:30 PM, but there are two information offices in Bologna offering advice and assistance in English (open daily from 9 AM to 7 PM; Sundays from 9 AM to 12:30 PM. One is in the center of the city (6 Piazza Maggiore; phone: 239660), and the other is at the main railway station (in Piazza delle Medaglie d'Oro; phone: 246541). Both are closed Saturday afternoons and Sundays. The APT can arrange for visitors to have a guide for the day, at a modest price. A knowledgeable, multilingual guide is Herta Mulazzini (46 Via Venezia, San Lazzaro di Savena; phone: 463441).

Local Coverage – The bimonthly publication *A Guest in Bologna* is in English and Italian and is distributed free at hotels or the tourist office. Bologna's film, music, and gallery listings can be found in *Mongolfiera,* a biweekly magazine. Published in Italian, it can be bought at newsstands for $1.75. The newspaper that serves Bologna and the rest of the province is *Il Resto del Carlino,* one of Italy's oldest dailies. The Italian-language newspaper, *L'Unità,* has a special insert on Fridays that lists the following week's special events. The *International Herald Tribune* can be purchased on the day of publication at the larger newsstands around Piazza Maggiore and at the train station. A colorful local guidebook published in English, *Bologna: A City to Discover,* can be bought at newsstands, bookshops, and souvenir stands.

TELEPHONE: The city code for Bologna is 51. When calling from within Italy, dial 051 before the local number.

GETTING AROUND: Bologna is a city best seen on foot. Almost all the sights of note are near the city center, and the porticoes make pedestrian traffic easy in any weather.

Airport – Aeroporto Civile Guglielmo Marconi (38 Via Aeroporto, 4 miles/6 km northwest of the city center; phone: 311578, 312259 for information, 312297 for reservations, and 311810 for baggage problems) serves domestic and international flights.

Bus – Service is excellent, comprehensive, fast, and inexpensive. Most lines run 24 hours a day, although frequency drops off considerably after midnight. A ticket must be purchased at tobacco shops or newsstands before boarding. Passengers cancel their own tickets once on board. For information, call 248374.

Car Rental – The major firms have rental offices both in the city itself and at the airport: *Hertz* (17 Via Amendola; phone: 524648); *Avis* (5 Via Pietramellara; phone: 551528), very close to the train station; and *Europcar* (3A/B Via Boldrini; phone: 247101).

Taxi – Hail taxis as they cruise, or reserve them in advance by calling 534141 or 372727. There are major taxi stands in Piazza Nettuno, Piazza Galvani, and many other locations, as well as at the main train station.

Train – The main train station, Bologna Centrale, is an important rail hub for central Italy. It's at Piazza delle Medaglie d'Oro, along Viale Pietro Pietramellara, at the head of Via dell'Indipendenza (phone: 246490).

SPECIAL EVENTS: At any given time of the year, Bologna is probably playing host to some industrial fair, convention, or congress. They range from the popular, such as the *International Fair of Contemporary Art* in late January, to the esoteric, such as the *Packaging Machines and Materials Exhibition* in September. The important, international *Children's Book Fair* (April) and the *Bologna Motor Show* (December) are perhaps the best known. More traditional events are definitely subordinate to such shows, but they do exist. For instance, every year, on the Sunday before *Ascension Thursday* in May, the 12th-century Madonna that's usually in the Santuario della Madonna di San Luca is carried down to the city amid great fanfare to be displayed in the Cattedrale di San Pietro (Metropolitana). She receives the homage of the faithful while there, attended by men in tuxedos, and then returns home the following Sunday at the head of a procession, an event that began in the early 15th century.

MUSEUMS: Besides those mentioned in *Special Places,* a number of other museums in Bologna may be of interest. All have an admission charge.

Galleria Comunale d'Arte Moderna (Modern Art Museum) – An impressive exhibition of 20th-century art includes works by the surrealists, the *scuola romana,* Pollock, Sutherland, and an entire collection of paintings by Giorgio Morandi that is housed in a new wing. Near the *Fiera di Milano,* the convention center at the edge of town. Open daily, except Mondays, from 10 AM to 1 PM and 3 to 7 PM. 3 Piazza della Costituzione (phone: 502329).

Museo Carducci – The home of the poet, as he left it, with his library and manuscripts. The *Museo del Risorgimento,* also here, has a collection of historical memorabilia from the mid-19th century. Open Tuesdays through Sundays from 9 AM to 1 PM. The wing with Carducci's memorabilia is closed indefinitely because of a lack of funds. 5 Piazza Carducci (phone: 347592).

Museo Civico Archeologico (Civic Archaeological Museum) – Egyptian and Greco-Roman antiquities, plus a notable collection of local Etruscan finds. Open Tuesdays through Fridays from 9 AM to 2 PM, Saturdays and Sundays to 1 PM. 2 Via dell'Archiginnasio (phone: 233849).

SHOPPING: Bologna is one of the richest cities in Italy, and the quality and quantity of the merchandise for sale reflect its taste for the good life. The main shopping streets are Via Rizzoli, Via Ugo Bassi, Via dell'Indipendenza, Via D'Azeglio, and Via Farini. Virtually all the side streets running off these contain more shops stocking everything from puppets to high-fashion wear. Local handicrafts tend to be of the edible variety, and if there exists a more lavish foodshop in Italy than *Tamburini* (corner of Via Caprarie and Via Drapperie; phone: 234354), it has yet to be found. Always busy, it stocks an unbelievable assortment of prepared meats, salads, vegetables, fish, soups, and sweets — everything fresh and delicious and ready to go for a picnic. Even if you are not hungry, it is a sight worth seeing. A walk along nearby Via Orefici is a delight for food market browsers where an open-air food market sprawls through all neighboring streets Monday through Saturday mornings. Near Via Indipendenza is a street market, half of which (*La Piazzola*) sells new items; the other half (*La Montagnola*) secondhand goods.

Regular shop hours are from 9 or 9:30 AM to 1 PM and 3:30 or 4 to 7:30 or 8 PM. Stores are closed Sundays and many do not reopen on Saturday afternoons.

Bongiovanni's – Rare operatic recordings, tapes, and disks. 28/E Via Rizzoli (phone: 225722).

***Bordoli* (*SAIA*)** – Fine, rare art objects; very expensive, but high quality. 1 Piazza Galvani (phone: 222603).

Demitrio Presini – A famous puppeteer makes delightful puppets with handmade costumes. 12 Via Vittorio Veneto (phone: 434605).

Donati – One of Bologna's best-known outfitters for men. 18 Via Rizzoli (phone: 227422).

Galleria Marescalchi – Bologna's finest art gallery, featuring important paintings by modern Italian masters such as De Chirico and Morandi. 116/B Via Mascarella (phone: 240368).

Marisell – Clothes for women, including some of the best-known Italian designers. 4 Via Farini (phone: 234670). For men: just around the corner at 13 Via D'Azeglio (phone: 234909).

Palazzo Lupari – An extensive complex of small boutiques selling jewelry, objets d'art, fur, luggage, perfume, and sportswear — all under one roof in a beautifully designed structure incorporating bits and pieces of the original 14th-century palazzo and blessed with a small luxurious tearoom for weary shoppers. 11 Strada Maggiore.

Schiavina – A wide selection of Italian and imported cookware and utensils in a city that's kitchen-crazy. 16 Via Clavature (phone: 223-3438).

SPORTS AND FITNESS: Golf – There's an 18-hole course at *Chiesa Nuova di Monte San Pietro,* about 10 miles (16 km) west of town (phone: 969100).

Horseback Riding – For a lazy afternoon canter through the park, contact the *Gruppo Emiliano Sport Equestre,* 126 Via Jussi, San Lazzaro (phone: 469452).

Horse Racing – Trotting races take place year-round at the *Ippodromo Arcoveggio,* 37/2 Via Arcoveggio (phone: 371505).

Soccer – The Bolognese are passionate supporters of their home team (*Bologna*), which plays from September to May at the *Stadio Comunale,* 174 Via Andrea Costa (phone: 411651 or 411818).

Swimming – Try *Record,* 8 Via Pilastro (phone: 503311).

Tennis – *Virtus Tennis Club* has well-equipped facilities, 1 Via Galimberti (phone: 412408).

THEATER: The major theater in town, *Teatro Duse* (42 Via Cartoleria; phone: 231836), stages an eclectic repertoire of modern and classical plays by both Italian and foreign playwrights. Avant-garde and experimental productions are presented at *Teatro Testoni* (2 Via Tiarini; phone: 368708) and *Teatro Dehon* (59 Via Libia; phone: 344772). The *Dehon* also stages more traditional modern drama, as does the *Teatro Moline* (1 Via delle Moline; phone: 235288) and the *Teatro Soffitta* (41 Via D'Azeglio; phone: 331425).

MUSIC: Bologna's opera season takes place (usually from November or December through March) at the magnificent restored 18th-century *Teatro Comunale* (Piazza Verdi; phone: 529011; for tickets: 1 Largo Respighi; phone: 522999). Both before and after that period, the orchestra presents a season of symphonic concerts. World class singers, instrumentalists, conductors, and guest orchestras regularly appear, so tickets sell out quickly. More intimate musical events, such as chamber music concerts and recitals, take place at the *Teatro delle Celebrazioni* (236 Via Saragozza; phone: 529993 for information, 529994 for tickets), an adjunct of the *Teatro Comunale.* Also check the programs of the *Sala Bossi* at the *Conservatorio* (2 Piazza Rossini; phone: 221483) and the *Sala Mozart, Accademia Filarmonica* (13 Via Guerrazzi; phone: 235346).

NIGHTCLUBS AND NIGHTLIFE: Bologna's nighttime social scene is very active, but tends to be crowded with students from the university. The best discos are *Living* (218 Via di Corticella; phone: 321043), *Flamengo* (1/C Via Direttissima; phone: 471951), and *La Campanina* (29 Via San Vittore; phone: 581115), which has dancing outdoors in the summer. No reservations are necessary. Good music can be heard at *Desiree Club* (1/D Via Paradiso; phone: 261648) and *Kaos Discoteca* (2/F Via delle Moline; phone: 228971). A typical night out consists of dinner at one of the city's fine restaurants or neighborhood trattorie, followed by animated conversation over grappa and coffee, or a bottle of wine in one of the many *osterie* and *enoteche* (wine bars that usually serve food). In summer, cabaret and vintage movies occasionally can be seen at the *Archiginnasio* (1 Piazza Galvani; phone: 236353), the *Civic Archaeological Museum* next door (2 Via dell'Archiginnasio; phone: 233849), the *Museo Civico Medievale* (*Medieval Renaissance Civic Museum;* Palazzo Ghislardi, 4 Via Manzoni; phone: 228912), and other places. Ticket prices include museum admission. Contact the APT for a schedule of events.

BEST IN TOWN

CHECKING IN: Hotels in Bologna fall into two distinct categories. The larger, commercial hotels are oriented to the needs of businesspeople and conventioneers, and the smaller, more intimate hostelries cater to visitors at leisure. Most hotels in the first category are in the newer part of town, where streets are wider, traffic is heavier, and access to and from the train station, airport, and convention center is easy. The smaller hotels are mostly on quieter, narrower streets in the historic center, perfectly located for the tourist. The top hotels in town, listed as very expensive, cost over $300 for a double room; expensive is $225 to $300; moderate means $125 to $175; and inexpensive is $100 or less. All telephone numbers are in the 51 city code unless otherwise indicated.

Baglioni – The grande dame of Bologna hotels, this 17th-century palace-turned-hotel has undergone extensive restoration. The 117 rooms are exquisitely decorated, the service is impeccable, and *I Carracci* restaurant (see *Eating Out*) is one of the city's finest. 8 Via Indipendenza (phone: 225445; fax: 234840). Very expensive.

Royal Hotel Carlton – This modern 250-room establishment is geared primarily to international businesspeople. It offers spacious, airy rooms, all with bath, mini-bar, color TV sets, air conditioning, and the well-known *Royal Grill* restaurant. The staff is particularly attentive and eager to preserve the hotel's high standing in this very competitive city. The location, in the newer section of town near the busy Piazza dei Martiri, is good but not great. Ample parking. 8 Via Montebello (phone: 249361; fax: 249724). Very expensive.

Albergo al Cappello Rosso – Very near Piazza Maggiore, this is one of Bologna's most sophisticated and intimate stopping places. The building itself is a 16th-century palazzo, but the ultramodern interiors seem closer to the 21st than to the 16th century. Each room has a TV set, mini-bar, radio, and a small kitchenette. Most of the 35 rooms are grouped around an interior courtyard that has a tiny, vest-pocket garden. Service is excellent. 9 Via de' Fusari (phone: 261891; fax: 227179). Expensive.

Corona d'Oro – A special hotel in the very center of town, with a 14th-century portico, some of the 35 rooms have wooden beams from the original building, exceptional paintings and decor, sparkling white walls, palms, masses of carefully arranged flowers, and even a meeting room with a medieval coffered ceiling. Nearby parking available. 12 Via Oberdan (phone: 236456; fax: 262679). Expensive.

Elite – Just beyond the city gates, this very sophisticated hotel has 86 tastefully furnished rooms, mini-apartments, a splendid restaurant (see *Eating Out*), a piano bar, and parking. 36 Via Aurelio Saffi (phone: 437417; fax: 424968). Expensive.

Internazionale – First-rate and old-fashioned, with a convenient location, it has 140 fully appointed rooms with all the amenities the business traveler expects. The service is efficient and parking is available. 60 Via dell'Indipendenza (phone: 245544; fax: 249544). Expensive.

Dei Commercianti – A very modern hotel housed in a converted medieval building right next to St. Petronius. In the city center, this quiet 31-room property features side views of the Gothic basilica. Parking available. 11 Via de' Pignattari (phone: 233052; fax: 224733). Moderate.

Orologio – Small and pleasant in decor and price, it offers basic, clean accommodation. Recently restored, it's perfectly located in the Piazza Maggiore, facing the Palazzo Comunale, and some of the 29 rooms have excellent views of the piazza or that beautiful building. Well run (owned by the *Corona d'Oro*), it has a private garage. 10 Via IV Novembre (phone: 231253; fax: 260552). Moderate.

Roma – One of the rarest birds around, a first-rate hotel at a moderate price, and it's on a pedestrian street only a block away from Piazza Maggiore. This best buy for the non-business traveler has 84 comfortable rooms, most of which are refurbished, plus a fine dining room and a small indoor bar. There is good English-speaking service and ample — but not free — parking. 9 Via D'Azeglio (phone: 231330; fax: 239909). Moderate.

Accademia – In the heart of the busy university area, this clean 28-room hostelry costs surprisingly little and is well placed for sightseeing, dining, and shopping. 6 Via delle Belle Arti (phone: 232318). Inexpensive.

EATING OUT: Bologna's celebrity as the home of some of the best food in Italy gives its restaurateurs something of a big reputation to justify. But on the whole, though some fail outright, most live up to the challenge, and others surpass expectations. Tortellini, mortadella, and sauces *alla bolognese* are the items most closely associated with the city, but other culinary inventions are worth sampling as well. Lasagna, it is said, was born here, and most restaurants are sure to have *lasagne al forno* on their menus. Another pasta the Bolognese are credited with devising is *tagliatelle,* ribbons of golden noodles usually served with a sauce made of onions, carrots, chopped pork, and tomatoes — the traditional *ragù* served with any pasta ordered *alla bolognese.* Favorite second courses are *cotolette alla bolognese,* breaded veal cutlets baked with a dressing of ham, white wine, and white truffles; *maiale al latte alla bolognese,* pork roast simmered in milk with mushrooms; and *involtini alla bolognese,* little slices of veal wrapped around a stuffing of chopped pork and served in a sauce of onions, tomatoes, and butter. The best-known wine of the region is lambrusco, a sparkling red that comes semisweet and dry. Lambrusco reggiano is particularly good. Also consider trying pagadebit, a dry white, and trebbiano di Romagna, a characteristic white. In the list below, an expensive meal for two will cost $100 and up; a moderate one, $50 to $100; and an inexpensive one, $50 or less. Prices include service and a carafe of house wine. All telephone numbers are in the 51 city code unless otherwise indicated.

I Carracci – One of the city's best, in the deluxe *Baglioni* hotel, featuring fine traditional cooking, a selection of excellent national specialties, and a topnotch wine cellar. It has 15th-century, frescoed ceilings. Open year-round. Reservations necessary. Major credit cards accepted. 2 Via Manzoni (phone: 229476). Expensive.

Cordon Bleu – This excellent restaurant in the *Elite* hotel has a reputation for serving *piatti antichissimi,* very old traditional dishes, that still tantalize the palate — such as filet of beef flambéed with a sauce of puréed strawberries, a bit of ricotta, and cognac that comes from an old Estense recipe, and a 1,000-year-old Pugliese dish, *purea di fave con la cicoria* (puréed beans with chicory). It also has an excellent wine list. Closed Sundays, Monday lunch, and from late July to late August. Reservations necessary. 38 Via Aurelio Saffi (phone: 437417). Expensive.

Notai – This big, beautiful, turn-of-the-century restaurant near the main square stands apart from the crowd for two reasons: It has waitresses (very rare in Italy) and a circle of fans who say it is the best and most elegant dining place in the city, if not the country. Decide for yourself by sampling traditional Bolognese dishes such as *tagliatelle Notai* and scaloppine of veal with *porcini* mushrooms. Trebbiano and sangiovese are the best of an excellent collection of local wines. Closed Sundays (except during trade fairs). Reservations necessary. Major credit cards accepted. 1 Via de' Pignattari (phone: 228694). Expensive.

Al Pappagallo – Once trumpeted as the best eating place in Italy, it is still famous but no longer the best, though critics say the quality has improved under the new ownership of a young and enthusiastic Bolognese. The vaulted, dramatically decorated dining room is extremely elegant and boasts excellent service, with black-tied waiters hovering about to refill your glass the moment it is empty. Try the delicious *tagliatelle* with basil and mushrooms, the excellent breast of turkey, or the braised chicken in white wine sauce. Closed Sunday nights, Mondays, and the first half of August. Reservations necessary. Major credit cards accepted. 30 Piazza della Mercanzia (phone: 232807). Expensive.

Taverna delle Tre Frecce – Sleek, reserved, and well-established, this restaurant in the Old City is housed in an 800-year-old palazzo. Another of Bologna's best, where quality and innovation stand equally high. The menu changes every month. Closed Sunday evenings, Mondays, *Easter* weekend, during August, and 2 weeks after *Christmas.* Reservations necessary. 19 Strada Maggiore (phone: 231200). Expensive.

Cantina Bentivoglio – This delightful, cavernous *enoteca* is filled with the *ambiente* and effervescent clientele that give an idea of what Bologna really is like — casual, but sophisticated. Choose from the thousands of wine bottles around you, and the many soups, cheeses, and meats on the menu. Open from 8 PM to 2 AM; closed

Mondays and 1 week in mid-August. Reservations advised. Major credit cards accepted. Close to the university. 4/B Via Mascarella (phone: 265416). Moderate.

Da Carlo – A wonderful place for a modestly priced dinner or lunch — particularly in summer when meals are served outdoors under a medieval loggia. The sausages, minestrone, braised pigeon — *piccione brasato* — or guinea hen with artichokes, and the desserts are all good, as is the service. Closed Tuesdays, 3 weeks in January, and a week in late August. Reservations advised. Major credit cards accepted. 6 Via Marchesana (phone: 233227). Moderate.

Da Cesari – An informal, relaxed atmosphere as well as fine pasta dishes, superlative veal kidneys in balsamic vinegar (*rognoncini con aceto balsamico*), and good grilled meats make this a favorite among the Bolognese literati. After a dessert of delicate half-moon pastries filled with fresh fruit, try a smooth *grappa mirtilli* (made from blueberries) as a special "digestive" drink. Closed Sundays. Reservations advised. Major credit cards accepted. 8 Via Carbonesi (phone: 237710). Moderate.

Osteria de' Poeti – Bologna not only stands for Italy's best food, but its never-ending desire to eat it late. Of the dozens of *osterie* where the kitchens are still open well after midnight, this is the most celebrated. The food served on the 15th-century premises is good enough to inspire diners at times to break into song. If that is too tall an order, then there's always entertainment in the in-house cabaret. Open to 4 AM; closed Mondays. Reservations advised. Major credit cards accepted. 1/B Via Poeti (phone: 236166). Moderate.

Al Portichetto – A delightful hillside trattoria, with terrace dining in warm weather, just a few miles from town. Regional country cooking features frequent use of wild truffles and mushrooms. Closed Sunday evenings, Mondays, and during January. Reservations advised. Visa accepted. 21 Via dei Colli, beyond the town's favorite park, Giardini Margherita (phone: 581110). Moderate.

Rosteria da Luciano – This is a genuine anomaly — a high-quality restaurant that doesn't make diners pay an arm and a leg. As the name suggests, roast and baked meats are the specialty, the centerpiece being a very tender pork dish, *maialino di latte al forno.* Also try the "royal" salad of mushrooms and truffles, if it's on the menu (which is limited to a few items available on specific nights). Closed Tuesday evenings, Wednesdays, the month of August, and at *Christmas.* Reservations necessary. Major credit cards accepted. 19 Via Nazario Sauro (phone: 231249). Moderate.

Da Bertino – One of the last of a dying breed — the reliable neighborhood trattoria. It serves good, old-fashioned Italian cooking to regular customers who know exactly what to expect: nothing exotic, but good value for the money. Excellent fresh pasta. Closed Sundays, *Christmas* through *Epiphany* (January 6), and 3 weeks in August. Reservations unnecessary. Major credit cards accepted. 55 Via delle Lame (phone: 522230). Inexpensive.

Birreria Lamme – A Bolognese institution, which once kept students fed and active and now attracts businesspeople and locals in the know. There are good pasta dishes as well as chops, steaks, sausages, and roasts. Service tends to bustle along — you won't make friends with your waiter, but you won't wait long for your food either. Just a few steps from the twin towers and a great place for lunch (be sure to go before or after the 1–2:30 PM rush. It's open continuously from 11:30 AM to 11:30 PM — almost unheard of in Italy. There is counter service, too. Closed Wednesdays and during August. No reservations. Major credit cards accepted. 4 Via de' Giudei (phone: 236537). Inexpensive.

FLORENCE

Florence, city of the arts, jewel of the Renaissance, symbol of the Tuscan pride in grace and refinement, is for many an acquired taste. Rome has romance, Venice intrigue, and Naples a poignant gaiety; Florence may seem too austere, too serious, too severe. The elegance that is Florence does not seize you immediately — not like the splashing fountains of Rome, the noisy laughter and song of Naples, the pastel chandeliers peeking out of patrician palaces along Venice's Grand Canal.

Next to the mellow tangerine hues of Rome, the pinks of Venice, and the orgy of color that is Naples, Florence is a study in neutral shades: blacks and whites, beiges and browns, a splattering of dark green. Its people seem less spontaneous and exuberant than Romans or Neapolitans, more hardworking and reserved, with a sort of innate sense of dignity and pride.

Florentine palaces are more like fortresses, at first glance rather forbidding and uninviting to the visitor; the city's somber streets are lined with solid, direct architecture; its civic sculpture is noble and restrained. But this is only a superficial view of Florence. Step into the palaces and you will be awed by the beauty of fine details as well as by some of the world's greatest art treasures. Look at the fine Florentine crafts in gold and leather and exquisite fabrics in the elegant but classically serious shops. It won't take long before you will understand why the culture and art of Florence have attracted people from around the world through the centuries, and why it is as much a favorite of artists, students, and expatriates today as it was at its apogee under the Medicis in the 15th century.

Florence was the home of Cimabue and Giotto, the fathers of Italian painting; of Brunelleschi, Donatello, and Masaccio, who paved the way for the Renaissance; of the Della Robbias, Botticelli, Leonardo da Vinci, and Michelangelo; of Dante Alighieri, Petrarch, and Boccaccio; of Machiavelli and Galileo. Art, science, and life found their finest, most powerful expression in Florence, and records of this splendid past fill the city's many galleries, museums, churches, and palaces, demanding attention.

Florence — *Firenze* in Italian — probably originated as an Etruscan center, but it was only under the Romans in the 1st century BC that it became a true city. Like so many other cities of its time, Roman Florence grew up along the fertile banks of a river, in this case the Arno, amid the rolling green hills of Tuscany. Its Latin name, *Florentia* ("flowering"), probably referred to the city's florid growth, although some ancient historians attributed it to Florinus, the Roman general who besieged the nearby Etruscan hill town of Fiesole in 63 BC.

During the Roman rule, Florence became a thriving military and trading center, with its share of temples, baths, a Town Hall, and an amphitheater, but few architectural monuments of that epoch have survived. After the fall of the Roman Empire, Florence sank into the decadence of the Dark Ages, and despite a temporary reprieve during Charlemagne's 8th- and 9th-century European empire, it did not really flourish again until the late 11th century. It was then that the great guilds were developed and the florin-based currency began to appear, and Florence became a powerful, self-governing republic.

In the 12th century, interfamily feuds were widespread, and over 150 square stone towers — built for defense by influential families right next to their houses — dominated the city's skyline. Even so, during that and the next century, the Florentine population of about 60,000 (twice that of London at the time) was busily engaged in trade with the rest of the Mediterranean. The amazing building boom that followed, bringing about the demolition of the fortified houses in favor of more gracious public and private palazzi and magnificent churches, reflected the great prosperity of the city's trading and banking families, its wool and silk industries, and the enormous strength of the florin.

As a free city-state or *comune,* Florence managed to maintain a balance between the authority of the Germanic emperors and that of the popes, overcoming the difficulties of internal struggles between the burgher Guelphs (who supported the pope) and the aristocratic Ghibellines (who were behind the Holy Roman Emperor). Eventually, by the late 13th century, the Guelphs won power and a democratic government was inaugurated with the famous Ordinances of Justice. So began Florence's ascent, which spanned 3 centuries and reached its height and greatest splendor under the Medici family.

Owing in large measure to the patronage of the Medicis, Florence became the liveliest and most creative city in Europe. While this certainly pertained during the time of Giovanni di Bicci de' Medici (1360–1429) and his illustrious dynasty of merchants, bankers, and art patrons, as well as that of his son Cosimo the Elder (1389–1464), who continued to gather artists around him, it was Cosimo's grandson Lorenzo the Magnificent (1449–1492) who put Florence in the forefront of the Italian Renaissance. An elaborate celebration will take place this year to mark the 500th anniversary of Lorenzo's death (see *Special Events*). Today, the Medici might be thought of as something of a political machine, since they controlled — through their wealth and personal power alone — a city that was, in theory at least, still a democratic republic governed by members of the trade guilds. Their de facto rule was not uncontested, however. They suffered reversals, such as the Pazzi Conspiracy in 1478, and twice they were expelled — from 1494 to 1512, when a revolution brought the religious reformer Savonarola briefly to power (and an attempt was made to reestablish democracy), and again from 1527 to 1530, when another republic was set up, only to fall to the troops of Emperor Charles V and lead to the Medici restoration.

Finally, in the late 16th century, their glory days behind them, the Medici gained an official title. They became grand dukes (Cosimo I was the first), and Florence became the capital of the grand duchy of Tuscany. In the 18th century, the grand duchy of the Medici was succeeded by that of the house of Lorraine, until Tuscany became part of the kingdom of Italy in 1860. From 1865 to 1871, Florence reigned as temporary capital of the kingdom, but with the capital's transfer to Rome, the history of Florence merges with that of the rest of Italy.

Two catastrophes in this century have caused inestimable damage to Florence's art treasures. In 1944, all the beloved bridges crossing the Arno — except for the Ponte Vecchio — were blown up by the Nazis. Reconstruction began as soon as the Germans retreated. Then, 2 decades later, in November 1966, the Arno burst its banks, covering the historic center with a muddy slime. Over 1,400 works of art, 2 million valuable books, and countless homes were damaged by floodwaters that reached depths of 23 feet. The people of Florence, with help from all over the world, rose to the challenge. Before the floodwaters had receded, they began the painstaking chore of rescuing their treasures from 600,000 tons of mud, oil, and debris.

Today, the city of Florence — with a population of slightly less than half a million — still is a vital force in the arts, in culture, and in science, as well as an industrial, commercial, and university center and a leader in the fields of handicrafts and fashion. Note, indeed, how the Florentines dress, their fine attention to detail and the remarkable sense of style that turns an ordinary outfit into something personal and very special. And note the almost arrogant local swagger. Then realize that these are people who wake up every morning to the marvels of Michelangelo, who literally live in a 15th-century Renaissance textbook. Their artistic and cultural heritage is unsurpassed, truly unique in the world. No doubt you'll agree that they have every reason to be proud.

FLORENCE AT-A-GLANCE

SEEING THE CITY: The picture-postcard view of Florence is the one from Piazzale Michelangelo, on the far side of the Arno. From here, more than 300 feet above sea level, the eye embraces the entire city and neighboring hill towns as far as Pistoia, but it is the foreground that rivets the attention. The Arno, with all its bridges, from Ponte San Niccolò to Ponte della Vittoria, the Palazzo Vecchio, with its tower and crenelations, the *Uffizi,* the flank of Santa Croce, numerous spires and domes — all are in the picture. And looming over the whole, like a whale washed ashore in the land of Lilliput, is the massive Duomo, with its bell tower and giant red cupola. The *piazzale* is reached by a splendid tree-lined avenue, called the Viale dei Colli, which begins at Ponte San Niccolò and winds up to the enormous square under the name of Viale Michelangelo. It then proceeds beyond the square as far as the Porta Romana under the names of Viale Galileo and Viale Machiavelli. From the bridge to the Roman Gate is a scenic 4-mile walk, but it's also possible to trace the same route aboard bus No. 13 from the station. Another extraordinary view, of Florence and the entire Arno Valley, can be enjoyed from the lookout terrace just before the Church of St. Francis, perched on a hill studded with cypress trees and sumptuous villas in neighboring Fiesole (see *Special Places*).

SPECIAL PLACES: The Arno is a good orientation point for first-time visitors to Florence. Most of the city sits on the north, or right, bank of the river, including its principal squares: Piazza del Duomo, the religious heart of Florence; Piazza della Repubblica, its bustling commercial center; and Piazza della Signoria, the ancient political center and today a favorite meeting place because of its outdoor cafés. The most elegant shopping street, Via Tornabuoni, runs from the Arno to Piazza Antinori. The other side of the river is known as the Oltrarno, literally, "beyond the Arno." Sights here include the *Pitti Palace* and Boboli Gardens, the churches of Santo Spirito and Santa Maria del Carmine, and Piazzale Michelangelo.

THE CATHEDRAL (DUOMO) COMPLEX

Il Duomo (The Cathedral) – The Cathedral of Santa Maria del Fiore was begun in 1296 by the Sienese architect Arnolfo di Cambio and took 173 years to complete. Dominating a large double square, it is the fourth-longest church in the world (after St. Peter's in Rome, St. Paul's in London, and the Duomo of Milan) and is said to be capable of holding over 20,000 people. The gigantic project was financed by the Florentine republic and the Clothmakers Guild in an age of faith when every city-state aspired to claim the biggest and most important cathedral as its own. Besides religious services, the Duomo has served as the site of major civic ceremonies and many noteworthy historical events, such as the Pazzi Conspiracy, when Giuliano de' Medici was assassinated in 1478. The original façade, never completed, was destroyed in the 16th century and replaced in the late 19th century. Whereas the exterior walls are encased in colorful marble (white from Carrara, green from Prato, and pink from Siena), the interior seems plain and cold by comparison, a brownish-gray sandstone called *pietra forte* and soberly decorated in keeping with the Florentine character. Most of the original statuary that adorned the Duomo, including Michelangelo's unfinished *Pietà,* has been moved to the *Museo dell'Opera del Duomo* (see below). The remains of the ancient Church of Santa Reparata, the original cathedral of Florence, which came to light under the Duomo during the extensive excavation after the 1966 flood, are very interesting (take the staircase near the entrance on the right side of the nave). The crypt is particularly haunting. Closed Sunday and holiday afternoons; admission charge.

The public competition for the design of the dome was won by a Florentine, Filippo Brunelleschi, who had marveled at the great engineering feat of ancient Rome, the dome of the Pantheon. The Renaissance architect's mighty cupola, built between 1420 and 1436, the first since antiquity, subsequently inspired Michelangelo as he faced the important task of designing the dome of St. Peter's in Rome. Brunelleschi's dome surpasses both the Pantheon and St. Peter's, although today it is seriously cracked and monitored by computer. Over 371 feet high and 148 feet across, it has double walls between which a 463-step staircase leads to a lantern at the top (also a Brunelleschi design). Restorations have been under way for more than a decade and, due to the necessity of scaffolding — not to mention the huge green canvas drape — there is little available light for viewing the dome's immense fresco (begun by Vasari). Still, the 40-minute climb up and down is well worth the effort for the breathtaking panorama from the top and for a true sense of the awesome size of this artistic and technical masterpiece. No, Virginia, there is no elevator. Closed Sundays and holidays. Admission charge.

Il Campanile (Bell Tower) – The graceful freestanding belfry of the Duomo, one of the most unusual in Italy, was begun by Giotto in 1334 (when he was 67) and eventually completed by Francesco Talenti. The bas-reliefs adorning the base are copies of originals by Giotto and Luca della Robbia that have been removed to the *Duomo Museum,* as have the statues of the Prophets (done by various artists, including Donatello) that stood in the niches. The 414-stair climb to the top leads to a terrace with another bird's-eye view of Florence. There's no elevator. Closed Sunday and holiday afternoons; admission charge.

Il Battistero (The Baptistry) – Dedicated to St. John the Baptist, the patron saint of Florence, the baptistry is a unique treasure, the origins of which are lost in time. The octagonal building may date to the 4th century, contemporary with the Church of Santa Reparata, while the exterior of white and green marble dates to the 12th century and is typical of the Tuscan Romanesque style, with an Oriental influence. To this day, the baptistry still is used for baptisms, and many a famous Florentine (such as Dante

Alighieri) has been baptized here. On the *Feast of St. John* (June 24), the relics of the saint are displayed in the building and candles are lit in his honor (see *Special Events*). The interior is covered with magnificent Byzantine mosaics by 13th- and 14th-century Florentine and Venetian masters, but it is the three gilded bronze doorways that are the main tourist attraction. The South Door, by Andrea Pisano, is the oldest, dating from the early 14th century. In the Gothic style, it has 28 panels with reliefs of the life of St. John the Baptist and the cardinal and theological virtues. The North Door (1403–1424), in late Gothic style, was the result of a competition in which the unanimous winner was Lorenzo Ghiberti (Brunelleschi was among the competitors). It, too, is divided into 28 panels depicting scenes from the life of Christ, the Evangelists, and the Doctors of the Church. Ghiberti's East Door, however, facing the cathedral, is his masterpiece. In full Renaissance style, it was defined by Michelangelo as worthy of being the "gate of paradise." Begun in 1425 and completed in 1452, when Ghiberti was 74 years old, it consists of 10 panels illustrating Old Testament stories and medallions containing self-portraits of Ghiberti and his adopted son, Vittorio (who designed the frame), as well as portraits of their principal contemporaries.

Museo dell'Opera del Duomo (Duomo Museum) – Masterpieces from the cathedral, the baptistry, and the bell tower are here, especially sculpture: Michelangelo's unfinished *Pietà* (third of his four), Donatello's *Mary Magdalene,* the famous choir lofts (*cantorie*) by Luca della Robbia and Donatello, the precious silver altar frontal from the baptistry, fragments from the original cathedral façade, even the original wooden scale model of Brunelleschi's dome. Closed Sunday afternoons; admission charge. 9 Piazza del Duomo (no phone).

ELSEWHERE DOWNTOWN

Galleria degli Uffizi (Uffizi Museum and Gallery) – Italy's most important art museum is in a Renaissance palace built on the site of an 11th-century church (San Piero Scheraggio), the remains of which are incorporated in the palazzo and may still be seen. The splendor of this museum derives not only from the great works it contains but also from the 16th-century building itself, which was commissioned by Cosimo I and designed by Vasari (completed by Buontalenti) to house the Medicis' administrative offices, or *Uffizi.* In 1581, Francesco I began converting the top floor into an art museum destined to become one of the world's greatest. The three corridors, with light streaming through their great windows, are a spectacle in themselves, and the collection they contain is so vast — the most important Italian and European paintings of the 13th through the 18th century — that we suggest taking along a good guide or guidebook (Luciano Berti's is excellent) and comfortable shoes. Remember also to allow more time for a visit here than you think you'll need. At the top of the monumental staircase (there also is an elevator) on the second floor is the Prints and Drawings Collection; the museum proper (painting and sculpture) is on the third floor. Fifteen rooms are devoted to Florentine and Tuscan masterpieces, including the work of Cimabue, Giotto, Fra Filippo Lippi, Paolo Uccello, Fra Angelico, Da Vinci, and Michelangelo, not to mention such other non-Florentine masters as Raphael, Titian, Tintoretto, Caravaggio, Rubens, Van Dyck, and Rembrandt. The Botticelli Room contains the master's *Birth of Venus* and his restored *Allegoria della Primavera* (Allegory of Spring) as well as other allegorical and mythological works that make this the most important Botticelli collection in the world. Open Tuesdays through Saturdays from 9 AM to 7 PM. Admission charge. Piazza della Signoria (phone: 218341).

For diehards, there is an important collection of self-portraits lining the Corridoio Vasariano (Vasari Corridor) that may be visited by special arrangement. The portraits include those of Raphael, Rubens, Van Dyck, Velázquez, Bernini, Canova, Corot, Fattori, and Chagall. Even without the portraits, the half-mile walk would be fascinating. The corridor actually is a raised passageway built in the 1560s to allow members of the Medici court to move from their old palace and offices (Palazzo Vecchio and Uffizi) to their new palace (*Palazzo Pitti*) without having to resort to the streets. It crosses the river on the tops of shops on the Ponte Vecchio and affords splendid views of the Arno, the Church of Santa Felicità, and the Boboli Gardens. Closed Mondays and Sunday and holiday afternoons; admission charge. To visit the Vasari Corridor, write to the *Uffizi* well in advance of your arrival (there's no extra fee). 6 Loggiato degli Uffizi (phone: 218341).

Palazzo della Signoria or Palazzo Vecchio (Old Palace) – This fortress-like palace, built by Arnolfo di Cambio between 1298 and 1314 as the seat of Florence's new democratic government of *priori,* or guild leaders, began as Florence's Town Hall and is still just that. From 1540 to 1550, it was temporarily the residence of the Medicis as they progressed from their ancestral home, the Medici-Riccardi Palace, to their new home in the *Palazzo Pitti.* Although in a rather severe Gothic style, it is at once powerful and graceful, with a lofty tower 308 feet high. Beyond its rusticated façade is an elaborately ornate courtyard highlighted by Verrocchio's delightful fountain of a bronze cherub holding a dolphin (1476). The medieval austerity of the exterior also contrasts with the sumptuous apartments inside. The massive Salone dei Cinquecento (Salon of the Five Hundred) on the first floor, built in 1496 for Savonarola's short-lived republican Council of Five Hundred, is decorated with frescoes by Vasari. Also, don't miss Vasari's *studiolo,* Francesco de' Medici's gem of a study, with magnificent *armadio* doors painted by artists of the schools of Bronzino and Vasari. On the third floor is an exhibition of 140 works of art removed from Italy by the Nazis and recovered by Rodolfo Siviero, the famed Italian art sleuth. Open Mondays through Fridays from 9 AM to 7 PM; no admission charge Sundays. Piazza della Signoria (phone: 276-8465).

Loggia dei Lanzi or Loggia della Signoria – Built between 1376 and 1382 for the election and proclamation of public officials and other ceremonies, it took its name in the 16th century from Cosimo I's Germano-Swiss mercenary soldiers (known in Italian as *lanzichenecchi*), who were stationed here. Today the loggia is a delightful open-air museum with masterpieces of sculpture from various periods under its arches. Particularly noteworthy are Cellini's *Perseus* and Giambologna's *Rape of the Sabines.* Piazza della Signoria.

Ponte Vecchio – The "old bridge" is indeed Florence's oldest and the only one to survive the Nazi destruction in 1944, although the houses at either end were blown up by the Germans. Built on the site of a Roman crossing, the first stone version was swept away in a flood in 1333 and rebuilt in 1345 as it is now, with rows of shops lining both sides (the backs of which, supported on brackets, overhang the Arno). They were occupied by butchers until Cosimo I assigned them to gold- and silversmiths in the late 16th century.

Palazzo Pitti e Galleria Palatina (Pitti Palace and Palatine Gallery) – On the side of the Arno opposite the *Uffizi,* and a few blocks from the riverbank, is a rugged, austere, 15th-century palace built to the plans of Brunelleschi, originally for the Pitti family. When it was bought by Cosimo I and his wife, Eleonora of Toledo, in the 16th century, it was enlarged and became the seat of the Medici grand dukes and later of the Savoy royal family until 1871. The enormous building now houses several museums: The *Galleria Palatina,* upstairs on the first floor and one of the must-sees, is devoted to 16th- and 17th-century art — works by Raphael (11 in all), Rubens, Murillo, Andrea del Sarto, Fra Filippo Lippi, Titian, Veronese, and Tintoretto, to name a few (there are over 650) — arranged in no apparent order. The gallery, in fact, still resembles a sumptuous apartment in a palace more than a museum. Priceless masterpieces seem to hang at random in elaborately decorated rooms filled with tapestries, frescoes, and gilded stuccoes. The Appartamenti Monumentali (Royal Apartments), in another wing of the same floor and once inhabited in turn by the Medici, Lorraine, and Savoy families, reopened in 1989 after 2 years of restoration work. The *Museo degli Argenti* (Silver Museum), occupying 16 rooms on the ground floor and another must-see, is filled not only with silverware but also with gold, jewels, cameos, tapestries, furniture, crystal, and ivory of the Medicis. Still another museum, the *Galleria d'Arte Moderna,* on the second floor, houses mainly 19th-century Tuscan works. There is also a *Coach and Carriage Museum* (temporarily closed). An entrance on the left side of the palace leads to the Boboli Gardens, which extend for acres and are open until dusk. A delightful example of a 16th-century Italian garden, they were laid out for Eleonora of Toledo and are studded with cypress trees, unusual statuary, grottoes, and fountains — plus the *Museo delle Porcellane* (Porcelain Museum) and the *Galleria del Costume* (Costume Gallery) in the Palazzina della Meridiana.

The *Palatine Gallery* (phone: 210323), the *Gallery of Modern Art* (phone: 287096), the *Silver Museum* (phone: 212557), and the *Costume Gallery* (phone: 287096) are open Mondays through Saturdays from 9 AM to 2 PM; Sundays from 9 AM to 1 PM. One admission charge covers the *Palatine Gallery,* the *Silver Museum,* and the Royal Apartments. The *Gallery of Modern Art* charges a separate admission. No admission charge to the Boboli Gardens (phone: 213440), *Porcelain Museum,* and *Costume Gallery.* Piazza dei Pitti (phone: 213440).

Chiesa di Santo Spirito (Church of the Holy Spirit) – This is one of Brunelleschi's last works, and a gem, though you'll notice the church's stark façade is very different from its interior. Brunelleschi died before he could complete what is generally acknowledged as one of the finest examples of a Renaissance church, so a team of architects finished it. Inside there are 2 dozen chapels, with masterpieces by Donatello, Ghirlandaio, Filippino Lippi, Sansovino, and others. Piazza Santo Spirito itself is a charming quiet spot, surrounded by 16th-century buildings — the perfect place to escape from the bustle on the other side of the Arno. Open daily from 8:30 AM to noon and 3:30 to 6:30 PM. Piazza Santo Spirito (phone: 210030).

Palazzo del Bargello e Museo Nazionale (Bargello Palace and National Museum) – The *Bargello* is to sculpture what the *Uffizi* is to painting, yet for some reason it is visited far less frequently by tourists. Its most noteworthy piece just might be Florence's second-most famous *David* — the bronze by Donatello — sculpted in 1530. The building, the Palazzo del Podestà, is one of the finest and best-preserved examples of Florence's 13th- and 14th-century medieval architecture. Inside, all of the schools of Florentine and Tuscan sculpture are represented: Donatello, Verrocchio, Cellini, Michelangelo, the Della Robbias, and others. Open Tuesdays through Saturdays from 9 AM to 12:30 PM; Sundays from 9 AM to 1:30 PM. Admission charge. 4 Via del Proconsolo (phone: 210801).

Santa Croce (Church of the Holy Cross) – Italy's largest and best-known Franciscan church, Santa Croce was begun late in the 13th century and was enriched over the centuries with numerous works of art as well as tombs of many famous Italians, including Michelangelo, Machiavelli, Rossini, and Galileo (there is a funeral monument to Dante here, but he is buried in Ravenna). Under Santa Croce are the remains of an earlier chapel founded by St. Francis of Assisi in 1228. The church is particularly noteworthy for a wooden crucifix by Donatello, for chapels with frescoes by Taddeo and Agnolo Gaddi, and above all for the fresco cycles by Giotto in the Bardi and Peruzzi chapels. Go outside the church and turn left to visit the 14th-century cloister and the 15th-century Pazzi Chapel, a Renaissance gem by Brunelleschi, designed at the height of his career. During the 1966 flood, the waters reached the top of the cloister's arches and damage here was particularly severe. Piazza Santa Croce (phone: 244619).

Galleria dell'Accademia (Academy of Fine Arts Gallery) – Michelangelo's original *David* was brought here from Piazza della Signoria (where one of many first-rate copies takes its place) in 1873. Since then, millions of visitors have come just to see this monumental sculpture (about a million a year now—one of whom smashed a toe on *David's* left foot last fall; it was being pedicured at press time) carved from a single block of Carrara marble and, in the same room, the four unfinished *Slaves* that Michelangelo meant to adorn Pope Julius II's unrealized tomb for St. Peter's in Rome. In the summer, lines form down the street and the doors often close when it gets too crowded. Unfortunately, many visitors ignore the rich collection of Florentine paintings — from 13th-century primitives to 16th-century mannerists — and the five rooms opened in 1985 to display works that had never before been shown to the public. These include 14th- and 15th-century paintings and an extraordinary collection of Russian icons brought to Florence by the Lorraines when they succeeded the Medicis during the first half of the 18th century. Open Tuesdays through Saturdays from 9 AM to 2 PM; Sundays to 1 PM. Admission charge. 60 Via Ricasoli (phone: 214375).

Convento di San Marco (Museum of St. Mark) – Vasari described this monastery as a perfect example of monastic architecture. It was built in the 15th century by the Medici architect Michelozzo (who actually rebuilt a more ancient Dominican monastery) and its walls — as well as more than 40 monks' cells — were frescoed by Fra Angelico (and his assistants), who lived here as a monk from 1438 to 1445. Now a Fra Angelico museum, it contains panel paintings brought from various churches and galleries in addition to the painter's wonderful *Crucifixion* (in the chapter house across the cloister) and his exquisite *Annunciation* (at the top of the stairs leading to the dormitory). In addition to the cells decorated by Fra Angelico, see the one used by the reforming martyr Savonarola. There also are paintings by Fra Bartolomeo (see his portrait of Savonarola), Ghirlandaio, Paolo Uccello, and others. Open Tuesdays through Saturdays from 9 AM to 2 PM; Sundays to 1 PM. Admission charge. 1 Piazza San Marco (phone: 210741).

Piazza della Santissima Annunziata (Square of the Most Holy Annunciation) – This square best preserves the essence of the Florentine Renaissance spirit. It has porticoes on three sides, a 16th-century palace (by Ammannati) on the fourth, plus an early-17th-century equestrian statue of Ferdinando I de' Medici by Giambologna in the middle. Most interesting is the portico on the east side, that of the Spedale degli Innocenti (Hospital of the Innocents), built in the early 15th century by Brunelleschi as a home for orphans and abandoned children, one of Florence's oldest charity institutions and the world's first foundling hospital. Except for the two imitations at either end, the ceramic tondos of swaddled babies are by Andrea della Robbia. Inside, the *Galleria dello Spedale degli Innocenti* (closed Wednesdays; admission charge) contains works by Ghirlandaio and others.

The Chiesa della Santissima Annunziata (Church of the Most Holy Annunciation), on the north side of the square, is much loved by Florentine brides, who traditionally leave their bouquets at one of its altars after the wedding ceremony. The church was founded in the 13th century, but rebuilt in the 15th century by Michelozzo. The left door of the church portico leads into the Chiostro dei Morti (Cloister of the Dead), which contains the *Madonna del Sacco,* a famous fresco by Andrea del Sarto. The middle door leads into the church via the Chiostrino dei Voti (Little Cloister of the Vows), with frescoes by several famous artists of the 16th century, including Del Sarto, Pontormo, and Rosso Fiorentino. Of the numerous artworks in the church itself, Andrea del Castagno's fresco of the Trinity, over the altar of the second chapel on the left, is one of the most prized.

Chiesa di San Lorenzo (Church of St. Lawrence) – This 15th-century Renaissance building was designed by Brunelleschi as the Medici parish church. A later façade, by Michelangelo, was never completed. Make your way to the Sagrestia Vecchia (Old Sacristy), the earliest part of the church and one of Brunelleschi's most notable early creations, remarkable for the purity and harmony of the overall conception. It contains, besides decorations by Donatello, the tombs of several Medicis, including Giovanni di Bicci. Be sure to go outside and through a doorway to the left of the façade to the Chiostro di San Lorenzo and to the Biblioteca Mediceo-Laurenziana (Laurentian Library; closed Sundays and holidays), a Michelangelo masterpiece designed to hold the Medici collection of manuscripts — 10,000 precious volumes. Piazza San Lorenzo (phone: 216634).

Mercato di San Lorenzo – This colorful open-air market has stalls where everything — from a special wooden rolling pin for making ravioli to a handmade mohair sweater — is sold. And because this is Florence, the leather goods can be a good buy, especially belts, jackets, and handbags. There also is a 2-story covered building with a lovely glass dome, where all kinds of food products are on sale, including local meats, cheeses, and produce, and fresh eggs and homemade wine brought in by peasant farmers from the Tuscan countryside. The indoor market is closed Sundays. Piazza San Lorenzo.

Cappelle Medicee (Medici Chapels) – Once part of San Lorenzo, these famous Medici funerary chapels now have a separate entrance. The first of the chapels, the Cappella dei Principi (Chapel of the Princes), where Cosimo I and the other grand dukes of Tuscany lie, is the later of the two, and it is a family burial vault supreme: The elaborate baroque interior took all of the 17th and 18th centuries to complete. Note the fine examples of Florentine mosaic, fine inlay done with semi-precious stones. But the real attraction here is the other chapel, the Sagrestia Nuova (New Sacristy), a companion piece to the Sagrestia Vecchia (see above). This magnificent show is by Michelangelo, who was commissioned by Cardinal Giulio de' Medici (later Pope Clement VII) and Pope Leo X (another Medici) to design both the interior — Michelangelo's first architectural job — and the statuary as a fitting resting place for members of their family. Michelangelo worked on it from 1521 to 1533 and left two of the projected tombs incomplete, but those he finished — the tomb of Lorenzo II, Duke of Urbino, with the figures of Dawn and Dusk, and the tomb of Giuliano, Duke of Nemours, with the figures of Night and Day, are extraordinary. (Lorenzo il Magnifico and his brother Giuliano, the latter murdered in the Duomo, are buried in the tomb opposite the altar, which bears a splendid *Madonna with Child* by Michelangelo.) The Sagrestia Nuova was being restored at press time as part of the 500th anniversary celebration of Il Magnifico's death. Don't miss the feeling of this room as a whole; with its square plan and imposing dome (especially its unusual trapezoidal windows), one almost has a sensation of soaring upward! Open Tuesdays through Saturdays from 9 AM to 2 PM; Sundays to 1 PM. Admission charge. Piazza Madonna degli Aldobrandini (phone: 213206).

Palazzo Medici-Riccardi (Medici-Riccardi Palace) – Not far from San Lorenzo is the palace where the Medici family lived until 1540, when they moved to the Palazzo Vecchio. When Cosimo the Elder decided to build a mansion for the family, he first asked Brunelleschi to design it but rejected the architect's plans as too luxurious and likely to create excessive envy. So Michelozzo was the master responsible for what was to be the first authentic Renaissance mansion — as well as a barometer of the proper lifestyle for a Florentine banker. Be sure to visit the tiny chapel to see Benozzo Gozzoli's wonderful fresco of the Three Kings on their way to Bethlehem; admission charge. At press time, the palazzo was being restored for the Medici anniversary celebration. Open daily except Wednesdays from 9 AM to noon and from 3 to 5 PM; Sundays from 9 AM to noon. 1 Via Cavour (phone: 217601).

Santa Maria Novella – Designed by two Dominican monks in the late 13th century and largely completed by the mid-14th century (except for the façade, which was designed by Leon Battista Alberti and finished in the late 15th century), this church figures in Boccaccio's *Decameron* as the place where his protagonists discuss the plague of 1348, the Black Death. Michelangelo, at the age of 13, was sent here to study painting under Ghirlandaio, whose frescoes adorn the otherwise gloomy interior, as do others by Masaccio, Filippino Lippi, and followers of Giotto. See the Gondi and Strozzi chapels and the great Chiostro Verde (Green Cloister), so called for the predominance of green in the decoration by Paolo Uccello and his school. Piazza Santa Maria Novella (phone: 282187).

Orsanmichele – This solid, square 14th-century structure once housed wheat for emergency use on its upper floors, while the ground floor was a church, and the whole was adopted by the city's artisans and guilds and used as an oratory — an unusual combination. Outside, the 14 statues in the niches representing patron saints of the guilds were sculpted by the best Florentine artists of the 14th to 16th centuries. The interior is dominated by a huge 14th-century tabernacle of colored marble by Andrea Orcagna. On *St. Anne's Day,* July 26, the building is decorated with flags of the guilds to commemorate the expulsion of the tyrannical Duke of Athens from Florence on July 26, 1343. Via dei Calzaiuoli.

Sinagoga (Synagogue) – Built in the late 19th century by the Florentine Jewish community in the Sephardic-Moorish style, this is one of the world's most beautiful synagogues. It was severely damaged during the 1966 floods but was lovingly and accurately restored. Visits are permitted from 9 AM until half an hour before rites. Ring the bell at the smaller of the two gates, and an English-speaking woman will take you around. 4 Via Farini (phone: 284715).

ENVIRONS

San Miniato al Monte – Near Piazzale Michelangelo, this lovely church beloved by the Florentines dominates the hill of the same name and looks out over a broad panorama of Florence and the surrounding hills — a romantic setting that makes it a particular favorite for weddings. One of the best examples of Tuscan Romanesque architecture and design in the city, it was built from the 11th to the 13th century on the spot where St. Miniato, martyred in the 3rd century, is reputed to have placed his severed head after carrying it up from Florence. The façade is in the typical green and white marble of the Florentine Romanesque style, as is the pulpit inside, and the geometric patterns on the inlaid floor are Oriental. Art treasures include Michelozzo's Crucifix Chapel, with terra cotta decorations by Luca della Robbia; Spinello Aretino's frescoes in the sacristy; and the Chapel of the Cardinal of Portugal, a Renaissance addition that contains works by Baldovinetti, Antonio and Piero del Pollaiolo, and Luca della Robbia. The church was being restored as we went to press, in preparation for the festivities to mark the 500th anniversary of the death of Lorenzo de' Medici. The monks of San Miniato repeat vespers in Gregorian chant every day from 4:45 to 5:30 PM. Tourists are welcome if they plan to attend the entire mass (before the service, a monk asks visitors to leave if their time is short). By all means stop by the adjoining cemetery, a wonderful collection of Italian funerary art (the English painter Henry Savage Landor and Carlo Lorenzini, a.k.a. Carlo Collodi, author of *Pinocchio,* are buried here). The fortifications surrounding the church were designed by Michelangelo against the imperial troops of Charles V. Viale Galileo (phone: 234-2731).

Forte Belvedere – A 15-minute walk, or a short bus ride from the center of Florence will take you to this imposing 16th-century fort — built by the famous Florentine architect Buontalenti — which forms part of the Old City walls. There are splendid views of the city below and the fortress itself often has exhibitions of painting and sculpture inside. In summer the grounds become a makeshift open-air movie theater. It's a pleasant walk either up through the Boboli Gardens or up the steep Costa San Giorgio from the Ponte Vecchio. Alternatively, take bus Nos. 12 or 13 from the center. Open daily from 9 AM to 8 PM. Admission charge. Costa San Giorgio (phone: 234-2822).

Fiesole – This beautiful village on a hill overlooking Florence and the Arno was an ancient Etruscan settlement and, later, a Roman city. The Duomo, begun in the 11th century and radically restored in the 19th, is on the main square, Piazza Mino da Fiesole, and just off the square is the *Teatro Romano,* built about 80 BC, where classical plays are sometimes performed, especially during the summer festival (*L'Estate Fiesolana*), which is devoted primarily to music. Take the picturesque Via San Francesco leading out of the square and walk up to the Church of St. Francis, passing the public gardens along the way and stopping at the terrace to enjoy the splendid view of Florence. The church, built during the 14th and 15th centuries, contains some very charming cloisters, especially the tiny Choistrino di San Bernardino. Visit the monks' cells, furnished as they were in the 15th century. Fiesole's tourist office is at 37 Piazza Mino (phone: 598720). Fiesole is 5 miles (8 km) north of Florence and can be reached by bus No. 7 from the railway station or Piazza San Marco (be careful, as this bus is a notorious venue for pickpockets).

Certosa di Galluzzo – Southwest of downtown is this monastery 7 miles (11 km) away, where the monks have been growing herbs and making liqueurs from them for centuries. Visitors can tour this splendid working facility, set in a magnificent countryside of rolling Tuscan hills, and buy some of their products to take home. There also is a small museum with some beautiful frescoes, most notably those by Pontormo from the 16th century. The No. 37 bus from the center goes directly to the *certosa* (monastery). By car, it is a 15-minute trip. Follow the signs for Galluzzo, and you'll see the monastery loom up in front of you. Open daily except Mondays from 9 AM to noon and 3 to 5 PM; admission charge. Galluzzo (phone: 204-9226).

Casa di Machiavelli – In the small village of Sant'Andrea in Percussina, 12 miles (20 km) and a half-hour drive from the city, is this house (known as Albergaccio) where Niccolò Machiavelli lived after being exiled from Florence by the Medicis. He wrote his masterpiece *Il Principe* (The Prince) here. The house is furnished as it was when Machiavelli was in residence. Open daily from 9 AM to 12:30 PM and 3:30 to 6 PM. Admission charge. Across the road (you can't miss it) is a small trattoria where the writer apparently was wont to repair for a jug of wine in between chapters. It still serves an excellent dish of Tuscan beans and very good peasant bread. A private bus company, *Sita* (phone: 48365 weekdays, 211487 weekends), runs from Piazza Santa Maria Novella to the village; by car, take SS2 heading toward Siena and turn off at San Casciano Val di Pesa. The village is signposted from there. Sant'Andrea in Percussina (no phone).

■ **EXTRA SPECIAL:** Scattered about the Florentine countryside are a number of stately villas of the historic aristocracy of Florence, three of which are associated with the Medici family. On the road to Sesto Fiorentino, about 5 miles (8 km) north of the city, are the 16th-century Villa della Petraia (originally a castle of the Brunelleschi family, rebuilt in 1575 for a Medici cardinal by Buontalenti) and, just down the hill, the 15th-century Villa di Castello, which was taken over by the Medicis in 1477. Both have lovely gardens and fountains by Tribolo. The Villa Medici at Poggio a Caiano, at the foot of Monte Albano, about 10 miles (16 km) northwest of Florence, was rebuilt for Lorenzo the Magnificent by Giuliano da Sangallo from 1480 to 1485. The gardens of all three villas usually are open daily except Mondays; the interiors of the Petraia and Poggio a Caiano villas also may be visited (but hours and policies change; call 451208 for information regarding the former, 877012 for the latter). *Agriturist* runs organized excursions to the villas, as well as to country estates in the neighboring wine growing region. For information, contact *Agriturist,* 3 Piazza San Firenze (phone: 287838).

SOURCES AND RESOURCES

TOURIST INFORMATION: The Ente Provinciale per il Turismo (16 Via Alessandro Manzoni; phone: 247-8141/2/3/4/5) will provide general information, brochures, and maps of the city and the surrounding area. It is open Mondays through Saturdays from 8:30 AM to 1:30 PM. There's also a tourist information booth just outside the train station as well as an office at 15 Via Tornabuoni (phone: 217459), open Mondays through Saturdays from 9 AM to 1 PM. For information on Tuscany, contact the Regional Tourist Office (26 Via di Novoli; phone: 438-2111). Helpful for younger travelers is the *Student Travel Service* (*STS*) (18r Via Zannetti; phone: 268396 or 292067).

The US Consulate is at 38 Lungarno Amerigo Vespucci (phone: 298276).

Numerous maps and pocket-size guidebooks to Florence, such as the *Storti Guides*, are published in Italy and are available at newsstands throughout the city. Excellent guides in English available in bookstores are by Luciano Berti and by Rolando and Piero Fusi. Background reading before your trip might include Mary McCarthy's classic *The Stones of Florence* (Harcourt), a discussion of the history and character of the city as seen through its art, Christopher Hibbert's *The House of Medici: Its Rise and Fall* (Morrow), a study of the city's most influential family, and new this year, our own *Birnbaum's Florence* (HarperCollins).

Local Coverage – Check the brochure *Florence Concierge Information*, available at most hotels, or pick up a copy of *Florence Today* at the tourist information office. *Vista*, a free English-language magazine published every 3 months, also lists activities of interest to visitors. It is found at major hotels and tourist offices. Florence's daily newspaper is *La Nazione*. A national newspaper, *La Republicca*, has a section on Florence in which there is a daily calendar of events in English.

TELEPHONE: The city code for Florence is 55. When calling from within Italy, dial 055 before the local number.

GETTING AROUND: Most visitors find Florence one of the easiest of European cities to navigate. Although it is fairly large, the scale is rather intimate, and it's easy to get just about anywhere on foot. Almost all the major sites are on the north side, or right bank, of the river, but most of those on the Oltrarno side ("beyond the Arno") are within easy walking distance of the center. Part of the city's center is closed to traffic, except for those with permits, making it quite pleasant for pedestrians. Visitors sometimes are confused by the numbers on Florentine buildings, for houses are numbered according to a double system. Black (*nero*) numbers indicate dwellings, while red (*rosso*) numbers — indicated by an "r" after the number in street addresses — are commercial buildings (shops and such). The black and the red have little relationship to each other, so you may find a black 68 next to a red 5.

Airport – Florence has no international airport; the closest one is Pisa's Galileo Galilei Airport (phone: 50-28088), a 1-hour train ride from the city, but too often closed due to nearly ubiquitous early morning fog. Travelers destined for flights from Pisa's airport can check bags through to their final destination from Florence's train station, where a Pisa airport check-in counter has been set up on Quai 5. It's far safer, though, to take the train to Rome and fly out of Italy from there (although there are flights from

Milan, in winter, it is fog-bound even more frequently than Pisa). From Florence's main train station, the minibus operated by *Auto Alberghi* (phone: 261624) stops at most of the city's hotels for a fee.

Florence does have a domestic aiport, Peretola Civic Airport (11 Via Del Termine; phone: 373498), with some flights to Milan, Rome, Venice, Turin, and Trieste. Service to this airport has been expanded, with scheduled international flights arriving from Brussels, Frankfurt, London, Munich, Nice, Paris, Stuttgart, and Vienna. Peretola is a 10-minute drive from downtown; taxi fare into the city will run about $10.

Bicycles, Mopeds, and Motorbikes – *Ciao & Basta* (33 Via Bardi; phone: 234-2726), rents bicycles; *Bici-Città* (phone: 499319 or 296335) will furnish two free bikes for 2 hours upon presentation of a *SCAF* car park coupon, and has three locations: Fortezza da Basso, Piazza Pitti, and Stazione Centrale on Via Alamanni (by the stairway). Motorbikes are available from *Program* (135r Borgo Ognissanti; phone: 282916), *Motorent* (9r Via San Zanobi; phone: 490113), and *Sabra* (8 Via Artisti; phone: 576256 or 579609), which also rents mopeds. Ride carefully!

Buses – *ATAF* is the city bus company, running about 40 city and suburban routes. Bus routes are listed in the yellow pages of the telephone directory. Tickets — which should be purchased before boarding — can be bought at tobacco counters, in bars, and at some newsstands; they cost about $1 and can be used more than once, with a 1½-hour time limit. Children under 1 meter (39 inches) tall ride free. As there are no ticket collectors (only automatic stamping machines), many passengers do not buy tickets, but anybody caught without one by the occasional controller is fined on the spot. The back door of the bus is for boarding, the middle for disembarking; the front door is only for season ticket holders. At rush hour, buses are impossibly crowded and it's sometimes difficult to get off at the desired stop. Walking often is faster and more enjoyable, but pedestrians are cautioned to watch out for buses and taxis in special lanes permitting them to travel the wrong way on many one-way streets.

Car Rental – *Avis* (128r Borgo Ognissanti; phone: 289010 or 213629); *Europcar* (53 Borgo Ognissanti; phone: 293444); *Europedrive* (35-37 Via Bisenzio; phone: 437-6862 or 422-2839); *Garage S. Lucia* (9r Via Orti Oricellari; phone: 216583); *Hertz* (33 Via Maso Finiguerra; phone: 298295); *InterRent Autonoleggio* (1r Via il Prato; phone: 218665); *Italy by Car* (*Budget;* 134r Borgo Ognissanti; phone: 293021); *Maggiore* (11 Via Maso Finiguerra; phone: 210238); and *Program* (135r Borgo Ognissanti; phone: 289010). Be aware that parking is difficult in the center and the one-way system can be maddening. An alternative is to leave your car at one of the attended parking lots outside the center or at your hotel, and walk or take a taxi.

Taxi – You can hail a cruising taxi (it's available if the light on top is lit) or pick one up at one of the numerous cabstands around the city. You can call for a taxi by dialing 4798 or 4390. Cabs are metered, but there are extra charges for night rides, luggage, station pickups, and the like. It is customary to give a small tip. A general rule is to round off the fare to the nearest 1,000 lire (about 80¢).

Train – Stazione Centrale Santa Maria Novella, the city's main railway station, is near the church of the same name, at Piazza Stazione. Call 278785 from 7 AM to 9 PM for information.

LOCAL SERVICES: Dentist (English-Speaking) – Dr. Mario De Leo (1 Via Roma; phone: 215030); Dr. Giano Ricci (26 Via Gino Capponi; phone: 247-9471).

Dry Cleaner/Tailor – *Augusta,* 1-hour dry cleaning (16r Via delle Belle Donne and other locations; phone: 210249); *Sartoria Maiano,* for men's tailoring only (2 Piazza Antinori; phone: 284146).

Limousine Service – *Barocchi* (9 Via Orti Oricellari; phone: 216583); *Far-Autonoleggio,* also has minibus service (101 Via San Gallo; phone: 483410).

Medical Emergency – *Ambulanze Misericordie* (phone: 212222) or *Fratellanza Militare* (phone: 215555). For emergency heart problems, call the *Unità Coronarica Mobile* (Mobile Coronary Unit; phone: 283394). English-speaking doctors can be reached 24 hours a day at *Tourist Medical Service* (59 Via Lorenzo Il Magnifico; phone: 475411), or *Santa Chiara Clinic* (11 Piazza Indipendenza; phone: 496312 or 475230).

Messenger Service – *Amico Espresso,* Via Ponte All'asse (phone: 375108 or 375136).

National/International Courier – *DHL International* (243-45 Via della Cupola; phone: 318031); *Federal Express* (200 Via Sansovino; phone: 706460); *Universal Express* (1 Piazza Goldoni; phone: 296525).

Office Equipment Rental – *Sabbatini & Co.,* typewriters and calculators for a 15-day minimum. 16r Via Banchi (phone: 210103).

Pharmacy – *Taverna* (20r Piazza San Giovanni; phone: 284013); *Molteni* (7r Via Calzaiuoli; phone: 263490); *Comunale No. 13* (Stazione Santa Maria Novella; phone: 263435). All are open daily, 24 hours.

Photocopies – *Landini* (87/L Via Novoli; phone: 431308); *Centro 2P* (30 Via G. Bastianelli; phone: 417709 or 430783); *Eliocopia* (138r Via Cavour; phone: 210004). Some stationers (*cartolerie*) also provide this service.

Post Office – *PTT,* open weekdays from 8:15 AM to 7 PM and Saturdays from 8:15 AM to noon. 3 Via Pellicceria (phone: 211147).

Telex – *PTT,* open 24 hours. 3 Via Pellicceria (phone: 215364).

Translators/Interpreters – *International Service Inc.* (20 Via Palazzuolo; phone: 575371); *Tradv-Co* (27 Via Marconi; phone: 579657).

Other – Office space rental: *Centro Uffici Redco,* furnished and equipped. 11 Lungarno B. Cellini (phone: 681-1893).

SPECIAL EVENTS: Florence is bathed in medieval splendor each year for festivities surrounding the *Festa di San Giovanni Battista* (Feast of St. John the Baptist), June 24. Part of the tradition for the past several hundred years has been the *Calcio in Costume,* which consists of more than 500 men wearing colorful 16th-century costumes — with modern T-shirts — and playing a very rough game of soccer. Actually, because there are four teams, representing the old rival neighborhoods of San Giovanni, Santo Spirito, Santa Croce, and Santa Maria Novella (distinguishable by their green, white, blue, and red costumes, respectively), three games are played, two preliminaries and a final. One is usually scheduled on June 24 and the other two within a week or two before or after that date. The game, which resembles wrestling, rugby, and soccer, with the round leather ball thrown more often than kicked, originated in the Roman *arpasto,* played on sandy ground by soldiers training for war. It evolved through the Middle Ages and the Renaissance (in 1530 there was a most famous match played by the Florentines in defiance of the imperial troops of Charles V who were besieging the city), lapsed for about a century and a half, and then was revived in 1930. Also revived was the preliminary parade of Florentine guild officials, followed by the four teams led by their resident noblemen on horseback (the best known of whom is the Marchese Emilio Pucci di Barsento, the fashion designer). Because the game and its 8,000 or so spectators constitute some danger to the fountains and statuary of Florence's historic piazze, it was moved at one point to the Boboli Gardens, only to be banned there, too. This year (and probably every year to come) it will be held at its original site, Piazza Santa Croce.

Among the other folkloric events is the centuries-old ceremony called the *Scoppio del Carro,* literally "bursting the cart," which takes place traditionally on *Easter Sunday* in celebration of a Christian victory in one of the Crusades and culminates in a great fireworks display. A large cart drawn by white oxen is brought to Piazza del Duomo and connected to the main altar of the cathedral by a metal wire. At the stroke of noon, when the bells announce the Resurrection of Christ, the Cardinal Archbishop of Florence sets off a dove-shaped rocket that runs along the wire to the cart filled with firecrackers. When the cart explodes, the Florentine spectators jump with joy, taking the event and the flight of the "dove" as a good omen for the future. Occasionally the dove doesn't make it and sighs of something worse than disappointment fill the square, as this is considered a bad omen indeed. On *Ascension Day* each May, Florentines celebrate the *Festa del Grillo* by going to the Cascine, a park along the Arno at the edge of the center, and buying crickets in cages, only to set them free. The *Festa delle Rificolone,* September 7, is celebrated with a procession along the Arno and across the Ponte San Niccolò with colorful paper lanterns and torches.

At the *Fortezza del Basso* in June is the *Mostra Mercato degli Antiquari Toscani* where regional Tuscan antiques dealers sell everything from Etruscan relics to 19th-century antiques. The *Biennale Dell'Antiquariato,* an important international antiques fair, is held in odd-number years in the fall at the Palazzo Strozzi.

From April through the summer of this year, a series of events will take place to commemorate the 500th anniversary of the death of Lorenzo de' Medici — one of Florence's most famous and best-loved citizens. A series of exhibitions, talks, concerts, and costume parades will be held in the city and continue through the summer. Highlights include an exhibit at the *Palazzo Medici* of paintings, sculptures, majolica, and furnishings — collected from various museums around the world — that were part of Lorenzo's collection when he lived there. Another exhibit (the place had not been determined at press time) will re-create the workshops of some of the major artists who worked during Il Magnifico's lifetime, including Botticelli, Lippi, Ghirlandaio, and Perugino. For a detailed program of the festivities, contact the tourist office.

MUSEUMS: Since museums are possibly the city's top attraction, quite a few have already been described under *Special Places.* A few more of the 70 or so museums in the city are listed here, along with additional churches and palaces whose artwork makes them, in effect, museums, too. As hours may vary, contact the tourist information office (phone: 217459) or the Superintendent of Museums and Galleries (phone: 218341) for information about hours.

Badia Fiorentina – The church of a former Benedictine abbey (*badia*), with a part-Romanesque, part-Gothic campanile, it was founded in the 10th century, enlarged in the 13th, and rebuilt in the 17th. Opposite the *Bargello.* Via del Proconsolo (no phone).

Casa Buonarroti – The small house Michelangelo bought for his next of kin, containing some of the master's early works, as well as works done in his honor by some of the foremost artists of the 16th and 17th centuries. Open Tuesdays through Saturdays from 9:30 AM to 1:30 PM, Sundays from 9:30 AM to 12:30 PM. Admission charge. 70 Via Ghibellina (phone: 241752).

Casa di Dante – A small museum in what is believed to have been Dante's house, it documents his life, times, and work. Open from 9:30 AM to 12:30 PM and 3:30 to 6:30 PM, Sundays from 9:30 AM to 12:30 PM. Closed Wednesdays. No admission charge. 1 Via Santa Margherita (phone: 283343).

Casa Guidi – Robert and Elizabeth Barrett Browning lived on the first floor of this 15th-century palazzo at the corner of the *Pitti Palace* from shortly after their secret marriage in 1846 until Elizabeth's death in 1861. Now called the *Browning Institute,* it is an unfinished museum and a memorial to both poets. It's best to ask the tourist office about when the museum is open. Admission charge. 8 Piazza San Felice (no phone).

Cenacolo di Sant'Apollonia – The refectory of a former convent, containing Andrea del Castagno's remarkable fresco of the Last Supper (ca. 1450). Closed Mondays. Admission charge. 1 Via XXVII Aprile (phone: 287074).

Museo Archeologico (Archaeological Museum) – This fascinating museum contains a permanent jewelery exhibit of gold and gems from the Medici. There also is an outstanding collection of Etruscan, Greek, and Roman art housed in six halls (damaged during the 1966 flood) that were reopened after a lengthy, costly restoration. A topographical section features objects from ancient Etruria; and an Egyptian area has mummies, statues, and a well-preserved chariot found in Thebes. Open Tuesdays through Saturdays from 9 AM to 2 PM, Sundays from 9 AM to 1 PM. Admission charge. 38 Via Colonna (phone: 247-8641).

Museo Archeologico di Fiesole – A fine selection of treasures from both the Etruscan and Roman periods of Fiesolan history, including an especially rich collection of Etruscan pottery. The museum is part of a complex that also has a Roman theater — used for concerts in the summer — and the remains of an Etruscan temple. Open daily from 9AM to 7 PM. Admission charge. Piazza Mino, Fiesole (phone: 59477).

Museo di Antropologia ed Etnologia (Museum of Anthropology and Ethnology) – First of its genre in Italy, continually enlarged, now with more than 30 rooms and a vast collection divided by race, continent, and culture. Open Thursdays, Fridays, and Saturdays from 9 AM to 1 PM and the third Sunday of the month (except July through September). Admission charge. 12 Via del Proconsolo (phone: 296449).

Museo Bardini – Sculpture, tapestries, bronzes, furniture, and paintings. Open from 9 AM to 2 PM, Sundays from 9 AM to 1 PM. Closed Wednesdays. Admission charge. 1 Piazza dei Mozzi (phone: 234-2427).

Museo Firenze Com'Era (Florence "As It Was" Museum) – Collection of mainly 19th-century maps, paintings, documents, and photos illustrating aspects of the city over the centuries. There also is a permanent exhibition of works by the 20th-century artist Ottone Rosai. Open from 9 AM to 2 PM, Sundays from 9 AM to 1 PM. Closed Thursdays. Admission charge. 24 Via dell'Oriuolo (phone: 217305).

Museo della Fondazione Horne (Horne Museum) – A jewel of a museum — paintings, drawings, sculptures, furniture, ceramics, coins, and unusual old household utensils, the collection of an Englishman, Herbert Percy Horne, bequeathed to the city in 1916 and set up in his 15th-century *palazzetto.* Open from 9 AM to 1 PM. Closed Sundays and holidays. Admission charge. 6 Via de' Benci (phone: 244661).

Museo Stibbert – Vast collection (about 50,000 pieces) of art objects, antiques, arms from all over the world, and other curiosities left by the English collector Stibbert, with his villa and gardens. Open from 9 AM to 1 PM, Sundays from 9 AM to 12:30 PM. Closed Thursdays. Admission charge. 26 Via Federico Stibbert (phone: 486049).

Museo di Storia Naturale (Museum of Natural History) – Also known as "La Specola," it has a weird but interesting collection of wax anatomical models from the late 18th century. There also is an exhibit of waxed and stuffed animals. Open daily except Sundays from 9 AM to noon; second Sunday of the month from 9:30 AM to 12:30 PM. No admission charge. 17 Via Romana (phone: 222451).

Museo di Storia della Scienza (Museum of the History of Science) – Scientific instruments, including Galileo's telescopes, and odd items documenting the development of modern science from the Renaissance to the 20th century. Open Tuesdays, Thursdays, and Saturdays from 9:30 AM to 1 PM; Mondays, Wednesdays, and Fridays from 9:30 AM to 1 PM and from 2 to 5 PM. Admission charge. 1 Piazza de' Giudici (phone: 293493).

Ognissanti (All Saints' Church) – Built in the 13th century and rebuilt in the 17th, it contains extraordinary frescoes by Ghirlandaio and Botticelli and is the burial place of the latter as well as of the family of Amerigo Vespucci. 42 Piazza d'Ognissanti (phone: 239870).

Palazzo Davanzati – A well-preserved 14th-century palace with 15th-century furniture, tapestries, and ceramics, also known as the *Museo della Casa Fiorentina Antica* (Florentine House Museum). Open from 9 AM to 1 PM. Closed Saturdays. Admission charge. 13 Via Porta Rossa (phone: 216518).

Palazzo Strozzi – This masterpiece of Renaissance architecture is the scene of a biennial international antiques show, held in the fall (in odd-number years). Open from 9:30 AM to 1 PM and 3 to 7 PM. Closed Mondays. Admission charge. Piazza Strozzi (phone: 215990).

Santi Apostoli (Church of the Holy Apostles) – Built in the 11th century, redecorated in the 15th and 16th centuries, and restored in the 1930s, it holds the flints said to have been brought back from Jerusalem during the Crusades and still used to light the Holy Fire in the Duomo for the *Scoppio del Carro* at *Easter* (see *Special Events*).

Santa Maria del Carmine – Dating from the second half of the 13th century, this Carmelite church was mostly destroyed in a fire in 1771, but the Corsini and Brancacci chapels were spared. The latter, reopened after 10 years of restoration, contains the Masaccio frescoes that inspired Renaissance painters from Fra Angelico to Raphael. Piazza del Carmine.

Santa Trinita (Church of the Holy Trinity) – One of the oldest churches in Florence, built in the 11th century with a 16th-century façade. See the Ghirlandaio frescoes in the Sassetti Chapel — one shows the church with its original Romanesque façade. Piazza Santa Trinita.

SHOPPING: Shopping is absolutely wonderful in Florence, arguably Italy's most fashionable city. For clothing, the smartest streets are Via Tornabuoni, Via della Vigna Nuova, Via Calzaiuoli, and Via Roma. The shops lining the Ponte Vecchio have been selling beautiful gold and silver jewelry since 1593. Antiques, leather goods, and handmade lingerie are other specialties of Florentine shops. Winter store hours are 9 AM to 1 PM and 3:30 to 7:30 PM Tuesdays through Saturdays; 3:30 to 7:30 PM on Mondays. The summer finds these stores closed on Saturday afternoons rather than Monday mornings, and the evening closing hour is extended by a half hour to 8. Some shops that are geared to tourists (fashion, leather, souvenirs, and so on) stay open all day. Food shops traditionally close on Wednesdays.

Alex – The best in designer clothes for women — Gianni Versace, Yamamoto, Byblos, Claude Montana, Basile, Thierry Mugler. 19r and 5r Via della Vigna Nuova (phone: 210446).

Antico Setificio Fiorentino – Fabulous fabrics, all handloomed. 97r Via della Vigna Nuova (phone: 282700).

Befani & Tai – Quality gold craftsmanship at good prices. 13r Via Baccherecia (phone: 287825).

Beltrami – A chain of elegant, expensive leatherwear shops: shoes, bags, jackets, pants, and other items. 31r, 44r, and 202r Via Calzaiuoli (phone: 212418); 1r Via dei Pecori (phone: 216321); 11r Via Calimala (phone: 212288); and 28 Via Tornabuoni (phone: 287779).

Benetton – Colorful, reasonably priced casualwear for the young at heart. 66-68r Via Por Santa Maria (phone: 287111) and 2r Via Calimala (phone: 214878), and other locations.

Bijoux Cascio – Moderately priced jewelry, particularly in gold; the designs are the shop's own. 32r Via Tornabuoni (phone: 284709) and other locations).

BM – An English-language bookstore. 4r Borgo Ognissanti (phone: 294575).

Bottega Veneta – Exquisite leather goods, especially handbags. 3-4r Piazza Ognissanti (phone: 294265).

Cartier – Fantastic jewelry. 1 Piazza Santa Trinita (phone: 292347).

Casa de' Tessuti – *The* place to go to find wonderful Italian fabrics, including wool, silk, and linen. 20-24r Via de' Pecori (phone: 215961).

Cellerini – High-quality bags and suitcases made by a craftsman in a workshop above the store. 9 Via del Sole (phone: 282533).

Cirri – Lovely linen. 38-40r Via Por Santa Maria (phone: 296593).

C.O.I. – Gold jewelry sold by weight at affordable prices. 8 Via Por S. Maria (phone: 283970 or 293424).

David – Leather bags, luggage, shoes, clothes. 11-13r Via Roma (phone: 211884).

Emilio Paoli – Straw market with class — locally produced gift articles and imports. 26r Via della Vigna Nuova (phone: 214596).

Emilio Pucci Boutique – Pucci fashions — back in style. Palazzo Pucci, 6 Via de' Pucci (phone: 287622).

Falai – Florence is known for its jewelry shops, but this one will also copy much-loved items or help you design new ones from drawings or descriptions. 28r Via Por S. Maria (phone: 261688).

Feltrinelli – Art books. 12-20r Via Cavour (phone: 219524).

Ferragamo – The famous shoemaker's headquarters in Italy, with the widest selection of styles and colors. 12-16r Via Tornabuoni (phone: 292123).

Gants – Gloves of the highest quality; they make their own. 78r Via Porta Rossa.

Gerard – Way-out, punk, and exotic fashions for men and women. 18-20r Via Vacchereccia (phone: 215942).

Gherardini – A century-old leather shop, also selling sunglasses and perfume, run by an old Florentine family (the subject of the *Mona Lisa* was a Gherardini). 57r Via della Vigna Nuova (phone: 215678) and other locations.

Giulio Giannini e Figlio – This father-and-son store is one of the oldest selling the famous hand-crafted Florentine paper products, and its selection is one of the best in town. 37r Piazza Pitti (phone: 215342).

Gori Boutique – Santa Croce Leather School products, as well as articles by Italy's top-name designers. 13r Piazza Santa Croce (phone: 242935).

Gucci – The parent store of Italy's best known leather and fashion purveyor. Less expensive than in the US, but hardly inexpensive. 57-73-75r Via Tornabuoni (phone: 264011).

Happy Jack – A good, men's boutique; alterations done quickly. 7-13r Via della Vigna Nuova (phone: 284329).

Libreria Franco Maria Ricci – Fine books selected by the publishers of *FMR* magazine. 41r Via delle Belle Donne (phone: 283312).

Libreria Salimbeni – Specializes in art books. 14r Via Matteo Palmieri (phone: 234-0904).

Lily of Florence – Italian shoes in American sizes. 2r Via Guicciardini (phone: 294748).

Loretta Caponi – Exquisite handmade lingerie and linen by this second-generation shop that designs for Nina Ricci and Dior. 38-40r Borgo Ognissanti (phone: 213668).

Luisa Spagnoli – Women's high-quality clothing, made from the purest cotton and wool, at moderate prices. 20 Via Strozzi (phone: 211978).

Madova – Italy's most competent and incomparable glovemaker. 1r Via Guiccardini (phone: 296526).

Mario Buccellati – Fine jewelry and silverware in traditional Florentine designs. 71r Via Tornabuoni (phone: 296579).

Mario Valentino – Designer shoes and bags. 67r Via Tornabuoni (phone: 261338).

Melli – Antique jewelry, ivory, silver, and clocks. 48 Ponte Vecchio (phone: 211413).

***Mercato Nuovo* (Straw Market)** – The covered market, with all sorts of items made of straw, wood, and leather, as well as goods from Florence's growing immigrant community. Piazza del Mercato Nuovo.

Mujer – Original fashions for the adventurous woman. 6r Via Vacchereccia (phone: 210057).

Neuber – British and Italian wools. 32r Via Strozzi (phone: 215763).

Papiro – *Papier à cuve,* or marbled paper, a method of hand-decoration invented in the 17th century; lovely stationery. 55 Via Cavour (phone: 215262) and other locations.

Parson – Trendy women's boutique. 16-18r Via Tosinghi (phone: 282590).

La Pelle – Leather clothes made to order in two stores. 11-13r and 11-14r Via Guicciardini (phone: 292031).

Pineider – Italy's most famous stationers. 13r Piazza della Signoria (phone: 284655) and 76r Via Tornabuoni (phone: 211605).

Pratesi – Elegant and expensive linen. 8-10 Lungarno Amerigo Vespucci.

Primi Mesi – Embroidered crib and carriage sets; maternity, infants, and toddlers wear. 23r Via dei Cimatori (phone: 296372).

Principe – A small but elegant department store. 21-29r Piazza Strozzi (phone: 216821).

Renard – Leather, suede, and sheepskin clothing. 21-23r Via dei Martelli (phone: 284566).

Rosetta Belli – Specializes in handbags, and at relatively reasonable prices. 9r Via dei Fossi (phone: 293567).

Santa Croce Leather School – Top-quality leather goods (boxes, gloves, handbags, wallets, clothing, and shoes) from the school and shop inside the Monastery of Santa Croce. 16 Piazza Santa Croce or (through the garden) 5r Via San Giuseppe (phone: 244533 or 247-9913).

Schwicker – Quality gifts by Florentine artisans. 40r Piazza Pitti (phone: 211851).

Seeber – English-language bookshop. 70 Via Tornabuoni (phone: 215697).

Stefanel – Colorful casualwear. Via Borgo San Lorenzo (phone: 312578).

Tanino Crisci – The most stylish shoe shop (for men and women) in town. 43-45 Via Tornabuoni (phone: 216741).

Torrini – Exquisite jewelry. 10r Piazza Duomo (phone: 284506).

U. Gerardi – Best selection of coral jewelry in town. 5 Ponte Vecchio (phone: 211809).

Ugo Poggi – Florentine handicrafts in silver, china, glass. 26r Via degli Strozzi (phone: 216741).

Ungaro Parallèle – High fashion for women. 30r Via della Vigna Nuova (phone: 210129).

UPIM – A large, moderately priced department store. Piazza della Repubblica (phone: 298544).

Valmar – Tapestry items perfect for everything from upholstery to women's belts. 53r Via Porta Rossa (phone: 284493).

Zanobetti – Classic clothing and leather goods for men and women. 20-22r Via Calimala (phone: 210646).

SPORTS AND FITNESS: Check with your concierge to find out which sports facilities currently are open to the public. Most are private clubs, but a day visit often can be arranged for a fee.

Fitness Centers – *Indoor Club* (15 Via Bardazzi; phone: 430275); *Palestra Savasana* (26 Via J. da Diaccetto; phone: 287373); *Sauna Finlandese* (108 Via Cavour; phone: 587246); *Tropos* (20a Via Orcagna; phone: 661581).

Golf – There is a good 18-hole course (closed Mondays) at *Golf dell'Ugolino,* in nearby Impruneta, 3 Via Chiantigiana (phone: 230-1096).

Horseback Riding – For information, call *Piazzale Cascine* (phone: 360056) or *Agriturist* (phone: 287838). Just outside the city is *Badia Montescalari* (129 Via Montescalari at La Panca; phone: 959596).

Jogging – The best place to run is the Cascine, a very long, narrow park along the Arno west of the center. To get there, follow the river to Ponte della Vittoria.

Soccer – See the *Fiorentina* in action from September to May at the *Stadio Comunale,* designed by Pier Luigi Nervi. 4-6 Viale Manfredo Fanti (phone: 572625).

Squash – Courts can be reserved at the *Centro Squash Firenze;* 24-29 Viale Piombino (phone: 710055).

Swimming – Swimmers will do best to stay at one of the following hotels: *Crest, Croce di Malta* (although the pool is very small), *Jolly Carlton, Kraft, Minerva, Park Palace, Villa Belvedere, Villa Medici,* or *Villa sull'Arno* or, outside the city, at the *Grand Hotel Villa Cora, Villa La Massa, Villa San Michele,* or the *Villa Villoresi.* There also are a few indoor and outdoor public pools, including *Piscina Costoli* (Viale Paoli; phone: 669744); *Piscina Le Pavoniere,* an outdoor pool in a pleasant park (Viale degli Olmi; phone: 367506); and *Zodiac Sport* (2 Via A. Grandi; phone: 202-2847).

Tennis – Play tennis at the semi-public *Circolo Tennis alle Cascine* (1 Viale Visarno; phone: 356651); *Assi-Giglio-Rosso* (64 Viale Michelangelo; phone: 681-2686 or 687858); *Il Poggetto* (24/B Via Michele Mercati; phone: 460127); and *Match Ball* (Via della Massa; phone: 631752).

THEATER: If you'd like to see a play in Italian, the principal theaters in Florence are the *Teatro della Pergola* (32 Via della Pergola; phone: 247-9651); the *Teatro Niccolini* (5 Via Ricasoli; phone: 213282); and *Tenda Città di Firenze* (Via de Nicola; phone: 650-4112). *Teatro Variety* (47 Via del Madonnone; phone: 660632) offers singers and humorous contemporary pieces. Films in English are shown frequently at the *Cinema Astro* (Piazza San Simone near Santa Croce; phone: 222388).

MUSIC: Opera begins earlier in Florence than in most Italian cities. The season at the *Teatro Comunale* (Corso Italia; phone: 27791), the principal opera house and concert hall, runs from October to early January, with ballet in July. The annual *Maggio Musicale Fiorentino* festival, which attracts some of the world's finest musicians and singers, also is held here in May and June. Tickets can be purchased at the theater; *Universal Turismo* (7r Via Speziali; phone: 217241); or *Box Office* (10A/r Via della Pergola; phone: 241881). The *Teatro della Pergola* (see *Theater*) is the scene of Saturday afternoon concerts from autumn through spring. The *Orchestra da Camera Fiorentina* (Florentine Chamber Orchestra; 6 Via E. Poggi; phone: 470027) regularly stages classical concerts. Open-air concerts are held in the cloisters of the Badia Fiesolana (in Fiesole) and of the Ospedale degli Innocenti on summer evenings, and occasionally in other historic monuments such as the restored Church of Santo Stefano al Ponte Vecchio, now the seat of the *Regional Tuscan Orchestra.*

NIGHTCLUBS AND NIGHTLIFE: A Florentine evening usually begins with an *aperitivo* at one of the cafés on Piazza della Signoria (such as *Caffè Rivoire,* an elegant watering hole with wood-paneled walls and marble-top tables) or Piazza della Repubblica, at *Harry's Bar* (22r Lungarno Amerigo Vespucci; phone: 296700), or at *Bar Donatello,* on the main floor of the *Excelsior* hotel, the pre-dinner gathering place for Florence's smart set. Because nightspots come and go so quickly — and since most are closed at least 1 night of the week — it always is a good idea to check with your hotel concierge before going out. Discos and piano bars are among the most popular forms of evening entertainment, and tops among the former are *Tenax* (46 Via Pratese; phone: 373050) and *Jackie-O'* (24/A Via dell'Erta Canina; phone: 234-2442). Other discos include *Yab Yum* (5r Via Sassetti; phone: 282018); *Full-Up* (21r Via della Vigna Vecchia; phone: 293006); and *Plegyne* (26r Piazza Santa Maria Novella; phone: 211590). For the very young crowd, dancing happens at *Space Electronic* (37 Via Palazzuolo; phone: 293082). If a quieter evening is called for, there are numerous lovely piano bars from which to choose, such as the elegant *Loggia Tornaquinci,* nestled atop a 16th-century Medici building (6r Via Tornabuoni; phone: 219148). Others include the *Caffè* (9 Piazza Pitti; phone: 296241);

Oberon (12r Via dell'Erta Canina; phone: 216516), and *Prezzemolo* (5r Via della Caldaie; phone: 211530), a champagne bar for night owls. The elegant *Oliviero* (51r Via della Terme; phone: 287643), is a restaurant with piano bar, the place for a romantic evening. There also are piano bars at some of the hotels, such as the *Anglo-American,* the *Londra,* the *Majestic,* and the *Savoy. Il Salotto* is a "private" club open to everyone. Situated in a 15th-century palazzo at 33 Borgo Pinti, it's not surprising that it boasts a clientele of Florentine nobility, artists, and wealthy merchants. Popular for drinks is the *Caffè Strozzi* (16-19 Piazza Strozzi; phone: 212574), with outdoor tables for good people watching. Three other local favorites are *Gilli,* a *Belle Epoque* café with a lively outdoor terrace (39r Piazza della Repubblica; phone: 296310); *Giacosa* (83 Via Tornabuoni; phone: 296226), where the elite meet over truffle-paste sandwiches; and *Procacci* (33 Via Tornabuoni), a café/bar serving white truffle-paste sandwiches and other elegant snacks to a chic local crowd.

BEST IN TOWN

CHECKING IN: Florence is well organized for visitors, with more than 400 hotels to accommodate more than 20,000 travelers. Still, somehow, it's hard to find a room in high season. The hotel count above and the list below include former *pensioni,* something like boarding houses, but now officially designated as "hotels." A few still require that some meals be taken, a feature that is specified for those that do. (Half-board means you must take breakfast and either lunch or dinner at the establishment.) Very expensive establishments can charge above $500 a night. At an expensive hotel, plan on spending from $210 to more than $470 a night for a double room. Moderate-priced establishments cost between $95 and $210; inexpensive lodging ranges from $60 to $95. All telephone numbers are in the 55 city code unless otherwise indicated.

Villa San Michele – Dramatically set about 5 miles (8 km) from Florence, on the slopes below Fiesole. Originally an ancient monastery, built by the Davanzati family in the late 15th century and designed in part by Michelangelo, it became a private villa during Napoleon's day and was transformed into one of Tuscany's most romantic hotels in the 1950s. (Brigitte Bardot honeymooned here in the 1960s.) Restored to its former glory, it now has 28 rooms (most with Jacuzzis), intimate dining indoors or in the open-air loggia, fragrant gardens with splendid views, a pool, and limousine service into the city. Business facilities include 24-hour room service, meeting rooms for up to 40, English-speaking concierge, foreign currency exchange, secretarial services in English, audiovisual equipment, photocopiers, computers, cable television news, translation services, and express checkout. Half-board required. Open from March to mid-November. 4 Via Doccia, Fiesole (phone: 59451; in the US, 800-237-1236; fax: 598734; telex: 570643). Very expensive.

Villa Cora – A neo-classical villa built during the period when Florence was the capital of Italy. The name comes from one of the many former owners, an ambassador. As a private villa, it hosted Napoleon's widow, Eugénie, as well as Tchaikovsky's patron, the Baroness Von Meck. It offers spacious rooms and suites (56 rooms) decorated in the original style, grand public rooms, and a magnificent garden with heated pool, all about 2 miles (3 km) from the chaotic city center. On the other side of the Boboli Gardens. Business facilities include 24-hour room service, meeting rooms for up to 120, English-speaking concierge, foreign currency exchange, secretarial services in English, audiovisual equipment, photocopiers, computers, cable television news, translation services, and express checkout. 18

Viale Machiavelli (phone: 229-8451; fax: 229086; telex: 570604). Very expensive.

Excelsior – Beside the Arno, just a short walk from the city center, traditional in both style and service. Part of the reliably luxurious and efficient CIGA chain. The excellent terrace restaurant, *Il Cestello,* has a splendid view when the stained glass windows are opened. The 205-room hotel is a favorite of Florentines and their guests. Business facilities include 24-hour room service, meeting rooms for up to 350, English-speaking concierge, foreign currency exchange, secretarial services in English, audiovisual equipment, photocopiers, computers, cable television news, translation services, and express checkout. 3 Piazza Ognissanti (phone: 264201; fax: 210278; telex: 570022). Expensive.

Grand – Across the street from the *Excelsior,* this 109-room hostelry was renovated in 1990 to re-create its original 15th-century elegance. Brunelleschi is said to have designed the palazzo as a residence for one of Florence's noble families. Part of the CIGA chain, it has meeting and banquet rooms and a restaurant. Business facilities include 24-hour room service, meeting rooms for up to 230, English-speaking concierge, foreign currency exchange, secretarial services in English, audiovisual equipment, photocopiers, computers, cable television news, translation services, and express checkout. 1 Piazza Ognissanti (phone: 278781; fax: 217400; telex: 570055). Expensive.

Helvetia & Bristol – Considered one of Florence's best in the 19th century, this hotel has now been restored to all its former glory, with antique furniture, velvet drapes, and original oil paintings. All 50 rooms and suites are decorated in different styles, ranging from chinoiserie to Art Nouveau, and all have Jacuzzis. Ideally located on a tranquil street behind the Piazza della Repubblica. Business facilities include 24-hour room service, meeting rooms for up to 70, English-speaking concierge, foreign currency exchange, secretarial services in English, audiovisual equipment, photocopiers, computers, cable television news, translation services, and express checkout. 2 Via dei Pescioni (phone: 287814; fax: 288353; telex: 572696). Expensive.

Hotel de la Ville – Dark, quiet, and somber, the perfect place for light sleepers. Its double doors and storm windows provide a peaceful oasis in the center of Florence, just off the elegant Via Tornabuoni. There are 96 rooms. Business facilities include 24-hour room service, meeting rooms for up to 75, English-speaking concierge, foreign currency exchange, secretarial services in English, audiovisual equipment, photocopiers, computers, cable television news, translation services, and express checkout. 1 Piazza Antinori (phone: 261806; fax: 261809; telex: 570518). Expensive.

Regency Umbria – Small (31 rooms) patrician villa set in a quiet residential area and decorated with exquisite taste. Like its sister in Rome (the *Lord Byron*), it offers calm and privacy, discreetly displaying its Relais & Châteaux crest at the entrance. There is a charming garden and an excellent restaurant (see *Eating Out*). Business facilities include 24-hour room service, meeting rooms for up to 20, English-speaking concierge, foreign currency exchange, secretarial services in English, audiovisual equipment, photocopiers, computers, cable television news, translation services, and express checkout. 3 Piazza Massimo d'Azeglio (phone and fax: 245247; telex: 571058). Expensive.

Savoy – A classic gem in the heart of Florence, with most of its 100 rooms decorated in Venetian style. It also has a popular piano bar. Business facilities include 24-hour room service, meeting rooms for up to 150, English-speaking concierge, foreign currency exchange, secretarial services in English, audiovisual equipment, photocopiers, computers, cable television news, translation services, and express checkout. 7 Piazza della Repubblica (phone: 283313; fax: 284840; telex: 570220). Expensive.

Sheraton – Situated 3 miles (5 km) south of Florence, this 321-room member of the worldwide chain has tennis courts and an outdoor swimming pool (perfect for a dip after a hot day's sightseeing). A van transports guests into the city. Business facilities include 24-hour room service, meeting rooms for up to 1,300, English-speaking concierge, foreign currency exchange, secretarial services in English, audiovisual equipment, photocopiers, computers, cable television news, translation services, and express checkout. Just off the Firenze Sud autostrada exit. 33 Via G. Agnelli (phone: 64901; fax: 680747; telex: 575860). Expensive.

Torre di Bellosguardo – The majestic, cypress-framed site on a hill overlooking Florence's terra-cotta roofs makes this handsome, 16-room hostelry a special place to stay. A sunny verandah, lush gardens, and a swimming pool — plus rooms whose ceilings are punctuated by rough hewn beams and each of which is individually decorated with antiques — add to the charm. There is an English-speaking concierge and 24-hour room service. 2 Via Roti Michelozzi (phone: 229-8145). Expensive.

Villa Medici – A reconstruction of the 18th-century Sonnino de Renzis Palace, halfway between the railroad station and the River Arno. Many of the 110 charming, spacious rooms have balconies affording panoramic views. The grand public rooms, tranquil gardens, and elegant service all are worthy of a hotel of this class. The swimming pool is a bow to contemporary tastes. Business facilities include 24-hour room service, meeting rooms for up to 100, English-speaking concierge, foreign currency exchange, secretarial services in English, audiovisual equipment, photocopiers, computers, cable television news, translation services, and express checkout. 42 Via del Prato (phone: 261331; fax: 261336; telex: 570179). Expensive.

Anglo-American – Between the train station and the river, very near the *Teatro Comunale,* with 118 refurbished rooms. Business facilities include 24-hour room service, meeting rooms for up to 150, English-speaking concierge, foreign currency exchange, secretarial services in English, audiovisual equipment, photocopiers, computers, cable television news, translation services, and express checkout. 9 Via Garibaldi (phone: 282114; fax: 268513; telex: 570289). Expensive to moderate.

Croce di Malta – Housed in a former convent close to Santa Croce, the site actually harks back to Roman times — you'll see Roman columns and an ancient brick vaulted roof, all carefully restored by the hotel's architect-owner. There are 98 rooms, a pretty garden, and a small swimming pool — a luxury for a hotel in the center of town. Business facilities include 24-hour room service, meeting rooms for up to 70, English-speaking concierge, foreign currency exchange, secretarial services in English, audiovisual equipment, photocopiers, computers, cable television news, translation services, and express checkout. 7 Via della Scala (phone: 282600 or 211740; fax: 287121; telex: 570540). Expensive to moderate.

Fenice Palace – Recently renovated and restored, the 67 guestrooms occupy 4 floors in a 19th-century palazzo near the Duomo. The accommodations offer considerable comfort and some magnificent views of the city's major monuments. Business facilities include 24-hour room service, English-speaking concierge, foreign currency exchange, secretarial services in English, audiovisual equipment, photocopiers, computers, translation services, and express checkout. 10 Via Martelli (phone: 289942; fax: 210087; telex: 575580). Expensive to moderate.

Jolly Carlton – Large and modern, this 167-room member of the efficient Jolly chain has a pool and a wonderful view from the terrace. It's near the Cascine park. Business facilities include 24-hour room service, meeting rooms for up to 120, English-speaking concierge, foreign currency exchange, secretarial services in English, audiovisual equipment, photocopiers, computers, cable television news, translation services, and express checkout. 4/A Piazza Vittorio Veneto (phone: 2770; fax: 292794; telex: 571523). Expensive to moderate.

Kraft – This modern 66-room hotel in a nice area near the *Teatro Comunale* has a roof-garden restaurant sporting umbrella pines and a cypress tree as well as a splendid panorama and a rooftop swimming pool. Business facilities include 24-hour room service, meeting rooms for up to 60, English-speaking concierge, foreign currency exchange, secretarial services in English, audiovisual equipment, photocopiers, computers, translation services, and express checkout. 2 Via Solferino (phone: 284273; fax: 298267; telex: 571523). Expensive to moderate.

Lungarno – Comfortable, functional, and cheerful. Set between the Ponte Vecchio and the Ponte Santa Trinita on the Oltrarno side of town, with 70 modern rooms, the best of which have terraces and balconies overlooking the Arno (be sure to book one of these in advance). There also is a garage. Business facilities include 24-hour room service, meeting rooms for up to 60, English-speaking concierge, foreign currency exchange, secretarial services in English, audiovisual equipment, photocopiers, computers, cable television news, translation services, and express checkout. 14 Borgo San Jacopo (phone: 264211; fax: 268437; telex: 570129). Expensive to moderate.

Minerva – The 107 rooms here are large and comfortably furnished, all with private modern baths. The staff is pleasant, and the hotel is near the train station, convenient to shopping and the major museums. Business facilities include 24-hour room service, meeting rooms for up to 70, English-speaking concierge, foreign currency exchange, secretarial services in English, audiovisual equipment, photocopiers, computers, cable television news, translation services, and express checkout. 16 Piazza Santa Maria Novella (phone: 284555; fax: 268281; telex: 570414). Expensive to moderate.

Palazzo Antellesi – Visitors planning at least a 1-week stay in Florence might want to consider renting an apartment in this exquisite palazzo on Piazza Santa Croce. The owners have converted it into several self-contained units that can sleep from two to five people. It is one of the few buildings in the city with a frescoed façade and some of the apartments also have frescoes. All are beautifully furnished, most have fireplaces, and some have terraces. There also is a garden and several courtyards, making this place an oasis of peace when Florence is at its hottest and most crowded. 21-22 Piazza Santa Croce (phone: 244456; fax: 234-5552). Expensive to moderate.

Tornabuoni Beacci – This delightful former pensione occupies the top floors of a 14th-century palace on Florence's most elegant street. It's traditional yet cheerful and sunny, provides excellent service, and has a charming terrace. Guests are required to take breakfast and another meal (half-board) during high season. 3 Via Tornabuoni (phone: 212645; telex: 570215). Expensive to moderate.

Baglioni – A traditional hotel in refined Tuscan taste: parquet floors, solid furnishings, handsome carpets, sober — even somber — atmosphere and service, with nearly 200 rooms. It's near the railway station and only a short walk from the best shopping. The roof garden restaurant has an enviable view of the historic city. Business facilities include 24-hour room service, meeting rooms for up to 210, English-speaking concierge, foreign currency exchange, secretarial services in English, audiovisual equipment, photocopiers, computers, cable television news, translation services, and express checkout. 6 Piazza dell'Unità Italiana (phone: 218441; fax: 215695; telex: 580525). Moderate.

Continental – In an ideal, albeit sometimes noisy, spot overlooking the Ponte Vecchio, this is as efficient as its sister hotel across the river, the *Lungarno,* which you can see from the terrace. No restaurant. Business facilities include 24-hour room service, English-speaking concierge, and cable television news. 2 Lungarno Acciaiuoli (phone: 282392; fax: 268557; telex: 580525). Moderate.

Monna Lisa – On a tiny side street, this hostelry in an old renovated building offers Old World charm and style with modern comforts. Some of the 20 guestrooms have Jacuzzis. There is private parking for no extra charge during low season. 27 Borgo Pinti (phone: 247-9751). Moderate.

Villa Villoresi – About 5 miles (8 km) from the center of Florence, it's another noble home away from home. It dates to the 12th century, but for the last 200 years it has been the property of the Villoresi family, who turned it into a hotel in the 1960s. With only 28 rooms, they manage to impart a sense of family as well as history. Bedroom walls have frescoes and meals are good. There is a pool in the garden among the olive trees. 2 Via Ciampi, Località Colonnata, Sesto Fiorentino (phone: 448-9032; telex: 580567). Moderate.

Loggiato dei Serviti – Well located on the charming Piazza SS Annunziata, the 20 rooms in this Renaissance palazzo are a bargain, especially by Florentine standards. Most are furnished with antiques. Be sure to book well in advance. 3 Piazza SS Annunziata (phone: 219165; telex: 575808). Moderate to inexpensive.

Balestri – A clean, no-frills stopping place overlooking the Arno. It has 50 rooms, no restaurant. 7 Piazza Mentana (phone: 214743). Inexpensive.

Bencistà – This 35-room 15th-century villa, an inn among the olive trees near Fiesole, is a beautiful bargain for those whose shoestrings do not stretch as far as the *Villa San Michele.* Half-board is required. No phones in the rooms. A free minibus service is available to take guests into Florence. Open mid-March to November. 4 Via Benedetto da Maiano, between Fiesole and San Domenico (phone: 59163). Inexpensive.

Morandi alla Crocetta – A small but charming 15-room hotel, run by an Englishwoman and her Italian-born son in what used to be a Dominican convent. Rooms are furnished with Tuscan antiques and many guests become friends of the family, returning year after year. 50 Via Laura (phone: 234-4747; fax: 248-0954). Inexpensive.

Pendini – An old-style, family-run place, in operation for over 100 years in a building far older, but renovated. 2 Via degli Strozzi (phone: 211170; fax: 282179; telex: 570007). Inexpensive.

Porta Rossa – Said to be one of Florence's oldest (14th century, with a 13th-century tower), and perhaps in need of a little sprucing up. Balzac and Stendhal, they say, slept here. It has Renaissance public rooms (good for meetings in the commercial center of the city) and a terrace overlooking the Ponte Vecchio. 19 Via Porta Rossa (phone: 287551). Inexpensive.

Quisisana Ponte Vecchio – Between the Ponte Vecchio and the *Uffizi,* with a view of the former from a charming terrace. This was the setting for the film *A Room with a View,* adapted from E.M. Forster's novel. 4 Lungarno Archibusieri (phone: 216692; fax: 268303). Inexpensive.

La Residenza – A small, renovated hotel, with a lovely terrace, on Florence's best shopping street. Half-board is required during high season. 8 Via Tornabuoni (phone: 284197; telex: 570093). Inexpensive.

Silla – A quiet, charming, and friendly place, with 3 large newer rooms on the third floor. Its large flowered terrace overlooks the river and a park on the Oltrarno side of town. No restaurant; usually closed in December. 5 Via dei Renai (phone: 234-2889). Inexpensive.

EATING OUT: Back in the 16th century, Catherine de' Medici married King Henry II of France, and her cousin Maria de' Medici married Henry IV. The women took their cooks and their recipes for creams, sauces, pastries, and ice creams to the French court — along with their trousseaus. As an Elizabethan poet once said, "Tuscany provided creams and cakes and lively Florentine women to sweeten the taste and minds of the French."

Following their departure, the fanciness went out of Florentine food, and French cooking began to shine. But today, Florentine cooking, while simpler and more straightforward than it was during the Renaissance, is still at the top of the list of Italy's many varied regional dishes. No small contributing factor to this culinary art is the quality of the ingredients. Tuscany boasts excellent olive oil and wine, exquisite fruits and vegetables, good game in season, fresh fish from its coast, as well as salami, sausages, and every kind of meat. A *bistecca alla fiorentina,* thick and juicy on the bone and traditionally accompanied by new potatoes or white beans drenched in pure golden olive oil, is a meal fit for the fussiest of kings. Diners can roughly gauge the price of a restaurant before entering by the cost per kilo (2.2 pounds) of its Florentine steaks on the menu displayed outside. Fortunately, one steak is usually more than enough for two persons, and it is not considered a gaffe to order one steak for two or more.

Mealtimes in Florence begin earlier than in Rome, beginning by 12:30 or 1 PM for lunch, and by 8 PM for dinner. Many of the typical mamma 'n' papa restaurants are small, popular, and crowded. If you don't book, be prepared to wait and eventually share a table (single guests are often seated at a communal table — a respectable way of meeting residents). Also unlike Rome, you won't be encouraged to linger over your dessert wine if there are people waiting for your table. Food, like most everything else in Florentine life, is taken seriously; do your business and socializing elsewhere. A meal for two at the very expensive *Enoteca Pinchiorri* will vary (but will be at least $200), depending on what you eat and what wine you order. A full meal for two, including the house wine or the low-priced (but excellent) local chianti, at an expensive restaurant will cost between $95 and $180. Expect to pay between $60 and $95 at a moderate restaurant and under $60 at an inexpensive one. All telephone numbers are in the 55 city code unless otherwise indicated.

Enoteca Pinchiorri – In the 15th-century Ciofi-Iacometti Palace, with a delightful courtyard for dining alfresco, this is possibly Italy's best restaurant and certainly the place for that grand dinner in Florence. The service, however, can be very unfriendly — a major minus, considering the size of the check. The four chefs prepare exquisite traditional and nouvelle dishes with a Franco-Italian flavor, perhaps a mosaic of sweet and sour fish, sweetbread salad with shrimp sauce, ricotta and salami pie, or medallions of veal with capers and lime. The wine collection (60,000 bottles) is outstanding, understandably so, since the restaurant actually began as a wine showroom. Closed Sundays, Mondays at lunch, and August. Reservations necessary. Major credit cards accepted. 87 Via Ghibellina (phone: 242777). Very expensive.

Campidoglio – White tablecloths and elegant service set this attractive place apart from most Florentine trattorie, and the excellent Italian fare makes it worth the tab. Closed Thursdays. Reservations advised. Major credit cards accepted. 8r Via Campidoglio (phone: 287770). Expensive.

Il Cenacolo – "The Last Supper" continues to be the rage in refined restaurants. The ambience is ultra-cool, with a lovely garden for alfresco dining in fine weather. The cuisine is both traditional and new, featuring some old Florentine recipes with an innovative flair and a light touch for today's health-conscious patrons. There also is a bar in which to drown your sorrows after you settle the tab. Closed Sundays all day and Mondays at lunch. Reservations necessary. Major credit cards accepted. 34 Via Borgognissanti (phone: 219493). Expensive.

Harry's Bar – No relation to the famed eatery in Venice, but Americans tend to flock here just the same. Italian specialties are best, though it's also the place to find a hamburger and French fries. Closed Sundays and mid-December to mid-January. Reservations advised. Major credit cards accepted. 22r Lungarno Amerigo Vespucci (phone: 296700). Expensive.

Relais le Jardin – Located in the *Regency Umbria* hotel, well-heeled Florentines like to dine here, especially in summer when the tables are moved into the garden.

The tone is one of understated elegance, with first class service and faultless Florentine cooking. The menu changes frequently, and the chef turns out some interesting pasta variations. Open daily. Reservations advised. Major credit cards accepted. 3 Piazza Massimo d'Azeglio (phone: 245247). Expensive.

Sabatini – Once Florence's top dining room, but thoroughly outclassed in recent years. It's still quiet, dignified, and noted for its traditional fare, but the quality has slipped. Some may find the standard menu far less interesting than those of less expensive trattorie. Closed Mondays. Reservations advised. Major credit cards accepted. 9/A Via Panzani (phone: 211559 or 282802). Expensive.

Cantinetta Antinori – Not quite a restaurant, but a typically rustic yet fashionably chic cantina, with food designed to accompany the Antinori wines. Perfect for a light lunch of salami or *finocchiona* with bread, *crostini* (chicken liver canapés), soup, or a modest hot dish such as tripe or *bollito* (mixed boiled meats). Closed weekends and August. Reservations unnecessary. No credit cards accepted. 3 Piazza Antinori (phone: 292234). Expensive to moderate.

Cibreo – Also named after a historic Florentine dish, one so good it is said to have given Catherine de' Medici near fatal indigestion from overeating. Although the menu offers interesting old Tuscan dishes, it does not limit itself to the traditional Florentine fare it does so well. Genoese minestrone, eggplant parmesan from the south, polenta from the Veneto, plus savory appetizers such as walnut and *pecorino* cheese salad, soups, seafood with an unusual twist (mussel terrine, squid stew), and homemade desserts are all available, as are good wines. In summer, there's alfresco dining. Closed Sundays and from late July to mid-September. Reservations necessary. Major credit cards accepted. 118r Via de' Macci (phone: 234-1100). Expensive to moderate.

Coco Lezzone – Another Florentine favorite, serving authentic local food using the best ingredients and no pretenses. Try the *pappa al pomodoro,* a thick soup made of fresh tomatoes, herbs, and bread. This restaurant is crowded and hurried; don't expect to linger. Closed Sundays, Saturdays in the summer and Tuesdays in the winter, the last week in July, and August. Reservations advised. No credit cards accepted. 26r Via del Parioncino (phone: 287178). Expensive to moderate.

Taverna del Bronzino – Rustic yet elegant, set in a 16th-century palazzo furnished with antiques and a garden for alfresco dining in season. *Crostini ai funghi porcini* (wild mushroom canapés), *tortelloni al cedro,* and renowned Florentine beef with green peppers are specialties. Closed Sundays. Reservations advised. Major credit cards accepted. 25-27r Via delle Ruote (phone: 495220). Expensive to moderate.

La Vecchia Cucina – A bit out of the way, but with a *nuova cucina* worth trying when you've had your fill of wonderfully traditional Tuscan food. The innovative menu of a half-dozen first and second courses and three desserts is recited by the owner (tricky if you don't speak Italian), and it changes every week. Interesting wine list. Closed Sundays and August. Reservations advised. Major credit cards accepted. 1r Viale Edmondo De Amicis (phone: 660143). Expensive to moderate.

Buzzino – The perfect place for lunch or dinner after a cultural feast at the *Uffizi,* which is just a block away. The setting is warm, the waiters friendly, and the food good enough to put tired museumgoers back on their feet. The bill is sweetened by the arrival of the free *vin santo* (a sweet dessert wine). Open daily. Reservations advised. Major credit cards accepted. 8 Via dei Leoni (phone: 239-8013). Moderate.

Cammillo – An appealing, bustling spot near the Ponte S. Trinita, offering authentic dishes such as tripe *alla fiorentina* and, in season, pasta with white truffles. Closed Wednesdays and Thursdays. Reservations unnecessary. No credit cards accepted. 57r Borgo San Jacopo (phone: 212427). Moderate.

La Carabaccia – Named after an antique Florentine dish (none other than onion soup) loved by the Medicis, the menu changes daily according to what's good at the market. Five starters and five main courses generally are offered, occasionally featuring parts of an animal you never thought you could eat (don't ask!). Very popular, informal, and unrushed. Closed Sundays, Mondays at lunch, and August. Reservations advised. No credit cards accepted. 190r Via Palazzuolo (phone: 214782). Moderate.

Le Cave – A delightful stop in Fiesole and sheer magic in early summer and fall, when it's great to lunch under the linden trees and gaze out over the splendid valley. Indoors is warm, cozy, and rustic, as is the country-style cooking, beginning with excellent prosciutto, *finocchiona,* and other local salami, chicken and truffle croquettes, canapés of mozzarella and mushrooms, *crespelle* or ravioli, and the house specialty, *gallina al mattone,* spring chicken grilled on an open fire and seriously seasoned with black pepper and the purest of virgin olive oils. Closed Thursdays, Sunday evenings, and August. Reservations necessary. No credit cards accepted. 16 Via delle Cave, Località Maiano, Fiesole (phone: 59133). Moderate.

Da Ganino (Ex-Mario) – Long a Florentine favorite, this typically tiny Tuscan trattoria is run by a family. It still is small and cozy in the winter, with alfresco dining on the small square in fine weather. Here is some of the best Florentine *cucina,* including fresh mushrooms and truffles in season and a justifiably famous cheesecake. Closed Sundays, 3 weeks in August, and Christmas. Reservations advised. Major credit cards accepted. 4r Piazza dei Cimatori (phone: 214125). Moderate.

Garga – The unusual specialties of this establishment include *zuppa di cavoli neri* (soup of a bitter green local vegetable), risotto of leeks and bacon, and *gnocchetti verdi* (pasta of spinach and ricotta) — all exquisitely prepared. Absolutely terrific. Closed Sundays and Monday lunch. Reservations necessary. No credit cards accepted. 48-52 Via del Moro (phone: 239-8898). Moderate.

Il Latini – This popular eatery, in the former stables of the historic Palazzo Rucellai, serves such solid and abundant fare as hearty Tuscan soup, unpretentious meat platters, grilled fish, fresh vegetables, and traditional desserts. Not for romantic evenings, here you sit at long communal tables and the food keeps arriving. Good value. Closed Mondays and at lunch on Tuesdays. Reservations unnecessary. No credit cards accepted. 6r Via Palchetti (phone: 210916). Moderate.

La Loggia – On the most spectacular site in Florence, with a view over the entire city, it's run by some former *Sabatini* waiters who, by employing traditional Tuscan cuisine and efficient service despite the crowds, have transformed a once-mediocre restaurant into a Florentine favorite. The panorama from the terrace makes it especially pleasant during the summer. Closed Wednesdays. Reservations advised. Major credit cards accepted. 1 Piazzale Michelangelo (phone: 287032 or 234-2832). Moderate.

Omero – The menu here hasn't changed in decades, and all the regulars who flock to this eatery are grateful. In the front is a grocery store where Florentines buy staples or stop for a glass of wine. The restaurant in the back has beautiful views of the Tuscan hills, and the small garden downstairs is wonderful for summer dining, although the service tends to be slow and the sound of the insect zapper may be distracting. Still, the exceptional *fettunta* (Tuscan garlic bread), ravioli, grilled chicken, ubiquitous *bistecca alla fiorentina,* fried artichokes or zucchini blossoms (in season), and meringue dessert are worth the wait. Closed Tuesdays and August. Reservations advised. Major credit cards accepted. 11r Via Pian dei Guillari (phone: 220053). Moderate.

Osteria da Quinto – A longtime favorite with Florentines, in large part because owner Leo Codacci is a great music lover and often treats customers to bursts of song when the mood strikes him. The *bistecca alla fiorentina* is among the biggest and best in town. It's always packed, so be sure to reserve ahead. Closed Mondays. Major credit cards accepted. 5 Piazza Peruzzi (phone: 213323). Moderate.

Pallottino – One of Florence's newest, this rising star on the gastronomic scene offers a good selection of Tuscan food, including many hard-to-find dishes. Specialties like spaghetti with fresh tomatoes and arugula, stuffed chicken neck (tastes much better than it sounds), and *bistecca alla fiorentina* are not to be missed. Closed Mondays and Tuesdays for lunch. Reservations necessary. Major credit cards accepted. 1r Via Isola delle Stinche (phone: 289573). Moderate.

Pierot – The specialty is seafood, especially on Tuesdays and Fridays. The menu is long and ever changing, depending on the availability of ingredients, but if you spot the traditional squid and beet dish called *inzimino di calamari e bietoline,* try it; ditto the chestnut ice cream for dessert. Open later than most. Closed Sundays and the last 3 weeks of July. Reservations advised. Major credit cards accepted. 25r Piazza Taddeo Gaddi (phone: 702100). Moderate.

La Sostanza – Popularly called *Troia,* literally a hog (also a woman of easy virtue), this is one of Florence's oldest and most cherished trattorie, serving some of the best steaks in town. If you haven't had a *bistecca alla fiorentina* with Tuscan beans, get here early. The place is picturesquely plain and tiny, the turnover as fast as the service (which can be rude if you try to linger). Communal tables. Closed Saturday evenings, Sundays, and August. Reservations necessary. 25r Via del Porcellana (phone: 212691). Moderate.

Trattoria del Francescano – Lovers of hearty Florentine fare such as *tagliatelle con funghi porcini* (wide noodles with mushrooms) and *pappa al pomodoro* (thick fresh tomato and bread soup) will appreciate this family-run place. Great store is set by fresh ingredients and time-honored recipes. Closed Wednesdays. Reservations necessary. Major credit cards accepted. 26r Via San Giuseppe (phone: 241605). Moderate.

Tredici Gobbi – Once known for Hungarian cooking, which still simmers on the back burner, Tuscan specialties have come to the fore. Closed Sunday evenings, Mondays, and August. Reservations advised. Major credit cards accepted. 9r Via del Porcellana (phone: 298769). Moderate.

Antico Fattore – In the shadow of the *Uffizi,* it's famous for its *ribollita,* a vegetable soup so thick with broccoli, bread, and white beans a spoon stands up in it. The rest of the menu is equally hearty peasant fare. Closed Sundays, Mondays, and mid-July to early August. Reservations advised. Major credit cards accepted. 1r Via Lambertesca (phone: 261215). Moderate to inexpensive.

Angiolino – Very good potluck and very economical. This is on the Pitti side of the river and the ambience is cozy. Closed Sundays and Mondays. Reservations unnecessary. No credit cards accepted. 36r Via di Santo Spirito (phone: 239-8976). Inexpensive.

Cinghiale Bianco – Cozy and hospitable, this trattoria serves great pasta and other tasty Florentine specialties at very reasonable prices. Don't miss the *fettunta farcita,* an old peasant recipe of garlic-rubbed bread layered with spinach and white beans. Closed Tuesdays, Wednesdays, and January. Reservations advised. No credit cards accepted. 43r Borgo San Jacopo (phone: 215706). Inexpensive.

Fagioli – A cheery, rustic ambience and a full bar. Enjoy the *passato di fagioli con pasta,* a thick soup of white beans and pasta. Closed weekends and August. Reservations unnecessary. No credit cards accepted. 47r Corso Tintori (phone: 244285). Inexpensive.

Le Mossacce – Still largely frequented by habitués, it's filled with long paper-covered tables and serves good country cooking. Try the *ribollita,* a thick and hearty vegetable soup. Closed Saturday nights, Sundays, and August. Reservations unnecessary. No credit cards accepted. 55r Via del Proconsolo (phone: 294361). Inexpensive.

Ruggero – This simple trattoria serves some of the best Florentine food in the city — well-prepared, rustic fare. The *pasta alla carrettiera* (in a spicy tomato sauce), the traditional *pappa al pomodoro* (thick tomato soup), *ribollita,* and meat dishes are all tasty. The tables are filled with members of the Florentine nobility during Sunday lunchtime. Closed Tuesdays, Wednesdays, and July 7 to August 7. Reservations necessary. No credit cards accepted. 89 Via Senese (phone: 220542). Inexpensive.

Trattoria da Graziella – When you are tired of Florentine fare, head to this eatery in Fiesole where Sardinian-born Ugo Salis offers well-cooked island dishes, such as the spectacular and mouth-watering suckling pig. There are good Sardinian wines to wash down the meal, though chianti fans also will be satisfied. There is a large terrace for alfresco dining. Closed Mondays. Reservations advised. Major credit cards accepted. 20 Via Cave di Maiano, Fiesole (phone: 599963). Inexpensive.

Vecchia Bettola – A typical Tuscan trattoria with quality home-style cooking and marble tabletops. Closed Mondays and Tuesdays. Reservations unnecessary. No credit cards accepted. 32-34r Viale Ariosto (phone: 224158). Inexpensive.

Note: When the urge for something delectably *dolce* becomes irresistible, we head for one of our two overwhelming favorites. *Vivoli* (7 Via Isola della Stinche) serves some of the best gelati in town, in flavors from chocolate to grapefruit, fresh strawberry to tea. Another good place is *Perchè No* (19r Via dei Tavolini), on a side street near Piazza della Signoria, where all the fruit flavors are made with fresh fruit. *Rivoire* (on the Piazza della Signoria), a combination coffeehouse/candy shop, sells a confection of creamed chocolate that you literally eat with a spoon. It's sold in individual boxes — with spoon attached! And if for some reason your tastebuds get homesick, head for *CarLie's* (12r Via della Brache). Started by two Smith College graduates, these Yankees offer brownies, cupcakes, strawberry shortcake, and at *Thanksgiving,* pumpkin or apple pie.

GENOA

Two centuries ago, Genoa, along with Rome, Florence, and Venice, occupied a prime position on the itinerary of any Grand Tour of Europe. Today's visitors to Italy, however, often bypass the city entirely, little realizing that behind the sprawling port lies one of the country's most elegant, interesting, and sophisticated cities. The evidence of past wealth and power is still visible in its many monuments, great churches, countless palaces, lavish courtyards, and rich art treasures. The composer Richard Wagner even considered that "Paris and London, compared with this divine city, seem simply an agglomeration of houses and streets without any form."

Genoa — *La Superba* ("the proud") — was a flourishing port several hundred years before Christ. With a natural harbor on its southern flank and a semicircle of mountains as a landside frontier, its location has always been ripe for occupation and development. Since its steep terrain was obviously unsuitable for cultivation, the Genoese turned naturally to the sea — but not in the halfhearted style of a modest fishing community. For centuries the Genoese navy, along with the Venetian fleet on the far side of the peninsula, ruled the waves while its merchants traded with, and established outposts in, far-flung countries (the ruins of a Genoese fort have even been found in the Soviet Union, on the banks of the river Dniester).

The capital of Liguria and the fifth-largest city in Italy, Genoa has a population of around 815,000. It stretches 25 miles along the coast and spreads up the hills that rise around the bay — the only flat place in town is the sea. Shipping is still the major industry, with related business — in communications, electronics, banking, insurance, and general commerce — also highly developed, making the city one of the most prosperous in Italy. But, remarkably, Genoa has managed to retain its historical legacy. The medieval city center is one of the largest in Europe (surpassed only by that of its archrival, Venice), and it is maintained not as a relic of the past or as a tourist attraction but as an active, thriving part of contemporary life. The vivid contrasts between, say, the *caruggi* — the winding ancient streets, most so narrow that you can touch opposite walls with outstretched arms — and the orderly planning of the modern town, with the elegant Piazza de Ferrari at its center, somehow seem entirely harmonious.

The etymological origin of the word *Genoa* is not certain. It probably derives from the Latin *janua,* meaning "door." This explanation is satisfactory at least in a figurative sense, since Genoa forms a natural inlet along the rocky and sometimes inaccessible Riviera coastline. Long before the Romans, the Greeks, and the Etruscans used this place as a harbor; from here they traded goods and ideas, and penetrated inland. Pre-Roman Ligurians, the original Genoese inhabitants, had a settlement on the hill now called Santa Maria di Castello. By the 5th century BC the city was already an important port and trading center and an ally of Rome. Although Genoa was sacked and its inhabitants massacred in 205 BC by Magone, Hannibal's son, it soon reasserted itself, as it would each time it was plundered in the following centuries. With strong Byzantine and Christian connections, Genoa became a bishopric as early as AD 381. An invasion by barbarians in about AD 640, during which the original city walls were destroyed, roughly marked the end of the Roman era and the beginning of the Middle Ages. From the 7th century, when the Arabs conquered Spain, Genoese shipping — and indeed all Mediterranean trading — was continually under attack by Saracen pirates. Ironically, it was the city's constant struggle to maintain itself and survive Saracen attacks that led to the gradual rise of its powerful fleet. By the middle of the 11th century, many Genoese were selling their landholdings and going over to shipping. By the 12th century, the proud Genoese felt protected enough by their economy and their new city walls to refuse to pay tribute to Emperor Frederick Barbarossa.

Between the 11th and 13th centuries, Genoa's rivals for sea power were Pisa, Venice, and Amalfi, the other three ancient maritime republics. But with the defeat of Pisa in 1284, Genoa ensured its mastery over the Tyrrhenian Sea. The city had also begun a campaign to conquer the two Rivieras lying to its west and east. This was not fully achieved until the 14th century, and even thereafter some of the Ligurian cities periodically rebelled, especially Savona, which did not concede final surrender until 1541.

Genoa's prosperity was at its peak from the middle of the 13th to the 15th century, but politically it was continually threatened by external forces. After 1529, when the great leader Andrea Doria drew up a constitution that was to work effectively for the next 200 years, the city achieved relative peace under the protection of Spain. At its peak, it had settlements all over the Middle East — in Constantinople, Beirut, Syria, and Armenia, as well as in Egypt. Its merchants dealt in numerous profitable commodities, such as wheat, fish, fur, silk, wool, oil, wine, spices, and slaves. The Genoese were unusually tolerant to foreigners and foreign religions. In the 16th century they built a mosque in the port for galley slaves captured from the Barbary pirates. From as early as the 5th century, a large Jewish community existed in the city and was treated with comparative tolerance.

The ruins of the family house of Genoa's most famous citizen, Christopher Columbus, still stand at the bottom of the Vico Diritto di Ponticello, below the impressive medieval Porta Soprana. A thorough restoration of the house is scheduled to be completed this year. Columbus came from a family of humble weavers but earned a place for himself in world history when, on behalf of the Spanish queen, he discovered the New World in 1492. He also changed the fortunes of his native city, which up to that time had been a maritime power. Ironically, after the discovery of the Americas, Genoa was increasingly cut off from what came to be the most important trade routes; after its commercial loss, the city also lost much of its political power. Nevertheless, cordial relations with Spain, which had begun between Andrea Doria and Charles V, continued. For another 2 centuries Genoa provided Spain with outstanding military and naval leaders and handled vast amounts of trading between the mother country and the colonies. Genoese banks also financed many Spanish ventures in the New World. With their long-established, if highly secretive, strength, the banks ensured that the city would remain materially rich long after it had ceased to be a visible political power. Foremost among them was the Banco San Giorgio, which the Genoese hold as the world's first bank.

Although Genoa retained its own government until the beginning of the 19th century, in actuality it was overshadowed by other powers that controlled the politics and economics of Europe. When Napoleon defeated the Austrians and annexed the Genoese Republic to France, he effectively ended its independent history. But even after Napoleon's final defeat in 1815, when Genoa was united with the kingdom of Sardinia, the nationalistic fervor within the city remained strong. Genoa, in fact, had been a center for the radical new politics of Jacobinism since 1796, and from then on it played a leading part in the Young Italy Movement. Founded in Genoa by Mazzini, the movement led to the Risorgimento and finally to the unity and independence of the whole of Italy. On September 20, 1870, Rome was finally liberated by Italian troops, thus completing the last stage of the unification. It is not surprising that this proud city, after contributing so much to Italy's unity, named its main thoroughfare — Via XX Settembre — to commemorate that date.

Today, Genoa continues to be Italy's most active port, and the second largest in the Mediterranean after Marseilles. Perched in curious layers, hewn and clinging on like a limpet to its particular position, it is a complex of steps, tunnels, overpasses, and public elevators, and by night it becomes a study in neon. Here are monuments of all kinds: ranging from the once bombarded, today beautifully restored opera house to the medieval lighthouse said to be modeled on that of Alexandria. Two years ago, the city underwent much restoration, construction, and a general sprucing up of the city's piazze in time for the *1990 World Soccer Cup* (Genoa was one of the host cities). The overriding impression of Genoa is of a city that works hard and plays hard. It will play especially hard this year during the celebrations marking the 500th anniversary of Columbus's discovery of America (see *Special Events,* below).

GENOA AT-A-GLANCE

SEEING THE CITY: Access by road or rail is via a series of tunnels carved through the rocks and under the houses; within the city, the hills that form a natural amphitheater entail plenty of slopes, steps, and underground passageways, as well as a number of elevators and funicular railways to get visitors to the city's best vantage points. A funicular runs every 15 minutes from Largo della Zecca up Monte Righi, where, at nearly 1,000 feet above sea level, the panorama spans several miles of the Riviera. This is also the best place from which to view the old city fortifications. From Via San Benedetto, another funicular climbs to Granarolo for an equally stunning view of the city, while a third funicular, scheduled to open as we went to press, goes from Piazza Portello to Sant'Anna.

SPECIAL PLACES: Although Genoa proper is vast, the city center, which includes the historic section, is exceptionally concentrated, crisscrossed with steep, narrow, winding passages. It is, therefore, possible to see most of the interesting features of the town on foot, with occasional recourse to funiculars. In fact, many of the sights cannot be seen or reached by car.

Cattedrale di San Lorenzo (Cathedral of Saint Lawrence) – Although it is not the oldest church in Genoa, San Lorenzo is the heart of the medieval city. For many centuries it was the scene of the principal acts of both church and state: ceremonies, celebrations, investitures, negotiations, judgments, and elections. Construction of the church began in 1099; consecration was in 1118. Saint Lawrence, to whom it was dedicated, is said to have passed through the city in the 3rd century on his way to Rome. An earthquake in 1222 damaged the building, and some years later a new Gothic façade was built to replace the Romanesque original. The alternating bands of black slate and white marble create an imposing and monumental effect. Entering the cathedral, a visitor is immediately impressed by the size of the interior and the richness of its design. The eye is led by the black-and-white pattern down the aisle and toward the nave and the spacious apse of the sanctuary. Renaissance frescoes depict moments in the life of Saint Lawrence. Also of interest is the Chapel of Saint John the Baptist, which houses sculptures by Sansovino and Guglielmo Della Porta, among others. It formerly held a silver casket containing the saint's ashes, brought from Jerusalem by Genoese crusaders; this is now in the treasury. The treasury also contains the plate, made out of the precious stone chalcedony, said to have held the head of St. John the Baptist, and the chalice that was used at the Last Supper. Elsewhere in the cathedral is an unexploded bomb (now defused) that fell during World War II. The cathedral is open daily from 7 AM to 7:45 PM; the chapel is open Tuesdays through Saturdays from 9:30 to 11:30 AM, and 3 to 5:30 PM. Piazza San Lorenzo (phone: 296695).

Chiesa di San Donato (Church of Saint Donato) – This 11th-century church, a few minutes' walk from the cathedral, also exemplifies the transition from Romanesque to Gothic architecture. Its octagonal tower, rising above the conical roof, is formed by a central nave and flanking aisles. At the front of the church are heavy Roman columns; at the back, black and white medieval columns with imitation classical capitals. A splendid triptych hangs on the wall in the apse, making up for the lack of other ornamentation. Its panels, depicting the Adoration of the Magi, are attributed to the Flemish painter Joos van Cleve, who probably painted the work on a visit to Genoa in the early 16th century. The simplicity of this church inspires quiet reverence. Piazza San Donato (phone: 29269).

Oratorio di San Filippo Neri (Oratory of St. Philip the Black) – Located in the northwest part of the Old City in a piazza of the same name, this church and its adjoining oratory are exceptional examples of Genoese baroque art. San Filippo founded the order known as the Oratorians in Rome in the mid-16th century. One of the founding fathers left a sum of money to the order to establish an oratory in his native Genoa. Construction of the church proper was completed in 1700. The chief features of the exterior are the *Virgin of the Immaculate Conception* marble group and a medallion with a portrait of San Filippo by Carlo Cacciatori of Carrara. The interior of the church is formed by a single nave with highly ornamental walls and vault. Next to the church is the oratory, built in 1750 by the architect Giovanni Battista Montaldo. This elaborate, impressive building is the home of a remarkable sculpture of the Virgin by Pierre Puget. With its swirling draperies and delicate execution, it is one of the artist's finest works. An outstanding mural by Giuseppe Davolio that continues from the wall onto the ceiling creates an impressive illusionistic vision. Piazza San Filippo Neri.

Via Garibaldi – Originally known as Strada Nuova (New Street), this is the only street in Europe composed entirely of palazzi. In the early 16th century, wealthy patrician families of Genoa expanded their living quarters beyond the severely cramped medieval city. The plan of the street, said to have been devised by the Perugian architect Alessi, eventually included 14 palaces. Some are still owned and inhabited by descendants of the original powerful families, several are now used for local government and commercial functions, and one or two are important museums. Of these, the following are the most interesting and accessible:

Palazzo Tursi – Now the Town Hall, this is the largest and perhaps the most beautiful of all the palaces. Its façade is of the lovely roseate stone quarried in Finale Ligure. Among the many treasures housed within are a violin of Paganini's that is played every year on *Columbus Day* (October 12) and what are said to be Columbus's ashes. Apply to the director of public relations inside the building to see the violin. Open to the general public weekdays from 8:30 AM to 4:30 PM. Groups can arrange visits on weekends by contacting the public relations director. Admission charge. 9 Via Garibaldi (phone: 20981).

Palazzo Carrega-Cataldi – This building was commissioned by one of the greatest Genoese financiers, Tobia Pallavicino. Its exterior is severe, its interior very richly decorated. Among its most dazzling features is the Sala degli Specchi (Room of Mirrors), designed by Lorenzo de Ferrari. The glitter and sparkle of this wonderful room provide the setting, ironically, for the sober decisions of the Genoa Chamber of Commerce, which now owns the building. Open Mondays through Fridays from 9 AM to 6 PM; Saturdays from 9 AM to noon. The Room of Mirrors is not open to visitors when meetings are in progress. Admission charge. 4 Via Garibaldi (phone: 20941).

Palazzo Bianco – A sumptuous palace that contains a fine collection of paintings from the Genoese and Flemish schools, among them *Venus and Mars* by Rubens and *The Tribute Money* by Van Dyck. Many of the works, however, are in the process of being restored. Open Tuesdays through Saturdays from 9 AM to 6 PM, Sundays from 9:15 AM to 12:45 PM. For group visits, call 282641. Admission charge. 11 Via Garibaldi (phone: 291803).

Palazzo Rosso – Van Dyck lived in Genoa and was one of the city's most sought-after portrait painters. Many of his full-length portraits of Genoese citizens are housed here, along with some fine examples of Venetian works, including masterpieces by Titian and Veronese. Open Tuesdays through Saturdays from 9 AM to 6 PM; Sundays from 9 AM to noon. Guided tours in Italian can be booked in advance. Admission charge. 18 Via Garibaldi (phone: 282641).

Palazzo Spinola – Bequeathed to the state as a national gallery by the Spinola family in 1958, the building contains mainly 17th-century Genoese works but also some important ones by non-Italian artists. *Ecce Homo* by Antonello da Messina, one of the many hauntingly beautiful works at the palazzo, is also historically interesting as an example of painting techniques. It was Messina who introduced oil painting to Italy after his travels in the north. Restoration of the palazzo was scheduled to be completed as we went to press. When finished, the first two floors will house these works, and the third and fourth floors will contain a collection of works by Ligurian painters. Open Tuesdays through Saturdays from 9 AM to 5 PM (in the summer until 7 PM), Sundays and Mondays from 9 AM to 1 PM. 1 Piazza di Pellicceria Superiore (phone: 294661).

■ **EXTRA SPECIAL:** To the east of the medieval city are ancient fishing villages that seem virtually untouched by time. Boccadasse is noteworthy not only for its historical significance, but also for its many fine trattorias and lively bars. Nervi offers a delightful promenade along the sea to the left of the harbor with a view of the nearby Portofino promontory, and borders the lush Parco Nervi, where visitors can enjoy open-air theater and ballet in the summer. Other easily accessible coastal towns include San Remo, Camogli, Rapallo, Santa Margherita Ligure, Portofino, Chiavari, and Sestri Levante, all of which can be reached in less than an hour by train from Stazione Brignole, Piazza Verdi (also see *The Italian Riviera,* DIRECTIONS). In summer, many of the towns are accessible by boat. Some destinations involve an easy bus connection from their inland stations to the coast.

SOURCES AND RESOURCES

TOURIST INFORMATION: The Azienda Autonoma di Soggiorno e Turismo (AAST) provides tourist information about the city of Genoa at its two locations. One is in the center of town (10 Via Porta degli Archi; phone: 541541) and is open weekdays from 8 AM to 1:30 PM and 2 to 5 PM, Saturdays from 8 AM to 1:30 PM. The other is near the Stazione Brignole (18r Piazza Verdi; phone: 562056) and is open Mondays to Saturdays from 8 AM to 8 PM. The Ente Provinciale per il Turismo (EPT; 11 Via Roma; phone: 581371) offers information about the region surrounding Genoa. Its office hours are Mondays through Thursdays from 8:30 AM to 1:30 PM and 2:30 to 5:30 PM, Fridays from 8:30 AM to 1:30 PM, and Saturdays from 8 AM to 12:30 PM. The tourist offices provide various pamphlets on museum exhibits and hours, tours of the city and the surrounding area, and hotel accommodations. They also have the most up-to-date information on the Columbus festivities. *Un Ospite in Liguria* (A Guest in Liguria), a free multilingual booklet, sometimes is available at the tourist offices. A surer bet is to find a copy at the better hotels, where the pamphlet is distributed regularly.

The US Consulate is in the Banca d'America Building, 6 Piazza Portello (phone: 282741).

Local Coverage – *Il Secolo XIX* (The 19th Century) is the most popular Genoese newspaper and also the most useful to visitors, as it has a good section on local events. Like many Italian newspapers, it is not published on Mondays; an alternative is *La Gazzetta del Lunedì.* Another daily, Genoa's oldest, is *Il Lavoro Nuovo.* Newsstands with English-language newspapers are all over the city. For general guidebooks or other reading material, try the English bookstore, *Bozzi* (6 Via Cairoli; phone: 298742), which is closed the first half of August, or the *Libreria di Stefano* (40r Via Ceccardi; phone: 593821).

TELEPHONE: The city code for Genoa is 10. When calling from within Italy, dial 010 before the local number.

GETTING AROUND: In the center of the city, walking is best, since many places of interest are in pedestrian zones or on very narrow streets. Street numbering can be confusing: According to the importance of an entrance, numbers may be black (for palaces, office blocks, banks) or red (for cafés, trattorie, hotels). Black and red numbers do not run consecutively; for example, the number 3 black may be followed by 14 red.

Airport – The Aeroporto Internazionale di Genova Cristoforo Colombo (at Sestri Ponente) is a 20-minute taxi ride from the city center. Bus service is available to the airport as well. The city terminal is in Piazza Verdi at the Stazione Brignole. For *AMT* information, call 59971. The airport serves most of the main Italian cities, plus London, Frankfurt, Paris, and Zurich. For airport information, call 2411.

Boat – Various kinds of yachts can be hired by experienced sailors for 1–2 weeks from the *Sailor's Center* (19-26 Via C. Beralino; phone: 592089; fax: 553-3177). Tickets for hour-long boat tours around the harbor, organized by the *Cooperative Battelieri* (sailors' cooperative), are available at the landing stage to the right of the main marine station in Calata Zingari, not far from Stazione Principe; for groups, call 265712 for bookings. There are roughly a half-dozen trips a day, organized on an ad hoc basis and costing roughly 4,000 lire (about $3) per person. They also offer daily mini-cruises along the Riviera. Ferries run daily to Sardinia, and boats sail to Corsica, Sicily, and Tunisia. For information on ferries to Sardinia, Sicily, and Tunisia, contact *Tirrenia* (phone: 26981); for Corsica, *Corsica Ferries* (phone: 593301).

Bus and Tram – Services are frequent and reliable. Tickets (which also cover the funicular and lifts) can be bought for 1,000 lire (77¢) at tobacconists and newsstands displaying the *AMT* sign; they are valid for any number of journeys within a 1¼-hour period (misuse can result in an on-the-spot 25,000 lire — $19 fine). A day-long tourist bus ticket (valid until midnight), *biglietto turistico,* costs 3,000 lire ($2.30). For schedule and services information, (including a special "Art Bus" tour for 18,000 lire — $13.85 — contact *AMT* (phone: 59971).

At main hotel desks, as well as at a kiosk beside the Stazione Principe, travelers can buy tickets for short guided coach tours of Genoa. The cost is 18,000 lire ($13.85) for roughly 3 hours, departing daily at 3:30 PM (3:45 PM in winter) from Stazione Principe. The tours are a good way to get an overview of the city before starting out on an individual itinerary.

Car Rental – Cars are useful for day trips from Genoa but are more trouble than they're worth for touring within the city. All the major car rental firms have offices at the airport: *Avis* (phone: 607280) and *Hertz* (phone: 651-2422). Other locations include: *Avis* (190r Via Balbi; phone: 257065; and at the train station, Porta Principe; phone: 255598); and *Hertz* (3 Via delle Casacce; phone: 540906).

Taxi – For 24-hour service, call 2696. During the day, pay only the price registered on the meter; at night and on Sundays, there is a surcharge.

Train – There are two main stations in Genoa — Stazione Porta Principe (Piazza Principe; phone: 284081) and the newer Stazione Brignole (Piazza Verdi; phone: 586350). Connecting bus and train services between them are fast and frequent, so this is a good way to hop from one side of town to the other. Both stations have frequent service to Milan (90 minutes on a fast train) and to towns along the Riviera.

SPECIAL EVENTS: This year is a very special one for Genoa, commemorating the 500th anniversary of native son Columbus's discovery of America. From May 15 to August 15, in addition to Italy, 32 countries — especially those from the Americas, Spain, and Portugal — will participate in the celebration. The theme of the festivities is "Christopher Columbus: The Ship and the Sea." Although there will be events all over the city, the focal point will be the Porto Vecchio (Old Port), the 15-acre site of an elaborate restoration project. Launched in 1989 and designed by the esteemed, local architect Renzo Piano, whose *Beaubourg* success in Paris established his prominence worldwide, this large exhibition area with international pavilions explores Genoa's — and people's — relationship with the sea. Buildings at the Porto Vecchio include an enormous aquarium (the largest in Europe and the site — together with a large schooner — of the Italian Pavilion), an open-air theater, a reception area and convention center in a former cotton warehouse, as well as many outdoor colorful cafés and restaurants. A number of cultural events will recreate 15th-century Genoa from which Columbus set out and changed the course of history. For the latest information, contact one of the AAST offices (see *Tourist Information* above).

The *Fiera Internazionale di Genova,* a vast exposition center on the sea, usually has an interesting fair or show. *Euroflora,* held there in the spring every 5 years (the next is scheduled for 1996), transforms the vast *Fiera* into an immense field of flowers (1 Piazzale Kennedy; phone: 53911; fax: 539-1270). Every 4 years in late spring the city hosts the *Regata Storica delle Repubbliche Marinare,* the race and procession of historic boats and costumes that hark back to the 11th century when Genoa was one of the ancient maritime republics (the others are Venice, Pisa, and Amalfi). This year is Venice's turn, but there also will be a regatta in Genoa as part of the Columbus festivities. The *International Festival of Ballet* is held in the beautiful Parco Nervi (see *Extra Special* and *Music*) in July. The *Salone Nautico* (International Boat Show), the biggest of its kind in Europe, is held at the *Fiera* every October. The *Niccolò Paganini* violin contest, another annual international event, is held in October.

MUSEUMS: Genoa has many fine galleries, palaces, and museums. Admission is 1,000 lire (77¢), Sundays are free, and all are closed Mondays. The following are among the best:

Museo del Risorgimento (Museum of the Risorgimento) – Visitors will have a better understanding of recent Italian history after visiting this museum, situated in the house where Mazzini was born. The building is 17th century, with original frescoes. Open Tuesdays through Saturdays from 9 AM to 7 PM, Sundays from 9 AM to 12:15 PM. 11 Via Lomellini (phone: 207553).

Lunardi Museum of American Studies – Displays on life in America illuminate the European view of contemporary American culture. The museum, housed in the 17th-century Villa Grüber, has a fine collection of pre-Columbian art. Open Tuesdays through Fridays from 9:30 AM to noon and from 3 to 5:30 PM; weekends from 3 to 5:30 PM. Villa de Mari-Grüber, 39 Corso Solferino (phone: 814737).

Museo d'Arte Orientale (Museum of Oriental Art) – Here is one of Europe's largest collections of Oriental art, and undoubtedly the best in Italy. The original Japanese, Chinese, and Thai collections were donated by the painter Edoardo Chiossone. Open Tuesdays through Saturdays from 9 AM to 5 PM, Sundays from 9 AM to 12:30 PM. Villetta di Negro, Via Piaggio (phone: 542285).

SHOPPING: There are two good department stores in Genoa: *La Rinascente* (1 Via Vernazza; phone: 586995) and *Coin* (4 Via XII Ottobre; phone: 543126). Many of the smaller, more exclusive stores are on the Via XX Settembre and the pedestrian-only Via Lucolli, while others are to be stumbled on while exploring the narrow streets of the medieval city. Food and clothing, as well as the crafts for which the region is famous — ceramics from Sestri Levante, fine lace, and silver and gold filigree — are all found here. Between Piazza Fontane Marose and Piazza della Zecca are a number of antiques shops that sell, among other things, curious objects relating to Genoa's seafaring past. In Piazza Lavagna a small, permanent flea market is worth a visit even if you are not looking for a bargain. The Genoese are great snackers, like most Italians, and it is not unusual to munch and shop at the same time. Look especially for shops bearing the sign *Torte e Farinate,* which feature local specialties. The majority of shops are closed on Sundays and on Monday mornings.

Antica Erboristeria San Giorgio – An old, well-known herbal shop stocked with everything from old-recipe panaceas to natural cosmetics, health foods, and teas. 47r Via Luccoli (phone: 206888).

Berti – The classic English look the Genoese so love, from high-quality English and Italian manufacturers of clothing for both sexes. 94r Via Ottobre (phone: 540026).

Chiarella – Amusing, moderate-price Italian and European clothing for men and women. 224r Via XX Settembre (phone: 562868).

"Come tu mi vuoi" – Unique women's clothing. 8 Vico Casana (phone: 208920).

Dallai Libreria Antiquaria – Large selection of antique books, unusual or first editions, and interesting old prints in this small store in the *centro storico.* 11r Piazza de Marini.

L'Enoteca – A small but rare selection of wines, particularly the better Ligurian wines not always available in restaurants. 31 Via Porta degli Archi (phone: 564071).

Il Fornaio di Sattarnino – The perfect place to sample the local staple, *focaccia,* in all its glory — simple or filled with any of a myriad of ingredients. Other breads, rolls, and baked sweets are made around the clock. 18r Via Fiasella (phone: 580972).

Giglio Bagnara – A refurbished, upscale department store offering everything for women, men, and children, as well as home furnishings and textiles. 46 Via Sestri (phone: 624841).

Klainguti – Homemade ice creams and cakes to rival the perfection of Romanengo's chocolates (see below). There also is a pleasant tearoom, open since 1828. 100 Piazza Soziglia (phone: 296502).

Lucarda – Exceptional nautical clothing and accessories for both men and women. 61 Via Sottoripa (phone: 297963).

Le Mimose – A small, delightful store full of exquisite women's lingerie. 58r Via XXV Aprile (phone: 292619).

Pecchioli – Ceramics, crystal, and other fine gift items. 126 Via XX Settembre (phone: 564914).

Pietro Romanengo fu Stefano – For 2 centuries, the best handmade chocolates and other confections in Genoa. 74r Via Soziglia (phone: 297869) and 51r Via Roma (phone: 580257).

Pittaluga – A historic florist shop with attentive service. 18 Piazza Portello (phone: 298787).

Prini – Offering shoes, bags, and all accessories as well as quality clothing since 1860. 155r Via XX Settembre (phone: 594421) for men; 17r Via XX Settembre for women (phone: 561984).

SPORTS AND FITNESS: As might be expected, water sports are the most popular here. Genoa competes in an annual regatta during the first week in June against the three other ancient maritime republics — Pisa, Venice, and Amalfi. The contest alternates each year among the cities. Although this year is Venice's turn, the regatta will also be held in Genoa, in celebration of the 500th anniversary of Columbus's discovery of America (see *Special Events*).

Bocce – One of the most popular ball games in Italy, a bit like French *boules,* it is played in parks and squares all over the city. Contact the *Associazione Bocciofila Genovese,* 2 Passa Zerbino (phone: 810770).

Sailing – *Club Vela Pegli,* 40 Via Lungomare di Pegli (phone: 683213).

Soccer – Matches take place from September to May at the *Luigi Ferraris Stadium* (Piazza Ferraris). The Genoese have two teams for which they root: *Genoa* (phone: 892431) and *Sampdoria,* or "La Samp" (phone: 813252).

Squash – *Squash Club Genova,* 7/A Corso Italia (phone: 303718).

Swimming – Pools are at *Stadio del Nuoto* (39 Via de Gaspari; phone: 362-8409) and *Sportiva Sturla* (2 Via V Maggio; phone: 389325), both indoors; and in summer only at *Gropallo* (Passeggiata Anita Garibaldi, Nervi; phone: 321311). The most popular (and crowded) beach for swimming is the Bagno Nuovo Lido (13 Corso Italia; phone: 308079); take bus No. 31 from the city center. The nearby Ligurian resorts offer more attractive beaches.

Tennis – Courts are at *Stadio del Tennis* (74 Via Albaro; phone: 317604), *Campo Tennis* (4 Via Campanella; phone: 313056), and *Tennis Club Genova* (5 Salita Misericordia; phone: 586662).

THEATER: The acclaimed *Teatro Stabile di Genoa* company performs in two theaters. The *Politeama Genovese* (4 Via Piaggio; phone: 893589) is the principal building, but productions also take place at the smaller *Sala Eleonora Duse* (6 Via Bacigalupo; phone: 873420). Various experimental works, as well as traditional Italian and international productions, can be seen in the small, well-established theaters *Teatro delle Tosse* (2 Piazza Negri; phone: 247-0793) and *Carignano* (8r Viale Villa Glori; phone: 593533). The tiny *Teatro dell'Archivolto* (1 Piazzetta Chighizola; phone: 281409) often presents works by traveling companies. During the summer, the *Comune di Genova* stages open-air programs under the title *Acquasola* in the public park near Piazza Corvetto. Detailed information about specific performances can be obtained from the theaters (box offices open from 3 PM) or from the main tourist offices.

MUSIC: The Genoese love music, and although their early 19th-century opera house, *Teatro Carlo Felice* (Piazza de Ferrari; phone: 53811) was bombed during World War II, the mere shell that remained was fiercely protected and was rebuilt in time for this year's Columbus celebration. In addition to opera (the season is from mid-January to mid-June), the theater also hosts classical concerts and rock shows. Other musical performances are given in the century-old *Politeama Margherita* (33 Via XX Settembre; phone: 589329). In late June and July, concerts and international music and ballet festivals are held in the public gardens at Nervi. Genoa is also something of a hothouse of a particular brand of folk music, typified by present-day singer Francesco de Gregori's laconic, *cantastoria* style. The city still has something of a medieval madrigal tradition. Concerts by the *I Madrigalisti* group, under the direction of Nevio Zanardi, can be heard at the *Oratorio San Filippo Neri* (10 Via Lomellini; phone: 292241).

NIGHTCLUBS AND NIGHTLIFE: The best bet is to find a congenial restaurant, of which there are many, and settle in comfortably and enjoy a chat with your neighbors. There are two established nightclubs in Genoa: the *Orchidea* (28 Via Casaregis; phone: 591559) and the *Astoria Club* (7 Via Quarnaro; phone: 361195). Discos come and go, so it is best to ask at your hotel about popular places. *Xenos* (152 Via XX Settembre; phone: 542480) is a lively spot. The *Louisiana Jazz Club* (1 Corso Aurelio Saffi; phone: 585067) swings on Thursday nights only. For a late-night drink or just to hear some lullabies, try the piano bars: *American Bar La Marinetta* (19 Corso Italia; phone: 310093), nightly except Tuesdays; or *Mix in Glass* (2 Piazza Leopardi; phone: 310319), closed Sundays.

BEST IN TOWN

CHECKING IN: There are fewer hotels in Genoa than might be expected of a large, busy city. This is perhaps because most visitors stay nearby in the smaller resort towns, which are connected to the city by frequent train service and by two main roads. Nevertheless, Genoa has more than adequate facilities. The main tourist offices can help with arrangements. Hotels listed here as very expensive charge $200 and up for a double room with bath; expensive, between $125 and $200; moderate, from $75 to $125; and inexpensive, $75 or less. All telephone numbers are in the 10 city code unless otherwise indicated.

Bristol Palace – Although lacking the convenience of a restaurant, it is understandably one of the most popular (and expensive) hotels in Genoa because of its fashionable location and friendly, bustling atmosphere. Located in a handsome 19th-century palazzo, there are 130 rooms and its 5 floors are linked by a grand marble staircase. 35 Via XX Settembre (phone: 592541; fax: 561756). Very expensive.

Pagoda – This ornate building, a real pagoda, built in the early 19th century by an eccentric sea captain returned from the Orient, has 21 tastefully furnished, modern rooms (although not all are air conditioned) and an ambience more of a private home than of a hotel. There is a large lounge, decorated with baroque mirrors from Venice, as well as a restaurant and an attractive garden. Located in nearby Nervi, a 10-minute walk from Nervi station, which has frequent train service to Brignole, in the center of Genoa, and about 10 to 15 minutes by car from the city center. 15 Via Capolungo, Nervi (phone: 326161; fax: 321218). Very expensive.

Astor – In a small, lovely park, this modern, comfortable (air conditioned) hotel with 55 rooms, a restaurant, and bar is only a brief stroll from the sea and the public gardens and open-air theater. 16 Viale delle Palme, Nervi (phone: 328325). Expensive.

City – Completely refurbished in 1989 in anticipation of the Columbus festivities, this member of the Best Western chain has 70 soundproof, tastefully decorated rooms that promise a quiet and pleasant stay in the very heart of town. 6 Via San Sebastiano (phone: 5545; fax: 586301). Expensive.

Jolly Hotel Plaza – Although rather reserved, this 97-room modern hostelry (a link in the well-known hotel chain) is quiet and well located. All the rooms are air conditioned, and have television sets and mini-bars. 11 Via Martin Piaggio (phone: 893642; fax: 891850). Expensive.

Savoia Majestic – Also facing the Stazione Principe and near the historic center, this place is very comfortable, with 120 air conditioned rooms and a good restaurant as well as a grillroom and American bar. 5 Via Arsenale di Terra (phone: 261641; fax: 261883). Expensive.

Metropoli – A homey, friendly 50-room establishment, with a sweet, pervasive fragrance of fresh polish and a central, though noisy, location (ask for a quiet room at the back). 8 Vico Migliorini (phone: 284141; fax: 281816). Moderate.

Park – Many of the 19 rooms in this place face the ocean. A beautiful garden surrounds the hotel and shady trees give you the sense of being at a cool, seaside retreat. Note: If things are slow, the hotel shuts down in August. 10 Corso Italia (phone: 311040). Moderate.

Bel Soggiorno – There are 18 rooms in this rare find on the city's main palazzo-lined street — be sure to ask for a quiet one. Closed mid-December to mid-January. 19 Via XX Settembre (phone: 581418). Moderate to inexpensive.

Rio – For those who wish to sleep in the medieval section of town, this 47-room place is just off the port, very near the ancient Church of San Siro. Comfortable and simple, it does lack a restaurant. Closed during January. 5 Via al Ponte Calvi (phone: 290551; fax: 290554). Moderate to inexpensive.

Vittoria Orlandini – Simple and comfortable (60 rooms), though not luxurious, with its own restaurant. Air conditioning is $15 extra a day. Near Genoa's historic center, just minutes away from the magnificent Via Garibaldi, and across from the main train station. 33-45 Via Balbi (phone: 261923; fax: 268552). Moderate to inexpensive.

Agnello D'Oro – The "Golden Lamb" is a bargain, one of the better hotels in its price category. All 38 rooms have air conditioning and telephones. Its restaurant is for guests only (closed October to March). 6 Vico delle Monachette (phone: 262084; fax: 561124). Inexpensive.

Assarotti – Twenty-five clean rooms, an accommodating staff, parking, and low prices make this a good value. 40/C Via Assarotti (phone: 885822). Inexpensive.

Minerva Italia – Despite its very central location near the Piazza de Ferrari, this 45-room hotel with a pleasant staff is one of the least expensive in its category. 14 Via XXV Aprile (phone: 200941). Inexpensive.

EATING OUT: Ligurian culinary arts include many special dishes normally found only within the region; Genoese restaurants offer these either exclusively or combined with better known national dishes. Some can be a little heavy — with lots of garlic and olive oil — but because they are so well prepared, they may not seem so. One such specialty, for example, is pesto, which is made from a variety of basil native only to Liguria, along with pine nuts, garlic, olive oil, and often parmesan cheese, and is served on rice, gnocchi, locally made *trofie* noodles, or flat spaghetti known as *trenette. Focaccia,* a simpler version of pizza as we know it (there is no sauce), is topped or more often filled with local delicacies ranging from vegetables to cheese, served as a first course, appetizer, or snack — whereas other Italian towns have pizzerias, Genoa abounds with *focaccerie.* Other Ligurian treats are *pansotti alla salsa di noce,* plump tortellini-like pasta with a creamy walnut sauce; *polpettone,* a meat and vegetable loaf; and *torta Pasqualina,* an *Easter* pie (though it's eaten year-round) traditionally made with Swiss chard or artichokes. There are 33 flaky layers of dough — one for each year of Christ's life. Another cake, *farinata,* contains ground chick-peas; baked in the oven, it is flat and served in slices. Veal is the most popular meat, though beef and other meats are plentiful. Naturally, the sea provides fresh fish and shellfish in abundance. The Genoese take great pride in their desserts, so most are homemade — *cucina casalinga.* Like other Italians, they eat out a lot, often with large family groups, ranging from infants to ancients. As a consequence, there are many restaurants in Genoa and nearby Boccadasse and Nervi, and prices are competitive. Prices given below are based on a meal for two, including wine but not liquor. Meals for two at restaurants categorized as very expensive are $175 and up; expensive, $125 to $175; moderate, from $60 to $120; inexpensive, less than $60. The price usually includes at least three courses with side dishes. All telephone numbers are in the 10 city code unless otherwise indicated.

Le Fate – Originally a shop that sold wine and oil, this restaurant serves some of the best food in Genoa, especially the fish cooked with herbs, homemade pasta, and desserts. Closed Saturday lunch and Sundays. Reservations necessary. Major credit cards accepted. 31 Via Ruspoli (phone: 546402). Very expensive.

Da Giacomo – An unusually formal restaurant by Genoese standards. In a deluxe, modern environment, with spacious seating arrangements and first class service, this establishment is popular with the cognoscenti. Dishes tend toward international favorites, though there are also many Ligurian specialties, especially seafood. An excellent wine selection is available, and the waiters are happy to offer advice. The menu changes daily but always includes both fish and meat. Closed Sundays and most of August. Reservations necessary. Major credit cards accepted. 1 Corso Italia (phone: 369647). Very expensive.

Gran Gotto – This small, elegantly appointed place has an exceptional kitchen specializing in seasonal regional dishes. The pesto and the *ripieni* (stuffed) dishes are especially good. Try the fresh *pesce ripieno.* Homemade desserts such as cinnamon sorbet and *antica torta di mele* (apple pie) are a fitting end to a sublime meal. Closed Saturday lunch, Sundays, public holidays, and the last 3 weeks in August. Reservations advised. Major credit cards accepted. 11 Via Fiume (phone: 564344). Very expensive.

Aladino – The central location, warm atmosphere, and chef Vincenzo's fine artistry in the kitchen make this an ideal stopover for lunch. Try the *trenette al pesto,* any of the superbly presented seafood dishes, and the desserts. Closed Sundays. Reservations necessary. Major credit cards accepted. 8 Via E. Vernazza (phone: 566788). Expensive.

Cardinali da Ermanno – Decorated with wooden figures and Tuscan terra cotta, this intimate, family-run bistro offers few Ligurian specialties, concentrating instead on international dishes such as French crêpes and Swiss fondue, with a particularly good truffle fondue in season. Closed Sundays and the latter part of July. Reservations advised. Major credit cards accepted. 60 Via Assarotti (phone: 870380). Expensive.

Harry's Bar – Informally chic decor and international food is found here. Enjoy a cocktail at the lively bar before moving on to dinner. A first course worth noting is the *riso mantecato,* a light rice dish resembling a soufflé. Chicken *alla* Harry's is stuffed with prosciutto and cheese. Good French and Italian wines. Closed Wednesdays and part of July. Reservations necessary. Major credit cards accepted. 13 Via Donato Somma, Nervi (phone: 326074). Expensive.

Manuelina – For travelers along the coastal road to the east of the city, this is an ideal place to stop for a meal. (A few guestrooms were scheduled to open as we went to press). It is one of the region's best seafood restaurants, specializing in dishes grilled on an open fire and mushroom dishes when in season. Closed Wednesdays, mid-January to mid-February, and the latter half of July. Reservations advised. Major credit cards accepted. 278 Via Roma, Recco (phone: 185-74128). Expensive.

Il Primo Piano – In the center of the modern city, this well-established and pleasant place serves Genoese specialties, particularly fish. The *risotto di scampi* is very good, as are all the other rice dishes, and the *lasagne al pesto* is excellent. Also try the delicate fish tartare and the unusual *gelato di riso* (rice ice cream). Closed Sundays and during August. Reservations necessary. Major credit cards accepted. 36 Via XX Settembre (phone: 540284). Expensive.

Saint Cyr – Elegant and modern, but not spacious, this friendly, lively restaurant is particularly popular with the Genoese for lunch. Innovative selections include *timballo Arlecchino,* a casserole with spinach, fontina cheese, and tomato; *risotto ai funghi* (rice with mushrooms); and *filetto al barolo* (steak smothered in a delicious red wine sauce). Light desserts include fresh fruit terrine and orange mousse. Closed Saturdays, Sundays, the last 3 weeks of August, and 1 week at *Christmas.* Reservations advised. Major credit cards accepted. 8 Piazza Marsala (phone: 886897). Expensive.

La Santa – This restaurant is in the 12th-century palace that once housed Saint Catherine of Genoa. Dining in its intimate, rather small environment, with soft lighting and traditional Ligurian furnishings, it's easy to feel transported to a bygone time. The food is outstanding: various *aragosta* (lobster) or *gamberi* (shrimp) dishes, ravioli stuffed with fish, and *tagliatelle* (noodle-like pasta) smothered in walnut sauce are fabulous possibilities. Don't miss *tiramisù* (pick-me-up), a chocolate confection with liberal splashings of marsala. Closed Sundays. Reservations advised. Major credit cards accepted. 1-3r Vico degli Indoratori (phone: 293613). Expensive.

Zeffirino – The five Belloni brothers run their restaurant in the tradition of their father, Zeffirino. Their sisters and wives make the homemade pasta in the *stirata,* or pulled, fashion — by hand with long rollers. *Passutelli* is a ravioli stuffed with ricotta and fruit, a recipe known only to the family. The *lasagne al pesto* is another longtime favorite. Other specialties are added daily to the ample menu, which includes a good regional wine list. A large upstairs room is often used for receptions and banquets; the smaller room downstairs is more intimate. Both are decorated in a traditional style, all in wood, combining old Genoa with old America. Closed Wednesdays. Reservations advised. Major credit cards accepted. 20 Via XX Settembre (phone: 591990). Expensive.

Antica Osteria del Bai – From the outside, you never want to go in; from the inside, you never want to leave. Within this crumbling building on the sea, which was a port of call for Garibaldi 125 years ago before he set sail for Sicily, the decor is warm, attractively redone in wood, with windows facing the sea. Gianni Malagoli's Genoese fare is good and includes ravioli stuffed with fish, *zuppa di pesce* (a hearty fish soup), and many other delectables, including fine desserts. Closed Mondays and the first 3 weeks of August. Reservations advised. Major credit cards accepted. On the way to Nervi, 12 Via Quarto (phone: 387478). Expensive to moderate.

Il Cucciolo – Spacious and modern, specializing in Tuscan dishes such as *pasta e fagioli* (with beans) and *fritto alla livornese* (fish fried with lots of garlic). Closed Mondays and August 1–27. Reservations advised. American Express accepted. 33 Viale Sauli (phone: 546470). Moderate.

Europa – This restaurant distinguishes itself not only with its relaxed atmosphere, but because guests are welcome for a late meal. People are still arriving at midnight, and the place is buzzing until closing time at 2:30 AM. Everything from pizza to Genoese specialties — such as grilled local seafood and *pasta al pesto* — are available. Reservations unnecessary. No credit cards accepted. Inside the arcade at No. 53 in the *Galleria Mazzini* (phone: 581259). Moderate.

Gheise – The name of this quaint dining spot derives from the chants of the washerwomen at a once nearby laundry. Genoese specialties and some excellent meat dishes, particularly Florentine steaks, are served. Closed Mondays and August. Reservations advised. American Express accepted. 29 Via Boccadasse, Boccadasse (phone: 377-0086). Moderate.

Napoleon – Always bustling, always full, this modern eatery is two steps from the Piazza de Ferrari. Intimate it's not, but an extensive stock of vintage olive oil and wine and a number of traditional local specialties keep everyone coming back. The *menù degustazione* (minimum 2 people) is more expensive, but is a crash course in fine *cucina genovese.* Closed Sundays and 3 weeks in the summer. Reservations advised. Major credit cards accepted. 33r Via XXV Aprile (phone: 541888). Moderate.

Santa Chiara – Dine outdoors at this wonderfully located fish restaurant on the coast. The crêpes and seafood risotto are especially good, the pasta homemade. Closed Sundays and during August. Reservations necessary on weekends. American Express accepted. 69 Via al Capo di Santa Chiara, just beyond Boccadasse (phone: 377-0081). Moderate.

Sette Nasi – Enrico Nasi is one of seven children — hence the name of his eatery, which literally means "Seven Noses." It's a friendly place on the beach offering its own pool and terrace, fresh fish daily, and very good homemade desserts. Closed Tuesdays. Reservations advised. Major credit cards accepted. 16 Via Quarto (phone: 337357). Moderate.

Del Mario – Housed in a 13th-century building, once the loggia, or assembly hall, and now a national monument. Its menu is traditional and seasonal, with many mushroom and truffle dishes. A very good *cima* (veal joint stuffed with vegetables and eggs) and *stoccafisso* (stockfish soup), plus other Ligurian specialties, are served in an extremely courteous and relaxed atmosphere. Closed Saturdays and August. Reservations unnecessary. Major credit cards accepted. 35r Via Conservatori del Mare (phone: 298467). Moderate to inexpensive.

Mario Rivaro – A few charming rooms decorated with light wood paneling, traditional Genoese fare, and a devoted clientele make this centrally located eatery a guaranteed favorite. Closed Sundays and holidays. No reservations. No credit cards accepted. 16r Via del Portello (phone: 201554). Inexpensive.

Il Melograno – This small place is delightfully decorated in the Art Nouveau style and personally supervised by the charming, energetic couple who also do the cooking. The menu changes daily, with occasional Tuscan and other regional specialties as well as Ligurian. Ice creams and desserts are homemade. Closed Sundays and the last 3 weeks of August. Reservations unnecessary. American Express accepted. 62r Via Maccaggi (phone: 546407). Inexpensive.

BARS AND CAFÉS: For lighter meals, snacks, and to satisfy those with a sweet tooth, Genoa's many *caffès* are worth trying and all are inexpensive. The following are a few of our favorites:

Antica Gelateria Balilla – The handsome *ambiente* of old-fashioned mirrors and cushioned chairs goes unnoticed when the gelato arrives. The specialty is the many varieties of *semifreddo* (soft ice cream). There also are dozens of flavors of freshly made ice cream and hard-to-find Sicilian *granita* (refreshing shaved-ice drinks served in a glass or cone). No reservations. No credit cards accepted. 84r Via Maccaggi (phone: 542161). Inexpensive.

Bar Romanengo – Founded in 1805, the original location of this Genoese tradition on Via Orefici is the oldest bar in the city. Now at two sites, each offers old-fashioned, wood-trimmed display counters are loaded with homemade candies, hand-dipped chocolates, glazed chestnuts, and candied fruits. Closed Sundays. No reservations. No credit cards accepted. 31 Via Orefici (phone: 203915) and 74r Piazza Soziglia (phone: 297869). Inexpensive.

Cremeria Augusto – All the traditional and in-season fruit varieties of gelato are served here, but the custardy *crema* and cappuccino-flavored *panera* (a must for coffee lovers) are the best. Closed Saturdays and the last 3 weeks of August. No reservations. No credit cards accepted. 3r Via Nino Bixio (phone: 591884). Inexpensive.

Grattacielo – Situated below Porta Soprana, this smart café serves coffee, snacks, and ice cream (with photographs of various concoctions featured in an album-menu on each table) and occasionally features a pianist. No reservations. No credit cards accepted. 26 Piazza Dante (phone: 590402). Inexpensive.

Mangini – Sweets, pastries, and candies that will make your mouth water and your head swim, in a handsome Old World *ambiente.* Closed Mondays. No reservations. No credit cards accepted. 91r Via Roma (phone: 564013). Inexpensive.

Tonitto – A popular coffeehouse and *gelateria* that sells a host of tempting flavors all made on the spot (and supplied to several other restaurants in town). No reservations. No credit cards accepted. 31 Piazza Dante (phone: 581077). Inexpensive.

MILAN

Milan is the financial and commercial hub of Italy, and one of the most important business centers in the world. At first glance, it is a city of cold, uninspired skyscrapers, a city whose energizing force is money. Even the museum devoted to Leonardo da Vinci here testifies as much to his scientific and technical genius as to his artistic spirit. The people of Milan are industrious, sophisticated, chic, serious — not inclined to watch the world pass by from a sunny café table.

Although with nearly 1.6 million people Milan is a distant second in size to Rome, many Milanese think of their city as Italy's real capital; it is arguably more powerful than Rome. It boasts 400 banks and a silk market that rivals the one in Lyons. Its *International Trade Fair* each spring draws hundreds of thousands of businesspeople from all over the world, as do its autumn and spring showings of luxury fashions. Milan is the home of the prestigious Luigi Bocconi Commercial University, whose graduates include successful international economists, bankers, and company presidents. The city also is the center of Italian publishing and of trendsetting furniture design.

Still, Milan's economic preoccupation is tempered by an appreciation of less mundane pursuits. It is the *La Scala* opera house, with its perfect acoustics and grand traditions, not the Milan Stock Exchange (Borsa Valori), that is the pride of the city. The opening of the opera season each December is a national event, when newspapers print even the menus for the traditional midnight supper parties in the tony restaurants.

The very heart of Milan is its rose-tinted white marble Gothic Duomo; the spires of Milan's magnificent cathedral seem to soar in defiance of the less ethereal buildings around it, though many of them often boast lovely fin de siècle architectural details and delightful, secret courtyard gardens. At the same time, Milan is the gateway to the Lombardy lake region, to ski resorts along the Swiss border to the north, and to the mist-veiled charm of the broad Po River — with its rice paddies, fishermen, and even a school of naïf painters — to the south.

So it is unfortunate that many visitors who look for the Italy of sunny skies, outdoor cafés, and quaint villages may hurry through Milan. The early-19th-century French writer Stendahl lived here for 4 decades; when he died in 1842, there were instructions for his tombstone to read: "Arrigo [Henri] Beyle [his real surname], Milanese — Lived, Wrote, Loved." Stendahl's enthusiasm for Milan, which in 1800 was one of Europe's wealthiest and most luxurious cities, was boundless: "For me this city is the most beautiful place on earth," he wrote. The Milanese themselves passionately ascribe to this view. They point with pride to the city's symbols of its illustrious past: the 16 Corinthian columns outside the 4th-century San Lorenzo Basilica, the remains of the

16th-century Spanish ramparts, and the traces of *navigli* (canals) that once crisscrossed the city and linked it to other regions of Italy.

Milan has had a tumultuous history. Invading armies continually descended upon it from the time it was a Celtic settlement. The Romans subdued the city they called "Mediolanum" in 222 BC, and it was the capital of the Roman Empire from AD 286 to 402. In AD 313, Constantine the Great officially recognized Christianity in the famous Edict of Milan, and with the coming of Christianity, Milan found a spiritual father in Bishop Ambrose (later proclaimed a saint), who accomplished the seemingly impossible task of conciliating church and state. After a series of invasions by Huns and Goths, the Lombards (Lungobardi), who had originated in northwest Germany, pushed their way southward to cross the Alps and invade the Po Valley towns, including Milan, in 568. They ruled for more than 2 centuries, giving their name to the region, and they left their imprint on the art and architecture, language, and laws. Tyrranical Frankish rulers followed, but around the year 1000 the Milanese bishops wrested temporal power from them, and Milan became one of the first Italian city-states to be ruled by the church. Constant wars followed, and after a 9-month siege Milan fell to Frederick Barbarossa. In 1176, all the cities in the area united in the Lombard League to defeat the German invader and win recognition of its independence.

This ushered in a century of prosperity and power, as local family dynasties, beginning with the Torriani, assumed power in 1260. The Visconti then seized power from them in 1277. Under the Visconti, particularly Gian Galeazzo (1345–1402), Milan grew in wealth and splendor. When the Visconti died out in 1447, Milan experienced 3 years of Republican government before Francesco Sforza proclaimed himself duke. The most famous of the Sforzas was Ludovico il Moro (1451–1508), who brought Leonardo da Vinci, Donato Bramante, and other artists to Milan to enhance the city. After Ludovico's death, Milan fell to the invading French, to the Spanish in 1535, and, then, in 1713, to the Austrian Empire. At the beginning of the 19th century, Napoleon made Milan the capital of the Cisalpine Republic, but the tyrannic Austrian rulers returned when Napoleon fell.

The succession of foreign rulers began to ebb in 1848, when the Milanese staged a glorious 5-day revolution, known as the Cinque Giornate. But it was nearly 10 years before Milan was liberated and could throw its support to the Piedmontese King Victor Emmanuel of Savoy, who would become king of a unified Italy in 1860.

During World War II, Milan was the site of bitter partisan fighting; it was bombed 15 times and many of its historic buildings were damaged extensively. But restoration work and new construction began immediately after the war. Bomb damage required the complete rebuilding of about half the region's factories, which proved a blessing in disguise since the new plants were extremely modern manufacturing entities, making them especially competitive and spawning the boom of the 1950s and 1960s.

Contemporary Milan is surrounded by a massive, smoke-belching industrial belt — producing auto parts, chemicals, manmade fibers, appliances and rubber. The consequent smog has been somewhat reduced in recent years, but still remains a problem, as do polluted waterways. The city's air is constantly monitored, and when it reaches the risky level, automobile driving is severely curtailed. A large downtown stretch of shopping area is totally traffic-free. Milan is a virtual maze of four-lane highways connecting it with the other northern industrial cities — Genoa, Turin, Venice, and Brescia — and, by the Autostrada del Sole, to Rome and southern Italy.

The center of Italy's publishing and advertising industry and private TV networks, Milan specializes in innovative industrial design and avant-garde graphics. Its textile design and fashions are on a par with those of Paris. The city itself is prosperous and elegant; its people enjoy a high standard of living and a stimulating cultural and intellectual life. Whether you come on business, to attend the opera, to patronize the elegant Milanese fashion houses, or to admire the city's art treasures, you will find Milan's sophistication equal to that of London or Paris or New York, but always uncompromisingly Italian.

MILAN AT-A-GLANCE

SEEING THE CITY: For a grand view of Milan, the surrounding Lombard plain, the Alps, and the Apennines, climb the 166 steps, or take an elevator, to the roof of the cathedral (see *Special Places*). From here, more stairs take you to the topmost gallery at the base of the cathedral's central spire, 354 feet from the ground. The stairway to the roof is entered from the south transept near the Medici tomb; the elevator is entered from outside the church, on the north side (toward the *Rinascente* department store); an elevator on the south side is sometimes also in operation. Both are open daily and charge admission. A new seventh-floor addition to *Rinascente* boasts a café whose vast windows bring the Duomo's gargoyles within, it would seem, sipping distance of your *aperitivo.* Here your admission charge for a unique view is the price of a cup of coffee. There is also a 350-foot viewing tower in Sempione Park, just beyond the Castello Sforzesco (see *Special Places*).

SPECIAL PLACES: The huge Piazza del Duomo (Cathedral Square), with its perennial pigeons and ever-present pensioners, is one of the city's few pedestrian oases and the heart of this bustling metropolis. Leading north from Piazza del Duomo to Piazza della Scala is the elegant glass-domed arcade, the *Galleria Vittorio Emanuele.* Built between 1865 and 1877 under the direction of architect Giuseppe Mengoni, it has for decades been considered the *salotto,* or salon, of Milan for its exclusive shops, bookstores, cafés, and restaurants.

Some of the city's tourist attractions are too far from the center to reach comfortably on foot, but *ATM,* the local bus and tram system, connects these sites efficiently, as does the relatively new and clean subway system.

DOWNTOWN

Il Duomo (Cathedral) – The most magnificent Milanese monument is the shimmering marble cathedral, with 135 spires and more than 2,200 sculptures decorating its exterior. From the roof, reached by an elevator or a 166-step climb, you can study the details of its pinnacles and flying buttresses. The interior of the cathedral, divided into five main aisles by an imposing stand of 58 columns, contains another 2,000 sculptures. The cathedral, on the site of an early Christian church located in the center of the then

Roman city of Mediolanum, is considered the finest example of Gothic architecture in northern Italy, although its own architectural peculiarities — it was begun in 1386 but not completed until 1813 — prevent it from being pure Gothic. Only St. Peter's in Rome is larger. Next to the cathedral at 14 Piazza del Duomo is the *Museo del Duomo,* which beautifully displays Milanese artifacts from the early Middle Ages, including illuminated manuscripts, parchments, statuary, architectural plans, and tapestries. A plus is the air conditioned *ambiente.* Open Tuesdays through Sundays from 9:30 AM to 12:30 PM and 3 to 6 PM. Admission charge. Piazza del Duomo.

Teatro alla Scala (La Scala) – The most famous opera house in the world was built between 1776 and 1778 on the site of the Church of Santa Maria della Scala. It was here that works by Donizetti, Rossini, Bellini, and Verdi were first acclaimed and where Arturo Toscanini conducted and was artistic director for many years. The neo-classic building, damaged extensively during World War II, was reopened in 1946. Its acoustics are perfect. Traditionally, *La Scala*'s season begins on December 7, the feast day of Milan's patron saint, St. Ambrose, and lasts until the end of May. The box office (phone: 807041/42/43/44) is open daily, 10 AM to 1 PM and 3:30 to 5:30 PM (until 9:30 PM on the day of a performance); closed Mondays. (For information, call 809129; for credit card purchases, call 809126.) Agencies do not exist, and opera tickets are extremely difficult to obtain (even for Milanesi), but the theater can be visited by appointment (phone: 887-9377). A sure way to get tickets is to give large amounts of lire to the *portiere* at your hotel. The adjacent *Museo della Scala* (La Scala Museum) houses a rich collection of manuscripts, costumes, and other memorabilia from the theater's history. Open Mondays through Fridays from 9 AM to noon and 2 to 6 PM; Saturdays from 9 AM to noon and 2 to 3:30 PM; Sundays from 9 AM to noon from May through September. Admission charge. The theater and museum are north of Piazza del Duomo, through the *Galleria Vittorio Emanuele,* on Piazza della Scala (phone: 805-3418).

Museo Poldi-Pezzoli (Poldi-Pezzoli Museum) – The Milanese nobleman Gian Giacomo Poldi-Pezzoli bequeathed his home and exquisite private art collection to the city in 1879. It includes some prime examples of Renaissance to 17th-century paintings and sculpture, Oriental porcelain, Persian carpets, and tapestries. There also are a Botticelli portrait of the Madonna, paintings by Giovanni Battista Tiepolo, Pollaiolo and Fra Bartolomeo, as well as Giovanni Bellini's *Pietà.* Open Mondays through Fridays from 9:30 AM to 12:30 PM and 2:30 to 6 PM; Saturdays from 9:30 AM to 12:30 PM and 2:30 to 7:30 PM. Admission charge. A short walk from *La Scala.* 12 Via Manzoni (phone: 794889).

Palazzo e Pinacoteca di Brera (Brera Palace and Art Gallery) – One of the most important state-owned galleries in Italy, and Milan's finest, is housed in the 17th-century Brera Palace. Its 38 rooms contain a broad representation of Italian painting, with particularly good examples from the Venetian and Lombard schools, including such masterpieces as Andrea Mantegna's *Dead Christ,* Raphael's *Wedding Feast of the Virgin,* and Caravaggio's *Dinner at Emmaus.* The palace also has an important library (founded in 1770) of incunabula and manuscripts, plus a collection of all books printed in the Milanese province since 1788. In the courtyard is a monumental statue of Napoleon I, depicted as a conquering Caesar. The art gallery is open Mondays through Saturdays from 9 AM to 1:45 PM; Sundays from 9 AM to 12:45 PM; closed the last Tuesday each month. Admission charge. The library is closed Sundays. A few blocks north of *La Scala.* 28 Via Brera (phone: 808387).

Castello Sforzesco e Museo d'Arte Antica (Sforza Castle and Museum of Antique Art) – In the mid-15th century, Duke Francesco Sforza built this large, square brick castle on the site of a castle of the Visconti that had been destroyed. It became a fortress after the fall of the Sforzas and was damaged repeatedly in sieges before restoration began in the 19th century. Further damaged during World War II, it has been repaired, and today houses the *Museo d'Arte Antica* (Museum of Antique Art) whose treasures include the unfinished *Rondanini Pietà,* the last work of Michelangelo. The museum is entered from the courtyard of the residential part of the castle, the Corte Ducale. Open Tuesdays through Sundays from 9:30 AM to 12:30 PM; closed the last Tuesday of each month. No admission charge. West of the Brera. Piazza Castello (phone: 6236, ext. 3940).

The castle also houses exhibits of art, musical instruments, and manuscripts. Well-publicized temporary exhibitions often are set up in other rooms. (Same hours as the *Museo d'Arte Antica.*) Beyond the castle is the beautiful 116-acre Parco Sempione (Sempione Park), with an aquarium, sports arena, and neo-classic Arco della Pace (Arch of Peace), a triumphal arch with statues and bas-relief. The arch, on the model of Septimius Severus at Rome, marks the beginning of the historic Corso Sempione (Simplon Road) through the Alps to France, which was built by order of Napoleon.

Basilica e Museo di Sant'Ambrogio (St. Ambrose's Basilica and Museum) – The basilica was founded in the 4th century by Bishop Ambrose (later St. Ambrose), who baptized St. Augustine here. The bas-relief on the doorway dates from the time of St. Ambrose, and the two bronze doors are from the 9th century. The basilica was enlarged in the 11th century, and its superb atrium was added in the 12th century. Two other early Christian saints — Gervase and Protasius — are buried with St. Ambrose in the crypt. The ceiling of the apse is decorated with 10th-century mosaics. Above the portico is the *Museo di Sant'Ambrogio* (Museum of St. Ambrose), where you can see a 12th-century cross, a missal of Gian Galeazzo Visconti, and other religious treasures. The museum is open Wednesdays, Thursdays, Fridays, and Mondays from 10 AM to noon and 3 to 5 PM; Saturdays and Sundays from 3 to 5 PM; closed in August. Admission charge. South of the Sforza Castle. 15 Piazza Sant'Ambrogio (phone: 872059).

Santa Maria delle Grazie (The Church of St. Mary of Grace) – The interior of this restored brick and terra cotta church, representing a period of transition from Gothic to Renaissance, is decorated with some fine 15th-century frescoes. But the church, though beautiful in itself, usually is visited because Leonardo da Vinci's *The Last Supper* (known as the *Cenacolo Vinciano*) is on a wall of the refectory of the former Dominican convent next to it. *The Last Supper* was painted in tempera, which is not particularly durable, and though it has been restored several times, it has suffered considerable deterioration. The current restoration keeps viewers at a frustrating distance from the dim painting, and the nearly ubiquitous scaffolding doesn't help; meanwhile, the refectory remains open to visitors. Open Tuesdays through Saturdays from 9 AM to 1:15 PM and 2 to 6:15 PM; Sundays and Mondays from 9 AM to 1:15 PM. Admission charge. A few blocks northwest of Sant'Ambrogio. Piazza Santa Maria delle Grazie (phone: 498-7588).

ENVIRONS

Certosa di Pavia (Carthusian Monastery) – Gian Galeazzo Visconti founded this monastery in 1396 as a family mausoleum. With its façade of multicolored marble sculpture and its interior heavily decorated with frescoes, baroque grillwork, and other ornamentation, the monastery is one of the most remarkable buildings in Italy. It is conveniently reached from Milan by coach excursion or by road. Closed Mondays. No admission charge, but donations are welcome. Sixteen miles (26 km) from Milan, just off the Milan-Pavia Road (call 925613 for information on guided tours).

Pavia – On the banks of the Ticino, this gracious city was the capital of the Lombard kingdom and later a free commune, until it fell to the Visconti in 1359. The famous University of Pavia was officially founded in the same century, although its origins go back to the 9th century. The 15th-century Duomo (with a 19th-century façade, however) is flanked by an 11th-century tower and backed by the 16th-century Broletto

(Town Hall). An admirable church (Leonardo da Vinci and Bramante helped with the plans), it is nevertheless a relative newcomer — not far away is the Romanesque Basilica di San Michele, a 12th-century rebuilding of the 7th-century church where Charlemagne and Frederick Barbarossa were crowned Lombard kings. Still another Romanesque church, San Pietro in Ciel d'Oro, holds the tomb of St. Augustine. Pavia's main street, the Strada Nuova, is lined with elegant shops and ends at the river, which is crossed by a postwar reconstruction of a 14th-century covered bridge. Five miles (8 km) south of the Certosa di Pavia.

Monza – The world-famous Monza *Autodromo* is the scene of the Italian *Grand Prix Formula One* race early in September each year. Except during race preparation times, visitors can drive around the course, with its well-known seven corners (admission charge). The *Autodromo* is in a splendid park that was once part of the Villa Reale (Royal Villa), and now has golf courses, a racecourse, and a swimming pool, as well as the auto track. The historic cathedral at Monza (Piazza del Duomo) also is worth a visit. Built during the 13th and 14th centuries, it has a façade of white, green, and black marble, notable for its harmonious proportions and decorations. The *Museo Serpero* (Piazza del Duomo; phone: 393-23404) houses an interesting collection of precious medieval works in gold from the cathedral. It is open daily, except Sunday mornings and Mondays, from 9 AM to noon and 3 to 5 PM; admission charge. Monza is easily reached by bus or train; by road, it is 7 miles (11 km) northeast of Milan on SS 36.

■ **EXTRA SPECIAL:** Until the early part of this century, Milan was crisscrossed by canals (*navigli*). Today only two remain, and their environs (it's a fair walk; from the Piazza del Duomo take Via Torino and Corso di Porta Ticinese) are perhaps the most picturesque in Milan. A stroll through this quarter provides a marked contrast to the rest of this modern, bustling city. On the last Sunday of every month, there is a huge and fascinating antiques market, the *Mercatone del Naviglio,* along the *navigli.*

SOURCES AND RESOURCES

TOURIST INFORMATION: General tourist information is available at the extremely helpful Provincial Tourist Board (Ente Provinciale per il Turismo, or EPT), conveniently located at the corner of Piazza del Duomo (2 Via Marconi; phone: 809662 or 870016), and at the central train terminal (phone: 669-0432 or 669-0532)). The EPT will make hotel reservations within Milan (phone: 706095) and provide information on current exhibits and events in the city, and to a lesser extent, on other regions of Italy. A good way to be introduced to the city is to view the free video presentation at the EPT office by the Duomo (address above).

Agenzia Autostradale conducts a 3-hour bus tour in English of the city that leaves daily from the Piazzetta Reale. Tickets are available from most hotels and travel agencies, or directly on board. From April to October, the company also offers an all-day tour of the Lombardy lakes. Pick-up points are at Piazza Castello and the Stazione Centrale (the main train station). For information on prices and hours for both tours, call 801161. The *Gestione Governative Navigazione Laghi* (21 Via Ariosto; phone: 481-6230 or 481-2086) arranges boat trips on the lakes.

A welcome convenience to travelers low on lire are automatic foreign exchange machines where you can change $5, $10, and $20 bills (as well as many other currencies) into local tender. The exchange rate is usually about what banks offer and there is a fixed commission charge comparable to what financial institutions charge. A few of the many locations for these ATMs are at the airports; the tourist office (1 Via Marconi); and the Banca Cesare Ponti (19 Piazza Duomo).

The US Consulate is at 2-10 Piazza Amedeo (phone: 290-09841).

Local Coverage – The tourist board can provide copies of *Milan Is,* a useful guide in English, which includes activities, facts, phone numbers, and listings of restaurants and discos. The monthly *Night & Day Milano,* distributed by many hotels, has bulletins on special events, and *Viva Milano,* a weekly entertainment newspaper in Italian, provides up-to-date information on shops, fairs, restaurants, and discos. Other publications, such as the monthly *Milano Mese* and *Un Ospite di Milano* (A Guest in Milano), produced by the Hotel Concierges Association, often are available in hotels. *Yes please* is an English-language monthly about Milan, available at newsstands.

The *Milan Trade Fair Center* is at 1 Largo Domodossola (phone: 49971). During fair events, an office is set up at Linate Airport (phone: 738-2431).

Food – There are several books in Italian that provide listings of restaurants and food and wine shops throughout Italy. Some of the better guides are *La Guida d'Italia* (published annually by *L'Espresso*), *I Ristoranti di Bell'Italia* (published annually by Mondadori), and *Gambero Rosso* (published by *Il Manifesto*). They all are sold on newsstands.

TELEPHONE: The city code for Milan is 2. When calling from within Italy, dial 02 before the local number.

GETTING AROUND: Much of the center of Milan has been closed to traffic, so it is far more convenient for visitors to use public transportation. Inexpensive day tickets that allow unlimited travel on the public transportation system can be purchased at the *ATM* Ufficio Abbonamenti at the Piazza del Duomo subway station, at the Stazione Centrale, and at the EPT on Via Marconi.

Airports – Malpensa Airport is about 28 miles (45 km) and less than an hour's drive from the center of Milan; a taxi ride into town can cost as much as $70. Buses to Malpensa leave from Stazione Centrale, on the east side of the *Galleria delle Carrozze,* every half hour and cost about $7 (phone: 868008 or 331-797480). They also stop at the east entrance of Porta Garibaldi Station en route. For flight information, call 748-52200, and for lost luggage, call 748-54215.

Linate Airport handles domestic traffic, as well as some international — but not intercontinental — flights. Linate is 5 miles (8 km) and 15 minutes (longer if traffic is heavy) from downtown Milan; taxi fare into the center of the city is about $16. *ATM* bus No. 73 leaves for the airport from Corso Europa (near Piazza San Babila), and Porta Garibaldi Station every 10 minutes between 5:40 AM and midnight, and costs about $1 (phone: 748-52200). For lost luggage, call 748-54215. *Doria Agenzia* has buses that leave from Stazione Centrale every 20 minutes from 5:40 AM to 8:30 PM. Tickets cost about $2.

Although there is no regular transportation between Malpensa and Linate airports, *Alitalia* occasionally provides group transfers when two connecting *Alitalia* flights are involved. For information on domestic flights, call 28361; for international flights, call 28371.

Bus and Tram – The local bus and tram service, *ATM,* efficiently connects various points of this sprawling city. Tickets are sold at tobacconists and newsstands throughout the city and must be purchased in advance. They are valid for 75 minutes, thus permitting transfer to other lines, and can be used for the subway as well.

Car Rental – Most international firms are represented. *Avis, Europcar, Hertz,* and

Maggiore all have counters at both Malpensa and Linate airports and at several locations in the city. Central reservations numbers are *Avis* (phone: 6981); *Europcar* (phone: 607-1051); *Hertz* (phone: 20483 or 654929); *Maggiore* (phone: 760-04238). Also try *Budget* (13 Via Vittor Pisani; phone: 670-3151) and at Malpensa (phone: 868221) and Linate (phone: 738-5639); *InterRent* (4 Corso Como; phone: 657-0477 or 659-9417) and at Malpensa (phone: 868124) and Linate (phone: 733585). *Avis, Hertz,* and *Maggiore* also have branches at the train station. Note that Malpensa Airport has desks at which tourists may buy coupons that can be redeemed at gas stations around Italy. Coupons must be purchased in foreign currency. Another option is *Limousine Service* (phone: 344752).

Subway – The efficient, clean *Metropolitana Milanese* (*MM*) now has three lines (a third was inaugurated last year). The most useful for tourists is line M3, which directly links the main railway station, through Piazza del Duomo, and the Porta Romana. Tickets are sold at coin-operated machines in each station and at many tobacconists.

Taxi – Taxis can be hailed while cruising, picked up at a cabstand, or called by radio taxi (phone: 8388, 8585, 6767, or 5251). Meters begin at about $5 plus arrival and waiting time if the cab is called by phone. Do not be surprised if the driver asks for a surcharge after 10 PM or on Sundays or holidays. There is an additional small charge for baggage.

Train – Milan's main train station is Stazione Centrale (Piazzale Duca d'Aosta; phone: 67500). Several smaller stations serve local commuter lines. The largest of these is Porta Garibaldi, the departure point for trains to Turin, Pavia, Monza, Bergamo, and other points (phone: 655-2078). Several new, comfortable, high-speed trains make the trip to Rome in 5 hours or less. The *Pendolino* clocks it in 4 hours, and the ticket price includes dinner. Some of the fast trains (the *rapidi*) have comfortable second class accommodations. Book ahead.

LOCAL SERVICES: Credit Card Offices – *American Express* (3 Via Brera; phone: 85571; for lost traveler's checks, phone: 1678-720-0024, toll-free in Italy); *Diners Club* (32 Piazza della Repubblica; phone: 669-81203); *MasterCard* and *Visa* (toll-free phone: 1678-68086); *AT&T* (for calls to the US, dial 172-1011).

Dentist (English-Speaking) – Dr. Lucia Calinescu (7 Piazza Giovanni delle Bande Nere; phone: 406241); Dr. Massimo Rossi (121 Porta Romana; phone: 546-4664).

Dry Cleaner – *Guritz,* 7-9 Via Sant'Andrea (phone: 760-02129).

Limousine Service – *Garage Principe e Savoia* (1 Via Cartesio; phone: 650220); *Autonoleggi Del Sole* (120 Viale Umbria; phone: 714023); *Auto VIP* (7 Via Aldrovandi; phone: 204-9817).

Medical Emergency – *Ospedale Maggiore Policlinico* (35 Via Francesco Sforza; phone: 551-1655); *Ospedale Fatebenefratelli* (23 Corso di Porta Nuova; phone: 63631). In cases of extreme emergency, call 3883 for a house call, 7733 or 113 for an ambulance or medical assistance. Two English-speaking physicians are Dr. Larry Burdick (4 Corso XXII Marzo; phone: 204-9167) and Dr. Bettina Sturlese (19 Via S. Eufemia; phone: 805-7831 or 279167).

Messenger Service – *Rinaldi* (10 Via Sant'Andrea; phone: 796851; fax: 782160); *Agenzia Scutto* (21 Via Bramante; phone: 316441); *Pony Express* (39 Via Bernardino Vero; phone: 8441); *City Cross* (phone: 404-8241).

National/International Courier – *DHL International* (15 Via Agnello and 21 Via Fantoli; phone: 50781); *Emery Air Freight* (in Segrate; phone: 213-4613); *Italcargo* (214 Via Cassanese, Segrate; phone: 213-99510); *Moto Mondo* (phone: 738-3310); *Federal Express* (10 Via Albricci; phone: 863222 or 506-4076; fax: 502341).

Office Equipment Rental – Most of the city's better hotels can arrange for short-term rental (a day or two) of typewriters and other items. Companies that rent such equipment usually do so only on a monthly basis. For long-term rental, contact *ARS* (5 Piazza della Repubblica; phone: 799151); *Executive Services Business Center* (8 Via Monti; phone: 345-2211, and 14 Via Leopardi; phone: 498-2251); *Managing Center* (12 Via Washington; phone: 481-93012).

Pharmacy – The main floor of Stazione Centrale (the main railway station), *Galleria delle Partenze,* has a 24-hour pharmacy (phone: 669-0735). *Cooperative Farmaceutica* (1 Via Orefici, Piazza del Duomo; phone: 872266) is open day and night but closed at mealtimes. Call 192 for information regarding pharmacies that are open at night, Sundays, and holidays (*farmacia di turno*). Local newspapers list which pharmacies are open on holidays.

Photocopies – *Fotocolors Duplicating Service* (6 Largo Promessi Sposi; phone: 846-5176); *Fotoriproduzione Documenti* (Via Larga; phone: 862319); *De Poli* (27 Corso Vercelli; phone: 487438); *Copisteria Tecnocopy* (17 Via Grossich; phone: 236-0475), which stays open in August. Some photocopy centers also will send and receive faxes.

Post Office – The main post office is open weekdays from 8 AM to 8 PM and Saturdays from 8 AM to noon (4 Piazza Cordusio; phone: 160). The railway post office is open for registered letters weekdays from 8 AM to 10 PM and Saturdays from 8 AM to noon (8-10 Via Aporti; phone: 663-0649).

Secretary/Stenographer (English-Speaking) – *Congress Service* (7 Piazza Massari; phone: 608-0983); *Copisteria Manara* (28 Porta Vittoria; phone: 540-1047).

Tailor – *Caraceni* (16 Via Fatebenefratelli; phone: 655-1972); *Luisa Corvino* (6 Corso Concordia; phone: 795147).

Telex/Telefaxes – Main post office (4 Piazza Cordusio; phone: 869-2874), open 24 hours daily. For information about telefax service, call 866702.

Translator – *Associazione Italiana Traduttori Interpreti* (*ANTI,* 75 Via B. d'Alviano; phone: 415-9846); *Centro Serbelloni* (1 Via Serbelloni; phone: 760-00248); *Congress Service* (7 Piazza Massari; phone: 608-0983); *Translator/Interpreter Center* (10 Via Lambrate; phone: 287-0336); *Pronto-Mondo,* telephone interpreter (phone: 669-84862); *Simultanea* (phone: 720-01266).

Other – Milan has numerous "congress centers" that are equipped with audiovisual devices, simultaneous translation systems, and other services: *Athena* (4 Via Serbelloni; phone: 741253); *Centro Congressi Milanofiori* (Viale Milano Fiori, Assago; phone: 825-2969 or 824791); *Castello di Macconago Meeting Center,* a 14th-century castle 15 minutes from downtown (38 Via Macconago; phone: 539-1053 or 569-4819); *Centro Mitec* (49 Via Vittorio Colonna; phone: 439-0383); and *Tekno Congress* (1 Via Marazzini; phone: 282-2730). Fully equipped offices can be rented through *Executive Service* (8 Via V. Monti; phone: 345-2211); *International Business Centre* (12 Corso Europa; phone: 545-6331); *Centro Bonsaglio* (1a Via Borromei; phone: 805-1898); *Centro Italiano Congressi* (121/A Corso di Porta Romana; phone: 551-87057); *ES Assistance* (8 Corso Venezia; phone: 784812). Other helpful places for business travelers: *US International Marketing Center* (5 Via Gattamelata; phone: 469-6451); *Camera di Commercio Americana in Italia* (12 Via Agnello; phone: 869-0661). Formal wear rental: *Lo Bosco Casa d'Arte* (7 Corso Venezia; phone: 760-00585).

SPECIAL EVENTS: The annual *International Trade Fair* held in late April since the 1920s has put Milan squarely on the international business map. Although this is the city's biggest, there are various other trade fairs and exhibitions (including the showings of designer collections, the twice yearly fashion fair, and the September furniture fair) almost every month except July and August, making advance hotel reservations essential. Information, a copy of the useful bilingual periodical *In Fiera,* and a year-round calendar of events can be obtained from the main *Trade Fair* office (1 Largo Domodossola; phone: 49971). In July and August, the city sponsors a variety of outdoor cultural events; sometimes restaurants join in by serving regional specialties in the parks. The opening of the opera season at *La Scala,* which takes place each year on December 7, is the city's major cultural event.

MUSEUMS: In addition to those listed in *Special Places,* there are several other museums in Milan worth a visit. All, except the Basilica di San Lorenzo Maggiore, have an admission charge.

Basilica di San Lorenzo Maggiore – This 4th-century church is the oldest in the West. 39 Corso di Porta Ticinese.

Galleria d'Arte Moderna (Modern Art Gallery) – Open Wednesdays through Mondays from 9:30 AM to 7:30 PM. Villa Comunale, 16 Via Palestro (phone: 702819).

Museo e Casa di Manzoni (Manzoni Museum and House) – The former home of Alessandro Manzoni, author of the 19th-century classic *I Promessi Sposi* (The Betrothed). Open Tuesdays through Fridays from 9 AM to noon and 2 to 4 PM. 1 Via Morone (phone: 871019).

Museo di Milano (Museum of Milan) – Open Tuesdays through Sundays from 9:30 AM to 7:30 PM; closed the last Tuesday of each month. 6 Via Sant' Andrea (phone: 706245).

Museo del Risorgimento Nazionale (National Museum of the Risorgimento) – Open daily from 9:30 AM to 7:30 PM. 23 Via Borgonuovo (phone: 869-3549).

Museo della Scienza e della Tecnica Leonardo da Vinci (Leonardo da Vinci Museum of Science and Technology) – Open daily except Mondays from 9:30 AM to 4:50 PM. 21 Via San Vittore (phone: 480-10040).

Museo di Storia Contemporanea (Museum of Contemporary History) – Open Tuesdays through Sundays from 9:30 AM to 7:30 PM; closed the last Tuesday of each month. 6 Via Sant' Andrea (phone: 760-06245).

Palazzo Reale (Royal Palace) – A beautiful 18th-century building that houses the *Museum of Contemporary Art* and prestigious temporary exhibitions. Open daily from 9:30 AM to 7:30 PM. Piazza del Duomo (phone: 6236).

GALLERIES: Milan also has scores of art galleries with interesting shows. They generally are open from 10:30 AM to 1 PM and 4 to 8 PM except Mondays. The following offer an excellent selection of contemporary and early-20th-century Italian art:

Arte Centro – 11 Via Brera (phone: 865888).

Centro Annunciata – 44 Via Manzoni (phone: 796026).

Christie's – 9 Via Borgogna (phone: 794712).

Galleria Fonte d'Abisso – 7 Via del Carmine (phone: 873050).

Salvatore Ala – 3 Via Mameli (phone: 716500).

Sotheby's – 3 Via Montenapoleone (phone: 783907).

Studio Marconi – 15-17 Via Tadino (phone: 294-04373 or 225543).

Toselli – 9 Via del Carmine (phone: 805-0434).

SHOPPING: With the explosion of Italian design and fashion over the last 20 years, Milan is an international style center full of enticing, if expensive, shops, including showrooms and boutiques of many of Italy's major contemporary clothing designers, such as Milan's own *Mila Schön* (2 Via Montenapoleone); her store for men is a few steps away. It also is a center for antiques and home furnishings. The main shopping area comprises the streets near Piazza del Duomo and *La Scala,* particularly the elegant Via Montenapoleone, Via della Spiga, and Via Sant'Andrea. Here you'll find the boutiques of top Italian designers *Giorgio Armani* (9 Via Sant'Andrea); *Gianni Versace* (4 and 25 Via della Spiga); *Enrico Coveri* (Via San Pietro all'Orto); *Missoni* (1 Via Montenapoleone); *Ferragamo* (3 Via Montenapoleone); and *Krizia* (23 Via della Spiga), most of whom are based in Milan. The

Galleria Vittorio Emanuele (between the Piazza del Duomo and the Piazza della Scala) is a good place to window shop and stop at one of its many cafés for a coffee or cool drink in summer. Boutiques offering modern fashions and antique clothes also are scattered throughout the old Brera quarter — Milan's Left Bank — and around St. Ambrose's Basilica. *Caffè Moda Durini* (14 Via Durini), the only mini-shopping mall in the city, is filled with fashions by designers such as Valentino (for men); there's also a café on the lower level. Shop hours generally are from 9 or 9:30 AM to 12:30 PM and 3:30 to 7:30 PM. Most shops are closed Sundays and Monday mornings.

Milan also has several outdoor markets. Tuesday mornings and Saturdays, there are clothing stalls on Viale Papiniano and Via V. Marcello. On the third Saturday of the month the *Mercato di Brera* sells antiques, real and otherwise, from 10 AM to 11 PM in and around Piazza Formentini. Early in December, a flea market and fair near the *Basilica e Museo di Sant'Ambrogio* features a wide selection of clothes, antiques, old books, and knickknacks.

Accademia – Fine menswear and accessories. 11 Via Solferino.

Alberto Subert – Fine Italian and imported antiques. 22 Via della Spiga.

Arflex – Armchairs and chaises that are produced by top designers and are among the best known in Italy. 28 Via Durini.

Arte Antica – One of the city's best-known antiques stores, with French porcelain, clocks, and furniture. 11 Via Sant'Andrea.

Beltrami – Shoes, handbags, and beautifully styled, ready-to-wear. 16 Via Montenapoleone.

Bottega Veneta – Basket-woven fine leather goods are the hallmark of this famed store. 5 Via della Spiga.

Brigatti – Considered Milan's finest men's sportswear shop. Also has a ski boutique for the entire family. 15 Corso Venezia.

Bulgari – World-famous high-style jewelry designer, offering masterpieces made from gold, silver, platinum, and precious stones. 6 Via Sant'Andrea.

Calderoni – Exquisite jewelry and silver. 8 Via Montenapoleone.

Carrano – Stylish women's shoes. 21 Via Sant'Andrea.

Centenari – Fine old prints and paintings. 92 *Galleria Vittorio Emanuele II.*

Cignarelli – Wonderful homemade herbal liqueurs. 65 Corso Buenos Aires.

Decomania – Art Deco objects and furniture. 5-9 Via Fiori Chiari.

Dispensa Gualtiero Marchesi – The maestro of Italian nouvelle cooking sells culinary items from pâté to placemats. 6 Via San Giovanni sul Muro.

Ermenegildo Zegna – Designer menswear. 3 Via Verri.

Fendi – High-fashion silk shirts, purses, and furs designed by Karl Lagerfeld. 16 Via Sant' Andrea.

Fontana – Furniture with a flair by the famous avant-garde Memphis Milano School. 3 Via Montenapoleone.

Franco and Aldo Lorenzi – Elegant travel and smoking accessories for men. 9 Via Montenapoleone.

Frette – Luxurious linen for bed and bath, as well as silk negligees. 21 Via Montenapoleone.

Galtrucco – Shimmering silks from Como, by the meter or ready-to-wear. 27 Via Montenapoleone.

Gherardini – Florentine leather goods and sportswear. 8 Via della Spiga.

Guanti Berni – Beautiful leather gloves for men and women. Via Sant'Andrea.

Gucci – Leatherwear, clothing, and shoes from the famous maker. 5 Via Montenapoleone.

Mario Buccellati – Jeweler famed for his finely chased, engraved gold. Inside the courtyard at 12 Via Montenapoleone.

Mastro Geppetto – Dolls, toys, models, plus a life-size Pinocchio. 14 Corso Matteotti.

Moschino – High fashion ready-to-wear for women. 12 Via Sant'Andrea.

Naj-Oleari – Vibrant-colored animal prints. 8 Via Brera.

Officina Alessi – The ultimate in wooden and stainless steel household objects, in a tiny shop designed by Sottsass, Italy's most famous architect. 9 Corso Matteotti.

L'Oro dei Farlocchi – The place for unique presents — ivory penknives, crystal knickknacks, and so on. 5 Via Madonnina.

Orsi – A small but highly regarded antiques shop, with lovely 17th- and 18th-century furniture. 14 Via Bagutta.

Peck – This fancy food store should not be missed, especially by those eager for the best in dried *porcini* mushrooms, truffles, and other Italian specialties. Its restaurant is next door (see *Eating Out*). 9 Via Spadari.

Philippe Daverio – Prestigious antiques dealer. 6/A Via Montenapoleone.

Prada – Fashion insiders know that this is the place for shoes with the shape of things to come. 1 Via della Spiga.

Pratesi – Luxurious linen. 21 Via Montenapoleone.

Provera – Top-quality wines sold in a 1920s' shop that specializes in wines from the north. Sold by the bottle or the glass; there are a few tables for tasting. 7 Corso Magenta.

Richard Ginori – Fine bone china in traditional or contemporary styles, such as the popular "Italian Fruit" design. 1 Corso Matteotti.

Rubinacci – Top French designers and the store's own elegant line of women's fashions. 10 Via Sant'Andrea.

Salviati – Exquisite hand-blown Venetian glass in decorator bottles, designer desk lamps, and vases. Corner of Via Manzoni and Via Montenapoleone.

Scavia – Sleek and supemely elegant jewelry, especially the satin-smooth gold bracelets in a variety of widths. 9 Via Spiga.

Shara Pagano – The bijoux are not the real thing, but are gems nonetheless. 7 Via della Spiga.

Stationery – The city's best-stocked stationery store, with interesting gadgets and office accessories. 3 Via Solferino.

T & J Vestor – For Missoni's carpets and wall hangings, and tablecloth and napkin sets. 38 Via Manzoni.

Tanino Crisci – The best in finely crafted men's and women's footwear. 3 Via Montenapoleone.

Trussardi – High-fashion leatherwear, luggage, and briefcases for men and women. 7 Via Sant'Andrea.

Valentino Donna – Women's clothing by the famous designer. 3 Via Santo Spirito. Men's fashions sold at *Valentino Uomo.* 20 Via Montenapoleone.

Venini – Hand-blown glass — from perfume bottles to chandeliers, made by one of Venice's foremost artisans. 9 Via Montenapoleone.

Vittorio Siniscalchi – One of Milan's best custom shirtmakers for men. 8 Via Gesù.

DISCOUNT SHOPS

If you're one of those — like us — who tries to make every lira go a long, long way, here are some select discount outlets where fine Italian goods and fashions are often found at far less than the prices in fancier shops. For indefatigable bargain hunters, a good guide is *Bargain Hunting in Milan, Le Occasioni di Milano,* available at bookstores and some newsstands.

Diecidecimi – Men's and women's fashions, all discounted 50%, including a large selection of leather jackets and sheepskin coats. 34 Via Plino.

Emporio – Discounted classic, spirited clothing from previous and current seasons; *not* part of *Emporio Armani.* 11 Via Prini, near Corso Sempione.

Emporio Armani – His less expensive line. 24 Via Durini.

Mimosa – Samples from the salons of name designers. 12 Piazza Santo Stefano.

Misul – Women's clothes in luxurious fabrics, often sold at far less than retail prices. Call for an appointment. 3 Via San Calocero.

Niki – Elegant women's clothes at half the usual price. 78 Viale Montenero.

Il Salvagente – Armani, Valentino, and other famous designer clothes for men, women, and children; in a warehouse-like store offering excellent discounts. 16 Via Fratelli Bronzetti and 28 Via Balzaretti.

SPORTS AND FITNESS: Downtown Milan is small, and has little green space, few gyms, and a scarcity of public parks. But it has an efficient municipal sports organization. For specific information on what sports are offered, and where, contact the Ufficio Sport e Tempo Libero (2 Via Marconi; phone: 6236) to consult their listings on golf courses, horseback riding, squash courts, etc. The staff (some English-speaking) either will make reservations for you (in the case of municipal tennis courts) or explain how you can do it yourself (alternatively, ask your hotel concierge to do it for you). The closest and largest green space for jogging, paddling a boat, swimming in a large public pool, picnicking, sunbathing, and café sitting with Milanese families is the Idroscalo Parco Azzurro (Azzurro Park and Boat Landing), whose artificial lake served the city's seaplanes until the 1970s. The waters are now filtered and reportedly not polluted. The city bus No. ID leaves from Piazza Fontana for the park at frequent intervals, including on Sundays.

Bicycling – Rentals by the hour, day, or month at *Vittorio Comizzoli* (60 Via Washington; phone: 498-4694) and *Cooperativa Il Picchio* (49 Corso San Gottardo; phone: 837-7926 or 837-2757).

Fitness Centers – *Skorpion Center* (24 Corso Vittorio Emanuele; phone: 796098); *Club Francesco Conti* (7 Via de Toqueville; phone: 657-0297, and 4 Via Cerva; phone: 760-00141); *American Contourella* (six locations, including 10 Via Montenapoleone; phone: 760-05290); *Health Center Club* (33 Via Kramer; phone: 272372); *Skorpion Center* (24 Corso Vittorio Emanuele; phone: 796098).

Golf – There are several golf courses in the Milan area, the largest and most accessible of which is the 27-hole course at the *Golf Club Milano,* in the park at nearby Monza (phone: 39-703081/2).

Horseback Riding – There are two riding stables in Milan: the *Centro Ippico Lombardo* (21 Via Fetonte; phone: 408-4270) and the *Centro Ippico Milanese* (20 Via Macconago; phone: 539-2013). For more information, get in touch with the Milan branch of *ANTE,* the national equestrian society (44/B Via Piranesi; phone: 738-4615).

Horse Racing – Thoroughbred and trotting races are run at the internationally famous *Ippodromo San Siro* (phone: 452-1854), on the eastern outskirts of Milan.

Ice Skating – There is a rink in operation from September through May at the Palazzo del Ghiaccio (14 Via Piranesi; phone: 7398). Skates can be rented at *Saini* (136 Via Corelli; phone: 738-0841).

Jogging – Try Parco Sempione, the Giardini Pubblici (Public Gardens), or the Idroscala Parco Azzurro.

Soccer – From September to May, both *Inter* and *Milan* play at *Stadio Comunale Giuseppe Meazza* (5 Via Piccolomini; phone: 454123 or 408-4123).

Squash – Courts are available at the *Giambellino Squash Club,* 5 Via Giambellino; (phone: 422-5979).

Swimming – Public indoor pools include *Cozzi* (35 Viale Tunisia); *Mincio* (13 Via Mincio); and *Solari* (11 Via Montevideo). Open-air pools include *Lido* (15 Piazzale Lotto, near the *San Siro Stadium;* phone: 7398); Romano (35 Via Ponzio); *Piscina Olimpica* (in the park at Monza); and *Argelati* (6 Via Segantini; phone: 835-0012).

Tennis – Public courts should be booked well ahead of time. Some of the main courts are at *Bonacossa* (74 Via Mecenate; phone: 506-1277); *Centro Polisportivo* (48 Via

Valvassori Peroni; phone: 236-6254); *Lido di Milano* (15 Piazzale Lotto; phone: 391667); and *Ripamonti* (4 Via Iseo; phone: 645-9253).

THEATER: You can take in classical Italian theater productions, including ones by world-famous director Giorgio Strehler, at the *Piccolo Teatro* (2 Via Rovello; phone: 869-0631); the *Manzoni* (40 Via Manzoni; phone: 790543); the *Salone Pier Lombardo* (14 Via Pierlombardo; phone: 584410); or the *Teatro Lirico* (14 Via Larga; phone: 866418). For avant-garde and experimental theater, try the *Carcano* (63 Corso di Porto Romana; phone: 551-81377); or the *Centro Ricerca Teatro* (7 Via Ulisse Dini; phone: 846-6592 or 846-5693). Three theaters now offer English-language films: *Anteo* (9 Via Milazzo; phone: 659-7773) on Mondays; *Arcobaleno* (11 Viale Tunisia; phone: 294-06054) on Wednesdays; and *Mexico* (57 Via Savona; phone: 479802) on Thursdays.

MUSIC: The renowned *La Scala* (see *Special Places*) is an obvious must for an opera fan lucky enough to have tickets in hand (or to have made the acquaintance of a sharp concierge who knows the ropes), but ballet and concerts also are held here; Piazza della Scala (phone: 807041). Concerts also are held at the *Auditorium Angelicum* (2 Piazza Sant'Angelo; phone: 632748), and the *Conservatorio di Musica* (12 Via Conservatorio; phone: 760-01755). Tickets to the *Angelicum* are sold at 4 Via Gustavo Favo or at *Ricordi Music Shop* (2 Via Berchet).

NIGHTCLUBS AND NIGHTLIFE: Milan has a variety of nightclubs offering both dinner and dancing. The most popular of these include *Charley Max* (2 Via Marconi; phone: 871416); *Caffè Roma* (4 Via Ancona; phone: 876960); and *Nepentha,* open until 3 AM (1 Piazza Diaz; phone: 804837). Top discos include *American Disaster* (48 Via Boscovich; phone: 225728); *Good Mood* (29 Via Turati; phone: 669349); *Plastic* — a favorite with the young, avant-garde crowd — (120 Via Umbria; phone: 733993); and *Calipso Club* (120 Viale Umbria; phone: 256-0553). Live music, including jazz, can be heard regularly at numerous clubs, among them *Capolinea* (119 Via Ludovico il Moro; phone: 428602), the city's oldest jazz spot, where internationally acclaimed musicians perform; *Ca'Bianca,* an excellent music and cabaret spot near the Naviglio Grande (117 Via Ludovico il Moro); and the loud, loud *Le Scimmie* (49 Via Ascanio Sforza; phone: 839-1874). The latter also has rock or blues, as does *Live Music* (4 Via Ciaia; phone: 668-8738). Milanese folk tunes and ballads are performed at *Osteria Amici Miei* (14 Via Nicola d'Apulia; phone: 285-0001). *Apollo Danze* (17 Via Procaccini), a 25-year-old dance hall, has live music on Monday afternoons (at cut rates), Saturday nights, and Sundays.

Milan has many cozy piano bars that are ideal for a late drink and snack. Try *Bistrot Piano Bar di Gualtiero Marchesi* (Piazza del Duomo; phone: 877120); *Golden Memory* (22 Via Lazzaro Papi; phone: 548-4209); *Gershwin's* (10 Via Corrado il Salico; phone: 849-7722); or the elegant *Momus* (8 Via Fiori Chiari; phone: 896227). There are striptease shows at *Teatrino* (3 Corsia dei Servi; phone: 793716), *Maschere* (7 Via Borgogna; phone: 705584), *Venus* (1 Via Giardino; phone: 805-0330); and *Smeraldo* (Piazza 25 Aprile; phone: 662768).

BEST IN TOWN

CHECKING IN: As an international business center, Milan offers a wide range of accommodations for the visitor, from traditional, old-fashioned hotels to efficient, modern, commercial ones. The number of hotels grew last year, just in time to help the city promote its bid to host the *2000 Olympic*

Games. Because of the many fairs and fashion showings, some hotels are fully booked in peak periods a year ahead. Summer reservations are easier to obtain. Milan's hotel prices are quite high. In high season (summer, *Easter*), very expensive hotels here will cost $550 or more a night for a double room; expensive hotels will cost from $350 to $500 a night; moderate hotels charge $200 to $350 for a double; and inexpensive hotels will charge between $100 and $200. Off-season rates are about 10% lower. Unless otherwise noted, all Milan hotels accept major credit cards. All telephone numbers are in the 2 city code unless otherwise indicated.

Excelsior Gallia – Built by the Gallia family in the early 1930s, this luxury place — decorated in the grand style — with 241 rooms and 12 suites is spacious, efficient, and friendly. Its restaurant ranks among the city's very finest (see *Eating Out*). Near the central train station. Business facilities include meeting rooms for up to 400, English-speaking concierge, foreign currency exchange, secretarial services in English, audiovisual equipment, photocopiers, computers, translation services, and express checkout. 9 Piazza Duca D'Aosta (phone: 6785; fax: 656306; telex: 311160GALLIA I). Very expensive.

Pierre Milano – Slightly off the beaten track, nevertheless, this luxurious 47-room hotel is a favorite of the VIP business crowd. There is an American bar on the premises, but no restaurant. Business facilities include 24-hour room service, meeting rooms for up to 20, English-speaking concierge, foreign currency exchange, secretarial services in English, audiovisual equipment, photocopiers, cable television news, translation services, and express checkout. 32 Via de Amicis (phone: 805-6221; fax: 805-2157; telex: 333303PIER MI). Very expensive.

Duomo – Much favored by the movers and shakers of Italian commerce. Bi-level rooms provide a businesslike sitting room, while touches of marble and Oriental carpets add swank to the contemporary decor. In the heart of town, just off Piazza del Duomo, but on a pedestrian street that ensures quiet. Business facilities include 24-hour room service, meeting rooms for up to 20, English-speaking concierge, foreign currency exchange, secretarial services in English, audiovisual equipment, photocopiers, computers, and translation services. 1 Via San Raffaele (phone: 8833; fax: 864-62027; telex: 312086). Expensive.

Hilton International – An attractive 332-room hotel in the new commercial center facing the main railway station, about a mile north of the center and the cathedral, it is tastefully decorated in a mixture of Italian provincial and modern styles. There is also a colorful, moderately priced Italian restaurant and a discotheque. The service is first-rate. Business facilities include 24-hour room service, meeting rooms for up to 240, English-speaking concierge, foreign currency exchange, secretarial services in English, audiovisual equipment, photocopiers, computers, cable television news, translation services, and express checkout. 12 Via Galvani (phone: 698331; fax: 607-1904; telex: 330433HILTEL I). Expensive.

Palace – Transformed by a $2.5-million renovation, each floor has a different color scheme and the rooms are decorated in ultramodern style. The smaller new wing is more conventional than the renovated old wing. Dining is on the roof garden or in the famous and attractive *Casanova Grill,* with its refined decor. 20 Piazza della Repubblica (phone: 6336; fax: 654485). Expensive.

Principe di Savoia – An ambitious renovation recently took place at this classic deluxe hotel, including a new façade, lobby, and reception areas. Enlarged and redecorated guestrooms boast antiques, thick rugs, marble baths, and air conditioning. There are kitchenette apartments with balconies in the new wing. The location is excellent: just north of the cathedral on a fashionable street away from the busy main road, yet within walking distance of Milan's boutique-lined Via Montenapoleone. 17 Piazza della Repubblica (phone: 6230). Expensive.

Spadari al Duomo – Under new management (and formerly called the *Lord Internazionale*), this tiny hostelry is on a busy little shopping street near the cathedral.

All 18 rooms are decorated with Memphis-style furniture, with attention paid to architectural details. Although the guestrooms are soundproofed, be sure to ask for one on the top floor — the plumbing is quite noisy farther down. There is no restaurant, but a small café serves light meals. Business facilities include 24-hour room service, meeting rooms for up to 30, cable television news, translation services, and express checkout. It also is possible to have a fax machine in your room. 11 Via Spadari (phone: 720-02371; fax: 720-02371). Expensive.

Blaise & Francis – New and conveniently close to the main train station (and 10 minutes from the center), it has 110 rooms, but no restaurant. It also has a garage. Business facilities include 24-hour room service and meeting rooms for up to 250. 9 Via Butti (phone: 668-02366; fax: 668-02909). Expensive to moderate.

Bonaparte – Formerly a residential hotel (now fully refurbished), this smallish property (56 rooms) is luxuriously appointed. 13 Via Cusani (phone: 8560; fax: 869-3601). Expensive to moderate.

Century Tower – This new, very comfortable, 198-room hotel has a garden, restaurant, and bar. 25/B Via Fabio Filzi (phone: 67504; fax: 669-80602). Expensive to moderate.

Executive – Next to the old airport bus terminal, about a mile from downtown Milan, this American-style hotel has a pleasant staff, deluxe rooms, a good restaurant and bar, saunas, and a swimming pool. 45 Via Don Luigi Sturzo (phone: 6294). Expensive to moderate.

Fiera Milano – Across the street from the fairgrounds, this 238-room hostelry has air conditioning and private parking. Business facilities include meeting rooms for up to 50, English-speaking concierge, foreign currency exchange, secretarial services in English, audiovisual equipment, photocopiers, cable television news, translation services, and express checkout. 20 Viale Boezio (phone: 3105; fax: 314119; telex: 331426HOTFIE). Expensive to moderate.

Jolly President – So centrally located that you can see the gargoyles on top of the Duomo from some windows, it has 201 comfortable rooms and a restaurant. 10 Largo Augusto (phone: 7746; fax: 783449). Expensive to moderate.

Europeo – Not far from the center of town, this fine hotel has its own peaceful garden and pool, all the modern conveniences, and very good service. 38 Via Canonica (phone: 331-4751; fax: 331-05410). Moderate.

Ibis Ca'Grande – Not centrally located, but new, with 132 rooms, a restaurant, bar, and garden. It has parking facilities, and also is well connected to the city center by bus. 13-15 Viale Suzzani (phone: 661-03000; fax: 661-02797). Moderate.

Manin – This small, first class hostelry is about a half mile from *La Scala.* Some of the rooms have been redecorated in a modern style; the older rooms are not impressive but are spacious and comfortable. There's also a very good restaurant and bar. Business facilities include meeting rooms for up to 100, English-speaking concierge, foreign currency exchange, audiovisual equipment, photocopiers, cable television news, and express checkout. 7 Via Manin (phone: 659-6511; fax: 655-2160; telex: 320385MANIN I). Moderate.

Mirage – Renovated last year, this high-quality, 50-room establishment has a bar, but no restaurant. 61 Via Casella (phone: 392-10471; fax: 392-10589). Moderate.

Nasco – An American-style place, it's an excellent choice when downtown hotels are full. Business facilities include meeting rooms for up to 150, English-speaking concierge, foreign currency exchange, audiovisual equipment, and photocopiers. 40 Via Spallanzani (phone: 204-3841). Moderate.

Novotel Milano Est Aeroporto – Near Linate Airport, this Fiat investment has 208 rooms and is one of the few to offer a swimming pool and garden, as well as a restaurant. Business facilities include meeting rooms for up to 320, English-speaking concierge, foreign currency exchange, secretarial services in English, audiovisual equipment, photocopiers, computers, cable television news, translation services, and express checkout. 12 Via Mecenate (phone: 580-11085; fax: 580-11086; telex: 331237NOVMIE). Moderate.

Novotel Milano Nord – Another newcomer, with 172 rooms, swimming pool, garden, restaurant, and bar. Business facilities include meeting rooms for up to 500, English-speaking concierge, foreign currency exchange, secretarial services in English, audiovisual equipment, photocopiers, computers, cable television news, translation services, and express checkout. 13 Viale Suzzani (phone: 661-01861; fax: 566-101961; telex: 331292). Moderate.

Manzoni – Small, pleasant and quiet, it's right in the city's center, and boasts a garage. No restaurant, but room service provides snacks. There's a shopping mall nearby. No credit cards accepted. 20 Via Santo Spirito (phone: 794045). Moderate to inexpensive.

Antica Locanda Solferino – Delightful tiny place, with only 11 rooms, in the old Brera quarter a few blocks north of *La Scala.* This once was a tavern and retains much of the Old World fin-de-siècle charm in its furniture and decor. No credit cards accepted. Book far in advance. 2 Via Castelfidardo (phone: 657-0129). Inexpensive.

Casa Svizzera – Near the Duomo, well maintained, and with air conditioning to boot. This 45-room place is a good value for the money and location. 3 Via San Raffaele (phone: 869-2246; fax: 349-8190). Inexpensive.

Centro – A small budget hotel in the heart of downtown Milan. 46 Via Broletto (phone: 875232; fax: 875578). Inexpensive.

EATING OUT: It is a time of special grace for dining out in Milan. Its restaurants today are among the world's finest. Milanese food, like much of northern fare, differs from other Italian food in that butter is used more often than olive oil. Look for special dishes made with the fabulous *tartufi bianchi* (Italian white truffles) from the neighboring Piedmont region, when they are in season between September and *Christmas.* Rice from the region's own plantations is used as a food base, with saffron-perfumed *risotto alla milanese* the favorite provender — best eaten with a steaming osso buco (veal shank). The Milanese also love fresh fish and know how to prepare it. In September, try delicious white peaches. Expect to pay $200 or more for dinner for two at one of Milan's expensive restaurants — among the most expensive in Italy; $80 to $130 at a moderately priced restaurant; and $50 to $75 at an inexpensive one. Prices don't include drinks, wine, or tips. It is a good idea to check whether the restaurant you select accepts credit cards. All telephone numbers are in the 2 city code unless otherwise indicated.

Antica Osteria del Ponte – At last, a real challenge to *Gualtiero Marchese,* 10 miles (16 km) outside Milan in an old-fashioned inn by a bridge along a picturesque *naviglio.* Here since 1976, it is one of only two restaurants in Italy (both, significantly, in Milan) to be awarded three Michelin stars. It's a family affair — Ezio Santin and his son Maurizio perform wonders in the kitchen and wife Renata is hostess in the intimate dining room with a fireplace and antique furnishings. Look for expert, creative ways with the classic risotto and ravioli — including one dish that has them stuffed with lobster and covered with a lobster sauce — and new and interesting ways of preparing fine fresh fish. Truffles in season make their appearance, and for lovers of sweets, a hot chocolate soufflé arrives blanketed in a white chocolate sauce. Closed *Christmas* to January 12 and August. Reservations necessary. Major credit cards accepted. 9 Piazza G. Negri, Cassinetta di Lugagnano (phone: 942-0034). Very expensive.

Gualtiero Marchesi – Owned by one of Italy's most eminent chefs (Michelin has given him three stars), this restaurant provides an elegant setting for an Italian nouvelle cuisine that many consider the best in Italy — though some critics fault the tiny portions and somewhat staid atmosphere. The open-face ravioli are a triumph, the risotto sublime, though the edible gold-leaf topping is a real case of gilding the lily. A single dish can be ordered as a sampler. Closed Sundays, Mondays for lunch, and August. Reservations necessary. Major credit cards accepted. 9 Via Bonvesin della Riva (phone: 741246). Very expensive.

El Toulà – One of Milan's finest dining places, created by the noted restaurateur Alfredo Beltrame and situated behind *La Scala.* The pasta specialty is *manicaretti,* but the chef, Daniel Droudaine is French; so is much of the menu. Closed Sundays; from June to August, closed Saturdays in winter. Reservations necessary. Major credit cards accepted. 6 Piazza Paolo Ferrari (phone: 870302). Very expensive.

Aimo and Nadia – A husband and wife team from Tuscany run this restaurant, one of Italy's top ten and renowned for its creative fare, in an unprepossessing area of Milan. *Ovoli* (mushrooms) and Alba truffles abound, but the real culinary triumph is the risotto with zucchini blossoms and truffles; the desserts are luscious. Closed Sundays and August. Reservations necessary. Major credit cards accepted. 6 Via Montecuccoli (phone: 416886). Expensive.

Biffi Scala – A favorite place for late-night suppers, particularly after the opera. The decor is extravagant, the fare Lombard and international. Closed Sundays, last 2 weeks in August, and *Christmas* week. Reservations necessary. Major credit cards accepted. Piazza della Scala (phone: 866651). Expensive.

Calajunco Milano – The Aeolian Islands inspire its fine Sicilian restaurant's menu, which includes zucchini blossom–stuffed ravioli with squid sauce and, for an antipasto, seashell "plates" brimming with linguini in a mixed shellfish sauce. The unique fish sausage also is worth trying. There is a fixed price sampler menu (*menù degustazione*). Closed Sundays and some holidays. Reservations necessary. Major credit cards accepted. 5 Via Stoppani (phone: 204-6003). Expensive.

Gallia's – Some of Milan's hotels provide fine dining, and here is one of the best. At the *Excelsior Gallia,* diners can savor traditional dishes, such as the delicious tournedos Rossini, in an elegant setting. Open daily. Reservations necessary. Major credit cards accepted. Piazza Duca d'Aosta (phone: 6785). Expensive.

Giannino – So famous that some people reserve 6 months in advance, this is a beloved bastion of traditional Italian fare, including homemade pasta and pastries. The fish also is excellent. Elegant private dining rooms can be provided. Closed Sundays and August. Reservations necessary. Major credit cards accepted. 8 Via Amatore Sciesa (phone: 545-2948). Expensive.

Saint Andrews – This elegant downtown dining place with dark paneled walls and plush upholstery is a favorite of Milanese executives. Romantic atmosphere and an imaginative menu. Closed Sundays and August. Reservations advised. Major credit cards accepted. 23 Via Sant'Andrea (phone: 793132). Expensive.

Savini – Everything here, from the service to the decor, including the crystal chandeliers and silk lampshades, is classic and exquisite. After a brief lapse, the restaurant is once again topnotch, with mostly Lombard fare (although there is a smattering of international dishes), excellent fresh fish, and fine wines. VIPs like the private rooms; Onassis and Callas dined together in the small, gilded downstairs room. Closed Sundays and August. Reservations necessary. Major credit cards accepted. 11 *Galleria Vittorio Emanuele* (phone: 805-8343). Expensive.

La Scaletta – The Italian *nuova cucina* at this outstanding, elegantly appointed 2-room restaurant is so popular among Milanese diners that reservations are essential. Closed Sundays, Mondays, *Christmas, New Year's,* and August. No credit cards accepted. 3 Piazza Stazione Porta Genova (phone: 581-00290). Expensive.

Alfio – It has a central location, an enclosed winter garden, and very good antipasti, risotto, and fish and meat dishes. Closed Saturdays, Sunday lunch, and August. Reservations advised. Major credit cards accepted. 31 Via Senato (phone: 780731). Expensive to moderate.

Da Alfredo Gran San Bernardo – Alfredo Valli serves some of the best regional cooking in town in this large and friendly place. Try the *risotto alla milanese,* the veal cutlet, or the classic Lombardy stew of pork, sausages, carrots, and white wine, *casseoeula,* served with cornbread, or polenta. Closed weekends and August. Reservations advised. Major credit cards accepted. 14 Via Borgese (phone: 331-9000). Expensive to moderate.

Boeucc – Artists dine next to financiers in this traditional downtown restaurant. In the local dialect, the name means "hole-in-the-wall," but the clientele, service, traditional menu (here's the place for the real Milanese, saffron-perfumed risotto), and vast wine list belie the name. Closed Saturdays. Reservations advised. Major credit cards accepted. 2 Piazza Belgioioso (phone: 790224). Expensive to moderate.

La Briciola – High-fashion models, journalists, and young Milanese-about-town enjoy the light touch of host Gianni Valveri's homemade pasta, salads, and fresh fish. Good value for the money. Closed Sundays and Monday afternoons. Reservations necessary. Major credit cards accepted. 25 Via Solferino (phone: 655-1012). Expensive to moderate.

Don Lisander – On summer evenings, downtown diners can enjoy the courtyard garden at this reliable old favorite. It offers a sampler menu of impeccably prepared traditional Italian dishes year-round. Closed Saturday evenings and Sundays. Reservations advised. Major credit cards accepted. 12/A Via Manzoni (phone: 790130). Expensive to moderate.

Gli Orti di Leonardo – In this smart, brick-vaulted eatery, fish hors d'oeuvres are served and followed by "little risotti," made with surprising ingredients. A rich choice of wines is available. Closed Sundays and most of August. Reservations advised. Major credit cards accepted. 6-8 Via Aristide de Togni (phone: 498-3476). Expensive to moderate.

Osteria del Binari – Elegant, with an impressive choice of traditional dishes from several Italian regions. The hot soup is topped with an incredibly light puff pastry. Closed Sundays and mid-August. Reservations advised. Major credit cards accepted. 1 Via Tortona (phone: 894-09428). Expensive to moderate.

Peck – Around the corner from the Duomo, this is an offshoot of the eponymous, elegant, food emporium. With its masterful blend of the classics and the creative, it is taking over the block, with an adjacent delicatessen (see *Shopping*), a pricey takeout, and separate counter service also worth trying. Closed the first 3 weeks of July and in early January. Reservations advised. Major credit cards accepted. 4 Via Victor Hugo (phone: 876774). Expensive to moderate.

Il Porto – The specialties at this family-run eatery are fresh fish and friendly service. Closed Sundays and August. Reservations necessary. Major credit cards accepted. Piazzale Cantore (phone: 832-1481). Expensive to moderate.

Stendhal – Named for the French author (who lived in the area), the menu offers Brera's finest dining. It's everything a fancy restaurant should be: intimate, candle-lit, beautiful. The French antiques are authentic; so is the cuisine — from fresh *porcini* mushrooms to delectable desserts. Closed Saturday lunch and Sundays. Reservations necessary. Major credit cards accepted. Via San Marco near Via Ancona (phone: 653917 or 655-5587). Expensive to moderate.

Torre del Mangia – The tennis pros and other movers and shakers like the healthy approach to food here, such as the fresh fish prepared by Tuscan chef Peppino. Try the *tagliolini allo scorfano,* stuffed pasta with fish sauce, and light fried zucchini. Closed Sunday evenings and Mondays. Reservations necessary. Major credit cards accepted. 27 Via Procaccini (phone: 314871). Expensive to moderate.

Bice – Years ago, Tuscan-bred Bice Mungai opened a tiny shop in which she served staples from home, such as *la ribollita* (vegetable soup made with purple cabbage). From such beginnings came an evolution into one of Milan's chicest restaurants, with branches in Paris and New York, and today's wide menu of both meat and fish specialties, including *risotto al pesce* (risotto with fish). In season, wild mushrooms, stuffed pheasant, and truffle toppings are also served. Closed Mondays, Tuesday lunch, and July 22 to August 30. Reservations advised. Major credit cards accepted. 23 Via Borgospesso (phone: 760-02572). Moderate.

La Brisa – In the heart of the city, though hidden away, with a garden and a first class kitchen. Popular with financiers and artists. Closed for lunch on weekends. Reservations advised. Major credit cards accepted. 15 Via Brisa (phone: 864-50521). Moderate.

Canovianio – Right in the Duomo's shadow, highly creative dishes are served in a stunning interior. Closed Saturday lunch and Sundays. Reservations advised. Major credit cards accepted. 6 Via Hoepli (phone: 864-60147). Moderate.

Cavallini – With a garden for summer dining, this cosmopolitan trattoria reflects decades of sober culinary industry. Fresh fish is served daily, and the *tortellini in brodo* (small stuffed pasta in broth) is outstanding. Closed Sundays, during mid-August, and some holidays. Reservations advised. Major credit cards accepted. 2 Via Mauro Macchi (phone: 669-3174). Moderate.

Le Colline Pisane – This lively Tuscan trattoria serves fine food in pleasant surroundings. Closed Sundays and August. Reservations advised. Major credit cards accepted. 5 Largo La Fobba (phone: 659-9136). Moderate.

Decio Carugati – The food critic and author Decio himself is the host here. His creative, adventurous culinary compositions and fine wines are widely admired. Closed Sundays. Reservations advised. Major credit cards accepted. 2 Via Corsica at the corner of Via Vigevano (phone: 832-3970). Moderate.

Al Garibaldi – An unpretentious eatery catering to Milan's young professional crowd. The kitchen dispenses topnotch inventive food with great professionalism. Closed Fridays, *Christmas,* and August. Reservations advised. Major credit cards accepted. 7 Viale Montegrappa (phone: 659-8006). Moderate.

Alle Langhe – A family-style, popular trattoria serving Piedmontese fare that makes visitors feel welcome. Closed Sundays. Reservations advised. Major credit cards accepted. 6 Corso Como (phone: 655-4279). Moderate.

Malatesta Il Punto – Quail eggs with truffles, eel pâté with pine nuts, and Chinese fondue for two are among the specialties of this popular restaurant, one of several in Milan offering a fixed price sampler menu (*menù degustazione*). Closed Sundays and part of August. Reservations advised. Major credit cards accepted. 29 Via Bianca di Savoia (phone: 546-1079). Moderate.

Al Materel – It's rustic Lombardy at its best, with old family recipes, homemade pasta, and wild game and wild mushrooms in season. Closed Tuesdays. Reservations advised. No credit cards accepted. Corner of Via Laura Solera Montegazza and Corso Garibaldi (phone: 654204). Moderate.

Osteria di Porta Cicca – In one of the oldest parts of the city, with only 11 tables, be prepared for truly innovative dining. Favorites are *tagliolini* with zucchini blossoms and chunks of salmon, and poppy-seed-coated salmon steaks served with a whipped horseradish cream. Closed Sundays and alternate Mondays when the restaurant offers cooking classes, January 1 to 10, and August. Reservations advised. Major credit cards accepted. 51 Ripa di Porta Ticinese (phone: 581-04451). Moderate.

Osteria del Vecchio Canneto – It's definitely the place to try wonderful seafood and fine wines from Abruzzi. There is only a prix fixe menu. Closed Sundays and

August. Reservations advised. Major credit cards accepted. 56 Via Solferino, but the entrance is around the corner on Via del Porto Nuovo (phone: 659-8498). Moderate.

La Pantera – Near Milan University, this Tuscan-style restaurant is run with loving care by Tina Lucchesi and her family. The *involtini* (stuffed veal slices), *farro* (a staple grain eaten by the ancient Romans), chick-peas in olive oil, and *la ribollita* (hearty vegetable soup) are among the specialties. Closed Tuesdays. Reservations advised. Major credit cards accepted. 12 Via Festa del Perdono (phone: 583-307408). Moderate.

Paper Moon – The city's first high-style pizzeria, where the show business, fashion business, and business business crowds rub elbows. Very trendy, and the people watching makes up for the slow service. Closed Sundays, 3 weeks in August, and 2 weeks around *Christmas.* Reservations advised. No credit cards accepted. 1 Via Bagutta (phone: 760-222297). Moderate.

Al Piccolo Teatro – Milan insiders enjoy this casual, traditional, and reliable trattoria, which they describe as simpatico (congenial). Especially good for lunch. Closed Sundays. Reservations advised. Major credit cards accepted. 8 Viale Pasubio (phone: 657-5648). Moderate.

Prospero – Though this eatery has been around since 1900, its dining room now is sleek and modern. The *ravioloni* with eggplant, bacon, and *porcini* mushrooms or the *risotto saltato* are great starters for lunch or dinnner. Closed Sundays. Reservations advised. Major credit cards accepted. 20 Via Chiosetto (phone: 551-87646). Moderate.

Quattro Mori – Near the Sforza Castle, this elegant, family-run eatery serves traditional Milanese food. It has a garden. Closed Saturday lunch, Sundays, and August. Reservations advised. Major credit cards accepted. 2 Via San Giovanni sul Muro (phone: 870617). Moderate.

Ribot – Set in a splendid garden, here's where the horsey set comes before the races at nearby *Ippodromo San Siro;* pictures of horses adorn the dark, paneled walls. In season, the spaghetti comes with the prized wild mushrooms, *ovoli.* Steaks are a specialty, and the chef makes his own cookies. Closed Mondays and most of August. Reservations necessary. Major credit cards accepted. 41 Via Cremosano (phone: 330-01646). Moderate.

Rigolo – A large, friendly place that's a favorite of local journalists and businesspeople, it serves Tuscan specialties (such as thick, grilled steaks) and a superb selection of homemade desserts. Closed Mondays and August. Reservations advised. Major credit cards accepted. 11 Via Solferino (phone: 864-63220). Moderate.

Il Sole – A favorite with Milanese, thanks to its relaxed atmosphere and air conditioning. Try the ricotta-based *gnocchetti* (little dumplings) in herb butter and homemade *tagliatelle* in a yellow bell pepper cream sauce. Dinner only. Closed Mondays. Reservations advised. Major credit cards accepted. 5 Via Curtatone (phone: 551-88500). Moderate.

Solferino – Milanese tradition holds sway in this pleasant eatery in La Brera, the artists' quarter. The potato soup with wild mushrooms is intriguing. Also try the house specialty, *risotto alla milanese* (rice doused in saffron), and the real thing when it comes to the Milanese cutlet. Closed Saturday lunch, Sundays, and the last 2 weeks in August. Reservations advised. Major credit cards accepted. 2 Via Castelfidardo (phone: 659-9886). Moderate.

Torre di Pisa – Everybody dines here, jamming into five rooms to enjoy host Romano's trendy fare of Tuscan specialties. Closed Saturday lunch, Sundays, and the first 3 weeks of August. Reservations necessary. Major credit cards accepted. 26 Via Mercato (phone: 874877). Moderate.

L'Ulmet – Milanese adore this place for its successful combination of traditional and creative Italian fare. Built on ancient Roman foundations, its roof incorporates a 1,600-year-old plinth. Wild game is served in season. For dessert, try the crêpes with honey and pine nuts. Closed Sundays and Mondays for lunch. Reservations advised. Major credit cards accepted. At the corner of Via Disciplini and Via Olmetto (phone: 805-9260). Moderate.

Il Verdi – *The* place for lunch these days. The menu offers a choice of 24 salads, ranging from the seafaring *innamorata* with trout, octopus, and potatoes to a mango, corn, and bamboo-based *orientale.* There is a full regular menu as well, and the restaurant also is open for dinner. Closed Saturday lunch and Sundays. No reservations. No credit cards accepted. 5 Piazza Mirabello (phone: 651412). Moderate.

La Vittoria – Opened in 1905, this friendly *ristorante* has kept pace with the times. It offers an ever-changing menu, and the selection of olive oils makes salad dressings an adventure. Closed Saturday lunch and Sundays. Reservations advised. Major credit cards accepted. 6 Via Anfiteatro (phone: 860726). Moderate.

Il Brigadino – The menu includes a variety of creative dishes, including fruit-based risottos. A prix fixe lunch makes this a popular spot with fashion models and photographers. Closed Sundays. Reservations unnecessary. No credit cards accepted. 14 Via Savona (phone: 835-4812). Moderate to inexpensive.

Giardino – Near the banks of the Naviglio River, this restaurant in the 19th-century courtyard spreads out under surrounding trees in summer and is enlivened by passing musicians. The food is simple but delicious and the atmosphere is reminiscent of a 19th-century Milanese tavern or *osteria.* Closed Tuesdays. Reservations unnecessary. No credit cards accepted. 36 Alzaia Naviglio Grande (phone: 894-09321). Moderate to inexpensive.

El Pouliereu – Summer diners delight in the century-old trees in the garden here, and in winter guests savor the mixed boiled meats. Fish, game, and other hearty, well-prepared dishes also are served. Closed Wednesdays and in mid-August. Reservations unnecessary. No credit cards accepted. 337 Via Rapiamonti (phone: 569-0954). Moderate to inexpensive.

San Fermo – The main lure is a wide selection of fixed price lunches, as well as its signature *insalatone.* Closed Sundays and Monday lunch from September through mid-June; Saturday nights and Sundays from mid-June through August. Reservations advised. Major credit cards accepted. 1 Via San Fermo della Battaglia (phone: 655-1784). Moderate to inexpensive.

La Topaia – Run by a multi-ethnic couple, the menu includes specialties from the Liguria region (near Genoa), Yugoslavia, and the French countryside. This spot is a summertime favorite. Dinner only. Closed Sundays. Reservations advised. Major credit cards accepted. 46 Via Argelati (phone: 837-3469). Inexpensive.

Along with its fine restaurants, Milan now boasts some of Italy's best *paninerie* (sandwich shops), which offer a variety of hot and cold sandwiches of sometimes unusual combinations. Try *Bar Magenta* (13 Via Carducci; phone: 805-3808) or *Paninomania* (Corso Porta Romana; phone: 576827). Most frequented by local office and fashion industry workers are the tiny coffee bars inside some of downtown Milan's charming courtyards. They also offer inexpensive, pleasant lunches — a plate of pasta, a cooked vegetable, and a glass of wine. Try the *Montanelli American Bar* (inside the courtyard by *Buccellati* at 12 Via Montenapoleone).

For Milan's best coffee, visit *Marches* (Via Meravighi); customers must stand at the bar, but they linger over hand-dipped chocolates and the Milanese *Christmas* specialty, the *panettone* (fruitcake). For tea and chocolates, the *Sant'Ambroeus* (7 Corso Matteotti) is the place to go — big, old-fashioned, and charming, with immense Venetian chandeliers and matrons in furs. The 164-year-old *Cova* (near

La Scala at 8 Via Montenapoleone) similarly has pink damask tablecloths and waiters in black tie; try the hand-dipped *kikingerli*-filled (sour cherry) chocolates, and take home some candied violets. *Babington's* (8 Via Sant'Andrea), a sister to the English tearoom in Rome, has just opened. Conveniently located in the shopping district, it's off a courtyard and has Victorian decor. At the *Café Radetzky* (105 Corso Garibaldi), a 15-minute walk from downtown, the atmosphere of Milan 150 years ago when the Austrians ruled has been lovingly re-created in a coffee shop with style. *Note:* After a full day of gallery-hopping or nonstop shopping, unwind at *Cucchi* (closed Mondays; 1 Corso Genova), and sip a Bellini (fresh peach juice and champagne) outdoors in summer, or in winter nurse a Negroni (red vermouth and gin) surrounded by pink velvet and chandeliers. Should you want to start your day with a fresh-from-the-oven brioche, stop by at 7:45 AM.

NAPLES

Naples, Gothic and baroque under an azure sky, intellectual capital of the Mezzogiorno, and Italy's third-most populated city, with nearly 1.7 million inhabitants, has often been described as one of the world's most beautiful seaports. Indeed, the magnificent Bay of Naples has long been lauded by its many illustrious visitors for its gently curving shoreline and palm-lined seaside avenues, its mild climate, sunny beaches, and romantic islands.

But Naples has always had a darker side. The brooding Mt. Vesuvius, "its terror and its pride," ever hovering over the city, buried neighboring Pompeii and Herculaneum when it erupted in AD 79. And the eerie Campi Flegrei (Phlegrean Fields), a steaming volcanic area just to the north, whose violent beauty inspired both Homer and Virgil, was regarded by the ancients as the entrance to the underworld. More recently, the earthquake that devastated southern Italy in November 1980 took a tragic toll in Naples, adding yet another major problem to the city's permanent ills of unemployment, crime, and disease.

For some visitors today, Naples is a disappointment. The old quarter is among the most densely populated areas in the world; infant mortality and unemployment rates here are among the highest in Italy — almost a fifth of the city's labor force is unemployed, and another estimated 40,000 persons derive their livelihood from smuggling. When a cholera outbreak in 1973 revealed that Naples had no sewers and was living on a beautiful but poisoned bay, "See Naples and die," once a popular saying beckoning visitors to the seductive charms of the city, suddenly acquired a morbid and foreboding significance.

But the poor of Naples continue to survive with a surprising stoicism, and the people themselves are one of the city's attractions, laughing off their many problems, helping each other with an extraordinary sense of warmth and humanity — they are a people incapable of hatred, of any kind of discrimination, yet strongly emotional, sensitive, full of fantasy. Just remember the best movies of the postwar school of Italian neo-realism, directed by Roberto Rossellini, Vittorio De Sica, and Francesco Rosi, or the theatrical masterpieces of the famed Eduardo De Filippo, the voluptuous figure of Sophia Loren representing the Neapolitan woman — madonna, mother, and *puttana* (whore) all in one.

Watch them live: Naples is like a theater of life. Stroll along Via Caracciolo and see the fishermen pulling in their nets, oblivious to the traffic behind them; buy lemons and oranges or sulfur water from men and women who transact their business across 17th-century marble tabletops; give in to the importuning of pizza vendors hawking their wares; or, when the jostling of the small, crowded streets becomes too much to bear, retire to a table in the elegant *Galleria Umberto I* or to the old *Caffè Gambrinus* on Via Chiaia and watch well-dressed Neapolitans socialize over an afternoon coffee or *aperitivo.*

Naples also is famous for its music, its festivals, its colorful arts. Neapolitan popular songs are, short of operatic arias, the best-known tunes to have come out of Italy; anyone who can strum a guitar or a mandolin knows at least one, and nearly everyone can sing along, at least the refrain. In the 17th and 18th centuries, the works of a Neapolitan school of composers — Alessandro Scarlatti was its leader — were just as well known; Pergolesi, Paisiello, and Cimarosa drew capacity crowds. The city's opera house, *Teatro San Carlo,* built in 1737, remains one of the world's finest. A Neapolitan school of painting, characterized by realism and warm colors, flourished in the 18th and 19th centuries. In the 18th century, too, the famous Capodimonte porcelain factory was turning out highly elaborate pieces for members of the royal court, while less exalted folk artists were raising the making of nativity scenes, or *Christmas* cribs, into an art. The shepherds and angels of many an *ignoto Napoletano* (unknown Neapolitan) live on in museums, and at *Christmastime,* an entire street — Via San Gregorio Armeno — is taken over by artisans selling their hand-crafted *presepi* or crèche scenes.

The city that was to spawn so much natural talent was founded as a Greek colony, probably in the 7th century BC, and was first called Parthenope, later Neapolis. Little remains of its earliest period. Then, along with the rest of the Italian peninsula, it became part of the great Roman Empire, and its intensely green countryside and sunny shores were soon studded with palatial villas of wealthy Romans who chose to spend the winters in Naples's milder climate.

But the tranquillity of the Roman period came to an end with the fall of the empire, and Naples sank into the abyss of the Dark Ages, as did all of Italy. The city came into its own again under the French rulers of the House of Anjou, who made it the capital of their Angevin kingdom of southern Italy in the 13th century and continued its progress under the Catalonian rulers of the House of Aragón, who took over in 1442. Then, in 1503, Naples (with Sicily) became a part of Spain, ruled for more than 2 centuries by Spanish viceroys who exploited the Italian provinces for the benefit of the Spanish treasury; so heavily taxed were the commoners (nobles and clergy were exempt) that in 1647 they rose up, led by Masaniello, but the revolution was crushed. After a short period under Austrian rule, it was the turn of the Bourbons, who arrived in 1734 and established the Kingdom of the Two Sicilies, with Naples as the capital. Its ancient dignity restored, Naples became one of Europe's major cities, attracting leaders in art, music, and literature until the unification of Italy in 1860. Economic and political problems gradually diminished its prestige, however, and damage from World War II dealt a severe blow to an already sick economy.

Today, thanks to a busy port, Naples is an important industrial and commercial center. It is a city both wise and violent, religious and pagan, magical and dirty, old and new. It attracts thieves, tourists, artists, and lovers of beauty with a contagious gaiety and exuberant, if chaotic, vitality. Its wealth of historical monuments; proximity to the Amalfi Coast, Capri, and the archaeological treasures of Pompeii and Herculaneum; and the magnificent — if somewhat tarnished — splendors of the romantic Bay of Naples, make it one of the world's great cities and a perennial tourist attraction.

NAPLES AT-A-GLANCE

SEEING THE CITY: Panoramic views of Naples and the bay are at every turn. Within the city, the outstanding view is from Room 25 of the *Certosa di San Martino* (Carthusian Monastery of St. Martin), now a museum. Depending on the weather and the visibility, however, the most spectacular view is from Mt. Vesuvius, some 15 miles (24 km) southeast of Naples. For more information on both these vantage points, see *Special Places,* below.

SPECIAL PLACES: To make sightseeing easier, think of Naples as divided into the following sections: In the area roughly between Piazza Municipio and Piazza del Plebiscito, there are monumental buildings and relatively wide-open spaces. The old quarter is near narrow Spacca-Napoli Street (the classic photos of streets strung with washing are taken here) and the historic center is to the northeast. Farther inland is Naples on the hills, the Vomero being the principal hill and an elegant residential district. To the west of the Piazza del Plebiscito area is Naples by the bay. Where the workaday port ends, a lovely promenade begins along the shore before the port of Santa Lucia and extends as far as another port area, Mergellina. Museums in Naples are open 9 AM to 2 PM Tuesdays through Saturdays, and 9 AM to 1 PM Sundays and holidays, unless otherwise noted.

DOWNTOWN

Castel Nuovo (New Castle) – This landmark on the Neapolitan waterfront, more often called the Castel Angioino (Angevin Castle) or Maschio Angioino, was built in the late 13th century by Charles I of Anjou, who modeled it on the castle at Angers. In the mid-15th century, Alphonse I of Aragón made substantial alterations. The triumphal arch sandwiched between two towers at the entry celebrates his entrance into Naples in 1443 and is an early example of Renaissance art in Naples. Inside the courtyard, the doorway to the Chapel of St. Barbara (or the Palatine Chapel), the only part of the castle remaining from Angevin times, is noteworthy, but the castle proper is not open to visitors. Piazza Municipio.

Palazzo Reale (Royal Palace) – Built in the early 17th century by Domenico Fontana for the Spanish viceroys, later enlarged and restored, this became the home of the Bourbon Kings of Naples and was then inhabited from time to time by the Kings of Italy. The niches on the façade contain statues of eight famous kings of the various dynasties that ruled Naples, including Charles I of Anjou, Alphonse I of Aragón, and Victor Emmanuel II of Italy. The palace is now a museum whose rooms contain original Bourbon furnishings, paintings, statues, and porcelain. Closed Mondays; in August and September, the museum stays open weekdays until 7:30 PM. Admission charge. Piazza del Plebiscito (phone: 413888).

Piazza del Plebiscito – This vast semicircle cut off on one side by the Palazzo Reale is the center of public life in Naples. Directly opposite the palace is the Church of San Francesco di Paola, a copy of the Pantheon in Rome, built by order of Ferdinand I of Bourbon in the late 18th century. Equestrian statues in the center of the square are of Ferdinand (by Canova) and Charles III of Bourbon.

Teatro San Carlo – Italy's second-most famous opera house is just off Piazza del Plebiscito and 40 years older than *La Scala.* Built under Charles of Bourbon in 1737 and inaugurated on the feast day of St. Charles Borromeo (whence its name), it was destroyed by fire in 1816 and thoroughly rebuilt in neo classic style within 6 months, with Ionic columns, niches, and bas-reliefs on the outside and a fresco of Apollo and the Muses on the ceiling of the sumptuous auditorium — which seats 3,000 and has perfect acoustics. *San Carlo* audiences were the first ever to hear Bellini's *La Sonnambula,* Donizetti's *Lucia di Lammermoor,* and many other great works. Those not attending a performance can tour the theater in the morning, by prior arrangement. Closed Mondays. Via San Carlo (phone: 797-2111).

Galleria Umberto I – Across the street from *San Carlo,* this is the perfect place to sit down for a *caffè* or an ice cream. The Victorian arcade of glass and steel, topped with a cupola, was built from 1887 to 1890, and is younger than the one in Milan.

Chiesa di Sant'Anna dei Lombardi (Church of St. Anne of the Lombards) – This church was built in the 15th century and rebuilt in the 17th century. It is best known for its Renaissance sculptures, particularly for the eight life-size terra cotta figures of the *Pietà* (1492) by Guido Mazzoni — extremely realistic and rather eerie when seen from the main part of the church (it's in a chapel to the right at the far end). Via Monteoliveto.

Chiesa di Santa Chiara (Church of St. Clare) – The Church of the Poor Clares was built by order of Sancia of Majorca, wife of Robert I of Anjou, in the early 14th century. From the beginning, it was the church of the Neapolitan nobility. By the 18th century, it was covered with baroque decoration, but following serious damage in World War II, it has been rebuilt in its original Provençal-Gothic style. Be sure to see the 14th-century tomb of Robert of Anjou behind the altar and then go out to see the adjoining Chiostro delle Clarisse (Cloister of the Poor Clares). This unique 18th-century cloister is a lovely bower of greenery and flowers studded with columns and lined with seats entirely covered with majolica tiles — a colorful, welcome surprise. Via Benedetto Croce.

Chiesa del Gesù Nuovo – Just across the square from Santa Chiara on land surrounding the Palazzo Sanseverino. The interior of this late-16th-century church is full of baroque marblework and painting. The unusual façade originally was built in the 15th century for the palace. Piazza del Gesù Nuovo.

Chiesa di San Lorenzo Maggiore (Church of St. Lawrence Major) – One of the most important medieval churches in Naples, it was begun in the late 13th century by French architects, who did the polygonal Gothic apse, and was finished in the next century by local architects. Boccaccio fell in love with Fiammetta in this church in 1334 and Petrarch, who was living in the adjoining monastery, came here to pray during a terrible storm in 1345. Excavations at this site in 1990 uncovered some Greek and Roman ruins. Piazza San Gaetano.

Duomo (Cathedral) – The cathedral of Naples is dedicated to the city's patron saint, San Gennaro. It was built by the Angevins (in the late 13th and early 14th centuries) on the site of a previous basilica dedicated to Santa Stefania, which in its turn had been built on the foundations of a Roman temple dedicated to Apollo. It also incorporates a smaller basilica dating from the 5th century and dedicated to Santa Restituta. Rebuilt several times, the Duomo's 19th-century façade still sports 15th-century doorways. It contains the famous Chapel of San Gennaro (third chapel on the right), a triumph of 17th-century baroque art built in fulfillment of a vow made by Neapolitans for the passing of a plague. (The Latin inscription notes that the chapel is consecrated to the saint for his having saved the city not only from plague but also from hunger, war, and the fires of Vesuvius, by virtue of his miraculous blood.) Two vials of San Gennaro's dried blood are stored in a reliquary in the chapel, and twice a year, in May and September, all of Naples — or as many people as the church and the street in front can hold — gather to await the miracle of the liquefaction of the blood (see *Special Events*). If the miracle happens, all is well with the city. Via del Duomo.

Museo Archeologico Nazionale (National Archaeological Museum) – One of the most important museums in the world dedicated to Greco-Roman antiquity.

Among its precious artworks are sculptures collected by Pope Paul III of the Farnese family during 16th-century excavations of the ruins of Rome, including two huge statues found at the Baths of Caracalla: the *Farnese Hercules,* a Greek copy of a bronze original by Lysippus, and the *Farnese Bull,* a Roman copy of a Hellenistic bronze, carved from a single block of marble. The museum also is the repository of art and artifacts removed from Pompeii and Herculaneum since the 18th century. Most impressive of these are the exquisite mosaics from Pompeii and the bronzes from the Villa dei Papiri at Herculaneum, especially the water carriers (or dancers) and the two athletes. Other items removed from Pompeii and Herculaneum include silverware and glassware, combs, mirrors, and other toiletry articles, some furniture, and foodstuffs, such as carbonized bread, olives, grapes, onions, figs, and dates. Two other important collections to see in this 16th-century palace — which was first a barracks and then the seat of the university until the Bourbon King of Naples turned it into a museum in 1777 — are the Santangelo collection of ancient coins and the Borgia collection of Egyptian and Etruscan art. Closed Mondays. Admission charge. Piazza Museo (phone: 440166).

Catacombe di San Gennaro (Catacombs of St. Januarius) – The remains of San Gennaro lay in these catacombs from the 5th to the 9th century. On two levels, they date from the 2nd century and probably began as the tomb of a noble family that was later donated to the Christian community as a burial place. They are important for their early Christian wall paintings. Guided visits (most are in Italian, but some English-speaking guides are available) take place on Friday, Saturday, and Sunday mornings at 9:30, 10:15, 11:00, and 11:45. Admission charge. Off Via di Capodimonte, past the Church of the Madre del Buon Consiglio (no phone).

Museo e Gallerie Nazionali di Capodimonte (Capodimonte Museum and Picture Gallery) – One of Italy's best collections of paintings from the 14th through the 16th century is displayed in the grandiose 18th-century palace of a former royal estate on the hills in the northeastern part of the city. A Simone Martini panel (1317) of Robert of Anjou being crowned King of Naples is one of the museum's treasures; other masters represented are Bellini, Masaccio, Botticelli, Correggio, and Titian, among whose portraits of the Farnese family is a well-known one of Pope Paul III. The royal apartments on the first floor include a marvelous parlor, the Salottino di Maria Amalia, completely built and decorated in Capodimonte ceramics (some of which were shattered in the 1980 earthquake). In the park surrounding the palace a wedding party is often having pictures taken — it's one of the Neapolitans' favorite backgrounds. Open Tuesdays through Saturdays from 9 AM to 7:30 PM, June through September; 9 AM to 2 PM the rest of the year; and Sundays from 9 AM to 1 PM year-round. Admission charge. Parco di Capodimonte (phone: 741-0881).

Certosa di San Martino (Carthusian Monastery and National Museum of St. Martin) – Now a museum, this enormous monastery founded by the Angevin dynasty is beautifully situated on the Vomero Hill, next to an Angevin fortress, the Castel Sant'Elmo. The monastery was renovated in the 16th and 17th centuries (in the latter period by Cosimo Fanzago), so it is today a monument to the baroque. The church immediately to the left as you enter is lavishly done in baroque inlay of variously colored marbles and stones (see, too, the rooms behind the altar, including the one to the left with the intricate inlay of wood). In the museum, the marvelous view from the belvedere of room 25 is said to have inspired the saying "See Naples and die." The museum contains a collection of 19th-century Neapolitan painting, a naval section, a collection of memorabilia from the kingdom of Naples, and some striking 18th- and 19th-century *presepi,* or nativity scenes. The most famous is the Presepe Cuciniello, a room-size installation with countless figures and particularly graceful angels. Another *presepe* fits in an eggshell. Closed Mondays; in August and September it remains open until 8 PM Tuesdays, Thursdays, and Saturdays. Admission charge. Via Tito Angelini (phone: 578-1769).

Porto di Santa Lucia e il Lungomare (Santa Lucia Port and the Waterfront) – One of the best-known Neapolitan songs has immortalized this tiny port abob with picturesque fishing and pleasure boats. It is formed by a jetty that leads out from the mainland to a small island entirely occupied by the Borgo Marinaro, a so-called fishing village now populated largely with restaurants, and the Castel dell'Ovo (Egg Castle, not to be confused with the Castel Nuovo, described above). The fortress dates from the 12th century, but monks lived here even earlier, and in Roman times a patrician villa occupied the site. Santa Lucia is the focal point of seaside Naples: Via Nazario Sauro approaches it from the east; Via Partenope passes in front of it; and Via Caracciolo leads away from it to the west. The three together constitute Naples's *lungomare,* a broad promenade along the water that is *the* place in Naples to take the early evening *passeggiata* (stroll) and watch the sun go down. For at least a half mile of its length, Via Caracciolo is backed by the greenery of the Villa Comunale, or public park, which is stuffed with life — young lovers hugging, kids playing ball, grandparents taking the air with the grandchildren, fathers renting miniature cars for mere toddlers who are learning to become Neapolitan drivers. Ice cream is consumed by all.

ENVIRONS

Campi Flegrei (Phlegrean Fields) – Hot springs and sulfurous gases rise from this dark, violent volcanic area that extends west of Naples from Capo Posillipo to Capo Miseno, along the Gulf of Pozzuoli. Its name comes from the Greek, meaning "burning," and it is an area as rich in archaeological remains as in geophysical phenomena. The remains of the Greek colony of Cuma, founded in the 8th century BC (the oldest archaeological site in Italy), are about 12 miles (19 km) west of Naples (closed Mondays; admission charge), as are remains of Roman baths at Baia (closed Mondays; admission charge). In Sophia Loren's hometown, Pozzuoli (8 miles/13 km west), the third-largest amphitheater in Italy, built when the town was a major port in Roman times, can be visited (closed Mondays; admission charge). Also in Pozzuoli is a Roman temple, partially submerged in water, that reveals the effects of bradyseism, or "slow earthquake," to which the whole area is subject; less or more of the pillars is visible as the earth rises and falls. Lakes — such as Lago d'Averno (said to have been the entrance to the underworld) and Lago Miseno — have formed in the craters of extinct volcanoes in the Campi Flegrei, but the Solfatara crater just north of Pozzuoli is merely dormant (its last eruption was in the 12th century). Full of steaming fumaroles and containing the remains of a Roman spa, it is open daily (admission charge). Pozzuoli is the last stop of the *metropolitana* from Piazza Garibaldi in Naples; Baia and Cuma are stops of the Ferrovia Cumana suburban train line leaving from Piazza Montesanto.

Vesuvio (Mount Vesuvius) – This still-active volcano about 15 miles (24 km) southeast of Naples last erupted in 1944 and has averaged one eruption every 35 years over the past 300. Its most famous eruption was the one that buried Pompeii and Herculaneum in AD 79 (see *Campania and the Amalfi Coast* in DIRECTIONS). That explosion came from Monte Somma, 3,713 feet high, one of the volcano's two present summits; some 200 years later, another summit, Monte Nuovo, 4,189 feet high, formed, and this is the one that now is called Mount Vesuvius. There is no longer a chair lift to the top of Monte Nuovo, but the ascent still can be made on foot along the path that follows the edge of the crater, from which there are views down into the enormous cavity or out toward the sea and the surrounding towns. All that is visible of Vesuvius's cataclysmic power, however, are the vapors rising from fumaroles, and the guide occasionally descends a bit into the crater for a better look at these vents. Take the Naples-Salerno autostrada to Ercolano. From there it is an 8-mile (13-km) drive with spectacular views. To reach Vesuvius by public transportation, take the *Circumvesuviana* railway (*Napoli–Barra–Torre del Greco–Torre Annunziata* line) from Stazione Circumvesuviana on Corso Garibaldi (it is reached by means of the down escalator from the main train station in Naples). Get off at Herculaneum (Ercolano) or Pugliano, then take a bus to the *stazione inferiore,* where an English-speaking guide may be hired. Be prepared for a long, steep climb; take comfortable shoes. Don't bother going on an overcast day.

■ **EXTRA SPECIAL:** No stay in Naples is complete without a sunny drive up the famed promontory of Posillipo, a few miles southwest of the center, perhaps culminating in an alfresco lunch at Marechiaro (a most picturesque fishing village built high above the sea), which overlooks the southern end of the Bay of Naples. The road from Mergellina climbs past villas and fragrant gardens, becoming Via Nuova di Posillipo, which was begun by order of Murat, King of Naples, and completed in 1830. Don't miss the view of Cape Posillipo (from Via Ferdinando Russo just past Piazza Salvatore di Giacomo) before continuing up Via Nuova di Posillipo, which ends at Marechiaro. It was made famous by a song of the same name written by Salvatore di Giacomo, the first line of which is inscribed in the wall of an old house overlooking the water, marking the window celebrated in the song. On the way back, take Via Nuova di Posilippo, turn right onto Via Giovanni Boccaccio, and stop at the Parco della Rimembranza for spectacular views of the Bay of Naples on one side and the Bay of Pozzuoli on the other.

SOURCES AND RESOURCES

TOURIST INFORMATION: For general information, brochures, and maps of Naples and its environs, contact the Ente Provinciale per il Turismo (EPT; 58 Piazza dei Martiri, Scala B/Staircase B; phone: 405311); branches or booths are at the Stazione Centrale, the Stazione di Mergellina, and at the Aeroporto di Capodichino. The Azienda Autonoma di Turismo di Napoli (AAST), or local tourist office, is based in the Palazzo Reale (Piazza del Plebiscito; phone: 418744), but it has branches, including one at Piazza del Gesù Nuovo, one at the Castel dell'Ovo (phone: 552-3328), and one at the hydrofoil terminal in Mergellina (phone: 761-4585). The *Associazione Alberghi per la Gioventù* (Association of Youth Hostels) is at 40 Piazza Carità (phone: 551-3151).

The US Consulate is at Piazza della Repubblica (phone: 761-4303).

Local Coverage – Among its other brochures, the AAST puts out an interesting one entitled *Naples — The Old City: A Stratified Multiple Itinerary Map* that traces four itineraries through the historic center (roughly the area between Piazza del Gesù Nuovo and the Duomo), each route corresponding to a period in Neapolitan art: medieval, Renaissance, baroque, and rococo. The office also publishes a useful booklet, *Qui Napoli,* which is distributed monthly to the better hotels. Listings are in Italian and English. Another good monthly guide is *Napoli Top,* available in bars, hotels and at newsstands. The Neapolitans' daily newspaper is *Il Mattino.*

TELEPHONE: The city code for Naples is 81. When calling from within Italy, dial 081 before the local number.

GETTING AROUND: Many of the major sights are easily accessible by foot. For others, such as the Parco di Capodimonte and sights on the Vomero, alternate means of transportation are desirable. Do everything you can to avoid driving in the city: Neapolitan traffic jams belong in the *Guinness Book*

of World Records. If you do drive, *never* leave anything in your car, even for the shortest period of time. Neapolitan car thieves are among the most resourceful in the world and can open and empty a car trunk in a matter of seconds.

Airport – Capodichino Airport serves mostly domestic and some international flights. A taxi ride from downtown takes anywhere from 15 to 45 minutes, depending on the traffic, and costs about $27; from the airport to downtown, the fare is double the meter. Night and holiday rides cost extra, as does baggage; ask to see the *tabella* (fare table). There is no special airport bus, but bus No. 14 from the main train station, Stazione Centrale, stops at the airport. The trip takes 30 minutes to an hour depending on traffic. Tickets cost about 75¢ and must be purchased in advance at a tobacco shop or newsstand.

Boats – Ferries and hydrofoils for Capri, Ischia, and Procida leave from the Molo Beverello, in front of Piazza Municipio and the Castel Nuovo, or from Mergellina's Porto Sannazaro. In summer, hydrofoils also depart from Mergellina to Sorrento, Positano, Amalfi, the islands of Ponza and Ventotene, Sicily, and the Lipari Islands. Sailing times are listed in *Il Mattino* and at tourist offices.

Bus and Tram – Main routes and schedules are listed in the supplement to the telephone directory, *Tutto Città.* Tickets cost 800 lire (about 65¢) and must be bought in advance at a tobacco shop or newsstand.

Car Rental – Major international firms are on Via Partenope: *Avis* (32 Via Partenope; phone: 764-5600); *Eurodollar* (14 Via Partenope; phone: 764-6364 or 764-5464); *Europcar* (38 Via Partenope; phone: 401454); *Hertz* (29 Via Partenope; phone: 764-5533, and 69 Piazza Garibaldi; phone: 206228); and *Maggiore* (92 Via Cervantes; phone: 522-1900, and the railway station). In addition, most of these companies have branches elsewhere in the city, including the railway station at Piazza Garibaldi and Capodichino Airport. Only a few gas stations are open at night. Check with your hotel or see the listings in *Qui Napoli* or *Napoli Top.*

Funicular – Four funicular lines connect lower-lying parts of Naples to neighborhoods on the hills. Of the three that go to the Vomero, the *Funicolare Centrale,* from Via Toledo to Piazza Fuga, and the *Funicolare di Montesanto,* from Piazza Montesanto to Via Morghen, are useful for visiting the Certosa di San Martino. The fourth funicular connects the Mergellina area to the Posillipo area.

Subway – The *metropolitana* runs from Napoli Gianturco to Pozzuoli Solfatara, making useful stops at the Stazione Centrale, Piazza Cavour (near the *National Archaeological Museum*), Piazza Montesanto and Piazza Amedeo (near funiculars), Mergellina, Campi Flegrei, and elsewhere en route.

Taxi – Taxis can be hailed while they cruise or may be picked up at any cabstand. For a radio-dispatched taxi call 556-4444 or 556-0202. Do not use unmetered taxis.

Train – Naples's main train station is Stazione Centrale (Piazza Garibaldi; phone: 553-4188). Trains to Herculaneum, Pompeii, and Sorrento, operated by the suburban railway, *Ferrovia Circemvesuviana,* leave from the nearby Stazione Circumvesuviana (Corso Garibaldi; phone: 779-2444), and can be reached by the down escalator from Stazione Centrale. Trains to Campi Flegrei points, operated by *Ferrovia Cumana,* another suburban railway, leave from Piazza Montesanto (phone: 551-3328).

LOCAL SERVICES: Dentist (English-Speaking) – Dr. Antonio Siciliano (156 Via Toledo; phone: 552-2264); *Oral Rehabilitation Center* (141 Via Manzoni; phone: 640971 or 640932).

Dry Cleaner – *Lavanderia Sanmarco,* 41 Via Santa Lucia (phone: 421396).

Limousine Service – *Garage Dubbio* (6 Via Petronio; phone: 407138); *Autonoleggio Spigno* (13 Via Carrozzieri Alla Posta; phone: 552-4337).

Medical Emergency – *Policlinico, Facolta di Medicina e Chirurgia* (5 Via Sergio

Pansini; phone: 746-1111). One English-speaking doctor in private practice is Dr. Vincenzo D'Antonio (5-8 Vico Satriano; phone: 414452); 24-hour ambulance service (phone: 752-0696); 24-hour medical service, doctor on call (phone: 751-3177).

Messenger Service – *Recapito Espresso Città,* 8 Via Nardones (phone: 418766 or 421904).

National/International Courier – *DHL International,* 94 Via Padula (phone: 540-1111).

Office Equipment Rental – *Aletta* (two locations: 6 Vicolo Campanile Al SS Apostoli; phone: 297100; and 130 Via Rossi; phone: 773-2976); *Scuotto,* audiovisual equipment (47 Via Padre Rocco; phone: 281073 or 734-9311); typewriters can usually be rented through your hotel concierge. Fully equipped offices for short-term rental (along with multilingual secretarial services, photocopy and telex machines, and meeting rooms) are available through *Centro Ufficio Attrezzati* (50/A Via Gianturco; phone: 205444) and *Tiempo Spa* (19-23 Via Sannio; phone: 785-9111).

Pharmacy – *Carducci,* open 24 hours daily (21-23 Via Carducci; phone: 417283); or dial 192 for recorded message of all-night pharmacies.

Photocopies – *Copy Rapid Galbiati* (18-20 Via S. Fusco; phone: 551-8437); and at most stationery shops.

Post Office – Central Post Office, open from 8 AM to 8 PM Mondays through Saturdays, to noon on Sundays. Piazza Matteotti (phone: 551-1456).

Secretary/Stenographer (English-Speaking) – *Tiempo Spa* (19-23 Via Sannio; phone: 785-9111); *Centro Ufficio Attrezzati* (50/A Via Gianturco; phone: 205444).

Tailor – *Ciardulli,* 109 Via Santa Lucia (phone: 421716).

Telex – Central post office, open daily from 8 AM to 8 PM; open 24 hours for telegrams. Piazza Matteotti (phone: 551-3446).

Translator – *European Secretarial Services* (126 Via Scarlatti; phone: 368925); *Associazione Interpreti e Traduttori* (88 Via Depretis; phone: 551-3507); *Centro Interpreti di Congressi e Traduttori* (63 Via Ventaglieri; phone: 412796); *Translation Center* (74 Via Cilea; phone: 647217).

Other – Convention equipment and personnel: *Centro Congressi Napoli* (146 Riviera di Chiaia; phone: 682420). Formal wear and costume rental: *Abiti Società* (6 Via Santa Brigida; phone: 323646).

SPECIAL EVENTS: Twice a year (on the Saturday before the first Sunday in May and on September 19), Neapolitans crowd into the Duomo of San Gennaro and pray for the *Miracle,* the liquefying of the dried blood of their patron saint that is kept in two vials in a chapel of the church. The miracle is supposed to have first occurred on the hands of a bishop transporting the body after San Gennaro's martyrdom in Pozzuoli on September 19, 305, and it has been happening regularly since the first recorded recurrence in 1389 — regularly, but not *always.* The event is something of a mass fortune telling, because when it fails, some disaster is expected to befall the city — in the past it might have been plague, in the future it could be Vesuvius. (The blood failed to liquefy during the last eruption of Vesuvius in 1944). The miracle lets Naples know that the saint still is with them, and nowhere is the atmosphere more alive with anticipation than in the chapel downstairs, where San Gennaro's bones are kept and the people plead for a sign. For information on details of the liquefaction, call 449097). Other important festivals celebrate the feast of *Santa Maria del Carmine* on July 16, and the *Madonna di Piedigrotta,* which lasts several days in early September.

MUSEUMS: In addition to those mentioned in *Special Places,* a number of other museums and churches are impressive.

Aquarium – One of the oldest, if not *the* oldest, in Europe (1872), housing some 200 species of Mediterranean marine life, all collected from the Bay of Naples. Open daily except Mondays from 9 AM to 5 PM; admission charge. Villa Comunale (phone: 583-3111).

Cappella Sansevero (Sansevero Chapel) – The funerary chapel of the Sangro family, containing the *Veiled Christ* by Giuseppe Sammartino and many other 18th-century sculptures. Since its recent renovation, visits are by appointment only. 19 Via Francesco De Sanctis (phone: 454684).

Chiesa di San Domenico Maggiore (Church of St. Dominic Major) – A 13th-century church, frequently restored, containing the famous crucifix of St. Thomas Aquinas (who lived and taught in the adjoining monastery) and paintings by Titian, Luca Giordano, Solimena, Simone Martini, and others. Piazza San Domenico.

Chiesa di San Gregorio Armeno (Church of St. Gregory of Armenia) – A baroque church worth a visit for its famous nativity scene (only on view during the *Christmas* period). Via San Gregorio Armeno.

Chiesa di San Paolo Maggiore (Church of St. Paul Major) – A church of the late 16th century, wonderfully Neapolitan baroque in style, with paintings by Stanzione, Solimena, and Paolo de Matteis. Piazza San Gaetano.

Chiesa di Santa Maria del Carmine (Church of Santa Maria del Carmine) – Built in the 12th century and substantially reconstructed between 1283 and 1300, this church is home to a venerated image of the Madonna. An adjacent tower is the scene of a mock burning and other celebrations on the saint's day, July 16 (see *Special Events*). Piazza del Carmine.

Museo Civico Filangieri (Filangieri Civic Museum) – Arms, furniture, porcelain, costumes, and paintings, housed in the 15th-century Palazzo Cuomo. Open Tuesdays through Saturdays 9AM to 2PM; Sundays and holidays 9AM to 1PM. Admission charge. 288 Via Duomo (phone: 203175).

Museo Duca di Martina (Duke of Martina Museum) – Ivories, enamels, china, and majolica, European and Oriental, are displayed in the Villa Floridiana, a small neo-classical palace in the Vomero section, with splendid gardens and a panoramic view of the bay. Closed Mondays. Admission charge. Via Cimarosa (phone: 578-8418).

Museo Principe Aragona Pignatelli Cortes (Prince of Aragón Pignatelli Cortes Museum) – A collection of 19th-century furniture and china, plus a coach museum in the park's pavilion, with French and English carriages. Closed Mondays. Admission charge. Riviera di Chiaia (phone: 669675).

SHOPPING: For shopping purposes, Naples is commonly divided into a *zona elegante* (elegant zone) and a *zona commerciale* (commercial zone). The most fashionable shopping area, the *zona elegante,* is centered around Piazza dei Martiri, along Via Calabritto, Via Filangieri, Via dei Mille, and Via Chiaia. The latter leads to the more commercial zone between Piazza Trieste e Trento and Piazza Dante along Via Roma (also called Via Toledo after the viceroy who opened it in 1536) and toward the main railroad station along Corso Umberto I. Ceramics and porcelains have been sold here since the Bourbon kings founded the Capodimonte school and factory in the 18th century. Although original Capodimonte pieces are collectors' items and Capodimonte-style figurines are produced by companies all over Italy, the production of more traditional ceramics, in popular folk styles, continues to thrive in Naples and the vicinity. Another important product of the area is coral, much of which, it is said, is now imported from Southeast Asia but handcrafted nevertheless in nearby Torre del Greco, where there are several large factories and showrooms (*Giovanni Apa,* in Torre del Greco, just off the Naples-Pompeii Highway, is one source of coral and cameos). Neapolitan street markets are very colorful (always beware of pickpockets and *scippatori,* who speed by on motorbikes, grabbing bags and gold chains from shoulders and necks as they go). Markets are in the neighborhoods of Resina, for new or used clothing and fabrics; *Spacca-Napoli,* for books and silver objects; *Antignano,* for fabric, household goods, and food; and, at *Christmas,* Via San

Gregorio, for traditional Neapolitan nativity figures. Antiques shops are found mostly in the area around Piazza dei Martiri and Via Santa Maria di Costantinopoli.

Baracca e Burattini – Opposite the entrance to the archaeological museum, an artisans' shop selling masks, marionettes, and lovely dolls. 2 Piazza del Museo (no phone).

Berisio – Antique books. 28 Via Port'Alba (phone: 544-7639).

Bowinkle – Lovely old prints of Naples — among other places — framed and unframed. 24 Piazza dei Martiri (no phone).

Chiurazzi – Bronze reproductions of sculptures in the archaeological museum. 271 Via ai Ponti Rossi (phone: 751-2685).

Coin – A good department store. 10 Via Scarlatti (phone: 578-0111).

Ospedale delle Bambole – Handcrafted dolls. 81 Via San Biagio dei Librai (phone: 203067).

La Rinascente – Another good and reasonably priced department store. 343 Via Roma (phone: 411511).

Il Sagittario – Curious leather goods (masks, sculptures). 10/A Via Santa Chiara (no phone).

Simplement – Top-quality women's shoes, ranging from classic to more unusual styles. 27 Via Calabritto (no phone).

La Soffitta – Hand-painted ceramics. 12 Via Benedetto Croce (no phone).

SPORTS AND FITNESS: Most sports facilities belong to private clubs, so check with the concierge of your hotel about which may be open to the public.

Fitness Centers – *Athletic Club* for men and *Silhouette* for women, both at 21 Via Fiorentini (phone: 313160 or 313342).

Jogging – One good place to run is the *lungomare* (seafront promenade) along Via Caracciolo and Via Partenope from the port of Santa Lucia to the Mergellina. The Villa Comunale, the park behind Via Caracciolo, is another good spot.

Soccer – From September to May, *Napoli* plays at the *Stadio San Paolo* (Piazzale Vincenzo Tecchio, Fuorigrotta; phone: 615623 or 619205). Its capacity is 100,000 often fierce fans, although Neapolitans have the reputation of being the least rowdy among Italians.

Swimming – The polluted Bay of Naples is not the best spot for water sports, but there are fine seaside resorts on the nearby islands and along the Amalfi Coast.

Tennis – There are public courts at several tennis clubs, including the *Sporting Club Virgilio* (6 Via Tito Lucrezio Caro; phone: 769-5261); the *Tennis Club Vomero* (8 Via Rossini; phone: 658912); and the *Tennis Club Napoli* (Villa Comunale, Viale Dohrn; phone: 761-4656).

THEATER: Even those who speak Italian probably won't readily understand the Neapolitan dialect, but just for the color and sheer vitality, take in a performance by the renowned *Repertory Group of Eduardo de Filippo* at the *Teatro San Ferdinando* (Piazza Teatro San Ferdinando; phone: 444500). A fine place to sample Neapolitan music and folklore is the *Circolo della Stampa* (reserve seats through your concierge). Other theatrical groups perform at the *Politeama* (Via Monte di Dio; phone: 764-5016); *Cilea* (Via San Domenico, at Corso Europa; phone: 656265); *Sannazaro* (157 Via Chiaia; phone: 411723); and *Bracco* (40 Via Tarsia; phone: 340234).

MUSIC: The season at the *Teatro San Carlo* (Via San Carlo; box office closed Mondays; phone: 797-2370 or 797-2111), one of the finest opera houses in the world, generally runs from December through most of June. Then, from mid-September through mid-November, the theater is the scene of a series of symphonic concerts, the *Concerti d'Autunno* (Autumn Concerts). The *Associazione Alessandro Scarlatti* performs at 58 Piazza dei Martiri (phone: 406011). Still more symphony and chamber concerts, by groups such as the *Accademia Musicale Napoletana* and others, are scheduled frequently at the *Auditorium RAI-TV* (Via Guglielmo Marconi; phone: 610122); in the church or cloisters of Santa Chiara (Via Benedetto Croce; phone: 522-6209); and in numerous other churches about town. The *Conservatorio di Musica* (Via San Pietro a Maiella; phone: 459255). In the summer, concerts are also held in the gardens at Capodimonte.

NIGHTCLUBS AND NIGHTLIFE: Like most port towns, Naples has a number of seedy bars and rip-off joints to be avoided. *Il Gabbiano,* near the principal hotels (26 Via Partenope; phone: 411666), is a piano bar that serves late snacks. One of the most elegant nightclubs in town is the *Virgilio* (6 Via Tito Lucrezio Caro; phone: 769-5261), up on the exquisite Posillipo Hill, one of the poshest areas in Naples. Another swanky nightspot is *Rosolino* (5-7 Via Nazario Sauro; phone: 415873), which also is a piano bar and restaurant. Worth looking into are *Chez Moi* (Parco Margherita 13; phone: 407526); *Boomerang* (Via Giotto; phone: 365185); *My Way* (Via Cappella Vecchia; no phone); *Casablanca* (101 Via Petrarca; no phone); and *Villa Scipione* (4 Via Scipione Capece; no phone).

BEST IN TOWN

CHECKING IN: An expensive hotel in Naples will charge from $145 to $220 a night for a double room; moderately priced hotels range from $100 to $145; and in the inexpensive category you'll be charged $45 to $100. All telephone numbers are in the 81 city code unless otherwise indicated.

Britannique – Offering Swiss management and efficiency, it's hospitable and very clean. Most of the 86 rooms in this old converted villa are large, and since it's set on a hillside up and back from the waterfront, most of them have attractive views. Business facilities include 24-hour room service, meeting rooms for up to 150, English-speaking concierge, foreign currency exchange, secretarial services in English, audiovisual equipment, photocopiers, computers, translation services, and express checkout. 133 Corso Vittorio Emanuele (phone: 761-4145; fax: 669760; telex: 722281). Expensive.

Continental – This ultramodern hotel has none of the charm of its older rivals, but what it lacks in style, it makes up for in efficiency. It is big (716 rooms), centrally located, and particularly geared to the business traveler. Business facilities include 24-hour room service, meeting rooms for up to 600, English-speaking concierge, foreign currency exchange, secretarial services in English, audiovisual equipment, photocopiers, computers, cable television news, translation services (including simultaneous interpreters), and express checkout. 46 Via Partenope (phone: 764-4636; fax: 764-4661; telex: 710244). Expensive.

Excelsior – Naples's only truly deluxe hotel, part of the reliable CIGA chain, it dominates the port of Santa Lucia, with terraced seaside rooms overlooking the 12th-century Castel dell'Ovo, the old fishing village of Borgo Marinaro, and the whole bay. The *Casanova Grill* takes some prizes, too (see *Eating Out*). There are 138 air conditioned rooms and a garage nearby. Business facilities include 24-hour room service, meeting rooms for up to 200, English-speaking concierge, foreign currency exchange, secretarial services in English, audiovisual equipment, photocopiers, computers, cable television news, translation services, and express checkout. 48 Via Partenope (phone: 417111; fax: 411743; telex: 710043). Expensive.

Miramare – Also conveniently located, with the added attraction of the waterfront, this hotel is reputable, comfortable, and small (30 rooms). Although it has no restaurant, there is a lovely breakfast terrace, and it is very near *La Cantinella* (see *Eating Out*). 24 Via Nazario Sauro (phone: 427388; fax: 416775; telex: 710121). Expensive.

Parker – This fine, renovated 96-room *Belle Epoque*-style property has a sweeping staircase, chandeliers, and old-fashioned elevators. Business facilities include 24-hour room service, meeting rooms for up to 220, English-speaking concierge, foreign currency exchange, secretarial services in English, audiovisual equipment, photocopiers, computers, translation services, and express checkout. 135 Corso Vittorio Emanuele (phone: 761-2474; fax: 663527; telex: 710578). Expensive.

Royal – Also on the Santa Lucia waterfront, this one is Naples's biggest (300 rooms). It's modern and busy, and it has a rooftop pool, garage, and air conditioning. Business facilities include 24-hour room service, meeting rooms for up to 550, English-speaking concierge, foreign currency exchange, secretarial services in English, audiovisual equipment, photocopiers, computers, cable television news, translation services, and express checkout. 38 Via Partenope (phone: 764-4800; fax: 764-5707; telex: 710167). Expensive.

Santa Lucia – This once shabby seafront property has been spruced up with considerable taste to match its smarter neighbors, which include the *Excelsior* and the *Vesuvio.* Old paintings and antiques lend an Old World touch to this 107-room hostelry, but the amenities are strictly 20th century. Business facilities include 24-hour room service, meeting rooms for up to 250, English-speaking concierge, foreign currency exchange, secretarial services in English, audiovisual equipment, photocopiers, computers, cable television news, translation services, and express checkout. 46 Via Partenope (phone and fax: 416566; telex: 710595). Expensive.

Vesuvio – Close to the *Excelsior,* Naples's second hotel also faces the picturesque port of Santa Lucia. It has 174 rooms, good baths, a decor ranging from period style to modern, a garage, and air conditioning. Business facilities include 24-hour room service, meeting rooms for up to 280, English-speaking concierge, foreign currency exchange, secretarial services in English, audiovisual equipment, photocopiers, computers, cable television news, translation services, and express checkout. 45 Via Partenope (phone and fax: 417044; telex: 710127). Expensive.

Paradiso – The breathtaking panoramic view of the entire Bay of Naples, seen from the front bedrooms and the roof terrace, make this place particularly appealing. Business facilities include 24-hour room service, meeting rooms for up to 35, English-speaking concierge, foreign currency exchange, secretarial services in English, audiovisual equipment, photocopiers, computers, translation services, and express checkout. 11 Via Catullo (phone: 761-4161; fax: 761-3449; telex: 722049). Expensive to moderate.

Mediterraneo – Not very romantic, but conveniently located in the commercial center of town, behind Piazza Municipio. More than 250 rooms, all air conditioned; garage. Via Nuova Ponte di Tappia (phone: 551-2240; fax: 552-5868; telex: 721615). Moderate.

San Germano – A few miles drive from the center of Naples, it's in rather nondescript surroundings at the crossroads for the *Ippodromo di Agnano* racecourse. This efficient hotel has some 100 pleasant rooms (each with TV set and air conditioning), a lovely garden, swimming pool, tennis courts, and a garage. 41 Via Beccadelli (phone: 570-5422; telex: 720080). Moderate.

Le Fontane al Mare – Nicely located (close to the seafront) and a very good value. Its 21 rooms are tastefully furnished in keeping with the 19th-century palazzo in which it is housed, but there's no restaurant. Be sure to keep a supply of coins on hand to feed the elevator. 14 Via N. Tommaseo (phone: 764-3470 or 764-3811). Inexpensive.

EATING OUT: While Italian food is not all pasta and pizza, both originated in Naples and are a staple of southern Italy. Here pasta is almost always eaten as a first course at lunch, while it is usually replaced at the evening meal by a light broth or soup (if the evening meal itself hasn't been replaced altogether by a pizza, which is generally served only in the evenings). Naples is the home of *spaghetti c'a pummarola* (*spaghetti al pomodoro* in Italian), born of the mating of pasta with the tomato not too long after the latter arrived in Italy from South America in the 16th century. It is still the most popular pasta dish, easily prepared, vividly colorful, fragrant with additions of basil or parsley, oregano, and garlic, and topped with tangy parmesan cheese. Other Neapolitan favorites are *vermicelli con le vongole* (pasta with clams, with or without tomatoes, in a garlic and olive oil sauce), or *con zucchine* (with zucchini, garlic, and oil), and *pasta e fagioli* (a very thick white bean soup with short pasta).

As Naples is seafood country, the best main course here is simple fresh fish grilled and seasoned with olive oil and lemon. But if you're watching your budget, be careful. Most quality fish is sold by weight at restaurants, and you'd do well to avoid those whose prices are listed on the menu *al chilo* (per kilogram), which can turn an otherwise modest bill into a major monetary setback. Exceptions to this rule are lesser fish such as *alici* (anchovies), which, when fresh, can be tastefully prepared in oil, garlic, and parsley, and *fritto misto,* a mixture of fried shrimp, squid, and small local fish. One piece of advice: Don't ever eat raw seafood that may have come from the polluted Bay of Naples. Dinner for two with a house wine will run from $85 to well over $110 at a restaurant listed as expensive, from $55 to $85 at a moderate one, and from $25 to $55 at an inexpensive place. All telephone numbers are in the 81 city code unless otherwise indicated.

La Cantinella – A favorite of Neapolitans, visiting dignitaries, and tourists staying nearby along the picturesque port of Santa Lucia. Fresh fish, as everywhere, is at a premium, but local clams and mussels mated with a hint of garlic, parsley, and *pummarola* or tomato and lavished on a steaming plate of linguine constitute one of the great pleasures of southern Italian life, within reach of everyone's pocket. The service is friendly and efficient. Closed Sundays. Reservations advised. Major credit cards accepted. 23 Via Nazario Sauro (phone: 404884 or 405375). Expensive.

Casanova Grill – A delightfully intimate dining room for such a grand hotel as the *Excelsior,* it offers a wide selection of enticing antipasti, plenty of fresh fish, Neapolitan specialties such as pasta with seafood, a remarkable fish soup, and roast baby lamb with rosemary and garlic — all prepared and served with care and refinement. Open daily. Reservations advised. Major credit cards accepted. 48 Via Partenope (phone: 417111). Expensive.

Ciro a Mergillina – For 150 years, this has been *the* place to see and be seen in Naples. Its fish always is top quality, and the pizza is among the best in town. Closed Mondays. Reservations advised. Major credit cards accepted. 21 Via Mergellina (phone: 681780). Expensive.

Giuseppone a Mare – Traditionally one of Naples's best fish restaurants, with incomparable views from Cape Posillipo, it seems to have its ups and downs in quality, service, and price. Still, it's worth trying if you're in the Posillipo area. Closed Sundays and from *Christmas* through *New Year's.* Reservations advised. Major credit cards accepted. 13 Via Ferdinando Russo, Capo Posillipo (phone: 769-6002). Expensive.

Rosolino – An elegant supper club, piano bar, and nightclub in the Santa Lucia quarter, just a skip and a jump from the *Excelsior* and *Vesuvio* hotels. The restaurant is open at lunch, too; closed Sundays. Reservations necessary at dinner. Major credit cards accepted. 5-7 Via Nazario Sauro (phone: 415873). Expensive.

La Sacrestia – Dine alfresco here on delicious Neapolitan dishes such as homemade pasta stuffed with ricotta cheese, *scazzette di Fra' Leopoldo,* or any of the fresh fish dishes. On a hillside beyond Mergellina that affords splendid views from the terrace, it is closed Mondays from September through June, and Sundays in July and August. Reservations advised. Major credit cards accepted. 116 Via Orazio (phone: 664186). Expensive.

La Fazenda – Very Neapolitan, serving homemade garlic bread, wonderful pasta dishes, fresh fish, home-raised chickens, and exquisite desserts. In the Posillipo area, the surroundings are rustic, with spectacular views of the bay and flowers everywhere. Closed Sundays and 2 weeks in August. Reservations advised. Major credit cards accepted. 58 Calata Marechiaro (phone: 769-7420). Expensive to moderate.

Amici Miei – Traditional Neapolitan fare is served in a traditionally elegant ambience in one of the elegant residential zones of Naples, near the *Politeama Theater.* Closed Mondays and August. Reservations advised. Major credit cards accepted. 78 Via Monte di Dio (phone: 764-6063). Moderate.

La Bersagliera – In good weather, the Borgo Marinaro facing the Castel dell'Ovo can't be beat for local color. And this is the only one of these portside restaurants that makes it: Sometimes a dose of sun in a spectacular setting is worth more than a flawless meal. Specialties include good varied antipasti, fresh octopus salad, and a surprisingly inexpensive mixed grill of seafood that includes a tender and tasty fresh squid — a dish certainly worth a repeat visit. Naples' famous *scugnizzi* (streetwise waifs) ask for pieces of bread as they pass by between swims in the polluted bay. Closed Tuesdays. Reservations advised. Major credit cards accepted. 10 Borgo Marinaro, Santa Lucia (phone: 764-6016). Moderate.

Ciro a Santa Brigida – In the center of town, this has been one of the best and busiest of Naples' trattorie/*pizzerie* since the 1920s. Sample the great variety of fresh fish or pasta such as *lasagna imbottita* and *maccheroni alla siciliana.* This is also a good place for *pastiera,* a typical Neapolitan dessert made of ricotta cheese and wheat. Closed Sundays. Reservations advised. No credit cards accepted. 71 Via Santa Brigida (phone: 552-4072). Moderate.

Don Salvatore – It has been said that "Mergellina without Don Salvatore would be like Naples without Vesuvius." It's a longtime Neapolitan favorite where everything is good, from antipasto to pasta, fish, meat, and pizza (served evenings only). Closed Wednesdays. Reservations advised. Visa accepted. 5 Via Mergellina (phone: 681817). Moderate.

Dora – The ambience here is that of a small fishing boat and the fish served is first class. Try the *linguine all'aragosta* (pasta with crayfish). Closed Sundays and August. Reservations advised. No credit cards accepted. 30 Via Ferdinando Palasciano, Riviera di Chiaia (phone: 680519). Moderate.

Il Gallo Nero – Elegant dining in an antiques-filled 19th-century villa or on a terrace with a splendid view of Mergellina. Classic favorites as well as sensible innovations are on the menu, plus fresh fish and imaginative meat dishes. Open evenings only, except Sundays, when it's open for lunch; closed Mondays and August. Reservations advised. Major credit cards accepted. 466 Via Tasso (phone: 643012). Moderate.

Al Poeta – The Varriale brothers come from a long line of Neapolitan restaurateurs, and their flair has won them a dedicated following at this busy eatery, high up on Posilippo hill. The specialty is fish, and customers know it will be fresh (which is not always true in Naples). Closed Mondays. Reservations advised. Visa accepted. 134 Piazza Salvatore di Giacomo (phone: 769-6936). Moderate.

Osteria al Canterbury – Like many Neapolitan eating places, this one keeps its doors locked to ward off holdups. But don't be put off — inside, the atmosphere is warm and welcoming, with walls lined with wine bottles. Try the *maccheroni di casa Canterbury* (homemade pasta topped with mozzarella, eggplant, and a tomatoey meat sauce). The set lunchtime menu is particularly inexpensive. Closed Sundays. Reservations advised on weekends. Major credit cards accepted. 6 Via Ascensione a Chiajà (phone: 413584). Moderate to inexpensive.

Osteria Castello – This small trattoria beckons you with its terra cotta tile floors, cheerful red-and-white check tablecloths, and the wafting aroma of homemade pasta sauces. Owner Carmine Castello also waits on tables and is always ready to explain the menu, which changes every 3 days. The emphasis is on traditional, no-frills Neapolitan cooking, at down-to-earth prices. Closed Sundays. Reservations advised. American Express accepted. 38 Via Santa Teresa a Chiaia (no phone). Moderate to inexpensive.

Pizzeria Bellini – One of the city's oldest *pizzerie.* Besides a vast assortment of pizza (the most famous, with fresh basil and tomato), there are pasta, fish, and meat dishes. Closed Wednesdays. Reservations unnecessary. No credit cards accepted. 80 Via Santa Maria di Costantinopoli (phone: 459774). Moderate to inexpensive.

Il Pulcinella – A genuine family-style restaurant, cozy, friendly, and delicious. Closed Mondays and from July to September — but it's really a winter ambience anyway. Reservations unnecessary. No credit cards accepted. 4 Vico Ischitella (phone: 764-2216). Moderate to inexpensive.

Gorizia – One of the Vomero's older *pizzerie,* now a full restaurant with traditional Neapolitan cuisine. The pizza is still noteworthy (available evenings only). Closed Wednesdays and August. Reservations unnecessary. No credit cards accepted. 29 Via Bernini (phone: 644662). Inexpensive.

Vini e Cucina – The food is delicious — real home cooking, Neapolitan style — and so this little Mergellina restaurant is increasingly popular and often impossibly crowded. Closed Sundays. Reservations unnecessary. No credit cards accepted. 762 Corso Vittorio Emanuele (no phone). Inexpensive.

PALERMO

Capital of Sicily, Palermo (from the Greek *panormos,* meaning "broad harbor") is bordered on one side by the blue Tyrrhenian Sea and on the other by dusty-brown mountains. It nestles on the edge of a fertile valley known as the Conca D'Oro, literally "Golden Conch Shell," said to be named for the exquisitely scented orange and lemon groves that once encircled the city.

Throughout history, Palermo has drawn from its twin heritages, European and Mediterranean. Unlike much of Sicily, it was never Greek, but was founded in the 6th century BC by seafaring Phoenicians from Carthage. In AD 254, it was conquered by the Romans. Over succeeding centuries, it was invaded by Saracens, Normans, Swabians, Angevins, and Spaniards, each of whom influenced the city's monuments and customs. Under the Arabs, who conquered the city in AD 831 and ruled it until their defeat in 1072 by the Norman King Roger I, Palermo became a major Mediterranean center (in the 10th century the city reportedly had 300,000 inhabitants). Subsequent wars among the European monarchs led to alternating periods of prosperity and decline (including a 19th-century "wine boom," spurred by British fondness for wines like marsala) until the city was annexed by Italy in 1860. Scholars date the birth of the contemporary Mafia to the mountain banditry of that turbulent era.

Since Garibaldi's day, Palermo — like much of Sicily — has been under the influence of the Mafia, Sicily's secret criminal organization. Allied bombings racked Palermo during World War II, and during the ensuing military occupation some members of the Mafia were installed as mayors of Sicilian towns. Since World War II — and during the semi-autonomy that Sicily enjoyed for the following 3 decades — the Mafia has exerted significant economic as well as political influence, and subjected the city to a succession of bloody gang wars. During the last decade, however, much of the Mafia's activity has shifted toward the more financially active city of Catania in the eastern part of the island.

Today, the historic center of Sicily's major port city, with a population of nearly 800,000, is a hodgepodge of narrow streets, broad squares, bustling outdoor markets, luxuriant subtropical gardens, Arab mosques with red domes, Gothic churches and cathedrals, Spanish baroque chapels, and decaying 17th-century palaces. In some areas, such as the *Vucciria* market, which resembles an Arab bazaar, the cries of fishmongers and greengrocers can be heard over the cacophony of automobile horns from snarled traffic. In this and other markets, like the Capo or Ballaro, women dressed in black pick and choose among ripe red tomatoes, deep purple eggplants, bell peppers, artichokes, zucchini, onions, oranges and lemons, pumpkins, persimmons, and prickly pears piled high alongside tables of fresh-killed kid or lamb and the seafood catch of the day.

Downtown, in the business and exclusive shopping district along Viale della Libertà, courtly gentlemen with appreciative roving eyes still stroll unhurriedly, or linger over their *caffè,* the better to admire the ladies. Prince Guiseppe Tomasi di Lampedusa wrote his early-20th-century masterpiece *Il Gattopardo* (The Leopard) while seated in a café near Piazza Politeama. The tale still is considered the best introduction to Sicily as cultivated Sicilians see it. Lampedusa's world of clubs and palazzi still survives behind Palermo's drawn shutters. Traditions die hard here.

The Sicilian regional government sits in a 12th-century Arab-Norman palace (known as Palazzo dei Normanni, or Palazzo Reale). And the best sweets in town — such as the Arab-derived "joy of the throat," a mound of pistachio-flavored almond paste — are still made by a small group of Benedictine nuns cloistered in the central downtown area. Long neglected, the downtown area is at last getting a face-lift, and several shopping streets have been closed to automobiles.

Palermo has many points of international artistic interest. The imposing Norman cathedral, from which Cardinal Salvatore Pappalardo now frequently rails against the city's criminals, dates back to the 12th century. The center of town is the four-cornered Quattro Canti intersection, with its Spanish baroque design. And the majestic baroque fountain in Piazza del Municipio casts a spell of the past in the fading evening light. The small Martorana church in central Piazza Bellini has beautiful Byzantine-influenced mosaics, as does the incomparable cathedral in the nearby town of Monreale. The 8,000 mummies that line the walls of the Capuchin convent's catacombs are an eerie reminder of those who came before.

But if the waves of invaders left their mark on the city's art and architecture (as well as on the local dialect, many words of which are derived from the Arabic, and on the physical traits of its populace — witness the blond, blue-eyed Sicilians who claim descent from Normans), they have left an even more obvious imprint on the island's distinctive dishes. Because of its hot, sunny climate and variable topography, which includes some extremely fertile areas, Sicily has always been blessed with a surfeit of high-quality culinary resources. Its vegetables and fruits are among the tastiest in Italy.

PALERMO AT-A-GLANCE

SEEING THE CITY: Palermo is bordered on the north by 1,800-foot Monte Pellegrino (Pilgrim's Mountain), which Goethe described as "the most beautiful promontory in the world." The headland, defended by Carthage against Rome for 3 years during the First Punic War, is 9 miles (14 km) from Palermo by car and can be reached by the winding Via P. Bonanno. There are impressive views of the city below and of the fertile Conca d'Oro Valley beyond at almost every turning. The best view is from the terrace of the abandoned *Castello Utveggio* hotel. The road continues to the Sanctuary of Santa Rosalia, the patron saint of Palermo, and then down to the beach of the resort of Mondello.

SPECIAL PLACES: The Old City center, near the bay, can be covered fairly easily on foot, but some of the sites worth seeing require transportation. When touring, remember that some churches close at noon or earlier and do not reopen until 4 or 5 PM. Carry a handful of 100- or 200-lire pieces to operate the machines that provide extra lighting or recorded explanations.

Quattro Canti (Four Corners) – This four-cornered crossroads (sometimes called Piazza Vigliena) is the heart of the Old City. It is the intersection of Via Maqueda and Corso Vittorio Emanuele; from here it is a short walk to many of Palermo's principal monuments. The four façades at Quattro Canti, built in the early 17th century, are fine examples of Spanish baroque architecture. The fountains are decorated at ground level with statues representing the four seasons; at the next level, with four of Sicily's Spanish kings; and yet higher, with four of the city's women saints.

Chiesa di San Giuseppe dei Teatini (Church of Saint Joseph of the Theatine Fathers) – St. Joseph's Church stands on the southwest corner of the Quattro Canti; its entrance is on Corso Vittorio Emanuele. The Genoese façade is simple, but the Spanish baroque interior is notable for its rich detail. The frescoes on the roof of the vault are copies of the originals that were destroyed when the church was bombed in 1943.

Piazza Pretoria, or Piazza del Municipio (City Hall Square) – From the Quattro Canti, just a few steps along Via Maqueda, is Piazza Pretoria. In its center is a huge, slightly elevated fountain designed by 16th-century Florentine sculptors. Beautifully illuminated at night, the fountain is known by local residents as the Fountain of Shame because the statues are very explicitly naked. The City Hall, originally called Palazzo delle Aquile (Palace of the Eagles), dates from 1463 and has been restored several times. A small street on the left of the palace leads to Piazza Bellini, the third part of this central monumental complex.

Chiesa di Santa Caterina (Church of Saint Catherine) – If you enter Piazza Bellini from Piazza Pretoria, Santa Caterina, built between 1580 and 1596, is to the left. Its late Renaissance façade (the cupola is especially lovely) suggests little of the polychrome marble decoration within, a splendid example of Spanish baroque. Except for Sunday mornings from 10 AM to noon, the church is rarely used for services.

La Martorana, or Chiesa di Santa Maria dell'Ammiraglio (Church of Saint Mary of the Admiral) – Facing Santa Caterina in Piazza Bellini is Palermo's single most famous church and one of the few Greek Orthodox churches in Italy today. The first visible feature is the strikingly beautiful campanile, which dates from the 12th century. The interior, where the original central Greek cross plan can still be detected, is decorated with intricate Norman mosaics. Originally named for its founder, George of Antioch, admiral to the fleet of King Roger II, the church was later ceded to the nearby Benedictine convent founded in 1193 by Eloisa Martorana. Open daily, 8:30 AM to 1 PM and 3 to 5 PM; closed 8:30 AM to 1 PM on weekends; it closes earlier in winter (phone: 616692).

Chiesa di San Cataldo (Church of Saint Cataldo) – Opposite La Martorana, this tiny church, which dates from the Norman period, shows its Arab heritage in its three small red domes. Because of the untimely death of its founder, Admiral Maione of Bari, it was never fully decorated. It does have its original mosaic floor and rows of original columns, and the altar still bears the ancient symbols of the lamb and the cross. This church has no electricity, so it must be seen during daylight. Ask the caretaker of La Martorana for the key (which you must remember to return when you leave).

Chiesa del Gesù (Church of Jesus) and Casa Professa – Across Via Maqueda, the narrow Via Ponticello leads to the first church built by the Jesuits in Sicily (1564), now their local headquarters. The church, which was completely restored after being badly bombed in 1943, has a sober façade and a richly decorated interior. Located in the heart of the Alberghiera quarter of Palermo, one of the city's poorest and liveliest neighborhoods, it is only a few steps from Piazza Ballaro, where a colorful morning market flourishes. Open 7 to 10 AM and 5 to 6 PM. Also nearby is the Chiesa del Carmine. Piazza Casa Professa (phone: 329878).

Duomo (Cathedral) – From Quattro Canti, Corso Vittorio Emanuele leads to Piazza della Cattedrale. There, a small park with palm and other trees stands before the imposing Cattedrale di Santa Maria Assunta (Cathedral of Saint Mary of the Assumption). Dedicated in 1185 by an English archbishop, the cathedral blends northern European Gothic (the original towers to the east) with Arab styling, but was much altered in the late 18th century by baroque architect Ferdinando Fuga, who added a large dome and a transept. The main entrance, from the park, is through the great south porch with its carved wooden doors; the column on the left is inscribed with a verse from the Koran. The spacious interior houses the tombs of the great King Frederick II and five other former Sicilian monarchs and their relatives. The Duomo, originally a mosque, is interesting, too, for its exceptionally long nave, its choir, and treasury. Usually open daily, 7 AM to noon and 5 to 7 PM (phone: 334373).

Palazzo dei Normanni, or Palazzo Reale (Palace of the Normans, or Royal Palace) – Connected by a bridge to the Duomo is the Palazzo Arcivescovile, or archbishopric. Piazza della Vittoria, a square traditionally used for public celebrations, lies just beyond, on the left, and is the setting for the splendid Palazzo dei Normanni. Originally built by the city's Arab occupiers and subsequently modified by both the Normans and the Spaniards, this building has always been the residence of Sicilian rulers. The restored palazzo houses the Sicilian regional government. The royal apartments on the top floor have beautiful mosaics. The Cappella Palatina (Palace Chapel), with its Saracen carved ceilings and columns and Greek Byzantine mosaics, is considered one of the finest examples of Arab-Norman art in Sicily. Visiting hours may vary because of political use. The royal apartments are generally open Mondays, Fridays, and Saturdays from 9 AM to 12:30 PM. The chapel is open daily, 9 AM to noon and 3 to 5 PM and is closed Saturday afternoons and holidays. No admission charge. Piazza del Parlamento (phone: 488449).

Chiesa di San Giovanni degli Eremiti (Church of Saint John of the Hermits) – Not far from the Palazzo dei Normanni is a lovely Arab-Norman church built in 1132 at the request of the Norman King Roger II. It has picturesque pink domes and a cloister with elegantly wrought columns and a luxuriant tropical garden. Open Mondays, Thursdays, and Saturdays from 9 AM to 2 PM, Sundays from 9 AM to 1 PM. 18 Via dei Benedettini (phone: 426900).

Chiesa di San Domenico (Church of Saint Dominic) – Taking Corso Vittorio Emanuele from the Quattro Canti toward the port (and away from the Duomo), turn left onto Via Roma. Past the entrance to the *Vucciria* market are the Piazza and the Church of San Domenico. Many well-known Sicilians are buried inside this large church. The Oratorio del Rosario di San Domenico behind it boasts a masterpiece, the *Madonna del Rosario,* painted by Van Dyck after he fled the plague in Palermo in 1628. Open daily 7:30 to 11:30 AM, and also 5 to 6 PM on weekends. Piazza di San Domenico (phone: 584872).

Museo Archeologico Nazionale (National Archaeological Museum) – Next to the post office on Via Roma is one of the most important historical museums in Italy. It is not large (only 2 floors) but has an excellent collection of Phoenician, Egyptian, Punic, Greek, and Roman artifacts, including the famed metopes of the Selinunte Greek temples. Open Tuesdays through Saturdays from 9 AM to 1:30 PM and 3 to 5:30 PM; admission charge. 4 Via Olivella (phone: 587825).

Oratorio di San Lorenzo (Oratory of Saint Lawrence) – Walking east on Corso Vittorio Emanuele, beyond Via Roma, the narrow Via Immacolatella is on the left. The oratory, at No. 5, contains a sculpture by Serpotta. The custodian will let visitors in.

Galleria Regionale della Sicilia (Regional Gallery of Sicily) – The Palazzo

Patella, or Abatellis — a late Gothic-Catalan structure on the edge of the Kalsa neighborhood near the port — houses the *Regional Gallery.* Tastefully arranged, its exhibits well documented, the gallery contains interesting paintings and sculptures from many Sicilian periods, including a superb half-length *Annunciation,* by Antonello da Messina (1430–79). Open weekdays from 9 AM to 1:30 PM and from 3 to 7:30 PM; weekends from 9 AM to 12:30 PM. Admission charge. 4 Via Alloro (phone: 6164317).

Convento dei Cappuccini (Convent of the Capuchin Friars) – For even the most unimpressionable, the catacombs of this ancient convent are an amazing sight, containing the desiccated bodies, some naturally mummified, of more than 8,000 priests, professionals, workers, women, and children of Old Palermo. Donations requested. Open daily, 9 AM to noon and 3 to 5 PM. Via Cappuccini (phone: 212633).

Orto Botanico (Botanical Garden) – The garden is situated alongside Villa Giulia, off Via Lincoln on the eastern edge of Palermo. The design is 17th century and the vegetation is lush and subtropical. Open Mondays through Fridays from 9 AM to noon, and Saturdays from 9 to 11 AM. Closed holidays. 2/B Via Lincoln (phone: 6166540).

Palazzo della Zisa (Palace of Zisa) – La Zisa, from the Arabic *El Aziz* (The Magnificent), is one of several pleasure palaces built by the Norman kings outside the city proper. The former residence of King William, who reigned from 1156 to 1166, it is a splendid example of Arab-Fatimid architecture, one of the most important of the surviving Arab-Norman secular monuments in Sicily. At press time, the palace was closed for restoration. Vicolo Zisa (Bus No. 24).

■ **EXTRA SPECIAL:** Palermo has several colorful open-air street markets that hark back to the days of the Arabs. The biggest of these, and the best known — immortalized in a painting by Sicily's most celebrated 20th-century artist, Renato Guttuso — is the *Vucciria.* The name comes from the French, *boucherie,* or slaughterhouse, and it was first a meat market. Now it sells foods of all kinds: fish of varied stripes and sizes, meats, cheeses, fresh fruits and vegetables, dried herbs, fried balls of stuffed rice, dried fruits and nuts, and even some non-food products, such as transistor radios and cassettes. Not far from the port, the *Vucciria* stretches from Via Roma to the sea and from the Church of San Domenico to Corso Vittorio Emanuele. It is noisy and crowded (be careful with your wallet or purse) but wonderfully vivid and alive. Although it is open all day (except Sundays), the mornings are cleaner and more colorful.

Added attractions in the *Vucciria* are a small restaurant called the *Maestro del Brodo* (the Broth Master; 7 Via Pannieri), where various broths can provide an inexpensive meal for about $8 or $9; the *Shangai* (34 Vicolo dei Mezzani), where in warm weather diners sit on a terrace overlooking Piazza Caracciolo while sampling pasta *con le sarde* (sardines), *con broccoli,* or *alla norma* (with eggplant) and delicious baked squid; and the tiny *Taverna Azzurra* (on Discesa dei Maccheronai), where locals gather for a glass of *zibibbo* (sweet wine), sangue siciliano (sicilian blood, another sweet wine), or marsala.

ENVIRONS

There are several interesting day trips from Palermo. Most can be made by bus, but for speed and convenience we suggest a taxi or private car. Beware of poor sign posting, commonplace in Sicily.

Piana degli Albanesi – This Albanian settlement, one of the island's most interesting, was founded in 1488. Its inhabitants retain their ancient dialect and observe Greek Orthodox traditions. *Easter* and *Epiphany* are especially colorful celebrations. About 14½ miles (23 km) from Palermo; buses leave several times a day from Stazione Centrale on Piazza G. Cesare.

Casteldaccia – Situated on the coastal road (SS113), just after Bagheria, a town famous for its wealth of 18th-century villas (see *Sicily and the Lipari Islands,* DIREC-

TIONS), are the presses of the Duke of Salaparuta's vino corvo, Sicily's most famous wine, which is exported abroad. Corvo now conducts tours and tastings. As the hours and tours vary according to season, ask your hotel concierge to call first (phone: 91-953988).

■ **Monreale:** Five miles (8 km) southwest of Palermo is the hilltop town of Monreale, site of the famous Cathedral of Santa Maria la Nuova, built by King William II between 1172 and 1176. This is indisputably the most important Norman church in Sicily and contains some of the most impressive medieval artwork. The façade is grand, but nothing to compare with the vast interior, the walls of which are almost entirely covered with mosaic scenes from the Old and New Testaments. One of the most stunning depictions, the full-length figure of Christ kneeling in benediction, is in the apse. The wooden choir is beautiful, as are the sarcophagi of several Sicilian kings and queens. (One hundred–lire coins will operate temporary lights for viewing the art.) There is an admission charge for access to the roof, from which it's possible to view the cloister next door and the fertile Conca D'Oro Valley below the town. Open daily, 8:30 AM to 12:30 PM and 3:30 to 6:30 PM.

On the south side of the cathedral is the 12th-century *chiostro* — Cloister of the Benedictines — which is enclosed by double rows of individually designed columns, many of which are decorated with reliefs or mosaics. Open weekdays from 9 AM to 1:30 PM, weekends from 9 AM to 12:30 PM. Buses leave from 8-9 Via Stabile in downtown Palermo.

During a visit to Monreale, travelers may want to shop for ceramics (there is a local school), less expensive here than in Palermo. For inexpensive dining, try *La Botte* (Contrada Lenzitti, SS186416; phone: 414051) with its vast selection of antipasti, plus old-time Sicilian dishes such as artichokes with tuna and shrimp; spaghetti with ricotta cheese or with tuna, capers, and olives; and *falsomagro,* the classic Sicilian meat loaf. Closed Mondays and in August and September.

FULL-DAY EXCURSIONS

Erice and Segesta – Erice is a lovely medieval village 62 miles (99 km) west of Palermo along the coast road toward Trapani. It was known in antiquity throughout the Mediterranean for its temple to the goddess of fertility, Venus Erycina. It also has two interesting castles and the lovely Chiesa Matrice. Its mountain perch above the sea provides a number of impressive views, but the little town is often shrouded in fog, particularly in winter, so try to visit in good weather and early in the day. On the way back to Palermo, stop at Segesta, where there are well-preserved ruins of a Doric temple dating from the 5th century BC.

Cefalù – A pleasant drive or train journey (1 hour; about $3.50, round trip) about 47 miles (75 km) along the coast road east of Palermo includes the picturesque town of Cefalù, an ancient Greek cliffside seaport, with fine beaches. Its 12th-century cathedral has mosaics to rival those of Monreale. The Old Town, dating from 1130, consists of nine parallel streets.

SOURCES AND RESOURCES

TOURIST INFORMATION: General tourist information regarding Palermo and its environs is available at the Ente Provinciale per il Turismo (EPT) office (35 Piazza Castelnuovo in downtown Palermo; phone: 583847). It is open weekdays from 8 AM to 8 PM, Saturday from 8 AM to 2 PM. The EPT also has lists of hotels. Other EPT branches are at the international terminal of the airport (phone: 591698), and at the train station (phone: 616-5914). The *CIT* travel agency (Via Libertà; phone: 586333 or 586782) offers tours of the city and of the island.

The US Consulate is at 1 Via Vaccarini (phone: 343917 or 343532).

Local Coverage – Two daily papers are published in Palermo: *Giornale di Sicilia* and *L'Ora.* The EPT also produces its own magazine, *Ciao Sicilia,* a monthly, in Italian, available at newsstands. *Libreria Flaccovio* (37 Via Ruggero Settimo) has a good selection of guidebooks and other books in English.

TELEPHONE: The city code for Palermo is 91. When calling from within Italy, dial 091 before the local number.

GETTING AROUND: Downtown thoroughfares are few, so traffic in Palermo is, to say the least, chaotic. Rush hour often lasts for most of the day. Allow plenty of time to get where you're going.

Airport – Domestic and international flights operate from two terminals at the Punta Raisi Airport, 20 miles (32 km) outside the city. Buses to the airport run from the terminal (59 Via Mazzini). Taxis are available but are very expensive: To or from the airport, one-way cab fare may exceed $50. Airport buses, which cost about $4, leave from the train station and Via Amari Terminal (corner of Via Isidoro La Lumia, behind the *Politeama Garibaldi Theater*) roughly every hour from 5:40 AM to 10:20 PM; from the airport, from 6:15 AM to 11 PM or later, depending on the arrival of the last flight. Travel time is about 45 minutes. For information call 580457 or *Alitalia* (phone: 601-9111).

Boat – Boats to Naples (daily), Sardinia (1 day a week), Tunisia (1 day a week), and some of the Sicilian Islands leave the maritime station at the Vittorio Veneto dock. Principal carriers are *Adriatica-Italia/Tirrenia* (385 Via Roma; phone: 585733) and *Siremar* (120 Via Francesco Crispi; phone: 582403). Boats and hydrofoils also depart daily for Ustica, an unspoiled island off the Palermo coast, and in summer, for the Lipari Islands. Contact *SNAV* (55 Via Principe di Belmonte; phone: 333322). Also check local newspapers for schedules.

Bus – Because of the traffic jams, city travel by crowded public bus can be hard work and a waste of time. Tickets are 750 lire (about 55¢) per ride and can be bought at shops with a sign reading "Biglietti A.M.A.T." Efficient by contrast (especially to Catania), the Sicilian intercity bus company, *SAIS* (16 Via Balsamo; phone: 235527 or 235722), provides daily bus service between Palermo and most Sicilian cities; *Dionisio* (16 Via Balsamo; phone: 616-6028) serves Catania and Siracusa. *AST* (*Azienda Siciliana Transporti*) operates services between Palermo and nearby towns. Buses depart from Piazza Lolli (phone: 577120) and Piazza Marina (phone: 589636). *Giornale di Sicilia* publishes daily schedules.

Carrozze – Sometimes called *carrozzelle,* these ever-less-frequent horse-drawn cabs are pleasant when there is little traffic. Work out the price with the driver beforehand; otherwise you may find the hansom's meter conveniently broken when your drive is over.

Car Rental – Driving a car is recommended for excursions outside Palermo, but not in the city itself, given traffic and parking difficulties. Main companies are *Hertz* (7/E Via Messina; phone: 331668; and at the airport; phone: 591682); *Avis* (12 Via Principe di Scordia; phone: 586940; and at the airport; phone: 591684); and *InterRent* (6l Via Cavour; phone: 328631).

Taxi – Cabs are relatively affordable and can be picked up at a downtown stand or called by your hotel, though this costs slightly more (radio taxi phone: 513311, 513198, 625-5911/2, and 625-5933). Taxi meters start at 3,000 lire ($2.30); the fare rises in increments of 900 lire (70¢), with an additional charge of 2,000 lire ($1.50) on Sundays, holidays, and evenings after 10 PM. Luggage costs 1,000 lire (80¢) per bag. Since it is often hard to find taxis outside the immediate central city, it is a good idea to ask a cab to wait while you visit a site.

Train – The main train station is the Stazione Centrale (Piazza Giulio Cesare; phone: 616-1806 or 616-4808). Main trains are listed in daily local newspapers. Train service is less efficient in Sicily than elsewhere in Italy; better to try one of the bus companies listed above.

SPECIAL EVENTS: In March, drivers from around the world leave Palermo for Cefalù in the *Targa Florio* car rally. On March 18, bonfires rage throughout the city in celebration of *St. Joseph's Day,* which follows. In nearby Piano degli Albanesi, *Epiphany* and *Easter* are celebrated according to Greek Orthodox rites. In Prizzi, also near Palermo, the special *Ballo dei Diavoli* (Dance of the Devils) takes place just before *Easter. Festino di Santa Rosalia,* the *Feast Days of Santa Rosalia,* the patron saint of Palermo, a 3-day event, culminating on July 15 with a street procession in which a statue of the saint is carried joyfully through the city. In early September there is a procession to the sanctuary on nearby Monte Pellegrino. The *Palermo Grand Prix* tournament is held in October. Every November there is a 2-week *Marionette Festival* at the *Museo Internazionale delle Marionette* (19 Piazza Marina; phone: 328060) and other theaters.

MUSEUMS: Besides those mentioned in *Special Places,* Palermo has a number of museums of special interest.

Galleria d'Arte Moderna (Gallery of Modern Art) – Collection of works by painters from Sicily and elsewhere in southern Italy. Open Tuesdays through Sundays from 9 AM to 1 PM; also Tuesdays and Thursdays from 4:30 to 7:30 PM. Admission charge. 10 Via F. Turati (phone: 588951).

Museo Archeologico della Fondazione Mormino (Mormino Foundation Archaeological Museum) – In the Banco di Sicilia building. Prehistoric and ancient pottery. Open from 9 AM to 1 PM and 3 to 5 PM; closed Saturday afternoons, Sundays, and holidays. Admission charge. 185 Via Roma (phone: 585144).

Museo Etnografico Pitrè (Pitrè Ethnological Museum) – Art, crafts, and folklore collection illustrating all aspects of Sicilian life. Near the Palazzina Cinese (Chinese Palace) in the Parco della Favorita estate, which can be reached by taxi or public bus No. 14 or 15. Open daily, 8:30 AM to 1:30 PM (Sundays to 1 PM) and 3 to 5 PM; closed Friday mornings. Admission charge. Via Duca degli Abruzzi (phone: 6710900).

Museo Internazionale delle Marionette (International Museum of Marionettes) – Collection of puppets from various parts of Sicily. (See also *Italy's Museums and Monuments,* DIVERSIONS.) Open Mondays through Saturdays from 9 AM to 1 PM and 4 to 7 PM. Admission charge. 1 Via Butera (phone: 328060).

SHOPPING: Like many smaller Italian cities, Palermo has a compact, central shopping district with several stores as elegant as those in Rome, Florence, and Milan. Some streets off Via della Libertà are closed to traffic. All the famous Italian designers have shops or outlets here. Hand-crafted items include ceramics, willow baskets, embroidered fabrics, clay crèche figures, and replicas of the famed Sicilian puppets and horse carts. For fun and perhaps a serendipitous find, try your luck at the colorful morning flea market, *Il Mercato delle Pulci* (just behind the cathedral); closed Mondays. Marsala wine and marzipan candy are two of the prime gastronomic products available. Some pastry shops prepare *cassatte,* traditional Sicilian sponge cakes, for air shipment.

Most Palermo stores are open daily, 9 AM to 1 PM and 4 to 7:30 PM. Most stores are closed on Monday mornings, food stores on Wednesday afternoons. All shops are closed on Sundays and holidays, including January 1 and 6, April 25, May 1, August 15, November 1 and 4, and December 8, 25, and 26.

Aguglia Tanio – A good ladies' salon run by a dynasty of hairdressers. 59 Via Ricasoli (phone: 581740).

Battaglia – Where Palermo's high society shops for top-label women's and men's clothing. 74 Via Ruggero Settimo (phone: 580224).

La Botteguccia – Women's sportswear; imaginative and innovative daytime and evening wear. No credit cards accepted. 11 Piazza Ungheria (phone: 334200).

Convento di San Benedetto – Traditional Palermo cakes and cookies prepared and sold by the Benedictine nuns. Open daily, 9:30 AM to 6:30 PM; closed Wednesday afternoons. 38/A Piazza Venezia.

Fecarotta – Fine Sicilian, Italian, and other European antiques. 108/A Via Principe di Belmonte (phone: 331518).

Fecarotta Gioielli – Jewelers with top-label watches and high-quality gifts. 68 Via Ruggiero Settimo (phone: 586282).

Fendi – Handbags, furs, and fabulous accessories from the famous sisters. 35 Via della Libertà (phone: 332894).

Fratelli Magrì – One of the city's oldest and best-known bakeries. 42 Via Isidoro Carini (phone: 584788).

Frette – A vast array of fine linen in a city where the dowry still has its cult. 12 Via Ruggero Settimo (phone: 585166), 85 Via G. Sciutti (phone: 343288), and 36/B Via della Libertà (phone: 625-0075).

Giovanni Alongi – Menswear, from shoes to evening wear. 46/A Via Ruggero Settimo (phone: 582927).

Harabel's – Elegant women's wear. 189 Via M. Stabile (phone: 584136).

Harper – Small, well-organized department store carrying men's, women's, and children's clothing as well as housewares and gift items. 31 Via Ruggero Settimo (phone: 583703).

Libreria Flaccovio – The best bookstore in town; wide selection of art books, guidebooks, and books in English. 37 Via Ruggero Settimo

Lorizzo – Attractive men's clothing. 114 Via Principe di Belmonte (phone: 589468).

Ma Gi – Fine jewelry and silver. No credit cards accepted. 45 Via Ruggero Settimo (phone: 585446).

Mangia, R – Fine regional food products, well packaged and fresh, as well as an international charcuterie. 116 Via Principe di Belmonte (phone: 587651).

Max Mara – Stylish, moderately priced women's sportswear. 22 and 167 Via della Libertà.

Napoleon – An elegant shop with a vast range of styles and labels, as well as leather jackets and handbags. 1 Via della Libertà (phone: 587173).

Prezioso – Fine women's clothing and leather goods. 14/A Via della Libertà (phone: 329941).

Pustorino – The next best thing to visiting London's Savile Row is a visit to this oldest of gentlemen's haberdashers, where even King George V shopped when he came to town over 60 years ago. 174 Via Maqueda (phone: 580984).

De Simone – Colorful, even gaudy, decorative ceramics. 636 Via Messina Marine (phone: 622-1662) and 2 Piazza Leoni (phone: 363190).

Spatafora Calzature – Moderately priced Italian shoes are offered at this branch of a well-known chain. 111 and 365 Via Maqueda (phone: 6165887).

Trussardi – Up-to-the-minute clothes for men and women. 33 Via V.E. Albanese (phone: 332354).

Tullio – Beautiful furs, suitcases, and leather goods. 104/B Via Principe di Belmonte (phone: 584005).

Vicenzo Argento – The last of the great *pupari,* Sicilian puppet makers, sells his exquisite work in this tiny shop in the shadow of the cathedral. 445 Via Vittorio Emanuele (no phone).

SPORTS AND FITNESS: Horseback Riding – For information, reservations, and directions for day trips call *Mano Stalla* in Ballestrate at 878-7033.

Horse Racing – Trotters and bettors assemble at *La Favorita* racecourse (phone: 510961) Wednesdays and Saturdays at 2:30 PM from January to June; in summer, races are in the evening. Entrance on Viale del Fante.

Scuba Diving – Information on this and underwater fishing is obtainable from *FIPS* (93 Via Terrasanta; phone: 302302); favored areas are Punta Raisi, Sferracavallo, and the lovely island of Ustica, site of international diving competitions.

Skiing – Information on lifts and slopes (including one for beginners) in the nearby Madonie Mountains is available from the *Club Alpino Italiano* (*CAI,* 30 Via Agrigento; phone: 250875) and *Club Alpino Siciliano* (43 Via Paternostro; phone: 581323).

Soccer – From September to May, *Palermo* — in the pink shirts and black shorts — plays at the *Stadio Comunale,* 11 Viale del Fante (phone: 513643 or 523869).

Swimming – The many pleasant beaches in Palermo are the city's pride and joy, but watch for pollution warnings, posted on signs. The beaches tend to be overcrowded in August. The city's main beach resort is Mondello, 7 miles (11 km) north. Most of the long, sandy beach is taken up by *stabilimenti balneari* (bathing establishments), which charge an entrance fee. By Italian law, anyone is free to use the beach without paying, as long as he or she stays within 15 feet of the shoreline. Those who pay the admission fee, however, may also rent chairs, take showers, and use the pool if there is one. Another beach, in the small fishing village of Sferracavallo, lies beyond the rocky spur of Monte Gallo, a few miles farther west. It is somewhat less commercial, and the water is delightfully clear. Solunto and Porticello, east of Palermo, also have good beaches. One hour away are the popular beaches of Cefalù.

The *Piscina Olimpica Comunale* (a city swimming pool) is at 11 Viale del Fante (phone: 510558).

Tennis – *Circolo del Tennis* (3 Viale del Fante; phone: 544517). The regional *Federazione Italiana di Tennis* (*FIT,* 115 Via Alpi; phone: 501266) can provide additional information.

Water Sports – For information on sailing, try the exclusive *Circolo della Vela Sicilia* (1 Viale Regina Elena, Mondello Valdesi; phone: 450182 or 450333). *Club Sci Nautico Mondello* (Via Piano Gallo, Mondello; phone: 455500) will get you onto water skis. For windsurfing, there's *Albaria Windsurfing Club* (9 Viale Regina Elena, Mondello; phone: 454034). At Cefalù there is a popular summer sports resort complex, the *Club Valtur.* Reservations must be made in advance in Rome (phone: 6-678629).

THEATER AND MUSIC: Since the closing of the 19th-century *Teatro Massimo* for restoration, the major theaters in Palermo are the *Politeama Garibaldi* (Piazza Ruggero Settimo; phone: 584334), which generally produces classical theater or concerts; *Teatro Biondo* (Via Roma; phone: 588755); and *Teatro Golden* (60 Via Terrasanta; phone: 302377). In summer, a program of ballet, jazz, and classical music is offered at the *Teatro del Parco di Villa Castelnuovo* (Viale del Fante; phone: 518287), an open-air theater by the sea. Tickets are available through the *Politeama.* Concerts are also held at the *Sala Scarlatti* of the Music Conservatory (45 Via Squarcialupo; phone: 240241) or at *SS Salvatore Auditorium* (396 Corso Vittorio Emanuele; phone: 26654).

Palermo has a century-long history and tradition of puppet theaters. Performances are held at the *Museo Internazionale delle Marionette* (1 Via Butera; phone: 328060).

Call to find out schedule of performances. Other theaters sometimes used for puppet shows are *Figli d'Arte Cuticchio* — the name is from a family of puppet makers (95 Via Bara all'Olivella; phone: 323400 or 323400); the *Teatro Ippogrifo* (6 Vicolo Ragusi; phone: 329194); *Compagnia A. Mancuso* (Piazza Luigi Sturzo; phone: 329697); and *Bradamante* (25 Via Lombardia; phone: 625-9223).

NIGHTCLUBS AND NIGHTLIFE: There are several small piano bars, where conversation and liquid (and sometimes solid) refreshments can be enjoyed against a musical background. The best piano bars are at *Grande Albergo e delle Palme* and *Villa Igiea* (see *Checking In*) and at *Mazzara* (15 Via Generale Magliocco; phone: 321366) and the *Collica* (6 Via Notarbartolo; phone: 625-2040). *Villa Verde Mondello* (36 Via Piano Gallo; phone: 454237) also has a piano bar. Wine bars are fashionable in Palermo; some are open late. *Genova* (54 Via Patania; phone: 587883) operates until after midnight, serving crêpes and snacks along with wine and beer in an attractive outdoor courtyard. For live music, try *Il Ritrovo degli Artisti Golosi* (37 Via Gerbasi; phone: 325742; it serves food too), *Metropolis* (Piazza Marina; no phone), and *L'Onix* (Via Fattori; no phone). For those with a yearning to dance, there are discotheques: *Speak Easy* (34 Viale Strasburgo; phone: 518486; popular with the younger set); and *Pare Choc* (55 Via dei Nebrodi; phone: 501056). The *Coca Cola Club* (also called *Waikiki,* Viale Galatea, at Mondello Beach; phone: 454196) is a popular, outdoor discotheque, open in summer. But you will find that most Sicilian nightlife takes place at home. There is much socializing among families and friends, either at each other's homes or in the many fine neighborhood restaurants.

BEST IN TOWN

CHECKING IN: In Palermo, as throughout Sicily, hotels are less expensive than elsewhere in Italy. The hotel below rated as expensive charges $300 and up for a double room; moderate hotels, from $120 to $200; and inexpensive, less than $120. All telephone numbers are in the 91 city code unless otherwise indicated.

Villa Igiea Grand – Europe's visiting monarchs once stayed in this sprawling, turn-of-the-century villa in a seaside park 2 miles (3 km) out of the city center. Palermo's only luxury hotel, it boasts 117 rooms, tennis courts, a swimming pool, and beach. Rooms are beautifully decorated; service is excellent; and the dining room and piano bar are first rate. The only disadvantage is the need for transportation into town. 43 Via Principe di Belmonte (phone: 543744; fax: 547654). Expensive.

Astoria – This 325-room hotel is efficient, modern, and fairly close to downtown (though not within walking distance). The restaurant is pleasant. 62 Via Monte Pellegrino (phone: 637-1820; fax: 337-2128). Moderate.

Europa – Small (35 rooms) and comfortable, with a convenient downtown location. 3 Via Agrigento (phone: 625-6323; fax: 625-6323). Moderate.

Excelsior Palace – Once a convent, now refurbished and refurnished, this 128-room downtown establishment has been turned into a jewel of comfort. A short walk from the main shopping center. Some rooms overlook the fashionable Via della Libertà, one of Palermo's busiest (and noisiest) streets. The dining room is small and windowless, but the food is good. 3 Via Marchese Ugo (phone: 625-6176; fax: 342139). Moderate.

Grande Albergo e delle Palme – Richard Wagner stayed here, formerly the Palazzo Ingham, in 1882, just after he completed *Parsifal,* and the word is that

Mafia bigwigs once held summit meetings here. Today, this 187-room, centrally located hotel is a home away from home for Italian businesspeople, politicians, and traveling journalists (not to mention tourists). Good service, good food (see *Eating Out*), good piano bar, but some guestrooms are small. 398 Via Roma (phone: 583933; fax: 33154). Moderate.

Jolly – Located near the Villa Giulia and the botanical gardens, this large, modern member of the well-known chain offers 273 rooms, many with ocean views. There also is a swimming pool (rare in Palermo) and a pleasant restaurant with alfresco dining. Slightly outside the center (and therefore away from the noise), but the hotel has a van that regularly transports guests downtown. 22 Foro Italico (phone: 616-5090; fax: 616-1441). Moderate.

Mondello Palace – Just 7 miles (11 km) north of town, this is a pleasant, 83-room resort hotel with a pool, garden, and private beach. Mondello's best. Viale Principe di Scalea, Mondello (phone: 450001; fax: 450657). Moderate.

Politeama Palace – Across the street from the *Politeama Theater* and fine for short stays. All of its 102 rooms have TV sets and air conditioning. 15 Piazza Ruggero Settimo (phone: 322777; fax: 611-1589). Moderate.

President – Business travelers will appreciate this clean, modern hotel with 129 rooms, excellent rooftop restaurant offering Sicilian specialties at reasonable prices, private parking lot with attendant, and harbor view. Closer to the port and less central than some others mentioned, but still conveniently downtown. 230 Via Francesco Crispi (phone: 580733; fax: 611-1588). Moderate.

Splendid Hotel La Torre – On the far end of the Mondello Beach, about 7 miles (11 km) from town, this modern 177-room hotel has all private outdoor facilities, including a pool, a park, and a beach. 11 Via Piano Gallo, Mondello (phone: 450222; fax: 450033). Moderate.

Cristal Palace – Just 2 years old, this centrally located, very modern hotel is a good value. All the 90 rooms are air conditioned and there is a fine restaurant and parking. 447/D Via Roma (phone: 611-2580; fax: 611-2589). Inexpensive.

Ponte – Although the 137 rooms are simple, they are all air conditioned. Conveniently located in downtown. 99 Via Crispi (phone: 583744; fax: 581845). Inexpensive.

EATING OUT: Food in Palermo is distinctive for its combination of Arab, Norman, and Spanish influences, and for the quality of its super-fresh ingredients (provided by the markets described in *Extra Special*). Local fish is fresh and abundant and sometimes is prepared in unusual ways — slivers of swordfish stuffed with raisins and pine nuts, sardines *a beccafico* (stuffed and flavored with laurel), and *neonato,* a fish cake made from minnows. (The local meats, primarily kid and lamb, are a little less plentiful but excellent.) Two centuries of Arab domination, along with the influence of other "visitors," left an exotic gustatory heritage. Many Sicilian recipes include pine nuts, raisins, and sweet-and-sour condiments. Desserts of almond paste, ricotta cheese, and candied fruits may also be of Arab origin. Besides homemade sorbets, the best known desserts are the *cassatta siciliana* (sponge cake with a filling of ricotta and candied fruits), cannoli (pastry cones filled with sweet ricotta cream), and *frutta della Martorana* (marzipan), in the shapes of fruits, vegetables, and even pasta.

Sicily's best dishes are probably its pasta — with a sardine and wild herb sauce, with tomatoes and eggplant, or with broccoli and pine nuts. Swordfish, sliced in steaks or formed into meatballs or cold stuffed rolls, is also among the island's favorites, as is the famous *falsomagro* ("falsely thin"), a veal roll stuffed with eggs, cheese, tomatoes, and fresh herbs.

Expect to pay over $70 for a meal for two, including wine, at the city's few luxury eating places, listed as expensive; from $40 to $70 in the moderate category; and less than $40 for an inexpensive meal. All telephone numbers are in the 91 city code unless otherwise indicated.

Charleston – This elegant downtown restaurant is considered Sicily's best, with an Art Nouveau decor and excellent food. Specialties include eggplant Charleston (stuffed with pasta), pasta with sardines, and grilled stuffed swordfish rolls. All go well with feudo dei fori white wine. Closed Sundays and from mid-June to mid-October. Reservations advised. Major credit cards accepted. 30 Piazza Ungheria (phone: 321366). In summer, this place has a branch at seaside Mondello (*Le Terrazze*). Viale Regina Elena (phone: 450171). Expensive.

Gourmand's – Palermo businesspeople and politicians favor its modern decor, discreet service, good Sicilian cooking, and small bar. Try the *fettuccine alla Nelson* (homemade pasta in a sauce of zucchini, eggplant, tomato, basil, oregano, anchovies, and mozzarella). Closed Sundays and August 10–20. Reservations advised. Major credit cards accepted. 37 Via della Libertà (phone: 323431). Expensive.

Renato–L'Approdo – One feature of this attractive restaurant is its excellent wine cellar, with some 70,000 bottles from which to choose. Another is its varied menu of traditional Sicilian dishes. Closed Wednesdays. Reservations advised. American Express accepted. 224 Via Messina Marine (phone: 6302881). Expensive.

Friend's Bar Reginella – Despite its out-of-the-way location, this place is favored by Palermo's smart set for its outdoor dining and lavish menu. Book first, then take a taxi. Closed Mondays. Reservations necessary. No credit cards accepted. 138 Via Brunelleschi (phone: 201401). Expensive to moderate.

Il Gambero Rosso – The imaginative menu includes such interesting selections as pasta with oysters, risotto with seafood sausage, and delectable imperial shrimp. Closed Mondays and during November. Reservations necessary. Major credit cards accepted. 30-32 Via Piano Gallo, Mondello (phone: 454685). Expensive to moderate.

Regine – This downtown eatery offers an array of international dishes, made with the local fish and produce. Specialties include *pasta alla Lido* (with chunks of swordfish, clams, shrimps, and tomato) and mixed grilled fish. Closed Sundays and 2 weeks in August. Reservations advised. Major credit cards accepted. 4/A Via Trapani (phone: 586566). Expensive to moderate.

Savoya – Imaginatively prepared Sicilian fare and its hospitable atmosphere make this a popular place with the locals. Try the vegetable appetizers or one of the delicate pasta dishes followed by the wonderfully fresh grilled swordfish. Closed Mondays. Reservations advised. Major credit cards accepted. 22 Via Torrearsa (phone: 582173). Expensive to moderate.

Sympathy Trattoria – At this eatery on the Mondello waterfront, Brooklynese is spoken as well as Sicilian. The fish is excellent in this tiny, colorful place, and you can never be sure just what the person at the next table does for a living. Reservations advised. Major credit cards accepted. 18 Via Piano Gallo, Mondello (phone: 454470). Expensive to moderate.

Sympathy 2 – Great fish dishes at this sister eatery to *Sympathy Trattoria.* Reservations necessary in summer. Major credit cards accepted. Near the beach, 30 minutes from town. Piazza Sferracavallo (phone: 532389). Expensive to moderate.

A'Cuccagna – This well-known, relaxing trattoria is right downtown and features an impressive self-serve antipasto display and typical Palermo dishes. Closed Fridays and 2 weeks in August. No reservations. Major credit cards accepted. 21/A Via Principe di Granatelli (phone: 587267). Moderate.

Terrazza Fiorita – On a summer evening in the city, try this rooftop garden restaurant where the choice of both antipasti and main dishes is enticing. Open for dinner, only in July and August. Reservations necessary. Major credit cards accepted. In the *Grande Albergo e delle Palme,* 389 Via Roma (phone: 583933). Moderate.

La N'grasciata – Habitués of this simple, harborside restaurant call first to ask if the catch is in, and the proprietor has been known to tell customers to come on a better day. You could start with tiny fried baby fish (*u'sciabbacheddu,* in Sicilian dialect) or slices of *bottarga* (pressed tuna roe). Pasta with *bottarga* is also a specialty. Closed Sundays. Reservations advised. Major credit cards accepted. 12 Via Tiro a Segno, in the Sant'Erasmo neighborhood (phone: 6161947). Moderate to inexpensive.

La Playa – Only 3 years old, this seaside restaurant has a warm tone. The seafood antipasto and smoked swordfish are special; so is the lemon sorbet. Open daily. Reservations necessary. Major credit cards accepted. 120 Viale Europa in Ficarazzi, on the outskirts of town (phone: 496538). Moderate to inexpensive.

La Scuderia – The name means "the stable," but this is more a carriage house offering elegantly prepared Sicilian rustic specialties. You'll need to take a taxi. Closed Sundays. Reservations advised. Major credit cards accepted. 9 Viale del Fante (phone: 520323). Moderate to inexpensive.

Da Totuccio – Very popular with locals, this newly renovated, vast, and boisterous trattoria conceals an entire floor above with a patio overlooking the sea. Impressive array of antipasti and desserts. Closed Mondays. Reservations advised. Visa accepted. 26 Via Torre, Mondello (phone: 450151). Moderate to inexpensive.

Il Mirto e la Rosa – Vegetarian dishes with a Sicilian accent. This co-op restaurant opened several years ago with serious culinary ambitions. It offers interesting selections such as pumpkin dishes and vegetable couscous. Closed Sundays. Reservations advised on Saturdays. No credit cards accepted. 30 Via Principe Granelli (phone: 324353). Inexpensive.

Primavera – For sampling basic and beautifully prepared Sicilian dishes such as pasta with sardines, broccoli, or eggplant, this small, family-run trattoria is ideal. Go early. Closed Fridays and Sunday evenings. No reservations. No credit cards accepted. 4 Piazza Bologni (phone: 329408). Inexpensive.

Roney – Known for its people watching, this self-service restaurant serves a wide range of dishes, including pasta, omelettes, and roast meats. Try some of the island's best cannoli and other sweets in its café. No credit cards accepted. 13 Viale della Libertà (phone: 328427). Inexpensive.

Shangai – This small Chinese-red trattoria overlooking the heart of the *Vucciria* market has become a landmark (see *Extra Special*) for its atmosphere and location. The food, however, is notably less exciting. The fish get hauled up from the market below with a basket and rope. Classic Sicilian antipasti and pasta dishes, at times accompanied by owner Benedetto Basile's verses. Closed Wednesdays. Reservations advised. No credit cards accepted. 34 Vicolo dei Mezzani (phone: 589702). Inexpensive.

ROME

If you're traveling from the north, you'll quickly understand why *Italia meridionale,* or southern Italy, begins in Rome. ancient stone ruins basking in the southern sun, baroque swirls teasing the senses at every turn, religious art exploding with color and Catholic sensuality — celebrating life with the conspicuous joie de vivre (here known as *gioia di vivere*) of southern Europe. Rome reaches out to your senses, blinding you with colors, beckoning you to stay. Its appeal is gripping and obviously romantic, inspiring throughout history many an illustrious northern visitor — such as Goethe, Keats, Byron, and Shelley — though today these romantic souls might be repelled by the insufferable noise, the screaming traffic, the exasperating strikes, political demonstrations, and general chaos of modern Rome. Yet despite the familiar symptoms of contemporary blight, Rome remains the Eternal City, ancient capital of the Western world, and center of Christianity for nearly 2,000 years.

Rome lies roughly in the center of the region of Lazio (Latium), just below the knee of boot-shaped Italy, between the Tyrrhenian Sea to the west and the Apennine Mountains to the east. The Tiber River gently curves through the city, with ancient Rome on its left bank, Vatican City and Trastevere (*tras* means across; *tevere,* Tiber) on its right. The original seven hills of Rome are all on the left bank, as is its modern center — the shopping areas that surround Piazza di Spagna (the so-called Spanish Steps), Piazza del Popolo, Via del Corso, Via del Tritone, and the legendary Via Veneto, celebrated in Fellini's film *La Dolce Vita.*

The 3rd-century Aurelian Walls still surround ancient Rome as well as most of papal and modern Rome. The city is unique because its fine buildings span so many centuries of history. There are Etruscan and ancient Roman remains, the most famous of which are the Colosseum and the Forum; buildings from the early Christian period such as the Castel Sant'Angelo; and a wealth of dazzling Renaissance and baroque architecture — from St. Peter's itself to Piazza del Campidoglio, the square designed by Michelangelo. The city abounds in churches, palaces, parks, piazze, statues, and fountains — all of which sparkle in the golden light and clear blue sky of the region.

Rome's beginnings are shrouded in a romantic legend that attributes the city's birth to Romulus and Remus, twin sons of the war god Mars and Rhea, a Vestal Virgin, who encountered Mars in a forest one day. The babies, left to die on the shore of the Tiber River at the foot of the Palatine Hill, were rescued and suckled through infancy by an old she-wolf and grew up to lead a band of adventurers and outlaws. Romulus, the stronger leader of the two, is said to have founded Rome in 753 BC, killing his brother to become its first king.

But earlier traces of habitation have been found on the Palatine Hill — one of the original seven hills — the site of Roma Quadrata, a primitive Rome squared off by a surrounding rectangular wall. Below were the shallows of the Tiber River, where flocks of animals crossed, and trading took place in earlier times. The traditional founding date perhaps refers to when the first settlements of shepherds and farmers on the Palatine took on the shape of a city and the Latins, Sabines, and Etruscans who peopled the area had fused under one system of laws. The name *Roma* was probably a derivation of *Ruma,* an Etruscan noble name.

Following a succession of seven legendary kings, a republic was declared in 509 BC, and a period of expansion began. By 270 BC or so, the entire Italian peninsula was under the protection of Rome, and the resulting political unification brought about a cultural unity as well, a new Roman style in art and literature. Hannibal's defeat at Zama in 201 BC, an event that brought the Second Punic War to an end, prepared the way for further expansion: Rome's dominion over the Mediterranean and its eventual supremacy over Alexander the Great's empire in the East and over Spain and Gaul in the West.

A long period of civil war ended with Julius Caesar's defeat of Pompey in 48 BC, but the brilliant conqueror of Gaul was assassinated in the Senate 4 years later. His great-nephew and heir, Octavian, continued in the victorious vein, becoming, with the honorific name of Augustus, Rome's first emperor and one of its best administrators. Augustus is said to have found Rome a city of brick and to have left it a city of marble; the Theater of Marcellus and the Mausoleum of Augustus are among his many fine constructions that survive today.

The reign of Augustus (27 BC–AD 14) saw Roman civilization at its peak, and it ushered in 2 centuries of peace known as the Pax Romana. Wherever they went, the Romans introduced brilliant feats of engineering and architecture, as well as their own culture, government, and law. Persecution of the Christians, which had begun as early as Nero's reign — he blamed the burning of Rome on the new sect and executed large numbers of them in AD 64 — came to an end in the early 4th century, when Constantine the Great issued the Edict of Milan, guaranteeing freedom of worship for all religions. But Rome by now had become top-heavy with its own administration; the empire was divided in 395, with an eastern section in Byzantium (Constantinople, now Istanbul). This was the beginning of the end.

Rome's grandeur had long passed by the 5th century, when a series of economic crises, internal decadence and corruption, and repeated barbarian invasions led to the final fall of the empire with the deposition of her last emperor, Romulus Augustulus, in 476.

Thus began the Dark Ages, fraught with struggles between the empire and the church, which was centered in the papacy at Rome. Struggles between empire and papacy ensued. The Holy See, under Pope Clement V, actually fled Rome in the 14th century, taking up residence in Avignon, France, for 70 years. During that period, the city of Rome declined, and its population, which had been as many as a million at the time of Augustus, shrank to less than 50,000. The Capitoline Hill and once-bustling Roman Forum became pastures for goats and cows. Sheep grazed in St. Peter's.

The popes returned in 1377, and Rome again became the capital of the

Catholic world. Under papal patronage it was soon reborn artistically and culturally. During the 15th century, restoration of St. Peter's began, prior to its complete reconstruction; the Vatican complex was built; and new palaces, churches, and well-planned streets changed the face of the city. Powerful popes commissioned artists and architects to beautify Rome, and their genius created sumptuous palaces, splendid villas, and squares adorned with fountains and obelisks, until a second city grew out of the ruins of ancient Rome to match its former splendor. The 17th century brought the birth of baroque Rome, with its dominating figure, architect, sculptor, and painter Gian Lorenzo Bernini, whose masterpieces perhaps still best symbolize the spirit of this magnificent and undeniably theatrical city.

The comfortable security of the popes was shaken by the arrival of Napoleon Bonaparte in 1798. He soon set up a republic of Rome, deporting Pope Pius VI briefly to France, and in 1805 he was crowned King of Italy, proclaiming Rome a sort of second capital of the French Empire. In 1809, Napoleon declared the papal territories a part of France and in return was excommunicated by Pope Pius VII, who was deported to Fontainebleau. By 1815, the Napoleonic regime had collapsed, the papal kingdom was reconciled with France, and the pope was back in Rome, but the sparks of nationalistic passion had already been ignited in Italian hearts.

Friction between papal neutralism and patriotic fervor drove Pope Pius IX out of Rome to Gaeta in 1848. In 1849, Rome was again proclaimed a republic under the leadership of patriot Giuseppe Mazzini. Twice the French tried to restore the temporal power of the pope in Rome, meeting strong resistance from Republican forces led by Garibaldi. Finally, in 1870, the Italians entered Rome through a breach in the Aurelian Walls at Porta Pia and incorporated the city into the kingdom of Italy. That act dissolved the pontifical state and made Italian unity complete. A year later, Rome became the capital of the kingdom.

Mussolini's march on Rome in 1922 began the infamous Fascist regime that lasted until his downfall some 20 years later. The city was then occupied by the Germans until its liberation in 1944 by the Allies. In 1946, a referendum was held and Italy was declared a republic — just as it had been nearly 2½ millennia earlier.

Today, Rome is still the capital of Italy and of the Catholic church, as well as the home of some 3.5 million people (up from 260,000 inhabitants in 1870). Many Romans are employed in tourism-related industries and in government — in a city often strangled by bureaucratic problems. Besides filmmaking (in its cinematic heyday, Rome was called "Hollywood on the Tiber") and a certain amount of printing, there is some small-scale production of foodstuffs, pharmaceuticals, building materials, armaments, plastics, glass, clothing, religious articles, and handmade crafts. Thousands of artisans work in *botteghe* (shops) that open onto the streets in the area around Piazza Navona and in Trastevere.

For a society with significant problems — insufficient housing, impossible traffic, a soaring cost of living, and worrisome pollution — today's Romans still enjoy a relaxed way of life, as they have done for centuries. Perhaps nowhere north of Naples is the *arte di arrangiarsi* — the art of making do, or surviving with style — learned with such skill and practiced with such a timeless sense of resignation.

The *dolce vita* nightlife, more a figment of Fellini's imagination than a reality for any more than a handful of rich and/or famous Romans, has become subdued, but an unmistakable air of conviviality still prevails.

Not even soaring prices have limited the traditional Roman pastime of lingering lunches and late-night dinners at the city's 5,000 or so restaurants and trattorie. A sunny day at any time of the year still fills the cobblestone squares with diners at open-air eateries. They usually are engaged in animated conversation over their robust Roman food and inexpensive carafe wine from the Castelli (the surrounding hill towns such as Frascati). Most visitors are pleased to "do as the Romans do." No sense worrying about high prices and pollution if the inhabitants don't.

Roma, Non Basta Una Vita (Rome, A Lifetime Is Not Enough), by the late Italian author and journalist Silvio Negro, hints, with justification, at the impossibility of ever knowing everything about this city. For visitors who harbor the illusion of having seen all the ruins, churches, and monuments of Rome's glorious past, it may be time to begin discovering her countless hidden treasures, best done by walking the back streets and alleyways of the historic center (cars have limited access to many of them). Returning visitors will notice a spruced-up look — there are newly renovated palazzi everywhere, painted in the pale pastels popular in the early years of this century. And the *1990 World Cup* soccer games spurred on some transportation improvements as well — a new tram line and an efficient train service from Fiumicino Airport to downtown Rome.

If you feel suffocated by city life, try a day or two in the neighboring countryside. The surrounding Lazio region, sandwiched between the Tyrrhenian Sea and the Apennine Mountains, offers seaside resorts, rolling hills topped by medieval towns, picturesque lakes, rivers, and green meadows studded with umbrella pines, cypress trees, and wildflowers. Take an organized excursion to the Villa d'Este and Hadrian's Villa in Tivoli; to the Castelli Romani, or Roman hill towns, where the pope has his summer home; or to the excavations of Ostia Antica, the ancient port of Rome.

But take time to sit back and enjoy Rome. Visit the Forum and the Colosseum by day, and return at night when the ruins are bathed in gentler light to meditate over the rise and fall of ancient Rome. Watch the play of water in the Trevi Fountain or any of Rome's nearly 1,000 other fountains of every size and shape. See the ancient Roman Theater of Marcellus, which has been a Roman amphitheater, a medieval fort, a Renaissance palace, and which now contains apartments. Enjoy the savory cooking of the Lazio region. Ride a rented bicycle or jog in the Villa Borghese. Sip an *aperitivo* on the famed Via Veneto or at one of the many *caffès* that suddenly appear in unexpected corners of the historic city center.

Locally it is believed that on the last day of the world, while all the rest of humankind broods and repents, the Romans will throw a great farewell party, a gastronomic feast to end them all, with wine flowing from the city's many fountains. With the apocalypse not yet at hand, and despite the agonies besetting the country at large, the Eternal City remains eternally inviting.

ROME AT-A-GLANCE

SEEING THE CITY: Enjoy the magnificent view of all of Rome and the surrounding hill towns from Piazzale Garibaldi at the top of the Giancolo (Janiculum hill). It's best at sunset. Another panorama is visible from the top of St. Peter's dome. For a view of Rome dominated by St. Peter's, go to the terrace of the Pincio, next to the Villa Borghese, above Piazza del Popolo. And the most unusual view is of the dome of St. Peter's as seen in miniature through the keyhole of the gate to the priory of the Knights of Malta, on Piazza dei Cavalieri di Malta at the end of Via di Santa Sabina, on the Aventine hill. The picturesque piazza was designed by engraver Piranesi, a surrealist in spirit though he lived in the 18th century. For a real treat, a bird's-eye view of Rome is available via helicopter. Leaving from the Centro Sperimentale d'Aviazione at Urbe Airport (825 Via Salaria; phone: 812-3017), the $125 per-person fee yields 15 minutes of breathtaking spectacle. (Minimum of five passengers; reserve 1 week in advance.)

SPECIAL PLACES: Rome cannot be seen in a day, 3 days, a week, or even a year. If your time is limited to a few days, an organized bus tour is your best bet. (A quick and interesting one covers some 45 major sights in 3 hours. Although there is no guide, a short brochure gives the highlights. It leaves Piazza dei Cinquecento at 3:30 PM and, in winter, at 2:30 PM and costs about $6. Check the *ATAC* booth in the square for bus No. 110; it operates daily in season, weekends only out of season.) The Dutch Roman Catholic sisters of Foyer Unitas (30 Via Santa Maria dell'Anima; phone: 686-5951) lead free (though an offering is appreciated) tours to many sites around the city and the Vatican, and give slide presentations on various subjects (not always religious in nature). In addition, they offer information about Rome to anyone who drops in. Walking tours (usually in English) generally take place on Tuesdays, Thursdays, and some Saturdays. Then, when you've seen where your interests lie, grab your most comfortable walking shoes and a map. Most of historic Rome, which also is the city's center today, is within the 3rd-century Aurelian Walls and is delightfully walkable.

For practical purposes, the "must-sees" below are divided into ancient, papal, and modern Rome, but elements of two or all three categories often are found in one site — such as a sleek modern furniture shop in a Renaissance palace built with stones from the Colosseum. A further heading focuses on the palaces, fountains, splendid piazzas, and streets of Rome. The ancient center of the city is very close to Piazza Venezia, the heart of the modern city, and most of the sights of ancient Rome are around the Capitoline, Palatine, and Aventine hills. They can be seen on foot — though they were not built — in 1 day. Much of papal Rome is centered in the Vatican, but since all of Rome is a religious center, some of its many fascinating and beautiful churches are included under this heading. (For other churches, and for museums not mentioned below, see "Museums" in *Sources and Resources.*) Two bits of trivia worth noting: Throughout Rome, you will come across the initials *SPQR,* which stand for *Senatus Populusque Romanus* (the senate and the people of Rome). Ancient Romans used these letters to distinguish public works from private holdings, and as part of the city's inheritance they are still to be seen today — on everything from a magnificent monument to a mundane manhole cover. What's more, there really are seven hills of ancient Rome, and for the record they are called the Palatine, Capitoline, Quirinal, Viminal, Esquiline, Caelian, and the Aventine.

Virtually all the museums, monuments, and archaeological sites run by the state or city are closed on Sunday afternoons, and many on Mondays. Opening and closing hours change often (some are closed indefinitely because of strikes, personnel shortages, or restorations — it is estimated that only a third of Italy's artworks are exhibited), so check with your hotel, the tourist office, or the daily newspapers before starting out. Where possible, we have listed hours that seem relatively reliable.

Warning: Pickpockets work all around the city, but are especially numerous on such bus lines as the No. 56 to Via Veneto, and the Nos. 62 and 64 to the Vatican, and at the most popular tourist spots, even though plainclothes police scour these areas. Watch out especially for gangs of Gypsy children who will surround you and make straight for your wallet or purse. They haunt the Tiber bridges and the quayside walk to Porta Portese. Carry your shoulder bag on the arm *away* from passing vehicular traffic to avoid bag snatchers on motor scooters. Do not hang purses on café or restaurant chairs. Avoid carrying your passport and any significant amount of money around with you, and be sure to store valuables in a hotel safe-deposit box.

ANCIENT ROME

Colosseo (Colosseum) – It's said that when the Colosseum falls, Rome will fall — and the world will follow. This symbol of the eternity of Rome, the grandest and most celebrated of all its monuments, was completed in AD 80, and it is a logical starting point for a visitor to ancient Rome. See it in daylight, and return to see it by moonlight. The enormous arena, ⅓ mile in circumference and 137 feet high, once accommodated 50,000 spectators. To provide shade in the summer, a special detachment of sailors stretched a great awning over the top. There were 80 entrances (progressively numbered, except for the four main ones), allowing the crowds to quickly claim their marble seats. Underneath were subterranean passages where animals and other apparatus were hidden from view. In the arena itself, Christians were thrown to lions, wild beasts destroyed one another, and gladiators fought to the death. Gladiatorial combats lasted until 404, when Honorius put an end to them (possibly after a monk had thrown himself into the arena in protest and was killed by the angry crowd); animal combats were stopped toward the middle of the 6th century.

The Colosseum was abused by later generations. It was a fort in the Middle Ages; something of a quarry during the Renaissance, when its marble and travertine were used in the construction of St. Peter's and other buildings; and in the 18th century it even became a manure depot for the production of saltpeter. Yet it remains a symbol of the grandeur of Rome. Open daily. Admission charge for the upper level. Piazzale del Colosseo.

Palatino (Palatine Hill) – Adjacent to the Colosseum and the Roman Forum, the Palatine is where Rome began. Its Latin name is the source of the word *palace.* In fact, great men — Cicero, Crassus, Marc Antony — lived on this regal hill, and the Emperors of Rome — Augustus, Tiberius, Caligula, Nero, Domitian, Septimius Severus — built their palaces here, turning the hill into an imperial preserve. A 12th-century author called the spot the "palace of the Monarchy of the Earth, wherein is the capital seat of the whole world." In ruins by the Middle Ages, the ancient structures were incorporated into the sumptuous Villa Farnese in the 16th century, and the Farnese Gardens were laid out, the first botanical gardens in the world.

The Palatine is a lovely spot for a walk or a picnic. See especially the so-called House of Livia (actually of her husband, Augustus), with its remarkable frescoes; Domitian's Palace of the Flavians, built by his favorite architect, Rabirius; the impressive stadium; the view from the terrace of the Palace of Septimius Severus; and the remains of the Farnese Gardens at the top with another superb panorama of the nearby Forums. Closed Tuesdays; admission charge includes the Roman Forum. Enter at Via di San Gregorio or by way of the Roman Forum on Via dei Fori Imperiali.

Foro Romano (Roman Forum) – Adjoining the Palatine Hill is the Roman Forum, a mass of ruins overgrown with weeds and trees that was the commercial, civil, and religious center of ancient Rome. Its large ceremonial buildings included three triumphal arches, two public halls, half a dozen temples, and numerous monuments and statues. Set in what was once a marshy valley at the foot of the Capitoline Hill, the Forum was abandoned after the barbarian invasions and had become a cattle pasture by the Renaissance. When excavations began during the last century, it was under 20 feet of dirt.

Highlights of the Forum include the triumphal Arch of Septimius Severus, built by that emperor in AD 203; the Arch of Titus (AD 81), adorned with scenes depicting the victories of Titus, especially his conquest of Jerusalem and the spoils of Solomon's Temple; the ten magnificent marble columns — with a 16th-century baroque façade — of the Temple of Antoninus and Faustina; the eight columns of the Temple of Saturn (497 BC), site of the *Saturnalia,* the precursor of our *Mardi Gras;* three splendid Corinthian columns of the Temple of Castor and Pollux (484 BC); the Temple of Vesta and the nearby House of the Vestal Virgins, where highly esteemed virgins guarded the sacred flame of Vesta and their virginity — under the threat of being buried alive if they lost the latter. The once imposing Basilica of Maxentius (Basilica di Massenzio), otherwise known as the Basilica of Constantine, because it was begun by one and finished by the other, still has imposing proportions: 328 by 249 feet. Only the north aisle and three huge arches remain of this former law court and exchange.

As this is one of the most bewildering archaeological sites, a guide is extremely useful, especially for short-term visitors. A detailed plan and portable sound guide are available (in English) at the entrance. Open from 9 AM to 3 PM. Closed Tuesdays. Admission charge includes the Palatine Hill. Entrance on Via dei Fori Imperiali, opposite Via Cavour.

Fori Imperiali (Imperial Forums) – Next to the Roman Forum and now divided in two by Via dei Fori Imperiali is the civic center begun by Caesar to meet the demands of the expanding city when the Roman Forum became too congested. It was completed by Augustus, with further additions by later emperors. Abandoned in the Middle Ages, the Imperial Forums were revived by Mussolini, who constructed Via dei Fori Imperiali in 1932.

Two of the major sights are Trajan's Forum and Trajan's Market. Trajan's Forum, although not open to visitors, can be seen from the sidewalk surrounding it. It is memorable for the formidable 138-foot-high Trajan's Column, composed of 19 blocks of marble, now beautifully restored. The column is decorated with a spiral frieze depicting the Roman army under Trajan during the campaign against the Dacians — some 2,500 figures climbing toward the top where, since 1588, a statue of St. Peter has stood instead of the original one of Trajan. The Market (entered at 94 Via IV Novembre) is a 3-story construction with about 150 shops and commercial exchanges, some newly restored. Admission charge for Trajan's Market (closed Sunday afternoons and Mondays). Via dei Fori Imperiali.

Carcere Mamertino (Mamertine Prison) – Just off Via dei Fori Imperiali between the Roman Forum and the Campidoglio is the prison where Vercingetorix died and where, according to legend, St. Peter was imprisoned by Nero and used a miraculous spring to baptize his fellow inmates. From 509 to 27 BC it was a state prison where many were tortured and slaughtered. Much later, the prison became a chapel consecrated to St. Peter (called San Pietro in Carcere). To Charles Dickens it was a "ponderous, obdurate old prison . . . hideous and fearsome to behold." The gloomy dungeons below, made of enormous blocks of stone, are among the oldest structures in Rome. Via San Pietro in Carcere off Via dei Fori Imperiali.

Circo Massimo (Circus Maximus) – A few ruins dot the open grassy valley that once was the site of the great 4th-century BC arena. Originally ⅓ of a mile long and big enough to accommodate 250,000 spectators, the horseshoe shape of this racetrack served as a pattern for the other circuses that later arose in the Roman world. Today, the obelisks that decorated a long central shelf can be seen in Rome's Piazza del Laterano and Piazza del Popolo. The medieval tower that still stands is one of the few remains of the great fortresses built by the Frangipane family. Behind the Palatine Hill.

Pantheon – This, the best preserved of Roman buildings, was founded in 27 BC by Agrippa, who probably dedicated it to the seven planetary divinities, and rebuilt by Hadrian in AD 125. It became a Christian church in 606 and contains the tombs of Raphael and the first two Kings of Italy. The building is remarkable for its round plan combined with a Greek-style rectangular porch of 16 Corinthian columns (three were replaced in the Renaissance), for the ingenuity evident in the construction of the dome, and for its balanced proportions (the diameter of the interior and the height of the dome are the same). Closed Mondays. No admission charge. Piazza della Rotonda.

Terme di Caracalla (Baths of Caracalla) – These ruins are in the southern part of the city, near the beginning of the Appia Antica. Built in the 3rd century, they accommodated 1,600 bathers, but all that's left are sunbaked walls and some wall paintings. The vast scale makes a picturesque ruin, however, and Shelley composed "Prometheus Unbound" here. Operas are staged here in the summer. Baths open daily from 9 AM to 1:30 PM. Admission charge. Enter on Viale delle Terme di Caracalla, just short of Piazzale Numa Pompilio.

Porta San Sebastiano (St. Sebastian Gate) – This majestic opening in the 3rd-century Aurelian Walls (which encircle the city of Rome for 12 miles, with 383 defense towers) marks the beginning of the Appia Antica. It was, in fact, originally called the Porta Appia, and was rebuilt in the 5th century and restored again in the 6th century. Every Sunday morning, guided tours walk along the walls from Porta San Sebastiano to Porta Latina, affording good views of the Baths of Caracalla, the Appia Antica, and the Alban hills in the distance. The *Museo delle Mura* (Museum of the Walls), incorporated into the two medieval towers of the gate, contains local archaeological finds. Open Tuesdays through Saturdays from 9 AM to 1:30 PM; Tuesdays, Thursdays, and Saturdays from 4 to 7 PM; and Sundays from 9 AM to 1 PM. Admission charge. 18 Porta San Sebastiano (phone: 788-7035).

Via Appia Antica (Appian Way) – Portions of this famous 2,300-year-old road are still paved with the well-laid stones of the Romans. By 190 BC the Appian Way extended all the way from Rome to Capua, Benevento, and Brindisi on Italy's southeastern coast. Although its most famous sights are the Catacombs (see below), many other interesting ruins are scattered along the first 10 miles (16 km) of the route, which were used as a graveyard by patrician families because Roman law forbade burial (but not cremation) within the walls. Among the sights worth seeing is the Domine Quo Vadis chapel, about ½ mile beyond Porta San Sebastiano. It was built in the mid-9th century on the site where St. Peter, fleeing from Nero, had a vision of Christ. St. Peter said "Domine quo vadis?" ("Lord, whither goest thou?"). Christ replied that he was going back to Rome to be crucified again because Peter had abandoned the Christians in a moment of danger. Peter then returned to Rome to face his own martyrdom. Also see the Tomb of Cecilia Metella, daughter of a Roman general, a very picturesque ruin not quite 2 miles (3 km) from Porta San Sebastiano. Open daily from 9 AM to 1:30 PM. Admission charge.

Catacombe di San Callisto (Catacombs of St. Calixtus) – Of all the catacombs in Rome, these are the most famous. Catacombs are burial places in the form of galleries, or tunnels — miles of them, arranged in as many as 5 tiers — carved underground. Marble or terracotta slabs mark the openings where the bodies were laid to rest. Early Christians hid, prayed, and were buried in them from the 1st through the 4th centuries. After Christianity became the official religion of Rome, they were no longer necessary, but they remained places of pilgrimage because they contain the remains of so many early martyrs. St. Cecilia, St. Eusebius, and many martyred popes are buried here. Take a guided bus tour or a public bus. At the catacombs, guides, who are often priests, conduct regular tours in several languages. Closed Wednesdays. Admission charge. 110 Via Appia Antica.

Terme di Diocleziano (Baths of Diocletian) – West of the center of Rome, not far from the train station, are the largest baths in the empire, built in AD 305 to hold 3,000 people. The site now houses both the Church of Santa Maria degli Angeli, adapted by Michelangelo from the hall of the tepidarium of the baths, and the *Museo Nazionale Romano delle Terme* (National Museum of Rome of the Baths). The museum, one of the great archaeological museums of the world, contains numerous objects from ancient Rome — paintings, statuary, stuccowork, bronzes, objects of art, and even a mummy of a young girl. Admission charge to the museum, which is open Tuesdays through Saturdays from 9 AM to 1:45 PM and Sundays from 9 AM to 1 PM. The church is on Piazza della Repubblica; museum entrance is on Piazza dei Cinquecento (phone: 460530).

Castel Sant'Angelo – Dramatically facing the 2nd-century Ponte Sant'Angelo (St. Angelo Bridge — lined with statues of angels, including two originals by Bernini), this imposing monument was built by Hadrian in AD 139 as a burial place for himself and his family, but it has undergone many alterations, including the addition of the square wall with bastions at each corner named after the four evangelists. Later, as a fortress and prison, it saw a lot of history, especially in the 16th century. Some of the victims of the Borgias met their end here, popes took refuge here from antipapal forces (an underground passage connects it to the Vatican), and Benvenuto Cellini spent time as a prisoner on the premises. The last act of Puccini's opera *Tosca* takes place here. It is now a museum containing relics, works of art, ancient weapons, a prison cell, and a recently restored, 300-year-old papal bathtub. Open Mondays from 2 to 7:30 PM, Tuesdays through Saturdays from 9 AM to 7:30 PM, Sundays and holidays from 9 AM to 1 PM. Admission charge. Lungotevere Castello.

Teatro di Marcello (Theater of Marcellus) – Begun by Caesar, completed by Augustus, and named after the latter's nephew, this was the first stone theater in Rome and was said to have been the model for the Colosseum. It seated from 10,000 to 14,000 spectators and was in use for over 300 years. During the Middle Ages, what remained of the edifice became a fortress, and during the 16th century, the Savelli family transformed it into a palace, which later passed to the powerful Orsini family. The sumptuous apartments at the top still are inhabited by the Orsinis, whose emblem of a bear (*orso*) appears on the gateway in Via di Monte Savello, where the theater's stage once stood. Via del Teatro di Marcello. The palace can be visited only with a permit from City Hall: *Comune di Roma,* Ripartizione X, 29 Via del Portico d'Ottavia.

Largo Argentina – Just west of Piazza Venezia are the remains of four Roman temples, which, still unidentified, are among the oldest relics in Rome. It was at this site that Julius Caesar actually was assassinated (the Senate was meeting here temporarily because of fire damage to the Forum). The area, also the home of Rome's largest stray cat colony, is slated for much-needed archaeological excavation and restoration. Corso Vittorio Emanuele II.

Piramide di Caio Cestio (Pyramid of Caius Cestius) – In the southern part of the city, near the Protestant cemetery, is Rome's only pyramid. Completely covered with white marble, 121 feet high, it has a burial chamber inside decorated with frescoes and inscriptions. (Note: the interior can be visited only with special permission from the *Sovrintendenza Comunale ai Musei,* Monumenti, 3 Piazza Caffarelli.) Piazzale Ostiense.

PAPAL ROME

Città del Vaticano (Vatican City) – The Vatican City State, the world's second-smallest country (the smallest is also in Rome, the Sovereign Military Order of Malta, on Via Condotti), fits into a land area of less than 1 square mile within the city of Rome.

Headquarters of the Roman Catholic church, the Vatican has been an independent state under the sovereignty of the pope since the Lateran Treaties were concluded in 1929. The Vatican has its own printing press and newspaper (*Osservatore Romano*), its own currency, railway, and radio station, as well as its own post office and postage stamps (thriving right now, with the surrounding Italian post offices functioning so badly, so do all your mailing from here! Vatican stamps may be used in Rome but not elsewhere in Italy, while Italian stamps may *not* be used in Vatican mailboxes). Souvenir packets of stamps can be purchased at the Philatelic Service in the office building on the left side of St. Peter's Church, entered under the Arch of the Bells. The Vatican's extraterritorial rights cover the other major basilicas (Santa Maria Maggiore, San Giovanni in Laterano, and San Paolo Fuori le Mura), the pope's summer home at Castel Gandolfo, and a few other buildings. It is governed politically by the pope and protected by an army of Swiss Guards (since 1506 when the corps was formed by Pope Julius II) whose uniforms were designed by Raphael. The changing of the guards takes place daily — at 9:30 and 11 AM, and 12:30, 2, 3:30, 4:30, and 5:30 PM.

General audiences are held by the pope every Wednesday on St. Peter's Square (at 10 AM during the summer; 11 AM in winter); in bad weather they are held in the Sala Udienza Paolo VI. Special audiences can be arranged for groups of 25 to 50 persons. Given John Paul II's propensity for travel, however, it is a good idea to check on his whereabouts before trekking off to the Vatican to see him. To arrange for free tickets to papal audiences, write to Bishop Dino Monduzzi (Prefettura della Casa Pontificia, Vatican City 00120, Italy). Be sure to include your address in Rome. Reservations will be confirmed by mail before the audience, but tickets will be delivered by messenger the day before. Last-minute bookings can be made in person from 9 AM to noon, up to 24 hours in advance, space permitting. They are available at the Prefettura office, located at the bronze doors of the right wing of the colonnade of St. Peter's Square.

Guided tours in English are offered year-round of Vatican City, including the underground excavations, the gardens, the Sistine Chapel, and the radio station. Sign up at the Ufficio Scavi (Excavations Office; near the Arch of the Bells; phone: 698-5318) for a 90-minute tour of the pre-Constantine necropolis in the Vatican, where it is believed that St. Peter is buried (closed Sundays; admission charge). Book a tour of the gardens at the *Vatican Tourist Information Office* (on the left side of St. Peter's Square, facing the church; phone: 698-4866). They are offered daily except Wednesdays and Sundays, from 10 AM to noon; in English on Thursdays. Admission charge. Also ask at the information office about tours of the Sistine Chapel (or make prior arrangements for a group visit through a travel agency). Weekdays from 8:30 AM to 1 PM there is a free 1-hour tour of Vatican Radio (3 Piazza Pia; phone: 698-34643), which broadcasts in 33 languages to 100 countries. Tickets also are available through Foyer Unitas (30 Via Santa Maria dell'Anima; phone: 686-5951) and Santa Susanna Catholic Church (14 Via XX Settembre; phone: 482-7510). Visits to the famous *Vatican Mosaic Workshop,* a school where students have been making miniature and full-size mosaic pictures for centuries, can be arranged by writing to Mons. Virgilio Noe (*Studio del Mosaico Vaticano,* Vatican City 00120, Italy; phone: 698-4466).

Piazza San Pietro (St. Peter's Square) – This 17th-century architectural masterpiece was created by Gian Lorenzo Bernini, the originator of the baroque style in Rome. The vast, open area is elliptical, with two semicircular colonnades, each four deep in Doric columns, framing the façade of St. Peter's Basilica. The colonnades are surmounted with statues of saints. An 83½-foot obelisk, shipped in a specially made boat from Heliopolis to Rome by Caligula, marks the center of the square and is flanked by two fountains that are still fed by the nearly 4-century-old Acqua Paola aqueduct which brings water from just north of Rome. Find the circular paving stone between the obelisk and one of the fountains and turn toward a colonnade: From that vantage point it will appear to be only a single row of columns.

Basilica di San Pietro (St. Peter's Basilica) – The first church here was built by

Constantine on the site where St. Peter was martyred and subsequently buried. Some 11 centuries later it was the worse for wear, so renovation and then total reconstruction were undertaken. Michelangelo deserves a great deal of the credit for the existing church, but not all of it: Bramante began the plans in the early 16th century, with the dome of the Pantheon in mind; Michelangelo finished them in mid-century, thinking of Brunelleschi's dome in Florence. Giacomo della Porta took over the project at Michelangelo's death, actually raising the dome by the end of the century. In the early 17th century, Carlo Maderno made some modifications to the structure and completed the façade, and by the middle of the century Bernini was working on his colonnades. Open daily in summer from 7 AM to 7 PM, in winter from 7 AM to 6 PM. The vast dome of St. Peter's is visible from nearly everywhere in the city, just as the entire city is visible from the summit of the dome. For a fee, a visitor may go up into the dome by elevator, then take a staircase to the top for a panoramic view of Rome or a bird's-eye view of the pope's backyard. Also inside the basilica is the *Museo Storico* (Historical Museum; phone: 698-3410) which houses part of the Vatican's treasures. The dome and museum are open daily in summer from 8:30 AM to 5:30 PM, in winter from 8:30 AM to 4:30 PM. No admission charge.

The door farthest to the right of the portico is the Holy Door, opened and closed by the pope at the beginning and end of each *Jubilee Year,* usually only four times a century. The door farthest to the left is by the modern Italian sculptor Giacomo Manzù and dates from the 1960s. Among the treasures and masterpieces inside the basilica are the famous *Pietà* by Michelangelo (now encased in bulletproof glass since its mutilation and restoration a decade ago); the *Baldacchino* by Bernini, a colossal baroque amalgam of architecture and decorative sculpture weighing 46 tons; and the 13th-century statue of St. Peter by Arnolfo Di Cambio, his toes kissed smooth by the faithful. The interior of St. Peter's is gigantic and so overloaded with decoration that it takes some time to get a sense of the whole. Piazza San Pietro.

Musei Vaticani (Vatican Museums) – The Vatican's museum complex houses one of the most impressive collections in the world, embracing works of art of every epoch. It also contains some masterpieces created on the spot, foremost of which is the extraordinary Sistine Chapel, with Michelangelo's frescoes of the *Creation* on the ceiling (painted from 1508 to 1512) and his *Last Judgment* on the altar wall (1534 to 1541). The highly controversial restoration of the ceiling (sponsored by Japan's largest TV network) — only the first phase of the project — was completed 2 years ago after 10 years of work, and the removal of centuries of soot revealed unexpected vibrancy in Michelangelo's colors. A new lighting system also was installed in the chapel, and footnotes are being added to art histories. The second phase — restoration of the *Last Judgment* — is expected to take at least another year. The chapel is open in summer from 9 AM to 4 PM, the rest of the year from 9 AM to 1 PM.

While Michelangelo was painting the Sistine Chapel ceiling for Pope Julius II, the 25-year-old Raphael was working on the Stanza della Segnatura, one of the magnificent Raphael Rooms commissioned by the same pope, which would occupy the painter until his death. Also part of the Vatican museum complex are the *Pio-Clementino Museum of Greco-Roman Antiquities,* which houses such marvelous statues as *Laocoön and His Sons* and the *Apollo Belvedere;* the *Gregorian Etruscan Museum;* the *Pinacoteca* (Picture Gallery); the Library; and the Gregorian Profane, Pio-Cristiano, and Missionary-Ethnological sectors. Open 8:45 AM to 1:45 PM (longer in summer); closed Sundays except the last Sunday of the month, when the complex is open at no charge; other times there is an admission charge. Entrance on Viale Vaticano (phone: 698-3333).

San Giovanni in Laterano (Church of St. John Lateran) – Founded by Pope Melchiades in the 4th century, this is the cathedral of Rome, the pope's parish church, in effect. It suffered barbarian vandalism, an earthquake, and several fires across the centuries; its interior was largely rebuilt in the 17th century by Borromini, who maintained the 16th-century wooden ceiling (the principal façade belongs to the 18th century). Older sections are the lovely cloisters, dating from the 13th century, and the baptistry, from the time of Constantine. The adjoining Lateran Palace was built in the 15th century on the site of an earlier one that had been the home of the popes from Constantine's day to the Avignon Captivity and that had been destroyed by fire. In front of the palace and church are the Scala Santa (Holy Stairs), traditionally believed to have come from the palace of Pontius Pilate in Jerusalem and to have been climbed by Christ at the time of the Passion. The 28 marble steps, climbed by worshipers on their knees, lead to the Sancta Sanctorum, once the popes' private chapel (not open to the public, but visible through the grating). Both the chapel and the stairs were part of the earlier Lateran Palace but survived the fire. Also in the piazza is the oldest obelisk in Rome. Piazza di San Giovanni in Laterano.

Santa Maria Maggiore (Church of St. Mary Major) – A 5th-century church, rebuilt in the 13th century, with an 18th-century façade and the tallest campanile in Rome. It has particularly interesting 5th-century mosaics and a ceiling that was, according to tradition, gilded with the first gold to arrive from the New World. Piazza di Santa Maria Maggiore.

PIAZZAS, PALACES, AND OTHER SIGHTS

Piazza del Campidoglio – The Capitoline was the smallest of the original seven hills, but since it was the political and religious center of ancient Rome, it was also the most important. When the need arose in the 16th century for some modern city planning, the task was given to someone worthy of the setting. Thus, the harmonious square seen today, with its delicate, elliptical, star-patterned pavement centered on a magnificent 2nd-century bronze equestrian statue of Marcus Aurelius (removed for restoration), is the design of none other than Michelangelo. The piazza is flanked by palaces on three sides: Palazzo Nuovo and Palazzo dei Conservatori, facing each other and together making up the *Musei Capitolini* (Capitoline Museums), and the Palazzo Senatorio, between the two, which houses officials of the municipal government. The *Capitoline Museums* are famous for an especially valuable collection of antique sculptures, including the *Capitoline Venus,* the *Dying Gaul,* a bronze statue (known as the *Spinario*) of a boy removing a thorn from his foot, and the *Capitoline Wolf,* an Etruscan bronze to which Romulus and Remus were added during the Renaissance. Open Tuesdays through Saturdays from 9 AM to 1:30 PM, and Sundays from 9 AM to 1 PM. Admission charge.

Piazza di Spagna (Spanish Steps) – One of the most picturesque settings of 18th-century Rome was named after a palace that housed the Spanish Embassy to the Holy See. The famous Spanish Steps actually were built by the French to connect the French quarter above with the Spanish area below. One of Rome's fine French churches, Trinità dei Monti, hovers over the 138 steps at the top, as does an ancient obelisk placed there by Pius VI in 1789. At the bottom of the steps — which in the spring are covered with hundreds of pots of azaleas — is the Barcaccia Fountain, depicting a sinking barge, inspired by the Tiber's flooding in 1589. Modern art historians disagree on whether this fountain, the oldest architectural feature of the square, was designed by Pietro Bernini or his son, the famous Gian Lorenzo Bernini.

Over the years, the steps have become a haunt of large crowds of young visitors, and all manner of crafts sales, caricature sketchers, and musicians contribute to the throng. The house where John Keats spent the last 3 months of his life and died, in February 1821, is next to the Spanish Steps at No. 26. It is now the *Keats-Shelley Memorial House* (phone: 678-4235), a museum dedicated to the English Romantic poets, especially Keats, Shelley, Byron, and Leigh Hunt, with a library of more than 9,000 volumes of their works. Open weekdays from 9 AM to 5:30 PM (with a lunchbreak). Admission charge.

Via Condotti – A sort of Fifth Avenue of Rome, lined with the city's most exclusive shops, including *Gucci, Bulgari,* and *Ferragamo.* Only a few blocks long, it begins at the foot of the Spanish Steps, ends at Via del Corso, and is a favorite street for window shopping and the ritual evening *passeggiata,* or promenade, since it is — like much of the area — closed to traffic. Via Condotti's name derives from the water conduits built under it by Gregory XIII in the 16th century.

One of Via Condotti's landmarks is the famous *Antico Caffè Greco,* at No. 86, long a hangout for Romans and foreigners. Among its habitués were Goethe, Byron, Liszt, Buffalo Bill, Mark Twain, Oscar Wilde, and the Italian painter Giorgio de Chirico. The place is full of busts, statues, and varied mementos of its clientele, and the somber waiters still dress in tails. Another landmark, at No. 68, is the smallest sovereign state in the world, consisting of one historic palazzo. If you peek into its charming courtyard, you'll see cars with number plates bearing the letters SMOM (the Sovereign Military Order of Malta). Besides its own licenses, the order, founded during the Crusades, also issues a few passports and has its own diplomatic service and small merchant fleet.

Piazza del Popolo – This semicircular square at the foot of the Pincio was designed in neo-classical style by Valadier between 1816 and 1820. At its center is the second-oldest obelisk in Rome, dating from the 13th century BC. Twin-domed churches (Santa Maria di Montesanto and Santa Maria dei Miracoli) face a ceremonial gate where the Via Flaminia enters Rome. Next to the gate is the remarkable early Renaissance Church of Santa Maria del Popolo, an artistic treasure containing two paintings by Caravaggio, sculptures by Bernini, and frescoes by Pinturicchio, among others. The piazza's two open-air cafés, *Rosati* and *Canova,* are favorite meeting places.

Piazza Navona – This harmonious ensemble of Roman baroque is today a favorite haunt of Romans and tourists alike. It is also one of Rome's most historic squares, built on the site of Domitian's stadium. In the center is Bernini's fine Fontana dei Quattro Fiumi (Fountain of the Four Rivers), the huge figures representing the Nile, Ganges, Danube, and Plata. On the west side of the square is the Church of Sant'Agnese in Agone, much of it the work of a Bernini assistant, Borromini. There was little love lost between the two men, and according to a popular local legend, the hand of the Plata figure is raised in self-defense, just in case the façade of the church falls down, while the Nile figure hides under a veil to avoid seeing Borromini's mistakes. However, since the fountain was completed a year before the church was begun, the story doesn't hold water. From the 17th to the mid-19th century, the square would be flooded on August weekends, and the aristocrats of the city would cool off by splashing through the water in their carriages. Nowadays, during the *Christmas* season, until *Epiphany,* it is lined with booths selling sweets, toys, and nativity figures.

Piazza Farnese – This square is dominated by Palazzo Farnese, the most beautiful 16th-century palace in Rome. Commissioned by Cardinal Alessandro Farnese (later Pope Paul III), it was begun in 1514 by Sangallo the Younger, continued by Michelangelo, and completed by Della Porta in 1589. Opera fans will know it as the location of Scarpia's apartment in the second act of Puccini's *Tosca.* Today it is occupied by the French Embassy and can be visited only with special permission. The two fountains on the square incorporate bathtubs of Egyptian granite brought from the Baths of Caracalla.

Piazza Campo dei Fiori – Very near Piazza Farnese, one of Rome's most colorful squares is the scene of a general market every morning. In the center — surrounded by delicious cheeses, salamis, ripe fruit and vegetables, and *fiori* (flowers) of every kind — is a statue of the philosopher Giordano Bruno, who was burned at the stake here for heresy in 1600. Watch your wallet — this is a favorite hangout for thieves.

Piazza Mattei – A delightful clearing on the edge of the ancient Jewish ghetto, this small square's famous Fontana delle Tartarughe (Fountain of the Tortoises), sculpted in 1585 by Taddeo Landini, is one of Rome's most delightful. Four naked boys lean against the base and toss life-size bronze tortoises into a marble bowl above. The water moves in several directions, creating a magical effect in the tiny square.

Piazza del Quirinale – The Quirinal Palace was built by the popes in the late 16th to early 17th century as a summer residence, became the royal palace after the unification of Italy, and is now the official residence of the president of Italy. The so-called Monte Cavallo (Horse Tamers') Fountain is composed of two groups of statues depicting Castor and Pollux with their horses and a granite basin from the Forum once used as a cattle trough. The obelisk in the center is from the Mausoleum of Augustus. The square affords a marvelous view of Rome and St. Peter's. A band plays daily during the changing of the guard at 4 PM in winter, 4:30 PM in summer.

Fontana di Trevi (Trevi Fountain) – Designed by Nicola Salvi and completed in 1762, the Trevi Fountain (newly renovated after more than 2 years of work) took 30 years to build and is the last important monumental baroque work in Rome. Incongruously situated in a tiny square tucked away amidst narrow, cobblestoned streets, the magnificent fountain is quite striking when you suddenly come upon it at the turn of a corner. The colossal Oceanus in stone rides a chariot drawn by seahorses and is surrounded by a fantasy of gods, tritons, and horses. A low-voltage electronic field has been installed to discourage (but not injure) pigeons from perching on the fountain. According to legend, you will return to Rome if you stand with your back to the fountain and throw a coin over your left shoulder into the fountain. Young Roman men like to congregate in the small square on summer evenings, trying to pick up foreign women. Some prefer to pick your pocket — so be careful. Piazza di Trevi.

Piazza Barberini – At the foot of Via Veneto, this square in northern Rome has two of Bernini's famous fountains: the Triton Fountain in travertine, representing a triton sitting upon a scallop shell supported by four dolphins and blowing a conch shell; and the Fountain of the Bees on the corner of the Veneto, with three Barberini bees (of that family's crest) on the edge of a pool spurting thin jets of water into the basin below.

Villa Borghese (Borghese Gardens) – In the northern section of the city, this is Rome's most magnificent park, with hills, lakes, villas, and vistas. It is the former estate of Cardinal Scipione Borghese, designed for him in the 17th century and enlarged in the 18th century. Two museums are here: the *Galleria Borghese,* housed in the cardinal's small palace and noted for its Caravaggios, its Bernini sculptures, and Antonio Canova's statue of the reclining *Pauline Borghese;* and the *Galleria Nazionale d'Arte Moderna,* with its Italian modern works. Open Tuesdays through Saturdays from 9 AM to 2 PM, Sundays from 9 AM to 1 PM. No admission charge. The Villa Borghese is a wonderful place to sit and picnic in the shade of an umbrella pine on a hot summer day. Enter through the Porta Pinciana, at the top of Via Veneto, or walk up to the Pincio from Piazza del Popolo. The main entrance is at Piazzale Flaminio, just outside the Porta del Popolo.

Cimitero Protestante (Protestant Cemetery) – In the southern part of the city, behind the pyramid of Caius Cestius, the Protestant cemetery is principally a foreign enclave that harbors the remains of many adopted non-Catholics who chose to live and die in Rome: Keats, Shelley, Trelawny, Goethe's bastard son, and the Italian Communist leader Gramsci. There is nothing sad here — no pathos, no morbid sense of death — and few gardens are so delightful on a spring morning. 6 Via Caio Cestio.

Jewish Ghetto and Synagogue – On the banks of the Tiber River, near the Garibaldi Bridge, is this vibrant section of town, once a walled area, that is rich with restaurants offering Roman-Jewish specialties and tiny shops. The synagogue, located on the Lungotevere Cenci by the Tiber, houses a permanent exhibition of ritual objects from the 16th to the 19th century, plus documents of recent history. Open daily except Saturdays and on Jewish holidays.

Tiber Island – In the oldest part of the city, between Trastavere and the Jewish Ghetto, is this small, 900-foot-long island in the Tiber River. Roman legend has it that the island grew from a seed of grain tossed in after the Etruscan kings were forced out. Noteworthy is the Chiesa di San Bartolomeo (Church of St. Bartholomew) — set into its steps is a medieval marble font carved from an ancient column said to mark a sacred spring and early temple to Asclepius, the Greek god of healing. Victims of the city's 3rd-century plague were sent here and today a hospital here still cares for sick Romans. A small historical museum devoted to the island (*Museo Storico dell'Isola Tiberina*) was set to open as we went to press. There also is a tiny park on the marble-paved point of the island, a good spot to read or enjoy a picnic. The *Antico Caffè dell'Isola* has 2 rooms inside with tables for snacks. Next door is the popular trattoria *Sora Lella.*

MODERN ROME

Monumento a Vittorio Emanuele II (Monument to Victor Emmanuel II) – Sometimes called the Vittoriano, this most conspicuous landmark of questionable taste was completed in 1911 to celebrate the unification of Italy. Built of white Brescian marble and overwhelming the Capitoline Hill, it is often derided by Romans as the "wedding cake" or the "typewriter." It contains Italy's Tomb of the Unknown Soldier from World War I, and from the top you can see the network of modern boulevards built by Mussolini to open out the site of ancient Rome: Via dei Fori Imperiali, Via di San Gregorio, Via del Teatro di Marcello, and Via Nazionale — a busy and somewhat chaotic shopping street leading to the railroad station. Turn your back to the monument and note the 15th-century Palazzo Venezia to your left. It was from the small balcony of this building, his official residence, that Mussolini made his speeches. Piazza Venezia.

Via Vittorio Veneto – Popularly known as Via Veneto, this wide, café-lined street winds from a gate in the ancient Roman wall, the Porta Pinciana, down past the American Embassy to Piazza Barberini. The portion around Via Boncompagni is elegant, but the street also attracts a mixed crowd — from down-and-out actors and decadent Roman nobility to seedy gigolos and male prostitutes. Well-to-do Americans still stay in the fine hotels. The entire area, including the adjacent Via Bissolati with its many foreign airline offices, is well patrolled by police.

Porta Portese – Rome's flea market takes place on the edge of Trastevere on Sundays from dawn to about 1 or 2 PM. It's a colorful, crowded, and chaotic happening. Genuine antiques are few and far between, quickly scooped up before most people are out of bed. Still, you'll find some interesting junk, new and secondhand clothes, shoes, jeans, items brought by Eastern European immigrants, pop records, used tires and car parts, black market cigarettes — everything from Sicilian puppets to old postcards, sheet music, and broken bidets. Some say that if your wallet is stolen at the entrance, you'll find it for sale near the exit. Via Portuense.

OUT OF TOWN

Esposizione Universale di Roma (EUR) – Mussolini's ultramodern quarter was designed southwest of the center for an international exhibition that was supposed to take place in 1942 but never did. It's now a fashionable garden suburb and the site of international congresses and trade shows as well as of some remarkable sports installations built for the *1960 Olympic Games,* including the *Palazzo dello Sport,* with a dome by Pier Luigi Nervi. The *Museo della Civiltà Romana* (Museum of Roman Civilization) is worth seeing for its thorough reconstruction of ancient Rome at the time of Constantine. Open Tuesdays, Wednesdays, Fridays, and Saturdays from 9 AM to 1:30 PM, Thursdays from 4 to 7 PM, and Sundays from 9 AM to 1 PM. Admission charge. 10 Piazza Giovanni Agnelli (phone: 592-6135).

Ostia Antica – This immense excavation site about 15 miles (24 km) southwest of Rome was once the great trading port of ancient Rome, much closer to the mouth of the Tiber than it is today. The ruins — picturesquely set among pines and cypresses —

first were uncovered in 1914 and new treasures are being discovered constantly. They have not had much chance to crumble, and they reveal a great deal about the building methods of the Romans and the management of a far-flung empire.

A visit takes at least half a day. Among the chief sites are the Piazzale delle Corporazioni (Corporations' Square), once 70 commercial offices, with mottoes and emblems in mosaics revealing that the merchants were shipwrights, caulkers, ropemakers, furriers, and shipowners from all over the ancient world; the capitolium and forum, baths, apartment blocks, and several private houses, especially the House of Cupid and Psyche; and the restored theater. Recent excavations have brought evidence of the town's Jewish community. Take the Decumanus Maximus to the end, turn left, and a few hundred yards away, on what was once the seashore, a synagogue stands, a moving testimonial to the Jewish presence in Rome in earliest times. Open daily except Mondays from 9 AM to 1 hour before sunset. A local museum (phone: 565-0022) traces the development of Ostia Antica and displays some outstanding statues, busts, and frescoes. Open daily except Mondays from 9 AM to 5 PM. Admission charge. To reach Ostia Antica, take the *metropolitana* from Stazione Termini, a train from Stazione Ostiense (the best choice), an *ACOTRAL* bus from Via Giolitti, or the *Tiber II* boat, daily from March through September (see *Getting Around*).

Lido di Ostia (also known as Lido di Roma) – Located 2½ miles (4 km) southwest of Ostia, it's a popular, polluted, and crowded seaside resort. Here and at other pleasant beaches both north and south of Rome, pollution has been so bad in recent years that swimming has been banned at many of them, but the view and the restaurants are pleasant, especially on summer evenings.

Castelli Romani – Rome's "castles" are actually 13 hill towns set in the lovely Alban Hills region southeast of Rome, an area where popes and powerful families of the past built fortresses, palaces, and other retreats. The mountains, the volcanic lakes of Nemi and Albano, chestnut groves, olive trees, and vines producing the famous Castelli wine continue to make the area a favorite destination of Romans who want to get away from the city on a fine day. Particularly charming are Frascati, known for its villas and its wines; Grottaferrata, famous for its fortified monastery, which can be visited; beautiful Lake Nemi, with its vivid blue waters and wooded surroundings, where Diana was worshiped; and Monte Cavo, a mountain whose summit can be reached by a toll road and which offers a panorama of the Castelli from a height of 3,124 feet. The Castelli Romani are best seen on an organized tour or by car — but beware of Sunday traffic. (For more information and a suggested itinerary, see Lazio in DIRECTIONS.)

■ **EXTRA SPECIAL:** Fountain fans should not miss Tivoli, a charming town perched on a hill and on a tributary of the Tiber (the Aniene) about 20 miles (32 km) east of Rome. It's famous for its villas, gardens, and, above all, cascading waters — all immortalized by Fragonard's 18th-century landscapes. Called *Tibur* by the ancient Romans, it was even then a resort for wealthy citizens, who bathed in its thermal waters, which remain therepeutic to this day.

The Villa d'Este, built for a cardinal in the 16th century, is the prime attraction — or, rather, its terraced gardens are. They contain some 500 fountains, large and small, including the jets of water lining the famous Avenue of the Hundred Fountains and the huge Organ Fountain, so named because it once worked a hydraulic organ. The villa and gardens are open to the public daily (admission charge). The fountains are gushing once again after being turned off because of fears that the water was polluted, but you'll have to look at them from behind a railing. On summer nights the fountains are beautifully illuminated, and there's a sound-and-light show. Nearby, the Villa Gregoriana, built by Pope Gregory XVI in the 19th century, has sloping gardens and lovely cascades (which are best on Sundays, since most of the water is used for industrial purposes on other days), but it is definitely to be seen only after you have seen the Villa d'Este. It, too, is open daily; admission charge.

Only 4 miles (6 km) southwest of Tivoli is Villa Adriana (Hadrian's Villa), the most sumptuous of the villas left from ancient Roman times. It was built from AD 125 to 134 by the Emperor Hadrian, whose pleasure was to strew the grounds with replicas of famous buildings he had seen elsewhere in his empire. Extensively excavated and surrounded by greenery, the ruins of the villa include the Maritime Theater, built on an island and surrounded by a canal; the Golden Square in front of the remains of the palace; and the Terrace of Tempe, with a view of the valley of the same name. There are statues, fountains, cypress-lined avenues, pools, lakes, and canals. Closed Mondays; admission charge. You can see Tivoli with a guided tour or take an *ACOTRAL* bus from Via Gaeta or a train from Stazione Termini. Villa Adriana also can be reached by bus from Via Gaeta, but note that while one bus, leaving every hour, stops first at Villa Adriana and then at Tivoli, the other, leaving every half hour, goes directly to Tivoli and entails getting off at a crossroads and walking about a half-mile to Villa Adriana. If you rent a car (a wise choice), take the "autostrada per l'Aquila" to the Tivoli exit, then follow the signs.

SOURCES AND RESOURCES

TOURIST INFORMATION: The Ente Provinciale per il Turismo (EPT) for Rome and Lazio (headquartered at 11 Via Parigi; phone: 488-1851), has a main information office (5 Via Parigi; phone: 488-3748), with branches at Stazione Termini and in the customs area at Leonardo da Vinci Airport at Fiumicino. There also are branches at the Feronia "Punto Blu" and Frascati Est service areas of the A1 and A2 highways, respectively, for those arriving by car. All branches stock various booklets, maps, and hotel listings, all free. Ask for the English language monthly listing of events, *Carnet.*

The US Embassy and Consulate are at 119/A and 121 Via Vittorio Veneto respectively (phone: 46741).

For some good background material about Rome, see Georgina Masson's *Companion Guide to Rome* and Eleanor Clark's *Rome and a Villa,* both useful and amusing. A locally published book on the city's hidden treasures, *In Rome They Say,* by Margherita Naval, is also good reading; 30 walks through the city are described and mapped in *The Heart of Rome.* There are several English-language bookstores in the Spanish Steps area: the *Lion Bookshop* (181 Via del Babuino), *Anglo-American Book Company* (57 Via della Vite), and the *Bookshelf* (in the *Tritone Gallery,* 23 Via Due Macelli). The *Economy Book Center* (136 Via Torino) is particularly good for paperbacks.

For those especially interested in art history and archaeology, a team of professionals in both fields is available to take individuals or groups on private English-language tours of Rome, as well as 1- and 2-day trips outside the city. For information, contact Peter Zalewski (6 Via Cristoforo Colombo, Marcellina di Roma; phone: 774-425451; fax: 774-425122). An English-speaking German, Ruben Popper (12 Via dei Levii; phone: 761-0901), who has lived in Rome for 30 years, also leads tours (mostly walking) of the city.

Local Coverage – The *International Herald Tribune,* now also printed in Rome, is available at most newsstands each morning; it often lists major events in Italy in its Saturday "Weekend" section. *A Guest in Rome* is published by the Golden Key Association of Concierges. *La Repubblica, Corriere della Sera,* and *Il Messaggero* are daily newspapers that list local events on weekends; *La Repubblica* has an interesting

Thursday supplement called "TrovaRoma" that lists the week's events, shows, theater, new movies, and more. *Wanted in Rome* is a useful handout found in American shops and schools.

Food – *La Guida d'Italia* — updated annually — is a comprehensive guide to restaurants and wine shops in Rome and throughout Italy. In Italian, it is published by *L'Espresso* and is available at newsstands. Another popular book — and with a fresher and zestier approach (but also in Italian) — is *Roma,* a restaurant guide published by Gambero Rosso.

TELEPHONE: The city code for Rome is 6. When calling from within Italy, dial 06 before the local number.

GETTING AROUND: Airports – Leonardo da Vinci Airport in Fiumicino (phone: 601-24455 or 601-23640), about 21 miles (33 km) from downtown Rome, handles both international and domestic traffic. Check in at least 45 minutes before flights and allow waiting time in line, or you risk losing your reservation. In only moderate traffic, taxi travel time to the city is about 45 minutes and will cost up to $55, with additional costs for baggage, nighttime — after 10 PM — and holiday trips. The quickest and least expensive way to get to and from the airport is to take the train. Completed in 1990, an efficient and clean train line carries passengers between Leonardo da Vinci and the Piazza Piramide *metropolitana* station in Rome — 1 mile (1.6 km) south of the Colosseum — (where transfers can be made for *Linea A* and *Linea B*). The one-way fare is $5; service runs from 6:30 AM to 12:15 AM. A moving sidewalk from the airport's main terminal carries passengers to the *metropolitana*'s station near the airport. Taxis at the Piramide station can be hard to find; if you have lots of luggage, a better way to go is by cab from the airport. There no longer are any buses between the airport and the central railway station; however, from 6:30 AM to 12:15 AM, bus No. 176 departs from in front of the train station for Stazione Ostiense where it connects with the train to the airport. The fare is 1,000 lire (about 75¢). Ciampino Airport handles mostly charter traffic (phone: 794941). Urbe Airport is for private planes; it's a 15-minutes taxi ride from the center, and public transport (by bus) also is available from Piazza Vescorio; 825 Via Salaria (phone: 886-2075).

Bicycle and Moped – Pollution and insufferable traffic jams have made bicycling a popular, if sometimes dangerous, alternative to driving for many Romans. *Collati* (82 Via del Pellegrino; phone: 654-1084) rents bikes. Others can be found at Piazza San Silvestro, Piazza del Popolo, Piazza di Spagna, Piazza Augusto Imperatore, Lungotevere Marzio, and at Viale della Pineta and Viale dei Bambini in the Villa Borghese Gardens. To rent a moped, scooter, or motorbike, try *Scoot-a-long* (304 Via Cavour; phone: 678-0206); *Scooters for Rent* (66 Via della Purificazione, near Piazza Barberini; phone: 488-5485), which also rents bikes; and *St. Peter Moto* (43 Via Porta Castello, near St. Peter's; phone: 687-5714). By law, helmets must be worn while riding scooters or motorbikes.

Boat – From March through September, weather and water level permitting, the *Tiber II* carries 300 passengers on cruises along the river to Ostia Antica and back. It departs at 9:30 AM on Tuesdays, Thursdays, and Saturdays. For information and reservations, call *Tourvisa* at 445-3224 or the *Associazione Amici del Tevere* (Friends of the Tiber Society) at 637-0268. From May to September, the *Acquabus* plies the river daily, except Mondays, beating the road traffic, from Tiber Island to Duca d'Aosta Bridge near the *Olympic Stadium.* The trip takes 45 minutes each way and runs every 25 minutes. Pay the 1,000 lire (about 75¢) fare on board. Contact *Tourvisa* for information. For boat charters, contact *Aquarius* (32 Corso Vittorio Emanuele; phone: 687-1437).

Bus – *ATAC* (*Azienda Tramvie e Autobus Comune di Roma*), the city bus company, is the rather weak backbone of Rome's public transportation system. During August the number of buses in use is greatly reduced while drivers are on vacation. Most central routes are extremely crowded, getting off where you'd like is sometimes impossible, pickpockets are rampant, and some lines discontinue service after 9 PM, midnight, or 1 AM. Tickets, which currently cost about 75¢, must be purchased before boarding and are available at certain newsstands, tobacco shops, and bars. (Be aware that these outlets frequently exhaust their ticket supply, and the fine for riding without a ticket is about $40.) Remember to get on the bus via the back doors, stamp your ticket in the machine, and exit via the middle doors (the front doors are used only by *abbonati,* season ticket holders). There are no transfer tickets, but visitors can save money by buying 90-minute or full-day tickets, called "Big," at the *ATAC* information booth in Piazza dei Cinquecento or at principal bus stations, such as those at Piazza San Silvestro and Piazza Risorgimento. Tourists will appreciate the tiny, electric-powered No. 119, which loops through downtown Rome between Piazza del Popolo and close to Piazza Navona, passing the Spanish Steps. A weekly bus pass also is available, and route maps — *Roma in Metrobus* — are sold at the *ATAC* information booth and at the Ufficio Abbonamenti of *ATAC* at Largo Giovanni Montemartini and at some newsstands. For information, call 46951. Bus service to points out of town is run by *ACOTRAL* (including buses to Leonardo da Vinci Airport at Fiumicino). For information, call 593-5551. The Rome telephone directory's *TuttoCittà* supplement lists every street in the city and contains detailed maps of each zone as well as zip codes, bus routes, and taxi stands.

Car Rental – Major car rental firms such as *Avis* (38/A Via Sardegna; phone: 470-1229 in Rome, 167-863063 toll-free in Italy); *Budget* (24 Via Sistina; phone: 461905); *Europcar* (7 Via Lombardia; phone: 465802); and *Hertz* (156 Via Veneto; phone: 321-6831 or 321-6834); as well as several reliable Italian companies such as *Maggiore* (8/A Via Po; phone: 851620), have offices in the city and at the airport and railway stations. *Tropea* (1 Piazza Barberini; phone: 488-4682; fax: 482-8336) has rental and chauffeur-driven cars.

Leonardo da Vinci Airport (outside Rome) has desks at which tourists may buy coupons that can be redeemed at gas stations around Italy. Coupons must be purchased in foreign currency. Note that gas stations close for 2 hours at lunch and at 7 PM in winter, 7:30 PM in summer. Most are closed Sundays. Self-service stations operate with 10,000-lire ($8) notes. An efficient — and often economic — way to tour is by limousine. Hotels can suggest some, but a few to contact are *Capitol* (33 Via del Galoppatoio; phone: 360-5866); *Coop. UARA* (261 Via Panisperna; phone: 679-2320); and *Italo Mazzei Roma* (123 Via Trionfale; phone: 310963). Generally, it's not a good idea to hire free-lance taxis; drivers usually are unlicensed, ahd charge up to double the price of the regular taxi fare.

Horse-Drawn Carriages – Rome's *carrozzelle* accommodate up to five passengers and are available at major city squares (Piazza San Pietro, di Spagna, Venezia, and Navona), in front of the Colosseum, near the Trevi Fountain, on Via Veneto, and in the Villa Borghese. They can be hired by the half hour, hour, half day, or full day. Arrange the price with the driver before boarding — 1 hour currently costs about $50 minimum.

Subway – The *metropolitana,* Rome's subway, consists of two lines. *Linea A* runs roughly east-west, from an area close to the Vatican, across the Tiber, through the historic center (Piazza di Spagna, Piazza Barberini, Stazione Termini), and over to the eastern edge of the city past Cinecittà, the filmmaking center; a branch goes to the Tiburtina train station, where numerous long-distance trains stop. *Linea B,* which is partly an underground and partly a surface railroad, runs north-south, from Stazione Termini to the Colosseum and, with a stop at the Ostiense station at Piazza Piramide to connect with the train to Leonardo da Vinci Airport, down to the southern suburb of EUR. The fare is about 80¢, and tickets are sold at certain newsstands, tobacco shops, and bars, as well as at most stations. Only a few stations are staffed with ticket sellers; there also are ticket-dispensing machines, but they only accept coins, so be prepared. Subway entrances are marked by a large red "M."

Taxi – Cabs can be hailed or found at numerous stands, which are listed in the yellow pages with their phone numbers. The *Radio Taxi* telephone numbers are 3570, 3875, 4994, and 8433. Taxi rates are increasing regularly, and drivers are obliged to show you, if asked, the current list of added charges. The current minimum fare is about $5 for the first 2 miles (3 km) or (if stalled in traffic) the first 9 minutes. After 10 PM, a night charge is added, and there are surcharges for holidays and for suitcases.

Train – Rome's main train station is Stazione Termini (phone: 4775 for information). There are several suburban stations, but the visitor is unlikely to use them except for Stazione Ostiense, from where trains depart for Ostia Antica and the Lido di Ostia (phone: 575-0732).

LOCAL SERVICES: Dentist (English-Speaking) – Dr. Peter Althoff (280 Via Salaria; phone: 844-3317); Dr. Charles Kennedy (29 Via della Fonte di Fauno; phone: 578-3639).

Dry Cleaner – *Tintoria Maddalena* (40 Piazza Maddalena; phone: 654-3348); *Minerva* (71/A Via del Gesù; phone: 679-2310); and *Mosca* (23 Via Belisario; phone: 482-7255).

Limousine Service – *Biancocavallo* (126 Via Tiburtina; phone: 520-2957); *Nazionale* (32/B Via Milano; phone: 481-8587; fax: 481-4530); *International* (60 Via Ludovisi; phone: 474-6078 or 475-0872); *Traiano* (19 Via Sant'Agata dei Goti; phone: 679-1518; fax: 678-7996).

Medical Emergency – *Policlinico* (1 Umberto, Viale Policlinico; phone: 492341); *Red Cross Ambulances* (phone: 5100). English-speaking physicians: Dr. Ettore Lollini (Salvador Mundi International Hospital, 67-77 Viale della Mura Gianicolensi; phone: 586041 or 839-3154); Dr. Frank Silvestri (36 Via Ludovisi; phone: 485706 or 332-2017); Dr. Susan Levenstein (Via Tritone; phone: 654-5708 or 475-8429); Dr. Vincenzo Baci (43 Via Cesare Balbo; phone: 474-1021). For an emergency house visit, around the clock, call 482-6741. In downtown Rome, the *San Giacomo Hospital* (off Via del Corso; phone: 67261) has an efficient first-aid service. The *Croce Rossa* (Red Cross; phone: 5100) provides ambulances.

Messenger Service – *Romana Recapiti* (two locations: 38 Via Vicenza; phone: 559-0917 or 559-0993; and 68 Via Palestro; phone: 495-6990); *Pony Express* (phone: 3309).

National/International Courier – National: *Carlo Ciucci* (18-20 Viale del Vignola; phone: 360-7803 or 360-5622). International: *DHL International* (two locations: Ciampino Airport, phone: 79491; and at the air terminal at the central railway station, 36 Via Giolitti; phone: 724-0641); *Stelci & Tavani* (103 Via Alessandro Severo; phone: 541-4460; fax: 541-1334); *Federal Express* will pick up at your hotel (phone: 675-2673; fax: 791-5831); *Fast Cargo* (141 Via dell'Omo; phone: 228-8305; fax: 228-8340); *XP-Express Parcel Systems Italy* (Ciampino Airport; phone: 796-0382); *Rinaldi* (34 Via Smerillo; phone: 410911; fax: 411-1565); *UPS/Alimondo* (329 Via della Magliana; phone: 527-3371; fax: 528-4859).

Office Equipment Rental – *Centro Macchina Ufficio* (48b-52 Via Tagliamento; phone: 867465 or 869233); *Executive Service* (68 Via Savoia; phone: 853241); *International Services Agency* (35 Piazza di Spagna; phone: 684-0287 or 684-0288).

Pharmacy – *Internazionale* (49 Piazza Barberini; phone: 462996); *Cola di Rienzo*

(213 Via Cola di Rienzo; phone: 351816). Both are open nights. To find out about drugstores open on Saturday afternoons and holidays, call 1921, or check the newspapers for their listings of *farmacie di turno.*

Photocopies – *Sandy* (58-59 Via San Basilio; phone: 475-8533 or 461346); *Centro Eliografico Prati* (7 Piazza dei Quiriti, near the Lepanto subway stop; phone: 389657 or 316643); *Centro Rank Xerox* (28 Largo delle Stimmate; phone: 654-1898; fax: 686-7542).

Post Office – The main post office (19 Piazza San Silvestro; phone: 6771) is open from 8:30 AM to 8 PM weekdays (until noon Saturdays). An express service called CAI (Corriere Accelerato Italiano) Post is now available at major post offices. Otherwise, Rome's most efficient post office for mail going out of Italy is the Vatican Post Office (Piazza San Pietro), open from 8:30 AM to 7 PM weekdays (until 6 PM Saturdays).

Secretary/Stenographer (English-Speaking) – *Rome At Your Service* (75 Via Orlando; phone: 484583 or 484429); *Executive Service* (78 Via Savoia; phone: 853241). Both can provide translation services. *Copisteria al Tritone* (17 Via Crispi; phone: 679-7190) has word processing facilities, fax machine, and secretarial services in English.

Tailor – *Cifonelli* (68 Via Sella; phone: 488-1827); *Caraceni* (two locations: 61/B Via Campania, phone: 488-2594; and 50 Via Sardegna, phone: 474-4023); *Coccurello,* for smaller budgets (7 Via Manfredi; phone: 802360 or 534-7038).

Telex/Facsimile Transmissions – Telexes and telegrams can be sent 24 hours daily from 18 Piazza San Silvestro (phone: 679-5530), next to the main post office. Fax service also is available there weekdays from 8:30 AM to 8 PM and from 8:30 AM to noon on Saturdays.

Translator – *World Translation Centre* (181 Via di Santa Maria Maggiore; phone: 475-5986, 461039, or 485922); *Agenzia Barberini* (5 Piazza Barberini; phone: 474-1738 or 488-1497; fax: 488-5491); *Alfa International* (29 Via Lucrezio Caro; phone: 323-0077; fax: 322-2038); *Rome at Your Service* (75 Via Orlando; phone: 484583); *Outer Relations Office* (123 Via Sistina; phone: 463951); *Executive Service* (78 Via Savoia; phone: 854-3241; fax: 844-0738). For simultaneous translations, contact *Centro Congressi* (23 Via Sallustiana; phone: 485990 or 465392); or *STOC* (two locations: 44 Via G. de Ruggiero, phone: 540-5621; and 203 Via Laurentina, phone: 540-3741).

Other – Convention Centers: *Palazzo dei Congressi* has 30 meeting rooms for up to 4,000 (Piazzale Kennedy in EUR; phone: 591-2735; fax: 592-4044); *Centro Internazionale Roma* (*CIR*) has 8 meeting rooms for up to 8,000 (619 Via Aurelia; phone: 6644; fax: 663-2689); *Palazzo dello Sport* has meeting rooms for up to 5,000 (Piazzale dello Sport; phone: 592-5107); *Palazzo Brancaccio* is available for conferences and is centrally located (7 Via Monte Oppio; phone: 487-3177). Also centrally located is the Renaissance *Palazzo Taverna* (37 Via di Monte Giordano; phone: 683-3785), which is available for receptions and business lunches. The Orsini-Odescalchi Castle (25 miles from Rome, in Bracciano) is a 15th-century castle, richly furnished and decorated with frescoes, that can be rented for receptions of up to 500. Office Space Rental (fully equipped): *Amministrazione Principe Livio Odescalchi* (80 Piazza SS. Apostoli; phone: 679-2154); *Executive Service* (68 Via Savoia; phone: 853241; fax: 844-0738); *International Business Centre* (121 Piazzale di Porta Pia; phone: 886-3051); *Tiempo* (50 Via Barberini; phone: 482-5151 or 482-1456); and *Center Office* (132 Via del Tritone; phone: 488-1995 or 474-7641). Desktop Publishing: *Scribe Desktop Publishing* (45 Via Paola Falconieri; phone: 531-5050). Tuxedo Rental: *Misano* (88 Via Nazionale; phone: 488-2005).

SPECIAL EVENTS: The events of the church calendar — too numerous to mention here — are extra special in Rome. For *Natale* (*Christmas*), relatively modest decorations go up around the city, almost all churches display their sometimes movable, elaborate *presepi* (nativity scenes), and a colorful toy and candy fair begins in Piazza Navona. The season, including the fair, lasts until January 6, *Epiphany,* when children receive gifts from a witch known as the Befana to add to those Babbo Natale (Father Christmas) or the Bambìn Gesù (Baby Jesus) brought them at *Christmas.* The intervening *Capodanno* or *New Year* is celebrated with a bang here as in much of the rest of Italy — firecrackers snap, crackle, and pop from early evening, and (though less than in the past) at midnight all manner of old, discarded objects come flying out of open windows. (Don't be on the street!) During the *Settimana Santa* (Holy Week), the city swarms with visitors. Religious ceremonies abound, particularly on *Good Friday,* when pilgrims, on their knees, climb the Scala Santa at St. John Lateran and the pope conducts the famous *Via Crucis* (Way of the Cross) procession between the Colosseum and the Palatine Hill. At noon on *Easter Sunday,* he pronounces the *Urbi et Orbi* blessing in St. Peter's Square. The day after *Easter* is *Pasquetta* (Little Easter), when Romans usually go out to the country for a picnic or an extended lunch in a rustic trattoria. The arrival of spring is celebrated in April with a colorful display of potted azaleas covering the Spanish Steps, and in May a picturesque street nearby, Via Margutta, is filled with an exhibition of paintings by artists of varied talents. (The Via Margutta art fair is repeated in the fall.) In May, too, Villa Borghese's lush Piazza di Siena becomes the site of the *International Horse Show,* and soon after that is the *International Tennis Championship* at *Foro Italico.* An antiques show also takes place in spring and fall along the charming Via dei Coronari (near Piazza Navona), and there's an *International Rose Show* in late spring at the delightful Roseto di Valle Murcia on the Aventine Hill. In late May or June the vast *Fiera di Roma,* a national industrial exhibition, takes place at the fairgrounds along Via Cristoforo Colombo. In mid-July the *Festa di Noiantri* is celebrated in one of Rome's oldest quarters, Trastevere. This is a great pagan feast, involving plenty of eating, music, and fireworks — as filmed by Fellini in his surrealistic/realistic *Roma.*

There are also innumerable characteristic *feste* or *sagre* (festivals, usually celebrating some local food or beverage at the height of its season) in the many hill towns surrounding Rome. The *Sagra dell'Uva* (Grape Festival) is the first Sunday in October at Marino celebrates the new vintage with grapes sold from stalls set up in the quaint old streets and wine instead of water gushing out of the fountain in the main square! Also worth seeing is the *Infiorata* at Genzano di Roma. On a Sunday in mid-June, a brightly colored carpet of beautifully arranged flowers is laid along the entire Via Livia. Both towns are about 15 miles (24 km) south of Rome in the *Castelli Romani* (see "Out of Town" in *Special Places*).

MUSEUMS: Many museums are described in *Special Places.* Included in the following list of additional museums are churches that should be seen because of their artistic value. Many museums are closed on Mondays and some charge no admission on Sundays. Always check the hours before setting out (although most open at 9 AM and close for lunch).

Galleria Colonna – The Colonna family collection (in their home) of mainly 17th-century Italian paintings. Open Saturdays only, from 9 AM to 1 PM. Palazzo Colonna, 17 Via della Pilotta (phone: 679-4362).

Galleria Doria Pamphili – The private collection of the Doria family, housed in a sculpture hall and apartments, of Italian and foreign paintings from the 15th to the 17th century, including a portrait of Christopher Columbus. Open Tuesdays, Fridays, Saturdays, and Sundays, 10 AM to 1PM. Palazzo Doria, 1/A Piazza del Collegio Romano (phone: 679-4365).

Galleria Nazionale d'Arte Antica (National Gallery of Ancient Art) – Recently renovated, this museum exhibits paintings by Italian artists from the 13th to the 18th century, plus some Dutch and Flemish works. Open Mondays through Saturdays from 9 AM to 2 PM, Sundays from 9 AM to 12:30 PM. Palazzo Barberini, 13 Via delle Quattro Fontane (phone: 481-4591).

Galleria Nazionale d'Arte Moderna (National Gallery of Modern Art) – Particularly noteworthy are the pre-World War I Italian painters and the futurists. Open daily from 9 AM to 1:30 PM; on Thursdays and Fridays, it also is open from 3 to 7 PM. 131 Viale Belle Arti (phone: 802751).

Galleria Spada – Renaissance art and Roman marble work from the 2nd and 3rd centuries; also two huge rare antique globes that were used on Dutch ships in the 16th century. Open Mondays and Tuesdays from 9 AM to 2 PM, Wednesdays and Saturdays from 9 AM to 2 PM and 3 to 7 PM, and Sundays and holidays from 9 AM to 1 PM. Palazzo Spada, 13 Piazza Capo di Ferro (phone: 686-1158).

Keats-Shelley Memorial House – A shrine to the romantics. Keats lived (briefly) and died here. Open weekdays from 9 AM to 1 PM and 2:30 to 5:30 PM. 26 Piazza di Spagna (phone: 678-4235).

Museo Napoleonico (Napoleonic Museum) – Memorabilia of the emperor's family during their rule in Rome. 1 Via Umberto I (phone: 654-0286).

Museo Nazionale d'Arte Orientale (National Museum of Oriental Art) – Pottery, bronzes, stone, and wooden sculpture from the Middle and Far East. Open Mondays through Saturdays from 9 AM to 2 PM, Sundays and holidays from 9 AM to 1 PM. 248 Via Merulana (phone: 737948).

Museo Nazionale Etrusco di Valle Giulia (National Etruscan Museum of the Giulia Valley – The country's most important Etruscan collection in a 16th-century villa by Vignola. Open Tuesdays through Saturdays from 9 AM to 7 PM, Sundays from 9 AM to 1 PM. 9 Piazzale di Valle Giulia (phone: 360-1951).

Museo di Palazzo Venezia (Palazzo Venezia Museum) – Tapestries, paintings, sculpture, and varied objects, as well as important temporary exhibits. Open Mondays from 9 AM to 2 PM, Tuesdays through Saturdays from 9 AM to 7 PM, and Sundays from 9 AM to 1 PM. 118 Via del Plebescito (phone: 679-8865).

Museo Preistorico ed Etnografico Luigi Pigorini (Luigi Pigorini Prehistoric and Ethnographic Museum) – A unique collection of objects from Italy's early history. Open Mondays from 2 to 7 PM, Wednesdays through Saturdays from 9 AM to 7 PM, and Sundays from 9 AM to 1 PM. 1 Via Lincoln (phone: 591-0702).

Museo di Roma (Museum of Rome) – Paintings, sculptures, and other objects illustrating the history of Rome from the Middle Ages to the present. Open daily from 9 AM to 1:30 PM. 10 Piazza San Pantaleo (phone: 687-5880).

Museo della Sinagoga (Synagogue Permanent Collection) – Adjacent to the synagogue is this small museum with exhibits on the arts and history of Rome's Jewish community through the centuries. Open Mondays through Thursdays from 9:30 AM to 2 PM and 3 to 5 PM, Fridays from 9:30 AM to 2:30 PM, and Sundays from 9:30 AM to 12:30 PM. Lungotevere Cenci (phone: 686-4193).

San Carlo alle Quattro Fontane (St. Charles at the Four Fountains) – A small baroque church by Borromini, it was designed to fit into one of the pilasters of St. Peter's. Via del Quirinale, corner Via delle Quattro Fontane.

San Clemente – An early Christian basilica with frescoes and a remarkable mosaic. Piazza di San Clemente.

San Luigi dei Francesi (St. Louis of the French) – The French national church, built in the 16th century and containing three Caravaggios. Piazza San Luigi dei Francesi.

Sant'Agostino (St. Augustine) – A 15th-century church containing the *Madonna of the Pilgrims* by Caravaggio and the *Prophet Isaiah* by Raphael. Piazza di Sant'Agostino.

Sant'Andrea al Quirinale (St. Andrew at the Quirinale) – A baroque church by Bernini, to be compared with Borromini's church on the same street. Via del Quirinale.

Santa Maria d'Aracoeli (St. Mary of the Altar of Heaven) – A Romanesque-Gothic church with frescoes by Pinturicchio and a 14th-century staircase built in thanksgiving for the lifting of a plague. Piazza d'Aracoeli.

Santa Maria in Cosmedin – A Romanesque church known for the *Bocca della Verità* (Mouth of Truth) in its portico — a Roman drain cover in the shape of a face whose mouth, according to legend, will bite off the hand of anyone who has told a lie. Piazza della Bocca della Verità.

Santa Maria sopra Minerva (St. Mary over Minerva) – Built over a Roman temple, with (unusual for Rome) a Gothic interior, frescoes by Filippino Lippi, and Michelangelo's statue of St. John the Baptist. Piazza della Minerva.

Santa Maria in Trastevere – An ancient church, the first in Rome dedicated to the Virgin, with 12th- and 13th-century mosaics. Piazza Santa Maria in Trastevere.

Santa Maria della Vittoria (St. Mary of the Victory) – Baroque to the core, especially in Bernini's Cornaro Chapel. Via XX Settembre.

San Pietro in Vincoli (St. Peter in Chains) – Erected in the 5th century to preserve St. Peter's chains, this church contains Michelangelo's magnificent statue of Moses. Piazza di San Pietro in Vincoli.

Santa Sabina – A simple 5th-century basilica, with its original cypress doors, a 13th-century cloister and bell tower, and stunning views of the city. Piazza Pietro d'Illiria.

SHOPPING: Rome is a wonderful place to shop. You'll find the great couturiers, many of whom have boutiques as well, and most important Italian firms have branches here. While elegant clothing by top Italian designers will cost less here than back home, don't expect any bargain-basement finds. The best buys are in quality, hand-finished leather goods, jewelry, fabrics, shoes, and sweaters.

The chicest shopping area is around the bottom of the Spanish Steps, beginning with the elegant Via Condotti, which runs east to west and is lined with Rome's most exclusive shops, such as *Gucci* and *Ferragamo* for leather goods, and *Bulgari, Beltrami, Cartier, Di Consiglio, Massoni, Merli, Rapi,* and *Van Cleef* for exquisite jewelry. Via del Babuino, which connects the Spanish Steps to Piazza del Popolo, has traditionally been better known for its antiques shops, but is coming into its own as a high-fashion street, as is nearby Via Bocca di Leone, where there are such designers' boutiques as *Valentino, Ungaro, Versace, Trussardi,* and *Yves Saint Laurent.* Running parallel to Via Condotti are several more streets, most closed to traffic, with fashionable boutiques, such as Via Borgognona (*Fendi, Versace, Missoni, Laura Biagiotti,* and *Testa*), Via delle Carrozze, Via Frattina (for men's fashions at *Testa,* women's at *Max Mara,* as well as costume jewelry, lingerie, and some ceramics), Via Vittoria, and Via della Croce (known particularly for its delicious but pricey delicatessens such as *Ercoli,* or *Fior Fiore* for cheese, bread, and cookies). All of these streets end at Via del Corso, the main street of Rome, which runs north to south and is lined with shops tending to resemble each other more and more with their offerings of the latest fashions in shoes, handbags, and sportswear, particularly along the stretch between Piazza del Popolo and Largo Chigi, where Via del Tritone begins. There are some fine shops along Via del Tritone, Via Sistina, and in the Via Veneto area.

On the other side of the river toward the Vatican are two popular shopping streets that are slightly less expensive, Via Cola di Rienzo and Via Ottaviano. Also somewhat less expensive is Via Nazionale, near the railroad station. For inexpensive new and secondhand clothes, visit the daily market on Via Sannio, near San Giovanni, and the flea market on Sunday mornings at Porta Portese. For old prints and odds and ends, try the market at Piazza della Fontanella Borghese every morning except Sunday; antiques can be found along Via del Babuino, Via dei Coronari, Via del Boverno Vecchio, Via del Governo Vecchio, Via Margutta, and Via Giulia.

Fairly new on the Roman shopping scene is *Cinecittà Due,* an air conditioned shopping mall that has over 100 shops. Easily accessible by subway, it is open daily except Sundays from 9 AM to 8:30 PM.

Store hours are capricious. Shops usually are open in winter from 10 AM to 1 PM and 4 to 7:30 PM; closed Monday mornings. Summer morning hours are the same, but in the afternoon, stores are open from 4:30 to 8 PM; closed Saturday afternoons. A few, such as the popular department store *UPIM* on Via Tritone, are open all day.

The following are a few recommended shops in Rome:

Arte – Household and hope-chest linen, such as tablecloths, and hand-embroidered curtains at this shop near the Campo de' Fiori. 39 Via dei Giubbonari.

Balloon – Chinese silk is used to make Italian-style women's shirts in this store that is so popular that there are six in Rome and one in Paris. 35 Piazza di Spagna, 495 Via Flaminia Vecchia, and other locations.

Battistoni – Men's conservative clothing. The Duke of Windsor had his shirts made here — secretly, so as not to offend Britain's shirtmakers. 61A Via Condotti.

Bertè – Old and new toys. 108 Piazza Navona.

Bises – A place for fine fabrics. 93 Via del Gesù. *Bises' Boutique Uomo,* for men, is at 1-3-5 Corso Vittorio Emanuele.

Bomba e De Clercq – Exclusive sweaters and blouses with hand-crafted details. 39 Via dell'Oca, behind Piazza del Popolo.

Borsalino – World-renowned hats. 157/B Via IV Novembre.

Bruno Magli – Top-quality shoes and boots of classical elegance. 70 Via Veneto, 1 Via del Gambero, and 237 Via Cola di Rienzo.

Buccellati – For connoisseurs: A fine jeweler with a unique way of working with gold. 31 Via Condotti.

Bulgari – One of the world's most famous high-style jewelers, offering fabulous creations in gold, silver, platinum, and precious stones. 10 Via Condotti.

Capodarte – The latest styles in shoes and boots — many with matching bags — and some stylish fashions for women. 14/A Via Sistina.

Carlo Palazzi – Creative, high-quality fashions for men. 7/C Via Borgognona.

Carlo Pasquali – Old prints, engravings, original lithographs, and drawings. Near the Trevi Fountain. 25 Largo di Brazzà.

Cartoleria al Pantheon – Marbelized paper, some handmade and suitable for framing. Ask to see the one-of-a-kind paper mosaic-covered diaries and notebooks. Ideal for small gifts. 15 Via della Rotonda (phone: 687-5313).

Cascianelli – Old maps of Rome as well as prints and rare books. 14 Largo Febo.

Cerruti 1881 – Favorite fashions for Italian yuppies of all ages. Their jackets last a lifetime. 20 Piazza San Lorenzo in Lucina.

Cesari – Two locations, with fine household linen, including tablecloths and placemats, lingerie and beachwear at 1 Via Barberini; exquisite upholstery fabrics by the meter at 96 Via Frattina.

Cicogna – The ultimate (or nearly) in children's clothing. 138 Via Frattina and 268 Via Cola di Rienzo.

Croff Centro Casa – Inexpensive household items and gifts, some of Italian design. 197 Via Cola di Rienzo, 137 Via Tomacelli, and 52 Via XX Settembre.

Davide Cenci – Classic elegance for men and women. Italian diplomats buy their pinstripe suits and trenchcoats here. 4-7 Via Campo Marzio.

Discount dell'Alta Moda – Last season's *alta moda* at discount prices. 16/A Via Gesù.

Discount System – A high-fashion discount store, featuring clothing, shoes, and leather goods up to 50% off retail. 35 Via Viminale.

Essences – Natural fragrances and the house's own blends of toilet water and perfume. 88 Piazza della Cancelleria.

Ex Libris – Antique books, prints, and rare maps are found in this charming shop. 77/A Via dell'Umiltà.

Fendi – Canvas and leather bags, luggage, and clothing. 39 Via Borgognona. Shoes and purse accessories. 4/E Via Borgognona and 55.A Largo Goldoni.

Ferragamo – For high-style women's shoes. 66 Via Condotti.

Filippo – An avant-garde boutique for men and women. 7 *bis* Via Borgognona and 6 Via Condotti.

Fiorucci – Famed, funky sportswear and shoes. 12 Via Genova, 19 Via della Farnesina, 236 Via Nazionale, 27 Via della Maddalena, and elsewhere.

Fornari – Fine silver and other gifts. 71-72 Via Frattina.

Franco Maria Ricci – Sumptuously printed books by a discriminating publisher, sold in an elegant setting. 4D Via Borgognona.

Funke – Top-quality shoes for men and women plus cordial service. Near the Pantheon. 52 Piazza della Maddalena.

Gabbiano – Modern artworks by Italians and others (there's also a branch in New York City). 51 Via della Frezza.

Galtrucco – All kinds of fabrics, especially pure silk. 23 Via del Tritone.

Genny – Ever-popular boutique for women. 27 Piazza di Spagna.

Gianfranco Ferré – High fashion for women. 6 Via Borgognona.

Gianni Versace – The Milanese designer's Rome outlets. 41 Via Borgognona and 29 Via Bocca di Leone.

Giorgio Armani – High fashion for men and women. 102 and 139 Via del Babuino.

Gucci – Be ready to wait in line for men's and women's shoes, luggage, handbags, and other leather goods. 8 Via Condotti.

Krizia – Elegant women's boutique. 11/B Piazza di Spagna.

Laura Biagiotti – Elegant women's wear. 43 Via Borgognona, corner of Via Belsiana.

Laurent – Good buys in leatherwear. 3 Via Frattina.

Libreria Archeologica – For the bookworm whose passion is the past. The specialty is Rome and Italy, but a few of the books on archaeology and ancient history have a broader reach. 2 Via Palermo.

Libreria Editrice Vaticana – A vast selection of art and archaeological books as well as books on religion and theology at the Vatican's own publisher's outlet. Next to the Vatican's post office in Piazza San Pietro.

Lio Bazaar – Amusing women's shoes. 35 Via Borgognona.

Lion Bookshop – The city's oldest English-language bookstore, chock full of volumes on Rome's history, travel, and food. 181 Via del Babuino.

Luna di Carta – All types of crafts made from paper — handmade papier-mâché fruit, small sculptures, and hand-colored prints. Il Vicolo dell'Atleta.

Maccalè – Yet another fine boutique for women. 69 Via della Croce.

Mail – English and western saddlery and other riding gear. 154 Via Germanico.

Marisa Pignataro – Outstanding knit dresses and tops in pure wool with interesting color combinations. 20 Via dei Greci.

Mario Lucchese – Everything for the golfer, including handmade spike-soled shoes and other tee-time apparel. 162 Via del Babuino.

Mario Valentino – Fine shoes and leather goods. 58 and 84 Via Frattina.

Maud Frizon – Highly original shoes for women, with corresponding prices. 38 Via Borgognona.

Miranda – Colorful women's woven shawls and jackets. 220 Via delle Carrozze.

Missoni – High-fashion knitwear in unique weaves of often costly blended yarns, such as linen with wool and silk. Via Borgognona 38/B. *Missoni Uomo,* for men, is at 78 Piazza di Spagna.

Ai Monasteri – Products ranging from bath oils to honey and liqueurs from more than 20 monasteries. 72 Corso del Rinascimento.

Moriondo & Gariglio – Delicious hand-dipped chocolates and violets crystallized in sugar. 2 Via della Pilotta.

Myricae – Hand-painted ceramics and such, made by Italian craftsmen from Sardinia to Deruta. 36 Via Frattina.

Naj Oleari – Famed cotton fabrics and accessories from bags to lampshades. 25A Via di San Giacomo and 32 Via dei Greci.

Nazareno Gabrielli – Excellent leather goods. 3-5 Via Sant'Andrea delle Fratte and 29 Via Borgognona.

Dell'Orologio – Decorative and figurative 20th-century art, including Art Deco, Futurist, and right now. 8 Piazza dell'Orologio.

Ottica Scientifica – Eyeglasses and contact lenses, fitted by one of Rome's best and most scrupulous optometrists; camera supplies and electronic equipment,too. 19 Via delle Convertite, near Piazza San Silvestro.

Ottocento Italiano – The 19th-century look in Italian furniture made from antique wood. They also make bookcases to order. 26 Via Nizza (near Piazza Fiume).

Perla – Avant-garde looks for young women. 88 Piazza di Spagna.

Perrone – Gloves — leather and other. 92 Piazza di Spagna.

Petochi – A treasure trove of fine jewelry and old and new tea services. 72 Piazza di Spagna.

Pineider – Italy's famed stationer. 68-69 Via Due Macelli and Piazza Cardelli.

Polidori – Exclusive menswear and tailoring at 84 Via Condotti and 4C Via Borgognona; finest pure silks and other fabrics at 4A Via Borgognona.

Le Quattro Stagioni – A delightful array of handmade ceramics by artisans from all over Italy. US shipping can be arranged. 30B Via dell'Umiltà.

Ramírez – Latest shoe fashions at reasonable prices. 73 Via del Corso and 85 Via Frattina.

Raphael Salato – For famous-maker Italian men's and women's shoes. 104 and 149 Via Veneto; 34 Piazza di Spagna.

Rinascente – One of the few department stores, offering good buys on gloves, scarves, and clothing for all ages. Piazza Colonna and Piazza Fiume.

Roland's – The specialty here is luxury coats for men and women. Piazza di Spagna.

Salotto – Made-to-order shirts for both sexes. 18 Via di Parione.

Sansone – Large selection of Italian and imported luggage, trunks, and travel bags, as well as wallets, purses, knapsacks, etc. Repairs and custom designs. 4 Via XX Settembre.

Schostal – Since 1870, traditional supplier of stockings (in silk, linen, cotton, etc.) and other undergarments for men and women. Moderate prices. 158 Via del Corso.

Soggetti – A 2-story showroom of Italy's famed high-style home furnishings and decorating objects — not easy to find in Rome. Near the Piazza Venezia on Via IV Novembre.

Al Sogno Giocattoli – Toys, including huge stuffed animals in amusing window displays. 53 Piazza Navona.

Spazio Sette – Two stories of Italian and imported fine design — everything from potholders to teapots, placemats, lamps, notebooks, quilts, and furniture. Just off Largo Argentina. 7 Via dei Barbieri.

Stefanel – Lively, youthful sportswear at a dozen branches, the most central of which are 148 Via del Corso, 31-32 Via Frattina, 41 Via Tritone, 227 Via Nazionale, and 191-193 Via Cola di Rienzo.

Testa – For offbeat, resort, and casual clothes for men. 13 Via Borgognona, and 42 and 104-106 Via Frattina.

Trevi Moda – Best buy for moderately priced, quality leather shoes and handbags, located in a favorite tourist area. 33 Via Lavatore.

Trimani – Founded in 1821, this is Rome's oldest wine shop. Its marble decorations are a national monument. 20 Via Goito.

L'Ulivo – Ceramics, handmade by the owner as well as by artisans from Puglia. 61 Via del Monte della Farina.

Valentino – Bold, high-fashion clothes for men and women. 13 Via Condotti for men, 15-18 Via Bocca di Leone for women; haute couture salon at 24 Via Gregoriana.

Vertecchi – Rome's most important stationer and artists' supplier, also gifts and design products. 38 and 70 Via della Croce, 18 Via Pietro da Cortona, and 12/F Via Attilio Regolo.

SPORTS AND FITNESS: Auto Racing – The *Autodromo di Roma* (*Valle Lunga* racetrack, Campagnano di Roma, Via Cassia, Km 34; phone: 904-1027). Take a bus from Via Lepanto.

Fitness Centers – Rome has relatively few fitness centers and gyms, and those that exist tend to be cramped. An exception is the roomy, well-equipped, and (unusual for Rome) air conditioned *Roman Sport Center* (in the underground passage to the *metropolitana* stop at the top of Via Veneto in the Villa Borghese, 33 Via del Galoppatoio; phone: 320-1667). Although it is a private club, its American owner makes special arrangements for visitors to use the pool, squash court, aerosol room, sauna, Jacuzzi, and two workout gyms, as well as aerobics classes. Another private club, the *Navona Health Center* (39 Via dei Banchi Vecchi; phone: 689-6104), also will open its 3-room gym in an ancient historical palazzo to non-members. Fitness centers accessible to the public include: *Aldrovandi Health Center* (11 Via Michele Mercati; phone: 322-1435); *American Workout Studio* (5 Via Giovanni Amendola; phone: 474-6299), run by a former Jane Fonda Workshop instructor; and *Barbara Bouchet Body-shop* (162 Viale Parioli; phone: 807-5049). Most others are by membership only.

Golf – Both the *Circolo del Golf Roma* (716/A Via Appia Nuova; phone: 794-6219), about 8 miles (12 km) from the center, and the *Olgiata Golf Club* (15 Largo Olgiata; phone: 378-9141), about 12 miles (19 km), have 18-hole courses and extend guest privileges to members of foreign clubs. The former is open to guests Tuesdays through Saturdays; the latter, Tuesdays to Fridays. There also is the 9-hole *Golf Club Fioranello* (Via Appia Nuova, Santa Maria delle Mole; phone: 608058). At *Acquasanta* (Via Appia Nuova; phone: 780-4307), visitors can play Tuesdays through Fridays (if they show a home club membership card) on an 18-hole course. Tee off with spectacular views of ancient ruins in the background; the club also has a lovely swimming pool and an excellent restaurant.

Horse Racing – Trotting races take place at the *Ippodromo Tor di Valle* (Via del Mare, Km 13; phone: 592-6786). Flat races take place at the *Ippodromo delle Capannelle* (1255 Via Appia, Km 12; phone: 799-3143) in the spring and fall.

Horseback Riding – For lessons at various levels of proficiency, rentals by the hour (sometimes a subscription for several hours is required), or guided rides in the country, contact the *Circolo Ippico Appia Antica* (Via Appia Nuova, Km 16.5; phone: 724-0197); *Società Ippica Romana* (30 Via dei Monti della Farnesina; phone: 396-6214); *Scuola d'Equitazione Le Piane* (Campagnano; phone: 904-2478 or 904-1925), or *Circolo Buttero Fontana Nuova* (near Sacrofano, outside Rome; phone: 903-6040). For weekend or weeklong riding vacations, contact *Agriturist* (phone: 651-2342) or *Turismo Verde* (phone: 396-9931).

Jogging – There are two tracks at the *Galoppatoio* in the Villa Borghese; enter at the top of Via Veneto or from Piazza del Popolo. Villa Glori has a 1,180-meter track which is illuminated at night; the large Villa Pamphili has three tracks, as does Villa Ada, and Villa Torlonia has one pretty track flanked by palm and acacia trees; at *Acqua Acetosa* there is also a dressing room open until 5 PM; and the Baths of Caracalla provide another good running spot (between the road and the Terme).

Soccer – Two highly competitive teams, *Roma* and *Lazio,* play on Sundays from September to May at the *Olympic Stadium* (site of the final game of the *1990 World Cup*), *Foro Italico* (phone: 36851).

Swimming – The pools at the *Cavalieri Hilton* (101 Via Cadlolo; phone: 3151) and the *Aldrovandi Palace* hotel (15 Via Ulisse Aldrovandi; phone: 322-3993) are open to non-guests for a fee. Public pools include the *Piscina Olimpica* (*Foro Italico;* phone: 360-8591, 360-1498) and the *Piscina delle Rose* (EUR; phone: 592-6717). Swimming in the sea near Rome has become dangerous due to very high levels of pollution; signs prohibiting swimming speckle many nearby beaches. The beach nearest Rome is at Ostia, and it's among the most polluted, very crowded, and strung from end to end with bathing establishments charging admission for entry and use of changing rooms. There are stretches of free beach at Castel Fusano and Castel Porziano, southeast of Ostia; the first is reachable by subway from Stazione Termini. Fregene, farther north along the coast, is very popular with fashionable (and mostly topless) Romans. There's also swimming at Lake Bracciano, about 20 miles (32 km) north of Rome, but no changing facilities. Avoid Sunday crowds.

Tennis – Most courts belong to private clubs. Those at the *Cavalieri Hilton* (101 Via Cadlolo; phone: 3151) and at the *Sheraton Roma* (Viale del Pattinaggio; phone: 5453) are open to non-guests for a fee. There are public courts occasionally available at the *Foro Italico* (phone: 361-9021). Also open to the public is the *Società Ginnastica Roma* (5 Via del Moro Torto; phone: 488-5566) which has 21 courts that are open from 9 AM to 9 PM and in the Appia Antica area, the 4-court *Oasi di Pace* (2 Via degli Eugenii; phone: 718-4550), which also has a swimming pool.

Windsurfing – Windsurf boards and lessons are available at *Castel Porziano* (*primo cancello,* or first gate); at the *Stabilimento La Baia* (phone: 646-1647) and the *Miraggio Sporting Club* (in Fregene; phone: 646-1802); and at the *Centro Surf Bracciano* (Lake Bracciano; phone: 902-4568).

THEATER: During the theater season, approximately October through May, check *A Guest in Rome* or any daily newspaper for listings. Most theater in Italian consists of revivals of the classics (including Goldoni's and Pirandello's works and English and French classics in translation) and some lively avant-garde works. The principal theaters are the *Teatro Eliseo* (183 Via Nazionale; phone: 488-2114), the *Teatro Argentina* (Largo Argentina; phone: 654-4601), the *Teatro Valle* (23 Via Teatro Valle; phone: 654-3794), and the *Teatro Quirino* (1 Via Minghetti; phone: 679-4585). A season of classical drama (in Italian, and sometimes in Greek) is held in July each year in the open-air *Teatro Romano di Ostia Antica* (phone: 565-1913). The *Teatro Sistina* (129 Via Sistina; phone: 482-6841) is Rome's best music hall, offering top class, often imported, musical entertainment on Monday nights, when the regular rep is resting (in the fall, they usually run top-name Brazilian entertainment Monday nights). The charming, turn-of-the-century cabaret theater *Salone Margarita* (75 Via Due Macelli; phone: 679-8269) offers late-night shows and Sunday afternoon concerts. For films in English, check the newspapers for *Cinema Pasquino* (in Trastevere, Vicolo del Piede; phone: 580-3622) and the *Cinema Alcazar* (14 Via Merry del Val; phone: 588-0099), which often has English-language movies on Mondays and Thursdays.

MUSIC: Again, for current schedules, check *A Guest in Rome* or the daily newspapers. The regular opera season at the *Teatro dell'Opera* (1 Piazza Beniamino Gigli, corner Via Firenze; phone: 461755 or 463641), runs from December through May. The best way to get tickets for good seats is through your hotel concierge or major travel agencies. If you choose to buy them yourself, go to the box office at 10 AM, no more than 3 days prior to the performance. Be prepared to wait — the line moves slowly. During July and August there is a summer opera season at the Baths of Caracalla. (Tickets are on sale at the *Teatro dell'Opera* box office or, on the day of performance, at Caracalla.) The *Rome Ballet* Company also performs at the *Teatro dell'Opera.* Rome's *RAI* symphony orchestra, one of four orchestras run by Radiotelevisione Italiana, the state television network, holds its concert season at the *Auditorio del Foro Italico* (1 Piazza Lauro de Bosis; phone: 365625), from October to June. At roughly the same time, the venerable *Accademia Nazionale di Santa Cecilia* gives first class concerts with international guest artists, either at the *Auditorio Santa Cecilia* (4 Via della Conciliazione; phone: 654-1044), or at the smaller *Sala Concerti* (Concert Hall; 18 Via dei Greci; box office, 6 Via Vittoria; phone: 679-0389). Between October and May, the *Accademia Filarmonica Romana* sponsors a series of concerts at the *Teatro Olimpico* (17 Piazza Gentile da Fabriano; phone: 396-2635 or 393304) — its summer season is held in the garden at the academy headquarters (118 Via Flaminia; phone: 360-1752) — and the *Istituzione Universitaria dei Concerti* holds concerts at the *Auditorium San Leone Magno* (38 Via Bolzano; phone: 853216), and at the university's *Aula Magna* (1 Piazzale Aldo Moro; phone: 361-0051). Other concerts occasionally are held at the *Auditorio del Gonfalone* (32 Via del Gonfalone; phone: 687-5952), and around Rome by the *Coro Polifonico Romano.* Still other musical groups use the *Teatro Ghione* (37 Via delle Fornaci; phone: 637-2294). Finally, there are concerts in many, many churches throughout the year, especially around *Christmas,* and music festivals — classical, jazz, pop, and folk — outdoors in the parks and picturesque piazze during the summer. For jazz and other modern music in clubs, see *Nightclubs and Nightlife* below.

NIGHTCLUBS AND NIGHTLIFE: Nightspots are born and die so quickly, slip into and out of fashion so easily, so that visitors would do well to check with Thursday's "Trova Roma" supplement to the daily *La Repubblica* for an up-to-date idea of what's going on. Since the 1950s, the few nightclubs are clustered around the big hotel/tourist office area of Via Veneto (although obviously there are exceptions). By US standards, their prices are high. In most, the drink minimum is about $25, and a bottle of champagne will cost at least $125. For the younger set on the lookout for disco, jazz, and general hanging out spots with a few extras — sometimes as much as a piano bar or as little as a dart board — a walk through Trastevere or the Testaccio area around Rome's old general markets and slaughterhouse (the newer bohemian area now that Trastevere has become gentrified) will turn up a host of intriguing places.

Among the nightclubs, small, swanky, expensive *Tartarughino* (near Piazza Navona, 1 Via della Scrofa; phone: 678-6037) is popular with the political set. Everyone seems to know each other, so it seems like a private club. A slightly younger crowd gathers at *Gilda* (near the Spanish Steps, 97 Via Mario de' Fiore; phone: 678-4838), known for its live music and pricey restaurant. *Cica Cica Bum* (pronounced *Chee*-ka *Chee*-ka *Boom* (38 Via Liguria; phone: 464745), with 1940s decor and both easy listening and disco music. Also fashionable is *Open Gate* (22 Via San Nicola da Tolentino; phone: 475-0464), which also has a restaurant and is not far from the Via Veneto. Also fashionable are *Open Gate* (22 Via San Nicola da Tolento; phone: 474-6301), not far from the Via Veneto; and *Jackie O'* (11 Via Boncompagni; phone: 461401). Both are restaurants, but prepare to spend.

The disco *Piper '90* (9 Via Tagliamento; phone: 841-4459) has been packing people in literally for generations. It changes its show every night, so be sure to call ahead to find out if there's a fashion show or break dance demonstration. *La Makumba* (19 Via degli Olimpionici; phone: 396-4392) plays African, Caribbean, and Latin music. The *Kripton* (52 Via Luciani; phone: 870504) is very in with the gilded younger set. It has a bar and restaurant. *La Tentazione* (Km 17.2 on Via Domentana; no phone) goes in for disco happenings, while *Vicolo delle Stelle* (22 Via Cesare Beccaria; phone: 361-1240) plays disco, rap, soul, and funk music until dawn. *Bulli e Pupi* (on the Aventine Hill, 11/A Via San Saba; phone: 578-2022) is not for executives, but for their offspring. The posh *Hosteria dell'Orso* (33 Via dell'Orso; phone: 656-4904) is a surefire and dignified solution to everyone's musical tastes — the dimly lit, comfortable *Blue Bar* on the main floor offers laid-back piano or guitar music, and *La Cabala* upstairs is a disco scene for title young Romans. It's in one of Rome's loveliest, centuries-old buildings, not far from the Piazza Navona (closed Sundays). There also is a restaurant (see *Eating Out*). *Hysteria* (3 Via Giovanelli; phone: 864-4587) is the newest "in" spot for dancing and drinking; it has the same owner as the swanky *Jackie O',* Beatrice Jannozzi. There is live music some weekends and a VIP corner where only celebrities are seated. The locals love it. *Veleno* (27 Via Sardegna, off Via Veneto; phone: 493583) packs in the motorscooter crowd rather than the jet set. For live music and disco dancing in downtown historical Romè is the very special *Casanova* (36 Piazza Rondanini; phone: 654-7314). *Notorious* (22 Via San Nicola da Tolentino; phone: 474-6888) mingles disco with dining. *L'Incontro* (near Piazza del Popolo; phone: 361-0934) has a piano bar and disco.

Especially good jazz can be heard (despite the noise of diners in its restaurant) at *Saint Louis Music City* (13/A Via del Cardello; phone: 474-5076) and *Alexanderplatz* (9 Via Ostia; phone: 372-9398). Also try the well-regarded *Café Caruso* (36 Via Monte Testaccio; phone: 574-7720). *Yes Brazil* (in Trastavere, Via San Francesco a Ripa; phone: 581-6267) has live music from 7 to 9 PM and Latin disco after until 1 AM. Two other favorites for live music are *Caffè Latino* (96 Via di Monte Testaccio; phone: 574-4020) and *Grigio Notte* (30/B Via dei Fenaroli; phone: 686-8340) for jazz, salsa, and drinks.

If you're just an amiable barfly who might like to strike up a pleasant conversation in English, the place to go is the bar at the *Inghilterra* hotel (14 Via Bocca di Leoni; phone: 672161); there is no music except for the tinkling of ice cubes, but the bartender is the nicest in town. Also drop by another occasional American haunt, *Little Bar* (54/A Via Gregoriana — the street where the big fashion houses are located).

For those with a *funiculi funicola* idea of Italy as peasant exuberance expressed through music, you can spend an evening joining in with the singing waiters and waitresses at the twin restaurants (opened in the 1960s in Trastevere by two American brothers) *Da Meo Patacca* (30 Piazza dei Mercanti; phone: 581-6198) and *Da Ciceraucchio* (1 Via del Porto; phone: 580-6046). You might think that you won't be able to stand all the noise, but the wine flows freely and fun is on the house; so take the kids along and enjoy.

BEST IN TOWN

CHECKING IN: Of the more than 500 hotels in Rome, the following are recommended either for some special charm, location, or bargain price in their category. Those without restaurants are noted, although all serve breakfast if desired, and all have heating and telephones in the rooms unless otherwise stated. In high season prices can be staggering; expect to pay from $550 up to $700 for a double room with bath in the hotels listed as very expensive, from $350 to $550 for hotels in the expensive price range, from $150 to $350 in the moderate category, and under $150 (to as low as $90) in the inexpensive category. Off-season rates are about 10% lower. All telephone numbers are in the 6 city code unless otherwise indicated.

Cavalieri Hilton International – Far from the historic center of Rome at the top of a lovely hill (Monte Mario) overlooking much of the city, with shuttle buses to Via Veneto and Piazza di Spagna running hourly during shopping hours only. But the swimming pool is especially desirable in summer, and the rooftop restaurant, *La Pergola* wins high praise from food critics. A resort property with year-round swimming, tennis, a sauna, and other diversions, it has 387 rooms. Business facilities include meeting rooms for up to 2,100, English-speaking concierge, foreign currency exchange, secretarial services in English, audiovisual equipment, photocopiers, cable television news, translation services, and express checkout. 101 Via Cadlolo (phone: 31511; fax: 315-12241; telex: 625337HILTRO I). Very expensive.

Eden – Among the most elegant in Rome, this hotel has excellent service, an intimate roof garden restaurant (see *Eating Out*), and a panoramic bar. There are 116 air conditioned rooms with TV sets. Business facilities include meeting rooms for up to 214, English-speaking concierge, foreign currency exchange, secretarial services in English, audiovisual equipment, photocopiers, cable television news, translation services, and express checkout. 49 Via Ludovisi (phone: 474-3551; fax: 482-1584; telex: 610567EDENRM I). Very expensive.

Excelsior – Big, bustling, but efficient, it dominates the Via Veneto, next to the US Embassy. It's a favorite with Americans, and the bar is a popular meeting place. There are 383 rooms in this member of the CIGA chain. Business facilities include 24-hour room service, meeting rooms for up to 400, English-speaking concierge, foreign currency exchange, secretarial services in English, audiovisual equipment, photocopiers, computers, cable television news, translation services, and express checkout. 125 Via Vittorio Veneto (phone: 4708; fax: 482-6205; telex: 610232EXCEROI). Very expensive.

Grand – The pride of the CIGA chain in Rome, and traditionally the capital's most dignified hotel. It is truly grand — formal, well run, and elegant in style and service. It has 175 rooms and a central (if not exactly prime) location between the railroad station and Via Veneto areas. Its *Le Restaurant* is pretty near perfect (see *Eating Out*) and the two bars are cozy and chic — indeed, perfect, according to a recent industry poll on Roman watering holes. Afternoon tea also is served, with harp music. Business facilities include 24-hour room service, meeting rooms for up to 400, English-speaking concierge, foreign currency exchange, secretarial services in English, audiovisual equipment, photocopiers, computers, cable television news, translation services, and express checkout. 3 Via Vittorio Emanuele Orlando (phone: 4709; fax: 474-7307; telex: 610210GRANDRO I). Very expensive.

Hassler — Villa Medici – At the top of the Spanish Steps and within easy striking distance of the best shopping in Rome, favored by a loyal clientele. Guestrooms could stand some refurbishing, and the public rooms have seen better days. Each of the 108 rooms is individually decorated, and manager Albert Wirth is an attentive host. The roof garden restaurant has only so-so food, but splendid views, and offers Sunday brunch. Business facilities include meeting rooms for up to 180, English-speaking concierge, foreign currency exchange, secretarial services in English, audiovisual equipment, photocopiers, cable television news, translation services, and express checkout. 6 Piazza Trinità dei Monti (phone: 679-0770; fax: 678-9991; telex: 61028 HASLER I). Very expensive.

Aldrovandi Palace – Quiet, with 139 rooms in a fashionable residential area next to the Villa Borghese, and not far from Via Veneto, it has a delightful park with a swimming pool and a full-facility health club. Its restaurant, *Relais le Piscine,* is next door at 6 Via Mangili. Business facilities include 24-hour room service, meeting rooms for up to 400, English-speaking concierge, foreign currency exchange, secretarial services in English, audiovisual equipment, photocopiers, computers, cable television news, translation services, and express checkout. The hotel is at 15 Via Ulisse Aldrovandi (phone: 322-3993; fax: 322-1435; telex: 616141ALDROV I). Expensive.

Ambasciatori Palace – Across the street from the US Embassy, it has 145 generally spacious rooms, old-fashioned amenities, and a very convenient location. Business facilities include 24-hour room service, meeting rooms for up to 200, English-speaking concierge, foreign currency exchange, secretarial services in English, audiovisual equipment, photocopiers, cable television news, translation services, and express checkout. 70 Via Veneto (phone: 47493; fax: 474-3601; telex: 610241HOTAMB I). Expensive.

Atlante Star – Near the Vatican, this large, modern hotel boasts a roof garden with a splendid view of St. Peter's dome, an excellent restaurant, and an efficiently equipped business center. Parking is available, as is the rental of a private plane for island-hopping. Business facilities include 24-hour room service, meeting rooms for up to 83, English-speaking concierge, foreign currency exchange, secretarial services in English, audiovisual equipment, photocopiers, computers, cable television news, translation services, and express checkout. 34 Via Vitelleschi (phone: 687-9558; fax: 687-2300; telex: 622355). Expensive.

Holiday Inn Crowne Plaza Minerva – The reopening of this 134-room, well-located hotel where Stendhal used to stay, was something of an event for downtown Rome. Its pricey restoration preserved the old baroque adornment. *La Cesta,* its restaurant (see *Eating Out*), has not yet won over all the food experts, but is quite good. Near the Pantheon. Business facilities include meeting rooms for up to 250, English-speaking concierge, foreign currency exchange, secretarial services in English, audiovisual equipment, photocopiers, cable television news, translation services, and express checkout. Piazza della Minerva (phone: 684-1888; fax: 679-4165; telex: 620091). Expensive.

Lord Byron – A small (47 rooms) first-rate place in the fashionable Parioli residential district, this once was a private villa, and it maintains the atmosphere of a private club. It has a celebrated restaurant, *Relais Le Jardin* (see *Eating Out*). Business facilities include 24-hour room service, meeting rooms for up to 100, English-speaking concierge, foreign currency exchange, secretarial services in English, audiovisual equipment, photocopiers, cable television news, translation services, and express checkout. 5 Via Giuseppe de Notaris (phone: 360-9541; fax: 322-0405; telex: 611216HBYRON I). Expensive.

Majestic – Completely restored with 100 rooms and suites, this air conditioned, century-old hostelry (the oldest on Via Veneto) is across the street from the American Embassy. Its opulently decorated reception room has a handsome fresco ceiling. There is a restaurant and the terrace bar offers a fine view of the Roman skyline. Business facilities include 24-hour room service, meeting rooms for up to 150, English-speaking concierge, secretarial services in English, audiovisual equipment, photocopiers, computers, cable television news, translation services, and express checkout. 50 Via Veneto (phone: 486841; fax: 488-0984; telex: 622262). Expensive.

Nazionale – Another old favorite (of Sartre and de Beauvoir, among others), the 86 renovated rooms here are very central, next to the Chamber of Deputies, between Via del Corso and the Pantheon. Business facilities include meeting rooms for up to 900, English-speaking concierge, foreign currency exchange, secretarial services in English, audiovisual equipment, photocopiers, and express checkout. 131 Piazza Montecitorio (phone: 678-9251; fax: 678-6677; telex: 6211427NATEL I). Expensive.

Parco dei Principi – This modern hotel is on the edge of Villa Borghese in the Parioli residential district, not far from Via Veneto. It has 203 rooms and a small swimming pool in a lovely garden. Business facilities include meeting rooms for up to 500, English-speaking concierge, foreign currency exchange, secretarial services in English, audiovisual equipment, photocopiers, computers, translation services, and express checkout. 5 Via Girolamo Frescobaldi (phone: 855-1758; fax: 884-5104; telex: 610517PRISOM I). Expensive.

Raphael – Behind Piazza Navona, it's a favorite of Italian politicians (it's near the Senate and the Chamber of Deputies), with 83 rooms. Some are small, some could use a bit of refurbishing, but loyal patrons love the antiques in the lobby, the cozy bar, and the location. The roof terrace has one of Rome's finest views. Business facilities include 2 English-speaking concierges, foreign currency exchange, secretarial services in English, photocopiers, cable television news, translation services, and express checkout. 2 Largo Febo (phone: 650881; fax: 687-8993; telex: 622396RHOTEL). Expensive.

Sheraton Roma – With 631 rooms and 25 suites, air conditioning, and a conference center that can handle up to 1,200 people, this modern, efficient hotel is also the one with the most sports facilities. Located in the suburb of EUR about 25 minutes south of central Rome, it has ample parking and regular shuttle-bus service to downtown and to the nearby Leonardo da Vinci Airport. There are 2 restaurants and a piano bar. Pluses include a health club, squash and tennis courts, outdoor pool, jogging circuit, sauna, and masseur. Business facilities include 24-hour room service, English-speaking concierge, foreign currency exchange, secretarial services in English, audiovisual equipment, photocopiers, computers, cable television news, translation services, and express checkout. Viale del Pattinaggio (phone: 5453; fax: 594-3281; telex: 626077SHEROM I). Expensive.

Sole al Pantheon – For those without a car, this 400-year-old, 25-room hostelry is in a perfect location. Lavishly renovated from the days when the poet Ariosto stayed here, today's conveniences include air conditioning and some spacious rooms (a few of the guestrooms have Jacuzzis). Shut your eyes to the garish decor in the lobby, and focus instead on the fine views from the upper rooms. Business facilities include an English-speaking concierge, foreign currency exchange, photocopiers, translation services, and express checkout. 73 Piazza della Rotonda (phone: 678-0441; fax: 684-0689). Expensive.

Cicerone – In the residential and commercial area of Prati on the Vatican side of the river, but convenient nevertheless because it's just across from Piazza del Popolo and the Spanish Steps. It has modern and spacious public areas, 237 well-appointed rooms, friendly, attentive service, and a large garage. Business facilities include meeting rooms for up to 200, English-speaking concierge, foreign currency exchange, secretarial services in English, audiovisual equipment, photocopiers, cable television news, translation services, and express checkout. 55/C Via Cicerone (phone: 3576; fax: 654-1383; telex: 622498CICER I). Expensive to moderate.

Columbus – In a restored 15th-century palace right in front of St. Peter's, this 107-room hotel offers antique furniture, paintings, and a garden — a lot of atmosphere for the price. 33 Via della Conciliazione (phone: 686-4874). Expensive to moderate.

Eliseo – Just off Via Veneto, this has traditional furnishings (with a slightly French air) in the public rooms and in some of the 50 guestrooms; others are super modern. A roof restaurant looks out over the tops of the umbrella pines in the Villa Borghese. 30 Via di Porta Pinciana (phone: 460556). Expensive to moderate.

Flora – At the top of Via Veneto, right next to the Villa Borghese, the 174 rooms are traditional, reliable, and not without charm. Business facilities include meeting rooms for up to 200, English-speaking concierge, foreign currency exchange, secretarial services in English, audiovisual equipment, photocopiers, computers, translation services, and express checkout. 191 Via Vittorio Veneto (phone: 497281). Expensive to moderate.

Forum – Built around a medieval tower in the middle of the Imperial Forums, this charming 79-room hotel is a bit out of the way but worth any inconvenience for the spectacular view of ancient Rome from its roof garden. The food here is less spectacular. 25 Via Tor de' Conti (phone: 679-2446). Expensive to moderate.

Inghilterra – Extremely popular with knowledgeable travelers, its 102 rooms have numbered Anatole France, Mark Twain, and Ernest Hemingway among many illustrious guests. Particularly attractive are the top-floor suites, some with flowered terraces. Be sure to ask for a spacious room; some are small, inevitable in older, downtown hotels. There is a small and simpatico restaurant (the *Roman Garden*), and the ever-crowded bar is a cozy haven for Roman patricians. Business facilities include meeting rooms for up to 50, English-speaking concierge, audiovisual equipment, photocopiers, computers, cable television news, and express checkout. Near the Spanish Steps, in the middle of the central shopping area. 14 Via Bocca di Leone (phone: 672161; fax: 684-0828; telex: 614552). Expensive to moderate.

Anglo-Americano – Just off Piazza Barberini, it has 115 rooms, and the back ones look out on the garden of Palazzo Barberini. Business facilities include English-speaking concierge, and photocopiers. 12 Via delle Quattro Fontane (phone: 472941; fax: 474-6428; telex: 626147ANCAM I). Moderate.

Degli Aranci – Small and quiet, it's in the Parioli residential district and has 48 rooms, a bar, and a lovely garden restaurant. Business facilities include 24-hour room service, meeting rooms for up to 40, English-speaking concierge, secretarial services in English, audiovisual equipment, photocopiers, translation services, and express checkout. 11 Via Barnaba Oriani (phone: 879774; fax: 879774; telex: 621071). Moderate.

Atlas – With 45 rooms and a flowered roof garden, this place has a central location. 3 Via Rasella (phone: 488-2140). Moderate.

Campo dei Fiori – Near the Campo dei Fiori square — a market area since the 1500s — the Renaissance palaces, the giant Palazzo Cancelleria, and the Palazzo Farnese (French Embassy), which was partly designed by Michelangelo, it is one of the coziest (and narrowest) in the area. The rustic rooms are small and sparsely decorated, but the exposed brick walls, hand-painted bathroom ceilings, and detailed architecture make up for the lack of space. For guests willing to climb 6 flights, there's a wonderful view of the city from the roof garden. No restaurant or bar. Business facilities include meeting rooms for up to 40, translation services, and express checkout. 6 Via del Biscione (phone: 687-4886). Moderate.

Cardinal – On Renaissance Rome's stateliest street, this restored 66-room palace (attributed to Bramante) is convenient for exploring some of the city's hidden treasures, but less so for shopping in the city center. No restaurant. 62 Via Giulia (phone: 654-2719). Moderate.

Fontana – A restored, air conditioned 13th-century monastery next to the Trevi Fountain, with cell-like rooms — though 10 of the 30 rooms have great views of the fabulous fountain — and a lovely rooftop bar. A bargain in every way. Business facilities include meeting rooms for up to 35, English-speaking concierge, and secretarial services in English. 96 Piazza di Trevi (phone: 678-6113). Moderate.

Pullman Boston – The roof garden is just one of the selling points of this carefully renovated 120-room hostelry, well located between Via Veneto and the Spanish Steps. Business travelers will appreciate the services. Business facilities include meeting rooms for up to 90, English-speaking concierge, secretarial services in English, audiovisual equipment, cable television news, translation services, and express checkout. The breakfast buffet is a serendipitous plus. Good value. 47 Via Lombardia (phone: 473951; in the US, 800-223-9862; fax: 482-1019; telex: 622247ETAPRM I). Moderate.

La Residenza – An exceptional bargain on a quiet street just behind Via Veneto. Old-fashioned and well-maintained, it has 27 rooms and feels much more like a private villa than a hotel. Book well in advance. Full American breakfast, but no restaurant per se. Business facilities include meeting rooms for up to 25, English-speaking concierge, foreign currency exchange, secretarial services in English, photocopiers, cable television news, and translation services. No credit cards accepted. 22 Via Emilia (phone: 488-0789; fax: 485721; telex: 410423). Moderate.

Santa Chiara – Beautifully renovated last year, this centrally located, 94-room hostelry has been in the Corteggiani family since 1834. No dining room, but close to many restaurants. Business facilities include meeting rooms for up to 40, English-speaking concierge, audiovisual equipment, photocopiers, cable television news, and express checkout. 21 Via Santa Chiara (phone: 683-3763; fax: 687-3144). Moderate.

Scalinata di Spagna – Tiny, but spectacularly placed overlooking the Spanish Steps, it's opposite the pricey *Hassler.* There are 14 rooms, no restaurant. 17 Piazza Trinità dei Monti (phone: 684-0598). Moderate.

Senato – Newly renovated, this 50-room hotel with delightful views of the Pantheon from the front rooms has air conditioning. A good value. Business facilities include English-speaking concierge, foreign currency exchange, photocopiers, and express checkout. 73 Piazza della Rotonda (phone: 679-3231; fax: 684-0297). Moderate.

Sitea – Gianni de Luca and his Scottish wife, Shirley, have bestowed the coziness of a private home on their 40-room, 5-floor hotel opposite the *Grand.* Rooms have high ceilings, crystal chandeliers, and hand-painted Florentine dressers. Other amenities: sitting rooms and a sun-drenched penthouse bar. 90 Via Vittorio Emanuele Orlando (phone: 482-7560). Moderate.

Trevi – Located in a recently renovated palazzo only a few steps from the fabled fountain. Tiny (20 rooms, all with private baths), this 4-story hotel offers many amenities, including air conditioning. 20 Vicolo del Babuccio (phone: 684-1406). Moderate.

Villa Florence – A charming 19th-century patrician villa in a residential area a few minutes' drive from the Via Veneto. The comfortable, modern rooms have TV sets, radio, and mini-bar, and are complemented by touches of ancient Rome in the public areas. Parking facilities and nice gardens. 28 Via Nomentana (phone: 440-3036). Moderate.

Aberdeen – Small and unpretentious, this completely renovated 26-room inn stars for its prime location near Parliament. Some rooms are air conditioned and there's a buffet breakfast. 48 Via Firenze (phone: 481-9340; fax: 482-1092). Moderate to inexpensive.

Canova – All 15 comfortable rooms in this quiet hostelry are air conditioned. There is a small café on the roof and an inexpensive restaurant next door. Well located between the Roman Forum and Santa Maria Maggiore. 10/A Via Urbana (phone: 481-9123; fax: 481-9123). Moderate to inexpensive.

Clodio – A modern 61-room hotel on the Prati side of the river, close to RAI's headquarters and to the *Foro Italico,* where the *International Tennis Championship* is held every May. 10 Via Santa Lucia (phone: 317541; telex: 625050). Moderate to inexpensive.

Coronet – Guests won't find luxurious accommodations at this pensione, but it is in a central area just a few blocks from the Piazza Venezia. Inside the Palazzo Doria, a palace which still is the home of the family who built it, some of its rooms have private baths. No restaurant. Business facilities include English-speaking concierge and foreign currency exchange. 5 Piazza Grazioli (phone: 679-2341). Inexpensive.

Dinesen – Off Via Veneto and next to the Villa Borghese, the 20 rooms in this charming place with a 19th-century air are a real bargain. Breakfast is included. No restaurant. 18 Via di Porta Pinciana (phone: 460932). Inexpensive.

Fabrello White – For basic, affordable accommodations, this pensione is a good bet. Not all of the 33 rooms have baths, but some have terrace views of the river. On the right bank of the Tiber, it's a 10-minute walk to the Spanish Steps. 11 Via Vittoria Colonna (phone: 360-4446/7). Inexpensive.

Gregoriana – On the street of the same name — high fashion's headquarters in Rome — this tiny (19 air conditioned rooms) gem attracts the fashionable. Its decor is reminiscent of Art Deco, with room letters (rather than numbers) by the late fashion illustrator Erté. No restaurant, though a continental breakfast is included. No credit cards accepted. 18 Via Gregoriana (phone: 679-4269 or 679-7988). Inexpensive.

King – The 61 rooms in this well-positioned, immaculate hotel are reasonably priced. No restaurant, though breakfast is served. Business facilities include English-speaking concierge, foreign currency exchange, secretarial services in English, photocopiers, cable television news, translation services, and express checkout. 131 Via Sistina (phone: 474-1515; fax: 487-1813; telex: 626236KINGHO I). Inexpensive.

Locarno – Near the Piazza del Popolo and the Spanish Steps, this Belle Epoque hotel often attracts artists, writers, and intellectuals. The 35 rooms have Victorian furniture, and many are large enough to include couches and desks. A clever touch here — guest bikes for getting around. During winter, a fire burns in the lounge, and in the summer drinks and breakfast are served on the terrace. Business facilities include meeting rooms for up to 15, English-speaking concierge, secretarial services in English, photocopiers, and express checkout. 22 Via della Penna (phone: 361-0841; fax: 321-5249; telex: 622251HOTLOC I). Inexpensive.

Margutta – Try for the two rooms on the roof (Nos. 50 and 51), complete with fireplaces and surrounded by a terrace. This 21-room hotel is near Piazza del Popolo and has an English-speaking concierge. No restaurant. 34 Via Laurina (phone: 679-8440). Inexpensive.

Sant'Anselmo – In a small villa on the Aventine Hill, this beflowered bargain has 26 rooms, a family atmosphere, but no restaurant. (Nearby are 4 other villas — with this one, totaling about 120 rooms — each with similar accommodations and prices, and all run by the same management.) Reservations necessary well in advance. Business facilities include meeting rooms for up to 50, English-speaking concierge, foreign currency exchange, secretarial services in English, and photocopiers. 2 Piazza di Sant'Anselmo (phone: 574-5174; fax: 578-3604; telex: 622812). Inexpensive.

Teatro di Pompeo – History, literally, is at the root of this hotel, as its foundation was originally laid in 55 BC and is said to have supported the Theater of Pompey, where Julius Caesar met his untimely end. On a quiet street, its 12 charming rooms have hand-painted tiles and beamed ceilings. No restaurant. Business facilities include meeting rooms for up to 20, English-speaking concierge, foreign currency exchange, audiovisual quipment, and photocopiers. 8 Largo del Pallaro (phone: 687-2566; fax: 687-2566). Inexpensive. 1

EATING OUT: The ancient Romans were the originators of the first fully developed cuisine of the Western world. Drawing on an abundance of fine, natural ingredients from the fertile Roman countryside and influenced by Greece and Asia Minor, they evolved a gastronomic tradition still felt in kitchens the world over.

While the lavish and exotic banquets of exaggerated proportions described in detail by Roman writers such as Petronius and Pliny no doubt existed, they were relatively infrequent and probably more a vulgar show of *nouveaux riches* than typical examples of local custom. The old nobility, then as now, must have found such conspicuous consumption in poor taste, and in fact, the beginnings of genuine Roman gastronomic traditions were more likely among the humble masses, who dined on such staples as lentils and chick-peas, still regularly offered in Roman trattorie. Even the ancient Romans' beloved sauce of rotted fish, *garum,* is echoed in the olive oil, crushed anchovy bits, and garlic sauce that anoints the quintessential Roman salad green, crisp and curly *puntarelle.*

Unfortunately, today's authentically Roman kitchens are dwindling in number. One by one, the old-fashioned, inexpensive mamma-papa trattorie are becoming Chinese restaurants, of which Rome now boasts 140 — none of them too terrific. In addition, fast-food joints have arrived with a vengeance and with the *1990 World Cup* soccer games, every restaurateur renovated his or her locale — and the price list as well. So don't be surprised if an old favorite trattoria now is all tarted up and pricey.

Rome's traditional fare is further threatened by the standardized fad menus, which include such vogues as *rughetta* (rugola), tucked everywhere and often cooked to little effect. Watch out, too, for the new handy way to deal with leftover carpaccio (raw slivers of beef), sautéed *stracci* ("rags"). The trendy dessert continues to be *tiramisù,* a Tyrolean calorie bomb of mascarpone cheese, liqueur, and coffee. The very ease of its preparation, with no cooking involved, is elbowing out better and more interesting desserts.

The bright side is that a new generation of well-trained cooks is bringing back forgotten regional dishes and devising new versions of old standbys. These relative youngsters call their fare "creative cuisine," the fruit of their labors, and are well worth seeking out. The decreasing number of authentic Roman kitchens makes the survivors all the more precious, and it means that while a careful diner will test the new, he or she also will seek out and cherish the authentic old.

Real Roman cooking is quite like the real Roman people — robust and hearty, imbued with a total disregard for tomorrow. There's no room in the popular Roman philosophy of *carpe diem* for thoughts of cholesterol or calories or preoccupations with heartburn, hangovers, or garlic-laden breath. These considerations disappear before a steaming dish of fragrant *spaghetti all'amatriciana* (tomato, special bacon, and tangy *pecorino* — ewe's milk cheese), deep-fried *filetti di baccalà* (salt cod fillet), or *coda alla vaccinara* (oxtail stewed in tomato, onion and celery) — all accompanied by the abundant wines of the surrounding hill towns, the Castelli Romani.

Since Rome is close to the sea, its restaurants offer abundant fresh fish — particularly on Tuesdays and Fridays — but it is costly. All restaurants are required to identify frozen fish as well as other frozen ingredients. Don't hesitate to try the *antipasta marinara* (a mixture of seafoods in a light sauce of olive oil, lemon, parsley, and garlic), the *spaghetti alle vongole* (spaghetti with clam sauce — the clam shells come as well), and as a main course, trout from the nearby lakes or rock fish from the Mediterranean.

Veal is typically Roman, served as *saltimbocca alla romana* (literally, "hop-into-the-mouth," flavored with ham, sage, and marsala wine) or roasted with the fresh rosemary that grows in every garden. *Abbacchio al forno* is milk-fed baby lamb roasted with garlic and rosemary, and *abbacchio brodettato,* ever harder to find, is cooked in a sauce of egg yolks and lemon juice. *Abbacchio scottadito* ("finger burning") are tiny grilled lamb chops. On festive occasions, *maialetto* (suckling pig) appears on the menu; it is stuffed with herbs, roasted, and thickly sliced. Its street-stand version is eaten betweeen thick slabs of country bread. Watch, too, for such Roman specialties as *tripa* (tripe flavored with mint, parmesan cheese, and tomato sauce), *coniglio* (rabbit), *capretto* (kid), *coratella* (lamb's heart), *animelle* (sweetbreads), and, in season, *cinghiale* (wild boar). Wild boar dried sausages are popular as an antipasto course, along with salamis; the local Roman salami is prepared with tasty fennel seeds.

Pasta dishes include the incredibly simple *spaghetti alla carbonara* (with egg, salt pork, and *pecorino* cheese). *Penne all'arrabbiata* are short pasta in a tomato and garlic sauce "rabid" with hot peppers. The familiar *fettuccine all'Alfredo* depends upon the quality of the homemade strips of egg pasta in a rich sauce of cream, butter, and parmesan.

Fresh, seasonal vegetables, which often are treated as a separate course, provide the base for many a savory antipasto, accompany the main dish, and are even munched raw — for instance, *finocchio al pinzimonio* (fennel dipped into the purest of olive oil seasoned with salt and pepper) — after a particularly heavy meal to "clean the palate." Several local greens are unknown to visitors, such as *agretti, bieta, cicoria,* and *broccolo romano* — the last two often boiled briefly, then sautéed with olive oil, garlic, and hot red peppers. Salad ingredients include red radicchio, wild aromatic herbs, and the juicy tomatoes so cherished during the sultry summer months when they are served with ultra-aromatic basil — the sun's special gift to Mediterranean terraces and gardens. Tomatoes are also stuffed with rice and roasted; yellow, red, and green sweet peppers, eggplant, mushrooms, green and broad beans, and zucchini are favorite vegetables for antipasto; while asparagus and artichokes are especially prized in season. The latter is stuffed with mint and garlic and is stewed with olive oil seasoning *alla romana,* or opened out like a flower and deep-fried *alla giudia* (Jewish-style).

After such a meal, Romans normally have fresh fruit for dessert, although there is no shortage of sweet desserts (such as *montebianco, zuppa inglese,* and, of course, *gelato* (ice cream). For a final *digestivo,* bottles brought to the table may include *Sambuca Romana* (it has an aniseed base), *grappa* (made from the third and fourth grape pressings and normally over 60 proof!), and some sort of *amaro* (which means bitter, but is more often quite sweet).

A full meal, including house wine, may cost between $50 and $60 for two in a modest restaurant, while the same fare may cost twice that amount if the restaurant is even marginally fashionable. Most dining is à la carte, although a *menù turistico* is offered at some unpretentious trattorie for very reasonable prices, and a few tony establishments now serve sampler menus (*menù degustazione*) at a slightly lower price. Less expensive are the quick service, often cafeteria-style, *rosticcerie* and *tavole calde* (literally "hot tables"). A delightful novelty is the spate of small wine tasting establishments that offer light snacks at lunch with a glass of fine wine; some also provide pasta or a mixed vegetable platter. Most café-bars serve sandwiches as well as that delicious and filling health snack, *frullato di frutta* (a mixture of frothy blended fruit and milk). Be careful when ordering fresh fish or Florentine steaks *al chilo* — by weight — as this may swell a bill way out of proportion, even at average-priced restaurants. When in Rome, start your day as the Romans do with a tiny, but terrific cup of coffee at one of the many coffee-bars like *Antico Caffè Greco* (86 Via Condotti); *Rosati* (4-5 Piazza del Popolo); *Sant' Eustachio Il Caffè* (82 Piazza Sant' Eustachio); or *Tazzo a'Oro* (6 Via degli Orfani). Also, always ask prices when ordering wine. Good Italian wines can cost as much as $30 and up per bottle. Dinner for two (with wine) costs from $170 to $250 in restaurants listed below as very expensive, $100 to $175 in restaurants classed as expensive; $60 to $100 is moderate; and below $60 is inexpensive. All telephone numbers are in the 6 area code unless otherwise indicated.

Alberto Ciarla – Alberto, long an impassioned diver and spearfisherman, is another restaurateur who knows where to find fresh oysters (which he sometimes serves raw), lobster, and fish. Ciarla is rated one of Rome's finest chefs; the *L'Espresso* guide gives him its highest marks, three chef's toques. His herbed pasta sauces are a welcome change from the more usual ways of preparing Italy's favorite food. For meat lovers, the "Alter Ego" menu offers a pâté of wild pigeon, baby lamb, and game — including venison — in season. The ever-large, noisy crowd brightens up the black decor (even down to the tablecloths). In good weather, there's alfresco dining on a little piece of a Trastevere street. Dinner only; closed Sundays. Reservations advised. Major credit cards accepted. 40 Piazza San Cosimato (phone: 581-8668). Very expensive.

Il Pianeta Terra – This Planet Earth comes close to paradise. A young couple, half Tuscan and half Sicilian, has created an elegant, traditional, yet adventurous dining place in the heart of Rome. Starters such as ravioli stuffed with sea bass in a pistachio sauce or pasta with clams and broccoli lead to exciting main courses, such as the squab stuffed with artichokes or with oysters and clams, and to delicate desserts. The wine list is intelligently chosen. Note: the *menù degustazione* can cost more than an à la carte meal. Dinner only; closed Mondays and from mid-July through August. Reservations necessary. Major credit cards accepted. 94-95 Via Arco del Monte (phone: 686-9893 or 679-9828). Very expensive.

Relais Le Jardin – The sumptuous dining room of the *Lord Byron* hotel is still Rome's foremost restaurant. Chef Antonio Sciullo's creations blend the unlikely into the surprising and sometime sublime. The menu follows the seasons — you will find zucchini blossoms stuffed with bean purée, ravioli with a delicate pigeon ragout, and scallops lurking in a watercress flan. The dessert soufflé has a crunchy hazelnut topping. Service is appropriately sophisticated, as are the wines. Closed Sundays and August. Reservations necessary. Major credit cards accepted. *Lord Byron Hotel,* 5 Via Giuseppe De Notaris (phone: 322-4541). Very expensive.

La Rosetta – One of Rome's most famed fish restaurants, it is small, jam-packed, and chic. The chef grills, fries, boils, or bakes to perfection any — or a mixture of all — of the fish and seafood flown in from his native Sicily. A favorite specialty is *pappardelle al pescatore* (wide noodles in a piquant tomato sauce with mussels, clams, and parsley) or Sicilian-style *pasta con le sarde,* flavored with wild fennel. Closed Sundays, Mondays at lunchtime, and August. Reservations necessary. Major credit cards accepted. 9 Via della Rosetta (phone: 686-1002). Very expensive.

El Toulà – The well-heeled, well-traveled, and aristocratic assemble here for Cortina- and Venice-inspired fare; in winter that means hearty game dishes such as venison and, year-round, fish, such as the poppyseed-daubed salmon in oyster sauce. A favorite dessert is a large shortbread biscuit. There's an impressive wine list, but you might have to put up with hearing the man at the next table negotiating a major deal as the tables are quite close together. Closed Saturday lunch, Sundays, and August. Reservations necessary. Major credit cards accepted. 29/B Via della Lupa (phone: 687-3498). Very expensive.

Andrea – Tops for the Via Veneto area. In season, fettuccine with artichoke sauce; always on the menu, ricotta-stuffed fresh ravioli. Pleasant service, a serviceable house wine, and sweeties to sweeten the bill. Closed Sundays and 3 weeks in August. Reservations necessary. Major credit cards accepted. 26 Via Sardegna (phone: 446-3707). Expensive.

Le Cabanon – French and Tunisian food are served in an intimate ambience accompanied by Mediterranean melodies sung by the well-traveled owner, Enzo Rallo. South American or French singers ably fill in the gaps. The usual onion soup and escargots, as well as a delicious Tunisian *brik à l'oeuf* (a pastry concealing a challengingly dripping egg within), couscous, and *merguez* sausages are among the choices. Open evenings only, and until late. Closed Sundays and August. Reservations necessary. No credit cards accepted. 4 Vicolo della Luce (phone: 581-8106). Expensive.

La Cesta – Centrally located in the *Holiday Inn Crowne Plaza Minerva* is this delightfully restored 19th-century restaurant. You can enjoy quiet dining for business as well as pleasure under splendid Venetian glass chandeliers. Beside a somewhat standard menu, there is a daily list of Roman and international specialties. The fare is excellent if not brilliant. Open daily. Reservations advised. Major credit cards accepted. 69 Piazza della Minerva (phone: 684-1888). Expensive.

Charles Roof Garden – A breathtaking view and creative Italian fare is offered at this restaurant on top of the *Eden* hotel. Regional specialties include homemade *tonnarelli* (thick noodles) with lemon sauce, while the café on the terrace offers a snacks menu. Open daily. Reservations necessary. Major credit cards accepted. 49 Via Ludovisi (phone: 474-3551). Expensive.

Il Convivio – A welcome addition on a street of artisans and antiques dealers, chef Angelo Trioiani and his brother Massimo have just 10 tables on which to lavish their version of "creative cuisine." A special menu (with lower prices) is available at lunchtime. A fine wine list. Closed Sundays. Reservations advised. Major credit cards accepted. 44 Via dell'Orso (phone: 686-9432). Expensive.

Girarrosto Toscano – Old fashioned and serious, it's a fine eatery for lovers of classic Tuscan fare. The sizzling Florentine steaks and fresh fish are grilled to perfection. The rest is perfect, too, but this is not always a restful place. Closed Wednesdays. Reservations necessary. Major credit cards accepted. 29 Via Campania (phone: 482-1899). Expensive.

Hosteria dell'Orso – Although this is widely known as a tourist place, the traditional Italian fare offered in an elegant 13th-century building is quite good. Upstairs is a disco (see *Nightclubs and Nightlife*), and downstairs is a piano bar. Closed Sundays. Reservations necessary. Major credit cards accepted. 33 Via dell'Orso (phone: 656-4904). Expensive.

La Lampada – This is the only Roman restaurant that specializes in truffles and wild mushrooms, but don't anticipate bargains, and don't expect the truffles to be fresh beyond the autumn/winter season. The risotto is made with white truffles, and the carpaccio with a grating of both black and white truffles (from Norcia and Alba, respectively). Closed Sundays. Reservations necessary. Major credit cards accepted. 25 Via Quintino Sella (phone: 474-4323). Expensive.

Papà Giovanni – It's small and intimate, with paintings and wine bottles lining the walls, and the bar is very well stocked — sip a *kir* as an *aperitivo* while choosing from over 700 wines. The highly praised fare is basically refined Roman, with truffles a seasonal specialty. Try *panzerotti al tartufo* (small ravioli with truffles). The interesting menu varies, so ask your waiter for current specialties. Closed Sundays. Reservations necessary. Major credit cards accepted. 4 Via dei Sediari (phone: 686-5308). Expensive.

Passetto – For classical Roman cooking, this Belle Epoque restaurant is a beloved local institution. In addition to the excellent antipasto, try the *filetto con carciofi* (steak with artichokes) and *porcini* mushrooms with asparagus, if they're in season. Closed Sundays and Monday afternoons. Reservations advised. Major credit cards accepted. 13-14 Via Zanardelli (phone: 654-0569 or 687-9937). Expensive.

Il Peristilio – The decor is sumptuous, with fine objets d'art, tasteful cutlery and china, and a refined aura. Air conditioning, a piano bar, and polite waiters complete the picture; the quality of the food may blur it. Closed Mondays. Reservations necessary. Major credit cards accepted. 6/B Via Col di Lana (phone: 322-3623). Expensive.

Pino e Dino – Although the founders have gone, current management continues their menu of interesting regional dishes. The restaurant is on one of Rome's more picturesque squares, but a cozy winter meal indoors, surrounded by wine bottles and artisan products from all over Italy, is just as enticing. Closed Mondays and most of August. Reservations necessary. Major credit cards accepted. 22 Piazza di Montevecchio (phone: 656-1319). Expensive.

Quinzi e Gabrieli – Seafood is a very serious subject here. It is prepared as naturally as possible for a maximum of 22 diners. In season, the oyster bar is popular. Closed Sundays and August. Reservations necessary. Major credit cards accepted. Near the Pantheon, at 5 Via delle Coppelle (phone: 687-9389). Expensive.

Le Restaurant – This elegant dining room at the *Grand* hotel serves continental cuisine and has a menu that changes with the season. Decor, flowers, and waiters in tails, all reflect the *Grand* approach to luxury. Open daily. Reservations necessary. Major credit cards accepted. 3 Via Vittorio Emanuele Orlando (phone: 4709). Expensive.

Ai Tre Scalini – Not to be confused with the renowned *gelateria* and café *Tre Scalini*, the food and wines here are special. Owners Roanna Dupre and Matteo Cicala change the menu frequently, but you'll be lucky if you find the fish soup or the fish-stuffed ravioli. A sampler menu is offered. The decor is simple; there are only seven tables, 30 diners in all, so reservations are necessary. Closed Mondays. Major credit cards accepted. 16 Via dei Santi Quattro (phone: 732695). Expensive.

Alvaro al Circo Massimo – Let Alvaro suggest what's best that day and you'll not go wrong, whether it's fresh fish, game such as *fagiano* (pheasant) or *faraona* (guinea hen), or mushrooms (try grilled *porcini*). The ambience is rustic indoors, and there are tables outdoors during the summer. Closed Mondays. Reservations generally are not necessary. Major credit cards accepted. 53 Via dei Cerchi (phone: 678-6112). Expensive to moderate.

Dal Bolognese – Strategically set next to the popular *Caffè Rosati* on Piazza del Popolo and with a menu nearly as long as the list of celebrities who frequent this fashionable eatery, it's run by two brothers from Bologna. Stargazers will still enjoy such specialties as homemade *tortelloni* (pasta twists stuffed with ricotta cheese) and the *bollito misto* (boiled beef, tongue, chicken, pig's trotter). There are tables outdoors in good weather. Closed Sunday evenings, Mondays, and most of August. Reservations necessary. Major credit cards accepted. 1 Piazza del Popolo (phone: 361-1426). Expensive to moderate.

Il Canto del Riso – There are two, actually — summer and winter. In warmer days it's a gussied-up river barge lurking under the Ponte Cavour, while in winter the restaurant makes its home in a historic building in old Rome. The name means "the Rice Song," and a northern connection (Veneto/Friuli) explains the preponderance of rice dishes: *risotto ai capasanti* (rice with scallops) is only one of more than a dozen rice starters. There is live music in the evening. Closed Sunday nights, Mondays, and in bad weather. Reservations advised in summer. Major credit cards accepted. Summer: Walk down to the river from Lungotevere Mellini, on the Vatican side (phone: 361-0430); winter: 21 Cordonata (phone: 678-6227) Expensive to moderate.

Cesarina – Year in, year out, here's the place to enjoy a well-prepared *bollito misto* from the rich cart of meats and sausage, with the green sauce *comme il faut.* In summer, the fresh fish may appeal more, as will the air conditioning. Year-round, the pasta Bolognese-style is a traditional favorite. Closed Sundays. Reservations necessary. Major credit cards accepted. 109 Via Piemonte (phone: 488-0828). Expensive to moderate.

Checchino dal 1887 – Among the most traditional of all dining places, it's renowned for its light touch with such Roman staples as oxtail, tripe, brains with artichokes, and *spaghetti con pajatta* (spaghetti in a tomato sauce with lamb's intestines). Try the *bucatini all'amatriciana* (a hearty pasta dish with bacon). Closed Sunday evenings and Mondays. Reservations advised. Major credit cards accepted. 30 Via Monte Testaccio (phone: 574-6318 or 574-3816). Expensive to moderate.

Comparone – Roomy and cheery, with plenty of tables outside in the piazza, this is an old favorite of *trasteverini* and visitors alike. The menu is traditional Roman. Closed Mondays. Reservations necessary. Major credit cards accepted. 47 Piazza in Piscinula (phone: 581-6249). Expensive to moderate.

Cornucopia – At this eatery in Trastevere, the few tables outdoors in this lovely piazza offer a view of medieval buildings. Inside, it is air conditioned, small, and inviting. The fare is seafood only, except in winter, when game also is on the menu. At lunchtime, a special limited menu (a choice of seven dishes with a glass of sparkling white wine, mineral water, and coffee) is available at an especially low price. Closed Mondays. Reservations necessary. Major credit cards accepted. 18 Piazza in Piscinula (phone: 580-0380). Expensive to moderate.

Cul de Sac 2 – On a tiny street in Trastevere, the owners of the wine shop *Cul de Sac 1* have created an elegant and attractive restaurant offering *cucina creativa.* Dishes such as lobster with creamed broccoli are carefully prepared, as is the wine list. Closed Sunday evenings, Mondays, and August. Reservations advised. Major credit cards accepted. 21 Vicolo dell'Atleta (phone: 581-3324). Expensive to moderate.

Fortunato al Pantheon – Barely a block from the Pantheon, this eatery is a favorite among politicos and writers. Fish in all ways — grilled, in risotto or pasta — is the specialty, and it is usually as fine as this eatery's long-standing reputation. Tables outside in summer. Closed Sundays and August 15–30. Reservations necessary. American Express accepted. 55 Via del Pantheon (phone: 679-2788). Expensive to moderate.

Al Gladiatore – This old-fashioned, cozy trattoria overlooking the Colosseum is known for its fresh fish. Closed Wednesdays. No reservations. Major credit cards accepted. 5 Piazza Colosseo (phone: 700-0533). Expensive to moderate.

La Maiella – On a delightful square colorfully illuminated in the summer for outdoor dining, this efficient organization with delicious food owes its fame and popularity to owner/manager Signor Antonio. The pope (while still a cardinal) was among his clientele, and the Roman-Abruzzian menu is nearly as long as the Bible. Fresh seafood, truffles, and the alfresco dining are the major attractions. Closed Sundays and a week in August. Reservations advised in the evenings. Major credit cards accepted. 45 Piazza Sant'Apollinare (phone: 686-4174). Expensive to moderate.

Nino – A reliable place, frequented by artists, actors, and aristocrats, and near the Spanish Steps, it is truly Tuscan. The cuisine is composed of the best ingredients, ably yet simply prepared, and the service is serious. Specialties: *zuppa di fagioli alla Francovich* (thick Tuscan white bean soup with garlic), *bistecca alla fiorentina* (thick succulent T-bone steak), and for dessert *castagnaccio* (semisweet chestnut cake). Excellent wine list. Closed Sundays. Reservations advised. Major credit cards accepted. 11 Via Borgognona (phone: 679-5676). Expensive to moderate.

Orient Express – Italians in the know dine here. Antique railway fixtures and menu items that track the famous route from Istanbul (shish kebab) to Paris (delicious onion soup) are what gives this small, pleasant eatery its name. The owners are a former Italian diplomat and his ex-schoolteacher wife. In Trastevere. Closed Sundays. Reservations necessary. American Express accepted. 80 Via Ponte Sisto (phone: 580-9868). Expensive to moderate.

Osteria dell'Antiquario – This small dining spot on a picturesque little square along the antiques-shop-lined Via dei Coronari prides itself on genuine Roman fare, well prepared with the finest seasonal ingredients. Alfresco dining in fine weather. Closed Sundays. Reservations advised. Major credit cards accepted. 27 Piazza San Simeone (phone: 687-9694). Expensive to moderate.

Paris – The Cappellanti family of chefs adds a creative zing to traditional Roman-Jewish and strictly Roman dishes such as *pasta e ceci* (pasta with chick-peas). Closed Sunday evenings, Mondays, and August. Reservations necessary. Major credit cards acepted. 7/A Piazza San Calisto (phone: 581-5378). Expensive to moderate.

Piccolo Mondo – Not exactly a "find," this cheerful and busy restaurant behind Via Veneto has been popular with Italians and foreigners alike for decades. Among the many varied antipasti displayed at the entrance are exquisite *mozzarellini alla* *panna* (small balls of fresh buffalo's milk cheese swimming in cream), as well as eggplant and peppers prepared in several tempting ways. There are sidewalk tables in good weather. Closed Sundays and the first 3 weeks of August. Reservations advised. Major credit cards accepted. 39 Via Aurora (phone: 481-4595). Expensive to moderate.

Piperno – A summer dinner outdoors on this quiet Renaissance *piazzetta,* next to the Palazzo Cenci — which still reeks "of ancient evil and nameless crimes" — is sheer magic. Indoors it is modern and less magical, and the classic Roman-Jewish cooking can be a bit heavy. The great specialty is *fritto vegetariano* (zucchini flowers, mozzarella cheese, salt cod, rice and potato balls, and artichokes — the latter *alla giudia,* or "Jewish-style"). Closed Sunday nights, Mondays, and August. Reservations necessary. Major credit cards accepted. 9 Monte de' Cenci (phone: 654-2772). Expensive to moderate.

Romolo – Summer dining is alfresco, in the dappled sunlight of a 450-year-old arbor, but eating is a delight year-round in this famed tavern in Trastevere where the painter Raphael courted the baker's daughter, la Fornarina. A favorite of Romans and tourists alike is the tasty *spaghetti alla bocaiola* (with a sauce of tomatoes, mushrooms, and tuna) and the grilled, herbed scampi kebabs. Another specialty is *mozzarella alla Fornarina* (melted cheese wrapped in prosciutto and accompanied by a fried artichoke). The wine list is excellent. Closed Mondays and August. Reservations necessary in summer. Major credit cards accepted. 8 Via di Porta Settimiana (phone: 581-8284). Expensive to moderate.

Taverna Flavia – It's been fashionable with the movie crowd, journalists, and politicians for over 30 years. Owner Mimmo likes autographed pictures — one entire room is devoted to Elizabeth Taylor — and the *Sardi's* style survives, despite the crash of "Hollywood on the Tiber" long ago. Near the *Grand* hotel, and open quite late. Good pasta dishes and fine grilled fish. Closed Saturday lunch, all day Sundays, and August. Reservations necessary. Major credit cards accepted. 9-11 Via Flavia (phone: 474-5214). Expensive to moderate.

Taverna Giulia – This reliable old favorite is set in a 600-year-old building. Genoese specialties include pesto served over the traditional *troffie* noodles, and smoked fish. Closed Sundays and August. Reservations advised. Major credit cards accepted. Vicolo dell'Oro (phone: 686-4089). Expensive to moderate.

Vecchia Roma – The setting is truly out of a midsummer night's dream on magical Piazza Campitelli on the fringe of Rome's Jewish quarter. The menu is traditional, the ingredients fresh, the salads pleasing, and the waiters courteous. We love it. Closed Wednesdays and 2 weeks in August. Reservations advised. No credit cards accepted. 18 Piazza Campitelli (phone: 686-4604). Expensive to moderate.

Apuleius – Near Rome's United Nations office complex, this tavern serves seafood in amiable, if kitschy, surroundings. Its Aventine hill location is a plus. *Spaghetti alla pescatore* (fish sauce) is special. Closed Sundays. Reservations advised. Major credit cards accepted. 15 Via Tempio di Diana (phone: 574-2160). Moderate.

La Campana – This unprepossessing, 400-year-old truly Roman restaurant, is favored by everyone from local folk to the stars and staff of RAI, Italian radio-television. Waiters help decipher the handwritten menu, which tempts most with *carciofi alla romana* (fresh artichokes in garlic and oil), *tonnarelli alla chitarra* (homemade pasta in an egg and cheese sauce), and lamb, and truffle-topped poultry dishes. Closed Mondays and August. Reservations advised. Major credit cards accepted. 18 Vicolo della Campana (phone: 686-7820). Moderate.

La Carbonara – On the square where Rome's most colorful morning food market has been held for centuries, this is where *spaghetti alla carbonara* (the sauce is eggs and bacon) is said to have been invented. The windows of the ancient palazzo look out over the scene; indoors is no less authentically Roman, from menu to decor.

Closed Tuesdays. Reservations unnecessary. Major credit cards accepted. 23 Campo dei Fiori (phone: 686-4783). Moderate.

Il Cardinale – In a restored bicycle shop off the stately Via Giulia, decorated in a somewhat precious turn-of-the-century style, this popular evening spot specializes in regional dishes: pasta with green tomato or artichoke sauce, grilled eels, a sweetbread casserole with mushrooms, and *aliciotti con l'indivia* (an anchovy and endive dish). Closed Sundays and August. Reservations advised. Visa accepted. 6 Via delle Carceri (phone: 686-9336). Moderate.

Checco er Carettiere – In the Trastevere area — the Greenwich Village of Rome — this eatery has a large and friendly interior, with a garden in a courtyard, and a wood-paneled dining room. A guitarist strolls among the tables, a flower girl proffers blossoms, and a fledgling artist opens her portfolio to display sketches of surrounding landmarks. The food's super. An antipasto made entirely of seafood is a specialty, and there's a unique mixture of tomatoes and potatoes. Closed Sunday evenings and Mondays. Reservations advised in the evenings. American Express and Visa accepted. 10-13 Via Benedetta, Piazza Trilussa (phone: 581-7018). Moderate.

Le Colline Emiliane – With Tuscan inspiration and truffle toppings, an eatery like this is becoming a rarity. Service is prompt, decor simple, and the *maccheroncini al funghetto* delicious. It has a well-deserved reputation for consistency over the years. Closed Fridays and August. Reservations advised. Major credit cards accepted. Near Via Veneto. 22 Via degli Avignonesi (phone: 481-7538). Moderate.

Costanza – For those who prize a bit of history with their supper, these vaulted dining rooms are in a 2,000-year-old entryway to the ancient Theater of Pompeii. Now wildly chic, it has an interesting menu and is pleasant in winter; the service in summer is irritatingly slow. Closed Sundays and August. Reservations advised. American Express and Visa accepted. 63 Piazza Paradiso (phone: 686-1717 or 654-1002). Moderate.

Cuccurucù – A garden overlooking the Tiber provides one of Rome's most pleasant summer settings for dining alfresco, while inside it's cozy and rustic. The antipasti are good, and so are the meats grilled on an open fire. Ask for *bruschetta con pomodori* (toasted country bread smothered in fresh tomatoes and oregano), and a *spiedino misto,* a sort of shish kebab bearing great chunks of veal, pork, and sausage, all interspersed with onions and peppers and grilled. Closed Sunday evenings and Mondays year-round, Sundays in the summer, and August. Reservations advised. Major credit cards accepted. 10 Via Capoprati (phone: 325257). Moderate.

Il Dito e la Luna – Sicilian fare and *la cucina creativa* (Italy's answer to France's nouvelle cuisine) are featured at this lovely restaurant with white walls, terra cotta floors, and antique furnishings. Specialties include *lasagnette con scampi, pomodori, e zucchini* (flat pasta with shrimp, tomatoes, and zucchini), *anitra in pasta sfoglia* (duck in puff pastry with an orange sauce), and a good selection of homemade desserts. Open for dinner only; closed Sundays and August. Reservations advised. No credit cards accepted. 51 Via dei Sabelli (phone: 494-0276). Moderate.

Il Drappo – Drapes softly frame the two small rooms of this *ristorantino* run by the brother-sister team of Paolo and Valentina Tolu from Sardinia. They offer delicate dishes based on robust island fare, fragrant with wild fennel, myrtle, and herbs. The innovative menu, recited by Paolo and artfully prepared by Valentina, always begins with mixed antipasti including *carta di musica* (hors d'oeuvres on crisp Sardinian wafers). Closed Sundays and 2 weeks in August. Reservations necessary. American Express accepted. 9 Vicolo del Malpasso (phone: 687-7365). Moderate.

Giulio II – Fish baked in parchment and Sicilian-style stuffed swordfish are the specialties at this stylish new eatery in the Parioli quarter. It is within walking distance of the *Coppede'* fine arts complex, with its lovely fountain and architectural curiosities. Closed Saturday lunch, Sundays, and August. Reservations unnecessary. Major credit cards accepted. 80 Via Arno (phone: 841-5535 or 855-1002). Moderate.

Isola del Sole – A converted houseboat on the Tiber offers a variation on the theme of alfresco dining — with lunches under a welcome winter sun, or candlelit dining with the summer stars as backdrop. Try pasta with eggplant and ricotta, ravioli stuffed with *porcini* mushrooms, or carpaccio (thin slices of raw beef seasoned with olive oil, lemon, and flaked parmesan cheese). Extra-special chocolate mousse. From 11 PM to 4 AM there's a piano bar and dancing. Closed Mondays. Reservations advised (for best service, get there by 8:30 PM). Major credit cards accepted. Between Ponte Matteotti and the *metropolitana* train bridge; walk down to the river from Lungotevere Arnaldo da Brescia (phone: 320-1400). Moderate.

Mario – A Tuscan favorite, with the usual Tuscan specialties such as Francovich soup, Florentine steaks, and delicious game in season, all prepared with admirable care and dedication by Mario himself, but served by only three overworked waiters. Closed Sundays and August. Reservations advised. Major credit cards accepted. 55 Via della Vite (phone: 678-3818). Moderate.

Al Moro – Not far from the Trevi Fountain, this is a quiet, dignified place, very "in" with the theater crowd and the powers-that-be at the nearby Parliament. Traditional Roman specialties and seasonal dishes such as pasta with truffles are a must, as is the *fritta vegetariana,* a mix of deep-fried vegetables and cheeses. Closed Sundays and August. Reservations advised. No credit cards accepted. 13 Vicola delle Bollette (phone: 678-3495). Moderate.

Osteria Picchioni – The most expensive pizza in town, but it could also be the best, and it's a whole meal. Only top-quality ingredients are used in this family-style, old-fashioned trattoria, but the decor runs to plastic flowers. Fortunately, they don't tell the whole story. Watch out for the prices — a plate of spaghetti with truffles can run around $100! Be sure to make reservations — there are only 50 places. Closed Wednesdays. No credit cards accepted. 16 Via del Boschetto (phone: 465261). Moderate.

Osteria Sant'Ana – The locale was a convent in the 18th century, and Elio, the owner, is the third generation to run a restaurant. The vegetable hors d'oeuvres array is admirable, while carnivores will enjoy the charcoal grill; everyone likes the marron glacé ice cream, the location near Piazza del Popolo, the somewhat austere tone, and the moderate price considering the quality. Closed Saturday afternoons, Sundays, and 1 week in August. Reservations necessary in the evenings. Major credit cards accepted. 68 Via della Penna (phone: 361-0291). Moderate.

Otello alla Concordia – A delightful trattoria in the middle of the Piazza di Spagna shopping area, with certain tables reserved for habitués and a colorful courtyard for fine weather dining. The menu is Roman, and it changes daily, depending a great deal on the season. Closed Sundays, *Christmas* week, and the first week in January. No reservations. Major credit cards accepted. 81 Via della Croce (phone: 679-1178). Moderate.

Pierluigi – The fish is fresh, the piazza is charming, the price is a bargain, and in summer, the dining is alfresco. Reservations, therefore, are necessary at this popular trattoria in the heart of old Rome. Closed Mondays and Tuesday lunch. Reservations advised. Major credit cards accepted. 144 Piazza de' Ricci (phone: 686-1302). Moderate.

Al Pompiere – Visiting firemen and travelers adore this bright, old-fashioned restaurant in an ancient palazzo near the Campo dei Fiori, whose name means "The

Fireman." The menu includes deep-fried artichokes and mozzarella-stuffed zucchini blossoms. Closed Sundays. Reservations advised in the evenings. No credit cards accepted. 38 Via Santa Maria Calderari (phone: 686-8377). Moderate.

Su Recreu – Finding this spot isn't easy, but the Sardinian food is worth the expedition. The large buffet antipasto is a "take all you want" affair, and there are about a dozen hot and cold choices. The authentic mozzarella (made with buffalo milk) is marvelous, as is anything cooked on the large wood fire right at the entrance. The fresh fish will add to the price. Closed Mondays. Reservations advised. Major credit cards accepted. 17 Via de Buon Consiglo; one block off the Via Cavour, not far from the Forum and the Via del Colosseo (phone: 684-1507). Moderate.

Shangri Là-Corsetti – In the EUR suburb, it's much favored by American businessmen who like the fresh fish. The public pool alongside can be agreeable despite the loud, loud music. Closed August. Reservations advised. Major credit cards accepted. 141 Viale Algeria (phone: 592-8861). Moderate.

Sora Cecilia – Founded in 1898, this modest trattoria offers homemade *agnolotti* (large ravioli) and good *penne all'arrabiata* (pasta with a peppery tomato sauce). Closed Sundays. Reservations advised. American Express accepted. 27 Via Poli (phone: 678-9096). Moderate.

Specchio Antico – Young people run this 6-year-old restaurant that is decorated with fine antiques from their father's prestigious shop. They have won kudos for the spaghetti with seafood *in cartoccio* (a paper bag), delicious array of vegetable hors d'oeuvres, and grilled meats. Closed Sundays. Reservations necessary in the evenings. Major credit cards accepted. 17 Via dei Pastini (phone: 679-7273). Moderate.

Toto alle Carrozze – It has hardly changed after all these years, but we liked it then and we like it now — a trattoria with a banquet spread of strictly Roman antipasti, good pasta, and Roman fish and meat dishes. This is a *giovedì gnocchi, sabato tripa* (Thursday gnocchi, Saturday tripe) kind of traditional Roman place. Closed Sundays. No reservations. Major credit cards accepted. Just off Via del Corso at 10 Via delle Carrozze (phone: 678558). Moderate.

Tullio – Up a narrow hill, just a few yards from the Via Veneto is this just refurbished Tuscan trattoria that serves superb *ribollita* (Tuscan vegetable soup) and baked beans *al fiasco* (in the bottle). It's a custom to place a straw-covered bottle of chianti on the table — diners pay only for what is drunk — and if you're not planning to visit Florence, this is a good place to try a grilled steak Florentine-style. Closed Sundays and August. Reservations advised. Major credit cards. 26 Via di San Nicola da Tolentino (phone: 481-8564 or 474-5560). Moderate.

Le Volte – Carlo Castrucci ran the renowned restaurant at the *Eden* hotel, and now has struck out on his own, in the 16th-century Palazzo Rondanini. Under its frescoed ceiling, diners can enjoy linguini in a lobster sauce, pizza baked in a wood-burning oven, and wild boar with polenta in autumn and winter. Closed Tuesdays and for 15 days in August. Reservations advised. Major credit cards accepted. 47 Piazza Rondanini (phone: 687-7408). Moderate.

Altrove – A new trattoria in the old Subura quarter between Trajan's Market and the Basilica of Santa Maria Maggiore. In one of the downstairs rooms, there is a patch of original Servian wall from ancient Rome. Open until 1 AM; closed Sundays. No reservations. Major credit cards accepted. 35 Via Cimarra (phone: 474-2923). Moderate to inexpensive.

Il Barroccio – *Pane rùstico,* crusty country-style bread, is made here every day, and beans are baked in a wood-burning oven. On a side street not far from the Pantheon, this is a prime place to try *crostini* in all its infinite permutations, and if you want to sample Roman-style pizza, do it here. Across the street at No. 123

is its twin, *Er Faciolaro,* owned by the same people. One or the other always is open. Reservations unnecessary. Major credit cards accepted. 13 Via dei Pastini (phone: 679-3797). Moderate to inexpensive.

Il Falchetto – Conveniently set off Via del Corso, with a few tables outdoors in fine weather, this might seem a tourist haven. But knowledgeable Romans fill the small rooms even in the gray days of winter. The imaginative game, veal, and fish dishes are delicious. Closed Fridays. Reservations advised. Major credit cards accepted. 12-14 Via Montecatini (phone: 679-1160). Moderate to inexpensive.

La Fiorentina – This favorite Roman pizzeria, with its wood-burning oven and grill, is in residential Prati on the Vatican side of the river. It serves pizza even at lunchtime, a rarity in Italy. Tables on the street in good weather. Closed Wednesdays all day, Thursdays at lunch. Reservations advised. Major credit cards accepted. 22 Via Andrea Doria (phone: 312310). Moderate to inexpensive.

Il Giardinetto – Not far from Piazza Navona is this quiet and charming newcomer with a few outdoor tables. The owner is Tunisian, speaks English, and cooks creditable Italian fare, including the ever-popular *spaghetti alla carbonara* (with egg and bacon), onion soup, and tiny *gnocchetti sardi* (an eggless Sardinian pasta with a sauce of fresh tomato and aromatic basil). A good value. Closed Mondays. Reservations necessary in summer. Major credit cards accepted. 125 Via del Governo Vecchio (phone: 686-8693). Moderate to inexpensive.

Giggetto al Portico d'Ottavia – In Rome's Jewish ghetto, this is the place to sample the delicious and well-prepared fried artichokes that most Roman menus identify as *alla giudeo,* "Jewish-style," as well as zucchini flowers stuffed with mozzarella and *crostini* (fried bread offered with an assortment of toppings). But don't take the waiters' occasional lack of attention personally; they ignore everybody. The food is first-rate and the experience absolutely authentic. Closed Mondays. Reservations advised. Major credit cards accepted. 21A Via del Portico d'Ottavia (phone: 686-1105). Moderate to inexpensive.

La Luna sul Tevere – A river restaurant, the "Moon on the Tiber" brought their chef from the Via Veneto's famed *Café de Paris.* Set on the banks of the Tiber, beneath the Duca d'Aosta Bridge, it has alfresco dining in summer and a rustic barge for indoor meals during inclement weather. Specialties include fettuccine with tuna and wild *porcini* mushrooms, breast of chicken with almonds, and petits fours of *tartufini* and *cremini.* Closed Mondays and the last 2 weeks of November. Reservations advised. Major credit cards accepted. Via Capoprati (phone: 323-6456). Moderate to inexpensive.

Le Maschere – For a taste of Calabria's Costa Viola, fragrant with garlic and devilish with red peppers, try this rustic and charming 17th- century cellar behind Largo Argentina. The fare is not for fragile stomachs: antipasti of tangy salamis, marinated anchovies, and stuffed, pickled, or highly seasoned vegetables of every sort; pasta with broccoli or eggplant, or the traditional *struncatura* (handmade whole-wheat pasta with anchovies, garlic, and breadcrumbs); fresh swordfish harpooned off the Calabrian coast, *stoccafisso* (salt cod stew with potatoes), or meats grilled on an open fire; pizza, southern sweets, 100-proof fresh fruit salad, and *tuma* (Calabrian sheep's milk cheese). Dinner only. Closed Mondays and part of August. Reservations necessary on weekends. Major credit cards accepted. 29 Via Monte della Farina (phone: 687-9444). Moderate to inexpensive.

L'Orso '80 – An old-fashioned trattoria close to Piazza Navona and with good traditional fare such as *spaghetti all'amatriciana* (with bacon, cheese, and tomatoes). Meats are grilled over a wood fire. Closed Mondays and August. Reservations unnecessary. Major credit cards accepted. 33 Via dell'Orso (phone: 686-4904). Moderate to inexpensive.

Al Piedone – Tiny and unpretentious, this spot is much favored by newsmen and politicos from nearby Parliament. Try the rigatoni with broccoli, sausage, and bacon, or the Puglia-style *orecchietti* (pasta) with hot red pepper, broccoli, and anchovies. When available, the roast veal stuffed with almonds, pine nuts, and raisins is truly special. A good wine list for a modest restaurant. Closed Sundays and late August. Reservations advised in the evenings. Major credit cards accepted. 28 Via del Piè di Marco (phone: 679-8628). Moderate to inexpensive.

Polese – This is a good value any time of the year, either outside under the trees of the spacious square or inside the intimate rooms of the Borgia palace. A great summer starter is *bresaola con rughetta* (cured beef with arugula, seasoned with olive oil, lemon, and freshly grated black peppeı), and the *pasta al pesto* is fine year-round. Closed Tuesdays. Reservations taken reluctantly (come and wait your turn). Major credit cards accepted. 40 Piazza Sforza Cesarini (phone: 686-1709). Moderate to inexpensive.

Ponentino – A pizzeria in Trastevere, it has the ubiquitous wood-burning oven. The youthful owners also serve spaghetti old-Trastavere-style (with tuna, anchovies, and capers), vegetarian antipasto (the best choice), and grilled meat including lamb chops. Closed Mondays. Reservations necessary in summer for tables outside in the piazza. Major credit cards accepted. Off Via della Lungaretta near Tiber Island. 10 Piazza del Drago (phone: 588-0680). Moderate to inexpensive.

Sora Lella – In the heart of Rome on Tiber Island is this trattoria serving authentic Roman dishes such as *penne all'arrabiata* (quill-shaped pasta with spicy tomato sauce), *pasta e ceci* (pasta and chick-peas) with clams, tiny sautéed lamb chops, and beans with pork rind. Closed Sundays. No reservations. No credit cards accepted. 16 Via di Quattro Capi (phone: 686-1601). Moderate to inexpensive.

La Tavernetta – It looks like a take-out pasta shop, but there are actually four narrow dining rooms set one above the other. This is a tiny, tidy spot, barely a block from the Spanish Steps (toward the Piazza Barberini), where the homemade pasta is pretty near perfect and seafood is the specialty. Closed Sundays and August. Reservations advised. Major credit cards accepted. 147 Via Sistina (phone: 679-3124). Moderate to inexpensive.

Trearchi da Gioachino – Among the declining numbers of true Roman trattorie, this one stands out, thanks to Mamma Colomba Giammiuti's loving cooking. She comes from the Abruzzi region and specialties include homemade ravioli, *pappardelle* noodles with hare sauce and lamb, and other pasta made in various delectable ways. Closed Sundays and late August. Reservations advised. Major credit cards accepted. 233 Via dei Coronari (phone: 686-5890). Moderate to inexpensive.

Ettore Lo Sgobbone – A trattoria popular with newspaper and TV journalists, noted for its unpretentious northern Italian home-style cooking. Pasta and risotto courses are excellent: Try the simple *tonnarelli al pomodoro e basilico* (pasta with fresh tomato and basil sauce) or *risotto nero di seppie* (rice cooked with cuttlefish in its ink). Reservations advised for the few tables outdoors on the rather dreary, typically working class street. Closed Tuesdays. Reservations necessary. Major credit cards accepted. 8-10 Via dei Podesti (phone: 323-2994). Inexpensive.

Da Giulio – Another bargain for budget-minded travelers, on a tiny street off Via Giulia in a historic building. A few tables line the sunless street in the summer, but inside is most pleasant — if a bit noisy — with an original vaulted ceiling and paintings by local artists. Roman family-style cooking. Closed Sundays and late August. Reservations advised in summer. Major credit cards accepted. 19 Via della Barchetta (phone: 654-0466). Inexpensive.

Grotte Teatro di Pompeo – One of several places in this tiny, packed neighborhood that claims to be the place where Julius Caesar met his untimely end. On any chilly day, the *zuppa di verdura* (vegetable soup) can keep one's inner self warm, and the *fettuccine verdi alla gorgonzola* (green noodles in a rich cheese sauce) is a wonderful pasta choice. The colorful but unprepossessing premises don't bother guests. This is the perfect place for cost-conscious visitors to try *osso buco con funghi* (veal shank with wild mushrooms) and *saltimbocca alla romana* (small pieces of veal with prosciutto). Closed Mondays and August. Reservations unnecessary. Visa accepted. 73 Via del Biscione (phone: 654-3686). Inexpensive.

La Sagrestia – Lots of places claim the best pizza in town, and this one is a top contender, with pies fresh from the wood-burning oven. Good pasta, good draft beer, ever-crowded and cheery, with kitschy decor. Near the Pantheon. Closed Wednesdays and 1 week in mid-August. Reservations advised for large groups. Major credit cards accepted. 89 Via del Seminario (phone: 679-7581). Inexpensive.

Lo Scopettaro – On the Tiber River, right near the Porta Portese flea market, is this popular, noisy neighborhood spot that serves traditional Roman fare such as *pasta e fagioli* (pasta and beans) and simple grilled meat. Closed Tuesdays and August. Reservations unnecessary. No credit cards accepted. 7 Lungotevere Testaccio (phone: 574-2408). Inexpensive.

Settimio all'Arancio – Simple but good, right in the heart of downtown Rome, near the old Jewish ghetto. It's always crowded. Particularly noteworthy is the *fusili con melanzane* (pasta with eggplant). Closed Sundays and August. Reservations advised. Major credit cards accepted. 50 Via dell'Arancio (phone: 687-6119). Inexpensive.

La Villetta al Piramide – Near the Protestant cemetery and the marble pyramid, this cheery, large trattoria is run by owner-cook Ada Mercuri Olivetti, who once took first prize over 4,000 other Roman cooks for her *spaghetti all'amatriciana,* made with special bacon, tomato, and cheese. She serves other wholesome, hearty dishes, including vegetable antipasti. Closed Wednesdays. Reservations unnecessary. No credit cards accepted. 53 Viale Piramide Cestia (phone: 574-0204). Inexpensive.

A novelty for Rome are the less expensive eateries as an alternative to pizza; one such is the *Lucifero Pub* (28 Via dei Cappellari; phone: 654-5536), a fondue-and-beer tavern tucked into a side street off the Campo dei Fiori.

BARS AND CAFÉS: For lighter meals, Rome's many *caffès* are also well worth trying. The most fashionable spots for the lunch or pre-dinner *aperitivo* are the *Antico Caffè Greco* or the *Baretto* (Via Condotti), *Rosati* or *Canova* (Piazza del Popolo), and *Harry's Bar, Carpes,* the *Café de Paris, Doney's,* or others on Via Veneto. Best for light lunches are *Canova* and *Café de Paris. Babington's* (Piazza di Spagna) is an English tearoom that serves expensive snacks and luscious cakes. Currently *alla moda* is the little *Bar della Pace* (Piazza della Pace behind Piazza Navona), which is frequented by vendors from the nearby market in the morning and pre-lunch period, and then later in the day (until 3 AM) by all types, from artists and filmmakers to punks, poets, and students who, when the little marble tables fill up, rest their drinks and their bottoms on cars parked in the square.

At the tiny, busy Piazza Sant'Eustachio, the *Bar Eustachio* serves what is reputed to be the best coffee in town. It is an Italian-style espresso bar where a quick coffee is downed while standing. In the Jewish ghetto, lovers of sweets stand on line to get pastries fresh from an ancient oven, in the tiny, shabby, and excellent *Forno del Ghetto* (119 Via Portico d'Ottavia), where the production follows the religious holiday tradition.

As rising prices (and the influx of Chinese restaurants) oblige the more inexpensive trattorie either to upgrade to *ristorante* status or simply to disappear, they are being replaced by wine shops–cum–wine bars. In addition to being able to buy the traditional glass, bottle, or case of wine, these establishments also now offer a light lunch of artfully prepared vegetables or pasta and a glass of good wine (from November through March, try the wonders of the *vini novelli*) for $10–$12 per person. They are scattered all over old Rome, and are tiny and dark. Simply look for their sign — *Enoteca.* The shops have only a few tables, do not take reservations, honor no credit cards, and close before 8 PM. Try the *Bottega del Vino da Bleve* (9/A Via Santa Maria del Pianto; phone: 686-5970) in downtown Rome; the tiny *Cul de Sac I* (73 Piazza Pasquino; phone: 654-1094), which re-creates the atmosphere of an old *osteria; Il Piccolo* (74 Via del Governo Vecchio; phone: 654-1746) near Piazza Navona; and *Spiriti* (5 Via di Sant'Eustachio; phone: 689-2499).

On summer evenings, the after-dinner crowd often moves toward one of the many *gelaterie* in Rome, some of which are much more than ice cream parlors, since they serve exotic long drinks and *semifreddi* (like the famous *tartufo* — a double chocolate truffle — at Piazza Navona's *Tre Scalini,* where they sell 800 a day), and a few have lovely gardens and even live music. *Selarum,* (12 Via dei Fienaroli), and *Fassi* (45 Corso d'Italia), have both gardens and music. Perhaps the best-known *gelateria,* however, is the very crowded *Giolitti* (40 Via Uffici del Vicario), not far from Piazza Colonna — try any of the fresh fruit flavors; it boasts a tearoom (closed Mondays). Others are the sleek, high-tech *Gelateria della Palma* (which is also a piano bar, at the corner of Via della Maddalena and Via delle Coppelle); *Fiocco di Neve* (51 Via del Pantheon); and *Di Rienzo* (5 Piazza della Rotonda). They're all near the Pantheon; *Gelofestival* (29 Viale Trastevere, in Trastevere); and *Biancaneve* (1 Piazza Pasquale Paoli, where Corso Vittorio Emanuele II meets the Lungotevere dei Fiorentini). Favorites in the fashionable Parioli residential district are *Gelateria Duse* (also called *Giovanni;* 1 Via Eleonora Duse) and *Bar San Filippo* (8 Via San Filippo), both specializing in *semifreddi; Bar Gelateria Cile* (1–2 Piazza Santiago del Cile); the nearby *Giardino Ferranti* (29 Via Giovanni Pacini); and the *Casina delle Muse* (Piazzale delle Muse) for a fabulous *granità di caffè con panna* (coffee ice with cream). In the Jewish ghetto, try *Dolce Roma* (20/B Via Portico d'Ottavio; phone: 689-2196) for chocolate chip cookies and Austrian pastries. *Europeo Gran Caffè* (33 Piazza San Lorenzo in Lucina) is the place for indulging in high-calorie pastries.

SIENA

True to the traditional pattern of settlement in Tuscany, Siena sits on top of a hill or, rather, on top of three hills, enclosed within high walls — an age-old vision, the exact color of which every one of us has known since opening our first box of crayons. Approaching these walls, it is easy to feel like a medieval traveler looking for access through a gateway or portico carved with the Sienese coat of arms. Inside, drawn into the labyrinth of narrow steets that snake through the medieval fabric of the city, the feeling does not dissipate. Few modern buildings disturb the illusion; it's as though medieval Siena were merely playing host to modern life.

After Florence, Siena has probably the richest artistic heritage in Tuscany, but unlike Florence it remains more of a medieval than a Renaissance city, its overall 13th- and 14th-century Italian Gothic look a result of certain vicissitudes of its history. But there are other differences between the two cities. Siena is a lot smaller. It has the friendly spirit of a well-to-do provincial town in the midst of an agricultural region, not the refinements and sophistication of the region's cultural capital. Also, while the elegance and pride of the Florentines are sometimes seen as verging on arrogance, the quality most frequently attributed to the Sienese is a kind of sincere politeness, a soft-spoken charm — *gentilezza.*

The late Italian writer Curzio Malaparte points out in his wonderfully satirical evaluation of his fellow Tuscans that if you ask a Florentine saint some news about heaven, you will get an answer, but in a tone of voice that casts doubt on your worthiness to go there. Ask San Bernardino of Siena, however, and you will be told not only what heaven is, where it is, and the shortest road to take, but also how many rooms it has, how many kitchens, and what's cooking in the pot. Something of the same air of affectionate intimacy pervades Sienese speech, peppered with diminutives (it is said the Sienese speak Italy's purest Italian), and Sienese painting, which continued to delight in pretty Madonnas while the Florentines wrestled with problems of depth and perspective. (Look closely at the backgrounds of those lovingly rendered Sienese panels, and you sometimes *can* see what's on the back burner.)

Florence was a menacing presence through much of Siena's history, and in a certain sense it was Florence that arrested Siena's development and caused it to remain the medieval gem it is today. One legend has it that Siena was founded by the Senes Gauls; another recounts that it was founded by Senio, son of Remus, one of the founding brothers of Rome, and hence the Roman she-wolf on the Sienese emblem. Regardless of its origin, Siena was certainly an Etruscan city and then a military stronghold under the Romans until it finally began to flourish as a center of commerce, finance, and culture in the Middle Ages. At the same time, Siena's wealth and trade became the envy of her Tuscan neighbors, prompting continual warfare with the Florentine city-state in particular. By 1235, the mightier military strength of Florence forced Siena to accept harsh peace terms.

But that was merely round one. On September 4, 1260, the Sienese dealt the Florentines such a resounding defeat at Montaperti, a hill east of the city, that it is remembered to this day. Having exorcized Florentine dominance, good sense prevailed, and under a nine-member government of merchant families (Governo dei Nove), peace was made and Siena embarked on one of its most enlightened and prosperous periods. Some of the city's most noteworthy buildings, such as the Palazzo Comunale, the Palazzo Chigi-Saracini, and the Palazzo Sansedoni, as well as plans to enlarge the cathedral, date from this time. It was a golden age for painting, too — Duccio di Buoninsegna and Simone Martini were making names for themselves beautifying palaces and churches.

The good times lasted until 1355, when, following a severe drought and then a terrible outbreak of plague in 1348, civil discontent brought about a rebellion of leading noble families and a series of short-lived governments. Would-be conquerors came from farther afield until, in 1554, a 24,000-man army of Spanish, German, and Italian troops under the command of the Florentine Medici family laid siege to the city. A year later, Siena fell. Cosimo I de' Medici became its ruler and Siena was taken as a part of the Grand Duchy of Tuscany, first under the Medicis and then under the French house of Lorraine, until it passed, with Tuscany, to the kingdom of Italy in 1860.

It was probably due to Siena's absorption by Florence that the city stayed as small and as resolutely medieval-looking as it is. What's more, it was probably due to their loss of independence that the Sienese invested their annual *Palio* — the reckless bareback horse race around the treacherous Piazza del Campo — with so much civic passion. There are two runnings of this madcap race, one on July 2 and one on August 16. Both originated long ago as the popular part of religious festivities, the former in honor of the Madonna di Provenzano, the latter in honor of Our Lady of the Assumption. The August 16 *Palio,* the more important of the two, has been documented as far back as 1310; the July 2 *Palio* was instituted in 1656.

Then, as now, the city was divided into *contrade,* or districts, which compete against each other with one horse and rider each. The city once had 59 *contrade;* now it has 17, with allegorical names such as Bruco (caterpillar), Tartuca (tortoise), Chiocciola (snail), Drago (dragon), and Leocorno (unicorn). Keep an eye on the corners of buildings as you walk around town, and you'll see the *contrade* marked off with their symbols, just as streets are with their names. Each *contrada* has its own patron saint, a church where the saint is worshiped, and a feast day in the saint's honor, and each *contrada* has its own fountain, outside the church, where its babies are baptized a second time.

A Sienese is born into his *contrada* and roots for it all his life, so when the day of the *Palio* rolls around, after months of preparation, spirits are as high as they are in a neighborhood *favela* in Rio during *Carnaval.* The day begins, now as then, with a mass in the Cappella di Piazza and the hanging of the *contrada* banners in either the church of Santa Maria di Provenzano or in the Duomo. Among the banners is the *palio* itself, the banner that goes to the victor. (A *palio* is a banner, but since it is one that is the prize of a competition, the word now also refers to the competition itself and has a double meaning, something like "stakes.") In the early afternoon, each horse is taken to its local *contrada* church to be blessed (it's considered a good omen if the horse leaves something behind). Then, later in the afternoon, comes the most magnificent historical procession in Italy — a parade of dignitaries such as might have taken place in the days of the Sienese republic, delegations from all the *contrade* in full 15th-century regalia, trumpeters, and *sbandieratori* (flag bearers) who wave, toss, and manipulate their flags in intricate synchronized routines.

The race takes 3 minutes at most, but it's hardly an anticlimax. While thousands of the spectators are tourists, the enthusiasm and joy shown by the winning *contrada* indicate that this is not merely an attraction staged for tourists but a deeply felt tradition. The victorious jockey is carried around town in triumph, and at the subsequent outdoor banquet in the winning *contrada,* the winning horse is treated as an honored guest. *Palio* time is definitely the time to visit Siena *if* you don't mind massive crowds and *if* you make all reservations and other arrangements well in advance. If you miss it, well, you still might catch sight of a clutch of little boys, perhaps standing in a slice of late afternoon shade by the Duomo, wielding, waving, throwing the flag, practicing. The image will stay with you. All the *Palio* pageantry may be only one expression of Siena's past, but it's the one that most vividly captures the imagination.

SIENA AT-A-GLANCE

SEEING THE CITY: The best spot for a bird's-eye view of Siena is the top of the Torre del Mangia, next to the Palazzo Comunale in Piazza del Campo, from which one can see not only all of the Campo below and across a sweep of red tile roofs to Siena's other major monumental complex, the Duomo, but also out to the surrounding hills. Another vantage point for bringing it all into focus is from the top of what the Sienese call the Facciatone, or big façade, actually the façade of the never-finished Duomo Nuovo (New Cathedral), which now houses the *Museo dell'Opera del Duomo.* Among other things, there's a good view of Piazza del Campo and the Torre del Mangia from here. Still another view is that from the Fortezza Medicea (see *Extra Special*), which should be saved for the end of a visit. *Note:* Cars are not permitted in much of the downtown area.

SPECIAL PLACES: A glance at the map shows that all of Siena seems to gravitate toward the seashell-shaped Piazza del Campo. In fact, since Siena's *centro storico* is no bigger than a large provincial town, almost all of its sights are within walking distance of this center of gravity. Be aware, however, that the town's narrow streets wind uphill and downhill, and sometimes turn into steps, so comfortable walking shoes are necessary.

Piazza del Campo – Siena's main square is certainly one of the beautiful old squares of Europe. It's on a slant, and its brick paving is divided into nine sectors, a number that harks back to the 13th and 14th centuries, when the city was ruled by a government of nine men who did much to create the cityscape that remains today. The nine sectors converge on the piazza's lower side, in front of the Palazzo Comunale and the adjacent Torre del Mangia. Facing them on the higher side is the Fonte Gaia, a monumental fountain that was decorated with reliefs by Jacopo della Quercia (reproductions take the place of the 15th-century originals, which are now in the *Museo Civico* in the Palazzo Comunale). Its name — the "gay" fountain — alludes to the fact that the arrival of water in the piazza sparked no end of festivity in the 14th century. All around the semicircular edge of the piazza are medieval and Renaissance palaces, one of the most noteworthy of which is the Palazzo Sansedoni, with a curved façade. It dates from the 13th and 14th centuries but became a single residence in the 18th century. At *Palio* time, the windows of the palaces are hung with ancient banners, the center of the piazza is stuffed with spectators, and the roadway all around turns into the route of the historical procession — and then the *Palio* racetrack.

Palazzo Comunale – The elegant façade of this Gothic building is slightly curved, in keeping with the unusual outline of the Campo. It is Siena's City Hall, as it has been since it was built between 1297 and 1310, but because part of it has become a museum, it is accessible to visitors. The adjacent bell tower, the Torre del Mangia, was added in the mid-13th century. It takes its name from a onetime bell ringer, Giovanni di Duccio, who was evidently a man of prodigal habits and better known to the Sienese as Mangiaguadagni (Spendthrift). The pillared and roofed structure at the base of the tower is the Cappella di Piazza, built from 1352 to 1376 to fulfill a vow made during the plague of 1348.

Inside the Palazzo Comunale are beautifully proportioned rooms that give a sense of tangible authority rather than grandeur, and the frescoes with which they were decorated remain, although not in their pristine state. The world map that gave the Sala del Mappamondo its name is gone, but in the same room it's still possible to see the *Maestà* (1315) of Simone Martini, the great Sienese painter's first masterpiece. (Unfortunately, it has deteriorated a great deal.) The fresco of Guidoriccio da Fogliano (1328) in the same room has long been attributed to Martini, although its authenticity has recently become a point of controversy. Below that is a Madonna and Child by the earlier Sienese painter Guido da Siena, dated 1221 but commonly held to have been done in the latter half of that century and to have been repainted in part by another great master of the Sienese school, Duccio di Buoninsegna. The next room, the Sala della Pace, is decorated with a series of allegorical frescoes on the subject of good and bad government. Painted between 1338 and 1340, they are the most extensive fresco cycle of the Italian medieval period with a secular subject and the most important works of their creator, Ambrogio Lorenzetti, a painter who was much influenced by Giotto and who probably died during the plague not too many years after completing them. One of the frescoes is particularly noteworthy for its early rendering of the Sienese urban scene and for its early use of landscape as a subject rather than a background. The museum also contains the originals of Jacopo della Quercia's reliefs for the Fonte Gaia. Open daily, 9:30 AM to 1:30 PM from November 16 to March 15; 9:30 AM to 7:45 PM (1:30 PM Sundays and most holidays) the rest of the year. Admission charge. Piazza del Campo (phone: 292111).

Duomo – This landmark, dedicated to Santa Maria dell'Assunta (Our Lady of the Assumption), is one of the most beautiful medieval churches in Italy. In many ways, it is a chronicle of the artistic and political history of Siena. It was begun in 1196, during the early stages of Siena's development as a city-state, and much of what is seen today was completed in the 13th century. But in the 14th century, with a growing population and the example of Florence's huge Duomo, the city's plans for the cathedral also grew. It was decided that the existing church should form the transept of a newer, much larger church, so construction began again, in 1339. By 1355, money problems and the plague had put an end to the super-church dream but not before the façade of the new church had been built. (It is this piece of unfinished architecture, off to the right of the Duomo, that the Sienese call the Facciatone, or big façade.) Attention returned in the late 14th century to finishing the old Duomo, and the result is an imposing, if somewhat irregular, white marble basilica with characteristic black stripes. The lower level of the façade, largely Romanesque, is dominated by the stone carving of Giovanni Pisano, whose work decorates many Tuscan churches. The upper level, Siena's response to the magnificent façade of the Duomo in Orvieto, is full 14th-century Gothic. The mosaics at the top, whose gold backgrounds catch the sun like mirrors playing with a beam of light, are from the 19th century.

The interior of the church is rich in art treasures, not the least of which is the floor, done from the mid-14th century to the mid-16th century and divided into 56 squares, each recounting a different biblical story in inlaid marblework. The scenes are the work of more than 40 different, mostly Sienese, artists (there are several by Beccafumi), and although many are visible all year, the most precious are kept covered in the interests of conservation and can be seen only from August 15 to September 15. Another treasure is the magnificent marble and porphyry pulpit by Nicola Pisano, Giovanni's father, sculpted with the help of his son and Arnolfo di Cambio. (Giovanni's own great pulpit sits in the Duomo at Pisa.) Lovers of the Renaissance should look at the chapel, Cappella di San Giovanni Battista, which has frescoes by Pinturicchio (note the two portraits of Alberto Aringhieri). Pinturicchio also painted the lively, vivid frescoes recounting the life of Pope Pius II (Enea Silvio Piccolomini) in the Libreria Piccolomini, off the left side of the nave. The library, built in 1495 by the pope's nephew (who later became Pope Pius III) to house the uncle's precious collection of books, also contains a famous Roman statue of the Three Graces. The Duomo is open until sunset, but closed for 1 hour at lunchtime, except during the summer. The library is open 9 AM to 7:30 PM from March 9 to September 30, and 10 AM to 1 PM and 2:30 to 5 PM the rest of the year. Admission charge for the library. Piazza del Duomo.

Battistero – Siena's baptistry is down a flight of stairs to the right of the cathedral, behind the apse. A 14th-century building, it is best known for its baptismal font, designed by Jacopo della Quercia and considered a work of transition from the Gothic to the Renaissance. A collaborative effort, it has two bronze angels by Donatello, as well as bas-reliefs around the basin by Donatello, Lorenzo Ghiberti, and others. Piazza San Giovanni.

Museo dell'Opera del Duomo (Cathedral Museum) – Also known as the *Museo dell'Opera Metropolitana,* this contains mainly works that have been taken from the cathedral. Almost as interesting as the works themselves is their setting: the Duomo Nuovo, the unfinished extension of the cathedral that was planned and then abandoned in the mid-14th century. A visitor can only imagine its potential magnificence from the five huge Gothic arches that still stand and would have been the nave. Three of these have been closed off to form the museum. On the ground floor are ten statues of Old Testament figures carved by Giovanni Pisano for the Duomo façade (the statues on the façade now are reproductions) and a stone relief panel of the Madonna and Child carved by Jacopo della Quercia for one of the side altars. Upstairs is the masterpiece that made Duccio di Buoninsegna's career, the *Maestà* (1308–11), which was carried from his workshop to the high altar of the cathedral in solemn procession. Originally it showed the Madonna and Child on the front and the 26 scenes of the Passion on the back (it was sawed in two in the 18th century), with smaller scenes of the life of Christ and the Virgin above and below. (Nineteen of these smaller panels remain; others are in museums in the US and Great Britain.) Still another masterpiece is Simone Martini's *Blessed Agostino Novello and Four of His Miracles* (1330). From the museum it's possible to climb to the top of the Duomo Nuovo façade — the Facciatone — for a splendid view of the town. Open daily from 9 AM to 7:30 PM March 9 to September 30, and from 9 AM to 1:30 PM the rest of the year. Admission charge. Piazza Jacopo della Quercia.

Pinacoteca Nazionale – The *National Picture Gallery* is a must for a clear understanding of Sienese art from the 12th to the 17th century. Housed in the beautiful 15th-century Palazzo Buonsignori, here are 40 rooms filled with Sienese masterpieces — from Guido da Siena, Duccio, Simone Martini, Pietro and Ambrogio Lorenzetti, Beccafumi, and more. Open Tuesdays through Saturdays from 8:30 AM to 7 PM, Sundays and holidays from 8:30 AM to 1 PM. Admission charge. 29 Via San Pietro (phone: 281161).

Chiesa di Sant'Agostino – This ancient church houses Perugino's *Crucifix and Saints* (1506) and, in one of the chapels, the *Slaughter of the Innocents* (1482) by Matteo di Giovanni, *Madonna with Child and Saints* by Ambrogio Lorenzetti, and the *Epiphany* by Sodoma over the altar. The church was built during the 13th and 14th centuries and underwent baroque modifications in the 18th century. Prato di Sant'Agostino.

Palazzo Chigi-Saracini – Like many Sienese palaces and churches, this was begun in the 12th century, finished in the Gothic style in the 14th century, and later altered and restored. Originally built for one of the leading families of Siena, it is now the seat of the Accademia Musicale Chigiana and a music school whose international summer students congregate around the carved stone well in the delightful courtyard. The interior can be visited on request: Its lofty ornate rooms are decorated with some of the gems of Sienese art of the 13th to 17th centuries. Concerts are held in the palace's music room, which is adapted from the noble apartments and is Siena's main concert hall. Closed Mondays. No admission charge. To visit the interior, apply to the Accademia, 89 Via di Città (phone: 46152).

Palazzo Piccolomini – A mid-15th-century Renaissance palace in the midst of medieval Siena, this was once the home of the family of Pope Pius II and now houses the state archives, with a wealth of documents and statutes pertaining to Siena's turbulent history. (Archives closed Sundays.) Farther down the street are the Logge del Papa, three graceful Renaissance arches that Pius II had built in his family's honor. No admission charge. Via Banchi di Sotto.

Museo Archeologico Nazionale (National Archaeological Museum) – Exhibits range from prehistory to the Roman period and include Etruscan funeral urns from the 3rd century BC and Greek and Roman statues and statuettes dating from the 6th century BC. The museum was temporarily closed at press time to prepare for its move to new quarters. Check with the tourist office for an update. 3 Via della Sapienza (phone: 44293).

Basilica di San Domenico – Approach from Via della Sapienza for a breathtaking glimpse of the Duomo and its bell tower as well as of the Torre del Mangia next to the Palazzo Comunale. San Domenico is a massive, severe-looking monastic Gothic building begun in 1226 and completed in the 15th century, while the graceful bell tower next to it was built in 1340. Inside, the spacious, simple majesty of this austere church — in the unusual T-shape of an Egyptian cross — is interrupted with shafts of light from modern stained glass windows. See the Chapel of St. Catherine, which is adorned with Sodoma's early 16th-century frescoes of the mystic Sienese saint who was a member of the Dominican order and who eventually became one of the two patron saints of Italy (with St. Francis of Assisi). A reliquary in the same chapel contains the head of St. Catherine, while another chapel, the Cappella delle Volte, contains a fresco of her by a contemporary, Andrea Vanni, which is held to be the only authentic portrait of the saint in existence. Piazza San Domenico.

Santuario Cateriniano (St. Catherine's Sanctuary) – St. Catherine lived from 1347 to 1380, and by 1464, only a few years after her canonization, her house was turned into a sanctuary. Despite the sacred transformation, the addition of chapels, and the 15th- and 16th-century paintings showing scenes from her life, there is still a homey atmosphere about what was once an ordinary household. The adjoining Church of Santa Caterina in Fontebranda, facing Via Santa Caterina, is part of the sanctuary; once the dyer's shop of her father, it too contains frescoes and statues of the saint. Open daily from 9 AM to 12:30 PM. No admission charge. Costa di Sant' Antonio.

Fonte Branda – One of Siena's oldest and best-loved fountains stands at the end of

Via Santa Caterina, not far from the sanctuary. There are references to it as far back as 1081, but it was rebuilt in the mid-13th century, when it was given its present triple-arched mini-fortress form with the emblem of Siena in the middle.

Basilica di San Francesco – Begun in the 14th century and originally Gothic in style, this was much changed externally by later building, baroque additions following a 17th-century fire, and a modern façade. Still, the interior, in the shape of an Egyptian cross, retains the characteristic alternating layers of black and white marble. Detached frescoes by Pietro Lorenzetti (the *Crucifixion*) and Ambrogio Lorenzetti (the other two) are in the side chapels. The church opens onto the former Convent of St. Francis and a wonderful Renaissance cloister. Piazza San Francesco.

Oratorio di San Bernardino – This 2-tiered oratory was built in the 15th century on the spot where Siena's beloved second saint, the Franciscan San Bernardino (1380–1444), preached his sermons (quite lively ones, evidently — his gift for persuasion caused him to be made the patron saint of advertising and public relations by Pope John XXIII). The upper floor of the oratory is gracefully decorated with stuccoes and is frescoed with images of the Madonna and saints (including San Bernardino himself) by some notable 16th-century artists: Sodoma, Girolamo del Pacchia, and Beccafumi. Not open to the public; to visit, you must contact the custodian (phone: 289081). 6 Piazza San Francesco.

Basilica di Santa Maria dei Servi – Set away from the center, on a rise that offers a splendid view of the Duomo, it has a simple 13th-century façade and bell tower, and an interior that mixes Gothic with Renaissance splendor. Among the works of art are a *Madonna* (1261) by Coppo di Marcovaldo and one by Lippo Memmi. Piazza Alessandro Manzoni.

■ **EXTRA SPECIAL:** Besides the Torre del Mangia and the Facciatone, one other special spot in Siena offers a panoramic view of all the palaces and churches, the red-roofed expanse cut through by winding streets. This is the Fortezza Medicea, also known as the Forte di Santa Barbara, a defensive fortress built in 1560 by Cosimo I of the Florentine Medici family shortly after his arrival in Siena as the city's conquerer. Now it's a city park, and although anyone standing on its battlements is no longer master of all he or she surveys, he or she does still survey quite a lot, both of the city and of the surrounding countryside, in all directions. But the view is not the only reason to visit this well-preserved fort at the end of a long day's sightseeing. Inside, part of the space is given over to the *Enoteca Italica Permanente,* a showroom and outlet for all the best Italian wines, including the excellent chianti bottlings for which the province is famous. The most demanding restaurateurs do their shopping here, but so can the enthusiastic individual, and wine tasting is encouraged, for a small charge. With advance notice, a guided visit to a vintner's farm also can be arranged here for $35 and up a person; the price varies with the excursion. The cellars are open daily, 3 PM to midnight. Fortezza Medicea (phone: 288497).

SOURCES AND RESOURCES

TOURIST INFORMATION: Siena's tourist office, Azienda di Promozione Turistica (APT; 56 Piazza del Campo; phone: 280551) is an information office and travel agency. Open weekdays, 9 AM to 12:30 PM and 3:30 to 7 PM (in summer, open all day); closed Saturday afternoons and Sundays. The services of Donatella Grilli, a private guide, are recommended (phone: 285188). The

APT has a list of other English-speaking, licensed guides and of drivers with cars.

Local Coverage – The Sienese read Florence's daily newspaper, *La Nazione.* The weekly *La Voce del Campo* lists local events. Many shops in the heart of town carry guidebooks in English.

TELEPHONE: The city code for Siena is 577. When calling from within Italy, dial 0577 before the local number.

GETTING AROUND: Since so many of the narrow streets in the center of this city are closed to traffic, the only way to get around is on foot. Several car parks situated around the walls make any walk to the center easy enough for even the most reluctant pedestrian.

Bus – Siena has local bus service; one of the main stops for most of the buses is Piazza Matteotti. Buses for destinations in and around Tuscany usually leave from Piazza San Domenico. Call *TRAIN* (pronounced Trah-*een;* phone: 221221) for information on the latter.

Car Rental – Most big international chains are not represented, but there are many smaller firms. Try *Auto Noleggi ACI* (47 Viale Vittorio Veneto; phone: 49118), run by Italy's main automobile club, or *Auto Noleggio Intercar Eurodrive* (96 Via San Marco; phone: 41148), affiliated with *Hertz,* which also rents motor scooters and will arrange chauffeured trips in the area.

Taxi – There are cabstands at the train station and at Piazza Matteotti (phone: 289350), or call *Consorzio Taxisti Senesi* (phone: 49222).

Train – The main train station is at the foot of the hills, a short taxi ride from the city center, Piazzale Fratelli Rosselli (phone: 280115).

SPECIAL EVENTS: The *Palio,* Siena's famous bareback horse race around the outer edge of the Piazza del Campo, has been going on since the 14th century. One of Italy's major traditional events, it is run twice, once on July 2 for the *Feast of Santa Maria di Provenzano* and once on August 16 in honor of Maria Santissima Assunta in Cielo (Our Lady of the Assumption), to whom the cathedral is dedicated. The races involve months of preparation on the part of each *contrada,* but the actual *Palio* activities begin 3 days or so before each race, with the selection of horses, a lottery to choose which of the 17 *contrade* will run (the Campo track can accommodate only 10 horses), and several rehearsals (called *prove*). The night before the race a banquet is held in each of the participating *contrade* (visitors with tickets may attend). The next day, various religious activities fill up the morning; then, in the afternoon, horses are blessed in the local churches. In late afternoon, the Torre del Mangia bell sounds, and one of the most spectacular parades imaginable files into Piazza del Campo — representatives of the city and of all the *contrade,* every marcher in historic costume. This is followed by the race itself. There are no rules, so rumors of the drugging of horses and bribing of jockeys goes on right up to post time. The Sienese are by now worked up to a fever pitch, and even though the race is over in only a few minutes, celebration in the winning *contrada* goes on all night and the next day. Finally, in September, the two winning *contrade* of the July and August *Palio* hold a huge outdoor banquet, with the winning horses at the head of the table — understandably, since more horses than riders finish the race, and it can be won by a riderless horse.

Tickets for the *Palio* are not easy to come by. Most of the grandstand seats on the perimeter of the course belong to the Sienese, almost by birthright. Remaining seats sell out many months in advance, and are expensive in the rare instances that they are available. Merchants in the town's better shops are the best source; ask around the

Piazza del Campo. In 1991, the cost was about $180 per ticket. The demand for them is so great that spaces at the windows of homes around the Campo are sold, too, and scalping is rampant. Non-ticket holders can stand in the mass of humanity in the middle of the piazza without charge, but early arrival (before noon) is imperative to ensure a view (pick a high spot near the Fonte Gaia). Another alternative is to buy a ticket for one of the *prove,* or rehearsals, that take place on the 3 days preceding each *Palio,* though this is becoming increasingly impossible as city officials usually buy up all the tickets. The regal pageantry is missing at these trial heats, but it's still possible to feel a bit of the spirit. Occasionally, too, a third *Palio* may be declared for some special reason (as in 1986, in honor of a local government anniversary).

For those not planning to visit Siena at *Palio* time, but still looking for a taste of it, note that each *contrada* has its own feast day when its church and the museum in which it keeps the silk *Palio* banners are open to the public. The tourist information office can provide a list of these days, all of which occur between April and October.

MUSEUMS: The most important museums of Siena are listed under *Special Places.* In addition, the following (none charges admission) are also of interest:

Biblioteca Comunale degli Intronati – Ancient religious and civic manuscripts and beautifully illuminated sacred books. Open weekdays from 9 AM to 8 PM; Saturdays from 9 AM to 2 PM. 5 Via della Sapienza (phone: 280704).

Musei dell'Accademia dei Fisiocritici – A geomineralogical museum and a zoological museum with prehistoric fossils, shells, and skeletons found in the surrounding area. Open weekdays from 9 AM to 1 PM and 3 to 6:30 PM; closed Thursday afternoons. 4 Piazza Sant'Agostino (phone: 47002).

Orto Botanico – Botanical garden. Open Mondays through Fridays from 8 AM to 1 PM and 3 PM to 5 PM. 4 Via Pier Andrea Mattioli (phone: 281248).

SHOPPING: Sienese shops are a mixture of extreme sophistication and rustic simplicity. While leading names in Italian fashion are in evidence in clothing and shoe stores, local craftsmanship can be found in the numerous ceramic and pottery shops selling original designs, as well as excellent copies of medieval and Renaissance Sienese items. The shops lining the main streets — Banchi di Sopra, Banchi di Sotto, and Via di Città — in the vicinity of Piazza del Campo are fertile ground for all of Siena's specialties, including the numerous culinary delicacies to be found in this area. Siena is particularly famous for *panforte,* a rich, spiced fruit and nut cake; *ricciarelli* (almond cookies); and salami. Wines can be bought at the *Enoteca Italica Permanente* in the Fortezza Medicea (see *Extra Special*) or at any local grocer. Siena also has branches of the all-purpose *Upim* and *Standa* department stores that are found in every major Italian city. One favorite souvenir quest is the attempt to collect a set of flags, mugs, or plates that carry each of the crests of Siena's 17 surviving *contrade.*

There is a colorful outdoor market every Wednesday at Piazza La Lizza (near the Basilica of San Domenico) where you can buy everything from flowers to handbags, dresses, kitchenware, and pottery.

Regular shop hours are usually from 9 AM to 12:30 PM and 3:30 to 7:30 PM daily in winter, from 9 AM to 12:30 or 1 PM and 4 to 8 PM daily in summer.

Antica Drogheria Manganelli – This 102-year-old shop is the best place to buy Tuscan fruitcakes and vin santo. 71 Via di Città.

Antichità Saena Vetus – High-quality antiques and some small pieces for the bargain hunter. 53 Via di Città.

Arabesque – Fashions for the younger set, from students at the local seamstress school. 6 Via Stalloreggi.

Art Shop – Exquisitely made paper products — notebook covers, picture frames, large folders, tiny boxes — made with 17th-century methods. 17 Via di Città.

La Balzana – An antiques shop, selling Tuscan and other Italian antiques and bric-a-brac. 26 Via della Sapienza.

Le Botteghe Piccole – Custom-made jewelry. 83 Via dei Rossi.

Ceccuzzi – Beautiful Italian fabrics as well as made-to-measure and ready-made clothes. 1 Banchi di Sopra and 32-36 Via dei Montanini.

Ceramiche Santa Caterina – One-of-a-kind hand-painted ceramics. 12 Via Pier Andrea Mattioli (workshop); 9A Via Camporegio and 51 Via di Città (stores).

Fendi – Clothing, accessories, and leather goods by the world-famous designers. 62 Via Banchi di Sopra.

Luisa Spagnoli – A good place for classic women's clothing. 65-67 Banchi di Sopra.

Marina Rinaldi – Good styling for the not-so-slender woman. 77 Via Banchi di Sopra.

Max Mara – Very smart women's apparel. 81-83 Via Banchi di Sopra.

Mercatissimo della Calzatura e Pelletteria – Fine, reasonably priced leatherwork. 1 Viale Curtatone and 3 Via Doccia.

Mori – An extensive selection of shoes, bags, and belts. 30-32 and 68-70 Via Banchi di Sopra.

Il Papiro – Hand-decorated paper — including the unusual *papier à cuvé* — and marbleized paper designs applied to fabrics that are then affixed to wallets, handbags, etc. 37 Via di Città.

Provvedi – One of the best stocked of the many ceramics shops in this area. 96 Via di Città.

Quercioli – Jewelry, some of it from the nearby workshops of Arezzo, a leading jewelry making town. 5 Via Banchi di Sopra.

Scapecchi – Classic women's fashions, both made-to-order and ready-to-wear, made from fine silks from Como and other quality fabrics. 120-122 Via di Città.

Siena Ricama – Hand-embroidered table linen and pillow covers in the colors and designs of Renaissance Siena. 61 Via di Città.

SPORTS AND FITNESS: Bicycling – *Autonoleggi Borgogni* (18 Via S. Bandini; phone: 281096), a car rental office, also rents bicycles.

Horseback Riding – The *Club Ippico Senese* (Località Pian del Lago; phone: 53277) offers riding lessons and countryside treks.

Soccer – From September to May, *Siena* plays at *Stadio Comunale Artemio Franchi* (3 Viale dei Mille; phone: 281084), near the Fortezza Medicea.

Swimming – The outdoor municipal swimming pool in *Piazza Amendola* (phone: 47496), on the northwest edge of the city, is open in the summer months. There also is *Piscina Quattro Querce* (31 Stada di Marciano; phone: 40013).

Tennis – There are clay courts at *Circolo Tennis Siena* (Località Vico Alto; phone: 44925 or 283397), just outside the walls on the northwest side of the city.

MUSIC: Siena has no opera company, but the highly active *Accademia Musicale Chigiana* more than makes up for this deficit in July and August, when its summer school for professional and advanced musicians is in session. For the duration of the program, students make regular concert appearances, as soloists or in ensembles, and at the same time the Academy sponsors a series of concerts, the *Estate Musicale Chigiana,* featuring well-known guest artists. An annual week-long festival in late August, the *Settimana Musicale Senese,* features rarely played or forgotten works as well as those of contemporary composers. The events take place in the Palazzo Chigi-Saracini music room — Siena's main concert hall for performances at other times of the year as well — or in any of the city's innumerable palaces and churches. For information, contact the *Fondazione Accademia Musicale Chigiana,* 89 Via di Città (phone: 46152).

NIGHTCLUBS AND NIGHTLIFE: As in most Italian cities, at least in the summer, nightlife to the average Sienese simply means wandering through the city and stopping at the occasional café that's open late in the Campo. There are always groups of people congregated around the fountain here or elsewhere in some small piazza, in animated discussion. Greater stimulation is possible at three discotheques, *Club Enoteca,* adjacent to the wine cellars of the Fortezza Medicea (phone: 285466), open Thursdays through Sundays; *Tom Cat* (Via dei Termini; phone: 280152); and the more centrally located *Jet Set* (13 Via Pantaneto; phone: 288378), closed Wednesdays. *Al Cambio* (48 Via Pantaneto; phone: 43183), open to 2 AM and closed Sundays, is a gathering place for drinking, music, and conversation. *Porta Giustizia* (11 Porta Giustizia; phone: 222753) is an after-dinner gathering place that sometimes has live music, and *L'Officina* (3 Piazza del Sale; phone: 286301) is a piano bar watering hole.

BEST IN TOWN

CHECKING IN: It is unwise to arrive in Siena without a hotel reservation between May and October. Because of the small size and popularity of the town, its 30 or so hotels, both inside and outside the walls, usually are booked solid for most of the prime tourism season. It is definitely a mistake to arrive in town unexpectedly on *Palio* days and the days immediately preceding them. Prices in the larger out-of-town hotels, some of which are converted Renaissance villas, are expensive, from $250 all the way up to $600 for a double room with bath. Moderate means prices ranging from $125 to $250 for a double, and inexpensive means $65 to $125. All telephone numbers are in the 577 city code unless otherwise indicated.

Certosa di Maggiano – Among the cypress trees and vineyards, this hotel has a unique atmosphere of seclusion and meditation, which is not surprising because it began in the 14th century as a Carthusian monastery. A short taxi or bus ride outside the city walls, it has several spacious sitting rooms, Renaissance furniture, and a permanent show of ancient manuscripts and documents. A large, well-kept garden contains a heated swimming pool and tennis courts, and there is a highly recommended restaurant (see *Eating Out*). The rooms are few (only 14), however, so book well in advance. Member of the Relais & Châteaux group. 82 Via di Certosa (phone: 288180; fax: 288189; telex: 574221). Expensive.

Park – The building originally held a castle-cum-villa, built in 1530, of the local well-to-do Gori family. They chose the spot for its dominating position (and, therefore, its easy defendability) as well as for the healthy air and attractive countryside views of olive trees and rolling hills. Today's traveler can enjoy the same, with the addition of a swimming pool and tennis courts unobtrusively integrated into a romantic, slightly decadent-looking Italian garden surrounded by a small wood of oak and beech trees. There are 69 rooms in this link in the CIGA chain, all with air conditioning (color TV set on request), and the restaurant is good (see *Eating Out*). A short taxi or bus ride from the city center. 18 Via di Marciano (phone: 44803; fax: 49020; telex: 571005). Expensive.

Villa Scacciapensieri – A bit over a mile (1.6 km) from the city center, this handsome family villa, built a little over 100 years ago, is another romantic spot in the Sienese countryside. With its large garden and outlook onto both the city and the surrounding vineclad hills, tennis court, swimming pool, color TV sets in all rooms, and excellent cuisine, plus regular bus service into town, this is an ideal stopping-place from which to enjoy sightseeing trips in Siena or forays into the Chianti hills. Closed November to mid-March. Its chic restaurant is closed Wednesdays. 10 Via di Scacciapensieri (phone: 41441; fax: 270854; telex: 573390). Expensive.

Garden – Housed under two roofs — 50 rooms altogether between the main building and the new, posher annex. This hostelry has plenty of charm, a swimming pool, garden, and restaurant. 2 Via Custosa (phone: 47056; fax: 46050; telex: 574239). Expensive to moderate.

Jolly Excelsior – There are 126 well-appointed rooms in this comfortable, traditional hotel with a restaurant and bar. Centrally located near the town gate. Piazza La Lizza (phone: 288448; fax: 41272; telex: 573345). Expensive to moderate.

Villa Belvedere – Just 7 miles (11 km) outside Siena in Colle Val d'Elsa, this beautifully restored 15-room villa — built in 1795 — was once the residence of the Grand Duke of Tuscany. There is a lovely garden and a good restaurant. Località Belvedere, Colle Val d'Elsa (phone: 920966). Expensive to moderate.

Villa Liberty – Another renovated villa, this one 100 years old and in the center of town. Very attractive, all of the 15 rooms are decorated in contemporary style. No restaurant, but a bar. 11 Via Veneto (phone: 44966). Expensive to moderate.

Residence Catignano – On a hilltop 15 minutes from town, a meticulously restored series of suites are available for weekly rental in a 16th-century villa's renovated farm buildings. There is a splendid view, a formal Renaissance garden, and a swimming pool under ancient cypress trees. No restaurant, but each suite includes a kitchenette. Pianella, Castelnuovo Berardenga (phone: 356744 or 356755). Moderate.

Castagneto – Set below the city walls at the foot of the western side of Siena, this small but comfortable hotel offers splendid panoramas from its own garden. There are 11 rooms with private showers; no restaurant. Closed December through mid-March. 39 Via dei Cappuccini (phone: 45103). Moderate to inexpensive.

Duomo – An attractive, good hotel that's perfect for a comfortable, reasonably priced stay in town. It's in the heart of medieval Siena, a 5-minute walk from the Duomo, and within easy reach of Via di Città, one of the main shopping streets. There are 23 quiet rooms, many with a view of the Duomo; no restaurant. 38 Via Stalloreggi (phone: 289088; fax: 44043; telex: 583035). Moderate to inexpensive.

Palazzo Ravizza – This 17th-century villa is an old-fashioned pensione within easy walking distance of the main sights of Siena. It is surrounded by its own garden and provides a peaceful, yet central, vantage point from which to enjoy the city. There are 30 rooms (be sure to ask for one with bath) and a pleasant restaurant for guests only, open evenings (in high season, guests must take breakfast and dinner daily). The restaurant is closed November to March, but the hotel is open year-round. 34 Pian dei Mantellini (phone: 280462; fax: 271370; telex: 570252). Moderate to inexpensive.

Santa Caterina – Opened in 1986 in an 18th-century palazzo, with 19 tastefully furnished rooms, each with a private bath and air conditioning. There's a large, pleasant verandah for breakfast and a delightful garden for an aperitif. Located just outside the city walls, but only a minute's walk from the city center. 7 Via Enea Silvio Piccolomini (phone: 221105; fax: 271087; telex: 575304). Moderate to inexpensive.

Chiusarelli – Set just below the imposing walls of the Basilica di San Domenico and the Fonte Branda on the western outskirts of the city, yet within easy reach of the center. There are 50 rooms, a restaurant, and a small garden. 9 Viale Curtatone (phone: 280562). Inexpensive.

EATING OUT: Tuscan cooking is celebrated throughout Italy for its robust and simple dishes and excellent wines, and Siena is a choice city in which to sample it. This is one of the few parts of Italy where diners can enjoy good beef as well as game — venison, wild boar, hare, pheasant, quail, wild pigeon. Whether in salamis, in rustic pâtés to be spread on rounds of toasted bread, or served with lentils or beans, these seasonal delights are a staple of the area's hearty country fare. Sienese cooks are also handy with vegetable dishes and are well versed in the making of soups, such as the rich vegetable broth with bread and poached egg known as *acqua cotta* (literally, "cooked water") and the *ribollita* ("reboiled"), the Rolls-Royce of vegetable soups. Wild mushrooms, gathered fresh from the surrounding wooded areas and served in a variety of ways, can be a main course or a side dish. Cheeses are traditionally made from sheep's and cow's milk, the most prevalent being *caciotta* or *pecorino,* which can be mild and soft or seasoned to become salty and hard. Wines range from the local chianti to the very finest — arguably, the red wine from the brunello grapes of nearby Montalcino. The dry but robust Tuscan whites include vernaccia from San Gimignano and bianco vergine della Valdichiana. And then there is the traditional sweet dessert wine, vin santo.

Siena is essentially an informal city, and while the more expensive hotels offer an elegant ambience befitting their ratings, the average restaurant tends to be more homey — though the food is no less delectable for being served in relaxed surroundings. Service is friendly, and waiters are happy to help bewildered foreigners through the menu. In the listings below, a meal for two in an expensive restaurant will cost $150 and up, including wine, while the moderate restaurants charge from $70 to $120. Inexpensive is under $70. All telephone numbers are in the 577 city code unless otherwise indicated.

Certosa di Maggiano – The cuisine in this sophisticated country hotel, transformed from a 14th-century monastery into a restaurant seating 30, ranges far beyond the Tuscan border to include such nouvelle-style dishes as tortellini soufflé, shrimp fricassee, and sole with asparagus. Most of the dishes are made from locally grown ingredients, the choice of dessert changes daily, and there is an excellent selection wines. Closed Tuesdays except to hotel guests. Limited seating; reservations advised. Major credit cards accepted. 82 Via di Certosa (phone: 288180). Expensive.

Magnolia Terrace – For traditional Tuscan cooking, try this restaurant in a 16th-century villa hotel. Original salads of mushrooms and white beans are bathed in the purest olive oil, soups are made from freshly gathered mushrooms, and fresh fish is brought in from the Tuscan coast. Homemade cheeses and cakes, and a vast selection of wines. Reliable, if uninspired. Closed Wednesdays. Reservations advised. Major credit cards accepted. In the *Park* hotel, at 18 Via di Marciano (phone: 44803). Expensive.

Al Mangia – Since it's right in Piazza del Campo, this well-known Sienese eatery, with alfresco dining in the summer, is inundated in summer by *Palio* fans and other visitors. At other times, however, it makes a pleasant eating place, with tables outside looking toward the handsome Palazzo Comunale. The menu is particularly good for game and mushroom dishes, and there's a good wine selection. Closed Mondays. Reservations advised. Major credit cards accepted. 43 Piazza del Campo (phone: 281121). Expensive.

Da Guido – In the heart of the Old City, and one of the most characteristic of the inner city's wood-beamed restaurants, with an equally characteristic Tuscan cuisine. This is one of Siena's favorite haunts, and photos of its famous habitués cover its brick walls. Closed Wednesdays. Reservations advised. Major credit cards accepted. 7 Vicolo Pier Pettinaio (phone: 280042). Expensive to moderate.

Il Biondo – This large, modern restaurant, with an outdoor terrace at the edge of the Old City center, adds fresh fish dishes, such as homemade spaghetti with shrimp, to an otherwise Tuscan menu, which often features roast lamb with artichokes, grilled pork liver, and pork and sausage on skewers. Closed Wednesdays. Reservations advised. Major credit cards accepted. 10 Vicolo del Rustichetto (phone: 280739). Moderate.

Botteganova – A creative approach to traditional Tuscan fare in an elegant setting. Truffles abound and owner Ettore Silvestri's wife makes all the desserts. Closed Sundays and Monday afternoons and from July 20 to August 10. Reservations advised. Major credit cards accepted. 29 Via Chiantigiana (phone: 284230). Moderate.

Le Campane – Between the Duomo and Piazza del Campo, its menu includes house variations on classic Tuscan soups such as *ribollita* and an artichoke quiche. Fresh fish, charcoal-grilled meat, and veal scaloppine with fresh tarragon are other entrées. Closed Mondays. Reservations advised. Major credit cards accepted. 6 Via delle Campane (phone: 284035). Moderate.

Cane e Gatto – Owners Paolo and Sonia Senni have their collection of modern lithographs by, among others, Picasso hung on the pristine walls of this chic, tiny, very personal eatery. There is no menu, but there is art in the creative cooking and fine wines. Closed Thursdays and after the August 16 *Palio* for about 1 week. Reservations necessary. Major credit cards accepted. 6 Via Pagliaresi (phone: 220751). Moderate.

Al Marsili – A handsome 15th-century vaulted restaurant near the Duomo, this is another prime Sienese eating place rooted in Tuscan tradition, but it has its own original dishes as well. Fresh vegetables form the basis of some of the regulars' favorites: zucchini in casserole, chick-peas with garlic and rosemary, and vegetable *sformati* (mousses). Mushroom pâté is spread on toasted country bread for an hors d'oeuvre, and game — guinea fowl, wild duck, or pigeon, roasted or served with one of the inimitable house sauces — is prominent among the meat dishes. Closed Mondays. Reservations advised. Major credit cards accepted. 3 Via del Castoro (phone: 47154). Moderate.

Mugolone – Serving excellent Tuscan fare in a rustic setting, it's a favorite of local society. Closed Thursdays and 10 days in mid-July. Reservations advised. Major credit cards accepted. 8 Via dei Pellegrini (phone: 283235). Moderate.

Nello La Taverna – The informal, friendly atmosphere makes this a popular place with the Sienese as well as with visitors. A good place to try traditional Tuscan game and also Tuscan pasta served with a sauce or, as in the *tagliatelle* with tarragon, simply with fresh herbs. Try the *menù gastronomico sienese.* Closed Sunday evenings, Mondays, and during February. Reservations advised. Major credit cards accepted. 28 Via del Porrione (phone: 289043). Moderate.

Osteria Le Logge – Farther down the street and slightly more upscale, this is where the connoisseurs congregate. Taste host Gianni Brunelli's delectible rustic Sienese bean soup, *crostini* (toasted rounds of bread) with game and mushroom pâté, or classic meat and game dishes with a sprinkling of truffles, in season. A home-produced *caciotta* dominates the cheese selection. A word of caution — don't order the house wine. Closed Sundays, June 1–15, and November 15–30. Reservations necessary. Major credit cards accepted. 33 Via del Porrione (phone: 48013). Moderate.

Turrido – Dine in the garden in warm weather, on Tuscan fare such as *pappardelle alla lepre* (wide noodles in hare sauce), grilled lamb, and wild *porcini* mushrooms in various guises. There is an inexpensive tourist menu. Closed Mondays. Reservations necessary during *Palio* season. No credit cards accepted. 60-62 Via Stalloreggi (phone: 282121). Moderate.

Grotta di Santa Caterina–Da Bagoga – This lively restaurant founded by a former *Palio* jockey (Bagoga) is jammed during *Palio* time and often during the rest of the season as well, so it's preferable off-season. *Palio* mementos decorate the walls, and the menu is classic Tuscan fare — pasta with hare sauce, roast meats, and game. Closed Sunday evenings, Mondays, and 10 days in mid-July. Reservations advised. Major credit cards accepted. 26 Via della Galluzza (phone: 282208). Moderate to inexpensive.

Papei – The perfect place to try home-style Sienese cooking — homemade pasta, beans, steaks *alla fiorentina* — in a friendly trattoria that locals frequent. There is alfresco dining in the summer. A real find. Closed Mondays and in late June. Reservations advised. No credit cards accepted. 6 Piazza del Mercato (phone: 280894). Inexpensive.

TAORMINA

Set on the slopes of Monte Tauro (Mountain of the Bull), looking out at snow-capped Mount Etna and the blue Ionian Sea, this little town is easily one of the world's loveliest resorts. For 20 centuries, Taormina has offered visitors the amenities of a restful vacation against the backdrop of exquisite natural beauty. Its purpose is reflected in its current composition: a year-round population of fewer than 11,000 people with more than 70 hotels and *pensioni* in the town itself and another 25 in the seaside suburb of Mazzarò. Along with swarms of day visitors, in a typical year, Taormina hosts nearly three-quarters of a million overnight travelers.

A peacefully beautiful place — ancient and medieval stone buildings are framed by palm trees and vivid bougainvillea vines — in recent times Taormina has been known primarily as a refuge for rich and cultured Europeans. The first modern hotel was built in 1874; others followed, many built with British capital. After a stay by Emperor Wilhelm II of Prussia, it became a well-known aristocratic watering spot. By the turn of the century, it was popular not just with crowned heads but with the families of European financiers. It was not unusual for the Rothschilds, the Krupps, and the Vanderbilts to take vacations here, while still later it became a favorite spot for artistic personalities such as British writer D. H. Lawrence and German photographer Wilhelm von Gloeden. (Von Gloeden shocked the locals when he took to photographing local lads, often in the nude, posed as small Greek gods.)

Taormina has historical roots that reach far back in time. Tombs built by the Siculi (Italian tribes that migrated to Sicily 1,300 years before Christ) have been discovered nearby, proving that the area has long been settled. In 735 BC, Greek sailors founded the nearby city of Naxos. For several centuries, there was bitter rivalry among Greek colonies in Sicily. After Naxos was destroyed by Dionysius of Syracuse in 403 BC, the Siculi survivors founded Tauromenium. This town, too, was wiped out by Dionysius but was soon refounded. In 358 BC, with the support of the Naxian survivors, a new state was established by Andromachus. His son, Timaeus of Tauromenion, became the city's chief historian.

The Romans gave Taormina considerable autonomy. Despite the vicissitudes of the empire (and the emperors' internal rivalries), it seems to have enjoyed centuries of peace and prosperity, attracting patrician vacationers. The area was known for its fruits, vegetables, olives, and grapes, as well as for its marble, but its primary importance was military — the natural harbors below and the rocky lookout points above were a strategic advantage.

After the fall of Rome and the brief period of domination by barbarian tribes, Taormina — like the rest of Sicily — fell under the influence of the Byzantine Empire. It became an archbishopric and, for a while, was the most important city in eastern Sicily. It fell to the Arabs in 902, and for the next several centuries it was variously dominated by the Swabians, the Normans, the Angevins, and the Aragonese. When King Martin died without heirs in 1410, King Ferdinand sent his son John to the island, and for the next 3 centuries all of Sicily was ruled by Spanish viceroys. During the latter part of this period, Taormina suffered a major fire and a severe earthquake; it lost population and sank into obscurity. Little changed during the 18th and 19th centuries under the Spanish Bourbons, the Savoys of Piedmont, and the Hapsburgs of Austria.

The town's fortunes began to turn after Italian unification in 1860. With the stabilization of government and development of transportation, it was soon discovered by wealthy German and British travelers. In a short time, its hotel industry burgeoned. Taormina today is known for the cultivation of citrus fruits, olives, and the wine commonly known as the "red wine of Etna," but there is no doubt that mass tourism is the city's principal source of revenue, which has led to some problems. The traffic jams on the few narrow, steep roads leading from the sea to Taormina's position on a rocky balcony or the long lines for the cable car from Mazzarò to the center can be overwhelming, especially in August. Steps are being taken, however, to alleviate some of the congestion — a new road and underground parking facilities are being built below the town, as well as elevators to carry people up to Taormina. It is expected that the project will take a few years to complete. Fortunately, its price tag and governors have succeeded in protecting Taormina from the defacement that can result from invasions of vacationers. It has taken on a role in Italian cultural life as well — theater, film, and literary festivals are held here annually — so this enchanting city of gardens and medieval monuments continues to offer its visitors, in the words of Guy de Maupassant, "all that seems made on the earth to entice eyes, spirit, and imagination."

TAORMINA AT-A-GLANCE

SEEING THE CITY: Taormina, with its stone buildings, flowered balconies, and lush subtropical vegetation, appears to be a physical outgrowth of the surrounding mountainous landscape. There is a good view of the town from the ruins of the Castello (Castle) on the summit of Monte Tauro; the sea is accessible from here by foot or by car along the road descending from the village of Castel Mola, or by cable car from the center of Taormina just beyond Porta Messina. There's an even better view from Castel Mola itself, about 3 miles (5 km) away. Taormina, however, is best known for the stunning view of the town, the sea, and — in the distance — volcanic Mount Etna, visible from the well-preserved Greek theater. In town, from Piazza IX Aprile, off the central Corso Umberto I, there is a lovely view of the sea and coastline below.

SPECIAL PLACES: The town itself is tiny, with most shops, restaurants, and other attractions on or just off the main street, Corso Umberto I. The smaller crossroads are often merely pedestrian staircases hewn into the rock.

Corso Umberto I (Umberto I Avenue) – The central street of Taormina, now closed to automobiles, runs horizontally through the town from Porta

Messina to Porta Catania. The street marks the outskirts of what was the ancient Greek city of Tauromenion and what is still known as the Borgo Medioevale (Medieval Township). With its many cafés and benches, this street is where the locals take their evening and Sunday strolls. It is undoubtedly the best place in Taormina for watching neighbors and strangers alike, a favorite Sicilian pastime.

Teatro Greco (Greek Theater) – A short walk along the *corso* from Porta Messina is Piazza Vittorio Emanuele. From this square, turn left and walk along Via del Teatro Greco directly to one of Sicily's most impressive and well-preserved archaeological ruins. The original structure, probably built in the 3rd century BC, is the second-largest ancient amphitheater in Sicily after the one in Syracuse. The *cavea,* the graduated rows of seats, was carved out of the hillside and surmounted by a portico of marble columns. Under the Romans, the theater was significantly rebuilt for use as a gladiatorial arena. The view from the theater is fine, and the acoustics are so good that it is still used during summer arts and film festivals. Next door is a small antiquarium with relics of the ancient city. The theater is open daily, 9 AM to shortly before sunset. Admission charge. 40 Via Teatro Greco (phone: 23220).

Palazzo Corvaja (Corvaja Palace) – In Piazza Vittorio Emanuele stands Palazzo Corvaja, an impressive late-14th-century building with a crenelated façade. Built on the site of the ancient Roman forum, the palazzo is Taormina's most important medieval building and originally housed the first Sicilian parliament. It is also thought to have been the residence of Queen Bianca of Navarre. In the 16th century it was passed on to the Corvaja family. Windows and other decorations, such as the black and white lava inlay ornamentation, are typically Catalán-Gothic in style. There is a picturesque inner courtyard with a 13th-century stone staircase. Palazzo Corvaja today houses the Azienda Autonoma di Soggiorno e Turismo (tourist information office).

Chiesa di Santa Caterina (Church of Saint Catherine) – This small church next to Palazzo Corvaja has a fine statue of Saint Catherine, three handsome baroque altars, and a gloomy downstairs funeral chamber. Behind the church are the remains of a small Roman theater, or *odeon,* where musical performances were held in ancient times.

Naumachiae – Farther west along Corso Umberto I is the Via Naumachia, which leads to the remains of an ancient cistern and its arcaded retaining wall. The Romans used naumachiae (artificial ponds or lakes, surrounded by seating for spectators) to stage mock sea battles. Some archaeologists believe this one may have been part of a gymnasium.

Piazza IX Aprile (Ninth of April Square) – Corso Umberto I continues west to a charming square, complete with jacaranda trees and a lovely 19th-century iron lamppost. Passersby stop here for an *aperitivo* at one of the several outdoor cafés or to enjoy the panoramic view of the Greek theater, Mount Etna, and the sea below. To the left as one enters the square (which is simply a broadening of the *corso*) is the tiny 15th-century Chiesa di Sant'Agostino, now the public library (phone: 23310), which often hosts temporary exhibits, including contemporary paintings, antique books and sculptures, and photographs. Open daily from 9 AM to 8 PM. On the right, up a double staircase, is the Chiesa di San Giuseppe, with its charming baroque façade. And at the end of the square stands the Torre dell'Orologio (Clock Tower), which is the entranceway to the Borgo Medioevale (Medieval Township). The present tower dates from the 12th century, but its foundations are believed to be much older.

Borgo Medioevale (Medieval Township) – This district preserves many architectural details from the Middle Ages. Note especially the Gothic windows and doors at Nos. 122, 176, 190, 228, and 241. Up a staircase on the right is Palazzo Ciampoli, which dates back to 1412.

Duomo (Cathedral) – San Nicola di Bari (Saint Nicholas of Bari), the Duomo of Taormina, on Piazza del Municipio, is a severe 14th-century church of rough-hewn stone. Its crenelated walls have a decidedly Norman appearance. Its interior is in the form of a Latin cross — the nave and two aisles are separated by columns of Taormina rose marble. Note the 15th-century triptych, *Visitation of Mary to Elizabeth, Saint Joseph, and Saint Zachariah* by Antonio Giuffrè, and other medieval religious paintings.

Piazza del Municipio and Porta Catania (Municipal Square and Catania Gate) – The Duomo's main portal opens out onto Palazzo Municipio, where there is a baroque fountain supporting a female centaur, symbol of the town. Across the *corso* is what is left of the Chiesa del Carmine, including its campanile. The *corso* comes to an end at the arch of Porta Catania, which is also called Porta del Tocco (Tolling Gate) because in Norman times the people of Taormina gathered here when the bells were rung. It is inscribed with the date 1440, as well as the Taormina and Aragón coats of arms. To the left is the Palazzo del Duca di Santo Stefano, a massive Gothic residence.

Convento di San Domenico (Convent of Saint Domenic) – Just downhill from Piazza del Municipio is the Chiesa di San Domenico, whose campanile commands a lovely view. The nearby convent has been a hotel — the *San Domenico Palace* — since 1896 and is today probably one of the most luxurious and beautiful resorts in all of Italy (see *Checking In*). The hotel has preserved the original monastic furnishings and is a treasure trove of art objects. The 15th-century cloister with its fine marble well has been glass enclosed. The gardens are lush; the views of the sea and Mount Etna are spectacular. (The management does not encourage uninvited guests — especially those who are too casually dressed, although both bar and restaurant are open to non-residents.)

Giardino Pubblico (Public Garden) – Via Roma winds down from San Domenico, providing a viewer with exceptional panoramas. At the end, turn right into Via Bagnoli Croce, which leads to the Giardino Pubblico. Once part of the nearby Villa Cacciola, the park was taken over by the city in 1923 and has been open to the public ever since. Not only are the views from the park splendid, but the colorful Mediterranean subtropical vegetation is enhanced by odd Babylonian-style structures erected in the last century for the villa's owner, Lady Trevelyn. A springtime stroll in these well-tended formal gardens is truly a sensual experience.

ENVIRONS

Lido di Mazzarò (Mazzarò Beach) – A summer vacation in Taormina also means sun and sea, with the accompanying gastronomic delights. Most people staying in Taormina swim at the Lido di Mazzarò, a long, well-equipped beach lined with numerous hotels, cafés, and restaurants. There are footpaths to the beach, and a *funivia* (cable car) operates every 15 minutes from 8 AM to midnight July through September and from 8 AM to 8:30 PM the rest of the year between Mazzarò and a point just outside Porta Messina. A one-way ticket for the 3-minute ride costs 1,000 lire (about 75¢). If there is a long line (which there is sure to be in August), a taxi ride up to Taormina from the stand next to the *funivia* can (if negotiated beforehand) cost about the same per person. Other pleasant beaches in the area are Spisone and Giardini-Naxos, for which there is regular bus service, and Capo Schisò.

Castel Mola – Three miles (5 km) away and 1,800 feet above sea level is a tiny village that overlooks Taormina and the ruins of its medieval castle. Historians believe Castel Mola may have been the ancient city of Mylai, which was used as a place of hiding by refugees of various wars in the area. It was destroyed by the Arabs in AD 902. *SAIS* buses (phone: 625301) run to the top from the terminal on Via Luigi Pirandello. The ride takes 20 minutes and costs 1,300 lire (about $1).

Giardini-Naxos – Naxos was the oldest Greek colony in Sicily. There are few traces of the ancient city, but excavations begun in 1967 have unearthed some of the basalt blocks from the town's defense walls. Its location on Capo Schisò, a peninsula of lava rock, is striking. Giardini, the new sea resort, is less than 3 miles (5 km) south of Taormina. It was from this spot that the Italian patriot Giuseppe Garibaldi sailed with about 5,000 troops to fight for Italian unification in 1860.

Forza D'Agrò and Capo Sant'Alessio – The tiny medieval town of Forza D'Agrò is only a short drive north of Taormina. Both the Chiesa della Trinità (Church of the Trinity) and the Chiesa di San Francesco (Church of Saint Francis) contain interesting paintings and artifacts. Capo Sant'Alessio, a twin-peaked rock cliff separating two beaches and topped by a medieval castle, is nearby.

Alcantara Gorge – A winding road toward the interior (SS195, signposted "Francavilla") from Giardini leads to the scenic Alcantara Valley, the setting for various Greek myths. After the viaduct in Contrada Larderia, one comes to the gorge, a narrow split in the lava rock, plunging precipitously down to the river.

Mount Etna – The biggest volcano in Europe — and still very active — Etna was believed by the ancients to be the forge of Hephaestus, the Greek god of fire. It was also associated with the legend of the Cyclops Polyphemus, who waylaid Ulysses on his way through the Straits of Messina. (*Etna* comes from the Greek *aitho,* or "eye burn.") The mountain's earliest known eruption, in 475 BC, was recorded by Pindar and Aeschylus. We know of 135 eruptions since. Several times — notably in 1669 when it destroyed Catania — its lava has reached the sea, and in 1983 eruptions lasted a full 3 months. It still smokes and rumbles frequently — Etna was particularly active in 1990 — indicating that a major eruption is possible at any time. Its several craters, especially the main caldera, are fascinating geologically, and the view from the summit, including most of Sicily, the Lipari Islands, and Calabria, is awesome. A consideration of weather conditions and the volcano's current activity is advisable before going up the mountain, however.

There are several approaches to Etna from Taormina. The nearest is by way of Fiumefreddo. Drive south on SS114, then take SS120 northwest to Linguaglossa; bear left to the village of Mareneve. A minibus carrying visitors from there to within a short walk of the caldera costs about 30,000 lire ($23). Fee includes guide. There also is a small train that goes around the base. Farther south there are easy approaches from either Nicolosi or Zafferana. At Nicolosi-Nord a cable car climbs to within about 8,500 feet; 4-wheel-drive vehicles are available from there to the top, where visitors can get to within 900 feet of the central crater. Plan to spend at least half a day on the volcano; wear warm clothing and sturdy shoes. It's also fun to make the trip at night, when lava glows eerily red in the caldera, and then stay to see the sunrise — a poetic experience. Locals make a habit of skiing on the volcano in winter. The *CIT* bus company offers all-day excursions to Etna with English-speaking guides. The cost is 25,000 lire (about $19) for an ascent of approximately 3,280 feet; for an additional 35,000 lire (about $27), you can leave the guide behind and continue up by four-wheel-drive (with a driver) an additional 1,640 feet toward the crater. *CIT* also has an afternoon trip (same cost as the all-day excursion) for those who wish to watch the sun set from Etna. Call 23301 for reservations. (For further information on Mount Etna, see *Sicily (and the Lipari Islands,* DIRECTIONS.)

SOURCES AND RESOURCES

TOURIST INFORMATION: The Taormina Azienda Autonoma di Soggiorno e Turismo (in the back of Palazzo Corvaja, Piazza Santa Caterina; phone: 23243; fax: 24941) is open weekdays from 8 AM to 2 PM and 4 to 7 PM, Saturday from 8 AM to noon and 4 to 7 PM. The office provides several brochures and pamphlets on Taormina, its services, and surroundings, as well as information about hotels, although it does not make reservations. Do this directly or through the *Compagnia Italiana Turismo* (*CIT,* 101 Corso Umberto I; phone: 23301, 23302, and 23303), or any private agency.

Local Coverage – Newspapers published in Palermo, *Giornale di Sicilia* and *L'Ora,* are the best sources of local information. Taormina visitors should also consult *Best of Taormina,* a free monthly magazine in Italian and English published by the regional tourism office, and available at Palazzo Corvaja.

TELEPHONE: The city code for Taormina is 942. When calling from within Italy, dial 0942 before the local number.

GETTING AROUND: Walking is the easiest and most enjoyable way around town. A car is useful for excursions.

Buses – There is regular bus service from the terminal on Via Luigi Pirandello, in front of the *Miramare* hotel, to most nearby towns, including Mazzarò, Castel Mola, Forza d'Agrò, and Giardini-Naxos. The bus company, *SAIS,* also offers tours to Agrigento, Alcantara, and Siracusa (phone: 625301). Many hotels also have minibuses that make round trips to the beach.

Car Rental – The major car rental companies all have offices in Taormina. Some also rent scooters.

Taxi – Taxis can be hired for special excursions. Stands are at Piazza Badia (phone: 23000), Piazza Duomo (phone: 23800), the Taormina–Giardini-Naxos train station (phone: 51150), and Mazzarò (phone: 21266). A taxi ride to the Catania Airport takes about 1 hour. Prices are by meter or negotiable beforehand.

Trains – Trains to and from Messina and Catania and other points arrive regularly at nearby Taormina–Giardini-Naxos Station (phone: 51026), where taxi and bus services to Taormina are available.

SPECIAL EVENTS: Every summer, beginning in mid-July, Taormina hosts *Taormina Arte,* a 2-month arts festival that consists of about 10 days of films and a month or more of theatrical and dance productions, many of which are held in the *Teatro Greco* (see *Special Places*). Although less important than in the past, it is still very much a part of the international film festival circuit and draws critics, directors, and stars. The program and tickets for the festival are available in June from *Taormina Arte* (Palazzo Congressi; phone: 21142).

SHOPPING: Taormina has perhaps the best selection of antiques, ceramics, jewelry, and lace handiwork in all of Sicily. Conveniently, most of the shops are concentrated on the main street, Corso Umberto I, which stretches from one end of the old town to the other. The *corso* is off limits to cars (beware — Taormina's traffic wardens are the least lenient in Italy), making it ideal for leisurely strolls and window shopping. It is also an unusually beautiful street, with bougainvillea-filled balconies, shady piazzas, outdoor cafés, and irresistible pastry shops. Don't be afraid to browse farther afield, such as around the area just below the *corso,* which can provide some interesting finds.

The *Bar Mocambo* (in Piazza IX Aprile) is a favorite spot for a cappuccino or an *aperitivo.* Its outdoor tables are perfect for people watching. Inside, the café's walls are decorated with enlargements of Wilhelm von Gloeden's famous turn-of-the-century photographs of Sicilian boys — some dressed as ancient Greeks or as girls, some semi-nude or nude.

The ubiquitous *Benetton* has an outlet on the *corso,* but far more interesting are the scores of small stores selling antiques and ceramics. Shops are open daily, including Sundays, 9 AM to 1 PM and 4 to 9:30 PM in summer, or 3:30 to 7:30 PM in winter. Most accept major credit cards and will send packages out of the country.

Antichità Pandora – Quality antiques, often outlandish. 2 Salita Lucio Denti (no phone).

La Baronessa – Extremely tasteful clothes and accessories for men and women. 148 Corso Umberto I (phone: 24960).

Carlo Panarello – A tasteful selection of decorative Sicilian ceramics and antiques. 122 Corso Umberto I (phone: 23910).

Casa d'Arte M. Forin – Fine silver, porcelain, antique furniture, and other art objects. 148 Corso Umberto I (phone: 23060).

Daneu – Unusual and imaginative gift shop, especially the handmade pottery and local prints. 126 Corso Umberto I (no phone).

Estro – High-quality gems and gold jewelry. 205 Corso Umberto I (phone: 24981).

Extreme – A range of stylish and modern dress labels. Corner of Via Fratelli Bandiera, which leads down from the *corso,* and Via Bastone (no phone).

Galeano (Concetta) – Beautiful hand-embroidered lace tablecloths and bedspreads in linen and cotton. 233 Corso Umberto I (phone: 625144).

Il Gaucho – Casual and dressy shoes for men and women. 118 Corso Umberto I (no phone).

Gioielleria Giuseppe Stroscio – Finely crafted modern and antique jewelry. 169 Corso Umberto I (phone: 24865).

Giovanni Panarello – Taormina's version of a thrift shop filled with antique bits (pieces of marble, candlesticks, etc.) from local churches at reasonable prices. 110 Corso Umberto I (phone: 23823).

Giovanni Vadalà – Designer clothes for men and women. 189-191 Corso Umberto I (phone: 625163).

Granduca – Pastries made on the premises (and supplied to the sister restaurant next door — see *Eating Out*), elegant surroundings, and breathtaking views make this tea-room a delightful oasis. Closed Mondays. 170 Corso Umberto I (phone: 625446).

Lepezze – Tucked away in the street that winds from Piazza Vittorio Emanuele below the Greek theater, this shop has an excellent selection of ready-to-wear women's clothing. 39 Via Giovanni di Giovanni (phone: 625175).

Maru – For Fendi furs and leathers. 83 Corso Umberto I (phone: 24218).

Mazzullo – Elegant clothing and accessories for men and women. 35 Corso Umberto I (phone: 23152).

Parrucchiere Elle – Taormina's best beauty salon. 99 Corso Umberto I (phone: 23997).

Ritrovo Tamako – A café and pastry shop, known for homemade marzipan in the form of fruits and vegetables, delicious cannoli, praline almonds, and other Sicilian sweets. 141 Corso Umberto I (phone: 24782).

Stefanel – Moderately priced sportswear for men and women. 117 Corso Umberto I (phone: 24886). Across the *corso* at No. 144, *Stefanel* caters to children.

Valentino – Room after lofty room of gracious antiques. Wander into the garden built in the remains of the Naumachiae at the back. 46 Corso Umberto I (phone: 23162).

SPORTS AND FITNESS: Activities here are limited mainly to water sports and tennis. Most major hotels have arrangements with bathing establishments at Mazzarò, Spisone, Isolabella, and Mazzeo; a list is available at the tourist information office.

Horseback Riding – This is an excellent, though slightly pricey, way to explore Mount Etna's strange lava terrain, much as Goethe did. Sturdy beasts depart from Villa Maria near Linguaglossa at 9:30 AM sharp. For rentals, contact *Ippotour Etna* (Località Villa Maria, Piano Ciocche, 6½ miles/11 km) from Linguaglossa on the left turnoff to Mareneve). For further information, contact the Linguaglossa Tourist Office (8 Piazza Annunziata, Linguaglossa; phone: 95-643094).

Skiing – In winter, when tourism and Etna are dormant, the volcano provides 13 miles of slopes at the Linguaglossa pine forest (see *Sicily and the Lipari Islands,* DIRECTIONS, for information).

Tennis – Book a court through the *Taormina Sporting Club Campi Tennis,* Via Bagnoli Crocel (phone: 23282).

Water Skiing – Arrangements can be made with the *Water Ski Club,* Villagonia, Via Nazionale (phone: 52283).

THEATER AND MUSIC: In August a concert and ballet series is offered at the *Teatro Greco* (see *Special Places*). A schedule of performances is usually available from the tourist information office or *Taormina Arte* (Palazzo Congressi) at the beginning of the summer.

NIGHTCLUBS AND NIGHTLIFE: Taormina's classiest nightclub is *Tout Va* (70 Via Luigi Pirandello; phone: 23824), a former gambling casino set in a huge park. It has a restaurant (see *Eating Out*), piano bar, and discotheque. Open daily to 4 AM, June through September, and on weekends year-round. Other nightclubs with live music and dancing are *La Giara* (1 Vico Floresta; phone: 23360; a very good meal can also be had here) and *L'Ombrello* (Piazza Duomo; phone: 23733). For traditional Sicilian music, visit *Grotta Di Ulisse* (3 Salita Dente; phone: 23394). In the evenings, people gather until late either at *Mocambo* (8 Piazza IX Aprile; phone: 23350) or at *Wunderbar Caffè Concerto* (across the piazza; phone: 23502). Both have Belle Epoque salons. Taormina also has a host of pubs. At the *Casanova* (Vico Francesco Paladini, an alley off the *corso;* phone: 23965), young people and music spill out of the interior as the sun goes down, or crowd the painted benches outside the *Sycilian* on nearby Via Amari. A popular late-night discotheque is *Le Perroquet* (Piazza San Domenico; phone: 24808); open daily in summer and weekends only the rest of the year.

BEST IN TOWN

CHECKING IN: Hotels are Taormina's major commercial resource. Usually modern, comfortable, attractive, and well equipped, they are occasionally elegant as well. Service is generally good to excellent. A double room at the one hotel listed as very expensive will run $400 and up; expect to pay between $175 and $300 at hotels rated expensive; around $90 to $175 in a place listed as moderate; and under $90 at those rated as inexpensive. Many hotels encourage guests to take half board; it's worth considering as it usually is a good value. Note that many of the hotels close for several months during the winter. All telephone numbers are in the 942 city code unless otherwise indicated.

San Domenico Palace – A superlative hotel, one of Italy's best, this former 15th-century Dominican monastery has 101 luxurious rooms, lounges, and an assortment of public spaces — including courtyards and hallways — all furnished with antiques, a huge baronial parlor transformed into an elegant bar, some of Taormina's most beautiful gardens, a restaurant, *Les Bougainvilles* (see *Eating Out*), a heated swimming pool, and private beach facilities. (See also *Special Places.*) The service is impeccable. Open year-round. 5 Piazza San Domenico (phone: 23701; fax: 625506). Very expensive.

Grand Albergo Capo Taormina – Right on the beach, this large and modern property offers 207 comfortable rooms, each with an ocean view. There is a beautiful saltwater swimming pool with a vista of Mount Etna, excellent beach facilities, a good restaurant, and bar. Run by the same management as the *San Domenico.* Closed January through *Easter.* 105 Via Nazionale, Capo Taormina, Mazzarò (phone: 24000; fax: 625467). Expensive.

Mazzarò Sea Palace – Luxurious with 81 rooms, and right on the beach, with a good restaurant and a swimming pool. Closed November through March. 147 Via Nazionale, Mazzarò (phone: 24004; fax: 626237). Expensive.

Villa Sant'Andrea – Once the summer home of a British family, this small hotel overlooking the bay has 58 charming rooms, most with sea views, a beautiful terrace restaurant (see *Eating Out*), and a lush private garden. Closed January and February. 137 Via Nazionale, Mazzarò (phone: 23125; fax: 24838). Expensive.

Bristol Park – Elegant, with 50 rooms, a good restaurant, swimming pool, splendid views of the Ionian and Mount Etna, and a private beach. Half board is encouraged. Closed November through February. 92 Via Bagnoli Croce (phone: 23006; fax: 24519). Moderate.

Excelsior Palace – Located at the edge of town by the Porta Catania, this property offers beautiful views of Etna and the hotel's exquisite garden. The 89 rooms are tastefully arranged. There is a low-key atmosphere, a private pool, and a beach. Open year-round. 8 Via Toselli (phone: 23975; fax: 23978). Moderate.

Villa Belvedere – True to its name, this simple hotel offers great views of Mount Etna and the sea. Its 40 rooms are sparely decorated, but comfortable; its swimming pool is set in a tranquil garden. Closed November through *Easter.* 79 Via Bagnoli Croce (phone: 23791; fax: 625830). Moderate.

Villa Paradiso – Small (33 rooms) and centrally located, overlooking the sea, with an excellent restaurant and one of the best views of Mount Etna. Half board is encouraged. Closed November to mid-December. 2 Via Roma (phone: 23922; fax: 625800). Moderate.

Pensione Svizzera – Splendid vistas of the Ionian Sea from most of the 18 rooms in this clean, comfortable property. Some rooms have terraces and all have baths. Lovely garden. Breakfast included. Closed mid-November to mid-December and mid-January to March 1. 26 Via Luigi Pirandello (phone: 23790; fax: 625906). Inexpensive.

Villa Fiorita – This small (24-room) hostelry offers restful stays and magnificent views (many rooms look onto the sea and some have balconies) for a modest price. There is a garden, swimming pool, comfortable lounges, and excellent service in a clean, but somewhat worn, environment. Open year-round. 39 Via Luigi Pirandello (phone: 24122; fax: 625967). Inexpensive.

EATING OUT: Most of the local hotels have their own dining rooms, but don't hesitate to sample the local restaurants as well. These, for the most part, are pleasant, often have lovely views, and can offer better value than comparable restaurants in northern Italy. Whenever possible, try the local specialties, particularly the fish and succulent fresh vegetables such as eggplant, artichokes, and squash. The pasta is delicious. Expect to pay $70 to $100 or more for a meal for two at restaurants categorized as expensive; between $45 to $70 at those listed as moderate; and under $45 at inexpensive restaurants. Prices do not include wine or tip. Generally, restaurants in Taormina are open 7 days a week in summer and take their appointed day off only when the season slumps. All telephone numbers are in the 942 city code unless otherwise indicated.

Les Bougainvilles – In the *San Domenico,* Taormina's most elegant hotel, this dining room has an assortment of refined Sicilian dishes (although the quality is uneven) and elegant decor. Open year-round. Reservations necessary. Major credit cards accepted. 5 Piazza San Domenico (phone: 23701). Expensive.

La Giara – Just a few steps down from the *corso* is this fashionable late-night restaurant and nightclub that is frequented by locals and visitors alike. The menu features both continental and Sicilian fare, all prepared with attention. Excellent Sicilian wines. Closed Mondays. Reservations advised. Major credit cards accepted. 1 Vico Floresta (phone: 23360). Expensive.

Granduca – Opened in 1987, this has quickly become *the* place to be seen and to dine. Smart interiors and lovely views are matched by personal service and the stylish Sicilian cooking of Antonio d'Ambra. Try the *stinco di manzo di Casale* (beef served on the shank) and the dessert crêpes. Closed Mondays except in summer, when dining is alfresco. Reservations advised. Major credit cards accepted. 170 Corso Umberto I (phone: 24420). Expensive.

Oliviero – By the sea, housed in the *Villa Sant'Andrea* hotel, with a lush outdoor terrace and a piano bar. Specialties include crabmeat risotto, grilled mixed fish, filet of beef, and dessert crêpes. Excellent Sicilian wines. Closed January and February. Reservations advised, particularly on weekends. Major credit cards accepted. 137 Via Nazionale, Mazzarò (phone: 23125). Expensive.

Da Lorenzo – Located in the center of town, with a pleasant garden for outdoor dining, it is noted for its fresh fish and traditional Sicilian cuisine, including an excellent *spaghetti alla Norma* (with eggplant). Closed Tuesdays. Reservations advised for parties of more than two people. Major credit cards accepted. 4 Via M. Amari (phone: 23480). Expensive to moderate.

Il Pescatore – Perched above the bay and considered by many to be Taormina's best trattoria. The menu features mainly fish, usually caught in the restaurant's own boat, with very good cannelloni and *risotto alla pescatora* (rice with seafood). Closed Monday afternoons and November through February. Reservations unnecessary. Visa accepted. Via Nazionale, Isolabella (phone: 23460). Expensive to moderate.

Tout Va – A fashionable establishment in a private park, with a piano bar and discotheque, this restaurant serves continental and Italian cuisine. Closed mid-September through May. Reservations advised. Major credit cards accepted. 70 Via Luigi Pirandello (phone: 23824). Expensive to moderate.

La Ginestra – About a 15-minute walk from Taormina's south gate brings you to this restaurant/pizzeria, managed by a retired chef from *Les Bougainvilles.* The menu includes a variety of pizza, tasty pasta specials, and many well-prepared, fresh Sicilian fish and meat dishes. The hearty house wine is made by the management. Closed Wednesdays except in summer. Reservations advised. Visa accepted. Via Crocifisso (phone: 625751). Moderate.

La Botte – This favorite late-night spot serves excellent pizza, a vast assortment of Sicilian appetizers and main courses, and grilled meat and fish, at reasonable prices. Closed Mondays in winter. Reservations advised. Major credit cards accepted. 4 Piazza Santa Domenica (phone: 24198). Moderate to inexpensive.

La Buca – Pleasant outdoor dining on typical Sicilian cuisine — grilled meats and fish, good homemade pasta. Closed Mondays and December. Reservations advised for parties of more than two people. Visa accepted. 140 Corso Umberto I (phone: 24314). Moderate to inexpensive.

La Bussola – An attractive establishment that serves very good food and affords a great view. Closed Wednesdays. Reservations unnecessary. Major credit cards accepted. Via Nazionale, Isolabella (phone: 21276). Moderate to inexpensive.

Il Ficodindia – A beachside eatery featuring pasta with sardines and an excellent entrée of fish simmered in a sauce of capers, tomatoes, and olives. Closed Mondays, January, and February. Reservations unnecessary. Major credit cards accepted. Via Appiano Mazzeo, Letojanni (phone: 36301). Moderate to inexpensive.

Da Giovanni – This bright, family-run restaurant, with a spectacular view of the sea, offers good fish dishes. The enormous fish soup, made with the catch of the day, is a meal in itself. Closed Mondays. Reservations advised weekends and in high season. Major credit cards accepted. Via Nazionale, Isolabella (phone: 23531). Moderate to inexpensive.

Il Maniero – The ambience and food make this a favorite retreat for locals who prefer to head for the hills in high season. Closed Wednesdays. Reservations advised on weekends, especially lunchtime. Major credit cards accepted. Salita Castello, Castel Mola (phone: 28180). Moderate to inexpensive.

Da Antonio – It's never a bad idea to follow the locals, and in Taormina they all come here. The trattoria's strict family interest — mother, father, three sons, and numerous in-laws — and excellent local seafood is why. Try the *risotto alla frutta di mare.* Closed Mondays. Reservations advised on weekends. Major credit cards accepted. Via Crocifisso, along the descent by road to Giardini-Naxos, soon after leaving the Duomo end of the *corso* (phone: 24570). Inexpensive.

Il Barcaiolo – This wonderful local beachfront place produces great food at great prices; hence it has a big following in summer. Closed in winter. Reservations advised in summer. No credit cards accepted. Spiaggia Mazzarò, reached from Via Castellucio (turn off Via Nazionale at the *Atlantis Bay* hotel), then down the steps (phone: 625633). Inexpensive.

TRIESTE

At one time the major port of the Hapsburg Empire, this once-glamorous commercial and cultural center on the Adriatic suffered a steady decline after World War I and today is a city far overshadowed by its past. All but forgotten by the rest of Italy, it is tucked away in the northeasternmost corner of the peninsula, 90 miles (144 km) northeast of Venice and right on the border of Yugoslavia. But if present-day Trieste seems faded compared with the bustling seaport of a century ago, much of its old fascination still lingers.

Tourists find very few of the great monuments, antiquity, and art treasures that are so plentiful in other Italian cities. Trieste's special appeal is its ambience and people, Old World elegance, and interesting mixture of cultures. Triestines say that their city has two souls, one worldly and the other provincial, and the pleasure of a visit lies in experiencing these contrasts. Traces of Trieste's cosmopolitan past are evident in its religious and ethnic diversity, its grand old hotels, the strong Slavic flavor, a richly varied local cuisine, and its Viennese-style cafés. Yet it is essentially a quiet little town, which the Italian Census Bureau has ranked as the most livable in Italy. This distinction hardly qualifies as a major tourist attraction, but it does suggest the easy pace and tranquillity that can make a visitor's stay here so pleasant.

Trieste also boasts a wonderful natural setting, from the beautiful harbor and coastline to the surrounding mountains in the Carso, Trieste's limestone highlands (which include some of the most spectacular caves in Europe). Its handsome examples of 18th- and 19th-century neo-classical architecture are interesting, including the *Teatro Verdi* (the opera house), the old Stock Exchange, the Offices of the Captain of the Port, and the splendid Church of Sant'Antonio. Its magnificent Piazza dell'Unità d'Italia, with one side open to the sea, is unique in Italy, and the lively Piazza Ponte Rosso (see *Extra Special*) has to be one of the most picturesque squares in the world. And no visitor should leave the city without taking a long and leisurely stroll along the seafront.

To understand Trieste is to grasp the sense of loss that permeates the air, creating a nostalgic, somewhat romantic mood. The city still laments the transferral of its environs to Yugoslavia after World War II, and there is a growing sense of isolation from the rest of Italy. Much like the local weather, which can be gloriously sunny in summer but suffers from a cold, sometimes fierce, wind from the north called the bora, the Triestine character is a curious blend of Mediterranean and more northern elements. In casual contact this comes across as exuberance tempered by melancholy.

Trieste's origins go back to Roman times, when it was a small port known as Tergestum. By the Middle Ages it had become an independent municipality that periodically fell under domination by Venice, then the major power in the Adriatic. In 1382, Trieste placed itself under the protection of the

Austro-Hungarian Empire, where it remained for more than 500 years (interrupted briefly when Napoleon's armies occupied the town during the early 1800s). Only after the Hapsburg Emperor Charles VI declared the city a free port in 1719 did Trieste attain real importance. The decree launched the city's fortunes as the empire's major gateway to the world. But it was Charles's daughter, Empress Maria Theresa, who is generally credited with creating modern Trieste. In the mid-18th century the empress enlarged the seaport and revamped the city, laying out a neat grid of streets in the quarter named after her, the Borgo Teresiano, which is still considered the "new" part of town. She improved public education, encouraged local industry, and lifted the constraints that confined Trieste's Jewish community to a ghetto.

The lure of commerce attracted foreign merchants and entrepreneurs from all over the Mediterranean and central Europe. By the mid-1800s, Trieste's population had soared to over 150,000, nearly ten times that of the previous century. The newcomers blended into the city's fabric without losing their distinct identities. This mutual tolerance is evident in the variety of churches in Trieste: Catholic, Protestant, Serbian Orthodox, Waldensian, Anglican, and Methodist. A magnificent synagogue built in 1912 is still active, although the once sizable Jewish community, whose roots in Trieste go back at least 7 centuries, has shrunk to only a few hundred.

By the end of the 19th century, Trieste had become a center of trade, finance, and banking, the birthplace of the modern insurance company, and Austria-Hungary's great emporium for central Europe. A prosperous bourgeoisie built stately homes in the Teresiano quarter, several of which can be visited as museums today. The city also nurtured some great writers, including James Joyce, who lived here with his family from 1904 to 1915, supporting himself by teaching English. Much of his autobiographical novel *A Portrait of the Artist as a Young Man* was written here, as well as parts of his masterpiece *Ulysses.* The local tourist board distributes a small booklet in English that provides a "Joycean" walking tour of the city, pointing out his haunts and homes. One of Joyce's most devoted pupils, the businessman Ettore Schmitz, launched a writing career of his own under the name Italo Svevo and together with fellow Triestine writer Umberto Saba helped launch a new trend in Italian literature. In a letter that looks back at his time in Trieste, Joyce says: "I cannot begin to give you the flavor of the old Austrian Empire. It was a ramshackle affair, but it was charming, gay, and I experienced more kindness in Trieste than ever before or since in my life."

Although Trieste had strong Austrian and Slavic overtones, it remained essentially Italian. In the late 1800s the struggle for union with Italy gained force. The Italian composer Giuseppe Verdi (who created two works for Trieste's opera house) became a symbol of this cause, and disorders usually erupted wherever his music was played. Trieste also had a local martyr, Guglielmo Oberdan, a deserter from the Austrian army who returned to the city with the goal of assassinating Emperor Franz Joseph, but was arrested and executed before he could carry out his plan.

Sadly, unification with Italy in 1918 signaled the city's demise. The new frontier severed Trieste from its German and Slavic hinterland, leaving it, in the words of historian Denis Mack Smith, "a head without a body." World War I seriously damaged the port and local industry, and Trieste never regained the prosperity of its pre-war days. The Nazis occupied it in 1943 and established a concentration camp at an old rice-processing plant outside town (the Risiera di San Sabba has become a memorial to the Resistance and is open to visitors). After the war, the territory bordering Trieste — most of the Istrian Peninsula and the Karst (Carso), predominantly Slovenian — was transferred to Yugoslavia, and in 1947 the city itself, also in dispute, was proclaimed a free territory under United Nations administration. Trieste remained a city without a country for 7 years until it was finally returned to Italy in 1954, along with a sliver of Istrian coast. Ten years later it became the capital of the region known as Friuli–Venezia Giulia.

Today, about a quarter of the city's 140,000 residents are retired (it has the highest per capita pensioner population in the country). Most of the others are involved in Trieste's traditional occupations: banking, insurance (it is the insurance capital of Italy), trade, and import-export. In an effort to attract new business to the city, last year the Italian government granted tax incentives to companies choosing to invest in Trieste. A large Slovenian minority continues to run its own cultural and educational facilities, while the location here of the prestigious International Center for Nuclear Physics has given Trieste a certain stature in the scientific community, too.

As the dividing point between East and West, Trieste is vulnerable to policies on both sides of its frontier. Its port has suffered from the crisis in Italy's steel and shipbuilding industries, and a 1982 travel tax imposed by the Belgrade government all but eliminated the regular influx of Yugoslav shoppers, bringing many Trieste stores to the verge of bankruptcy. After lengthy negotiations, Belgrade lifted the tax, and until the recent civil unrest in their home country, more Yugoslavs were crossing the border to buy blue jeans, coffee, appliances, and machine replacement parts.

Visitors, however, have a hard time perceiving these economic hardships. The city is full of elegant shops and fine restaurants, and Triestines enjoy a comparatively high standard of living. Most important, Trieste's appealing ambience and the echoes of its glorious past are still here for all to savor.

TRIESTE AT-A-GLANCE

SEEING THE CITY: For a spectacular panorama of Trieste, its harbor, coast, and the mountains of Istria, take the No. 2 tram or the No. 4 bus from Piazza Oberdan to the village of Opicina, 1,000 feet above sea level. Get off two stops before the end, at the Obelisco di Opicina. Both the tram and the bus run every 20 minutes. Another good vantage point is the hilltop Castello di San Giusto (see *Special Places*), which can be reached by foot, taxi, or the No. 24 bus. The Molo Audace, a pier that juts out into the harbor near Piazza dell'Unità d'Italia, is a favorite promenade and offers a beautiful view of the city, sea, and hills.

SPECIAL PLACES: Piazza dell'Unità d'Italia is the heart of Trieste and the natural starting point for a walking tour of the city, as most of the major attractions are nearby. To the north of it is the area called Borgo Teresiano, the business, cultural, and commercial center, encompassing Trieste's opera house in Piazza Verdi, the neo-classical palace of the Borsa Vecchia (the former Stock

Exchange) in Piazza della Borsa, and avenues and side streets lined with elegant boutiques, old cafés, and colorful food shops. The district is bisected by the Canal Grande, which once allowed ships to sail right into Piazza Ponte Rosso. To the south of Piazza Unità, the winding streets of the old medieval city lead past the Roman amphitheater and a Roman gateway, the so-called Arco di Riccardo, to the Colle di San Giusto, a hill named after Trieste's patron saint. Perched on top of the hill are the old fortress and the 14th-century church that dominate the town. It's a good walk to the hill (or, better, take bus No. 24 up and walk down), but vehicular transportation is needed to get to Miramare Castle, the most unusual and spectacular of Trieste's sights, as well as to the Grotta Gigante (see *Environs,* below).

CENTER

Piazza dell'Unità d'Italia – A spacious, truly breathtaking square. Enclosed on three sides by stately 19th-century palazzi — the Palazzo Comunale (Town Hall), the Palazzo del Governo (Prefecture), and the building housing the once powerful *Lloyd Triestino* shipping line — the piazza is open to the sea on its west side, which sweeps right up to the Adriatic. By all means, find an outside table at *Caffè degli Specchi* and take it all in.

Castello di San Giusto – This 15th-century castle was built by the Venetians on the site of a Roman fort. Its bastions command a wonderful view of Trieste. In recent decades, the castle has been tastefully restored, and today it houses the city's tourist information office as well as an extensive collection of old arms and armor. The museum is open mornings only and closed Mondays. Admission charge. Piazza della Cattedrale, Colle di San Giusto.

Cattedrale di San Giusto – Dedicated to the city's patron saint, the 14th-century cathedral is a curious amalgam of two earlier churches, from the 5th and 11th centuries, which in turn were built on the site of an ancient Roman temple. The decision to incorporate the previous structures into the new, grander cathedral reflects the characteristic practicality of the Triestines, and the result is a unique but appealing blend of styles. The simple, Romanesque façade is embellished by a Venetian Gothic rose window. The five-nave interior contains some handsome Byzantine mosaics, a 9th-century baptismal font, a 16th-century wooden pietà, and a small collection of holy relics and artworks. Piazza della Cattedrale, Colle di San Giusto (phone: 766956).

Orto Lapidario (Lapidary Garden) – Just downhill from San Giusto, this is one of the most romantic spots in Trieste, with a Byronesque feel to it. Formerly the church's graveyard, it was transformed in the middle of the last century into a stone garden of archaeological finds. Strolling among the ruins one comes across Roman tombstones, fragments of altars, memorial tablets, urns, and other statuary. Off to one side, a neo-classical temple, built in the last century, houses a sculptured monument to the German archaeologist Johann Winckelmann, who was murdered in Trieste in 1768. The garden also contains the *Museo Civico di Storia e d'Arte,* which has a small, eclectic collection of ancient art and artifacts. Of particular interest are Egyptian burial objects and several mummies; Roman jewelry, busts, and urns; pre-Roman bronzes; and an extensive coin and medal exhibit. Open mornings only; closed Mondays. Admission charge. 1 Piazza della Cattedrale (phone: 362531).

Civico Museo Revoltella – The Baron Pasquale Revoltella, a Venetian financial tycoon of the mid-19th century and one of the main financiers of the Suez Canal, bequeathed his palazzo and private art collection to the city. Revoltella specified, however, that his home should also be used as a showcase for contemporary art, and the gallery, reopened after an extensive renovation, now ranks among the best modern art galleries in Italy, with works by Picasso, Braque, and Kokoschka. Of particular interest are the museum's upper floors, which have been maintained as they were in the baron's day. The ornate furnishings and luxurious quarters give a good idea of how affluent families lived in the last century. Open mornings only; closed Mondays. No admission charge. 27 Via Diaz (phone: 302742).

Museo del Mare (Maritime Museum) – This delightful museum, tastefully modernized, contains all kinds of objects that illustrate the history of navigation and fishing. In addition to nautical instruments and maps, there are wonderful scale models of a wide variety of vessels. One room is devoted to Guglielmo Marconi, and upstairs there are superbly crafted three-dimensional scenes depicting various kinds of fishing. Open mornings only; closed Mondays. Admission charge. 1 Via Campo Marzio (phone: 304885).

Museo Morpurgo – The home of a wealthy family has been turned into a museum, complete with original furniture, gilded mirrors, Venetian chandeliers, paintings, and sculpture. Although officially open every morning except Mondays, museum hours are extremely erratic, depending on the availability of its small staff. Visitors have to ring a downstairs doorbell to be admitted. Admission charge. 5 Via Imbriani (phone: 773713).

ENVIRONS

Castello di Miramare (Miramare Castle) – At the tip of a wooded promontory overlooking the Bay of Grignano and surrounded by a magnificent park, this white turreted castle has a past as romantic as its setting. It was built in 1860 for Archduke Maximilian and his wife, Princess Carlotta of Belgium, who spent 3 happy years here before Maximilian was persuaded to take over as Emperor of Mexico. The ill-fated Hapsburg prince was soon executed by the Mexican republican army of Benito Juárez, and his wife went insane. The sumptuous rooms of the castle are maintained exactly as they were when the royal couple was in residence. The throne room, chapel, several parlors, the royal bedrooms, and Maximilian's fine library — all filled with precious furniture, paintings, antique vases, and art objects — are open to the public. Visitors are also free to stroll through the beautiful 55-acre park, which contains a small café. The castle is open mornings year-round; admission charge, except on Sundays. The guided tours in English are a must. On summer evenings, the royal couple's sad tale is told in a dramatic hour-long sound-and-light show. Miramare is about 5 miles (8 km) north of Trieste, a 10-minute taxi ride that costs about $15. An alternative is to take the No. 6 bus from the train station to Barcola, and then change to the No. 36 bus. In summer, transportation to the castle from Trieste is available by boat (phone: 224143).

Grotta Gigante (Giant Grotto) – About 10 miles (16 km) north of Trieste, this enormous cave is the largest natural cavern known today, and it is considered a speleological wonder. The cave has been equipped with stairways and lighting, and there are 45-minute guided tours in English every half hour. There is also a small museum of local archaeological finds. Closed Mondays. Admission charge (phone: 327312). The cave can be reached by the bus or tram to Opicina.

■ **EXTRA SPECIAL:** To fully grasp the special nature of Trieste, every visitor must stroll along the *riva,* its waterfront promenade, and take in the harbor, the ships, the surrounding hills, the fishermen's shops, and the restaurants. This was one of James Joyce's favorite walks, and it has been an inspiration to generations of Trieste writers. The stroll should include a stop at the huge enclosed fish market — the *Grande Pescheria* — on the waterfront just south of Piazza dell'Unità d'Italia. Another must is a visit to Piazza Ponte Rosso. The Grand Canal that bisects this unusual square was dug in the 18th century to allow trading ships to sail into the business district. Today it serves as a dock for pleasure craft. But the piazza is still a lively center of commerce, with outdoor food and flower markets, and numerous clothing stalls frequented primarily by Yugoslav shoppers. Rising like an ancient

Greek temple at its far end is the Church of Sant'Antonio, one of Trieste's most striking neo-classical monuments.

Some 7 miles (11 km) southwest of the city (about a 20-minute ride by car or the No. 20 bus), the tiny fishing village of Muggia is well worth a visit. This jewel of a harbor, once part of the Republic of Venice, is virtually unknown to tourists and, indeed, to most Italians outside Trieste. It has a miniature main square with an exquisite 13th-century cathedral. There are several excellent seafood restaurants, which make this a perfect lunchtime excursion. Its *Carnevale* celebration is famous throughout Italy (see *Special Events*).

Nine miles (14 km) east of Trieste is the small village of Monrupino, worth the 10-minute taxi ride from the city's center. The village is dominated by the Rocca di Monrupino, a castle built by local inhabitants in 1300 to defend themselves against Turkish incursions. The castle offers an extraordinary panorama of the spectacular Carso region. At the end of August in even-numbered years, the village's Slovenian population hosts the *Nozze Carsiche* (Weddings of the Carso), 4 days of dancing, merrymaking, and other costumed festivities.

SOURCES AND RESOURCES

TOURIST INFORMATION: General tourist information is available at Trieste's Azienda Autonoma di Soggiorno e Turismo, which has its main office inside the Castello di San Giusto (phone: 309298 or 309242). Travelers can cross into Yugoslavia by bus, train, boat, or car. Tourist visas are issued at the border for a nominal fee. For fares and schedules, inquire at the tourist information office, at the Trieste bus terminal (11 Piazza Libertà; phone: 368804), near the central railroad station, or at the Opicina train station (phone: 211682). For other train information, contact Trieste's main railway station (8 Piazza Libertà; phone: 418207).

The US Consulate (42 Via dei Pellegrini; phone: 911784) is open Mondays, Wednesdays, and Fridays only, 10 AM to noon.

Local Coverage – The tourist office publishes an excellent free guide, *Discovering Trieste,* written in English and listing museums, special events, theater and concert halls, and day excursions. Hotels have information about evening activities. The local Italian-language daily newpaper is *Il Piccolo.*

TELEPHONE: The city code for Trieste is 40. When calling from within Italy, dial 040 before the local number.

GETTING AROUND: The city is small, and most of the main points of interest are easily accessible on foot.

Airports – Trieste's airport, Ronchi dei Legionari (phone: 481-7731), is 20 miles (32 km) northwest of the city and served by domestic flights only. An airport bus operates between the airport and the central railroad station on Viale Miramare. The nearest international airport is Venice's Marco Polo.

Bus – Service is good within the city and to nearby points of interest. Tickets are sold at newsstands and tobacconists and must be purchased before boarding.

Car Rental – *Hertz* (1 Via Mazzini; phone: 777600); *Avis* (12 San Nicolò; phone: 777085); *Eurodollar* (at the airport; phone: 481-779866); *Europcar* (at the airport; phone: 481-778920); and *Maggiore* (2 Viale Miramare; phone: 421323).

Taxi – Taxis are quite expensive, but given the city's small size, rides to the most likely tourist spots should be less than $15. There are numerous cabstands, and two 24-hour taxi services: *Taxi Radio Trieste* (phone: 307730) and *Radio Taxi* (phone: 54533).

Train – Stazione Trieste Centrale is at 8 Piazza Libertà (phone: 418207).

SPECIAL EVENTS: Each February, on or near *Pentecost Sunday,* the nearby fishing port of Muggia (about a 20-minute car ride from Trieste) holds a colorful *Carnevale,* with huge floats (the whole city participates in building them) and costumed parades through the town. Trieste's annual *International Trade Fair* is held the last 2 weeks in June. From July through mid-August, a popular *Festival dell'Operetta* takes place at the *Teatro Stabile–Politeama Rossetti.* Other summer events include outdoor concerts, ballets, and plays at the *Castello di San Giusto;* classical drama performances amid the ruins of the *Teatro Romano;* and evening sound-and-light shows at *Miramare Castle.* Every September, the *Settembre Musicale* festival features classical concerts by first-rate guest musicians and ensembles in the city's churches.

MUSEUMS: The museums of most interest to visitors are discussed in *Special Places.* But time permitting, several others are worth a visit. Unless otherwise indicated, they are open mornings only and closed Mondays.

Acquario Marino – A public aquarium on the waterfront with a wide variety of Adriatic marine life. 1 Riva Nazario Sauro (phone: 306201).

Museo del Risorgimento – A small collection of artifacts and paintings illustrating Trieste's struggle to become part of Italy. 4 Via XXIV Maggio (phone: 361675).

Museo Teatrale (Theater Museum) – Housed in the *Teatro Verdi,* this small museum contains several thousand old librettos, manuscripts, books, and photographs related to opera, and a fine collection of musical instruments. Open during intermissions and Tuesday and Thursday mornings. 1 Piazza Verdi (phone: 366636).

SHOPPING: Trieste is less a shopper's paradise than Milan or Rome, but it has a fine selection of the designer clothes, sportswear, shoes, and leather goods for which Italy is famous. It is also an easy and extremely pleasant place to shop. Most of the best boutiques are concentrated in the area from Piazza della Borsa to Piazza Goldoni, including the main avenue Corso Italia, the elegant 19th-century *Galleria Tergesteo* shopping arcade (on the Piazza della Borsa), and numerous side streets. An added attraction are the nautical shops that line the waterfront, selling boating accessories and clothing. Two hidden alleyways (Via del Ponte and Via delle Beccherie) behind Piazza dell'Unità d'Italia are lined with antiques shops and old curio shops — a kind of mini–flea market — that are great for browsing and for some good buys. If you want to check out the blue jeans that bring Yugoslav shoppers to Trieste, stop by Piazza Ponte Rosso any morning. It's also the best place to buy fresh fruit and vegetables. Although Trieste is not particularly known for handicrafts, a few bottles of the excellent wines produced in the region make a worthwhile purchase. In addition to the shops listed below, *Gucci* (21 Corso Italia) and *Fendi* (1 Capo di Piazza) are also represented in Trieste. Shop hours are 8:30 AM to 1 PM and 3:30 to 7:30 PM (7 PM in winter). Most are closed Monday mornings.

Ambassador – Wide selection of designer clothes (including Armani, Missoni, and Valentino) for men. 3 Piazza della Borsa (phone: 366500).

Beltrame – A large store for the whole family, selling casual and designer clothes, coats, and furs. 25 Corso Italia (phone: 62648).

La Bomboniera – This tiny, 120-year-old, jewel of a sweets shop has etched glass doors, carved walnut shelves, and an original Bohemian glass chandelier. It sells pastries and beautifully wrapped chocolates. 3 Via XXX Ottobre (phone: 62752).

Christine Pelletterie – Fine leather clothes, shoes, and accessories for men and women. 15 Piazza della Borsa (phone: 366212).

Coin – A good, general-purpose department store. 16 Corso Italia (phone: 61431).

Max Mara – Fine sportswear for women at significantly less than what this fashionable label costs in the US. 23 Via Carducci (phone: 631334).

Le Monde – Trendy fashions for men and women. 1 Passo San Giovanni (phone: 62237).

Spangher – This large, slickly modern waterfront shop sells the latest in nautical equipment and elegant sailing clothes, shoes (including designer rubber boots), and accessories. 8 Riva Gulli (phone: 305158).

Stefanel – A *Benetton*-type chain with a lively selection of moderately priced sweaters and slacks for both sexes. Corso Italia (phone: 61659).

Trussardi – Elegant sportswear and accessories for men and women by the well-known Milanese designer. 27 Via San Nicolò (phone: 68087).

Vecchia Europa – A tasteful selection of antique objects, art, furniture, and jewelry. 1/C Via Armando Diaz (phone: 366852).

V. Zandegiacomo – Elegant smoking and grooming articles for men, and quality silver, china, and glassware. 1 Corso Italia (phone: 60974).

SPORTS AND FITNESS: The tourist office (inside Castello di San Giusto; phone: 309298 or 309242) has information on sports facilities in the city.

Golf – The *Golf Club Trieste* (80 Padriciano; phone: 226159) has an 18-hole course about 4 miles (6 km; 20 minutes) from the city center. Closed Tuesdays.

Horse Racing – Trotting races are run Wednesdays and Sundays at the *Ippodromo di Montebello,* 4 Piazzale de Gasperi (phone: 393176 or 947100).

Sailing – In the summer, sailboats can be rented at *Società Triestina della Vela* (8 Pontile Istria; phone: 305999) and at *Società Triestina Sport del Mare* (1/D Molo Venezia; phone: 303580).

Soccer – From September to May, *Triestina* plays at *Stadio Comunale Grezar,* 2 Via Macelli (phone: 812210).

Swimming – There's an indoor municipal pool (3 Riva Gulli; phone: 367816). The Trieste coastline is dotted with rocky beaches (the ones in Muggia and the resort town of Barcola are particularly nice), several of which have water sport facilities in the summer.

Tennis – Courts can be booked by the hour at *Tennis Club Park Hotel Obelisco* (1 Via Nazionale, Opicina; phone: 212756), and at the *Tennis Club Triestino* (Padriciano; phone: 226179).

THEATER: The *Teatro Stabile–Politeama Rossetti* (45 Viale XX Settembre; phone: 567201) is Trieste's major theater for top national productions. *Teatro Cristallo* (also known as *Teatro Popolare la Contrade,* 12 Via Ghirlandaio; phone: 948471) offers a mixture of avant-garde and traditional theater by repertory groups from all over Italy. Plays for the local Slovene community are staged at the *Teatro Sloveno* (4 Via Petronio; phone: 734265).

MUSIC: Trieste is a music-loving city, with classical concerts year-round. But its major attraction is the beautiful 19th-century opera house *Teatro Comunale Giuseppe Verdi* (1 Piazza Verdi; phone: 367816), similar to Milan's *La Scala* and one of the best run in Italy. The opera season lasts from mid-October through April. Concerts and other musical events are held at the *Conservatorio Tartini* (12 Via Ghega; phone: 363508), and at the *Teatro Cristallo* (12 Via Ghirlandaio; phone: 948471).

NIGHTCLUBS AND NIGHTLIFE: Despite its cosmopolitan aspects, Trieste is still a town that closes down rather early in the evening. But it does have its pockets of after-hours vitality. The hot discotheque is *Il Mandracchio* (1 Passo di Piazza; phone: 64464). Other good discos are *Big Ben* (285 Viale Miramare, about 5 miles (8 km) outside the city in Barcola; phone: 421452) and *Nepenthes* (67 Duino, near the airport; phone: 208607). The *Bottega del Vino* (phone: 309750), an elegant piano bar and restaurant occupying the former stables of the Castello di San Giusto, offers romantic dining and dancing until 1 AM, except Tuesdays (see *Eating Out*). Another popular late-night restaurant is the stylish *Elefante Bianco* (on the waterfront near Piazza dell'Unità d'Italia, at 3 Riva Tre Novembre; phone: 60889).

BEST IN TOWN

CHECKING IN: For a small city, Trieste has a surprisingly varied selection of hotels, some of which recall its glamorous past. As it is still relatively undiscovered by foreign tourists, local prices are quite reasonable. The best hotels in town, listed as expensive, cost up to about $200 for a double room. Hotels in the moderate category charge $60 to $90 for a double; inexpensive ones, $60 or less. The hotels listed below as moderate and inexpensive do not have air conditioning, but keep in mind that summers are rarely very hot here. All telephone numbers are in the 40 city code unless otherwise indicated.

Duchi d'Aosta – Small and truly elegant, with an ideal location right on Piazza dell'Unità d'Italia. Built in the late 19th century, the 52 rooms have been tastefully modernized and equipped with air conditioning, television sets, and a small refrigerator bar. Exquisite decor and friendly service (the hotel is part of the prestigious CIGA chain) make it a jewel of a place to stay. Ask for a corner room looking out at the square and the waterfront. The ground-floor *Harry's Bar* offers an intimate setting for cocktails, and the adjoining *Grill Room* (see *Eating Out*) is one of the city's finest restaurants. 2 Piazza dell'Unità d'Italia (phone: 7351). Expensive.

Jolly Cavour – Near the station, this 274-room, modern efficient hotel is part of a national chain that caters mainly to businesspeople. It lacks the special character and decor of the other good accommodations, and be aware that service tends to be impersonal. 7 Corso Cavour (phone: 7694). Expensive.

Savoia Excelsior Palace – Some critics claim the modernization of this grand old hotel overlooking the waterfront has destroyed its Old World elegance, but guests will find the rooms more comfortable and equipped with all the amenities. Nostalgic patrons can still find some of the former ambience in the spacious lobby. Many of the 150 rooms (including several suites and apartments) have wonderful views. There is also a restaurant and piano bar. 4 Riva Mandracchio (phone: 7690). Expensive.

Abbazia – This renovated small hostelry near the train station is nicely decorated for its genre. Most of the 21 rooms have private baths. It seems to be a favorite of Italian businesspeople. 20 Via della Geppa (phone: 369464). Moderate.

Colombia – The pick of properties in the moderate-priced category. A real value, with 40 modern, carpeted rooms and tiled baths, an attractive lobby and bar, and a particularly nice concierge. It's near the train station. 18 Via della Geppa (phone: 369191). Moderate.

Continentale – Pleasant and small, opposite a house where James Joyce once lived, on a quiet side street in the center of town. Rooms are spacious and very clean, and about 20 of the 53 have baths. There's a bar and a small breakfast room. 25 Via San Nicolò (phone: 65444). Moderate.

Al Teatro – An old-fashioned hotel near the opera and thus popular with musicians. The rooms are simple but comfortable, some with wood parquet floors. Only 12 of the doubles have private baths. 1 Capo di Piazza (phone: 366220). Inexpensive.

EATING OUT: Trieste's cuisine is a hearty blend of northern Italian and middle-European cooking, and it offers a wide variety of characteristic dishes. As might be expected in a port city, the fish is superb, and there are plenty of fine seafood restaurants. But pork, beef, veal, and venison are also local specialties. One pleasant Triestine tradition that's especially convenient for visitors is the informal "buffet," which offers home-cooked meals that are consumed with beer or wine at stand-up counters (some have stools) or at small tables. Buffets offer the best sausages, ham, and salami, in addition to such typical dishes as goulash, *tafelspitz* (tender cuts of boiled beef), and *jota,* a thick bean soup with sauerkraut, served at room temperature. Trieste has the added advantage of being in good wine producing country. Excellent regional wines include pinot grigio, tocai, and merlot. Beer is also extremely popular; in addition to the full range of Italian brands, there are plenty of imports from Germany and Austria. Desserts are decidedly Austro-Hungarian in origin: rich cakes and strudels, coffee rings, and sacher tortes. Among the restaurants listed, expect to pay $50 to $70 and up for a three-course meal for two without wine at restaurants categorized as expensive; $35 to $45 at moderately priced restaurants; and under $30 at inexpensive ones. All telephone numbers are in the 40 city code unless otherwise indicated.

Antica Trattoria Suban – A well-known restaurant in a country house a few miles from the center of town, it has been in the same family for over 100 years. It has a lively, elegantly rustic atmosphere and an excellent menu and wine list. Try the *crespelle al radicchio rosso* (crêpes with grilled radicchio) or the crêpes with basil and cream sauce as an appetizer, followed by one of the superb steak or veal dishes. This is regional cooking at its best. Closed Monday lunch, Tuesdays, and during August. Reservations advised. Major credit cards accepted. 2 Via Comici (phone: 54368). Expensive.

Grill Room – This elegant hotel restaurant once belonged to the Cipriani family that runs the famous *Harry's Bar* in Venice. The current owners have maintained its Old World charm and offer a refined cuisine of regional and international inspiration. The filet mignon is excellent, and there is a good selection of pasta and fish dishes. More indulgent diners might want to try some beluga caviar at about $120 per portion, but there are other appealing appetizers that cost considerably less. Open daily. Reservations advised. Major credit cards accepted. *Hotel Duchi d'Aosta,* 2 Via dell'Orologio (phone: 7351). Expensive.

Marinella – A pleasant, 10-minute walk from Miramare Castle, this huge restaurant on the sea has a beautiful view of the coast and excellent seafood. The risotto with scampi is particularly good. Closed Sunday evenings and Mondays. Reservations advised. Major credit cards accepted. 323 Viale Miramare, Barcola (phone: 410986). Expensive.

La Bottega del Vino – This medieval-style restaurant is actually inside the Castello di San Giusto, with superb views of the city. The chef specializes in meat cooked over a charcoal fire. One part of the restaurant is given over to wine tasting. Closed Tuesdays. Reservations unnecessary. Visa accepted. 3 Piazza Cattedrale (phone: 309142). Moderate.

Al Bragozzo – Fish is the specialty of this cheerful, wood-paneled restaurant along the waterfront. Customers can help themselves to a wide variety of fish antipasti and choose their main dish from the fresh catch of the day. The homemade *ravioli Miramare,* stuffed with shrimp, salmon, and heavy cream, is not to be missed. Closed Mondays. Reservations unnecessary. No credit cards accepted. 22 Riva Nazario Sauro (phone: 303001). Moderate.

Buffet Benedetto – One of the best buffets in town, it also has ample room for sit-down dining, and its homey, wood-paneled decor, much like an Alpine tavern, is nicely complemented by the friendly service. This is a place for hearty meat and potato dishes such as goulash and *stinco di maiale* (roast shank of pork), and it also serves excellent gnocchi, with a meat or cheese sauce. For quicker, stand-up meals, the buffet offers a tantalizing array of salamis, cold meats, and salads. Try the exquisite marrons glacés (candied chestnuts) made fresh every day, for dessert. Closed Mondays and during August. Reservations unnecessary. No credit cards accepted. 19 Via XXX Ottobre (phone: 61655 or 62964). Moderate.

Elefante Bianco – This excellent restaurant's menu has a distinctly Central European flavor. Interesting specialties include *gamberoni all'arancia* (shrimps cooked in an orange sauce) and *costate di cervo gratinate* (ribs of venison served au gratin). There's also a tempting selection of homemade desserts. Closed Sundays. Reservations advised. Major credit cards accepted. Riva III Novembre (phone: 60889). Moderate.

Ai Fiori – Traditional food with a touch of fantasy is served in a charming and intimate setting. The menu changes daily, but the focus remains finely prepared fish and pasta dishes. Try the artichoke soup or the exquisite risotto made with oysters and champagne. Closed Sunday evenings, Mondays, *Christmas* through *New Year's Day,* and mid-June to mid-August. Reservations advised. Major credit cards accepted. 7 Piazza Hortis (phone: 300633). Moderate.

Le Giarre – The former *All'Adriatico da Camillo,* once a family-style trattoria, has been transformed into a much more sophisticated eatery. It boasts an impressive wine list and an ambitious menu that changes daily. Fish is the specialty, and the chef prepares it with flair. When it's offered, the *spaghetti con granchi* (spaghetti with crabmeat) is hard to beat. Closed Sunday evenings and Mondays. Reservations advised. Major credit cards accepted. 7 Via San Lazzaro (phone: 65680). Moderate.

Al Granzo – A favorite seafood place, with a waterfront terrace overlooking the huge, enclosed fish market. Specialties include spaghetti with crabmeat, fish soup, and a delicate seafood risotto, as well as delicious homemade desserts — particularly the chocolate cream pastry called *rigojanci,* a local specialty of Hungarian origin. Owners Dario and Tullio, who both speak English, are exuberant hosts. Closed Wednesdays. Reservations advised. Major credit cards accepted. 7 Piazza Venezia (phone: 306788). Moderate.

Nastro Azzurro – A popular lunch spot for businesspeople, and considered one of the best seafood restaurants in town. It consists of one large room with brass chandeliers and a sumptuous display of shellfish appetizers, the catches of the day, and rich desserts. Fish is prepared in every way possible and also appears in delicious pasta and risotto dishes. Closed Saturday evenings and Sundays. Reservations advised. Major credit cards accepted. 10 Riva Nazario Sauro (phone: 305789). Moderate.

Sacra Osteria – Housed in a former inn where a Hapsburg prince once slept, this landmark restaurant, a block from the sea, has the feel of an old tavern that has been tastefully modernized. Open all day for drinks and cold-cut snacks, the restaurant has a fine menu of fish and meat dishes, a legendary homemade sacher torte, and an exceptional wine list. Meals are served until midnight, and there is a pleasant outdoor garden for summer dining. Closed Mondays. Reservations advised. Major credit cards accepted. 13 Via Campo Marzio (phone: 304791). Moderate.

Da Ciano e Maria – Excellent home cooking in a friendly atmosphere, at very reasonable prices. Highly recommended are the *pappardelle con lepre* (homemade noodles with a rich hare sauce) and the gnocchi with game sauce. Good local wine from the barrel. Closed Wednesdays. Reservations unnecessary. No credit cards accepted. Località San Giuseppe della Chiusa (phone: 823285). Moderate to inexpensive.

Buffet Borsa – A popular lunchtime spot for downtown shoppers and office workers eating on the run. The fare consists of good goulash, sandwiches, and grilled meat. It's friendly but tiny — just a few tables and some counters with stools. Closed Sundays. Reservations unnecessary. No credit cards accepted. 2 Via Cassa di Risparmio (phone: 630165). Inexpensive.

La Cantina Sociale – Another good seafood restaurant, with a down-to-earth style and extremely reasonable prices. The house specialty is a very good *zuppa di pesce* (fish soup). Reservations unnecessary. Closed Tuesdays. No credit cards accepted. 18 Riva Nazario Sauro (phone: 300689). Inexpensive.

Siora Rosa – This small, lively neighborhood buffet has a cozy atmosphere and an irresistible aroma wafting from its kitchen. The food is genuine Triestine fare: roast pork, *cotechino* (a kind of cooked salami), hot boiled ham with horseradish, and liver with onions. This is a good place to try *jota* soup, and for a light lunch there are sandwiches and salads. Closed Saturday evenings and Sundays. Reservations unnecessary. No credit cards accepted. 6 Piazza Hortis (phone: 301460). Inexpensive.

Trieste Pick – Trieste's most famous buffet and a favorite with the locals, who come here to sample this spot's main fare — pork. It is cooked in every way imaginable, served with *crauti* (sauerkraut) and washed down with jugs of wine or beer. It's good fun, if you don't mind the crowded tables, and a very good value. Closed Sundays and the last 2 weeks of July. Reservations unnecessary. No credit cards accepted. 3 Via della Cassa di Risparmio (phone: 366858). Inexpensive.

CAFÉS AND BARS: The coffeehouse tradition is an important part of Trieste life, and there are several historic cafés in which to enjoy a leisurely coffee or light snack. When ordering, keep in mind that, here, cappuccino means an espresso in a small cup with a bit of steamed milk. For the standard large cup of cappuccino served in the rest of Italy, ask for a *caffè latte.* The 155-year-old *Caffè degli Specchi* (in Piazza dell'Unità d'Italia) was modernized in the 1960s and remains the fashionable meeting place. Its splendid outdoor setting makes it the best place to see and be seen while sipping an *aperitivo* or savoring a gelato. It's open until 11:30 PM daily, except Mondays. For true Old World atmosphere, nothing beats the recently restored *Caffè San Marco* (18 Via Cesare Battisti), two cavernous rooms with high ceilings, black wrought-iron lamps, golden wall friezes, and red marble tables where regulars play cards or read newspapers all day. Writers Italo Svevo and Umberto Saba used to come here. Linger for hours over a cup of coffee or toasted sandwich any day except Wednesdays, from 7:30 AM until midnight. Unfortunately, there are no notable pastries other than a large jam-filled cookie. The elegant *Bar Tergesteo* (in the *Galleria Tergesteo* shopping arcade, 15 Piazza della Borsa) has antique wooden tables and glittering Venetian crystal chandeliers. It's a good spot for a light snack or pastry, or a late drink after the opera. Open daily, except Mondays, from 7:30 AM to 11:30 PM.

TURIN

Turin (Torino) is one of the richest cities in Italy — and any Italian will tell you why: The Turinese simply work harder than most of their compatriots. This should not give the visitor the idea that Turin is an all work and no play industrial city. Far from it. A stroll down Turin's main shopping street, Via Roma, proves that the inhabitants are blessed with excellent taste and the means to indulge it. Block after block on Via Roma — and elsewhere in the city — features luxury shops selling everything from the latest fashions to antique treasures.

It is obvious that the almost 1 million Turinese work hard to enjoy the fruits of their labors. But to be entirely honest, the people of Turin do tend to go to bed a little earlier than in the rest of Italy — the dinner hour begins closer to seven o'clock than to eight; many restaurants close by ten — but the locals seem to feel that this is a small price to pay for the rewards their labors afford them.

Still, the favorite image the Turinese present to the rest of the country is one of hardworking sobriety, though this is not quite accurate. In fact, there seems to be a curious dichotomy at work in this city — a second face carefully concealed from outsiders. For example: the vast wealth of Turin derives from the massive heavy industrial projects that ring the city, notably the enormous plants producing Italy's low-priced Fiat automobiles; yet Turin is also home to the finest names in automotive haute couture, car designers like Bertone, Pininfarina, and Giugiaro — names that quicken the pulse of car buffs the world over. The Turinese are not famous for being big drinkers, yet they have invented some of the best-known drinks in the world: Martini, Cinzano, and Carpano vermouths were invented and are still made in Turin. Turinese cuisine is elaborate and delicious; fanciful pastries and sweet, sweet chocolate concoctions are prized, yet Turin is the proud birthplace of the simple *grissino* — the breadstick.

Perhaps the oddest example of Turin's split personality is that the city is the undisputed capital of black magic in Italy. These same no-nonsense Turinese who seem so down-to-earth and efficient by day are dedicated followers of their horoscopes. The more superstitious regularly seek out the wisdom of fortunetellers and soothsayers, known as *maghi* and *chiromanti.* If they are in need of some serious black magic, they might go in search of a *stregone* who will cast a spell — for a healthy fee. Practitioners of the black arts are not hard to find. They advertise in newspapers, there are several pages of them in the Turin yellow pages, and they even operate on the streets. The various first class exorcists who are said to make Turin their base are harder to find — presumably they will contact you. Native-born Turinese claim that none of this necromancy is homegrown but rather that it was imported by the suspicious southerners who came north in droves after the war to work in the newly rebuilt car factories. Nevertheless, a certain portion of the native Turinese have also taken to the occult in a big way.

Turin's roots lie deep in history. Conveniently placed on the banks of the Po River, the original city was laid out as a garrison town for the Romans who were working their way north in their ultimate conquest of Gaul. These ancient founders have left a notable legacy. The grid street pattern still visible today was laid out by the Romans. Successive rulers of the city saw no need to alter it — in fact, they added to it.

The Roman heritage of the city notwithstanding, it is impossible to divorce the history of Turin from a great noble family, the House of Savoy. This aristocratic clan, possessed of a lineage longer, it is said, than that of any other nobility in Europe, made Turin the capital of its vast duchy in the 11th century. Over a span of 9 centuries, the citizens of Turin saw their fortunes soar under such enlightened rulers as Charles Emmanuel III and at times sink to sickening depths as their city was threatened by many enemies. For every enlightened Savoyard ruler, however, there seemed to be a dozen soldier-dukes. The history of Turin is, therefore, a martial rather than a cultural one.

Twice in its history Turin experienced lengthy and severe sieges at the hands of the French. Both sieges lasted months, yet at neither time was the city taken (once the French were turned back by the heroism of a single man; see *Pietro Micca Museum,* in *Museums*). From their strong capital, the House of Savoy spent much of their tenure conquering additional territory (they acquired the kingdom of Sardinia in the 18th century) or repulsing invaders. Charles Albert of Savoy expelled the Austrians from his lands in the early 19th century, although Turin did fall (like the rest of northern Italy) to the armies of Napoleon in 1798.

But Turin and the House of Savoy had a greater role to play in the destiny of nations. It was here that the first murmurs of the new Italian state — a unified Italy — were heard. The able and intelligent Victor Emmanuel II and his wise, if rather cold, prime minister, Count Camillo Cavour, became the chief movers and shakers of Italian unity. If Garibaldi can be considered the George Washington of Italian independence, then Cavour was its Thomas Jefferson. Cavour enlisted the aid of the French in a war against Austria (which was the major impediment to Italian unity) and, following two stunning victories at Magenta and Solferino (battles said to have been so bloody that the blood-soaked earth gave their names to dark red pigments on a painter's palette), broke the power of foreign interventionists in Italy. By 1861 the kingdom of Italy had been proclaimed, with Turin as its capital. In 1870 Rome was given that honor, but the king who ruled in Rome was Turinese, Vittorio Emanuele II of the House of Savoy.

The dynamic struggles for independence did not leave Turin spent, doomed to look back on the good old days forever. The Piedmontese faction was a power with which to reckon in Rome — a Turin-born son of the new kingdom would always have a voice in the running of the country. But more important, Turin rapidly caught up with its European economic rivals, whose industrial revolutions had a 2-decade start on Italy's. Fiat and, later, Lancia were the leaders of this industrialization. It was the influx of workers to a traditionally independent-minded town that made Turin sit rather uneasily with fascism.

Through the fascist period anti-fascist cells were at work in the city; when, in 1943, the Germans assumed control of northern Italy, open warfare broke out between partisan bands and the Nazis in and around the city. In addition, there were almost daily air attacks by the Allied air forces.

Yet the city survived and ultimately prospered. It was the cornerstone of the Italian Economic Miracle that followed World War II, and it became the center of modern Italian writing. First published out of Turin were such important authors as Italo Calvino (*If on a Winter's Night a Traveller*), Primo Levi (*The Truce, Survival in Auschwitz, The Periodic Table*), and Cesare Pavese (*The Good Summer*).

It's an old joke in Italy: "If the government needs more money, we'll just make them work harder in Turin." It might be true, but the rest of the country can be sure that the "somber," high-living, superstitious, well-fed Turinese will do their part — and keep the lion's share for themselves.

TURIN AT-A-GLANCE

SEEING THE CITY: In the heart of the city is the dramatic and rather oddly designed tower of the Mole Antonelliana. It is some 500 feet high, and the viewing platform at the 275-foot mark provides a commanding view of the city and the Alps beyond. Begun by Alessandro Antonelli in 1863 as part of Turin's synagogue, the congregation that commissioned it objected to its unorthodox design (it looks like a cross between a very large greenhouse and a very thin pagoda), leaving it to the city to either demolish or finish it. It was completed in 1897. An elevator takes visitors to the base of the spire. Open daily, except Mondays, from 9 AM to 7 PM. Admission charge. 20 Via Montebello (phone: 839-8314).

A magical nocturnal view of the city is available from the terrace of the Convento dei Cappuccini, situated on the far bank of the Po. (Cross the river at Ponte Vittorio Emanuele I and follow signs for Via M. Giardino.)

SPECIAL PLACES: Piazza San Carlo is the heart of this busy town, and the square itself is an impressive architectural unity, incorporating the twin churches of Santa Cristina and San Carlo, which frame Via Roma. The equestrian statue dominating the square is of Emanuele Filiberto, the first of the House of Savoy to make Turin a capital. Elegant shops front the square, particularly some fine antiques shops and antiquarian bookshops. Weather permitting, the cafés that ring the square put out tables and chairs for their customers. Piazza San Carlo is *the* place to sip one of Turin's famous *aperitivi* and feel the vibrant city bustling all around. Not far away is the smaller, quieter Piazza Carignano. Packed into this tranquil square are some of Turin's best-known sights: the massive baroque Palazzo Carignano, home of the first Italian parliament, and the Academy of Sciences, which houses the world-famous Egyptian collection. There is also the ancient and venerable *Cambio* restaurant (see *Eating Out*), a favorite haunt of Cavour. (Most of the places noted here are in the city center, an area flanked on the south by Corso Vittorio Emanuele, on the east by Corso Inghilterra, on the north by Corso Regina Margherita, and on the west by the Po River. Many sites are within walking distance of each other.)

Cappella della Santa Sindone (Chapel of the Holy Shroud) – Within the 15th-century Duomo di San Giovanni (Saint John's Cathedral) is the chapel containing

Turin's most famous possession, the Holy Shroud. Behind the apse stands the awesome black marble chapel of the *santissima sindone.* On the altar is a black marble urn containing the Holy Shroud, in which it is said the body of Christ was wrapped following his crucifixion. The shroud has not always been in Turin. Although specifically mentioned in the Gospel of Matthew, no trace of cloth was known until it turned up in Cyprus centuries after Christ's death. From Cyprus it traveled to France, where it is thought to have been acquired by the Savoys in 1578. The sheet, rarely exhibited, does show the features of a man who suffered crucifixion — specifically in the manner described in the Gospels. While millions believe the features to be those of Christ, the Vatican has been reluctant to acknowledge them as such. The church, however, treats the shroud as a holy relic, and belief in its validity has been enhanced since the present pope agreed to accept the shroud as a gift from the Archbishop of Turin to the Holy See. Tests have been performed on the cloth, and some say there is evidence to suggest that the cloth is of the correct age (early 1st century) and that its origins are in the Middle East. But tests of the cloth conducted at Oxford University in England in 1988 place its date of origin at about 1350. As for the imprint of the man on the cloth itself, how and when it appeared, dozens of theories exist (none is irrefutably supported by scientific data). Although technically belonging to the Vatican, the shroud will always remain in Turin. It is kept in a silver casket, within an iron box enclosed in the marble urn on display. The only two keys are held by the Archbishop of Turin and the Palatine Cardinals, the group of senior churchmen based permanently at the Vatican. A large reproduction of the shroud, itself shown to the public on very rare occasions, stands in the chapel (which currently is undergoing renovation). Open daily, except Mondays and Sunday and holiday afternoons, from 7 AM to noon and 3 to 6 PM. Piazza San Giovanni (phone: 436-6101).

Palazzo dell'Accademia delle Scienze (Academy of Sciences) – A 17th-century palace designed by Guarino Guarini houses the two collections which follow. Admission charge. 6 Via Accademia delle Scienze.

Museo Egizio (Egyptian Museum) – It is said that Turin's collection of Egyptian artifacts is second only to that of the *National Museum* in Cairo. By far the most exciting exhibit in the museum is the entire Temple of Ellessya (dating from 15 BC). The presentation of this stone temple to the museum was a reward for the museum's work in saving ancient sites lost forever by the building of the Aswan High Dam (which created Lake Nasser, submerging hundreds of square miles in Upper Egypt). Overall, the museum includes precious and rare objects dating from the earliest civilization in Egypt to the full flowering of its culture in the 17th and 18th Dynasties. Open daily except Mondays and holidays from 9 AM to 2 PM (phone: 537581).

Galleria Sabauda (Savoy Gallery) – The gallery houses a fine collection of Flemish and Dutch paintings, including works by Van Eyck, Memling, and Rembrandt. Italy is well represented by various Piedmontese, Tuscan, and Venetian masters, among them Mantegna, Guardi, Fra Angelico, and Veronese. Of particular interest are Palladio's *Tobias and the Angel* and Bronzino's *Eleonora of Toledo.* Open Tuesdays, Thursdays, Saturdays, and Sundays from 9 AM to 2 PM, Wednesdays and Fridays from 2:30 to 7:30 PM (phone: 547440).

Palazzo Madama (Madama Palace) – It is possible to see every phase of Turin's history in the architecture of this, one of the town's most imposing buildings. It incorporates the remains of a gate dating from the time of the Roman founders. In the Middle Ages, the palazzo became a Savoy stronghold, and over the years it was enlarged until, in the 17th century, its military value diminished and it became the household of the "Madama Reale" (loosely, dowager duchess) Maria Cristina, widow of Vittorio Amedeo II of Savoy. In 1721, the baroque façade was added by the brilliant Sicilian architect Filippo Juvarra. The palazzo now houses the *Museo d'Arte Antica* (Museum of Ancient Art), something of a misnomer, as the bulk of the collection —

certainly the masterpieces — dates from the late Middle Ages, the Renaissance, and the 17th and 18th centuries. One large gallery contains a Venetian state barge that once belonged to the King of Sardinia. As we went to press, the palazzo was closed for restoration; call to check if it has reopened. When open, its hours are 9 AM to 7 PM weekdays, 10 AM to 1 PM and 2 to 7 PM Sundays; closed Mondays and public holidays. Admission charge, except on Fridays. Piazza Castello (phone: 5765).

Palazzo Reale (Royal Palace) – This rather plain 17th-century building was the home of Savoy rulers until 1865. The first floor has excellent examples of furniture and decoration from the 17th and 18th centuries. There is a fanciful Chinese room with some excellent porcelains. In the gallery attached to the library is a Leonardo da Vinci self-portrait. Open Tuesdays through Sundays in winter from 9 AM to 2 PM; Tuesdays, Wednesdays, Fridays, and Sundays in summer from 9 AM to 1:45 PM, Thursdays and Saturdays from 2 to 6:45 PM. Admission charge. Piazza Castello (phone: 436-1455).

Chiesa di San Lorenzo (Church of Saint Lawrence) – Near the Palazzo Reale is a 17th-century church that served as chapel for the ruling family. Designed by Guarini, its somber façade belies its sumptuous baroque interior. Piazza Castello.

Armeria Reale (Royal Armory) – Nowhere is the martial past of the House of Savoy more clearly documented than in the Royal Armory, which houses a rich collection of arms and armor dating from Roman times to the Napoleonic era. Open Tuesdays and Thursdays from 2:30 to 7:30 PM and Saturdays from 9 AM to 2 PM. Admission charge. 191 Piazza Castello (phone: 543889).

Parco del Valentino (Valentino Park) – In the southern part of the city, set along the banks of the Po River, is a broad swatch of park containing an imitation castle constructed in the mid-1600s by the Francophile Maria Cristina. The castle is an almost perfect reproduction of a French château. Nearby is a newer (1884) reproduction, the Borgo Medioevale (Medieval Village). The houses of the village are patterned after those in the Piedmont region, the castle after Valle d'Aosta. Open daily except Mondays and holidays, 9:30 AM to 4 PM, until 5:30 PM in the summer. Admission charge, except on Fridays.

Museo Nazionale d'Artiglieria (National Artillery Museum) – Housed in the Mastio della Cittadella, the only remaining tower of the 16th-century citadel, this collection contains firearms from the history of Turin. Open Tuesdays and Thursdays from 9 AM to 2 PM, Saturdays and Sundays from 9 to 11:50 AM; closed Mondays, Wednesdays, and Fridays. Corso Galileo Ferraris (phone: 553925).

Palazzo Carignano (Carignano Palace) – Originally built for the Carignano princes in the 17th century, this palace has two noteworthy façades: The one toward Piazza Carignano was designed in the baroque style by Guarini; the other, toward Piazza Carlo Alberto, was added nearly 2 centuries later by Ferri and Bollati. The palazzo was the seat of the first Italian parliament and the birthplace of Victor Emmanuel II. It houses the *Museo Nazionale del Risorgimento* (National Museum of the Risorgimento), which displays documents and relics of the Italian unification movement. Open Tuesdays through Saturdays from 9 AM to 6:30 PM, Sundays to 12:30 PM. Admission charge, except on Sundays. 5 Via Accademia delle Scienze (phone: 511147).

Museo dell'Automobile (Automobile Museum) – A huge collection of auto memorabilia, including 160 cars, documenting the entire history of the internal combustion engine. There is a vast research library as well. Open daily, except Mondays, 9 AM to 12:30 PM and 3 to 7 PM. Admission charge. 40 Corso Unità d'Italia, south of the city center (phone: 677666).

Museo Nazionale della Montagna (National Alpine Museum) – Located on the Monte dei Cappuccini, overlooking the river and the city, is a small museum devoted to Piedmontese alpinism, mountain life and culture. Open Saturdays, Sundays, and Mondays from 9 AM to 12:30 PM and from 2:45 to 7:15 PM; Tuesdays through Fridays from 8:30 AM to 7:15 PM (evening closing time is 1 hour earlier in winter). Admission charge. 39 Via G. Giardino (phone: 688737).

ENVIRONS

Sacra di San Michele – Perched on the edge of the San Michele ravine, this ancient Benedictine monastery was built by a group of French monks in 998. It takes its name from the miraculous appearance of Saint Michael, who is said to have appeared in midair to catch a falling child. The abbey, now overseen by Rosminian priests, commands an astonishingly beautiful position high above the Dora Riparia Valley. The "staircase of the dead" leads to the marble portal, which has strong Romanesque bas-reliefs — some decidedly more profane than sacred (symbols of the zodiac, women offering their breasts to serpents, and the like) — as well as the stories of Cain and Abel and of Samson and Delilah. From the esplanade surrounding the Romanesque Gothic church at the summit are beautiful views of the Dora Valley, the Po Plain, and the Turin Plain. Open daily, 9 AM to noon and 2 to 5 PM, until 6 PM in the summer. On Route SS25, 23 miles (37 km; about a half-hour drive) west of the city.

Palazzo Stupinigi (Stupinigi Palace) – Built in the 18th century as a hunting lodge for the Savoy family, the design of this beautiful palace (sometimes called the Villa Reale or *la palazzina di caccia*) was based on that of Versailles and has all the clarity and authority of a great work of art. Filippo Juvarra, whose signature is indelibly stamped on Turin, was the architect. Although "merely" a hunting lodge, it was Napoleon's home before he assumed the crown of Italy. It is now a museum of 18th-century furniture — some of it lovely — but it is the building, with its frescoes and noble sculpture of a stag stamped against the Alpine sky, that one comes to see. Visitors must take guided tours which are offered only in Italian. Open Tuesdays through Saturdays from 9:30 AM to 5 PM, Sundays from 10 AM to 12:30 PM and 2 to 5 PM. Admission charge. On the Pinerolo road (SS23), less than 7 miles (11 km) south of Turin. Groups should book in advance (phone: 358-1220).

Basilica di Superga – In 1706, when King Vittorio Amedeo II feared defeat at the hands of a French army that was besieging Turin, he promised to have a basilica built if the Turinese forces won. They did, and the result is this baroque jewel designed by Juvara that sits on top of Superga — one of Turin's highest hills. It then became the Savoy royal family's mausoleum. The basilica is open daily from 8:30 AM to 12:30 PM and from 2:30 to 5:30 PM The royal tombs are open daily, except Fridays and holidays from 9:30 AM to 12:30 PM and 2:30 to 6:30 PM from April to September; from 10 AM to 12:30 PM and 3 to 5 PM from October to March. No admission charge. SS590, 15 miles (25 km) east of Turin (phone: 890083).

Castello di Rivoli – In this industrial suburb west of town is this baroque castle, designed in part by Juvarra. Recently restored and now a contemporary art museum (*Museo d'Arte Contemporanea*) that houses special shows and a permanent collection emphasizing the Italian school known as "Arte Povera": In the 1950s, conceptual and minimalist artists used worthless material — rags, stones, paper, etc. — in an attempt to escape commercialism; judge for yourself. Open Tuesdays through Sundays from 10 AM to 7 PM. Admission charge. On SS25, 13 miles (21 km) west of Turin. Piazza Castello (phone: 958-1547).

SOURCES AND RESOURCES

TOURIST INFORMATION: The main tourist office in Turin (222-226 Via Roma; phone: 535901) offers advice and assistance in English. It is open daily 8 AM to 8 PM.

Local Coverage – The Turin daily newspaper is *La Stampa,* considered one of the finest papers in Italy. Its readership and influence extend well beyond the city. The *International Herald Tribune* can be purchased on its day of publication at the larger newsstands or at the train station. A useful booklet, *A Guest in Turin,* is available free at hotels, tourist offices, the train station, and the airport.

TELEPHONE: The city code for Turin is 11. When calling from within Italy, dial 011 before the local number.

GETTING AROUND: Airport – There are daily connecting flights to all major European cities from the Turin international airport, Città di Torino, in Caselle (phone: 577-8361/2/3/4). Bus service and taxis to Turin are available.

Bus and Tram – Turin has an extensive bus and tram service. There is even a country trolley line serving the outskirts of the city. Very few of the buses, trams, or trolleys run all night. Tickets must be purchased before boarding at tobacco shops or some newsstands and are validated on board. For information about schedules, call *Trasporti Torinesi* (*T.T.,* phone: 531327) or ask at the information office (19 *bis* Corso Turati).

Car Rental – The major firms have offices at the airport and in Turin: *Avis* (15/G Via Corso Turati; phone: 500852 or 501107; at the airport; phone: 470-1528; and at the railway station; phone: 669-9800); *Budget/Italy by Car* (85 Piazza Carlo Felice; phone: 547160; at the airport; phone: 512425); *Europcar* (17 Via Buonarroti; phone: 650-3603); *Hertz* (19 Corso Marconi; phone: 650-4504; at the railway station; phone: 669-9658; and at the airport; phone: 470-1103).

Taxi – Taxis can be hailed as they cruise or found at one of the taxi stands on the major streets — Via Po, Via Roma, and so on — or call 5730, 5737, 5744, or 5748.

Trains – Turin is an important railway center for northern Italy. The Stazione Porta Nuova is on the Corso Vittorio Emanuele II, one of the city's most important streets (phone: 517551).

SPECIAL EVENTS: As might be expected in a city that makes much of its living from automobiles, the biggest event is the *International Car Show,* held in even-numbered years at the *Lingotto Exhibition Center* (61 Corso G. Ferraris). The show takes place in the spring, usually in late April or early May. Since the city is overrun with conventioneers who crowd every hotel, restaurant, and shop, it is suggested that only devoted autophiles visit Turin during this period. Other events at the fairgrounds (15 Corso Massimo D'Azeglio) include the *International Salon of Domestic Arts* (February); the *International Show on Vacations, Sport and Leisure* (March); the *Oscar Award* competition for the best shoes (June); the *International Shows of Technology and Mountain Sports* (October); and the *International Industrial Vehicle Expositions* (November). May marks an annual book show at the *Torino Esposizioni* (15 Corso Massimo d'Azeglio). In September, the annual 4-week *Settembre Musica* takes place. This major cultural event focuses on classical and contemporary music; concerts are performed in churches and theaters around the city (phone: 576-5564; fax: 644927).

MUSEUMS: Besides those mentioned in *Special Places,* Turin has a number of galleries and museums of special interest:

Galleria dell'Accademia Albertina delle Belle Arti (Gallery of the Albertine Academy of Fine Arts) – Small, with paintings by Piedmontese masters. Open by appointment only. 6 Via Accademia Albertina (phone: 839-7008).

Galleria Civica d'Arte Moderna (Gallery of Modern Art) – 19th- and 20th-century paintings, many by French artists. Closed for restoration at press time; call for information 31 Via Magenta (phone: 488343).

Museo d'Antropologia ed Etnologia (Anthropology and Ethnology Museum) – Open by appointment only. 17 Via Accademia Albertina (phone: 832196).

Museo della Marionetta (Puppet Museum) – The Lupi family has been staging shows for 200 years with the puppets exhibited here. Open Tuesdays through Fridays from 9 AM to noon, Saturdays and Sundays from 9 AM to 1 PM and 3 to 6 PM Closed June through August. Admission charge. 5 Via Santa Teresa (phone: 530238).

Museo Nazionale del Cinema (National Cinema Museum) – Memorabilia and occasional films. At press time, the museum was closed for restoration, but movies were being shown at *Massimo,* 8 Via Montebello (phone: 871048), a multi-screen theater. 2 Piazza San Giovanni (phone: 510370).

Museo Pietro Micca (Pietro Micca Museum) – Illustrates the history of Turin. Open daily, except Mondays and holidays, from 9 AM to 2 PM. 7 Via Guicciardini (phone: 546317).

Museo di Storia Naturale "Don Bosco" (Don Bosco Natural History Museum) – Open Sundays from 2:30 to 6:30 PM, Mondays through Saturdays for groups on request; no admission charge. 37 Viale Thovez (phone: 650-5094).

SHOPPING: The most elegant shopping street is Via Roma, which runs from the Porta Nuova railway station to Piazza Castello. Along this busy thoroughfare, or just off it, are a number of the shops that allow the hard-working Turinese to enjoy the fruits of their labors, as well as local branches of the *Standa* department store (56 Via Roma) and *Upim* (305 Via Roma). Via Garibaldi is also a mother lode of fine shops, some less expensive than those on Via Roma. As Via Garibaldi is closed to motor traffic, shopping here can be a bit less frantic than elsewhere. Turin also has a colorful, sprawling flea market called *Il Balon* (in the Porta Palazzo area).

The Turinese are artists when it comes to producing and consuming chocolate. *Peyrano* (47 Corso Moncalieri; phone: 660-2202 and 76 Corso Vittorio Emanuelle II; phone: 543940) has been making chocolate for a number of royal houses for centuries. The firm specializes in bitter and liqueur chocolates; the prices, unfortunately, are rather high. Other top-quality makers of Turin's favorite sweet are *Stratta* (191 Piazza San Carlo; phone: 541567) and *Caffarel* (distributors to the city's best cafés and *pasticcerie*), the original creator of the velvety-smooth, hazelnut-flavored *gianduiotto,* the Turinese chocolate candy.

Regular shop hours are from 9 or 9:30 AM to 1 PM and from 3:30 or 4 to 7:30 or 8 PM. Stores are closed Sundays and many are closed on Saturday afternoons.

Bambi – High-quality children's shoes at good prices. 15 Via Gramsci (phone: 510166), 4 Via Garibaldi (phone: 436-6073), 70 Via XX Settembre (phone: 530916).

De Candia – For the well-dressed Turinese male. 175 Piazza San Carlo (phone: 543800).

Durando – Large selection of the finest furs — capes, jackets, stoles, and full-length coats — well suited to the Alpine air or a first night at the theater. This is Turin's sole retailer of Fendi furs. 77 Via Roma (phone: 537087).

Mariangela – One of the city's best boutiques for top designer women's clothing. 149 Piazza San Carlo (phone: 519380).

Olympic – Extremely elegant shop known for its classic women's and men's clothing. 182 Piazza San Carlo (phone: 518090).

Visetti – A breathtaking selection of lingerie in silks, satins, crêpes de Chine, and good old-fashioned cotton to keep out the Alpine chill. 247 Piazza C. L. N. (Via Roma; phone: 546120).

SPORTS AND FITNESS: Golf – The *Torino Golf Club* (137 Via Granje, Fiano Torinese; phone: 923-5440) maintains a championship course at Mandria Park (see *Great Italian Golf,* DIVERSIONS). In addition, there are courses at *E Roveri* (24 Rotta Cerbiatta, Fiano Torinese; phone: 923-5719),

Stupinigi (506 Corso Unione Sovietica in Turin; phone: 347-2895), *Vinovo* (182 Via Stupinigi, Vinovo; phone: 965-3880), and *Le Fronde* (68 Via Sant'Agostino, Avigliana; phone: 938053).

Horse Racing – There are flat races most of the year, except during August and the dead of the winter, at *Vinovo,* near Stupinigi (phone: 965-3285).

Soccer – From September to May, both *Torino* (phone: 393496, 327474) and *Juventus* (phone: 390292) — "la Juve" in headlines and graffiti — play at *Stadio delle Alpi* (131 Strada Altessano; phone: 455-9066).

Swimming – The municipal swimming center (113 Corso Sebastopoli; phone: 329-9836) has both covered and uncovered pools. Admission charge.

THEATER AND MUSIC: Operas, symphonies, ballets, and any number of plays may be running concurrently. There is no "season" as such — productions go on year-round. The best way to find out what Turin is offering on a daily basis is to consult *La Stampa* or your hotel desk. Activities usually are centered on the *Teatro Regio* (Royal Theater; 215 Piazza Castello; phone: 881-5241 or 881-5242; fax: 881-5214), which publishes extensive calendars of events. Other theaters of note are *Teatro Nuovo* (17 Corso Massimo D'Azeglio; phone: 655552 or 669-0668), *Teatro Carignano* (6 Piazza Carignano; phone: 547048; the booking office is on 49 Via Roma; phone: 544562), and *Teatro Alfieri* (4 Piazza Solferino; phone: 545352). Symphony concerts and chamber music can be heard at the *Auditorium della RAI* (15 Via Rossini; phone: 880-74961). In summer, opera and other productions are offered outside in the Palazzo Reale gardens.

NIGHTCLUBS AND NIGHTLIFE: The Turinese do not generally dance the night away, and what nightlife there is seems to be restricted to those lucky few in the know. Such nightclubs as the city possesses are located mostly in the area around the Porta Nuova railway station. Some clubs come and go so fast that they are known by word of mouth only. Hotel porters are the best sources of information on the discotheques, pubs, and piano bars that have brilliant, but brief, life spans. Several worth noting are *Vogue* (9 Via Doria; phone: 553771), the aptly named *Pick Up* (8 Via Barge; phone: 447-2204), and *Jazz Club* (8 Via Volta; phone: 545458). The piano bar, *Casanova* (4 Via Volta; phone: 543713) also houses a discotheque.

CHECKING IN: Turin has a parking problem, so visitors who are driving should ask the management of any hotel (or a travel agent) whether garage space is available. Hotels that charge more than $275 a night and up for a double room are classified here as very expensive; those that charge between $175 and $250 are expensive; $125 and $175 are moderate; $90 or less, inexpensive. All telephone numbers are in the 11 city code unless otherwise indicated.

City – Small (44 rooms) and modern, with an attractive little garden and a late-night grill that serves hot snacks (no restaurant). 25 Via F. Juvarra (phone: 540546; fax: 548188). Very expensive.

Jolly Principi di Piemonte – One of Turin's finest hotels is in the heart of town, not far from the train station. The 107 rooms are large, some grand, and the service is superlative. 15 Via P. Gobetti (phone: 532153; fax: 510270). Very expensive.

Villa Sassi – A good choice for those who want to escape the noise and bustle of the city center. Three miles (5 km) from downtown (follow signs for Pino Torinese and Chieri), this 17th-century country house is set in a beautifully landscaped park. There are 12 elegant rooms filled with antiques, and its restaurant, *El Toulà,* is one of the best in Turin (see *Eating Out*). 47 Strada al Traforo del Pino (phone: 890556; fax: 890095). Very expensive.

Turin Palace – It has all of the elegance you'd expect of the city's leading hotel. Many of the 125 rooms have been renovated, and the restaurant has an excellent reputation. 8 Via Sacchi (phone: 515511; fax: 561-2187). Very expensive to expensive.

Jolly Ligure – This contemporary 169-room hotel offers every modern amenity. It is directly opposite the Porta Nuova Station. 85 Piazza Carlo Felice (phone: 55641; fax: 535438). Expensive.

Sitea – Each of the 119 spacious rooms has air conditioning, a color television set, a mini-bar, and a direct-dial phone. It has a central location and excellent service. Buffet breakfast included. Discounted rate on weekends. 35 Via Carlo Alberto (phone: 5570171; fax: 548090). Expensive.

President – Several of the 72 rooms overlook an enclosed garden. The hotel boasts a cheerful, modern environment and a helpful staff. Only breakfast is served, and there is a small bar. 67 Via A. Cecchi (phone: 859555; fax: 248-0465). Moderate.

Europa – Once the haunt of local nobility, this 28-room hostelry fell on hard times for a while. It was renovated, however, and again has become a pleasant place to stay. Ask for a quiet room with a bath. 99 Piazza Castello (phone: 544238 or 534448). Inexpensive.

EATING OUT: The cuisine of Turin, like northern Italian cooking in general, is similar to that of the French in method — but very different in ingredients. Piedmont is especially rich in special delicacies, some as simple as the breadstick. Others are more exotic: fabulous white truffles, for instance, are hunted at night, not by pigs, as in France, but by dogs — in fact, there is a special school at Rodi that does nothing but turn ordinary hounds into truffle hunters. This range of culinary delights and a plethora of cheeses and hot appetizers make dining in Turin a distinctly different experience.

Meals for two that cost more than $120 are categorized here as expensive; those between $60 and $110, moderate; and $50 or less, inexpensive. All telephone numbers are in the 11 city code unless otherwise indicated.

Bontan – On the city's outskirts, this more than 70-year-old villa is decorated with Oriental carpets and Gobelin tapestries. Piedmontese cooking is the order of the day, with such specialties as tortellini stuffed with robiole cheese and green squash. Fish and vegetarian menus available. Closed Sundays and Mondays. Reservations necessary. Major credit cards accepted. 55 Via Canua, San Mauro Torinese (phone: 822-2680). Expensive.

Del Cambio – A little piece of Turin history. A scarf in the Italian colors still marks the table that Cavour frequented, and some of the waiters, who wear black tails, white gloves, and aprons, look as if they could have waited on him. Although the braised beef in barolo wine is exceptional, diners come here most for the history and the atmosphere. Closed Sundays and August. Reservations necessary. Major credit cards accepted. 2 Piazza Carignano (phone: 546690). Expensive.

Neuv Caval d'Brons – This very stylish restaurant is right in the center of town. The food here — including many sublime vegetarian dishes — is excellent, the menu at times a little daring. Go for it! Closed Sundays and early July. Reservations necessary. Major credit cards accepted. 157 Piazza San Carlo (phone: 553491). Expensive.

La Smarrita – This former country inn has become a downtown meeting place for executives, and offers variations on traditional dishes such as *ovoli* mushroom and watercress salad and pasta stuffed with *porcini* mushrooms. The service, by waiters dressed in burlap tunics, is excellent. Closed Mondays. Reservations necessary. Major credit cards accepted. 244 Corso Unione Sovietica (phone: 390657 or 328488). Expensive.

El Toulà – One of the best restaurants in Turin, in the *Villa Sassi* hotel, 3 miles (5 km) from the city center but well worth the short drive. Specialties include salmon marinated in raspberry vinegar, and breast of duck with local herbs. Any pork dish is sure to be outstanding, while the wine list boasts an excellent selection of exclusive house wines, including champagne. The service is excellent. Closed Sundays and in August. Reservations necessary. Major credit cards accepted. 47 Strada al Traforo del Pino (phone: 890556). Expensive.

Vecchia Lanterna – Quiet and hospitable, this place makes the most of the local duck and pork dishes. Any meal begun with a terrine of duck foie gras is bound to be a success. Duck even finds its way into stuffed pasta such as *agnolotti* (large ravioli). Closed Saturday lunch and Sundays. Reservations necessary. Major credit cards accepted. 21 Corso Re Umberto (phone: 537047). Expensive.

Balbo – A stone's throw from the train station, this attractive spot has 2 levels. For starters, try the *tortelloni* stuffed with asparagus. Closed Mondays and mid-July to mid-August. Reservations advised. Major credit cards accepted. 11 Via Andrea Doria (phone: 571743). Expensive to moderate.

I Due Lampioni – The atmosphere recalls a 19th-century drawing room, with a high, barrel-vaulted ceiling and rather somber decor. A wide range of Piedmontese hot appetizers are served, as well as excellent *agnolotti* (large ravioli) stuffed with pheasant. Typical Tuscan cuisine. Closed Sundays and during August. Reservations advised. Major credit cards accepted. 45 Via Carlo Alberto (phone: 839-7409). Expensive to moderate.

Al Gatto Nero – Turin's best fish restaurant is an inconspicuous place. It has no street sign, but behind its large windows there usually are some 80 diners enjoying excellent fish, shellfish, and steaks. Closed Sundays and during August. Reservations advised. Major credit cards accepted. 14 Corso Filippo Turati (phone: 590414). Expensive to moderate.

L'Oca Nera – Recently opened, this eatery is devoted to "slow food," a culinary movement committed to combining traditional cuisine with a creative presentation. The vegetable flans and *branzino* (bass) marinated in basil make this place worth visiting, but there's an added attraction — for a small charge, you can enjoy an after-dinner cabaret or puppet show. Closed daily for lunch, Sundays, and August. Reservations advised. Visa accepted. 14 Via San Massimo (phone: 882336). Expensive to moderate.

San Giorgio – Enjoy an evening of dining and dancing at this lakeside restaurant with a lovely view. Closed Tuesdays and Wednesday afternoons. Reservations advised. Major credit cards accepted. Borgo Medioevale al Valentino (phone: 6692131). Expensive to moderate.

Montecarlo – This wonderful find turns out abundant portions of food, such as *orzo e fagioli,* as *la nonna* (grandmother) used to make. The surroundings are worthy of a film set. Closed Saturday afternoons and Sundays. Reservations advised. Major credit cards accepted. 37 Via San Francesco da Paola (phone: 830815). Moderate.

Buca di San Francesco – A popular spot near the train station serving a wide choice of pasta and meat dishes that are prepared in northern Italian and Tuscan styles. Closed Mondays and August. No reservations. Major credit cards accepted. 27 Via San Francesca da Paola (phone: 839-8464). Inexpensive.

Porto di Savona – Sample herb omelettes, risotto with radicchio, and homemade desserts at this pleasant, family-style trattoria. Closed Tuesdays and mid-July through mid-August. No reservations. No credit cards accepted. 2 Piazza Vittorio Veneto (phone: 831453). Inexpensive.

COFFEEHOUSES: Turin is home to some of Italy's most celebrated coffeehouses — many of which are 19th-century palaces — where customers can overdose on pastries and chocolates. Among the best known, and certainly the oldest, is *Baratti & Milano* (29 Piazza Castello). This grand old establishment is dark and intimate — and a great place to people watch, and to try its famous fruit jellies, candies, and chocolates. Dating from the same era, yet ages away in decor, are the *San Carlo* and the *Torino* (both in Piazza San Carlo). The interiors of these two are a riot of mirrored gilt and stucco. Another historical place is *Florio* (8 Via Po), a *caffè/gelateria* that also has some of the city's best ice cream. Not to be forgotten is *Platti* (72 Corso Vittorio Emanuele II). First opened in 1876, the original structure, decor, and sign *liquoreria* (liquor store) have all been preserved. In addition to a vast assortment of sandwiches, cocktails, and freshly baked pastries, you can enjoy lunch in its buffet and restaurant rooms. Off Via Garibaldi is the *Confetteria al Bicerin* (5 Piazza della Consolata). Its name comes from the traditional blend of hot coffee, chocolate, and milk — *bicerin* — that once was served in all the best coffeehouses in Turin, but today can only be sipped here. With its small white tables and the old wooden counter overflowing with colorful candies, this establishment maintains the atmosphere of a 19th-century *cioccolateria* (a coffeehouse that specialized in chocolate drinks). Heaven!

VENICE

Venice is one of the world's most photic — and photographic — cities. As the sun sets, it burnishes the old buildings with a splendid, rosy glow that is reflected, then refracted, in the waters of the canals. The city is luminously beautiful, both in radiant, peak-season August and in bleak, wet November. And it is painfully beautiful when suddenly, on some late-winter morning, the rain trickles to a halt, the cloud curtains part, and trapezoids of sunlight reheat the ancient stones. Then there is an ineffable sense of renewal as the café tables are set up again in Piazza San Marco, and pigeons and waiters alike swoop out from the dark arcades while an orchestra begins another airy melody. Little wonder that, long before photography, Romantic painting flourished here.

Venice is 117 islets separated by 177 canals and joined by 400 bridges on Italy's northeastern Adriatic coast. A 3-mile bridge reaches across the Laguna Veneta (Venetian Lagoon), connecting it to the mainland near the small town of Mestre. The city is protected from the force of the Adriatic Sea by the natural breakwater of the Lido, a long, narrow sandbar that is one of the most fashionable resorts on the Adriatic.

The lagoon city began as a place of refuge from the violent barbarian invasions of the 5th century; mainland inhabitants fled to the isolated islands. As communities grew up, the islands became connected to one another, and Venice developed into a powerful, flourishing city-state. During the Crusades, this little maritime republic came to dominate the entire Mediterranean, and the winged Venetian lion, symbol of St. Mark, the city's protector, stood guard over a network of palaces from the Strait of Gibraltar to the Bosporus. This was the city of Marco Polo.

Renaissance Venice was the focal point for the great trade routes from the Middle East, and the markets beside the city's Ponte di Rialto (Rialto Bridge) were a pulse of European commerce. The doges — the city's rulers — celebrated their mastery of the Mediterranean with an annual ceremony of marriage to the sea, and the golden ducats that overflowed the city's coffers financed some of the world's most spectacular art and architecture. The Venetian school of painting, which produced magnificent colorists, began with Giorgione and achieved its apogee in the 16th century with Titian Vecellio, Paolo Veronese, and Jacopo Tintoretto. The proud, 1,000-year Venetian independence (La Serenissima) ended with the Treaty of Campoformio in 1797, when Napoleon traded the territory to Austria. In 1866, after nearly 70 years of Bonaparte and Hapsburg domination, the city was joined to newly unified Italy.

Today, Venice proper has a population of nearly 122,000 — 316,000 including the metropolitan area — which is steadily decreasing due to the city's extraordinarily high cost of living. The millions of tourists who swarm through its narrow streets and tiny squares make up Venice's chief industry — and they leave behind well over $100 million a year. A gaudy party atmosphere reigns from *Easter* to October, with a midsummer explosion sometimes as crass as it is colorful: the landing stages jammed and listing with tour groups, long lines waiting for frozen custard beside the Doge's Palace, and the big Lido ferries packed with sun-scorched day-trippers. Hawkers and hustlers populate every corner. (In 1990, after both national and international cries of outrage, Venice took itself out of the running as the site of *Expo 2000,* a proposed world's fair at the turn of the century that's expected to attract as many as 45 million visitors during a 4-month period!) In its way the scene is as vibrant, insistent, chaotic, and vulgar as anything from the days of the international market on the Ponte di Rialto.

And yet, even on *Ferragosto* weekend, Italy's state holiday in mid-August, it's still possible to turn deliberately from the main thoroughfare and string together a few random rights and lefts to find yourself in a haven of quiet back alleys, on a tiny bridge across a deserted canal, in the middle of a silent, sunbaked *campo,* with a fruit stall — and not a tourist in sight.

Venice in winter is a totally different experience: placid, gray, and startlingly visual. Suddenly, there is no one between you and the noble palaces, the soaring churches, the dark canals. Only the mysterious masked merriment of *Carnevale* (a month-long celebration, ending March 3 this year) interrupts the chilly repose of the time when Venice is most emphatically a community of Venetians.

Not everyone loves Venice. D. H. Lawrence called it "an abhorrent, green, slippery city," and it does have a dark, decadent quality, sometimes a damp depressiveness. (An inscription on a sundial says, "I count only the happy hours.") But few cities have attracted so many illustrious admirers. Shakespeare set one of his best-known plays, *The Merchant of Venice,* here. Galileo Galilei used the bell tower in Piazza San Marco to test his telescope. Richard Wagner composed here. Lord Byron and Henry James wrote here. It's not hard to feel the ghosts of these and others who, as James said, "have seemed to find [here] something that no other place could give."

VENICE AT-A-GLANCE

SEEING THE CITY: The traditional vantage point from which to admire Venice is the summit of the 324-foot red campanile (bell tower) in Piazza San Marco. The view on all sides is breathtaking — from the red-shingled rooftops and countless domes of the city to the distant islands that dot the wide lagoon. There's an elevator to the top or, for the heartier, a ramp. Open daily. Admission charge.

For a bird's-eye view of Piazza San Marco itself (and the rest of the lagoon city), take a short boat ride to the Isola San Giorgio (No. 5 ferryboat from the Riva degli Schiavoni — one stop) and ride the elevator to the top of the church tower. The church itself, a masterpiece by Andrea Palladio, contains two major works by Tintoretto. It also has beautiful carved wooden choir stalls depicting the life of St. Benedict. Open daily. Admission charge.

SPECIAL PLACES: Piazza San Marco is the center of life in Venice; from here sightseers can board steamers to the Lido and other islands as well as to the various quarters of the city. The Corso della Gente — a phrase Venetians use to describe the "flow of people" — is, in fact, the route that roughly parallels the Grand Canal, snaking through the heart of the city from the bridge (Ponte degli Scalzi) near the Santa Lucia railway station to Piazza San Marco and from there to the *Accademia.* You can follow it instinctively without once asking for directions.

DOWNTOWN

Piazza San Marco (St. Mark's Square) – Napoleon called this huge marble square the finest drawing room in Europe. Bells chime, flocks of pigeons crisscross the sky, violins play, couples embrace in the sunset — while the visitor takes it all in from a congenial café. A mere turn of the head allows you to admire St. Mark's Basilica, the Doge's Palace, the early 20th-century copy of the original 9th-century bell tower, the clock tower where giant bronze Moors have struck the hours for 5 centuries, the old administration offices, and the old library, which now houses the archaeological museum. In the *piazzetta,* through which the square opens onto the Grand Canal, there are two granite columns — one topped by the Lion of St. Mark (returned on April 25, 1991 — *St. Mark's Day* — after 6 years of restoration in the Netherlands), the other by a statue of St. Theodore.

Basilica di San Marco (St. Mark's Basilica) – This masterpiece of Venetian-Byzantine architecture was built in 830 to shelter the tomb of St. Mark, whose bones had been smuggled out of Alexandria. When first built, it was not a cathedral but a chapel for the doges. The present basilica was constructed during the 11th century, but the phenomenal decoration of the interior and exterior continued well into the 16th century. The basilica has a large dome and four smaller ones; its imposing façade of variegated marble and sculpture has five large doorways. The four famous bronze horses that have adorned the central doorway since 1207, when they were brought here after the sack of Constantinople, were removed in 1980 for restoration. Bronze replicas have taken their place in the doorway, and the originals are now on permanent display in the basilica's museum. Inside, the walls are encrusted with precious art, rare marbles, and magnificent mosaics. Behind the high altar in the chancel is the famous gold altarpiece, the *Pala d'Oro,* and the basilica's treasury includes rare relics as well as Byzantine goldwork and enamels. Much of the treasury has been on tour for some time. It is expected to be back in Venice at the end of this year. Open daily. Admission charge for the chancel and treasury. *Vaporetto* stop San Marco. Piazza San Marco.

Palazzo Ducale (Doge's Palace) – Next to the basilica is the pink and white palace with an unusual double loggia that served as the residence of the doges and the seat of government. The finest room in the palace is the Grand Council Chamber, containing paintings by Tintoretto and Veronese. You may also visit the doge's apartments and the armory. The palace is connected to the old prisons by the famous Ponte dei Sospiri (Bridge of Sighs), whose name comes from the lamentations of prisoners supposedly taken across the bridge to be executed. Open daily. Admission charge. *Vaporetto* stop San Marco. Piazza San Marco (phone: 522-4951).

Grand Canal – Lined with some 200 marble palaces built between the 12th and the 18th century, the occasionally drought-plagued Grand Canal has been called the finest street with the finest houses in the world. On the right (east bank) are the Palazzo Vendramin-Calergi, where Wagner died, now the winter home of the *Municipal Casino;* the Ca' d'Oro (Golden House), so called because its ornate façade once was entirely gilded; the Palazzo Mocenigo, where Lord Byron lived; and *Palazzo Grassi,* an art museum bought and refurbished by the Agnelli family of Fiat fame. On the left (west bank) are the *Palazzo Pesaro,* which houses the modern art gallery, and the Ca' Rezzonico, an architectural jewel that contains the civic museum of 18th-century art.

A good way to see all of these beautiful palazzi is to take a slow boat ride over the entire 2-mile length of the Grand Canal with the No. 1 line.

Chiesa di Santa Maria della Salute – Dedicated to the Madonna for delivering Venice from a plague, this 17th-century baroque church is just across the Grand Canal from Piazza San Marco. Its octagonal shape and white Istrian limestone façade are easily recognizable in innumerable paintings of Venetian scenes and panoramas. Inside are paintings of the New Testament by Titian and Tintoretto. *Vaporetto* stop Salute. Campo della Salute, Dorsoduro.

Chiesa del Redentore (Church of the Redeemer) – Also built to thank the Madonna for rescuing the Venetians from an earlier plague, and a must for architectural enthusiasts, this 16th-century church is known for its perfect proportions and remarkable harmony both inside and out. It was constructed by Andrea Palladio on a point of the Giudecca Island, a short ferry ride (take a No. 5) from St. Mark's by way of Isola San Giorgio. The yearly *Feast of the Redeemer* (the third Sunday in July; see *Special Events*) used to be attended by the doge, who reached the church across a bridge of boats. Open daily. *Vaporetto* stop Redentore. Campo Redentore. Isola della Giudecca, Dorsoduro.

Galleria dell'Accademia (Gallery of Fine Arts) – Brief but frequent visits are the best way to savor the rich contents of this great art gallery. Of particular interest are Veronese's *Supper in the House of Levi,* Titian's *Presentation of the Virgin,* Tintoretto's *Transport of the Body of St. Mark,* and Giorgione's *Tempesta.* The paintings of Venice by Antonio Canaletto, Francesco Guardi, and Gentile Bellini are the academy's most Venetian selections, both by subject and artist, and meld all impressions of the city. Open daily. Admission charge. *Vaporetto* stop Accademia. Campo della Carità, Dorsoduro (phone: 522-2247).

Museo del Settecento Veneziano (Museum of Eighteenth-Century Venice) – Built in the 17th century, Ca' Rezzonico — the palace that has housed the museum since 1936 — has a magnificent exterior that is best observed from the Grand Canal (in turn, its windows afford superb views of the canal). A splendid backdrop for some of the most sumptuous treasures of 18th-century Venetian art, the palace itself is known for its grandiose decor and its frescoes by Giandomenico Tiepolo and his son Giambattista. Closed Fridays. Admission charge. *Vaporetto* stop Rezzonico. Ca' Rezzonico, Dorsoduro (phone: 522-4543).

Scuola Grande di San Rocco (Great School of San Rocco) – The Venetian *scuola* was not a school, but something of a cross between a trade guild and a religious brotherhood that did works of charity and supplied wealthy patronage for the arts. San Rocco contains a rich collection of Tintorettos — some 56 canvases depicting stories from the Old and New Testaments. Open daily. Admission charge. *Vaporetto* stop San Tomà. Campo San Rocco, San Polo (phone: 523-4864).

Chiesa di Santa Maria Gloriosa dei Frari (St. Mary's Church) – Known simply as *Frari,* this Gothic Franciscan church is considered by many to be the most splendid in Venice after St. Mark's. It contains three unquestioned masterpieces: the *Assumption* and the *Madonna of Ca' Pesaro,* both by Titian, and Giovanni Bellini's triptych on the sacristy altar. An excellent way to appreciate its beauty is to attend an early morning mass before the tourists come. Open daily. Next to the *Scuola Grande di San Rocco. Vaporetto* stop San Tomà. Campo dei Frari, San Polo.

Chiesa di Santa Maria del Carmelo (Church of Our Lady of Mount Carmel) – Also known as the Chiesa dei Carmini (Church of the Carmelites), this 14th-century Gothic church with a 17th-century campanile — crowned by a statue of the Virgin — still has original gilded wooden ornamentation in its nave. Also worthy of attention are the church walls, which are lined with many 17th- and 18th-century paintings. The cloister adjacent to the church (see the next entry) now belongs to the State Institute of Art. Open daily. *Vaporetto* stop Rezzonico. Campo Santa Margherita, Dorsoduro.

Scuola Grande dei Carmini (Great School of the Carmelites) – Next to the Carmelite church, this gracious 17th-century palace contains the most extensive collection of works by Giambattista Tiepolo anywhere in Venice. Paintings and frescoes adorn the interior. Closed Sundays. Admission charge. *Vaporetto* stop Rezzonico. Campo Santa Margherita, Dorsoduro.

Scuola San Giorgio degli Schiavoni (School of St. George of the Slavonians) – This small building, beyond Piazza San Marco in a part of the city most visitors do not tour, contains one of the city's most overlooked treasures: the frieze of paintings by Vittore Carpaccio depicting stories of St. George, St. Jerome, and St. Tryphon. Closed Mondays. Admission charge. *Vaporetto* stop San Zaccaria. Calle dei Furlani, Castello.

Jewish Ghetto – Venice's ghetto — the world's first — gave its name to all other confined Jewish communities. The word comes from *geto,* which in the Venetian dialect means foundry. Prior to 1516, when Venice's Jewish population was forced to move to an abandoned arsenal on a small, naturally isolated island in the *sestiere* of Cannaregio, they had lived predominantly on the island of Giudecca, "Island of the Jews." The 700 Jews who moved to the Ghetto Nuovo (New Ghetto) grew to 5,000 within a century. In 1541, an adjoining area, the Ghetto Vecchio (Old Ghetto) was annexed, followed by the Ghetto Nuovissimo (Newest Ghetto) in 1633. All three areas are characterized by "skyscrapers" — 7 stories high — that utilize the limited space. It was not until Napoleon arrived in 1797 that Venice's Jews were declared free citizens and allowed to live where they pleased. Five synagogues in the ghetto (the oldest is the German Synagogue — built in 1528 — and home of the *Museo Ebraico* — Jewish Museum) still stand in the three ghettos, where a small number of Jewish families continue to live. Take *vaporetto* No. 1 to San Marcuola. It's a 5-minute walk northeast from the train station.

ENVIRONS

Lido – For most of the 20th century, this shoestring island — across the lagoon from Venice proper — has been one of the world's most extravagant resorts. Indeed, the word *lido* has come to mean, in much of the world's lexicon, any fashionable, luxuriously equipped beach resort. There has always been a touch of decadence to the Venetian Lido with its elegant rambling hotels, sumptuous villas, swank casino, and world-weary, wealthy clientele. Thomas Mann used the Lido's posh *Grand Hotel des Bains* (see *Checking In*) as a background for his haunting novella *Death in Venice.* Today, hundreds of cabins and cabanas line the Lido's fine sandy beaches, and purists assert that the old resort has lost much of its glamour. But the tourists still come by the thousands — some drawn by the tinsel of an international film festival, others by the trendiness of a pop music celebration, but most lured by the legendary Lido ambience. There are buses on the island, which can be reached by frequent boat service from several different stops, including Riva degli Schiavoni (lines Nos. 1, 2, 6, and 34). There also is a car ferry (*tronchetto* No. 17) from Piazzale Roma.

Murano – This island has been the home of Venetian glass making since the 13th century. Visitors can watch the glass blowing and molding processes at one of the island factories but should be aware of the high-pressure tactics used to sell the glass. Murano is 15 minutes by the No. 5 or No. 12 *vaporetto* from Fondamenta Nuove.

Burano – The colorful homes, small boats, and nets and tackle of the fishermen who live here add charm to this little island, best known as a center of lace making, still practiced by some island women. Burano is 40 minutes by the No. 12 *vaporetto* from Fondamenta Nuove.

Torcello – This was one of the most prosperous colonies on the lagoon in the 5th and 6th centuries, but as Venice grew, Torcello declined. The main square is overgrown with grass. Most of the cathedral, as it appears today, dates from the 7th to 13th centuries. It has several fine Byzantine mosaics, an interesting iconostasis, and a couple of noteworthy restaurants (see *Eating Out*). The island is 45 minutes by the No. 12 *vaporetto* from Fondamenta Nuove.

■ **EXTRA SPECIAL:** West of Venice the so-called Brenta Riviera was where many wealthy Venetian merchants built luxury summer residences in the 16th century, many designed by Andrea Palladio or Andrea Sansovino. During the 17th and 18th centuries a luxurious barge, *Il Burchiello,* made a daily trip along the lazy Brenta, which links Venice and Padua. Today's tourist can enjoy the same cruise, from April through October, by motorized boat from Pontile Giardinetto near Piazza San Marco. The excursion, which includes lunch in Oriago and a bus return from Padua, takes a full day. The boat leaves from Venice to Padua on Tuesdays, Thursdays, and Saturdays, and it returns from Padua to Venice on Sundays, Wednesdays, and Fridays. Apply at *Compagnia Italiana Turismo* (*CIT*), open year-round (48 Piazza San Marco; phone: 528-5480), for information. (It also is possible to tour the area by car on a road that roughly parallels the canal.)

South of Venice is the seaside town of Chioggia, once a major stronghold of the Venetian Republic. Now little more than a fishing port, it retains tantalizing traces of its past glory. The 13th-century Church of San Domenico displays works by Carpaccio and Tintoretto; the highly decorated baroque altar contrasts with its simpler surroundings. There are numerous other small churches in Chioggia, some in a poor state of repair, but all with significant works of Venetian art. The Duomo, or cathedral and bishopric, which stands at the end of Corso del Popolo, is a grandiose 17th-century building reconstructed on the ruins of the original 12th-century church. Inside are paintings that recount some of the history and sacred legends of Chioggia. Around the corner is the celebrated Piazza Vescovile. Bordered by plane trees and an ornamented balustrade, it has been a favorite subject for painters through the ages. Chioggia can be reached by boat, passing several other lagoon islands on the way, or by bus from the Piazzale Roma bus station. On the waterfront is *El Gato,* an excellent, inexpensive restaurant which specializes in local fish from the Adriatic Sea, served with fresh salads and local wines.

SOURCES AND RESOURCES

TOURIST INFORMATION: Stop in at the Azienda di Promozione Turistica in the southwest corner of Piazza San Marco (APT; 71/C Ascensione; phone: 522-6356) or the APT office at Santa Lucia train station (phone: 719078) for maps, and listings of hotels, museum hours, and special events. The Assessorato al Turismo (nearby in the Ca' Giustinian; phone: 522-4842) has information about the city's cultural events. The *Biennale* organization also is housed here. The *Associazione Guide Turistiche* (5267 Calle delle Bande, Castello; phone: 529-8730) has a list of multilingual tour guides whose fixed rates are approved by the local tourist board (about $90 for 3 hours, maximum 20 people). For information about winter activities, particularly cultural events, contact *Promove* (Corte del Teatro San Moisè, San Marco; phone: 521-0200).

The nearest US Consulate is in Milan, at 2-10 Piazza Amedeo (phone: 2-900-1841).

Local Coverage – The weekly *Un Ospite a Venezia* (A Guest in Venice) is a useful multilingual booklet published weekly and available at newsstands and hotels; it lists up-to-date museum schedules, special events, entertainment programs, and other activities. The glossy magazine *Marco Polo* covers all special events and cultural issues.

Published monthly in Italian and English, it is available at newsstands and most hotels. *The Companion Guide to Venice* by Hugh Honour (London: Collins; $29.50) is a sensitive, well-written guide to the city; it is available in many bookstores.

TELEPHONE: The city code for Venice is 41. When calling from within Italy, dial 041 before the local number.

GETTING AROUND: Losing yourself in Venice is inevitable — and recommended. However, major confusion can be avoided by knowing a few facts. Since 1711, Venice has been divided into six *sestieri* or wards, namely San Marco, Castello, Canareggio, San Polo, Dorsoduro, and Santa Croce. "Downtown" Venice — the largest of the six — is San Marco. The *sestieri* are used as points of reference and are part of a location's address. All locations have two: One is the official mailing address and the other is a specific street address. A store's mailing address, for instance, could be 2250 San Marco, while its street address is 2250 Calle dei Fuseri.

There are no cars in Venice. After crossing the Ponte della Libertà, visitors leave their cars in the lots and garages at Piazzale Roma. *Note:* don't leave anything in your car; even though there are attendants and a "security patrol" at the *piazzale,* things have been known to disappear. An even better idea for those arriving by car — to avoid the terrible congestion of the high season — is to park in mainland Mestre and catch the train to Venice, a journey of only 10 minutes or so. An added advantage of this strategy is that the sight of Venice has a far greater impact when one steps out of the train terminal into the midst of the city's beauty.

Airport – Marco Polo Airport (phone: 661111) serves both domestic and international flights. It is 8 miles (13 km) from the city and is reachable by *motoscafo* (motorboat) service, which leaves from the airport or Piazza San Marco and costs about $11 per person. A motorboat taxi (*taxi acquei*) for up to four people is about $60, including bags. *ATVO* bus No. 5 from the parking area of Piazzale Roma (across the Grand Canal from the Santa Lucia train station) costs about $4 per person. Ask for time schedules at *Compagnia Italiana Turismo (CIT),* Piazza San Marco, or at the tourist office in Piazzale Roma. Also consult the weekly booklet *Un Ospite a Venezia* (A Guest in Venice), available at newsstands and hotels.

Bus and Train – The bus station (phone: 528-7886) is at Piazzale Roma; the train station, Stazione Santa Lucia (phone: 715555), is on the Grand Canal not far from the bus station.

Gondola – A 50-minute tour of the city in one of these sleek, black boats will cost you as much as $60 (although five people can fit in each) and the price rises to $75 if you take one after 8 PM. Each additional 25 minutes will increase the bill by $30. Unless you give the gondolier specific directions, he will determine the route and may or may not play tour guide (at no extra cost). Sing, he won't. If you're looking for those romantic *barcaroli* you saw in Katherine Hepburn's *Summertime,* you'll have to sign up with *CIT* (48 Piazza San Marco; phone: 528-5480) or make arrangements through your hotel for a nighttime "Gondola Serenade" (about $25 per person). Depending on the request, a number of gondolas (from two to ten) will travel together, sharing the accordion music and Italian songs of an accompanying duo. It won't be intimate, but it will be fun. A less costly alternative is the gondola-ferry, called a *traghetto,* that crosses the Grand Canal at seven points for a bargain 50¢. The ride only lasts a minute, but it can be exciting as the drivers dodge *vaporetti* and *taxi acquei.*

Motoscafi and Vaporetti – The little steamers that make up the municipal transit system are inexpensive and fun. The *motoscafi* are express boats, making only a few important stops. The *vaporetti* are much slower; No. 1 chugs leisurely along the whole length of the Grand Canal, and No. 5 meanders for more than an hour through interesting parts of the city. Tickets cost between $1.50 and $2.50. If you're in a rush to get to the station or elsewhere, you can ask your hotel to call a *taxi acquei.* Although they're almost as expensive as gondolas, they're faster (phone: 522-2303). There is a movement afoot by environmentalists to replace them all with electric boats (sob!).

LOCAL SERVICES: Dentist (English-Speaking) – Dr. Pietro Ambrosini, Calle Bembo, San Marco (phone: 528-7736).

Dry Cleaner/Tailor – *Centro Pulisecco,* 6262/D Calle Della Testa, Cannaregio (phone: 522-5011).

Limousine Service – *International Rent-a-Car* (468/B Piazzale Roma; phone: 522-1159; fax: 520-8396); *Avis* (4964 Piazzale Roma; phone: 522-5825).

Medical Emergency – Ambulance service for *Ospedali Civili Riuniti* (phone: 523-0000). An English-speaking physician is Dr. Salvatore Saccardo (Calle Ostreghe, San Marco; phone: 522-1370).

Messenger Service – *Agenzia Espressi* (Ponte dell'Olio, San Marco; phone: 522-3719); *Nuova Serenissima* (496 Piazzale Roma; phone: 523-5415).

National/International Courier – *DHL International* (111 Via Torino, in Mestre; phone: 531-2666) will arrange hotel pickup.

Office Equipment Rental – *ENDAR* (*Centro Congressi,* Via Castello, Castello; phone: 523-8440); *Venezia Congressi* (1056 Accademia Dorsoduro, San Marco; phone: 522-8400) rents audiovisual equipment as well as other office equipment, and can help arrange meetings and conferences.

Pharmacy – Pharmacies take turns for 24-hour service; every week at least six stay open all night. Each pharmacy posts a list; dial 192 to find out which ones are on duty.

Photocopies – *Graphoprint* (Fondamenta Tolentini, Santa Croce; phone: 528-7035); *Christian Micoud* (Campo de San Luca, San Marco; phone: 528-9275).

Post Office – *PTT* (Rialto, Fontego dei Tedeschi; phone: 528-6212), open from 8:30 AM to 7 PM Mondays through Saturdays. More centrally located, though with shorter hours, is *PTT* (Calle Larga de l'Ascension, just off St. Mark's Square), open 8:10 AM to 1:40 PM weekdays, and from 8:10 AM to noon on Saturdays.

Secretary/Stenographer (English-Speaking) – *ENDAR* (*Centro Congressi,* Via Castello, Castello; phone: 523-8440); *Venezia Congressi* (1056 Accademia Dorsoduro, San Marco; phone: 522-8400).

Telex/Facsimile Transmissions – *PTT* (Rialto, Fontego dei Tedeschi; phone: 528-62320), open 24 hours daily.

Translator – *ENDAR* (*Centro Congressi,* Via Castello, Castello; phone: 523-8440); *Venezia Congressi* (1056 Accademia Dorsoduro, San Marco; phone: 522-8400); *TER* (3640/A Castello; phone: 528-9879).

Other – Formal wear and *Carnevale* costume rental: *Il Baule (di Pertini e Roditi),* Calle Lion, Castello (phone: 528-7788).

SPECIAL EVENTS: Starting about a month before *Ash Wednesday* (March 4, 1992), Venetians celebrate *Carnevale,* a pre-*Lenten* fete that includes outdoor masked balls, 24-hour street theater, and pop music. Every 4 years in June, the city hosts the *Regata Storica delle Repubbliche Marinare,* the race and procession of historic boats and costumes that hark back to the 11th century when Venice was one of the ancient maritime republics (the others were Amalfi, Genoa, and Pisa). This year is Venice's turn, although there also will be a regatta in Genoa to commemorate the 500th anniversary of Columbus's discovery of America. On the night between the third Saturday and Sunday in July, illuminated gondolas glide along the canals while musicians play from barges on the lagoon and fireworks paint the sky. This is the *Festa del Redentore* (Feast of the Redeemer), one of the most special celebrations of the year in Venice. That Sunday, a "bridge" of boats from Dorsoduro to the Chiesa del Redentore commemorates the end of the 1576 epidemic. On the first Sunday in September, gondola races and a procession of decorated barges filled with Venetians in Renaissance dress highlight the *Regata Storica* (Historic Regatta) on the Grand Canal. The annual *International Film Festival* is held on the Lido in late August and early September, and in even-numbered years the important *Esposizione Internazionale d'Arte Moderna* (International Exposition of Modern Art), better known as *Biennale d'Arte,* takes place in a small park beyond the Riva dei Sette Martiri from June through October. Every September, there is a marathon that starts along the Veneto's Brenta Canal and follows the tow paths into and through the center of Venice, ending at the Basilica San Marco. To celebrate the *Festa della Salute* on November 21, another "bridge" of boats is formed from Santa Maria del Giglio to the Chiesa di Santa Maria della Salute.

MUSEUMS: Besides those mentioned in *Special Places,* Venice has a number of museums of special interest. The days and hours vary with the season. Check with the APT in Piazza San Marco (phone: 522-6356) for current schedules or look in *Un Ospite a Venezia.*

Civico Museo Correr (Correr Civic Museum) – A collection of historical curios from the Venetian Republic. Also, a picture gallery with works from the 13th to the 18th century, along with prints, sketches, and ceramics. Admission charge. *Vaporetto* stop San Marco. Piazza San Marco (phone: 522-5625).

Galleria Giorgio Franchetti (Franchetti Gallery) – Bronze sculpture from the 12th through the 16th century as well as an important collection of Renaissance paintings from Venice and Tuscany. Admission charge. *Vaporetto* stop Ca' d'Oro. Ca' D'Oro, 3932 Grand Canal, Cannareggio (phone: 523-8790).

Museo Archeologico (Archaeological Museum) – Recently reopened after extensive renovation, this museum houses ancient Greek and Roman statues, Greek and Etruscan vases, Egyptian and Assyrian jewels and antiques. Admission charge. *Vaporetto* stop San Marco. Piazza San Marco (phone: 522-5978).

Museo Ebraico (Jewish Museum) – A visit to the Jewish Ghetto is incomplete without time spent at this small museum that houses a collection of memorabilia from the ghetto's origins. The museum also organizes tours of the museum itself as well as to a number of the ghetto's synagogues otherwise closed to the public. Admission charge. *Vaporetto* stop Ponte delle Guglie or San Marcuola. 2902 Campo del Ghetto Nuovo, Cannaregio (phone: 715359).

Museo Fortuny (Fortuny Museum) – The sketches, pleated silk fabrics, and personal belongings of the Spanish-born material master Mariano Fortuny, who made this 15th-century Gothic palazzo his home for 42 years. Admission charge. *Vaporetto* stop Sant'Angelo. 3780 Campo San Benedetto, San Marco (phone: 520-0995).

Museo Guggenheim (Guggenheim Museum) – The private modern art collection of Peggy Guggenheim, including works from the cubist, abstract, surrealist, and expressionist movements. Artists represented include Picasso, Braque, Max Ernst (one of Peggy's husbands), and Jackson Pollock (her discovery). Admission charge. *Vaporetto* stop Accademia. Palazzo Venier dei Leoni, 701 Calle Cristoforo, Dorsoduro (phone: 520-6288).

Palazzo Grassi (also called Palazzo Fiat) – Splendidly restored, it's the site of important artistic expositions of international themes. Admission charge. *Vaporetto* stop San Samuele. 3231 Campo San Samuele, San Marco (phone: 523-1680).

SHOPPING: Venetian glass is a seductive item, but most of it made today is of poor quality and design. Do a bit of comparison shopping first, and if you can, visit the museum and factories on Murano (see *Special Places*). With a keen eye to cut through the trinkets, you'll find winning souvenirs —

from inexpensive necklaces of colorful Venetian glass beads to a simple, handsome decanter or perfume flacon. Other items worth purchasing are the traditional handmade papier-mâché *Carnevale* masks, which have been enjoying a renaissance since the fete was reinstated in 1980. Almost all souvenir shops carry a sampling — from the authentic and historical to the modern and bizarre. Handmade lace can be exorbitantly expensive, but some of the smaller and simpler pieces can be charming and affordable. The widest selection can be found on Burano and in the shops around Piazza San Marco. In addition, marbleized paper products make lovely and easily transportable gifts.

Two of the city's most colorful outdoor food markets — the *Erberia* for produce and the *Pescheria* for fish — are near the Ponte di Rialto (Rialto Bridge). It is fascinating to wander here, even if you aren't shopping. During the Middle Ages, this area was the Wall Street of Europe, since Venice was queen of the seas and, therefore, queen of trade. In those days, spices, silver, and silks from the overland Eastern trade route all were sold here, and banks surrounded the area. Now it is more the staples of life that are sold from the small stalls — fruits and vegetables, coffee and cheeses, fresh game and seafood. The sounds and smells are pure Venice.

Venice's main shopping district is the area directly surrounding and west of Piazza San Marco or in the adjacent Mercerie to the north. While most shops are open in the mornings from 9 AM to 1 PM, they close for a long lunch, reopen around 3:30 PM, and remain open until 7 or 7:30. Most Venetian merchants accept major American credit cards.

Barozzi – Antique furniture, mainly 18th-century Venetian. One of the best in town. 2052 Calle delle Veste, San Marco (phone: 528-9615).

Domini – Fine silverware and china. 659-664 Calle Larga San Marco, San Marco (phone: 522-3892).

Al Duca d'Aosta – Sports clothes and accessories for men; women's wear is available across the street. 4946 Mercerie del Capitello, San Marco (phone: 534-4525).

Elysée – Elegant footwear and designer wear for men and women. 4485 Calle Goldoni, San Marco (phone: 523-6948).

Fendi – Chic clothing and leather goods for women. 1474 Salizzada San Moisè, San Marco (phone: 520-5733).

L'Isola – Contemporary museum-quality glassware designed by the Carlo Moretti firm — pieces are simple and lightweight. Some objects are displayed in the *Museum of Modern Art* in New York City. 1468 Campo San Moisè, San Marco (phone: 523-1973).

Jesurum & Co. – Exquisite lace and other handmade needlework. Ponte Canonica, Castello (phone: 706177) and a much smaller selection at its branch in Piazza San Marco.

Libreria Antiquaria La Fenice – Old books and prints. Campo San Fantin and 1850 Piazza San Marco, San Marco (phone: 523-8006).

Luigi Bevilacqua – Silk brocade, damask, and printed velvet fabrics that have draped European courts, the Vatican, and the White House. 1320 Campiello Comare, Santa Croce (phone: 23384).

Mondo Novo – The city's best *mascheraio* (mask maker). Papier-mâché masks — alligators, camels, and mummies — for *Carnevale.* 3063 Campo Santa Margherita, Dorsoduro (phone: 528-7344).

Nardi – Beautiful high-quality jewelry in the Venetian tradition — both new and antique. 69 Piazza San Marco, San Marco (phone: 522-5733).

Paola Carraro – Unique oversize sweaters made of silk, mohair, or cotton that are hand-knit renditions of some of the world's great contemporary masterpieces — from Klee to Picasso, Magritte to Warhol. On the street from the *Accademia* to the *Guggenheim,* Dorsoduro (phone: 520-6070).

Pauly – Venetian glass by one of the star producers. Ponte dei Consorzi, Castello (phone: 529899).

Piazzesi – Notebooks, boxes, albums, and other gift articles crafted from handmade marbleized papers in classic Italian style. 2511 Campiello della Feltrina, San Marco (phone: 522-1202).

Rubelli – A Venetian landmark and one of Europe's most celebrated names in exquisite fabrics, some still made by hand on 15th-century looms. 1089 Campo San Gallo, San Marco (phone: 523-6110).

Salviati – A 100-year-old firm with the highest traditions of craftsmanship in Venetian glass. Largest collection at 195 San Gregorio, Dorsoduro (phone: 522-2523); other stores at 78 Piazza San Marco, San Marco, and the glassworks museum in Murano.

Veneziartigiana – A consortium of 60 local artisans housed in a beautiful wood-paneled building that used to be a pharmacy. 412 Calle Larga San Marco, San Marco (phone: 523-5032).

Venini – The only Venetian retail store for this world-famous glass design company of contemporary hand-blown glass. 314 Piazzetta dei Leoncini, San Marco (phone: 522-4045).

V. Trois – An exclusive representative of luxurious Fortuny fabrics as well as other exquisite new and antique Venetian fabrics. 2666 Campo San Maurizio, San Marco (phone: 522-2905).

SPORTS AND FITNESS: The visitor to Venice gets plenty of exercise climbing up and down and across its hundreds of bridges. For more organized sports, one must move to the open spaces of the Lido, where the CIGA chain pretty much has the monopoly on sports activities. What they don't own, they manage, and with one phone call or fax, you can book tennis, windsurfing, water skiing, golf, or a beach cabaña. Contact them from April through October at 52 Lungomare Marconi, Lido (phone: 526-7194; fax: 526-0058).

Bicycling – A well-stocked place to rent bikes, including two-, three-, and four-seaters, as well as conventional two-wheelers, is *Giorgio Barbieri,* 5 Via Zara (no phone).

Fitness Center – *Palestra Europ* (6661/V Castello; phone: 520-7475), is the only fitness center in Venice open to visitors.

Golf – The *Golf Club Lido di Venezia* is a championship 18-hole course at the far southern end of the Lido (phone: 526-7194). It's reached by the the *C* bus from the main Lido *vaporetto* landing or the No. 11 bus, just a block away.

Jogging – Just east of Piazza San Marco, the Riva degli Schiavoni runs southeast along the water toward the Riva dei Sette Martiri and the Giardini Pubblici (public gardens) — a good 20-minute jog. Runners also may jog on the Lido beach.

Sailing – If you arrive in Venice by boat, you can moor it at one of two marinas. The most picturesque is the *Marina San Giorgio* at the island just across from Piazza San Marco. Renting a boat in Venice is almost impossible now because there have been too many accidents in the past with tourists at the helm.

Soccer – From September to May, *Venezia* plays at *Stadio Comunale P. L. Penzo,* S. Elena (phone: 522-5770).

Swimming – The northern end of the Lido has municipal beaches, all of which charge admission. Other beaches are the domain of the great luxury hotels of the Lido, but cabañas are available for an entrance fee. There is also a public pool at *Piscina Comunale Sacca Fisola,* Guidecca (phone: 528-5430).

Tennis – On the Lido, the *Tennis Club* (41/D Lungomare Marconi; phone: 526-7194) has 7 courts (2 covered; 2 lighted). Visitors also can play at the *Henkell Club* (Via Malamocco; phone: 526-0122) or the *Tennis Club Lido* (163 Via Sandro Gallo; phone: 526-0954).

THEATER: Music, rather than drama, is the performing art of Venice. If the language is not a problem, a pleasant theater for traditional and contemporary productions is *Teatro Goldoni* (4650/B Calle Goldoni, San Marco; phone: 520-5422). *Teatro Ridotto,* a delightful little rococo theater, hosts dance performances as well as drama. It's just off Piazza San Marco (Calle Vallaresso; phone: 522-2939).

MUSIC: Venice is a city with a rich musical tradition and a full calendar of musical events — as you will see from the wall posters that announce forthcoming concerts. *Teatro La Fenice* (1977 Campo San Fantin; phone: 521-0161), which celebrates its 200th anniversary this year, is the city's main auditorium. A first night at the *Fenice,* site of world premieres of opera classics by such composers as Verdi and Rossini, is a highlight of the social season. Its gold and pink plush interior is pure Venetian; tours are permitted when rehearsals are not in progress. In summer, there are concerts in various churches (where the acoustics are fabulous). If possible, attend a performance by either of the city's stellar chamber music groups: the *Solisti Veneti* or the *Sestetto a Fiati di Venezia* (Venice Wind Sextet). In winter, too, you can attend concerts in churches and in the ornate salons of palaces such as the 17th-century Palazzo Labia (now the Venice office of Italian state radio and television). Many church concerts are free, though contributions are welcome. The Chiesa della Pietà (Church of the Pietà), in the Castello *sestiere* where Vivaldi lived and worked, holds many concerts throughout the year featuring his music. Look for posters advertising these musical events along the main route between the Rialto and St. Mark's and in the weekly *Un Ospite a Venezia.*

NIGHTLIFE: *Martini Scala Piano Bar* (1980 San Marco; phone: 522-4121), is Venice's chicest nightspot and open until 3 AM. It has the same kitchen as *Antico Martini* (see *Eating Out*); the light fare is great and the prices much lower. Next to the *Teatro La Fenice,* which supplies it with a glossy, after-theater crowd, is *Antico Martini* (1983 Campo San Fantin; phone: 522-4121) a pleasant outdoor terrace and good, although very expensive, food. *Linea D'Ombra* is a lively jazz club (Fondamento Zattere, Dorsoduro; phone: 528-5295). As long as the weather holds, the city's best nightlife is the nonstop show in Piazza San Marco. Take up residence in one of the cafés, listen to the schmaltzy orchestra, and watch the world go by. Popular places for rock and disco are the *Acropolis* on the Lido (Lungomare Marconi; phone: 536-0466) and *El Souk Disco* (1056/A Accademia; phone: 520-0371). For gambling enthusiasts, the *Municipal Casino* (at the Lido; phone: 526-0626) is open from April through September — its winter home is the handsome *Palazzo Vendramin-Calergi* (on the Grand Canal; phone: 710211), open from October through March or April. Go for the opulent setting, if not to toss some chips. Both open 4 PM to 3 AM.

BEST IN TOWN

CHECKING IN: Your first decision is whether to stay out at the Lido or right in the center of town. Staying in the city might make your Venetian experience complete — you can look out onto a small picturesque canal or catch a sweeping view of the grand lagoon. But being on the Lido gets you away from the crowds. Be forewarned — Venice has some of Italy's most expensive hotels. Very expensive hotels here will charge $400 and up per night for a double; expensively priced hotels, $250 to $400; those in the moderate category, $150 to $250; inexpensive places, $80 to $150; and very inexpensive ones, $50 to $80. Most moderate hotels tack on a daily supplemental rate for air conditioning (about $15). Many hotels offer significant discounts in winter, and even in July and August.

During peak season (*Christmas* to January 6, around *Carnevale,* March 15 through June, and September and October), finding accommodations in Venice may be a problem. A pleasant solution is to stay in Padua, 20 miles and a 30-minute train ride away (see *Veneto,* DIRECTIONS) or in Ferrara, only slightly farther away (see *Emilia-Romagna,* DIRECTIONS). All telephone numbers are in the 41 city code unless otherwise indicated.

Cipriani **–** On the serene Isola della Giudecca, this luxurious, charming 3-acre oasis has a beautiful garden surrounding an Olympic-size swimming pool, and stunning views of the nearby Isola San Giorgio. Immaculate but relaxed service and such details as silk Fortuny wallpaper and heavy matching drapes are redolent of other times. Last year 9 private apartments in an exquisite old palazzo next door — each with a private butler — were added to the existing elegant rooms in the main building. All offer very formal, very capable service that's a throwback to a more formally opulent age. A sleek mahogony motorboat whisks guests to and from Piazza San Marco in 5 minutes, 24-hours a day. There is a fine restaurant in an idyllic setting. Open mid-March through mid-November. Business facilities include 24-hour room service, meeting rooms for up to 200, English-speaking concierge, foreign currency exchange, secretarial services in English, audiovisual equipment, photocopiers, computers, cable television news, translation services, and express checkout. *Vaporetto* stop San Marco. 10 Isola della Giudecca, Dorsoduro (phone: 520-7744; in the US, 800-524-2420; fax: 520-3930; telex: 410162). Very expensive.

Danieli **–** Once the residence of a 14th-century doge, this is one of Venice's largest hotels, with 222 rooms in three adjoining buildings. It is one of CIGA's crown jewels and you'll understand why just by walking into the historic palazzo's Gothic courtyard, now the hotel lobby in the Casa Vecchia. On the right is the Casa Nuova, where rooms are just as opulent but less theatrical, and on the left is the Danielino, which boasts a wonderful terrace restaurant on the top floor with a bird's-eye view of Isola San Giorgio. Service at times, however, can be less than gracious. Business facilities include 24-hour room service, meeting rooms for up to 300, English-speaking concierge, foreign currency exchange, secretarial services in English, audiovisual equipment, photocopiers, computers, cable television news, translation services, and express checkout. *Vaporetto* stop San Zaccaria. 4196 Riva degli Schiavoni, Castello (phone: 522-6480; fax: 520-0208; telex: 410077). Very expensive.

Gritti Palace **–** There are those — Ernest Hemingway was one, and we are two and three, as well as many crowned heads, film stars, and day dreamers — who would rather stay in this one-of-a-kind CIGA gem than anywhere else in Europe. Once the Renaissance residence of the Venetian doge Andrea Gritti who died here in 1538, it is one of the world's most celebrated hotels — famous for excellent service, a classic dining room (see *Eating Out*), and a beautiful dining terrace overlooking the Grand Canal. It also offers its guests use of the CIGA sports facilities — private beach, tennis, golf, and horseback riding — on the Lido. Exquisite interiors capture quintessential historical Venice at its best. Business facilities include 24-hour room service, meeting rooms for up to 80, English-speaking concierge, foreign currency exchange, secretarial services in English, audiovisual equipment, photocopiers, computers, cable television news, translation services, and express checkout. *Vaporetto* stop Santa Maria del Giglio. 2467 Campo Santa Maria del Giglio, San Marco (phone: 794611; fax: 520-0942; telex: 410125). Very expensive.

Locanda Cipriani **–** Even Venetians dream of honeymooning here on the peaceful, otherworldly island of Torcello, 40 minutes from Piazza San Marco. Most settle for a memorable meal (see *Eating Out*), for even though the inn's 6 country-style rooms are charmingly simple (so agreed Winston Churchill), obligatory half board makes this a costly escape. You'll never feel so removed from civilization, yet you'll have the luxury of first class dining just downstairs. Opened in 1936 by the man who gave the world *Harry's Bar* and now managed by his daughter and grandson. Closed in winter. *Vaporetto* stop Torcello. 29 Piazza San Fosca, Torcello (phone: 730150; fax: 735433). Very expensive.

Bauer Grünwald and Grand – Visiting royalty often stays in the poshest suites in this Grand Canal hotel, near Piazza San Marco. The hotel's other 200 rooms and junior suites are primarily populated by tour groups. There have been complaints recently about the service, but its roof garden, piano bar, and fine restaurant offer some of the loveliest vantage points from which to admire the city. Business facilities include 24-hour room service, meeting rooms for up to 160, English-speaking concierge, foreign currency exchange, secretarial services in English, audiovisual equipment, photocopiers, cable television news, translation services, and express checkout. *Vaporetto* stop San Marco. 1459 Campo San Moisè, San Marco (phone: 523-1520; fax: 520-7557; telex: 410075). Very expensive to expensive.

Monaco and Grand Canal – The intimate seclusion of this elegant yet homey hotel is just a minute's walk from Piazza San Marco and was constructed from three 18th-century family houses. Its acclaimed restaurant, suitably named *Grand Canal,* has a lovely flowered terrace directly across from the beautiful Chiesa di Santa Maria della Salute. Business facilities include 24-hour room service, meeting rooms for up to 50, English-speaking concierge, foreign currency exchange, secretarial services in English, audiovisual equipment, photocopiers, computers, cable television news, translation services, and express checkout. *Vaporetto* stop San Marco. 1325 Vallaresso, San Marco (phone: 520-0211; fax: 520-0501; telex: 410450). Very expensive to expensive.

Cavalletto e Doge Orseolo – Wonderfully situated two steps from Piazza San Marco, most of the 40 rooms overlook the colorful Bacino Orseolo, a kind of parking lot for gondolas (be sure to ask for one). Originally the home of Doge Orseolo, this completely restored 12th-century palazzo is stately and handsome and has a restaurant. Business facilities include meeting rooms for up to 40, English-speaking concierge, foreign currency exchange, secretarial services in English, audiovisual equipment, photocopiers, computers, translation services, and express checkout. *Vaporetto* stop San Marco. 1107 Bacino Orseolo, San Marco (phone: 520-0955; fax: 523-8184; telex: 410684). Expensive.

Excelsior Palace – This luxurious Old World property, refurbished in an exotic Hispano-Moorish style, established the Lido as a luxury seaside resort for Europe's monied set. Since 1937 it has played a key role in the prestigious *International Film Festival* held across the street. It has its own fine restaurant, private beach, tennis courts, and transportation to CIGA's horseback riding and a golf course off the hotel's property. Open *Easter* through October. Business facilities include 24-hour room service, meeting rooms for up to 600, English-speaking concierge, foreign currency exchange, secretarial services in English, audiovisual equipment, photocopiers, cable television news, translation services, and express checkout. *Vaporetto* stop Lido. 41 Lungomare Marconi, Lido (phone: 526-0201; fax: 526-7276; telex: 4210023). Expensive.

Grand Hotel des Bains – On the Lido, this stately, porticoed, luxurious, and gracefully old-fashioned hotel is where Luchino Visconti filmed much of *Death in Venice.* Its painstaking renovations were completed last year. It has spacious rooms and bathrooms, and is across the road from its private beach and luxurious cabañas. Part of the CIGA chain, it shares tennis, golf, and horseback riding facilities with the *Excelsior* down the road. Open *Easter* through October. Business facilities include meeting rooms for up to 400, English-speaking concierge, foreign currency exchange, secretarial services in English, audiovisual equipment, photocopiers, cable television news, translation services, and express checkout. *Vaporetto* stop Lido. 17 Lungomare Marconi, Lido (phone: 526-5921; fax: 526-0113; telex: 410142). Expensive.

Londra Palace – This charming place on a popular promenade offers the wonderful, romantic views of the Bacino di San Marco and the Byzantine Chiesa di San Zaccaria that inspired Tchaikovsky to write his *Fourth Symphony.* All 69 rooms have modern bathrooms, and a few have private balconies. Other amenities include a very good restaurant, an elegant bar, and a sixth-floor panoramic sun deck. Guests have a Mercedes at their disposal for a 1-day jaunt through the Veneto. Business facilities include meeting rooms for up to 200, English-speaking concierge, foreign currency exchange, secretarial services in English, audiovisual equipment, photocopiers, computers, cable television news, translation services, and express checkout. *Vaporetto* stop San Zaccaria. 4171 Riva degli Schiavoni, San Marco (phone: 520-0533; fax: 522-5032; telex: 431315). Expensive.

Luna Baglioni – Years of restoration have transformed this regal 115-room hotel into a cool marble palace with frescoed ceilings and imposing chandeliers made from Murano glass. Upper floors look out on the Giardinetti Reali (a lovely park) and neighboring *Harry's Bar* and over to the island of San Giorgio. There is a restaurant, and guests have access to numerous sports facilities on the Lido. Business facilities include meeting rooms for up to 150, English-speaking concierge, foreign currency exchange, secretarial services in English, audiovisual equipment, photocopiers, computers, cable television news, translation services, and express checkout. *Vaporetto* stop San Marco. 1243 Calle Vallaresso, San Marco (phone: 528-9840; in the US, 800-448-8355; fax: 528-7160; telex: 410236). Expensive.

Metropole – One of the last big hotels along the stretch of Riva degli Schiavoni toward the Arsenale, this hostelry offers exceptionally amiable service and an owner who is an avid antiques collector (each of the 64 rooms is decorated differently). Room 349 on the top floor may not overlook the lagoon as many of the others do, but a huge, elaborately hand-carved wooden bed and one of Venice's famed *altana* (wooden terraces) make you feel as if you're on top of the world. Vivaldi once lived here in far more monastic surroundings when the palazzo belonged to the adjacent Pietà Church. Free parking at the Piazzale Roma is available for hotel guests. Business facilities include 24-hour room service, meeting rooms for up to 80, English-speaking concierge, foreign currency exchange, secretarial services in English, audiovisual equipment, photocopiers, computers, translation services, and express checkout. *Vaporetto* stop San Zaccaria. 4149 Riva degli Schiavoni, Castello (phone: 520-5044; fax: 522-3679; telex: 410340). Expensive.

Bellini – Elegant Venetian decor replete with inlaid marble, matching silk wallpaper and drapes, authentic period pieces, and impressive Murano chandeliers. Just a block from the train station, this first class 70-room hotel was recently reopened after a major overhaul. It has a restaurant and sun deck with a view of the Grand Canal. Business facilities include meeting rooms for up to 80, English-speaking concierge, foreign currency exchange, secretarial services in English, audiovisual equipment, photocopiers, computers, cable television news, translation services, and express checkout. *Vaporetto* stop Ferrovia. 116 Lista di Spagna, Cannaregio (phone: 524-2488; in the US, 800-448-8355; fax: 715193; telex: 420374). Expensive to moderate.

Pullman Park – On the outskirts of the Papodopoli Gardens, this large, attractive hotel with efficient service is on a small canal. It is a very short walk from Piazzale Roma (the first stop for everyone en route from the airport by bus or car), the train station, and all the must-sees in the Santa Croce neighborhood. All 100 rooms are furnished in 18th-century Venetian style and those on the top floor have private balconies. It has easy access to the main *vaporetto* lines to all parts of Venice. Business facilities include 24-hour room service, meeting rooms for up to 110, English-speaking concierge, foreign currency exchange, secretarial services in English, audiovisual equipment, photocopiers, computers, cable television news, and translation services. *Vaporetto* stop Piazzale Roma. 245 Giardino Papadopoli, Santa Croce (phone: 528-5394; in the US, 800-223-9862; fax: 523-0043; telex: 410310). Expensive to moderate.

Accademia – In the 17th-century Villa Maravegie, this tranquil, rather stately, family-run establishment is near the *Galleria dell'Accademia.* It has a lovely garden where breakfast is served, with a view down a small canal to the Grand Canal. Wide vestibules, high ceilings, and the ambience of a private home from another era are slowly getting a much-needed uplift while leaving the informal *ambiente* intact. *Vaporetto* stop Accademia. 1058 Fondamenta Maravegie, Dorsoduro (phone: 523-7846; fax: 523-9152). Moderate.

Ala – In a charming *campo* directly behind its grand luxe neighbor, the *Gritti,* is this gracious and traditional hotel. Restoration of its 85 rooms is scheduled to be completed this year. It's about equidistant from Piazza San Marco and the *Galleria dell'Accademia. Vaporetto* stop Santa Maria del Giglio. 2494 Campo Santa Maria del Giglio, San Marco (phone: 520-8333; fax: 520-6390). Moderate.

Bisanzio – Although it is tucked away in one of the oldest and quietest corners of town, this hostelry is nevertheless close to everything. Of the 40 rooms decorated in the grand manner of Old Venice (Murano chandeliers, damask curtains, and so on), 6 of them have private terraces, some overlooking the nearby Chiesa della Pietà on the Riva degli Schiavoni. It has a private mooring for gondolas. *Vaporetto* stop San Zaccaria. 3651 Calle della Pietà, Castello (phone: 520-3100; in the US, 800-528-1234; fax: 520-4114). Moderate.

Bonvecchiati – Comfortable, with 86 rooms, midway between Piazza San Marco and the Rialto, it boasts an impressive collection of contemporary art. A bar and lovely terrace restaurant overlook a lively canal (as do 12 of the guestrooms). *Vaporetto* stop San Marco or Rialto. 4488 Calle Goldoni, San Marco (phone: 528-5017; fax: 528-5230). Moderate.

Cassiano – There are 36 rooms in this restored 15th-century Gothic palazzo on the Grand Canal; 6 of them (all triples, but they can be booked as doubles for a small supplement) look out on the *Canalazzo* (as the Venetians call their beloved canal). Decor is the predictable 18th-century Venetian, but leave it all behind and bring your lemonade out on the hotel's private landing overlooking the glorious façade of the Ca' d'Oro. *Vaporetto* stop San Stae. On the Grand Canal, Santa Croce (phone: 524-1735; fax: 721033). Moderate.

La Fenice et des Artistes – Behind the *Teatro La Fenice* in a lively, popular neighborhood, this refined 61-room hotel has always appealed to opera buffs, performers, and musicians. There is a pretty garden, and marble, beam ceilings, and antique Venetian decor throughout. Its new management recently reopened the wonderful *La Taverna La Fenice* restaurant next door (see *Eating Out*). *Vaporetto* stop Santa Maria del Giglio or San Marco. 1936 Campo San Fantin, San Marco (phone: 523-2333; fax: 520-3721). Moderate.

Flora – This small jewel of a hotel (44 rooms) has a beautiful, flowered patio where you can eat breakfast or have afternoon tea or an evening *aperitivo.* Located 5 minutes west of Piazza San Marco, the atmosphere is tranquil and gracious. Ask for No. 47, a corner room on the top floor — it looks out onto Desdemona's palazzo (of *Otello* fame) with the dome of Santa Maria della Salute in the background. *Vaporetto* stop San Marco. 2283 Calle Larga XXII Marzo, San Marco (phone: 520-5844; fax: 522-8217). Moderate.

Giorgione – A top-to-bottom refurbishment completed last year (as well as the addition of more rooms this year) has left this 75-room hotel fresh, attractive, and inviting. It's located on a quiet side street off the popular Campo Santi Apostoli and is a minute's walk from the Ca' d'Oro and the Rialto. *Vaporetto* stop Ca' d'Oro. 4587 Salizada del Pistor, Campo SS. Apostoli, Cannaregio (phone: 522-5810; fax: 523-9092). Moderate.

Hungaria – Built in 1906, the mosaic façade of this 100-room hotel is a riveting focus of one of the Lido's main streets. The guestrooms are large, clean, and simple, and it has a comfortable Old World charm enlivened by a predominantly European clientele. A private beach shared by a number of the smaller hotels and the lagoon-side *vaporetto* dock are just 5 minutes away. Parking is available. *Vaporetto* stop Lido. 28 Gran Viale, Lido (phone: 526-1212; fax: 526-7619). Moderate.

Kette – Tucked in a quiet spot between *La Fenice* and Piazza San Marco, this charming and efficient hostelry is within strolling distance of everything, and has its own private dock for gondolas. *Vaporetto* stop San Marco. 2053 Piscina San Moisè, San Marco (phone: 522-7766; fax: 522-8964). Moderate.

Mapaba – There are 60 rooms in this property on the Lido. Your stay here will be tranquil and relaxing, whether reading in the hotel's wonderful garden or biking to nearby beach facilities arranged by the hotel. Open *Easter* to October. *Vaporetto* stop Lido. 16 Riviera San Nicolò, Lido (phone: 526-0590; fax: 526-9441). Moderate.

Panada – Renovations 3 years ago spruced up all of the 48 old Venetian-decorated rooms, 3 of which boast Jacuzzis. Common areas are modern and marble, all a minute's walk north of Piazza San Marco. There is no restaurant, but there is a cocktail lounge. *Vaporetto* stop San Marco. 646 Calle Specchieri, San Marco (phone: 520-9088; in the US, 800-221-6509; fax: 520-9619). Moderate.

Do Pozzi – Small, attractive, and just a minute west of Piazza San Marco, it has a pleasant atmosphere and a lively canalside restaurant, *Da Raffaele.* Breakfast is served in a charming courtyard. *Vaporetto* stop Santa Maria del Giglio or San Marco. 2373 Calle Larga XXII Marzo, San Marco (phone: 520-7855; fax: 522-9413). Moderate.

Quattro Fontane – Transformed from a 19th-century villa, this quiet 68-room hostelry with excellent service offers the peace of an English country garden. It still has the air of a family dwelling, with antique furniture of various origins and a pleasant alfresco restaurant. Set back from the main street, midway between the *Excelsior* and the *Grand Hotel des Bains.* Closed most of October through the end of April. *Vaporetto* stop Lido. 16 Via Quattro Fontane, Lido (phone: 526-0227; fax: 526-0726). Moderate.

Rialto – You can almost touch Venice's world-famous bridge from half of this hotel's 70 rooms; some of them with small wrought-iron balconies afford incomparable views. Double-paned windows and air conditioning (for an extra charge) keep out the inevitable cacophony of the busiest spot in town. The decor is a cross between modern and 18th-century Venice, with handsome beam ceilings; there is a restaurant. *Vaporetto* stop Rialto. 5149 Ponte di Rialto, San Marco (phone: 520-9166; fax: 523-8958). Moderate.

San Stefano – Last year's renovation of this former 15th-century watchtower-cum-hotel has created an intimate and immaculate oasis in one of the city's most elegant squares. There are only 11 rooms (8 overlooking the *campo*), each with brand-new, tiled bathrooms and lovingly decorated by the owner's wife. Very friendly service, excellent location, but no restaurant. *Vaporetto* stop San Samuele. 2947 Campo San Stefano, San Marco (phone: 520-0166; fax: 522-4460). Moderate.

Santa Chiara – With 28 rooms and a Grand Canal location — with beamed ceilings, antique furniture, and many views of the canal — it is particularly convenient for guests arriving by car (you can pull up to the back door before dropping it off at the car park across the street — a rare amenity in Venice). *Vaporetto* stop Piazzale Roma. 548 Piazzale Roma, Santa Croce (phone: 520-6955; fax: 522-8799). Moderate.

Savoia e Jolanda – This 78-room hotel, reopened last year after an extensive renovation, has two buildings. All the guestrooms in the main palazzo have a balcony and face the Grand Canal, but air conditioning hasn't been added yet. In the warm weather, you might want to stay in the *dependence* (where there is a cooling system) that overlooks a quiet piazza and the important Church of San Zaccaria. It has a restaurant. *Vaporetto* stop San Zaccaria. 4187 Riva degli Schiavoni, Castello (phone: 522-4130; fax: 520-7494). Moderate.

Seguso – Obligatory half board doesn't seem to daunt any of the regular guests, making this otherwise inexpensive family-run hotel moderate in price. Children are welcome in this 33-room hostelry on the sunny, Zattere promenade, with sweeping views of Giudecca island. *Vaporetto* stop Zattere. 779 Zattere, Dorsoduro (phone and fax: 522-2340). Moderate.

Torino – Tucked in a corner near fancier hotels, close to Piazza San Marco, this comfortable 20-room place located in a 16th-century palazzo is within easy reach of *La Fenice. Vaporetto* stop Santa Maria del Giglio or San Marco. 2356 Calle delle Ostreghe, San Marco (phone: 520-5222; fax: 522-8227). Moderate.

Campiello – In the shadow of big, well-known hotels sits this small family-run property in a quiet little piazza off the Riva degli Schiavoni. There are 15 clean and simple rooms. *Vaporetto* stop San Zaccaria. 4647 Calle del Vin, Castello (phone: 520-5764; fax: 520-5798). Inexpensive.

Canada – There's no elevator here, and the lobby is on the third floor, but if you have good legs, ask for either of the top floor's 2 rooms with beamed ceilings, a terrace, and roofscape. It is a minute's walk from the Rialto on one of the main arteries to Piazza San Marco. *Vaporetto* stop Rialto. 5659 Calle San Lio, Castello (phone: 522-9912; fax: 523-5852). Inexpensive.

Novo Teson – This 30-room hotel is located in a lively neighborhood near the Arsenale, across the street from the popular *Al Covo* restaurant (see *Eating Out*) and a stone's throw from the waterfront. Small, simple rooms with shower, though no air conditioning. *Vaporetto* stop Arsenale. 3980 Riva degli Schiavoni, Castello (phone: 522-9929; fax: 528-5335). Inexpensive.

Paganelli – This hostelry encompasses two buildings, each with 11 rooms. One has been renovated — all the rooms are air conditioned and have beautifully tiled bathrooms. In the other, less quiet half, the rooms offer character, wooden beams, occasionally a view of the Grand Canal, and air conditioning. Great value for Venice. *Vaporetto* stop San Zaccaria. 4183 Riva degli Schiavoni (phone: 522-4324; fax: 523-9267). Inexpensive.

La Residenza – A delightful 14th-century building that is little more than a stone's throw from the busy Riva degli Schiavoni. An enormous salon and 15 less dramatic guestrooms for lovers of faded grandeur and the drama of centuries past. Closed mid-November to mid-February. *Vaporetto* stop Arsenale. 3608 Campo Bandiera e Moro, Castello (phone: 528-5315; fax: 523-8859). Inexpensive.

Serenissima – Midway between the Rialto and Piazza San Marco, this hotel has 37 rooms, both with and without bath. Over 400 works of contemporary art make this place a magnet for those who appreciate the blend of modern painting and old-style decor. Closed mid-November to *Carnevale. Vaporetto* stop Rialto or San

Marco. 4486 Calle Goldoni, San Marco (phone: 520-0011; fax: 522-3292). Inexpensive.

Locanda Montin – This 7-room place overlooking a charming stretch of canal with flower-covered balconies is ideal for those who want to spend little and be in a quiet, centrally located neighborhood. Ask for the room where Eleonora Duse and Gabriele D'Annunzio stayed. You'll sacrifice a private bathroom, but the payoff is the good food served in the far more expensive restaurant downstairs that used to be frequented by artists and intellectuals before it became trendy. There is a collection of original paintings by Venetian artists of the 1950s and 1960s, many of whom were regulars. *Vaporetto* stop Accademia. 1147 Fondamenta Eremite, Dorsoduro (phone: 522-7151). Very inexpensive.

Noemi – None of the 15 rooms here has private baths, but the shared facilities are clean and you'll feel as if you're visiting a dear Venetian aunt with your gracious octogenarian host, Signora Noemi. Downstairs is the well-known restaurant named after her (see *Eating Out*). Most guestrooms have impressive antique pieces that once graced the signora's home, and the stair's banister is an unusual tribute to Murano glasswork. *Vaporetto* stop San Marco. 909 Calle dei Fabbri, San Marco (phone: 523-8144). Very inexpensive.

EATING OUT: One of life's great pleasures is dining out in Venice in good weather — alongside a canal on one of the wide, sunny squares, or in a little garden shaded by vine leaves. But in winter the crowded tables and warm interiors offer refuge from the misty, melancholy streets. As for the fare, everyone's perfect idea of Venice is eating a delicious seafood dinner and drinking a good wine from Veneto. It might be easier to find the idyllic setting than reliably good, fresh seafood dinners that have become quite expensive and hard to find. Frozen fish is too often served when an unknowing tourist doesn't ask about whether it is *fresco,* although a city law requires that menus specify which are *surgelato* (frozen) and which are fresh (often they don't). It is not uncommon to see Venetians at the next table eating fresher fish for lower prices. Be forewarned — the fish market is closed on Mondays, so the restaurant's pickings are slim. Prices for dinner for two, with wine, range from $150 to a whopping $225 at a very expensive restaurant; $100 to $175 at an expensive one; $50 to $100 at a moderate place; and $40 to $50 in the inexpensive category. Don't plan to linger too late; most restaurants take their last orders at about 10:30 PM or earlier. All telephone numbers are in the 41 city code unless otherwise indicated.

Antico Martini – One of Venice's classiest restaurants, across the square from the fabled *Teatro La Fenice,* serves both international and Venetian specialties in a *Belle Epoque* setting. It has a fine wine list and the kitchen accepts orders until 11:30 PM for the sophisticated after-theater crowd. Closed Tuesdays, Wednesday lunch, and December to mid-March. Reservations necessary. Major credit cards accepted. *Vaporetto* stop San Marco. 1983 Campo San Fantin, San Marco (phone: 522-4121). Very expensive.

Club del Doge – In the *Gritti Palace* hotel, right on the Grand Canal, this is the place for a delicious selection of both traditional Venetian and continental dishes served in deluxe surroundings. In good weather, diners are served on a flower-bedecked canalside terrace across from the Chiesa di Santa Maria della Salute. Open daily. Reservations necessary. Major credit cards accepted. *Vaporetto* stop Santa Maria del Giglio. 2467 Campo Santa Maria del Giglio, San Marco (phone: 794611). Very expensive.

Harry's Bar – The original establishment to carry this moniker and long a Venetian landmark, it is also the city's only restaurant to be awarded one Michelin star. This popular spot is crowded with tourists in summer, and during the film and art festivals, it is the place to celebrity watch. The food is splendid, though it may be a bit overpriced. The Bellini cocktail was born here. Closed Mondays and most of January. Reservations necessary for the upstairs restaurant. Major credit cards accepted. Directly in front of the San Marco *vaporetto* stop. 1323 Calle Vallaresso, San Marco (phone: 523-6797). Very expensive.

Locanda Cipriani – The almost pastoral tranquillity of the garden makes this a perfect place for a leisurely lunch, or serene stay (see *Checking In*). The restaurant, under the same management as *Harry's Bar,* sits on an ancient piazza on the sleepy island of Torcello. Closed Tuesdays and in the winter. Reservations advised. Major credit cards accepted. *Vaporetto* stop Torcello. 29 Piazza San Fosca, Torcello (phone: 730757). Very expensive.

Quadri – A formal dinner here brings you back in time to the days of La Serenissima when lavish surroundings, deft service, and excellent *cucina veneta* was befitting a doge, with prices to match. Surprisingly, it is the only full-blown restaurant in the whole of Piazza San Marco. There also is a café downstairs. Closed Mondays. Reservations advised. Major credit cards accepted. *Vaporetto* stop San Marco. 120 Piazza San Marco (phone: 528-9299). Very expensive.

La Colomba – Sooner or later, everyone drops in at this favorite Venetian hangout near *La Fenice,* as folks have since the 1700s. Large, elegant, and always crowded, it has a lovely outside terrace, a renowned collection of modern art on the walls, and an equally creative array of meat and seafood specialties. Try *cartoccio Colomba,* Adriatic fish baked in a paper bag. Closed Wednesdays from November through June. Reservations advised. Major credit cards accepted. *Vaporetto* stop Santa Maria del Giglio or San Marco. 1665 Piscina di Frezzeria, San Marco (phone: 522-1175). Expensive.

Corte Sconta – Despite its steadily increasing prices, this old neighborhood *bacaro* (wine bar) has held onto its welcoming atmosphere. Old-timers still congregate at the bar, leaving the bare wooden tables to the savvy clientele who've found this hidden spot for inventive and traditional fish dishes prepared by the young chef. Closed Sundays, Mondays, January, and mid-July to mid-August. Reservations advised. Major credit cards accepted. *Vaporetto* stop Arsenale. 3886 Calle del Pestrin, Castello (phone: 522-7024). Expensive.

Da Fiore – This venerable establishment is a Venetian tradition for its simple treatment of fresh fish and shellfish, as well as fresh vegetable specialties and home-baked breads and desserts. Closed Sundays, Mondays, the last 3 weeks of August, and from *Christmas* to January 6. Reservations necessary. Major credit cards accepted. *Vaporetto* stop San Tomà. 2202 Calle del Scaleter, San Polo (phone: 721308). Expensive.

Al Graspo de Ua – This colorful and popular place is in a 19th-century blacksmith's shop and has been a restaurant for over 100 years. It offers very good Venetian and regional dishes, fresh fish, and a good selection of wines. Closed Mondays, Tuesdays, mid-December to mid-January, and late July to mid-August. Reservations advised. Major credit cards accepted. *Vaporetto* stop Rialto. 5094 Calle Bombaseri, San Marco. (phone: 522-3647). Expensive.

Malamocco – A favorite of after-theater crowds (one of those rare few in town to stay open until midnight), it has elegant 18th-century decor, beamed ceilings, and is set in a pretty little square for outdoor eating. Closed Wednesdays, and early January to early February. Reservations advised. Major credit cards accepted. *Vaporetto* stop San Zaccaria. 4650 Campiello del Vin, Castello (phone: 522-7438). Expensive.

Taverna La Fenice – New management, young blood, undaunted enthusiasm, and a talented chef from the *Gritti* hotel promise to resuscitate this refined restaurant in the shadow of the *Teatro La Fenice.* For openers, try the *fettuccine alla Pavarotti* (with a cream base, escarole, and slivers of chicken breast and tongue), then move on to the fresh *sogliola alla Fenice* (filet of sole with zucchini, shrimp, and clams). There also are delicious meat entrées. Closed Wednesdays and January. Reservations advised. Major credit cards accepted. *Vaporetto* stop San Marco or Santa Maria del Giglio. 1938 Campo de la Fenice, San Marco (phone: 522-3856). Expensive.

Al Covo – Both owners — the Texan Diane and the Venetian Cesare — are reason enough to come here every night of your stay in Venice. She's as friendly and enthusiastic as he is talented and creative. Both are passionately dedicated to offering the freshest fish their suppliers can provide. Relatively new on the scene, the setting is handsome and relaxed and the staff exceptionally friendly. Although it is considered one of the best places in town for fresh fish and shellfish, carnivores will be just as delighted. Closed Wednesdays and Thursdays. Reservations advised. Major credit cards accepted. *Vaporetto* stop Arsenale. 3968 Campiello della Pescaria, Castello (phone: 522-3812). Expensive to moderate.

Osteria del Ponte del Diavolo – With two restaurants on the charming island of Torcello, it won't be hard to find this popular eatery owned by Corrado Alfonso, the former chef at the *Locanda Cipriani.* What's on the menu, from appetizers to desserts, is determined by what's in season. Open for lunch only, except June through August when dinner also is served; closed Thursdays. Reservations advised, especially on weekends. Major credit cards accepted. *Vaporetto* stop Torcello. Torcello (phone: 730401). Expensive to moderate.

Antica Bessetta – Venetian home-cooking is hard to beat, and here it is at its best in the fresh vegetable and homemade pasta dishes as well as in the more sophisticated (and expensive) fish specialties. Closed Tuesdays, Wednesdays, and mid-July to mid-August. No reservations. No credit cards accepted. *Vaporetto* stop Riva Biasio. 1395 Calle Salvio, Santa Croce (phone: 721687). Moderate.

Caffè Orientale – In a particularly delightful spot near the Chiesa Dei Frari with a romantic terrace on the Rio Marin, this family-run restaurant is as popular with the local Venetians as with foot-weary tourists for lunch. The menu (be prepared for Venetian dialect) includes reliably fresh Adriatic fish. Closed Mondays, January, and 2 weeks in August. Reservations advised. Major credit cards accepted. *Vaporetto* stop San Tomà. 2426 Calle dell' Olio, San Polo (phone: 719804). Moderate.

Ai Gondolieri – This dining spot serves a menu of traditional meat dishes to a full house of predominantly Italian patrons in a typical trattoria setting. The fresh pasta ushers in a memorable meal. Closed Wednesdays. Reservations advised. Major credit cards accepted. *Vaporetto* stop Accademia or Salute. 366 Ponte del Formager, Dorsoduro (phone: 528-6396). Moderate.

Da Ivo – When Venetians can't look another sea bass in the face, they head here to enjoy chef Ivo's renowned *bistecca alla fiorentina.* If you've just come from Florence, the menu's specialties will look familiar — and inviting. Try the *pappardelle alla marinara* (thick, flat pasta in tomato, caper, and black olive sauce). Open until 11:30 PM. Closed Sundays and 3 weeks in January. Reservations advised. Major credit cards accepted. *Vaporetto* stop San Marco or Rialto. 1809 Calle dei Fuseri, San Marco (phone: 528-5004). Moderate.

Noemi – Salmon mousse, *risotto nero* (made with squid), and shrimp pâté are some of the many specialties at this well-known, family-run eatery. The elderly Signora Noemi now runs the show upstairs where 15 rooms are rented to lucky visitors (see *Checking In*), while her son efficiently takes care of things in the kitchen. Closed Sundays, Monday afternoons, and January 5 to February 15. Reservations advised. Major credit cards accepted. *Vaporetto* stop Rialto or San Marco. 909 Calle dei Fabbri, San Marco (phone: 522-5238). Moderate.

Riviera – Possibly the best restaurant on the wide Zattere promenade overlooking the Giudecca Canal. With decades of experience at the legendary *Harry's Bar,* the owner serves some homemade pasta that gives that institution a run for its money. The delicious *gnocchi alla gorgonzola* has a creamy cheese sauce with a bite. Closed Sunday evenings and Mondays. Reservations advised. Major credit cards accepted. *Vaporetto* stop San Basilio. 1474 Fondamenta le Zattere, Dorsoduro (phone: 522-7621). Moderate.

Da Valentino – On the Lido, this small dining spot with garden and terrace serves Venetian fish and meat specialties, including game in season. Homemade desserts and good local wines are an integral part of any meal here. Closed Mondays, Tuesdays, and Wednesdays during off-season, and October through mid-November. Seating is limited, so reservations are advised. Major credit cards accepted. *Vaporetto* stop Lido. 81 San Sandro Gallo, Lido (phone: 526-0128). Moderate.

Al Vecio Cantier – If you're on the Lido, it's worth the 10-minute taxi ride south to Alberoni and this lovely trattoria known for its fresh fish dishes. Try the enormous array of fish-based antipasti, or any of the daily specials, including *branzino,* sweeter than the American sea bass, expertly prepared *alla griglia* (grilled), and served outdoors when the weather is good. Closed Monday and Tuesday lunch, and November through January. Reservations advised. Visa accepted. *Vaporetto* stop Lido. 76 Via della Droma, Alberoni, Lido (phone: 731130). Moderate.

Alla Madonna – Brightly lit and lively, on a little side street on the San Polo (not San Marco) side of the Ponte di Rialto, it is a consistent favorite with Venetians because of its professional service (despite the bustle), reasonable prices, and reliably good food in unpretentious surroundings. Closed Wednesdays, 2 weeks in August, and December 24 to January 31. No reservations. Major credit cards accepted. *Vaporetto* stop Rialto. 594 Calle della Madonna, San Polo (phone: 522-3824). Moderate to inexpensive.

Al Mascaron – A great place for a meal after a visit to the nearby churches of Santa Maria Formosa or Santissimi Giovanni e Paolo. Join the food-wise habitués for a good, reasonably priced meal. Closed Sundays. No reservations. No credit cards accepted. *Vaporetto* stop Rialto. 5225 Calle Lunga Santa Maria Formosa, Castello (phone: 522-5995). Moderate to inexpensive.

Osteria Ca' d'Oro alla Vedova – This attractive place has successfully made the transition from *bacaro* (wine bar) to trattoria. It boasts a particularly well stocked wine cellar to accompany its Venetian fish and vegetable dishes, polenta (not always so easy to find in Venice), and Veneto cheeses. Closed Thursdays. No reservations. No credit cards accepted. *Vaporetto* stop Ca' d'Oro. 3912 Via Nova, Cannaregio (phone: 528-5324). Moderate to inexpensive.

Al Teatro – No place stays open so late (1 AM) and offers so much. Its neighbor, *Teatro La Fenice,* supplies much of the late-night crowd, but lots of others stop by for an *aperitivo,* a pizza, or full-course dinner. There is a piano bar, *Club la Mansarda,* on the top floor that stays open until 3 AM. Closed Mondays. No reservations. Major credit cards accepted. *Vaporetto* stop Santa Maria del Giglio. 1916 Campo San Fantin, San Marco (phone: 523-7214). Moderate to inexpensive.

Altanella – Four generations have been producing nothing but the freshest fish in a homey, no-frills ambience on the island of Giudecca, one of the least touristy areas of Venice. Try any of the daily specials, mostly grilled fresh fish, or the very light *fritto misto.* There are a few tables on a charming *altanella* (wooden terrace) over a small, pretty canal, so book in advance. Closed Monday evenings, Tuesdays, and most of August. No credit cards accepted. *Vaporetto* stop Redentore or Traghetto. 264 Calle dell'Erbe, Giudecca (phone: 522-7780). Inexpensive.

Al Bacareto – Near Campo Santo Stefano, this rustic trattoria has a few tables outside and a welcoming dining room inside where you can sample traditional local dishes, such as *bigoli in salsa* (whole wheat spaghetti with anchovy and onion sauce) or *fegato alla veneziana* (sautéed liver with onions). This is a home away from home for the artisans and residents of the Salizzada San Samuele area. Closed Saturday dinner and Sundays. No reservations. Major credit cards accepted. *Vaporetto* stop San Samuele. 3447 Calle Crosera, San Marco (phone: 89336). Inexpensive.

Dona Onesta – After a few hours at the Frari and the nearby Scuola di San Rocco, it's an easy walk to this congenial trattoria with simple, reliable food. The nearby university supplies a regular clientele of happy patrons. Closed Sundays. No reservations. Visa accepted. *Vaporetto* stop San Tomà. 3922 Calle de Dona Onesta, Dorsoduro (phone: 522-9586). Inexpensive.

Al Milion – Marco Polo's memoirs — he lived nearby — gave this *bacaro* (wine bar) its name. The food and *ambiente* are simple and unpretentious, yet enjoyable, and the selection of wines impressive. Closed Wednesdays and most of August. Reservations advised. No credit cards accepted. *Vaporetto* stop Rialto. 5841 San Giovanni Crisostomo, Cannaregio (phone: 522-9302). Inexpensive.

Pizzeria le Oche – With an incredible 40 varieties to choose from, this is the Baskin-Robbins of Venice's pizzerias. There's a pleasant garden in the back, but if you're lucky, there will be a free table out in front, the better to enjoy your *disco volante* (flying saucer) — two pizzas face to face like a giant sandwich — or the *mangiafuoco* with spicy salami and chili peppers. Closed Sundays. No reservations. Major credit cards accepted. *Vaporetto* stop San Stae or Rio Biasio. 1552 Calle del Tinto, Santa Croce (phone: 27559). Inexpensive.

Pizzeria alla Zattere – This is the favorite of pizza aficionados as much for its lengthy list of delicious pies as for its idyllic views of the Giudecca Canal. Closed Tuesdays. No reservations. No credit cards accepted. *Vaporetto* stop Zattere. 795 Zattere ai Gesuati, Dorsoduro (phone: 704224). Inexpensive.

Da Remigio – The food at this neighborhood trattoria is reliably good and the prices surprisingly low for a place so close to San Marco. Fresh fish, however, will hike your otherwise conservative bill. Closed Monday evenings and Tuesdays. No reservations. No credit cards aceptrd. *Vaporetto* stop Arsenale. 3416 Salizzada dei Greci, Castello (phone: 523-0083). Inexpensive.

Trattoria San Tomà – You might see pasta hanging out to dry in the sun, but most neighborhood regulars seem to return here for pizza while sitting in the lovely garden in the back. There also are a few tables in front in a charming little piazza. Closed Tuesdays. No reservations. Major credit cards accepted. *Vaporetto* stop San Tomà. 2864 Campo San Tomà, San Polo (phone: 523-8819). Inexpensive.

La Zucca – The name, "The Pumpkin," hints at its vegetarian menu and some of its specialties, such as cream of pumpkin soup and pumpkin bread. It is always packed with a young, sophisticated, and interesting crowd that is mostly Venetian, as this place is off the tourist track. Desserts are homemade and delicious. Closed Sundays. No reservations. No credit cards accepted. *Vaporetto* stop San Stae or Rialto. 1761 Remo del Maggio, Santa Croce (phone: 524-1570). Inexpensive.

WINE BARS AND CAFÉS: Join the Venetians in their ritual of drinking an *ombra* (a glass of wine) any time during the day from late morning to late at night at a *bacaro,* a pub named after a pugliese wine once very popular in Venice, or an *enoteca,* a cheerful neighborhood wine bar usually offering simple hors d'oeuvres (*cichetti*) in the style of Spanish *tapas.* You'll also find hearty sandwiches, the occasional hot pasta dish, and if you're lucky, a few tables. *Bacari* are generally priced very modestly according to the wine choice — the reliable house wine (usually around 50¢ a glass) is de rigueur — while *enoteche* offer more extensive selections for some interesting wine tasting. Venice will sink before you can get to even a small sampling of these ubiquitous, unofficial social clubs. The following are the best known and most characteristic. None of the *enoteche* accepts credit cards. Also included are two of the most famous cafés in Venice, where you also can get a light meal.

Caffè Florian – Open since 1720, this beautiful, slightly frayed café looks out on the entire Piazza San Marco scene. It's the perfect site from which to watch the world go by while sipping coffee and nibbling a sandwich or sweet confection. Closed Wednesdays. No reservations. Major credit cards accepted. *Vaporetto* stop San Marco. 57 Piazza San Marco (phone: 528-5338). Expensive.

Lavena Caffè – One of the Piazza San Marco's historical cafés, it is said that Richard Wagner found inspiration here. Specializes in light food, but don't miss the "Lavena's Cup" ice cream extravaganza. An orchestra plays until midnight from early March through mid-November. Closed Tuesdays. No reservations. Major credit cards accepted. *Vaporetto* stop San Marco. 133 Piazza San Marco (phone: 522-4070). Moderate.

Leon Bianco – Grab a toothpick and spear any number of delicious potato, rice, or cheese croquettes. This is one of Venice's best-stocked sandwich bars, with a wine list to match. Closed Sundays. Near the busy Campo San Luca. *Vaporetto* stop Rialto. 4153 Salizzada San Luca, San Marco (phone: 522-1180). Inexpensive.

Do Mori – Open since 1750, this is one of the most characteristic of the traditional *bacari* — sandwiches, croquettes, and other fresh *cichetti,* but it's standing room only; there's no place to sit. Open daily until 10:30 PM; closed Wednesday afternoons and Sundays. *Vaporetto* stop Rialto. 429 Ramo Primo Calle Galiazza, San Polo (phone: 522-5401). Inexpensive.

Do Spade – This unspoiled, authentic *enoteca* is frequented by market vendors and high-brow connoisseurs alike. A variety of delicious sandwiches are made daily and there are a few wooden tables, although the crowd prefers to stand. Closed Sunday and most of July. *Vaporetto* stop Rialto. 860 Sotoportego delle Do Spade, San Polo (phone: 521-0574). Inexpensive.

Vino Vino – Purposely low-key and neighborhoody, this fashionable wine bar near *La Fenice* is owned by the upscale *Antico Martini.* Enjoy light meals at marble-top tables. Open until 1 AM for the after-theater set; closed Tuesdays. *Vaporetto* stop Santa Maria del Giglio. 2007 Ponte delle Veste, San Marco (phone: 522-4121). Inexpensive.

Al Volto – Considered the best in town, offering over 2,000 different wine labels from all over the world and 70 foreign beers. There are rare and costly wines as well as the more current and affordable vintages. Open until 9 PM; closed Sundays. *Vaporetto* stop Rialto. 4081 Calle Cavalli, San Marco (phone: 28945). Inexpensive.

On summer evenings, locals and visitors alike stroll through Venice, stopping for a gelato at one of the many ice cream shops in the city. Two that are worth a visit are *Paolin* (2962 Campo Santo Stefano, San Marco; phone: 25576), the oldest and best *gelateria* in town, and *Gelateria Nico,* behind the Accademia and on the Zattere promenade (922 Zattere ai Gesuati, Dorsoduro; phone: 25293), where gelato is made fresh daily.

VERONA

While the Venetians are all *gran signori* (fine gentlemen) and the people of Padua are *gran dottori* (very learned), the Veronese — as the old saying goes — are all *tutti matti* (quite mad). We don't mean insane, but mad as in March hares, enjoying a rollicking good time. Even the statues, somber in some cities, smile here, evidently enjoying some local joke.

The Veronese love to drink their excellent wines, the soaves and valpolicellas of the region, and when they have had a little to drink, they love to sing. A favorite meetingplace for drinking and singing is any local *osteria* (inn), and there seems to be one on almost every street in Old Verona. Here a glass of wine costs about 75¢, and the conversation is very loud, usually because the Veronese are discussing the exploits of their soccer team, of which — as in all Italian cities — they are inordinately proud.

Or if it is January or February, the uproar could be about the election of the Gnocchi King of *Carnevale.* This is a tradition that goes back to the 16th century, when a rich lord of Verona distributed flour among the poor of the city to make gnocchi, a local pasta dish. To this day, *Gnocchi Friday* is the height of *Carnevale,* when the fun-loving Veronese are even madder than usual!

Although Verona was known as *piccola Roma* (little Rome) during Roman times — as the massive Arena, the arched stone doors such as the Porta Borsari, and the fragments of ancient pillars and walls amply attest — the overwhelming impression today is medieval. There are battlements, turrets, slits in the walls from which archers fired their arrows, and cobbled streets that seem left over from the times of the Montagues and Capulets, whom visitors can easily imagine clattering across the Ponte di Castelvecchio.

As a border town, Verona played a key role in Italy's past. After the Romans, the city was ruled by the Goths and King Theodoric, followed by 2 centuries of Lombards, until it was conquered by the Franks and Charlemagne in 774. The grand masters left their imprints on the city, especially under the doges and their Venetian republic, a time known as the Serenissima, during which Verona contributed to the Italian Renaissance with painters such as Paolo Veronese and architects like Michele Sanmicheli. The Venetians were ousted in 1797 by Napoleon, whose government was in turn ousted in 1814 by the European coalition. Verona was then ruled by the Hapsburgs until the Italian unification in 1860.

The rule of the Della Scala family had the most lingering effect on Verona. Known as the Scaligeri, the family reigned from 1262 to 1387, during which time Romeo is supposed to have courted Juliet and "with love's light wings did o'erperch these walls" into the Capulet garden. It was the Scaligeri who gave Verona so many of the city's monuments, such as the Arche Scaligere, above-ground tombs where the family is buried; the *Castelvecchio,* now the city's main museum; the old Town Hall; and Piazza dei Signori (Lords' Square). Many of the churches grew in splendor during the rule of the Scaligeri, and it was a time of great cultural awareness. The poet Dante Alighieri stayed in the Palazzo Scaligero during his Florentine exile as a guest of Cangrande I della Scala, whom he immortalized in the 17th canto of his *Paradiso.*

Long before Romeo and Juliet, Verona claimed to be Italy's city of love. A legend tells how the Adige River, cascading down from the glacier in the mountains above the city, fell in love with Verona. The love was fiercely contested by the goddess Diana — to whom Verona had pledged a vow of chastity. Diana condemned the city to die in the watery embrace of its suitor, which wound lovingly around the city in the shape of an "S" for *sposa* (bride). But love prevailed. Verona did not die, and to this day it remains enclosed within the wide curves of the river and within the series of city walls built by succeeding overlords.

During the 13th century, the poor people actually lived under the arches of the Roman Arena and had to pay rent for their humble dwellings, until they were turned out to make way for the city's red-light ladies, who in those days had to wear a cap with a rattle on the peak to differentiate them from honest women. In fact, Verona has always been "lived in" by the Veronese, and the city's monuments, however ancient and revered, are still just as much a part of day-to-day life as they always were. The Arena, which once featured gladiators and lions and, later, medieval jousters, still dominates the city; during its world-famous opera season, it is an important part of civic life. The Scaligeri palaces have become government offices. The daily market is held in Piazza delle Erbe on the site of the old Roman forum. Lawyers and judges still ascend the Scala della Ragione (Stair of Reason) as they did in the 15th century.

Verona is a small, compact city, only a half-hour walk end to end. But it has much to see. The visitor should come equipped with comfortable shoes and be prepared to walk, walk, walk the cobbled streets, taking time to look up at the façades of the buildings (some of them, like No. 4 on Via San Cosimo, are almost grotesque). The diligent roamer will soon discover that not only Romeo and Juliet but everyone in Verona had a balcony. It will also quickly become apparent that Romeo and Juliet are only one reason to come to Verona, and the least haunting of the impressions visitors will carry home.

VERONA AT-A-GLANCE

SEEING THE CITY: The Torre Lamberti (Lamberti Tower) rises to 272 feet in Piazza delle Erbe in the heart of Old Verona. Fortunately, there is an elevator as well as stairs to the top, from which there is a fine view of the city. Open daily, except Mondays, 8:30 AM to 2 PM in winter, to 7:30 PM in summer. Admission charge (discounted for those who climb the stairs). Piazza delle Erbe (phone: 32726).

On the other side of the Ponte di Pietra (Stone Bridge) from the Torre Lamberti are the Teatro Romano (Roman Theater), founded by Augustus, and the Castel San Pietro (St. Peter's Castle), built by the Austrians in the 19th century. Both places afford good views of Verona. The Scalone di San Pietro (St. Peter's Stairway) is steeped in legend. The higher one climbs, the more of the city is visible on the horizon. Here King Albion, King of the Lombards, was killed at the instigation of his wife, Rosamund. On the same side of the river is the lovely Giusti Garden, a 16th-century formal Italian garden with terraces overlooking the city (see *Special Places*).

SPECIAL PLACES: Other cities have their museums and picture galleries. Verona has churches, although many are so dimly lit that one can only guess at the artistic and architectural wonders lurking in the transepts and side chapels. There are so many churches, so large, so awe-inspiring, that it is hard to believe there were ever enough Veronese to fill them (most churches were affiliated with monasteries). They all close for a long lunch, usually from 1 to 3 PM.

Duomo (Cathedral) – The most important church in Verona is this 12th-century Romanesque basilica with a 15th-century Gothic nave. It is located in the old section of the city near the Ponte di Pietra and was probably built on the site of a paleochristian church dating from the late Roman Empire. The choir screen separating the altar from the rest of the church is attributed to Sanmicheli. At the end of the nave, in the Nichesola chapel, is Titian's *Assumption of the Virgin Mary.* Behind the cathedral is the little 12th-century Church of San Giovanni in Fonte, one of the most important examples of Romanesque architecture in Verona. It is named for the huge octagonal baptismal font in red stone, its eight sides showing scenes from the life of Christ. Open daily from 7 AM to noon and 3 to 7 PM. Piazza Duomo (phone: 595627).

Chiesa di Sant'Anastasia (Church of Saint Anastasia) – This basilica was built on the site of a much older church. Although the foundations were laid in 1290 by the Dominicans, the basilica was not finished until 1481. The vaulted ceiling is supported by massive red Veronese marble columns. Two *gobbi,* or hunchbacks, support the holy water fonts at the foot of the first column on either side of the nave. There is something uncannily realistic in the resigned expressions and torn trousers of the *gobbi,* as if they were carrying the weight of the church on their shoulders. In the sacristy to the left is *St. George and the Princess,* the famous fresco by Pisanello. Illuminate the picture by putting a 100-lire coin into the machine. It is like a fairy-tale painting with a knight in armor, a damsel in distress, a castle in the clouds, and, in the foreground, the unexpectedly large rump of a white charger. Open daily from 7 AM to noon and 3:30 to 6:30 PM. Corso Sant'Anastasia (phone: 34325).

Chiesa di San Zeno Maggiore (Church of Saint Zeno Major) – This is the only site around town that requires a bus or a taxi to reach. Zeno is the patron saint of Verona. His black-faced, laughing statue is seated on its bishop's throne in a small apse to the left of the altar. The 48 panels of the magnificent bronze doors show scenes of the Old and New Testaments, and the triptych above the main altar is a depiction of the Madonna with angel musicians and saints by Andrea Mantegna. The ceiling of the nave looks like an upturned wooden ship's keel. Open daily from 7 AM to noon and 3 to 7 PM. 2 Piazza San Zeno.

This basilica is not to be confused with the tiny church called San Zeno in Oratorio on Via A. Provolo, near the *Castelvecchio Museum.* The smaller church contains an enormous boulder that is supposedly the stone on which the laughing Saint Zeno used to sit fishing by the Adige River.

Chiesa di San Fermo Maggiore (Church of Saint Firmanus Major) – This is, in fact, two churches in one. Both, in the form of a Latin cross, are considered a turning point in local ecclesiastical architecture; this type of plan is also found in Normandy. The lower church, which parishioners use in winter, is pure Romanesque; the upper and larger church, altered by the Franciscans in the 13th century, has a more Gothic aspect. The interior is decorated with frescoes by Veronese painters from Turone (see his *Crucifixion*) to Pisanello (the *Annunciation*). The ceiling here, as at San Zeno, looks like a ship's keel. Open daily from 7 AM to noon and 3 to 7 PM. 2 Via Dogana (phone: 800-7287).

Chiesa di San Lorenzo (Church of Saint Lawrence) – Still remaining here are the *matronei,* or women's galleries, running above the two lateral naves. (Men and women used to worship separately.) Two cylindrical towers of striped stone and brick were the entrances to the galleries. Open Sunday only for mass at 9:30 PM. 28 Via Cavour.

Chiesa di Santo Stefano (Church of Saint Stephen) – Time permitting, walk over the Ponte di Pietra and visit this church, believed to have been built in the time of Theodoric the Goth. The church was built in a mixture of styles, tradition dating its foundations to around AD 415. It is thought to have been the cathedral of Verona for more than 3 centuries. More than 20 Veronese bishops are buried here, and the façade is inscribed with records of important events, as they are in a family Bible. Open daily from 7 AM to noon and 3 to 7 PM. Via Vicino Ponte di Pietra (phone: 48529).

Chiesa di Santa Maria in Organo (Church of Saint Mary in Organo) – Known for the remarkable marquetry (inlaid designs in wood) on the backs of the wooden choir stalls and in the sacristy. Executed around 1499 by Fra Giovanni da Verona, they contain 32 types of wood, endowing them with extraordinary nuances of light and color. Open daily from 7 AM to noon and 3:30 to 6:30 PM. Piazza Santa Maria (phone: 591440).

Chiesa di San Giorgio Maggiore in Braida (Church of Saint George in Braida) – This later building, constructed from 1536 to 1543, lacks the powerful atmosphere of some of the earlier Romanesque churches, but it is rich in artwork (Goethe once termed the church "a fine gallery"). Paintings include a large Tintoretto, *The Baptism of Christ,* over the entrance and a Veronese, *The Martyrdom of St. George,* on the end wall of the apse. The design of the cupola and the unfinished campanile are attributed to Sanmicheli. Open daily from 7 AM to noon and 3:30 to 6:30 PM. Lungadige San Giorgio.

Giardino Giusti (Giusti Garden) – Across the Adige from the Old City is a formal garden that was designed by its 16th-century owner, Count Agostino Giusti. Laid out behind a palazzo of the same name, the garden is composed of formal walks with box-hedge mazes geometrically arranged around statues and fountains. The place is a child's (and adult's) delight, a series of terraces and stairs leading to what in gardening terms are called follies and hahas. Open daily from 8:30 AM to 8 PM. Admission charge. Via Giardino Giusti (phone: 38029).

Piazza delle Erbe (Square of the Herbs) – Every morning, except Sundays, octagonal white umbrellas shade the stalls of this market square, where you can buy food, especially fruits and vegetables, flowers, and clothing. There is even an *arrotino* (knife grinder). On the fountain is a Roman statue known as Madonna Verona, who holds a scroll declaiming, *Est iusti latrix urbs haec et laudis amatrix* ("The city is proud of her justice and fond of praise"). The statue is the only visible remains of the Roman forum that was at this site. Evidence of the forum was discovered about 10 feet belowground when a hole was being dug for the flagpole. At the northwest end of the square is the baroque façade of Palazzo Maffei, with statues of Greek gods along the roof. At the same corner is the beautifully frescoed 14th-century Casa Mazzanti. Next to the Casa Mazzanti, leading into the Mercato Vecchio square, is the Arco della Costa, an arch from which hangs a prehistoric whalebone, also discovered under the square during excavations, evidence that millennia ago this entire area was under the sea.

Case e Tombe di Romeo e Giulietta (Romeo and Juliet's Homes and Tombs) – Juliet's house, with its famous balcony, is beautiful, but it is empty of anything except its graffiti-covered walls. Romeo's house is but a façade, albeit with battlements. It is easier to be caught up in the immortal love story at Juliet's tomb, which, although also empty, is in the evocative crypt of the Cloisters of San Francesco al Corso. Lord Byron found it so romantic that he purloined little pieces of marble from the tomb to make into jewelry for his current *innamorata.* Juliet's house is at 23 Via Cappello, in the middle of a shopping street (phone: 38303). Open daily, except Mondays, 7:30 AM to 6:40 PM. Romeo's house, on Via Arche Scaligere near Piazza Indipendenza, can be viewed from the street only. The tomb is on Via del Pontiere (phone: 800-0361). Open daily, except Mondays, 7:30 AM to 6:45 PM in winter, to 7 PM in summer; admission charge.

Castelvecchio Museum – Verona does not have many museums, but this one is very special. Also called the *Museum of Art,* it is in the Scaligeri Castle, which looks like a set for *The Prisoner of Zenda.* Like the Castello Sforzesco in Milan, this 14th-century building is as interesting as its exhibits. The galleries span its battlements and its buttresses and lead over a little bridge where the famous statue of Cangrande della Scala, Lord of Verona from 1311 until 1329, sits smiling on its horse. The museum houses a large collection of Romanesque, Gothic, and Renaissance sculpture, as well as an impressive array of Madonnas — of the Fan, of the Rose Tree, of the Quail, of the Goldfinch, and of the Passion. Famous Italian painters are well represented here — Crivelli, Tintoretto, Guardi, Tiepolo, and the great Veronese painter Paolo Caliari, known as Il Veronese. Open daily, except Mondays, 7:30 AM to 6:45 PM. Admission charge. Via Castelvecchio (phone: 594734).

Caffè Dante – This old-fashioned coffeehouse is in the heart of Old Verona, in Piazza dei Signori, with Scaligeri monuments all around and a statue of the family's most famous guest, Dante Alighieri, in the middle of the square. The restaurant has marble tables and plush armchairs, a little worse for wear. In the afternoons the tables in the back room are taken by chess players. In 1866, to mark the annexing of Verona to a unified Italy, the ceiling was painted with oval portraits of Italy's great patriots — Garibaldi, Mazzini, Cavour, et al. Light refreshments, as well as history, are to be had here. Closed Mondays. 2 Piazza dei Signori (phone: 595249).

Arena – Nowadays, the enormous Roman arena in Piazza Brà is the opera house and remains an important component of Veronese life. It was still intact in the 11th century when an earthquake caused its outside wall to collapse, and now only a piece remains to show of the original structure. Since then, the Veronese have been assiduous in their conservation efforts, maintaining their arena as one of the better preserved Roman amphitheaters. Its acoustics are excellent, too. The outdoor opera season presented here each summer has been well known to music lovers since it began in 1913 with a staging of *Aïda* in honor of the 100th anniversary of Giuseppe Verdi's birth. Piazza Brà is the largest square in Verona. From a balcony in this square, Garibaldi declared *Roma o morte* — "Rome or die." Today the square is filled with sidewalk cafés. The Arena is closed to visitors on Mondays. In opera season (July and August), it is open 8 AM to 1:30 PM; otherwise, 7:30 AM to 6:45 PM (phone: 800-3204). See also *Theater and Music,* below.

ENVIRONS

Lago di Garda (Lake Garda) – Less than 25 miles (40 km) from Verona is one of the most beautiful Italian lakes. The climate in this area is mild, and in the warmer months there are facilities for bathing and sailing. In high summer it gets crowded. The lake is surrounded by picturesque villages and vineyards, and there are plenty of good restaurants.

Bolca – This town and the surrounding area, about 30 miles (48 km) northeast of Verona, is one of the most important geological sites in Italy. Stunning marine fossils found here date back 50 million years when the area was a vast lagoon, languishing in a tropical climate; now it's hilly. The town has a *Museo dei Fossili* (Fossil Museum), which draws visitors from all over the world. Open daily, except Mondays, from 10 AM to noon and 2 to 6 PM. Admission charge (phone: 747-0068).

The trip from Verona, driving east on the SS11 about 10 miles (16 km) before turning off north toward Tregnago, goes through the Val d'Illasi, overrun with cherry blossoms and patrician villas. Many can be visited, though they don't advertise the fact. For information, contact the central office of the Azienda di Promozione Turistica (APT), 42 Piazza delle Erbe (phone: 803-0086).

SOURCES AND RESOURCES

TOURIST INFORMATION: General tourist information is available at the Azienda di Promozione Turistica (APT, 6/B Via Dietro Anfiteatro; phone: 592828); open daily except Sundays from 8 AM to 8 PM; during July and August, open all week. Another APT branch (42 Piazza delle Erbe; phone: 803-0086) is open from May through October from 8 AM to 8 PM. Ask for free publications: the four-language guide, *Passport Verona;* the hotel-restaurant guide and the city map that locates principal monuments, *Verona Anni 90.* The *Verona Trade Fair Center* is at the gates of the city on the Bologna side (phone: 588111).

Verona has nearly 2 dozen officially accredited guides, most of whom speak excellent English. If time is short, a morning spent with one of these guides can be invaluable. Contact the *Associazione di Guide Turistiche,* 7 Via di Mosta (phone: 576852).

Local Coverage – The daily paper of Verona and its province is *L'Arena di Verona.*

TELEPHONE: The city code for Verona is 45. When dialing from within Italy, dial 045 before the local number.

GETTING AROUND: This is a town for walking. Park outside the gates and walk from there. (It is unlikely that a car would be stolen, but it would be unwise to leave anything of value visible in it.)

Airport – Verona is served by Verona-Villafranca Airport, about 7 miles (11 km) out of town (phone: 513700). Bus and taxi service into Verona is available.

Bus – Verona has an extensive municipal bus service. Tickets are inexpensive; buy them beforehand at tobacconists. Buses that serve the province and Lake Garda depart from Piazza Brà, Piazza Cittadella, and Piazza Isolo (phone: 521200).

Car Rental – Representatives of the major car rental firms are at Porta Nuova, the main train station at the south end of Corso Porta Nuova.

Taxi – Feet do wear out sometimes; fortunately, a taxi is not expensive. There is a cabstand at Piazza Brà; or call *Radio Taxi* from 6 AM to midnight (phone: 532666).

Train – Insist on *rapido,* or at least direct, trains. The main station, Porta Nuova, is at the south end of the Corso Porta Nuova (phone: 590688 for information from 7 AM to 10 PM).

SPECIAL EVENTS: Verona has a large trade fair center with an international following. Although some of the exhibitions are of limited interest to the layperson (such as the fair for agricultural machinery), many others are well worth browsing. In April, *VinItaly,* Italy's most important wine fair offers a complete panorama of Italy's wines — and a taste of them as well. *Herbora,* in May, specializes in herb-based products. In September, *Marmomaccine* shows all the marble, granite, and other stone produced in Italy today, much of which comes from the Verona area. In November, *Fieracavalli* is very popular with horse buffs from all over the country.

In odd-numbered years, an *Antiques Fair* is held in the Palazzo della Gran Guardia. Another very special event is the *Rassegna del Presepe* (*Christmas* Crèche Exhibition), which is held in the Arena from December 5 to February 7. There's no need to celebrate *Christmas* to be fascinated by this international collection of historic crèches.

MUSEUMS: Apart from the *Castelvecchio Museum,* mentioned in *Special Places,* Verona has a few smaller museums.

Biblioteca Capitolare (Capital Library) – The oldest functioning library in Europe, with manuscripts, parchments, codices, and so on. Open weekdays except Thursdays from 9:30 AM to 12:30 PM, and Tuesdays and Fridays from 4 to 6 PM. No admission charge. 13 Piazza Duomo (phone: 596516).

Museo Civico di Scienze Naturali (Natural Sciences Museum) – In Sanmicheli's Palazzo Pompei. Open daily, except Fridays, 8 AM to 7 PM. Admission charge, except on Sundays. 9 Lungadige Porta Vittoria (phone: 807-7711).

Museo Lapidario Maffeiano (Maffeiano Lapidary Museum) – The oldest in Europe, with stone plaques, statues, urns, and reliefs. Open daily, except Mondays, 8 AM to 6:45 PM. Admission charge. 28 Piazza Brà (phone: 590087).

Teatro Romano e Museo Archeologico (Roman Theater and Archaeological Museum) – An ancient theater and antiquity museum. Open daily, except Mondays, from 8 AM to 1:30 PM in winter and from 8 AM to 6:45 PM in summer (to 1:30 PM during opera season). Admission charge. Lungadige Regaste Redentore (phone: 33974).

SHOPPING: The province of Verona produces shoes for all of Italy and abroad — one-tenth of the country's entire production. Drive along the main road toward Lake Garda, through Bussolengo, and buy directly from the factories at very low prices. Verona is also known for its reproductions of antique furniture. Drive the *strada dei mobli* (furniture road) toward Legnago and visit the artisans' workshops.

In the center of town are two streets devoted almost exclusively to authentic antiques, Via Sant'Anastasia and Via Sottoriva, especially the latter. Stores here are tucked away under medieval arches. Their façades date from the 3rd and 4th centuries.

The main shopping street is Via Mazzini, which branches right into Via Cappello, the site of Juliet's home. Like most of the historic center, this is a pedestrian zone. All the big names in Italian fashion are here: *Pollini, Gianni Versace,* and *Ritzino,* for example, as well as the big department stores *Coin* and *Upim.* Many of the shops have outlets in other towns, but the stores listed below are found only in Verona. Most are closed on Monday mornings and during lunch, from 1 to 3:30 or 4 PM.

Alloni – Spectacular flower shop specializing in dried herbal and floral arrangements. A self-service vending machine outside the shop offers a limited selection 24 hours a day. 11 Corso Porta Nuova (phone: 596077).

Bon Bon – For children's clothes. 25 Via Cappello (phone: 594727).

Calimala – Embroidered linen and lace. 6/B Via E. Noris (phone: 800-2427).

Canestrari – The oldest jeweler in Verona. The shop looks a bit like Aladdin's cave. 35 Via Cappello (phone: 594763).

Casa Mia di Montaldo – Wall-to-ceiling housewares as well as some toys. Via 17 IX Novembre (phone: 914362).

Il Cassettone – More embroidered linen and lace. 3 Vicolo Crocioni (phone: 590077).

Cose di E. Passeroni & S. Tapparini – New and antique silver. 63 Via Mazzini (phone: 596596).

Faraoni – A fashion boutique specializing in Kenzo designs. 9 Via Ponte Nuovo (phone: 590989).

Fulmine del Guanto – For great gloves. 44 Via Mazzini (phone: 595512).

Libreria Ghelfi & Barbato – An old-fashioned bookstore; many books are in English. 21 Via Mazzini (phone: 597732 or 800-2306).

Mantellero – High class men's hats and women's hosiery in a hallowed atmosphere. 59 Via Mazzini (phone: 31607).

New Galles – Fashion, including Emporio Armani styles. 4 Via A. Cantore (phone: 31555).

Pasticceria Cordioli – A traditional coffee bar and pastry shop. 39 Via Cappello (phone: 800-3055).

Principe – Verona's local shoe store. 80 Via Mazzini (phone: 800-7165).

Sinico – One of Verona's best *salumerie,* or fine food stores. 5 Via Leoni (phone: 800-2581).

Spega – A *salumeria,* selling freshly prepared delicacies that are perfect for a picnic by the banks of the Adige River. 11 Via Stella (phone: 34998).

SPORTS AND FITNESS: Sports do not seem to be very high on the agenda for visitors to the city, perhaps because they get quite enough exercise just walking around. The Veronese ski in the mountains above the city, about an hour away by car (see *Italy's Unparalleled Skiing,* DIVERSIONS), and in summer they go sailing on Lake Garda (see *Special Places*).

Golf – *Golf Club Verona,* Ca' del Sale, Sommacampagna (phone: 510060).

Horseback Riding – *Società Ippica Veronese* (Boschetto, Lungadige Galtarossa; phone: 31854).

Soccer – Every other Sunday, from September to May, *Verona* plays at *Stadio Comunale, Marc'Antonio Bentegodi,* Piazzale Olimpia (phone: 564063).

Swimming – *Piscina Comunale,* Via Galliano (phone: 567622).

Tennis – *Associazione Tennis Verona,* 4 Via Colonello (phone: 565900).

THEATER AND MUSIC: The *Arena di Verona* opera season, spanning July and August, is a major musical phenomenon in Europe. World-famous stars perform in the Arena's vast oval auditorium that seats 22,000. Although the soprano can look very small if you're sitting near the lip of the Arena, she's still visible and, more important, more audible than in the higher-priced seats farther down. Prices for the best seats are expensive; higher up and to the sides, they are more reasonable. The rest of the year there is excellent music, including opera, at the *Teatro Filarmonico* (4 Via dei Mutilati; phone: 800-2880), where the tickets are less expensive. In summer, ballet performances are given in the Teatro Romano on the other side of the river. The theater also hosts a summer Shakespeare festival. All bookings are made through the *Ente Lirico Arena di Verona* (28 Piazza Brà, Verona 37100; phone: 590109, 590966, or 590726). You can book months in advance by mail or phone.

NIGHTCLUBS AND NIGHTLIFE: Popular nightclubs in the city center are *A'nzao* (7 Via Tezone; phone: 595545), which doubles as a piano bar (closed Wednesdays); *Excalibur Club* (24 Stradone A. Provolo; phone: 594614), which welcomes non-members and is the best in town (closed Mondays); *Campidoglio* (4 Piazzetta Tirabosco; phone: 594448), a piano bar specializing in 1960s music, with live music after midnight (closed Mondays); and *Café Jazz Beer Jose* (8 Via Sant'Egidio; phone: 592958), offering jazz in a 14th-century palazzo (closed Tuesdays).

BEST IN TOWN

CHECKING IN: Verona hotels are very reasonably priced, except for the one listed below as very expensive where double rooms start at $425! Those rated expensive are between $175 and $250; moderate $85 to $150; inexpensive, $85 and less. Verona's hotels usually give guests a discount if they choose not to have breakfast. The difference can amount to $15 a day or more, and you might want to enjoy it in a café in the piazza anyway. All telephone numbers are in the 45 city code unless otherwise indicated.

Due Torri – The entrance hall is like the throne room of a doge's palace, and other rooms are furnished with expensive antiques. Mozart once stayed here. This 96-room luxury hotel is one of Italy's finest, though some guestrooms are on the small side. Its restaurant, *L'Aquila* (see *Eating Out*), is excellent. 4 Piazza Sant'Anastasia (phone: 595381). Very expensive.

Accademia – Just off Via Mazzini, the main shopping street, this 100-room place is traditionally *the* hotel for visitors in Verona. 10-12 Via Scala (phone: 596222; fax: 596222). Expensive.

Colomba d'Oro – Excellently maintained and just around the corner from the Roman arena, this comfortable, 50-room hotel has a bath in every room and a garage. 10 Via Cattaneo (phone: 595367; fax: 594974). Expensive.

Antica Porta Leona – Around the corner from Juliet's house and Via degli Amanti (Lovers' Street), this charmingly redecorated, 36-room hotel is on one of the quaintest corners in Verona. 3 Corticella Leoni (phone: 595499; fax: 595499). Moderate.

Bologna – Ideally located just off Piazza Brà, this unpretentious, modern 30-room hostelry has a very good restaurant, *Rubiani,* with a sidewalk terrace looking out toward the Arena. 3 Piazzetta Scalette Rubiani (phone: 800-6830; fax: 801-0602). Moderate.

Touring – A turn-of-the-century 40-room hotel in the heart of Old Verona. 5 Via Q. Sella (phone and fax: 590944). Moderate.

Aurora – Economical accommodations for those who appreciate a hotel's view more than its comforts (only double rooms have bathrooms). There are 20 rooms — ask for one overlooking the white umbrellas of the market square. 2 Via Pelliciai (phone: 594717; fax: 801-0860). Inexpensive.

Torcolo – Just a few steps away from the Arena is this 20-room hostelry. The guestrooms are decorated in a variety of styles — from 18th century to modern. Breakfast is served on a shady terrace. 3 Vicolo Listone (phone: 800-7512).

EATING OUT: Veronese menus differ only slightly from those elsewhere in northern Italy, and the overall standard is high. Local specialties include gnocchi, little dumplings made of flour and potatoes (best when handmade — *fatti a mano*) and that come with a variety of sauces, from the classic meat or tomato to butter and sage. An interesting local pasta dressing is made with *ortiche* (nettles), which taste a little like broccoli. For the main course, Verona is famous for its boiled meat, not just the usual cuts, but less expected parts of different animals — such as *testina* (head), which is always served with *pearà,* a bread sauce spiced with pepper. If you are not squeamish, you might try another typical dish, *pastissada,* a horse meat stew, served with polenta, yellow cornmeal pudding, a staple served all over the Veneto region. In the Veronese version, it is served in solid strips, usually toasted. The town has become synonymous with the *pandoro,* a simple but delicious cake that resembles panettone.

On the whole, eating out in Verona is not very expensive, especially in simple trattorie and small restaurants. In the restaurants listed as very expensive, expect to spend about $150 for two, including wine. Restaurants rated as expensive cost about $100; moderate cost about $50 to $100. It is possible for two people to have a full meal with wine at an inexpensive place for under $50. All telephone numbers are in the 45 city code unless otherwise indicated.

L'Aquila – Located in Verona's oldest and finest hotel, this formal restaurant turns out some of the best classic dishes in town — all done with a great deal of style. Try the *pasta alle cozze con zucchini* (with mussels and zucchini), the trout au gratin served with leeks, or the magnificent duck with sweet-and-sour sauce, washed down with an excellent red valpolicella wine taken from the hotel's impressive cellars. Open daily. Reservations necessary. Major credit cards accepted. *Due Torri,* 4 Piazza Sant'Anastasia (phone: 595381). Very expensive.

Le Arche – Excellent fish, served imaginatively in an aristocratic atmosphere. Considered one of the two best dining places in Verona (the other is *Il Desco* below). Closed Sundays, Mondays at lunchtime, and the first 3 weeks of July. Reservations advised. Major credit cards accepted. 6 Via Arche Scaligere (phone: 800-7415). Very expensive.

Il Desco – Save this elegant restaurant for a romantic evening; it's now considered one of Verona's best. Begin with the fondue specialty, *budino di formaggio con fonduta.* Closed Sundays and the second half of June; open after opera performances during August. Reservations advised. Major credit cards accepted. 5-7 Via Dietro San Sebastiano (phone: 595358). Very expensive.

12 Apostoli – One of Italy's most celebrated dining spots, dating back 200 years. It's still a wonderful experience — original recipes and soups, excellent wines, Renaissance-style decor. Closed Sunday evenings, Mondays, mid-June through the first week of July, and during *Christmas.* Reservations advised. Major credit cards accepted. 3 Vicolo Corticella San Marco (phone: 596999). Very expensive.

Groto de Corgnan – It's worth driving the 12½ miles (20 km) to Sant'Ambrogio to experience this eatery, with a lengthy, variable menu. Closed Sunday evenings and Mondays. Reservations advised. No credit cards accepted. 41 Via Corgnano, Sant'Ambrogio di Valpolicella (phone: 773-1372). Expensive.

Nuovo Marconi – Elegant Belle Epoque decor is the backdrop for painstakingly prepared Veronese specialties. Fish is the specialty, though everything is delicious. Closed Sundays, Monday lunch, and early July. Reservations advised. Major credit cards accepted. 4 Via Fogge (phone: 591910). Expensive.

Ciopeta – Centrally located, behind the Arena and Piazza Brà, this is a family restaurant serving simple, healthy fare (closed Saturdays). There is alfresco dining in the summer. It also has 5 rooms above, none with private bath. It has lots of atmosphere, though. Reservations advised. No credit cards accepted. 2 Vicolo Teatro Filarmonico (phone: 800-6843). Restaurant, expensive to moderate; hotel, inexpensive.

Il Cenacolo – Choose from a wide selection of entrées and grilled meat; the fixed-price menu seems endless (even though its name means "The Last Supper"). Closed Saturday lunch and Tuesdays. Reservations advised for dinner. Major credit cards accepted. 10 Via Teatro Filarmonico (phone: 592288). Moderate.

Torcoloti – Old-fashioned elegance, perfect for a quiet dinner. Appetizers are excellent, especially the combination *tris della casa,* three kinds of stuffed pasta. Closed Sundays, Monday evenings, and during June. Reservations advised. Major credit cards accepted. 24 Via Zambelli (phone: 30945). Moderate.

La Greppia – Imaginatively renovated, this very old restaurant is ideal for lunch;

try the fresh pasta and boiled meats. Closed Mondays and the second half of June. Reservations unnecessary. Major credit cards accepted. 3 Vicolo Samaritana (phone: 800-4577). Moderate to inexpensive.

Armando – Unassuming (but excellent) fish restaurant next to an *osteria* of the same name. Closed Mondays. Reservations unnecessary. No credit cards accepted. 8 Via Macello (phone: 800-0892). Inexpensive.

Osteria la Fontanina – The menu changes daily in this friendly trattoria run by two brothers. The food is great and the prices can't be beat. Closed Sundays, Monday lunch, most of August, and *Christmas.* Reservations necessary. No credit cards accepted. 3 Portichette Fontanelle (phone: 913305). Inexpensive.

Pizzeria Marechiaro – We give this place a zero for atmosphere and a ten for pizza (all of Verona thinks so too!). Closed Wednesdays. No reservations. No credit cards accepted. 15 Via Sant'Antonio (phone: 34506). Inexpensive.

CAFÉS AND WINE BARS: To better enjoy the local wines, join the Veronese in one of their *osterie,* of which there are no fewer than 26 between the bends of the Adige River. Many have a history almost as old as Verona itself, and some have given their names to the streets on which they stand, such as *Osteria La Pigna* (4/B Via Pigna; phone: 800-4080; closed Thursday and Friday lunch). *Osterie* usually serve food — such as little open sandwiches with anchovies, cheese, or ham — to ballast the wine. Some now offer a full, medium-priced meal, although they have lost the traditional atmosphere of hubbub and camaraderie in the process. Try *Bottega del Vino* (3 Via Scudo di Francia; phone: 800-4535; closed Tuesdays). More typical is *Osteria Le Vecete* (32 Via Pellicciai; phone: 594681; closed afternoons and Sundays), where the emphasis is on drinking. The quality of the local house wines is surprising, even in the humblest *osteria.* This is one of the few regions of Italy where red and white wines are equally good. On the sweeter side, try Verona's best gelato maker, *Da Paolo* (1 Via Risorgimento; phone: 918429; closed Mondays, January, and August) who specializes in fruit flavors.

DIVERSIONS

For the Experience

Quintessential Italy

Italians are such *maestri* of pleasure that they consider it foolish to venture far afield for the thrill of a Kenyan safari or for the peaceful pleasure of a seashell hunt in the Seychelles. Italy still is a country where the smallest unit of time is the "while," and only since the concept of *lo stress* was imported from America have Italians needed the noun *il relax* (pronounced re-leck-e-*say*) to describe the state of being that they have always taken for granted. Any visitor can savor the quintessence of this nation, which has entranced travelers since the Visigoths first applied for a visa, simply by getting away from it all in any one of the selection of vintage destinations and diversions that follow. So remember, before you trot off to the Great Wall or sail for Bora Bora, there's no place like Rome.

SOCCER SUNDAY: One of the best-selling newspapers in Italy is *La Gazzetta dello Sport,* and the possibility that his dearly beloved soccer team might fall back into the B-League is far more ominous to Italy's Everyman than any governmental collapse; *calcio* is a national religion (it seems fitting that the *1990 World Cup* was held here — matches took place in 12 cities throughout the country, although Italy placed a heart-breaking third), and the Sunday afternoon *partita* its rite. During the 2 hours when these games are played all through the country, an eerie hush, broken only by periodic roars of raw joy, falls over town and country alike. After a team has won a home game and the stadiums empty out, triumphant fans wrap themselves in team colors and wave banners from buses and cars; the streets are raucous with honking. Where teams share a home town and a stadium, as in Turin, rivalries are particularly intense; they climax during the twice-yearly meeting known as the *derby,* when parents who root for, say, *Inter* disown children who favor, say, *Milan.* By all means go to see a match, even if you don't know a corner from a striker. But take care about the colors you wear. And if you like to express your sympathies exuberantly, don't sit in the wrong part of the bleachers.

CROSSING THE ALPS TO CORTINA D'AMPEZZO, Trentino–Alto Adige: The drive into the Trentino, across the Brenner Pass, unveils a skier's-eye view of the peninsula that seems to extend almost to the Sicilian shore and, in winter, the spectacle of Cortina: an urbane populace in mauve ski outfits and matching goggles, the civilized smell of suede mingling with pine and cedar, elbow rubbing with some of Milan's most elegant citizens, narrow valleys, figure-eight roads flanked by giant evergreens, and precipitous drops into snowy nothingness. Where the road stops, the chair lift carries you, legs dangling, up to the thin air of the top of Italy, where it's merely magical to loll on the sun-warmed deck of a mountain restaurant, the craggy pink Dolomites all around, or wait for your ears to thaw while nursing a *caffè corretto* (a coffee "adjusted" with brandy).

VILLAGE ON A VOLCANO, Etna, Sicily: In the diminutive metropolis of Catania, vendors with muddy dialects hawk postcards of villages being destroyed by burning lava and tell of incautious tourists seeking sights too near the crater. In the plaza, the men play a placid game of after-dinner cards, offer glasses of the smoky wine from which they make their living, ask after long-lost cousins in Teaneck and Toledo, show off the ruined Norman church that is their local treasure, and otherwise demonstrate their Sicilian pride in home. Ride the tiny train that runs around the base of Mount Etna, Europe's largest active volcano, to get a better look at the agricultural heart of the area: dark slopes braided with rich vineyards; moonlike hills of hardened rock and ash; farmers, commuting from the towns to their fields, disembarking now and again, to all appearances, in the middle of nowhere. When raging Etna drives them away, they will return to build again.

HARVEST TIME, Orvieto, Umbria: The serene hills below Orvieto begin bustling in September, as harvest workers armed with shears fan out into the disciplined rows of vines, clip away the clusters of fat trebbiano and malvasia grapes hiding under their protective leaves, and haul away crate upon crate of rich fruit. At noon, these laborers can be seen resting on blankets scattered through the fields, gnawing slabs of prosciutto between bread, and downing swigs of last year's wine. Later, their clothes and hands stained a rich scarlet, they bring the piled fruit to be crushed — in some villages by the oaken *torchio.* Some of the larger vineyards offer public tours of the cool cellars where the grapes are pressed by machine and the product is fermented, aged, bottled, and labeled; for weeks, whole villages reek of new wine. Meanwhile, everyone hopes: Maybe some fluke in the weather or an all too rare smile from the gods will have made this vintage *speciale.*

A PROVINCIAL PASSEGGIATA, Perugia, Umbria: The Sunday evening stroll, the *passeggiata,* is an Italian ritual, but it is particularly colorful on the handsome Corso Vannucci, the main street of Umbria's attractive regional capital. Bearded university students argue as they amble. A grinning maiden in her first-communion lace leads a retinue of proud sisters, aunts, cousins, parents, and grandparents. A blaring town marching band trumps the violinist squeakily serenading café-sitters in exchange for small change. A clique of teenagers coolly holds court on motor scooters parked in front of a restaurant sign offering "Fast Food All' Italiana," and a group of olive-uniformed soldiers in tasseled caps trace the progress of a cluster of girls sauntering along, arm in arm, sharing self-conscious giggles. Flow with the crowd along the city's curved Renaissance façades to the fountain in the cathedral piazza. Or take a front row seat in a café. The cost of this entertaining procession? The price of a Campari and soda.

PORTO SANTO STEFANO IN AUTUMN, Tuscany: In the middle of some week in late September, when all of Italy has gone back to work after its summer holiday, the warm beaches here are deserted, except for a few diehard Nordic vacationers and a handful of dedicated windsurfers. Take a lazy drive on the empty roads leading to the Tuscan sea and sleepy Porto Santo Stefano, and stroll along the town's marina. The discos are muted and the hotels vacant, worn out by bustling August and the long summer simmer; the autumn air is beginning to nip. But the lifeguard dutifully puts up row after row of deck chairs and candy cane-striped umbrellas that flap gently in the breeze. The wandering trinket peddler demonstrates the virtues of his beads and shawls to the scattered customers. Beach-browned children buttress a sand castle against the tide and the inexorable start of the school year. On a languid afternoon, wash down *pesce spada* (swordfish), just unloaded in the port, with an amber liter of the local white on the sun-washed patios of seashore restaurants, have a swim in the still-tepid waters under the lengthening shadow of Monte Argentario, and stay a while.

ROME AT CHRISTMAS: Spirits soar along with prices, and stores stay open on Sundays during Italy's holiday jubilee, which lasts from early December until the arrival of La Befana, the national answer to Santa Claus, on January 6. A giant *Christmas* tree stands guard at Piazza Venezia. Windows are dressed in glitter and Styrofoam snow (as close as Rome ever gets to the real thing). A near life-size crèche is built into the steps of Piazza di Spagna, complete with bagpipers; nearby, live Abruzzi shepherds in leggings and leather vests are playing their pipes. Shoppers wrapped in showy furs inspect the king's ransom in gold and jewels along Via Condotti, and Piazza Navona is jammed with stalls selling records, toys, ready-stuffed stockings, and the freshly mined hunks of coal-colored rock candy known as *carbone.* The city fathers offer an elegant gift to visitors and Romans — free concerts in selected ancient churches and palazzi, their organs tuned and frescoes brilliantly illuminated for the occasion. Wear warm clothes, and later, heat your hands on a fistful of roasted chestnuts from a street-corner vendor, or sip an espresso with whipped cream in the antique *Antico Caffè Greco* (86 Via Condotti; phone: 6-678-2554), aromatic with freshly ground coffee, Diorissimo, Gucci leather, and the sweet smell of prosperity.

FOUNTAINS OF ROME: In the thick heat of a Roman August, flocks of bare-legged tourists and the few natives who have not migrated to the teeming beaches converge under the spray of the city's innumerable fountains. Clutching fast-liquefying ice cream cones and soaking their feet in the recently restored Fontana di Trevi, these chill-seekers stare enviously at Neptune riding his marine chariot through cool waves of marble and water, or they enjoy the water, water everywhere, alongside the Four Rivers at Piazza Navona, the Roman bathtubs at Campo dei Fiori, the horses at Piazza Esedra, the fish at the Pantheon, or the climbing turtles at Piazza Mattei. Those with the energy to wander find comfort at corner cast-iron fountains spouting drinking water that has been piped from springs outside the city ever since the ancients built the aqueducts. And in the evening, when the temperature has receded to the level of long sleeves and slacks, the fountains provide a soothing background gurgle and a civilized place to rinse off the stickiness of that irresistible watermelon nightcap.

TRASTEVERE, Rome: The people who live in Trastevere, the medieval maze of curving alleys and *piazzette* on the right bank of the Tiber, believe that their neighborhood is the only true Rome and its inhabitants the only true Romans. Gentrification has set in, but it still teems and throbs with life Italian style, particularly on Saturday nights in summer. Visit it then and walk across the river by way of the boat-shaped Tiber island known as the Isola Tiberina. Get there when dusk gilds the medieval mosaics in Piazza Santa Maria, and hunt around for one of the area's basement theaters, mini-jazz clubs, and tiny art cinemas, their signs camouflaged by laundry hung out to dry. Then have supper outdoors at one of the chaotic *pizzerie* that appropriate sidewalks and parking spaces all summer long. After midnight, stop at the back door of an unassuming bakery a block from Piazza Trilussa to sate yourself on tomorrow's *cornetti* and hot, cream-filled bombe. And at dawn on Sunday, show up at the immense flea market at Porta Portese, which closes by lunchtime, to comb through piles of early Renaissance Levis, stucco busts of Mussolini, and priceless and prongless silver forks. You just might find something you couldn't live without haggling for.

MASS IN ST. PETER'S, Vatican City: There is an opulent sense of secrecy and devotion in the penitent hum seeping from the confessionals, the permanent smell of incense, the smoky glow of candles on gilt-framed paintings and glinting baroque statues in St. Peter's Cathedral. Here's where the elegant faithful of Rome share pews with shoddy pilgrims from Lithuania, Poland, and Zaire, and stately processions of white-robed men and boys perpetually reenact a ritual that only the initiated can fully understand. The air undulates with murmured prayers and mumbled chants, the voice of the priest filtered through ancient loudspeakers, the organ's mellow buzz, the harsh treble of the occasional impious baby. Sometimes the dark whispers of the mass are broken by a bright burst of sound as orchestra and chorus deliver the Bach *Magnificat,* the soloists' voices rebounding off the fluted columns and convoluted walls. At the final cadence, the hush sets in again.

GRAND CANAL, Venice: Drift down the lavish 2-mile length of the Grand Canal in a sleek gondola — yes, a touristy, expensive gondola. There's more to see than even the observant have time to notice: hundreds of wrought-stone, pink-tinted, marble-edged Gothic and Renaissance palaces; mahogany motor launches moored in front of equally princely hotels with the best of addresses; lumbering boat-buses unloading passengers onto listing docks; a skein of alleyways and slender, twisting canals winding away from this broad boulevard of water. Anyone beholding it all for the first time without a lump in his or her throat surely has a heart of stone.

Italy's Most Memorable Hostelries

Sooner or later, whenever the world was too much with them, the Greta Garbos and Winston Churchills, Richard Wagners and Liz Taylors of every era slept here. Even the pleasure-loathing Lenin couldn't resist a season on Capri.

None of this should come as a surprise to anyone who has ever experienced the pleasures of the best Italian hostelries. Like one big room with a view, Italy is full of princely villas, magnificent monasteries, and other handsome accommodations lovingly and lavishly ransomed from the past. These historic hostelries supply the perfect excuse to avoid the anonymous glass-and-concrete business domes of postwar Italy.

HOTEL DEI TRULLI, Alberobello, Puglia: One of the main attractions of little-visited Apulia, the narrow streets of Alberobello are lined with clusters of more than 1,000 *trulli* — tiny whitewashed, beehive-shaped houses. Found only in this part of southern Italy, the design is prehistoric and pagan and conjures up images of gnomes' houses or Tolkien land. This hostelry provides the opportunity to actually lodge in one of them. Each cozy room is an authentic individual *trullo,* complete with patio, bathroom, bedroom, and miniature living room with fireplace. When you emerge from your room, the Castellana Grottoes and the antique town of Martina Franca nearby are worthy destinations for Apulian jaunts; the Gargano promontory to the north and the Gulf of Taranto to the south, both within day-tripping distance, offer some of Italy's least footprinted beaches. Details: *Hotel dei Trulli,* 32 Via Cadore, Alberobello (Bari) 70011 (phone: 80-721130; fax: 80-721044).

QUISISANA, Capri, Campania: When Doctor Clark, a British physician, founded his little sanatorium in the middle of the last century, he chose the sunniest and least windy corner of Capri — and named the spot *Qui Si Sana,* meaning "Here you get well." The hotel grew and prospered, and today enjoys perfect health in the heart of Capri as one of Italy's best-known and most glamorous holiday spots. The notion of a vacation curing anything seems quaint now, so it's to the well-off — not the ill — that this hotel currently caters, a crowd that wouldn't shop anywhere but at Fendi or Armani, except maybe Valentino. Only the service is still superbly old-fashioned, and its three-star oval swimming pool, celebrated terrace bar, and international parade of guests are great for what ails you. Capri itself makes the rest of the world and its problems seem sweetly irrelevant; the vital issues here are the flawless sea, the endless bouquet of flowers, the wish-you-were-here sunny-Italy sunshine. Closed November through March. Details: *Quisisana,* 2 Via Camerelle, Capri (Napoli) 80073 (phone: 81-837-0788).

VILLA D'ESTE, Cernobbio, Lombardy: Between its construction by luxury-loving Cardinal Tolomeo Gallio in 1568 and its conversion to a hotel in 1873, this sumptuous tandem of villas on mountain-framed Lake Como passed through the hands of those noble families, Torlonia and Orsini, who seem to have owned every worthwhile piece of Renaissance real estate under the Italian sun. Its residents have numbered bluebloods by the score — among them George IV's wife, Princess Caroline, whose behavior inspired this ditty: "Most gracious Queen, we thee implore/To go away and sin no more/Or if that effort be too great/To go away at any rate." Now nudged into the 20th century with grace and style, the place must rank with the top half-dozen resort hotels on the planet. And you don't have to be a prince of the church, or even a princess, to stroll through the 20-acre park on pathways across velvet lawns or through groves of pine and cypress, promenade under the lindens alongside the lake, mount the monumental staircase, wander through the columned-and-chandeliered corridors, and hold court in the sauna. Days begin here as all days should in the best of all possible worlds, with a lakeside chalice of orange juice and champagne. There's a squash court, 3 swimming pools (one of which miraculously floats raft-like in the waters of the lake), 8 tennis courts, and a nightclub to offer dizzying possibilities for distraction during the remaining hours. Every inch of the place is absolutely gorgeous and superbly maintained, and the level of service is never less than impeccable. The nearby mountains and lake guarantee cool weather even during the hottest of Italian summers (though air conditioning has been added). The food in the less formal grillroom (called the "Sporting Club" by some) is even better at dinner than the dining room fare. And if you feel like changing lakes in mid-visit, lovely, lively Lugano is just across the Swiss border. Closed December through February. Details: *Villa d'Este,* 40 Via Regina, Cernobbio (Como) 22010 (phone: 31-511471; fax: 31-512027).

MIRAMONTI MAJESTIC, Cortina d'Ampezzo, Veneto: In the craggy heart of the Dolomites, a few kilometers above the glitter of Italy's most sophisticated and *very* expensive mountain resort, surrounded by a parkful of pines, this venerable hotel still has one courtly toe in the 19th century. But the sybaritic guests of the fin de siècle did without such modern delights as the year-round swimming pool, tennis courts, the fully equipped sports center, and the 9-hole golf course. If the gabled roofs and romantic balconies look familiar, it's because you saw them in a James Bond film. Greater proof of glamour hath no hotel. There are two seasons — December to March (for Cortina's incomparable skiing) and June to September (for inspiring mountain rambling). Details: *Miramonti Majestic,* 103 Peziè, Cortina d'Ampezzo (Belluno) 32043 (phone: 436-4201; fax: 436-867019).

CALA DI VOLPE, Costa Smeralda, Sardinia: The crown jewel of the complex that the far-sighted and then young Aga Khan developed on a grand scale, yacht basin and all. It is discreetly tucked into a vividly turquoise cove, just at the water's edge on the once-remote island of Sardinia, is deluxe in comfort and management, and rustic in style — a mixture of Moorish and medieval, farmhouse and Hollywood, full of arches, pillars, beams, stucco, and such. The sheer natural beauty of the place has made it a favorite shooting location for fashion photographers and filmmakers (*Diamonds Are Forever,* among others, was filmed here). Rooms come in all shapes and sizes, some with balconies. Tennis, boating, swimming in the sea or in an Olympic-size pool, skin diving, golf on one of the country's best courses (described in "Great Italian Golf," *For the Body*), and one of the Mediterranean's most fascinating islands is just outside your door. Closed October through April. Details: *Cala di Volpe,* Cala di Volpe, Porto Cervo (Sassari) 07020 (phone: 789-96083).

VILLA SAN MICHELE, Fiesole, Tuscany: Michelangelo designed the façade for a spartan monastery, but this 28-room hostelry in the hills above Florence, under the same careful ownership as the *Cipriani* in Venice, is a place of aristocratic dinners by candlelight in an open-air restaurant, state-of-the-art Jacuzzis, manicured gardens, canopied beds and other antiques, and princely prices. A limousine is available to whisk guests back and forth to see Michelangelo's other creations in the museums and churches of Florence. Art critic Bernard Berenson's famed villa and painting collection, *I Tatti* — now the property of Harvard University — is only a Titian's throw away. Closed mid-November through February. Details: *Villa San Michele,* Via di Doccia, Fiesole (Firenze) 50014 (phone: 55-59451).

GRAND HOTEL PALAZZO DELLA FONTE, Fiuggi, Lazio: Lord Charles Forte, founder of the Trusthouse Forte hotel chain, was born near here, and partly for personal satisfaction, he lavished $30 million to bring back to life and luster the famed pre-World War I property that was once a royal favorite. Close to the renowned Fiuggi springs, guests at this 153-room luxury hotel also can enjoy a fitness center, indoor and outdoor swimming pools, 2 tennis courts, with a nearby 9-hole golf course (with another 9 holes planned at press time), and equestrian center complete with a polo field. The dining room offers refined versions of local and regional Italian dishes and a superior selection of wine. Details: *Grand Hotel Palazzo della Fonte,* Via dei Villini, Fiuggi (Frosinone) 03015 (phone: 775-55001; in the US, 800-255-5843).

SANTAVENERE, Maratea, Basilicata: The white-arcaded façade, set in a verdant fabric of olive and pine trees, and its dramatic position between Saracen tower and turquoise Tyrrhenian would ensure a nomination for an Oscar among Mediterranean hostelries. So it's surprising that this structure, built when Maratea was an innocent fishing village and no one who counted vacationed in the tumbledown region, remained such a well-kept secret for so many years. The fact is that those who knew about it wouldn't tell even their best friends. Maratea's narrow streets, rising and falling over well-trod steps and twisting and turning under ancient arches, bustle nowadays, but the hotel is as pretty as ever — elegant but not stuffy, scattered with reproduction antiques, model sailboats, and other nautical touches, rather like a comfortable country home. The disco-and-boutique option is there when you want it. Closed from October to May. Details: *Santavenere,* Fiumicello di Santa Venere, Maratea (Potenza) 85040 (phone: 973-876910).

DUOMO, Milan: If modern industrial Italy has a heart, you can watch it beating in this hotel right next to the cathedral, that mad Gothic confection at the center of Milan. It's here that the country's *pezzi grossi* (big businessmen) meet to make the country's biggest deals. The upwardly mobile rooms are arranged on two levels, with the lower living room section providing a suitable atmosphere for the signing of contracts. The furnishings are contemporary, but elegant notes of marble, Oriental carpeting, and burnished wood enliven the background. An added attraction is the companionable silence of the pedestrian zone outside the hotel — which also happens to be the most animated part of town, and leads into what is arguably the smartest single acre of fashion in all of Europe. Details: *Duomo,* 1 Via San Raffaele, Milano 20121 (phone: 2-8833).

SPLENDIDO, Portofino, Liguria: Since its transformation from private aristocratic residence at the turn of the century, this very special hotel has pampered both well-to-do and ne'er-do-well; and the view from its terraces and balconies — of many-colored cottages and bobbing boats in Portofino and its aquamarine port down below — has remained so miraculously unchanged that the late Duke and Duchess of Windsor would feel right at home, as they did long ago. The perfectly tended grounds, atwitter with birds and perpetually scented with mimosa and orange blossoms, modestly conceal tennis court and swimming pool. A romantic path leads down to town and the irresistible *aperitivo* hour at dockside, where ruddy fishermen mend their nets and bronzed gigolos cast theirs. Groucho Marx summed it up: "Wonderful place, wonderful people," he scrawled in the visitors' book. A 5-year, meticulous renovation was recently completed, making it even more heavenly. Closed November through March. Details: *Splendido,* Portofino (Genova) 16034 (phone: 185-269551; fax: 185-269614).

ALBERGO SAN PIETRO, Positano, Campania: Even the bathrooms in this stunning and supremely romantic hilltop hotel have views over the Amalfi Coast, so that not one moment of visual pleasure is wasted. The building seems tied to the cliff that plunges into the Bay of Salerno, its architecture and furnishings a colorful blend of the Italian and the Moorish. Rooms are tucked into the hillsidc, layer upon layer of them. Their walls are white and dazzling, their floors tiled and scattered with Oriental rugs, and each is embellished with antiques and sea-view balconies. And there are flowers at every turn, inside and out. The swimming pool is on top, with more of the stunning view, and an elevator that pierces the rock carries guests to the private beach and tennis courts below in style. Chic little Positano is a couple of kilometers away; visit it at the ice cream cone hour to browse through the shops brimming with kaleidoscopic summer cottons and to people watch in streets teeming with Italian magazine cover folk. Film and opera director Franco Zeffirelli has his summer palace here and gives the town a kind of perpetual opening-night air when he and his retinue are in residence. Closed November through mid-April. Details: *Albergo San Pietro,* Positano (Salerno) 84017 (phone: 89-875454).

SAN DOMENICO, Taormina, Sicily: Most people visit Taormina for the clear air, the ridiculously clear water, the good food, the strolling, the Greek theater, the haunting tour to the moonscape of Mount Etna, or the summer film festival. If you can, knock all that off in an hour — and then never again set foot outside this house of gilded repute. In 1896, after 500 years as a Dominican monastery, this regal Renaissance construction, dramatically positioned high above the Mediterranean, was reborn as a singularly unascetic hotel, and has been playing host to the famous ever since. Luminaries like Sophia Loren and Marlene Dietrich have marveled at the spectacle of sunset from the terrace and inhaled the scents of lemon and jasmine in the garden overlooking the azure Ionian and nearby Etna. Elsewhere, shady cloisters, immense salons, tapestry-hung corridors, and sober bedrooms artfully mix the extravagant and the severe. Life at the arcaded edge of a heated pool is a side of earthly existence the friars never even imagined. Details: *Palace Hotel San Domenico,* 5 Piazza San Domenico, Taormina (Messina) 98039 (phone: 942-23701; fax: 942-625506).

VILLA SASSI, Turin, Piedmont: In the wooded hills just outside the city, where the local patrician industrialists have their homes — Italy's answer to "Dallas" and "Dynasty" country — it's fun to live the life of Agnelli at this noble and splendidly restored 12-room mansion set in an immense park. Then, amid marble floors and antique furnishings, wine and dine in the villa's eminent restaurant, *El Toulà,* (with perhaps a bottle of heady, crimson barbaresco to accompany the tender, truffled roast beef). The trip home afterward lasts only as long as it takes to climb the stairs. Details: *Villa Sassi,* 47 Strada al Traforo del Pino, Torino 10132 (phone: 11-890556).

CIPRIANI, Venice: On the serene island of Giudecca, light years away from the hubbub of San Marco, this is the ultimate posh country club. It exudes Venetian polish and poise, presenting a secluded paradise comprising a peaceful garden, spa, heated Olympic-size saltwater swimming pool and tennis court, and stunning views of the lagoon. The hotel's 2 restaurants, from the dynasty that brought you *Harry's Bar,* make it worthwhile to eat six or seven meals a day, not counting a buffet at poolside, a dazzling spread of shrimp, spiny lobsters, Adriatic crabs, desserts by the dozen — everything perfectly cooked and immaculately served. Some of the hundred-odd superbly decorated rooms have Jacuzzis of their own. Others offer gold-leaf-trimmed furniture, lace curtains, vast windows, circular bathtubs, and more.Scheduled to open this year is the adjacent 15th-century wing, Palazzo Vendramin, that will house 9 deluxe apartments, complete with butler service. Some guests are relieved to discover that there's a private yacht harbor; if you're slumming, you will enjoy the free shuttle service by brass-fitted, sheer-curtained, mahogany-hulled boats to St. Mark's Square, 5 minutes away. Closed November through mid-March. Details: *Cipriani,* 10 Giudecca, Venezia 30123 (phone: 41-520-7744; fax: 41-520-3939).

GRITTI PALACE, Venice: Dramatically situated on the Grand Canal, this polished and sumptuous 99-room Renaissance palazzo, a compact version of the Doge's Palace, has been a favorite destination of Maria Callas, Charlie Chaplin, Charles de Gaulle, Paul Newman, and a procession of authors from Somerset Maugham to Ernest Hemingway to Judith Krantz. One of its most notable features is its greenery-edged dining terrace, which floats on the Grand Canal in the middle of the gondola traffic, just opposite the great baroque Church of Santa Maria della Salute — the perfect place to down quantities of beluga and drink museum-quality wines. The rooms have high ceilings, damask couches, Venetian mirrors, antique tables and chests, elaborate parquet floors, huge down pillows, and comfortable beds practically paved in crisp linen. No two are alike, and all are wonderful. Many overlook the canals, so just hang out your window to listen to the occasional tenor of a gondolier and watch most of Venice float by. Details: *Gritti Palace,* 2467 Campo Santa Maria del Giglio, Venezia 30124 (phone: 41-794611; fax: 41-5200942).

DUE TORRI, Verona, Veneto: A magnificent living museum fitted out entirely with antiques, this deluxe centuries-old inn, constructed as the official guesthouse for Verona's Scaligeri family, is *the* place to be during the summer opera festival at the *Arena di Verona* (described in "Theater, Music, and Opera," *For the Mind*). The management and the mood are highly personal. There's a roomy lounge full of antiques on each floor, and each guestroom is furnished in a different style (Louis XVI, Greco-Roman, Charles X, Biedermeier) — the object being to re-create the hotel that Grand Touring Americans might have found at the turn of the century. Enrico Wallner, the man responsible for refitting the palazzo, not only knows his antiques but also exhibits exquisite good taste: Even his ashtrays are handsome. When the hotel isn't full, guests may choose a room from a set of slides in the marbled, columned, and frescoed lobby. Music lovers will be gratified to note a plaque in the lobby commemorating the sojourn of "Wolfgango Amadeo Mozart" in 1770. Details: *Due Torri,* 4 Piazza Sant'Anastasia, Verona 37121 (phone: 45-595381; fax: 45-800-4130).

AGRITURIST

When you've had your fill of marble bidets, Raphaels, and four-posters, try taking the cure under the auspices of the nonprofit purveyor of simple accommodations known as *Agriturist.* Spend a week tasting the wines of the Chianti region, walk in the mountains of Trentino, go cross-country skiing a half-hour drive from the Italian Riviera, canoe in Campania, or hunt in Tuscany — and return each night to a quiet place in the country.

Each year, *Agriturist* publishes an enthrallingly detailed index to hundreds of private farms, villas, even castles that accept paying guests. Some offer independent mini-apartments, others room and homey country board. Still others will turn the whole house over to a traveler and ten friends for, say, *Christmas Week.* Send for the catalogue, or abbreviate matters by writing your exact requirements, and the organization will send a short list of places to contact directly. You may never allow yourself to be snubbed by a frock-coated concierge again. Details: *Agriturist,* 101 Corso Vittorio Emanuele, Roma 00186 (phone: 6-651-2342).

Buon Appetito: The Best Restaurants of Italy

While all those mad dogs and Englishmen are running around in the noonday sun, Italians are lolling in the shade of a spaghetti tree by the banks of a river of chianti. Every afternoon, they sit happily and hungrily at table for 3 or 4 hours. Almost every evening, dinner is the principal entertainment. The country is full of family trattorie that make the most of their comestible bounties, wonderful establishments that offer a mix of homeyness, sophistication, and generally superb foods made from whatever was in the market that morning (usually written in purple ink in an almost indecipherable scrawl). At places like these, it's great fun to share the Italians' zest in their culinary heritage — those below are just the *crema della crema.*

La cucina creativa — Italy's answer to the nouvelle cuisine of France — is firmly established. And unlike the food found at the United States of McDonald, Italian specialties change significantly from area to area. Centuries-old regional dishes are being rediscovered and presented in modernized versions. Old-fashioned cereal staples like barley and *faro* are new culinary fashions; give them a try. Just as you've memorized one menu, you're forced to master a whole new culinary vocabulary. Forge ahead. With 5,000 miles of coastline, there are plenty of fish in the Italian seas. There are more pasta dishes in Italy than there are forks (see *Dining in Italy,* PERSPECTIVES, for a glossary of the most common types of pasta). We suggest making an effort to try them all. (Be sure to phone ahead for reservations.) And if you overeat, a shot of the pungent little herbal horror known as Fernet-Branca, available in most bars and restaurants, normally will chase away all evil abdominal spirits. *Buon appetito.*

PARACUCCHI–LOCANDA DELL'ANGELO, Ameglia, Liguria: A modern, unprepossessing hotel near the buzzing beaches of Liguria's Riviera is the modest backdrop for Angelo Paracucchi's nationally acclaimed seafood workshop, one of the culinary landmarks of Italy. Traditional marine staples like clams, rock lobster, shrimp, and sea bass all appear here in enticing and original guises. The pasta is tossed with asparagus or seafood or the simplest tomato and olive oil sauces. Game in the fall and winter, raspberries and wild strawberries in early summer, and honey-and-vinegar-flavored duck for all seasons. Be sure to wait three days before going in the water. Closed Mondays and 3 weeks in January. Details: *Paracucchi–Locanda dell'Angelo,* 60 Via XXV Aprile, Ameglia, La Spezia 19031 (phone: 187-64391; fax: 187-64393).

CAVALLO BIANCO, Aosta, Valle d'Aosta: Coaches and carriages clattered up to the door of this wood-balconied restaurant for hundreds of years before cars ever whizzed through the nearby Alpine tunnels to France and Switzerland; the foundations go back to Roman times. The table decor is pure and perfect — linen cloths from Flanders, crocheted centerpieces, underplates of silver, porcelain covers. The six-page menu is as innovative as the setting is traditional. Make your own choices or simply nod and they'll be made for you. Selections cover terrine, quiche, *spuma di trota* (trout mousse), *sformato di verdura* (vegetable timbale), delicately sauced lamb, turkey, pheasant, and guinea hen. And accompanying each course are small loaves of home-baked breads chunked with olives, nuts, or herbs. Closed Sunday evenings, Mondays, and from mid-June to mid-July. Details: *Cavallo Bianco,* 15 Via Aubert, Aosta 11100 (phone: 165-362214).

PAPPAGALLO, Bologna, Emilia-Romagna: In a city widely known as a destination of choice for the Italian *buongustaio,* this restaurant set in Bologna's ochre porticos is worth a visit. The great but weighty traditional dishes are still star players — lasagna, boiled meats — but newer, more feathery dishes are pulling in the crowds. Red radicchio in the crêpes, chives on the ravioli, nuts on the *tortelloni* are more the style now. Whether you choose the time-tested classics or sample the newer variations, the region's simple sparkling lambrusco is the perfect complement to your meal. Closed Sunday dinner and Mondays. Details: *Pappagallo,* 30 Piazza della Mercanzia, Bologna 40125 (phone: 51-232807).

ANTICA OSTERIA DEL PONTE, Cassinetta di Lugagnano, Lombardy: When you're ready to take pastoral refuge from the clatter of brisk, commercial Milan, make the short drive to this fetching and photogenic *osteria* — an old country inn near a bridge and a bubbling stream, with a pretty landscape in the distance. The walls are white, the floors dark, the fire crackling, the flowers cheery, and the atmosphere decidedly warm and comfortable. Owners and kitchen-masters Ezio and Renata Santin create according to the calendar, and diners unswervingly trust the day's fixed-price selections. Highlights may include wild mushroom soup, lobster risotto, beef with artichoke mousse. Closed Sundays and Mondays. Details: *Antica Osteria del Ponte,* Cassinetta di Lugagnano, Abbiategrasso (Milano) 20081 (phone: 2-942-0034).

LA FRASCA, Castrocaro Terme, Emilia-Romagna: That proprietor Gianfranco Bolognesi began life as a sommelier is evident here. The stone walls of the cozy dining room are upholstered with empty wine bottles, the cellars are pavement-to-beams with the best vintages from around the world, and Bolognesi himself still delights in helping guests match, say, a thickly perfumed cannonau from Sardinia with the lobster ravioli in sweet pepper sauce; an ardent aglianico del vulture from Potenza to accompany the stuffed rabbit; a pale blond müller thurgau to honor the seafood-and-truffle salad. End the celebration with a grappa *digestivo* and stroll around this graceful spa town in the Apennine foothills. The air blowing in from the nearby Adriatic coast is as cool and tangy as a 1983 Colli Morenici Mantovani del Garda. Closed Tuesdays, 3 weeks in January, and 2 weeks in August. Details: *La Frasca,* 34 Via Matteotti, Castrocaro Terme (Forli) 47011 (phone: 543-767471).

LOCANDA DELL'ISOLA COMACINA, Comacina Island, Lombardy: For close to 30 years, this restaurant perched on a hilltop on the only island in Lake Como has featured the same memorable menu. The feast begins with a bottle of wine and an entire loaf of warm freshly baked bread placed on the table. Now comes a thick slice of tomato topped with a sliver of lemon drizzled with olive oil and a touch of oregano. Then on to praga ham and melon and tissue thin slices of *bresola* (dried beef). Next comes a procession of bowls that would send a vegetarian into ecstasy, and everyone else as well: roast onions (our favorites), zucchini, marinated carrots (sheer ambrosia), cauliflower, red, yellow, and green peppers, and sensational celery. On to "Smuggler's Trout" (perfectly grilled salmon trout with just the right touches of olive oil, lemon juice, and rough salt), followed by perfectly grilled chicken served with a green salad. The parmesan cheese that comes next is fresh (not at all the kind of dry, tasteless stuff that most folks eat at home), hacked off a wheel that weighs more than 70 pounds. Dessert is ice cream (a prodigious portion) atop slices of fresh peaches, all doused in peach liqueur. The meal is concluded with a coffee ceremony calculated to keep the island's old Evil Spirits at bay; host Benvenuto Puricelli dons a ritual rainbow cap to ladle huge quantities of brandy and sugar into freshly brewed coffee. It's not the sort of libation around which a prudent person would light a match. One of the matchless meals of Italy, consumed in a sublime setting (all at a fixed price). Open March through October for lunch and dinner; closed Tuesdays, except in June and July. Reservations advised. Information: *Locanda dell'Isola Comacina,* Uff. Postale 22010, Sala Comacina, Lago di Como, Italy (phone: 344-55083).

ENOTECA PINCHIORRI, Florence: Michelangelo, Botticelli, and this place make a perfect Florentine day. The edible art here changes with the market's offerings but often exhibits such masterworks as foie gras with pomegranate salad, sole with onion-and-parsley purée, tiny gnocchi (potato dumplings) with basil, veal with caper-and-lime sauce, duck in red wine. The charming 15th-century-palace setting and the flawlessly appointed tables complete the picture. An *enoteca* is a kind of wine merchant's show-room — that's how the restaurant got its start — and red, white, and rosé are still its flying colors. One ingredient that should be left out: Service is very stuffy these days and the $300 check for two does make you think twice before being snubbed by Italy's haughtiest waiters. Closed Sundays, Mondays at lunch, and August. Details: *Enoteca Pinchiorri,* 87 Via Ghibellina, Firenze 50122 (phone: 55-242777).

SAN DOMENICO, Imola, Emilia-Romagna: Probably more superlatives have been slung at *San Domenico* than at any restaurant in Italy. Make the half-hour pilgrimage from Bologna to the shady, tree-lined square beneath the castle in Imola, and you, too, will want to coin a few "issimos" of your own. The ambience is refined without being precious, and every harmonious detail has been attended to, right down to the waiters' buttons. The warm and winning proprietor, Gianluigi Morini, makes guests feel as though all this luxury were their due. The chief pleasures: the *garganelli in salsa primavera* (twisted pasta in a fresh vegetable sauce), the green gnocchi adrift in sage-flavored cream, shrimp salad with truffle butter, trout mousse in shrimp sauce, stuffed chicken thighs, sole in mushroom-and-champagne sauce, beef with basil and white wine. Your just desserts: apples baked with almonds and cider, zabaglione with vanilla and hazelnuts. For a postprandial, have a prowl through the wine cellar in the old convent tunnels beneath the restaurant. Closed Mondays and the first 2 weeks in January, and from the last week in July to about mid-August. Details: *San Domenico,* 1 Via Sacchi, Imola (Bologna) 40026 (phone: 542-29000).

IL SOLE, Maleo, Lombardy: This rustic converted farmhouse — in the same family for a century — rises among grapevines, birds' nests, and gentle church bells. The ceilings are wooden and the walls whitewashed, and the menu's offerings suit the setting. Minestrone precedes traditional Milanese *maccheroni alla verdura* (giant macaroni with vegetables), pheasant with apples, osso buco with fresh peas — all country foods, urbanely prepared. Proprietor Colombani collects antique recipes and delights in researching and re-creating long-ignored regional dishes from other eras. In summer, you can drink your coffee and grappa on the shady loggia, watch the flight of the swallows, and breathe the herb-scented country air. Closed Sunday evenings, Mondays, January, and August. Details: *Albergo del Sole,* 22 Via Trabattoni, Maleo (Milano) 20076 (phone: 377-58142).

GIANNINO, Milan: The foods of Tuscany are featured here, despite a Lombard location, and the noted large and elegant restaurant on two floors first made its name in the 19th century with a simple plate of beans, and delicacies like *olivette di vitello tartufate* (slices of veal wrapped around ham and seasoned with truffles), *panzerotti* (mozzarella in grilled pasta), and *tortelloni al basilico* (stuffed pasta with basil) still are the most popular offerings. The fish is outstanding, whether it's crisply fried or served in salad and lightly dressed with olive oil and lemon. Visible from the foyer is the spectacular and spotlessly clean kitchen — so before the gastronomic performance, take a peek at the actors in the wings. Closed Sundays and August. Details: *Giannino,* 8 Via Amatore Sciesa, Milano 20135 (phone: 2-545-2948; fax: 2-545-2765).

GUALTIERO MARCHESI, Milan: If a country as rich in restaurants and culinary tradition has a single best restaurant, this might be it. The quality of the meal guests enjoy in the domain of television idol and cookbook king Gualtiero Marchesi fully supports his reputation. Responsible for introducing notions of nouvelle cuisine to Italy, he now demonstrates this inventive cooking at its unfussy best in one of only two three-Michelin-star establishments in Italy. Choose from a wide selection of seafoods, often joined with vegetables — lobster with peppers, shrimp with cucumbers, hake with potatoes. The meat dishes are more traditional; when thyme and rosemary work sorcery on rare roasted rack of lamb here, the result is enchanting. Sherbets of imaginative flavors are one closing note; or it's possible to depart with a mountain of white and dark chocolate mousse with chocolate sauce under your belt, or perhaps a dollop or two of Grand Marnier ice cream. For a simpler, less expensive version, try the genial chef's newest endeavor, the *Bistrot,* on the seventh floor of the Piazza del Duomo department store *La Rinascente,* open for lunch and dinner weekdays. The main restaurant is closed Sundays, Monday lunch, and August. Details: *Gualtiero Marchesi,* 9 Via Bonvesin de la Riva, Milano 20129 (phone: 2-741246).

GIRARROSTO TOSCANO, Rome: The cramped staircase entrance to this popular restaurant (whose name means simply "Tuscan roast spit") doesn't prepare first-time guests for the spacious, cave-like rooms around the corner. From Roman *haute bour-*

geoisie and movie producers to Middle Eastern yuppies and American cardiologists on convention, the clientele waits patiently at the entrance and then sits down zestfully to enjoy the eavesdropping, the people watching, and the bustle — and to dine excellently on ultra-traditional Tuscan specialties. Waiters automatically serve platterfuls of well-aged hams, mortadella, salami, prosciutto, mozzarella, stuffed tomatoes, meatballs, baked eggplant, and other antipasti. Then, right after you've eaten enough to last at least a couple of days, dinner begins. Gigantic Florentine steaks grilled to perfection stand out in any season; spaghetti with fresh tomato and basil is a worthy summer offering. Menus with prices are sometime things at best, and if you don't want antipasto, which costs extra, say so as soon as you sit down. Closed Wednesdays. Details: *Girarrosto Toscano,* 29 Via Campania, Roma 00187 (phone: 6-482-1899).

RELAIS LE JARDIN, Rome: Though this superlatively comfortable and elegant dining room is a bit out of the way, once there, you'll agree that the food deserves the fuss. The menu is dizzying yet engaging: Zucchini flowers stuffed with bean purée, ravioli filled with pigeon, and watercress flan with scallops were among the recent offerings. Closed Sundays. Reservations are essential. Details: *Relais Le Jardin,* 5 Via Giuseppe de Notaris, Roma 00197 (phone: 6-360-9541; fax: 6-322-0405).

EL TOULÀ, Rome: Completely unlike the plain, brightly lit restaurants so typical of Rome, this one boasts decor that is at once plush and subtle, a clientele that is aristocratic and well traveled, a staff as warm and easygoing as the local trattoria's, and a menu that takes diners through Paris, Vienna, and a score of other European capitals. Stick to the dishes of Venice, the restaurant's culinary starting place. Try the *radicchio di Treviso ai ferri,* a slightly bitter red lettuce served grilled. Go on to black risotto, a rice dish perfumed with squid and its ink. Try calves' liver with onions or sage butter or the famous *baccalà mantecato* (creamy codfish). And finish up with *tiramisù,* a creamy coffee-and-chocolate-flavored confection whose name means "pick-me-up." Skiers and hikers headed for the Dolomites should look up the sister restaurant by the same name in Cortina d'Ampezzo. Closed Saturdays at lunchtime, Sundays, and August. Details: *El Toulà,* 29B Via della Lupa, Roma 00186 (phone: 6-687-3750).

LE TRE VASELLE, Torgiano, Umbria: In the center of a quiet village rising gently above the soft, reassuring Umbrian countryside, this restaurant is the latest effort of the Lungarotti family, the area's most highly regarded wine producers, and their own home-bottled torre di giano, rubesco, and san giorgio grace tables full of rabbit with laurel, arugula-and-mushroom salad, zucchini with basil and parmesan, and more. Details: *Le Tre Vaselle,* 48 Via Garibaldi, Torgiano (Perugia) 06089 (phone: 75-982447). See also *Most Visitable Vineyards.*

Cafés

Perhaps no other institution reflects the relaxed Italian lifestyle as much as the ubiquitous café (or bar, as it is called in Italy). From village emporia with three tin tables where the black-hatted pensioners perpetually argue the Sunday soccer results, to the sprawling outdoor drawing rooms of Venice's Piazza San Marco, life slows to a sit-and-sip. Italians order Campari or cappuccino and put the world on hold. Inside, Italian cafés are for receiving friends and suitors, reading the paper, and writing the great Calabrian novel. Some regulars even get their mail at their local café. Outside, in summer, the café is for appraising and supervising the spectacle. Puccini set a whole act of his opera *La Bohème* in a café.

When you visit those below — a few of the most evocative of the breed — remember that cafés are not necessarily inexpensive. Table prices are usually far higher than what you pay for the same items standing at the bar. So when you're charged $5 for an espresso, don't grumble — just think of it as rent.

RIVOIRE, Florence: Established over 100 years ago, this café is across the square from the stern façade of the Palazzo Vecchio. From its outdoor tables, you may contemplate the austere architecture of the fortress-like palace and the copy of Michelangelo's *David* while literally spooning up the decidedly wicked chocolate confection that is the specialty of the house. It was in this piazza that the charming Lucy in Forster's *A Room with a View* fell in love, beneath "a pillar of roughened gold." Piazza della Signoria (phone: 55-214412).

CUCCHI, Milan: Sip your Bellini (fresh peach juice and champagne) outdoors in the summer and eye the Armani-clad executives who have maneuvered Italy into one of the top economic slots in the world. Nurse a Negroni (red vermouth and gin) indoors in the winter amidst the pink velvet and chandeliers preserved from the 1930s when *tutto* Milano came here to dance. Or time your visit for 7:45 AM to sample brioche fresh from the oven. Closed Mondays. 1 Corso Genova (phone: 2-839-9793).

PEDROCCHI, Padua: This sedate neo-classical gathering place in the center of Padua, built in 1831 long before Italy became a unified state, once reverberated with revolutionary patriotic fervor, and its three rooms — open from early morning until after midnight — are still painted red, white, and green like the Italian flag. A bullet hole in the wall of the White is a cherished reminder of the 1848 student uprisings against the city's Austrian rulers. Earnest young people come to the Green to study, talk, and celebrate graduation from the nearby university. The Red? It's where local businesspeople, intent on their double espresso, plot to preserve the status quo. Via 8 Febbraio (phone: 49-875-2020).

RONEY, Palermo: The best stand-up food in Sicily is served at one end of its immense bar; at the other, a hundred different sweets, including the island's special cannoli. In between is a coffee bar that serves a particularly black and potent espresso. In the spacious tent-like pavilion outdoors, patrons lean back in their wicker chairs, look out on the tree-lined avenue, and ponder the mystery of Palermo. How can a city whose per capita income is one of Italy's lowest be among the country's top ten consumers? The answer — the rumor is that it's hidden Mafia money — may give people watching in this café an added dimension. 13 Viale della Libertà (phone: 91-328427).

GRECO, Rome: When this café was opened in 1760 by the Greek-born Nicola della Maddalena, its clients were local working people. Later, the tranquil little marble tables in the three back rooms were a place for Stendhal and Schopenhauer to pause and reflect. They prompted Hans Christian Andersen to characterize Rome as the only city in the world that made him feel instantly at home. Casanova mentioned the establishment in his memoirs, Mark Twain loved the place, Nicolai Gogol scribbled *Dead Souls* seated on its austere benches, and the painter Giorgio de Chirico said he couldn't paint without stopping here for his daily dose of the Italian drink Punt e Mes. After World War II, local intellectuals dubbed the narrow elongated room where John Keats, Washington Irving, and Oscar Wilde had taken coffee "The Omnibus." Today, the place is full of busts and statues of such famous habitués, and the front bar is jammed with expensive furs and suede slippers whose owners are catching their breath between jaunts to Fendi and Ferragamo. Couturier Valentino comes here, as do members of the Bulgari clan, whose shop is nearby. *Antico Caffè Greco* has been declared a part of Italy's national patrimony, and even the waiters, who dress in tails, look as if they're being preserved for posterity. 86 Via Condotti (phone: 6-679-1700).

TRE SCALINI, Rome: Not surprisingly, this place is a perennial favorite with both Romans and foreigners, particularly in summer, when the cone-seekers are often three deep at the ice cream counter inside. The setting — right at the center of Rome's beautiful and fume-free Piazza Navona, staring at Bernini's famous Fountain of the Rivers — is incomparable; the cast of characters colorful; and the ice cream the finest in Rome. The renowned specialty is *tartufo,* a kind of chocolate-covered chocolate with chocolate in the middle, under an avalanche of whipped cream, named for its resemblance to the knobby truffle. 28 Piazza Navona (phone: 6-654-1996).

SAN MARCO, Trieste: With its newspapers draped over bamboo poles, its card tables surrounded by intent retired government employees, its corners occupied by solitary readers and scribblers, this holdover of pre–World War I days, when Trieste had 56 coffeehouses, was like something out of the late great Austro-Hungarian Empire. Its fin de siècle Viennese atmosphere was treasured by habitués, many of whom regularly met and chatted with friends here as if it were their own living room. A sprightly refurbishing has lightened the mood, but the friendly ghosts linger. 18 Via Battisti (phone: 40-727216).

TOMMASEO, Trieste: Lovingly restored, this Trieste café is a landmark located along the blowy seafront. The marble tables, on their cast-iron bases, the ornate coat stands, the mirrors, and the cupids are all as they were when James Joyce was living in the city, hanging out at the *Tommaseo,* teaching at Berlitz, and trying to scrounge a few lire for a glass of *birra.* On Riva 3 Novembre (phone: 40-366765).

FIORIO, Turin: Only a few steps from Piazza Castello, tucked into the famous *portici* — those roofed-over sidewalks so welcome in intemperate northern Italian cities — this century-old café hums and clinks with top-drawer Turinese, from tailored Fiat executives to old Piedmont aristocrats and their well-groomed offspring just back from skiing in the mountains at the end of the street. No less than Friedrich Nietzsche was a habitué, and the zabaglione with whipped cream that was a favorite in his day is still on the menu. Closed Mondays. 8 Via Po (phone: 11-839-6585).

FLORIAN, Venice: The show first opened in 1720 and has been running here ever since — both outdoors, on the dizzyingly ornamental and people-packed Piazza San Marco, and indoors, among the salons full of red velvet, parquet, and intricate paneling and painting. To enjoy it all, order a cappuccino on an early April morning, when the pigeons and the first trans-Alpine arrivals herald Venice's spring opening. Or sip a cold white soave on a balmy summer night when the crowds seem to sway in unison to the lilting rhythm of Strauss or Rossini or Offenbach, as interpreted by the *Florian* orchestra from late April until October. Or enjoy a rum punch on a windy November afternoon, standing shoulder to shoulder with soigné Venetians in the coffee-fragrant bar. Or experience this café with a Brandy Alexander in hand and a pale winter sun outside. Venice is for all seasons, and this favorite of Casanova and Madame de Staël is as important a stop on a Venice itinerary as the Doge's Palace, whose superb Gothic pastel façade is clearly visible from most tables. 57 Piazza San Marco (phone: 41-528-5338).

Shopping in Italy

In the beginning, Italians created marble statues, stone palazzi, and alabaster altarpieces. In our era, the national talent has turned from the eternal to the ephemeral, from the permanent to the portable. As a result, the descendants of Cellini and Michelangelo lavish their genius for design, their sure instinct for what is simply beautiful, on the creation of objects for daily use that delight the senses. The result has come to be known as "Italian style."

Most shops practice the Anglo-Saxon rite of *prezzi fissi* (fixed prices). Or at least they claim to. But it never hurts to try for the traditional *sconto* (discount) on the grounds that you're paying in cash, that you're buying in quantity, that the price is outrageous, or that you were sent by the owner's brother-in-law in Buffalo.

For information on the value added tax (VAT) refund scheme, see *Shopping,* GETTING READY TO GO. For information about the best buys and where to find them, read on.

WHERE TO SHOP

CHAIN STORES: In a nation dedicated to the proposition that boutique is best, the department store and one-stop shopping site are only a minor part of the scene. *La Rinascente* recently has upgraded its collections in Rome and Milan, and its newly remodeled Milanese establishment is an outstanding store by world standards — don't miss the seventh floor with its *Bistrot* restaurant, café, hair dresser, and cosmetician. *Coin* and *Upim,* the nationwide major leaguers, both sell middle-priced clothing and household items of decent quality. The former has over 2 dozen shops all over the country, many in wonderful old palaces in the historic town centers. The latter is in major cities; the store in downtown Rome, on Via del Tritone, is a comfortable place to begin conspicuous consuming within the city limits of the capital. *Standa* resembles a glorified *Woolworth's* and is found in every important town or city. Clothing is a good buy, especially at *Upim;* prices are fair, and many items are pure cotton or all wool. Housewares are also attractive and inexpensive.

Since all four chains are self-service and have fitting rooms, they're convenient places to figure out your Italian size and get a feel for price or fit — without having to sign-language with salespeople.

STREET MARKETS: If shopping is entertainment, Italy's street markets are its best theater. Most of the country's most intriguing goods can be found here. High-quality shoes show up at Rome's gigantic Sunday morning labyrinth at the Porta Portese. Top designers are remaindered on Turin's Via della Crocetta. Imitations of all the big names in leather will fool you at the daily *Mercato Nuovo* in Florence. Forget the four walls and shop as the Italians do — alfresco.

Amantea, Calabria – A typical southern market heaped high with technicolor fruits and vegetables, this cheerful weekly happening shows off stands of therapeutic herbs, handmade baskets, embroidered fabrics, wooden sculpture, and mountains of hot red peppers. Sunday mornings.

L'Aquila, Abruzzo – Besides the usual fruits, vegetables, and inexpensive housewares, this 600-year-old market in the main downtown square sells good quality lace, ceramics, hand-worked leather, and metal goods. Look into the many little artisans' shops nearby for baskets, fabrics, wood sculpture, and wrought iron. Daily except Sundays.

Bari, Puglia – The flea market on Via Calefati offers mostly new and used clothing, antique beds, antebellum fur coats, old shoes, garish crockery, and the overflow from the nearby American navy base. Monday mornings.

Campobasso, Molise – Local cheese, earthenware, lace, embroidery, wrought iron, and knives are the specialties of this traditional provincial market. Daily except Sundays.

Florence, Tuscany – Florence's two markets make an exhilarating contrast to the sober beauty of its narrow streets. Exuberant *San Lorenzo* teems with low-cost temptations: mohair and Shetland sweaters, prim and practical underwear, costume jewelry, brilliantly colored scarves. The *Straw Market,* also known as *Il Mercato Nuovo* or *Il Mercato del Porcellino* — centrally located on Via Calimata — is covered over and graced with a bronze wild-boar fountain. On sale here are all the usual fake Fendi, Gucci, and Gherardini handbags and belts, and a medley of straw hats, bags, and baskets, plus a wide range of African wares. Daily except Sundays and Mondays.

Forte dei Marmi, Tuscany – Everything for the beach life — wooden clogs, novelty T-shirts, and straw hats — plus the latest and glossiest Chinese trinkets. Wednesdays until 2 PM.

Isernia, Molise – Since the 1984 earthquake, the houses on the tiny streets of this town are shored up with posts, and the women sit outside on low chairs embroidering goods soon to appear in the market. These, together with rustic woolen stockings, wild chamomile and oregano, and over 2 dozen different qualities of olives, impart a genuine country feeling. Saturday mornings.

Naples, Campania – Sicilian puppets, German shepherd puppies, wooden polenta plates, broken mandolins, tubes for wireless sets, shiny new electrical appliances: The old, the new, the borrowed, the blue, and the stolen enliven this chaotic conglomeration of hundreds of stands and thousands of voices that sprawls between Via del Vicinale and Santa Maria del Pianto. Sunday mornings.

On Via Forcella, between Via Duoma and Piazza Calenda, a daily market of gigantic proportions offers everything from soap to stereos. Bathroom products, lighters, records, electrical appliances, and every sort of cigarette, cigar, and pipe tobacco are all at prices half of those in the shops. But check carefully to be sure the box you take home really contains what you bought. And watch your purse!

Palermo, Sicily – *La Vucceria* — the place of the voices — is the name of this colorful city's brightest and noisiest market that most resembles an Arab souk. Hide your wallet, and enjoy the excitement; you'll see stalls heaped high with foods you've never seen before, herbs, and delicious edibles being fried on the spot. Closed Sundays.

Rimini, Emilia-Romagna – Dried mushrooms and freshly gathered wild salad greens flourish next to a colorful maritime assortment of sandals, sand toys, sun togs, and seashells by the seashore. In Piazza Malatesta. Wednesday and Saturday mornings.

Rome – For every Roman who goes to mass on Sunday morning, a dozen go shopping with the masses at Porta Portese. To join them, stuff a little naked cash in a tight pocket, leave camera and purse at home, and prepare to shuffle through the packed streets. Sundays from 5 AM (the bargain hour) until 1 PM.

The vast clothing market at the daily shops and stands at Via Sannio, near San Giovanni, is the place for good buys and a wide assortment of rough stuff — army surplus, jeans, down jackets, mode-of-the-moment sweaters. Beware of imitation Levis, Wranglers, and such, and be sure to check out Rome's mini-*Macy's* across the street — the *Coin* department store.

The air conditioned shopping mall has finally appeared on the Roman scene. *Cinecittà Due,* with over 100 shops, reachable by subway, is open daily except Sundays, from 9 AM to 8:30 PM. Don't expect bargains.

One of the most rewarding Roman experiences is to take the time to pore over the new and used books, occasionally authentic antique prints, and modern reproductions of etchings of Rome's monuments — all offered weekdays in the stalls at the Piazza di Fontanella Borghese. Many of the reproductions (some rare booksellers also stock originals) are the work of Giambattista Piranesi, whose first plates of Roman antiquities were printed in 1743. Piranesi was a forerunner in his age's rediscovery of Roman antiquities. He was followed by other engravers who have left us documents of romantic ruins and the Roman palazzi and piazze as they must have looked looked in the Renaissance and baroque eras.

San Remo, Liguria – Piazza del Mercato in this flower capital of the Riviera blooms with carnations, roses, gladioli, local herbs, and spices. Pungently overshadowing it all is the perfume of fragrant masses of *basilico* (basil): This is the region for pesto, the green, basil-based spaghetti sauce. This open-air market also sells clothing and accessories. Tuesday and Saturday mornings from 8 AM to 1 PM.

Turin, Piedmont – The flea market known as *Il Balon* is open all day Saturday and the second Sunday of every month; the best time is dawn. The dealers' stock in trade ranges from furniture and prewar spark plugs to stamp collections, bicycles, and Mussolini relics. Tourists seldom visit.

In Via Marco Polo, at *Il Mercato della Crocetta,* right next to the fruit and vegetables, eagle-eyed shoppers can find model-size cashmere, silk, and leather goods left over from last year's fashion shows — their labels neatly removed. Monday through Friday mornings and all day Saturday.

BEST BUYS

CERAMICS AND POTTERY: In the days when earthenware was made from local clay to stock local kitchens, towns in every corner of Italy created their own pottery designs and have continued the traditions down through the centuries. Consequently, the search for pottery and ceramics can lead a traveler to far-flung villages, and for those who see shopping as simply an excuse to explore, the search for ceramics and pottery is particularly gratifying.

Albisola, Liguria – Dozens of factories and workshops produce hundreds of windows full of the baroque blue style that has been traditional since the 17th century. Little figures for *Christmas* crèches are a specialty, and there's a museum at the Villa Faraggiana; open from mid-April to mid-September.

Deruta, Umbria – Lavishly supplied showrooms are scattered all along the main road, but some of the best shopping is in the *botteghe* (studios) uphill in town, where you can see the artists at work. Look at the museum in town and at the Church of Madonna dei Bagni a mile south of the city before making a selection.

Faenza, Emilia-Romagna – The French word faïence has come to signify any ceramic tableware. But the trademark of Faenza is a cheerful red, blue, and green flower pattern. The local museum (2 Via Campidoro; phone: 546-21240) has antique pottery from all regions of Italy.

Fratte Rosa, Marches – Pots made of the iron-rich local clay, often painted a rich eggplant color, come in many sizes and shapes. Sturdy pots suitable for cooking are particularly attractive, albeit a challenge to carry home.

Grottaglie, Puglia – In this town not far from Taranto, an entire quarter is dedicated to ceramics. You can find everything from doll-size pitchers to gigantic urns with the local pattern of blue flowers on a beige background.

Terlizzi, Puglia – Royal blue and rust glazes characterize the ceramics of this town.

Vietri sul Mare, Campania – The last town (or the first, depending on direction) on the Amalfi Drive is still full of potters. Pass the picturesquely tiled food stores en route to the huddle of shops around the main square. Naively painted goats are one motif among the many on the plates, vases, and colorful whatnots for sale.

CLOTHING: The prospect of picking up an entire wardrobe in Italy is so tempting that some travelers dream of an airline losing their luggage permanently.

Giorgio Armani creates clothing for women in styles not unlike those he makes for men. The star of both shows has always been the broad-shouldered, loose-fitting jacket and slacks that manage to be at once comfortably baggy and elegant of line. The designer's Emporio models can be found in many outlets; his boutiques have exclusive models at triple the price. A shopper's prime destination is 102 Via del Babuino in Rome.

Laura Biagiotti's spare, linear clothes in softly off-beat colors, are displayed against a dazzling white backdrop in her Rome shop on dark, narrow Via Borgognona. Her shops can also be found in Milan, Venice, and Florence.

Luisa Spagnoli offers high-quality, moderately priced clothing for women in the purest cotton and wool — which is why this designer's more than 100 shops are popular in every corner of the country. In Florence, stop at 20 Via Strozzi. In Rome on the Via Frattina and at 84 Via Barberini.

Missoni started with knitwear, but the unexpected patchworks can now be found as shirts, slacks, bathing suits, and even belts for men and women. The all-time classic is a heavy cardigan sweater for men, suitable as outerwear, in sophisticated color mixes. The newest wrinkle: handsome sheets, bedspreads, stunning area rugs, and wall hangings. On a rainy day, it's cheering just to pop into a *Missoni* shop. You'll find them in Milan, Turin, Venice, and Rome.

Valentino has ready-to-wear for men and women with a sophisticated look that is both timeless and elegant. Women's dresses are slim and tailored or full and definitively romantic. If money doesn't matter, bypass the boutiques and go for the *alta moda* (haute couture). It's all under one roof at 3 Via Santo Spirito in Milan; there are also shops in Rome.

Il Discount dell'Alta Moda (16/A Via Gesù) sells last season's high fashions at down-to-earth prices in Rome. *Bassetti Confezioni* (5 Via Monterone) also has high fashion ready-to-wear for both men and women at discounted prices and is the best fashion bargain in the Eternal City.

EMBROIDERY AND LACE: These still are produced and prized in Italy.

Isola Maggiore, Lake Trasimeno, Umbria – Fine handiwork is still practiced in a workshop on an island in the middle of Lake Trasimeno. A permanent exhibition and sale near the castle on the island is accessible by boat from the town of Passignano.

Offida, The Marches – When the warm weather comes, the women of this town near Ascoli Piceno sit in their doorways and make lace, sometimes spending as much as a year on a single tablecloth. Meanwhile, local monasteries exhibit 500-year-old examples.

San Caterina Villermosa, Sicily – A thousand pairs of hands carry on old traditions in this small town near Caltanisetta, where the entire female population is employed in embroidering precious household linens. The customary purchasers, still-powerful aristocratic Sicilian families, may pay over $500 for a single magnificent heirloom sheet.

FABRICS: Italy is known around the world for its velvet, linen, silk, and other fabrics.

Città di Castello, Umbria – Tablecloths, towels, and sheets are worked on Renaissance looms in *Tela Umbra* on Piazza Costa in this small city on the left bank of the Tiber.

Como, Lombardy – Como has always been *the* Italian silk center, and *Il Centro della Seta* (64 Via Volta or 2 Via Zamenhof) stocks yard goods as well as scarves, ties, and classic shirts that demonstrate the range of the Italian imagination. Stop by *Ratti* (19 Via Cernobbio) for great prices on silk designer scarves and shawls and fabric.

Rome – *Cesari* has a dizzying selection of upholstery material in its Via del Babuino building, as well as regally impractical lingerie and home linen at the branch on Via Barberini. Branches are in Florence, Milan, and Turin; all stores offer good prices during January white sales.

Sant'Arcangelo, Forlì (Emilia-Romagna) – Linen is still hand-printed here with great wooden blocks that have been used since the 17th century. The antique tools and techniques are still visible at *Alfonso Marchi,* the shop in Via Battisti.

Venice – *Rubelli* manufactures and markets its own elegant upholstery fabrics in Venice, Florence, and Rome.

FOOD: In Rome, there is a wide selection of Italy's finest food products in the shops along Via della Croce or at *Franchi* (204 Via Cola di Rienzo). And when Italians travel around their own country — and they rarely bother with any other — they pride themselves on knowing when and where to find each special food at its golden moment.

Asparagus – A tender white variety, delicately tipped with violet, is grown from March to May. Eat it raw, sliced into salad. The best place: *Cooperativa Asparagi,* 14

Vicolo Mattiussi, Tavagnacco (Udine), Friuli–Venezia Giulia. In Rome and Sicily, wild asparagus is a fleeting treat, often served in a *frittata* (omelette).

Cheese – Most shops throughout the country stock gift boxes of *parmigiano reggiano,* the perfect cheese — natural and wholesome — for snacks and grating. Made of pure buffalo milk, fresh mozzarella is delicate and soft — not the rubbery square stuff seen in American supermarkets. True mozzarella must have a minimum of 30% buffalo milk, the rich ingredient that gives this cheese its unique taste; the rest is properly (and legally) called *fior di latte,* and is cow's milk. Stands line the streets in Mondragone and Formia on the coast between Rome and Naples; sample before deciding. Or go to Battipaglia, near Salerno, and buy it at *La Bufarella,* Via Belvedere.

Excellent varieties of local cheeses also can be sampled in the covered market at Piazza Cavalieri di Vittorio Veneto in Aosta.

Fruit – A sour cherry known as the *amarena* appears in Cantiano, near Pesaro in the Marches, in late spring. Out of season, buy the homemade jam. The year's first peaches ripen in Monte San Biagio, near Latina in Lazio, in mid-May, and the town celebrates with a peach festival in late June. This is also the place to try white peaches, Italy's most succulent fruit. Nemi, near Rome, is known for its strawberries; Trento, for its apples, untreated with chemicals; and Sicily, for its ruddy blood oranges, available from January through April.

Grappa – In any season, the best of this powerful grape-based liquor is found in the north. Visit the *Distilleria Rossi d'Angera,* in Angera (Varese) in Lombardy, for a look at the venerable slow methods of maturing it in oak barrels. Or shop at *Romano Levi,* Via XX Settembre, Neive (Piedmont).

Olive Oil – Balestrino (Savona) in Liguria grows 17 different types of olives. To compare the oil made from each type, visit in March, when samples are offered to the public for tasting. Bitonto, near Bari in Puglia, is another olive capital; the local oil can be bought in little shops all over town.

Pasta – It's available in every imaginable size, shape, and composition at *De Filippis,* 39 Via Lagrange (phone: 11-596953), in Turin.

Pastries – In Assisi in Umbria, eat *mostaccioli di San Francesco,* a honey-and-almond cake that the saint is said to have requested on his deathbed. And especially on Sunday, all Palermo lines up in tiny Piazza Venezia, behind the *Teatro Biondo,* for cookies and cakes made by the cloistered nuns, who take orders and hand out sweets through a curtained, wrought-iron grating. In Rome, *Krechel* is a tiny Swiss pastry shop at 134 Via Frattina, where the matrons in mink jostle with the fashion-house salesmen for a cream-filled *lippenrollen* or *vol au vent* eaten at the counter.

Truffles – Acqualagna, near Pesaro in the Marches, is fragrant with pungent truffles, especially at the end of October. The white truffles reign in the Thursday and Sunday markets in Piazza Mattei. To enjoy them in a meal, visit the *Ristorante Ginestra* on Passo del Furlo. A major effort is underway to make truffles a year-round treat. They are being frozen for restaurant menus, and used to flavor spreads sold in toothpaste-type tubes in delicatessens.

Vinegar – Balsamic vinegar is the champagne of its breed, and a tiny bottle of the real thing, a result of years of distillation, sells for over $10. The best is found in Modena, made by the Giusti family, who have been in the business for 4 centuries. *Giuseppe Giusti,* 77 Via Farini.

FURS: The youthful look of family-owned *Fendi* became famous around the world when the company introduced the fur-lined raincoat over 25 years ago. Since then, the five Fendi sisters have made squirrel and shearling as sexy as sable, and put their double-F symbol on leather goods of every description, from key chains to suitcases. There are 22 boutiques from Palermo to Venice, and the whole range of Fendi design can be seen in the firm's six separate shops on Rome's Via Borgognona, near the Spanish Steps.

JEWELRY: Italians have been working with precious stones and metals since the time of the Etruscans. So if you make only one Italian purchase, it ought to be a small (but fine) piece of jewelry. Your Gucci shoes may lose their charm, but gold never seems to go out of style. Arezzo is the capital of gold manufacturing in the country, a tradition dating back to Etruscan times. For the prized hand-chased, Florentine effect, shop at one of the *Buccellati* boutiques in Rome, Florence, and Milan.

Campoligure, Liguria – The score of family-run workshops in this tiny mountain town export almost all of their precious handmade filigree, a braid of two threads of gold or silver woven into delicate webs and then connected to make feathery jewelry and decorative objects. A silver-and-gold filigree show is held every Saturday and Sunday throughout September in the Palazzo Comunale. Beware of factory-made imitations sold throughout the rest of the country. For information, call the tourist office (phone: 10-921055).

Florence – A line of minuscule jewelry shops tempts strollers on the Ponte Vecchio, the oldest bridge across the Arno. Other outstanding jewelers are strategically stationed in the center of town: *Cartier* at 1 Piazza Santa Trinità and *Torrini* at 10r Piazza Duomo.

Milan – Gold bracelets in a variety of widths and other elegant jewelry reign supreme at *Scavia,* 9 Via Spiga.

Rome – A quarter of Via Condotti's windows glow with gold. Look for *Bulgari* and *Buccellati* (still reigning supreme), *Cartier* and *Van Cleef,* and, nearby, *Di Consiglio, Massoni, Merli,* and *Rapi.* Knowledgeable buyers also seek out the exclusive shops tucked discreetly into corners of the neighboring Piazza di Spagna district: *Capuano,* inside the courtyard of the Palazzo Caffarelli (61 Via Condotti); *Vincenzo Arcesi,* whose contemporary designs are made on the premises (86 Via della Vite); and *Petochi,* which sells imaginative jewelry and lordly old clocks (23 Piazza di Spagna, above Babington's *Tea Room*). For irresistibly convincing costume jewelry, stop at *Bijoux de Paris* (27 Via Condotti).

Torre del Greco, Campania – The cameo and coral capital of Italy is just outside Naples. But unless your eye is infallible, trust only reputable shops, such as *Orafa International* (35 Via de Nicola); *Coral Orafa International* (17 Via de Guevera); *Cameos at Cammei* (32 Via de Nicola; phone: 882-4582); or *Apa* (1 Via de Nicola).

Valenza Po, Piedmont – With more than 1,200 companies and studios, this one-industry town works (and then exports along with Arezzo) almost all the gold that Italy imports. Professional jewelers and passionate amateurs should aim to visit during the annual October exhibition. Near Turin.

KNITWEAR: The knitted creations of Italian factories are famous for reasons that can be immediately seen in almost every clothing store all over the country.

Benetton is a prime destination for anyone who wants to take home an armload or two. In the last few years, the streets of Italy have sprouted hundreds of *Benetton* shops, and their windows are full of the informal, brilliantly colored, and inexpensive sweaters, shirts, pants, and accessories for men, women, and children.

Albertina hand-finishes glamorous knit clothes in a tiny workroom above the store (20 Via Lazio in Rome). The best of her works have been exhibited in the *Metropolitan Museum of Art;* the merchandise is a paragon of Italian craftsmanship.

LEATHER GOODS: Just as France's Louis Vuitton made his initials the hallmark of luxury luggage, Italy's big G's — *Gherardini, Gucci,* and *Nazareno Gabrielli* — have become synonymous with Italian leather fashion. Each company makes and markets its own lines, emblazoning its initials on boots, briefcases, key rings, umbrellas, bags, and baggage. Since the quality is high (with prices to match), any one of these items is sure to impress. Shops are located in the major cities — on or near Via Condotti in Rome, Via Tornabuoni in Florence, and Piazza del Duomo in Milan.

Bottega Veneta's advertising suggests that your own initials are enough. But the firm's buttery soft, basket-weave leather is their own unmistakable statement, as you can see for yourself in the many company shops — most notably those on Piazza Ognissanti in Florence and 18 Via San Sebastianello in Rome. And for those whose fingers do the walking, *Madova* in Florence (1r Via Guiccardini) remains the country's foremost glove maker.

For less expensive versions of Italy's luxury lines, visit *Armando Rioda,* 90 Via Belsiana — on the second floor — in Rome. You'll find hand-crafted copies of all the greats at impressively discounted prices.

MUSICAL INSTRUMENTS: The antique tradition of hand-crafted musical instruments is alive and well in a few renowned centers all over Italy.

Accordions – The first accordion was made in 1863 in Castelfidardo, near Ancona in the Marches, and the streets of the town still echo with the sounds of tuning and testing from a dozen workshops. Watch the 8,300 pieces being assembled at the *Brandoni* shop (38 Via Sauro) and see 100 vintage instruments from all over the world in a museum in Piazza della Repubblica.

Bagpipes – Simple bagpipes, fifes, drums, and other folk instruments have been made with the same techniques for some 2,000 years in the town of Scapoli, near Isernia in the Molise. Look for those made of cherry wood and goatskin.

Lutes and Violins – Cremona, a sizable town in Lombardy, was the home of Antonio Stradivari, the greatest violin maker of all time, and the art of creating stringed instruments has not been forgotten. On the Corso Garibaldi, look for the *Scuola Internazionale di Liuteria* and the workshops of a number of master lute makers and, at No. 95, the workshop of world class violin maker Istvan Konja, a Hungarian, now boasting the newly Italianized name of Stefano Conia.

Whistles – Comic terra cotta figures of priests, roosters, and puppets are made into whistles in Rutigliano 24 miles (38 km) outside of Bari in Puglia.

Wind Instruments – The traditional craft goes back to the 18th century in the small town of Quarna, near Novara in Piedmont, where 600 workers turn brass, silver, and ebony into clarinets, flutes, and saxophones in family-run workshops. A small museum, the *Museum of Quarnese History* (near Lake Orta; phone: 323-026141), shows off the town's historical best.

SHOES: You'll find a shoe shop on virtually every corner in Italy, but it's the rare Anglo-Saxon foot that matches an Italian last. Price is generally a clue to what you're getting — as usual, you get just what you pay for. When in doubt about the composition, just sniff. The aroma of real leather is inimitable.

Beltrami dresses its windows at 19 Via Condotti in Rome with a moneyed gleam every bit as splendid as those of the jeweler *Bulgari* down the street. Sleek and sophisticated women's clothing rounds out the picture. You also can buy Beltrami designs in Florence, Milan, and Bologna.

Ferragamo made Italian shoes a byword of elegance in the US when its namesake and founder fitted John Barrymore, Mary Pickford, and Gloria Swanson in Hollywood in the 1920s. Still largely handmade today, the firm's shoes are available in various widths — which makes them a rarity in Italy. Soft and comfortable men's and women's loafers are top sellers despite prices that will take your breath away. Shops are found in the major Italian cities; the headquarters are at 16r Via Tornabuoni in Florence.

Raphael Salato offers sparkly sandals, glossy moccasins, and other attention-getters for men, women, and children at three shops in Rome. Best bets: 149 and 104 Via Veneto.

Tanino Crisci's many outlets in Rome, Milan, and Florence are our choice when searching for the finest, most classically fashionable men's and women's shoes and boots.

Spas

In Italy, real water-immersion addicts wouldn't even think about a trip to the Riviera or the Greek isles when they could wallow happily in the mud of Salsomaggiore. Consequently, Italy's water — and its mud — are the base of one of the country's most lucrative industries. There are *terme* (spas) all over the country. Some flourish on the sites of thermal springs first exploited by those imperial water-worshipers, the ancient Romans, who built baths with great fervor. Others trace their origins to antique legends of healing streams spurting from the warm blood of slain princes and miraculous geysers that gushed forth from the tears of abandoned maidens.

Today, for those who are "taking the waters," there is a whole menu of steamrooms and saunas, sprays and whirlpool baths, mud tubs and honey rubs, paraffin packs and vapor inhalations, underwater gymnastics and regimens of just plain drinking. Every spa has its specialty, and things are so clinical that if a doctor prescribes the cure, the patient's health insurance plan may well cover it. In any event, checkups generally are required before any steam treatments or submersions can be undertaken.

As important to the cure as the sipping is what's done afterward. After all, who's to say whether the healing comes from the waters that bubble or from the diversions that have proliferated alongside the spas and springs — golf and tennis and horseback riding, casinos and discos and boutiques, not to mention abundant fine dining. And some spas feature wonderful, fat-free haute cuisine menus for dieters. Some of the most salutary of total vacation destinations — for whatever reason — are described below. For a complete map of spas in Italy, write to *ACI,* 8 Via Marsala, Rome 00185.

ABANO, Veneto: *Mud* is the magic word at this favorite of the ancient Roman aristocracy and military, whose name derives from the Greek for "pain remover." And after mud, which is mineral-enriched volcanic material at about 189F, comes massage — all available as part of the facilities of most hotels. Then the rest of the day is free for swimming in thermal waters or for golf, riding, tennis, and touring. Abano is a pretty, bustling town of tree-lined streets, just outside Padua and a half hour from Venice. The Brenta River is nearby, and a boat trip on *Il Burchiello* that sails by the more than 70 harmonious and gloriously frescoed villas built in the 17th and 18th centuries for the great Venetian families (visitors are permitted only in three). The cities of Verona and Vicenza are within reach as well. In fact, with so much to see in the area, the distractions may leave only limited time for wallowing. Of the dozens of comfortable hotels, the exclusive *Orologio* and the less expensive *Quisisana Terme* have the best food and the most cosmopolitan clientele. Details: *Azienda di Promozione Turistica,* 18 Via Pietro d'Abano, Abano Terme (Padova) 35031 (phone: 49-669455).

CHIANCIANO TERME, Tuscany: The origins of this red-roofed town can be traced to the Etruscans and a pre-Roman era, and, like many other Italian spas, its springs were much appreciated in ancient times. Today, the lure of the rich Tuscan and Umbrian countryside distracts some visitors from the venerated water regimen that proposes to return their livers to their original pristine state. Nearby is Arezzo, with its serene frescoes of Piero della Francesca and a lively, irresistible antiques market on the first Sunday of every month. Siena, home of the raucous, twice-yearly horse race known as the *Palio* (see "Italy's Most Colorful Festas," *For the Mind*), is an hour distant, as are the churches of Assisi and the towers of San Gimignano. Body and soul will both thrive in the unhurried atmosphere, the fine air, and the cypress- and pine-trimmed landscapes of this beautifully groomed region, whether or not guests decide to drink the waters with the clockwork regularity that a proper cure demands. The season runs from mid-April to mid-November. For low-key comfort, stay at the *Excelsior* hotel. Details: *Azienda Autonoma di Cura,* 7 Via Giuseppe Sabatini, Chianciano Terme (Siena) 53042 (phone: 578-63538).

FIUGGI, Lazio: When Michelangelo felt the need to flee Rome and the rigors of painting the ceiling of the Sistine Chapel — for a breath of clean air and a sip of purifying water — it was to this town (an hour south of Rome and 2,500 feet above sea level) that he came. Carried by papal couriers to Boniface VIII in Rome during the Middle Ages, this water is now bottled and sold all over Italy, but many Italians still consider a summer holiday at the source essential to year-round health. The two springs, each set in a lush garden, are known nationally as surefire cures for kidney disturbances; one is recommended for morning therapy, the other for postprandial. Open April through November. During the interval, leave the spa area and explore the Old Town with its high walls, stone staircases, and evocative aromas of wine cellars, wood fires, and grilled meat; one of its charming outdoor restaurants makes a pleasant stop before a tour of the surrounding Ciociara hills. Hotels range from the simply splendid — Italy's kings summered here — to the simple and economical, with full facilities for the disabled. The splendid *Grand Hotel Palazzo della Fonte* (phone: 775-5081) — built in 1913 — recently underwent a $30-million renovation. Italy's kings and queens used to take the waters here. In addition to the usual luxury hotel and spa amenities, there is a fitness center with personalized exercise program, haute weight-watching cuisine, golf course, riding, and tennis. Details: *Azienda Autonoma di Soggiorno,* 4 Via Gorizia, Fiuggi (Frosinone) 03015 (phone: 775-55446).

GRADO, Friuli–Venezia Giulia: Up the coast from Trieste and the Yugoslav border, this island town, now linked to the mainland by a 3-mile causeway, has a great deal in common with many other Adriatic resorts. The beach is broad, sandy, and umbrella-gaudy; the old medieval mariners' quarters have been upstaged by spacious avenues, and sailboats and water skiers outnumber fishing craft offshore. What distinguishes it from the pack is its marine thermal establishment and the renowned *sabbiatura* treatments. Here's the place to get buried up to your neck in sun-warmed sand for relief from the aches and pains of arthritis and rheumatism, or simply for the pleasure of the immersion. There are also the classical warm seawater procedures — pool and tub soaks, inhalations, and the like. When all that palls, this far corner of Italy is also a good jumping-off point for visits to Trieste, the Roman ruins of Aquileia, or the unique Yugoslavian grottoes of Postojna. Details: *Azienda Autonoma di Soggiorno e Cura,* 58 Viale Dante Alighieri, Grado (Gorizia) 34073 (phone: 431-80234).

ISCHIA, Campania: The largest island in the Bay of Naples is volcanic, and it bubbles with hot springs and naturally radioactive water. The steamy mud is good for aching bones, and the vapors do wonders for respiratory disorders. All the sloshing and sniffing can be done right in your hotel — and in some cases in your own room, if that's what you want. Of the four main thermal centers, Lacco Ameno is the best supplied with luxury hotels with their own thermal establishments: *San Montano,* whose furnishings re-create the atmosphere of a transatlantic ship, right by the sea, with its own private beach; and the outstanding *Regina Isabella,* which offers the most elaborate medical menu of all. Taking the cure at Ischia is a favorite activity of burghers from the north eager to bake the chill out of their bones, but the island attracts sun seekers of every age and type, as well as those who come mainly for mud during its prime season, from April to October. Auto access is limited but not banned, and the peak summer months are peak indeed. Slip away to the promontory of Sant'Angelo, a tiny village on the far side of the island, and enjoy a tranquil, freshly fished meal on the square. Details: *Azienda Autonoma di Soggiorno,* Via Iasolino, Porto d'Ischia (Napoli) 80077 (phone: 81-991146).

LEVICO TERME, Trentino: Just 13 miles (21 km) from the mountain city of Trento, Levico Terme is set on an idyllic, tree-bordered lake at the foot of Monte Fronte at an altitude of 1,800 feet; its sister town, Vetriolo Terme, is about 7 miles away (11 km) at about 4,900 feet. Both offer a wide variety of sports; sailing and windsurfing in summer at Levico and skiing in winter at Vetriolo are the main draws. The colonnaded thermal complex, set in a botanical park remarkable for its variety of exotic trees, dates from the turn of the century; the high arsenic and iron content of spring waters available here is reputed to benefit blood and nerves, cure skin diseases, and even resolve various ailments of the reproductive system. Details: *Azienda di Promozione Turistica,* 3 Via Vittorio Emanuele, Levico Terme (Trento) 38056 (phone: 461-706101).

MERANO, Alto Adige: Not far from the Brenner Pass and Austria, the mountain town of Merano glows with Tyrolean charms — steep-roofed houses with painted façades, oak-beamed wine cellars with wrought-iron signs, flower-bordered streets and balconies, café-lined promenades, 6,560-foot-high trails that can be reached by skiers or hikers by cable car in a few minutes. The spa is across the river from the tightly packed streets of the old town. Mud baths and masks, radioactive waters, vigorous rubdowns, and steamy saunas administered at the spacious, greenery-rimmed thermal center not only pamper those in good health but also bring relief to sufferers of arthritis, allergies, and asthma. The *Meranerhof* hotel is next to the thermal center and its lake and swimming pool; the *Schloss Rundegg* has all the facilities of a health and beauty farm; and the *Villa Mozart,* renovated in perfect *Jugendstil* (Art Nouveau), where there also are 4-day wine seminars and 6-day courses in Italian and Tyrolean cooking. Details: *Azienda Autonoma di Soggiorno e Cura,* 45 Corso Libertà, Merano (Bolzano) 39012 (phone: 473-35223).

MONTECATINI, Tuscany: Time passes with Olympian calm in this most celebrated of Italian spas, an elegant enclave that once belonged to the Medicis and that has hosted princes and pashas, dukes and duchesses, marquises and their betters since it became popular in the late 19th century. Giuseppe Verdi wrote the last act of *Otello* while taking the waters here, Samuel Barber readied his opera *Vanessa* for production between sips, and Kostelanetz, Cole Porter, and Von Karajan all found inspiration in the soothing routines. Visitors stop at the grandest of the grand spa pavilions, the Tettuccio Terme, all columns, caryatids, and ceramic tile murals, and then stroll for hours in the splendid and serendipitous gardens, sipping the medicinal waters before lunch as many a Henry Jamesian character has done on the pages of his period novels, and peregrinating past the nine other pavilions — they look more like castles, palaces, and monasteries. The straight, tree-lined streets are silent as a siesta for much of the afternoon. Only in the evening do the crowds emerge, glowing and rested — the provincial grocer's liver purified, the jet-lagged nerves of the overfed nobility untangled. The cultural calendar that attracts this cross section of Italian society is chockablock with theater, films, concerts, dance performances, and even auctions, after which the refreshed spa-goers find their way to little cafés where they sip an espresso to the waltzes of a local orchestra. Stay in the venerable *Grand Hotel e La Pace,* an establishment as regal as the town itself. The more energetic routinely travel to Arezzo, Florence, Pisa, Lucca, Pistoia, or Siena, all less than an hour away. Details: *Azienda Autonoma di Cura e Soggiorno,* 66 Viale Verdi, Montecatini (Pistoia) 51016 (phone: 572-70109).

SAINT-VINCENT, Valle d'Aosta: All the deep relaxation of the day's thermal treatments can be cheerfully undone each evening in the gambling casino of this Alpine town. But if guests can resist the charm of chips and late nights around the wheel, they may discover the myriad benefits that Saint-Vincent's waters are said to offer the digestive system. These powers are put to the test with the ravioli and salmon mousse of the town's top restaurant, *Batezar da Renato* (1 Via Marconi). The *Billia* hotel, set in its own pretty park, has a swimming pool and medical staff to advise guests on the optimal diet-dissolution ratio. There are footpaths for quiet post-sip rambles; high-altitude hiking trails are just a short drive away. Details: *Azienda Autonoma di Soggiorno e Turismo,* 50 Via Roma, Saint-Vincent (Aosta) 11027 (phone: 166-2239).

SALSOMAGGIORE, Emilia-Romagna: When a local doctor named Lorenzo Berzieri successfully used the local warm salt springs to cure an ailing young patient in 1839, he little imagined the parade of screen folk, royalty, and Miss Italy candidates that would descend on this garden-greened town in the years to come. Equidistant from Milan and Bologna (in the hills between Lake Garda and the Italian Riviera), Salsomaggiore was where Italy's crowned heads of the 19th and early 20th centuries recovered from overdoses of champagne and rheumatism induced by damp palaces. (The *Grand Hotel des Thermes,* their destination, is now a convention hall.) Said to be efficacious in treating chronic inflammations of every sort, the local regimen of massages, baths, mud packs, and irrigations — which often attract singers looking after abused vocal chords — is administered at major hotels with their own thermal facilities. But most visitors patronize the huge baroque spa center and splash along with the masses. More worldly than most Italian spas, Salsomaggiore brims with boutiques and discos, and cafés are shoulder to shoulder in the traffic-free town center. The busy morning market and the frequent evening auctions staged by one or the other of the numerous antiques shops give Salsomaggiore a cheerful animation missing at many other Italian health resorts. Details: *Azienda Autonoma di Cura e Soggiorno,* 4 Viale Romagnosi, Salsomaggiore Terme (Parma) 43039 (phone: 524-78265).

SATURNIA, Tuscany: This tiny spot in the Tuscan hills between the Aurelia coast road and the Via Cassia, near a less tiny place named Manciano (on Rte. 74), is simply a warm thermal waterfall where 2,000 years of bathers have smoothed and hollowed out sitting places among the rocks. Swimming and soaking here can be done comfortably even on a crisp day in February by anyone brave enough to race from car to springs. If you prefer to soak in greater style, check into the only hotel — *Terme di Saturnia* — whose two grandiose sulfur-pungent pools are more elegantly accessible. The hot fumes float above the warm water, and, when the evening chill sets in, they swirl foggily above the grass-edged basins, mysteriously concealing, then revealing, their borders. Details: *Terme di Saturnia,* Saturnia (Grosseto) 58050 (phone: 564-601061).

Most Visitable Vineyards

Italy has been producing wines since long before the ancient Greeks knew the local landscape as "Enotria" — the land of wines — and wine making is still big business from the cool Alpine terraces of South Tyrol to the sun-scorched Sicilian isles off the coast of North Africa. With 4 million acres planted in vineyards, 220 zones of controlled name and origin (known as Denominazione di Origine Controllata or, simply, DOC) established by law in 1963, and another five regions bearing the prestigious government guarantee (Denominazione di Origine Controllata e Garantita or DOCG), the nation produces more liters of wine than any other country in the world — and more varieties.

Touring Italy's countless wineries shows off this oenological spectacle in all its many facets. Visitors will encounter vast modern plants turning out tens of millions of bottles annually — as well as cramped cellars presided over by a farmer who puts out just a barrel or two in a good year. Signs reading *vendita diretta* (direct sales) invite visitors to stop, sample, and buy wine to take away. Wine shops, some very upscale with marble furnishing, or public displays denoted by the term *enoteca* (wine library) welcome browsers; in many cases tastings are offered by the glass for a nominal fee. The more humble establishments are known as *bottiglierie.* And exceptional hospitality is everywhere.

Spring and fall are the most pleasant times to travel and taste, but winters are fine as well because wine makers may have more time to devote to visitors. Even in July or August, when urban Italy nearly closes down, there is always somebody on hand to look after a wine estate. Whenever you go, try to phone ahead to make sure there will be someone to show you around when you get there.

Unexpected treasures can be turned up in vineyards nearly everywhere in Italy; many very fine Italian bottlings are sold as simple *vini da tavola* (table wines) — perhaps because the wines are relatively new and a DOC standard has not yet been codified or because they don't fit an existing DOC statute and are depending on word of mouth and critical acclaim for their business. However, serious oenophiles may want to start in an area where the wines are of premium quality. So the following representative selection of visitable wineries is culled from a handful of top wine making areas — Veneto, Friuli–Venezia Giulia, and Alto Adige in the northeast; Piedmont and Lombardy in the northwest; and Tuscany and Umbria in central Italy.

THE NORTHEAST

ALTO ADIGE: In the province of Bolzano, known as Bozen by the area's German-speakers and as South Tyrol to the rest of the world, many wineries are located along the Weinstrasse (Wine Road) that runs from Bolzano south past Lago di Caldaro to Roverè della Luna. With the Dolomites towering over valleys of neatly kept apple orchards and vineyards, cozy guesthouses, and hearty Austrian food, the area presents an inviting contrast to Mediterranean Italy. It is also one of the few parts of the country where white wines are treated with as much care as reds. There are many fragrant and well-balanced rieslings, sylvaners, and pinots; the traminer aromatico grape originated near Termino (Tramin to the Germans), and the best Italian gewürztraminers still come from here — pale gold and spicily aromatic but more restrained than their Alsatian cousins. The area also makes, in fairly small quantities, cabernets that are delightfully perfumed, clear-flavored, supremely fresh, and notably well balanced.

Schloss Turmhof, Entiklar, Bolzano – This winery run by Herbert Tiefenbrunner and his family occupies a shady glen with a castle that looks as if it belongs in the Vienna woods. The wines are first-rate — particularly the white pinots, chardonnays, rieslings, sylvaners, gewürztraminers, and goldenmuskatellers; the müller thurgau, which goes by the name of feldmarschall and comes from 3,300-foot vineyards that are the highest in South Tyrol, is exquisite. Plates of cold cuts, sausages, and sauerkraut are served with the wines in the gardens and the cozy, wood-paneled *Weinstuben.* Details: *Schlosskellerei Turmhof,* Entiklar, Kurtatsch (Bolzano) 39040 (phone: 471-880122).

FRIULI–VENEZIA GIULIA: With Trentino–Alto Adige, this area of northeastern Italy is the center of Italy's white wine production. The hilly areas known as the Collio Goriziano and Colli Orientali del Friuli, near the Yugoslav border, produce some remarkably fruity and flowery whites that range from delicate to light to substantial and full-bodied and rich (depending on the producer). They are generally known by their varietal grape names — pinot bianco, pinot grigio, riesling Renano. Charming, nicely rounded reds, simple and rather light because they are not wood-aged as in France and California, are made with merlot and cabernet grapes in these two areas and in the flatter districts known as Grave del Friuli and Isonzo. The *Enoteca La Serenissima* at Gradisca d'Isonzo, 7½ miles (12 km) southwest of Gorizia, was Italy's first public wine library and remains one of the most impressive. Details: *La Serenissima,* 26 Via Battisti, Gradisca d'Isonzo (phone: 481-99528).

Russiz Superiore, Capriva del Friuli, Gorizia – This estate founded 25 years ago by Marco Felluga, in the Collio Goriziano just west of Gorizia, is a model of its genre in Italy. Everything about its manicured vineyards and up-to-the-minute cellars is designed to bring out the most from the local grapes. The white tocai friulano, sauvignon, pinot bianco, and pinot grigio wines epitomize the finesse of the regional style, while the red cabernet and merlot are as elegant as they are easy to drink. Details: *Russiz Superiore,* Capriva del Friuli (Gorizia) 34070 (phone: 481-80328).

VENETO: This pretty area of hills and villas produces more DOC wines than any other, and the bulk of them are the Veronese trio of bardolino and valpolicella (reds) and soave (white). Known worldwide as everyday wines par excellence, they are never tastier than when drunk young and fresh at the vineyard in which their grapes were grown. Oeonological-minded visitors should make the pilgrimage to Verona in April, when the nation's most important wine fair, *VinItaly,* is in full swing. Above all, sample the costly, majestic valpolicella known as amarone. This deep garnet-red, almost port-like wine derives its intense fruity flavors (and an alcohol content of up to 17%) from grapes crushed only after weeks-long aging off the vine on straw pallets. Tourists in Venice may be tempted by a side trip to nearby Treviso province, where a number of Italy's best country restaurants serve good local pinot, cabernet, merlot, and the fizzy white prosecco di Conegliano–Valdobbiadene — dry but fruity and distinctively aromatic.

Masi, Gargagnago di Valpolicella, Verona, Veneto – In a zone dominated by the industrialized giants among wine producers, Masi treads a civilized middle ground and draws on choice vineyards of the area to produce highly individualistic wines — soave classico col baraca, valpolicella classico Serego Alighieri, sweet recioto, and two unusual table wines known as masianco and campo fiorin. The latter, a distinctive, dark red, is elegantly flavored and long-lived as a result of having been partly fermented on the skins of grapes pressed to make amarone. The amarones, made in several styles, rank among Italy's most distinguished red wines. Some of the area's wine *cantine* are open to the public. Details: *APT,* 42 Piazza delle Erbe, Verona (phone: 45-30086).

Col Sandago, Pieve di Soligo, Treviso – The modern cellars in the town of Pieve di Soligo are used to transform grapes from 197 acres of estate vineyards in the nearby Marca Trevigiana hills into a wide range of wines — from bubbly prosecco and pinot bianco to chardonnay, pinot grigio, cabernet, merlot, and the unique red wildbacher. *Agriturismo* — the renting of converted farmhouses or small apartments in the midst of vineyards for a minimum stay of 1 week — was recently started here. (Also see "Farmhouses, *Accommodations,* GETTING READY TO GO.) Details: *Col Sandago,* 79 Via Chisini, Pieve di Soligo (Treviso) 31053 (phone: 438-841608; fax: 438-980001).

THE NORTHWEST

PIEDMONT: Well known for its robust, complex, dry reds — authoritative barolo, barbaresco, gattinara, and others like them that develop greatness with aging — this area also makes two whites of renown, the sweetish and sparkling asti spumante and the bone-dry still wine called gavi, as well as delightful lighter reds that are meant to be drunk young. These most notably include barbera and dolcetto. Far from being sweet (as its name might suggest), dolcetto is a soft, intensely fruity, low-acid wine. Well-marked wine roads lead through major DOC zones, including barolo, barbaresco, and asti spumante, and there are impressive public *enoteche* at Barolo, Grinzane Cavour (near Alba), Costigliole d'Asti, and Vignale Monferrato.

Fontanafredda, Serralunga d'Alba, Cuneo – This handsome wine estate began its life in 1878 as the hunting lodge of Conte Emanuele Guerrieri, son of King Vittorio Emanuele II, and his wife, Contessa Rosa Mirafiori. Today it is a major producer of barolo (with several single-vineyard bottlings), barbaresco, barbera d'alba, the rugged and astringent dolcetto d'alba, asti spumante, and two impressive champagne-style whites — Contessa Rosa and brut gattinera. Located near Alba, about 46½ miles (74 km) southeast of Turin. Details: *Fontanafredda,* Serralunga d'Alba (Cuneo) 12050 (phone: 173-53161).

Abbazia dell'Annunziata, La Morra, Cuneo – This 15th-century abbey, south of Alba in the heart of the barolo zone, houses a wine museum and produces noteworthy barolo, nebbiolo, barbera, and dolcetto in the cellars adjoining the museum. Details: *Ratti,* Antiche Cantine dell'Annunziata, La Morra (Cuneo) 12064 (phone: 173-50185).

Martini & Rossi, Pessione, Turin – Among Piedmont's large wine and vermouth houses, Martini & Rossi is perhaps the most visitable. A wine museum on the premises has pieces that date to the times of the Etruscans and Greeks, and the hospitality is impeccable. Guided tours and tastings at the main cellars in Pessione, about 9 miles (14 km) southeast of Turin, may be arranged by appointment. Details: *Martini & Rossi, S.p.A.,* 42 Corso Vittorio Emanuele, Torino 10123 (phone: 11-57451).

LOMBARDY: This area around Milan makes wine of virtually every style. There are dry spumanti and fruity whites, light rosés, and reds of all styles. Rugged and mountainous Valtellina to the north — a growing area praised by Pliny, Virgil, and Leonardo da Vinci, among others — starts with the hard-to-cultivate nebbiolo grape, grown on south-facing vineyards. Then the pressings are wood-aged to produce a simple, substantial red with rich color and deep flavor that is less austere and more immediate than the barolo, barbaresco, and other nebbiolo-based wines from Piedmont. Valtellina sfursat is produced by methods similar to those used for Veneto's amarone. Oltrepò Pavese, to the southwest, makes a number of full, grapey reds, plus clean, crisp, fruity whites that range stylistically from müller thurgaus to pinots. Franciacorta to the east is the home of some of Italy's best sparkling wines. Some of these are dry, some sweet; those made by the *metodo champenois* (champagne method) tend to be less yeasty than their French counterparts.

Guido Berlucchi, Borgonato di Cortefranca, Brescia – Some 12½ miles (about 20 km) northwest of Brescia, near Lake Iseo at the nation's largest producer of champagne-style wines, visitors are welcome to witness the intricacies of the *metodo champenois* and sample the product — Berlucchi cuvée imperiale brut, brut millesimata, pas dosé, grand cremant, and Max Rosé — all made from pinot or chardonnay grapes from Franciacorta, Oltrepò Pavese, and Trentino–Alto Adige. Nearby, the firm also has a small estate known as Antica Cantina Fratta. Details: *Guido Berlucchi & Compagnia, S.p.A.,* 4 Via Don Secondo Duranti, Borgonato di Cortefranca (Brescia) 25040 (phone: 30-984381).

CENTRAL ITALY

TUSCANY: Tuscan wine makers have been building their reputations of late on the strength of imposing reds such as brunello di Montalcino, vino nobile di Montepulciano, and a variety of new *vini da tavola.*

Still, chianti remains the quintessential Italian wine, and Tuscany is its home. You'll find it here in all its many styles — from light and easy-drinking *classicos* to spicy and assertive *riservas.* Don't miss the vineyards of the *classico* zone between Florence and Siena, some of the most picturesque in all of Italy, particularly the Castelnuovo Berardenga, Radda, and Gaiole townships. And be sure to stop at the towered town of San Gimignano, known for its white vernaccia. The *Enoteca Italica Permanente* in the Fortezza Medicea in Siena displays and serves choice wines from all over Italy.

Badia a Coltibuono, Gaiole in Chianti, Siena – This ancient abbey, amid a forest of pine and fir overlooking the valley of the Arno, may have been the place where the first chianti was made nearly 1,000 years ago. Today the Gaiole township is known for the delicacy of its chianti classicos, particularly in good years; the estate itself is noted for its stocks of fine chianti riserva, as well as good red and white table wines. The local vin santo toscano, made of trebbiano and malvasia grapes that have been left to dry before pressing and then allowed to ferment in small oak barrels for three or four years, is especially interesting; it is dark gold, has a lively bouquet, a velvety texture, and more or less sweetness depending on the sugar content of the original grapes. The establishment also produces a delicious extra-virgin olive oil. Wines and oils can be tasted at a restaurant on the grounds; visits to the abbey and cellars are by appointment only. Details: *Badia a Coltibuono,* Gaiole in Chianti (Siena) 53013 (phone: 577-749424).

Ruffino, Pontassieve, Florence – A large but widely respected producer of chianti and other wines, Ruffino welcomes visitors to its main cellars at Pontassieve, 10½ miles (17 km) east of Florence. There, and in the restaurant *Girarrosto* in Pontassieve, tasters may sample the white galestro and orvieto classico, chianti classico aziano, the aged riserva ducale, and chianti torgaio di San Salvatore, as well as a new line of premium table wines with the designation Alto Predicato. In a region whose wines usually vary radically from year to year, Ruffino chianti has the distinction of maintaining its quality from one vintage to the next. Details: *Ruffino, S.p.A.,* 42-44 Via Aretina, Pontassieve (Firenze) 50065 (phone: 55-830-2307).

Villa Banfi, Sant'Angelo Montalcino, Siena – This vast estate belonging to Villa Banfi, one of the leading US wine importers, which California's Robert Mondavi described as "the world's most modern winery," is open to the public by appointment. Wines use the fruit of more than 2,000 acres of vines. Notable products include an austere and full brunello di Montalcino, rosso di Montalcino centine, santa costanza, the bubbly-and-sweet moscadello di Montalcino, and the California-style chardonnay fontanelle and cabernet sauvignon tavarnelle. A medieval castle has been restored to house a wine museum. Details: *Villa Banfi, S.p.A.,* Castello Bianfi, Sant'Angelo Montalcino 53020 (phone: 577-864111).

UMBRIA: Known as "the green heart of Italy," this region was noted in the past for the sweet white wine from Orvieto. In the last several years its wine makers have experimented with non-Italian grapes like chardonnay and cabernet sauvignon, with the result that Umbria promises to one day produce some of Italy's finest modern wines. The areas of special interest are Orvieto and the hills along the Tiber between Perugia and Todi.

Cantine Lungarotti, Torgiano, Perugia – This estate winery about 6 miles (10 km) south of Perugia has become something of a contemporary legend under the supervision of Giorgio Lungarotti, who made his name with the Torgiano DOC white and red wines (most notably the single-vineyard reserve Rubesco red). He has recently taken on prestigious chardonnay, cabernet sauvignon, and San Giorgio wines — this last a blend of cabernet and sangiovese, the grape on which chianti is based. The family also owns *Le Tre Vaselle* (described in *Buon Appetito: The Best Restaurants of Italy*). A major national wine competition known as the *Banco d'Assaggio* is held here each fall. Nearby are an attractive wine museum and a display of local ceramics. Details: *Cantine Lungarotti,* Torgiano (Perugia) 06089 (phone: 75-982348).

Azienda Vallesanta di Luigi Barberani, Baschi, Terni – Right off the autostrada that goes from Rome to Orvieto (A1), in the beautiful town of Baschi, Barberani has restored ancient wine making traditions using very modern equipment and methods in an establishment graced with charming old-fashioned Umbrian country furniture. His orvieto muffa nobile "calcaia" is a venerable dessert wine, whose production depends on the most careful balance of damp growing conditions, a regal variety of mold, and rigid temperature controls. The results are intriguing. Visit his shop in Orvieto itself, across from the Duomo, if you're short of exploring time. Details: *Azienda Agricola Vallesanta,* Loc. Cerreto, Baschi (Terni) 05023 (phone: 744-950113).

Cooking Schools

Until recently, every Italian kitchen was a cooking school, *la professoressa* was *la Mamma,* and the student body was restricted to family members. However, Italians have discovered the pleasures of their own nation's regional cooking right along with the rest of the world: Neapolitans now eat Tuscan food at home and Venetians down Sicily's cannoli and cannelloni — foods which, as often as not, *Mamma*'s *mamma* told her nothing at all about. Enter the cooking school.

Some are taught by superstars of Italian cooking like Marcella Hazan and Giuliano Bugialli. Some are in Italian with translation on the spot. Others are in English. Most are staged in spring and summer, and early booking is a must. Some of the best include the following:

CLASSIC ITALIAN COOKING, Bologna: Marcella Hazan's well-established school in Bologna, the master classes at her home in Venice, and her annual November class hosted by the legendary Venetian *Cipriani* hotel are so popular that reservations are made as much as 2 years in advance. In Bologna, a 3-week course leading to a diploma teaches the essentials of making pasta, antipasti, and country breads, as well as traditional main courses. In English. Details: *Hazan Classics,* PO Box 285, Circleville, NY 10919 (phone: 914-692-7104).

VILLA TABLE, Coltibuono: This weeklong cooking experience permits total immersion in the way of life on a Tuscany country estate. Lorenza Medici, author of many cookbooks published in Italy, teaches cooking using simple ingredients, including wine and olive oil produced on the estate (see *Most Visitable Vineyards*). Students sleep in the 15th-century guestrooms of the villa. In English. Details: *The Villa Table,* Badia a Coltibuono, Gaiole in Chianti (Siena) 53013 (phone: 577-749498); or *The Villa Table,* Judy Terrell, 2405 Clublake Trail, McKinney, TX 75070 (phone: 214-542-1500).

COOKING IN FLORENCE, Florence: Giuliano Bugialli is well known as the author of four definitive books on Italian cuisine. However, every year in Florence, he also offers several hands-on courses that cover the culinary delights of all Italy. Each of the five classes in each course involves supervised preparation of a complete meal planned by Bugialli — a different menu for each class. In English. Details: *Giuliano Bugialli's Cooking in Florence,* PO Box 1650, Canal Street Station, New York, NY 10013 (phone: 212-966-5325).

ITALIAN CUISINE IN FLORENCE, Florence: Teacher Masha Innocenti offers classes in English on haute Italian cuisine, as well as special pastry and dessert courses. Most last 4 to 5 days and are held year-round in Signora Innocenti's apartment. Course organizers will help students find suitable lodgings. Details: *William Grossi,* RD 1, Ancramdale, NY 12503 (phone: 518-329-1141).

RUFFINO TUSCAN EXPERIENCE, near Florence: Chefs such as Maria Salcuni and Rosario Santoro who demonstrate their culinary expertise and a group of sommeliers that includes Ruffino Wine Company owner Ambrogio Folonari Ruffino are the lure of this adventure in the wine and food of chianti country. In English. Accommodations are in the *Excelsior* hotel in the heart of Florence. Details: *Annemarie Victory Organization, Inc.,* 136 E. 64th St., New York, NY 10021 (phone: 212-486-0353).

ITALIAN COUNTRY COOKING, Positano, Campania: In the classes of this 8-day full-participation course in fabled seaside Positano, on the Amalfi Coast, the emphasis is on country cooking with locally available ingredients. Each of the various spring, summer, and fall sessions emphasizes a specific area — pasta and other first courses, meat, fish, desserts. All instruction is in English in director Diana Folonari's cliffside home. Lodging is in nearby hotels. Details: *Folonari Country Cooking Classes,* c/o *E&M Associates,* 211 E. 43rd St., New York, NY 10017 (phone: 212-599-8280 in New York State; 800-223-9832 elsewhere).

SCALDAVIVANDE COOKING SCHOOL, Rome: After Jo Bettoja, an American from Georgia, exhibited her good taste by marrying into a distinguished Italian family that still cures its own prosciutto and salami, she soon came to realize that other Italians were not learning what she had learned from her new *Mamma*-in-law. So she began combing the countryside for great classic Italian recipes. With this knowledge under her belt, she wrote a cookbook and is now sharing her culinary expertise at her cooking school (*lo scaldavivande* means "the covered dish"). The English-language course is held in a 17th-century Roman palazzo, with a farewell graduation luncheon at the family's 18th-century hunting villa outside the city and lodging in the first class *Mediterraneo* hotel, which her husband's family also owns. Details: *E&M Associates,* 211 E. 43rd St., New York, NY 10017 (phone: 212-599-3994 in New York State; 800-223-9832 elsewhere).

COOKING SCHOOL OF UMBRIA, Todi: A father-and-son team, Donaldo and Dino Soviero, presides over a world class kitchen in the dreamy Umbrian countryside and instructs small groups of students in everything from pizza to pastry. Accommodations are in a deluxe hotel in the charming medieval town of Todi. Courses last from 1 day to 1 week and are popular with the Roman diplomatic community. In English. Details: *The Cooking School of Umbria,* 127 Casella Postale, Todi (Perugia) 06059 (phone: 75-887370).

GRITTI PALACE COOKING COURSES, Venice: Every year in July or August, this splendid old hotel, once the palace of a Venetian doge, is home to a month of 5-day cooking courses. Each is taught by a different master chef invited for his or her knowledge of some regional cuisine — from Tuscany, Liguria, Emilia-Romagna, and other prime Italian gastronomic areas. The venue is the hotel's own ultra-professional kitchen. Students may sign up for just one or stay for all four courses; it's not necessary to stay in the hotel to participate. In Italian with English translations. Details: *Mauro Scoccimarro, Gritti Palace Hotel,* 2467 San Marco, Venezia (phone: 41-794611; fax: 41-520-0942). See also *Italy's Most Memorable Hostelries.*

For the Body

Italy's Unparalleled Skiing

Not so long ago a pastime of privilege solely for sporty Milanese industrialists and *alpini* mountain troops on furlough, skiing has exploded into high fashion in Italy. Nowhere else in Europe are the moon boots as furry, the faces as bronzed, and the styles as avant-garde. Some large international resorts like Cervinia, Cortina, and Sestriere have it all — a vast array of runs and lifts, troops of multilingual instructors, a selection of winter sporting opportunities such as ice skating and tobogganing, cornucopias of shops, shimmering hotels, high-speed nightlife, and the glossy aura of Europe's leisured classes. But there are also lots of cozier, *famiglia*-oriented villages, many of them linked to a constellation of neighbors by far-reaching networks of chair lifts and cable cars.

Increasingly available is the all-region *tessera,* a pass that permits a skier to schuss hundreds of miles of trails with a single document. One of the best, the Superski Dolomiti Pass, offers access to more than 450 lifts serving more than 675 miles of ski trails, an authentic orgy of Alpine ski touring from village to mountain pass and mountain pass to village. District passes that permit use of some portion of these 450 lifts — as much territory as most intermediates would be able to cover in a couple of weeks of skiing — are also available and are somewhat less expensive.

The best of Italy's ski towns are strung through the Alps across the northern tier of the country. Resorts in the French-flavored Valle d'Aosta are situated on natural balconies with stunning views of Mont-Blanc (Monte Bianco here), the Matterhorn (which Italians know as Monte Cervino), Italy's own Monte Rosa, and other celebrated Alpine peaks; the opening of the Mont-Blanc and Great St. Bernard tunnels and the construction of the Aosta–Po Valley autostradas have made the area easily accessible.

There's also the German-speaking Alto Adige and the craggy pink peaks of the Dolomites — named for the 18th-century French geologist Déodat de Dolomieu — which rise fantastically out of valleys. With their spires and towers, deeply grooved boulders and huge terraces, and sheer vertical faces on all sides, the Dolomites do not look particularly skiable. But wide-open ledges and snowfields above, and tree-covered lower slopes below, provide sport enough to last a lifetime. That this area also is known as South Tyrol gives a clue to the culture here — equal parts Teutonic and Mediterranean.

Surprisingly, there also is some very serviceable skiing within striking distance of southerly cities better known for their sunny summer languor — Abetone near Florence; Terminillo, Campo Imperatore, and Ovindoli near Rome; and Roccaraso, equidistant from Rome and Naples. It's even possible to ski on Mount Etna — volcanic activity permitting — and cool off afterward in the Sicilian sea.

Throughout most of these regions, those who like their luxury rugged can hire a helicopter for a quick trip up to their choice of high-altitude moonscape and the subsequent opportunity to carve their way back through miles of glittery virgin powder. If your special pleasure is the trudgery known as *sci di fondo* — cross-country skiing —

be aware that the sport is booming here; a wide choice of trails and excursions (and a good supply of the relatively inexpensive necessary equipment) are readily available. And no matter where you go, there's a very high standard of cooking in the dining rooms adjacent to the slopes. Italians demand that of their resorts (or why go?).

Words of caution: If you need an English-speaking instructor from the area's ski school, say so when signing up or risk having to learn to recognize "Bend your knees" when spoken in all too faultless Italian. Know the local trail markings — green for novice, blue for intermediate, red for competent, and black for the very best skiers. Be prepared for sometimes hair-raising traffic — both on the mountain roads and on the slopes. Since skiing as a mass activity is a Gianni-come-lately in Italy, the average level of expertise is lower than in Switzerland or Austria, and traditions of slope safety and etiquette are not at all hallowed. Avoid crowded *Christmastime* if you can (when the snow conditions in recent years have been less than ideal); and remember that the Italian school vacation extends through *Epiphany,* January 6. Take advantage of lunchtime — the quiet time in all seasons as skiers *all'italiana* down their regulation portions of pasta. Don't overlook the interesting opportunities for summer skiing on glaciers, such as at Bormio in Lombardy. June and September are its prime times for snow, sunny skies, and smaller, fewer crowds. And remember that the same ebullience that makes an Italian so vocal in a lift line also leads to easily made friendships elsewhere in the resort.

For each ski center, we have included a few favorite hotels, generally in each price range: Expensive (E), Moderate (M), Inexpensive (I) — or at least, more moderate.

BORMIO, Lombardy: In ancient times, Romans traveled to Bormio to cure gout, diabetes, and allergies in the natural hot water bubbling from its nine springs. Now Italians from every corner take to the heights in a two-stage cable lift that carries them above the lower mountain and its soft snow and forest-edged runs to 6,500 feet and on to the wide-open snowfields at about 9,800 feet. Then, at the end of each bracing day's runs, they return to agreeably relaxed Bormio and a warm reception, Bormio-style. That means enjoying the tumble of buildings and cobbled streets that infuses the town with charm throughout the year, with or without the snow, and doing as those ancient Romans did — in the thermal center in town or, a 15-minute taxi ride into the mountains, at the original Roman baths. (The original sauna is in a cave, and the pools are naturally heated — hot, hotter, hottest.) At nearby Passo dello Stelvio, summer skiing is a serious business, and no fewer than 16 schools help keep the high-altitude glaciers populated even at high noon in July — which, incidentally, is the time of year for a would-be sybarite to learn to ski. Details: *Azienda Autonoma di Soggiorno, Cura e Turismo,* 10 Via allo Stelvio, Bormio (Sondrio) 23032 (phone: 342-903300). Hotels: *Palace* (E), *Miramonti Clementi* (M), *Everest* (I).

CANAZEI, Trentino: Busy, friendly, and not overly chic, surrounded by the most decorative mountains in Italy — the Sella, Marmolada, and Sassolungo sections of the distinctively dramatic Dolomite range. The more than 60 miles of trails here are linked with the extensive networks of neighboring Val Gardena and Val Badia, so there's no shortage of skiable terrain, and the valley ski schools are known for their professionalism and highly developed teaching methods. The covered swimming pool and the up-to-date skating rink will burn off any unused energy. Details: *Azienda Autonoma di Soggiorno e Turismo,* 16 Via Roma, Canazei (Trento) 38032 (phone: 462-61113). Hotels: *Diana* (M), *Tyrol* (M to I).

CERVINIA, Valle d'Aosta: In the Italian shadow of the Matterhorn, this is one of the most popular Italian mountain resorts — partly because of its open, sunbathed position; partly because of its majestic mountain-rimmed setting on the Monte Rosa plateau; partly because of its altitude, which begins at over 6,500 feet and guarantees an abundant harvest of snow in an average year; and, last, because the spring skiing is superb. The trails are mostly smooth and forgiving — it's possible to stay on the slopes all day without ever bending your knees. The lift system is also one of Italy's most sophisticated, and the town is linked to neighboring Valtournenche; on a clear day it's possible to ski to Switzerland, passport in parka, over the saddle to Zermatt. Every type of winter sport is on tap, from cross-country skiing to ice hockey and bobsledding, and if the looks of the place are unexceptional, the atmosphere is agreeably frenetic; chic shops, discos, skiers dressed at least to maim (both on and off the slopes), and Maseratis with roof racks full of Rossignols. Quaint it ain't. Details: *Azienda Autonoma di Soggiorno e Turismo di Breuil-Cervinia,* 29 Via J. A. Carrel, Cervinia (Aosta) 11021 (phone: 166-949136). Hotels: *Cristallo* (E), *President* (M), *Europa* (I).

CHAMPOLUC, Valle d'Aosta: Tucked into the end of the sunny Val d'Ayas under Monte Rosa, Champoluc has been mercifully ignored by the great mass of European skiers; the fur-coated folks with year-round suntans gravitate to nearby Cervinia and Courmayeur, also in the Aosta Valley, so Champoluc has kept its countrified air. But the facilities are as complete as the town life is simple. Including the facilities of the neighboring areas of Frachey, Staval, Orsia, and Gressoney, 30 lifts serve over 120 miles of trails, offering skiing for every level. There's even an 18-mile cross-country trail. Glamorous hotels are not part of Champoluc life, and quiet is the order of the evening. High school French aids communication with the hospitable natives, whose dialect is heavily Gallicized. Details: *Azienda Autonoma di Soggiorno,* 16 Route Varasc, Champoluc (Aosta) 11020 (phone: 125-307113). Hotels: *Anna Maria, Castor* (M), *Monte Cervino* (I).

CORTINA D'AMPEZZO, Veneto: The country's number-one ski resort attracted its first tourists — English, German, and Austrian mountain climbers — in the mid-19th century; skiing began here early in the 20th century. But the ski trade didn't really boom until the town hosted Italy's first *Winter Olympics* in 1956. Now among the Alps' best-equipped and most cosmopolitan ski resorts, it counts a huge, open, blond-wood *Stadio Olimpico del Ghiaccio* (Olympic Ice Stadium) among its special offerings, along with a location amidst the toothy spikes of the Dolomites at the heart of the Superski Dolomiti region. Add the resort's own network of four ski areas, and the resulting package draws a stylish international set that nourishes the department stores, big hotels, and scores of smart boutiques and eateries that crowd the long, narrow main street, Corso d'Italia. As a reminder that Venice and the Mediterranean are only a few hours away, a powerful sun is always present, even in February and March. Details: *Azienda Autonoma di Soggiorno e Turismo,* 8 Piazzetta San Francesco, Cortina d'Ampezzo (Belluno) 32043 (phone: 436-3231). Hotels: *Cristallo, Miramonti, De la Poste* (E).

CORVARA, Alto Adige: Corvara is the principal departure point for the Sella Ronda, the Dolomite circuit that connects five downhill areas and countless skiing experiences and that, together with a mega ski pass, provides access to about 250 miles of linked trails. Located in one of the few valleys where residents still speak Ladin (a language said to have come down from the Latin of Romans who came here in the 4th century, similar to Switzerland's *Romansch*), Corvara itself has a bucolic flavor, despite the modish tone of its shops, cafés, and discotheques. For those who prefer the Great Indoors, there's heated swimming, covered tennis, and high-Alpine bowling. Details: *Azienda Autonoma di Soggiorno e Turismo,* Palazzo Comunale, Corvara in Badia (Bolzano) 39033 (phone: 471-836176). Hotels: *La Perla* (E), *Posta Zirm* (M), *Tablè* (M to I).

COURMAYEUR, Valle d'Aosta: Among the most glamorous of Italian ski resorts, and one that some call the friendliest in the Alps, it is stunningly situated in the middle of 12 peaks above 13,000 feet, the magical tag of mountain supremacy in Europe. The dramatic south-facing side of the Mont-Blanc massif looms above, and over 2 dozen lifts make more than 60 miles of ski runs accessible to both beginners and experts; the area is heaven for intermediates, with enough autostrada-on-snow trails to boost any ego and enough moguls to show that there's always more to learn. Meanwhile, snow pioneers accompanied by guides can ski across Monte Bianco and over the French border to Chamonix. Such facilities and terrain attract important skiing competitions all winter and, with them, the sleek international set and modern Milan-Turin managerial money. The even more upwardly mobile use helicopters as transport to powdery plateaus. The beauties of the old-fashioned town itself will satisfy valley types: four cross-country circuits ranging in length from 3½ to 12 miles, the snow-golf course, an arpeggio of high-decibel discotheques, and a simpatico watering hole called the *American Bar* (Via Roma). Summer skiing keeps the Gigante glacier from getting lonely during the off-season. Details: *Azienda Autonoma di Soggiorno e Turismo,* Piazzale Monte Bianco, Courmayeur (Aosta) 11013 (phone: 165-842060). Hotels: *Palace Bron* (E), *Chetif* (M), *Centrale* (I).

LIVIGNO, Lombardy: Not so long ago, this curious, little-known village of distinctive wooden houses strung out along a valley on the Swiss-Italian border was exclusively the domain of cross-country ski wanderers; its only road was regularly blocked by heavy snowfalls. Now, thanks to enthusiastic, but not excessive, development and the construction of a tunnel into Switzerland as an alternative means of egress, it offers a good deal of attractive skiing and accommodation, plus ice skating, tobogganing, a pretty lake, gentle landscape, and a pleasantly lost horizon. Yet it still caters to a reasonably limited clientele, particularly compared with some of the great ski mills across the border. Diehards can shop for duty-free items in the chalets-turned-shops along the main street, thanks to Livigno's special border-town dispensation. Details: *Azienda Autonoma di Soggiorno e Turismo,* Plaza dal Comun, Livigno (Sondrio) 23030 (phone: 342-996379). Hotels: *Du Lac* (E), *Alpina* (M), *Verde Lago* (I).

MADONNA DI CAMPIGLIO, Trentino: The least cosmopolitan of Italy's Big Five — a group that also includes Cervinia, Cortina, Courmayeur, and Sestriere — this resort is not widely known outside the country. So instead of the high-powered international set, the slopes are full of sleek and stylish northern Italians who are serious about their snow. The facilities for which they come are world class: helicopters to ascend to the farthest peaks for guided all-day descents and three dozen lifts fanning out from the town to serve four separate areas with 60 miles of slopes and trails. The possibilities run the gamut from ballroom slopes for novice snowplowers to the steep and bumpy terrain favored by high-tech slalomers. The town itself is Tyrolean in style, though there are modern structures in the Campo Carlo Magno section, and it is surrounded by beautiful pine forests and lakes — all dominated by the awesome sawtooth skyline of the Brenta Dolomites. Snowcats can haul hardy skiers up to one of the slopeside refuges for dinner and then back down in time for action in one of the town's discos, if that's your pleasure. Details: *Azienda Autonoma di Soggiorno,* Madonna di Campiglio (Trento) 38084 (phone: 465-42000). Hotels: *Golf* (E), *Grifone* (E to M), *Il Caminetto* (M).

MOENA, Trentino: This Italian capital of cross-country skiing, in a sunny valley at the bull's-eye of the Dolomites, is the starting point for the annual competition known as the Marcialonga, a circuit of 43 miles that attracts cross-country fans from all over Europe. During the rest of the season, trails are exceptionally well maintained, and the town is cheerful, bustling, and unpretentious. A favorite of vacationing families, it offers an order of luxury lower than that of some of its glossy neighbors, and prices are the opposite of exorbitant. Details: *Azienda Autonoma di Soggiorno,* 33 Piazza Cesare Battisti, Moena (Trento) 38035 (phone: 462-53122). Hotels: *Leonardo* (M), *Catinaccio* (M), *Alpi* (I).

ORTISEI/VAL GARDENA, Alto Adige: Tucked below the broad open plateau of the Alpe di Siusi in the lushly wooded Val Gardena, sunny Ortisei is lively and pretty, with ornately decorated houses and shops overflowing with woodcarvings. The atmosphere is decidedly South Tyrolean — in addition to the local Ladin language, German is also spoken here — and the food is more Teutonic than Mediterranean. From the main square, buses fan out to all adjacent valleys, and a 5-minute cable car ride hoists skiers 2,625 feet to a bounty of ski trails linked to the 675 miles of the Superski Dolomiti facilities. One of the most attractive sections is the Sella Ronda, over 16 miles of lift-connected runs around the Sella mountain massif; easy enough even for beginners, it's best done on Tuesdays or Wednesdays, when less-trafficked lifts make it possible to cover the maximum territory. Those who care more about serious skiing than village life should stay at Alpe di Siusi itself at 5,900 feet, where there are 9 hours of sunlight in January and guaranteed snow. Details: *Azienda Autonoma di Soggiorno e Turismo,* 1 Via Rezia, Ortisei (Bolzano) 39046 (phone: 471-76328). Hotels: *Adler* (E), *Villa Emilia* (M), *Ronce* (I).

SAN MARTINO DI CASTROZZA, Trentino: Under the rose-colored peaks of the Dolomites' theatrical Pale di San Martino, this long-established center in the Valle del Cismon enjoys the twin Italian advantages of a southern exposure and protection from icy northern winds. Yet at 4,760 feet (about 1,450 meters), there is reliable snow on the piney trails that skirt the village, and the local master ski pass admits skiers to the multiple joys of the Superski Dolomiti system. The *Drei Tannen* (Via Passo Rolle, near the *Savoia* hotel) has the best food in town; don't depart without the traditional *polenta e salsiccie* — cornmeal and sausage in tomato sauce, served on homemade wooden trenchers. It is also almost obligatory to swig a little of the incendiary local grappa, especially on gelid early-morning runs from the high Rosetta. Details: *Azienda Autonoma di Soggiorno e Turismo,* 165 Via Passo Rolle, San Martino di Castrozza (Trento) 38058 (phone: 439-68101). Hotels: *Savoia* (E), *Rosetta* (M), *Bel Sito* (I).

SAN SICARIO, Piedmont: Designed and built from scratch in the late 1960s with the hard-core skier in mind, this high-powered, very Italian ski center offers not one whit of the quaint, and its complex of hotels and mini-apartment residences, accessible by silent monorail from the covered parking lot, is the ultimate in contemporaneity. The no-traffic regime guarantees stressless days and sleepful nights, and the location in the middle of an extensive trail network known as the Via Lattea (Milky Way) — a consortium of nine ski towns and their collective lift systems — takes care of the skiing. The comfort, convenience, and quality of the facilities more than make up for the lack of local color — especially for 9-to-5 trailaholics. Details: *Azienda Autonoma di Soggiorno,* 3 Piazza Vittorio Amedeo, Cesana (Torino) 10054 (phone: 122-89202). Hotels: *Rio Envers* (E), *San Sicario* (M).

SAPPADA, Veneto: The language is German and the food Austrian. But the currency is still Italian in this town off the beaten trails just south of the border. Ideal for seekers of the small but *bello,* Sappada has 30 miles of varied and well-groomed skiing as well as opportunities for cross-country trekking. The friendly hotels are mostly pocket-sized and family-run, and there is a broad selection of short-term apartment rentals in balconied chalets. Evening entertainment centers on hot *vino brulé* (mulled wine) or cold beer, not brassy disco dancing. The costumed *Carnevale* merriment of February is an added dividend. Details: *Azienda Autonoma di Soggiorno e Turismo,* 20 Borgata Bach, Sappada (Belluno) 32047 (phone: 435-69131). Hotels: *Bladen* (E), *Oberthaler Park* (M), *Sorgenti del Piave* (I).

SAUZE D'OULX, Piedmont: Lift-linked to the bigger, brassier centers of Sestriere and San Sicario, and thereby to the 240 trail miles of the Via Lattea, Sauze d'Oulx itself is a smaller, more easygoing, and less sophisticated snow haven — an excellent choice for those preferring ski-borne access to the widest possible range of trails with less conspicuous merriment off-trail. Close to the border, Sauze d'Oulx has been a favorite with the French since the early part of the century. It is also very popular with the British, and English — of a sort — is widely spoken. The mountain terrace of the Val di Susa, at 4,900 feet, is a wind-free suntrap — ideal for mid-winter tanning, and rows of comely maidens in deck chairs can usually be seen cupping aluminum reflectors under their chins while turning their tawny faces phototropically. Wide north-facing slopes and open larch woods mean a long season of powder and fine trails of the calendar art variety. The town itself is a charmer — buildings leaning this way and that over the twisting streets, a 15th-century fountain in the plaza. Dedicate evenings to the *fonduta* — the Italian answer to Swiss fondue, chased with a local arneis or erbaluce di Caluso wine. Details: *Azienda Autonoma di Soggiorno e Turismo,* 18 Piazza Assietta, Sauze d'Oulx (Torino) 10050 (phone: 122-85009). Hotels: *Gran Baita* (E), *Sauze* (M), *Miosotys* (I).

SESTRIERE, Piedmont: Like Courcheval in France, Sestriere was carved out of snowy emptiness expressly to create a fabulous location for skiing, "a kind of skiing university in which the ordinary ski runner who usually knows nothing at all about mountains can graduate to an expert winter mountaineer" by working through its runs, according to a 1934 guidebook to the area. "Here," the guidebook goes on, "all is for the ski, for the slope . . . the most satisfying creation of the industrial revolution on the snows of the Alps." The main square is named for Fiat founding father Giovanni Agnelli, whose vision spawned the whole thing. His ideas have held up remarkably well. In season, excellent high-altitude runs rise from a base of about 9,200 feet for all levels of skier, and it's possible to ski here for a week without ever repeating a run — especially when you take advantage of the facilities of other Via Lattea resorts. The ski instruction is excellent, the mood chic and modern, and the condos comfortable. The sun shines abundantly, and there are large terraces with plenty of deck chairs and umbrella tables from which to enjoy it. And although there's no sense of village life, Sestriere is eminently lively in season. It's an especially marvelous place to ski on weekdays. High-season weekends, when big tour buses arrive from Turin, 55 miles (88 km) distant, are another matter. Details: *Azienda Autonoma di Soggiorno e Turismo,* 11 Piazza Giovanni Agnelli, Sestriere (Torino) 10058 (phone: 122-76865). Hotels: *Cristallo* (E), *Belvedere* (M), *Olimpic* (I).

VALGRISENCHE, Valle d'Aosta: A tiny two-tow valley, a bit off the highway that speeds the world to chic Courmayeur, with no nightlife, and no grand hotels. It simply offers the opportunity to travel back in time, to see the Italian mountains as they were 40 years ago before Italy high-styled skiing for the new leisure class. Go before it's too late, and be prepared for off-trail exploring, strapping on sealskins for steep ascents, and quaffing thermosfuls of *vino brulé* (but bring your own). If all this is too serene and relaxing, rest assured that high society is only a sleigh ride away. Details: *Pro Loco Valgrisenche,* Aosta 11010 (phone: 165-97105). Hotel: *Perret* (I).

Tennis

It wasn't too long ago that only a select group of Italians donned tennis whites for an afternoon of tennis, 5 o'clock tea, and 7 o'clock cocktails. Tennis was the game of the elite.

Then, after Italy produced a few champions during the 1950s, Italians began viewing tennis through new eyes. Hundreds of clubs were established all over the country and everyone rushed to join. Networks broadcast major international tournaments, and now it's often very hard to find a free court.

The traveling tennis player will find most of the activity at private tennis clubs, admission to which can usually be arranged by the better hotels for their guests. In addition, many hotels, particularly those in prime resort areas, have at least a court or two. Clay is the preferred surface everywhere, and regulation tennis shoes, as well as accepted tennis attire, are usually required.

At a number of tennis instruction camps, both adults and children can work on their strokes in gorgeous surroundings — by the sea, in the mountains, or in the countryside. Fitness centers, swimming pools, saunas, and solaria are the usual companions to serious instruction (usually in Italian) by *Federazione Italiana Tennis* (Italian Tennis Federation) coaches. And the atmosphere is always friendly and relaxed.

For a complete listing of Italian tennis clubs and for general information about the game in Italy, contact the *Federation* (70 Viale Tiziano, Roma 00100; phone: 6-323-3807). Here are some of the best net bets.

BAIA DI CONTE, Alghero, Sardinia: The clearly Catalonian port-and-resort of Alghero, set amid olive and eucalyptus trees, and the attractive seaside *Baia di Conte* hotel at Porto Conte, 4 miles (7 km) from town, are ideal for spicing stroke drills with Sardinian scenery. At hotel tennis camps, available for adults and children from April through October, certified instructors and coaches divide participants into groups of eight according to ability and work on their games using videotape analyses and ball machines as necessary. A fitness room, sauna and whirlpool bath, windsurfing boards, and horseback riding are available; guests can unwind in the evening in the hotel's disco. Details: *Baia di Conte,* Alghero (Sardegna) 07040 (phone: 79-952003 or 79-951109).

CAPO RIZZUTO, Catanzaro, Calabria: Following the French *Club Med* model of sports-oriented vacation villages, the 10 *Italian Valtur* complexes have cornered the market in the peninsula's glamorous locations. They guarantee luxurious accommodations and provide the same round-the-clock roster of activities as their Gallic counterparts. Near Cefalù, on the northern coast of Sicily, is *Pollina,* with 8 tennis courts, 4 of them lighted, so it's possible to water-ski all day and save tennis for a nightcap. *Capo Rizzuto,* on the Ionian coast of Calabria, has 8 courts, 3 lighted, and *Brucoli,* not far from the Sicilian city of Syracuse, has 6 courts, 3 lighted. Special tennis weeks with top-ranking coaches are featured in June and July. *Valtur* centers are open from May through September. Details: *Valtur,* 42 Via Milano, Roma 00184 (phone: 6-482-1000).

IL CIOCCO, Lucca, Tuscany: The summer tennis camps of this international vacation center in a vast natural reserve in the Garfagnana hills are organized primarily for 8- to 15-year-olds. However, adults can use the courts and arrange coaching sessions with the instructor, and, off the courts, enjoy the solarium, sauna, health club, pool, horseback riding, and hiking. Lodging is in the hotel or in cozy little chalets in the surrounding woods. Details: *Il Ciocco,* Centro Turistico Internazionale, Castelvecchio Pascoli (Lucca) 55020 (phone: 583-7191).

KAMARINA, Scoglitti, Sicily: An outstanding spot to play is at one of more than a hundred vacation villages of *Club Med. Le Club,* as it's known in its native France, is founded on the formula of Leisure — Sport, so the villages' facilities are extensive, their instruction first-rate, and their settings consistently attractive. The *Club Med Kamarina,* on the Ionian Sea in Sicily, is a fine place to mix tennis and beach life. There are 28 courts, of which 21 are clay. Accommodations are in a hotel or in separate bungalows. In May, June, and September, you're assured 2½ hours of instruction daily. Two pools, a sandy shore, sailing and windsurfing, archery, and biking will compete with the cultural pull of the Greek and Roman ruins that are within easy excursion distance. Open from early May through September. Details: *Club Med Kamarina,* BP25, Scoglitti (Ragusa) 97100 (phone: 932-911333; fax: 932-911719 — or contact the *Club*'s New York office at 40 W. 57th St., New York, NY 10019; phone: 1-800-CLUBMED).

METAPONTO, Marina di Pisticci, Basilicata: Located near pine woods and the gentle waters of the Gulf of Taranto, this *Club Med* collection of village-style houses has 18 tennis courts. An 18-hole golf course is 20 minutes away, with free transportation provided. There's plenty of opportunity for sailing and swimming, and, as at many

Club Med establishments, children's groups for every age level ensure amusement for every member of the family. Details: *Club Med Metaponto,* San Basilio Mare, Marina di Pisticci (Taranto; phone: 835-470160) — or contact the *Club* in New York (see *Club Med Kamarina,* above).

INTERNATIONAL TOURNAMENTS

For those accustomed to the respectful hush of *Wimbledon,* the noisy Italian crowds can strike a jarring note. But if you just think of the noise as heartfelt enthusiasm, attending a tournament in Italy can be a cultural as well as a sporting experience. The top tournaments at which this very Mediterranean show of excitement is most evident take place in the following cities and in the tiny republic of San Marino:

Milan, February.
Rome and Bologna, May.
Florence, June.
San Remo, July.
San Marino, July or August.
Palermo, September.

For exact dates and information on purchasing tickets, contact the *Federazione Italiana Tennis* (70 Viale Tiziano, Roma 00100; phone: 6-321-9897). For news about the sport in Italy, consult the country's major tennis publications: *Matchball, Il Tennista,* and *Tennis Italiano,* available on newsstands.

Great Italian Golf

The British brought golf to Italy around the turn of the century, but it was another 50 years before the game acquired any degree of popularity — and then it remained an activity of the very social or the very rich. Now an increasing number of foreign golfers have discovered that Italy's 100 or so courses offer the perfect formula for a golfing vacation: a beautiful natural setting, an ideal climate nearly year-round, and some rather challenging sport. The result is that 30 new courses have recently been completed or are currently being built, and the Italian golf devotees' explanation of the nation's relatively small number of courses — that they're looking for quality rather than quantity — is beginning to gain some credibility. It is also increasingly possible to find layouts that begin to measure up to the criteria for a great course articulated over 45 years ago by Bobby Jones: It should "give pleasure . . . to the greatest number of players . . . because it will offer problems many may attempt according to [their] ability. It will never become hopeless for the duffer nor fail to concern and interest the expert; and it will be found, like the *Old Course* at *St. Andrews,* to become more delightful the more it is studied and played."

As Italy becomes more involved with golf, it has become more apparent that the country is full of spots that seem to have been created just to hold a golf course: layouts by the sea, courses in the mountains, and more.

Some of the best are listed below. Greens fees begin at $60 on weekdays, considerably more on weekends; some courses do not allow visitors to play on weekends, and most are closed Mondays. Some, but not all, accept credit cards. The courses are very crowded on weekends, so reserve a tee time well ahead, either through your hotel or by contacting the club directly. All Italian golf clubs extend reciprocal privileges to foreigners with a membership card or other evidence of club membership at home.

For complete information about golf in Italy and Italian golf clubs, contact the *Italian Golf Federation,* 388 Via Flaminia, Roma 00196 (phone: 6-323-1825; fax: 6-322-0250).

BY THE SEA

ALBERONI, Venice: At 6,356 yards, this spectacular 18-hole seaside layout at the far western end of Venice's famed Lido is long for a continental course. And with tees and greens surrounded by groves of pines, olives, and poplars, it can also be demanding. However, it is extraordinarily well balanced. There are par 5 holes that call for long hitting, as well as other holes that require all the other golfing skills. Concentration is paramount, especially at the 7th hole, the longest par 4, where two bunkers guard the green; the 8th hole, which has a blind approach; and the 14th, which forces a player to avoid a gaggle of scattered traps. Details: *Golf Club Lido di Venezia,* Via del Forte, Alberoni (Venezia) 30011 (phone: 41-731333).

GARLENDA, Garlenda, Liguria: Winters are mild, springs gentle, and summers temperate on the Italian Riviera, so there's no season to the pleasures and challenges of this course. Just as the first holes have lulled you into relaxation, the 12th hole comes along, a long and very treacherous par 4. It's followed by a long par 3 that crosses a stream, and, three holes later, a par 4 with a left-hand dogleg. Even then, the average duffer has a good chance of making a few pars here. The course, 31 miles (50 km) from Savona, is open year-round, and is closed on Wednesdays. The most convenient lodging is next door at the *Golf Hotel La Meridiana* (11 Via ai Castelli, Garlenda; phone: 182-580271; fax: 182-580150). Details: *Garlenda Golf Club,* 7 Via del Golf, Garlenda (Savona) 17030 (phone: 182-580012 or 182-580013; fax: 182-580561).

PEVERO, Porto Cervo, Sardinia: When Robert Trent Jones, Sr. created this "emerald jewel in the Costa Smeralda crown," one of the world's great seaside courses 15 miles (9 km) from Olbia Airport, he gave free rein to his sense of the dramatic, and the resulting layout is a direct reflection of his raw materials — a narrow, rising and plunging, sea-edged neck of land patched with granite outcrops, pine, broom, gorse, lavender, poppy, lupin, and juniper that blazes with color in the spring. This is a tiger of a course, and perhaps the greatest difficulty is making a good recovery shot out of the rough. Major traps are found at the 3rd, 11th, and 15th holes. Rated tops by the Italian *Golf* magazine. Closed Tuesdays in winter. Details: *Pevero Golf Club,* Porto Cervo (Sassari) 07020 (phone: 789-96072 or 789-96210).

PUNTA ALA, Punta Ala, Tuscany: Set in southern Tuscany's Maremma, near the meeting place of the Tyrrhenian and the Ligurian seas opposite the isle of Elba, this 6,720-yard course has been a standout among Italian layouts since 1964, when it was carved out of a pine woods on rolling terrain that stretches down to the sea. Long and tough from start to finish, it has been seeded with a special Korean grass known for its even growth, so players are almost able to hit a driver off the fairways. Caution is required on the 5th and 12th holes; the 8th confronts players with a long par 4 on a steep uphill slope. High summer temperatures (albeit tempered by sea breezes) add to the challenge. Open daily. Punta Ala itself is a prime destination for sports of all types, particularly swimming, sailing, and riding. Details: *Punta Ala Golf Club,* 1 Via del Golf, Punta Ala (Grosseto) 58040 (phone: 564-922121).

SAN REMO, San Remo, Liguria: Known for the olive groves through which the course unfolds, this 6,020-yard layout, rebuilt in 1972, offers panoramic sea views, narrow fairways, undulating greens, and a valley location that protects players from the sea winds. Tee shots must be precise, but otherwise this is a course for relaxation. Located 3 miles (5 km) north of San Remo. Closed Tuesdays. Details: *Golf Club San Remo,* 59 Strada Campo Golf, San Remo (Imperia) 18038 (phone: 184-557093).

NEAR MAJOR CITIES

MILANO, Milan: These 27 holes are in the heart of Monza Park, a few miles north of Milan, on the former estate of Umberto I (who was assassinated here in 1900). The site of several major tournaments, it also has pros who rank among Italy's best, and the physical facilities are first rate. Closed Mondays. Details: *Golf Club Milano,* Parco di Monza (Milano) 20052 (phone: 39-703081 or 39-703082).

OLGIATA, Rome: The preferred Italian venue for most major international tournaments, the *West* course is tough and demanding — particularly for the power golfer who may be short on precision. British course architect C. K. Cotton started with plenty of space, so there's never a feeling of congestion. At the same time, he gave every hole a character all its own, balancing the course as a whole to challenge every facet of a player's skill and strategic abilities. The large greens have narrow bunkered entrances, the levels change (though never too drastically), and there's scarcely a straight hole on the course. There's also a 3,092-yard, 9-hole *East* course. Closed Mondays; visitors may not play on weekends. Details: *Olgiata Golf Club,* 15 Largo Olgiata, Roma 00123 (phone: 6-378-9141).

ROMA, Rome: Rome's golf devotees, from cardinals to caddies, love this undulating 6,344-yard layout near the Acquasanta Springs 9 miles (14 km) north of Rome. It is probably the most prestigious course in all of Italy. The most strenuous test of shot making is posed by the strong winds that normally sweep across its pines, cypresses, and oaks. Accuracy is a must. Closed Mondays; book well ahead for weekends. Details: *Golf Club Roma,* 716/A Via Appia Nuova, Località Acquasanta, Roma 00178 (phone: 6-783407 or 6-788-6159).

TORINO, Turin, Piedmont: On a classic championship layout with wide fairways, these 36 holes in Mandria Park unwind along flat terrain scattered with trees and water hazards. Even Sunday players have a fighting chance here; the course is fairly forgiving and allows for errors and recovery. Site of many Italian championships, the club is considered very exclusive. The clubhouse is quite charming. Closed Mondays. Details: *Golf Club Torino,* 137 Via Grange, Fiano Torinese (Torino) 10070 (phone: 11-923-5670 or 11-923-5440).

IN THE HILLS

CANSIGLIO, Vittorio Veneto, Veneto: Robert Trent Jones, Jr. designed this 9-hole course on a limestone plateau with a good deal of wide-open space peppered by natural obstacles and double tees. Careful shots are in order. As we went to press, another 9 holes were nearing completion. Open daily, May through October. The course is 41 miles (65 km) from Treviso; 16 miles (25 km) from Vittorio Veneto. Details: *Golf Club Cansiglio,* Casella Postale 152, Vittorio Veneto (Treviso) 31029 (phone: 438-585398).

SESTRIERE, Sestriere, Piedmont: Known as the highest 18-hole course in Europe, this one in the western Alps is open only in July and August. After then, it's snow, snow, snow. Major challenges are the strong winds that often start up when players least expect them; be prepared. Watch out for the 9th hole, a long, uphill par 4 that plays to a very small green, and the 18th hole, where it's all uphill — and steep. Details: *Golf Club Sestriere,* 4 Piazza Agnelli, Sestriere (Torino) 10058 (phone: 122-76276 or 122-76243).

DELL'UGOLINO, Florence: Nestled in the Chianti hills, this layout is not very long, but its many trees and bushes, bunkers, and out-of-bounds require concentration and accuracy. The 4th hole is a long, downhill par 3, the 5th a long par 4 through an olive grove. Wine tasting before a round is not advised. Closed Mondays. Details: *Circolo Golf dell'Ugolino,* 3 Via Chiantigiana, Grassina (Firenze) 50015 (phone: 55-230-1009).

VILLA D'ESTE, Como, Lombardy: This interesting hillside course, on the banks of

Lake Montorfano, is an arduous test of shot making that some consider the toughest par 69 in Europe. It has hosted several major international tournaments since it was constructed in 1926. Unwinding through chestnut, birch, and pine groves, its 6,066 yards offer not a single opportunity for relaxation. The fairways, while not cramped, are bordered by trees and roll and dip inexorably toward the lake, so that both accuracy and power are essential every step of the way. The layout was built by the lush *Villa d'Este* hotel, though it is no longer involved in the club's operation. It does, however, still provide the perfect pampering headquarters at which to find succor from soaring scores. Open daily, March to December. Details: *Circolo Golf Villa d'Este,* 13 Via per Cantù, Montorfano (Como) 22030 (phone: 31-200200). (See also "Italy's Most Memorable Hostelries," *For the Experience.*)

Beaches

Italy's 5,000 miles of coastline are continually washed by the historic dark waves of the Ligurian, the Tyrrhenian, the Ionian, the Adriatic, and the Mediterranean. From Portofino to Trapani, the choice of beaches is as dazzling as the midsummer sun. Sun worshipers can sprawl on wide swaths of downy sand at Viareggio, hike down a cliff-hanging path to a craggy Calabrian cove, share a dry martini with a titled fellow beachcomber, plunge off a pedal boat on the far side of Sardinia, or overdo it on fish and Frascati at suburban Rome's Fregene. To get away from everybody else who's getting away from it all, it's a simple matter to head for the northern coast of the Gargano, near the obscure fishing village of Vieste, where a 40-mile-long strand is punctuated at either end by two huge dunes, or travel to the garland of islands that rings Italy's coast — Elba, Giglio, Ponza, Ischia & Co. — for the country's freshest fish and crystal-clearest waters. Sardinia, wind swept and flower scented, is a beach paradise in May, June, July, and even after August 16. Waters are warmest in the Cagliari bays and capes at the southern end of the rocky isle.

Most of Italy's best beachfronts are listed below. But wherever you decide to establish your beachhead, do it in June, July, September, or October. In August, all of Italy seems to slide down to the sea, and on even the tiniest postage stamps of sandy coastline, coconut-scented sun seekers jockey aggressively for meager patches of sand and salt water. But on a balmy *Columbus Day,* a beach-loving visitor can savor a semiprivate Capri and be positively lonely on the Lido.

AMALFI COAST, Salerno, Campania: The Sorrento Peninsula — the finger of land curling around the Bay of Naples and pointing to the island of Capri — is mountainous and brilliant with flowers. Its southern exposure is edged by a narrow road that has been famous for breathtaking views and heart-stopping curves since it was carved out of the rock in the mid-19th century. Break up the dizzying drive through its tunnels, over its bridges, and atop its cliffs with a stay in Positano, where cubist chunks of houses cling to the hillside that dives down to the busy seafront, and minuscule boutiques display rainbows of trendy summer styles. For the best swimming, rent a boat with enough motor to take you a few miles away from the gladding crowd. Yachts anchor off the coast at the privately owned islands of I Galli. One of the sleekest hotels in Italy, the *San Pietro* (described in "Italy's Most Memorable Hostelries," *For the Experience*), perched south of town, has its own private beach.

Once an independent republic with a population of over 100,000, Amalfi rivaled cities such as Genoa and Pisa during the medieval struggle for power in the Mediterranean. It remains small and charming despite its grandiose history and today's continued assaults by Nordic tour buses, whose merry regiments briefly besiege the shops and cafés but blissfully decamp (usually) by nightfall. The best beaching is to be enjoyed in early morning before the carnival comes to town. Details: *Azienda Autonoma di Soggiorno e Turismo,* 2 Via del Saracino, Positano (Salerno) 84017 (phone: 89-875067); or *Azienda Autonoma di Soggiorno e Turismo,* 19 Corsa Roma, Amalfi (Salerno) 84011 (phone: 89-871107).

CAPRI, near Naples, Campania: The most famous, most expensive, and most crowded of all Italian islands, Capri (pronounced *Kah*-pri, not Kah-*pree*) is also one of the most beautiful places in the world. To be sure, it's necessary to keep your distance in July and August, when the little main square and the Marina Piccola beach become twin cans of Mediterranean sardines. But during the off-season, on a sunny November Wednesday, say, it's absolutely incomparable, with sapphire sky and sea, heady aromas from hillside lemon groves perfuming the air, lush purple explosions of wisteria at every turn. The principal pleasures: funicular rides from the boat dock, lazy morning orange juice in one of the *caffès* in the *piazzetta,* afternoon jaunts to the marina, rowboat rides out around the grottoes, the hair-raising minibus ride back up the hairpin road to town, and spooky moon-shadowed rambles to the pagan shrine of the Matromania cave. The Roman Emperor Tiberius built 12 villas here to honor the 12 Olympian deities, and his Villa Jovis — from which he ruled the empire for a decade — is a wonderful walk with a view. From the peak of the island it's possible to see all the way to Calabria. Details: *Azienda Autonoma di Soggiorno,* 1 Piazza Umberto, Capri (Napoli; phone: 81-837-0686).

COSTA SMERALDA, Sardinia: It's remarkable what the Aga Khan and $200 million did for a primitive island coastline. Centuries of invasions by Libyans, Phoenicians, Saracens, Romans, and Spaniards had driven Sardinians into the mountains, leaving the island's rugged, rocky coastline largely uninhabited. Then, in the space of just a few years, the stretch between the port of Olbia and the island's tip at La Maddalena went from wasteland to Emerald Coast — now the country's most glamorous beach complex. The boulders are still here and the water is still an incredibly cloudless cobalt, but scattered from cove to cove are four elegant hotels tastefully designed so that they seem to grow gracefully out of the landscape — the Moorish-style, chalk-white *Romazzino* (90 rooms); the *Cervo* (family-oriented and Spanish-inspired); the 25-bungalow, ultra-private *Pitrizza;* and the biggest of all, the *Cala di Volpe* (described in "Italy's Most Memorable Hostelries," *For the Experience*). Each has its own beaches, which are separated from the main hotel grounds so that guests can enjoy total seclusion. And when one crescent of sand gets crowded, it's only a short hike around the bend to find another, equally pretty — one statistics maven counted 83 strands on the Costa Smeralda's 35 miles of coast. When there is a crowd, it can get very fancy, particularly when the yacht fleet's in at Porto Cervo (you might see movie stars, sheiks, and bluebloods). The million-dollar yachts jostle for space at the Porto Cervo basin. But everyone on the Costa Smeralda comes here for the laid-back sun-and-sea life, so it all stays superbly simple (and savagely expensive). Facilities off the beach include golf on one of Italy's best courses, tennis, boating, windsurfing, and water skiing, all shared by the four hotels. Boat and air connections with several mainland cities are available — but remember to make midsummer reservations well in advance or you may vacation in a sleeping bag on the dock at Civitavecchia. Details: *Azienda Autonoma di Soggiorno e Turismo,* Via 19 Brigata Sassari, Sassari 07100 (phone: 79-233534).

ELBA, near Piombino, Tuscany: Known mainly for Napoleon's brief stay on the island, Elba has many marvelous beaches — some sandy for swimmers and toe-dippers, others rocky and suitable for scuba divers. Sandy beaches in the north include Spartaia, Procchio, Campo all'Aia, Biodola, and Scaglieri; in the south, Stella Bay, Lacona, Marina di Campo, Cavoli, Fetovaia, and Seccheto (sand and rock); and on the east coast, Barbarossa Reale, Cavo (sand and rock), Calamita Peninsula, Naregno, Pareti, Morcone, and Straccoligno. The *Hermitage* hotel in Biodola is one of the island's most elegant resorts. Details: *Azienda di Promozione Turistica dell'Arcipelago Toscano,* 26 Calata Italia, Portoferraio 57037 (phone: 565-914671; fax: 565-916350).

FORTE DEI MARMI, Lucca, Tuscany: The Italian Riviera is really like a gigantic seaside café, and the chief amusement is watching the passing — or sprawling — parade: the phalanxes of candy cane–striped umbrellas, deck chairs, and beach cabins, the fleets of pedal boats, the sippers of Campari, the builders of sand castles, the narcissistic waders, the ostentatious players of volleyball. And the whole expanse of coast between the Lido di Camaiore and the bustling resort town of Viareggio is really one long marina. Patrician families from Rome, Florence, and Turin have been coming here every summer since the last century, though many of their pined and palmed seafront villas have been transformed into small hotels (the *Augustus* once belonged to the Agnelli clan). Though the air is perfumed with mimosa and eucalyptus, never expect romantic solitude (though by comparison with other parts of the coast, Forte Dei Marmi is almost sedate). Details: *Azienda Autonoma di Soggiorno,* 8 Via Franceschi, Forte dei Marmi (Lucca) 55042 (phone: 584-80901).

LIPARI, or AEOLIAN, ISLANDS, Sicily: Movie buffs know this chain of ancient volcanoes north of Milazzo, off the Sicilian coast, as the setting for Roberto Rossellini's *Stromboli,* starring Ingrid Bergman; classics majors may remember it as the home of Aeolus, the god of the winds, and a notable stop on Odysseus's grand tour. Each of the landfalls has its own magic. Lipari, the busiest and easiest to reach, is a subtle mosaic of pastel houses, buff-colored beaches, and turquoise waters. At Vulcano, the more adventurous can climb to the summit of the broad crater for fine views over the archipelago and splash in the thermal springs near the shore of Porto di Levante. On Stromboli, hike up the cone-shaped crater on a moonlit night to see the fiery bubbles of lava and showers of stone explode against the sky and then fall tamely back into the crater. Scuba divers choose the clear waters of Panarea or Salina, and those seeking solitude visit wild and secluded Alicudi or Filicudi. The archipelago can be reached by boat from six mainland cities, including Naples. Go early in the season; the water is warm enough for swimming by late May. Details: *Azienda Autonoma di Soggiorno e Turismo dell'Isole Eolie,* 231 Corso Vittorio Emanuele, Lipari (Messina) 98055 (phone: 90-988-0095).

MARATEA, Potenza, Basilicata: Fishermen have plied the transparent waters of this enchanted coastline since Greek times, but the pleasantly unpretentious town of Maratea, at the ankle of Italy's boot, was virtually unknown 25 years ago; even today few foreigners make their way this far down the coast. Those who do find beaches ranging from blanket-size to roomy and a shoreline jagged with cliffs, crags, coves, and caves. The Apennines reach almost to the sea here, leaving just enough space for a huddle of russet roofs and a riot of low-growing rosemary, myrtle, and broom between the pines and olive trees. Maratea harbors the sumptuous *Santavenere* hotel, whose affluent northern clientele sometimes seems an anomaly surrounded by the simplicity of the town; there are also more modest accommodations, plus *pensioni* and private rooms, for beachcombers of other classes. Details: *Azienda Autonoma di Soggiorno e Turismo,* 32 Piazza del Gesù, Maratea (Potenza) 85040 (phone: 973-876908).

MONTE ARGENTARIO, Grosseto, Tuscany: Halfway between Rome and Pisa on the Tyrrhenian coast, Monte Argentario has all the advantages of an island, but none of the drawbacks. The air is clear and tangy, the vegetation lush and fragrant, the sea spreads out on all sides, and, with a narrow causeway linking the promontory to Orbetello and the mainland coast road, there's no fuss over ferries. The Porto Ercole side of the mountain is frequented by nouveau-*ricco* Roman and landed aristocracy; Holland's Queen Beatrice has her vacation home here, the "White Elephant." Summer at the secluded, exclusive *Pellicano* hotel, and you won't have to worry your uncrowned head about villa upkeep. Rent a boat at *Cala Galera* nearby, one of the largest marinas on the coast, with space for 750 boats. Try to lunch at Porto Santo Stefano when the swordfish catch comes in. And should the water seem bluer on the other side of the strait, catch a ferry to the unblemished isles of Giglio and Giannutri. Details: *Azienda Autonoma di Soggiorno e Turismo della Costa d'Argento,* 55/A Corso Umberto, Porto Santo Stefano (Grosseto) 58019 (phone: 564-814208); or *Azienda Autonoma di Soggiorno e Turismo,* Isola del Giglio, Giglio Porto, 148 Via Umberto, Isola del Giglio (Grosseto) 58013 (phone: 564-809265).

PORTOFINO, Genoa, Liguria: Genoa divides the 180-mile-long marina known as the Italian Riviera midway along its gentle curve; Portofino is the jewel in the crown of the glittering Riviera di Levante (Riviera of the Rising Sun), which stretches east and south of the sprawling port city. A motley tumble of little houses clustered around a miniature natural harbor where yachts purr in at sunset in time for Campari-and-soda hour, Portofino mixes the scenically savage and the luxuriously manicured. Set like a chunk of coral on its hilly perch above the town, the *Splendido* hotel, a 3-tiered pink and white manse that once belonged to one of Liguria's noblest families, and today is owned by the luxury hotel chain Orient-Express, is a case in point. Don't miss the 2-hour walk to the Benedictine Abbey at San Fruttuoso and the grilled shrimp at *Da Giovanni,* the little restaurant and inn on the beach. Details: *Azienda Autonoma di Soggiorno,* 35 Via Roma, Portofino (Genova) 16034 (phone: 185-269078).

SENIGALLIA, Ancona, Marches: With miles of pale, velvety sand sloping gently into a warm and shallow sea, the Adriatic coast offers Italy's most immaculate strands. Less frantic in high season than more northerly parts, Senigallia is a prime destination for the sand castle set. Hundreds of family-run *pensioni* and hotels, in all price ranges, are scattered along a tidily modern beachfront; the historic old center represents the Renaissance and the baroque in pleasing harmony with a fortress, a palace, a church, a cathedral, and a papal wall that can be visited each day after a swim and lunch. An aged synagogue is a poignant reminder of a once-flourishing Jewish community. Details: *Azienda Autonoma di Soggiorno,* 2 Piazzale Morandi, Senigallia (Ancona) 60019 (phone: 71-792-2725).

SPERLONGA, Latina, Lazio: Attracting an intensely casual young crowd in June and July, and families with station wagons during the national holiday month of August, this tiny village is a Moorish labyrinth of white buildings, staircases, and alleyways stacked compactly on a seaside ledge, with the beach stretching below in a silken crescent. A few miles away is the Grotto of Tiberius, where the emperor maintained a huge marine theater and his own personal pleasure dome. A little-known museum there, the *Museo Nazionale Archeologico di Sperlonga,* houses several ancient monumental sculptures pieced together from thousands of fragments found buried in the grotto's pools and sands. Especially note the 2nd-century BC Greek sculptural depictions of Homer's *Odyssey.* Sperlonga itself, easily reached from both Rome and Naples, has only a handful of modest hotels; the lively, moderately priced *Corallo,* right in town, has a staircase that plummets to the beach. Also in the center is the *Florenza Residence,* a renovated palazzo with modern apartments. *La Playa* at Fiorelle on the beach is well equipped with creature comforts. After you climb back up at day's end, you'll be ready for a swim or a meal at *La Siesta.* Details: *Associazione Pro Loco,* 22 Corso San Leone, Sperlonga (Latina) 04029 (phone: 771-54796).

TAORMINA, Messina, Sicily: In Taormina, a medieval city carved into the side of Monte Tauro, visitors look up to the puffing, snow-covered Mount Etna and down into the warm, transparent seas of Sicily. It's also a place for exploring Greek and Roman ruins; trekking to the tower of Castel Mola for the last word in panoramic views; glancing at the lace and embroidery shops; then settling in for some serious *aperitivo* sipping and *passeggiata* ogling at a café on the Corso Umberto, where sleek Latin lover-boys still try to rub elbows with fetching blond maidens from the north. Evenings are for concerts or dance recitals at the outdoor Greek theater, as flowers perfume the soft air and reflections of the lights of fishing boats dance in the midnight sea. In August, the town tinsels with film festival followers, and the movie-set terrace of the glamorous *San Domenico* hotel (described in "Italy's Most Memorable Hostelries," *For the Experience*) blossoms with semi-famous faces. Details: *Azienda Autonoma di Soggiorno,* Piazza Santa Caterina, Taormina 98039 (phone: 942-23243; fax: 942-24941).

LIDO OF VENICE, Veneto: Just a reminder that while travelers are closely examining the most beautiful city in the world, it's also possible to swim, windsurf, sunbathe, and eat fresh shrimp on the Lido, a long, skinny island bordered on one side by the sea and on the other by the lagoon, just a short boat ride from downtown Venice. Besides golf, tennis, riding, biking, and boating, there are acres and acres of fine, soft sand — some handsome and public, some the combed-and-groomed-and-cabaña-lined private reserves of the great rambling seafront hotels that give the resort its air of slight decadence (the *Grand Hotel des Bains* was the setting for Thomas Mann's novella *Death in Venice*). Whichever patch of beach you choose for morning sun worship, it's still a snap to be strolling along the Venetian canals or sitting at a café in Piazza San Marco by late afternoon — and that sure beats the usual range of après-swim choices. (If you're willing to travel just a little farther afield, try the Lido di Jesolo. It lacks the Lido's tradition, but it's more charming in other ways. And the waters are bluer.) Details: *Azienda Autonoma di Soggiorno,* 71/C Ascensione, Piazza San Marco, Venezia 30127 (phone: 41-522-6356).

Sailing the Seas of Italy

Some of the greatest sailors who ever lived were Italians: Christopher Columbus, Amerigo Vespucci, Giovanni da Verrazano, and Giovanni Caboto, whom the world knew better as John Cabot. When these daring men set sail, the sea was a way of life. And since three-fourths of their country is surrounded by water, it should come as no surprise that Italians still take to the sea with great gusto. The country's four seas — the Tyrrhenian, the Ligurian, the Adriatic, and the Ionian — are each adventures that include charming ports, picturesque villages, crumbling ruins, historical monuments, elegant resorts, secluded coves, and incomparable beaches. Dock at any harbor and sample some of the country's finest cuisine or relax in a waterfront café. Or leave the crowds behind entirely and set sail for remote beaches on nearby islands.

Here are some of the best waters for sailing around Italy, as well as our selection of the prime ports of call.

TYRRHENIAN SEA: The most difficult sailing in the Mediterranean, the Tyrrhenian can be dangerous to small craft because of strong breezes, strong waves, and the *libeccio* — a treacherous southwest wind that strikes terror in the hearts of even the most competent experts. But as any sea enthusiast will tell you, the coastline here has what it takes to make those fears conquerable: sandy beaches, high peaks and promontories, quaint fishing villages, fine resorts, and the world's most beautiful islands. Capri, Ischia, and Sardinia alone can transform a simple cruise into a romantic and spectacular escapade. (However, not in July or August, when human hordes turn this watery paradise into a garbage dump.)

Indeed, approaching Ischia or Capri from the sea is one of the most breathtaking sailing experiences in Italy. As you sail on and through the sapphire sea that surrounds these fabulous islands, the scene framed by a cloudless sky, you have no doubt why even the most jaded travelers call this one of the most gorgeous places on earth. It's a special treat to explore hidden coves, visit the famed Blue Grotto (try to avoid the August crowds), call at the less known (but equally dramatic) Green Grotto, and stop at the Tiberian Baths.

The coast near Naples is all cliffs, fantastically sea-carved promontories, Saracen towers, and peaceful seaside towns — legendary Sorrento, villa-studded Posillipo, Moorish-looking Amalfi, and Positano ("a dream place that isn't quite real," according to John Steinbeck).

In Tuscany, farther north, visit Monte Argentario and Porto Ercole, walk along centuries-old cobblestone streets, or climb to high lookout points for bird's-eye views of the littoral.

And don't forget the Tuscan Archipelago. Sail around the island of Monte Cristo — "Treasure Island" to Alexandre Dumas — now a nature reserve. On the island of Giannutri, there are Roman remains to prowl and, on Giglio Island, an ancient castle and its fortifications to tour.

The knobby island of Elba, a gigantic, half-submerged mountain that is the largest landfall in this island group, is a splendid combination of rocky shores, sandy beaches, impressive mountains that descend straight to the sea, and clean waters whose depths hide ancient wrecks, rusted anchors, broken amphoras, and other relics of eras long past. The area around Sant'Andrea is particularly favored among boaters equipped with scuba gear.

The ultimate Tyrrhenian sailor's destination may be sun-washed Sardinia. The island's Costa Smeralda (Emerald Coast) radiates wealth and sophistication. Don't miss Porto Cervo, Porto Rotondo, Porto Conte, Stintino, and Golfo degli Aranci.

For charters in the Tyrrhenian: *Organizzazione Mare,* 172 Via Oderisi da Gubbio, Roma 00146 (phone: 6-559-3170).

For sailing along the Tuscan coast and Sardinia: *Top Service,* 40 Viale Duse, Firenze 50100 (phone: 55-608334).

For sailing in the Tuscan Archipelago and around Sardinia: *Renato Lessi,* Località Porto, Punta Ala, Grosseto 58040 (phone: 564-922793 or 564-920710).

For sailing around Sicily: *Salpancore,* Via Banchina Lupa la Cala, Palermo, Sicilia 90100 (phone: 91-331055; fax: 91-332128).

A few cautionary words: Although there is no test or license required for sailing the Italian seas, one crew member should be able to understand sufficient Italian to comprehend and to take notes from the radio *bollettino del mare,* and to deal with the local tourist port authorities. Dock space for overnighters becomes iffy in August. Many tourist ports are small, so arrive by 5 PM in peak season, when it's first-come, first-served.

LIGURIAN SEA: The going is a bit smoother in this body of water that laps at the strands of the Italian Riviera in central and northern Italy. Along the Tuscan and Ligurian coasts, beautiful old villas stand proudly on seaside cliffs, as if craning their necks to get a better glimpse of the view. Portovenere, an important harbor in Roman times and now a reference point for all sailors, is dreamy and picturesque — worth a special trip. The sight of the Genoese Gothic Church of San Pietro, rising dramatically out of sheer rock, overwhelms most visitors when first seen from the water. Ancient houses dating back 600 years (and more) line the tiny port and its pedestrian-only main street.

The other must is the more sophisticated Portofino, the celebrated port and resort near Genoa, extravagantly praised among globetrotters as "the world's pearl."

The rich and famous come here for the luxurious *Splendido* hotel, superb restaurants, and stylish boutiques; everyone enjoys the scenery — the tumble of brightly colored houses, and fisherfolk's boats, crystal-clear blue sea, olive trees, sea pines, and a lighthouse.

ADRIATIC AND IONIAN SEAS: The coastline here is linear and sandy rather than rocky and craggy, except in the south, so avid sailors usually prefer the Ligurian and Tyrrhenian alternatives. For this very reason, given the crowds, several ports can make a cruise here eminently enjoyable.

Muggia, an ancient Venetian village near Trieste is justly famous for its summer music festivals and folklore exhibits. The ancient seaside fishing town of Chioggia, in the Veneto region, has one of the largest and most picturesque fish markets in Italy and two canals photogenically packed with fishing boats.

In Puglia, to the south, fishing villages, historical sites, and archaeological remains abound. The mountain promontory of Gargano, the spur of Italy's boot, is edged with long, luxuriant strands, exotic rock formations, fantastic caves, and tiny coves perfect for picnicking. Vieste, an ancient fishing village with a medieval castle, is coming into its own as a resort. Manfredonia, Rodi Garganico, and whitewashed, cliff-top Peschici are other worthy ports of call. Just off shore are the jewel-like Tremiti Islands, virtually beachless fragments of rock that attract snorkelers and divers.

As the Adriatic flows into the Ionian, it becomes the Mediterranean's deepest sea, extending from Puglia to Basilicata and Calabria over to Sicily. Be sure to visit Gallipoli (in Puglia). This "Venus of the Ionian" shows off a wealth of historical, artistic, and archaeological treasures, not the least of which is the *Marechiaro* (phone: 833-476143) the city's best restaurant, perched on a large rock surrounded by water and connected to the mainland only by wooden planks. Details: *Skimar,* 4 Piazzetta Pattari, Milano 20122 (phone: 2-809166). There is also an office in Chioggia.

MORE SAILING INFORMATION

Local yacht clubs can be very helpful. In addition, there are several other reliable sources of information, among them:

Agenzia Nautica Altura (22/B Via Mecenate, Roma 00184; phone: 6-733242).

Federazione Italiana Vela (2 Viale Brigate Bisagno, Genova 16129; phone: 10-565723; fax: 10-592864).

Med-Rent a Boat (52 Via Piave, Roma 00187; phone: 6-422729). Rents sailboats with or without a skipper.

Renato Lessi (Località Porto, Punta Ala, Grossetto 58040; phone: 564-922793 or 564-920710). For sailing in many parts of Italy.

Velamareclub (12 Alzaia Naviglio Grande, Milano 20144; phone: 2-832-1739). Rents sailboats with or without skipper.

CANOEING

Canoeing is rapidly becoming a popular sport in Italy, and 250 clubs are currently affiliated with the *Italian Canoe Federation* (phone: 6-368-58215) in Rome. Each year from March to September, these organizations host a number of regional, national, and international competitions. In addition, they sponsor instructional programs for canoeists of all abilities on the best canoeing waters of the country — those in northern Italy, particularly in the Alpine regions. One of the better schools is *Centro Canoa Valle Anzasca* (3 Via San Pellico, Bernate fraz Casate (Milano) 20010; phone: 2-975-6282), which offers weekend and week-long sessions on the Anza River.

LAKE AND CANAL CRUISING

With the exception of the Po River, Italy's largest, Italian rivers are so shallow and rocky that river cruising is virtually nonexistent. The lakes are another matter, though, and the country's several organized boat excursions may well prove a highlight of your Italian sojourn.

LAKE MAGGIORE, Piedmont: The shores of this 40-mile-long, island-studded expanse of blue, nestled at the foot of the northern Italian mountains, are sometimes rugged, sometimes lush with subtropical vegetation — magnolias, azaleas, palms, and orange and lemon trees. Lake cruises here provide a view of the 14th-century castle of Rocca di Angera, the lovely town of Ispra, and the sanctuary of Santa Caterina del Sasso. In the center of the lake are the sweetly scented Borromean Islands. The baroque gem known as Isola Bella (Beautiful Island), the busiest and most famous, is capped by gracious gardens and inhabited by lacy albino peacocks; if you can somehow overlook the covey of tacky souvenir stands, it is a worthwhile sight. Isola Madre (Mother Island) has even more splendid gardens, luxuriant with 140-year-old cypress, massive palms, and 80-yard-long wisterias. Isola dei Pescatori (Fishermen's Island) is a simple folk legend of a place, with narrow alleyways and a pretty port full of little red and yellow houses. On the mainland is Stresa, a slightly stuffy, stately resort that livens up in September, when the annual festival of lyrical music comes to town. Details: *Skimar,* 4 Piazzetta Pattari, Milano 20122 (phone: 2-809166).

CANALS OF VENICE: It may be hard to swallow the instinctive reluctance to do anything so expressly aimed at innocent tourists as hiring one of the gondolas that, elegant as black swans, ply the Venetian canals. But once you overcome your misgivings, you're in for an experience that is poetic, mysterious — and worth every lira that it will cost. It's a unique experience, particularly at night, when the pale moonlight drapes the city's Gothic palaces in silver, and the island of San Giorgio Maggiore and the Giudecca all become a heart-stopping stage that calls to mind Robert Browning's *In a Gondola* and Thomas Mann's *Death in Venice.* Rates — 30% higher after dark — should not vary from one gondolier to another; choose one who is pleasant (and perhaps not too talkative, since twisting around to keep up your end of the conversation can be a bother). And if you choose against the gondola because of price or principle, remember that Venice boasts the only public transportation system that actually adds to the joy of the city. With five in a gondola, the cost of the 50-minute ride is less intimidating. Take your pick of *traghetti, motoscafi,* and *vaporetti,* depending on where you want to go and how fast. With a good map, it's possible to master the transportation system in about 10 minutes. To get started, see "Getting Around" in *Venice,* THE CITIES.

VENETO WATERWAYS, Veneto: During the 16th century, every Venetian who could afford it built a summer residence along the Brenta Canal, and the so-called Brenta Riviera was born. A cruise from Venice inland toward Padua along its peaceful green waters conjures up images of the trip as it doubtless was made regularly by the nobility during the 17th and 18th centuries. The vessel is the modern *Il Burchiello,* and the scenery is a string of classical villas, many of which were designed by Andrea Palladio and his contemporaries. The excursion, which includes a bus return from Padua, begins just after 9 AM at the Pontile Giardinetto near Piazza San Marco and takes a full day. Lunch is available on board. Details: *Compagnia Italiana Turismo (CIT),* Piazza San Marco (phone: 41-528-5480); or *Siamic Express,* 42 Via Trieste, Padova 35100 (phone: 49-660944). See also *Villa Foscari* in "Twenty-five Centuries of History: Italy's Museums and Monuments," *For the Mind.*

Fishing

The truth is that catching a fish in Italian waters is tougher than elsewhere in the world. The indiscriminate angling of the past and the pollution of the present have taken their toll, not only on countless Italian rivers, streams, and lakes, but also on its seas — the Tyrrhenian, the Adriatic, the Ligurian, and the Ionian. So the mere act of reeling in a live one in Italy brands the sportsman as a force to be reckoned with.

Nonetheless, fishing can provide some real adventure during an Italian tour. The Alps and the Apennines give life to diverse water systems, and with a bit of patience and some luck, there's a fish waiting to be caught somewhere. If not, there's always peace and quiet — and the delightful Italian scenery.

SEA ANGLING

Three-fourths of Italian territory is coastal, and on many islands the fishing is actually quite good — most notably around Sicily and Sardinia.

No license is needed to fish in these waters. However, there are regulations on size, species, seasons, and the like. Divers with oxygen tanks may not spearfish. For the particulars, check with the *Federazione Italiana Pesca Sportiva e Attività Subacquea,* or *FIPS* (Italian Fishing Federation; 16/A Piazza Emporio, Roma; phone: 6-575-5253). For local information, ask for the address and phone number of the *FIPS* office nearest the area where you plan to fish. Information about charter and party boats is readily available from yacht clubs, and it's easy to rendezvous with local fishermen (and hear a few good yarns) at local bait-and-tackle shops. Don't worry about the language barrier. The Italian who speaks no English will probably rush off to grab a countryman who does.

Other good information sources are the magazines *Il Subacqueo,* about spearfishing and scuba diving, and *Pesca Mare,* available on newsstands or through its offices at *Edizioni Aeronautiche Italiane* (4 Via Guinicelli, Firenze 501131; phone: 55-574774 or 55-570144). The staff can be quite helpful.

ADRIATIC SEA: Most Italian anglers know this body of water as Old Faithful — especially for blue shark (May through September) and giant tuna (late July through late October). Porto Barricata and Albarella are the chief angling centers, and the *Porto Barricata Fishing Club* (Scardovari; Rovigo; phone: 426-89125) organizes numerous annual tournaments.

For information about charters and fishing schools, contact *Gianni Bison,* GIBI, 4 Via Firenze, Tencarola (Padova) 35030 (phone: 49-624881).

LIGURIAN SEA: Here, along the Italian Riviera, the resorts of Alassio, Rapallo, and busy, sometimes chaotic San Remo are the best centers for big-game fishing. For details, contact the local yacht clubs and the Azienda Autonoma di Soggiorno e Turismo (AAST; Tourist Board) of each town or Azienda Promozionale di Turismo (APT).

TYRRHENIAN SEA: Punta Ala, in southern Tuscany, is an angling hot spot, especially in September and October, when hundreds of giant tuna pass offshore. For details on fishing trips and charters, contact *Renato Lessi* (Località Porto, 58040 Punta Ala, Grosseto; phone: 564-922793 or 564-920710). Mr. Lessi can introduce traveling anglers to local fishermen equipped to take them out fishing — and share their secrets.

Near the islands, where the waters are generally cleaner, fishing is even better. Sardinian action centers on Cagliari in Carlo Forte and the Asinara Gulf. For details, contact the *Ente Provinciale per il Turismo–Cagliari* (9 Piazza Deffenu, Cagliari 09100; phone: 70-663207). In Sicily, the best fishing, especially for tuna, is near the port of Milazzo. Your best contact is the *Associazione Turistica Pro Loco–Milazzo* (14 Piazza Caio Duilio, Milazzo; phone: 90-928-1231). Waters off the island of Ischia, near Naples, can also yield full creels. For information, contact the *Ente Provinciale per il Turismo–Naples* (Piazza dei Martiri 58, Scala B/Staircase B; phone: 81-405311) or the *Azienda Autonoma di Soggiorno e Turismo–Ischia* (116 Corso Vittoria Colonna, Ischia 8077; phone: 81-991464).

The Tyrrhenian Sea is also the best place for surf casting — shore fishing from rocks, beaches, and piers — or rod fishing from small boats. Quarry include bass, bogue, conger, cuttlefish, grouper, moray eel, mullet, saddled bream, and scad.

FRESHWATER ANGLING

Italy's prime freshwater sport is in northern Italy, especially in the Alps, Piedmont, Lombardy, Venetia, and Emilia-Romagna.

The northern Italian lakes — Como, Maggiore, Garda, and Iseo — are good for perch, pike, trout, and carp, shiners, and other fish of the cyprinid family. Mountain streams and rivers can produce good catches of brown and tiger trout. The fish population of valley rivers is varied. Sturgeon can be found in abundance in the Ticino and Po; in the former, you'll also find tiger trout. Canals, ponds, coves, and creeks of flatter areas are full of perch and pike.

Italy's main lakes are populated by those species and others — *Fallax lacustris,* twaite shad, and brown trout. The latter can be caught from shore with minnows during the hotter months. Lake Garda is the place to cast for carp. The Magra River, between the regions of Liguria, Tuscany, and Emilia-Romagna, is home to a variety of trout, as are the Abruzzo and Molise regions, where numerous slow-current rivers are found.

Lazio is fine for pike and perch, whereas the rest of central Italy offers an abundance of salmonoid *Coregonus italicus* — a member of the family that also includes trout and whitefish.

Licenses are required for freshwater fishing. They cost approximately $5 and can be obtained in any comune (Town Hall) or municipality, in the section called Ufficio Caccia e Pesca (Office of Hunting and Fishing). A temporary fishing license can also be obtained through the *Italian Fishing Federation* (*FIPS,* 16/A Piazza Emporio, Roma; phone: 6-575-5253), or at its provincial offices, which can be found in every city and large town.

FIPS also can give advice on all the open and closed seasons, creel limits, and permitted bait and tackle — which vary from one species (and region) to another. In addition, the organization owns fishing rights to many streams and small lakes. To fish them, simply apply to one of its offices. Be sure not to attempt to fish its waterways without membership as they are well patrolled and the fines are steep — even for foreigners who have made an honest mistake.

For further information, consult the publication *Pescare,* available on newsstands or from the publishers (Editoriale Olimpia, 7 Viale Milton, Firenze 50129; phone: 55-473843). Staff members will gladly answer any question you might have on Italian freshwater fishing. Once you've decided on a location for your angling expedition, get additional details from the nearest Azienda Autonoma di Soggiorno e Turismo (Tourist Board), fishing club (get addresses from *FIPS*), or bait-and-tackle shop.

Horsing Around, Italian Style

When you begin to believe that Italians are irretrievably wedded to their automobiles body and soul, remember that Italy's equestrian tradition goes back to the *condottieri* — the great mounted warrior-princes of the Renaissance. Notice, too, sometime just how many *Olympic* medals the Italians gallop off with in the four-footed competition. And then consider how many fine places there are for the horse-loving tourist to pursue his or her avocation, from the Alpine top of the boot to the Sicilian stirrup. You may change your mind about Italians and autos.

There are manicured manors where counts cantered, completely informal farmhouses converted to equitation to supplement faltering agricultural income, and all manner of establishments in between. For extensive information about simple, rustic accommodations throughout Italy, contact *Agriturist* (101 Corso Vittorio Emanuele, Roma 00186; phone: 6-651-2342) and the *National Association for Equestrian Tourism* (*ANTE;* 5 Via Alfonso Borelli, Roma 00161; phone: 6-444-1179). In Sardinia, contact *Agriturismo a Cavallo* (Casella Postale 107, Oristano 09170; phone: 783-418066). A representative selection of Italy's equitation establishments follows.

ALABIRDI, Arborea, Sardinia: Surrounded by pine woods near the beach on Sardinia's west coast, this complex of hotel, bungalows, and mini-apartments — one of Italy's best-equipped equitation centers — offers dedicated riders a choice of 45 horses and three first-rate instructors. The training is high-powered, with an emphasis on acquiring close-to-professional expertise. But there are also rambling excursions along the shore and into the neighboring countryside. That the sea is always at your stirrup tips is especially welcome in summer at the end of a tough day in the saddle. In spring and fall, there are vast flocks of migrating birds to observe, and the exotic flamingo and heron are regular winter visitors. Details: *Alabirdi,* 24 Strada a Mare, Arborea (Oristano) 09092 (phone: 783-801086; fax: 783-791167).

LE CANNELLE, Parco dell'Uccellina, Tuscany: The atmosphere at this parkland establishment is rough and ready, and the devotion to riding is single-minded. Paths wander through wild Mediterranean brush or along vast deserted expanses of parkland beach. Wild boar, fox, and horned white cattle are the only intruders. Housing is in 8 unadorned bungalows, and guests bring and prepare their own provisions. Since only one Land Rover is permitted on the single bumpy road connecting *Le Cannelle* to civilization, visitors must call ahead to request pickup at the entrance to the protected area. Details: *Le Cannelle,* Parco dell'Uccellina, Talamone (Grosseto) 58010 (phone: 564-887020).

FATTORIA CERRETO, Mosciano Sant'Angelo, Abruzzo: For those who want sea and saddle as a daily double, here is the best bet. Whether guests headquarter in one of the four rooms at the farm itself or at the *Smeraldo* hotel, in a grove of pine and eucalyptus at Giulianova on the Adriatic a few miles away, it's a delight to ride all morning and then while away entire afternoons stretched out in the sun. The atmosphere is cheerful and countrified; the town of Giulianova (pop. 15,000), which has several good restaurants, is the destination of choice for those seeking something a bit more worldly. The farm's 20 horses are well trained, with good mounts for riders of any level of skill. The horses are also excellent for mounted exploration of the area, and week-long trips that cover 100 miles or more in the Abruzzo foothills can be arranged. Details: *Fattoria Cerreto,* Colle Cacio, Mosciano Sant'Angelo (Teramo) 64025 (phone: 85-864-8197).

FONTANA PILA, Pontelatone, Campania: Set on 4,000 acres of vineyard, orchard, and pastureland, this establishment just north of Naples, near the medieval town of Caserta, has some 15 horses for visiting riders and another score that local owners board permanently in the well-groomed stables. Opportunities for manège, jumping, instruction, and mounted excursions are varied and ample. Forty guests can be housed in the center's comfortable double rooms, and there are facilities for campers as well. For un-reiny days, there's boating and fishing on the nearby Volturno River; hunting for boar, pheasant, and fox in the area; and sightseeing aplenty (the Norman cathedral at Capua, the royal palace at Caserta). When in Caserta, try the spaghetti with eggplant and mozzarella at the *Antica Locanda Massa* (55 Via Mazzini) and the assortment of game at *La Castellana* (4 Via Torre, in Caserta Vecchia). Details: *Fontana Pila,* 69 Via Ponte Pellegrino, Pontelatone (Caserta) 81050 (phone: 823-878107).

LA MANDRIA, Candelo, Piedmont: There really was gold in them thar hills, and in a day's ride from La Mandria you'll still see hopefuls panning for it in shallow riverbeds that cross the wild Baraggia plateau, where this equestrian holiday center is situated. The skilled and exacting management offers holidays in all-sized portions, from the equivalent of an afternoon's snack to a fortnight-long banquet that has riders traveling past ancient Roman gold mines or recently reclaimed trails between abandoned medieval castles. The plateau is on thousands of acres of state property, all forest-covered and uninhabited, and riding out from this once-fortified medieval village seems almost like time travel, though Candelo is only about an hour's drive from either Turin or Milan. Some 20 horses and a half dozen ponies are available to the 15 guests who can be accommodated in the restored farmhouse and the 10 who lodge in the annex; overnight trips include accommodations in modest inns en route. Expert riders can go wherever they wish and leave their youngsters in experienced hands. The food here features local country dishes, complemented by some very urbane wines. Details: *Tenuta La Mandria,* Candelo (Vercelli) 13062 (phone: 15-53078).

RENDOLA RIDING, Montevarchi, Tuscany: The proprietor of this pastoral riding center goes by the very Anglo-Saxon name of Jenny Bawtree. But the setting, the food, and the gracious simplicity of the farmhouse accommodations are pure Tuscan, and the bridle paths rise and fall over the vineyard-clad hills of Chianti itself. This is art and wine country, and Arezzo, Florence, and Siena are comfortable day trips away — by motorized horsepower for the saddle-weary. In the sunbaked summer months, the party moves to a mountain lodge in the cool woods of Vallombrosa, and the excursions wind through forests and greener pastures. Beginners start with a few lessons in the training ring (*maneggio*) before going out for brief outings; experts join 2- to 5-day trips around the area. *Rendola Riding* has 20 horses and can house 15 people in seven bedrooms year-round. Details: *Rendola Riding,* Rendola Valdarno (Arezzo) 52020 (phone: 55-970-7045); in summer, Centro Equitazione Vallombrosa, Saltino (Firenze) 50060 (phone: 55-862018).

RIFUGIO PRATEGIANO, Montieri, Tuscany: At this stone-faced, wooden-shuttered hotel high in the hills between Siena and the Tyrrhenian coast, beginners can alternate riding lessons with lounging sessions around the swimming pool and garden, while more experienced equestrians can range over the establishment's woods and meadows, along Etruscan roads, across burbling streams, and to hidden ruins. Tiny lakes, miniature churches, stark castles, and winding pathways to the sea, discovered during the day's ride, are the topics of dinnertime conversation. Choose from a dozen guided itineraries, with the mountaintop village of Gerfalco, the glorious abandoned abbey of San Galgano, and the river Merse, where riders can swim in late spring and summer, as prime points of interest. There also are longer organized trips to various places such as Volterra. The area is perfect for hiking and biking as well, though the hills are awesome in the heat of July and August. Montieri itself is attractive and unspoiled, and Siena, Volterra, and San Gimignano are all within easy reach by car. Details: *Rifugio Prategiano,* Montieri (Grosseto) 50026 (phone: 566-997703).

LA SUBIDA, Cormons, Friuli–Venezia Giulia: The countryside in this rural northeast corner of Italy, bordering Yugoslavia, is a patchwork of meadows and pastures, orchards and vineyards, chestnut forests and rustic churches, farms and mountain views; and this center is in perfect keeping with its surroundings. A handful of little houses, set on a verdant hillside, provide apartment lodgings, and the handsome family-run trattoria provides grilled specialties typical of the nearby Julian Alps, as well as the local polenta, lightly smoked hams, potato-and-fruit dumplings (*knödel*), and all manner of game. The main business of every day is riding, and a saunter up to the ruins of the castle at Monte Quarin opens a view that stretches from the Alps to the Adriatic. However, *La Subida* also has a pool, a children's playground, a stable of bicycles, and a lighted tennis court. Guests normally require long hours in the saddle to work off the richness of the cuisine. The wine of the local Collio area is superb, and in short supply elsewhere, and it makes a very festive end to a day on the trail. Details: *La Subida,* 22 Località Monte Subida, Cormons (Gorizia) 34071 (phone: 481-60531).

VALLEBONA, Pontassieve, Tuscany: Visitors to Vallebona can spend mornings on horseback and afternoons on foot exploring Florence, only a 20-minute drive away. A maximum of 15 guests stay in the simple rooms in this restored Tuscan farmhouse, help care for one of the 25 horses, putter in the garden, and generally participate in the busy, informal life on the farm. The center also organizes 3- to 10-day excursions to Etruscan sites, mountain trail rides, and sightseeing along the river valleys between Siena and Grosseto. Accommodations along these routes is in tents or on farms. Details: *Centro Ippico Vallebona,* Fattoria Lavaccho, 32 Via di Grignano, Pontassieve (Firenze) 50064 (phone: 55-839246).

ROME, Lazio: There are several riding schools and clubs inside the capital, and dozens more in the countryside surrounding the city. A regional branch of the *National Association for Equestrian Tourism* (*ANTE*) arranges special events for riders and can provide a complete list of local facilities. Better than almost any other Italian experience anywhere, a day trip through woods and vineyards to a tiny Roman amphitheater will help a visitor envision what Italy was like before the Fiat Age. Details: *ANTE,* 5 Via A. Borelli, Roma (phone: 6-444-1179).

Elsewhere in and around Rome, a number of establishments can provide information on sporting opportunities:

Centro Ippico Monte del Pavone organizes summer nighttime rides around the nature reserve of Lake Martignano. Via Valle di Baccano, Campagnano (Roma) 00194 (phone: 6-904-1378).

Società Ippica Romana (30 Via Monti della Farnesina, Roma; phone: 6-396-6386).

OTHER EXPERIENCES OF EQUINE ITALY

In addition to equestrian vacations such as those detailed above, another handful of Italian experiences should be on every horse lover's Italian must-see list:

Palio – A no-holds-barred race around the packed Piazza del Campo in Siena, with every rider garbed in Renaissance costume. Twice yearly, July 2 and August 16. Make plans far ahead, see *Siena* in THE CITIES.

Fieracavalli – A gigantic 4-day fair and market in mid-November that turns Verona into a thousand-horse town, with colorful sales and auctions, races, exhibitions, and a show of everything that's new and stylish in riding equipment.

Annual Horse Show, Rome – Held in the Piazza di Siena in the Villa Borghese park every May, it offers some of Europe's best and most aristocratic jumping competitions and ends with a breathtaking *carabinieri* cavalry charge. A real event.

Le Capannelle Racetrack – If you have a free sunny Sunday afternoon in Rome and a couple of dollars burning a hole in your pocket, blow the whole packet here, just beyond Ciampino Airport. The atmosphere is Italy's turfiest.

Biking

With the Alps across the top and the Apennines down the middle, there's not a great deal of flat terrain left for leisurely pedaling. But this is a nation of great bicycling traditions, and every Sunday on country roads all over the boot legions of capped and uniformed bicyclists hunch over their handlebars, pretending to be Saronni or Fausto Coppi.

The bicycle is also the nimblest transportation through the traffic-strangled cities, and most foreign pedalers can easily manage the Seven Hills of Rome in low gear. But a word to the two-wheeled: Italian automobile drivers consider cyclists more a nuisance than folks entitled to a share of the roadway. Ride with extreme caution — and a solid helmet. (For more details, see "Biking" in *Camping and Caravanning, Hiking and Biking,* GETTING READY TO GO.)

ITALIAN LAKES: The Italian lake region provides some of Italy's best cycling. The roadways are fairly flat, particularly around the lakes themselves, the summer temperatures moderate, the towns attractive and well spaced, and the landscape a lyrical mix of lemon groves, palm trees, and other subtropical vegetation against an Alpine backdrop. Visitors can stop at each of the five lakes, one by one, or cyclists with 2 weeks' vacation and the stamina to go 500 miles (800 km) can take a once-in-a-lifetime two-wheel ride around them all.

This circuit begins on Lake Como at Menaggio, an inviting resort town of considerable charm, then travels north to Gravedona, follows the lake shore around its northern tip, and heads southward, skirting Lago di Lecco's eastern shore.

To visit Lake d'Iseo and Lake Garda, the next lakeland destinations, the route passes through the busy center of Bergamo. Make a stop in the charming medieval part of the town, set high above the Lombardy plain, before continuing on to Lake d'Iseo, where George Sand's heroine Lucrezia came to live with her Prince Karol, and the dominant scenic elements are wild mountainsides and lots of shimmering gray-green olive trees. Circle this scenic, less-developed lake, passing through Sarnico, Lovere, and Iseo, and then head for Garda.

The largest and arguably the most spectacular of the Italian lakes (the poet Virgil called it a sea), Garda is wild and Alpine in the north, softer and greener to the south. The stretch between Salò, Mussolini's last headquarters, and Riva del Garda is lush, verdant, and entirely spectacular, particularly when the late afternoon sunlight gilds the eastern shore; in 27 miles, this road follows the corniche over 56 bridges and burrows through 70 tunnels.

Having pedaled through the olive groves, vineyards, and cypress stands of the eastern shore, head back to Como and admire its shores crowded with fig and mulberry trees. Pedal alongside wilder and more exotic Lake Lugano and finally to Lake Maggiore, where Hemingway set *Farewell to Arms,* and the little town of Luino. From there, circle broad Maggiore, weaving in and out of Switzerland, or bike to Lavena and take the ferry to the western shore. Hostels, campgrounds, and hotels dot the way. Just stay out of the area in August, Italy's vacation rush hour. Details: *Ente Provinciale per il Turismo,* 17 Piazza Cavour, Como 22100 (phone: 31-262091).

TUSCANY: An interesting circuit of about 50 miles (80 km) starts in the busy medieval city of Prato, not far from Florence. Take the road to Figline, Schignano, Migliana, Vernio, and Montepiano, all charming country towns way off the tourist track. From Montepiano the road passes through green and golden farmland to Barberino, Calenzano, and back to Prato, itself worth a good long look. You'll find many suggested itineraries for trips all over the country in *Cicloturismo,* a monthly biking magazine in Italian, available at newsstands.

ROME: Few tourists (and fewer Romans) ever see the verdant Rome it's possible to enjoy on the Villa Circuit, which travels 18 miles (29 km) from one major public park to another, all former private estates. Start on the silent residential Aventine Hill, cross the Tiber, and climb up the Gianicolo to the vast Villa Doria Pamphili. Dozens of muskrats, descendants of a single pair brought here as part of an experiment, waddle and paddle around the lake in the parks' center. Pass by St. Peter's, cross the river again, and pedal through the Villa Borghese gardens. The Pincio terrace, overlooking Piazza del Popolo, offers the classic view of Rome captured by northern painters in love with the city's unique light. From the Borghese park due north to Via Salaria, it's a short ride to the Villa Ada, wooded and aristocratic — our final suggested stop. *Nino Collati* (82 Via del Pellegrino, Roma; phone: 6-654-1084) has rental bikes, including tandems with two, three, and even four places. There are also rentals at the entrance to the Metro at Piazza di Spagna, at Piazza del Popolo, and on Lungotevere Marzio. Along the Via Flaminia, leading down from Piazza del Popolo, is the city's first bike trail that follows the Tiber.

PARCO NAZIONALE D'ABRUZZO: Two hours east of Rome, this national park is crisscrossed by 50 miles (80 km) of an almost carless asphalt road, as well as by a network of neglected country roads that are good for those with mountain bikes. The park has a healthy population of bears, foxes, mountain goats, and even wolves — all of which you're more likely to get a glimpse of if you plan an early morning ride in the spring or fall. Wonderful for walking, too. Good maps are available from the park authorities. From *Easter* through early autumn (depending on snow), mountain bikes are available for rent from *Coop. Ecotur,* 13 Via Santa Lucia, Pescasseroli (Aquila) 67032 (phone: 863-912760).

IL GIRO D'ITALIA: If you happen to have a spare semester to train, a 10-speed Bianchi bike, and the stamina of Stallone, you might attempt to follow in the tire treads of the speed demons who participate in this 3-week-long May (or early June) bike race — one of the great sports events of Italy's year. The competition has been going on for 70 years, covering 2,400 miles and climbing a grueling assortment of Alpine passes. Followed passionately both on television and by cheering crowds along the nation's roads, this galvanizing marathon is the *Wimbledon* and *Kentucky Derby* of biking champions. The route changes each year and is announced in February by its newspaper sponsor, *La Gazzetta dello Sport.* Details: *Federazione Ciclistica Italiana,* 25 Viale Tecnica, Roma 00196 (phone: 6-593-5462).

Walking

Despite the more familiar images of thronged piazze and medieval quarters as compact as a box of stone dominoes, a striking 21% of all Italy is still wooded, and wild mountains loom over a good deal more. The Aosta Valley alone offers a dozen peaks over 13,000 feet (4,000 meters) and a hundred-odd glaciers. The available wilderness ranges from northern tundras to subtropical woods and is home to wolf, brown bear, moufflon, ibex, and other fauna largely extinct in the rest of Europe. Despite the web of autostradas that now laces this passionately automotive country, hikeable, bikeable dirt roads still veer off the most beaten tourist tracks. In the Alps, many of these are dotted with mountain huts (*rifugi*) that provide bed, blankets, and board tasty enough that you don't forget where you are.

So hurry and see the countryside while the supply lasts — let your feet rush in where your Fiat cannot tread. Tromp from Tuscan hill town to Tuscan hill town, with a loaf of bread under your arm and a wineskin of brunello di Montalcino over your shoulder. Trek from *rifugio* to *rifugio* along the spiky, soaring ridges of the Dolomites. Wander from cliffside pasta to seaside gelato along the old Roman mule paths of Capri.

For simple, rustic accommodations in some of Italy's most walkable areas, consult the directory of farms and chalets published by *Agriturist* (101 Corso Vittorio Emanuele, Roma 00186 (phone: 6-651-2342), and for ecology and farming camps, get in touch with the *World Wildlife Fund National Headquarters* (290 Via Salaria, Roma; phone: 6-852492). For more details on accommodations, see *Camping and Caravanning, Hiking and Biking,* GETTING READY TO GO.

PARCO NAZIONALE DEL GRAN PARADISO, Aosta, Valle d'Aosta: Some of Europe's highest mountains — Monte Bianco (a.k.a. Mont-Blanc), Monte Cervino (known outside Italy as the Matterhorn), and Monte Rosa — stand on the border between Italy, France, and Switzerland and protect this green ribbon of valley from the colder, wetter weather of the north. But the relatively mild climate is only one reason that the spacious Gran Paradiso National Park, tucked in a large corner of the Valle d'Aosta, lives up to its name for dedicated walkers.

When Italy was a kingdom, the royal hunting parties rode in these hills along 43 miles of high-altitude bridle paths — and all of these can be hiked today. There are also a number of well-appointed mountain huts (open all summer) and wildlife galore, which is most often visible at day's end by those who lodge in one of the *rifugi:* when the day-trippers have gone, the ibex and chamois that populate the park come loping down the mountainsides, and it's very pleasant to spend the evening hours watching them leap and wrestle in the fading light. Otherwise, the best base for walking is either small, quiet Degioz in the neighboring Valsavaranche, or busy, cheerful Cogne, which organizes guided mountain excursions for visitors. Details: *Ufficio Informazioni Turistiche Regionale,* Piazza Narbonne, Aosta 11100 (phone: 165-303725).

PARCO NAZIONALE DELLO STELVIO, Bormio, Lombardy: The largest protected area in Italy, this park just south of Switzerland offers some of the most attractive hiking in the Alps. Deer, chamois, ibex, marmots, and wild goats populate the park, and hikers have occasion to encounter many of them on most local rambles. One particularly interesting tour is the 5-day trip to the massif of the Gran Zebrù, which represents about 25 hours of solid trekking from Sant'Antonio near Bormio, up the Gran Zebrù, and back to Santa Caterina Valfurva. En route, there are several refuges and marvelously varied scenery — glaciers, Alpine tundra, evergreen forests. However, since the paths can be steep, this is definitely for experienced walkers only. For other treks for lesser levels of expertise, and for information about expert guides, contact the park management: *Direzione Parco Nazionale dello Stelvio,* 54 Via Monte Braulio, Bormio (Sondrio) 23032 (phone: 342-905151).

ISOLA DI CAPRAIA, Livorno, Tuscany: When you make the 2-hour ferry ride here from Livorno and the teeming Italian Riviera, expect a tiny port village, a castle, no boutiques, no nightlife, very few tourists, and some wonderful walking through an untouched Mediterranean landscape. One path leads to the Punta della Bella Vista, a perfect wide-angle view of coast and shimmering Ligurian Sea. Other walking routes wind along hillsides perfumed with wild lilies and jasmine, brilliant with heather, rosemary, and cyclamen. Bird watchers will find kindred souls and expert guides. The rare Corsican gull nests on these shores; it can live only where the sea is pure and limpid. For swimming, rent a boat to sail to the tiny secluded coves a few minutes from the port. The prettiest among the handful of hotels and *pensioni* is *Il Saracino.* Private rooms are available, especially after August 20 or in the early summer. Details: *Pro Loco,* Isola di Capraia (Livorno) 57032 (phone: 586-905138); *Il Saracino,* Isola di Capraia (Livorno) 57032 (phone: 586-905018).

LAGO DEL MIAGE, Courmayeur, Valle d'Aosta: A 3-hour ramble from the mountain town of Courmayeur leads to this sky-blue glacier lake surrounded by beautiful woods. The vista of the neighboring Monte Bianco group is stupendous. The area offers many other mountain hikes, including a demanding 10-day circuit of Monte Bianco itself. Details: *Azienda Autonoma di Soggiorno e Turismo,* Piazzale Monte Bianco, Courmayeur (Aosta) 11013 (phone: 165-842060).

CINQUE TERRE, La Spezia, Liguria: Perched on the rocky coast north of La Spezia, these five villages, world-famous for their wine, once were accessible only by dirt road or by sea, and are now reachable by paved road or train. Once there, paths and trails along the beach, or high up through the vineyards and olive groves, will lead you from one to the other in the course of a day or two (although if you want to walk between two of villages, it will take you only a couple of hours; be careful — some of the paths are narrow and without railings). There's a chance to ogle the magnificent, craggy coast views all along the way. From Riomaggiore, a favorite walk is along the Via dell'Amore, the most picturesque and most beautiful. The northernmost town, Monterosso al Mare, has a few hotels; but simple accommodations can be found in the other four. Details: *Ente Provinciale per il Turismo,* 47 Viale Mazzini, La Spezia 19100 (phone: 187-770900).

BRENTA DOLOMITES, Madonna di Campiglio, Trentino: Only the most fearless walkers will want to tackle the hiking trails of this region. Along these *vie ferrate* (iron trails), bracelets and necklaces of iron cable have been anchored to the mountain at just the point that most sensible mortals would elect to turn back. (A prime example is the Via delle Bocchette — the "route of tiny passageways" — where the path clings precariously to the sides of sheer rock wall hundreds of feet above the gashes between the mountains.) Elsewhere, ladders are embedded in scrambles too steep for hands and knees. If the illusion, generally of grave danger, becomes too real, retreat to the delights of the *Madonna di Campiglio* resort, where golf and swimming keep guests risklessly active at close to the same altitude. Details: *Azienda Autonoma di Soggiorno,* Madonna di Campiglio (Trento) 38084 (phone: 465-42000). See also *Italy's Unparalleled Skiing.*

MONTE BALDO, Malcesine, Veneto: The little chain of mountains that separates Lake Garda from the Adige River is a haven for walkers interested in plants and flowers. The unusual varieties found here attract professional as well as amateur botanists. Dramatic views over the lake are an added delight at this spot approximately 25 miles (40 km) north of Verona. Details: *Azienda Promozionale di Turismo (APT),* 6-8 Via Capitanato, Malcesine, Verona (phone: 45-740-0044).

CATINACCIO DOLOMITES, Nova Levante, Alto Adige: Located about 12 miles (19 km) north of Bolzano, this sturdy, simple mountain town, known as Welschnofen by its German-speaking population, makes a fine base for walkers of every degree of expertise. Gentle, shady forest paths strike out in all directions. To the west is hill country and a descent to the Adige Valley and civilization. The rugged Latemar massif is to the south. Eastward are the long, rose-colored ridges of the Dolomites' Catinaccio range. Cable cars and chair lifts have made approaches to their dramatic footpaths much easier, and strenuous climbs are no longer a necessary ingredient of a trek here. But the ambitious and experienced will find challenging *vie ferrate,* with cables and ladders at crucial points; real experts can try the towering spirits of the Vaiolet. Refuges at frequent intervals provide both lunches and overnight lodging. Plan on half a day in engaging Bolzano, which is more Austrian than Italian — like most of the Alto Adige region. Details: *Azienda Autonoma di Soggiorno e Turismo,* 5 Via Carezza, Nova Levante (Bolzano) 39056 (phone: 471-613126; fax: 471-613360).

SAN FRUTTUOSO, Portofino, Liguria: Instead of the pleasant half-hour boat ride from the resort town of Camogli (55 minutes from Portofino) to this fascinating medieval abbey, walk an extraordinary hour and a half from Portofino with the sea and shoreline at your feet around every bend. The final reward is a picture-book inn, *Da Giovanni,* on the beach and accessible only by water or on foot. Details: *Azienda Autonoma di Soggiorno,* 35 Via Roma, Portofino (Genova) 16034 (phone: 185-269078).

PARCO NATURALE ALTA VAL SESIA, Rima, Piedmont: The austere trails of this protected mountain area lead out from several neighboring towns. The perfectly preserved village of Rima is the most beautiful starting point, with its carefully restored rustic houses of stone and wood, built to resist the heaviest snowfalls. Details: *Comunità Montana Val Sesia,* 5 Corso Roma, Varallo Sesia (Vercelli) 13019 (phone: 163-51555).

PARCO NAZIONALE DEL CIRCEO, Sabaudia, Lazio: A dangerous land of sorcery and spells when Odysseus passed through 3,000 years ago, the scene of Circe's mythical magic is now an enchanting national park on the edge of the Tyrrhenian Sea. In the landscape where Odysseus brought down a deer, the modern visitor can still catch glimpses of wild boar, fox, and hare. An experienced hiker can scramble over the promontory of Monte Circeo, which seems, when seen from the north, to rise from the sea like the figure of a reclining woman. From there, trekkers get to enjoy the fine view of the Pontine Islands, one of which, Zannone, is under park jurisdiction and can be visited by hiring a private boat from the popular resort island of Ponza. The park itself has a dozen or more easy walks through oak forests and low Mediterranean brush, often on trails used long ago by woodcutters and the *carbonai,* who once made charcoal here. The four coastal lakes, part of the park complex, teem with birdlife in spring and fall. Only about 49 miles (78 km) south of Rome, Circeo makes a fine overnight excursion from the capital, especially for those traveling with children and those needing a break from a rich diet of ruins. Open from 8 AM to 7 PM. Details: *Parco Nazionale del Circeo,* 107 Via C. Alberto, Sabaudia (Latina) 04016 (phone: 773-57251).

FORESTA UMBRA, near Vieste, Puglia: The Gargano promontory in the southern region of little-visited Puglia, on the spur of the boot, is best known for its beaches and animated resorts. But high above the coastal commotion is a shady, miraculously surviving 30,000-acre Eden of firs, oaks, maples, beeches, and giant ferns, such as Aeneas must have seen in his antique wanderings; even wild boar still roam free. Stay in the simple refuge-hotel and spend a piney and pensive day walking along the silent forest paths. Details: *Azienda Autonoma di Soggiorno e Turismo,* 1 Piazza Kennedy, Vieste (Foggia) 71019 (phone: 884-708806; fax: 884-707130).

LONG-DISTANCE HIKING

E-5 LONG-DISTANCE EUROPEAN FOOTPATH: The international long-distance footpaths that have been marked by modern pilgrims and crusaders since 1969, and are maintained by walking clubs and associations in 15 countries, are a fantasy come true for dedicated walkers through Europe. Two of the six that crisscross Europe from Denmark to Spain, Holland to Yugoslavia, pass through Italy. The E-1 is unmarked for most of its length in Italy, though about 24 miles (38 km) near Genoa are kept up with care. The E-5, a better choice, is 370 miles (592 km) and 26 days long. It begins in Konstanz, Germany, enters Austria at Bregenz, and reaches Italy at the Timmelsjoch, north of Merano. It then winds down the Passerier Valley, rich in fruit trees and vineyards; climbs into the Sarntal Alps; rolls and dips along a series of ridges and high valleys to Bolzano; heads south above the Adige River valley to just north of Trento, Lake Santo; and then swings through the southern Dolomites and heads southeast to Venice. Two compact German publications describe the complete route in detail, with maps, addresses, photos, and other information needed to walk each section: *Europäischer Fernwanderweg E-5,* published by Fink-Kümmerly & Frey (41 Gebelsbergstrasse, Stuttgart D-7000, Germany), and *Deutscher Wanderverlag,* c/o Dr. Mair & Schnabel & Co. (44/1 Zeppelinstrasse, Ostfildern, Germany D-7302). Details: *Provincia Autonoma di Trento, Assessorato al Turismo,* 132 Corso 3 Novembre, Trento 38100 (phone: 461-895111).

SENTIERO ITALIA: For serious trekkers, the newly blazed *Sentiero Italia* (about one-quarter completed at press time) will stretch all the way from Trieste, crossing the Alpine arch to Liguria on the Tyrrenian coast, down through the Appenine heart (or rib) of Italy to the Calabrian Aspromonte, and with extensions into Sicily, Sardinia, and Corsica, for an itinerary of 3,125 miles (5,000 km). Details: *Associazione Sentiero Italia,* 12 Piazza San Gervaso, Firenze 50131 (no phone).

GRANDE ESCURSIONE APPENNINICA: Inaugurated in 1983 by the celebrated Italian climber Reinhold Messner, this "green autostrada" through the central Apennines is evidence of a newly aroused Italian interest in hiking and the environment. Its approximately 250 miles (400 km) extend from the tricornered border of Umbria, the Marches, and Tuscany to the point where Tuscany joins Liguria and Emilia-Romagna, near the Tyrrhenian coast. It presents no particular technical difficulties and offers superb walking through the heartland of the most poetic areas of Italy. Details: *Gruppo Trekking Firenze,* 12 Piazza San Gervasio, Firenze 50100 (phone: 55-585320).

GRANDE TRAVERSATA DELLE ALPI: This challenging itinerary — the "Great Crossing of the Alps" — stretches east and north of Turin, from the Maritime Alps near the French border nearly to Switzerland, above Lake Maggiore. Its more than 400 marked miles (640 km) cross the region's most beautiful valley and take in 84 refuges (open July to September). One of the most interesting sections begins in Susa, a town easily reached from Turin, and leads north to Il Truc, Usseglio, Balme, and Ceresole. It's also possible to continue into the Valsavaranche in the Gran Paradiso National Park. All hiking is at fairly high altitudes, from 4,900 to 8,200 feet, and often follows old mule paths between abandoned mountain villages. The Grande Traversata does require a good level of physical fitness but is not a particularly difficult route. There are, however, a few strenuous ascents and descents that may inspire wistful memories of the mules. Details: *Comitato Promotore GTA,* 1 Via Barbaroux, Torino 10100 (phone: 11-514477).

Hunting

Whether out of love of sport or from necessity dictated by legendary appetites, the ancient Romans (as well as today's woodlands lovers) took their hunting very seriously. Special animal braking parks were created to make sure that everyone got his share, and there were no controls or restrictions at all on hunting (an anomaly in a nation that had laws for just about everything else).

Today, things are drastically different. To put the brakes on a situation in which hunting had become widely popular and game increasingly scarce, all kinds of regulations — both regional and national — are imposed on what can be hunted, how, when, and where (far too many regulations in the opinion of many). Whether you want to go for wildfowl, starling, partridge, pigeon, thrush, finch, skylark, hare, or wild boar — the most common quarry — or for other protected species of deer or fox, you will be confronted by a discouraging snarl of red tape.

However, hunting takes its enthusiasts into some of the country's wildest, most remote, and least-known areas — an experience rewarding enough in itself to justify the trouble. And a wild boar hunt is one of the ultimate hunting adventures.

While it is possible to hunt in almost every part of Italy except the Alpine regions, where hunting is for residents only, there are a handful that Italian hunters consider the best choices for visitors.

LOMBARDY: The low, marshy lands of this part of northern Italy are excellent for duck, pheasant, and gray partridge. Details: *Federazione Italiana della Caccia* (*FIDC*), Sezione Provinciale, 5 Via Santa Tecla, Milano 20122 (phone: 2-807996).

TUSCANY: Italian hunters are unanimous in acclaiming the Maremma, near the Tyrrhenian Sea in southern Tuscany, for its wild boar hunting — undoubtedly the most exciting quarry in Italy. The area is also one of the most beautiful and secluded spots in the country, and the hunting is in typical Mediterranean maquis and thick pine forests. Details: *Federazione Italiana della Caccia,* Sezione Provinciale, 3 Via Massimo d'Azeglio, Grosseto 58100 (phone: 564-22003).

Hunting holidays can be arranged through *Riserva Turistica di Caccia della Maremma Toscana,* Capalbio (Grosseto) 58011 (phone: 564-896024); or *Azienda Turistico–Venatoria "Il Bargello,"* Capalbio (Grosseto) 58011 (phone: 564-896020).

Tuscany is also a good choice for pheasant, wild rabbit, and partridge. Details: *Azienda Faunistico Venatorio, Ristorante La Bettola dal Prataiolo,* Badia di Susinana, Palazzuolo sul Senio, Firenze (phone: 55-804-9043); or *Federazione Italiana della Caccia,* Sezione Provinciale, 6 Via de' Banchi, Firenze 50122 (phone: 55-216875).

LAZIO: This part of central Italy is considered very good for pheasant shooting. There also is some wild boar (though the best bet is still the Maremma). Details: *Federazione Italiana della Caccia,* 70 Viale Tiziano, Roma 00196 (phone: 6-323-3784); or *Ente Produttori Selvaggina,* 69 Via L. Valerio, Roma 00146 (phone: 6-559-0832).

PUGLIA: Still a vast wilderness, Apulia probably has more game animals than any other region in Italy, so it's not surprising it's such a favorite with Italian hunters who go after wild boar, pheasant, gray partridge, hare, and deer. Details: *Federazione Sezione Comunale della Caccia,* Sezione Provinciale, 12 Via 25 Luglio, Lecce 73100 (phone: 832-46074); *Federazione Italiana della Caccia,* Sezione Provinciale, 111 Via Imbriani, Bari 70121 (phone: 80-540095). Also, contact the game reserve *Riserva di Pugno Chiuso,* c/o *Albergo del Faro,* Vieste (Foggia) 71019 (phone: 884-70911; fax: 884-709017).

SARDINIA: One of the most beautiful spots in all of Italy, Sardinia is more than a millionaire's playground and a sea lover's paradise. Its many secluded highland areas are also an ideal setting for the hunt. Game animals still abound, particularly pheasant and wild boar — here smaller than in Maremma but just as wild and wary. Details: *Federazione Italiana della Caccia,* 37 Via Sonnino, Cagliari 09100 (phone: 70-658966).

PROCEDURES AND INFORMATION

A hunting vacation must start out with an adventure into Italy's complex bureaucracy because organizations that can arrange hunting vacations or get together hunting parties are almost nonexistent. If you're still game for a hunting adventure, then this is what you must do:

First, decide when to go; Italian hunting season runs from September through February, with numerous interruptions depending on the quarry and the region.

Next, contact the *Federazione Italiana della Caccia,* also called *Federcaccia* (Italian Hunting Federation; 70 Viale Tiziano, Roma 00100; phone: 6-323-3779, 6-323-3784, or 6-323-3810). Find out what kinds of rifles are allowed, and with what permit,s if you want to bring your own. (Write or call well in advance of your trip.) Don't forget that Italian craftspeople have been making fine hunting weapons since firearms were invented. They are excellent buys, with handmade decorations.

For information about where to go, where to rent rifles, obtain permits, and find lodging, contact the *Ente Produttori Selvaggina,* which can be found in all Italian cities.

Then, equipped with a hunting license and gun permit from your country of origin and an export permit for your rifle, go to the *Ufficio Caccia e Pesca* (Office of Hunting and Fishing) in the provincial administration office or the town hall in the area or town where you plan to hunt. You will be asked to establish a temporary domicile, which will be at your hotel. Pay the state and regional tax (the cost depends on where you'll be hunting and what gun you use). Then, if your own insurance coverage for hunting accidents does not cover you for Italy, get an obligatory temporary policy through the *Italian Hunting Federation* in Rome (phone: 6-394871).

Also take a few minutes to stop in a shop that sells firearms and hunting equipment. You'll pick up precious bits and pieces of information and also learn something about Italian hunting customs and traditions. Language isn't a barrier — you're bound to find someone who speaks English.

Italian magazines are always a good source of information, and the staff of the hunting magazine *Diana,* available on newsstands, is more than willing to help visiting hunters. Offices are at Editoriale Olimpia, 7 Viale Milton, Firenze 50129 (phone: 55-473843).

For the Mind

Twenty-Five Centuries of History: Italy's Museums and Monuments

Napoleon determinedly exported a significant portion of Italy's art treasures to France, but even so, what remains easily could fill a planet or two. Parochial museums house ancient booty from local excavations. Villas from the 17th century overflow with 16th-century paintings, 1st-century sculptures, and quite a bit from all the centuries in between. The massive state museums have basements stuffed with the national artwork of 2,500 years ago.

Faced with all this, a visitor to Italy is well advised to master the fine art of museum-going. There is something essentially numbing about the means by which we normally view the world's greatest art, so when visiting the giant Italian warehouses of beauty, stop first to thumb through the catalogue or finger the postcards to get an idea of what the collection includes — and where to find it. Determine in advance what you want to see most, and don't try to cover everything. If you attempt a single heroic sweep of the 1,000 rooms of the *Vatican Museums,* you may well develop a case of the dread Titian-fission, where all the Madonnas blend into one polychromatic blur. And when you look at paintings at random, study a picture before you inspect the nameplate — that's the best way to quickly determine what you really like, as opposed to what you're supposed to like. And try to give luncheons and Leonardos equal attention.

Break away from the gargantuan museums in any way you can. Don't forget that single altarpiece in the empty village church, the grouping of portraits adorning the fireplace of the ancient mansion — art in the environment for which it was created. Try building an excursion around a manageable number of goals. For instance, cruise the gentle Tuscan countryside painted by Piero della Francesca, stopping to see his masterpieces in the Church of San Francesco in Arezzo and the Palazzo Comunale of Sansepolcro, his birthplace. Long after you're hazy on roomfuls of Raphaels, you'll remember della Francesca's solitary *Madonna del Parto* in the tiny pastoral chapel of Monterchi, 72 miles (115 km) south of Florence.

And visit a gallery or an auction house occasionally, just to remind yourself that once it was *all* for sale.

Note: Most of the opening and closing times listed here should be right most of the time. But museum hours in Italy are often rearranged because of personnel shortages, labor disputes, surprise restorations, and as many other causes as there are paintings in the *Uffizi.* Caveat visitor!

PARCO DEI MOSTRI, Bomarzo, Lazio: Cloistered by a protective forest and a placid countryside that's a day trip north of Rome, this sculpture park on the grounds of the Duke Paolo Giordano Orsini's 16th-century villa is like a 400-year-old spookhouse in the woods. Scholars believe that the house was built to reflect one of the religious beliefs of the time — that monsters from the underworld would materialize. Its forest seems somewhat sacred and Dantesque. Gargoyle doorways invite visitors to enter through gaping mouths. A lopsided miniature villa suggests an outdoor wax museum visited on a warm day. A cute baby elephant with hollowed-out eyes carries an eroded, androgynous figure on its back and a dead Roman soldier in its trunk. Open daily from dawn to dusk. Details: *Parco dei Mostri,* Bomarzo (Viterbo) 01020 (phone: 761-924029).

PALAZZO DEL BARGELLO AND MUSEO NAZIONALE, Florence: The impressively fortified exterior is an apt reminder of its earlier functions — first as a prison, then as the heavily guarded residence of the city's podestà, or chief magistrate. But within the severe 13th- and 14th-century ramparts is a gracious courtyard and a cornucopia of Florentine and Tuscan Renaissance sculpture. The collection's centerpiece is Donatello's effeminate *David,* sporting a helmet that looks like a flowered *Easter* hat and balancing with ballerina-like grace on Goliath's severed head. You'll also see several early Michelangelos and the Giambologna *Mercury,* who, poised precariously on one foot, looks as if he is about to launch himself into 16th-century space. Open Tuesdays through Saturdays from 9 AM to 1:30 PM, Sundays and holidays from 9 AM to 12:30 PM; closed Mondays. Details: *Palazzo del Bargello,* 4 Via del Proconsolo, Firenze 50100 (phone: 55-210801).

GALLERIA DELL'ACCADEMIA, Florence: Unlike the great, and often bewildering, warehouses that hold more than 700 years of art, this compact museum provides a single, unified experience — of perfection. Its core is the 19th-century hall built especially to fit around Michelangelo's majestic *David* (whose toe was smashed by a lunatic last fall, and was being pedicured at press time). No matter how many postcards and reproductions you may have seen of this gigantic boy, relaxed and self-confident in the moment before dispatching Goliath, the first in-person vision of him is always intensely dramatic. Don't ignore the rest of the rich collection. Retrace your steps through the hall to enter the tortured world of *The Prisoners.* Originally intended for the tomb of Pope Julius II, these figures try desperately to wrench themselves out of the rough stone blocks that Michelangelo never finished sculpting. In the next room is the splendid *Cassone Adimari,* a 15th-century Tuscan wedding chest, across whose delicately painted panels moves a procession of lavishly robed and coiffed gentlewomen and graceful, multicolored courtiers. Together, these three masterpieces seem to embody the spirit of the Renaissance — its boundless optimism and faith in humanity, its struggle toward freedom from the oppressive past, its festive joy in sheer physical beauty. Open Tuesdays through Saturdays from 9 AM to 2 PM, Sundays and holidays to 1 PM; closed Mondays. Details: *Galleria dell'Accademia,* 60 Via Ricasoli, Firenze 50100 (phone: 55-214375).

GALLERIA DEGLI UFFIZI, Florence: One of the world's great museums. While hiking through its glowing rooms, awash in the golden tides of the Italian Renaissance, reflect on the fact that over 90% of Italy's artistic patrimony is stacked in dingy storerooms, hanging in museum wings permanently closed for lack of personnel, and adorning the offices of petty bureaucrats in obscure ministries and consulates out of public view. Consequently, what is hung here is the *crema della crema della crema* by Botticelli, Caravaggio, Piero della Francesca, Giotto, Leonardo, Raphael, and virtually every other major Italian artist. Particularly beautiful, and often overlooked, are the 13th- and 14th-century religious paintings on wood panels. The Renaissance palace that houses these marvels was designed by Vasari in 1560 as the offices (*uffizi*) for Medici administrators. Open Tuesdays through Saturdays from 9 AM to 7 PM, Sundays to 1 PM; closed Mondays. Details: *Galleria degli Uffizi,* 6 Loggiato degli Uffizi, Firenze 50100 (phone: 55-218341). See also *Florence,* THE CITIES.

MUSEO DI SAN MARCO, Florence: Even this placid cedar-shaded cloister knew its share of the daily violence of 15th-century Florentine life. Until 1498, when he was burned at the stake, it was the home of Savonarola, the Dominican monk who declaimed against the arts and the pleasures of the senses, and even organized a bonfire for devilry such as books, paintings, and musical instruments (while the sensual and artistic Florentines quaked in their boots). Now the ideal museum, the monastery has remained just as it was at that time. Painted into the white wall of each plain cell is a single masterpiece intended by the artist Fra Angelico, another longtime Dominican, to encourage meditation. Stand in solitary silence, with a fresco of St. Francis preaching to the birds as your only companion, and it is not hard to imagine the monastic life. Better-known works by this pure and delicate artist — the *Annunciation,* for example — are more publicly displayed. Don't miss the airy, light-filled library, where Savonarola was arrested and which has a stunning collection of illuminated manuscripts. Open Tuesdays through Saturdays from 9 AM to 2 PM, Sundays and holidays to 1 PM; closed Mondays. Details: *Museo di San Marco,* 1 Piazza San Marco, Firenze 50100 (phone: 55-210741).

PALAZZO PITTI AND GIARDINI DI BOBOLI, Florence: With an appetite for exploring Italian Renaissance glories whetted at the *Uffizi,* a museumgoer is ready for the enormous banquet at this once-private estate, luxuriously sprawled across the Arno on an entire Florentine hillside. Five separate museums, including collections of Tuscan Impressionists and other modern art, plus a carriage display, are housed in the 104,000-square-foot *Palazzo Pitti* — a magnificent Renaissance villa designed by Brunelleschi under commission from banker Luca Pitti, with wings by other architects commissioned by its later owners the Medicis. Just the carefully selected collection of 16th- and 17th-century works in the *Galleria Palatina* includes 22 Raphaels and masterpieces by Rubens, Titian, Tintoretto, Van Dyck, Velázquez, and Fra Filippo Lippi. Behind the tri-level façades of rough-hewn rock are scores of resplendent drawing rooms, bedrooms, waiting rooms, reception rooms, and dining rooms. As the Medicis intended, the effect is nothing short of overwhelming. Walk off the rich diet of masterpieces with a stroll through the pleasantly asymmetrical *Giardini di Boboli* (Boboli Gardens), where the Medicis entertained their friends and Florentine matrons now pasture their children. This monument of sculpted and terraced nature, studded with cypress, unusual statuary, fountains, and grottoes, took half a century to complete. Be sure to take the 15-minute hike directly up the hill to the *Porcelain Museum.* Open Tuesdays through Saturdays from 9 AM to 2 PM, Sundays and holidays to 1 PM; closed Mondays. Details: *Palazzo Pitti,* Piazza Pitti, Firenze 50100 (phone: 55-213440).

VILLA FOSCARI, "LA MALCONTENTA," Malcontenta, Veneto: Sitting placidly on the shores of the Brenta Canal, this superbly simple villa, to which a Foscari family member banished his wife, is one of the three stops during the full-day boat cruise between Venice and Padua. Boxy, with the façade of a Greek temple on each side, it is one of many aristocratic homes in this area by the 16th-century local architect Palladio, whose classicism influenced notable 18th- and 19th-century English and American buildings from Knole to the White House. Open from 9 AM to noon Tuesdays, Saturdays, and the first Sunday of the month from May to October. (*The Veneto* in DIRECTIONS describes the road that roughly parallels this canal.)

The tourist vessel *Il Burchiello* follows the same route as its namesake, a luxurious 17th-century craft that shuttled back and forth between Venice and these terra firma country villas. Also along the canal are the Villa Pisani and its fine gardens and maze at Stra, where Hitler and Mussolini first met in 1934, and the Villa Foscarini at Mira, where Lord Byron wrote part of *Childe Harolde* in 1817. Relax and enjoy gliding along at the speed of the Renaissance. *Il Burchiello* operates daily (except Mondays), leaving Wednesdays, Fridays, and Sundays from Venice, and Tuesdays, Thursdays, and Saturdays from Padua, April through October.

Details: *Villa Foscarini,* Malcontenta (Venezia) 30030 (phone: 41-969012); *CIT Viaggi,* Piazza San Marco, Venezia 30124 (phone: 41-528-5480); or *Siamic Express,* 42 Via Trieste, Padova 35100 (phone: 49-660944).

MUSEO ARCHEOLOGICO NAZIONALE, Naples: Originally built as a 16th-century palace and later expanded for use as a university, Naples's prime museum now houses one of the most important archaeological collections in the world — one that's the size of a neighborhood. On a first visit, head past the hordes of ancient pots and pendants, baubles and busts, and concentrate on the finest part of its collection — the sculptures, paintings, and mosaics from Pompeii and Herculaneum. Except for the little that remains on these sites, this collection represents virtually everything that was buried under the tons of ash and pumice and the avalanche of hot gases and rocks that covered the two cities when Vesuvius erupted in the 1st century AD. Preserved in a blanket of volcanic debris for 1,800 years, everything was carefully excavated, allowing visitors to view wooden furniture, delicate surgical instruments, weighing scales, and even entire heating and lighting systems from the dead cities.

Among the marble sculptures that populate the museum's entire ground floor is a muscle-bound Hercules who once held up a hefty section of wall in Rome's Baths of Caracalla (described in *Remarkable Ruins*). Open Mondays through Saturdays from 9 AM to 2 PM; Sundays and holidays from 9 AM to 1 PM. Details: *Museo Archeologico Nazionale,* Piazza Museo, Napoli 80100 (phone: 81-440166).

CARAVAGGIO COUNTRY, Rome: If you wake to a Roman morning too sunbathed and gleaming to spend the day as a museum shut-in, combine some shopping, strolling, and snacking with a treasure hunt for the half dozen major works by the 17th-century painter and street-brawler Caravaggio, a notorious libertine who nonetheless revolutionized religious painting by setting his scenarios in lifelike locales and populating them with realistic, rather than idealized, characters. These are distributed throughout what art historian Howard Hibbard called "Caravaggio Country" — the alleys, markets, and sun-shot piazzas that provided his models during his brief, tempestuous Roman career.

Begin at the Church of Santa Maria del Popolo, just inside the Roman walls. On the sides of a dimly lit chapel are his *Conversion of St. Paul* and *Crucifixion of St. Peter.* After stopping for a cappuccino and a nut croissant at *Rosati's,* across the street, head for the once-suburban estate of the Borghese family. Wander through its huge park, then visit the *Galleria Borghese,* a fine, manageable museum whose roster of Caravaggios includes the dramatic *Madonna dei Palafrenieri* and a roomful of others. Then on to the virtual geometric center of Rome, Piazza Navona, where the hordes seem oblivious to the proximity of great art just a couple of blocks to the east at the recently restored and pristine mid-16th-century Church of San Luigi dei Francesi, on Via della Dogana Vecchia. Three paintings there portray the life of St. Matthew, among them the *Calling of St. Matthew,* arguably the single most famous of Caravaggio's images, and the *Martyrdom of St. Matthew.* Ten minutes away is the Church of Sant'Agostino, with its *Madonna of the Pilgrims,* a tender painting of a Madonna modeled on Caravaggio's mistress, cradling a round and energetic bambino; note the dirty feet of the pilgrims, a controversial note of realism at the time it was painted in 1604, 6 years before Caravaggio contracted malaria and died. Finish your tour with a pistachio ice cream cone at nearby *Giolitti's* (40 Via Uffici del Vicario). Churches are usually open daily from 7 AM to noon and from 4 to 6 PM.

For other Caravaggio explorations, visit the *Doria Pamphili Gallery* in the Palazzo Doria Pamphili near Piazza Venezia (at 1/A Piazza del Collegio Romano), and the *Palatine Gallery* in the *Vatican Museums,* which houses the famous *Entombment of Christ.*

PANTHEON, Rome: Come to this most perfectly preserved of ancient Roman buildings in the morning to witness the column of rain or sunshine that plunges through the giant round oculus in the middle of the roof. Visit again at twilight to sit on the steps of the fountain facing it, and watch the procession of clinging couples, soldiers on leave, families on tour, and the soccer players whose game in the portico has probably been going on since the fall of Rome. The Pantheon's proportions — its height equals the diameter of the dome — give it an aura of classical calm no matter who is coming or going. The structure was also a remarkable feat of engineering, the magnitude of which is suggested by the fact that the diameter of its dome was unsurpassed in the city until the construction (with prefab concrete) of the *Palazzo dello Sport* for Rome's *1960 Olympic Games.* The bronze doors are originals; the street level has risen since its construction by Hadrian in approximately AD 120, and the original staircase that led up to its colonnaded entrance has been replaced by a traffic-free piazza that slopes down to it. Initially a pagan temple to all the gods, the spacious, cylindrical Pantheon became a Christian church in 606; it now holds the tombs of the the first two kings of Italy and of the painter Raphael (whose epitaph reads "Here lies Raphael: While he lived the great mother of all things feared to be outdone; and when he died she feared too to die"). Open Tuesdays through Saturdays from 9 AM to 2 PM, Sundays and holidays to 1 PM; closed Mondays. Details: *Pantheon,* Piazza della Rotonda, Roma 00100 (phone: 6-369831).

MUSEI VATICANI, Rome: Occupying palaces constructed by popes from the 13th century onward, the Vatican collections are among the most impressive in the world, comprising works of every epoch. But seeing even a part of them poses a challenge. The pleasures are interspersed with a fair assortment of priceless objects in glass cases with which most people really don't want to bother. And there are not only the usual population of other museum visitors but also sizable bands of Vatican visitors and other pilgrims vying for space in front of the objects that one does want to see. The Sistine Chapel, in particular, sometimes seems more like a very tastefully decorated subway during rush hour, especially since part of its ceiling — Michelangelo's depiction of the *Creation* — now is brighter and more vivid as a result of a 10-year restoration project. Revitalization of *The Last Judgment* is expected to take at least another year. The solution: Visit at 9 AM sharp. Grab a ticket and scurry past what seems like kilometers of papal robes, old maps, and tomb inscriptions until you've left the school groups and Ecuadoran nuns far behind. Your destinations are the *Raphael Rooms;* the *Apollo Belvedere,* the *Laocöon Group,* and other classical statuary in the *Pio-Clementino Museum;* and the works of Fra Angelico, Giotto, and Filippo Lippi in the *Pinacoteca* (Picture Gallery). Open Mondays through Saturdays from 9 AM to 2 PM, to 5 PM around *Easter* and from July through September Mondays through Fridays, 9 AM to 2 PM Saturdays; on the last Sunday of every month from 9 AM to 1 PM (no admission charge); closed on other Sundays. Details: *Musei Vaticani,* Viale Vaticano, Roma 00100 (phone: 6-698-3333).

VILLA D'ESTE, Tivoli, Lazio: The seven terraced acres of gardens at this 16th-century villa are a tour de force of hydraulics, and the best time to visit is a warm summer afternoon when the more than 500 fountains, pools, and water jets seem a marvel of outdoor air conditioning. The gardens' centerpiece is a 2-story fountain that creates a sheet of water behind which visitors can walk and still stay relatively dry. The fountains are flowing again after fears that the water was polluted, but you'll have to look at them from behind a railing. In spring and summer, there is something almost tropical about the lush vegetation that climbs up walls and around statues but stays primly off the gravel paths. It makes an ideal excursion for kids with its endless possibilities for florid fantasy and damp mischief. Start earlier in the day from Rome and enjoy a double feature, with morning at the emperor Hadrian's spectacular Villa Adriana (described in *Remarkable Ruins*) and a lunchtime intermission in the engaging town of Tivoli. Open from 9 AM to an hour before sunset; closed Mondays. Details: *Azienda Autonoma Soggiòrno,* Tivoli (Roma) 00019 (phone: 774-21249).

MUSEO DELL'AUTOMOBILE CARLO BISCARETTI DI RUFFIA, Turin, Piedmont: Since Turin is in the heart of Italian car country, it is entirely appropriate that one of its major museums is devoted to the history of the automobile and its ancestors from 15th-century wind-powered contraptions to the development of the city's sprawling Fiat industrial complex. Started by an aficionado of things automotive in the mid-1950s, the museum now houses 150 vehicles, including a steam-powered tricycle from 1891 and the car that won the 1907 Paris-to-Peking motor race by covering the distance in 44 days. The first tentative efforts of such distinguished makers as Lancia, Ferrari, and Alfa Romeo are on display, along with some perfectly preserved legends — a 1916 Rolls-Royce Silver Ghost, a 1933 Bentley, a 1916 Model T Ford. Open daily, except Mondays, from 9 AM to 12:30 PM and 3 to 7 PM. Details: *Museo Dell'Automobile Carlo Biscaretti di Ruffia,* 40 Corso Unità d'Italia, Torino 10100 (phone: 11-677666).

Theater, Music, and Opera

Italy has been a land of patrons and performers since the flushest days of the Medicis. Noble courts throughout the peninsula maintained private orchestras. Comedians *dell'arte* found the palace gates flung wide open with welcome. Now, where the aristocracy is too impoverished to treat, the government has rushed in, and virtually every medium-size city has its publicly funded concert hall and *teatro stabile* (repertory theater), and some 40,000 subsidized musical events a year crowd the Italian calendar. As a result, ticket prices are far more reasonable than in the US — as long as they are purchased before the familiar *esaurito* ("all sold out") strip is pasted across the poster outside the theater.

Even outside Milan (the seat of music publishing and the home of a sophisticated and varied concert season) and Rome (the first city of Italian music), concerts are definitely a growth stock. Far from keeping audiences away, the widespread ownership of compact disc players and Walkman cassette players has actually brought down the average audience age. Increasingly, venues include not only staid and sterile local auditoriums but also Renaissance palazzi and medieval churches, piazzas, and flower-edged cloisters and courtyards. A recent Roman summer festival offered a string quartet concert on a barge moored off the tiny Tiber Island. And you've never really heard Bach until you've heard his music reverberating through a baroque basilica.

Long more popular than concert music in Italy, opera continues to boom. Bricklayers really do whistle *Traviata* as they trowel; your loge-mates may hum along with *Madame Butterfly.* Though the days have passed when fiascos automatically ended with a shower of rotten vegetables, there are still lots of lusty boos when the diva turns out to be a dog — and bravos when the tenor hits a string of flawless high C's. Lately, too, some of the country's dowager opera houses have been refitted with modish new finery.

In the theater, Goldoni and Pirandello are perennial favorites — with Guglielmo Shakespeare a close second. Theatrical activity is more national than metropolitan; companies usually do a limited run in major cities and then go out on tour — so travelers may well catch something in the provinces that they just missed in the capital. The stutter-and-mutter traditions that have reigned in much of the US since the rise of the Actors' Studio have no place here. The Italian stage style is definitely declamatory. Just think of it as reflecting the greater melodrama of daily Italian life.

SOCIETÀ AQUILANA DEI CONCERTI BARATTELLI, L'Aquila, Abruzzo: The nation's most impressive example of low-budget, high-quality music can be found in this Apennine city, the jumping-off point for visits to the Abruzzo National Park. That it has a musical reputation of a city many times its size is all the more impressive because this is the capital of one of Italy's poorer regions. Behind the reputation is an enterprising native lawyer, who not only founded the distinguished *Abruzzo Symphony Orchestra* but also has been able to recruit some of Europe's most prestigious artists for his Barattelli Society's chamber concert series, held in a tiny auditorium with state-of-the-art acoustics that is nestled picturesquely inside the city's 15th-century castle. An evening here is a perfect finale to a day's ramble in the neighboring wilderness. Details: *Ente Musicale Società Aquilana dei Concerti Barattelli,* Il Castello Cinquecentesco, L'Aquila 67100 (phone: 862-24262).

PICCOLO TEATRO, Milan: Since its creation just after World War II, the so-called *Little Theater* has been the most vital force of the Italian stage. The mission of its ever-active founder and godfather, Giorgio Strehler, was to make the theater a medium of popular culture; toward that end, the repertory is eclectic and international, the staging vigorous and imaginative, and its public the same patrician group glimpsed the evening before at *La Scala.* After a decade of debate, the *Piccolo* was expanded into new, less *piccolo* quarters. Details: *Piccolo Teatro,* 2 Via Rovello, Palazzo del Broletto, Milano 20100 (phone: 2-869-0631).

TEATRO ALLA SCALA, Milan: Built between 1776 and 1778 on the site of the Church of Santa Maria della Scala and then restored to rococo glory in 1948 after Allied bombing damaged it during World War II, *La Scala* has always been a prince among opera houses. Works by Donizetti, Rossini, Bellini, and Verdi were first acclaimed here, and Arturo Toscanini, conductor and artistic director for years, reintroduced the works of Verdi during his tenure. The house has never lost its aristocratic aura, and its opening night on *Saint Ambrose Day* (December 7) is a glittering, celebrity-studded gala, with special dinners offered by the toney Milanese restaurants who publish their opera soirée menus in the newspapers. Though the repertory tends toward the conservative, the glamorous tradition of world premieres continues: *L'Altra Storia,* co-produced by composer Luciano Berio and the eminent author Italo Calvino, opened in 1985 with all the hoopla bestowed on the debuts of *Otello* and *Pagliacci* a century ago. With legendary perfect acoustics, a performance here is truly exhilarating — and also expensive. Tickets for each season's performances, presented December through May, are passionately pursued and hard to come by — especially those to old favorites. Tickets can be purchased — with difficulty — from the box office in advance; at the last minute, concierges at the city's deluxe hotels often can get positive results for a consideration. There are also ballet performances during the summer as well as performances of the *Filarmonica della Scala,* perhaps Italy's finest orchestra, which has begun concertizing without vocals lately (although not in the summer). Details: *Teatro alla Scala,* 2 Via Filodrammatici, Milano 20100 (phone: 2-720-03744 from 10 AM to 1 PM and from 3 PM to 6 PM for information on prices and ticket availability).

RAI ORCHESTRAS, Milan, Naples, Rome, Turin: A household word from the Alps to the Ionian, *RAI* — which stands for *Radio Televisione Italiana,* the state network — is among the most influential organizations on the national music scene because it sponsors a symphony orchestra and chorus in each of Italy's four largest cities, each with its own full-length season and its own auditorium. Although the *Alessandro Scarlatti Orchestra* in Naples is probably best known, those in Milan and Turin are first-rate and produce some of Italy's finest recordings. The Rome orchestra produces a regular season at the *Foro Italico;* gives a special concert for the pope once a year, either in St. Peter's or in the Vatican's giant Sala Nervi; and premieres many contemporary works at the Villa Medici in an annual festival in September. Occasionally, all the *RAI* artists combine forces, as with the legendary triple-chorus-and-orchestra spectacular of Mahler's *Eighth Symphony* at St. Mark's Basilica in Venice. On the other hand, the parent organizations also break down into pocket-size chamber and choral groups. A chief mission of the *RAI* is to keep alive many little-performed works from past centuries. But it also has a virtual monopoly on symphonic pieces by contemporary composers. Tickets are kept at popular prices, and many concerts are televised. Details: *Auditorio del Foro Italico,* 1 Piazza Lauro de Bosis, Roma 00100 (phone: 6-365625; Thursdays through Saturdays only).

TEATRO SAN CARLO, Naples: Built under Charles III of Bourbon in 1737, destroyed by fire in 1816, and thoroughly rebuilt in neo-classical style within 6 months, Italy's second-most famous opera house would be worth a visit if only for a view of the flamboyant rococo reception hall. Talented and progressive direction of the theater where Bellini's *La sonnambula,* Donizetti's *Lucia di Lammermoor,* and many other operatic classics had their premieres has sparked a full-blown renaissance, with the consequence that an evening here is one of Italy's lushest musical experiences. Although *San Carlo* can seat twice as many as *La Scala,* it is perpetually packed. The spectators — as passionate about Pergolesi, Paisiello, and Puccini as they are about politics and soccer — tend to be vociferous. Join them: It's part of the fun, and the performers expect it (sometimes they've even paid for it). A bonus is the relatively low ticket prices compared to those found at other temples of European opera. Travelers not attending a performance can tour the theater in the morning, by prior arrangement. Box office closed Mondays. Details: *Teatro San Carlo,* 93/F Via San Carlo, Napoli 80100 (phone: 81-797-2111 or, for tickets, 81-797-2370).

MUSEO INTERNAZIONALE DELLE MARIONETTE, Palermo, Sicily: Marionette and puppet theater, which made its way to Sicily through Spain and Naples in the mid-19th century, has been a fundamental part of the island's peasant culture. But only recently has it begun to be acknowledged as a real art form. This entrancing museum, housed in an 18th-century baronial palace, contains specimens from China, Java, Burma, and points west, and a theater where marionette and puppet shows regularly take place. From mid-November to March, the annual *Sicilian Marionette Festival* held here and at the *Teatro Libero* brings performers from as far as Sweden and Malaysia, France and India. Open daily except Sundays from 9 AM to 1 PM and 4 to 7 PM. Details: *Museo Internazionale delle Marionette,* 1 Via Butera, Palermo 90100 (phone: 91-328060).

AMICI DELLA MUSICA, Perugia, Umbria: Held at the 13th-century Palazzo dei Priori, the chamber concert series of the *Amici della Musica* (friends of music) is both a rare musical experience and the highlight of the social season in this storybook 15th-century town surrounded by a soft gold and green patchwork of cornfields and olive groves. Despite its small size, the town is the capital of the flourishing Umbria region and, as such, attracts artists of the caliber of a Backhaus, Pollini, or Accardo; Claudio Abbado has conducted the *European Youth Orchestra* here. During August, the harmonies switch from Bach to bop for the *Umbria Jazz Festival,* and the cobbled streets swing to the likes of Miles Davis and Ornette Coleman as well as a number of younger jazz musicians and blues singers from all over Europe. The *amici della musica* are by this time on the Riviera listening to Stravinsky in stereo. Details: *Associazione Amici della Musica,* 63 Corso Vannucci, Perugia 06100 (phone: 75-25264).

ACCADEMIA NAZIONALE DI SANTA CECILIA, Rome: Named in dignified Latin style for the patron saint of music and established in 1566 by Pierluigi da Palestrina, this organization serves a host of functions: managing Rome's symphony orchestra in residence, staging its concerts in the Vatican's stark *Pio Auditorium* on Sunday afternoons (with reprises on Monday and Tuesday evenings) from October to June, and orchestrating Bach-to-Berg chamber performances in the academy's own delightful hall on Friday evenings. A guest conductor system brings visiting conductors such as Maazel, Abbado, Giulini, and Sawallisch. Yuppies and university students are swelling the once rather elderly ranks of the city's concertgoers, and large chunks of tickets are sold by subscription, so be prepared to queue to snare a seat. In summer, Santa Cecilia moves out into the open and presents evening concerts in the hilltop Piazza del Campidoglio. Since seats here are not numbered, it is wise to find your place an hour or more before the music begins, settle down with a picnic supper, and enjoy the summer sunset in the company of Michelangelo's majestic architecture. During the interval, stroll behind the square for Rome's best overview of the Forum by night. Details:

Accademia Nazionale di Santa Cecilia, 4 Via della Conciliazione, Roma 00100 (phone: 6-654-1044 or 6-689-3623).

TEATRO REGIO, Turin: Opera in Turin reflects the progressive spirit of the city, the first capital of modern Italy and currently its center of political liberalism. The *Teatro Regio,* an 1,800-seat hall that opened in 1973 with Maria Callas singing Verdi's *I Vespri Siciliani,* is the national testing ground for budding young vocal talent, and a significant portion of the works staged here are contemporary. When electronic opera arrives, this is where it will beep. Details: *Teatro Regio,* 215 Piazza del Castello, Torino 10124 (phone: 11-881-5241; fax: 11-881-5214).

TEATRO LA FENICE, Venice: An *istituzione nazionale,* this structure is celebrating its bicentennial this year. Unprepossessing in appearance, it is a titan on the local and national arts scene, and an architectural marvel within, from its wonderfully symmetrical grand staircase and mirrored corridors to the magnificent chandeliers, the scallop-topped velvet curtain, and the ceiling resplendent with rosy cherubs. Culturally there are performances for every taste and every season. *La Scala*'s greatest rival for national preeminence, the *Venice Opera,* which premiered Verdi's *Attila, Ernani, Rigoletto, La Traviata,* and *Simone Boccanegra* as well as Stravinsky's *Rake's Progress* and Britten's *Turn of the Screw,* raises its curtain annually in November, with all of the city's private gondola set in attendance. Chamber concerts are presented in the *Sale Apolline* throughout the year; the plums are the performances by the distinguished *I Solisti Veneti.* During the summer, music fills the languid Venetian evening in enthralling open-air venues such as the courtyard of the Doge's Palace, and in midautumn the city hosts the *International Contemporary Music Festival,* which has premiered works by the most renowned modern composers on either side of the Atlantic — Boulez and Berio, Cage and Carter, Stockhausen and Feldman and Maderna among their number. After concerts, the *Fenice*-side *Al Teatro* bar and pizzeria becomes the center of Europe's musical universe. Details: *Teatro La Fenice,* Campo San Fantin, Venezia 30124 (box office phone: 41-521-0161).

ARENA DI VERONA, Verona, Veneto: The most spectacular outdoor opera performances in Italy are dramatically set in a 1st-century amphitheater a stone's throw from the houses of Romeo and Juliet. This site has seen gladiators and lions and has served as fortress, marketplace, jousting field, and repertory theater before its bleachers first echoed with *Aïda* during the Verdi centenary celebrations of 1913. That prolific composer has remained the centerpiece of the Verona opera season, and every summer evening during July and August, Radames and Rigoletto, Alfredo and Otello belt out their passions on a stage twice the size of *La Scala*'s to sold-out audiences of 20,000 who have made pilgrimages here from every corner of the world. Three operas are grandiosely staged every season (Bizet, Donizetti, Gluck, Puccini, and Wagner are other mainstays), along with a densely populated ballet, and a few select concerts. The acoustics are perfect, directors and performances top rank, tickets expensive by anyone's standards, and lodgings hard to come by for the duration — so book well in advance. Afterward, stop for gelato on the piazza and study the contrast among the classical, medieval, and contemporary notes all around you. Details: *Arena di Verona,* 28 Piazza Brà, Verona 37100 (phone: 45-800-5151).

MUSEO PUCCINI, near Viareggio, Tuscany: A shrine for music devotees, this remarkable lakeside villa 15 minutes' drive from Viareggio was Puccini's home from 1891 until 1921 and is well worth a detour. Now a scrupulously maintained museum, the house and grounds where *La Bohème* was first hummed are exactly as they were when he died, and so is the Förster upright piano from which he conjured up a lifelong explosion of bel canto. You may visit the chapel where he and his family are buried, admire the rooms with their gloomy fin de siècle furniture, amble through the gardens, and, in the armory, admire the assortment of rifles that the maestro kept for hunting moorhens. Come on a sunny day and lunch on the wharf; better still, if you are in the area in late July or early August, combine an afternoon visit with dinner and an evening of the *Puccini Opera Festival,* glamorously staged at the edge of the lake. Open Tuesdays through Sundays from 9 AM to noon, 2:30 to 5:30 PM. Details: *Museo Puccini,* Villa Puccini, Belvedere Puccini, Torre del Lago (Lucca) 55048 (phone: 548-341445).

TEATRO OLIMPICO, Vicenza, Veneto: Designed by the late-Renaissance architect Palladio, this superb classical edifice, with its playful perspectives and orgy of ornament, was conceived to amuse the leisure class of 16th-century Vicenza and remains among the most stylish stages in Europe. Local repertory theater alternates with productions by touring companies during the June-through-September season; if you can't make it, visit the building anyway. Details: *Teatro Olimpico,* Piazza Matteotti, Vicenza 36100 (phone: 444-323781).

TEATRI STABILI: Italy has no single great national theater. It has instead 15 *teatri stabili* — regionally or municipally sponsored repertory companies that perform in their own theaters in most of the country's major cities as well as tour up and down the peninsula. In addition to premiering most contemporary Italian plays, they offer at least their share of foreign works — and thereby vary the diet of Goldoni and Pirandello that more traditional Italian companies serve the Sunday matinee crowd. Be on the lookout for the *Teatro di Genova,* the *Centro Teatrale Bresciano,* the *Teatro di Roma* at the *Argentina, Valle,* and *Quirino* theaters in Rome — splendid historic theater buildings all — and *ATER Emilia-Romagna* at the *Arena del Sole* in Bologna, and the *Piedmontese Gruppo della Rocca* (that tours around Piedmont), which some consider among the very best. Contact local or regional tourist offices for details.

Italy's Most Colorful Festas

The national delight in gregarious ritual means that hardly a day passes in Italy without some community of even a few hundred souls celebrating some village-shaking historical event, some traditional food, or some local saint. There are harvest festivals, banquets of music, masked carnival balls in candlelit palaces. Florence stages a medieval soccer match in its Piazza della Signoria, pungent Alba a *Festival of the Truffle,* Cavesana a feast consecrated to San Giorgio, the patron of oxen. Whether at the *Tournament of Noses* in Soragna, the live chess game at Marostica, the goose race of Lacchiarella, the *Mongrel Fair* in Mango, or the *Feast of Celibates* at Casto (which means "chaste"), banners are draped from every windowsill, lights are strung up, processions shuffle to the rejoicing of the town band, celebrants dance in the piazza — and everyone commemorates whatever it was with a *porchetta* sandwich.

Here are some of the most festive of Italian *feste.*

SAGRA DEL TARTUFO, Alba, Piedmont: This knobby cratered nugget, worth ten times its weight in silver, is the main pleasure of any food lover's autumn and the chief honoree in Alba, the truffle capital of Italy, at a series of October goings-on. The festivities culminate with an orgy of truffle madness: contests, auctions, truffle hound competitions, cooking demonstrations, and innumerable tastings and sniffings of the gloriously ugly fungus. Details: *Azienda di Promozione Turistica,* Piazza Medford, Alba (Cuneo) 12051 (phone: 173-35833).

FOIRE DE SAINT OURS, Aosta, Valle d'Aosta: At the end of every January, following a tradition that goes back 1,000 years, artisans from 12 mountain valleys around Aosta gather to show off the goods they've made by hand during the long winter months. Hundreds of stands exhibit items in wood, wrought iron, lace, wool, and straw — all for sale. Visitors can fight the cold with the region's famous cheese *fonduta* and its wicked *coppa dell'amicizia* (literally, the cup of friendship, since it is passed around a group) a spiked-and-spiced coffee served in strange, many-spouted wooden receptacles. The bright parkas and brown faces adorning fellow shoppers confirm that you're not far from Italy's finest skiing. Details: *Azienda Autonoma di Soggiorno,* 3 Piazza Narbonne, Aosta 11100 (phone: 165-303725).

VENDEMMIA DEL NONNO, Castagnole Monferrato, Piedmont: The second Sunday of October, while the tangy odor of pressed grapes suffuses the streets of small towns all over Italy, this village enacts an authentic old-fashioned grape harvest, a *Vendemmia del Nonno,* the way grandfather used to do it. Family groups work together in the vineyards, heap carts high with the richly colored fruit, trample it with bare feet, and feast raucously at day's end at a community supper that features the traditional *bagna cauda,* a savory anchovy and garlic vegetable dip. Don't miss the local wines — barbera, grignolino, dolcetto, and the precious ruché, a robust red produced only in small quantities and only in this area. Details: *Pro Loco,* Castagnole Monferrato (Asti) 14030 (phone: 141-292136).

RASSEGNA MEDITERRANEA DEGLI STRUMENTI POPOLARI, Erice, Sicily: Folk musicians from all over the Mediterranean — and as far abroad as Scotland and Scandinavia — descend on this pretty Sicilian hill town every year in late December to play and display bagpipes, flutes, lutes, tambourines, Jew's-harps, and other folk instruments. Two decades old, the festival is a fine time to visit ancient and mysterious Erice, where ivy-covered buildings of Arab, Gothic, and baroque design line the cobbled streets. The haunting music makes a perfect soundtrack for wide-screen views from the town's Norman castle overlooking Trapani and the Sicilian coast. Details: *Azienda Autonoma di Soggiorno e Turismo,* 11 Viale Conte Pepoli, Erice (Trapani) 91016 (phone: 923-869388).

MAGGIO MUSICALE FIORENTINO, Florence: Programs at this event, Italy's answer to the king of European music festivals at Salzburg, are so diverse that they seem a conscious attempt to avoid musical chauvinism; you're as likely to hear Berg and Stravinsky as Italian composers like Rossini and Puccini. Some of the concerts are held in the magical Boboli Gardens — lovely and quintessentially Italian, especially on a June evening. Despite a name that translates "Florentine Musical May," the goings-on continue right through June. Details: *Maggio Musicale Fiorentino, Teatro Comunale,* Corso Italia, Firenze 50123 (phone: 55-277-9236).

L'INFIORATA, Genzano, Lazio: On the Sunday after *Corpus Domini* in June, the long street that slopes up to the Church of Santa Maria della Cima in this hill town just outside Rome is completely, fragrantly carpeted with flowers worked into elaborate abstract designs, copies of famous artworks, or biblical scenes. Everyone in town, and visiting Romans by the score, turn out to see the pretty show and then pile into nearby country restaurants to fork down foothills of fettuccine with amber-hued liters of the local castelli wine. Follow their example. And don't leave Genzano without a wheel of the bread that bears the town's name — a dusky, rustic, crusty delight. Details: *Azienda Autonoma di Soggiorno e Turismo dei Laghi e Castelli Romani,* 1 Viale Risorgimento, Albano Laziale (Roma) 00041 (phone: 6-930-5798; fax: 6-932-0040).

LA CORSA DEI CERI, Gubbio, Umbria: This most beautiful and perfectly preserved of Italian towns honors its patron saint, Ubaldo, on May 15 with an unusual and spectacular event that brings native Gubbini back home from all over the world. Three *ceri* — gigantic wooden structures resembling Brobdingnagian candles that are topped with tiny, but resplendently attired, statues of St. George, St. Anthony, and St. Ubaldo — are fixed to mammoth litters. Then troupes of bearers tote them at top speed up and down through the town's steep, narrow medieval alleys to the summit of Monte Ingino, where St. Ubaldo's glass coffin occupies a crumbling basilica; St. Ubaldo's candle always arrives first. Townspeople and tourists pack the streets to watch the colorful event, and flags, food, and religious fetes are the order of the day. If you're in town on the last Sunday in May, stop by the Piazza della Signoria to see the showy annual crossbow contest, which carries on the tradition of rivalry between the men of Gubbio and those of nearby Sansepolcro. Details: *Azienda Autonoma di Soggiorno e Turismo,* 6 Piazza Oderisi, Gubbio (Perugia) 06024 (phone: 75-927-3693).

SAGRA DELL'UVA, Marino, Lazio: When this town on the slopes just southeast of Rome celebrates its grape harvest on the first Sunday of October, wine actually flows from its Fountain of the Moors. After the sacred thanksgiving rites of the morning (procession, grape offering to the Madonna, and ritual restaurant feasts), the day turns pleasantly pagan, with allegorical floats, roast suckling pigs, garish street stands, and gushing wine (gratis) — the straw-golden dry white of the Alban hills. Meanwhile, the mood builds from merry to mildly wild, and celebrants routinely stagger on until late at night. Details: *Ente Provinciale per il Turismo,* 11 Via Parigi, Roma 00185 (phone: 6-461851).

EASTER WEEK: The collective passion for ritual has all Italy in its grip during the 4 days preceding *Easter Sunday,* as nearly every village and town throughout the nation stages some special procession or ceremony. Some of these are derived from ancient pagan practices and some from medieval customs. The pageantry in Sicily is particularly colorful. All night long on *Good Friday* in Trapani, the air throbs with haunting Sicilian funeral music, and groups of men labor down the narrow streets carrying the weight of 20 huge platforms representing scenes of the Passion in an extraordinary display.

In Nocera Tirinese, near Catanzaro, Sicily, penitents cut their legs with shards of glass fixed into corks and dry the blood with wine and vinegar as they follow rough-hewn statues of the Madonna and Christ in procession.

In Cascia, near Perugia, hooded figures keep a 700-year-old tradition alive by carrying heavy crosses and wearing chains on their legs while trudging through the Stations of the Cross.

In Chieti, in Abruzzo, in one of the most ancient of rites, the whole town center is illuminated by torch and candlelight, and 150 musicians chant the *Miserere* as a solemn procession of men in black tunics and gray mantles slowly winds down the streets.

In Rome, the pope walks in a *Good Friday* procession in the ruins of the Colosseum, where Christian martyrs met their deaths.

Details: *Italian Government Travel Office.* For Trapani, *Azienda Provinciale Turismo,* 1/A Piazzetta Saturno, Trapani 91100 (phone: 923-29000).

SAN RANIERI E GIOCO DEL PONTE, Pisa, Tuscany: Every town in Italy has its own saint with his or her own special day and mode of celebration. In Pisa, the saint is Ranieri, and the celebrating begins on the night of June 16, as candles flicker enchantingly around the buildings along the Arno. The next day, 8-rower teams in 16th-century costume compete in a hotly contested race on the river and then scale a high post to claim the victory flag.

A few weeks later, the strongest men from each side of the river don medieval finery and join a gigantic tug of war on the Ponte di Mezzo — according to a tradition rooted in far more lethal local skirmishes. If you're inclined to visit the Leaning Tower, try to time your arrival to coincide with one of these two raucous happenings.

Details: *Ente Provinciale per il Turismo,* 42 Lungarno Mediceo, Pisa 56100 (phone: 50-542344).

LA FESTA DI NOIANTRI, Rome: For a boisterous week in mid-July, when the richest Romans have fled to the sea or the mountains, the teeming Trastevere quarter becomes one sprawling outdoor trattoria. As night falls and the air cools, streetlights illuminate rows of tables stretching for blocks, restaurant blending with pizzeria melting into café. Merrymakers pack the streets, musicians stroll, garish stands jam the main avenue, piazzas become dance floors and open-air cinemas, and — because there is a religious foundation to all this — the Madonna del Carmine Church stays open as late as the watermelon stands. The *noiantri* of the celebration are "we others" — the people of Trastevere who consider themselves the only true Romans and choose to honor their neighborhood when *those* others have fled the heat. Details: *Ente Provinciale per il Turismo,* 11 Via Parigi, Roma 00185 (phone: 6-461851).

IL PALIO, Siena, Tuscany: On July 2 and August 16 every year, the whole city comes alive with *Palio* fever for this wild and exciting medieval horse race around the central Piazza del Campo. The pageantry is incomparable, from the chapel blessing of the steed a couple of days before the event to the monumental costumed procession that kicks off the celebration the night before to the post-race all-night celebration of the victorious *contrada,* where the beast dines at a jubilant open-air banquet. The jockeys are notorious for their treachery, and there are absolutely no rules — even a riderless horse can finish in the money. Details: *Azienda Autonoma di Soggiorno e Turismo,* 43 Via di Città, Siena 53100 (phone: 577-42209). For further details, see *Siena,* THE CITIES.

FESTIVAL DEI DUE MONDI, Spoleto, Umbria: Founded in 1957 by Maestro Gian Carlo Menotti, this celebrated mid-June event brings together performers from both sides of the Atlantic for 3 weeks of dance, poetry readings, concerts, drama, opera, and art exhibits notable for their diversity, quality, and sizable number of new works. Equally noteworthy is the setting. The capital of the Dukes of Lombardy from the 6th to the 8th century, it is picturesque and full of narrow vaulted passages and interesting nooks and crannies, quaint old shops, and colorful markets. The final concert is traditionally held in front of the 12th-century cathedral, with the audience sitting on the majestic stairway that overlooks it in the shadow of handsome palaces and hanging gardens. Menotti himself is still actively involved. Details: *Festival dei Due Mondi,* 18 Via Beccaria, Roma (phone: 6-321-0288); or in Spoleto, Via del Duomo, Spoleto (phone: 743-40396).

FESTIVAL INTERNAZIONALE DI MUSICA ANTICA, Urbino, The Marches: For 10 days every year in late July, instrumentalists, dancers, singers, and theoreticians — both amateur and professional — from the four corners of Europe and the United States converge on this ancient hill town in the Marches, Raphael's birthplace, for the most important Renaissance and baroque music festival in Italy. The streets vibrate with the tootling of recorders, the strumming of lyres, the melodies of the viols, and the high C's of sopranos. Courses are offered at all levels and for all ages in the principal ancient instruments, voice, music history, and dance (both folk and courtly), and ambitious artisans can learn to construct their own harpsichords and lutes. There are ample opportunities to perform with other musicians, and the chorus, open to all, serenades in the main piazza on the last day. An evening concert series focusing on music composed before 1750 runs through the summer. Details: *Società Italiana del Flauto Dolce,* 5 Via Gonfalonieri, Roma 00195 (phone: 6-321-4206).

LA FESTA DEL REDENTORE, Venice: A deadly plague ravaged the city in the late 16th century, and this *Feast of the Redeemer* is how Venice has been commemorating its end every year for centuries, the night between the third Saturday and Sunday in July. It begins quietly enough with pilgrimages to Palladio's Church of the Redeemer on the Giudecca and with the mounting of two bridges of boats across the Giudecca Canal, and ends with a bang — the sound and light of Italy's most electrifying fireworks exhibition. Dazzling cascades, spinning wheels of sparks, and explosions of color surprise the night sky. The lagoon is almost solid with boats and floating midnight picnics, and the water's edge jammed with everyone who isn't afloat. At midnight, a grand and impressive barge full of flowers makes its stately way down the Grand Canal, and before dawn the hardy head for the Lido to greet the sunrise with a ritual swim. Details: *Azienda Autonoma di Soggiorno e Turismo,* 71/C Ascensione, Piazza San Marco, Venezia 30124 (phone: 415-522-6356).

LA FIERACAVALLI, Verona, Veneto: Whether you ride, raise, or simply relish horses, there's something for you at this mid-November fair, a 4-day medley of exhibitions, competitions, racing, jumping, dressage, and merchandising. Thousands of animals of all breeds compete for prizes and are sold at auction. The newest and best gear for the intelligent care and feeding of the horse is on display, and hundreds of dealers and shoppers from all over Europe are on hand to snap it up. Italy's best horsemen, the mounted carabinieri, are resplendent in their Napoleonic uniforms. Details: *Azienda di Promozione Turistica,* 42 Piazza delle Erbe, Verona 37122 (phone: 45-30086; for specific information on the fair, phone: 45-588211).

CARNEVALE, Viareggio, Tuscany: During the 3 weekends before *Lent,* this summer seaside resort is a whirl of *Carnevale* costumes, confetti, and floats that climaxes during a grand Sunday afternoon parade of leering dummies, pert majorettes, and immense floats that unequivocally demonstrate coastal Viareggio's shipbuilding expertise.

Such goings-on, plus theater, music, masked balls, sporting events, and fireworks displays, have always been *Carnevale* staples all over Italy. But in the last few years, a *Carnevale* mania seems to have swept Europe, and while the kindergarten crowd is dressing up as Superman and Cinderella, butchers and bankers don Rambo and Robespierre masks to dance down the roads, their spirits dampened not one whit by the unpredictable weather. Bassano del Grappa, Venice, and Verres (Valle d'Aosta) are other venues for *Carnevale* bacchanalia.

Details: *Azienda Autonoma di Soggiorno e Turismo,* 10 Viale Carducci, Viareggio (Lucca) 55049 (phone: 584-48881).

LA SAGRA DEI CUOCHI DEL SANGRO, Villa Santa Maria, Abruzzo: For 3 days every year in early October, gifted master chefs who hail from this small town in the Sangro River Valley, where some of the world's finest cooks learned their trade, return to their hometown to demonstrate their art in an appetizing festival that honors culinary talents stretching back to the Renaissance. Details: *Istituto Professionale Alberghiero di Stato,* Villa Santa Maria (Chieti) 66047 (phone: 872-944422).

An Antiques Lover's Guide to Italy

Though Italian cities preserve some of the finest collections of antiquities in the world, buying genuine antiques is not an easy matter. Plenty of dealers are willing to sell small relics of ancient Rome or Etruscan civilization, but even if these items were genuine, the strict control on exporting antiquities would make it impossible for foreign purchasers to take them out of the country. At the same time, the kinds of handsome household items of later periods that predominate in the antiques trade of countries like England and Scotland are uncommon in Italy; poorer than other European nations, it never had a large middle class to demand luxury goods in quantity. The objects of value that do exist were almost always made for large noble families who have passed them down — or sold them at prices far beyond the means of the average buyer.

Occasionally, there are fairs at the *Palazzo Pitti* in Florence; Viterbo's Palazzo del Concilio; and in Todi in Umbria. Arezzo holds an outdoor antiques fair the first Sunday of each month. Palermo's *Mercato delle Pulci* (flea market) may have a few bargains.

There is, however, a thriving antiques trade in Italy, particularly in Florence, Rome, and Milan. Many dealers trade in non-Italian goods. Many of the moderately priced antiques found here are English; silver is an especially common stock item. And since the antiques market in Italy is generally softer than that in London or New York, such items could well cost less than at home.

WHAT TO BUY

Italian antiques do exist in several categories. Candlestick holders and marionettes, Sicilian puppets, and lamps made from opaline are good finds, as are figurines from the traditional *Christmas presepe* (nativity scene). Also look for the following:

CHINA AND GLASS: There is a lot of Venetian glass about, but it is very hard to tell its age without expert advice (there are some master glass blowers who make excellent reproductions). The original Venetian crystal tended to be of a darker, smoky hue.

COPPER AND BRASS: You don't have to be an expert to find good pieces of domestic copper and brass. These metals were used for domestic utensils and, therefore, no imprints were used. The oldest pieces were shaped with a hammer and are of irregular thickness. Northern Italy is the most reliable source.

FURNITURE: Most genuinely old Italian furniture is very heavily restored or extremely expensive. What is available is often not nearly as beautifully finished as pieces made in England or France; design was generally considered more important. Renaissance furniture is particularly sought after and difficult to find at reasonable prices. Popular versions of *barocchetto* (baroque) furniture, however, as well as *rustico* (rustic furniture), are still available, usually in the provincial cities of central and northern Italy.

JEWELRY: Though Italy is one of the world's major centers of modern goldsmithing, much antique jewelry sold here is imported. However, the market offers some very beautiful and ornamental earrings — mostly produced in Gaeta in Lazio and largely found now in the south. Serving as a constant reminder of the beloved, these were traditionally used instead of engagement rings by peasant girls who worked in the fields, where a ring would have been a nuisance. Small mosaics that depict scenes of ancient Rome and are of great value can be spotted by a sharp eye in shop windows on Rome's Via Babuino and Via della Scrofa, some from the early 1800s. Many shops also sell old cameos.

PAINTINGS: Since Italians are the world's experts at restoration, there are plenty of appealing pictures on the market. But don't automatically assume they'll be as authentic (or as valuable) as they are handsome. Italian regional loyalties, which in past centuries gave rise to distinctive local schools of painting, are expressed today by the high demand among each region's collectors for the works created there. Consequently, dealers in Venice try to stock examples of the Venetian school, Genoese dealers works of the Genoese school. Works by non-Italian artists painted during Grand Tour days may be underpriced. Ask first about export restrictions.

PICTURE FRAMES: Gilded-and-carved wood-and-glass frames can still be found fairly easily — though you need a very large wall to hang them and a large bank account to pay for those made during the Renaissance. More practical are the little dressing table frames made in mahogany. They are not outrageously expensive and are widely sold.

POTTERY: Production of majolica — the tin-glazed and richly colored and ornamented earthenware pieces Italians know as maiolica or faïence — reached its zenith in the northern Italian towns of Deruta, Faenza, Gubbio, and in Urbino (the Marches) and Castelli (Abruzzo) during the Renaissance. In the middle of the 16th century, potters in Faenza introduced a lacy, baroque style of "white" pottery, called *bianchi di Faenza,* which remained popular well past the middle of the 17th century. Both types of pottery are much sought after. There are many clever copies, and antiques dealers tell of colleagues who commission pieces and then have them joined together with copper wire so that the finished vessel looks authentically old. Another trick is to glaze century-old bricks to give them an aged look before turning them into Castelli pottery.

PRINTS: The mapmaker of the medieval world, Italy created maps by the score beginning in the 14th century. Prints were also widely issued. Many of those available today have been reproduced on old paper or pulled out of old books. However, the stallholders in Rome's Piazza Borghese, as well as shops all over Italy, sell the real thing at favorable prices and are very helpful and knowledgeable. Venice, a center for engraving in the 15th century, also is a good source.

WHERE TO SHOP

For a comprehensive listing of antiques dealers by region and specialization and of major fairs, consult the *Guida OPI dell'Antiquariato Italiano,* published by Tony Metz, and the *Catalogo dell'Antiquariato Italiano,* published by Giorgio Mondadori. Both are in Italian.

FLORENCE: There are dozens of antiques shops in Florence, and the concentrations are highest along Via dei Fossi, Via Maggio, the Ponte Vecchio, and Borgognissanti. On the latter, the following establishments are good: *Bruzzichelli, Fioretto, Fratelli Romano, Palloni, Pierini, Romano, Ventura.*

Other good dealers include the following:

Bartolozzi – Furniture and works of art. 18 Via Maggio.

Berto Berti – Majolica. 29r Via dei Fossi.

Carlo Carnevali – Majolica. 64 Borgo San Jacopo.

Giuseppe Bellini – The doyen of local dealers, a generalist. 5 Lungarno Soderini.

There are junk markets in Piazza dei Ciompi (daily) and Piazza Tasso (Saturdays). Bargains are there for the finding, and haggling is the rule. Curiosities are also commonly found in the early morning under the loggias of the *Mercato Nuovo* (Straw Market), near Piazza della Signoria.

The premier Italian antiques fair is Florence's *Mostra d'Antiquariato,* held in mid-September of odd-numbered years in the Palazzo Strozzi.

MILAN: Shops are more spread out here than in other cities. However, there are some groupings concentrated on Via Bagutta, Via Bigli, Via Montenapoleone, Via Sant'Andrea, Via Santo Spirito, and Via della Spiga, a narrow pedestrian cul-de-sac lined with marble benches and trees. Try the following dealers:

Aldo Pavesi – Majolica. Via Vincenzo Monti.

Franco Sabatelli – Picture frames. 5 Via Fiori Chiavi.

A. Subert – Silver, faïence, scientific items. 22 Via della Spiga.

The local auction houses are *Christie's* (9 Via Borgogna; phone: 2-794712), and *Finarte* (4 Piazzetta Bossi; phone: 2-877041).

The city's most important antiques fair, the annual *Fiera di Sant'Ambrogio,* takes place in Piazza Sant'Ambrogio and adjoining streets for 15 days beginning December 7.

ROME: Italy's major center for antiques hunting is Rome, and most of the largest and most reliable dealers are on Via del Babuino, which runs from Piazza di Spagna to Piazza del Popolo. Among them are the following:

Apolloni – Antiques. 133 Via del Babuino.

Arturo Ferrante – Antiques. 42-43 Via del Babuino.

Fallani – Sculpture. 58a Via del Babuino.

Di Giorgio – Antiques. 182 Via del Babuino.

Olivi – Antiques. 136 Via del Babuino.

Browse in the venerable shops above, but the *Granmercato Antiquario Babuino* (150

Via del Babuino) is still the best bet for small, guaranteed items, most of which are English. Everything is clearly visible, priced, and explained.

Other good shopping streets are Via Margutta, behind Via del Babuino, Via del Governo Vecchio, Via di Panico, Via dei Coronari, Via Monserrato, Via dell'Orso, and the Campo Marzio area. (Via dei Coronari is especially delightful for strolling during the annual autumn antiques fair, when all the shops are open at night.) In the ancient Roman suburb known as the Suburra, near the Roman Forum between Via Cavour and Via Nazionale, there are a number of small, interesting shops — many of them selling Art Nouveau. The restorers in Via Boschetto are a good source of reasonably priced 19th-century furniture. The following dealers are worth a visit:

Bottega di Montevecchio – Small objects. 15 Piazza di Montevecchio.
Dakota – Small 1950s objects. 494 Via del Corso.
Enrico Fiorentini – Marble. 53/B Via Margutta.
Galleria Spada – Small objects. 3 Piazza Capo Ferro.
Galleria delle Stampe Antiche – Prints. 38 Via del Governo Vecchio.
Giacomo Cohen – Carpets. 83 Via Margutta.
Gussio – Majolica. 27/A Via Laurina.
Luciano Coen – Carpets. 65 Via Margutta.
La Mansarde – Furniture. 202-203 Via dei Coronari.
Pacifici – Bronzes and arms. 174 Via Giulia.
Rosario Lo Turco – Puppets. 17 Via dei Pianellari.
Lo Scrittoio – Furniture. 102-103 Via dei Coronari.
Tanca – Antique jewelry and silver. 12 Salita dei Crescenzi.

In addition, look for good prints, as well as other items, at the stalls in Piazza Borghese, and visit the following auction houses:

L'Antonina – 23 Piazza Mignanelli (phone: 679-4009).
Christie's – 114 Piazza Navona (phone: 654-1217).
Finarte – 54 Via Margutta (phone: 678-6557).
Semenzato – 93 Piazza di Spagna (phone: 676-6479).
Sotheby's – 90 Piazza di Spagna (phone: 678-1798).

Finally, the Sunday morning flea market at Porta Portese can be fun. However, it's said that anything you see there of real value has probably been stolen. Never pay the first price quoted.

RULES OF THE ROAD FOR AN ODYSSEY OF THE OLD

Buy for sheer pleasure, not for investment. Forget about the carrot of supposed retail values that dealers habitually dangle in front of amateur clients. If you love something, it will probably ornament your home until the Colosseum falls.

Buy the finest example you can afford of any item, in as close to mint condition as possible. Chipped or broken "bargains" will haunt you later with their shabbiness.

Train your eye in museums. These are the best schools for the acquisitive senses, particularly as you begin to develop special passions.

Get advice from specialists when contemplating major acquisitions. Much antique furniture and many paintings have been restored several times over, and Italian antiques salespeople, particularly in Rome, are more entertaining than knowledgeable. If you want to be absolutely certain that what you're buying is what you've been told it is, stick with the larger dealers. Most auction houses have an evaluation office whose experts will make appraisals for a fee. Even museums in some cities can be approached. In Rome, two useful contacts are Sally Improta, a member of the *Appraisers' Association of America,* at the *Bottega di Montevecchio* (15 Piazza Montevecchio; phone: 687-0497) and *Art Import* (a British firm specializing in British antiques but knowledgeable about the trade in general, 2 Piazza Borghese).

Don't be afraid to haggle. Only a few of the large dealers have *prezzi fissi* (fixed prices). The others will decide for themselves how much you can afford and charge accordingly. So the rule of thumb is to bargain wherever you don't see the *prezzi fissi* sign. A word of warning: While most larger dealers take credit cards, smaller shops do not.

When pricing an object, don't forget to figure the cost of shipping. Around 30% of the cost of the item is about right for large items. Italian firms are expensive, so the best idea is to stick to the bigger international shipping firms, which offer a door-to-door service to New York as well as advice about required export licenses. The following Rome firms could be helpful:

Bolliger – 61 Via dei Buonvisi (phone: 6-655-7161; fax: 6-651-7136).

Emery Air Freight – 48a Via Passo Buole, Fiumicino (phone: 6-658-1621).

Italian Moving Network – 132 Via del Tritone (phone: 6-690-2009).

Note that the Italian government requires that any object of possible historical interest to the Italian state be declared and has levied an export tax on goods exported to the United States.

Churches and Piazzas

Whether it's a sleek designer space ringed with chic cafés or a rustic square sprouting vegetable stalls, Italy's piazzas are the acknowledged centers of local activity. Revolutions are preached there, crowds harangued, heretics burned, confetti sprinkled. Every day marks a new period in the perennial urchin-league soccer match. Every evening, tables and chairs are hauled onto the sidewalk, and a new hand is dealt in some card game that seems to have been in progress since the sack of Rome. And every Sunday, at the end of mass in the late morning, a churchful of the faithful pours out onto the square for a round of local gossip before lunch. The church, drawing its patrons from the teeming society just outside its portals and representing a supremely Italian mix of diversion and devotion, is the raison d'être of almost every piazza in Italy. Their styles range from plain to grandiose, from peasant church tacked as afterthought onto the dusty piazza of a one-priest town to St. Peter's, with its oval square designed to allow optimum admiration of the basilica's façade.

So when making a list of touristy tasks, put "idleness" very near the top and spend a large, lazy slice of as many days as possible doing as the Romans do — sitting and sipping and stretching and strolling on a glorious Italian piazza in front of a lush Italian church like those listed below. Here, indeed, the *far niente* (doing nothing) for which Italy is well known is truly *dolce* (sweet).

BASILICA DI SAN FRANCESCO, Assisi, Umbria: This handsome, elaborate double church was erected for the greater glory of St. Francis in 1228, 2 years after his death, amid protests from Franciscans who thought such a structure inconsistent with their sect's consecration to a life of poverty. The colossal complex, which includes a Franciscan monastery and two churches (one on top of the other), towers over the roofs and alleys clustered on the Umbrian hillside town. The façade is a curious mixture of stolid squareness and Gothic fancy embroidered in light pink stone, and the windowless tower dissolves into a row of slender arches at the top. The rich artwork includes the portrait by Cimabue of a melancholy, slightly cross-eyed St. Francis and a famous series of 28 frescoes by Giotto depicting the saint's super-saintly life.

SANTA MARIA DEL FIORE AND PIAZZA DEL DUOMO, Florence: Henry James rhapsodized that this stupendous 13th-century structure — the fourth-largest cathedral in the world — was "the image of some mighty hillside enameled with blooming flowers." No less overwhelming today, a visit here is a series of vivid vignettes as unforgettable as Florence itself. Stand at the top of the cupola, and you're afloat in a realm of pink, green, and white marble, with a bird's-eye view of toy pigeons and toy people in the double-sized piazza below. Or climb the endless steps to the top of the bell tower designed by Giotto, and look out over a sea of shingles — those of the cathedral's own lordly Brunelleschi dome blending with those of the rusty rest of the roofs of Florence. Come to earth through the poised and soberly decorated gray and white *pietra forte* interior — stopping, perhaps, for a haunting few minutes at the crypt — and, before you know it, the piazza's rousing rabble is all around you. In front of the church is the octagonal baptistry of St. John the Baptist (San Giovanni), which was Florence's cathedral from the time it was built (in perhaps the 4th century) until the construction of Santa Maria del Fiore. It was clothed in its present marble stripes in the 12th century and is still used for baptisms — Dante Alighieri was baptized here. The royal gilded bronze-relief doors on the east, which Ghiberti spent 27 years of his life creating, rang in the Renaissance and were dubbed by Michelangelo as worthy of being "the gates of paradise." Just to the rear of the Duomo (at 9 Piazza del Duomo) is the *Museo dell'Opera del Duomo* (Duomo Museum), which houses two masterworks of Renaissance sculpture — Donatello's gaunt and tormented (but still elegant) statue of Mary Magdalene and an oddly powerful but unfinished Michelangelo *Pietà,* which the artist finally broke up in frustration. For further details, peruse the Duomo section in *Florence,* THE CITIES.

PIAZZA DELLA SIGNORIA, Florence: With the giant, needle-like tower of the Palazzo Vecchio shooting straight up from its base in Piazza della Signoria, this is a noteworthy spot, not least because of the towering, weathered copy of Michelangelo's *David,* the emblem of the city, that stands at its portal. It has also been the heart of Florence for a millennium. Over the troubled centuries of the Renaissance, the square was gradually expanded as powerful families razed the houses of the rivals they expelled. It was here, in the heart of what modern Italy knows as its prime magnet for consumer vanities, that the puritanical priest Savonarola organized his 1497 "Burning of the Vanities," a bonfire fed with purportedly lewd drawings, books, and other trinkets of worldly corruption. And it was also here that Savonarola himself was hanged and burned, on a spot now marked by an etched inscription. Now that the violence has given way to the peaceful ringing of the bells every quarter of an hour, which along with the throaty cooing of the pigeons are the dominant sounds, the piazza is shiningly beautiful, all the more so because of the adjacent Loggia dei Lanzi — so called because Cosimo the Younger stationed mercenary guards known as *lanzichenecchi* under its overhanging roof, where a small collection of statues now stands.

IL DUOMO, Milan: This frilly, glistening monument at the heart of Milan — Italy's largest cathedral next to St. Peter's — is something of an anomaly in modern, fast-paced Milan. With its arched flying buttresses, its gargoyles, and its statues perching perilously on narrow spires, it is the fullest-fledged example of Italian Gothic. Though nearly 150 feet high and big enough inside to seat 40,000, it manages to be less forbidding than its French counterparts because of the lightness of its off-white marble exterior. On the site of an early Christian church the cornerstone was laid in the late 14th century, and construction continued for more than 450 years, drawing on the talents of generations of architects, both Italian and imported, until it was completed in the early 19th century; statuary was added well into the 20th. Seen from the inside, the stained glass windows depicting Old and New Testament scenes are so huge that the roof seems supported by shafts of colored light. For an account of the cathedral's history and a look at some fine sculpture and reliefs, visit the beautifully displayed, modern *Museo del Duomo* (Cathedral Museum) across the piazza.

CERTOSA DI PAVIA (CHARTERHOUSE OF PAVIA), near Pavia, Lombardy:

This monumental monastery of glowing brick is wonderfully out of place in the quiet Lombard countryside just outside Pavia, on the banks of the Ticino, just an hour from Milan. When the dozens of architects, painters, sculptors, and builders who pieced it together during most of the 15th century were finished, it was an exuberantly decorated mini-city with its own unique urban sprawl. It has its own train station (station stop Certosa) and even a skyscraper of sorts (the octagonal cupola of its church, which towers 5 stories above everything else in the area). The arcades of its two cloisters are decorated with terra cotta reliefs, and the roofs are spiky with the chimneys of the Cistercian priests' cottages — tiny villas, each with 2 floors and a garden, which the religious occupants leave seven times daily to visit the church for prayers. They have taken a vow of silence; monks, who have not, are available to lead tours of the complex. The monastery is open to the public, and several of the cells can be visited.

CAMPO DEI MIRACOLI (FIELD OF MIRACLES), Pisa, Tuscany: The rakishly tilted bell tower (which is closed for repairs, and likely to be for some time) that attracts flocks of tourists in search of a new angle for their photography is only the most famous feature of this "Field of Miracles" at the edge of the city, where the cathedral, baptistry, and cemetery sit pensively on the emerald grass. Try to find a moment, perhaps at dusk, to peregrinate in solitude among the gleaming and magically simple buildings. They were built during the period that began in 1063 with the commencement of construction on the cathedral and ended in the mid-14th century with the completion of the cloistered cemetery. In the cathedral, be sure to see the ivory *Madonna with Child* leaning backward along the curve of the elephant's tusk out of which it is carved, and the intricately sculpted pulpit — both by the 14th-century artist Giovanni Pisano. And stroll through the Camposanto, the cemetery whose earth was brought by the Crusaders from Mount Calvary; the frescoes on the walls that surround it depict heaven, hell, life, death, and the cosmos, all in powerful style. Try to arrange to be here on June 17 for the *festa* of the city's patron, San Ranieri, when the piazza, Tower, and the Arno are dramatically aflicker with the light of dozens upon dozens of slow-burning torches known as *fiaccole.* For more details, see *Italy's Most Colorful Festas.*

BASILICA DI SAN VITALE, Ravenna, Emilia-Romagna: The naked brick exterior of this knobby, octagonal church, built between 526 and 547 — probably based on a much older church in Constantinople — conceals an Oriental treasure of an interior, brilliant with mosaics populated by royalty and gaudy birds and heavily embellished with columns whose capitals are encrusted with gingerbread curlicues. The imperial decoration climaxes in the apse. Depicted in a majestic fablescape of tiny colored stones at either side of the altar, Emperor Justinian and Empress Theodora, dressed in ornate Eastern robes and bearing the chalice containing the wine of the sacrifice of Christ in her hands, lead a stately procession toward Jesus. The infinitesimal stones are angled this way and that, and the effect as their blues, greens, golds, and whites catch the light is dazzling.

Installed during the 6th century, when the port of Ravenna was the capital of the western provinces of Justinian's Byzantine Empire — and at the height of its prosperity — this fabulous mosaic is one of the chief glories of Ravenna, a city whose early Christian churches are full of such wonders. To see more, don't fail to visit the adjacent 5th-century Tomb of Galla Placidia, Emperor Honorius's sister; the Orthodox baptistry; the 6th-century Church of Sant'Apollinare Nuovo; the small *Museo Arcivescovile,* near Piazza Duomo, whose collection is small but exquisite; and the 6th-century Sant'Apollinare in Classe. For further details, consult the Ravenna section in *Emilia-Romagna,* DIRECTIONS.

PIAZZA NAVONA, Rome: This pedestrian island in the middle of traffic-snarled Rome retains the elliptical shape, and much of the function, of the ancient Roman racetrack whose site it now occupies. But the chariots have been replaced by children on bicycles who cut nimble paths between unsuspecting photographers and rolling soccer balls. In summertime, people cluster to watch the progress of while-you-wait caricature artists or drop coins in the regiments of open guitar cases. Jugglers, fire-eaters, and long-haired bongo players vie for the attention of passersby. Hack artists peddle their watercolor cityscapes. In winter, from *Christmastime* through *Epiphany,* the piazza is crowded with booths full of sweets, toys, crèche figures, and goodies-stuffed stockings. In the middle of it all is the famous Pietro Bernini fountain, *Fontana dei Fiumi* (Fountain of the Rivers), which represents as powerful, writhing human figures what the 17th century considered the world's four great rivers — the Nile, Ganges, Danube, and Plata. There was no love lost between Bernini and his former pupil Borromini, who designed the Church of Sant'Agnese on the west side of the square. So the Rio della Plata is shrinking in horror from it, and the Nile has its head covered — some say to avoid seeing the church. (But in fact, it is because the Nile's source had not yet been discovered.)

PIAZZA SAN PIETRO, Vatican City, Rome: Since the first basilica of St. Peter's was built in the 3rd century by order of the emperor Constantine on the site where St. Peter was martyred and subsequently buried, millions of pilgrims have crossed continents by plane, train, car, carriage, and on foot to get to this vast elliptical space, the main square of Christendom. Every Wednesday morning in warm weather, thousands pack between the welcoming arms of Bernini's two semicircular statue-topped Doric colonnades to hear and see the pope on his Vatican Palace balcony. (The best comment on the efficiency of the Vatican is that, despite the hordes, the place is spotless.)

The present basilica, ordered after 11 centuries had left its predecessor somewhat the worse for wear, took a good chunk of the Renaissance to build and drew on the talents of Bramante, Michelangelo, and others. Among its myriad wonders are Michelangelo's *Pietà* (encased in bulletproof glass since its mutilation and restoration several years ago); Bernini's *Baldacchino,* a 46-ton bronze altar canopy so elaborate it is really more architecture than sculpture; and the climb through the innards of Michelangelo's cupola for a glorious view into the well-shielded Vatican gardens and out over the entire city. Visits to the subterranean vaults have become increasingly popular.

The whole place is overwhelming; save your first impression for a moment when you're fresh and firm-legged, and don't try to see it in tandem with the vast Vatican museums. For further details, consult "Special Places" in *Rome,* THE CITIES.

PIAZZA DI SPAGNA, Rome: The thing to do at this picturesque relic of 18th-century Rome can be summed up in a single word: nothing. Refresh yourself at Bernini's gushing, boat-shaped fountain, the *Barcaccia.* Recline on the voluptuous curving staircase. Almost magically, you'll find yourself impelled to stay right where you are. It has been this way for years. The stage-like set of 138 travertine stairs, known to everyone but locals as the Spanish Steps (after a palace that housed the Spanish Embassy to the Holy See), climbs to the twin-turreted Church of Trinità dei Monti and the green sprawl of the Villa Borghese park beyond. In the wings at No. 26, with a window onto the staircase, is the house where John Keats died in 1821, now a museum devoted to him and his fellow Romantics. In May, the stairs are covered with red, pink, and white azaleas; at *Christmastime,* the platform midway up is the site of an illuminated, near-life-size crèche. Rome's answer to New York's Fifth Avenue, Via Condotti runs from the foot of the Spanish Steps to Via del Corso and is a favorite spot for window shopping and the ritual evening *passeggiata* (promenade). (Also see "Special Places" in *Rome,* THE CITIES.)

PIAZZA DEL CAMPO, Siena, Tuscany: From the hazy horizon of Tuscan hills beyond the city walls, all Siena seems to slide down into the seashell-shaped Piazza del Campo, one of Europe's most beautiful old squares. Begin your visit on one of the streets that circle it slightly above. Walk down a flight of stairs, through a dark archway, and then into the splash of sunlight that washes the piazza. Look around you. Your dazzled gaze dips toward the Palazzo Comunale, halts momentarily against its stern, elegant battlements, and then soars up through the brown brick tower and its marble cap straight into the sky. All around the piazza's edge are medieval and Renaissance palaces — most notably the curved-fronted Palazzo Sansedoni, which dates from the 13th and 14th centuries. Twice each summer for 5 days in July and again in August, ancient banners hang from the windows of the palaces, the late-breakfast-takers give way to crowds of spectators, the piazza's usual languid atmosphere gives way to chaos, and the roadway all around turns into the route of a costumed procession and then becomes a racetrack for the *Palio* — hours of medieval pomp climaxed by a fierce horse race that follows traditions going back centuries. For further details, see "Special Places" in *Siena,* THE CITIES, and *Italy's Most Colorful Festas.*

IL DUOMO, Siena: Siena's cathedral, dedicated to Santa Maria dell'Assunta, rose mysteriously out of the 12th century and seems to be knotted into the thick skein of houses around it. Coated inside and out with the black and white marble stripes typical of Italian Gothic, it is both meticulously crafted down to the smallest detail and perfectly balanced — despite the shaggy remains of an abortive 14th-century attempt to double its size. Once inside, weave through the exquisitely carved patches of floor bathed in the amber light of the stained glass windows; each of the 56 squares tells a different biblical story in inlaid marble. (Some are so precious they are kept covered except from August 15 to September 15.) Next door is the *Museo dell'Opera del Duomo* (Cathedral Museum), which occupies what's left of the 14th-century enlargement. Its breathtaking collection of Sienese medieval paintings includes the *Maestà* of Duccio di Buoninsegna. For further details, see "Special Places" in *Siena,* THE CITIES.

PIAZZA SAN MARCO, Venice: Italy's square of squares, proudly placed at the entrance to the city on the Grand Canal and the center of Venetian life, is a glittering testimony to the opulence of the Venetian Empire in the East. The geometric pattern of inset marble on the façade of the Doge's Palace, the Islam-inspired basilica, the pair of giant bronze Moors that have struck the hours at the clock tower for 500 years, the granite columns topped by the lion of St. Mark and the statue of St. Theodore, the pigeons and the violins, and even the brightly tinted T-shirts and Murano glass trinkets, all give the piazza the gleam of some fairy-tale Oriental pavilion. It's not hard to understand why Napoleon called it Europe's finest drawing room and why, among all the squares of Venice, this is the only one that Venetians call a piazza (the other public spaces are known as *campi* — fields — because they were once unpaved). Galileo Galilei tested his telescope from the summit of the 324-foot-high, 9th-century red campanile (an early 20th-century copy now stands on the site), the traditional viewpoint over the city's red-shingled rooftops and domes to the lagoon and its distant islands; don't miss it. Also visit the 9th-century Venetian-Byzantine Basilica of San Marco, a masterpiece of mosaics and sinuous curves, massive domes, and a profusion of supportive pillars built as a chapel for the doges and a shelter for the tomb of St. Mark. When the Venetians sacked Constantinople in 1203, they carted back galleys full of gold, jewels, relics, the four famous bronze horses, and mosaic tiles with which to lavishly decorate this church — a process that continued through the 16th century. The bejeweled, miraculous 10th-century painting known as the *Madonna Nicopeia,* a part of this booty, is now exhibited in a chapel of its own.

Remarkable Ruins

The only museums in the world where picnics and dogs are allowed, and where sightseeing is ideally combined with a sunbath, a game of touch football, or a bottle of wine, historic ruins have always been part of Italian life. In the last century, cows grazed along protruding bits of now-priceless antique wall. The disfigured Roman street-corner torso called Pasquino served under Rome's more repressive popes as one of the "talking statues" on which sometimes witty protesters hung anonymous slogans and insults. And every government since Mussolini's has tried to dig up, fence off, and charge admission to the thousands of ruins peppering the peninsula.

But there are simply more of them than anyone can catalogue. In Rome alone, there are so many buried theaters and villas that building the city's skimpy subway system took 20 years — in good part because of the labyrinth of subterranean treasures that had to be dodged.

Each ruin is in its own distinctive state of decay, and the most romantic may not necessarily be the most historically significant. And each complex of ruins has its own particular mood and its own prime viewing time during the year. The spectacular hilltop temples, with views that plummet over rocks submerged 40 feet below the sea, belong to clear, hot summer days. For urban experiences like Pompeii or the Roman Forum, you won't feel crowded, even on Sundays, except during the peak tourist times at *Easter* and mid-summer. Whatever you do, by all means make the pilgrimage through the ice cream and soda peddlers at some time during your Italian sojourn to pay homage to these ancient places. Be sure to check schedules in advance; many of the most important sites are closed on Mondays or Tuesdays and on holidays; and many shut down Sunday afternoons as well. And always keep an eye peeled for the unobtrusive yellow signs that point down dusty roads. Together with the handful of superbly interesting destinations sketched below, the moss-covered stumps of column in the middle of the woods that are found in this fashion may turn out to be the best part of the journey.

NORA, Gonnesa, Sardinia: Jutting out into the sensuously limpid water for which Sardinia is famous, this area on the island's southern tip bears traces of 4,000 years of population. Primitive stone huts, called *nuraghi,* that date from 1500–2000 BC dot the countryside and make up the Bronze Age village of Seruci (not far from the modern town of Gonnesa). Remains of the ancient city of Nora, founded by the Phoenicians in the 9th century BC, are here as well, and above them are later, Roman ruins. At the center of the city is the temple to the Phoenician goddess Tamit, made of large, irregular blocks of stone. In addition, much of the Roman city remains, including a theater and some intricate decorative mosaics. A special bonus of a visit here: Nora is well off the path beaten by most tourists. Details: *Azienda Autonoma di Soggiorno e Turismo,* 9 Piazza Matteotti, Cagliari (Sardegna) 09100 (phone: 70-669255).

HERCULANEUM AND POMPEII, Campania: Shortly after noon on August 24, in the year AD 79, Mount Vesuvius erupted, and the busy port city of Pompeii and the smaller, quieter town of Herculaneum were buried under tons of ashes, pumice, and other volcanic debris. Pompeii, which was then, and is now, a thrumming business center of about 30,000, was effectively embalmed. Excavations that began in the 18th century have unearthed almost two-thirds of the place. Hundreds of buildings are still standing — cramped houses from poor neighborhoods as well as sumptuous villas complete with interior gardens, central heating, and libraries. It's like a set for a 1st-century period movie or a huge, three-dimensional still life. Much of the artwork is kept in nearby Naples's *Museo Archeologico Nazionale* (National Archaeological Museum), but there's enough here to leave a visitor thoroughly exhausted — and still feeling that there are a few blocks of marble unturned. Some high points: The Antiquarium building, which contains, among other things, the plaster casts of victims buried in the molten rock; the cross on the wall of Herculaneum's Casa del Bicentenario, possibly the oldest known example of Christian worship; the finely detailed frescoes at Pompeii's Villa dei Misteri, depicting the rites of initiation into the mysteries of the cult of Bacchus; and the obscene drawings and graffiti on the walls of the Lupanara, the town brothel. To get away from the tourist jam that snarls the city from

May to September, hike up to the still-steaming crater of Vesuvius, where it's possible to fry an egg on a rock for lunch. Closed Mondays. Details: *Azienda Autonoma di Soggiorno,* 1 Via Sacra, Pompeii (Napoli) 80045 (phone: 81-863-2401).

OSTIA ANTICA, Lazio: This much underrated and undervisited ruined sprawl at the mouth of the Tiber — in remarkably good condition because the excavations are relatively recent — was once among the most important trading centers of the empire. It had a population of 100,000, was a meeting place for sailors and merchants from all over Europe and northern Africa, and boasted remarkable cultural and religious diversity — obvious today from the remains of its synagogue, several Christian chapels, and the dozen or so temples to the Persian sun god, Mitra. A pile of columns marked with the name of their owner, Volusianus, and lying on what used to be a wharf, is a poignant symbol of its fall from prosperity, brought on by a malaria epidemic and the silting up of the harbor. Open daily except Mondays from 9 AM to 4 PM in winter, 9 AM to 6 PM in summer. Details: *Ente Provinciale per il Turismo,* 11 Via Parigi, Roma 00185 (phone: 6-461851); or *Museo di Ostia Antica,* Ostia (phone: 6-565-0022).

PAESTUM, Campania: The massive temples of Paestum, gleaming bone-white against the dark greens and browns of the brush-covered mountains south of Salerno, provide an almost unique opportunity to see a Greek town that has not been surrounded by modern structures. Founded by the Greeks in the late 7th century BC as Poseidonia, it was inhabited successively by the early Italic tribes, the Romans, and the early Christians. Consequently, the ruins are a catalogue of the changing styles of 700 years of art. The weathered, but ruggedly eternal, remains of three major temples — their parades of columns remarkably intact among the cypress trees, oleander, and fragrant herbs — show how quickly the Greeks solved aesthetic problems. They were built within a century of each other, and one of them is considered the most beautiful Doric temple in the world. Rediscovered only in the 18th century, after centuries of hiding among malarial swamps and giant trees, Paestum is also home to the only known examples of classical Greek painting. One fresco from the Tomba del Tuffatore (Tomb of the Diver), a 1968 discovery now housed in Paestum's museum, shows an athlete plunging into the water, a look of Olympic concentration on his face. Details: *Azienda Autonoma di Soggiorno,* Piazza Basilica Paleocristiana, Paestum (Salerno) 84063 (phone: 828-811016).

VILLA ROMANA DEL CASALE, Piazza Armerina, Sicily: This 4th-century Roman villa of a late Roman emperor named Maximian, located in the almost exact center of Sicily, is full of beautifully preserved mosaics depicting mythical acts of heroism, hunting scenes, races, and cupids harvesting grapes. The busy hunters, struggling heroes, and frightened running bulls and deer are powerfully realistic; tiny colored mosaic stones outline each tensed muscle. One scene of women bathing, remarkable for its subtle shadings of flesh color, shows that bikinis were already in style during the Roman Empire. No textbook of ancient history could ever tell the story of Roman life as vividly as this. Elsewhere in Sicily, there are almost more ruins than can be counted — to start, at Agrigento, Palermo, Segesta, Selinunte, and Syracuse. Details: *Azienda Autonoma di Soggiorno,* 15 Via Cavour, Piazza Armerina (Enna) 94015 (phone: 935-680201).

BATHS OF CARACALLA, Rome: This grandiose tribute to the human body was built on 27 acres by the emperor Caracalla in the 3rd century AD. Each of the sunken, mosaic-covered floors visible today was the bottom of a single pool. To get an idea of size, follow the curve of an imaginary arch up from one still-standing base; the other side is hundreds of feet away. Each one of these huge pools was heated to a different temperature by an elaborate underground central heating system, and the whole complex was open to the public. For a nominal fee, the citizens of Rome could pass from tub to tub, soaking in the steaming water of the circular *caldarium,* rubbing elbows with friends in the *tepidarium,* and talking brisk business in the *frigidarium.* Changing rooms, dry steamrooms, and gymnasia flanked the pool rooms. Everything about this glorified bathtub of ancient times is big — so it's entirely appropriate that the outdoor opera and ballet performances staged in the *caldarium* in July and August are blockbusters. (A legendary *Aïda,* for instance, was complete with prancing horses and a ponderous pachyderm.) It seems entirely fitting that Percy Bysshe Shelley composed his *Prometheus Unbound* here. Closed Mondays. Details: *Ente Provinciale per il Turismo,* 11 Via Parigi, Roma 00185 (phone: 6-461851; for information on summer performances, phone: 6-575-8302).

COLOSSEUM, Rome: Every week beginning in AD 80, at a time when Romans supplied free entertainment to their populace on a scale unique in the history of the planet, 50,000 spectators packed this stadium for an afternoon of gory Roman fun. Hundreds of gladiators did battle to the death, and unarmed Christians wrestled hungry lions; on state occasions, the Colosseum was flooded and naval battles staged. Since then, a large chunk of the outer wall has gone — Renaissance construction workers regularly chopped away at the structure when they needed marble for St. Peter's and assorted palazzi. Buttresses were erected by Pius VIII (1800–1823) to keep the structure from caving in on itself. Henry James's Daisy Miller came here against her elders' advice, caught Roman fever (as malaria was called then), and died of it. The luxuriant vegetation she came to see by moonlight (the 420 exotic species prompted two books on Colosseum flora and countless rhapsodies by Dickens, Byron, and other Victorians) has been entirely weeded out, a situation "much regretted by lovers of the picturesque," according to the 19th-century writer Augustus Hare. The floor was then excavated to reveal the locker rooms underneath — with separate but equal facilities for lions and Christians. The lions have long been replaced by stray cats, but the allure of the structure is as strong as ever, and visitors instinctively appreciate the genius of the engineers who found a way to erect such a gigantic structure on marshy ground (a challenge even today), and who designed it so that immense and often rowdy crowds could enter, claim seats, and exit with ease through its 80 *vomitoria.* Experiencing its immensity, it's easy to understand how Romans could think that were the Colosseum to fall, so would Rome — and the world itself. Until recently, contemporary visitors always have had to cross a potentially fatal torrent of traffic that promised to be no less lethal than Roman fever to get there, but when the piazza in front finally was closed to cars, this dangerous hazard was eliminated. Details: *Ente Provinciale per il Turismo,* 11 Via Parigi, Roma 00185 (phone: 6-461851 or 6-700-4261). See also "Special Places" in *Rome,* THE CITIES.

FORUM AND THE PALATINE, Rome: Begin your visit to ancient Rome on top of the first of Rome's seven hills, where Romulus and Remus were supposedly suckled by a she-wolf and where Rome began, because you'll be too tired to get up there *after* seeing the Forum. Bring picnic, kids, dogs, sketch pads, and cameras. The Palatine offers fine views through the framework of pine trees over ancient and modern Rome. Marble columns tower romantically over fields of flowers scattered with carved chunks of marble. Ruins of the luxurious imperial villas that once covered most of the hill — the reason that the Palatine is the namesake of all the world's palaces — stand next to the remains of the mud huts where Rome's founders settled in the 8th century BC. Painters such as Claude Lorrain and Jean-Baptiste Camille Corot created canvas after canvas depicting this ruin-scattered landscape; to judge from their work and that of their contemporaries, all Rome must have once looked like this. Seeing it inspired the English to pioneer a whole new style in landscape gardening.

Following in the footsteps of early Romans, climb down from the Palatine to the low area that grew from a neutral meeting ground of hilltop tribes into the center of downtown ancient Rome to become the Forum. Actually made up of many different fora, it was once an agglomeration of open-air markets, shopping malls, government buildings, temples, and public meeting spots, and their ruins can all be seen. Along its

Via Sacra, Julius Caesar returned from the wars in triumphal processions, and at its Basilica Julia, Mark Antony harangued the crowd after Caesar was killed. It was the business center of the empire as well as its religious and political center, and still embedded in the floor of the Basilica Emilia are the coins that melted in fires during the sack of Rome in the 5th century. During the Middle Ages, the Forum was covered with dirt and garbage and called Campo Vaccino (Cow Field); when excavations began in the 19th century, a good deal of it was 20 feet under. Today, much of the Forum lies beneath the roaring traffic of Via dei Fori Imperiali. What is left is a white, open jungle of fallen columns and headless statues; the detailed plan available at the entrance is a must. Don't miss the Forum of Trajan, which is separate from the rest and the best preserved of all. Keep in mind that this neighborhood becomes dangerously hot at midday in summer. Open daily at 9 AM to 1 hour before sunset; Closed Sundays and Tuesdays at 1 PM. Details: *Ente Provinciale per il Turismo,* 11 Via Parigi, Roma 00185 (phone: 6-461851). See also "Special Places" in *Rome,* THE CITIES.

VIA APPIA ANTICA AND THE CATACOMBS, Rome: Somber but refreshingly cool, the 2nd-century Catacombs are the miles of underground tunnels where the early Christians practiced their outlawed cult in secrecy, hid when necessary, and behind slabs of marble or terra cotta, buried their dead — among them St. Cecilia, St. Eusebius, martyred popes, and others. The Catacombs of St. Calixtus and St. Sebastian, two of the most striking, are both notable for their examples of early Christian painting. Both are on the Via Appia Antica (Appian Way), the former closed Wednesdays, the latter Thursdays.

Back with the sun and the pagans aboveground, explore the rest of the Appia Antica, one of the most important of all the roads that led to Rome. From the time of its construction between Brindisi and the capital, beginning in 312 BC, it was the primary link to distant outposts. Now lined with broken columns, headless statues, umbrella pines, and secluded villas, this sleepy haven for lovers and families is still partly paved by the same large, jagged slabs of stone that surfaced Roman roads from Egypt to Gaul during the empire. Off the road stand some of the arches whose sloping tops carried water, gravity-fed, from miles-distant springs to Rome's public fountains and houses of the wealthy. Have dinner at one of the many family-run trattorie that line the Appia as you approach the city walls. Details: *Ente Provinciale per il Turismo,* 11 Via Parigi, Roma 00185 (phone: 6-461851). See also "Special Places" in *Rome,* THE CITIES.

SEGESTA, Sicily: On the side of a barren, savage hill appropriately called the Monte Barbaro, the massive temple of Segesta sits eerie and solitary and silent, except for the clanging of boats' bells, and it dwarfs any mortal who braves the long staircase up from the road to see it. Destroyed by the Saracens in about AD 1000, it has no roof today and probably had none when it was built in the 5th century BC as a place of open-air sacrifices within a ring of 36 giant columns. The stark Greek amphitheater spread out in the sun-scorched wilderness above the temple would make an ideal spot for a UFO landing or a divine revelation. Details: *Azienda Provinciale di Turismo,* 1/A Piazzetta Saturno, Trapani (Sicilia) 91100 (phone: 923-27077).

TAORMINA, Sicily: Go to the Greek theater during July to watch the sunset. Peer through the breach in the scene where the wall has politely disintegrated, and look over the roofs of the steeply tiered town toward the sea and the natural fireworks coming from still-active Mount Etna. Though built by Hellenic colonizers in the 3rd century BC, the semicircular amphitheater seems an organic part of the landscape. In summer, however, there is also some manmade entertainment, and the outdoor concerts are superb. But then, even an organ-grinder would sound like Horowitz in this setting. Details: *Azienda Autonoma di Soggiorno,* Piazza Santa Caterina, Taormina (Messina) 98039 (phone: 942-23243; fax: 942-24941).

TARQUINIA AND CERVETERI, Lazio: Virtually all that is known of the remote, but hauntingly familiar, Etruscan civilization comes not from excavation of their cities but from excavation of their burial grounds (*necropoli*), virtual cities themselves of underground chambers and dome-shaped tombs. Though their inscriptions are written in a language that still baffles experts, the scenes of elaborate lovemaking and jovial banqueting inside tell a story equivalent to thousands of words. The *Vatican Museums* and the *Villa Giulia* in Rome both have extensive collections of the angular, modern-looking household objects the Etruscans buried with their dead. Equally worthwhile are the more intimate displays in the medieval towns of Tarquinia and Cerveteri, which superseded Tarquinii and Caere, two of the most important cities of ancient Etruria. The cozy museum buildings are so old it's easy to forget that they are 1,500 years younger than the tools, weapons, and pots they contain. Closed Mondays. Details: *Ente Provinciale per il Turismo,* 11 Via Parigi, Roma 00185 (phone: 6-461851); or the *Museo Nazionale Cerite,* Principe Ruspoli Castello, Cerveteri (phone: 6-995-0003); and the *Museo Nazionale di Tarquinia,* Palazzo Vitelleschi, Corso Emanuele, Tarquinia (phone: 766-856036).

VILLA ADRIANA, Tivoli, Lazio: The sophisticated emperor and amateur architect Hadrian enjoyed this stately pleasure dome just outside Rome for only 4 years before his death in AD 138. But it was a one-man city, and every detail of its two swimming pools, two libraries, gymnasium, theater, thermal baths, courtyards, tree-lined avenues, and dozens of buildings was perfect. Each window in each of the hundreds of rooms was placed for the best possible view of the gentlest of the estate's rolling hills. Jets of water spouted strategically in every corner, statues from all over the empire surrounded the pools, and romantic nooks for secluded contemplation were sculpted out of nature so as to appear that they'd always been there. Still standing in a huge, rambling, and somewhat abandoned archaeological park are numerous buildings, including a marine theater — a delightful little island construction accessible by bridges. The villa's sculpture is now in museums all over Europe, and many of the buildings have been replaced by beautiful olive groves, but copies of the statues are set between the Corinthian columns along one of the swimming pools, the Canopo, to suggest the magnitude of Hadrian's vision of home, sweet home; a scale model at the entrance gate reproduces the entire layout. Closed Mondays. Details: *Azienda Autonoma di Soggiorno,* 13 Piazzale Nazioni Unite, Tivoli (Roma) 00019 (phone: 774-20745 or 774-530203).

L'ARENA DI VERONA, Verona, Veneto: Rising majestically out of the sunny, noisy, populous Piazza Brà, a short walk through the quiet streets from the houses of Romeo and Juliet, this splendor of 1st-century classical Roman architecture is one of the few Roman amphitheaters still in use. During Verona's summer opera season, it is a showcase of splendid classical music. The audience sits on marble benches 2,000 years old; the inner wall, scenery, and staircase are intact; and the acoustics are perfect. In fact, the structure qualifies as a ruin only because of the crumbled state of the outer ring, of which only a small section remains. Sample some ice cream in one of the numerous cafés on the piazza and contemplate how the structure's giant pink and white marble arches contrast with the lights and darks of Verona's many medieval buildings. Closed Mondays. Details: *Azienda di Promozione Turistica,* 42 Piazza delle Erbe, Verona 30086 (phone: 45-592828). Also contact the arena box office (phone: 45-800-5151). If they are sold out, try the major travel agencies in town or at major hotels.

DIRECTIONS

Introduction

With its land a living and lively history text — and despite rumors (we admit, confirmed) of delinquent drivers — Italy lends itself to an infinite variety of driving tours. While visits to the major metropolitan areas reveal something of this diverse country and its people, there are other aspects of Italian life that can only be experienced outside city limits — in small fishing villages or mountain campsites in the Abruzzo, on rocky beaches along the Amalfi Coast or along hairpin turns in the Dolomites, through the lush hills of Tuscany or the rugged terrain of Sardinia, or in the wildlife preserve of Gran Paradiso National Park in the Valle d'Aosta.

Italy has captured the imagination of travelers for decades. Drawn to this land that offers a range of climates, scenery, and cultures, there is much for a visitor to absorb beyond its urban centers — museums, churches, ruins, and villas, to name the most obvious. Outdoor activities — from swimming off the shores of the eastern, southern, and western coasts (not to mention Italy's many islands) to skiing down Alpine slopes — also are a large part of the Italian experience.

On the following pages are 20 driving tours through Italy's varied regions, from mainland to irresistible islands. From Piedmont to Puglia, they traverse the country's most spectacular routes and roads, most magnificent historical sites, and most arresting natural wonders, offering unforgettable views of azure lakes, winding rivers, dramatic mountain peaks, and virgin forests. They are journeys, too, into Italy's fascinating past. Along the routes are monuments left by ancient civilizations — *sassi* (prehistoric caves), *trulli* (cylindrical limestone huts), and ruins of Greek, Etruscan, and Roman temples and houses — as well as structures built in later times — the churches, bell towers, and monasteries of the Middle Ages, the basilicas, chapels, and palazzi of the Renaissance, and modern-day *gallerie* and sports centers, to name only a few. Along these routes, too, are communities where traditional ways of life are still followed — fishing and farming support families as they have for centuries, dress and celebrations date back to the dimmest past, saints and sacred icons are religiously revered, and where people still speak dialects that reflect the numerous foreign invasions the country has endured.

Descriptions of each of the routes begin with an introduction to the region, then describe suggested driving tours, each designed to take 5 to 7 days. It is possible to string together several routes to form longer itineraries, but if you are pressed for time you will find that by following any single itinerary you'll see most of the sites and sights (and enjoy the best restaurants and accommodations) in the area. Each route offers suggestions for the most outstanding hotels and dining spots along the way, from simple *pensioni* to deluxe villas, from cozy trattorie to elegant restaurants (hotels are listed first, in order of expense, followed by restaurants).

These tours are not exhaustive — there is no effort to cover absolutely everything in each region. But the places recommended and activities described were chosen to make your trip a memorable one.

The Italian Riviera

What is pine green and bay blue, has over 18 million wisteria petals, and collects 3,000 annual hours of sunlight — most of which seem to be crammed into any average summer afternoon? Answer: The Italian Riviera. And as anyone who has spent a part of summer hereabouts will gladly agree, there is no satisfactory answer to the riddle of why this glorious arc of Mediterranean coast has remained so long in the shadow of its showy French cousin to the northwest.

Given a snorkel and a little wanderlust, it's really no trouble to polish off the itinerary offered below in a week — provided there's no dallying over lunch. But then, why *not* dally over lunch, letting your eye follow the frolicking gulls as they swoop among the yachts? With a little preplanning, the most strenuous afternoon activity could be ordering another bottle of chilled vermentino or a slushy *granita di caffè.* Who needs Nice? (With no preplanning in the summer, however, it's likely that you'll spend most of your time seeking accommodations.)

The backdrop for this *dolce vita* is a 220-mile-long crescent drizzled along the Ligurian Sea and divided in the middle by the sprawling port city of Genoa. Everything to the west is known as the Riviera di Ponente; everything to the east and south, as the Riviera di Levante — referring to whether the sun will be setting or rising as you gaze from your seafront window. In midsummer, the resident population of Liguria is outnumbered four to one by beach umbrellas, and from the air the whole province appears to be a series of blue-and-white-striped bumps. However, there are hundreds of wild, craggy coves carved into the wall of the coastline, and it takes only a 15-minute dinghy ride to be far from the paddling crowd.

Some of Italy's classiest vacationers indulge in cove hopping across the whole coast, from Ventimiglia to Lerici, via sleek sloops, eliminating the risk of being cast ashore at a less-than-hallowed hotel. Mahogany-legged signorinas in wet bikinis share dry martinis with titled beachcombers — they're normally found on the wharf at Santa Margherita during the Allegro Hour, or at the roulette wheels in San Remo. But this is a secondary attraction.

The Italian Riviera has a lot more to offer than superb climate and beaches. The narrow coastline is protected by a semicircle of mountain ranges, the Alps to the north and the Apennines to the east, making Liguria one of Italy's most scenically variable regions. The terraced hills that look like giant staircases are devoted to growing grapes for the region's delicate wines or olives for the olive oil industry. The seafood here is some of the best served anywhere in Europe. The Ligurians themselves are proud and reserved, but they welcome visitors to their many ancient festivals and pageants, as well as to the modern-day boat shows, flower fairs, and song contests.

Liguria has always been a seafaring region. Even today, 70% of the population of 1.7 million lives on the coast. Many of these people work at the ports, especially Genoa, or in the production of slate, olive oil, or pasta, but most are involved in tourism or related industries. Liguria is famous for handcrafted filigree, macramé, and ceramics, but even more famous for floriculture. As early as the 16th century, the Italian nobility of other regions sent to Liguria for fresh flowers — roses, carnations, strelitzias, gladioli, and daisies, to name only a few of the varieties grown here — to decorate weddings and festivals.

The most famous date in Ligurian history is the discovery of America in 1492 by the Genoese Christopher Columbus, and its 500th anniversary will be celebrated this year in Genoa. But the oldest evidence of Ligurian citizenry comes from the Balzi Rossi caves of Ventimiglia, near the French and Italian border. Over 200,000 years ago, men and women took shelter in these caves. Other parts of the western coast are also rich with traces of prehistory: Neanderthal people (who existed from about 100,000 to 30,000 BC) lived in caves in the San Remo and Finale districts. Farther inland, Paleolithic people (about 30,000 to 10,000 BC) left burial mounds and funeral artifacts. Coastal and hill tribes developed separately; their innate differences in temperament — coastal folk tend to be outgoing, hill people more reticent — are noticeable even today.

The Romans made their appearance after the first Punic War (3rd century BC). The fierce Ligurian tribes fought savagely for independence, but by 14 BC Augustus Caesar had conquered the whole Alpine arc region, and Liguria became completely Romanized. Towns sprang up at Albingaunum (Albenga) and Albintimilium (Ventimiglia) in the west and at Luna (Luni) in the east. Archaeological remains of these Roman towns are still in existence, most notably in Luni.

Liguria was considerably larger during antiquity than it is in modern times; its western borders stretched well into what is now France. However, the unity and prosperity of the region under the Romans was undermined by the collapse of the empire and the barbarian invasions that followed. Alaric, King of the Visigoths, destroyed Albenga in AD 409. Other barbarian tribes continued to wreak havoc in the area until the Lombards invaded in AD 568 and dominated for 200 years. Liguria's Middle Ages properly began only toward the end of the 8th century, when the Franks established a Tuscan-Ligurian feudal mark.

The ports along the coast had been important as trading centers. Genoa, in particular, from as early as the 5th century BC, had been a firm ally of Rome. After the fall of the Roman Empire and throughout the Middle Ages, the Arab Saracens, highly organized plunderers from North Africa and what is now the Middle East, repeatedly stormed the entire Ligurian coast. In AD 935 they sacked Genoa, and for the next 2 centuries, largely in response to the continuing Saracen threat, Genoa slowly built itself up as a powerful maritime center.

In the 12th century, Genoa began its conquest of the rest of the Riviera, although other independent Ligurian cities, particularly Savona and Ventimiglia, fought hard to retain their individual liberty. The conquest was complete by the end of the 14th century. Despite unification, however, trouble began to arise from within. Factions that supported the pope, the Guelphs, fought bitterly with those who supported the Holy Roman Empire, the Ghibellines, whether or not warring parties were members of the same city or even the same family. This, and the devastation caused by wars with Venice and Pisa, so weakened the region that, between 1499 and 1522, Louis XII of France was able to impose his authority over the area. A few years later, the French were ousted by the great Ligurian leader Andrea Doria, with the help of the Spanish. Doria, a brilliant admiral as well as a politician, known as Father of the Country, also framed a constitution and helped to create a unified Republic of Genoa that remained intact for nearly 200 years.

In 1746 the Austrians occupied the region and remained in control until the French Revolution. In 1797 the Ligurian republic became a battleground for the Napoleonic Wars. For the first decade of the 19th century the region was annexed to France, but with Napoleon's defeat in 1815, the newly titled duchy of Genoa became united to the kingdom of Sardinia.

The decades that followed witnessed the struggle for Italian unification. Ligurians contributed to its realization in a decisive way. In 1831, Giuseppe Mazzini founded the Young Italy movement, which led to the growth of a national spirit otherwise known as the Risorgimento, the "revival" or "rebirth." Another hero was Giuseppe Garibaldi (who was born in Nice), a charismatic military leader who was responsible for bringing Sicily and Naples into the growing union. Garibaldi achieved the liberation of the south with his famous "Thousand" Red Shirts, who were all fierce Ligurian sharpshooters.

Today's visitors to the Italian Riviera will see not the fierce and independent side of the Ligurians but only their hospitality, which, like the Ligurian sunshine, is rarely clouded over. All the towns and many of the villages have extremely efficient and friendly information offices that go under the lengthy name Aziende Autonome di Soggiorno Cura e Turismo, but just ask for "*informazione turistica*" and you can't go wrong. The offices will give advice on sights to see, hotels, tours, and festivals — also on where to find the best water skiing instructor or the best local wine.

This route, starting in Ventimiglia (near the French border not far from Nice), winds along the arc-shaped coast, passing through such chic resorts as San Remo and ancient fishing villages like Noli. It is bisected by the city of Genoa, then continues south toward such internationally famous playgrounds as Portofino. Halfway along the Riviera di Levante, the route turns slightly inland, skirting the insular Cinque Terre (Five Lands) to finish at Portovenere, on the peninsula just south of the port town of La Spezia.

Distances between towns are short — few are more than a 10-minute drive from one another, although Sunday traffic can be brutal. There are also a number of trains that stop at every village along the coast, and an energetic hiker could even cover some of the area on foot. There are two roads that traverse the Riviera, almost parallel to each other. Both have an average length of 164 miles (262 km; the coastline itself is closer to 200 miles/320 km). The autostrada (A10 west of Genoa and A12 east), which has some stunning views, generally runs inland and at a higher altitude. The older Via Aurelia (SS1) clings to the coast, running through all the towns and villages. The coast road can be congested with traffic, especially during the busy summer season, so unless you are a very patient driver, you probably should use the autostrada to make time, exiting to visit particular places.

Accommodations range from very expensive, where a double room with bath will cost $225 and up, to expensive hotels at around $150 to $225, to moderate places from $85 to $150, and inexpensive, under $85. (A warning here for visitors arriving during July and August: Sometimes as much as 4 to 6 months' advance booking is required by the more popular hotels, and that does not necessarily mean the most expensive.) Most hotels are not open year-round but those that are may offer discounts (unofficially) the winter months they accept guests. A very expensive dinner for two costs $200 or more; at an expensive restaurant, $100 to $200; at moderate, about $50 to $80; and at inexpensive places, less than $50. Prices include wine but not liquor.

En Route from the French Border – Coming from the French border, whether on A10 or SS1, stop at Mortola Inferiore, 3 miles (5 km) before Ventimiglia, to visit the Hanbury Gardens (phone: 184-229507). The gardens, which now have over 6,000 species of flora, were begun by the Englishman Sir Thomas Hanbury in 1867. They are regarded as one of the most important sites in Europe for the cultivation of exotic plants. The gardens are open daily, except Wednesdays, from 9 AM to 6 PM in the summer, and 10 AM to 4 PM in the winter; admission charge.

VENTIMIGLIA: The medieval section of Ventimiglia stands on a hill to the west of the River Roja, which divides this part of the town from the modern center below and to the east. This ancient port was independent until 180 BC, when it became subject to Rome. Invasions by Goths and other barbarians forced the citizens to move uphill from the coast, where some fine Roman archaeological sites, such as a well-preserved amphitheater, remain. The fortified hill city is very much as it was during the 13th century, when it was conquered by Genoa. The Church of San Michele is a large, sober Romanesque building (11th to 13th century), with the original crypt incorporating Roman columns and milestones. The modern section of Ventimiglia is important principally as a center for the production and sale of flowers. A yearly *Festival di Musica Antica* (Festival of Ancient Music) is held between July and August, and a colorful historical folk festival takes place around the middle of August. The nearby Balzi Rossi prehistoric caves (phone: 184-38113) are open to the public daily, except Mondays, from 9 AM to 1 PM and 2:30 to 6 PM; admission charge. Tourist information is available at 61 Via Cavour (phone: 184-351183). There is another tourist information office at the main train station that also has a travel agency (*AVAST;* phone: 184-358197).

CHECKING IN: ***Eden*** – Small (19 rooms) and quiet, this hotel owned by a Swedish concern has a lovely garden, pool, and a good restaurant. Within walking distance of the Hanbury Gardens. Open year-round. 68 Corso Montecarlo, Mortola Inferiore, Ventimiglia (phone: 184-38482; fax: 184-38481). Moderate.

La Riserva – Just on the outskirts of the medieval city, 1,300 feet above sea level, this secluded 30-room hotel offers a homey atmosphere, a superb restaurant next to a heated pool, and a wonderful panorama of the coast. Open from the end of March to the end of September and 3 weeks at *Christmas.* Castel d'Appio, Ventimiglia (phone: 184-229533; fax: 184-229712). Moderate.

EATING OUT: ***Balzi Rossi*** – If ever there was an outstanding restaurant at this end of the Riviera, surely this must be it. The cooking is topnotch and the terrace is a delight; considering the quality, so are the prices. Closed Sunday evenings in winter, Mondays, Tuesday lunch in summer, 2 weeks in March, and 2 weeks in November. Reservations advised. Major credit cards accepted. Piazzale de Gaspari, Ponte San Lucovico, Ventimiglia (phone: 184-38132). Expensive.

En Route from Ventimiglia – Only a mile or so out of Ventimiglia on A10, the exit to Pigna leads to Dolceacqua, which means "sweet water" (4 miles/6 km from the exit). In keeping with its name, the village produces some of the best wine in the region, a delicate, light red called rossese. Perched on a hill, with houses seemingly carved into it, are the impressive 12th-century ruins of the Doria family castle, open daily, except Tuesdays, from 9 AM to noon and 3 to 7 PM; admission charge (phone: 184-206561). Many of the narrow alleyways that run up to the castle are completely cut off from daylight, as the buildings through which they run engulf them on all sides. There are a number of traditional craft shops here, most notably that of Jean Perrino (43 Via Barberis; phone: 184-206090), who sculpts fantastic shapes from 300-year-old local wood.

Back on the autostrada, it is only 3 miles (5 km) to Bordighera where there are a number of good hotels and another 7 miles (11 km) to Ospedaletti. Both these small towns are popular winter resorts distinguished by their luxuriant vegetation and fin de siècle ambience. The British have been coming to Bordighera for over a century; Queen Margherita of Savoy chose this palm-shaded resort as her principal residence. The Vatican gets its supplies of palms for *Holy Week* exclusively from this district. Ospedaletti has always been important as a health resort and gets its name from a hospital founded there in the 14th century by the Knights of Rhodes.

CHECKING IN: ***Cap Ampelio*** – Set in a park with views of the sea, this well-established, elegant establishment has over 100 modern rooms as well as a pool, some spa services, and a good restaurant. Closed mid-October to mid-December. 5 Via Virgilio, Bordighera (phone: 184-264333). Expensive.

Del Mare – A large modern 100-room complex about 1 mile (1.6 km) outside the town center on Via Aurelia, including a pool, a restaurant, and a private beach. Closed October to mid-December. 34 Via Portico della Punta, Bordighera (phone: 184-262201). Expensive.

EATING OUT: ***Carletto*** – Delicious pasta, a mouth-watering selection of antipasti, fresh fish, and friendly owners make this attractively decorated spot a sure winner. Closed Wednesdays and mid-November to mid-December. Reservations advised. Major credit cards accepted. 339 Via Vittorio Emanuele, Bordighera (phone: 184-261725). Expensive to moderate.

Le Reserve Tastevin – Sublime seafood is served here, and the cooking standards are very high indeed. Try the *zuppa di pesce* (fish soup). Closed Sunday evenings, Mondays (except in summer), and mid-October to mid-December. Reservations advised. Major credit cards accepted. 20 Via Arziglia, Campo Ampelio, Bordighera (phone: 184-261322). Expensive to moderate.

SAN REMO: The capital of the Riviera di Fiori (Riviera of Flowers), San Remo is an elegant Edwardian resort reminiscent of Cannes. It is devoted to pampering visitors. Made fashionable at the turn of the century by Russian and German aristocrats, it is still a favorite watering spot of Italy's rich and powerful, as is evident from the number of luxurious yachts moored in the harbor.

The origins of the town are Roman, but its most potent period took place during the Middle Ages, when the Genoese bishops resided here. San Remo was, in fact, named after the first of the bishops, San Romolo. Over the centuries, the town was heavily fortified, having to endure persistent invasion by the Genoese, the pirate Barbarossa (who sacked the town in 1543), and the English. The medieval nucleus of the town, known as Pigna ("pine cone") due to its shape, is perched on a hill. Its tall houses, between which run dark flights of steps and alleyways, are joined by small arches for reinforcement against earthquakes. Sitting on top of this ancient pile of stones is the baroque Church of Madonna della Costa, the origins of which go back to the 6th century, when there was a sanctuary on the site; the façade of the church is particularly graceful. Another noteworthy building is the Russian Orthodox Church of Santa Maria degli Angeli; the building, on Via Nuvoloni, is not often open to visitors, but the colorful exterior is delightful in itself.

A visit to the *Mercato dei Fiori* (Flower Market) in Valle Arnica just outside of town, open weekdays, (the busiest months are from October to June), from about midnight to 8 AM, will reveal an abundance of roses, jasmine, carnations, narcissi, tulips, and countless other varieties: 20,000 tons of blossoms are shipped from the Riviera each year. The *Municipal Casino* (18 Corso Inglesi; phone: 184-534001) is one of only four in Italy; players must have some form of identification, such as a passport, to get in. Open daily from 11 to 2:30 AM. Winnings can be spent immediately at the fashionable boutiques on nearby Corso Matteotti, which is one of the most exclusive shopping areas in this part of the Riviera. An international song festival takes place here each year, usually between mid-January and mid-February. For a spectacular view of the coast, as well as Cannes on a clear day, which is nearly always, take the funicular (when it's working) from Via Isonzo up to Monte Bignone. The tourist office (at Palazzo Riviera, 1 Via Nuvoloni; phone: 184-571571) is open Mondays through Saturdays from 8 AM to 7 PM, and Sundays and holidays from 8 AM to 2 PM.

CHECKING IN: ***Royal*** – One of the most luxurious properties on the Riviera di Ponente, with 140 rooms and everything a guest might possibly desire, including air conditioning, a swimming pool, tennis courts, a nightly dance orchestra and impeccable service. At least one member of European royalty or international celebrity normally is in residence. Although the hotel is located in the center of town, the surrounding parks, with rare species of plants, lend a secluded atmosphere. Closed mid-October to mid-December. 80 Corso Imperatrice, San Remo (phone: 184-5391; fax: 184-61445). Very expensive.

Astoria West-End – This 120-room hotel is considerably more modern than the *Londra* next door; it has a high standard of service, a lovely park, and swimming pool. Open year-round. 8 Corso Matuzia, San Remo (phone: 184-667701; fax: 184-65616). Expensive.

Grand Hotel Londra – Dating from 1860, this large, elegant establishment was the first hotel to be built in San Remo, and it is still one of the great favorites. It has a park and swimming pool. Closed October to mid-December. 2 Corso Matuzia, San Remo (phone: 184-668000; fax: 880359). Expensive.

Mediterranée – A little outside of town, this modern but tastefully decorated hostelry has air conditioning and delightful gardens. Many of its 67 rooms have balconies overlooking the sea. 76 Corso Cavallotti, San Remo (phone: 184-571000; fax: 690106). Expensive to moderate.

EATING OUT: ***Casino*** – Compared with some Italian restaurants, the atmosphere here is formal, but this does not deter the devoted. Both the kitchen and the service are excellent. Open daily. Reservations advised. Major credit cards accepted. 13 Corso Inglesi, San Remo (phone: 184-534001). Expensive.

Pesce d'Oro – Once regarded as one of the best in the region, it is still an obligatory stop for its pasta dishes with pesto (a sauce made with fresh basil, pine nuts, and garlic) and excellent fresh fish. Try the *zuppa di frutti di mare* (seafood soup), with either the local pigato or rossese wine, for a particularly memorable experience. Closed Mondays and from mid-February to mid-March; reservations advised. Major credit cards accepted. 300 Corso Cavallotti, San Remo (phone: 184-576332). Expensive.

Da Giannino – A small, simple place particularly well known for its *tagliolini* *integrali al nero di seppia* (whole-wheat pasta in squid ink sauce). The *branzino in salsa di ribes* (sea bass with currant sauce) is another specialty. Closed Sundays and Monday lunch. Reservations advised. Major credit cards accepted. 23 Lungomare Trento e Trieste, San Remo (phone: 184-70843). Expensive to moderate.

En Route from San Remo – Take the short but worthwhile detour to Bussana Vecchia. Exit from A10 about 2 miles (3 km) out of San Remo; alternatively, take the Via Aurelia instead. This medieval village was leveled by an earthquake in 1887 and all its inhabitants, who were nicknamed, ironically, Bissana (Twice Healthy), were killed when the church where they had taken refuge collapsed. A community of artists work and live in the village; they have made charming homes and studios within the restored interiors of the old buildings without changing the exteriors. Beyond Bussana Vecchia, for the next 30 miles (48 km) or so, the route is lined with industrial developments, but there is a fine strip of beach at Alassio. There are also two very good restaurants along this stretch (see below).

EATING OUT: *Lanterna Blu–da Tonino* – This restaurant, with a friendly, relaxed atmosphere, is regarded as one of the best in the area. Its specialties are scampi (shrimp), *bianchetti* (tiny anchovies and sardines), a variety of fish soups, and delicious pasta. The building, one of the most attractive in an otherwise busy, modern harbor, dates from the 1700s. During the summer it's pleasant to eat outside and watch the fishing boats go by. Closed November to December 5; Tuesday and Wednesday lunchtimes in summer; and Wednesdays the rest of the year. Major credit cards accepted. 32 Via Scarincio, Borgo Marina, Porto Maurizio (phone: 183-63859). Expensive.

Salvo ai Cacciatori – Another great favorite with the Italians, this excellent restaurant is situated just to the east of Imperia. (*Lanterna Blu* lies to the west. If you happen to be en route from one to the other and it's June 24, you will have to make a detour because the Via Aurelia is closed in Imperia for the *Feast of St. John the Baptist,* when wild pigs are roasted in the street!) Fish is the thing to eat here, especially *bottarga* (fish eggs). Closed Mondays and the first half of November. Reservations advised. Major credit cards accepted. 14 Via Vieusseux, Oneglia (phone: 183-23763). Moderate to inexpensive.

ALBENGA: This small, flourishing market town, which lies just in from the sea on a fertile plain, is the most important historical site on the western Riviera. From the 6th century BC, Albenga was the seat of the Ingaunian tribes, until it was conquered by Rome in 181 BC. It then became a prosperous commercial center with territorial supremacy stretching from Finale in the east to San Remo in the west. The fortified walls of the historic center still are largely intact; the layout of the medieval buildings within reveals the early Roman influence. The most distinctive and evocative features of the town are the 50 brick tower houses, many still in excellent condition. Except for an early invasion by the Goths, the city enjoyed a long period of peace. This accounts for the preservation of the most important Christian monument extant in Liguria, the 5th-century cathedral baptistry, with its decagonal exterior and octagonal interior, and fine blue and white mosaic, *Christ Amidst Doves.* The cathedral, except for the baptistry, was reconstructed in the 13th century. With a somber and impressive interior and a graceful, rather than imposing, exterior, it has many little corners where architectural features have not changed for centuries, most notably the Piazzetta dei Leoni, which lies behind the apse. Although subject to Genoese authority since 1251, Albenga retained considerable independence; building continued here until the 15th century. Tickets to the baptistry are available at the *Museo Civico* (12 Piazza San Michele; phone: 182-51215)). The museum has a collection of prehistoric artifacts and Roman exhibits relating to the town. Also in the piazza and of interest are the *Museo Navale*

Romano and the *Museo Preistorico.* All three are open daily, except Mondays, 10 AM to noon and 3 to 6 PM;. The tourist office (1 Viale Martiri della Libertà; phone: 182-50475) has information on Albenga and nearby towns.

CHECKING IN/EATING OUT: ***Italia*** – Modest, with only 14 rooms, it also boasts a restaurant that turns out some of the best food in town. Restaurant closed Mondays and most of November and December. Major credit cards accepted. 8 Viale Martiri della Libertà, Albenga (phone: 182-50405). Hotel, inexpensive; restaurant, moderate.

En Route from Albenga – About 7 miles (11 km) from Albenga, take the exit for Borghetto. Just north of A10 is the village of Toirano, where at the Palazzo Communale (corner of Via Bernardo Ricci and Piazza San Michele) visitors can get tickets for a guided tour of the nearby Basura grottoes, filled with stalagmites and stalactites in pastel shades of rose and green. Admission charge. At the grotto's entrance is the *Museo Preistorico della Val Varatella "Nino Lamboglia"* (phone: 182-98062); no admission charge. The grotto and museum are open daily, 9 AM to noon and 2 to 5 PM. Tourist information is available in Albenga (address above).

FINALE-LIGURE: Ten miles (16 km) farther along the coast is the pleasant resort of Finale, which has a very good beach. On the west side of town is a charming historical section known as Finalborgo. The harshness of the surrounding countryside makes the ornate, colorful buildings, many with trompe l'oeil effects, all the more attractive. The Convent of Santa Caterina, with its serene inner courtyards, is in vivid architectural contrast to the ruins of the 12th-century Castel Govone, which stands above the town in massive isolation. Tourist information is available at 14 Via San Pietro (phone: 19-692581).

CHECKING IN: ***La Residenza Punta Est*** – One of the region's most delightful small hostelries is situated on the outskirts of Finale, in a shady hilltop garden. The elegant 18th-century complex of buildings with 37 rooms has been converted from a private residence, and its ambience still is more like that of a private villa than a hotel. There is a swimming pool. Closed October through April. 1 Via Aurelia, Finale (phone: 19-600612; fax: 19-600611). Expensive to moderate.

SAVONA: There are some attractive fishing villages, such as Noli and Spotorno, on the way to Savona, and nearby Garlenda has an excellent golf club (see *Great Italian Golf,* DIVERSIONS), but, for the most part, the coastline from here to Genoa is dominated by industry and shipping. Savona is the largest town on the Riviera di Ponente and is itself a large industrial complex. Well worth a visit in its small historic center is the *Pinacoteca Civica* (Civic Museum; 7 Via Quarda Superiore; phone: 19-828601) containing a rich collection of 14th- to 18th-century paintings that are well worth a visit. Most of the paintings are Lombard and Ligurian, including works by Foppa and Magnasco. Open daily, except Mondays, 9 AM to noon and 3 to 6 PM; Sundays, morning hours only. Tourist information is available at 23 Via Paleocapa (phone: 19-820522).

EATING OUT: ***Sodano*** – In the middle of the medieval section of town is an attractive, spacious Renaissance eatery with a black and white decor that manages to be cool in summer and cozy in winter. *Cima,* the specialty here, is a veal joint stuffed with vegetables and eggs, served warm rather than hot; it is a traditional dish and one of the most popular in Liguria. Closed Wednesdays and most of July. Reservations advised. Major credit cards accepted. 9 Piazza della Maddalena, Savona (phone: 19-38446). Moderate.

La Farinata – In this very lively, crowded spot, frequented mainly by locals, any fish dish will be delicious and fresh and should be eaten with *farinata,* roasted flat cakes made from corn and chick-peas. From the street this restaurant looks like a bakery only, but don't be put off, for there are two large rooms behind the shopfront. Open for lunch and dinner, or take away a *farinata* any time of day; closed weekends. Reservations advised. No credit cards accepted. 15 Via Montesisto, Savona (phone: 19-826458). Inexpensive.

GENOA: This dynamic city, sprawling up the Ligurian hillsides and along the coastline for nearly 25 miles (40 km), is the principal Italian port as well as one of the most important maritime centers on the Mediterranean. Many visitors to Liguria, intent on sun and sea, bypass Genoa, but it is a city of vivid contrasts, and a little exploration will reveal that it has many hidden treasures and a beauty of its own.

From the 5th century BC, when it became a Roman center of considerable importance, Genoa expanded in size and wealth. Gradually, by the 14th century, it reigned supreme over the entire Riviera, a position which in many ways it has never relinquished. Known as La Superba, for the pride of its inhabitants, it also played a major role in Italian unification. This year, the city will celebrate the 500th anniversary of the discovery of America by Genoa's most prominent son, Christopher Columbus. The narrow alleys (*caruggi*) and small piazzas of the city's historic center contrast with the orderly layout of its modern sections. Genoa has a number of exceptionally important galleries, museums, and palaces. For full details on sights, the Columbus festivities, hotels, and restaurants, see *Genoa,* THE CITIES.

RAPALLO: Only 17 miles (27 km) from the center of Genoa is one of Europe's most renowned resorts. Rapallo passed its peak before the last war, but the splendid yachts anchored in its perfect bay testify to the town's continuing, if largely nostalgic, popularity. Rapallo is a city of ancient origins. Hannibal is said to have passed through here after he crossed the Alps; the Roman single-span bridge on the east side of the bay has been named after him. The town was under the jurisdiction of the Bishops of Milan until 644, after which Genoese influence prevailed. Its most notable monuments are from the 14th to the 15th century. Examples from this period are the *Casa di San Lazarro* (Leper House of San Lazarus; on Via Bana), which still bears the original frescoes on its exterior, and the cathedral of Saints Gervasio and Protasio. The cathedral was founded in the 6th century, reaching its present proportions only in 1606. Behind the modern, palm and orange tree–lined promenade lie the remains of the medieval quarters, where over 500 years ago the wives of sailors and fishermen developed a lacemaking technique still in use today. In the quaint shop of *Emilio Gandolfi* (1 Piazza Cavour; phone: 185-50234), dedicated shoppers can still find exquisite lace, although extremely expensive, suitable to pass on as a family heirloom. Golfers can take advantage of the superb 18-hole course year-round at the *Rapallo Golf and Tennis Club* (377 Via Mamelli, Rapallo; phone: 185-261777); closed Tuesdays. Tourist information offices are at 9 Via Diaz (phone: 185-51282).

CHECKING IN: ***Bristol Rapallo*** – The town's most renowned hotel, with 93 air conditioned rooms, and the only ultramodern building on the Riviera. Besides seclusion, guests can enjoy all the usual comforts — including a heated pool, park, and a superb rooftop restaurant — in a luxurious and relaxing environment, as well as superb views of the bay. Closed January 7 to March 1. 369 Via Aurelia Orientale, Rapallo (phone: 185-273313; fax: 185-55800). Very expensive.

Eurotel – Well established but smaller than the *Bristol* and close to the harbor. It has a pool and a good restaurant. Open year-round. 22 Via Aurelia Ponente, Rapallo (phone: 185-60981; fax: 185-50635). Moderate.

EATING OUT: ***Da Ardito*** – *Pansotti* (stuffed pasta in a creamy walnut sauce) and *coniglio* (rabbit), are just two of many appetizing options in this popular trattoria. There is terrace dining in summer. Closed Mondays. Reservations advised. Major credit cards accepted. 9 Via Canale, San Pietro di Novella, Rapallo (phone: 185-51551). Moderate to inexpensive.

Santa Margherita Ligure: Penisola di Portofino (Portofino Peninsula) is a little off the beaten track, but far too good to miss. Its two main towns are Santa Margherita Ligure and Portofino. From Rapallo, detour onto southbound SS227. Only 2 miles (3 km) down the road is Santa Margherita Ligure, a more sedate, less developed version of Rapallo; many people prefer it to the busier Rapallo or the smaller, quieter Portofino. It has a beach (unlike Portofino) and a wide variety of hotels. The tourist office (2/B Via 25 Aprile; phone: 185-287485) is open daily except Sundays from 8:30 AM to noon and 3 to 6 PM.

CHECKING IN: ***Imperial Palace*** – Set in a spacious park, this 98-room luxury property combines all the modern comforts (including a heated pool) with Old World elegance — the bedrooms and public spaces are furnished with antiques. Once a favorite retreat for members of the aristocracy and still Santa Margherita's most elegant, it also has a very good restaurant. Closed November through March. 19 Via Pagana, Santa Margherita Ligure (phone: 185-288991; fax: 185-284651). Very expensive.

Miramare – There are 83 rooms in this slightly modern, lively, and still very tasteful building overlooking the sea from tropical gardens and a beautifully landscaped pool. Open year-round. 30 Via Milite Ignoto, Santa Margherita Ligure (phone: 185-287013; fax: 284651). Very expensive.

Minerva – There are 28 rooms with balconies overlooking the sea and surrounding green hills in one of this town's nicest middle-range hostelries. The tranquillity of the hotel contrasts with the lively waterfront just a minute away. There is a sun deck and parking. Open year-round. 34 Via Maragliano, Santa Margherita Ligure (phone: 185-286073). Moderate.

Ulivi – The perfect find for the traveler who revels in a family ambience. Each of the 8 rooms has a television set and it's a 2-minute walk to the beach and port. Half board required. Closed mid-October to mid-December and 2 weeks before *Easter*. 28 Via Maragliano, Santa Margherita Ligure (phone: 185-287890; fax: 185-282525). Moderate.

Fasce – In addition to 16 clean, modest rooms, there also is a pretty garden, rooftop sun deck, and parking. A good value. Open year-round. 3 Via Bozzo, Santa Margherita Ligure (phone: 185-286435; fax: 185-283580). Inexpensive.

EATING OUT: ***La Trattoria Cesarina*** – One of the best in the area, this place has a good cellar — the pigato wine is a favorite — and the specialties are regional fish and meat dishes. Closed Wednesdays, 2 weeks in March, and 2 weeks in December. Reservations advised. Visa accepted. 2/C Via Mameli, Santa Margherita Ligure (phone: 185-286059). Expensive.

Da Alfredo – Tucked away under arches in front of the port, this colorful trattoria has alfresco dining, and is where locals mix with visitors, including opera tenor Luciano Pavarotti, who often stops here when in town. The wonderful seafood risotto bears his name. Closed Thursdays and November. Reservations advised. Major credit cards accepted. 37 Piazza Martiri della Libertà, Santa Margherita Ligure (phone: 185-288140). Moderate.

PORTOFINO: Three miles (5 km) away is the exquisite fishing village of Portofino. It's best to leave your car at Santa Margherita (at times it's obligatory) and take one of the frequent boats to Portofino (contact *Servizi Marittimi del Tigullio,* 24 Via Marsala, Rapallo; phone: 185-55814) or regular buses (*Tigullio Pubblici Trasporti,* 36 Corso Italia, Rapallo; phone: 185-54509). Not only are the roads narrow here, but the roads often are closed during the summer and parking is impossible, and Monte Portofino is a national park (since 1980) with stringent regulations to protect its wildlife and lush vegetation.

A tiny place, Portofino is known as the Pearl of the Riviera for its unspoiled charm and romantic land- and seascapes. It has two castles: Castello Brown was renovated by an Englishman in the 19th century; Castello San Giorgio was completely rebuilt at the beginning of this century by an American millionaire. Each April 23, to commemorate St. George's feast day, Portofino residents burn a huge pine tree in the center of the village. Depending on whether the tree falls to the left or the right as it burns out, good luck will follow for one side of the town or the other. During the bonfire, villagers and visitors alike feast on wonderful food and delicious wines. Normally, however, the town is staid and fiercely concerned with repelling "barbarian" tourists; hence the high prices and restrictions. Dancing, for example, is forbidden, and would-be disco dancers are relegated to the *Carillon* restaurant (phone: 185-286721), out of town on the road to Santa Margherita Liguria. The tourist information office (35 Via Roma; phone: 185-269078) is open daily from 9 AM to 6 PM, Sundays from 9 AM to 1.

From Portofino, you might take one of the frequent 20-minute boat excursions to San Fruttuoso, also on the peninsula, but accessible only by sea. You can also get there on foot — it's a beautiful 1½ hour walk (about 2 miles/3 km). It is an even smaller village, with an abbey in its center. The original monastery, built in 711, was destroyed in a Saracen raid and then rebuilt after the 10th century. The church beside it is a young relation, having been founded only in the 13th century. Boat services are available to and from Rapallo and Santa Margherita Ligure, as well as to and from Camogli. For information, contact the local tourist office.

The Penisola di Portofino also has some delightful hiking routes. Detailed maps are available at various tourist information offices. But be aware that during the summer even a short walk (of an hour or so) can be fatiguing in the heat; good shoes and sensible planning are essential. (See *Camping and Caravanning, Hiking and Biking* in GETTING READY TO GO and *Walking* in DIVERSIONS.)

CHECKING IN: ***Nazionale*** – This small, delightful hotel was renovated 2 years ago, and offers 12 lovely suites that overlook the colorful, world-famous port and its *piazzetta.* Breakfast is served outdoors in good weather. Closed January through mid-March. 8 Via Roma, Portofino (phone: 185-269575; fax: 185-269578). Very expensive.

Splendido – Regarded as supreme among the many wonderful hotels along the Riviera or elsewhere, perhaps because the building with 61 guestrooms is situated in what can only be described as paradise, or because the standards of service set by a huge and efficient staff are simply the best. Whatever the cause, be prepared for the treat of a lifetime. A 5-year restoration was completed last year to keep things up to snuff. Closed November through March. Reservations necessary at least 3 months in advance for July and August. 10 Salita Baratta, Portofino (phone: 185-269551; fax: 185-269614). Very expensive.

Eden – Once a private home, this old villa has retained its charming *ambiente.* There are 9 rooms on a quiet side street behind the picturesque port and an enclosed garden where breakfast is served in good weather. Closed first 3 weeks of December. 18 Vico Dritto (phone and fax: 185-269091). Moderate.

Piccolo – Small, pleasant and considerably more modest than the *Splendido* higher up the slopes, it's a good alternative for leaner wallets. As we went to press, it was scheduled to reopen late this year after a complete overhaul. No restaurant, but there are plenty of dining places in the village. Closed November to late February. 31 Via Provinciale, Portofino (phone: 185-269015). Moderate.

Stella Maris – To describe this 15-room inn as secluded would be understating the case. From Portofino it takes a keen hiker 4 hours via a beautiful foot trail or, for those not so inclined, 55 minutes via boat. But the rustic setting and the freshly caught fish are worth it. Closed November through April. 68 Via San Nicolò, Punta Chiappa (phone: 185-772818). Moderate to inexpensive.

EATING OUT: ***Il Pitosforo*** – A very popular waterfront fish restaurant made famous by film stars who flocked here and even lent their names to some of the dishes, most of which are excellent. Reservations necessary. Closed Tuesdays, Wednesday lunch, January, and February. Reservations advised. Major credit cards accepted. 19 Molo Umberto, Portofino (phone: 185-269020). Expensive.

Puny – There is no better combination than the portside setting and acclaimed menu of this attractive restaurant. When weather permits, it's better to sit outside, but inside, the flat *pappardelle* noodles with a pesto and tomato sauce or the fresh fish sprinkled with fragrant laurel and baked in the oven taste just as delicious. Closed Thursdays, January, and February. Reservations advised. No credit cards accepted. 5 Piazza Martiri dell'Olivetta, Portofino (phone: 185-269037). Expensive.

CAMOGLI: Lying to the north of Rapallo on the peninsula, this charming fishing port, can be reached by car or boat from Genoa, Rapallo, Santa Margherita Ligure, and Portofino. The port is built in layers and looks like a palette of colors tumbling into the aquamarine sea. The tourist office is at 33r Via XX Settembre (phone: 185-770235).

CHECKING IN: ***Cenobio dei Dogi*** – Hard to beat, it has 88 rooms, each with its own bath, plus an excellent restaurant, a private beach, a pool, and tennis courts. Open March to early January. 34 Via Cuneo, Canogli (phone: 185-770041; fax: 185-772796). Very expensive to expensive.

EATING OUT: ***Da Rosa*** – Seafood served alfresco and portside, and marvelous views. Closed Tuesdays and from November to mid-December. Reservations advised. American Express accepted. 11 Largo Casa Bona, Canogli (phone: 185-771088). Expensive to moderate.

LEVANTO: Back on A10 or the SS1, another 12 miles (19 km) along the coast from Rapallo, the route turns inland, away from Sestri Levante (a tiny peninsula famous for its ceramics and ship models). Turn right at Passo del Bracco onto SS332 and drive 8 miles (13 km) south to Levanto.

A small resort with the last good stretch of beach for the next 20 miles (32 km), Levanto has a delightful historic section with a number of interesting buildings. One is the 13th-century Town Hall, with five arcades gracefully adorning its exterior. Another is the 15th-century Church of San Francesco, which contains an impressive painting of the miracle of San Diego by Bernardo Strozzi. There are also some very pleasant trompe l'oeil paintings on the exteriors of the townhouses. Levanto is the most convenient point — as an alternative to the larger town of La Spezia — to use as a base for touring the neighboring Cinque Terre, and there are some small hotels here. Tourist information is available at 12 Piazza Colombo (phone: 187-808125).

CHECKING IN: ***Stella d'Italia*** – A well-run 40-room hotel, the building itself is an elegant villa with a garden and a restaurant. Closed November 5 to mid-March, except for 2 weeks at *Christmas.* 26 Corso Italia, Levanto (phone: 187-808109; fax: 187-809044). Inexpensive.

Stella Maris – All the rooms in this tiny pensione have frescoes on the walls and are decorated with 18th-century furniture. The owners prepare all the delicious food themselves, including homemade ice cream. Closed November. Reservations well in advance are essential for this Italian family experience. 4 Via Marconi, Levanto (phone: 187-808258). Inexpensive.

EATING OUT: ***Da Franco*** – A wonderful selection of fresh seafood and local pasta. Try the *trenette* with pesto. Dining is alfresco. Closed Mondays and November. Reservations advised. No credit cards accepted. 8 Via Olivi, Levanto (phone: 187-808647). Expensive to moderate.

CINQUE TERRE: A string of five small fishing hamlets — nearly hidden between the mountains and the sea — Cinque Terre has changed very little over the centuries because, until recently, they were accessible only by donkey or by boat. Now all the villages can be reached relatively easily by train, and one (Monterosso al Mare), by car. Exit the Via Aurelia at the fork at Pian di Barca. This leads to the largest of the villages, Monterosso al Mare where the area's tourist office is located (Piazza Colombo; phone: 187-808125). It is also the only one with a beach. Park your car here and walk to the other villages (you could also take the local trains). An experienced hiker could cover all five villages on one long day's march (of about 12 miles/19 km), but it is more enjoyable to take your time, strolling over the steeply terraced, vine-covered slopes. Vernazza is the most colorful of the five villages. Like Manarola and Riomaggiore, two towns linked by the lovely, rock-hewn "Via dell'Amore" footpath, it sits on a tiny strip of coastline backed by a wall of sheer cliffs. Corniglia, in the center of the strip, is perched high on a hill, offering a fine view of the whole area. There are many little places in the Cinque Terre to take a break for a snack. Try a piece of the delicious *focaccia col formaggio* (a flat cheese-flavored bread) and a glass of sciacchetrà, the region's celebrated white wine. All the hotels are small, simple, and functional, and sometimes not as charming as you would imagine, but the hamlets more than make up for it, and the hiking trails are spectacular. The hostelries usually offer good dining — don't think of ordering anything other than pasta with pesto and seafood.

CHECKING IN: ***Porto Roca*** – Modern, with 43 rooms (most with dramatic views), and perched on a cliff above Monterosso surrounded by quiet, shady gardens, it offers first class service and cuisine. Closed mid-November to mid-March. Località Corone, Monterosso al Mare (phone: 187-817502). Very expensive to expensive.

Pasquale – As close to the sea as you can get, this hostelry has 15 rooms, all overlooking the water. Reserve ahead in season. Closed November to *Easter.* Via Fegina, Monterosso al Mare (phone: 187-817550). Moderate to inexpensive.

Cà d'Andrean – A small (10 rooms), simple hotel midway between the parking lot at the edge of Manarola (you'll see why cars aren't allowed) and the small port at the bottom of the town's winding main road. It is modern and clean and has an inviting garden to relax in after an afternoon's hike. Closed most of November. 25 Via Discovolo, Manarola (phone: 187-920040). Inexpensive.

EATING OUT: ***Il Gambero Rosso*** – High on the rocks of Vernazza, this establishment is worth a visit for its seafood and bustling atmosphere. Try the fish-stuffed ravioli. Closed Mondays, except in season; February, March, and mid-November to mid-December. Reserve well in advance and arrive early. Major credit cards accepted. 7 Piazza Marconi, Vernazza (phone: 187-812265). Expensive to moderate.

Aristide – Diners will have to walk to get to this attractive, old trattoria in the lower reaches of town, since cars are not permitted in the area in the evenings. Naturally, all the fish and seafood comes from the sea below. A popular spot. A specialty is a sampling of 12 antipasto dishes. Open year-round. Reservations advised. No credit cards accepted. 138 Via Discovolo, Manarola (phone: 187-920000). Moderate.

I Due Gemelli – There's fresh seafood from the neighboring coast and a dramatic view of the Ligurian Sea at this family-run place, as well as 14 rooms. Open year-round; restaurant closed Tuesdays. Reservations advised. No credit cards accepted. Six miles (9 km) outside of Riomaggiore on Via Litoranea, Località Campi, Riomaggiore (phone: 187-920111). Restaurant, moderate; hotel, inexpensive.

Franzi – This spot is a favorite with locals, day-tripping Genoese, and travelers alike, almost all of whom come here for the *penne con scampi* (quill-shaped pasta with shrimp) or *acciughe al forno* (local baked sardines). A seaview and the distinctive white wine from these terraced hills makes this place heaven indeed. Closed Wednesdays, January, and February. Reservations advised. Major credit cards accepted. 2 Via Visconti, Vernazza (phone: 187-812228). Moderate.

Il Gigante – Specialties at this restaurant include shellfish soup and risotto. Closed Tuesdays and November through February. Reservations advised. Major credit cards accepted. 9 Via IV Novembre, Monterosso (phone: 187-817401). Moderate.

Marina Piccola – This spot is a front row seat for the mesmerizing seascape at the foot of the vertical town of Manarola. Try the traditional *trenette con pesto* (thick pasta with pesto sauce) or *taglierini alla Marina Piccola* (pasta with seafood). There also are 10 simple rooms upstairs. Closed Thursdays and January. Reservations advised. Major credit cards accepted. 38 Via Discovolo, Manarola (phone: 187-920103). Restaurant, moderate; hotel, inexpensive.

LA SPEZIA: Return to SS1 or A12 and drive another 8 miles (13 km) or so to Italy's largest dockyard. The indented Golfo della Spezia is a natural safe harbor for the huge naval arsenal here, which can be visited only once a year — on March 19, the feast of the city's patron saint. La Spezia is a modern, highly industrialized city. Consequently it is often able to offer accommodations on short notice when smaller nearby resorts are booked. The city has an interesting naval museum (Piazza Chiodo; phone: 187-717600), exhibiting relics from the Battle of Lepanto as well as objects relating to sailing and steamships. Open Tuesdays, Wednesdays, Thursdays, and Saturdays from 9 AM to noon and 2 to 6 PM; Mondays and Fridays from 2 to 6 PM. The *Museo di Baldo Formentini,* known as the *Museo Civico* (9 Via Curtatone; phone: 187-27228), contains some remarkable statues from the Bronze and Iron ages and a collection of traditional costumes and household implements from the Cinque Terre. Open daily, except Mondays, from 9 AM to 1 PM and 2 to 7 PM; Sundays from 9 AM to 1 PM. Tourist information, boat tours, and information on ferries for Corsica, Cinque Terre, Portofino, San Fruttoso, and other destinations can be obtained at 47 Viale Mazzini (phone: 187-770900).

CHECKING IN: ***Jolly*** – Not beautiful, but the service is dependable and good, and the 110 rooms and facilities are modern. 2 Via XX Settembre, La Spezia (phone: 187-27200; fax: 187-22129). Expensive to moderate.

Residence "G" – Conveniently located on the edge of town, near the motorway, with 50 comfortable, pleasant rooms. There is a bar but no restaurant. 62 Via Tino, La Spezia (phone: 187-504141; fax: 187-514989). Moderate.

EATING OUT: ***Da Dino*** – A popular local restaurant specializing in seafood. Closed Sunday evenings, Mondays, and the last 2 weeks in July. Reservations are advised, particularly for lunch. Major credit cards accepted. 19 Via Da Passano, La Spezia (phone: 187-21360). Moderate.

La Posta – This traditional trattoria serves good food in a convivial atmosphere. Try the *lattuga ripiena* (stuffed lettuce) and the *frittelle di baccalà* (fried codfish), both house specialties. Closed Saturdays, Sundays, and August. Reservations advised. Major credit cards accepted. 24 Via Don Minzoni, La Spezia (phone: 187-34419). Moderate.

PORTOVENERE: A steeply pitched, pastel-colored little port town, 5 miles (8 km) southwest of La Spezia, reachable on the SS530. Just opposite, across a narrow strait, is Isola Palmaria. Prehistoric man first settled the area, and then came the Romans (Petrarch refers to it in his poetry). In the 12th century Genoa came into power and began to give the little town the heavily fortified appearance it maintains today. Although isolated, many poets and writers have made their way to this idyllic place. Among the famous who have sought inspiration here were D. H. Lawrence, Percy Bysshe Shelley (who drowned nearby), and Lord Byron. At the extreme edge of the village, standing high on a mass of rocks, is the Church of San Pietro, a 13th-century Gothic construction with 6th-century interior elements still visible. (Unfortunately, it is closed to the public.) Evidence suggests that the origins of the building were pagan and perhaps dedicated to the goddess of the sea. The town is dominated by the Genoese *castello,* which offers a panoramic view of the surrounding area (open 10 AM to noon and 2 to 6 PM in summer, 3 to 5 PM only in winter; phone: 187-900618). Portovenere also can be reached by boat, and from here the trip can be extended to Isola Palmaria, with its famous blue grotto; Isola del Tino, where the ruins of the 11th-century abbey of San Venerio stand; and Isola Tinetto and its 6th-century monastery. Gold-veined black marble is quarried on these islands; marble items can be purchased in Portovenere. This is an excellent place from which to tour other places on the Riviera. Boats leave for Portofino, Cinque Terre, and Lerici. Ask at the harbor.

CHECKING IN: ***Royal Sporting*** – A stay at this modern 62-room hostelry, with its lovely gardens and views, is a perfect alternative to the rush of nearby La Spezia. Located on the outskirts of town in an isolated spot, it has a private sand beach, a pool, and a restaurant. Closed October to April. Località Seno dell'Olivo, Portovenere (phone: 187-900326; fax: 514973). Expensive.

Locanda San Pietro – With fewer amenities than the *Royal,* this little hotel is nevertheless quite comfortable, and most of its rooms overlook the harbor. It has a very good restaurant and a lovely alfresco piano bar. Renovations to the hotel (including a pool) were expected to be completed this year. Closed January to mid-March. Near the Church of San Pietro, 117 Via Cappellini, Portovenere (phone: 187-900616). Moderate.

Della Baia – This modern 40-room hotel is popular with those who want a quieter stay than can be found at its better-known neighbor, Portovenere, just 2 miles (3 km) away. All the guestrooms have television sets, and many have small terraces looking out on the harbor and swimming pool. Open year-round. Via Lungomare, Le Grazie (phone: 187-900798; fax: 900034). Moderate to inexpensive.

EATING OUT: ***La Medusa*** – Slightly more formal than the waterfront restaurants, this eatery has an equally delicious fish-based menu. An alfresco terrace opens onto the tiny Piazzetta del Centario, a timeless spot in Portovenere. Closed Mondays and November. Reservations advised. Major credit cards accepted. 74 Via Cappellini, Portovenere (phone: 187-900603). Expensive to moderate.

Iseo – Located right on the harbor and considered the best in town, specialties at this restaurant include local fresh fish and seafood. Try the *spaghetti alla curry* (with olive oil, curry, herbs, and calamari) and the *spaghetti al Giuseppe* (with mussels, clams, squid in a tomato base). Closed Wednesdays and November through January. Reservations necessary. Major credit cards accepted. 9 Calata Doria, Portovenere (phone: 187-900610). Moderate.

LERICI: Take SS530 back to La Spezia, then head 7 miles (11 km) southeast to this seaside town with its 16th-century hilltop *castello.* Its imposing silhouette inspired Mary Wollstonecraft to write *Frankenstein* and it was in the Gulf of La Spezia (still known as the Gulf of the Poets) that her husband, Percy Bysshe Shelley, drowned after his sailboat capsized. Other literati drawn to the area include D.H. Lawrence, Lord Byron, and Baroness Orczy who wrote *The Scarlet Pimpernel* while in residence here.

The crowd today is less literary, but there is always a lively scene. In season, the port and its shops, restaurants, and bars stay open late. A drive to the nearby town of Ameglia offers coastal scenery as dramatic and memorable as the meal you'll have at *Paracucchi,* domaine of one of Italy's premier chefs (see *Eating Out*). Boats leave daily from Lerici to Cinque Terre and Portovenere and the Tuscan border is a minute's drive away. The tourist office (47 Via Roma; phone: 187-967346) can provide information on the area.

CHECKING IN: ***Europa*** – Shelley and Byron were not guests at this modern 37-room hotel, but the spectacular view from high atop this hill no doubt was the same. Climb down hundreds of stone stairs to a sandy beach or just stay put on the wide sun deck. This is a tranquil spot away from the center of town. 1 Via Carpanini, Lerici (phone: 187-967800; fax: 187-965957). Moderate.

Florida – Just outside of Lerici on the coast, this modern hostelry has access to a sandy beach directly in front of it. All 32 rooms have balconies with a view of the gulf. Closed mid-December to February. 35 Lungomare Biaggini, Lerici (phone and fax: 187-967332). Moderate.

EATING OUT: ***Paracucchi–Locanda dell'Angelo*** – Twenty minutes from Lerici is the backdrop for one of Italy's culinary landmarks. Traditional seafood and fish are present in delicious and original ways. The pasta is made with asparagus or simple tomato and olive oil sauces. Save room for the wild strawberries in early summer. There also are 37 modern rooms. Closed Mondays and the last 3 weeks of January. Reservations necessary. Major credit cards accepted. 60 Via XXV Aprile, Ameglia (phone: 187-64391; fax: 187-64393). Very expensive.

La Barcaccia – The morning's local catch will gladly be shown to you before it is prepared for your meal. Closed Thursdays and January. Reservations advised for the few tables outside. Major credit cards accepted. 8 Piazza Garibaldi, Lerici (phone: 187-96772). Expensive to moderate.

La Conchiglia – This small restaurant with alfresco dining offers pasta with any one of a number of fish-based sauces, and baked or grilled fish. Closed Wednesdays and February. Reservations advised. Major credit cards accepted. 3 Piazza del Molo, Lerici (phone: 187-967334). Expensive to moderate.

Due Corone – The pretty, outdoor dining area here is a good place to try homemade *gnocchetti in salsa di mare* (small pasta in a seafood sauce) or any of the fresh, simply grilled fish. Closed Thursdays and December 22 to January 22. Reservations advised. Major credit cards accepted. 1 Via Vespucci, Lerici (phone: 187-967417). Expensive to moderate.

SARZANA: A lovely 4-mile (7-km) drive leads to this ancient Roman site, founded in 177 BC. In addition to two interesting medieval fortresses, the town has a handsome Renaissance cathedral, original 15th-century ramparts, and narrow streets. The spring is a lovely time to visit when one of the town's three antiques fairs takes place for 4 days. Starting on *Good Friday,* hundreds of stalls offer everything from everyday collectibles to unusual and rare items. *La Soffitta nella Strada* (A Breath of Air in the Street), another fair, has drawn dealers and antiques buffs from all over Italy for 25 years. Beginning August 1, it lasts for 2 weeks, sprawling through narrow streets east of Piazza Matteotti in the center. The *Mostra Nazionale dell'Antiquariato* takes place at the same time in the Palazzo degli Studi (phone: 187-624095), but has more valuable, museum-quality pieces. The tourist office is at 1 Piazza Matteotti (phone: 187-623025).

EATING OUT: ***La Scalinetta*** – Less than a mile out of town in the Ligurian countryside is this family-run eatery that offers alfresco dining in a shaded garden in the summer. A refreshing change from the predictable fish-based menus at other restaurants in the area, this place offers *coniglio alle olive* (rabbit with olives) and delicious grilled steaks. Also worth trying are the homemade pasta and salami. It is rustic, but tastefully decorated with lots of artwork. Closed Tuesdays, September, and December 23 to January 2. Reservations unnecessary. Visa accepted. 3 Via Bradia, Sarzana (phone: 187-620585). Moderate.

Piedmont and Valle d'Aosta

Tucked into northwestern Italy and dominated by the Alps, these two regions impress visitors not only with their unique topography but also with the hearty spirit of their people. *Piemonte* (meaning "at the foot of the mountains") borders France in the west and abuts the Valle d'Aosta, a tiny, semi-autonomous region of green valleys and glaciers wedged among Piedmont, Switzerland, and France.

There is no typical Piedmont landscape — the whole area is crisscrossed by rivers fed by sources high in the Alps traversing a landscape of mountains, plains, woodlands, and rolling hills. The Valle d'Aosta, on the other hand, is a perfect example of an Alpine region, with farmlands in its deep valleys, pasture lands on the upper plateaus, and, higher, stately conifer forests and glittering glaciers overlooked by barren rocks and the snow-capped mountains.

The history of the two regions is linked, although not as closely as geography would suggest. The Valdostans — *valdostani* to the Italians — have always lived in a remote enclave, keeping themselves separate from the rest of Italy, both culturally and politically. They speak a patois closer to French than Italian, and their sense of their own national unity has generated a modest "independence movement," the intent of which is to loosen ties to the central Italian government. This separation movement does have an ancient historical precedent. Although both Piedmont and Valle d'Aosta were fiefs of the powerful House of Savoy, Piedmont was the personal possession of the Savoyard dukes, while Valle d'Aosta managed as early as the 12th century to gain a constitution granting it a degree of freedom. That is not to say that the House of Savoy did not make its presence felt — Valle d'Aosta was a favorite Savoy playground, so the area is littered with hunting lodges, castles, and sanctuaries all built to serve the ruling family.

Valle d'Aosta's strategic position has made it a crossroads of history. Recent road construction has revealed evidence of the original inhabitants, the Salassi, a pre-Roman tribe that may have drifted in from France. In the 3rd century BC, Hannibal, with his troops and elephants, passed through the region. The Romans, heading in the other direction, entered Gaul through one of the numerous passes in the Valdostan Alps. Part of the Roman road to Gaul can still be seen at various points, and the regional capital at Aosta (once known as "The Rome of the Alps") has extensive Roman remains. In 1800 Napoleon led his army through Valle d'Aosta on his way to conquer northern Italy.

For centuries pilgrims walked through Valle d'Aosta on their way to

Rome. It was here that the famous St. Bernard dogs were trained to rescue travelers lost in the snow. St. Bernard himself was a canon of the Cathedral of Aosta charged with keeping the Alpine passes cleared of robbers and keeping track of the pilgrims intent on making their way south. The famous St. Bernard dogs — the little flagons of brandy tied under their necks — do come from this region and were used for tracking, but (disappointing to learn) St. Bernard didn't think up the plan himself. The dogs were bred here many years after his death and only named in his honor. St. Bernard is the patron saint of alpinists and mountain climbers. The dogs are still bred and kept at the hospice of the Great St. Bernard Pass (the hospice was founded by the saint), but these days German shepherd dogs are favored for rescue operations, as they are lighter and fit more easily into a helicopter (no brandy either).

Formed millennia ago by a vast glacier, the Valle d'Aosta is shaped much like an oak leaf, with a main valley as its spine. Running laterally like veins from this central valley are side valleys, usually not more than 25 miles of twisting road, most of which end in soaring mountains 12,000 and 14,000 feet high: Monte Bianco (Mont-Blanc), the Matterhorn (Il Cervino in Italian), Monte Rosa (Mount Rosa), and the Gran Paradiso. Il Parco Nazionale del Gran Paradiso (the Gran Paradiso National Park) lies south of the central valley and runs over the mountains into Piedmont. The width of the central valley, the Vallata della Dora Baltea, varies in places, but wherever topography permits, local inhabitants make the best of a beautiful, if inhospitable, landscape. Where the valley is widest, there are vineyards and apple orchards.

The more than 100 castles that dot the valley served for defense as well as for residences, as the Valle d'Aosta was the beginning of the main "highway" into central Italy. Watchmen at the castles kept a sharp lookout for invaders, but they also kept a close watch on ordinary travelers — they were a source of taxes, and the Savoyard and local rulers wanted their due. So meticulous were the customs agents back then that they even set a tax on the import of monkeys and elephants (one assumes the tax on the latter was not imposed when Hannibal passed through!).

The route for this tour runs from the Piedmont capital of Turin through the major provincial town of Ivrea and on into Valle d'Aosta. The distance from Turin to Aosta, the capital city of the Valle d'Aosta region, is just under 80 miles (128 km). This ancient and charming town makes a good base for trips throughout the region. This itinerary explores the "lateral" valleys of Gressoney and Valtournenche and visits the most interesting castles along the way. From Aosta, our route travels south to Cogne in the Gran Paradiso National Park. From there, a little doubling back leads to the chic ski resort of Courmayeur, near the French border, for an Italian-side view of Mont-Blanc.

From June to October all but the highest roads can be negotiated without snow tires or chains, but these are essential from November to May. During the winter many of the passes are closed. The Great St. Bernard tunnel is open year-round. The autostrada (A5) runs direct from Turin to Aosta, but after Ivrea it might be best to take the state highway (SS26), which passes through many picturesque Valdostan towns and villages.

Those who are heading for Valle d'Aosta during prime ski season (advance booking essential from *Christmas* through *Easter*) might find themselves lucky enough to attend the 1,000-year-old *Festival of St. Orso.* Held in Aosta on January 31, its primary attraction is the array of fine local woodcarvings. Stone carving and lace making are also specialties of the region. The main ski resorts are Ayas, Breuil-Cervinia, Chamois, Champorcher, Cogne, Courmayeur, Gressoney, La Thuile, Pila (Aosta), Torgnon, and Valtournenche (see also "Italy's Unparalleled Skiing," *For the Body,* DIVERSIONS).

Expect to dine well and heartily in Valle d'Aosta. The climate encourages the stick-to-the-ribs sustenance of beef, game, and mountain trout. Also look forward to delicious dairy products, such as fondue of fontina cheese, polenta, and thick meat and vegetable soups. The best-known locally produced wine is the sang des salasses and that produced by the monks of the Great St. Bernard Abbey. In keeping with their appetites, *valdostani* drink a heady mixture of hot black coffee, grappa, genepy liqueur, and lemon peel from a giant beaker called *la grolla* or *la grolla d'amicizia* (cup of friendship), multi-spouted for passing round the table. The region's altitude and particular climate, one of the driest in Italy, are ideal for wine production. Noteworthy examples of the local vinoculture are the pinot noir, the rich ruby-red arnad-montjovet, fresh white wines from Morgex (near Courmayeur), and the coppery donnas (often spelled donnaz).

The Valle d'Aosta region has both a winter and a summer season, the winter season lasting from *Christmas* to *Easter* and the summer from June to the end of August. During both, hotel reservations are necessary. A double room in the hotel listed as very expensive in Courmayeur will cost about $220 a night; those rated as expensive charge $100 or more; moderate, from $65 to $100; inexpensive, under $65. Expensive meals are $85 and up for two; moderate, between $55 and $85; inexpensive meals, under $55.

TURIN: For a detailed report on the city, its sights, hotels, and restaurants, see *Turin,* THE CITIES.

En Route from Turin – Stop at Chivasso, Caluso, or Strambino to visit minor ruins. Otherwise, it is a quick drive north (about 35 miles/56 km) on A5 or SS26 through the Po Valley.

IVREA: Ivrea is considered the gateway to Valle d'Aosta, although still in the region of Piedmont. It has some industry (the main Olivetti plant is on the outskirts), a well-preserved Old Town, and a fine castle, built by the Savoys in the 14th century, that is still largely intact. One of the great attractions of Ivrea is its unique 2-week-long *Carnevale,* usually held at the end of February. It seems that in the 12th century the local lord insisted on droit du seigneur with a young miller's daughter. She pretended to agree to the marquis's demands, but when the opportunity presented itself, she decapitated her would-be lover and set fire to his castle. Far from decrying her actions, the local *ivreasi* — presumably sick of this sort of thing — supported her and celebrated her freedom. This story, greatly embellished over the years, is reenacted each year in a parade in which, oddly enough, Napoleonic generals and officers appear, along with medieval pipers and squires. A feature of the *Carnevale* is the battle of oranges, in which two teams — one on foot, the other mounted — pelt each other with fruit. If you are a spectator, be prepared to duck an unexpected dose of vitamin C.

CHECKING IN: ***Sirio*** – A little over a mile (1.6 km) north of Ivrea, overlooking Lake Sirio, this 53-room, modern hotel offers its guests rowing, swimming, fishing, and sailing. In addition, it houses the town's finest restaurant. 85 Via Lago Sirio, Ivrea (phone: 125-424247). Expensive to moderate.

EATING OUT: ***L'Aranciere*** – For tasty local cuisine and attentive service, try this cozy, wood-paneled restaurant set under the arcades of a fine neo-classical square. Closed Sundays. Reservations advised. Major credit cards accepted. Piazza Ottinetti, Ivrea (phone: 125-422443). Moderate.

Caffè del Teatro – Bask in period decor reminiscent of a 19th-century coffeehouse and, in the back room, indulge on excellent food amid furnishings that could belong to an English gentleman's club. Try the sandwiches. Closed Sundays. Reservations unnecessary. No credit cards accepted. 29 Via Palestro, Ivrea (phone: 125-422381). Moderate.

Monferrato – An attractive mountain ambience combined with delicious food and friendly owners make this trattoria (with a pensione across the street) a more than worthwhile stop. Especially good pasta, such as *fettuccine al limone* (noodles with lemon and cream), and mouth-watering local desserts vie with the regional *brasato* (beef sautéed with red barolo wine). On occasion, a guest will sit down to play the piano. Closed Mondays. Reservations unnecessary. Visa accepted. 1 Via Gariglietti, Ivrea (phone: 125-422059). Moderate to inexpensive.

Moro – A homey downtown establishment that serves a good prix fixe dinner. Reservations unnecessary. No credit cards accepted. 43 Corso Massimo D'Azeglio, Ivrea (phone: 125-422136 or 125-423136). Moderate to inexpensive.

Trattoria del Ponte – This pretty dining place, which takes its name from the 15th-century stone bridge close by, is a real bargain. A favorite of locals who come here for the excellent homecooked dishes such as polenta served with different cheeses and *coniglio in umido* (braised rabbit). Closed Fridays. Reservations unnecessary. No credit cards accepted. Fondo di Val Chiusella, Ivrea (phone: 125-749124). Inexpensive.

PONT-ST.-MARTIN: The climb into the Valle d'Aosta proper begins at the tiny hamlet of Pont-St.-Martin, a pretty little town that seems more French than Italian. Here a Roman bridge of the 1st century BC still spans the river Lys.

CHECKING IN/EATING OUT: ***Dora Stazione*** – A hotel-restaurant that, besides appetizing hot hors d'oeuvres and good game dishes, offers customers a painted ceramic plate as a souvenir of the meal. Closed Mondays and the second half of September. Reservations unnecessary. Visa accepted. Near the railway station, at 10 Via della Resistenza, Pont-St.-Martin (phone: 125-82035). Moderate.

Ponte Romano – Well maintained and well attended, this hostelry and its restaurant overlook the Roman bridge. Reservations unnecessary. Visa accepted. 10 Piazza IV Novembre, Pont-St.-Martin (phone: 125-82108 or 125-84329). Moderate.

En Route from Pont-St.-Martin – Drive north into the beautiful Gressoney Valley on a winding 25-mile (40-km) road that leads ever higher into the mountains and closer to the towering majesty of Monte Rosa, one of the principal peaks in this part of the country. The mountain is said to have acquired its name from its deep, rose-red color at sunset (although it probably derives from the local dialect word for "glacier"), a sight worth seeing despite the drive down afterward in total darkness (caution is advised). More Swiss than Italian, valley inhabitants are descended from the Walser people who crossed over from Switzerland during the Middle Ages — and have clung tenaciously to their old customs, colorful costumes at *festa* time, and language.

GRESSONEY-ST.-JEAN: The largest town in the valley, where the former villa of Queen Margherita of the Italian royal family now houses the local tourist authority (phone: 125-355185).

CHECKING IN: ***Lyskamm*** – Quiet and clean, with magnificent views of the surrounding countryside. Closed from the end of October to the beginning of December. Gressoney-St.-Jean (phone: 125-355436). Moderate.

EATING OUT: ***Lo Stambecco*** – Named for the local mountain goat (ibex in English), this is an excellent place to rest and "refuel" after a long drive in the mountains. The game dishes, open-fire roasted meats, and cornmeal polenta are guaranteed to revive the weariest traveler. Closed Wednesdays. Reservations unnecessary. No credit cards accepted. Via Deffeyes, Gressoney-St.-Jean (phone: 125-355201). Moderate to inexpensive.

En Route from Gressoney-St.-Jean – To visit the next valley, which runs parallel to the Gressoney, retrace the route to Pont-St.-Martin and then follow signs for Aosta. Near Donnas, famous for its rich, almost copper-colored wines, a yellow sign indicates the location of part of the Roman road to Gaul. (Because of the danger of falling rock, the section of ancient road is fenced off.) Just beyond Donnas is the great fortress of Bard. Built in the 10th century by Ottone of Bard, it commands the narrow gorge below. Napoleon had the road covered with straw and his troop's cart wheels wrapped in sacking and then led an entire army up the gorge at night without raising the alarm of the garrison.

ISSOGNE: Four miles (6 km) along the road from Bard a signpost marks the turnoff to the Issogne Castle. From the outside, the unprepossessing castle seems to be nothing more than the largest building in the village. Inside, it is fascinating, both historically and artistically. It was the residence of the Challont family, one of the most powerful in Valle d'Aosta, who in the 15th century created a cultured oasis here. The atrium and portico are decorated with frescoes which, because of the rarefied climate, have remained remarkably intact. The pictures are a charming record of local life, with scenes of butcher shops, tailors, fruit and vegetable markets, and the local pharmacy. As the exterior walls of the castle tell much about the life of the common folk of the age, so the interior is a marvelous record of the lives of their "betters." The noble bedrooms have attached chapels; there is a room for storage of the carpets and thick wall coverings that helped retain precious heat in the winter. Even here, in the remoteness of the Alps, protocol had an important part to play in the life of the nobility — elaborate assembly halls and opulent rooms were kept just in case the family had to entertain a passing Savoy duke or French king. Open daily, except Mondays, from 9:30 AM to noon and 2 to 4:30 PM March through November; 9:30 to 11:30 AM and 2 to 4 PM December through February. Admission charge.

VERRÈS: Immediately beyond Issogne on the main highway is the village of Verrès. The castle here was built by the same Challont family who constructed the manor at Issogne. A much earlier structure, however, it was built for defense rather than gracious living. A huge cube measuring some 90 feet along each wall, it has a square courtyard and a number of large high-ceilinged rooms. Completed in 1391, it was designed to display the power of Ibleto di Challont, the Duke of Savoy's regent in the district. It still makes a strong impression. Open daily, except Wednesdays, from 9:30 AM to noon and 2 to 4:30 PM March through November; 9:30 to 11:30 AM and 2 to 4 PM December through February. Admission charge.

CHECKING IN: ***Evançon*** – Pleasant and quiet, with a charming garden and a small restaurant. Rooms are spacious and bright, if a touch spartan. 9 Via Circonvallazione, Verrès (phone: 125-929035 or 125-929012). Moderate to inexpensive.

EATING OUT: ***Chez Pierre*** – The chef makes the most of good local ingredients, with outstanding selections that include mushroom and game dishes in season; homemade pâtés; delicious *agnolotti* (crescent-shaped ravioli) stuffed with a variety of fillings; and trout with almonds. The homemade desserts are excellent, especially the *gelato di crema con zabaglione caldo* (homemade vanilla ice cream with hot zabaglione). Closed Tuesdays. Also a hotel with 18 rooms. Reservations advised. Visa accepted. 43 Via Martorey, Verrès (phone: 125-929376). Restaurant, expensive to moderate; hotel, moderate.

SAINT-VINCENT: Before entering the Valtournenche, spend some time in Saint-Vincent, often called the Riviera of the Alps. Protected by the imposing bulk of Mount Zerbion, the town has a mild climate and lush vegetation. Its curative hot springs have drawn visitors since the 18th century. It is still one of the most fashionable communities in Valle d'Aosta, home to Europe's largest casino (*Casino de la Vallée;* open year-round) as well as fine hotels and a wide range of shops and restaurants.

CHECKING IN: ***Billia*** – Set in a lovely parkland, this recently renovated handsome, turn-of-the-century, 250-room hotel offers a heated swimming pool, 3 tennis courts, a fitness center with a sauna, a private fishing reserve, and direct access to the hot springs. There is a fine restaurant and a passageway that leads from the hotel to a nightclub and the *Casino de la Vallée.* The whole effect is not unlike discovering a miniature Palm Springs or Monte Carlo in the middle of the Alps. 18 Viale Piemonte, Saint-Vincent (phone: 166-3446). Expensive.

Elena – Small, extremely well run, and centrally located, this hostelry is less magnificent than the *Billia,* but luxurious in its own way. Piazza Zerbion, Saint-Vincent (phone: 166-2140 512140). Moderate.

Posta – Efficiently managed and well staffed, with an inexpensive but well-recommended restaurant in a good location. Piazza XXV Aprile, Saint-Vincent (phone: 166-512250). Moderate.

EATING OUT: ***Batezar–Da Renato*** – Small and elegant, with a limited but exquisite menu and the finest service. Specialties include *pazzarella* (a pizza garnished with mushrooms and truffles), cannelloni, and filet of lamb with mint. With only eight tables, reservations are essential. Closed Wednesday evenings and Thursday lunch. Major credit cards accepted. 1 Via Marconi, Saint-Vincent (phone: 166-3164). Expensive.

Le Grenier – After cocktails on the upper level, diners descend to the warm, rustic dining room for excellent fondues and trout. Closed Monday lunch and Tuesday evenings. Reservations advised. Major credit cards accepted. 1 Piazza Zerbion, Saint-Vincent (phone: 166-2224). Expensive.

En Route from Saint-Vincent – The entrance to the long, deep Valtournenche is approached from Chatillon on SS406, a few miles north of Saint-Vincent. The Matterhorn, rising to 14,700 feet, stands at the head of this valley, with the town of Breuil-Cervinia just beneath it.

BREUIL-CERVINIA: Most attempts on the mountain have been made from this base. Until 1937 the town had little importance as a resort, but in that year it was linked to the outside by the first proper roadway and a cable car. Since then, intrepid climbers have had to share the neighborhood with skiers, who come in droves to enjoy the Matterhorn's long ski runs, and with non-skiers, who come merely to see the magnificent mountain and the surrounding scenery. Development of the little town, unfortunately, has been too rapid to be entirely tasteful.

CHECKING IN: ***Cristallo*** – Amid quiet luxury and unobstructed views of the Matterhorn and its surrounding mountains, guests are pampered by an extremely attentive staff. There are an indoor swimming pool, tennis courts, and a lovely garden where guests can admire the view and take the mountain air. Open December to May, July, and August. Breuil-Cervinia (phone: 166-948121). Expensive.

Hermitage – The roaring fireplace in the lobby is indicative of the cozy and friendly mountain atmosphere throughout this restaurant. Giant windows look out at the Matterhorn and it is not unusual to find the owner seated at one of the tables following with his binoculars the progress of a climb on the mountain. Open mid-November to mid-May and early July to mid-September. Breuil-Cervinia (phone: 166-948998). Expensive.

Hostelerie des Guides – Opened to coincide with the 100th anniversary of the conquest of the Matterhorn, this establishment has the atmosphere of an English gentlemen's club. The lobby is a mini-museum to the feats of mountaineering; although emphasis is on the exploits of the Matterhorn guides (who have their office in the hotel), the museum also features mountaineering arcana from points as diverse as Canada and Nepal. There is a fine bar and billiard room. Via J. A. Carrel, Breuil-Cervinia (phone: 166-949473). Moderate.

EATING OUT: ***Copa Pan*** – Casual atmosphere and local Valdostan specialties; particularly good fondues. Closed Mondays. Reservations unnecessary. Visa accepted. Via Jumeaux, Breuil-Cervinia (phone: 166-949140). Moderate.

Les Neiges d'Antan – About 2½ miles (4 km) southwest of town, and one of those rare finds — a first class dining spot at a moderate price. In addition to friendly, attentive service, this family-run restaurant/guesthouse features delicious local antipasti, particularly sausages and pâtés, as well as an excellent onion soup. Good second courses are trout grilled in butter and tiny quail with polenta. There is a huge selection of local cheeses and lots of homemade puddings and pies. Closed Mondays. Reservations advised. Major credit cards accepted. 406 Strada Statale, Cret-Perrères, Breuil-Cervinia (phone: 166-948775). Moderate.

En Route from Breuil-Cervinia – Returning via SS406 to the state highway (E21–A5, in the direction of Aosta), you pass the village of St. Denis before reaching the 14th-century castle of Fénis, one of the best preserved and most picturesque in Europe. Its powerful double walls and jumble of squared and cylindrical towers make the castle look virtually impregnable. Within, surrounded by loggias and galleries, is a courtyard giving access to richly decorated rooms. The frescoes adorning the various apartments have been restored to some degree; in the State Room, a magnificent *St. George and the Dragon* is a first class example of Gothic painting. Open daily except Tuesdays from 9 AM to noon and 3 to 7 PM; admission charge.

AOSTA: The capital of the region is an ancient settlement; the Old Town (founded by the Emperor Augustus as Augusta Praetoria) is still contained within the walls built by the Romans 100 or so years before Christ. Among the many Roman remains are the Arch of Augustus, a fine theater with the *cavea* intact, the Porta Praetoria, and the single-arched bridge over the Buthier River. There are a number of imposing medieval sights as well. The town houses a fine archaeological museum, and its cathedral contains important Limoges enamels and reliquaries, as does the Church of St. Orso. St. Orso has a magnificent cloister, although the interior of this 10th-century structure has suffered two overzealous restorations. The medieval towers set in the city walls look as strong today as they must have been when they were built between the 12th and 13th centuries. One such tower is, sadly, called the Torre del Lebbroso, commemorating the internment there of a lone leper for the greater part of his life. The part of the city enclosed by Roman walls has been closed to cars, making it an enjoyable area for strolling. A variety of shops stock both Italian and French products, as well as typical Valdostan handicrafts — lace, wood and stone carvings, and such local delicacies as *tegole* (almond cookies) and, for those who fancy it, *mocetta* (dried meat) — which are featured at the *Festival of St. Orso* held on January 31. *Note:* As Aosta is not a ski resort, restaurants close early in winter. Arrive by 8 PM or make sure to reserve ahead if planning to eat later.

CHECKING IN: ***Valle d'Aosta*** – The best place to stay if you are traveling by car. Located less than a mile out of town, it even has a heated garage. Accommodations are clean, quiet, and comfortable. Its restaurant, *Le Foyer,* and bar are popular with *aostani* (closed Tuesdays; reservations advised). 146 Corso Ivrea, Aosta (phone: 165-41845). Expensive to moderate.

Europe – A clean, modest hostelry offering excellent service and a central location. 8 Piazza Narbonne, Aosta (phone: 165-236363). Moderate.

Turin – Spotlessly clean and cheerfully run, this establishment is in the middle of town. 14 Via Torino, Aosta (phone: 165-44593). Moderate to inexpensive.

EATING OUT: ***Cavallo Bianco*** – Once a 16th-century coach stop and now one of the best restaurants (with excellent service) in the entire province. A massive hearth in the middle of the room is the backdrop for excellent food, particularly chamois, fondue, and vegetable pie. There is an extensive list of regional wines. Closed Sunday evenings and Mondays. Reservations advised. Major credit cards accepted. 15 Via Aubert, Aosta (phone: 165-362214). Expensive.

Casale – Although it is a short distance from Aosta in the hamlet of St.-Christophe, many locals willingly make what is more of a pilgrimage than a drive to this justifiably famed restaurant. Make sure to arrive hungry as the waiters will bring you a huge array of local antipasti before you even get to the wide selection of pasta and meat courses. Closed Sunday evenings, Mondays, and December. Reservations advised. Major credit cards accepted. Take the E21–A5 highway toward St.-Vincent for 3 miles (5 km), and turn left at the St.-Christophe sign. 1 Regione Condemine, St.-Christophe (phone: 165-541203). Moderate to expensive.

Borgo Antico – A bustling restaurant on 2 floors, usually filled with locals of all ages who come for the large seafood menu, frogs' legs, or escargots. The pizza with fondue, wild mushrooms, and local fontina cheese is worth the wait if you've forgotten to reserve. Closed Mondays. Reservations advised, especially on weekends. Major credit cards accepted. 143 Via Sant'Anselmo, Aosta (phone: 165-42255). Moderate.

Valdôtaine – A typical mountain *birreria* (brasserie) with wood-paneled walls and a warm and inviting atmosphere, where local specialties such as good grilled meat and sausages and Valdostan fondue are featured. Closed Thursdays. Reservations unnecessary. Visa accepted. 8 Via Xavier de Maistre, Aosta (phone: 165-32076). Moderate.

Vecchia Aosta – Although fairly new, this family-run venture has built itself a reputation as one of the best eateries in town. The setting is a tastefully restored palazzo in the shadow of the ancient Porta Pretoria city gate. Try the house specialty — *trenette con sugo di trota* (flat pasta with trout sauce). Closed Wednesdays. Reservations advised. Major credit cards accepted. 4 Piazza Pretoria, Aosta (phone: 165-361186). Moderate.

Il Vecchio Ristoro – Housed in an old mill, and one of Aosta's prettiest restaurants, it produces some very good fish dishes, especially trout and salmon. Closed Sundays, the second half of July, and all of August. Reservations advised. Visa accepted. 4 Via Tourneuve, Aosta (phone: 165-33238). Moderate.

Piemonte – The owner/chef plies his trade in the kitchen, turning out dishes that include various home-cured hams and fresh *tagliatelle* and peppers in a *bagna caôda,* a "hot bath" of anchovies, oil, and garlic. Closed Sundays. Reservations advised. No credit cards accepted. 13 Via Porta Pretoria, Aosta (phone: 165-40111). Moderate to inexpensive.

En Route from Aosta – About 4 miles (6 km) west of Aosta toward Mont-Blanc on the SS26 is the sign for Cogne. Watch for the two magnificent castles visible from the turnoff. One, standing on an isolated rock, is St.-Pierre, the most fairy tale–like of all the Valdostan castles. The locals claim that this is the one that Walt Disney must have had in mind when he built *Disneyland.* Unfortunately, it is open only sporadically (a good time to visit is the summer, when there are archaeological exhibitions). Above St.-Pierre is the 13th-century fortress/castle of Sarre. This imposing building was once used as a hunting lodge by the Savoy family, a fact attested to by the enormous number of hunting trophies on display. The castle is open only in the summer. Nearby, also on the road to Cogne, is the four-towered castle of Aymaville, dating from the mid-15th century, and open to visitors.

COGNE: A mountain village known for lace making and woodcarving, Cogne is the gateway to the Gran Paradiso National Park. Founded in 1922, the park is the best-preserved Alpine nature reserve in the world. Its flora and fauna are representative of the Alps in general: Edelweiss, gentian, artemisia, and juniper grow in profusion or can be seen at the Giardino Alpino in the park itself. Chamois and the ibex — once threatened by extinction — are now quite plentiful here, as are fox, hare, marmot, and stoat. The rarest Alpine birds, notably the eagle, owl, and imperial raven, are occasionally visible. While hunting and scavenging are strictly forbidden in the park (fines are as high as $80,000!), hiking is encouraged. There are plenty of marked trails, but for a map and advice about routes, distances, and difficulty, stop in at the Cogne Tourist Office (Piazza E. Chanoux; phone: 165-74040). If you go on some of the longer hikes, you may want to stop in at a *rifugio* (mountain hut) where you can eat and sleep. Check with the tourist office before leaving, as they are not all open year-round. In winter, there are some 40 miles of cross-country skiing trails around Cogne. The Gran Paradiso National Park is open year-round.

CHECKING IN: ***Mont Blanc*** – Centrally located, this modern, clean, and comfortable hostelry has a good restaurant that turns out well-cooked local specialties. In high season (*Christmas, Easter,* July, and August), guests are required to take half or full board. 18 Via Gran Paradiso, Cogne (phone: 165-74211). Moderate to inexpensive.

Notre Maison – The restaurant attached to this small, 12-room hotel is a local favorite. Try the juniper-smoked trout caught nearby. Restaurant closed Mondays. Frazione Cretaz, Cogne (phone: 165-74104). Moderate to inexpensive.

Sant'Orso – Popular with skiers in winter and hikers in summer, this modern 30-room hotel is conveniently located close to the town's main piazza, but most guestrooms have views of the national park. There is a sauna and solarium. Half board required. 2 Via Bourgeois, Cogne (phone: 165-74821). Moderate to inexpensive.

EATING OUT: ***Lou Ressignon*** – Just beyond Cogne on the main road is a family-run restaurant that dispenses good local food. Chamois, served either as an hors d'oeuvre or as a main course, delicious polenta, an extremely filling rice and bread soup (*soupe à la cogneintze*), and veal *carbonada* (marinated in red wine) are specialties of the house. Closed Tuesdays. Reservations unnecessary. No credit cards accepted. 81 Via Bourgeois, Cogne (phone: 165-74034). Moderate.

En route from Cogne – Return along State Road 507 to St. Pierre and rejoin the SS26 to Courmayeur.

COURMAYEUR: Courmayeur was not popular as a resort until the British discovered it in the late 18th century. These prototypical alpinists came for the fine air, the beautiful views, and the excellent climbing and skiing on the slopes of Mont-Blanc (conquered in 1786) and environs. The town gained importance with the 1965 opening of the Mont-Blanc tunnel, which brought many more visitors. Today it is an elegant resort, an Italian equivalent of Gstaad or Klosters in Switzerland. But it is much more than a winter vacation spot; the sheltering effect of Mont-Blanc makes the summer climate far more agreeable than that of Chamonix on the other side of the border, so there is also an active season for walkers and hikers and those who just come to take the air, as well as for summer skiers. One of the most exciting cable car journeys in the Alps is that from La Palud, just 2 miles (3 km) away, over the Mont-Blanc massif, with views of the "sea of glaciers" that wend their way down the sides of the mountain. The highest point of the ride to Punta Helbronner is about 11,000 feet, easily worth the price of the round-trip ticket (about $26) for the breathtaking panorama of the entire Chamonix Valley.

Courmayeur attracts the sorts of vacationers that make it worthwhile for the best Roman, Milanese, and international retailers to keep permanent stores here, so the shopping is excellent. Especially on Via Roma, such names as *Cartier, Trussardi, Valentino, Fendi,* and *Armani* are easily found. In the center of town is the *Museo Duca degli Abruzzi* (no phone), one of the best mountaineering museums in Europe. Open daily except Mondays from 9 AM to noon and 3 to 7 PM.

CHECKING IN: Most hotels close for some weeks from after *Easter* to June and from late September to early December.

Royal e Golf – This is a sleek, modern place set in a lovely garden with beautiful views of the mountains and glaciers. Guests can swim in the heated swimming pool and are also provided with ski lift passes. 81-83 Via Roma, Courmayeur (phone: 165-843621). Very expensive.

Les Jumeaux – One of Courmayeur's newest and chicest hotels, it is the perfect place for the dedicated skier — the cable car is nearby. In addition to 86 rooms, there is a sauna and fitness center. 35 Strada Regionale, Courmayeur (phone: 165-844040). Expensive.

Pavillon – A member of the prestigious Relais & Châteaux group and the finest hotel in Courmayeur. All 40 rooms and suites have balconies with stupendous views. Beautifully situated, it is only 2 minutes from a ski lift, and for those who find a few miles of skiing on Mont-Blanc not enough exercise, there is a covered, heated swimming pool, complete with a lovely solarium and sauna. There is a relaxing bar for après-ski and a superb restaurant (see *Eating Out*). 60-62 Via Regionale, Courmayeur (phone: 165-842420). Expensive.

Brenva – Built in 1897 as a place for mountaineers to rest their weary limbs after attempts on Monte Bianco, this Old World–style hotel is in the picturesque village of Entrèves. The restaurant attracts many a diner away from Courmayeur proper, 2 miles (3 km) up the road. Entrèves, Courmayeur (phone: 165-89285). Moderate.

Le Bouton d'Or – Small but clean, comfortable, and nicely furnished rooms, some with views of Mont-Blanc and others facing the valley and less majestic mountains. Breakfast only, but it's very near *Le Vieux Pommier* (see *Eating Out*). 26 Strada Statale, Courmayeur (phone: 165-842380). Moderate to inexpensive.

Dolonne – Housed in a tastefully remodeled 17th-century house, with spacious and comfortably furnished rooms. A nearby cableway gives immediate access to the ski slopes of Val Veny. Breakfast only. 62 Via delle Vittorie, Courmayeur-Dolonne (phone: 165-841260). Moderate to inexpensive.

EATING OUT: *Le Bistroquet* – Housed in the *Pavillon* hotel, this is the grand, if small, restaurant of Courmayeur. In addition to delicious local delicacies, such as *bagna caôda,* a hot dipping sauce for vegetables that sometimes contains the local thistle, and a wide range of fondues, there are excellent pasta and risotto, as well as fine cuts of meat that have been grilled to perfection. Open evenings only. Closed Mondays. Reservations advised. Major credit cards accepted. 60-62 Via Regionale, Courmayeur (phone: 165-842420). Expensive.

Cadran Solaire – A serious rival to *Le Bistroquet* for the position as the best restaurant in the area. The difference is that this place, exquisitely decorated in a rambling old site replete with stone arches and wooden floors, is smack in the middle of town. Try the roast duck (locally raised) and the numerous delicate starters. Excellent service and value. Closed Mondays. Reservations advised. Major credit cards accepted. 122 Via Roma, Courmayeur (phone: 165-844609). Expensive to moderate.

La Maison de Filippo – The food is so good and the prices so low that even the grandees at the *Pavillon* and the *Royal* hotels, as well as skiers from France, come here to eat. It's known as the "most famous restaurant in the Alps." A prix fixe meal includes an incredible number of courses — dozens of appetizers which make up the bulk of the menu. The restaurant itself is rustic and intimate, with outdoor dining in the summer. Closed Tuesdays. Reservations necessary. Major credit cards accepted. There is also a pensione with 6 rooms (inexpensive) that are in big demand. Just north of Courmayeur in Entrèves (phone: 165-89968). Moderate.

Pierre Alexis – A bustling place, with a downstairs room that also has an attractive balcony. There is a good prix fixe menu, which may include dishes such as risotto with *porcini* mushrooms, *vitello alla carbonada* (veal cooked in a tangy wine sauce), and braised chamois. Closed Mondays. Reservations advised. Visa accepted. 54 Via Marconi, Courmayeur (phone: 165-843517). Moderate.

Vacherie – A few miles south, on the state highway between Morgex and Pré-Saint-Didier, this restaurant specializes in seafood, a nice change of pace for the region. The ground floor holds an expansive bar with an open fireplace, a charming place to sit before or after dinner. Closed Wednesdays. Reservations advised. Major credit cards accepted. Mont Bardon, between Morgex and Pré-Saint-Didier (phone: 165-809209). Moderate.

Le Vieux Pommier – An excellent family-run establishment, associated with *Le Bouton d'Or,* featuring various preparations of dried Alpine beef, pasta, fondue, and homemade desserts. Closed Mondays. Reservations unnecessary. Visa accepted. 25 Piazzale Monte Bianco, Courmayeur (phone: 165-842281). Moderate.

Moulin – Small and friendly, this restaurant is in the village of Entrèves. Try the homemade *agnolotti* (pasta triangles) stuffed with *porcini* mushrooms. The chef also produces a good *carbonada,* a ragout of veal in a piquant sauce. At the end of the meal, grappa lovers can look forward to sampling from the patron's vast selection. Closed Mondays. Reservations advised. No credit cards accepted. 6 Via Colle del Gigante, Entrèves, Courmayeur (phone: 165-89969). Moderate to inexpensive.

LA THUILE: A small resort town, a few miles along SS26 toward the Little St. Bernard Pass, with ski lifts linking directly with the La Rosière–Montvalenza resort area in France.

CHECKING IN: ***Planibel*** – This vast complex, which takes in the bulk of the skiers who come to La Thuile, has a skating rink, squash courts, restaurants, pubs, pizzerias, and a complete range of shops, including a supermarket. (Some rooms have cooking facilities.) Very much a "fun for the whole family" kind of place. La Thuile (phone: 165-884541). Expensive.

EATING OUT: ***La Bricole*** – Lively atmosphere and very good food make this a popular choice with residents of La Thuile, as well as those who live farther afield. Closed Mondays, May, June, September, October, and November.

Reservations advised. Visa accepted. Frazione Entrèves, La Thuile (phone: 165-884149). Moderate.

En Route from La Thuile – During the summer, drive through the Little St. Bernard Pass (it is closed in winter) to Bourg St.-Maurice in France and then descend the beautiful Val d'Isère. Re-enter Italy at the Colle di Liseran, in the Piedmont section of the Gran Paradiso National Park. At San Giorgio, just outside Ivrea, rejoin the Turin-Aosta autostrada (A5), which connects with highways leading to Milan and Genoa.

The Lombardy Lakes (including Lugano, Switzerland)

The Italian lakes have been a playground since the Romans conquered Gaul and Cicero set up a summer house on Lake Como. They continue to get good press: Wordsworth, Stendhal, D. H. Lawrence, and Hemingway were all inspired by the spectacular and majestic beauty of this most romantic of landscapes. Rossini, Donizetti, and Liszt were moved to compose music in response to its spellbinding natural beauty. The lakes are in the far north of Italy, in the region of Lombardy, although they also touch the region of Piedmont to the west and the Veneto and Trentino–Alto Adige regions to the east. South of them is the rest of Lombardy, a good deal larger than just its lake district, and north is Switzerland, into whose territory the topmost segment of Lake Maggiore projects and whose border dips to surround a good chunk of Lake Lugano. The lakes were originally formed by the same glaciers that cut the peaks and valleys of the nearby Alps into such fine relief, and up here the towering Swiss Alps are constantly in view.

The intense natural splendor of the landscape is embellished by some of the finest examples of manmade beauty. The lakeshores are dotted with palatial villas, the grandeur and opulence of which sometimes defy belief. And the lakes themselves are far from alike in mood and character. There are marked contrasts among the fine aristocratic bearing of Stresa on Lake Maggiore, the charm and intimacy of Lake Orta, the dreaminess of Lake Como, the more rugged scenery around Lake Iseo, and the magnificent mountain countryside around the highly sophisticated and developed Lake Garda.

The 2,000-year history of Lombardy has been scarred by war and domination, but the turbulent past has left a splendid heritage of castles, fortresses, and towers in the ancient cities and hill towns throughout the region. The earliest known invaders were the Etruscans, who came north from Tuscany to settle in the fertile plain of Lombardy, south of the lake district. Later came the Romans, who included Lombardy in their province of Cisalpine Gaul. The barbarian Longobard tribe invaded in the 6th century and, in retrospect, left the region a name. After their departure, Charlemagne, Bishops of Milan, the Holy Roman Emperor Otto I, sundry feudal lords, as well as some independent city-states, or communes, all had something to say about some part of Lombardy at some time. In the 12th century, in an effort to resist the authority of another Holy Roman Emperor, Frederick I, or, as he is better known, Barbarossa, some of these communes joined forces by forming the

Lombard League, and they did indeed defeat him at Legnano in 1176. But their newfound freedom was brief. Foreign domination was replaced by civil strife, and the territory was carved up among the powerful families whose names — Visconti, Sforza, Pallavicino, and Gonzaga, among others — are remembered today in the wealth of beautiful villas, castles, and works of art they built or acquired during this early Renaissance period.

At the beginning of the 15th century, the powerful Republic of Venice moved into the eastern part of the region, annexing Bergamo and Brescia, among other areas. The Venetians were followed by another wave of foreign invaders who penetrated farther afield: first the French, in the 16th century, then the Spanish, who stayed for 200 years, and finally the Austrian Hapsburgs. Apart from a brief hiatus under Napoleon in the early 19th century, Lombardy remained under Austrian control until 1859, when an allied French and Piedmontese victory finally ousted them. Lombardy thus became part of the independent kingdom of Italy just 1 year before Garibaldi and his 1,000 men achieved unification for most of the rest of the peninsula.

Perhaps because of their long history of domination, the people of Lombardy — the *lombardi* — are intensely proud of being Italian. Statues of Garibaldi are never more prominent than in the town squares of this region. Also very strong is a pride in the beauty of their homeland, which they are keen to show off to the visitor. Travelers who master even a few basic words of Italian will be rewarded by an extraordinary helpfulness and readiness to explain on the part of the people who live here.

Visitors to Italy and to Lombardy sometimes neglect the lakes in favor of towns with more established traditions as cultural and artistic capitals. But within the lake region itself are numerous fine cities whose architecture, museums, and monuments are wonderfully rich. The region has the bonus of a breathtaking natural landscape with clear air, piercingly blue water that usually is safe for swimming, and miles of glorious rolling hills, woods, and mountains to be explored or simply admired. This is an area endowed with all the natural beauty of Switzerland, combined with the unmistakable warmth of the Italian people.

Lombardy is also a fertile and very prosperous region, leagues apart from the poorer southern regions of the peninsula, and its cooking reflects the richness of the soil and the relative wealth of its people. The local cuisine is based on plentiful supplies of meat, game, and, naturally, lake fish, all prepared with skill and sophistication. Specialties include polenta, often inelegantly translated as cornmeal mush, plus venison and wild boar and other game, and fresh trout and the delicate *persico* (perch). The wines of the Franciacorta zone include a sparkling white the Italians claim rivals anything produced over the border in France.

Many of the fine villas around the lakes, especially those at Maggiore and Como, have magnificent gardens, so a visit in late April, May, or June will be rewarded with the spectacle of a riot of colors and scents. On Lake Garda, the peculiarly Mediterranean climate also makes spring a very attractive time of year. But to take advantage of all that the lakes have to offer — boat trips, swimming, water sports, evening strolls along the lakeshore, and dinners savored out of doors at the water's edge — the summer months are best. The majority of lakeside hotels and many restaurants close for the winter months from November to *Easter.*

The route outlined here heads northwest from Milan, the capital of Lombardy, to the attractive medieval town of Varese. It then proceeds west to Lake Maggiore, which is not the major lake of Lombardy, its name notwithstanding. After visiting both sides of Maggiore, and taking a short detour west to Lake Orta, it cuts east to explore Lake Lugano and a bit of its Swiss surroundings before arriving at Lake Como, of the distinctive upside-down "Y" shape. From here, the route continues eastward to the ancient hill town of Bergamo, to the smaller, lesser-known Lake Iseo, and to the historic city of Brescia. It ends still farther east, with a circle around the last, largest, and best known of the Lombardy lakes, Lake Garda, and then, not far away, stops at Mantua and Cremona.

A tour of the area would not be complete without the magical experience of spending at least 1 night in an aristocratic villa on the lakeshore, although travelers who savor the very grand will pay for it: Prices for a double room at the palatial *Villa d'Este* in Cernobbio on Lake Como *begin* at $400 a night and expect to pay $250 and up at other hotels listed as very expensive. But it is still perfectly possible to stay in hotels of great comfort, lakeside and otherwise, for far more reasonable rates. In the listings below, an expensive hotel is one charging $120 to $225 for a double room. A moderate one will cost between $70 and $120, and an inexpensive one will cost $55 or less. In the restaurant listings, the expensive category means dinner for two will come to more than $90; moderate means $50 to $80, and inexpensive, under $35. Prices do not include alcoholic drinks other than a basic house wine. In July and August, it's a good idea to make reservations at all restaurants. The rest of the year, follow our advice in the individual descriptions of hotels and restaurants.

MILAN: For a detailed report on the city, its sights, hotels, and restaurants, see *Milan,* THE CITIES.

En Route from Milan – Take SS233 northwest to Varese, 32 miles (51 km) from Milan and 3 miles (5 km) away from its own lake, Lago di Varese.

VARESE: An attractive market town of medieval origin, it is also a prosperous commercial center, known for its production of shoes and for its macaroons and liqueur. Like Rome, it is surrounded by seven hills. The town's most striking monument is the 254-foot-high bell tower of the Basilica di San Vittore, designed by Varese architect Giuseppe Bernascone in the early 17th century. At the foot of the tower stands Varese's most ancient building, the 12th-century Battistero di San Giovanni, which contains some interesting 14th- and 15th-century frescoes. Well worth a visit is the Palazzo Estense, built in the 18th century as the summer home of Francesco III d'Este, Duke of Modena and Lord of Varese. Today the palace is used as the Town Hall, but its splendid gardens are open to the public. The adjoining Villa Mirabello houses the *Museo Civico* (Municipal Museum; phone: 332-281590) and has impressive English-style gardens with good views of the Alps. It is open daily except Mondays from 9 AM to 1 PM and 3 to 5:30 PM; admission charge.

About 5 miles (8 km) outside town is the Sacro Monte (Sacred Mountain), for centuries a focal point for pilgrims. Follow the signs leading northwest out of Varese, passing the village of Sant'Ambrogio. At the Prima Cappella (First Chapel) a footpath begins that leads past 14 shrines to the rococo Santa Maria del Monte sanctuary. The shrines, designed by Bernascone in the early 17th century, contain frescoes and life-size terra cotta statues depicting the mysteries of the rosary. (Those in the tenth chapel — representing the Crucifixion — are by Dionigi Bussola.)

CHECKING IN: ***Palace*** – Built at the beginning of this century in Art Nouveau style and magnificently set in its own parkland in the hills overlooking Varese. In addition to spectacular views of the lake and Monte Rosa, this renovated 108-room hotel (50 of them deluxe, elegantly decorated and with marble bathrooms) offers grand Old World comfort, occasional classical concerts on the grounds, a good restaurant, tennis courts, and a swimming pool. Open year-round. 11 Via Manara, Varese (phone: 332-312600; fax: 332-312870). Expensive.

EATING OUT: ***Lago Maggiore*** – This small, popular restaurant in the historic center serves excellent Lombard food. Try *buon ricordo* (a chicken dish); you get to keep the ceramic plate it is served on as a souvenir. It also offers a good selection of wines. Closed Sundays, Monday lunch, first 2 weeks of July, and *Christmas.* Reservations advised. Major credit cards accepted. 19 Via Carrobbio, Varese (phone: 332-231183). Expensive.

Teatro – At Angelo Mario Mogavero's sophisticated establishment, diners enjoy delicious, imaginative dishes (many made with mushrooms, including truffles in season) and superb service. The restaurant was once the refreshment area of the *Teatro di Varese.* Although still housed in the same building, it now is an entity unto itself and the theater's history is inscribed on the walls. Closed Tuesdays and July 23 to August 25. Reservations advised. Major credit cards accepted. 3 Via C. Croce, Varese (phone: 332-241124). Moderate.

Al Tigli – A rustic, heartwarming restaurant featuring fine regional cooking. Closed Tuesday evenings, Wednesdays, and August. No reservations. Visa accepted. 128 Viale Valganna, Varese (phone: 332-283170). Inexpensive.

En Route from Varese – The road to Vergiate leads southwest out of Varese and passes through wooded scenery, with a view of Lake Varese to the right. Continue to the old Roman market town of Sesto Calende and pass over the bridge that spans the Ticino River. Ahead lies Lago Maggiore, with magnificent mountains in the background. Follow the road (SS33) up the western side (the Piedmont side) of the lake to Arona. The road proceeds northward through some of the loveliest scenery on Lake Maggiore, with villa after villa perched up on the left, most with spectacular gardens. At La Sacca, just before Stresa, a glance across the water will be rewarded with a view of the remarkable Santa Caterina del Sasso, a 13th-century Carmelite convent built into the sheer cliff face (see *En Route from Laveno*). A worthwhile side trip is to head north from Varese to Gavirate, where macaroons (*brutti e buoni*) are the local delicacy. Then visit the *Museo delle Pipe* (Pipe Museum; 1 Via del Chiostra; for an appointment, phone 332-747750), a private collection of over 20,000 pipes gathered from all over the world. Closed Sundays; no admission charge. At nearby Voltorre is the Church of San Michele's Roman cloister, an ancient jewel dating from the 11th to 12th century.

STRESA: Flanked by a belt of woods, surrounded by mountains, and facing the three Isole Borromee (Borromean Islands), one of the area's main attractions, this town enjoys a superb position on Lake Maggiore. Despite its long tradition as a resort, it has remained pleasantly small, its streets full of elegant townhouses and fine villas. This is the town where Ernest Hemingway's protagonist stayed in *A Farewell to Arms* before escaping by rowboat on the lake into Switzerland. The *Grand Hotel des Iles Borromées,* described in the novel, still dominates the waterfront (see *Checking In*). At the entrance to Stresa (coming up from Arona) is the Villa Pallavicino, a privately owned villa whose splendid gardens are open to the public from *Easter* through October (admission charge).

Boats for the Borromean Islands — Isola Madre (Mother Island), Isola Bella (literally Beautiful Island, but also a variation of the name Isabella), and Isola dei Pescatori (Fishermen's Island) — leave at frequent intervals from the landing stage. Be sure to take the public *traghetto* (ferry) as the small, private boats can be expensive.

The islands are named after the Borromeo family, one of the greatest among the Italian aristocracy, and except for the Isola dei Pescatori, they still belong to the family, as do the fishing rights to the lake. Isola Bella, the closest island to Stresa, is all but taken up by the 17th-century palace built by Count Charles III Borromeo for his wife Isabella (thus the name of the island). The terraced gardens of the palace are open from the end of March through October and are worth a visit (admission charge). Try not to let the countless tacky souvenir stands discourage you; once you're inside the palace grounds, the view improves perceptibly. The next island, Isola dei Pescatori, is a real fishing village, full of narrow cobbled alleys and many contented cats. The popular *Ristorante Italia* (no phone) is a good place to stop for a meal on the island. Isola Madre, the largest of the group, has the most spectacular gardens, especially in May, when the azaleas are in bloom. Both the gardens and the 18th-century palace are open to the public from the end of March through October for an admission charge.

Each year, from mid-August to mid-September, Stresa holds an international music festival, the *Settimane Musicali di Stresa* (Stresa Musical Weeks), 3 to 4 weeks of symphony and chamber concerts with world-famous soloists, as well as performances by young winners of international competitions. The concerts regularly take place at the Palazzo Borromeo on Isola Bella, in addition to other locations.

CHECKING IN: ***Des Iles Borromées*** – This gracious, 19th-century baroque villa on the lakefront is Stresa's most deluxe hotel. Part of the CIGA chain, it has 122 handsomely furnished rooms and suites, all with private baths (20 guestrooms were being added as we went to press). Along with superb gardens and an incomparable view of the Borromean Islands, there is a private beach on the lake, 2 heated outdoor swimming pools, tennis, a bar, and a restaurant. Open year-round. 67 Corso Umberto I, Stresa (phone: 323-30431; fax: 323-32405). Very expensive.

Regina Palace – An elegant, grand, 150-room lakeside hotel built in the 1890s and decorated in period style, it boasts exquisite gardens, a fitness center, tennis, squash, and the *Charleston* restaurant for fine dining. Closed January through March. Corso Umberto, Stresa (phone: 323-30171; fax: 323-30176). Expensive.

EATING OUT: ***Emiliano*** – Run by the Felisi family, its imaginative culinary repertoire has earned it a reputation as the best in town. Meals start with small samples of delicious appetizers to help guests decide which one to order. The fresh local produce and the desserts are particularly good. Closed Tuesdays and mid-November to mid-December. Reservations necessary. Major credit cards accepted. 48 Corso Italia, Stresa (phone: 323-31396). Expensive.

ORTA SAN GIULIO: Before continuing the exploration of Lake Maggiore, it is well worth the short detour to Lake Orta, which lies 9½ miles (15 km) due west of Stresa. SS56 leads up close to the peak of Mount Mottarone, a small popular ski resort with superb views, then down to the lake itself. Much smaller than Lake Maggiore, Orta is encircled by hills and mountains that give it an intimate and protected air. There are a number of charming little towns around the lake, all easily reached by road. There are day or evening boat excursions from the enchanting, petite, medieval town of Orta San Giulio. Narrow cobbled streets all lead to the town square on the lake. Sip an *aperitivo* at a café while enjoying the frescoed buildings, the Palazzo Comunale (built in 1582), a fairy-tale–like Town Hall, and the splendid lake view with the little island of San Giulio just a few hundred yards away. In April and May, Orta's gardens are illuminated as part of its annual flower festival. Sacro Monte (a hill dedicated to St. Francis of Assisi) overlooks the town. Twenty chapels were built from 1591 to 1770; they contain almost life-size terra cotta statues set in tableaux. The island of San Giulio has a 12th-century Romanesque basilica in its center, surrounded by small villas. Regular ferries leave Orta San Giulio for the island, or rowboats can be hired by the more adventurous. Every June, the town hosts a 10-day festival of ancient music, and in September there is a series of classical concerts. For details on the festival, as well as general information, contact the tourist office, 9-11 Via Olina (phone: 322-905614).

CHECKING IN: ***San Rocco*** – This luxurious 75-room hotel is the perfect place to idle summer days away. Ask for the more charming older rooms or one of the deluxe guestrooms. The swimming pool and terrace restaurant seem to float on the lake. There is a tennis court, a bar, and private parking. 11 Via Gippini, Orta San Giulio (phone: 322-905632; fax: 322-905635). Very expensive.

Orta – The somewhat elaborate 19th-century façade of this 36-room property that stands imposingly in the picturesque town piazza conceals what is actually a simple, family-run hostelry. There is a good traditional restaurant as well as a bar on the lake. Closed November to mid-March. 1 Piazza Motta, Orta San Giulio (phone: 322-90253; fax: 322-905646). Moderate to inexpensive.

EATING OUT: ***San Giulio*** – A large informal restaurant on the lake that offers both indoor and alfresco dining. Fresh fish from the lake is the specialty, but the pizza and gelato are also worth trying. Closed Mondays, November, and December. Reservations advised. Major credit cards accepted. 4 Via Basilica, Orta San Giulio (phone: 322-90234). Inexpensive.

En Route from Stresa – The lakeside road running north from Stresa passes through Baveno (Queen Victoria used to stay here when visiting cousins at their home, the Villa Branca) and over the bridge to Verbania, which includes the two centers of Pallanza and Intra. (The Roman name for Lake Maggiore was *Lacus Verbanus,* from the plant that grows abundantly on its shores, and even today the lake is sometimes called Lake Verbano.) From here, it is possible to follow the lakeside road (now SS34) all the way up to the Swiss town of Locarno and return via the lakeside road along the eastern shore. It is also possible to explore the upper part of the lake by boat. A steamer service from Arona to Locarno can be boarded at various interim points including Stresa and Intra (passports should be taken). A third option is to cross directly to the eastern shore of the lake, using the car ferry that leaves Intra every few minutes for the 20-minute ride to Laveno.

LAVENO: This picturesque port on the Lombardy side of Lake Maggiore has a harborfront of warm ocher buildings. A resort town, it is also known for its ceramics factories. Take the cable car that runs from Laveno almost to the summit of the Sasso del Ferro; it stops at Poggio Sant'Elsa and is worth the ride for the superb panorama over the lake and the mountains. Just short of 2 miles (3 km) south of town, in the fishing village of Cerro, a ceramics museum is housed in the 15th-century Palazzo Guilizzoni-Perabò (5 Lungolago), the courtyard of which is used for concerts during the summer.

CHECKING IN/EATING OUT: ***Bellevue*** – As its name suggests, this hotel/restaurant affords its guests splendid views of the lake and the little port of Laveno, with the car ferries plying from side to side in the foreground. The chef is a specialist in cooking lake fish and preparing sauces to bring out their flavor. Try the salmon trout in pink pepper sauce. Also heavenly are the *ravioli ripieni di pesce del lago,* homemade ravioli stuffed with fish. There are a small number of guestrooms, most with a spectacular panorama. The hotel is closed the last 2 weeks in November and the month of January; the restaurant is closed Wednesdays at lunch year-round and all day Wednesday during the winter. Reservations unnecessary. Major credit cards accepted. 40 Via Fortino, Laveno (phone: 332-667257; fax: 332-666753). Moderate.

En Route from Laveno – Luino is 10 miles (16 km) north of Laveno along Lake Maggiore's eastern shore. For those with time to spare, however, it's a very pleasant drive south from Laveno along the lakeside, passing through Cerro and continuing to Ispra, where you'll spot the Santa Caterina del Sasso, the 13th-century Carmelite convent built into a cliff. After Ispra, take the right turn to the enchanting village of Ranco, an idyllic spot with the bonus of an excellent restaurant (*Il Sole;* see below). The road continues south to the Rocca in Angera, a fortress owned by the noble Borromeo family (open from the end of March through October). Then return to Laveno and drive east along SS394 to Cittiglio. Turn left here into the hills toward Casalzuigno, and left again for Arcumeggia, an ancient village nestled in the woods and remarkable for the frescoes painted on the outside of its houses, all by contemporary artists. Continue through the hills to Sant'Antonio, where there is a marvelous view of Lake Maggiore and the Alps, and then down to Nasca. Once back on the lake, turn right to Castelveccana and follow the shore road north to Luino.

CHECKING IN/EATING OUT: *Il Sole* – A restaurant with a few rooms to rent — and such is the restaurant's reputation that Milanese industrialists often fly in by private helicopter. It is regarded by many as among the top ten dining spots in Italy. Nevertheless, it is a haven of peace and tranquillity, with a vine-covered terrace for outdoor eating. The menu changes every month, but there are always carefully prepared dishes based on lake fish, pigeon, and other local produce. Reservations necessary. The small hotel next to the restaurant consists of just 9 rooms (really miniature apartments), each beautifully decorated in modern style. Hotel closed January and early February; restaurant closed Monday evenings and Tuesdays. Major credit cards accepted. 5 Piazza Venezia, Ranco (phone: 331-976507; fax: 331-976620). Expensive.

LUINO: This attractive town at the mouth of the River Tresa, which connects Lake Maggiore to Lake Lugano, grew up as a fishing village but flourished during the 19th century as a textile manufacturing center, run mostly by Swiss proprietors — it's only a few miles from the Swiss border. Today most of the textile mills have closed, and many of the townspeople make the daily trip over the border to work in Swiss chocolate and watch making factories. The town has a long promenade along the lake, especially lovely in spring. Another attraction is its 200-year-old Wednesday market on the streets around the lake, which has some 900 stalls and draws bargain hunters from miles around.

CHECKING IN: *Camin* – A turn-of-the-century lakeside villa that has been converted with great taste and an eye to comfort into a very attractive hotel known for its exceptional service. There are only 13 rooms, so staying here is more like being a guest at a 19th-century nobleman's country residence than a customer. Beautiful gardens filled with camellias and rhododendron trees add to the illusion. The restaurant, the finest in the area, offers such specialties as gnocchi Camin (red, white, and green gnocchi with tomato and ham in a cream sauce), as well as a mouth-watering *carré d'agnello alle erbe aromatiche* (lamb roasted with herbs). Restaurant closed Tuesdays, except in the summer. Reservations advised. 35 Viale Dante, Luino (phone: 332-530118; fax: 332-537226). Hotel, expensive to moderate; restaurant, moderate.

EATING OUT: *Le Due Scale* – On the lakefront, overlooking the harbor, with a cloistered courtyard for outdoor dining during the summer. The fixed-price menus are a very good value. Closed Fridays, except during the summer, and the month of December. No reservations. Major credit cards accepted. 30 Piazza della Libertà, Luino (phone: 332-530396). Moderate.

I Tre Re – Housed in an attractive old building in the center of Luino. Patrons are invited to select their own trout if they care to. If not, there are also local delicacies such as *prosciutto di cervo* (venison ham) and *salame di cinghiale* (salami made from wild boar). Closed Mondays, and for 2 weeks in September and January. No reservations. No credit cards accepted. 29 Via Manzoni, Luino (phone: 332-531147). Moderate to inexpensive.

En Route from Luino – Take the road marked Fornasette. It climbs up out of the town through some lovely mountain pasture, crosses over the Swiss border, and leads into Ponte Tresa, a town at the Lago di Lugano end of the River Tresa and remarkable in that half of it is in Switzerland and half in Italy. Then turn northward along Strada Cantonale 23 toward Lugano.

LUGANO: The main city of Ticino, Switzerland's Italian-speaking canton, this is an elegant resort with a beautiful lakefront on the body of water from which it takes its name. Across the water lies the tiny enclave of Campione d'Italia, a bit of Italian soil entirely surrounded by Swiss territory — it even uses Swiss currency and the Swiss postal and telephone systems. Campione, best known for its casino, one of only four legal ones in Italy, can be reached by boat from Lugano or by road across the bridge at Melide, south of Lugano. A visit to *Villa Favorita* (on the outskirts of Lugano at Castagnola; phone: 91-521741 in Switzerland), is well worth the effort. The 17th-century villa is owned by Baron Thyssen-Bornemisza and contains his private art gallery with a collection including works from all the major European schools from the Middle Ages to the 19th century. An important part of the collection has been transferred to Madrid to a special building that is part of the *Prado Museum.* The remaining works, however, are supplemented regularly by major paintings borrowed from the world's leading museums. The villa can be reached by cab, bus, or boat from the main landing stage at Lugano. The hours vary, so be sure to call ahead; admission charge. While in Lugano, try to have either lunch or dinner at the splendid and recently renovated *Da Bianchi* restaurant (closed Sundays; 3 Via Pessina; phone: 91-228479 in Switzerland).

En Route from Lugano – The lakeside road leading northeast out of Lugano is one of the most spellbinding of the route, with calm blue water to the right and mountains and tiny perched villages to the left. It crosses the border back into Italy just before the town of Oria, which was the home of the Italian author Antonio Fogazzaro, and continues to hug the shore as far as Porlezza, at the eastern end of the lake. Then it leaves Lake Lugano behind and crosses the Porlezza plain to Lake Como, entirely in the Lombardy region. The first glimpse of the lake, whose praises were sung as early as Virgil's time (he gave it its other name, Larius, now Lario), comes as the road curves around above Menaggio, a little more than 7 miles (11 km) from Porlezza.

CHECKING IN: ***Stella d'Italia*** – The village of San Mamete, between Oria and Porlezza, is worth an overnight stop for the sheer pleasure of staying in a family-run establishment in the most romantic of settings. It, too, has links with Fogazzaro. The writer used to stay here soon after the present Signor Ortelli's grandfather opened the hotel early in this century. There are 37 rooms, a very attractive terraced garden for outdoor eating, a private beach, and even a hotel rowboat. Closed in winter. San Mamete (phone: 344-68139). Moderate to inexpensive.

Europa – The service is warm and personal at this comfortable hotel overlooking Lake Lugano. All rooms have private balconies, and there's also a good restaurant and plenty of parking. Closed January and early February. 17 Lungolago G. Matteotti, Porlezza (phone: 344-61142). Inexpensive.

EATING OUT: ***Regina*** **–** A splendid position overlooking the lake in Porlezza is one reason to eat here. In addition, the owners — Franco Vurro, who is head chef, and his Parisian wife, Dominique — provide a very warm welcome and excellent food. The antipasto Regina, a selection of mouth-watering, piping-hot hors d'oeuvres, is particularly recommended. Closed Mondays and mid-January to March. No reservations. Major credit cards accepted. Albergo Regina, 11 Piazza Matteotti, Porlezza (phone: 344-61228). Expensive to moderate.

MENAGGIO: This resort town is set on what many consider the most beautiful stretch of the Lago di Como. Just south of it, the lake splits into two, one branch pointing southwest, with Como itself at its southernmost tip, the other pointing southeast, with the town of Lecco at its tip. On a promontory across the water, in an angle between the two branches, is the picturesque town of Bellagio. Directly opposite, on the far shore, is the enchanting fishing village of Varenna. Menaggio, Varenna, and Bellagio are connected by car ferry.

CHECKING IN/EATING OUT: ***Victoria*** **–** A superbly situated lakeside property with an indoor swimming pool (uncovered in summer); most of the 53 rooms have spectacular views. The highly regarded restaurant, *Le Tout Paris,* features classic French as well as Italian dishes. Restaurant closed on Mondays. Reservations advised. Major credit cards accepted. 11 Via Castelli, Menaggio (phone: 344-32003; fax: 344-32992). Expensive to moderate.

En Route from Menaggio – The lakeside road south to Como passes through the resorts of Cadenabbia and Tremezzo, between which is the exquisite Villa Carlotta. Built in the mid-18th century and further embellished in the 19th century, it is open to the public from March through October (admission charge). The villa's garden is a spectacle, especially in April and May when its world-famous azaleas and rhododendrons are in bloom. The little hill town of Mezzegra, up on the right, is where Mussolini and his mistress Claretta Petacci were shot by partisans after they were captured farther north at Dongo as they were fleeing toward Switzerland. The lakeside road continues south to the town of Sala Comacina. Just offshore here is Lake Como's only island, Isola Comacina — with a sensational restaurant (see *Eating Out*), reached by a traditional lake boat called a *lucia* (they're the ones with the oval hoops over the hull), the local equivalent of a Venetian gondola. Farther on, just 3 miles (5 km) before it reaches Como, the road passes through another lake resort, Cernobbio, site of the exquisite *Villa d'Este,* built in the 16th century as a palace for Cardinal Tolomeo Gallio and now a fabulous (and fabulously expensive) hotel (see below).

CHECKING IN: ***Villa d'Este*** **–** The most elegant retreat in the lake district. Stay in the main building, the 16th-century cardinal's former palace, awash in marble pillars, crystal chandeliers, and winged staircases, or in the more secluded "annex," a 19th-century villa. In either case, guests luxuriate in the midst of acres of park, with superb formal gardens landscaped right to the edge of the lake. The 180 air conditioned rooms and suites are opulently decorated with period furniture and 19th-century antiques and come with cable television news. There are several restaurants (the *Grill/Sporting Club* is best), tennis courts, 3 pools (an indoor pool and 2 outdoors, one of which floats in the lake), and facilities for watersports. A new heating system has been installed to offset any chill in the off-season months. Open March through November. 40 Via Regina, Cernobbio (phone: 31-511471; fax: 31-512027). Very expensive.

Villa Flori **–** Not as grand as the *Villa d'Este,* but this pleasant 45-room (many with balconies) hotel, midway between Cernobbio and Como, also offers a sense of luxury. It has 19th-century elegance with modern comforts, lake views, and a good restaurant. 12 Via Cernobbio, Como (phone: 31-573105; fax: 31-570379). Expensive.

EATING OUT: ***Locanda dell'Isola*** – The menu at this rustic restaurant, a 5-minute boat ride from Sala Comacina (the landing stage is difficult to find; it's best to ask a local), hasn't changed much in half a century (thank goodness!). Be prepared for a unique dining experience as nonstop antipasti, trout smuggler's style (grilled and seasoned with salt, lemon juice, pepper, and olive oil), roast pressed chicken, salad, cheese, dessert, and brandy-laced coffee — approximately 3 hours' worth of indulgence — are served outdoors on tree-shaded, rough-hewn wooden tables. All meals are one set price. A tale of the island's "curse" is told during the coffee-brewing ceremony. Open March through October. Closed Tuesdays, except during June and July. Reservations necessary. Major credit cards accepted. Isola Comacina (phone: 344-55083). Expensive.

Terzo Grotto – One of the best restaurants on Lake Como for northern cuisine — a wide variety of soups, excellent meat, and pasta — and the spaghetti and seafood cooked in a paper bag is a treat. There are fresh mushrooms, truffles, wild strawberries, and blueberries in their respective seasons. Also several guestrooms upstairs. Closed Thursdays and November. Reservations advised. Major credit cards accepted. 21 Via Volta, Cernobbio (phone: 31-512304). Moderate.

Trattoria del Vapore – Small and friendly, this is a fine spot for pasta and fresh fish. Closed Tuesdays and December. Reservations advised. American Express accepted. 17 Via G. Garibaldi, Cernobbio (phone: 31-510308). Moderate.

Albergo Giardino – Though a variety of entrées are available, the many kinds of tasty pizza make this a pleasant place for dinner — try more than one in the garden under the stars. Closed December through February. Reservations advised. Major credit cards accepted. It also has 11 small rooms that are inexpensive (open year-round, except for 3 weeks at *Christmas*). 73 Via Regina, Cernobbio (phone: 31-511154). Inexpensive.

COMO: Twice a year, fashion buyers from all over the world flock to this bustling lakeside town to see what's new in silk fabrics. Como is not only one of the larger lake resorts — the largest on this lake — but also a famous silk producing town, and has been since the 16th century. Designer silk scarves and shawls, as well as fabric, are for sale at huge discounts at *Ratti* (open Mondays through Saturdays; 19 Via Cernobbio; phone: 31-233262). It enjoys a spectacular position at the southern end of the lake, with mountains all around and lovely villas scattered among the hills outside the city.

Como began as a Roman colony, and two famous Romans, Pliny the Elder and Pliny the Younger, were born here. In the medieval period, it was an independent commune. The old part of town is well preserved, despite a strife-torn history, with the three towers of the city walls still standing, several old churches, and a wealth of old cobbled streets and colonnades that house an array of irresistible shops. Piazza del Duomo is the heart of town. Here, side by side, are the black and white marble Broletto (the ancient Town Hall), built in 1215, with the Torre del Comune on one side and the Duomo on the other. Begun in 1396, the Duomo combines Gothic and Renaissance elements in its façade (the rose window is renowned) and interior, and it was finished in the 18th century with a baroque cupola. Among Como's other notable churches are the 11th-century Sant'Abbondio, in the Lombard Romanesque style, the 12th-century San Fedele, and the 14th-century Sant'Agostino.

Como is an excellent starting point for boat trips — by far the best way to explore the lake. A fleet of 50 or so paddle steamers and motor boats plies the water from here to the northern point of the lake at Colico, crisscrossing from bank to bank and stopping at lakeside villages on the way. A pass granting unlimited travel for one or more days can be purchased. Tickets and timetables are available at the office by the landing stage in Piazza Cavour, where there is also an information office of the Azienda di Promozione Turistica (17 Piazza Cavour; phone: 31-274064), or at the railway station (phone: 31-267214). It's also possible to enjoy the lake and eat at the same time by having lunch on board one of the boats that leave the landing stage twice daily, usually at 10:30 AM and at midday. The food is good, the scenery unparalleled, and the prices an extraordinarily good value. The boats go to the north of the lake, with stops en route, and return in the early evening.

CHECKING IN: ***Barchetta Excelsior*** – Conveniently situated on Como's lakefront main square, this recently renovated, 80-room and 3-suite property also has a restaurant. The guestrooms are attractively decorated in modern Italian style. 1 Piazza Cavour, Como (phone: 31-266531; fax: 31-302622). Expensive.

Santandrea Golf – Surrounded by lush greenery and woods on Lake Montorfano, just 10 minutes from Como, this small (12 rooms), elegant hotel offers tranquillity, a patch of private beach, and golf close by. It is patronized by American silk dealers who travel to Como on business. The excellent, expensive restaurant serves nouvelle cuisine alfresco during the summer. Closed January. Reservations necessary. Major credit cards accepted. 19 Via Como, Montorfano (phone: 31-200220; fax: 31-699529). Hotel, expensive to moderate; restaurant, expensive.

EATING OUT: ***Sant'Anna*** – Several charming wood panelled rooms offer intimate and delicious dining. The bill of fare lists unpretentious *nuova cucina*—try the fresh lake fish or *taglialini* with salmon and peppers, and the veal cutlet covered with diced tomato looks almost too good to eat—but not quite. The young waiters couldn't be more helpful. Closed Fridays, Saturday lunch, July 25 to August 25, and *Christmas.* Reservations advised in the evenings. Major credit cards accepted. 1-3 Via Filippo Turati, Como (phone: 31-505266). Expensive.

Imbarcadero – Good food in elegant surroundings, overlooking Lake Como. Closed the first week in January. No reservations. Major credit cards accepted. 20 Piazza Cavour, Como (phone: 31-277341). Expensive to moderate.

Da Angela – Owner/chef Mario Clovis carries on the tradition begun by his family 45 years ago. Elegant table settings, attractive decor, and an innovative menu make this one of Como's very best. Closed Mondays and August. No reservations. Major credit cards accepted. 16 Via Forsolo, Como (phone: 31-263460). Moderate.

En Route from Como – The slow, winding road leading up the eastern shore (of the western branch) of the lake passes through some of the smaller lakeside towns and villages such as Blevio, Torno (just beyond which is Pliny's Villa or, rather, a 16th-century villa with an unusual intermittent waterfall on its grounds that was described by both Pliny the Elder and the Younger and Leonardo da Vinci), Riva, Nesso (which has a dramatic waterfall), and Lezzeno. Beyond this is Bellagio, about 19 miles (30 km) from Como.

BELLAGIO: The town sits on a promontory at the inner angle of Lake Como's upside-down "Y," right where the eastern branch of the lake, commonly called the Lago di Lecco, or Lake Lecco, takes leave of the main branch, which retains the Como name. No more than a small village, Bellagio rises sharply from the lake, so that streets behind the flat area right at the waterfront are actually more like stairs. The gorgeous gardens of the Villa Serbelloni occupy much of the promontory itself. Built in the 16th century and redone in the 17th century, it passed into the hands of the Serbelloni family in the 18th century and was donated to the Rockefeller Foundation in this century. The villa is not open to the public, but the gardens, fortunately, are open twice daily from *Easter* to mid-October at 11 AM and 4 PM, for 2-hour guided tours; admission charge.

Nearby, the gardens of the Villa Melzi are also open to the public from mid-March to mid-October (admission charge), as is the early-19th-century palace they surround. This was built by Duke Francesco Melzi, vice president of the short-lived Italian Republic that was set up by Napoleon. The villa gardens are worth a visit, especially for the marvelous view across the lake toward Tremezzo, the same view Liszt had the year he spent here with his mistress, Countess Marie d'Agoult (one of their daughters, Cosima, who was to marry Wagner, was born here).

CHECKING IN: ***Grand Hotel Villa Serbelloni*** **–** This is not *the* Villa Serbelloni, but it is named for it, and it is *the* hotel in Bellagio to stay in. It's more than a century old, poised in a dramatic position on the headland. Public rooms, such as the dining room, have frescoed, vaulted ceilings, whereas the 95 guestrooms, with garden or lake views, are more homey. There are tennis courts, a heated pool, and a private beach. Open from mid-April to mid-October. 1 Via Roma, Bellagio (phone: 31-950216; fax: 31-951529). Very expensive.

En Route from Bellagio – Take the car ferry across the lake to Varenna, a colorful little marble quarrying port with pink and red houses in the harbor and steep, narrow alleyways leading up to the main piazza. It has a lovely lakeside promenade, shaded with fragrant bougainvillea. Also in town and worth a visit is the Villa Monastero, founded as a monastery in 1208 and today serving as the International Center of Physics. Both house and gardens are open to the public.

The steep backdrop of the Grigna Mountains, home to one of the most famous climbing schools in Europe, accompanies the route south from Varenna along the eastern arm of Lake Como (Lake Lecco). The landscape here differs sharply from that of the western arm, and it fascinated Leonardo da Vinci — it is believed to be the background for his famous *Mona Lisa.* At the end of the lake is the town of Lecco, now an iron manufacturing center but most notable as the setting for *I Promessi Sposi* (The Betrothed), the classic novel by the 19th-century author Alessandro Manzoni. Several places in and around Lecco are mentioned in the book, and the Villa Manzoni, where the author lived as a boy, houses the *Manzoni Museum* (open daily except Mondays from 9 AM to 1 PM and 3 to 5 PM; admission charge). Continue south of Lecco and then turn east to Bergamo, 20 miles (32 km) away from Lecco.

BERGAMO: The roads leading in and out of Bergamo may not be as beautiful as some of the lake routes, but this historic city is well worth a visit. From the 11th century to the 13th century Bergamo was a free commune but later came under the control of the squabbling noble families of Lombardy and later still belonged to Venice (from the early 15th to the late 18th century) and then to Austria. It is divided into a modern, busy Città Bassa, or Lower City, built largely during the Fascist period, and a quiet, medieval Città Alta, or Upper City, which stands majestically on a hill at the foot of the Bergamesque Alps. The *Accademia Carrara* (82/A Via San Tomaso; closed Tuesdays; admission charge), one of the best art museums in the country, with works by Botticelli, Canaletto, Bellini, Tiepolo, and Carpaccio, is in the Città Bassa; otherwise, the Città Alta, with its well-preserved fortifications, cobbled streets, and tiny shops, is by far the most interesting part of the city.

The Città Alta is reached by a funicular that drops its passengers in Piazza Mercato delle Scarpe, inside the walls of the Old City and not far from Piazza Vecchia, its heart, or by foot (cars are not permitted). In or around this square is a breathtaking collection of buildings, including the severe, medieval Palazzo della Ragione and its massive tower. Built in the 12th century, the palace was damaged by fire and restored in the 16th century (note the lion of St. Mark on the façade, a relic of the city's centuries as a Venetian possession). Through the archways of the palace is Piazza del Duomo, with the 15th-century Cappella Colleoni, actually a funerary chapel housing the tomb of Bartolomeo Colleoni, the famous *condottiere* (or soldier of fortune), a native *ber-*

gamasco. The chapel's façade, in Lombard Renaissance style, is a striking composition of colored marbles and delicate carving. Also on the square is the 12th-century Romanesque Basilica of Santa Maria Maggiore, to which the chapel is attached. It houses four beautiful inlaid wood panels partly designed by Lorenzo Lotto in the 16th century (they are in front of the choir and may be covered up — ask to see them); the small 14th-century baptistry, which was once inside the basilica but is now freestanding, behind the wrought-iron fence; and the Duomo, Bergamo's cathedral, which has a 19th-century façade. If you're an opera lover, be sure to go inside Santa Maria Maggiore to pay your respects at the tomb of Gaetano Donizetti, another native. It's covered with grieving cherubs looking for all the world as though they'd just seen Lucia unfold her wings to the sky.

Make your way back to Piazza Mercato delle Scarpe, from which Via Rocca leads off to the medieval lookout post, La Rocca, in the middle of a spacious park. From its height there's a glorious view of upper and lower Bergamo and over the surrounding mountains and plain.

EATING OUT: ***Trattoria da Ornella*** – A busy family-run restaurant in the heart of the Old City, a stone's throw from Piazza Vecchia. Its fixed-price lunch is a good idea in the midst of sightseeing. Try the *casonsei bergamaschi,* homemade ravioli filled with meat and served with butter, cheese, and sage. Closed Thursdays, Friday lunch, and during July. No reservations. No credit cards accepted. 15 Via Gombito, Bergamo Alta (phone: 35-232736). Inexpensive.

En Route from Bergamo – Take SS42 east out of Bergamo through the suburb of Seriate and the hilly Val Cavallina, past the tiny Lago di Endine to Lovere, on the shores of Lago d'Iseo.

LAGO D'ISEO: This is the smallest and most rugged of the main Lombardy lakes, and although it does not have the range of sophisticated amenities found on the larger lakes, the beauty and peace of the surroundings make forgoing luxury for at least one night worthwhile. Driving clockwise around the lake, you'll pass through some attractive towns, notably Pisogne, the gateway to the beautiful Valle Camonica, and the pleasant little port town of Iseo itself, with a 14th-century castle, Castello Oldofredi. But the main attraction of the lake is the beautiful island in it. At 2 square miles, Monte Isola is the largest of the Italian lake islands, but it is an oasis of peace, where only the local doctor, the veterinarian, and the priest are allowed cars. The island rises to a point, with four clustered fishing villages around its base and the sanctuary of the Madonna della Ceriola at the top. The islanders derive their income from fishing, tourism, and netmaking — some of the sports nets for the *Los Angeles Olympic Games* were made here. Boats to the island leave daily from Iseo and Sulzano, traveling north along the lakeshore from Iseo.

CHECKING IN: ***La Foresta*** – If you don't mind leaving your car behind and taking your luggage over on the boat to the island, this charming, if very simple, hotel has only 10 rooms, good food, friendly service, and blissful peace. Closed December through February. Peschiera, Monte Isola (phone: 30-988-6210). Inexpensive.

La Posada – In a small town about halfway between Lovere and Iseo, set in a garden of olive trees overlooking the lake, this small, family-run hotel, with a Spanish decor, has 17 clean, comfortable rooms, all with shower or bath, and a well-known restaurant. Closed Mondays, 2 weeks in November, and 2 weeks in January. 1 Via Provinciale, Sale Marasino (phone and fax: 30-986181). Inexpensive.

EATING OUT: ***Osteria Gallo Rosso*** – A warm, friendly restaurant loved by locals, who return time and again for the atmosphere, attractive rustic decor, and excellent cooking, supervised by two young brothers. Try the inviting array of *antipasti misti* and the remarkable *petto d'oca affumicato* (smoked goose breast). Meat is grilled over the open fire in the dining room, the salads are a work of art, and the wines are mostly from the family vineyard in the hills. Closed Tuesdays and 2 weeks in August. Reservations advised. No credit cards accepted. 19 Vicolo Nulli, Iseo (phone: 30-980505). Moderate.

Trattoria del Pesce – On Monte Isola, run by a very capable signora. Among the superb fish dishes are the *antipasto del lago,* which includes little *lavarello* fish in a sweet and sour sauce, home-cured lake sardines served with polenta, and baked eel. Also try the *tinca al forno,* a white fish baked with butter and parsley. There is a splendid view of the entire lake from the verandah. Closed Tuesdays and the first 2 weeks of November. Reservations advised on Sundays. No credit cards accepted. Peschiera, Monte Isola (phone: 30-988-6137). Moderate to inexpensive.

En Route from Iseo – To the south of Iseo lies the small wine producing area of Franciacorta, whose red, white, and sparkling wines are fast developing a well-deserved reputation. Don't miss a visit to one of the wine cellars. The largest is that of Fratelli Berlucchi, in the tiny village of Borgonato. The firm is family-run from a 16th-century farmhouse, where visitors are always welcome. Take the coast road westward from Iseo and turn left down through the village of Timoline to Borgonato, or call ahead (phone: 30-984381) for directions. Otherwise, drive southeast from Iseo to Brescia, about 15 miles (24 km) away.

BRESCIA: This ancient city is an important industrial center of modern Lombardy, but it is still rich in architectural monuments from its earlier days, from the Roman period through the Middle Ages to the Renaissance. Right at the center of town is Piazza della Vittoria, a modern square dating from the Fascist era; Mussolini gave public addresses from the red marble Arengario, or Rostrum, here. Just north is another square, Piazza della Loggia, the heart of the city since the Renaissance, surrounded by Renaissance buildings largely in the Venetian style. (Brescia, like Bergamo, was a Venetian possession for nearly 400 years.) One of these buildings, the Palazzo del Comune, also known as the Loggia, was begun during the late 15th century and finished in the late 16th century by numerous architects, sculptors, and painters, including Sansovino, Palladio, and Titian. In front of it is the exquisite Torre dell'Orologio, a clock tower designed on the model of the one in Piazza San Marco, Venice, with two statues striking the hours. Pass beyond the tower to Piazza del Duomo, which had been the civic as well as the religious center of town until it was superseded in the former capacity by Piazza della Loggia. Of interest here is the Duomo Nuovo (New Cathedral), whose huge cupola is the third largest in Italy. It was begun in the 17th century to replace the 11th-century Duomo Vecchio, the old cathedral next door, which is better known as the Rotonda because of its circular plan. Also in the square is the Broletto, a medieval Town Hall with an 11th-century tower, the Torre del Popolo.

The heart of Roman Brescia is Piazza del Foro, which covers part of the ancient forum and has in the background the spectacular remains of the Tempio Capitolino (Capitoline Temple), built in AD 73 and partially restored at the beginning of the 19th century. The *Museo Civico Età Romana* (open daily except Mondays from 9:30 AM to 12:30 PM and 2:30 to 4 PM; admission charge), an archaeological museum, has been installed in part of the temple. Next to it is the vast Teatro Romano, an amphitheater which held an audience of 15,000. Brescia has other monuments of interest, particularly churches dating from various periods (in fact, it used to be known as the "city of 100 convents" before the anticlerical Napoleon closed most of them). For information, stop in at the provincial tourist office (APT), 34 Corso Zanardelli (phone: 30-43418).

EATING OUT: *Pergolina* – A comfortably furnished trattoria near the Capitoline Temple with good home cooking, such as *tortellini di zucca* (pasta stuffed with pumpkin). An open fireplace in the middle of the restaurant is used to roast the meat served here. Closed Sunday evenings, Mondays, and during August. Reservations advised. No credit cards accepted. 65 Via Musei, Brescia (phone: 30-46350). Moderate.

Raffa – An elegant and refined restaurant (with a skylight in the dining area) in the heart of the city, especially popular at lunchtime for its good Brescian cooking. Closed Sundays and August. Reservations advised. Major credit cards accepted. 15 Corso Magenta, Brescia (phone: 30-49037). Moderate.

En Route from Brescia – The SS11 and the A4 lead to the southwestern corner of the Lago di Garda, the largest of all the Italian lakes. Its shores border the Lombardy, Veneto, and Trentino–Alto Adige regions and are dotted with cypresses, olive groves, vineyards, and flowering shrubs. Head first for Desenzano del Garda, which has an attractive harbor and Old Town center, and pick up SS572 north, the first leg of the Gardesana Occidentale (the road along the western shore). After passing through the Moniga area, known for its production of red chiaretto wine, take the turnoff for Salò. This beautiful spot was the seat of Mussolini's puppet government, the Republic of Salò, set up in September 1943. It is also the birthplace of Gasparo Bertolotti, held by some to have been the inventor of the violin. Much of the town was destroyed by an earthquake in 1901, but the two ancient town gates remain, as does the 15th-century late-Gothic cathedral. On Saturday mornings, a large market stretches along the lakefront. The resort town of Gardone Riviera is just 3 miles (5 km) north of Salò, but if you have time, leave the lake road at Barbarano, turning left into the Via Panoramica, which leads up into the hills, for a marvelous view over the lake and the tiny island Isola di Garda before winding down into Gardone.

CHECKING IN/EATING OUT: *Laurin* – An Art Nouveau villa used as Mussolini's Ministry of Foreign Affairs during World War II. Its owners have restored it beautifully, leaving many original features but furnishing the 36 large and airy guestrooms in a comfortable, modern style. Golf and tennis courts just 5 minutes away. The hotel restaurant, a wonderfully elegant, frescoed room, attracts customers from some distance, particularly for its exquisite fresh lake trout in a piquant wine sauce. The desserts are also very special. Closed for the last 2 weeks in December and the month of January. Reservations advised. Major credit cards accepted. 9 Viale Landi, Salò (phone: 365-22022; fax: 365-22382). Expensive to moderate.

GARDONE RIVIERA: The main point of interest in this lakeside resort is the villa built by the flamboyant poet and novelist Gabriele D'Annunzio and occupied by him until his death in 1938. D'Annunzio was also a hero of World War I. After the Treaty of Versailles failed to recognize Italy's claim to the port city of Fiume, on the Dalmatian coast, D'Annunzio rounded up a band of volunteers, captured the city himself, and ruled it for 15 months, much to the embarrassment of the Italian government. The estate is in the upper part of town — Gardone di Sopra — and it reflects all of its creator's eccentricities, not to mention his delusions of grandeur. Called Il Vittoriale degli Italiani, it is actually a complex of gardens, monuments, and memorials to his wartime and postwar achievements, containing the mausoleum where he and his comrades in the march on Fiume are buried, the car and airplane used in various exploits, and even a ship stuck into the flank of a hill. Visitors can walk around the grounds and are led through the memorabilia-stuffed villa, where the poet's study and his bathroom, chock-full of *objets,* including a marvelous, deep-blue glazed tub, are most interesting. Closed Mondays; admission charge.

En Route from Gardone – Traveling north through the former Roman colony of Maderno, one comes to Gargnano, where Mussolini had his villa (Villa Feltrinelli — not open to the public) and where a series of tunnels begins. Continue all the way up the Gardesana Occidentale (now SS45 *bis*) to Limone sul Garda and Riva del Garda, or, if time is no object, take the turn left toward Tignale, about 2 miles (3 km) beyond Gargnano. This winding mountain road is even more spectacular than the last, leading through magnificent scenery, with views of the lake stretching for 30 miles. (The sanctuary of the Madonna di Monte Castello is a superb panoramic point.) Following signs for Limone and Riva, the road eventually winds down through the pretty hill village of Tremosine into Limone sul Garda, an enchanting, old-fashioned town that was loved by Goethe and D. H. Lawrence, among others, and until a half century ago was accessible only by boat. Its steep mountain backdrop prevents it from expanding too much and also acts as a remarkable sun trap — which accounts for the lemons growing at this northerly point.

Continue north from Limone to Riva del Garda. A spectacular feat of engineering, the road passes through tunnel after tunnel hewn from the rock, with splendid vistas out over the lake. Riva itself has been Italian only since the defeat of the Austrians in World War I (you're now in the Trentino–Alto Adige region). At Riva, round the northern segment of the lake and turn southward along its eastern shore, most of which touches the Veneto region. The road (the Gardesana Orientale — SS249 the whole way) leads into Malcesine, which was a favorite holiday spot of Greta Garbo and has an impressive 13th-century castle housing a small museum. Another well-preserved castle is at Torri del Benaco, where the car ferry crosses over to Maderno. The road follows the outline of a lovely promontory — Punta di San Virgilio — where Winston Churchill painted just after the war and continues through the town of Garda and on to Bardolino, home of the delicious light, fruity wine of the same name. There are several wine cellars in the town where visitors are welcome. From here, drive south again, rounding the far end of the lake at Peschiera del Garda and into the spectacular walled town of Sirmione.

EATING OUT: ***Al Torcol*** – Housed in a converted stable, this lively, attractive restaurant specializes in meat and fish grilled on an outdoor barbecue. Closed late October and November. No reservations. No credit cards. 44 Via IV Novembre, Limone sul Garda (phone: 365-954169). Inexpensive.

SIRMIONE: This resort town is dramatically set; it runs the length of a narrow, 2-mile-long peninsula that projects into Lake Garda from the middle of its southern shore, dividing the water into the two bays of Desenzano and Peschiera. It has been a favorite holiday spot since Roman times, largely because of its hot sulphur springs, which have given rise to numerous spa clinics treating a wide variety of ailments. The Roman poet Catullus loved the place and wrote about it, although the Roman villa that has been excavated here — and is named for him — was not necessarily his. In the 13th century, the town, heretofore independent, fell to the powerful Della Scala, or Scaligeri, family of Verona, who immediately put a wall around it and built a fortress to guard the gate. This well-preserved castle, the Rocca Scaligera, its towers and crenelations intact, still stands right at the entrance, surrounded by water — it's actually built out onto the lake (open to the public daily in summer, except Mondays, from 9:30 AM to sundown; admission charge). Beyond it are the narrow streets of the old town, a pedestrian island, and at the very tip of the peninsula is the archaeological zone, where the so-called Grotte di Catullo (Grottoes of Catullus), actually the remains of a large, imperial-era Roman villa, can be visited (open daily, in summer except Mondays, from 9 AM to 4 PM; admission charge). Sirmione offers plenty of swimming and boating and other holiday activities, and there's a beautiful, well-posted walk, the Passeggiata Panoramica, that runs right around the headland.

CHECKING IN: ***Villa Cortine Palace*** – A league apart from the many other hotels in Sirmione, it is set in a cypress-studded park beyond the town on the way to the Grotte di Catullo, just where a nobleman would choose to put his summer residence. It has 50-plus rooms, a garden restaurant, swimming pool, private beach, and peace and quiet. Open March through October. 6 Via Grotte, Sirmione (phone: 30-916021; fax: 30-916568). Expensive.

Mon Repos – Set among the olive groves at the end of the promontory, this small hotel is a much more economical choice than the *Villa Cortine.* Most of the 25 rooms have a balcony for sunbathing and eating breakfast. Open mid-March to mid-November. 2 Via Arici, Sirmione (phone: 30-916260). Moderate.

EATING OUT: *Piccolo Castello* – Just inside the ramparts of the town, patrons enjoy a stunning location by the Scaligeri castle — and good cooking. Closed December through February. No reservations. No credit cards. 9 Via Dante, Sirmione (phone: 30-916138). Moderate to inexpensive.

Osteria del Pescatore – A popular restaurant specializing in carefully prepared fish dishes. This is a favorite meeting place for fisherfolk to eat and play cards. Closed Wednesdays, last 2 weeks of February, and December. No reservations. No credit cards. 24 Via Piana, Sirmione (phone: 30-916216). Inexpensive.

En Route from Sirmione – One of the main cities of the Veneto region is Verona, home of Romeo and Juliet and, more recently, of a summer opera season held in an ancient Roman arena less than 25 miles (40 km) to the east (see *Verona,* THE CITIES). For those with more time to spend in Lombardy, however, two historic towns beyond the lake district beckon: Mantua (Mantova in Italian) and Cremona. Leave Sirmione in the direction of Peschiera del Garda and there turn south, following signs for Ponti sul Mincio, Monzambano, Volta Mantovana, and Goito; from Goito, take SS236 into Mantua, a total of 30 miles (48 km) from Sirmione. After visiting Mantua, head west to Cremona, 38 miles (61 km) away via SS10. Set at the southernmost edge of Lombardy, Cremona is only a short distance from the banks of the Po River, on the other side of which is Emilia-Romagna. Piacenza, the starting point of our route through this region (see *Emilia-Romagna,* DIRECTIONS), is only 12 miles (19 km) from Cremona. Alternatively, from Cremona, drive back to Milan, 50 to 60 miles (80 to 96 km) depending on the road taken.

MANTUA: Although it is a city built of brick, Mantua is warm, its red and ocher buildings in contrast with the marsh lakes that surround it on three sides. What the Medici, Visconti, Sforza, Este, and Farnese families were to Florence and other Italian cities, the Gonzagas were to Mantua — a ruling dynasty that held sway for centuries and left behind a priceless heritage in works of art. Something of the grandeur of their court can be seen in the city's major attraction, the Palazzo Ducale, which is not one but several buildings, comprising, it is said, some 500 rooms, including 15 courtyards, gardens, and internal squares. The palace was begun in the 13th century by the powerful Bonacolsi family, who had imposed their rule on the formerly free commune of Mantua, and was later taken over by the Gonzagas after they ousted their Bonacolsi rivals in 1328. Thereafter, the building was continuously expanded and transformed until the early 18th century, although it was undoubtedly at its most resplendent at the height of the Renaissance, when the Gonzagas patronized such luminaries as the painter Andrea Mantegna, the architect Leon Battista Alberti, and the humanist Politian (the beautiful, refined, and learned Isabella d'Este, wife of Giovanni Francesco Gonzago II, herself became one of the era's leading lights). The family's glory endured through Vincenzo I, who was a friend to Tasso and who commissioned the world's first opera masterpiece, Monteverdi's *Orfeo,* and produced it at court. The glory declined after the senior branch of the family died out in 1627, and the last family member died in 1708.

The palace (open daily from 10 AM to 1 PM and 2 to 4:30 PM; admission charge) is entered from Piazza Sordello and, given its size, visits are by guided tour only. Since the tours are conducted in Italian, those wishing more than a cursory commentary may want to book a private guide through the Ente Provinciale per il Turismo (6 Piazza

Mantegna; phone: 376-350681), or the *Ufficio Guida* (Piazza Sordello, Casa di Rigoletto; phone: 376-368917). Either way, the highlight of the tour is the Camera degli Sposi, where Mantegna's famous frescoes (1472–74) of the family of Ludovico II (including a portrait of the painter himself) line the walls and his charming view of *putti* (children) and blue sky decorates the ceiling. Also of interest are the recently found remains of frescoes by an earlier painter, Antonio Pisanello; Rubens's portrait of Guglielmo and Vincenzo Gonzaga and their wives, Eleonora of Austria and Eleonora de' Medici; and the apartments of Isabella d'Este.

Before leaving Piazza Sordello, note the 18th-century façade of the Duomo and the 13th-century buildings opposite the Palazzo Ducale, especially the Palazzo Bonacolsi. Then walk under the archway to the adjacent Piazza Broletto and continue through the handsome porticoed Piazza delle Erbe, passing, to the left, the 13th-century Palazzo della Ragione, the 15th-century clock tower, and a tiny Romanesque church, the Rotonda di San Lorenzo, built by one of Mantua's 11th-century rulers, Countess Matilde di Canossa. Around the corner, in Piazza Mantegna, is the Basilica di Sant'Andrea, a Renaissance landmark designed by Leon Battista Alberti. Mantegna's tomb is inside, in the first chapel on the left.

One last sight in Mantua, not to be missed, is the Palazzo del Te (15 Viale Te; phone: 376-365886), designed and decorated by Giulio Romano as a summer palace for Federico II, an extremely cultured man with questionable moral standards, and completely restored in 1988. It is, not surprisingly, a long walk across town, since it was built, from 1525 to 1535, as a Gonzaga "country" retreat and horse-breeding farm. Its Mannerist style parodies the classicism of the previous generation. The Sala dei Cavalli, with frescoes depicting Federico's favorite horses, the Sala di Psiche, with its voluptuous scenes on the theme of the marriage of Love and Psyche, and the Sala dei Giganti, floor-to-ceiling with colossal giants, are among the most striking rooms painted by Romano and his collaborators. Open daily from 10 AM to 1 PM and 2 to 4:30 PM; admission charge. En route to the palace, or on the way back, stop to see Mantegna's house (47 Via Acerbi). A square building with a cylindrical courtyard, it's now used for art exhibits (open daily when there's a show).

A word of caution: Always drink mineral water in Mantua, as the tap water has a high sulfur content known to disagree with non-natives.

CHECKING IN: ***Albergo San Lorenzo*** – A comfortable hotel furnished with antiques and artworks. Although there are 40 rooms (some of which overlook the splendid Piazza delle Erbe), it feels more like a private home. 14 Piazza Concordia (phone: 376-220500; fax: 376-327194). Expensive to moderate.

Rechigi – Modest but comfortable quarters (50 rooms) conveniently located in the historic center of town. 30 Via Calvi, Mantua (phone: 376-320781; fax: 376-220291). Moderate.

EATING OUT: ***Il Cigno*** – Gaetano Martini and his wife, chef Alessandra, are renowned for their creative and outstanding Mantuan cooking, worthy of two Michelin stars. Closed Mondays, Tuesdays, and the first half of August. Reservations advised. Major credit cards accepted. Piazza Carlo d'Arco, Mantua (phone: 376-327101). Expensive.

Grifone Bianco – In summer, candlelit tables in a gently lit piazza make this a soothing place to dine. The restaurant's building dates from about 1400, making it one of the oldest in the city. The fare is typical Mantuan — try the *tortelli di zucca* (pasta stuffed with squash, macaroons, and grated cheese), then move on to the *filetto al pepe verde* (filet of beef with green peppercorns) or the carpaccio (thinly sliced raw beef), covered with chopped arugula and slices of parmesan cheese. Closed Thursdays. Reservations necessary. Major credit cards accepted. 6 Piazza delle Erbe, Mantua (phone: 376-365423). Moderate.

CREMONA: The world's first modern violin was made here in the 16th century by Andrea Amati, who passed the art on to his sons and particularly to his grandson, Niccolò. The latter taught his technique to Andrea Guarneri, whose grandnephew, Giuseppe Guarneri del Gesù, fashioned instruments that were surpassed only by those of Niccolò's other pupil, Antonio Stradivari, or, as he signed his work in Latin, Antonius Stradivarius. Even today, the world's finest violins continue to be those made in the 17th and 18th centuries by these two most celebrated masters of Cremona's three great violin making families. While examples of their superb Cremonese craftsmanship can be heard in concert around the world, five violins — by Andrea and Niccolò Amati, Giuseppe Guarneri (the father of "del Gesù"), Giuseppe Guarneri del Gesù ("of Jesus," so called because he signed his work with a cross and the letters IHS), and Stradivarius — have come home to Cremona and are on permanent display in the Palazzo Comunale (open daily) in Piazza del Comune.

Elsewhere, the city maintains a small *Stradivarius Museum* (see below) and the streets are dotted with the workshops of today's makers of stringed instruments. Even the most avid music mavens, however, are advised not to leave Piazza del Comune until they've taken taken full measure of Cremona's main square. Truly an open-air, municipal living room, it is also considered one of the most harmonious medieval squares in Italy. Next to the 13th-century Palazzo Comunale is the Loggia dei Militi (Soldiers' Loggia) of the same period. Across from them is the city's Duomo, founded in the 12th century in Lombard Romanesque style, enlarged with Gothic transepts in the 13th and 14th centuries, and later completed with Renaissance touches to the façade. The octagonal Baptistry, dating from the 12th century, is on one side of the church, while the 13th-century bell tower, better known as the Torrazzo, is on the other side. The latter is open March through September; in winter, contact the tourist office (in the *Galleria del Corso;* phone: 372-23233) for an appointment (admission charge). The intrepid who manage all 502 steps to the top are rewarded with a view that extends, on a clear day, to the Alps and Apennines. Those who make it only one-third of the way are rewarded with an inside view of the works of the 16th-century clock.

Cremona also has some other churches, such as Sant'Agostino and San Sigismondo (about 1½ miles/2 km from the center), that are worth a look, as well as several Renaissance palaces. One of these, the 16th-century Palazzo Affaitati (4 Via Ugolani Dati), houses the *Museo Civico* (closed Mondays, admission charge), with Cremonese paintings from the 13th through the 19th centuries, collections of ceramics and coins, and sections devoted to local archaeology, treasures from the cathedral, and the Risorgimento. The *Museo Stradivariano,* where the master's tools, paper patterns, and construction notes are displayed, is in the same building, but reached through an entrance around the corner at 17 Via Palestro (closed Mondays; admission charge).

CHECKING IN: ***Continental*** – The best hotel in town, it's centrally located, with ample parking, and its 57 rooms have all the modern amenities. There also is ample parking. 27 Piazzale Libertà, Cremona (phone and fax: 372-434141). Moderate.

Impero – Only a block away from Piazza del Comune, it has 36 well-kept rooms (many of which overlook the cathedral) with bath or shower, as well as a restaurant. Hotel open year-round; restaurant closed November through March. 21 Piazza della Pace, Cremona (phone: 372-20716; fax: 372-458785). Moderate to inexpensive.

EATING OUT: ***Ceresole*** – Reservations are advised for this very popular, pretty restaurant that serves various well-cooked fish dishes. Closed Sunday evenings, Mondays, the first 3 weeks in August, and *Christmas.* Reservations advised. Major credit cards accepted. 4 Via Ceresole, Cremona (phone: 372-23322). Expensive.

The Dolomites

The Italian Dolomites are one of Europe's most beautiful and striking mountain ranges. Part of the eastern Alps, they extend from the region of Trentino–Alto Adige and the Adige River Valley east to the Veneto region and the Piave River Valley, both only a short distance from the Austrian border. To the south, they continue as far as the Brenta River Valley. Named after Déodat Guy Silvani Tancrède Gratet de Dolomieu, an 18th-century French geologist who spent his life studying them, they are home to some of Italy's most popular ski resorts, including Cortina d'Ampezzo. Eighteen of the many Dolomite peaks rise above 10,000 feet. The highest, the Marmolada, "Queen of the Dolomites," a great glacier at its side, rises to 10,964 feet. The Marmolada range is one of the principal mountain groups of the western Dolomites, which also include the Pale di San Martino, Cima d'Asta, Latemar, Catinaccio, Sassolungo, and Sella groups. The principal mountain groups of the eastern Dolomites — the area around Cortina — are the Sorapis, Civetta, Pelmo, Antelao, Tofane, and Tre Cime di Lavaredo.

At certain times of the day, the majestic Dolomite peaks are definitely pink. According to legend, the peaks — the domain of a king named Laurin — were once covered by pink and red roses. Laurin fell in love with the daughter of a king who ruled nearby and kidnapped her. When her father found out where the princess was being held — no mistaking such a rose-colored world — he rescued his beloved daughter, taking her swain prisoner. Laurin escaped and returned home, but on seeing the roses that had betrayed him, he cursed them and turned them to stone so that no one would ever see them again, by day or by night. So it is that still today, they can be seen only at dawn and at sunset.

In geological terms, it is the mixture of dolomitic limestone and porphyry that transforms the Dolomites from a hundred shades of pink at dawn to an intense, almost inflamed red at sunset. In simpler terms, it is also the angle and intensity of the sun that breathes life into these massive and bizarre rocks. But the word "rock" doesn't really say it all. Pinnacles, towers and turrets, pyramids and columns, all pointing straight to the sky — they are truly a work of art sculpted by the forces of erosion.

Picture these bizarre rock formations surrounded by grassy pastures and plateaus, peaceful valleys, and dreamy mountain villages. It's an enchanted scenario, and part of the fascination these mountains hold for so many is that they are truly fabled. Legends linger everywhere. Today, as in the past, the children of the mountains love to sit by the fireplace in the evening to hear about Salvans and Ganes, the wild divinities who make their home in caves and appear only to protect the herds and the forests, or the Dragons of the Dolomites, who live at the bottom of mountain lakes, fighting other monsters for supremacy. The Gran Bracun, who saved the people of the valley by killing the evil dragon, is perhaps the noblest figure of all.

Historically, the Dolomite regions underwent countless vicissitudes. Stone weapons and utensils reveal that part of the area was inhabited as far back as the 5th millennium BC. Barbarian Celts then arrived, and in the year 15 BC they fell under Roman domination. Next came invasions by the Franks, Ostrogoths, Lombards and, last but not least, the Bavarians — a great deal of coming and going in a region where the mountains were insurmountable barriers. But credit must be given to the Romans, who as far back as 15 BC began opening roads in the Dolomites that were the forerunners of what is today considered one of the best networks of mountain highways in the world.

The invasions, lootings, and battles culminated when Charlemagne gained control, and then the ensuing events of several centuries eventually led to Austrian control. It wasn't until 1919 that the last of the area, now the autonomous region of Trentino–Alto Adige, returned to Italy.

The Dolomites remain a crossroads where different cultures, languages, and customs meet. En route, travelers come across Roman ruins, medieval castles, baroque churches, and Tyrolean chalets. The Trentino — the province of Trento — is predominantly Italian-speaking. But north of it, South Tyrol or Alto Adige — the province of Bolzano, which was Austrian until 1919 (the Italian name derives from the Adige River) — is predominantly German-speaking. Newspapers, radio, and television are bilingual, as are most road signs. If you know some German, use it, and you will be better received than if you were to speak Italian. (Inhabitants of the Südtirol still remember Mussolini's attempts to Italianize the area, and not kindly.)

Another population in the Alto Adige speaks Ladin, a mixture of Celtic dialect and the vernacular Latin brought to the area by the Roman soldiers and colonizers in the 1st century BC. The Rhaeto-Roman descendants of this historical encounter still live in the Ladin valleys of Badia, Gardena, Fassa, and Ampezzo. Numbering not quite 80,000, they are a proud people, currently engaged in a struggle to keep their heritage and national identity alive.

All of the mountain people, in fact, seem to have learned to benefit from the modern world while maintaining more than a fleeting attachment to centuries-old traditions. On holidays or even on Sundays, they don their ancient costumes and dance elaborately to the tune of yodled music. Their mountain folklore is a part of their lives, not something brought out for the sake of tourists. In short, the Dolomites are a way of life, not simply a region of natural beauty. So begin by exploring the villages, the museums of arts and crafts, and the local shops of the woodcarvers and sculptors. Walk through the tiny farm settlements that dot the valleys and look for signs of the past in the decorations encircling the windows, the carved symbols over the doors, and the painted façades. The balconies of these rustic houses are usually framed by geraniums, and even the *baite,* typical Alpine wood structures used to stack hay and stable animals, have a special charm.

As to the natural beauty, keep in mind that the almost unreal peaks and bizarre massifs that are fascinating when seen from the valley become an unparalleled reality up close. If time allows, take some hikes up the mountains or ride the chair lifts and tramways. And if possible, stop in at one of the many *rifugi,* or rustic lodges (at times little more than wood huts), scattered all over the mountains and at the base of the peaks. Some of them are repositories of another kind of mountain lore — that concerning the daring pioneer climbers who came from all over the world, especially England, in the mid-19th century to scale the exhilarating Dolomites. Their pictures hang on the walls and their old-fashioned climbing equipment is proudly displayed. Moreover, a hike up to a *rifugio* (in many places, the chair lift or tramway will also get you there) will allow you to watch as the modern-day climbers start out on their ascents or to enjoy a hearty mountaineer meal, and rather inexpensively, too.

Not surprisingly, the main attractions of the Dolomites in winter are the ski slopes. Adding luster to the region are the international *World Cup* races, held annually in Val Gardena, Val Badia, and Madonna di Campiglio. The network of lifts is exceptional, providing access to hundreds and hundreds of miles of great skiing. Most impressive of all is the Dolomiti Superski pass, available at all the resorts. With this one pass, skiers have access to some 650 miles of groomed runs and 464 lifts leading into and out of 38 separate facilities.

In the summer, the villages and the valleys come to life with music, folk, and wine festivals and parades in ancient costumes, while the mountains and the mountain lakes become a vast playground for young and old: Recreation includes swimming, sailing, windsurfing, fishing, jeep excursions, biking (mountain bikes — the current fad — can be rented at most resorts), tennis, golf and miniature golf, nature walks, and hiking. The largest group of visitors to the Dolomites are hikers and they can be seen on just about every peak. The climate is generally mild. Winters are cold but not frigid; summers are pleasantly warm and sunny. Storms, especially in August, do have a way of sneaking up, so hikers should be prepared with lightweight waterproof jackets and the like. A word of warning: These splendid mountains can also be very treacherous. It's easy to get lost, and darkness descends quite rapidly. All excursions are marked by painted symbols on stones or tree trunks. Before starting out, stop in at the local tourist board, where the helpful staff supplies detailed trail maps that also give the approximate time and distance of each excursion, as well as information on lodges and huts along the way. Only an expert mountaineer, or someone familiar with the area, should stray from the marked trails. The Dolomites also offer an excellent opportunity to experience the thrill of mountain climbing. Take note — as there have been numerous accidents in recent years, it's safer to go with a guide from one of the area's many rock climbing schools. Contact the local tourist boards or *Associazione Guide Alpine* in each of the resorts for more information. In addition, trekking on horseback is becoming increasingly popular, especially in the Alto Adige region, where locals boast of having their very own, homebred horse — the Avelignese, named after the village of Avelengo. As the story goes, this breed is the result of a romantic encounter between an Arabian steed passing through the area and a native horse. It is especially suited for mountain travel. For information, contact the tourist office in Bolzano (11-12 Piazza Parrocchia; phone: 471-993808; fax: 471-975448). Also: Though seemingly abundant, many of the multicolored flowers decorating the grassy plains and valleys are rare and some, such as the beautiful edelweiss, even face extinction. It's illegal to pick certain flowers; those who do face stiff fines. Note the signs posted on all hiking trails.

The most scenic and most popular driving route through the Dolomites is the Grande Strada delle Dolomiti (Great Dolomite Highway), from Bolzano to Cortina d'Ampezzo, which leads across grassy meadows and valleys, over famous mountain passes, close to majestic peaks, and into lovely Alpine villages. For the most part, the route outlined here follows the highway, with some detours to the most important and beautiful valleys and resorts. After Cortina, the route circles north and west to take in Brunico and Bressanone on its way back to Bolzano. A side trip to Merano is suggested before proceeding from Bolzano to Trento, after which another side trip is possible, to Madonna di Campiglio. The Great Dolomite Highway is fairly wide but, as with all mountain driving, bends and hairpin turns are unavoidable. Take it slowly. Visitors planning to be in the Dolomites in the winter should keep in mind that some of the higher passes may be closed due to snow. Numerous alternative routes are available, so check before starting out.

The local tourist offices have kept pace with the growing interest in mountain tourism. The staff is knowledgeable and friendly (most speak English) and can provide you with a wealth of information and printed materials (much of it in English) on activities, excursions, public buses, hotels, and restaurants. Some will handle reservations or put you in touch with a local travel agent.

There are literally hundreds of hotels all over the Dolomites, ranging from luxurious chalets to family-run *pensioni.* Another possibility that is kinder to the wallet and offers a chance to get a firsthand look at local life and customs are bed and breakfast accommodations (tourist offices have listings). Yet another way to fully savor local mountain life and discover authentic customs and traditions is to stay in a *maso,* a family-run farm. It affords a unique glimpse at the way mountain people live and work. The accommodations are charmingly rustic, the fare simple and hearty, much of it homegrown. For information, contact *Unione Agriturismo* (7/A Via Brennero, Bolzano; phone: 471-972145) or Bolzano's tourist office (see above). Restaurants are less numerous. Almost all of the hotels have dining facilities, and the food is generally quite good everywhere. The fare, mostly Austrian, includes specialties such as *knödel,* as they are called in Alto Adige, *canederli* in Trentino, and polenta (cornmeal mush), a good hearty dish served with assorted meats or mushrooms. *Speck* is an excellent smoked prosciutto, delicious in a sandwich. And last but not least, strudel — excellent all over. Pizzerias have experienced a boom in recent years. Besides pizza, you can enjoy a simple but excellent meal. Owing to their popularity, they tend to be crowded, especially on weekends, so it's best to dine early. Long before the Romans arrived, wine was being made in South Tyrol. Grape seeds and fragments of wine cups that date back to the 5th century BC have been found in the area. Wine growing originally was confined to the lower valleys, but later spread to the hills, which proved more suitable to cultivation. With some 2,500 years of experience in viniculture, the region produces some fine wines. The most renowned are teroldego rotaliano, pinot nero dell'Alto Adige, termeno aromatico, merlot dell'Alto Adige, and St. Magdalener.

Expect to pay $200 and up per night for a double room in those hotels listed as very expensive, $150 to $200 in the moderate category, $70 to $150 for a moderate lisiting, and under $70 in an inexpensive place. These rates almost always include breakfast. Weekly rates are available and include breakfast, lunch, and dinner or just breakfast and dinner. A meal for two in a restaurant listed as expensive will cost $90 and up; moderate means $60 to $90 for two; and inexpensive, $40 to $60. March to *Easter,* August, and *Christmas* are peak times, when prices may be higher and accommodations difficult to find, so it's prudent to reserve ahead. While some hotels stay open year-round, many close from May to the early part of June and from October to mid-December.

BOLZANO (BOZEN): Capital of the Alto Adige, Bolzano (or Bozen in German) is an important industrial and commercial city, as well as a tourist center. Its position on the way to the Brenner Pass has made it a gateway to northern Europe since its earliest days; now it is also the holiday maker's gateway to the western Dolomites. While modern highways have made it unnecessary to go through the city, it is a colorful and charming place; so plan to visit before heading for the mountains. Don't be surprised to hear the Italians speak German here or to eat the kind of food more common in Austria. Until the end of World War I, Bolzano was the capital of Austria's South Tyrol, and it is still bilingual and bicultural, predominantly Austrian in character and flavor, with interjections of contemporary Italian design. In fact, the sensation of being in two countries at once is one of its most distinctive (and attractive) features.

Life in Bolzano is pleasant and unhurried, as is immediately apparent while strolling through the Old Town. This district is set in an angle formed by the confluence of the Isarco and Talvera rivers (which then flow into the Adige south of town) and is entirely Tyrolean. Piazza Walther (Waltherplatz) is dominated by a splendid 14th- and 15th-century Gothic cathedral with a characteristic colored roof. Not far away is the 13th- and 14th-century Church of the Dominicans, also Gothic, containing a chapel with an important cycle of frescoes of the Giotto school. North of it is one of the main streets of Old Bolzano, Via dei Portici (Laubengasse), narrow and flanked by medieval arcades along which more modern buildings — 16th and 17th century — house modern shops offering the best Italian and German products. Shops are closed on Saturday afternoons. The buildings, the carved wood doors, and the elaborate windows are uniquely Tyrolean. Via dei Portici leads into Piazza delle Erbe, where a very colorful outdoor fruit market is held each day. Nearby is the 14th-century Franciscan church, noted for its altarpiece. After Piazza delle Erbe, Via dei Portici becomes Via del Museo, named after the *Museo Municipale* (Municipal Museum), which houses a vast archaeological and ethnographic collection as well as paintings and precious wood sculptures. Closed Mondays, admission charge. Last, take a walk across the Talvera River past the newer sections of the city into picturesque, suburban Gries. Once a resort town of its own, now a part of Bolzano, Gries has an old parish church with a 15th-century carved wood altarpiece by Michael Pacher, one of the most famous Tyrolean painters and sculptors of his time, as well as the 18th-century baroque church of the Benedictine monastery, noted for frescoes by Martin Knoller.

There are several interesting ancient castles in the immediate vicinity of Bolzano. One of the most famous is Castel Roncolo (Schloss Runkelstein), approximately 1½ miles (2 km) north, along the road to the Val Sarentina. Built in 1237, it rises high on a steep cliff and dominates the valley below, looking typically medieval. The interior is notable for its 14th- and 15th-century frescoes depicting feudal and court life (open for guided visits Tuesdays through Saturdays from 10 AM to noon and 3 to 5 PM; admission charge). For information on the other castles in the vicinity, some of which have been turned into fine hotels and restaurants, contact the Ufficio Provinciale del Turismo, 11-12 Piazza Parrocchia (phone: 471-993808; fax: 471-975448).

In Bolzano, as in the rest of Italy, wine plays an important role. In and around Bolzano's wine producing districts, all sorts of wine festivals are organized in the fall to celebrate the grape harvest. The most important one is called *Torggelen.* The name actually comes from "Torggl," meaning winepress, which refers to the tasting of the new wine. For aficionados of wine and wine making, a side trip along the "Strada del Vino" (wine route) is in order. To get there, take SS38, which goes from Bolzano to Merano. At the first intersection, there is a sign marked "Weinstrasse" (Wine Route). The route takes you south into the heart of wine making country, surrounded by hillside vineyards and picturesque castles. Don't miss the town of Caldaro (Kaltern). On its outskirts is the 12th-century Ringberg Castle (follow the signs) which now houses the *Museo del Vino* (Wine Museum), entirely devoted to wine making and its evolution through the centuries. Open daily from 2 to 6 PM from April to October; admission charge. In the castle's restaurant (phone: 471-960010), guests can enjoy a feast of local fare, and of course, the best regional wines. Closed Tuesdays.

In autumn (until November), try a wine tasting excursion or two. They include a roasted-chestnut feast and a tasting of *speck* (smoked prosciutto) and many other local specialties.

Lastly, if you enjoy outdoor markets, be sure to visit Bolzano's colorful and picturesque daily fruit market (in Piazza delle Erbe), as well as the delightful open-air flea market on Saturdays. The annual flower market is held from April 30 through May 1.

CHECKING IN: ***Park Hotel Laurin*** – Bolzano's most luxurious hotel, built in 1900, offers excellent service and a very elegant ambience. Set in a park in the old center of town, it has 115 rooms, a restaurant (appropriately called *La Belle Epoque*), and a heated swimming pool. Open year-round. 4 Via Laurin, Bolzano (phone: 471-980500; fax: 471-97095). Expensive.

Grifone-Greif – On the main square, near the cathedral. Guests enjoy modern comforts in an atmosphere that is elegantly reminiscent of the past, plus a very good restaurant (see *Eating Out*). There are 160 rooms and an outdoor swimming pool in the hotel-owned park. Open year-round. 7 Piazza Walther, Bolzano (phone: 471-977056; fax: 471-980613). Expensive to moderate.

Luna-Mondschein – Somewhat less refined than the other hotels in its category, it is nonetheless very pleasant and rustic. There are 85 rooms, a garden, and a restaurant. Open year-round. 15 Via Piave, Bolzano (phone: 471-975642; fax: 471-975577). Expensive to moderate.

Scala-Stiegl – A very Tyrolean 60-room hotel on the edge of town with extremely good service and an outdoor swimming pool. In summer, meals are served outside in a lovely garden. 60 rooms and an outdoor swimming pool. Open year-round. 11 Via Brennero, Bolzano (phone: 471-976222; fax: 471-976222). Moderate.

EATING OUT: ***Da Abramo*** – In a building that was once the Town Hall of Gries, enlivened by a multitude of flowers and plants. Traditional Italian dishes and seafood are served. Alfresco dining in summer months. Closed Sundays. No reservations. No credit cards accepted. 16 Piazza Gries, Bolzano (phone: 471-280141). Expensive.

Grifone – Old-fashioned Tyrolean elegance characterizes this hotel-restaurant. The cuisine, both regional and Italian, and the local wines — sylvaner, Santa Maddalena, and lago di caldaro — are very good. Closed Sundays. Reservations necessary. Major credit cards accepted. 7 Piazza Walther, Bolzano (phone: 471-977057). Expensive to moderate.

Chez Frederic – The ambience and style are French, the cuisine and wines are a combination of the best French and the best Italian, both of which can be savored outdoors in summer. Closed Mondays from October through April, Saturday evenings and Sundays from May through August, and July 5 to 27. Reservations necessary. Major credit cards accepted. 12 Via Armando Diaz, Bolzano (phone: 471-271011). Moderate.

En Route from Bolzano – Head northeast out of the city and pick up SS241 at Cardano (Kardaun), 1¾ miles (3 km) from Bolzano. For 5 miles (8 km), SS241 leads eastward through a narrow, and somewhat frightening, gorge called Val d'Ega (Eggental), whose entrance is guarded by the Castle of Cornedo. Continue through Nova Levante, a pretty summer resort surrounded by pine forests. As the road climbs, look up through the treetops for a glimpse of two impressive Dolomite peaks — the highest peak (9,236 feet) of the Latemar group and the 9,756-foot Catinaccio, in whose German name, Rosengarten (Rose Garden), the legend of Laurino lives on. Farther up the road is a grand view of Lago di Carezza (Karersee), a typical Alpine lake whose emerald green waters mirror the Latemar peaks. SS241 continues up and over the 5,671-foot Passo di Costalunga, also known as the Passo di Carezza (Karerpass), which marks the boundary between the provinces of Bolzano and Trento. On the approach to the top of the pass, the view suddenly opens up: To the west, in the far distance, are the Ortles and Venosta Alps; to the east, beyond the Fiemme and Fassa Dolomites, the renowned Pale di San Martino.

After the pass, the road descends into the Val di Fassa, and the Marmolada, or Queen of the Dolomites, the most majestic of all the mountains, comes into view. At Vigo di Fassa, time permitting, take the tramway to Ciampedie, where there is a natural panoramic terrace at the foot of the Rosengarten. From Vigo, take SS48 to Moena, the Italian capital of cross-country skiing and home to one of the world's most famous competitions — the *Marcialonga.* Because of its location in a very spacious and sunny valley, Moena is equally popular in summer and winter. Continue on SS48 north to Canazei.

CANAZEI: This summer and winter resort in the Alta Val di Fassa (High Val di Fassa) is surrounded by the peaks of three Dolomite groups — Sassolungo, Sella, and Marmolada — and is also central to three Dolomite passes — Passo del Pordoi, Passo di Sella, and Passo di Fedaia. In the center of town is the delightful late-Gothic Church of San Floriano, decorated with baroque wood altars. A hike or the chair lift takes visitors to scenic high spots such as Pecol and Col dei Rossi. The tourist board is located at 16 Via Roma (phone: 462-61113 or 462-61145; fax: 462-62502).

CHECKING IN/EATING OUT: ***Diana*** – Near a small pine forest, this very characteristic mountain lodge has 29 rooms and a restaurant. Open December 20 to April 20 and July to September 20. 84 Via Roma, Canazei (phone: 462-61477). Moderate.

Tyrol – A rather refined, 36-room chalet-like hotel near the center of town, on the edge of a pine forest. It also has a restaurant. Open December 20 to April 20 and June 20 to October 10. 3 Viale alla Cascata, Canazei (phone: 462-61156). Moderate to inexpensive.

En Route from Canazei – It would be a terrible mistake to leave Canazei without taking a side trip to Marmolada. Take SS641, a somewhat narrow but panoramic road, to the Fedaia Pass, which is also the boundary between the provinces of Trento and Belluno (the latter in the Veneto region), and continue on to Malga Ciapela. From here, catch the tramway that takes visitors as high up Marmolada as they can go short of mountain climbing for an unequaled view spanning the entire Dolomite range. The Marmolada glacier is also famous for some great summer skiing.

Return to Canazei and pick up SS48 northeast. Approximately 9 miles (14 km) from town, to the left, detour onto SS242, which travels over the Sella Pass, with the mountains of the Sella group to the east and Sassolungo to the west. The road then descends into tiny Plan de Gralba and right into the heart of the Val Gardena — one of the most beautiful resort areas in the Dolomites, a skiers' paradise in winter and a favorite summer playground for mountain climbers and hikers. The valley is part of the Ladin-speaking region of Alto Adige, and its inhabitants still conserve their enthusiasm for mountain culture and folklore. Its craftsmen are renowned — expert woodcarvers who are especially famous for hand-carved furniture, statues, and toys. The route (SS242) traverses the entire valley, passing through its three most important villages: Selva di Val Gardena, Santa Cristina, and Ortisei, all within a few miles of each other.

SELVA DI VAL GARDENA and SANTA CRISTINA: Known in German as Wolkenstein in Gröden and St. Christina, these two villages are equally charming. A number of excursions begin in each town. The Passo di Gardena can be reached by tramway from Selva di Val Gardena. After the 20-minute ride, passengers are rewarded with an incomparable view of the Sella, Sassolungo, and Sciliar mountains, and as far as the Ortles in the west, as well as of the Alpi di Siusi, a high Alpine plain. From Santa Cristina, a chair lift ride of less than 10 minutes leads to Monte Pana, where weary visitors can relax at the ski lodge *Sporthotel Monte Pana* and enjoy the magnificent view. For more altitude, another 10-minute chair ride carries visitors up to the Rifugio Mont de Soura at 6,565 feet, and a 3-hour hike reaches the top of the famed Sella Pass.

If you happen to be in Selva during the summer, there is a variety of musical events to enjoy, such as the *Gardenese Musical Weeks* in July and August, and the *Gardenese Folklore Festival* in August. For a list of events, check with the Azienda Autonoma di Soggiorno Selva/Gardena (phone: 471-75122; fax: 471-794245). For events in Santa Christina, call 471-73046 or send a fax, 471-73198.

For a delightful shopping experience, explore the colorful and picturesque outdoor markets, Wednesdays in Santa Cristina and Thursdays in Selva di Val Gardena.

ORTISEI (ST. ULRICH): This summer and winter resort village is the chief town of Val Gardena. It lies at the foot of the Alpe di Siusi, the most extensive plateau in the Alps. Grassy and wildflower-strewn in summer and snow-covered in winter, it can be reached by tramway from Ortisei and offers wonderful views. Ortisei is another village with a Ladin heritage (as are Selva di Val Gardena and Santa Cristina), and Ortisei's *Museo Ladin* (Ladin Museum; Antonius Pl., just behind the Sparkasse bank) also has a display of 300 years of the art of woodcarving. There are typical old wooden toys, as well as paintings by famous Gardena artists. In addition, the mineral and fossil collection also fascinates and provides some insight into the geological vicissitudes of the Dolomites. During July, August, and the first 2 weeks in September, open Mondays through Saturdays from 9 AM to noon and from 3 to 6 PM, Sundays from 9 AM to noon; the rest of the year from 10 AM to noon and 3 to 6 PM; admission charge. Ortisei is also a village of woodcarvers, and shops selling carvings are everywhere. For a more cultural glimpse of the artistry of local woodcarvers, visit the Permanent Exhibition of Gröden Handicraft at the Congress Hall; the tourist board (phone: 471-796328; fax: 471-796749) is also located there. Open daily from 8 AM to noon and 3 to 7 PM. And don't forget the outdoor market on Fridays.

CHECKING IN/EATING OUT: ***Aquila-Adler*** – Undoubtedly the best hotel in Ortisei. It boasts a golden book of famous guests and offers 85 rooms, a covered swimming pool, tennis, sauna, solarium, and a restaurant. Open June 15 to October 15 and December 23 to April 20. 7 Via Rezia, Ortisei (phone: 471-796203; fax: 471-796210). Expensive.

Angelo-Engel – A typical Alpine lodge, cozy and pleasant, with 35 rooms, good service, and a restaurant. Closed in November. 35 Via Petlin, Ortisei (phone: 471-796336; fax: 471-796323). Moderate.

Hell – Don't be deceived by the name. This hotel offers typical Tyrolean comfort in its 27 rooms, international cuisine, hearty breakfasts, a sauna, and a solarium. Open the beginning of June to mid-October and mid-December to mid-April. 3 Via Promenade, Ortisei (phone: 471-796-7850; fax: 471-796323). Moderate.

Ronce – A cozy family atmosphere, all wood decor, and it's near the ski slopes. There are 24 rooms and a restaurant. Open June through August and December 20 to April 20. 1 Via Ronce, Ortisei (phone: 471-76383). Moderate.

En Route from Ortisei – The next destination is Corvara in the Val Badia, but there are two ways to approach it. One way is to backtrack through Santa Cristina and Selva di Val Gardena to Plan de Gralba and pick up SS243 at the intersection. Travel north-northeast to the Gardena Pass (taking in yet another view of the Sella group as you climb) and into the village of Colfosco. To the right, after 1¼ miles (2 km), is Corvara in Badia.

Unfortunately, this approach cuts out what some consider the most splendid Dolomite pass of all — the 7,692-foot Pordoi Pass, which affords an exhilarating view of the Marmolada, Catinaccio, Sassolungo, and the Sella mountains. One way to see the Pordoi Pass is to head for Corvara straight from Canazei. Take SS48 over the pass and on to SS244, which leads into the Val Badia and to Corvara in Badia. Since the Val Gardena is only a stone's throw from Val Badia, side trips from Corvara are easy (via the Gardena Pass), or stop there after having visited the Val Badia.

CORVARA IN BADIA: This dreamy mountain village is in the heart of the Alta Val Badia, another Ladin valley. On the approach to town, the sight of a massive rock that seems to rise out of the earth is dazzling. This is the Sassongher (8,668 feet), Corvara's pride and joy. The small town sits at the foot of this lone giant, content to be dominated by it. Like the rest of the Val Badia, Corvara holds a special kind of appeal. Not as fashionable as the other resort areas, it is friendly, and probably as authentic today as it was in 1880 when visitors began to discover it.

Before then, Corvara was a tiny settlement of a few farmhouses and perhaps one or two taverns. The first tourists were English climbers, who came not only because of the challenging mountain but also because of the reputation of a local Alpine guide, Franz Kostner, who had spent much of his life as a guide in the Himalayas and was the first to lead the English to the top of the Matterhorn. The village rapidly became the place to go, especially to avoid frivolity and to live close to nature. Corvara is still basically the same. The people in town and in all of the valley take pride in an old-fashioned hospitality. In return, they — Ladins, as they consider themselves — ask only that visitors respect their mountains and learn to know and love them — not too much to ask considering the Val Badia's fabled setting.

The valley can be explored using Corvara as a base. The tiny town of Colfosco is literally around the bend and within walking distance (1¼ miles/2 km). Other villages — Pedraces, La Villa, and San Cassiano — are only a few miles away, easily reachable by daily, regularly scheduled bus service; accommodations in fine hotels or cozy, family-style, chalet-like *pensioni* are available to visitors. Short hikes into the mountains will turn up a variety of rustic farmhouses and barns or entire tiny settlements of mountain farmers — a very pretty sight, especially in summer when geraniums of all colors are in bloom. Some of the façades of the structures are frescoed, while the windows are framed by classic Ladin decorations. Look carefully for sundials or carved or painted flowers with six petals set inside a circle — the wheel of life, a Celtic symbol.

Hikes, excursions, and nature walks are organized 1 day each week by the *Azienda di Soggiorno Corvara/Colfosco* (located on the main thoroughfare; phone: 471-836176 or 471-401555). Check with them for schedules and reservations. Contact the *Arlan* hotel (phone: 471-836146) about tours on horseback. Bus excursions are also available. Again, inquire at the tourist board or at the *Tourdolomit* travel office (also on the main thoroughfare; phone: 471-836232). In summer, as part of its promotion of Ladin culture, the tourist board organizes weekly visits to *viles,* ancient Ladin settlements, and to *masi,* typical Ladin farmhouses, as well as Ladin cooking classes.

CHECKING IN: ***La Perla*** – This 50-room hotel introduces a touch of sophistication into a typically Tyrolean atmosphere. Besides a restaurant, it has an indoor pool, a sauna and solarium, a boutique, and an art gallery. Open from June 22 through August and from mid-December to mid-April. Corvara in Badia (phone: 471-836132; 471-796323). Expensive.

Posta-Zirm – Corvara's oldest and most prestigious hotel was opened in 1880 by the Alpine guide Franz Kostner after his return from the Himalayas. It has become an international gathering spot where friends meet again and again in a characteristically Ladin ambience. There are 48 rooms, a restaurant, indoor pool, sauna, and solarium. Closed in November. 16 Centro, Corvara in Badia (phone: 471-836175; fax: 471-836542). Expensive.

Sassongher – A 50-room hotel that combines rustic Tyrolean elegance and a cozy atmosphere. The finishing touches include locally produced antique furniture. There are a restaurant, indoor pool, sauna, solarium, hot tub, and a boutique. Open June 20 through August and from December 20 to April 20. 29 Via Pescosta, Corvara in Badia (phone: 471-836085). Expensive.

Tablè – Tastefully furnished according to the mountain tradition, this 27-room hotel organizes many special gastronomic evenings and candlelight dinners and is also renowned in the valley for its wonderful pastries and excellent homemade ice cream. Open May 20 to October 20 and December 20 to to April 15. 127 Via Pescosta, Corvara in Badia (phone: 471-836144; fax: 471-836313). Moderate.

EATING OUT: ***L'Fana*** – For beautiful mountain ambience and local fare presented with a touch of refinement, this is the place. It is especially popular among villagers as well as visitors for its vast selection of dishes and excellent service. Open June through September and December through March. Reservations necessary. Major credit cards accepted. In the nearby town of La Villa (phone: 471-847022). Moderate.

Speckstube Peter – The typical Tyroleon decor, with hand-carved wooden beams and all, is an appropriate backdrop for the excellent Ladin cuisine and the fine selection of vintage wines. A wonderful place to get tasty snacks or to indulge in some wine tasting, it is especially popular among the locals who enjoy coming here for midnight snacks. Open daily, from 2 PM to 1:30 AM June through September and December through March. No reservations. No credit cards accepted. In Colfosco, less than 2 miles (3 km) from Corvara (phone: 471-836071). Moderate.

La Tambra – A traditional Alpine chalet, small but lively, this is where the natives go for a good mountain meal. The cooking is regional, offering such dishes as barley soup, goulash, and game in season. Closed Wednesdays and April 25 to June 9 and September to December 6. No reservations. No credit cards. 159 Via Pescosta, Corvara in Badia (phone: 471-836281). Moderate.

En Route from Ccrvara – Head north to La Villa and then turn right into the Valle di San Cassiano. Travel through Armentarola to the Passo di Valparola (7,046 feet), past the foot of another mountain, Lagazuoi. The road then hooks into the Passo di Falzarego, a pass that is open only in summer. The next stop is Cortina d'Ampezzo, in the eastern Dolomites, about 21 miles (34 km) from Corvara.

CORTINA D'AMPEZZO: Of all the resorts in the Dolomites, Cortina is the only one that requires little introduction. The splendid town sits in a large basin called the Valle del Boite surrounded by majestic mountains. The Tofane, Pomagagnon, Cristallo, Sorapis, and many more gold-pink peaks frame it, making it picture-perfect. Cortina has been known as a mountaineers' paradise since the mid-19th century, although it wasn't until near the turn of this century that the first hotels were built. It then developed quickly, and even before World War I it was on the map as one of the best resorts in the Dolomites. The first ski competition in Italy took place here in 1902, and the *Winter Olympics* were held here in 1956. The town offers a huge variety of ski runs and facilities for all winter sports, including the *Stadio Olimpico del Ghiaccio* (Olympic Ice Stadium).

Much larger than other Dolomite villages, Cortina is actually a small but cosmopolitan city, with exclusive shops, luxury hotels, refined restaurants, nightclubs, and discos. Such glamorous and sophisticated accouterments have made it *the* place to be and ski in Italy, and at least once a year the jet-set crowds meet here to renew acquaintance. But Cortina is not glitter alone. It has a more rustic side sought by mountain climbers who test their courage on the high peaks and by hikers who pitch up at the quaint *rifugi,* small lone lodges, where the pioneer mountain spirit still lingers.

Corso Italia, the main avenue through the town, is largely a pedestrian island, where you'll find the *Ciasa de ra Regoles,* which houses an important museum of geology and mineralogy and the Rimoldi collection of modern art (67 Corso Italia; closed Mondays; admission charge). Stop in at the *Artigianato Artistico Ampezzano* (open daily), a permanent exhibit of the crafts of local artisans, also on Corso Italia, to see woodcarvings with precious inlays of ivory and mother-of-pearl; wrought-iron, brass, and copper objects; and splendid filigree necklaces, clasps, and brooches. After a day on the slopes, a visit to Cortina's most exclusive pastry shop, *Embassy* (44 Corso Italia), is definitely in order. Highly recommended is the "Embassy Cup," vanilla ice cream with sugar-coated walnuts. Three miles (5 km) from the center of town is one of Cortina's most colorful shops, *El Touladel* (in the village of Col), selling a whole range of items, including exquisite tablecloths, napkins, fabrics, loden-covered sofas, and marvelous terra cotta lamps.

But since Cortina's real wealth is the mountains, it would be a mistake not to take a few excursions to some of nature's best belvederes: The same mountains that are breathtaking when seen from the town will leave you absolutely speechless close up. There are tramways and chair lifts (not all of them depart from town, however) to some of the most scenic spots, such as the 10,673-foot summit of the Tofana di Mezzo or the foot of the Tofane group, west of Cortina, and the foot of the Cristallo group, east of town. The Rifugio Cinque Torri, the Rifugio Col Drusciè, and the Belvedere di Pocol shouldn't be missed. For more details about these and other excursions, contact the Azienda di Promozione Turistica (8 Piazzetta San Francesco, Cortina; phone: 436-3231), or the tourist information office (1 Piazza Roma; phone: 436-2711).

CHECKING IN: ***Cristallo*** – One of the many fine CIGA hotels in Italy, it offers real mountain-style luxury on a slope above town. The decor is both classic and Alpine, with beautiful paintings decorating the walls. There are 98 rooms and suites, a restaurant serving regional specialties, several bars, an outdoor heated swimming pool, a skating rink, tennis courts, and a shuttle bus to town. Open July to September 10 and December 18 to April 2. 42 Via Menardi, Cortina d'Ampezzo (phone: 436-4281; fax: 436-868058). Very expensive.

Cortina – Rustic yet refined, with Persian rugs adorning the floors, bed headboards hand-sculpted in Val Gardena, and 48 rooms furnished with beautiful objects made by Cortina's artisans. There also is a restaurant. Open June 15 to September 20 and December 18 to April 10. 94 Corso Italia, Cortina d'Ampezzo (phone: 436-4221; fax: 436-860760). Expensive.

De la Poste – Dating back to 1805, when the Manaigo family received permission to open an inn with only 4 bedrooms, this hotel has undergone many renovations over the years and now has 80 rooms. It is elegant, sophisticated, and fashionable, and no newer hostelry has been able to replace it as the chic place to congregate. Closed October 20 to December 10. 14 Piazza Roma, Cortina d'Ampezzo (phone: 436-4271; fax: 436-868435). Expensive.

Europa – The very rustic, Alpine atmosphere of this 52-room establishment is complemented by several beautiful pieces of antique furniture. The restaurant's international fare is highly recommended. Open December 10 through October. 207 Corso Italia, Cortina d'Ampezzo (phone: 436-3221; fax: 436-868204). Expensive to moderate.

Menardi – On the outskirts of town, this 40-room hotel was once a large, old farmhouse. Chalet-like furnishings give it a warm and cozy atmosphere. Open June 20 to September 22 and December 20 to April 7. 110 Via Majon, Cortina d'Ampezzo (phone: 436-2400; fax: 436-862183). Moderate.

Sport Tofana – An older 88-room, chalet-like hotel — located 3 miles (5 km) from Cortina — is in a peaceful spot away from the crowds. Open July to September 8 and December 21 to April 8. Via Pocol, Pocol (phone: 436-3281; fax: 436-440066). Moderate.

EATING OUT: *El Toulà* – Housed in a former hayloft, which is what its name means in the local dialect, this sister to *El Toulà* in Rome serves exceptional international cuisine. Closed Mondays and April 15 to July 15 and September 15 to December 20. Reservations necessary. Major credit cards accepted. 123 Via Ronco, Cortina d'Ampezzo (phone: 436-3339). Expensive.

Capannina – One of Cortina's best. The Venetian and Tyrolean dishes are excellent, as is the selection of fine wines (both regional and international). The dining room is small and cozy, but decorated with style and elegance. Closed Wednesdays. Reservations advised. Major credit cards accepted. 11 Via Stadio, Cortina d'Ampezzo (phone: 436-2950). Expensive to moderate.

Il Meloncino – Known for its remarkable grilled platters. Alfresco dining in the summer. Closed Tuesdays, June, and November. Reservations necessary. No credit cards accepted. Località Gillardon, Cortina d'Ampezzo (phone: 436-861043). Expensive to moderate.

Tanna della Volpe – The dark wood decor and pink accessories accentuate this eatery's quaintness. Make sure you reserve a table in the *Stube,* a typical Tyrolean dining area that is rustic, yet elegant. In summer months, dining alfresco on international fare is also an option. Closed Wednesdays in spring and fall, 1 week in January, and mid-June to mid-July. Reservations necessary. No credit cards accepted. 27A/B Via della Stadio (phone: 436-867494). Expensive to moderate.

Da Beppe Sello – Traditional but exquisite food is served in a rustic and cozy atmosphere. Closed Tuesdays, mid-April to mid-May, and September 20 through October 31. Reservations advised. No credit cards accepted. 68 Via Ronco, Cortina d'Ampezzo (phone: 436-3236). Moderate.

En Route from Cortina – Take SS48 east out of town through the Passo Tre Croci and enjoy an impressive view of Monte Cristallo. Continue on SS48 *bis* for Lago di Misurina. Although this lake is not as pretty as other, lesser-known Alpine lakes, it is famous for the way it mirrors the majestic 9,746-foot Tre Cime di Lavaredo (Drei Zinnen), a truly breathtaking visual effect. SS48 *bis* becomes SS51 and leads to the outskirts of Dobbiaco (Toblach), another lovely village in a very green valley, the Alta Val Pusteria. The parish church in Dobbiaco offers one of the best examples of baroque art in the whole Alto Adige. If all the glitz and glitter of Cortina have failed to meet your expectations of a rural and rustic ambience, a detour to Sesto in Val Pusteria will reward you. From Dobbiaco, head east on SS49 to San Candido. Take Route 52 southeast about 9 miles (15 km) to Sesto. Unmarred by any modern architecture, Sesto is a favorite in both winter and summer for those looking for quiet relaxation. The resort is surrounded by grassy plains and gentle peaks; less than a mile away is the tiny village of Moso which competes with Sesto for being the most picturesque and quaint. The tourist board in Sesto (9 Via Dolomiti; phone: 474-70318) can provide information about hotels. Return to Dobbiaco and pick up SS49 westbound for Brunico and then turn south on SS49 *bis* to Bressanone. A stroll through the old center of either town will reveal many old and elegant buildings, churches, porticoes, baroque palaces, typical Tyrolean homes with bays and pinnacles, and colorful courtyards.

BRUNICO (BRUNECK): The capital of the Val Pusteria, it is famous for the spacious and gentle slopes that surround it. Although dominated by a 13th-century castle, the area's greatest attraction is the panorama from the Plan de Corones, reached by cable car. On a plateau 7,460 feet high, Plan de Corones has an extensive network of lifts and offers great winter skiing.

The Azienda di Soggiorno di Brunico (at the bus station on Via Europa; phone: 474-85722; fax: 474-84544) organizes guided tours of the town every Friday at 5 PM, mid-June through August.

CHECKING IN/EATING OUT: ***Andreas Hofer*** – Pine-paneled walls and typical Tyrolean furniture are the most distinctive decorative features of this modern, 54-room hotel. The restaurant is cozy and friendly, and the Tyrolean cuisine is reputed to be the finest around (an entire dynasty of chefs comes from here). The specialty is game with polenta, Italy's signature cornmeal concoction. Hotel closed 2 weeks in May and from November 24 to December 16; restaurant closed Saturdays year-round. Visa accepted. 1 Via Campo Tures, Brunico (phone: 474-85469; fax: 474-85813). Moderate.

BRESSANONE (BRIXEN): On the road to the Brenner Pass, this most charming Alto Adige town claims an eclectic combination of architecture and monuments from the medieval to the baroque. From the 11th century to the first decade of the 19th century, it was ruled by prince-bishops, who also ruled much of the surrounding area. Its 13th-century cathedral, redone in the baroque style in the 18th century, is imposing, and it has an adjoining cloister covered with 14th- and 15th-century frescoes, as well as an even older (begun in the 11th century) frescoed baptistry. The Palazzo dei Principi Vescovi (Palace of the Prince-Bishops) is also worth a visit, but even if you see nothing else in Bressanone, stop at the *Elefante* hotel (see *Checking In/Eating Out*), a beautifully preserved 16th-century building with one of the best restaurants in the Dolomites. The tourist board is at 9 Viale Stazione (phone: 472-22401 or 472-36401; fax: 472-36067).

CHECKING IN/EATING OUT: ***Elefante*** – In the mid-16th century, this old inn stabled an elephant the King of Portugal was sending over the Brenner Pass as a gift to the Hapsburg emperors in Vienna. A fresco still remains on the hotel's façade to commemorate the event, and the inn looks as it did then, except for essential modernization such as heating, hot water, and phones. The public rooms and some of the 30-plus guestrooms have antique furnishings; across the street is an annex with 14 rooms and a heated swimming pool. The restaurant serves Tyrolean fare and homemade pastry, but no dish is as famous as its *Elefantenplatte* (*piatto elefante* in Italian), or elephant platter — a mountainous heap of meat and vegetables served to no fewer than four diners. The butter, eggs, milk, fruit, and vegetables served here all come from the hotel's own farm. Open March to November 10. Restaurant closed Mondays except from July 30 to November 10. Reservations advised. Visa accepted. 4 Via Rio Bianco, Bressanone (phone: 472-22288; fax: 472-36067). Expensive.

En Route from Bressanone – Pick up A22 to return quickly to Bolzano. Before leaving the Alto Adige, however, a side trip to charming Merano, approximately 18 miles (29 km) from Bolzano, is recommended for those who have the time. Take SS38 northwest.

MERANO (MERAN): This old-fashioned spa town has few major monuments but definite character. It is picturesque and quaint — see Via dei Portici in the old city center — as well as cosmopolitan. The town is also very lively, thanks to events such as international horse races, summer evenings of folk dancing, or the two concerts held each day from April to October along the Passeggiata Lungo Passirio (only one of Merano's promenades offering tranquillity or scenic views — others are the Passeggiata Tappeiner and the summer and winter promenades, the Passeggiata dell'Estate and the Passeggiata d'Inverno). Europeans also visit Merano for their health, since its mineral waters are supposed to be very beneficial, especially for digestive and circulatory problems as well as skin ailments. Others come for the beauty treatments: mud baths, massages, and diets. Contact Terme di Merano (9 Via Piave; phone: 473-37724) for information. In the summer, the town draws walkers; in the winter, skiers; but spring and autumn are the spa seasons. The *Gran Premio di Merano,* the most prestigious Italian horse race, is held here on the last Sunday of September. It is the Tyrolean equivalent of the *Kentucky Derby* and just as exciting. In fall, too, the town, in the center of a grape growing district, has been the traditional place to take the grape cure, although the distinction between grape cure and wine therapy is sometimes fuzzy.

Local grape festivals are organized in October, with the *Autumn Festival* taking place on the second Sunday of the month. Events include parades with allegorical floats, folk dances, a display of local costumes, and much more. For a delightful shopping experience, visit the city's outdoor market (on Via IV Novembre) on Fridays. Contact the tourist board (45 Corso Libertà; phone: 473-35223) for information about all events.

The *Museo Civico* (43 Via Galileo; phone: 473-37843) has several interesting collections, ranging from art and archaeology to local crafts, fossils, and minerals from the Alto Adige region. Noteworthy is the first wooden typewriter, conceived and built by Parcines Peter Mitterhofer, a local carpenter, in 1863. Closed Mondays; admission charge.

CHECKING IN: ***Castel Freiberg*** – Once upon a time, this hotel was a castle. Built in the 14th century, it stands on a hill in total isolation a bit more than 4 miles (6 km) southeast of Merano. Although reminiscent of very ancient times, the quality of service, the facilities, and the level of comfort in the 38 rooms are all up-to-date. Restaurant, sauna, solarium, indoor and outdoor pools, tennis. Open April 20 to November 4. Località Fragsburg, Merano (phone: 473-44196; fax: 473-44488). Expensive.

Kurhotel Schloss Rundegg – Another castle that has been transformed into a hotel, and since this one was built in the year 1100, a stay in one of the 30 rooms is like taking a leap into the past. Restaurant, indoor pool, tennis, garden, and spa facilities (sauna, solarium, diet consultation, and beauty treatments). Closed January 6 to 31. 2 Via Scena, Merano (phone: 473-34100; fax: 473-37200). Expensive.

Palace – A majestic structure with 124 rooms, set in a park and surrounded by exotic plants. It's furnished in the elegant Empire style and is both traditional and comfortable. There is a restaurant, spa, indoor and outdoor pools, sauna, and beauty treatments. Open March 20 to November 9 and mid-November to mid-

December. 2 Via Cavour, Merano (phone: 473-34734; fax: 473-34181). Expensive.

Villa Mozart – A refined 10-room hotel decorated in authentic turn-of-the-century Viennese Jugendstil (Art Nouveau). Although its restaurant now is closed, the owners have turned their attention to organizing wine seminars and courses in Italian and Tyrolean cooking (in English, Italian, and German). Open year-round. 26 Via San Marco, Merano (phone: 473-30630; fax: 473-211355). Expensive.

Schloss Labers – This medieval castle became a hotel in 1885, and the interior is highly evocative. An outdoor restaurant is used in warm weather; there is a typical Tyrolean bar, tennis courts, and a heated pool. 32 rooms. Open March 23 to November 3. 25 Via Labers, Merano (phone: 473-34484; fax: 473-31446). Expensive to moderate.

Augusta – A beautiful villa with 26 rooms and a restaurant. Open March 15 to November 15. 2 Via Otto Huber, Merano (phone: 473-49570; fax: 473-220029). Moderate.

EATING OUT: *Andrea* – The tone of this highly recommended restaurant is traditional; the cuisine is regional but with a modern twist. Spinach *Krapfen* and crêpes with parmesan and beer are among the specialties, and there is a very good selection of local and national wines. Closed Mondays and from January 6 to March 15. Reservations necessary. Major credit cards accepted. 44 Via Galilei, Merano (phone: 473-37400). Expensive.

Naif – A classic Austrian beer hall serving regional food. Closed Mondays and November 7–20. No reservations. No credit cards accepted. 35 Via Val di Nova, Merano (phone: 473-32216). Moderate.

Terlaner Weinstube – Located under the arches of a picturesque street, its furnishings are antique, and the food is regional and international. Closed Wednesdays, and January 10 to February 10. Reservations necessary. No credit cards accepted. 231 Via dei Portici, Merano (phone: 473-35571). Moderate.

En Route from Merano – Return to Bolzano on SS38 and switch there for the A22 southbound to Trento, only 18 miles (29 km) away.

TRENTO: A noble, although somewhat austere, city on the Adige River, Trento is surrounded by mountains — the Dolomites to the east and the Brenta group, a prolongation of the Dolomites, to the west. Roman in origin, Trento became an important town on the way to the Brenner Pass for the same strategic reasons its northern neighbor, Bolzano, did. From the 11th century until 1803, it, along with the rest of the Trentino province, was ruled by Prince-Bishops of Trent, whose rule extended into Alto Adige for part of that time. The city gained lasting fame in the mid-16th century as the seat of the Council of Trent, which sat from 1545 to 1563 in an attempt to reform the church and curtail the spread of the Protestant Reformation. After a brief stint of Napoleonic rule, Trento became Austrian until the end of World War I although, unlike Bolzano, it has always been largely Italian-speaking and Italian in character. Today it is the capital of the Trentino–Alto Adige region.

Much remains in Trento from the medieval period and much also from the early 16th century, due to the influence of a particularly humanistic prince-bishop, Bernardo Clesio. Among the city's highlights is the Duomo, 12th- and 13th-century Lombard Romanesque to Gothic in style. Inside is the Cappella del Crocefisso (Crucifix Chapel), containing the crucifix before which the Council of Trent's decrees were proclaimed. From the Duomo, walk north along Via Belenzani, the city's most beautiful avenue, lined with Venetian-style Renaissance palaces, some with frescoed façades. Turn right onto Via Manci, another notable street, and follow it to Trento's most celebrated monument, the Castello del Buonconsiglio (Castle of Good Counsel), the residence of the prince-bishops. It actually consists of several parts, including the 13th-century

Castelvecchio, the oldest, and the 16th-century Palazzo Magno, a Renaissance addition by Bernardo Clesio.

Trento has gained worldwide recognition for the *International Mountain and Exploration Film Festival* held here each year in April–May. For information, contact the tourist board (132 Corso III Novembre; phone: 461-895111; or in Piazza Duomo; phone: 461-981289; fax: 461-984508).

Trento also is close to many resorts. Take S47 south to Levico Terme, just 13 miles (21 km) away. At the foot of Monte Fronte, it is one of the most popular thermal and holiday spots in the area. Summer sports include sailing, windsurfing, and hiking. Seven miles (11 km) north of Levico is Vetriolo Terme with its thermal waters that have attracted visitors seeking cures for almost a century. At 4,900 feet, there also is decent winter skiing. For information about both towns, contact the tourist office (3 Via Vittorio Emanuele, Levico Terme; phone: 461-70601).

CHECKING IN: ***America*** – A very cordial family atmosphere is one of the pluses of this 43-room hotel. There also is a restaurant. 52 Via Torre Verde, Trento (phone: 461-983010; fax: 461-230603). Expensive to moderate.

Trento – A cozy place, with 94 rooms and a private garden. Its restaurant, *Il Caminetto,* is a good dining spot. 1 Via Alfieri, Trento (phone: 461-981010). Expensive to moderate.

Villa Madruzzo – Located 2 miles (3 km) east of Trento, in Cognola, this is a converted 18th-century villa, with 51 comfortable rooms and a pleasant garden. 26 Via Ponte Alto, Cognola (phone: 461-986220). Moderate.

EATING OUT: ***Chiesa*** – Housed in a 16th-century palace, with the accent on sophistication. The cuisine is regional Trentino but very refined, and a very select range of Trentino wines is served. Closed Sundays, Wednesday evenings, and the last 2 weeks of August. No reservations. Major credit cards accepted. Parco San Marco, Trento (phone: 461-985577). Expensive.

Birreria Forst – Don't miss the chance to eat in this very popular beer hall. The cooking is regional, as are the wines. Pizza is also served. Closed Mondays. No reservations. No credit cards accepted. 38 Via Oss Mazzurana, Trento (phone: 461-35590). Inexpensive.

En Route from Trento – One last side trip leads to the Dolomiti di Brenta and to the popular resort of Madonna di Campiglio. Take A22 north 9 miles (14 km) to Mezzolombardo. Exit and follow SS43 northbound to Cles. If its name rings a bell, it's because this pretty medieval village was once the home of the Clesio family, one of whose members figured prominently in Trento's past and whose ancestral castle is outside of town. After Cles, at the intersection, take SS42 westbound, through Male. At Dimaro, pick up SS239 southbound into Madonna di Campiglio.

MADONNA DI CAMPIGLIO: If ever a resort came close to competing with Cortina, it's Madonna di Campiglio. It has all the ingredients: first class hotels, excellent facilities, fashionable shops, and a marvelous setting at the bottom of a large valley, dominated to the east by the beautiful Brenta Dolomites and to the west by the magnificent Presanella and Adamello groups. Dense fir woods surround the village.

In 1110, Madonna di Campiglio was merely a shelter, built by a monk named Raimondo, for the few wayfarers who were brave enough to cross the Alpine passes with their cattle. It remained farmland for many centuries until 1862 when the entire Campiglio Valley was purchased by Giambattista Righi (an entrepreneur) in order to create a summer resort. And although the first hotel was built in Madonna di Campiglio in 1872, the resort became known in the years between the two world wars. It owes its popularity above all to skiers, but the area is also a real paradise for mountain climbers — it has one of the best mountain climbing schools in the Alps. For the less ambitious, there are countless excursions and hikes to some of the most scenic spots, and tramways and chair lifts are available for many of these. The best, by far, are trips to the Grosté, to Monte Spinale, and to Pradalago. For more information, check with the tourist board (4 Via Praealago; phone: 465-42000; fax: 465-40404) or *Trentino Holidays* (78 Via Soltieri, Trento; phone: 451-82200).

The accent in Madonna is on ecology. In keeping with this trend, local mountain guides organize nature excursions along some of the most beautiful trails in the area. Contact the *Ufficio Guide Alpine* (Madonna di Campiglio; phone: 465-42634) for information; be sure to reserve at least a day ahead for one of these trips.

CHECKING IN: ***Golf*** – This very fashionable 124-room hotel is 1½ miles (2 km) north of Madonna di Campiglio, in Campo Carlo Magno. A former summer residence of the Hapsburg family, it is both elegant and cozy, with an excellent restaurant, as well as a 9-hole golf course. Closed April through June and September through March. Campo Carlo Magno (phone: 465-41003; fax: 465-40294). Very expensive.

Relais Club des Alpes – Built on the spot where monk Raimondo built his refuge, and once the hunting retreat of the Hapsburgs is 105-room hotel. Its ancient splendor remains — frescoes adorn many walls, even in the guestrooms. The grand ballroom has been transformed into a theater decorated with frescoes and an elaborate wooden ceiling with curved, exposed beams. There's an indoor pool and a beauty center. Closed late spring and early fall. 1 Via Monte Spinale (phone: 465-40000; fax: 465-40186). Expensive.

Carlo Magno Zeledria – A cozy Alpine lodge that was a tavern in the 18th century. Set in a lovely pine forest, it has 94 rooms and an indoor pool. Closed May to June 24 and September 23 through April. Passo di Campo Carlo Magno (phone: 465-41010; fax: 465-40550). Expensive to moderate.

Grifone – Modern yet cozy, the atmosphere of a mountain lodge prevails in this 40-room hotel, which also has a nursery for children. Closed mid-April to mid-July and mid-September to December. 7 Via Vallesinella, Madonna di Campiglio (phone: 465-42002; fax: 465-40540). Expensive.

Il Caminetto – A cozy and warm air pervades this 33-room establishment, especially in the *caminetto* (fireplace) room. 17 Via Adamello, Madonna di Campiglio (phone: 465-41242). Moderate.

EATING OUT: ***Crozzon*** – Centrally located, this restaurant serves excellent regional dishes and wines. Carrot cake and strudel are two of the specialties in this wood-paneled rustic eatery. Fresh flowers on each table add elegance to the warm and friendly *ambiente.* Open daily. No reservations. Major credit cards accepted. Via Dolomiti di Brenta, Madonna di Campiglio (phone: 465-42217 or 465-42221). Moderate.

The Veneto

Ask a citizen of the Veneto to describe the area and, apart from showering the questioner with a well-used inventory of superlatives, the most likely reply will describe the region as having a little bit of everything. Such claims, far from being ill-founded boasts, are rooted solidly in the region's geography. Stretching from the soaring pink-hued peaks of the Dolomite Mountains to the flat, green plains of the Po River, the Veneto is one of the most diverse regions in all of Italy. Indeed, Truman Capote's description of Venice — "like eating an entire box of chocolate liqueurs in one go" — could equally apply to its namesake region.

Aside from the Dolomites and their rambling foothills, which define the Veneto's northern frontier with Austria, other highlands include the Asolan and Euganean hills, whose tranquil, vine-covered slopes have long been relished by writers, poets, painters, and others with a good excuse for escaping the often oppressive heat of the lowland summer. Even more typical of the region are the vast landscapes of its plains, ironed flat as a pizza by the sweeping maneuvers of mighty rivers like the Po, Italy's most important, the Adige, the country's third longest, the Brenta, Piave, Sile, and Livenza (all of which are touched and often intimately pursued by this itinerary).

The area is also abundantly rich in agriculture. Unlike the rural scenery found throughout much of Europe, the farms of the Veneto still retain a human scale, and many of the ingredients waiting to be savored on the local trattoria tables, especially the wines, have been grown on a small holding, probably no more than a few minutes' drive from the kitchen.

Vacationers, after touring the hinterlands of the Veneto, will invariably — and loudly — sing the praises of its beaches. Or rather its beach, for almost all the coastline constitutes one continuous, fine sand ribbon, interrupted only by the mouths of rivers and lagoons. But the flavor of its many parts does vary, from the heavily trafficked resorts of Jesolo and the Lido of Venice to miles of deserted horizons which remain the exclusive territory of birds that thrive in a low-profile world of reed beds and tall grasses. Inland the Veneto offers its visitors another bonus shoreline — more than 30 miles of beach on the eastern coast of Lake Garda, Italy's largest, and quite possibly its most beautiful, lake. Like the region's hillier retreats, the Riviera-like resorts of Garda have been popular since ancient times.

But the Veneto is more than a place of natural beauty. Historically and artistically it is the one region that reflects the Byzantine influences imported through Italy's eastern trading routes. Roman influence also left its mark, for the conquering legions of the emperor Augustus based themselves here to repulse the invading barbarian tribes of northeastern Europe. Later, during the Middle Ages, under the influence of rich local families who ruled the

Veneto cities (the Scaligeri of Verona, the Carraresi of Padua, the Camino of Treviso) the Veneto became, together with Tuscany, economically and artistically one of the richest areas of the peninsula.

The Veneto was also subject to the central government of Venice at the zenith of its career as a republic (during the 14th and 15th centuries). Venice's ascendancy resulted in the creation of some of the world's greatest works of art and supreme examples of serene architectural grandeur — most notably the magnificent Palladian villas, many of which still grace the Veneto landscape.

The rich, lively paintings and frescoes that adorn so many Venetian interiors are the work of such Renaissance greats as Giotto, Pisano, Andrea Mantegna, and Filippo Lippi in the 14th and 15th centuries, and the Tiepolo father and son Venetian painters of the 17th and 18th centuries, most of whom either lived or passed through the Veneto.

Venetian cooking is as diverse as its geography. The hearty mountain fare, featuring dumplings, soups, rich desserts, and cakes, shows a strong Austrian influence. The fertile hills and plains around Verona, Vicenza, and Treviso offer wonderful veal and vegetable dishes. In the hilly forests around Belluno, there is a wealth of wild mushrooms and game, while *cucina casalinga* (home cooking) on the coast boasts the culinary delights of Adriatic fish and shellfish, such as tuna, sardines, and lobster. Venetian wines are world famous, from the dry white pinot bianco and grigio to the red cabernet and merlot, not to mention the fiery, highly alcoholic grappa made from the final grape pressings.

So, being a land for the art lover or architecture buff, the winter sports enthusiast or beach bum, the mountaineer or the gourmet, the wine taster or the health nut, the Veneto is built to satisfy the most conservative tastes and the wildest whims. From Venice, our route follows the Brenta Canal, and the magnificent country villas that overlook it, to Padua (with an optional detour to the Euganean Hills) and, bypassing Vicenza, heads for Verona. After a stop at Verona on the Adige River, the route returns via Vicenza — the city of Palladio — branches out to the Dolomite foothills and Bassano del Grappa on the Brenta Canal, and then continues on to the mountain town of Belluno by way of the delightful panoramic setting of Asolo, before detouring down through the mountains to the town of Treviso. Nine or 10 days should be allowed for a leisurely drive since the countryside is as spectacular as the towns in this northeastern border region of Italy.

Prices in the Veneto vary greatly depending on whether an establishment is in the tourist honeypots like Venice and the historic centers like Padua, Verona, and Treviso, or slightly off the beaten track in Belluno, Bassano del Grappa, or the Euganean Hills. As a guideline, expect to pay $200 and up for a very expensive double room with breakfast, from $125 to $200 for an expensive room, $75 to $125 for moderate, and under $75, inexpensive. An expensive meal for two with wine will cost over $100; a moderate one, between $60 and $100; and inexpensive, under $60.

As in most other regions, the Veneto has a network of efficient tourist information offices. Most towns and cities have either an Azienda di Promozione Turistica (local tourist board) or an Ente Provinciale per il Turismo (provincial tourist board). The latter will have information not only on the town but also on the surrounding province.

VENICE: For a detailed report on the city, its sights, hotels, and restaurants, see *Venice,* THE CITIES.

En Route from Venice – Take the road for Porto Marghera and then follow signs for Malcontenta. Here the road follows the Brenta Canal, where, escaping the steamy heat of Venice, noble Venetian families took their ease in magnificent villas, some designed by the seminal local architect Andrea Palladio or his students. It is still possible to travel by boat to Padua aboard *Il Burchiello,* which makes the journey from Venice (from the waterfront at San Marco, 9 AM) on Tuesdays, Thursdays, and Saturdays, and the return trip (Piazzale Boschetti, Padua, 8AM) on Wednesdays, Fridays, and Sundays, from the end of March to the end of October, stopping off at three villas. The price (about $75) includes an English-speaking guide and entrance fees to three villas. Lunch on board is optional ($40). Bus and train service to Venice is frequent and efficient. Contact *Siamic Express* in Padua (42 Via Trieste; phone: 49-660944).

BRENTA RIVIERA: Villa La Malcontenta, the first of the grand villas, constructed by Andrea Palladio for the Foscari family in 1560, is a gracious masterpiece lying half hidden behind weeping willows. (Open Tuesdays, Saturdays, and the first Sunday of the month from 9 AM to noon, May to October.) The next villa worth stopping for is Widmann-Foscari, an impressive house with French baroque overtones to its original early-18th-century Venetian façade. Here the family portrait is a frescoed ceiling in the hall, and there are mythical frescoes by Giuseppe Angeli. The garden is a typical example of the Venetian mannerism of the 18th and 19th centuries, with its box hedges and statues. Open daily, except Mondays, from 9 AM to noon and 2 to 6 PM April through September; admission charge.

DOLO: This town is dotted with 17th- and 18th-century family villas, many of them still inhabited, as well as the domed and pillared 18th-century San Rocco parish church. Just beyond Dolo lies one of the Brenta's pièces de résistance, Villa Lazara Pisani, a romantic 18th-century construction, its creeper-covered façade facing the canal, its elegant porticoed back to the flat Veneto plains.

CHECKING IN: ***Villa Ducale*** – Staying at this stately, 18th-century country home is the perfect base for touring the neighboring aristocratic villas. There are 14 generous-size rooms, most with terraces overlooking formal gardens, and some with the original painted wall panels and frescoed ceililngs. Open year-round. 75 Riviera Martiri della Libertà, Dolo (phone and fax: 49-420094). Moderate.

STRA: The climax of this canalside tour is reached at Stra, on the outskirts of Padua, where the Villa Pisani (also called Villa Nazionale), now a national monument, dwarfs all other Brenta villas both in size and magnificence. Built in the mid-18th century for the Pisani family (who owned 50 villas in all), there are 164 rooms (only 8 of which are open to the public) bearing original frescoes, including the spectacular ballroom ceiling, a work by Giambattista Tiepolo that depicts the power and success of the Pisani family. As befits such a palatial residence, it was visited by several monarchs, grand dukes, and czars traveling around Europe. In 1807, Napoleon bought it and gave it to his brother, the Viceroy of Italy. Then, in 1934, it served as the first rendezvous for Hitler and Mussolini. The villa is open daily, except Mondays, from 9 AM to 1:30 PM; the park is open from 9 AM to 5 PM, to 6 PM in summer; admission charge.

PADUA: Padua's frenetic, noisy, unattractive approaches are a poor indication of what lies ahead. The city's heart is, like all the Venetian towns on this route, a historic jewel, its buildings looking more like a brilliant stage setting for some Shakespearean performance (in which no expense has been spared!). With a history dating back to the Trojan War, Padua (or Patavium, as it was known in 10 BC — Padova in modern Italian) is today one of the most important industrial, commercial, and agricultural centers in northern Italy. In 1200 the first wall around Padua was built and its university founded — one of the earliest in Europe and in Italy second in age only to Bologna.

Feudal rule in the mid-14th century culminated in virtual ownership of the town by the Da Carrara family, until they met their end in a war with the Venetians, under whose rule Padua prospered until it underwent the vicissitudes common to the Veneto region when it was ceded to the Austrians. The artistic landmarks of Padua are relics of its dramatic history, and today some of the major treasures of art and architecture in this part of the world are housed here.

The Scrovegni Chapel was erected by the noble Paduan family of the same name alongside the Piovego Canal (which runs through the city center) and is entirely decorated with 14th-century frescoes by Giotto. Considered to be among the most striking examples of the Tuscan painter's later works, they depict 38 scenes from the lives of the Virgin Mary and Jesus Christ. Off the Corso Garibaldi in Piazza Eremitani (phone: 49-650845). Open daily from 9 AM to 7 PM; admission charge.

When Padua's patron, Saint Anthony, died just behind the present train station in 1231, a Gothic basilica was erected around his tomb in Piazza del Santo. Known simply as the Santo, it is a wonderful mixture of Romanesque Gothic and Byzantine architecture, with arched doorways and eight-tiered domes. The main altar, notable for its ornate gold bas-reliefs, is the work of Donatello, a leading Renaissance artist, as are the nine sculpted reliefs along the top of the saint's enormous tomb. Open daily, from 6:30 AM to 7 PM October through March; to 7:30 PM April through September (phone: 49-663944). It is worth asking the sacristan for access to the cloisters, which were built between the 13th and the 16th century and which afford a fine view of the basilica. Saint Anthony's feast day (August 13) is enthusiastically celebrated with processions through the town.

In the square outside the Santo is Donatello's famed equestrian statue of a Venetian *condottiere* (military commander), Erasmo da Narni, better known as Gattamelata. Across the square (to the right as you face the church) is the Oratory of Saint George, a family burial chapel of the Soragna family frescoed by Jacopo Avanzi and Altichiero. Next door, the Scuola del Santo (School of Saint Anthony; phone: 49-663944) is lined with 16th-century frescoes, some by Titian. Both are open daily from 8:30 AM to 12:30 PM and 2:30 to 6:30 PM April through September, 9 AM to noon and 2:30 to 6 PM October through March; admission charge.

The neo-classical, "doorless" *Caffè Pedrocchi* is Padua's pride and its principal 19th-century monument, designed by Giuseppe Jappelli. Standing in Piazzetta Pedrocchi in the precincts of the university just off Piazza Cavour, it was bought by Antonio Pedrocchi in 1831. The ground floor is still used as a café, its outside seating a popular vantage point over the bustling heart of town. Open 8:30 AM to 12:30 PM and 2:30 to 6:30 PM April to September; 9 AM to 12:30 PM and 2:30 to 4:30 PM October–November and February–March; and 9 to 12:30 PM December–January (phone: 49-875-2020). Not far away are two interesting squares, Piazza delle Erbe and Piazza della Frutta, which, appropriately, contain outdoor fruit and vegetable markets. The huge building between them, girded with loggias and topped by a sloping roof, is the Palazzo della Ragione, built for municipal use during the 13th and 14th centuries. The interior frescoes, on religious and astrological themes, are 15th-century replacements of originals by Giotto and members of his school. Also inside is a large wooden statue of a horse, built for a tournament in the 15th century and for some time erroneously attributed to Donatello. Open for special occasions only (phone: 49-820-5006).

Another historic square not to be missed is Piazza dei Signori. It is surrounded by the onetime local government seat, the 14th-century Palazzo del Capitanio, the early-15th-century clock tower, and the Renaissance Loggia del Consiglio. In another of the city's beautiful squares, Prato della Valle, there is an open-air market every Saturday, selling, among other items, footwear manufactured along the Brenta River, including top-quality designer shoes for which Brenta is renowned.

CHECKING IN: ***Padovanelle*** – Situated just outside the city, in a park surrounding Padua's racecourse, this modern 40-room hotel complex has indoor and outdoor swimming pools, a tennis court, private parking, and lovely gardens. Its *Ippodromo* restaurant looks out onto the track, and if you're feeling lucky, bets can be placed during lunch or dinner when the course is open. Four miles (6 km) from the center of town. Via Ippodromo, Ponte di Brenta, Padua (phone: 49-625622). Expensive to moderate.

Europa – A large, centrally located, efficient establishment with 59 rooms and modern amenities, including a good restaurant offering local specialties. A short walk from the Scrovegni Chapel. 9 Largo Europa, Padua (phone: 49-661200; fax: 625320). Moderate.

Grande Italia – One of Padua's more popular hotels, it has 62 rooms and is directly opposite the main station. Its restaurant is closed Sundays. 81 Corso G.F. del Popolo, Padua (phone: 49-650877). Moderate.

EATING OUT: ***El Toulà*** – A line in the eclectic chain of very fine restaurants that specialize in Venetian cuisine, housed in a delightful 16th-century palace. Fish dishes make up the most important segment of the menu, supplemented by grilled vegetables, including the Venetian specialty, grilled radicchio (red lettuce), fresh salmon in a peppery marinade, grilled lamb and veal, and a variety of creamy desserts. Try Padua's special wine, the crisp, white moscato from Arquà Petrarca in the heart of the Euganean Hills, as an accompaniment. Closed Sundays, Monday lunch, and August. Reservations necessary. Major credit cards accepted. 11 Via Belle Parti, Padua (phone: 49-875-1822). Expensive.

Da Giovanni – A must for meat lovers, specializing in huge whole roasts or boiled meats (a specialty here) that are carved at the table and homemade pasta as a hearty first course. Vegetables and salads are fresh and dressed with pure olive oil. Wines, whether of the house or from local vineyards, are excellent. A short taxi ride from the center of town. Closed Sundays, Saturday lunch, the first 3 weeks of August, and from *Christmas* through *New Year's Day.* Reservations advised. American Express accepted. 22 Via Maroncelli, Padua (phone: 49-772620). Moderate.

En Route from Padua – Just south of Padua, in the middle of the plains, is an unexpected collection of small, cone-shaped, densely vegetated volcanic hills called the Colli Euganei (Euganean Hills). This is one of Italy's most romantic corners; its small villages, monasteries, vineyards, and villas have been visited by poets, writers, and artists over the centuries. From Padua's main station, follow the city's ancient walls to the turnoff for the airport (Via Sorio). First stop is the magnificent Abbey of Praglia, a Benedictine monastery founded in the 11th century set against a backdrop of sharply rising hills with a magnificent view over the surrounding plains. Facing the monastery is the Chiesa dell'Assunta, a church dedicated to the Madonna, reconstructed in the 15th century in Venetian Renaissance style. Ask one of the monks for permission to visit its art treasures and elegant cloisters.

From the abbey, return to the main road, turn right, and follow the signs to Torreglia, Galzignano, Valsanzibio — the site of *Golf Club Padova,* an excellent 18-hole course (47 Via Noiera; phone: 49-913-0215) and the beautiful gardens of the Villa Barbarigo — then on to Arquà Petrarca. The latter is one of the most picturesque medieval villages in the region and the retirement home of 14th-century poet Petrarch, whose house (15 Via Valleselle; phone: 429-718186) is open to visitors daily except Mondays (hours are erratic, so call ahead; admission charge). Return to Padua by way of Montegrotto Terme and Abano Terme, both important spa towns, so-called cities of miracles, where hotels continue the tradition of mud baths and similar therapies that have been enjoyed since Roman days. Today the area boasts over 100 indoor/outdoor swimming pools. It is also well endowed with simple trattorie — many offering quail and meat grilled on an open fire as specialties — and inexpensive *alberghi.*

The 55 miles (88 km) that separate Padua from Verona can be covered on either the state highway (SS11) or the autostrada (A4), which runs more or less parallel and gives splendid views of the luscious green vine-clad hills of one of the most fertile areas of the country.

VERONA: Verona, of *Romeo and Juliet* and *Two Gentlemen* fame, is one of Italy's oldest and most beautiful cities, already in existence when it was occupied by the pre-Roman Etruscans. By 89 BC it had become one of the most flourishing Roman colonies, strategically situated at the junction of three important roads on a U-bend of the Adige River.

Today the city, known as "little Rome," still stands in a historical time warp, or, rather, time *warps,* since there is a Roman, a medieval, and a "modern," or Renaissance, Verona to enjoy. Important Roman buildings and gateways are still visible, including the magnificent amphitheater dominating the heart of the city. The Roman walls surrounding Verona were added to and fortified through years of invasions and now offer splendid views of the Old City and the Adige River. Later, in the Middle Ages, Verona became an important feudal city of the Venetian Republic, under the 14th-century Scaligeri family, whose richly carved stone tombs figure largely on most itineraries. Veronese churches and museums house numerous samples of works by the grand masters of the "Serenissima" Republic of Venice — such as Paolo Veronese, Francesco Buonsignori, and Liberale da Verona. For a more detailed report on the city, its sights, hotels, and restaurants, see *Verona* in THE CITIES.

En Route from Verona – Before returning eastward to Vicenza, time permitting, take a brief 40-mile (64 km) excursion to Lake Garda, visiting Peschiera and returning to Verona via the impressive Gardens of Sigurta. Admission charge. Open Thursdays, Saturdays, Sundays, and public holidays, from 9 AM to 6 PM mid-March through November.

From the northern outskirts of Verona, follow the green signs for A4 to Vicenza (about 32 miles/51 km in the direction of Padua) and exit at Vicenza Ovest (west).

VICENZA: Beautiful enough to be dubbed "the Venice of terra firma," Vicenza is best known as the city of Andrea Palladio. Born in the city (though some experts contest this, maintaining his birthplace to be Padua), Palladio was to have a huge influence not only on Vicenza's architecture — hence its common name Città del Palladio — but also on the development of buildings throughout Europe and America.

The hub of activity is Piazza dei Signori, no less busy now than in the heyday of Vicenza's civic life. Like other Venetian cities, Vicenza was first and foremost a Roman colony which, having then suffered tyrannic ecclesiastical rule in the 11th century and coming close to destruction in medieval wars with neighboring armies in Padua and Verona, eventually flourished under the Venetian Republic. By the end of the 16th century the city was resplendent with new buildings, many of them built by Palladio, that survive to this day.

Piazza dei Signori is flanked on one side by what many consider this remarkable architect's masterpiece, the Basilica, formerly the Gothic Palazzo della Ragione (Town

Hall), which Palladio converted to High Renaissance style. Palladio simply enveloped the preexisting façade with his classic columns on 2 levels, the ground level in Doric form, the upper level in Ionic, transforming it into one of the finest Renaissance buildings in the world. Open Tuesdays through Saturdays from 10 AM to noon and 2:30 to 5 PM, Sundays from 9:30 AM to noon; no admission charge.

One corner of the Basilica is flanked by a tall, elegant clock tower, Torre Piazza, or Torre Bissari, dating from the 12th century. Across the square, the building with the enormous red brick columns is the Loggia del Capitaniato, the former residence of the Venetian local governor and one of Palladio's most imposing works, although he never completed it. The town's main shopping street, Corso Andrea Palladio, is a visual delight, with its pillar-fronted buildings on either side interspersed with Renaissance palaces.

Another of the architect's outstanding works of genius is the *Teatro Olimpico* (Piazza Matteotti). Modeled on an ancient Roman theater, it was begun in 1580, just a few months before the death of Palladio. The theater is an elliptical, rather than round, hemisphere made of wood and stucco, and the stage is surrounded by Corinthian columns and niches between painted street scenes with a masterly trompe l'oeil effect. Still in use, the theater is open to visitors daily, except Sunday afternoons, from 9:30 AM to 12:20 PM, 2 to 4:30 PM in winter and 3 to 5:30 PM in summer — unless rehearsals dictate otherwise; admission charge, except Sunday mornings. Tickets for performances can be purchased from the *Agenzia di Viaggi Palladio,* 16 Via Cavour (phone: 444-546111).

Palazzo Chiericati (Piazza Matteotti) is yet another of Palladio's imaginative projects, with its entire façade, except for the doorway, composed of 2 tiers of columns. This is now the home of the municipal museum and a fine collection of Venetian paintings by such artists as Paolo Veneziano, Battista da Vicenza, Carpaccio, Paolo Veronese, and Giovanni Buonconsiglio. Open daily, except Sunday afternoons and Mondays, from 9:30 AM to noon and 2:30 to 5 PM; admission charge.

Vicenza sits in the middle of a countryside peppered with Palladian villas — a total of 56 are included in a booklet, *The Villas,* produced by the regional tourist board (5 Piazza Duomo; phone: 444-544122 and 12 Piazza Matteotti; phone: 320854). One of the closest and most important is Villa Valmarana "ai Nani" ("of the dwarfs" because of the tiny statues on the garden wall). Built in the 17th century by Mattoni, a follower of Palladio, it is decorated with frescoes by Giambattista Tiepolo and his son Giandomenico. Open Thursdays, weekends, and holidays from 10 AM to noon and 2:30 to 5:30 PM March through April; 3 to 6 PM May through September; and 2 to 5 PM October through November. Closed December through February; admission charge. Another villa is La Rotonda, just beyond Villa Valmarana and usually visible only from the grounds; but this view is enough to admire the mastery of this perfectly proportioned villa begun by Palladio in the 16th century. Its four pillar-fronted façades have been copied by numerous English and French architects. The villa itself is open Tuesdays and Wednesdays only, from 10 AM to noon and 3 to 6 PM, and the grounds are open Tuesdays, Wednesdays, and Thursdays (same hours); closed from mid-October through mid-March. For special visits, call 2 weeks in advance (phone: 444-321793).

CHECKING IN: ***Campo Marzio*** **–** Considered the best in town, this modern, 35-room hotel stands at the edge of the Campo Marzio park, a short walk from the Duomo and Corso Andrea Palladio. 21 Viale Roma, Vicenza (phone: 444-545700; fax: 320495). Expensive.

Continental **–** A small, elegant 57-room hotel situated in front of the stadium, not far from the center of town. 89 Viale G.G. Trissino, Vicenza (phone: 0444-505476; fax: 513319). Moderate.

EATING OUT: ***Cinzia & Valerio*** **–** The best in town. The house specialty is Adriatic fish, prepared in inimitable Venetian pâté, risotto, or a casserole and accompanied by excellent local white wines. On the eastern outskirts of town.

Closed Mondays and during August. Reservations necessary. Major credit cards accepted. 65-67 Contrà Porta Padova, Vicenza (phone: 444-505213). Expensive.

Scudo di Francia – Housed in one of the city's many delightful old palazzi and dispensing cuisine as authentically local as its antique furniture. This is a good place to try the traditional dish of the area, *baccalà* (codfish) with polenta, or pasta with white beans, as well as game or a flight of fancy such as *faraona al forno in salsa al melograno* (pheasant with pomegranates). The wine list has an excellent selection of local vintages. Closed Sunday evenings, Mondays, August, and the last week of February. Reservations advised. Major credit cards accepted. 4 Contrà Piancoli, Vicenza (phone: 444-323322). Moderate.

En Route from Vicenza – Take a northeasterly route for Bassano del Grappa by following SS53. At the first main intersection turn left on SS47, which leads past the Villa Trissino at Cricoli and the Villa Casarotto and Villa Del Conte, both at Dueville and open only on Sundays. A 20-mile (32-km) drive, this road heads northward to the foothills of the Dolomites, which rise against the skyline, marking an abrupt boundary to the now familiar flat horizon. Before reaching Bassano del Grappa, it is worth taking a slight detour to the splendid medieval town of Marostica, a remarkable setting for a chess game played with living figures in Renaissance costume the first weekend of September in even-numbered years.

BASSANO DEL GRAPPA: On the banks of the Brenta River, Bassano del Grappa is a delightful little town filled with medieval and Renaissance streets, arcades, and houses with painted façades. From here, both the Venetian plains to the south and the mountains to the north, including Monte del Grappa, are visible. The town is famous for its 13th-century covered wooden bridge over the Brenta Canal. Designed to look like a ship moored between two quaysides, the bridge was immortalized in songs during World War I, when Bassano was at the center of fierce fighting between the Austrian and Italian armies (a war cemetery on Monte del Grappa holds the bodies of more than 20,000 victims). Bassano memorializes the war with Viale dei Martiri (Avenue of the Martyrs), which leads to the town's finest viewpoint, as well as with monuments to fallen soldiers. Bassano is also famous for its grappa, the fiery alcoholic drink made from the last grape pressings, as well as for its lovely white pottery.

The *Museo Civico* (Municipal Museum), housed in an old convent behind the medieval Church of Saint Francis (4 Via Museo) in Piazza Garibaldi, includes works by Jacopo dal Ponte, a local 16th-century realist painter known simply as Bassano, who excelled in trompe l'oeil painting. Open Tuesdays through Saturdays from 10 AM to 12:30 PM and 2:30 to 6:30 PM, Sundays from 10 AM to 12:30 PM; admission charge.

EATING OUT: *Ca'7* – Housed in an 18th-century Venetian villa about a mile (1.6 km) from town. Enjoy selections from the excellent fish-based menu either in the garden or in the gracious dining room, with a dry, sparkling, white prosecco. Closed Sunday evenings, Mondays, 10 days in mid-August, and the first week of November. Reservations necessary. Major credit cards accepted. 4 Via Cunizza da Romano, Bassano del Grappa (phone: 424-25005). Expensive.

Belvedere – A popular dining spot that attracts locals and travelers alike, it offers traditional *cucina veneta* with a light touch. Try the *bigola all' anatra* (tube-like spaghetti with duck sauce) for an appetizer; the unusual *insalata di granchio ed aparagi* (crab and asparagus salad); or the *brodetto di scampi* (shrimp consommé). A daily prix fixe menu offers a good meal at an equally appetizing price. Closed Sundays and August. Reservations advised. Major credit cards accepted. 1 Via delle Fosse, Bassano del Grappa (phone: 424-26602). Moderate to inexpensive.

ASOLO: From Bassano it is a 9-mile (14-km) drive eastward to Asolo, through countryside dotted with villas and green hills but lined mostly with unsightly ceramics factories (their showrooms, open to the public, are more interesting).

Known as "the town of 100 horizons" because of its immense panoramas, Asolo is a small farming market village. Perched on a hill and built around a small square filled with leafy horse-chestnut trees and 15th- to 17th-century buildings, it was much loved by Anglo-Saxon writers and painters in the last century. The local museum (irregular openings — inquire on the spot) has documents and manuscripts belonging to the English poet Robert Browning, who spent many years in Asolo (his son is buried here, as is the Italian actress Eleonora Duse), as well as works by the immensely successful 18th-century sculptor Antonio Canova (who was born 6 miles/10 km north of here in a village called Possagno).

CHECKING IN: ***Villa Cipriani*** – Among the green hills overlooking Asolo stands this 16th-century villa, embellished in the 18th century and now the epitome of rural romanticism and seclusion. It is a member of the luxury CIGA hotel chain, with 31 rooms and an excellent restaurant. Today's guests enjoy the same suggestive surroundings that seduced Anglo-Saxon travelers a century ago. 298 Via Canova, Asolo (phone: 423-55444; fax: 52095). Very expensive.

EATING OUT: ***Charly's One*** – Like the clientele, the menu is both local and foreign, with Scottish smoked salmon, onion soup, local smoked goose, or chateaubriand with tarragon and béarnaise sauce. Fresh fish served Tuesdays to Thursdays. Closed Thursday dinner, Fridays, and November. Reservations advised. Major credit cards accepted. 55 Via Roma, Asolo (phone: 423-52201). Moderate.

Hostaria Cà Derton – Enjoy excellent local fare in this 16th-century house with a 19th-century wood interior. The menu offers such traditional dishes as pasta with beans, risotto with fresh mushrooms, asparagus or radicchio from Treviso, and, according to season, game, suckling pig, and rabbit accompanied by fresh artichokes or peppers. Desserts are homemade and vary with the whim of the proprietor. Closed Monday evenings, Tuesdays, several days in February, and the last 2 weeks of August. No reservations. All major credit cards accepted. 11 Piazza D'Annunzio, Asolo (phone: 423-52730). Moderate to inexpensive.

En Route from Asolo – Follow the minor road that leads eastward for 5 miles (8 km) to Cornuda La Valle and the intersection of the main road to Belluno. Here turn left and head for the mountains. The road follows the Piave River of World War I fame and rises to fresher, purer mountain air. For some 30 miles (48 km), pastures, woods, and mountain peaks are occasionally interrupted by small villages of wooden chalets and smoking chimney pots.

BELLUNO: The approach to Belluno, as with a number of Italian towns, is a disappointing confusion of small industries and roadside billboards, with only glimpses of field and mountain between. Press on to the heart of the town, however, where its pretty piazze and cobbled streets, embodying the characteristic layout of a Roman city, lead to the market square and the 15th-century fountain with four water spouts. Some streets are still lined with shady, Renaissance porticoes.

Living up so high, Belluno's inhabitants are blessed with magnificent views of the northeastern Dolomites. Nearer home, the skyline is dominated by the huge baroque cathedral with its green, onion-shape dome and bell tower, which still has its 14th-century crypt. The 15th-century Palazzo dei Rettori (Rectors' Palace), with its carved stone balconies and huge clock, retains its Venetian splendor but is now an administration center and, unfortunately, is no longer open to the public. The same applies to the Bishops' Palace, across the square, which, although largely rebuilt in the 17th century, is the only town building with medieval characteristics.

The town's museum is in the ancient Lawyers' College and contains works by both famous (such as Bartolomeo Montagna) and lesser-known local artists, plus archaeological remains dating from prehistoric, Roman, and medieval times that were found in the area. In summer, open Mondays through Saturdays from 10 AM to noon and 3 to 6 PM; mornings only on Sundays. In winter, open Tuesdays through Fridays from 10 AM to noon and 3 to 6 PM, Mondays and Saturdays from 10 AM to noon (closed Sundays and holidays); admission charge. 16 Via Duomo (phone: 437-24836).

CHECKING IN: ***Villa Carpenada*** – Surrounded by a large garden and woodland, this 28-room 18th-century villa, 1½ miles (2 km) outside town, is an ideal spot from which to enjoy mountain jaunts year-round. 158 Via Mier, Belluno (phone: 437-28343; fax: 28345). Moderate to inexpensive.

Dolomiti – A neat, clean establishment with 32 rooms and tucked away down a side street off the main Piazza Vittorio Veneto and its arcaded shopping streets and cafés. 46 Via Carrera, Belluno (phone: 437-941660). Inexpensive.

EATING OUT: ***Al Borgo*** – Regional Veneto cooking is expertly prepared in this simple 18th-century villa. Highlights include soup, gnocchi (small, dumpling-like pasta) mixed with meat or ricotta cheese or with local radicchio, and pancakes made with field herbs or mushrooms, as well as local venison or goat, roasted or cooked with fresh vegetables. The homemade desserts are often based on local fruit, such as mountain blueberries or wild strawberries. Closed Monday evenings, Tuesdays, and 3 weeks in July. Reservations advised. Major credit cards accepted. 8 Via Anconetta, Belluno (phone: 437-926755). Moderate.

L'Hostaria – Specialties of the season make up the bill of fare at this small countryside eatery. The fixed price lunch menu makes a midday stop here a delightful, yet reasonably priced treat. Closed Monday, 2 weeks in August, and 2 weeks in February. Reservations advised. All major credit cards accepted. 1 Via Feltre, Belluno (phone: 0437-88228). Moderate to inexpensive.

En Route from Belluno – For a taste of the Dolomites, head north along the Piave River to Ponte nelle Alpi, then turn right, leaving the river behind, onto the main Venice road, and almost immediately take the left turn marked Cansiglio. Here the villages, meadows, and pine- and chestnut-covered mountains, their summits often hidden by cloud, make a refreshing change from the sultry summer heat of the towns and lagoons. The road winds around the mountains past the red, overhanging eaves of tiny holdings, sudden trattorie, and the occasional *albergo.* Continue across the flatter, lush meadows of the Alto Piano before descending steadily to Vittorio Veneto (where there is a good 9-hole golf course — *Golf Club Cansiglio;* another 9 holes are scheduled for completion early this year; open daily, May through October) and then follow the signposts to the attractive 15th-century town of Treviso.

TREVISO: This charming walled city is approached by straight-as-a-die, tree-lined avenues. One of Italy's industrial and agricultural centers and headquarters of Benetton and Stefanel, it stands where two rivers emerge (having traveled underground from the mountains), meet, and then divide into fast-flowing canals, giving the city a mini-Venice stamp of design, although with far more life and greenery.

Treviso suffered extensive damage during World War I, and nearly half its buildings were destroyed in an air raid in 1944; hence the general lack of antiquity in a town that was founded during the Roman Empire. Nevertheless, narrow streets and old houses decorated with frescoes, and flower-filled gardens are still evident. The central Piazza dei Signori is flanked on one side by the Romanesque Palazzo dei Trecento, named after the city's 13th-century governing council of 300 citizens. One of the buildings that needed scrupulous reconstruction after the bombing, it is now used for town administration.

A short walk down the Calmaggiore, the main street with its elegant shops semihidden behind elegant 15th-century porticoes, leads to the Duomo, with its seven hemispherical domes in lead and copper, its neo-classical façade a 17th-century addition to the original Romanesque design. Inside is an altar painting of the Annunciation by Titian.

The *Municipal Museum* (22 Borgo Cavour) contains frescoes and paintings by Venetian artists, including works by Cima da Conegliano, Titian, and Gino Rossi. Open Tuesdays through Fridays from 9 AM to noon and 2 to 5 PM, weekends from 9 AM to noon; admission charge.

CHECKING IN: ***Villa Corner della Regina*** – Magnificent golf courses and parks surround this 18th-century Palladian villa, with its 7 exquisite suites, 5 handsome rooms, and 35 new annex rooms, just 45 minutes from Venice. Amenities include lawn tennis, a pool, sauna, and air conditioning in a period setting, enhanced by a doting Venetian staff. The 50% fall/winter discounts make this a more affordable off-season choice. Eleven miles (18 km) west of Treviso on SS53, Cavasagra (phone: 423-481481; fax: 451100). Very expensive to expensive.

Villa Condulmer – Ten miles (16 km) south of Treviso in Zerman, on the outskirts of Mogliano Veneto, this 45-room 18th-century villa stands in its own parkland surrounded by such 20th-century luxuries as a swimming pool, 27 holes of golf, riding stables, and tennis courts. For a final act of indulgence in Venetian hospitality, this hotel is hard to beat, with the added pleasure of an excellent restaurant. Open year-round. Zerman (phone: 41-457100; fax: 457134). Expensive.

EATING OUT: ***Alfredo El Toulà*** – This is the original, from which the other members of this haute cuisine chain sprang. The highest traditions of *mittel*-European cuisine are respected and developed with local *trevigiano* flavor. Blinis with caviar, kidneys cooked with juniper berries, sirloin steaks with herbs, and veal with onions are just some of the culinary delights. Desserts include feather-light sorbets as well as more substantial creamy confections. Closed Mondays and August. Reservations necessary. Major credit cards accepted. 26 Via Collalto, Treviso (phone: 422-540275). Expensive.

Le Beccherie – Tucked away behind Piazza dei Signori, this is both a hotel and an immensely popular, traditional, family-run restaurant. The menu changes with the seasons, so all ingredients, whether vegetable or game, are garden- or field-fresh and exquisitely cooked. Staff members are fast and efficient as they steer between the tables at breakneck speed with steaks sizzling on marble slabs and with tempting dessert trolleys. Closed Thursday evenings, Fridays, and July 15–30. Reservations advised. Major credit cards accepted. 10 Piazza Ancilotto, Treviso (phone: 422-540871). Moderate.

A l'Oca Bianca – Near the central square, this is a must for lovers of *cucina casalinga* (home cooking). Closed Wednesdays and 3 weeks in August. No reservations. No credit cards accepted. 7 Vicolo della Torre, Treviso (phone: 422-541850). Moderate to inexpensive.

Toni del Spin – Located behind the magnificent Palazzo dei Signori, this trattoria is a family affair; its equally popular country restaurant and farm provides much of the fresh ingredients and meats served here. A blackboard menu features such dishes as *baccalà* (codfish), *pasta e fagioli* (pasta and bean soup), risotto, and game in season (look for *colombaccio,* wild pigeon). Closed Sundays, Monday lunch, and August. Reservations unnecessary. No credit cards. 7 Via Inferiore, Treviso (phone: 422-543829). Moderate to inexpensive.

En Route from Treviso – Follow A27 due south for 19 miles (30 km) to Venice.

Emilia-Romagna

The Emilia-Romagna region lies north of Tuscany and south of Lombardy and the Veneto, and from east to west it nearly stretches from sea to sea. Its eastern edge is on the Adriatic and its western tip reaches almost to the Ligurian coast, stopped short only by the Apennine range. Although part of the region is hill or mountain — a southerly strip that runs northwest to southeast along the Apennines — most of it is flat and low-lying, the fertile plain of the Po River, which forms the region's northern boundary. That geographical fact has made the region home to some of Italy's most abundant agriculture, which in turn has supported the rich and varied local cuisines. Bologna, the regional capital, fairly wallows in this abundance and revels in its nickname, *Bologna la Grassa* (Bologna the Fat).

The geographical reality of a low-lying wedge driven into an essentially mountainous country has also contributed to making Emilia-Romagna one of Italy's most prosperous commercial centers. The region takes its name in part from the Via Emilia, the ancient Roman road that runs, practically in a straight line, from Milan to the sea at Rimini. Laid out by Marcus Aemilius Lepidus in 187 BC to connect the Roman Empire with its newly acquired lands in northern Europe, the road proved to be the region's lifeblood, a communications link and a conduit for trade that played a role in virtually every social, political, and military development in the area from the days of the Roman Empire to World War II.

Despite the fact that modern Italy has made Emilia-Romagna one region, the area is, in fact, easily divided into two quite different sections. Emilia is the territory to the west, embracing the cities of Piacenza, Parma, Modena, Ferrara, and Bologna. Romagna is the smaller zone to the east, including Rimini and Ravenna. It is said in Italy that if you go to the house of an Emilian, he will offer you a glass of water; in Romagna, you will be offered wine. The gruffness inherent in the Emilian manner might have something to do with the fact that, until the unification of Italy in the 19th century, Emilia's cities and towns — first free communes, then medieval and Renaissance duchies or principalities — spent the greater part of their history fighting against outsiders and among themselves. The region that today is noted not only for its beautiful, flourishing cities but also for the small-town hospitality that prevails in them was not always so trusting of strangers.

The history of Romagna, on the other hand, tended toward internal cohesiveness and a wider identification with the world beyond its borders. The existence of the seaport at Rimini, once a major Western entrepôt for trade with the East, fostered a more cosmopolitan view of outsiders. That attitude lives on today: Rimini and the numerous seaside resorts nearby draw tens of thousands of holiday makers from Britain, France, Germany, and Scandinavia, all anxious to play on the wide beaches and swim in the warm

Adriatic. At high season in Rimini it is rare to hear Italian spoken in the streets.

A more detailed account of the separate past of the two areas might begin with the period from the 5th to the 8th century, when Emilia was invaded repeatedly by wild and bloodthirsty barbarians — Goths, Lombards, and Franks. Three centuries of foreign domination left the region's cities in ruins and completely disunited, so that no sooner had they driven the invaders out than they began warring with their neighbors. With the outbreak of the struggle between the Guelphs and the Ghibellines, the bloody and largely pointless internecine warfare gradually became codified along political lines. By the 13th century, there was hardly a city on the entire Italian peninsula that hadn't been drawn into this seemingly interminable dispute between the forces of the pope and the Holy Roman Empire, and Emilia was no exception. Cities formed allegiances, betrayed them, were subjugated, and rebelled throughout the medieval period. It was only with the establishment of some of the great ruling families that a semblance of order was restored. Parma and Piacenza initially fell under the sway of the Visconti of Milan. Ferrara became the seat of the Este clan, which gradually extended its power to Modena and Reggio. The Pepoli and the Bentivoglio families dominated Bologna.

Although the brilliant, erratic, and ruthless Malatesta family seized Rimini and held it from the 13th to the 16th century, most of Romagna managed to stay aloof from the torment experienced by the Emilian cities. In 402, after the division of the Roman Empire into an Empire of the East and an Empire of the West, Honorius made Ravenna the capital of the latter. After the fall of Rome in the West (476), a short-lived kingdom of the Goths, under Odoacer and Theodoric, maintained Ravenna as a capital city. In the 6th century, however, the great emperor of the East, Justinian, defeated the Goths, and Ravenna became part of the Byzantine, or Eastern Roman, Empire, ruled by exarchs (civil governors), with an eye to what was going on back home in Constantinople.

The world-famous, Byzantine-inspired mosaics of Ravenna are a legacy of that far-off time when the city, in effect, turned its back on Italy and looked to Byzantium for culture and guidance. By the 8th century, however, the Lombards had established themselves in much of northern Italy. They even took Ravenna, but only briefly, and Romagna owes its name to the fact that it remained Roman while the Lombards prevailed in the region that bears their name. Then, in a rapid turn of events, the pope asked the help of the Frankish Kings Pepin and Charlemagne in stemming the Lombard tide. Each proved willing and able, and Romagna came under papal domination, a condition that was to last until the nation of Italy was born in the 19th century.

Papal forces had, in the meantime, made some headway in Emilia, gaining a foothold in Bologna and its environs, but by and large this region remained fragmented and hard to handle. Then, in 1545, Pope Paul III, a member of the noble Farnese family, took control of Parma and Piacenza, creating a duchy for his illegitimate son to rule. By the 17th century, most of Emilia was in the hands of either the Farnese or the Este family, and the question of political power seemed more or less settled — until Napoleon invaded in the late 18th century, turning the balance of power upside down again. When the dust had settled, the Empress Marie Louise of France had become Duchess of Parma, and Austria had taken the rest of the province (along with Venice and a huge chunk of northern Italy). Romagna stayed safely in papal hands.

But it was not to last. By 1848, popular feeling for a united Italy, free of foreign occupiers, had become too great to suppress. Piacenza was the first city to throw in its lot with Piedmont (the birthplace of a unified Italy), and the rest of the region rapidly followed. In 1860, the area, now known as Emilia-Romagna, joined with Piedmont to form the nucleus of the modern Italian state.

Despite all the blood spilled in settling the fate of the region, Emilia-Romagna is today a peaceful, prosperous part of Italy. Some of the country's most famous exports originate here. Parma is the home of parmesan cheese and Parma ham. From Modena come such great Italian automobile marks as Ferrari and Maserati. Bologna has given the world *spaghetti alla bolognese* and mortadella, the granddaddy of American "baloney"; Faenza is the home of faïence pottery. Perhaps the most enduring gift of all is the genius of composer Giuseppe Verdi, who was born in the tiny hamlet of Le Roncole, just outside Piacenza.

Piacenza, in the west and only 40 miles (64 km) southeast of Milan, is the logical starting point for a tour of Emilia-Romagna. From here, following the ancient route — in some cases over the actual cobblestones — of the Via Emilia (SS9 on modern maps), our itinerary passes through Parma, Modena, Bologna, Imola, and Faenza to Rimini. From Rimini, it takes the coast road north to Ravenna and then turns inland to end in the majestic medieval town of Ferrara. In a hotel listed as very expensive, expect to spend $200 and up for two in high season. Other accommodations in the region range from expensive, where a room can cost $150 to $200, to many more moderate hotels ranging from $70 to $150. Inexpensive rooms are $70 and less. Expect to pay over $125 for a meal for two at the *San Domenico* in Imola; $90 to $125 at an expensive restaurant; $60 to $90 at moderate ones; and under $60 at inexpensive places.

PIACENZA: Originally founded by the Romans, Piacenza is now a modern industrial city, but the medieval underpinnings of the old town remain largely intact. The city has always had considerable strategic value — it lies at the point where the Via Emilia touches the Po River — and in keeping with the history of settlements in this region, a great deal of blood was shed over the centuries to keep it in one camp or another. In 1545, Alessandro Farnese, otherwise known as Pope Paul III, created the duchy of Parma and Piacenza, which the Farnese family ruled until the early 18th century. Piacenza, however, has a history of independent thinking, a trait that showed itself on two notable occasions. In 1547, a group of Piacenza nobles tired of the tyranny and debauchery of their overlord, Pier Luigi Farnese, and murdered him. Since the Farnese family was extraordinarily powerful and Pier Luigi was the (illegitimate) son of the pope, the tyrannicide was an action requiring great courage. Three hundred years later, in 1848, Piacenza took another step into the unknown as the first Italian city to vote for annexation to Piedmont, the nucleus of the new unified Italian nation, and for this it became known as the *primogenita,* or firstborn.

The medieval heart of the town is Piazza dei Cavalli, so called because of the two massive 17th-century equestrian statues (sculpted by Francesco Mochi, considered one of the great baroque masters), that dominate the square. Sixteen years in the making, the statues are of two Farnese dukes, Alessandro and Ranuccio I, both descendants of the murdered Pier Luigi but obviously held in higher esteem. Facing them, looming over the piazza, is the graceful Palazzo del Comune, built in 1281 in Lombard-Gothic style and also known as the Gotico. The Palazzo del Governatore, opposite, is a building of the late 18th century, and to one side of the square is the 13th-century Chiesa di San Francesco (Church of St. Francis), at the beginning of Via XX Settembre. Piacenza's Duomo, just down Via XX Settembre from Piazza dei Cavalli, is a towering Lombard-Romanesque building constructed between the 12th and 14th centuries. It appears to have been built more for fortification than for worship, and its most curious feature is a thick-barred iron cage set in the masonry at a dizzying height on the side of the soaring bell tower. Miscreants of the town were tossed naked into this *gabbia* and forced to endure the jeers and mockery of the townspeople in the marketplace below. Inside, the cathedral shows evidence of the evolution from Romanesque to Gothic style, and there are frescoes by Guercino.

The *Museo Civico* (Municipal Museum; Piazza Cittadella; phone: 523-28270), is housed in the renovated Palazzo Farnese, built in the latter part of the 16th century for that illustrious family. It contains paintings (especially an *Adoration* by Botticelli and other works of the 17th and 18th centuries) and a variety of archaeological specimens, one of which — the *fegato di Piacenza* — is a particularly odd relic of the days when Emilia was the land of the ancient Etruscans. This bronze cast of a liver inscribed with the names of various Etruscan deities is thought by archaeologists to have been a sort of religious road map, a guide to be consulted when Etruscan priests were called upon to read the entrails of a sacrificial beast. The museum also has an interesting collection of 18th- and 19th-century carriages and coaches. Closed Mondays; admission charge.

If time permits, some other sights to see in Piacenza include two Renaissance churches, San Sisto and Madonna di Campagna, the latter with frescoes by Pordenone, and Sant'Antonino, an 11th-century Romanesque church with 14th-century Gothic additions. The town also has a modern art gallery, *Galleria d'Arte Moderna "Ricci Oddi"* (15 Via San Siro; phone: 523-20742), whose collection of works ranging from Romanticism to the 1930s ranks among the best in Italy. Open daily except Mondays from 10 AM to noon and 3 to 5 PM in summer, with slight variations in spring and winter. The tourist office, Azienda di Promozione Turistica (APT; 17 Via San Siro; phone: 523-34347), or the tourist information office (IAT; 10 Piazzetta dei Mercanti; phone: 523-29324) can provide further information. Open 9 AM to 12:30 PM and 4:30 to 6:30 PM, except Thursday afternoons and Sundays.

CHECKING IN: ***Grande Albergo Roma*** – The best hotel in town, only a block from Piazza dei Cavalli, it has 90 rooms and an excellent restaurant with a good view of the city. This is a perfect location for exploring the city on foot, and there is ample parking for guests. Restaurant closed Saturdays and 1 week in August. 14 Via Cittadella, Piacenza (phone: 523-23201; fax: 523-30548). Expensive to moderate.

EATING OUT: ***Antica Osteria del Teatro*** – Easily the best in town and one of the best in the entire region, this quaintly elegant and atmospheric restaurant is set in a narrow, picturesque street in the oldest part of Piacenza. It's famous for ravioli stuffed with duck and, in season, *flan di ortiche ai dadini di pomodoro,* a mousse made of local greens and tomatoes. There is also a wide array of other local delicacies, meats, and produce. Service is excellent. Closed Sunday evenings, Mondays, the first 2 weeks of January, and most of August. Reservations necessary. Major credit cards accepted. 16 Via Verdi, Piacenza (phone: 523-23777). Expensive.

Antico Caffè – As an alternative to a heavy lunch, try this beautifully decorated café, a few blocks from Piazza dei Cavalli. It serves good sandwiches on crusty bread, delicious pastries, and the town's best cappuccino. Closed Sundays. Reservations unnecessary. No credit cards accepted. 49 Corso Garibaldi, Piacenza (phone: 523-24918). Inexpensive.

En Route from Piacenza – For a glimpse back in time, take SS654 southeast to Grazzano Visconti, a reconstruction of a medieval village just 8 miles (13 km) from Piacenza. Set against the backdrop of a 12th-century castle, Grazzano Visconti is a living museum and artisans' workshop; the region named it the "City of Art" in 1986. Craftspeople use traditional techniques and tools as old as their trades to create fine wrought-iron, ceramic, and silver objects, as well as elegant pieces of furniture. The last Sunday in May, the townspeople don medieval costumes and take part in a historical parade and a jousting tournament. For information, contact the tourist office (Piazza del Biscione; phone: 523-870205). For another medieval experience, head 18 miles (29 km) southeast of Piacenza to Castell' Arquato. High on a hilltop, the 1,000-year-old town's towers and monuments stand out above the terraced vineyards that surround the town. Most noteworthy are the Palazzo Pretorio with an outside staircase, loggia, and bell tower, the Collegiata (a Romanesque church), and the remains of a 14th-century castle. Its tourist office can provide information (phone: 523-80391).

Halfway to Parma (38 miles/61 km away by the direct route), a road running parallel to the Via Emilia travels through flat, bucolic countryside to the village of Busseto. The great opera composer Giuseppe Verdi was born in the tiny hamlet of Le Roncole (now known as Roncole-Verdi), about 3 miles (5 km) southeast of Busseto, lived for a time in Busseto itself, and later built an estate at Sant'Agata, about 2 miles (3 km) northwest of town. Every June, Busseto hosts one of the most prestigious international singing competitions in search of singers for Verdi's operas around the world. In July, there are performance in Busseto's piazzas and streets. For information, contact the *Gruppo Attività Verdiane* (Roncole-Verdi; phone: 524-91753). A ticket for admission to three Verdi landmarks can be bought at the Rocca (castle) of Busseto. It permits entry to the *Teatro Verdi* (Piazza Verdi), a small opera house built by the town in honor of its famous son; to a museum in the Villa Pallavicino, where a few rooms are given over to Verdi memorabilia, including a piano he played as a child; and to the rough stone farmhouse where he was born and raised in the center of Le Roncole. Part of the Verdi villa at Sant'Agata, still a private home, is also open to the public from April through October (admission charge). Visitors can see the composer's bedroom studio and a library, the bedroom of his second wife, singer Giuseppina Strepponi, a death chamber replicating the Milan hotel room where he died, and the surrounding gardens. For information, contact the tourist information office, 24 Piazza Giuseppe Verdi (phone: 524-92487).

Return to Via Emilia and continue east toward Parma 4 miles (6 km) to Fidenza and follow the signs to Salsomaggiore, one of Italy's most renowned spas. At the foot of the Appenine Mountains, the town has many boutiques, elegant cafés, antiques shops, and art galleries. In addition to the baroque spa center, many hotels offer their own thermal facilities, including massages, baths, and mudpacks. The tourist office (4 Viale Romagnosi; phone: 524-78265) can provide information on the town's events and hotels. (Also see *Spas,* DIVERSIONS.)

Return to Via Emilia and head east 13 miles (21 km) to Parma.

CHECKING IN: ***I Due Foscari*** – A small hotel in Gothic-Moorish style, owned by tenor Carlo Bergonzi and named after one of Verdi's operas, that offers 18 pleasant rooms near the center of town and has a restaurant with a terrace for outdoor dining in summer. Maestro Bergonzi also holds singing classes here. Restaurant closed Mondays and most of August. 15 Piazza Carlo Rossi, Busseto (phone: 524-92337; fax: 524-91625). Moderate.

EATING OUT: ***Guareschi*** – The brainchild of writer-cartoonist Giovannino Guareschi (the author of the famous *Don Camillo*), this place offers fabulous meals served with delightful informality. The restaurant, now more like a museum of Guareschi's work, is run by his son Alberto. All of the vegetables, meat, poultry, butter, and bread are produced on the property. Feast on the roast duck and polenta, the house specialty, but be sure to leave room for the coffee-flavored zabaglione — you've never tasted anything quite like it. Open only on request, mainly to groups large enough to make it worth the owner's while (at least 10). To see the artwork, call for an appointment. No credit cards accepted. 160 Via Processione, Roncole-Verdi, Busseto (phone: 524-92495). Expensive to moderate.

Ugo – A tastefully modern small restaurant where Ugo and family prepare delicious pasta, grilled meat, and excellent desserts. Closed Mondays, Tuesdays, and all of January. Reservations advised. Major credit cards accepted. 3 Via Mozart, Busseto (phone: 524-92307). Moderate to inexpensive.

PARMA: Despite heavy bombing during World War II, Parma retains the splendor it knew as the capital of the Farnese dukes from the mid-16th to the early 18th century. The French Bourbons succeeded the Farnese family, and then Napoleon annexed the duchy to France for a time. After his downfall, the Congress of Vienna awarded it to Marie Louise of Austria, Napoleon's second wife, who settled in for a long stay as duchess (1816–47) and added her own touches to the city.

Parma's elevated reputation among Italians is based largely on two factors. First, it is said to be one of Italy's most graceful and gracious towns, known not only for its architectural and artistic treasures but also for the courtly good manners of its people. Second, it has given Italy and the world *parmigiano* (parmesan cheese) and *prosciutto di Parma* (Parma ham). Free guided tours in English of the parmesan and prosciutto factories can be arranged by request. Contact *Il Prosciutto di Parma* (8 Via Marco dell'Arpa; phone: 521-208187) and *Consorzio il Parmigiano Reggiano* (26/C Via Gramsci; phone: 521-292700). Parma is so rich agriculturally that its new nickname is "Food Valley." One result is *Cibus,* a gastronomic fair held in May, said to rival those in Paris and Cologne.

Two painters of the early 16th century are associated particularly closely with Parma: Antonio Allegri (known as Correggio because he was born in that nearby town), who worked extensively in Parma, and Il Parmigianino, who was born and worked here. In addition, Parma provides the setting for Stendhal's classic novel *The Charterhouse of Parma,* and it has quite a few musical associations besides its nearby links to Verdi. Arturo Toscanini was born in Parma; Niccolò Paganini, the virtuoso violinist, was born elsewhere but is buried here. The opera house built by Marie Louise, the *Teatro Regio* (Via Garibaldi), is considered one of the most beautiful in Italy, and its audience is believed to be the toughest, perhaps in the world — the normal courtly good manners are nowhere in evidence if an operatic performance is merely mediocre.

The architectural beauty spots of the town are many, although the Duomo, the Baptistry, and the Chiesa di San Giovanni Evangelista (Church of St. John the Evangelist) — all part of the *centro episcopale,* on an ancient cobbled square in the historic heart of town — must have first claim to a visitor's attention. The Lombard-Romanesque Duomo was built in the 11th century, its campanile in the 13th century. Inside, the chief works of art are the *Deposition* bas-relief (on the west wall of the south transept) carved by sculptor Benedetto Antelami in 1176; the bishop's throne, which also has reliefs by Antelami; and Correggio's famous *Assumption of the Virgin* fresco (now restored) on the ceiling of the dome, painted from 1524 to 1530. This swirling ascent of concentric circles of figures is a stunning sight, anticipating the baroque in feeling, even though it was once unkindly described as a "hash of frogs' legs."

Building of the extraordinary, multi-tiered, octagonal Baptistry began in 1196, and when it was completed in the next century, Parma was graced by one of the finest ecclesiastical structures of the age. The work of Antelami adorns the doors, and the series of reliefs of the months and the seasons inside is also his, but some of the 13th-century ceiling frescoes are by an unknown hand. San Giovanni Evangelista, behind the Duomo, is noted for another ceiling fresco by Correggio, this time of St. John (the scene of St. John writing the Apocalypse over a doorway in the left transept is another Correggio), and for numerous frescoes by Parmigianino.

Not far from the *centro episcopale,* on the banks of the Parma River, is the giant and rather gloomy-looking Palazzo della Pilotta, begun as a complex of barns, an armory, and barracks by the Farnesi in the late 16th century but never finished. It is, however, big enough. The name derives from *pelota,* a Basque version of handball that was played in its vast, echoing chambers. Today the palace houses a complex of museums, including the *Galleria Nazionale* (National Gallery), the *Museo Nazionale Archeologico* (National Archaeological Museum), and the *Biblioteca Palatina* (Palatine Library), plus a theater, the *Teatro Farnese.* The *National Gallery* has some fine paintings by non-Emilian masters, such as Fra Angelico and Da Vinci, as well as a variety of works by Correggio and Parmigianino. It's considered one of Italy's finest art museums. The *Palatine Library* incorporates a museum dedicated to Giambattista Bodoni, the 18th-century printer, who worked in Parma. The most extraordinary sight in the Palazzo della Pilotta, however, is the *Teatro Farnese.* Although the original was lost when the palace was bombed in World War II, the precise reconstruction that now stands is more than enough to give 20th-century visitors a sense of the lavish life lived at a ducal court. This giant Palladian-style folly held 4,500 spectators and was in use from 1628 to 1732. Made entirely of wood, it's too much of a fire hazard to be used today. The palazzo is at Piazza Pilotta and is open daily except Mondays from 9 AM to 7:30 PM in summer and from 9:30 AM to 2 PM in other seasons (weekends to 1:30 PM); admission charge.

For more of Correggio's work, go to the Camera del Correggio (off Via Melloni, not far from Piazza Marconi). It's actually a room in the former Convent of San Paolo decorated with the artist's earliest frescoes, the spirit and subject matter of which (mythological scenes, greenery, and *putti*) hardly seem monastic. Tickets are available at the *National Gallery* entrance. Also worth a look is the majestic 16th-century Chiesa della Madonna della Steccata (Via Garibaldi), damaged by bombs in the last war but admirably restored; open 7 AM to noon and 3 to 7 PM (to 6 PM in winter). It contains Parmigianino frescoes, tombs of the Farnese family, and the tomb of Field Marshal Count Neipperg, Marie Louise's second husband. Parma's tourist office (APT, 5 Piazza del Duomo; phone: 521-233959 or 521-234735) has information on still other sights.

Just 9 miles (14 km) south of Parma via the provincial road signposted Traversetolo is an interesting spot for art lovers — the *Fondazione Magnani-Rocca* in the Villa di Corte di Mammiano (18 Via Vecchia di Sala, Traversetelo; phone: 521-848327 or 521-848148; fax: 521-848337). Opened in 1990, it houses a very rich collection of classic and contemporary paintings from artists such as Gentile da Fabriano, Fillippo Lippi, Tiziano, Dürer, Rubens, Van Dyck, Goya, Monet, Renoir, Cézanne, De Pisis, Morandi, and many others. Open daily except Mondays from 10 AM to 5 PM; closed mid-November to mid-February. Admission charge.

CHECKING IN: ***Palace Hotel Maria Luigia*** – Not far from the train station and within easy walking distance of the major sights, this modern, elegant hotel has 105 rooms and a well-regarded restaurant, *Maxim's* (no relation to the one in Paris). Closed Sundays and August. 140 Viale Mentana, Parma (phone: 521-281032; fax: 521-31126). Expensive.

Park Hotel Stendhal – Modern, comfortable, and well run, in the center of town. There are 60 rooms, all with bath and air conditioning. The restaurant, *La Pilotta,* is excellent; the bar next to the foyer is exceptionally friendly and well stocked.

Closed Sunday evenings, Mondays, and most of August. 3 Via Bodoni, Parma (phone: 521-208057; fax: 521-285655). Expensive.

Savoy – A good choice for budget travelers, on a quiet side street in the center of town. The 21 rooms are good value for the money, and the service is first rate. No restaurant. Closed December 23 to *New Year's Day* and August. 3 Via XX Settembre, Parma (phone: 521-281101; fax: 521-281103). Moderate.

EATING OUT: ***Angiol d'Or*** – The specialties that made Parma famous are served here, and any pasta dish *alla parmigiana* is sure to be a winner. Follow with one of the excellent beef, veal, or pork dishes as a second course. Closed Sunday evenings, Monday lunch, late August, and early January. Reservations necessary. No credit cards accepted. 1 Via Scutellari, Parma (phone: 521-282632). Expensive to moderate.

La Filoma – This stylish restaurant has been a favorite for so long that it's sometimes in and sometimes out of fashion. Try the *tortelli d'erbetta,* large ravioli-type pasta stuffed with beetroot greens, ricotta, and parmesan cheese. The *tortelli* traditionally were made for the town's *San Giovanni Festa* (June 24); due to popular demand, however, they are now produced year-round. Closed Sundays and during August. Reservations necessary. Major credit cards accepted. 15 Via XX Marzo, Parma (phone: 521-234269). Expensive to moderate.

Parizzi – One of Parma's best known — and busiest — restaurants. The local specialties are best; particularly delicious are the seafood and the crêpes stuffed with parmesan cheese. A good second is *stinco del santo,* a complicated pun (*stinco* is a cut of beef; in slang, a *stinco del santo* is someone who is too good to be true), but it adds up to a delicious beef casserole. Closed Sunday evenings, Mondays, and July 21 to August 17; open for lunch on weekends only. Reservations necessary. Major credit cards accepted. 71 Strada della Repubblica, Parma (phone: 521-285952). Expensive to moderate.

Vecchio Molinetto – A fine, old-fashioned, family-run dining place, with rustic decor and a menu that falls squarely in the hearty country category. There are excellent homemade pasta and veal dishes, and a delicious stuffed, boned chicken is the specialty of the house. All can be enjoyed in a nice little garden during the summer. There's a good choice of wines, especially the local colli di Parma selections, which include a refreshing malvasia white. Closed Fridays, Saturdays, and August. Reservations necessary. No credit cards accepted. 39 Viale Milazzo, Parma (phone: 521-52672). Moderate to inexpensive.

MODENA: Bypass Reggio Emilia and continue on to this large industrial city, the next stop along the Via Emilia (SS9), 35 miles (56 km) from Parma. The Este family brought it out of the bloody Middle Ages and conferred a long period of prosperity and prominence on it, through the Renaissance and beyond. The relative calm of the ducal period came to an abrupt end with the Napoleonic wars and subsequent Austrian domination, but the city rebelled twice and by the middle of the 19th century had dispatched the foreigners for good. Like Piacenza and Parma, it was an early member of the "new" Italy. Today, Modena is, above all, an automobile city. Three of the greatest names in Italian automobile design — Ferrari, Maserati, and De Tomaso — have their factories here. In addition, Modena is famous for its sparkling red lambrusco wine, for the walnut liqueur nocino, for *aceto balsamico* (balsamic vinegar), and for a local delicacy, *zampone* (stuffed pig's trotter), eaten all over Italy at *New Year's Eve* dinner. The great Italian opera singer Luciano Pavarotti is a local made good.

Today, most of Modena is newly built, a large part of it dating from the postwar period. However, a kernel of the Old Town remains around the Duomo. Begun in 1099 and consecrated in 1184, it was designed by Lanfranco, an architect from Lombardy, and decorated by Wiligelmo, a master sculptor who did the four friezes on the façade.

Dedicated to Modena's patron saint, St. Geminiano, it is one of Italy's best preserved Romanesque cathedrals. The Torre Ghirlandina, the tall, graceful Lombardian bell tower next to the cathedral, is one of the city's most conspicuous landmarks, completed in the early 14th century. Behind the cathedral is Modena's Piazza Grande, which has been the traditional marketplace of the city for centuries. Even today, on the last Sunday of every month (except in July and December), it is the focal point of a giant antiques market where it's fun to rummage through bric-a-brac, artwork, furniture, musical instruments, suits of armor, "genuine" religious relics, jewelry, and plain old junk, all available for prices far lower than those at comparable flea markets in Rome or Florence.

This town of motor racing and legendary factories is worth discovering from the factory floor. The Maserati operation offers tours on Mondays, Wednesdays, and Fridays after 5 PM by appointment only (English-speaking guides are available; admission charge). Contact *Maserati Automobile* (322 Via Ciro Menotti; phone: 59-21760; fax: 59-219669). Although only owners of Ferraris can gain access to its legendary plant (proof of ownership required), the next best thing is to visit the *Galleria Ferrari* (43 Via Dino Ferrari; no phone) in Maranello, just 7 miles (11 km) south of Modena via S12. Opened in 1990, this museum's 3 floors are a visual narration of the many stages the car has gone through over the years. On display are vintage vehicles, as well as the latest racing models. Open daily except Mondays from 9:30 AM to 12:30 PM and from 3 to 6 PM; admission charge.

One additional worthwhile sight is the *Palazzo dei Musei,* along Via Emilia at Largo Porta Sant'Agostino. It contains various museums and picture galleries, but the most noteworthy installation is that of the Biblioteca Estense (Este Library), which houses thousands of books and illuminated manuscripts. Among the treasures on display is the 1,200-page *Bible of Borso d'Este* — a tour de force of 15th-century illumination. Closed Mondays; admission charge. Modena's tourist office is at 3 Corso Canalgrande (phone: 59-222482; fax: 59-220686).

CHECKING IN: ***Fini*** – Modena's best hotel has 92 attractively decorated rooms and all the modern amenities, even hair dryers in the bathrooms. It's on the outskirts of town, in the direction of Bologna and thus not near the restaurant under the same management (see *Eating Out*). But guests can be shuttled back and forth via a complimentary limousine. Closed 3 days in August and at *Christmastime.* 441 Via Emilia Est, Modena (phone: 59-238091). Very expensive.

Roma – The ideal place to stay given its central, yet quiet, location. Its 55 rooms are spacious and comfortable. No restaurant. 44 Via Farini, Modena (phone: 59-222218 or 59-223618; fax: 59-223747). Moderate.

Villa Gaidello Club – In the beautiful countryside surrounding Modena, a charming stone farmhouse offers old-fashioned apartments for overnights or more. Superb simple meals are available upon request from the farm's own backyard. Closed August. About 9 miles (14 km) southwest of Modena. Reservations necessary. 20 Via Gaidello, Castelfranco, Emilia, Modena (phone: 59-926806). Inexpensive.

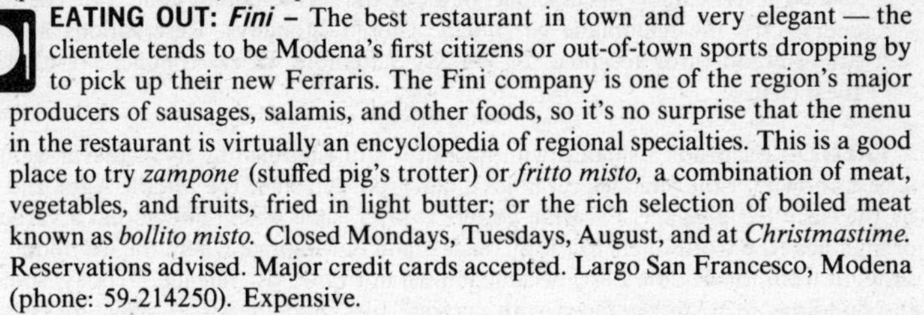

EATING OUT: ***Fini*** – The best restaurant in town and very elegant — the clientele tends to be Modena's first citizens or out-of-town sports dropping by to pick up their new Ferraris. The Fini company is one of the region's major producers of sausages, salamis, and other foods, so it's no surprise that the menu in the restaurant is virtually an encyclopedia of regional specialties. This is a good place to try *zampone* (stuffed pig's trotter) or *fritto misto,* a combination of meat, vegetables, and fruits, fried in light butter; or the rich selection of boiled meat known as *bollito misto.* Closed Mondays, Tuesdays, August, and at *Christmastime.* Reservations advised. Major credit cards accepted. Largo San Francesco, Modena (phone: 59-214250). Expensive.

Aurora – An intimate restaurant with good service and excellent food, very close to Piazza Grande. The roast veal is particularly good, as is the *pasta alla zucca* (pasta in squash sauce), and seafood dishes. Closed Mondays. Reservations necessary. Major credit cards accepted. 9 Via Taglio, Modena (phone: 59-225191). Moderate to inexpensive.

BOLOGNA: This historic city of red slate roofs, long arcades, and distinctive domes is roughly 24 miles (38 km) down the Via Emilia from Modena. It is a hub of commerce and learning, renowned for its university — one of the oldest in Europe — and a gastronomic center of no small repute. For a detailed report of the city, its sights, hotels, and restaurants, see *Bologna,* THE CITIES.

En Route from Bologna – Continue southeast in the direction of Imola and Faenza, respectively 20 miles (32 km) and 30 miles (48 km) from Bologna via the Via Emilia (SS9). About halfway between Castel San Pietro Terme and Imola is the turnoff for Dozza, a charming hill town crowned by a majestic castle built between 1200 and 1600. In September of odd-numbered years, the outside walls of many of Dozza's houses are painted with murals, the work of artists taking part in the *International Festival of the Painted Wall.* The best frescoes — and among them figure some of the works of important, internationally known artists — are eventually removed and put on display in a gallery in the castle. The onetime castle dungeons have become the headquarters of the wine growers' guild of Emilia-Romagna, an *enoteca* (cellar) where their wines can be sampled and purchased. Imola itself doesn't have quite the charm of some of the other cities in the region, although it does have a 14th-century castle housing a good collection of arms and armor, not to mention the famous Formula One racing circuit. Stop at the Palazzo Tozzoni to see a more realistic view of noble living than is usually apparent. The family memorabilia is touching, and the cultural life of the time is charmingly documented. For lovers of fine food, however, Imola is one of the most important stops in the entire Emilia-Romagna region, as it is the home of one of Italy's finest restaurants, the *San Domenico* (below).

EATING OUT: *San Domenico* – Housed in a little cottage — part of a former convent — facing the castle, this delightful restaurant consistently serves some of the best food in the country. The fare is a blend of festive dishes that would have been served at the aristocratic tables of yesteryear and latter-day nouvelle cuisine, and everything is always expertly prepared and beautifully presented. The prix fixe menu of seven courses changes with the season. Fresh grilled salmon with sour cream and caviar, braised pheasant with *porcini* mushrooms, tortellini with cream of goose liver, and Bavarian *semifreddo* for dessert might be among the choices. Closed Mondays, the first 2 weeks of January, and late July to mid-August. Reservations necessary. Major credit cards accepted. 1 Via Sacchi, Imola (phone: 542-29000). Very expensive.

Canè – A tiny hotel restaurant just down the street from the castle in Dozza. Its shaded terrace offers spectacular views of the fertile countryside. For the pasta course, try the handmade *garganelli.* Closed Mondays. Reservations advised. Major credit cards accepted. 27 Via XX Settembre, Dozza (phone: 542-678120). Inexpensive.

FAENZA: Faenza is a small town, most of it still encircled by its medieval walls. It is best known for the maiolica ceramics it has produced since the Middle Ages. Indeed, by the early Renaissance, Faentine potters enjoyed such wide renown that a variation of maiolica (the word refers to the Spanish island of Majorca, where the technique was brought from the Middle East) became known in France as "faïence." Today, some of the buildings in town are faced with ceramic tiles, and the street signs are ceramic plaques. Any number of artisans are at work in and around Faenza, and any number of shops offer vast assortments of their wares — among the best are *Bottega d'Arte Ceramica Gatti* (4 Via Pompignoli); *Morigi Mirta* (7 Via Barbavara); and *Geminiani Silvana* (52 Corso Mazzini), although generally, modern examples are but a shadow of the glory achieved in earlier work. The industry that put Faenza on the map has also spawned a museum, the *Museo Internazionale delle Ceramiche* (International Museum of Ceramics; 2 Via Campidoro; phone: 546-21240). Large and well designed, it covers the history, manufacture, and decoration of ceramics from every corner of the globe, from the dawn of time to the present, but the extensive collection of old Italian ceramics is particularly noteworthy. There is also a modern section, containing pieces by artists such as Matisse, Chagall, and Picasso. Closed Mondays; admission charge.

There also are a number of events highlighting ceramics. The *Estate Ceramica* (Summer of Ceramics), held annually from the fourth Sunday in June until the end of September in the Piazza del Popolo, offers a good opportunity to examine the latest creations and to endulge in a shopping spree. In addition, from July to October in even-numbered years, there is the *Exhibit of Antique Ceramics* at the Palazzo delle Esposizione (92 Corso Mazzini). The *International Show of Artistic Ceramics* takes place in odd-numbered years at the Piazza del Popolo. For information, contact the tourist office (1 Piazza del Popolo; phone: 546-25231).

En Route from Faenza – Keeping to the Via Emilia, the Adriatic coast at Rimini is now only 40 miles (64 km) away. A few small towns, however, make interesting deviations from the straight and narrow. One is the spa town of Brisighella, just south of Faenza, on SS302. This beautiful little hill hamlet is dominated on one peak by a 14th-century castle and on another by a 13th-century clock tower. The whole town is extremely picturesque, particularly its central piazza, which is overlooked by a curious, arcaded main street, Via del Borgo. Another detour can be made for Predappio, just south of Forlì. This tiny village has earned an unenviable place in history as the birthplace, and resting place, of the dictator Benito Mussolini. The Mussolini crypt at the cemetery of San Cassiano in Appennino, containing the tomb of Il Duce, as well as other family members, is open to the public. A spotlighted bust of the dictator glowers down at visitors, and a guestbook set before his tomb is filled with messages from the unrepentant few who continue to make the pilgrimage to their leader. From Predappio, drive over some rolling hill country (via the town of Meldola, then back to the Via Emilia, turning south off it just past Forlimpopoli) to another quaint town, Bertinoro, which produces some of the region's best known wines. In its main square the village has a *colonna dell'ospitalità* (hospitality post), which is actually a tall stone column with wide metal rings in its sides, each ring corresponding to the home of a local family. Although it is a modern reconstruction, its site is that of a post set up in the 13th century to settle disputes among the townsfolk as to who would play host to travelers (everyone, it seems, was only too eager to oblige). The idea was that a traveler would tie his horse to a particular ring, and that family would welcome the traveler for the night.

Note that just before Rimini comes the epic crossing of the Rubicon. Travelers pass over the legendary river just as Julius Caesar did in 49 BC, except that Caesar was moving south from Gaul to Rome when he forded it. Regrettably, the event is hardly notable these days, for the river is now an uninspiring ditch at Savignano, between Cesena and Rimini.

EATING OUT: ***Antica Cantina Pasini*** – This ancient wine cellar perched on a hillside serves a hearty lunch of good cold cuts, sausages, and crusty bread. It's also pleasant to sample some of the local wines: the sweet, white albana amabile, the drier albana secco, the medium-dry white pagadebit, and the full-bodied red sangiovese. Closed Tuesdays. Reservations unnecessary. No credit cards accepted. 3 Via Francesco Rossi, Bertinoro (phone: 543-445667). Inexpensive.

La Grotta – An intimate, first class eatery housed in a hollow scraped out of the giant rocks of the mountainside of Brisighella. The food is excellent, the service flawless, and the high overall quality of the place seems a bit out of sync with the modesty of the town (yet the prices are in keeping, because they're astonishingly reasonable). Three set menus are offered, ranging from a small sampling of one or two courses to a full four-course meal. Closed Tuesdays and the first 2 weeks in June. Reservations advised. Major credit cards accepted. 1 Via Metelli, Brisighella (phone: 546-81829). Inexpensive.

RIMINI: The Via Emilia comes to an end at Rimini, at once an ancient town and the most popular holiday resort on the Adriatic. The Lido di Rimini is a long, wide stretch of beach lined with hotels, bars, restaurants, souvenir stands, and discos that can be, by turns, sleazy, ultra-chic, or fun for the whole family. Foreigners descend on it by the tens of thousands each summer; in fact, Rimini gets so crowded that spur-of-the-moment visits in high season are probably a mistake — always have a reservation in hand unless you enjoy cruising crowded streets in desperate quest of accommodation. Bear in mind, too, that although there is much beach in Rimini, there is not much *public* beach (and there is a fee for the use of changing rooms, chairs, and umbrellas), so if the hotel you've selected has not staked a claim to its own portion of sand, there's a good chance you'll find yourself staring, hot and hostile, at all those tens of thousands of bathers enjoying beaches you can't visit. A sunny note: Most of the smaller hotels have recently joined forces to share beaches and make them available to their guests.

Difficulties notwithstanding, Rimini is just the place for those who like a fun-in-the-sun, dance-until-dawn summer vacation. While totally nude sunbathing is a no-no, topless women are the norm rather than the exception. At night, the beachfront main drags — Lungomare Tintori, Lungomare Murri, and parallel Viale Vespucci — draw hordes of boys and girls on the make, some "professional" talent, and carousers of every nationality. It almost looks like a scene from Federico Fellini, Rimini's most famous son. Those who like the Rimini scene come back again and again, as witnessed by the graffito near the train station that reads, in English: "Ciao Rimini, see you next year."

The historic center of Rimini, about half a mile (1 km) from the beachfront and separated from it by the railroad tracks, contains one sight of exceptional historic interest. This is the Tempio Malatestiano, a Gothic church converted in the 15th century into one of the most influential buildings of the Renaissance. Designed by the Florentine architect Leon Battista Alberti, who based the façade on Rimini's ancient Roman Arch of Augustus, it was one of the earliest Renaissance buildings to be based on an actual classical model. Alberti was in the employ of Sigismondo Malatesta, the tyrant of Rimini at the time but also a patron of the arts. Contemporaries have recorded that Malatesta was a brilliant man, with the ability to be very amiable when he chose, but it seems his wives saw little of that charm. He denounced one, poisoned the second, and strangled the third. Yet he was so full of love for his mistress Isotta that he raised the Tempio Malatestiano as a monument to her memory. The spacious interior is finely decorated with works of art and dotted here and there with the fanciful symbols of the Malatestas, the elephant and the rose. (The "S" superimposed by an "I" seen everywhere stands not for the dollar but for Sigismondo and Isotta.) The Tempio boasts, also, what must be the only souvenir stand in the world graced by a beautiful Piero della Francesca fresco.

The Arch of Augustus that inspired Alberti is the breach in the city wall at the end of Corso di Augusto. For other local sights, either the Azienda di Promozione Turistica (APT, Piazzale Cesare Battisti; phone: 541-27927), next to the train station, or the Azienda Autonoma di Turismo (Parco Indipendenza; phone: 541-24511) can provide information. Rimini is also one of the main jumping-off points for trips to the independent republic of San Marino, which is about 15 miles (24 km) away and which maintains its own information office in Rimini (Piazzale Cesare Battisti; phone: 541-56333), next to the APT. Many of the town's travel agencies organize excursions to this tiny country.

CHECKING IN: ***Grand*** – The grande dame of the Adriatic coast. Built in 1908, this giant 119-room Edwardian building still recalls the more opulent days of seaside resorts before World War I, even though it has been renovated from top to bottom. The entire hotel is decorated in lavish fin de siècle style, and the service is what would be expected of Rimini's premier hotel. As befits this premier position, the finest bit of Rimini seafront is reserved for its guests, but there is also a giant heated swimming pool on the extensive grounds for those who prefer fresh water. In addition, it has tennis courts and a sauna; the more sedentary will enjoy the fine bar. The restaurant, facing the water, serves very good food and also keeps a kosher kitchen. Closed November and December. 2 Piazzale Indipendenza, Rimini (phone: 541-56000; fax: 541-56866). Very expensive.

Club House – Squarely on the beach, each of its 28 rooms has a terrace, and the entire hotel is the last word in modern, high-tech convenience. From bed, guests can raise or lower the blinds, close the curtains, lock the door, and turn on a variety of gadgets, all at the touch of a button. No restaurant. Open year-round. 52 Viale Vespucci, Rimini (phone: 541-52166; fax: 541-391442). Expensive.

EATING OUT: ***Caffè delle Rose*** – The "Liberty" theme (as Art Nouveau is known in Italy) predominates in this very stylish place. Wicker tables and chairs, complemented by pink accessories, and dining on a large covered verandah amidst plants, help create a very pleasant *ambiente.* The food is well-prepared and refined, offering traditional fare with a sophisticated twist. There also is a piano bar where you can sip after-dinner coffee or a *digestivo.* Closed Tuesdays in low season. Reservations advised. Major credit cards accepted. 2 Viale Vespucci, Rimini (phone: 541-25416). Expensive to moderate.

Lo Squero – This attractive seaside dining spot has wonderful seafood and desserts. Closed Tuesdays. Reservations advised in high season. Major credit cards accepted. 7 Lungomare Tintori, Rimini (phone: 541-27676). Expensive to moderate.

Chicchibio – A small dining spot with wood paneling, reminiscent of an old English library, it serves typical local fare. Its specialties include homemade pasta and grilled and roast meat. Closed Sundays and August. Reservations necessary Saturday evenings. Major credit cards accepted. 11 Via Soardi, Rimini (phone: 541-26778). Moderate.

En Route from Rimini – Head north 5½ miles (9 km) on S9 to the small city of Cesena. Long overshadowed by its more famous neighbors, Bologna and Ravenna, Cesena is worth a stop, just to visit the Biblioteca Malatesta (Malatesta Library, 1 Piazza Bufalini; phone: 547-21297). Five centuries old, it is Europe's only perfectly preserved medieval library. Built by the Umbrian architect Matteo Nuti in 1452 for Prince Malatesta Novello, Cesena's enlightened ruler (1429–65), it steers away from rectangular halls and instead is a celebration of the arched vault, and naves and pillars. Multilingual guides take visitors past the *plutei* (reading desks made from cypress wood, carved with family crests), where you can stop and look at leaden tomes of superb illuminated manuscripts. The oldest is the *Etymologiae* of St. Isidore of Seville, dating from the 7th century. Open daily except Mondays from 8:30 AM to 12:30 PM and 4:30 to 7:30 PM from mid-June to mid-September. The rest of the year, it is open Mondays from 3 to 7 PM; Tuesdays through Fridays from 9 AM to 1 PM and 3 to 7 PM; Saturdays from 9 AM to 1 PM and 3 to 6 PM; and Sundays from 8:30 AM to 12:30 PM; admission charge.

Take S71 to Ravenna, 32 miles (51 km) north of Rimini via SS16. The Adriatic coast is lined with seaside resorts the whole way, each one, unfortunately, more tawdry than the last. A great exception is Cesenatico, 14 miles (22 km) north of Rimini. Today the town is a very pretty fishing village, but it was born in the early 14th century as a military port for the town of Cesena and can also claim to have been laid out in part by Leonardo da Vinci on behalf of Cesare Borgia. The central canal, dividing the town in two, is home to a permanently moored fleet of old fishing vessels and sailing barges. Farther along, Milano Marittima is an elegant resort. Just south of Ravenna, SS16 turns inland toward Ferrara, while the main coast road proceeds to Ravenna, passing the Chiesa di Sant'Apollinare in Classe, about 3 miles (5 km) south of the city. Stop here for a first look at Ravenna's magnificent mosaics. This beautiful building, standing where the ancient Roman port of Classis once stood, is notable for the simplicity of its 6th- and 7th-century designs. Ravenna's first bishop and martyr, Saint Apollinaris, is shown with the faithful depicted as lambs; Christ is surrounded by Apostles depicted as lambs; there is a great Latin cross surrounded by stars; and trees, birds, and flowers are in abundance.

EATING OUT: ***Gambero Rosso*** – A terraced restaurant that has won a Michelin star. Fresh fish is the specialty. Closed November through February. Reservations advised on weekends. Major credit cards accepted. 21 Molo Levante, Cesenatico (phone: 547-81260). Expensive.

Trattoria al Gallo – Try the mixed grill of fish in this friendly establishment that has been serving fresh seafood and mouth-watering homemade desserts for 20 years. Closed Wednesdays. Reservations advised. Major credit cards accepted. 21 Via Baldini, Cesenatico (phone: 547-81067). Expensive.

Gianni – This delightful and unusual spot is not only the best restaurant in Cesena, it's also the best value. The *zuppa di pesce* (fish soup) — locally known as *padella* — is unlike any other. The pasta dishes are superb. Closed Thursdays. Reservations advised. Major credit cards accepted. 9 Via Natale dell'Amore, Cesena (phone: 547-21328). Expensive to moderate.

La Buca – On the canal with tables outside in summer, this eatery is run by a seafaring family. The food is good, especially the fish and seafood, and the desserts are out of this world — but the prices are not. Closed Mondays, except in high season. Reservations advised. Major credit cards accepted. 41 Corso Garibaldi, Cesenatico (phone: 547-82474). Moderate.

RAVENNA: Ravenna's position in the history of Western Europe is unique. It existed as a Roman city even before Emperor Augustus founded the port of Classis just to the south. In the 5th century, after the Roman Empire had split into an eastern and a western section, it became the capital of the Empire of the West. It then went through a short period as a kingdom of the Goths. But at the height of its splendor, from the 6th century to the 8th century, while the western portion of the empire fell into the hands of many chiefs, it was part of the Eastern Roman Empire — the Byzantine Empire — and its dominant influence came not from the Italian peninsula, or even the rest of Europe, but from Constantinople. This eastern-facing stance marked the art and architecture of the city with the indelible imprint of Byzantium, first and foremost in the mosaic masterpieces that are the chief glory of Ravenna's early Christian churches. The most famous are in the Chiesa di San Vitale (17 Via San Vitale) and the adjacent Tomb of Galla Placidia, in the Orthodox Baptistry and the Arian Baptistry, and in the Chiesa di Sant'Apollinare Nuovo (Via di Roma).

San Vitale is an octagonal church built between 526 and 547, and probably based on a much older church in Constantinople. The upper gallery, beneath the dome, is the *matroneae,* an area once reserved for female worshipers. While the church itself is quite beautiful, the variety and complexity of the mosaics in the apse make San Vitale world famous. On the outer walls of the chancel are Old Testament scenes: on the left, Abraham and the three angels and the sacrifice of Isaac, and on the right, the death of Abel and the offering of Melchizedek. However, it is the inner part of the apse that is best known. Here presides the very grave figure of Empress Theodora with her retainers. Dressed in the ornate robes of the East, she looks out solemnly at the world, holding in her hands the chalice containing the wine of the sacrifice of Christ. Facing her, on the opposite wall, is Emperor Justinian, her husband, with his court, and by his side stands Archbishop Maximian, who consecrated San Vitale, holding the Eucharist. Blues, golds, and greens predominate, and the effect of the tiny mosaic tesserae, angled irregularly to catch and hold the light, is astonishingly beautiful.

In the same complex as San Vitale is the exquisite Tomb of Galla Placidia, the sister of the Emperor Honorius. It dates from the mid-5th century, and its mosaics are the oldest in Ravenna, still Roman rather than Byzantine in style. In some ways, the mosaics in this tiny, dark room are also more affecting than the ones in the main church, since they are closer to the eye and their symbolism is more personal, their execution more natural. The tomb is dominated by a tympanum mosaic of Christ the Good Shepherd and, facing that, one of St. Lawrence with the instrument of his martyrdom (a gridiron — he was roasted alive). In the transepts are some charming stags — representing souls — drinking from the Fountain of Life. The ceiling of the dome is deep blue, studded with countless stars. (*Note:* The coin box to light the tomb is outside, set in the wall facing the front door of the building.)

The Battistero degli Ortodossi (Orthodox Baptistry), also known as the Battistero Neoniano, adjoins the Duomo of Ravenna, which is largely an 18th-century baroque building. Originally a Roman-era bathhouse, it was dedicated to Christianity in the mid-5th century and is thus contemporary with the Galla Placidia tomb. The centerpiece of the mosaics in the dome here — betraying telltale signs of 19th-century restoration — is the baptism of Christ, the figures surrounded by Apostles as by the spokes of a wheel. The other baptistry, the Battistero degli Ariani (Arian Baptistry), is on a quiet side street (Via degli Ariani) not far from the main square of Ravenna, Piazza del Popolo. This structure, thought to have been built by Theodoric in the early 6th century, houses another set of brilliant mosaics with the sacrament of Baptism as a major theme.

The Basilica di Sant'Apollinare Nuovo is the last great treasurehouse of mosaics in the city. It was erected by Theodoric in the early 6th century and adapted for Christian use toward the mid-6th century by Justinian. Most, but not all, of the mosaics are from Theodoric's time — in fact, the transition from a classical Roman style to pure Byzantine is evident here. The mosaics of the two upper registers on either side (scenes from the life of Christ and prophets or saints) are from the era of Theodoric, as are the two city scenes on the lower friezes: the port of Classis, with its two lighthouse towers on the left frieze, and the palace of Theodoric, with the city of Ravenna behind it on the right frieze. The two glorious processions on the lower friezes, however, are from the time of Justinian, fully Byzantine. On the left is a procession of 22 virgins, preceded by the Magi marching toward the enthroned Virgin and Child. On the right, a procession of 26 martyrs moves toward Christ enthroned. They are the largest mosaics in Ravenna and are absolutely stunning.

A monument of an entirely different era is near the restored Church of San Francesco, not far from either Sant'Apollinare Nuovo or Piazza del Popolo. This is the Tomb of Dante, Italy's greatest poet. Exiled from his native Florence for political reasons, Dante spent his last years in Ravenna at the court of Guido da Polenta and finished his *Divine Comedy* here. He died on September 13, 1321, and his ashes are still in Ravenna (a portion of the ashes were kept in a Florence library until 1986, when they were proclaimed missing) — his tomb in Santa Croce in Florence is empty. Each year amid much pomp a Florentine delegation is dispatched to Ravenna to pay homage.

The tomb seen here today dates from 1780, covering another one of the late 15th century, beneath which is the actual resting place.

Ancient and modern mosaic tiles and figures remain a Ravenna art form. Two notable studios are *Studio Il Mosaico* (22 Via Argentario; phone: 544-36090) and *Artemosaico di Puglisi Liborio* (137 Via Cavour; phone: 544-23904). Check with the local APT (address below) for information on other studios. On the third Saturday and Sunday of each month, an antiques market is set up in the center of town.

The Ravenna Tourist Information Office is close to the town center (APT, 8 Via Salara; phone: 544-35404), north of Piazza del Popolo. A personal guide to the treasures of Ravenna is recommended: *Verdiana Conti Baioni* (9 Via Carrale; phone: 544-63154) grew up in one of Ravenna's museums, and her English is impeccable.

CHECKING IN: ***Park Hotel Ravenna*** – Slightly out of the way, in Marina di Ravenna, this large (146-room) resort hotel is a perfect compromise for those who want to do a little sightseeing in town and then relax on the beach, by the pool, or at tennis. Open April through October. 181 Viale delle Nazioni, Marina di Ravenna (phone: 544-531743; fax: 544-530430). Expensive.

Bisanzio – Comfortable rooms, a prime location for sightseeing and shopping, and free parking make this small, modern 36-room hotel an excellent choice. 30 Via Salara, Ravenna (phone: 544-27111; fax: 544-32539). Expensive to moderate.

Centrale Byron – For location rather than spacious quarters, try this very well run, simple hostelry with 57 rooms, only a step or two from the central piazza and in the midst of Ravenna's very good shopping district. No restaurant. 14 Via IV Novembre, Ravenna (phone: 544-22225; fax: 544-32539). Moderate to inexpensive.

EATING OUT: ***Tre Spade*** – Considered the best restaurant in town, its menu is vast, the food well prepared and very good. Try the turkey smothered in walnut sauce. The risotto with shrimp, *porcini* mushrooms, and saffron will appease even the most demanding palate. Closed Mondays, Sundays (from March through November), and July 25 to August 31. Reservations advised. Major credit cards accepted. 35 Via Rasponi, Ravenna (phone: 544-32382). Expensive.

Ca' de Ven – This huge old *enoteca* (wine cellar) is one of the nicest dining spots in town. A Ravenna institution, it's famous for a local creation called *piadina:* a bready pancake fried on a griddle and brought to the table warm, along with a huge platter of ham, salami, mortadella, and cheese. The wines served here, as might be expected, are exquisite, particularly the local pagadebit. Closed Mondays. Reservations unnecessary. No credit cards accepted. 5 Via Ricci, Ravenna (phone: 544-30163). Inexpensive.

En Route from Ravenna – Take SS16 north out of Ravenna to Ferrara, only 45 miles (72 km) away.

FERRARA: Like Bologna, 30 miles (48 km) to the south, Ferrara has — unjustly — been left off the itineraries of most foreign visitors to Italy, although it is familiar to some as the setting of Vittorio De Sica's *The Garden of the Finzi-Continis,* based on the book by Giorgio Bassani. While not a very large city, it has a colorful history and is rich in art and architecture, most of it in the beautiful, quaint medieval heart of town dominated by the giant Castello Estense (Castle of the Este Dukes). The size and prominence of the castle are telling reminders of the importance of the family in the history not only of the city but also well beyond its walls. Ferrara was the seat of the Este family from the 13th century to the very end of the 16th century, and during that time it was a cultural stronghold of the Renaissance in northern Italy. Few royal families lived with quite the splendor of the Dukes and Duchesses of Ferrara — they were famous for the luxury of the palaces they built, for the lavishness of their hospitality, and for the richness of their garb. They were also noted patrons of the arts, their court a meeting place for the most famous poets, painters, and philosophers of their age. Ludovico Ariosto and Torquato Tasso, writers of two of the great classics of Italian literature, were in the dukes' service.

The city flourished under Este patronage; in fact, at the end of the 15th century, Duke Ercole I embarked on a plan to double Ferrara's size by building a new urban quarter — the area known as the Herculean Addition — north of the castle. Later dukes consolidated the family's power and prestige. Ercole's son Alfonso I married Lucrezia Borgia; their son Ercole II married Renée, daughter of Louis XII of France (another son, an Este cardinal, built the Villa d'Este at Tivoli, near Rome). The marriage didn't work out, and Ercole exiled his royal wife for political reasons. That the move was accomplished without any repercussion is a sign of just how powerful the Estes had become. The end came swiftly, however. In 1598, the duchy was annexed to the Papal States, because the Estes failed to produce a legitimate male heir. A branch of the family lived on in Modena and Reggio Emilia, but with the loss of Ferrara its glory days were gone.

Begin by visiting the castle, right in the center of town (and just opposite the tourist office, which is at 22 Largo Castello; phone: 532-35017). Protected by a moat and three drawbridges, this giant building was begun in 1385 as a response to a revolt by the townspeople over a tax increase, in which the ducal tax collector was beheaded by the mob. The castle was finished some 2 centuries later. It now houses provincial offices, but some of the rooms in which the Estes lived are open to the public. Among these are the large and small Games Rooms, so called because of the theme of the frescoes decorating the ceiling — athletic games — and the Aurora Room, decorated with four frescoes showing different hours of the day. Beyond is the tiny chapel of the unhappy princess Renée (Renata, in Italian), one of the few old Protestant places of worship in Italy. (Princess Renée, an ardent Protestant, sheltered John Calvin in the city during the 1550s.) The last act of a particularly sordid chapter in Este family history was played out in the dungeons beneath the northeast tower. A 15th-century duke, Niccolò d'Este, discovered that his wife, Parisina Malatesta, was having an affair with Ugo, his illegitimate son. Niccolò imprisoned the two lovers in the dungeons and had them decapitated in 1425. The dungeons were in use as late as World War II, when first the Fascists and later the Nazis held political prisoners and resistance fighters there. Closed Mondays; admission charge. Behind the castle lies the old ghetto, which once housed one of the largest and most important Jewish populations in Italy.

A block from the castle is Ferrara's beautiful cathedral. Begun in 1135, it is remarkable for a wide marble triple façade, the upper portion of which is Gothic, the lower portion Romanesque. There is a stern Last Judgment over the main portal by a sculptor whose name has been lost to time. The cathedral museum inside contains two early-15th-century statues by the Sienese sculptor Jacopo della Quercia, late-15th-century works by Cosimo Tura, a master of the Ferrarese school of painting, as well as an unknown 12th-century master's sculptured reliefs of the months of the year that were part of a door on the south side of the cathedral. On the whole, the interior of the cathedral has been much altered, but outside, the cathedral itself, the beautiful and large adjacent piazza, and the towering campanile (a 15th-century addition) are so perfectly preserved they look as if they have been copied from a medieval painting illustrating the benefits of a just prince or good communal government. The façade of the Palazzo Comunale, however, is a 20th-century reproduction. Stroll down nearby Via San Romano and Via delle Volte ("Street of the Vaults," used to connect merchants' shops to sprawling warehouses in back) for a touch of medieval Ferrara.

On the edge of the historic center is the Palazzo Schifanoia (23 Via Scandiana), a home away from home for the ruling family. This noble building, begun in 1385 for Alberto V and greatly modified by Borso d'Este (whose famous Bible is in the museum in Modena) and by Ercole I in the late 15th century, was used primarily for the Estes' extravagant entertainments. It was their pleasure palace — hence the name, taken from the Italian words meaning "disgust" and "boredom." The frescoes in the Salone dei Mesi, by Francesco del Cossa, Ercole de' Roberti, and others of the Ferrarese school, make up one of the most important fresco cycles of the Renaissance with a profane theme. Zodiacal motifs and triumphs of the gods occupy the upper levels, but the lower levels, showing scenes of courtly life, with Borso d'Este figuring prominently in each one, are invaluable documents of the everyday existence of a great ducal family of the Renaissance. The palazzo now houses the numerous collections — illuminated manuscripts, ceramics, coins, medals, and so on — that make up the *Museo Civico.* Closed Mondays; admission charge.

Still another Este palace, the Palazzo dei Diamanti, stands at the corner of Corso Ercole I d'Este and Corso Rossetti. Built in the late 15th century by Duke Ercole I as the centerpiece of his Herculean Addition, the new Renaissance quarter he built (but never finished) to the north of the medieval part of town, it takes its name from the 8,500 diamond-shaped blocks of stone on its façade (the diamond was a symbol of the Este family). Inside the palace is the *Pinacoteca Nazionale,* the most important picture gallery in the city. The street is important in itself: Ercole I had it built and lined it with palaces, one after another, descending in height toward the end, where he had trees planted. From the castle, it looked like a long boulevard leading to the country, which was far from the truth. Closed Mondays; admission charge.

Other notable palaces built by members of the ruling family are not far from the Palazzo Schifanoia. The Palazzo di Ludovico il Moro (on Via XX Settembre) was built at the end of the 15th century by the Sforza husband of Beatrice d'Este. It is now the home of the *Museo Archeologico Nazionale* (National Archaeological Museum) and houses, among other curiosities, two Roman boats found in the region, each carved out of a single gigantic tree trunk, as well as Etruscan antiquities from the seaport of Spina. Also visit the Palazzina di Marfisa d'Este (at the far end of Corso della Giovecca), a small but beautiful 16th-century residence with elaborately painted ceilings, an outdoor theater, and a delightful garden. Both are closed Mondays; admission charge.

Today Ferrara is a uniquely friendly city, which with its perfect brick houses, swarms of bicycles (there isn't a hill in sight), and pea-soup fogs in winter resembles Bruges or Amsterdam rather than any place Italian. Because of its flat terrain and its green-bordered city walls, half the population jogs, more as an activity than a fitness regimen. Ferrara has produced winners in marathons the world over, including New York's. In the last week of August, the town hosts a curiosity, the *International Buskers Festival,* which draws street-corner musicians from all over the world. Don't miss the delightful open-air market with collector's items and "things from the past," held the first weekend of each month except August. For more information about the city, contact the tourist office at 19 Piazza Municipio (phone: 532-209370 or 419269).

CHECKING IN: ***Ripagrande*** – A restored 14th-century palazzo in the heart of the medieval section, it has 40 modern rooms, many with sitting rooms, kitchens, and second bathrooms. Ask for a room on the top floor — the rooms under the eaves have beautifully beamed ceilings and terraces with magnificent views. The attentive staff bends over backward to please. There is a good bar, quite a good restaurant, and a pleasant courtyard for alfresco breakfasts during the summertime. 21 Via Ripagrande, Ferrara (phone: 532-765250; fax: 532-764377). Expensive to moderate.

Ferrara – This modest 66-room hotel is perfectly situated just a stone's throw from the castle. 4 Piazza Repubblica, Ferrara (phone: 532-33015). Inexpensive.

EATING OUT: ***Buca San Domenico*** – The pizza here is the best in town, but there are many other good dishes as well. Closed Mondays, the first half of July, and the first half of January. Reservations advised. No credit cards accepted. 22 Piazza Sacrati, Ferrara (phone: 532-200018). Moderate.

La Provvidenza – The rustic atmosphere and a lovely garden provide a perfect setting in which to enjoy enormous quantities of fine fresh pasta, grilled meat, and great desserts. Closed Mondays and July. Reservations advised. Major credit cards accepted. 92 Corso Ercole d'Este, Ferrara (phone 532-21937). Moderate.

La Romantica – Across the street from the *Ripagrande,* this small spot lives up to its name, offering intimacy and discreet but attentive service. Start with *cappellacci di zucca alle noci,* a pasta stuffed with pumpkin and served with a walnut sauce. The filling harks back to the Middle Ages, when kosher cooking was prevalent around Ferrara — it has no dairy or meat in it and thus could be served with a meat second course. Closed Wednesdays, from January 25 to mid-February, and the last week in June. Reservations advised. Major credit cards accepted. 36 Via Ripagrande, Ferrara (phone: 532-765975). Moderate.

Grotta Azzurra – A popular place specializing in northern Italian cuisine. Closed Sundays and part of July. Reservations advised. Major credit cards accepted. 43 Piazza Sacrati, Ferrara (phone: 532-37320). Moderate to inexpensive.

San Marino

Every year, more than 3 million tourists visit San Marino, the oldest and smallest republic in the world. You might think that this number would overwhelm the country — considering that it has a population of only 22,000 and an area of only 23 square miles — and to a certain extent it does. At high noon on a midsummer day, it is sometimes hard to see San Marino's quaint charm beyond the droves of day-trippers and the gaudy displays of countless souvenir shops vying for their attention. But if that day is a clear one, look again. From any number of points in San Marino, the panorama embraces not only the Apennines to the south, expansive plains and hills to the north, the brilliant blue Adriatic to the east, but also the Yugoslav coast, 156 miles away. No doubt about it, San Marino's mountaintop setting is spectacular, and it is this, along with interesting historical sites and colorful remnants of the republic's long past, that makes a visit worthwhile.

San Marino lies 11 miles (18 km) from the Adriatic coast of north-central Italy, bordering the regions of Emilia-Romagna to the north and the Marche (Marches) to the south. Most visitors arrive from the coastal town of Rimini, and as you approach from this direction, the republic's distinctive "skyline" comes into view dramatically: Monte Titano (Mt. Titanus), at a height of 2,470 feet, with its three fortified peaks. The territory of San Marino consists of this mountain, with the capital, San Marino City, on top, and the surrounding hills, scattered with eight small villages or "castles" (*castelli*). The climate is temperate, thanks to its altitude and the ever-present "garbino" wind, with summer temperatures that rarely exceed 80F.

According to tradition, San Marino dates back almost 1,700 years, to AD 301 and the arrival of a Christian stonecutter from Dalmatia named Marinus. Fleeing the religious persecution of the Roman Emperor Diocletian, Marinus sought out the secluded safety of Monte Titano, where he built a chapel and began to live a saintly life. Other Christians soon followed him, giving rise to a free community that very early in its history developed the democratic institutions still governing it today.

San Marino's inaccessibility protected it throughout the period of the downfall of the Roman Empire and the subsequent barbarian invasions. Later, when covetous neighbors did cast eyes in its direction, it struggled valiantly to remain independent. Only twice was it unsuccessful, once in the 16th century, when it was occupied by Cesare Borgia, and again in the 18th century, when Cardinal Giulio Alberoni, legate in Romagna, took it upon himself to annex it to the Papal States. In each case, the loss of liberty lasted only a few months.

Along with its freedom, the country prides itself on a long tradition as a place of asylum. The Italian patriot Giuseppe Garibaldi was one of the most famous figures to have found refuge here, in 1849. During World War II, there were 100,000 refugees within its borders. Sadly, the republic was bombed in 1944, despite its proclaimed neutrality.

San Marino does have a small, picturesque, volunteer army. The blue uniforms, blue and white plumed headgear, and old-fashioned muskets and sabers of the militia and the Guardia del Consiglio Grande e Generale (the latter serves as an honor guard to the country's rulers) can be seen on special occasions. Guardsmen of the Guardia di Rocca, however, are on regular duty at the entrance to the government palace, and their green jackets, red trousers, red and white feathered caps, and vintage pistols are no less decorative.

The economy of the country is based on tourism, light industry, some farming, and the sale of postage stamps, which have considerable philatelic value. While the Italian lira is the local currency in common use, the minting of coins, mainly for collectors, is another source of revenue.

San Marino is accessible by bus, car, train, and even helicopter (see *Sources and Resources,* below).

The border is marked by a banner proclaiming, in Italian, "Welcome to the Ancient Land of Liberty." A passport is not needed to enter, and there is no customs control, despite the customs station.

Within minutes you are in Serravalle, the most populous of the *castelli.* Here there is evidence of industrial growth alongside one of the country's oldest and best-kept castles. Since the bestowal of Serravalle to San Marino in 1463, the republic's territory has not grown by a single inch. Not even Napoleon's offer to extend its borders in 1797 was accepted.

Continuing along the winding road is Domagnano, another of the "castles," to the left before arriving at Borgo Maggiore.

BORGO MAGGIORE: A market town established in the 12th century, and worth a stop. Originally known as Mercatale, its weekly open-air market, held on Thursdays, has been taking place since 1244. The porticoed Piazza di Sopra remains practically unchanged. Just off Piazza Grande, the main square, are two of San Marino's most important museums — the *Museo Postale, Filatelico e Numismatico* (Stamp and Coin Museum) and the *Museo delle Armi da Fuoco* (Firearms Museum; see *Museums*). Stop also for a look at the ultramodern Santuario della Beata Vergine della Consolazione (Sanctuary of the Blessed Virgin of Consolation), which was built in the 1960s and contrasts sharply with the town's medieval appearance.

En Route from Borgo Maggiore – San Marino City can be reached by foot along the shortcut called the Costa, by car, or by cable car.

SAN MARINO CITY: The Old City within the walls is entered through the Porta di San Francesco (St. Francis's Gate), begun in the 14th century as the doorway to a convent. Once inside, to the right, you will see the convent and the small Chiesa di San Francesco, both founded in 1361. Though this is the oldest church in the republic, only its façade gives away its age; much of the original character of the interior was lost in 17th- and 18th-century restorations. The cloister next door houses a gallery of changing exhibitions and a museum with some noteworthy old paintings, including one of St. Francis by Guercino.

From the Porta di San Francesco, San Marino's narrow streets must be explored on foot, and the ascent can be quite steep at times. Via Basilicius leads upward to the tiny Piazzetta del Titano, one of the social centers of the town. Not far off the square, on Contrada Omerelli, is the Palazzo Valloni, a structure partly of the 15th and partly of the 18th century. It houses the state archives, with documents dating from 885, as well as the government library. Until recently, it also contained the *Museo Pinacoteca di Stato* (State Art Gallery), which has been moved into storage until a decision is made about its permanent home. The street ends with the Porta della Rupe, the gate through which you enter the city if you take the shortcut from Borgo Maggiore.

To continue the ascent, return to Piazzetta del Titano and take the short walk up the hill to Piazza Garibaldi and the government stamp and coin office (Azienda Autonoma di Stato Filatelica e Numismatica; open daily except Sundays from 9 AM to 1 PM and 4:30 to 7:30 PM). Then turn and follow Contrada del Collegio up to Piazza della Libertà, the largest and most elegant of San Marino's squares. It takes its name from the 19th-century statue of liberty in the middle, but it's also known as the Pianello, since it's one of the few flat spaces within the walls. Off to the left is the mountain shelf and a spectacular view, while directly in front, dominating the square, is the Palazzo Pubblico, or government palace.

Although there has been a public building here since the early 14th century, today's Palazzo Pubblico dates only to the end of the 19th century, but it was built in an old-fashioned neo-Gothic style. If you want to arrive for the changing of the guard, stop at the nearby tourist office (on Contrada del Collegio; phone: 991435) for information on the time. It is open April through October. (For a fee, this office will also stamp your passport with an unnecessary, but official, San Marino visa.)

San Marino is governed by two captains regent chosen twice a year for 6-month terms by the Great and General Council, whose 60 members, in turn, are elected by popular vote and hold office for 5 years. When parliament is in session, your visit to the palace will be limited; otherwise, you will see its most important chamber, the richly decorated Sala del Consiglio, with the double throne of the two rulers at one end beneath a large allegorical painting featuring San Marino at its center. Two other rooms usually are on view, in addition to the atrium and the grand staircase, whose walls are covered with busts and inscriptions, works of art as well as symbols of the republic's past.

Among them is a bust of Abraham Lincoln, who was made an honorary citizen of San Marino in 1861. The *sammarinesi* (as the locals are known) are proud of the thank-you letter, preserved in the state archives, in which he said, "Although your dominion is small, nevertheless your State is one of the most honoured throughout history. . . ."

Beyond the Palazzo Pubblico, Contrada del Pianello leads to the cable car station. En route, it passes the Cava dei Balestrieri, the field on which the country's famous *Palio delle Balestre Grandi,* or crossbow competition, is held each year in September. From here, you can continue the climb by following Contrada Omagnano or by returning to Piazza delle Libertà. Either way, follow signs to the Basilica di San Marino. The mortal remains of the republic's founding saint are buried under the altar of this neo-classical church, which was built in the 19th century to replace an older church that stood on the spot.

From the basilica, more signs point through the oldest quarter of the city to the first of the three fortified towers that figure on the country's coat of arms. The tower, known as the Rocca or Guaita, dates from the 11th century, although in its overall appearance it is of the 15th century. San Marino is 2,465 feet above sea level at this point. You can climb to the top of the tower and enjoy the cool breezes blowing off the Adriatic as well as a splendid view. No admission charge.

The Rocca is joined by a watch path to the second tower, the Fratta or Cesta, on the highest point of Monte Titano (2,470 feet). This tower dates from the early 14th century and contains the *Museo delle Armi Bianche.*

If your legs have held out thus far, you may want to go along the less beaten path to the third tower, the Montale, although it is not open to the public. This narrow, graceful structure was in use from the 13th to the 16th century.

From the Montale Tower, a path leads down the slope to the modern Congress

Palace. Turn back toward the center along Viale J. F. Kennedy, Via Giacomo Matteotti, and Viale Antonio Onofri and you will see other modern buildings and, just up the hill, tennis facilities, all evidence of the present in this most ancient of states.

TOURIST INFORMATION: The main tourist office is in the historic center on Contrada Omagnano (phone: 882998). It is open weekdays from 8:15 AM to 2:15 PM and from 3 to 6 PM; closed Friday afternoons. Smaller outlets are at Piazza Mario Tini (phone: 905414; open May through September), Contrada del Collegio (phone: 991435), and Via XXVIII Luglio (phone: 902701). All are open weekdays from 8:30 AM to 12:30 PM and from 2:30 to 6:30 PM.

Local Coverage – The tourist office publishes *Practical Guide to San Marino,* an excellent free booklet in English, covering everything from cable car timetables to advice on how to cope with an overheated engine in traffic jams on the town's steep and narrow streets.

TELEPHONE: The area code for San Marino is 549. When calling from within Italy, dial 0549 before the local number.

GETTING AROUND: The nearest airports are at Miramare di Rimini (9 miles/14 km away) and Forlì (38 miles/61 km away). The closest train station is in Rimini. Travel by car is on the scenic four-lane highway from Rimini, though you also can reach the border along other well-paved but winding routes. San Marino is accessible by bus as well as by car, and even by helicopter.

Bus – The year-round bus service from Rimini departs several times a day, arriving about 45 minutes later in San Marino at either Piazzale della Stazione or Piazzale Marino Calcigni. Both stops are within easy walking distance of the historic center. Service within the country itself is good, with frequent buses available to most points of interest. Tickets, which cost 600 lire (about 46¢), must be purchased in advance from tobacconists or at newsstands.

Cable Car – Running nonstop in summer from Borgo-Maggiore to Contrada Omagnano — and on a reduced basis during winter — the service is headquartered right next door to the San Marino Tourist Office. Tickets cost 2,000 lire each (around $1.55), and can be bought at all cable car stops.

Car – You would do well to leave your vehicle in one of the 12 parking lots dotting the city. San Marino itself is small, with steep, winding streets, and is best explored on foot.

Helicopter – In summer, a helicopter service connects Rimini with Borgo Maggiore, one of San Marino's *castelli,* from which San Marino City is reachable via a cable car ride. For details, call Miramare Airport (phone: 337196), or contact a travel agent.

Taxi – The main taxi stand is in Piazzale della Repubblica (phone: 991441), but you also can order a cab by calling any of the following numbers: 903360, 900591, 902049, or 997444.

SPECIAL EVENTS: San Marino is at its traditional best during its holidays. In addition to the festivities at *Christmas* and *Easter,* two other choice days are April 1 and October 1, when members of San Marino's Great and General Council meet to elect two new captains regent to govern the republic for the next six months. The investiture ceremony, which takes place at these times, dates back to 1244 and attracts thousands of spectators. September 3 is set aside each year for a centuries-old crossbow competition, in which the people of San Marino gather at the Cava dei Balestieri, in the piazza near the main tourist office. The contest, complete with buglers and Renaissance costumes, celebrates the founding of the republic. Don't assume that this spectacle is staged for tourists alone. Actually, it was mandated by law in the early 17th century, even as crossbows were beginning to be superseded by more modern weaponry. Exhibitions are held at other times throughout the year as well, but even if you miss them, you still may catch sight of one of San Marino's crack crossbowmen engaged in target practice. Other public holidays that are recognized in San Marino include February 5, the *Feast of Saint Agatha,* the patron saint of San Marino; March 25, when the republic's small army marches through the streets, wearing colorful 18th-century costumes; and July 28, which marks the fall of fascism in Italy. Banks may be closed, but most shops tend to stay open on these days.

MUSEUMS: San Marino's museums are open daily from March through October from 8:30 AM to 12:30 PM and from 2:30 to 6 PM; from mid-June through mid-September from 8 AM to 8 PM; and in winter from 9 AM to 12:30 PM and from 2:30 to 5 PM. All have an admission charge. The following should not be missed:

Museo delle Armi Bianche – Housed in the Fratta (or Cesta) Tower, on the highest point of Monte Titano (2,470 feet), it features arms and armor from medieval times to the 20th century — as well as some magnificent views from its lookout points (phone: 882996).

Museo delle Armi da Fuoco (Firearms Museum) – An arms collection spanning the 14th to the 19th century, including a section dedicated to Garibaldi. Near Piazza Grande, Borgo Maggiore (phone: 882996).

Museo Auto Ferrari – For automobile enthusiasts, this small, but well-designed museum, contains a collection of gleaming Ferraris, from the earliest models to the famous Testarossa. Via Tonnini (phone: 990390).

Museo Pinacoteca di Stato (State Art Gallery) – The museum's collection of paintings and objects of historical and archaeological interest is temporarily closed to the public while a new home is being sought. Call the tourist office for current information.

Museo Postale, Filatelico e Numismatico (Stamp and Coin Museum) – One of San Marino's most important museums, it contains examples of all the stamps and coins issued by the republic, along with stamps from other countries. Borgo Maggiore, just off Piazza Grande (phone: 882996).

SHOPPING: Souvenirs of a very pedestrian nature are the most conspicuous items for sale in San Marino. Nevertheless, there are some legitimate buys. These include stamps and coins, as well as local wines (San Marino produces some excellent wines: sangiovese, a rich, robust red, and grilet, a naturally fermented sparkling dry white) and good liqueurs. You can sample, as well as purchase, these at the local wine cooperative, *Consorzio Vini Tipici* (Strada Serrabolino, 87 Valdragone, Borgo Maggiore; phone: 902124). For an idea of the local craft products available, go to the *Mostra dell'Artigianato* (Handicraft Exhibition) above the Piazzale Mario Giangi parking area, just off Viale Federico d'Urbino. Other stops to include on your shopping list include the following:

Costa Valerio e Susanna – Ceramics — both modern and antique — plus pottery, mostly hand-painted, by local craftsmen. 15 Salita della Rocca (phone: 991182).

Gioielleria Arzilli – A large, serious jewelry store, on a par with the best in Italy. The *Arzilli* links with goldsmithing go back several generations, and their wares — though certainly not inexpensive — are becoming known worldwide. 1 Via Donna Felicissima (phone: 992128 or 992038).

Marino Cesarini – One of San Marino's oldest dealers in stamps and coins, many of which are rare. Small antiques and objets d'art also are for sale. 2 Piazzale lo Stradone (phone: 991149).

Pasticceria Liberty – A bakery shop that features local cakes and pastries. You also can drop in for a spot of tea, or an aperitif before dinner. 1 Contrada San Francesco (phone: 991986).

Rafaella Antiquariato – Antique furniture and paintings — strictly Italian, French, and English. 104 Via 3 Settembre (phone: 905254).

Sir Paul – Men's and women's clothing, including some of Italy's best-known designer labels. 28 Contrada Santa Croce (phone: 992635).

SPORTS AND FITNESS: Fitness Centers – Workouts can be arranged at the *Palestra di Atletica Pesante* in Serravalle, one of the eight small towns just outside San Marino City. Strada la Ciarulla (phone: 901-1067).

Swimming – Not one but two pools (one's for kids) at the *Tavolucci* center, on the road from Borgo Maggiore to Serravalle. Via XXVIII Luglio (phone: 903354).

Tennis – Courts can be found at the *Tennis Club San Marino* (Via del Paron; phone: 991298) and the *Tavolucci* center (Via XXVIII Luglio; phone: 902011); and in Serravalle at *Tensport Serravalle* (Via Rancaglia; phone: 900111).

CHECKING IN: Expect to pay $55 or more per night for a double room in hotels rated as expensive; about $45 to $55 in those listed as moderate; and under $40 in inexpensive hotels. Note that most San Marino hotels close for a month or two in winter.

Grand Hotel San Marino – Just outside the Old City walls, this modern hotel is probably the most comfortable in town. Each of the 54 rooms has a private bath or shower and each of the front rooms has a balcony with a beautiful view of the Apennines. There is a restaurant, the *Arengo,* and a garage. Viale Antonio Onofri (phone: 992400; fax: 992274). Expensive.

Bolognese – There are only 5 rooms in this small, family-run hotel, but each is furnished with character, including some with solid wood antique bedsteads. The restaurant has a terrace for outdoor dining on warm summer evenings. 28 Via Basilicius (phone: 991056). Moderate.

Excelsior – Not as grand as its name suggests, but nevertheless a clean, comfortable 22-room hotel with an award-winning restaurant, as well as parking facilities. Viale J. Istriani (phone: 991163 or 991940; fax: 990399). Moderate.

La Grotta – This charming hostelry has 14 rooms, all with private bath or shower, and a pleasant restaurant. Contrada Santa Croce (phone: 991214). Moderate.

Joli – Just outside the city walls, this 20-room hotel is comfortable and friendly, with the added bonus of a garage. 38 Viale Federico D'Urbino, San Marino (phone: 991008). Moderate.

La Rocca – Most of the 10 rooms in this pleasant hotel on the way up to the Rocca have private balconies. It also boasts a swimming pool (albeit small), a rarity in San Marino hostelries. Salita della Rocca (phone: 991166). Moderate.

Titano – San Marino's first hotel, it opened in the 1890s, just a few steps from Piazza della Libertà. It has 50 rooms, all with bath or shower and some with a view. The panoramic terrace restaurant is one of the loveliest spots in town. 21 Contrada del Collegio (phone: 991006; fax: 991375). Moderate.

Diamond – Here are 7 inexpensive rooms for guests and one of the best restaurants in town. The building is quite unusual: it's been dug out of rock. Open daily from mid-March to mid-October. Contrada del Collegio (phone: 991003). Hotel, inexpensive; restaurant, moderate.

EATING OUT: A meal for two will cost from $45 to $70 in expensive restaurants and from $35 to $45 in moderate ones. All restaurants serve an economical tourist menu whose fixed price is prominently displayed. Most are closed for a month or two in winter.

Righi–La Taverna – In summer, the tables right on Piazza della Libertà are filled with tourists feasting on one-dish platters, pizza, and the grand view of the Palazzo Pubblico. But the local specialties also served at this 2-story restaurant make it very popular with the *sammarinesi* year-round. Open every day in summer; closed Wednesdays in winter and from mid-December through January. Reservations advised. Major credit cards accepted. Piazza della Libertà (phone: 991196). Expensive.

Il Beccafico – Centrally located and close to the Rocca, this eatery is decorated with crossbows and other ancient weapons with which the country has come to be identified. Specialties include typical San Marino dishes — ravioli stuffed with ricotta cheese and herbs, and *caciatello,* a dessert not unlike crème caramel and just as tasty. Open daily. Reservations unnecessary. Major credit cards accepted. 35 Via Salita alla Rocca (phone: 992430). Moderate.

Buca San Francesco – Straightforward cooking of San Marino and the neighboring Romagna region. Pasta dishes include *tagliatelle,* tortellini, and green lasagna, while second courses range from *scaloppine al formaggio e funghi* (with cheese and mushrooms) through grilled and mixed roast meat. Open daily from March through October. Reservations unnecessary. Major credit cards accepted. 3 Via Orafo (phone: 991462). Moderate.

La Fratta – This busy, cheerful restaurant specializes in spit-roasted meat, cooked over an open fire. It also turns out a very fine dish of homemade *tagliatelle con funghi porcini* (flat pasta with *porcini* mushrooms). A panoramic terrace offers alfresco dining. Open daily. Reservations advised. Major credit cards accepted. Salita alla Rocca (phone: 991594). Moderate.

Vecchia Stazione – Owned and operated by the Andreani brothers, who also operate the *Joli* hotel next door, this eatery has acquired a reputation for good traditional San Marino cooking. Try *nidi di rondine* (pasta rolls stuffed with ham, cheese, and tomato and baked in a bechamel sauce) and *coniglio porchetta disossato* (oven-roasted rabbit stuffed with fennel). Open daily. Reservations unnecessary. Major credit cards accepted. Viale Federico D'Urbino (phone: 991009). Moderate.

Tuscany

Nature has bestowed great gifts on almost every area of Italy, but it is widely agreed that Tuscany must surely be the most richly endowed region of all, the preferred child. There is nothing predictable about Tuscany's character — the open, cattle raising plains of the southern Maremma area are the perfect antithesis to the haughty grandeur of the Apennine Mountains — but there is one constant: a remarkable wealth of beauty, mellowed by history and tempered, ever so gently, by the hand of man.

If the landscape evokes a peculiar sense of familiarity, it is because it is almost inevitable that you have seen it all before. These gently undulating hills, punctuated by lone, dark cypresses and pines, and crowned by hilltop bastions, are the bucolic backdrop of every Raphael Madonna and every Botticelli nymph. The Renaissance masters superimposed the image of the Holy Land itself onto the Tuscan landscape — the same landscape that has triggered the genius and fired the soul of its people since the very earliest days of the pre-Roman Etruscans.

The ancient race that D. H. Lawrence described as "the long nosed, sensitive footed, subtly smiling Etruscans," first "appeared" in Tuscany. They were one of the most sophisticated Mediterranean civilizations of all times, yet only recently have advanced studies helped dispel our ignorance of them and lift a corner of the veil of mystery surrounding their lives and times. For centuries, Tuscan peasants left their land untilled, lest they disturb the Etruscans' reposing souls. What's more, nothing is left of their civilization aboveground, a result of the ephemeral wood with which they built their homes. Still, numerous brightly painted necropoli have been excavated beneath innocent forest-covered hills — the Etruscans, fortunately, were avid believers in a happy afterlife and left elaborate provisions for it. They were wise in the ways of agriculture, mining, and goldsmithing — three Tuscan inclinations that have survived well across the millennia — and they were surprisingly advanced (and not just for their time) in the manufacture of arms, for which they were known throughout Europe. Only now is it understood that they did not merely fade into oblivion but were gradually and perfectly integrated into a new Roman society sometime by the 1st century BC.

The Roman Empire grew from the seed of Etruria, the land of the Etruscans, actually a loose federation of 12 city-states that extended down into present-day Umbria and northern Lazio as well. The Roman Emperor Augustus declared Etruria a region, and then Diocletian reorganized it as Tuscia. Many centuries later, the regional perimeters were established as those we know today. That the towns of the region built their medieval walls upon Roman fortifications covering Etruscan foundations illustrates a process of continuing civilization that impresses even those who are not history buffs.

During the Middle Ages, Tuscany, as it came to be known (Toscana in

Italian), was a theater of constant warfare among the free communes of Lucca, Pisa, Florence, and Siena, with the continuing strife between the two medieval political factions — the pro-papal Guelphs and the pro-imperial Ghibellines — an added complication. Small, lofty hill towns, caught in the crossfire, fortified their naturally strategic positions with massive walls that became one with the hillside itself. Many of these towns never grew beyond their medieval walls or mentalities, having dreamed away the centuries. They tend to be tucked far back from the main arteries, but travelers who take the time to wend their way up to one of them are likely to find a one-tower, one-church settlement whose handful of families seem indifferent to the staggering view of mountains, valleys, and occasional plains that extend from their hushed *piazzetta.* Yet although their power and prestige are long gone, the Tuscans remain particularly proud of their resplendent patrimony. They are not entirely joking when they tell you that, while the Creator may be responsible for the beauty that is Tuscany, the designs were drawn up by Michelangelo.

Michelangelo and his contemporary Leonardo da Vinci were archetypal Tuscan and Renaissance men who headed an extensive roll call that was, without a doubt, the greatest company of genius ever assembled in one place at one time. It is difficult to circumscribe the Renaissance with actual dates. The 15th and 16th centuries were the indisputable apogee of this great period of art and thought. The 14th century, however, had already seen the arrival of the artist Giotto and three outstanding Florentine men of letters — Dante, Petrarch, and Boccaccio. They put the seal of approval on the Tuscan dialect by writing in the vernacular rather than in Latin, developed Italian literary style, and put Tuscan culture and manners on the map; they quite literally made Florence, and indeed all Tuscany, in D. H. Lawrence's words, "the perfect center of man's universe."

Florentine and other Italian artists, such as Donatello, Botticelli, and Raphael, later flourished under the tutelage of the Medici family, rulers of Florence and eventually Grand Dukes of Tuscany as well as insatiable patrons of the arts. The frescoes of Masaccio, Piero della Francesca, Fra Filippo Lippi, and Luca Signorelli can be found today in small country chapels or in the magnificent urban cathedrals that were the unprecedented engineering feats of architects such as Brunelleschi, the Pisano family, or Michelangelo (there was little he could *not* do).

For centuries, historians and curious travelers have marveled at the remarkable concentration of Renaissance genius that flowered within the confines of this small region. Why Tuscany? What was it about the Italian or Tuscan spirit that freed this avalanche of original thinking and artistic creativity and gave Western civilization its most fertile and exciting moment?

Italy had never completely forgotten its classical Roman heritage, whose rediscovery was the very essence of the Renaissance. Furthermore, the country had long been the crossroads for lucrative trade between the wealthy Orient and the merchants of the West, so that its cities grew rich financially as well as culturally. Tuscany, too, was the home of many prosperous monastic communities where advanced secular studies, such as the sciences and philosophy, were taken no less seriously than spiritual development. As a result, by the early 15th century, Florence had become an active and wealthy banking and commercial city whose political domain extended over most of the region. Florence's first family, the Medici, clever bankers themselves, even supplied the Vatican with a number of popes, and other family members soon assumed political positions. There is little doubt that the glorious period of the Renaissance was born as a result of the state of relative stability and unbounded prosperity the Medicis inspired and nurtured. The unusual enlightenment and enthusiastic support of Lorenzo de' Medici, called Lorenzo il Magnifico, and his personal attraction to the arts and humanities, assured that Florence would become a veritable hotbed of cultural innovation.

The sumptuous Medici courts rivaled those of Paris and Vienna; they were alive with theater, spectacle, banquets, salons, and important festivities such as weddings, baptisms, and celebrations of patron saints' feast days. To escape epidemics, summer heat, or urban ennui, the Medicis built regal country villas and hunting lodges in the cool, game-populated hills outside Florence. They elevated the garden to an art form that was soon imitated all over Europe as the "Renaissance garden" — embellished with geometric parterres and terraces, labyrinths, topiary hedges, Roman statues, pergolas, outdoor theaters, and manmade grottoes. Everywhere there were refreshing pools, fountains, and *giochi d'acqua* (practical jokes played with water) that revived the ancient Arab technique of tapping underground springs. Tuscany's aristocracy followed the new Medici mode, and the elite of Florence, Lucca, Siena, and other powerful Renaissance cities left their handsome palazzi within the protection of the fortified walls to carry rural villa life to the height of aristocratic refinement.

The Medici family ceased to exist with the death of Gian Gastone in 1737, and many of the aristocracy's country villas now stand empty, most Tuscans opting to live in the very cities their ancestors chose to leave behind. A more recent convergence on Tuscany of outstanding individuals in the arts, however, brought about a second and new kind of Renaissance. Goethe, Shelley, Stendhal, the Brownings, Dostoyevsky, Mark Twain, Gorky, Dylan Thomas — they all made Tuscany their home and escape, the goal of a spiritual pilgrimage that became a source of inspiration for some of their finest works. They spoke and wrote about art, history, love, God, and, always, the landscape. It is this same landscape that draws millions of lesser-known tourists who come to study the frescoes of Giotto or that treasure trove that is Florence's *Uffizi* and then return home remembering nothing but the gentle hills that the Tuscans call *dolci* (sweet).

More than 70% of Tuscany consists of these characteristic hills — only one-tenth of the region is flat plain, mostly in the Maremma, Pisa, and Lucca area — and entire tracts of land are works of art. They may not have been designed by Michelangelo, but human intervention and the farmer's resourcefulness are obvious everywhere. Slopes have been terraced to stop erosion, improve drainage, and increase the amount of arable land. Some forests have been cleared to provide more room for crops, while others have been planted in compensation. Mountains were (and still are) being carved away, their quarries supplying the needs of the world with the same white Carrara marble that supplied the geniuses of the Renaissance.

According to an ancient legend, the Etruscans introduced the one element that has come to be recognized as the most Tuscan of all: the cypress. Originally, the stately rows of these slender trees, so often seen in dark profile along the curve of a hill, had a specific function: They marked property boundaries and blocked the wind. Single, isolated cypresses that once stood as reference points to traveling pilgrims still stand sentinel, marking forks in the road and turnoffs.

Since ancient times, their longevity (many trees thrive for well over 1,000 years) and evergreen nature have lent them a sacred aura, and they have always been used to flank churches and adorn cemeteries. Unfortunately, a widespread fungus attacked this most recognizable feature of the Tuscan countryside, eating away at them from within and posing a serious threat. Unfortunately, too, tens of thousands of centuries-old olive trees, entire silvery groves of them, were destroyed by record-breaking cold temperatures in January 1986. The local farmers have left the gnarled stumps alongside new tender shoots that face long decades to maturation and have planted field after expansive field of sunflowers. Although the oil from these armies of *girasoli* will help soften the shortage of Tuscany's deep green, award-winning olive oil, they are a feeble, if colorful, substitute.

Besides the cypresses, the olive trees, the characteristic hills, and hilltop villages still peaked with fortified castles and church steeples — the two ever-contending symbols of power in medieval Italy — there are other characteristics of this very peaceful landscape, such as the vineyards. The heart of the region is braided with vines, row upon row of them, the only straight lines in what is otherwise a land of sinuous contour. Then there is the purest example of Romanesque art, the *pieve,* the country parish church, along with the cluster of buildings that served it. Often built on Etruscan or Roman foundations, they are today scattered across Tuscany like jewels, many still being used as religious seats.

The most indigenous architecture of all, however, is the *casa colonica,* or Tuscan farmhouse. Frequently set atop a hill, and built of whatever stone was immediately available, its style grew from a response to the simple needs of the *contadino* (peasant) into a natural, unpretentious elegance, its color and texture in rustic harmony with the tones and shapes of its surroundings. The extended family lived over the animal quarters for warmth, an outside staircase usually joining the 2 floors. For centuries, the farmers of the region had worked the land under a system known as *mezzadria,* where the laborers shared profits with the landowners. The practice finally died out in the early part of this century due to poor returns and a gradual exodus to the city, and the majority of these old country homes have been bought and restored by urbanites and foreigners who use them for weekend or summer homes. For those interested in a longer stay, renting one of these villas or an apartment in a home may prove to be a more attractive (and sometimes more economical) alternative to a hotel. There are several companies that handle rentals of properties, ranging from Renaissance castles to converted stables. Two reputable firms that have accommodations all over Tuscany are *Tuscan Enterprises* (Casella Postale 34, 1-53011 Castellina in Chianti; phone: 577-740623) and *Casaclub Toscana* (2 Piazza Indipendenza, 53100 Siena; phone: 577-

44041). Also see "Apartments, Houses, and Villas," *Accommodations,* GETTING READY TO GO.

It was from the economical hearth and frugal spirit of the Tuscan *contadino* that the regional cuisine evolved. Food was commonly cooked over a hearty fire, and today's high-quality Tuscan meats are cooked just that way, using only herbs (the frequent use of tarragon, sage, rosemary, and thyme came from the Etruscans) and a brushing of extra-virgin olive oil (unfiltered and from the first pressing). Long bouts of famine gave rise to *cucina povera* (poor cuisine), consisting of simple and unsophisticated dishes where everything was — and is — used. Stale bread thickens such winter soups as *pappa al pomodoro* (roughly, "tomato pap") and *ribollita* (literally, "reboiled"); chestnut flour is used for dessert breads such as *castagnaccio.* Game has always been important — the Tuscans are Italy's keenest hunters, and the region's thick woods are rich in wild boar (*cinghiale*), pheasant, wild pigeon, and hare — and the most beloved mushrooms of all are the *porcini* that grow wild, the size of T-bone steaks. With the discovery of America came white beans, an important source of protein in the peasant diet (Tuscans are insultingly called "bean eaters"). The favorite cheese, the pungent *pecorino,* originated in Roman times. Made from sheep's milk, it comes in over 100 surprisingly different varieties.

As with all aspects of Italian life, Tuscan cooking underwent a great change during the Renaissance. The Medicis hosted marathon feasts for popes and kings. In 1533, Catherine de' Medici was sent off to uncivilized France to marry the future Henry II and took along retinues of chefs, provisions of olive oil, and *la forchetta* (the fork). Even the great Escoffier was later moved to admit, "The French cuisine is an enriched recapitulation of Tuscan cooking." Such conspicuous consumption and innovative license have diminished, and it is the simple cooking of the farmer that has reached us today. The olive oil from the Lucchese hills vies with that of the Chianti area as the world's best. Chianti wines, both red and white, cost a fraction of their price abroad; many of the finest reserve bottlings never leave the country. Most restaurants also offer vin santo, a dessert wine something like old sherry that is difficult to find elsewhere.

As in much of Europe, Tuscany's prime touring months are May, June, September, and October. But with the exception of erratic rains and not-so-central heating systems, there are very few months of the year that do not have a certain beauty of their own. August is particularly hot, but Tuscany has 200 miles of long, sandy beaches lined with pine groves that alternate with a dramatic, rocky coast, and the Tuscan archipelago's eight islands offer delightful respite. During high season, ferries leave frequently for the islands from Livorno and Piombino. Summer is also the time when Tuscany's medieval *feste* take place — jousts, crossbow contests, Siena's wild bareback horse race, and other events that date back to the volatile Middle Ages. They are re-created with an attention to authenticity and detail that is amazing: Gleaming armor, luxe velvets and brocades, and brilliant plumes bring history out of the museums and into the piazzas.

The following circular itinerary begins 12 miles (19 km) northwest of Florence, in Prato, and continues west to Pistoia, Montecatini, and Lucca before almost touching the sea at Pisa. It then proceeds south and inland, to Volterra, and east to San Gimignano, in Chianti, and the glorious medieval city of Siena. From there it loops in a southeasterly direction, taking in several charming hill towns on its way up to Arezzo. At Arezzo, it's possible to return to Florence, to turn south into the neighboring region of Umbria (and pick up the *Umbria* route at Perugia), or to persevere and see the rarely visited northeastern corner of Tuscany, which offers cool mountains, monasteries, and solitude. The route is designed to be followed in full or sampled in bits and pieces, with optional detours for those who have the time or a particular interest. A detailed road map is necessary, but don't be inhibited for fear of getting lost — just follow your instincts and peek in the back door of Tuscany by following those turnoffs that appeal to your imagination.

Whenever possible, reserve both hotels and restaurants in advance. Hotels listed below as very expensive will cost $200 and up for a double room; those listed as expensive, from $120 to $180; moderate, from about $55 to $120; and inexpensive, less than $55. A meal for two (with house wine) will cost $75 and up in restaurants listed as expensive, while moderate means from $50 to $75, and inexpensive, under $50.

PRATO: Much medieval and Renaissance wealth went into the embellishment of this very prosperous town, which has been known for its high-quality textiles, especially its wool, since before the 8th century. Like all modern cities with ancient origins, however, there is an old and a new Prato. Bypass all the lifeless apartment buildings, textile factories, and peripheral reminders of the 20th century and head right to the heart of the well-preserved historic center, following signs for the *centro storico.* The imposing 13th-century Castello dell'Imperatore (Emperor's Castle) is the principal landmark. Medieval Prato was a staunch supporter of the Ghibellines (those favoring the emperor and opposing the temporal power of the pope), and in thanks for its loyalty the flattered Emperor Frederick II had this massive fortification with crenelated walls built, one of the very few examples of this type of architecture outside Sicily. A lofty view from any of its eight lookout towers is enchanting. Independent Prato eventually fell to the Florentine Guelphs (archenemies of the Ghibellines) in the 14th century, and the same Renaissance masters who lavished their arts on Florence were sent here to do the same. Witness the 15th-century Santa Maria delle Carceri (St. Mary of the Prisons), a fine Renaissance church by the noted Florentine architect Giuliano da Sangallo, just across the square from the castle. The magnificent interior is a study of harmonious proportions, highlighted with the beautiful white-on-blue glazed terra cottas by Andrea della Robbia.

Undoubtedly the most renowned of all the Renaissance artists to work in Prato was Fra Filippo Lippi, who was himself a native *pratese.* An orphan, he was put in a monastery at the age of 15, but, more suited to an unorthodox (and slightly licentious) life, he fled. He was captured by pirates, sold as a slave in Africa, and freed by the Saracens, who marveled at his artistic talents. Upon his return to Prato, he succumbed to the fair beauty of Lucrezia Buti, a young nun whose angelic face soon began appearing as that of the Madonna in most of his paintings. She gave birth to a son who would also become a prominent figure in Renaissance art; and Cosimo de' Medici had Fra Filippo released from his vows, freeing him to cover Prato's fine Duomo, and much of the rest of Tuscany, with his delicate frescoes.

The Duomo stands in Piazza del Duomo, on a site originally occupied by the 10th-century *pieve* (parish church) of Santo Stefano. One of the best examples of Romanesque-Gothic architecture in Tuscany, it has the typical white and green marble stripes adorning its façade, with a Della Robbia lunette over the entrance. To the right is an exterior pulpit, the work of Donatello and Michelozzo (1428–38); the *Dancing Putti* reliefs decorating it are copies of Donatello's originals, which are now in the *Museo dell'Opera del Duomo* (Cathedral Museum; phone: 574-29339; open daily except Mondays from 9 AM to 1 PM and 3:30 to 6:30 PM; admission charge). Several times a year, on special occasions (including May 1, August 15, and September 8), the Holy Girdle of the Virgin Mary is put on display in the pulpit. Said to have been given to the ever-doubting Apostle Thomas upon the Virgin's ascension into heaven, this precious relic was brought to Prato in the Middle Ages by a Tuscan merchant who had a Palestinian wife. Ordinarily, it's kept in a chapel of the Duomo, where frescoes by Agnolo Gaddi tell the story. The frescoes in the chancel of the church — stories of the lives of St. John the Baptist and of St. Stephen — are of greater significance, however. These early Renaissance masterpieces took Fra Filippo Lippi 14 years to finish and are considered his finest work. Frescoes by another master, Paolo Uccello, are in the Boccherini Chapel, to the right.

The old civil law court building, the 13th- and 14th-century Palazzo Pretorio, is in picturesque Piazza del Comune. It houses the *Galleria Comunale* (closed Mondays), one of the region's major collections of Renaissance, mainly Florentine, masters. Prato's tourist information office is at 48 Via Cairoli (phone: 574-24112).

CHECKING IN: ***Palace*** – Eighty-five rooms and well managed, with modern comforts — TV sets, air conditioning, and a pool — that are especially welcome after a day visiting the Middle Ages. The restaurant (closed August) is also highly regarded. Reservations advised. Major credit cards accepted. 230 Viale Repubblica, Prato (phone: 574-592841). Expensive.

Villa Santa Cristina – This 18th-century villa is a perfect introduction to Tuscan hospitality. It has 22 rooms with period furniture, as well as a pool, gardens, and modern features that only enhance its charm. Game, especially wild boar in season, is a specialty at the restaurant, which is closed Sunday evenings, Mondays, and August. Reservations advised. Major credit cards accepted. The hotel is closed in August. 58 Via Poggio Secco, Prato (phone: 574-595951). Expensive to moderate.

EATING OUT: ***Il Piraña*** – A modern yet elegant restaurant that is especially well — and widely — known for its specialties of fresh fish from nearby Tyrrhenian waters. Closed Saturdays, Sundays, August, and *Christmas* through *Epiphany* (January 6). Reservations advised. Major credit cards accepted. 110 Via Valentini, Prato (phone: 574-25746). Expensive.

Il Tonio – A rustic place, always busy and reliably good, in the *centro storico* on the picturesque piazza where Fra Filippo Lippi was born (in a building that is no longer standing). It includes fish specialties on its extensive menu of Tuscan dishes. Closed Sundays, Mondays, and August. Reservations advised. Major credit cards accepted. 161 Piazza il Mercatale, Prato (phone: 574-21266). Expensive.

En Route from Prato – Pistoia is due west, but about 10 miles (16 km) directly south from Prato is the village of Poggio a Caiano and the delightful wine producing zone of Carmignano. The village is the setting of one of the most splendid Medici summer villas, the Villa Medicea a Poggio a Caiano, which was originally a fortress but was transformed (from 1480 to 1485) into a showplace for Lorenzo il Magnifico by the very busy Giuliano da Sangallo. Lorenzo's son, the future Pope Leo X, was mostly responsible for the villa's impressive art collection. (The gardens of the villa are open daily, except Mondays and Sunday afternoons. For information on visiting the interior, call 55-877012.) From the villa, follow signs for the village of Artimino and a twisting, hairpin road through lovely, rolling countryside to another Medici outpost, the Villa di Artimino. This magnificent 16th-century structure, sometimes called the Villa of the

Hundred Chimneys (for obvious reasons) or La Ferdinanda, was designed by Buontalenti as a hunting lodge for Ferdinando I de' Medici. It sits atop a prominent hill overlooking elaborate gardens and olive groves, thick pine and ilex woods, and the vineyards that produce the famous red carmignano wines, lauded since the days of the Medici connoisseurs. The grounds of the villa are open to the public, and it is possible to actually eat and spend the night here, though not in the villa itself (see *Checking In* and *Eating Out,* below).

From the Poggio a Caiano area, it's a 20-minute, approximately 15-mile (24-km) ride (pick up SS66) to the important agricultural and commercial center of Pistoia.

CHECKING IN: ***Albergo Paggeria Medicea*** – A stay in the renovated pages' quarters of the Medicis' Villa di Artimino comes close to fulfilling any fantasy of being a guest of that illustrious family. The 37-room hotel is less opulent than the villa next door, but the utter silence, the bucolic surroundings, and the modern decor steeped in historical ambience are a magic combination. The management is very apologetic for the delayed completion of the swimming pool; it seems every time they break ground, they unearth another Etruscan ruin or Roman wall. But it does have tennis courts and a very good restaurant (see below). Via Papa Giovanni XXIII, Artimino (phone: 55-871-8081). Moderate.

EATING OUT: ***Biagio Pignatta*** – Just behind the *Paggeria,* in what was once the home of Ferdinando de' Medici's butler. Wild game from these very hills and recipes that purportedly pleased many a Medici palate are the specialties. Closed Wednesdays and Thursday lunch. Reservations advised. Major credit cards accepted. Via Papa Giovanni XXIII, Artimino (phone: 55-871-8086). Expensive to moderate.

Da Delfina – A rustic place within the medieval walls of the village of Artimino, a short walk down a tree-lined road from the *Paggeria,* where the local cooking is at its very finest. There is also a wide selection of carmignano wines. Closed Monday evenings, Tuesdays, early January, and August. Reservations advised. No credit cards accepted. 1 Via della Chiesa, Artimino (phone: 55-871-8074). Expensive to moderate.

PISTOIA: The treasures of this town easily merit a day's visit, but since they were created by the roll call of artists who performed similar artistic feats in Prato and Florence, and because the creative inspiration is again equaled in the great city of Pisa farther west, most visitors give short shrift to Pistoia. That is a shame, because it is a town full of character, still girdled by a handsome set of 14th-century walls that were fortified by the Medicis and once accommodated over 60 lookout towers. Like its neighbor, Prato, Pistoia was a firm supporter of the Ghibellines, and it, too, eventually fell to that most puissant of rivals, Florence.

From a map of the city, it is possible to pick out a square plan (harking back to Pistoia's Roman origins) inside a trapezoid (the walls), right in the center of which is Piazza del Duomo. The Duomo itself was built on 5th-century foundations during the 12th and 13th centuries, Pistoia's wealthier days. The Pisan-style façade has 3 tiers of arcades (as does the slim, adjacent bell tower, which was transformed, in the 13th century, from a Lombard military guard tower) and terra cotta decorations by Andrea della Robbia around the central door. The simple interior sets off an ecclesiastical masterpiece, the famous silver altar of St. James, housed in the Cappella di San Jacopo. Begun in the late 13th century, the altar contains more than 600 silver figures created by numerous artists through the mid-15th century — a compendium of Tuscan sculpture from the Gothic to the Renaissance. The Duomo's *Museo Capitolare* is worth a visit just for the dazzling array of antique gold plates, chalices, trays, and other treasures. It is open daily except Mondays from 9 AM to 1 PM and 3:30 to 6:30 PM; admission charge. The 14th-century white and green marble Baptistry, across from the

Duomo, was built according to the design of Andrea Pisano, a name behind much of northern Tuscany's finest architecture. Two other buildings in the same square are the austere 14th-century Palazzo del Podestà, adjoining the Baptistry, and the 13th- and 14th-century Palazzo del Comune.

Not far away from Piazza del Duomo is the 13th-century Ospedale del Ceppo, which takes its name from the *ceppo,* or box, in which offerings were once left. The hospital's most striking feature is the beautiful multicolored terra cotta frieze decorating the early-16th-century portico, a splendid work by Giovanni della Robbia and the Della Robbia workshop. Elsewhere among this labyrinth of medieval streets are the city's two oldest churches — the 12th-century Sant'Andrea and San Giovanni Fuorcivitas, which dates from the 8th century but was reconstructed from the 12th to the 14th centuries. Each is the proud possessor of an elaborate pulpit, the former a masterpiece carved (from 1298 to 1301) by Giovanni Pisano (as with the Della Robbias, the skilled Pisano family of architect-sculptors spanned several generations — another pulpit by Giovanni is in the Duomo at Pisa and one by his father, Nicola, is in the Pisa Baptistry), and the latter by Fra Guglielmo da Pisa, a student of the Pisanos, finished in 1270.

It's hard to believe today, but thousands of Pistoia's buildings were damaged during World War II. The city's pride, and a timeless expertise, have re-created history, however. The tourist information office (EPT, Piazza del Duomo; phone: 573-21622) can tell you all about it.

CHECKING IN/EATING OUT: *Il Convento* – One of the nicest places to stay when visiting Pistoia, this 24-room hostelry is 4 miles (6 km) outside town. Housed in a former convent, it is a peaceful spot, with a swimming pool to cool off in after a day's sightseeing. There also is a good restaurant. Reservations advised. Major credit cards accepted. 33 Via San Quirico (phone: 573-452651). Moderate.

En Route from Pistoia – Meticulously groomed *vivai,* extensive nurseries of fledgling trees, from exotic palms to the ubiquitous cypress and everything in between, compose the outskirts of Pistoia. Just beyond them, following SS435, lies the elegant spa town of Montecatini Terme, less than 10 miles (16 km) from Pistoia.

MONTECATINI TERME: What Vichy is to France and Baden-Baden is to Germany, Montecatini is to Italy. The resort's heralded mineral waters have had a salutary effect on many a stomach, liver, and intestine — including those of Giuseppe Verdi, Arturo Toscanini, and La Loren. To "take the waters" in Montecatini means to settle into a hotel, undergo an obligatory clinical consultation with a hydro expert, and make tracks each day, almost always in the morning and on an empty stomach, to one or the other of the town's *stabilimenti termali* (thermal establishments) to down the prescribed measure from any of the five springs — Tamerici, Torretta, Regina, Tettuccio, Rinfresco — that are used for drinking. About 2,000 immaculately clean WCs stand by, blending discreetly with the surroundings. The waters of two other springs — Leopoldina and Giulia — are for mineral baths, and an eighth spring, Grocco, is expressly for mud baths. The *termi* were once the private property of the Medicis, who undoubtedly appreciated the restorative treatments for gout and an excess of *la dolce vita,* but it was not until the late 1800s that the waters' curative powers became well known. Early in this century, all the various springs were taken over by the state, a massive building program was undertaken, and fashionable hotels were constructed to accommodate shahs, bluebloods, and Milanese industrialists. Now numbering well over 400, the hotels operate from *Easter* to the end of November.

A serious treatment should really last 12 days, so if you're here just a day or two, don't expect miracles (although it's possible to buy the bottled waters and schlep them home). But even for those who don't take the cure, a peek at one of the *stabilimenti,* all laid out in a vast green park, is enlightening. The most beautiful is the *Stabilimento Tettuccio,* built in 1927 in a classical style. Here, from early morning until noon, an orchestra plays under a frescoed dome, attendants fill cups at fountains spouting from counters of inlaid marble set before scenes of youth and beauty painted on walls of ceramic tile, and patrons stroll through the colonnades, peruse newspapers, or chat. The entrance fee is stiff because it includes water for those who are taking the cure (most who do, however, have a subscription) as well as the otherworldly atmosphere, and there is a lovely, conventional coffee bar inside. Off-season, only the less-impressive *Stabilimento Excelsior,* built in 1915 and with an ultramodern wing, is open.

Montecatini also has expensive boutiques, sports facilities, and seemingly endless flower gardens and forests of centuries-old oaks, pines, palms, cedars, magnolias, and oleanders. The tourist information office (66-68 Viale Verdi; phone: 572-70109, 572-78200, or 572-71284) has booklets on different walks through this luxurious vegetation as well as walks up into the nearby hills. Spa information can be found at 41 Viale Verdi (phone: 572-75851). The Old Town of Montecatini, Montecatini Alto, is another excursion. Set on top of a hill that dominates the spa town, it is reached by funicular from Viale Diaz or by a road winding 3 miles (5 km) through olive groves and orchards. (See also *Spas,* DIVERSIONS.)

CHECKING IN: ***Grand Hotel e La Pace*** – Open since 1870, this classic and quintessentially elegant Old World property still has a grandiose period decor and a pampering staff that keeps the clientele all feeling like VIPs. There are 150 air conditioned rooms, a heated pool set in an extensive park, and tennis courts, as well as its own natural health center. There are 3 restaurants, the most formal of which is graced with a frescoed ceiling, ornate chandeliers, and crisp napery, and serves a predictable continental menu. Closed November through March. Reservations advised. Major credit cards accepted. 3 Via della Torretta, Montecatini Terme (phone: 572-75801). Hotel very expensive; restaurant expensive.

G.H. Tamerici & Principe – Everything at this 157-room hotel is tasteful and has been chosen with care. The service is excellent, even by the high standards of Montecatini. There is a well-equipped fitness center with a gym, sauna, solarium, and indoor pool. The restaurant uses ingredients fresh from the owners' farm in the heart of chianti country. Closed December through March. Reservations advised. Major credit cards accepted. 2 Viale IV Novembre, Montecatini Terme (phone: 572-71041). Expensive.

Cappelli–Croce di Savoia – Far more intimate and affordable than the *Grand,* this very pleasant 72-room hotel has been run by the amiable Cappelli family since the 1930s. The spacious lobby, with marble floors, Persian carpets, and pots and vases of flowers, is a bit grander than the more modestly furnished rooms, but there is a beautiful back patio with a pool and a good restaurant, all only 100 yards or so from the spa facilities. Closed mid-November to April 1. 139 Viale Bicchierai, Montecatini Terme (phone: 572-71151). Moderate.

EATING OUT: ***Gourmet*** – What the *Grand Hotel e La Pace* is to hotels, the *Gourmet* is to restaurants. An exquisite meal here is worth every calorie (there's fresh fish, however, for truly determined dieters). Closed Tuesdays. Reservations advised. Major credit cards accepted. 6 Viale Amendola, Montecatini Terme (phone: 572-771012). Expensive.

En Route from Montecatini – Continue west toward Lucca on SS435, until a detour beckons at Pescia. If time permits, take the detour and turn south to Montecarlo (watch for signs). The drive to this hill town, only a short stretch of lovely rich farmland, should be made when there is still enough light to watch the Tuscan plains gradually spread out before you. The town's delightful isolation lends it a storybook quality, and it has some surprisingly fine restaurants. After the visit, return to SS435 and drive the remaining 10 miles (16 km) to Lucca.

EATING OUT: ***Forassiepi*** – Housed in an old, restored farmhouse, just outside the 15th-century walls of Montecarlo. Indoors everything is pink linen and orchids, but outdoors the unforgettable view vies with the menu for attention. For the first course, ask to try a variety of the delicious pasta specials. Then sample from the extensive menu of pheasant, thrush, quail, rabbit, and wild boar, as well as less gamey choices. Closed Mondays, Tuesdays; from January 1 to March 31, closed Mondays through Thursdays. Reservations advised. Major credit cards accepted. 800 Porta Belvedere, Montecarlo (phone: 583-22005). Expensive to moderate.

La Nina – Like *Forassiepi,* this pleasant restaurant also moves outdoors into a lovely garden at the first hint of warm weather. Find it by following the signs upon entering town. Closed Monday evenings, Tuesdays, 2 weeks following *Epiphany* (January 6), and a week in mid-August. Reservations advised. Visa accepted. 54 Via San Martino, Montecarlo (phone: 583-22178). Moderate.

LUCCA: A fair-size city with the air of an elegant town, Lucca, too, is often overlooked by travelers speeding on to nearby Pisa or the coast. But its gentle yet distinctive character makes it worth a stop. In the 9th century, the city already had 40 churches listed in its archives, and today there are more than 60 of them. During the 12th and 13th centuries, Lucca's power equaled that of Florence or Pisa, and its silk was considered the finest in all Europe. During the 16th and early 17th centuries, Lucca gained its third and final set of city walls, a girdle of ramparts that are intact today and constitute a unique feature — they are broad and low enough to be topped with a tree-lined promenade, a public thoroughfare that is an intrinsic part of city life.

Within the walls, Lucca's architecture is an interesting mélange of Roman to medieval to 16th century, with baroque, neo-classical, and Art Deco interventions. Winding streets, glimpses of internal courtyard gardens, 19th-century carved wood storefronts, and the extravagant wrought-iron street lamps are all relics of golden days. Giacomo Puccini was born here — the old-fashioned *Fanciulla del West* bar on Via Mordini is one of the gayer memorials to him, but Puccini himself preferred a bar (Via Fillungo), the *Caffè di Simo,* where excellent ice cream is still served amid marble, brass, and antique mirrors.

The center of town is Piazza Napoleone. Take Via del Duomo out of the square and pass the Church and Baptistry of San Giovanni to find Lucca's Duomo, dedicated to San Martino, in the piazza of the same name. Although a church has occupied the spot since the 6th century, this one dates only from the 13th century. It has an asymmetrical Romanesque façade of columned loggias and an interior of largely Gothic design, as a result of a 14th- and early-15th-century renovation. One of the treasures of the church is the very beautiful tomb of Ilaria del Carretto, wife of Paolo Giunigi, a powerful ruler of independent Lucca. The tomb, created in 1408, a few years after her death, is the marble masterpiece of Jacopo della Quercia, who breathed life into the silk-like folds of her gown and headrest. In the middle of the nave is another treasure: a small marble temple by Matteo Civitali that houses the Volto Santo (Holy Visage), a wooden crucifix with the image of Christ, probably of 12th-century Eastern origin. According to legend, however, it was carved by Nicodemus immediately following the Crucifixion and procured by a Lucchese bishop during a pilgrimage to the Holy Land; it was famous enough throughout Europe to have been mentioned by Dante in the *Inferno.* After dark each September 13, it is paraded through town in a candlelight procession.

After returning to Piazza Napoleone, head toward Piazza San Michele. The piazza that today hums with a colorful open-air market was once the old Roman Forum; in fact, the unusual church to one side of the piazza is called San Michele in Foro (St.

Michael in the Forum). Built in the 12th and 13th centuries, it has a Romanesque façade in the Pisan-Lucchese fashion, with four decorative arcades of sculpted columns (no two are alike), topped by a colossal statue of St. Michael. Inside the church are a *Madonna and Child* by Andrea della Robbia and a panel painting of four saints by Filippino Lippi. Follow Via Fillungo, one of Lucca's busiest streets, lined with medieval houses and towers, to reach another interesting church, San Frediano, in Piazza San Frediano. Have a look at the bell tower of this 12th-century church and, inside, in the Cappella Trenta, at the reliefs by Jacopo della Quercia, then cross over Via Fillungo to the 2nd-century Anfiteatro Romano, another of Lucca's Roman sites. Actually, all that remains is the oval outline, traced by soft yellow medieval-style houses, and the old amphitheater grounds are today the site of a daily fruit and vegetable market. Exit from the opposite side of the amphitheater and proceed to Via Giunigi, another medieval street containing several palazzi built by the Giunigi family in the 14th century. One of them is easily recognized, since it sports a tower with oak trees on top.

The wooded and olive-crowded hills outside Lucca produce the coveted *olio d'oliva lucchese* and are the home of a number of stately private villas that cropped up in the 16th and 17th centuries. The Villa Torrigiani, Villa Reale (once home of Napoleon's sister Maria Luisa), and Villa Mansi are just a few that are open to the public. The two tourist information offices (40 Via Vittorio Veneto; phone: 583-43639 and 2 Piazza Guidiccioni; phone: 583-41205) can help you plan an itinerary.

CHECKING IN: ***Villa La Principessa*** – A 13th-century villa turned into an elegant 44-room hotel and restaurant just 2 miles (3 km) outside Lucca on the road to Pisa. The spacious gardens, the large pool, the staff, and the total serenity make it an exquisite choice. Hotel closed January 7 to February 15. Restaurant closed Wednesdays. Via Nuova, Massa Pisana (phone: 583-370037). Very expensive.

Il Bottacio – Guests lucky enough to stay in one of the 5 suites in this former 17th-century olive oil mill in the village of Montignoso just northwest of Lucca, are cosseted from the moment they arrive to the minute they leave. Rooms are decorated with antique furnishings, the tile floors are heated, and the bed linen is made of Como silk. In season, baskets of freshly picked apricots, peaches, strawberries, and raspberries are left in the guestrooms. The one-Michelin-star restaurant lives up to the hotel's high standards. Neapolitan chef Pina Mosca turns out delicate and imaginative versions of traditional dishes such as ravioli stuffed with salmon and quail in a sauce made with fresh apricots. Meals are served at tables around a lotus-flower-strewn goldfish pond. Open daily. Reservations necessary. Major credit cards accepted. 1 Via Bottacio, Montignoso (phone: 585-34031). Expensive.

Napoleon – Just a few minutes' walk outside the walls is a clean, modern establishment with 63 air conditioned rooms. 1 Viale Europa, Lucca (phone: 583-53141). Expensive.

Universo – The best to be found within the walls. Its 60 rooms are clean and comfortable, if rather old-fashioned; the unbeatable advantage is its central location. 1 Piazza Puccini, Lucca (phone: 583-43678). Moderate.

Hambros – This 19th-century villa in the hamlet of Lunata, just 3 miles (5 km) from Lucca, has been converted into a country hotel. The 57 rooms are simply furnished and wonderfully quiet — the villa is set in its own parkland. No restaurant. 197 Via Banchierri, Lunata (phone: 583-935355). Inexpensive.

EATING OUT: ***Solferino*** – Another confirmation of Lucca's importance as a gastronomic center, this excellent, family-run establishment is 3 miles (5 km) outside town, on the road to Viareggio. The fare is basically local, but originality flares in dishes such as baby water buffalo and duck in cream sauce. Closed Wednesdays, Thursday lunch, January 7 to 14, and 2 weeks in August. Reservations advised. Major credit cards accepted. San Macario in Piano (phone: 583-59118). Expensive to moderate.

Buca di Sant'Antonio – Set in the medieval quarter near San Michele, with a largely Lucchese clientele that's been coming back for more than 200 years. It serves the best of local fare, including *porcini* mushrooms cooked *al cartoccio* (in paper wrapping) and game in season. Closed Sunday evenings, Mondays, and the last 2 weeks of July. Reservations advised. Major credit cards accepted. 1-3 Via della Cervia, Lucca (phone: 583-55881). Moderate.

Osteria Baralla – A medieval-style restaurant near the Roman amphitheater. Owner Renzo Fenili is something of a gastronomic historian and has hunted out ancient recipes, such as *risotto con i marroni* (risotto with chestnuts). There is also a well-stocked wine cellar. Closed Mondays. Reservations advised. Major credit cards accepted. 5 Via Anfiteatro, Lucca (phone: 583-47614). Moderate.

Vipore – Pietro Casella's welcoming hilltop eatery 5 miles (8 km) from Lucca is well worth the trip, as many locals will attest. Diners can choose between two *menù degustazioni* (tasting menus) or eat à la carte, selecting from dishes made from local ingredients, such as *tacconi* (homemade pasta with a wild mushroom sauce) and rabbit cooked in the famous Lucca olive oil. Perhaps what makes the food here so good is the more than 40 species of aromatic herbs that chef Pietro and his wife Rosa grow in the garden. Closed Mondays, Tuesday lunch, and January. Reservations advised. Major credit cards accepted. Leave Lucca from Ponte Monte San Quirico and go 3 miles (5 km) on the road to Via Sant'Alessio; and then take the road signposted Via Pieve Santo Stefano. Pieve Santo Stefano (phone: 583-59245). Moderate.

Da Giulio in Pelleria – A simple, informal, and first-rate trattoria in a relaxed setting. Lucchese specialties are served; try the *spezzatino di vitello con olive nere* (veal and black olive stew) or *farro,* a hearty country soup. Closed Sundays, Mondays, 2 weeks at *Christmas,* and August. Reservations advised. No credit cards accepted. 29 Via San Tommaso, Lucca (phone: 583-55948). Inexpensive.

En Route from Lucca – Take SS12R to Pisa, 14 miles (22 km) to the southwest.

PISA: Visitors invariably rush to Piazza del Duomo, otherwise known as the Campo dei Miracoli (Field of Miracles), to see the Leaning Tower. Then what to their wondering eyes should appear on this spacious green lawn but three stunning white buildings — the Leaning Tower, the Duomo, and the Baptistry — flanked by a fourth structure, the white wall of the Camposanto. The Duomo, especially, which set the style known as Pisan Romanesque, or simply Pisan, was one of the most influential buildings of its time; regardless of whether a visitor appreciates the fine points of architecture, it's hard not to be impressed by the Pisan triad.

This city on the Arno was a maritime power almost from the beginning. It was a naval base for the Romans, and during the darkest days of the Middle Ages it kept the Tyrrhenian coast free of Saracens. A fleet of Pisan ships sailed off to the First Crusade. By the 11th century, Pisa had developed into a maritime republic to rival Genoa and Venice. By the 12th century, it had reached the height of its supremacy — it defeated the maritime republic of Amalfi in 1135 — and also of artistic splendor, but the seeds of decline were already planted, in the form of internal rivalries and external strife with nearby Lucca, Genoa, and Florence (which was moving farther and farther along the Arno toward the sea). Pisa never fully recovered from a defeat by the Genoese in 1284, which decimated its fleet and aggravated its internal problems, and in 1406 it was defeated by the Florentines after a long siege. Although there was a period of well-being under the Medicis and even a brief period of independence at the turn of the century, from 1494 to 1509, from the early 1500s its history merges with that of Florence.

The Duomo was begun in 1064 and finished by the end of the 12th century. Its façade, consisting of four graceful galleries of columns, was much imitated (as visits to Lucca and Prato will attest). The bronze doors facing the Baptistry are from the 16th century, replacing originals lost in a fire, but the highly stylized bronze doors facing the Leaning Tower are by Bonanno Pisano and date from 1180. The interior is cavernous, close to 400 feet long and interrupted by 68 columns, but find the way to Giovanni Pisano's intricately carved pulpit (1302–11), perhaps the cathedral's greatest treasure. The 16th-century bronze "Galileo lamp" that hangs opposite is of special interest, too. According to the story, Pisa-born Galileo came up with his theory of pendulum movement by studying the swinging of the lamp set in motion by a sympathetic sacristan.

The Baptistry, begun in 1152 but not finished until the end of the 14th century, is most famous for its pulpit, carved by Nicola Pisano in 1260. Not long after construction had begun on the Baptistry, ground was broken for the elegant cylindrical campanile, the bell tower standing (or leaning) behind the Duomo. The tower rose quickly, but at the third floor, the complication that's very evident today appeared, suspending work for a century. Complications notwithstanding, construction was resumed in 1275, and the finishing touches were made between 1350 and 1372. A few romantic historians contend that the leaning was purposefully brought on by the architect who sought to prove his inordinate skill. Most, however, attribute it to a shifting of soil and the tilt continues to increase by an average of about 1 millimeter a year. A walk up the tower's 294 steps currently is not possible (the tower is closed indefinitely for extensive repairs), but tourists still are able to appreciate its tilt from outside. From the top terrace Galileo dabbled in his experiments to establish the laws of gravity.

The long, low rectangular building running along the side of the Pisan Triumvirate, its absolute simplicity relieved only by a tiny Gothic tabernacle, is actually a cemetery, the Camposanto, begun in 1277. It is said that some of the earth enclosed inside was brought from the Holy Land aboard Pisan ships. Many of the frescoes that once decorated the interior of the Camposanto walls were destroyed or heavily damaged in World War II, but some by Benozzo Gozzoli remain and enough remains of the famous *Triumph of Death, Last Judgment,* and *Inferno,* by the so-called Master of the Triumph of Death, to suggest the uneasy turn of the 14th-century mind. Sinopias (preparatory designs, drawn directly on the walls) of the frescoes, uncovered during postwar restoration, are now in the *Museo delle Sinopie,* across the street from the Duomo; open daily from 9 AM to 12:45 PM and 3 to 7 PM. The frescoes themselves can be seen in the nearby *Museo Camposanto Monumentale;* open daily in summer from 8 AM to 8 PM; in winter from 8 AM to 5 PM. On the other side of the cathedral is the fascinating and little-known *Museo dell'Opera del Duomo,* which opened in 1986 in a former Capuchin monastery. Fine examples of Islamic art — remnants of Pisa's tradition as a trading power — as well as sculptures by father and son Nicola and Giovanni Pisano, and a magnificent frescoed dining room are on display in the museum's 19 rooms. Open 8 AM to 8 PM in summer, 8 AM to 5 PM in winter. Admission charge for all museums. Piazza Arcivescovado (phone for all three museums: 50-560547).

Note, if pressed for time in Pisa, that the Duomo, the Baptistry, and the museum all close at lunchtime, while the Camposanto stays open. Even if pressed, make your way to the Arno for a look at Santa Maria della Spina (St. Mary of the Thorn; Lungarno Mediceo), a little jewel of a church in Pisan Gothic style. It was built in the early 14th century to house a relic from Christ's crown of thorns (no longer kept here), and it once stood much closer to the river — in the late 19th century it was moved piece by piece to its present spot. Another stop should be the *Museo Nazionale di San Matteo* (National Museum of St. Matthew; Piazza San Matteo in Soarta; phone: 50-541865), which contains many works of 12th- and 13th-century sculpture (the Pisano family is well represented) as well as a *Madonna and Child with Saints* by Simone Martini. It is open daily from 9 AM to 12:45 PM and 3 to 7 PM; no admission charge. The feast day of the city's patron saint, San Ranieri, is celebrated on June 17 with a regatta on the Arno, and the *Gioco del Ponte* (Battle of the Bridge), played in medieval costume by two teams from opposite sides of the river, also takes place in June (on the last Sunday). Another regatta, the *Regatta of the Four Ancient Maritime Republics,* rotates among Pisa, Venice, Amalfi, and Genoa, so that once every 4 years it takes place in Pisa (1995 will be Pisa's turn). The city's tourist information office is in Piazza del Duomo (phone: 50-560464) or at the station (phone: 50-42291).

CHECKING IN: ***Cavalieri*** – Named after the order of the Knights of St. Stephen, who had their seat here during the time of the Crusades, and now a member of the prestigious CIGA chain. Its international air, modern comforts, a bar, and a restaurant make its 100 rooms Pisa's best. 2 Piazza della Stazione, Pisa (phone: 50-43290). Expensive.

Duomo Grand – A large (94 rooms), busy establishment only a minute's walk from the Campo dei Miracoli. 94 Via Santa Maria, Pisa (phone: 50-561894). Expensive.

Villa Kinzica – Hard to beat in terms of position, this 30-room hotel is just a few steps from the major monuments — the tower can be seen from some of the rooms. The building once was a private villa. 2 Piazza Arcivescovado, Pisa (phone: 50-560419 or 50-561736). Moderate.

EATING OUT: ***Buzzino*** – Pisans are avid fish eaters, and this establishment keeps them happy with a fine selection of the day's freshest. The homemade pasta is also superb. Only a few blocks from the Campo dei Miracoli. Closed Tuesdays. Reservations advised. Major credit cards accepted. 44 Via C. Cammeo, Pisa (phone: 50-562141). Expensive.

Sergio – A small, hospitable restaurant on the banks of the Arno, long considered Pisa's best. Three menus are offered daily, including the suggested *menù degustazione,* as well as an extensive selection of à la carte meat and fish dishes. Closed Sundays, Monday lunch, January, and the latter half of July. Reservations advised. Major credit cards accepted. 1 Lungarno Pacinotti, Pisa (phone: 50-48245). Expensive.

Il Campano – A short stroll from the main Piazza dei Cavalieri will lead you to this picturesque trattoria, housed inside a 12th-century tower. In summer the tables are transferred outside. Traditional dishes are served, with the emphasis on fish from the coast close to Pisa. Closed Wednesdays. Reservations advised. Major credit cards accepted. 44 Via Cavalca, Pisa (phone: 50-46178). Moderate.

En Route from Pisa – Take SS67 for about 14 miles (22 km) southeast to Pontedera, then turn south onto SS439, following signs to Volterra. Much of the fertile land along this route was once swampland. The blue-green Cecina Hills on the right stretch for miles, and as Volterra (about 25 miles/40 km from Pontedera) comes closer, the countryside of green velvet hills turns lonely and scarred, with only an occasional flock of sheep to soften its appearance. The gashes marring the landscape are the alabaster quarries that have been Volterra's chief source of income since Etruscan days. More remarkable, however, are the yawning rifts, or *balze,* a peculiar earth flaw caused by intense erosion. The edges of the city have been eaten away by this unrestrainable and continuous movement, which has already consumed a portion of onetime Volterra — Etruscan and Roman temples and dwellings and the 7th-century Church of San Giusto.

VOLTERRA: Seen from a distance, Volterra rises up from abandoned countryside — isolated, gaunt, aloof. It has been the site of 3,000 years of continuous civilization, and the walled medieval city still stands within the perimeter of another, larger set of walls — Etruscan. Ancient Velathri was the northernmost and strongest of the 12 city-states of the Etrurian federation, three times larger than Volterra is today. The medieval city dates mostly from the 12th and 13th centuries. Built largely of a gray stone, *panchina,* it has taken on something of a golden hue, but Volterra is neither flirtatious nor charming as are some other Italian hill towns. It is, however, fiercely proud of its seemingly immortal disposition.

The beautiful, central Piazza dei Priori is bounded by sober medieval palaces, of which the Palazzo dei Priori (Town Hall), built from 1208 to 1254, is the most prominent. It is the oldest Town Hall in Tuscany still used as such, and from the top of its tower an unrivaled panorama can reach as far as the Tuscan coast on a clear day. The church behind the Town Hall is the Duomo, a Romanesque edifice consecrated in 1120, with Pisan touches that were added in the 13th century. The Baptistry, too, dates from the 13th century. Close by is the Porta all'Arco, an original Etruscan gate to the city, from which there are still more extensive and breathtaking views. The *Museo Etrusco Guarnacci* (Guarnacci Etruscan Museum, 15 Via Don Minzoni) has one of the best and largest collections of Etruscan objects in all Italy, including the famous elongated bronze figure known as the *Ombra della Sera* (Evening Shadow) and some 600 funerary urns of tufa, terra cotta, and alabaster that demonstrate that the Etruscans were already working the local alabaster in a skilled and imaginative way. (The alabaster industry still provides a third of Volterra's population with employment, and its myriad polychromatic products crowd most store windows.) Open daily 9:30 AM to 1 PM and 3 to 6:30 PM; phone: 588-86347). The climb to Volterra's 14th- and 15th-century Fortezza begins not far away from the museum. Lorenzo de' Medici was largely responsible for this massive installation, which serves as a reminder that independent Volterra, like many other Tuscan towns, eventually fell to the superior force of Florence. Lorenzo modified an existing 14th-century fortress (the Rocca Vecchia, or Old Fortress, which has a tower referred to as the Torre Femmina, Female Tower) and added a Rocca Nuova (New Fortress) of five towers, one of which is known as the Torre Maschio, Male Tower. Only the park of the Fortezza is open to the public (the rest is used as a prison), but the whole is an impressive feature of Volterra's silhouette.

The Volterra Tourist Information Office is at 2 Via Giusto Turazza (phone: 588-86150), just off Piazza dei Priori.

CHECKING IN: ***San Lino*** – Named after a Volterrano, the first pope to succeed St. Peter, and formerly a cloistered convent built in the 12th century, this is now a modern 44-room establishment with wide arches, handsome beamed ceilings, a delightful enclosed garden terrace, and swimming pool. The restaurant (open April through October) comes highly recommended. Major credit cards accepted. 26 Via San Lino, Volterra (phone: 588-85250). Hotel moderate; restaurant inexpensive.

EATING OUT: ***A Biscondola*** – A renovated rambling old farmhouse just a few minutes' drive southwest of the city walls on the road to Saline (watch for the signs). The service is friendly and the food — dishes such as *pappardelle alla lepre* (broad, flat noodles with hare sauce) and grilled or roasted meats — is straightforward and delicious. Closed Mondays. Reservations unnecessary. Major credit cards accepted. SS68 (phone: 588-85197). Moderate to inexpensive.

Ombra della Sera – This highly regarded restaurant is just 300 feet from the *Etruscan Museum.* Game is the specialty in season, but the whole Tuscan menu is delicious. Closed Mondays and the last 2 weeks of November. Reservations advised. Major credit cards accepted. 70 Via Gramsci, Volterra (phone: 588-86663). Inexpensive.

Il Porcellino – Tista, the gregarious owner, keeps the traditions of Tuscan home cooking vibrantly alive. Tables move outdoors during the spring, but the quaint pocket-size dining room inside is far more charming. Try the *piccata al funghetto* (roast lamb with mushroom sauce) or the *coniglio alla cacciatore* (rabbit with tomato sauce). Closed Tuesdays and October through March. Reservations advised. No credit cards accepted. 16 Canto delle Prigioni, Volterra (phone: 588-86392). Inexpensive.

En Route from Volterra – Proceed east on SS68 in the direction of Colle di Val d'Elsa. At Castel San Gimignano turn north onto a less-frequented road and travel through incomparable Tuscan countryside, above which rises the characteristic skyline of the small hill town of San Gimignano.

SAN GIMIGNANO: Ringed by three sets of historic walls, San Gimignano bristles with 14 (or 13 or 15, depending on exactly what you count) of its original 72 medieval towers and thus is known as San Gimignano delle Belle Torri — San Gimignano of the Beautiful Towers. Each tower was attached to the private palazzo of a patrician family and was used partly for defense against attack from without but also partly for defense against attack by feuding families from within the walls. As with today's skyscrapers, height was an indication of prestige, so "keeping up with the Joneses" is as old as the Tuscan hills.

The town's origins are Etruscan, but it takes its name from a Bishop of Modena who died here in the 4th century. It became a free commune in the 12th century, and life would have been tranquil had it not been for the destructive conflict between two families in particular, the Guelph Ardinghelli and the Ghibelline Salvucci (the city was predominantly Ghibelline). In 1300, Guelph Florence sent Dante as ambassador to make peace between the warring factions, but he was unsuccessful; internal strife grew so volatile that 53 years later, an exasperated San Gimignano willingly surrendered to the Florentines it had resisted for so many centuries.

Dante wouldn't be too overwhelmed by a return to 20th-century San Gimignano, so little have things changed. The two main streets of this perfectly preserved town, Via San Giovanni and Via San Matteo, feed into two splendid squares, Piazza della Cisterna and Piazza del Duomo. At the center of Piazza della Cisterna is the 13th-century well from which it takes its name. The piazza is paved with bricks inlaid in a herringbone pattern and surrounded by an assortment of medieval palazzi and towers. In the adjoining Piazza del Duomo, the 12th-century cathedral, known as the Collegiata, is flanked by more stately palazzi and seven towers. The Palazzo del Popolo, to one side of the cathedral, is the home of San Gimignano's small *Museo Civico* (phone: 577-940340). It contains, besides paintings from the 14th and 15th centuries, the room from which Dante delivered his harangue in favor of the Guelphs, and it provides access to one of San Gimignano's towers, from which there is a view of the town and hills in all directions. It is open daily except Mondays from 9 AM to 1 PM and 3:30 to 6:30 PM. The admission charge to the museum also permits entry to the Cappella di Santa Fina in the cathedral, a Renaissance addition that is decorated with Domenico Ghirlandaio's frescoes of the life of the saint, who was born here and died at the age of 15.

Stop in the 13th-century Church of Sant'Agostino at the far end of town to see the frescoes by Benozzo Gozzoli, and for another view out over the surrounding countryside — or back toward the town and towers — climb to La Rocca, a onetime fortress, now a public park (good pictures of the towers can be taken from the battlements here, but try to arrive early in the day to avoid direct sunlight). While away an hour at one of the sidewalk cafés with a glass of local *vino bianco* — San Gimignano's famous vernaccia is considered the finest white wine in the region and one of the finest whites in Italy. The tourist office is at Piazza Duomo (phone: 577-940008).

CHECKING IN: ***Bel Soggiorno* –** The former 13th-century Convento di San Francesco, its façade is barely distinguishable from the other medieval buildings on the street. It's comfortable in a simple Tuscan fashion. The back rooms afford a view of the morning mist swirling over the fields; even the restaurant has a view. There is a shower or bath in each of its 27 rooms. Restaurant closed

Mondays. 91 Via San Giovanni, San Gimignano (phone: 577-940375). Moderate.

La Cisterna – A rustic 50-room hotel in a 13th-century palazzo in one of the central piazzas of San Gimignano. The windows and large wooden balconies of some rooms overlook the surrounding valley and thus afford beautiful Tuscan views. The hotel's *Le Terrazze* restaurant has kept its age-old ambience, and the kitchen is the domain of some very fine chefs. Hotel closed November 10 to March 10; restaurant closed Tuesdays, Wednesdays at lunch, and November 10 to March 10. 23 Piazza della Cisterna, San Gimignano (phone: 577-940328). Moderate.

Leon Bianco – A comfortable, 24-room centrally located hotel, housed in an old palazzo on the 13th-century Piazza della Cisterna. No restaurant. 8 Piazza della Cisterna, San Gimignano (phone: 577-941294). Moderate.

Pescille – On a hilltop overlooking the towers of San Gimignano, this former farmhouse, now a 33-room country inn, is 2 miles (3 km) outside town. The owners have kept the rustic feeling, decorating rooms with terra cotta tiles, straw chairs, and good solid country furniture. Outdoors, the tennis courts and a swimming pool are set among olive trees. The restaurant turns out well-cooked dishes, making good use of the area's wealth of fresh, natural ingredients. Closed Wednesdays, January, and February. Reservations advised. Major credit cards accepted. Località Pescille (phone: 577-940186). Moderate.

Le Renaie – If San Gimignano is full — and it fills up very quickly — this attractive country hotel is a pleasant alternative, just 3 miles (5 km) out of town. It has 26 rooms, a restaurant, swimming pool, and fine views over the Tuscan countryside. Follow the signs for Certaldo and then for Pancole. Località Pancole, San Gimignano (phone: 577-955044). Moderate.

EATING OUT: *La Mangiatoia* – Cozy and candlelit, this trattoria specializes in a variety of excellent homemade pasta dishes. Closed Fridays and January. Reservations advised. No credit cards accepted. 5 Via Mainardi, San Gimignano (phone: 577-941528). Moderate.

En Route from San Gimignano – Siena is less than 25 miles (40 km) from San Gimignano and can be reached directly by taking the picturesque road east to Poggibonsi and then turning south and taking the old Roman consular road, the Via Cassia (SS2). Avoid the Florence-Siena superstrada. Nine miles (14 km) north of Siena is the tiny hill town of Monteriggioni, created by Siena as an elevated lookout fortress against the archenemy, Florence, in 1213. Ownership of Monteriggioni passed from one combatant to the other, and the town never grew beyond its original perimeters. Its walls have been left perfectly intact, although its 14 towers must have been considerably higher to have elicited Dante's likening them to looming giants.

A pleasant alternative to the direct route to Siena is to explore the chianti classico zone (where higher quality chiantis are produced), driving east from Poggibonsi to Castellina in Chianti, there picking up the SS222, romantically referred to as La Chiantigiana because it cuts through the heart of Chianti country. The chianti classico zone is not very large, measuring only 30 miles in length between Florence and Siena and 20 miles at its widest point, but the landscape is considered one of the most Italian in all Italy, exemplifying a wonderful harmony of color and form between the land and its provincial architecture. From Castellina, one option is to follow SS222 up to Greve, the unofficial capital of the wine producing region. Another is to simply zigzag through the network of country roads, visiting Radda in Chianti and Gaiole in Chianti, both east of Castellina, or any number of even more minor towns. The best way to explore this stretch is to drift from castle to roadside shrine, following the signs for *degustazione, vendita diretta,* or *cantina.* Producers at private, centuries-old *fattorie* (literally, "farmsteads") usually are happy to invite potential wine buyers for a taste (see *Most Visitable Vineyards,* DIVERSIONS). Afterward, take either the Chiantigiana or the Via Cassia south into Siena.

CHECKING IN: ***Residence San Luigi*** **–** Once a working *podere* (farm), this is 4 miles (6 km) west of Monteriggioni, at Strove. The old farm buildings have been tastefully restored and turned into 42 small apartments sleeping two, three, four, or five people, and they are surrounded by acres of peaceful grounds, including a swimming pool and tennis, basketball, and volleyball courts. Rustic elegance best describes the whole, which includes a restaurant that excels in local cuisine. Although the apartments are rented weekly in high season (May through September), single-night stays can be arranged when there is a vacancy, especially off-season or in the early spring or fall. Closed end of November to *Christmas* and mid-January to mid-March. Major credit cards accepted. 38 Strada della Cerreta, Strove (phone: 577-301055). Moderate.

EATING OUT: ***Il Pozzo*** **–** A very highly regarded restaurant in an idyllic setting within the walls of Monteriggioni. Like most rustic Tuscan establishments, the menu turns to game specialties such as *cinghiale in dolce e forte* (wild boar in a kind of sweet-and-sour sauce, a Sienese specialty) in season. The pasta and earthy *zuppa di fagioli* (bean soup) are other favorites. Closed Sunday evenings, Mondays, most of January, and the first 2 weeks of August. Reservations necessary. Major credit cards accepted. 2 Piazza Roma, Monteriggioni (phone: 577-304127). Expensive to moderate.

SIENA: A wonderfully well preserved medieval city laid out on three hilltops and surrounded by walls, Siena has an artistic heritage second only to that of Florence within Tuscany, and it is the site, twice each summer, of the running of the *Palio,* a famous bareback horse race that traces its origins to the Middle Ages. Siena is also a wine center, hardly remarkable considering its setting in the midst of chianti country and its proximity to the chianti classico zone. For a detailed report of the city and its sights, see *Siena* in THE CITIES.

En Route from Siena – To get to Montalcino, about 25 miles (40 km) south, follow the Via Cassia (SS2) past Buonconvento and turn off (either at Torrenieri or before) to Montalcino. If there is time for a detour along the way, however, turn east at Buonconvento to visit the Abbazia di Monte Oliveto Maggiore, a famous abbey that was a major cultural center in the 15th and 16th centuries. The few miles to the cypress-sheltered motherhouse of the Olivetan monks, a congregation of the Benedictine Order founded in 1319, is a marvelous drive, and readers who found Umberto Eco's *The Name of the Rose* intriguing (or those who liked the film) will be fascinated by this extensive compound still known for its skilled restoration of ancient illuminated manuscripts. Of greatest interest is the Chiostro Grande (Great Cloister), decorated with splendid frescoes on the life of St. Benedict by Luca Signorelli (nine frescoes, done from 1497 to 1498) and Sodom (the remainder, painted from 1505 on) that alone are worth the trip. The refectory and chapterhouse offer some faint indication of simple monastic life as it has always been, and there are beautifully manicured grounds, with gardens and meditation paths. The abbey is open daily, except at lunchtime.

EATING OUT: ***La Torre*** **–** The restored 16th-century tower that houses this restaurant run by the monks goes back to the abbey's earliest days. The food is simple and good. Open daily, except Tuesdays, for lunch and dinner. Reservations advised. No credit cards accepted. Abbazia di Monte Oliveto Maggiore (phone: 577-707022). Inexpensive.

MONTALCINO: The hill town of Montalcino is extraordinarily perched in the midst of a pretty area known for its noble wines and subtle light. In its early days, the site belonged to an abbey, the Abbazia di Sant'Antimo, 7 miles (11 km) to the south. Then Montalcino became a free commune — fought over by the Sienese and the Florentines, however, until the former defeated the latter in 1260 and the town became Sienese.

When Siena fell to Medici Florence in 1555, Sienese patriots fled to Montalcino to form a short-lived Sienese republic-in-exile, until Montalcino itself was forced into submission by Cosimo I. In recognition of this hospitality, a delegation from Montalcino occupies a place of honor in the historical procession that precedes Siena's twice-yearly *Palio* race. Most of Montalcino's stately architecture shows medieval Sienese influence. Be sure to visit the 14th-century Rocca, the fortress from whose aerial lookouts the city kept its enemies at bay and whose main attraction these days is its informal *enoteca* (wine bar), serving thick *panini* sandwiches, cheese, and glasses of the local brunello di Montalcino, one of the most celebrated (and costly) wines in all Italy. The other command post in town is the handsome 19th-century *Caffè Fiaschetteria Italiana* (in the central Piazza del Popolo) where the townsfolk converge to talk for hours, usually about the current status of the famous brunello grape. The *Sagra del Tordo* — part archery contest, part thrush festival (eating them, not listening to them sing) — is held here on the last Sunday in October, when colorful medieval costumes — and rivers of wine — bring the town to life. If visiting at this time, be sure to make your reservations well in advance.

To visit the Abbazia di Sant'Antimo, just follow signs along the drive south from Montalcino. The abbey, one of the most noted examples of medieval monastic architecture, is visible from afar, isolated in an open expanse of olive groves. According to legend, Charlemagne founded it in the 9th century, but most of what is seen today dates from the 12th century. Best preserved of the buildings is the church, built of travertine now turned golden, with alabaster used for much of the trim, column capitals, and windows — at sunset there is nothing quite as beautiful. To visit the church, contact the custodian at 12 Via del Centro, in Castelnuovo dell'Abate, at the top of the hill. And if at all possible, be on hand for early evening vespers (weekdays at 4 PM in winter; 5 PM in summer) when the monks walk down from their quarters in Castelnuovo for an hour of Gregorian chant that fills this sanctum sanctorum to its aged beams.

CHECKING IN: ***Giardino*** – Here are a dozen clean, modest rooms, as well as a good restaurant stocked with the best chianti and brunello vintages. Restaurant closed Wednesdays. 2 Piazza Cavour, Montalcino (phone: 577-848257). Inexpensive.

Il Giglio – A convenient, clean, and unpretentious hotel with about a dozen renovated rooms, an interesting restaurant, and a well-stocked wine cellar. Restaurant closed Mondays. 49 Via Soccorso Saloni, Montalcino (phone: 577-848167). Inexpensive.

Da Idolina – This small (3 rooms) pensione is exquisitely furnished, with canopied beds in some rooms. There is also a delightful attic apartment, complete with a small kitchen and a sun terrace. 70 Via Mazzini, Montalcino (phone: 577-848634). Inexpensive.

EATING OUT: ***La Cucina di Edgardo*** – Just up the street from the *Giglio,* it is the best choice in town — serving very good local cuisine. Closed Wednesdays and January. Reservations advised. Major credit cards accepted. 33 Via Soccorso Saloni, Montalcino (phone: 577-848232). Moderate.

Il Grappolo Blu – The perfect spot to get a late-night plate of pasta or linger over a jug of wine when every other place is closed — and restaurants tend to shut down early in these parts (especially off-season). There also is a simple, but good, cold buffet. Open 6 PM until early morning. Closed Tuesdays. Reservations unnecessary. No credit cards accepted. Scale di Moglio, Montalcino (phone: 577-849078). Moderate to inexpensive.

Sassetti Bassomondo – Just a stone's throw from the Abbazia di Sant'Antimo, 7 miles (11 km) outside of Montalcino is a country trattoria in the best Tuscan tradition, serving classics such as *zuppa di funghi* (soup made from wild mushrooms gathered from the nearby hills) and casserole of wild boar. The house wine is a very fine rosso di Montalcino. Closed Mondays. Reservations unnecessary. No credit cards accepted. Via Bassomondo, Castelnuovo dell'Abate (phone: 577-835619). Moderate to inexpensive.

En Route from Montalcino – Return to Torrenieri and the Via Cassia and follow it south to SS146, the turnoff for Pienza. After a visit, continue another 8 miles (13 km) east on SS146 to Montepulciano.

PIENZA: This little town was once called Corsignano and once belonged to the powerful Piccolomini family, one of whose number, Aeneas Sylvius Piccolomini, was born here and grew to be an exceptionally clever Renaissance man and, eventually, in 1458, Pope Pius II. An acclaimed humanist, he dreamed of creating the perfect Renaissance city, executed to a precise urban plan, and so he commissioned a famous architect, Bernardo Rossellino, to create this small jewel. It became a papal annex and summer home for Pius, who officially changed its name to Pienza in 1462. Today this unusual miniature city is so pristinely preserved that when director Franco Zeffirelli chose to film his *Romeo and Juliet* here, every set was already in place. White lace curtains grace the windows, flowers bloom on sills, and streets are curiously named del Bacio (of the Kiss), dell'Amore, and della Fortuna. A simple Renaissance cathedral stands in Piazza Pio II, the center of town, and to the right of it is the Palazzo Piccolomini, where the Piccolomini family lived until just after World War II when the last family member died. Also in the square are the Palazzo Vescovile, the Palazzo Comunale, and a small cathedral museum. Be sure to walk behind the church for a sweeping view of the whole Val d'Orcia and Monte Amiata, a dormant volcano.

EATING OUT: ***Dal Falco*** – A simple, rustic place, in a shady square just outside the town gate, it's always busy. Try the *pici,* very tasty homemade pasta of flour and water (no eggs). Wednesday is the day for fish, not commonly served in this landlocked, game-loving part of Tuscany. Closed Fridays and the last 2 weeks in November. Reservations advised. No credit cards accepted. 7 Piazza Dante Alighieri, Pienza (phone: 578-748551). Moderate to inexpensive.

MONTEPULCIANO: Famous for its wine — vino nobile di Montepulciano — and several times larger than Pienza, it is still something of a perfect miniature Renaissance city, except that it owes its harmonious aspect more to the continuing patronage of the Medicis than to the utopian dream of one man. A major determinant of the Medicis' favor, no doubt, was Agnolo Ambrogini, one of the great Renaissance poets and a friend and protégé of Giuliano de' Medici and Lorenzo il Magnifico. Born in Montepulciano, he was better known as Il Poliziano, from the ancient name of the town, which was in existence in Etruscan times. Montepulciano sits 2,000 feet above sea level, with the spacious and grandiose Piazza Grande at its highest point. Its major claim to fame is the number of handsome palazzi lining that square as well as the two main arteries — Via Roma, which begins at Porta al Prato but leads to the other end of town under several different names, and Via Ricci. Various architectural styles are represented, but Montepulciano is most noted for its monuments of the 16th century, as well as its flourishes of the baroque, and for the way these important buildings are superimposed on a town plan that goes back to the Middle Ages. There are few "must-see" attractions (discounting the view from the tower of the Palazzo Comunale, a 14th-century building with a 15th-century façade, possibly designed by Michelozzo, in Piazza Grande), but the town itself is a joy to discover, with its winding *vicoli* (alleys), majestic door knockers, window ironwork, and the aged clock tower with the masked Pulcinella striking the hours in front of the Church of Sant'Agostino (the Pulcinella is a 16th-century gift of a Neapolitan visitor, the church a definite Michelozzo design). Outside of town (a mile-long walk down the Strada di San Biagio) is the Tempio di San Biagio, a 16th-century church in pale gold travertine. A High Renaissance masterpiece by Antonio Sangallo the Elder, it sits in an open field, overlooking the whole valley.

CHECKING IN: ***Panoramic*** – A simple hostelry 1 mile (1.6 km) southeast of town, in the direction of Chianciano Terme. It offers 25 rooms, tennis courts, rural calm, pleasant gardens, a fishing lake, and expansive views. Closed November through March. SS146, 8 Via Villa Bianca (phone: 578-798398). Moderate.

Il Marzocco – This small, pretty hotel has two things going for it — its central location, which makes it ideal for exploring the town on foot, and the views of the countryside from many of the 18 rooms. 18 Piazza Savanarola, Montepulciano (phone: 578-757262). Inexpensive.

La Terrazza – This renovated 16th-century residence-turned-hotel is only a minute's walk from Piazza Grande. The name refers to two terraces that make it particularly enjoyable in warm weather. Each of the 13 rooms is furnished differently, most rather handsomely, and there are 3 mini-apartments with kitchenettes that sleep up to four people. 16 Via Piè al Sasso, Montepulciano (phone: 578-757440). Inexpensive.

EATING OUT: ***La Chiusa*** – This farmhouse restaurant can be reached by backtracking a few miles west of Montepulciano on SS146 and then turning north to the town of Montefollonico (which is roughly equidistant from Pienza and Montepulciano, so a meal here can be combined with a visit to either one). If the drive through hilly vineyards seems too far to go, consider that some discriminating diners make the trip from Paris, so the inconvenience is worth the culinary reward. Imaginative and creative cuisine is blended with rarely found Tuscan dishes, such as *gran farro* (a thick peasant soup of cracked wheat) and *piccione al vin santo* (wild pigeon in a sherry-based sauce). Try the heavenly *parfait al cioccolato.* Closed mid-January to end of March, November 5 to December 5, and Tuesdays from October through July. Reservations advised. Major credit cards accepted. Montefollonico (phone: 577-669668). Expensive.

Fattoria Pulcino – Out of town in the direction of Chianciano Terme, this is a medieval monastery-turned-farm that now also operates as a restaurant. Walk past the open wooden ovens and through a tempting maze of farm products (olive oil, wines, *pecorino* cheese, beans) before entering the large dining room, where meals are served at communal tables. The rustic menu is simple, and most of the choices are cooked on the grill. There are excellent steaks, sausages, and some very delicious first courses. Open daily for lunch, Saturdays and Sundays for dinner. Reservations unnecessary. No credit cards accepted. On SS146 (phone: 578-716905). Moderate.

Diva – A noisy, friendly, and unpretentious trattoria right in town. The decor may be a little nondescript, but the local dishes that grace the table make it a memorable dining experience. Closed Tuesdays and 2 weeks in July. Reservations unnecessary. No credit cards accepted. 92 Via di Gracciano nel Corso, Montepulciano (phone: 578-716951). Moderate to inexpensive.

En Route from Montepulciano – To reach Arezzo, take the winding, bucolic road to Nottola, and then head north toward Torrita di Siena and onward to Sinalunga. At Sinalunga, either head east and pick up the autostrada north (A1) to the exit for Arezzo, or continue northward along minor roads to Monte San Savino and then to Arezzo. The latter route passes by (or near) two tiny walled hamlets left over from the Middle Ages and, in a certain sense, from feudal times, because both are private property. Both have a farm family or two still living within the walls, and both are primarily visited now for the restaurants and hotels operating in some of the estate buildings. The first hamlet, the Fattoria dell'Amorosa, is seen from a distance, gently elevated above its own rolling farmlands south of Sinalunga. The second is another 20 minutes north to Gargonza, just outside of Monte San Savino.

CHECKING IN/EATING OUT: ***Locanda dell'Amorosa*** **–** A regal sweep of cypress trees leads up to this unique establishment, a tiny 14th-century walled village-cum-farming enclave turned into a restaurant with rooms to rent. Those who are only passing through can sit in the small, airy *piazzetta* in the warm Tuscan sun, nursing a long lemonade. Those staying in any of the 8 light and spacious rooms (once farmworkers' quarters) are more able to partake of the gastronomic genius of the kitchen, which is built into the old oxen's stalls and has garnered high praise for its local cuisine with an imaginative nouvelle twist. All in all, it is just as quaint as its name — Lover's Inn — implies, and it is a paradisiacal spot to call home while jaunting off to nearby Siena, Arezzo, and other Tuscan towns. Restaurant closed Mondays, Tuesday lunch, and mid-January through February. Reservations advised. Major credit cards accepted. Località l'Amorosa (phone: 577-679497). Hotel expensive to moderate; restaurant expensive.

Castello di Gargonza **–** A 13th-century walled hill town in miniature, Gargonza's claim to fame is that Dante used it as a refuge at some time during his exile from Florence. For over 300 years it has belonged to the noble Guicciardini family, which today runs it as a storybook hotel. There are spacious rooms in the simple, renovated *castello* (castle); otherwise, a score of skillfully renovated stone cottages, with kitchenettes and working fireplaces, sleep two to eight and can be rented weekly or nightly, depending on availability. Just beyond the town walls is the establishment's rustic restaurant, where tables are moved outside during the summer amid the fireflies and the scent of pine. Restaurant closed Mondays and January. Reservations advised. American Express accepted. Castello di Gargonza, Monte San Savino (hotel phone: 575-847021 or the Florence office, 55-296151; restaurant phone: 575-847065). Moderate.

AREZZO: A hill town set at the confluence of green valleys — the Valdarno, the Casentino (the upper valley of the Arno), the Valdichiana — ancient Arretium has been of strategic importance since its earliest Etruscan and Roman days. A free commune with Ghibelline leanings during the Middle Ages, it fell to Guelph Florence in 1289. Early in the next century, however, the short but decisive reign of Guido Tarlati, a bishop who ruled Arezzo from 1312 to 1327, lifted the city to prominence, and it is its early-14th-century character that remains most in evidence today. After Tarlati's death, Arezzo's fortunes waned, and in 1384 it fell once again, definitively this time, to Florence. Some very prominent Italians were born here: Guido d'Arezzo, the 11th-century Benedictine monk who invented the musical scale, the great Renaissance poet Petrarch, and Giorgio Vasari, Renaissance painter, architect, and historian. Piero della Francesca may have been born in nearby Sansepolcro, but Arezzo holds him as one of its dearest sons. The town's museums and churches are filled with his works.

At the top of the series of terraces on which the town is built stretches a spacious public park — the Passeggio del Prato — that overlooks the surrounding farmland. Arezzo's Romanesque-Gothic Duomo stands to one side of the Prato. Begun in the late 13th century and not finished until the beginning of the 16th century, it is home to a host of artworks, from the stained glass windows of Guillaume de Marcillat (a 15th-century French artist) to a famous fresco of Mary Magdalene by Piero della Francesca and, to the left of that, the tomb of Guido Tarlati, completed in 1330 by Giovanni and Agnolo di Ventura, possibly according to a design by Giotto. A few blocks north of the Duomo is the 13th-century Church of San Domenico (Piazza Fossombroni), which has a beautiful wooden crucifix, one of the earlier works of Cimabue. Not far away is the house (open to the public) of Giorgio Vasari (55 Via XX Settembre), who supervised the construction, took care of the furnishing, and decorated it himself with frescoes between 1540 and 1548.

Pace yourself, because Arezzo's main attractions are still to come. Piero della Francesca's remarkable fresco cycle illustrating the Legend of the True Cross (*La Storia della Croce*), a mature work and the one on which most of his fame rests, is behind the high altar of the Basilica di San Francesco, a large, barren 14th-century church that is the spiritual nucleus and geographical center of the old town. And not far from that is the Piazza Grande, center of urban life for centuries. This sloping, rhomboid piazza is surrounded by palazzi reflecting the architectural styles of several centuries: Giorgio Vasari's 16th-century Palazzo delle Logge (Loggia Palace), with its open portico of shops, is on the north side, flanked by several handsome Renaissance palazzi and medieval homes; the Palazzo della Fraternità dei Laici (Palace of the Lay Fraternity) has a Gothic-Renaissance façade; and the magnificent Pieve di Santa Maria, a 12th-to-14th-century church with a Pisan-Lucchese Romanesque façade of the 13th century, backs into the square, with its tall campanile of "100 holes" (it actually has 40 mullioned windows) standing alongside it. The first weekend of every month, Piazza Grande and the surrounding streets become the site of an antiques fair, with hundreds of vendors — of inexpensive bric-a-brac, sublime *objets* and furniture, and just plain junk — in attendance. On the first Sunday in September, the market moves elsewhere to make room for the annual *Giostra del Saracino,* a re-creation of a medieval jousting tournament in which eight knights representing the town's four quarters attack an effigy of the Saracen. Accompanying the joust is a historical procession of lance-bearing knights on brilliantly caparisoned horses, a fitting spectacle for this evocative and picturesque old square.

Other places of interest in Arezzo include the remains of a Roman amphitheater and the nearby *Museo Archeologico Mecenate* (Mecenate Archaeological Museum; phone: 575-20882), which contains a collection of the *corallini* vases made by Aretine artists from the 1st century BC to the 1st century AD. It is open daily except Mondays from 9 AM to 1 PM and 3:30 to 6:30 PM; admission charge. The Arezzo Tourist Information Office (116 Piazza Risorgimento; phone: 575-20839) can supply information on other attractions.

CHECKING IN: *Continentale* – Large (75 rooms), modern, and only a few minutes' walk from the medieval quarter. It has a restaurant. 7 Piazza Guido Monaco, Arezzo (phone: 575-20251). Moderate.

Minerva – Not as central as the *Continentale,* but modern, clean, and comfortable, with 118 rooms and a restaurant. 6 Via Fiorentina, Arezzo (phone: 575-27891). Moderate.

EATING OUT: *Buca di San Francesco* – The dining room is the beautifully frescoed former *cantina* (wine cellar) of a lovely 14th-century palazzo, and if that's not enough, the food here is some of the best in the region. In addition to thick, juicy steaks and roast lamb, there's a timbale of spinach and chicken livers, vegetable *sformati* (soufflés), and a hearty white bean soup. Closed Monday evenings, Tuesdays, and July. Reservations advised. Major credit cards accepted. 1 Via San Francesco, Arezzo (phone: 575-23271). Expensive to moderate.

Al Principe – Aretines love this warm and busy trattoria, one of the oldest still operating in the area. It's in the rural periphery, along SS71 northbound, a 5-minute drive from the center, but the ride is more than compensated by the pleasant culinary experience in store. It offers the whole roster of unpretentious local goodness, plus a few house specialties such as lamb cooked in a crust or baby eels (*cee*) in terra cotta casseroles. Closed Mondays and mid-July to mid-August. Reservations advised. No credit cards accepted. 25 Località Giovi (phone: 575-362046). Moderate.

En Route from Arezzo – To expedite the tour, hop on the A1, and be back in Florence in 45 minutes. Or, for those who intend to explore the neighboring region of Umbria, take SS71 south to Lake Trasimeno, then skirt the lake to Perugia, visiting a final Tuscan hill town, Cortona (18 miles/29 km from Arezzo), before reaching the lake. The birthplace of Luca Signorelli, Cortona has an Etruscan background and a medieval appearance, with steep, narrow streets, only one of which, Via Nazionale, the main street, is level. It leads into Piazza della Repubblica, with the Palazzo Comunale (Town Hall), and then on into the adjoining Piazza Signorelli, where the Palazzo Pretorio (or Palazzo Casali) houses the *Museo dell'Accademia Etrusca* (Etruscan Academy Museum; phone: 575-62767), most famous for its 5th-century BC bronze Etruscan chandelier, the largest and most richly decorated of its kind. The *Museo Diocesano* (Diocesan Museum; no phone), in a former church in front of the Duomo, contains — besides several Signorellis — an especially beautiful *Annunciation* by Fra Angelico. Both museums are open daily except Mondays from 9 AM to 1 PM and 3:30 to 6:30 PM; admission charge.

Otherwise, take SS71 north out of Arezzo to explore the northeastern corner of Tuscany. The road follows the Arno into a little-known, sparsely populated, forest-dense area known as the Casentino, site of powerful monastic developments in the late Middle Ages that were instrumental in paving the way for the Renaissance. The monasteries were usually set in inaccessible mountain sites along the backbone of the Apennines, and the overwhelming beauty of their natural surroundings predisposed residents to extraordinary meditational heights. Contact with the secular world was not totally severed, however, and artistic works and rich architecture are evident, if not abundant.

At Bibbiena, 20 miles (32 km) north of Arezzo, turn onto SS208 and climb another 17 miles (27 km) through pine and beech forests to the most famous of the Casentino monasteries, La Verna, at 3,500 feet. The noble Cattani family of Chiusi in Casentino donated this mountain to St. Francis in 1213, and it was here, in 1224, that the saint from Assisi received the stigmata. A cluster of churches sprang up in the century after his death (1226), many, as in the Chiesa Maggiore, filled with very beautiful terra cottas by Andrea della Robbia. A large community of Franciscans still lives in seclusion at La Verna, carrying on the 800-year-old tradition of the 3 PM procession and singing of vespers. The monks also maintain a modern but modest *foresteria* (quarters with accommodations for visitors); inexpensive, modest, clean rooms are available, and the price includes three obligatory meals (good and honest fare, and there really is no other place to eat). To reserve a room, contact the *Santuario della Verna,* Chiusi della Verna (AR) 52010; (phone: 575-599356 for general information, 575-599357 for price information).

Another monastery, Camaldoli, the oldest monastic center in all Tuscany, can be reached by a pine-shaded road from La Verna (about a 20-mile/32-km drive) or by returning to Bibbiena and there taking SS71 north (from Serravalle, follow signs to Camaldoli). What functions as the monastery today was founded in the 11th century as the *foresteria* for pilgrims visiting the renowned Eremo (Hermitage) of the Camaldolese division of Benedictine monks, another mile (1.6 km) up the road. Gradually it turned into a monastery itself and was a famed center of learning during the Renaissance — Giuliano and Lorenzo de' Medici used to meet here to discuss classical texts and philosophy with Marsilio Ficino, Leon Battista Alberti, and other 15th-century intellectuals. The monastery has an interesting 16th-century pharmacy with the original cabinets and ceramic containers, and still sells the herbal panaceas for which the monks have always been known. It also has its original 11th-century Hospitium Camalduli for receiving guests — simple, clean, renovated rooms, some with bath. (Unlike La Verna, there's no obligation to eat here because there are two other modest restaurants in the tiny town.) For reservations, contact the *Monastero di Camaldoli* (Foresteria,

Camaldoli (AR) 52010; phone: 575-556013). The Eremo, where the monks still live in seclusion under the Benedictine rule, is also open to the public. Founded in 1012 by St. Romualdo, it consists of 20 isolated, single cells, each with a sleeping area, study, and small outdoor garden.

Return to Bibbiena and take SS70 north to Poppi, where a quick slip through the Old Town will be of interest. Medieval home of the powerful Guidi counts, who ruled the Casentino from the 11th to the 14th century, Poppi has a superb castle (now the Palazzo Pretorio) with a small but elaborate courtyard and a tower offering sweeping views of all that was once the Guidi domain. From Poppi, bear west on SS70, up and over the Passo di Consuma, and then, after about 7 miles (11 km), turn left at the signs for Pelago and Vallombrosa. The latter, an ancient fir forest between the Casentino valley to the east and the Valdarno to the west, is a traditional summer escape for Florentines and the site of another ancient monastery, the seat of the Vallombrosian division of the Benedictines. The monastery dates from 1230, although the nucleus of monks founded by St. Giovanni Gualberto goes back to the year 1000. The body of buildings has undergone changes over time, but the 13th-century campanile and a 15th-century dungeon still exist. Nearby Saltino has a number of good restaurants and hotels, some with open vistas over the valley below.

To return to Florence, head south toward Reggello and then west to Leccio.

Elba

Known for the popular palindrome "Able was I ere I saw Elba" and for Napoleon's brief residence as an exile, the island of Elba remains a relatively undeveloped vacation paradise, with more than 50 beaches along its 90 miles of coastline, fine local food and wine, typical Tuscan hospitality, and great natural beauty. Five and a half miles from the mainland, Elba is just difficult enough to reach, and sufficiently out of the way, to deter hordes of package tour travelers (although the island does get very crowded in July and August). There are, however, many posh pleasure boats from the nearby Argentario peninsula yacht basin that make port at Elba during high season. Those travelers who come by ferry from Piombino — or on the flight from Pisa — find the journey well worth the effort. They tend to come back again and again, preferring Elba's quiet dignity to the more fashionable vacation spots along the frenetic Mediterranean-Ligurian coastline.

Despite its diminutive size, Elba has been known since the birth of history. Called *Ilva* by the Ligurians and *Aethalia* by the Greeks, it passed from the Etruscans and became part of the Roman Empire. It was ruled by the Pisans during the Middle Ages and served as a haven for the Barbary pirates in the 16th century. The Medicis, too, left their mark — their influence can be seen in the fortifications of Portoferraio, built after Cosimo I de' Medici bought Elba in the 16th century.

The island was perhaps most influenced by Napoleon Bonaparte, whose first exile from France, and short reign over Elba, began May 5, 1814 and ended February 26, 1815. Although he lived here less than a year, the emperor did much to improve the island, altering street plans and building new roads, modernizing agriculture, and developing iron mines. His summer home, the Villa di San Martino, can be visited and admired, and the hardy can climb the hillside beyond to the island's oldest fortress, Volterraio; situated atop ruins of an Etruscan temple site, it also is the place where local residents once gathered to protect themselves from the notorious pirates Barbarossa and Dragut.

Iron ore is still mined in the hills above Rio Marina and then shipped from Portoferraio ("Port of Iron") — with 11,500 inhabitants, the largest of the eight towns on the island and considered its "capital." Garnet, beryl, marcasite, tourmaline, and pollucite are just a few of the other 150 minerals and semiprecious stones to be found in Elban soil, the result of the seismic turmoil that created the island, and there are more varieties of granite here than anywhere in Europe. Geologists and gemstone collectors can often be found happily chipping away at the rock ledges along many of the island's winding roads. The astonishing range of colors of the island's hydrangeas is the result of the soil's rich mineral composition.

Elba bathes in sunshine most of the year. Although it is small, it is dramatic, with 3,000-foot-high mountains that create an east-west wind break from the prevailing scirocco, which brings hot air and sometimes dust from Africa, and a *maestrale,* which blows cool air south from the Alps. As a result of its peculiar formation, the eastern and northern parts of the island tend to be green and wooded, while the west is rocky and more barren (like Sardinia's coastline), and the south is buff-colored and sandy.

Most appropriately, the island is shaped like a fish, and Portoferraio's pretty port, marked by the stout ancient ramparts of the Fortezze Medicee, is tucked within the underside of the top fin. In ancient times, Elba had just two important towns, both set on high hills well inland because of the frequent incursions by pirates such as the notorious Barbarossa — Marciana (where the eye of the fish would be) and Rio nell'Elba (at the center of the tail). Both these tiny, gracious towns, whose somber medieval cast is enlivened by today's lush gardens, the many newly restored homes, and general air of prosperity, are only a half-hour drive from the splendid coastline.

The high season begins just before *Easter,* when the sea begins to warm and the island bursts into bloom — marguerites, broom, and other wildflowers cover the hills forested with pine, beech, chestnut, and ilex trees, and potted geraniums, bougainvilleas, roses, and hydrangeas brighten every doorstep and windowsill. It ends in mid-October, when the smell of autumn is in the air and many hotels close for the winter. Swimming is possible from mid-May through September. Sometimes the weather does become *brutto,* but the rain seldom lasts more than a day or two and provides a break from the normally hot and sunny weather.

Life here is governed by the seasons far more than by any other factor. For all the bustle of summer tourism, a largely agricultural existence creates a quiet atmosphere. Every town and village has its own well-cared-for *bocce* court, where the men (and more recently the women as well) play this traditional game almost every evening. The grass on the airport runway is kept trimmed by flocks of sheep and goats from a nearby farm that produces the extraordinary fresh ricotta cheese used in many of the island's dishes. At night, the lights of the island's fishing boats can be seen bobbing up and down at sea; in the morning, their catch — swordfish, cuttlefish, various white fish, clams and mussels, as well as prawns and small spiny lobsters — is displayed in ice-filled boxes on marble slabs at the market.

Whether a visitor chooses to relax on the island's wonderful beaches, to climb and picnic in the forests on the mountains, hike the inland roads with their breathtaking views of sea and wooded slopes, or to drive along the sometimes spectacular coastal roads, it's hard to miss Elba's natural charm, peaceful abundance, and timeless beauty.

TOURIST INFORMATION: Prices are generally higher from May to September, but tourist services are more plentiful during this time, too. Numerous free guides, including lists of hotels and restaurants, are available from the Azienda Autonoma di Cura Soggiorno e Turismo dell'Isola d'Elba (26 Calata Italia, Portoferraio; phone: 914671), which serves the entire island. In addition, information in Portoferraio and other towns is available from the following sources: *Portoferraio:* Agenzia Viaggi TESI (Calata Italia; phone: 914386) and *Centro Guide Isole d'Elba* (171 Viale

Elba; phone: 933017 or 914818); *Marina di Campo:* Ufficio Turistico CIPAT (Via Mascagni; phone: 976414); *Procchio:* Agenzia Viaggi Bruno (Via Provinciale; phone: 907716); *Marciana Marina:* Ufficio Turistico Brauntour (2 Via Mentana; phone: 996874); *Porto Azzurro:* Ufficio Turistico La Pianotta (Lungomare A. De Gasperi; phone: 95105); *Rio Marina:* Ufficio Turistico Forti (23 Via Palestro; phone: 962392); *Cavo:* Ufficio Turistico Estelba (Cavo; phone: 949934).

TELEPHONE: The area code for the entire island is 565. When calling from within Italy, dial 0565 before the local number.

FOOD AND WINE: Elba offers a particularly unusual combination of food — the fresh seafood dishes typical of a Mediterranean island plus the hearty peasant fare of the bountiful Tuscan farmland. The seafood dishes include *cacciucco,* a form of fish soup resembling bouillabaisse, and *gamberi* (prawns) or *polpi* (octopus), served in many ways, often together, dipped in batter and fried. Other fish offerings may include *dentice* (sea bream), *nasello* (whiting), and *triglia* (red mullet). There is a tradition of *cucina casalinga* (home cooking) with pasta, often handmade, combined with wonderful fish and shellfish — *alla margherita* (with spider crab), *all'aragosta* (with lobster), or *alle seppie* (with cuttlefish). More familiar is spaghetti with fish sauce, or *alle vongole* (with tiny clams), or *al pesto* (with fresh basil, oil, and parmesan cheese). *Gurguglione* is a tasty vegetable soup. *Cinghiale* (wild boar) may also appear on the menu. *Foccacia di pinoli,* a flat cake studded with pine nuts, is typical of Portoferraio. Don't be bashful about having the waiter explain the menu — many food names are in a colloquial dialect and incomprehensible even to Italians from the non-Tuscan mainland.

Be on the lookout for the colorful outdoor markets — food, household goods, clothing — held daily except Sundays in a different town: Rio Marina on Mondays, Marciana Marina on Tuesdays, Marina di Campo on Wednesdays, Procchio and Copliveri on Thursdays, Portoferrario (Piazza della Repubblica) on Fridays, and Porto Azzurro on Saturdays.

Elban wine is of high quality, even by Italian standards. The island produces a variety of table wines — white, red, rosé, and sparkling — and several sweet dessert wines. Of the former, the white is outstanding; try the procanico and elba bianco. A favorite red is sangiaveto. The moscato and aleatico dessert wines are delicious served with fresh fruits or with cookies called *crostate.* If you have a special interest in wines, drive to Marciana Marina and visit the bar-tasting platform at the end of the Lungo Mare. This is the place to sample locally made wines that complement Elban food. While on that side of the island, drive a little farther toward Poggio and taste the local brandy. The route is well marked, and the town is easy to find. Near Portoferraio is the century-old wine estate, La Chiusa, run by Giuliana Foresi, a top producer of the prized aleatico, which visitors can sample and purchase there. Another Elba specialty is its bracing white grappa, an after-dinner drink.

GETTING AROUND: Traveling to and around Elba often sounds more difficult than it really is. Transportation and route depend only on personal preference and available time.

Air – San Giusto Airport in Pisa is the international airport nearest Elba. There is a small airport at Marina di Campo in the southern part of the island near the coast (phone: 976011), but you'll have to fly on a regularly scheduled flight from Pisa or on a charter. *Alitalia* operates daily flights to Pisa from Rome, Milan, Turin, Sicily, and Sardinia, and there are daily flights to Pisa from other European cities such as London, Frankfurt, and Paris. From Pisa, *Transavio* (phone: 50-598096) flies to Elba Mondays through Saturdays, four flights per day, from June to September. *Transavio* also has service from Florence during the same months, operating three times each week. During the remainder of the year, travelers can get to Elba from Pisa by going down the coast and taking a boat at Piombino.

Boat Excursions – Regular excursions around the island operate from Portoferraio throughout the summer; inquiries may be made at the main tourist agencies (see *Tourist Information,* above), hotels, or the principal bar on the waterfront. A few excursions operate from Porto Azzurro as well. Contact *Agenzia Mantica* (at the port; phone: 95351) for information about 3-hour outings. Small motor boats can be hired at Porto Azzurro and Marina di Campo.

Bus – Regular bus service on the island is designed to meet the requirements of the inhabitants rather than those of visitors. Bus runs start very early in the morning; their frequency is reduced on Sundays and holidays. The main station in Portoferraio is next to the Grattacielo, Elba's 10-story "skyscraper." Pick up a schedule at *ATR*'s office (20 Viale Elba, Portoferraio; phone: 914392).

Car Rental – Cars can be rented at the airport in Pisa: *Avis* (phone: 50-42028), *Hertz* (phone: 50-44426), or *Europcar* (phone: 50-41017). The drive from Pisa to Piombino takes about 2 hours. There also are several major car rental agencies at the ferry terminal in Piombino. On all but weekdays in May, June, September, and October, you *must* have reservations to put your car on any of the ferries (see *Ferry,* below); reservations can be obtained through most travel agents.

Cars also can be rented on Elba. The main rental agency on the island is *Maggiore Autonoleggio* (8 Calata Italia, Portoferraio; phone: 915368). *Taglioni Giovanni-Aeroporto* (phone: 977150) is at the Elba airport. Arrangements can be made to have a car meet you at the ferry in Portoferraio or at the airport. However, renting on the island is considerably more expensive than on the mainland, where rates tend to be more competitive.

Ferry – There are ferries from Piombino to Portoferraio, and vice versa, about every 50 minutes from 5:15 AM to 9:30 PM during July and August (be sure to reserve in advance). Departures during other months are less frequent and more variable; inquire directly from the ferry companies (listed below). All the ferries accept cars and caravans; the journey takes an hour. The hydrofoil is for foot passengers and takes half an hour. All ferries and hydrofoils operate between Piombino and Portoferraio. Some ferries go to Cavo, Rio Marino, and Porto Azzurro as well.

Toremar has six offices (4 Via Calafati, Livorno; phone: 586-896113; 22 Calata Italia, Portoferraio; phone: 918080; 13-14 Piazzale Premuda, Piombino; phone: 31100; 9 Banchina dei Voltoni, Rio Marina, phone: 962073; Banchina IV Novembre, Porto Azzuro; phone: 95004; and 114 Via Appalto, Cavo; phone: 949871). *Navarma* can be found at three locations (13 Piazzale Premuda, Piombino; phone: 39775; 4 Viale Elba, Portoferraio; phone: 914133 or 918101; and 114 Via Appalto, Cavo; phone: 949871).

Guided Tours – The main travel agencies offer a number of half- and whole-day guided tours. Details may be obtained in Portoferraio from either *Aethaltour* (Viale Elba; phone: 915755) or *Intourelba* (162 Via Carducci; phone: 916034). There also is a guides' association (171 Viale Elba; phone: 933017, 914818, 914901, or 917223). For an individual guided tour in English, contact Lucia Pieri (phone: 914901).

Moped and Bike Rental – Either is a good alternative to a car for day trips on this small island. *Taglioni Giovanni-Aeroporto* (see *Car Rental,* above) also rents mopeds (phone: 977150). Also see *Brandi* (11 Via Manganaro; phone: 914359) and *Le Ghiaie Rental* (26 Via Cairoli; phone: 914666). Motorcycles can be rented at *Effepi Moto* (Viale Teseo Tesei; phone: 917543).

Taxi – Call *Molo Massimo* (phone: 915212).

Train – There are no trains on Elba, but to reach Piombino (and ferries) by train, take the main rail line that runs along the west coast of Italy and get off at Campiglia Marittima (be sure to take a train that stops in Campiglia). From Campiglia Marittima, a branch line runs the 9 miles (14 km) to Piombino Marittima, its quayside terminus. Leave plenty of time, and be careful not to get off at either of the two earlier stops in the town of Piombino. During the summer, there are several trains daily.

SPECIAL EVENTS: *Easter* is a very special time on Elba, but tourist services are severely limited at that time of year. On *Good Friday* evening, villagers gather at the local churches to organize processions. Young men carry the cross and an effigy of Christ through village streets, while others in the procession sing Gregorian chants. Early on *Easter* morning, villagers from Sant'Ilario and San Piero, hill towns above Marina di Campo, meet in procession on the way to worship in each other's churches. On *Easter Monday* worshipers make a pilgrimage to the Shrine of the Madonna del Monte above Marciana and, on *Ascension Thursday,* to the Shrine of Santa Lucia outside Portoferraio. A mass for Napoleon is celebrated annually on May 5 in Portoferraio.

On August 12 the island celebrates the *Feast of Santa Chiara,* the patron saint of Marciana Marina, with a religious procession, dancing in the piazza, and fireworks. Celebrations start in the evening and go on until the early hours. Similar rites are held on August 7 for San Gaetano in Marina di Campo. On August 16, San Rocco is feted with a rowboat competition with rowers in folkloric costumes, followed by a free meal of grilled sardines and wine served in the main piazza at Rio Marina.

SPORTS AND FITNESS: During the summer, there are a multitude of congenial competitions, such as boat races, tennis matches, and water skiing and windsurfing championships, all with vacationers in mind. These tend to be very friendly affairs, not serious tournaments. In general, water sports are the most popular. Equipment can be rented at most of the large beaches.

Beaches – Elba has a variety of wonderful beaches, some sandy and safe for swimmers and waders, others rocky and suitable for deep diving. The following are the best sandy beaches: on the north coast — Spartaia, Procchio, Campo all'Aia, La Biodola, and Scaglieri; on the south coast — Stella Bay, Lacona, Marina di Campo, Cavoli, Fetovaia, Seccheto (sand and rock); on the east coast — Barbarossa Reale, Cavo (sand and rock), Calamita Peninsula, Naregno, Pareti, Morcone, and Straccoligno. Usually, hotels and bars near the beaches own concessions for such facilities as deck chairs, umbrellas, changing cabins, and toilets; charges are by the day or week. During the high season, deck chairs at popular beaches are reserved months in advance by regular summer residents. For thermal waters, there is the well-equipped, modern *Terme San Giovanni* at Saline (phone: 914680).

Boating – For rentals, contact *Magazzini* (phone: 966-3936) and the *Tesi Agency* (Calata Italia; phone: 914386) in Portoferrario, and *Settemari* (*Circolo della Vela CVMM;* phone in Milan: 2-480-09403) in Marciana Marina.

Fishing – Both underwater and by boat, fishing is free except in the protected area between Le Ghiaie pebble beach at Portoferraio and the submarine nature reserve at Capo Bianco. Inquire at your hotel or at the waterfront. The village of Chiessi is a favorite base for spear fishers.

Golf – The *Acquabona Golf* hotel has a beautifully situated, well-maintained 9-hole golf course inland on the main road between Portoferraio and Acquabona (phone: 960064).

Horseback Riding – *Ranch Antonio* stables, Monte Orello (phone: 933132); *Paolo Rossi Fattoria* (Località Buraccio; phone: 940245); and *Azienda Agricola Sapere* (Località Mola Porto Azzurro; phone: 95033).

Sailing – For sailing lessons, contact *Segelschule Elba* (Località Magazzini; phone: 933288 or 933020 and Località Bagnaia; phone: 961012); and *Casa di Vela* (50 Schiopparello Spiaggia; phone: 933265 in summer; 74 Via del Mare, Livorno; phone: 586-50562 in winter). *Segelschule Elba* also has affiliations at some of the island's hotels — the *Feluca* (Località Bagnaia; phone: 933184); *Le Grotte del Paradiso* (Località Le Grotte; phone: 933057); and the *Garden* (Via Vittorio Emanuele, Schiopparello; phone: 933043).

Skin Diving – Elban waters are wonderful for skin diving, especially along the rocky northwest and west coasts and also along the east coast of the Calamita Peninsula, which is accessible only by boat. The fishing village of Chiessi is a favorite base. Oxygen tanks may be filled at the *Enfola* campsite (phone: 915390) and at *Armeria Elbana* (phone: 914770). In Marciana Marina, the *Centro Sub* (15 Via Aldo Moro; phone: 904256) offers courses in diving and underwater photography. They also rent boats to groups.

Tennis – It is hard to find courts near the beaches because of the steep terrain. Many of the hotels, however, have floodlit courts. In and around Portoferraio, non-guests may sometimes be able to play at the *Park Hotel Napoleone* (Località San Martino; phone: 916973); the *Hermitage* (Località Biodola; phone: 969932); *Le Grotte del Paradiso* (Località Acquabona; phone: 940065); *Picchiaie Residence* (Località Picchiaie; phone: 933072); *Galletti Fabrizio* (Località Schiopparello; phone: 933017); and *Fabricia* (Località Magazzini; phone: 933181). The island has one public tennis court — *Impianti Sportivi Comunali* (Località San Giovanni; no phone).

Windsurfing – This sport has taken hold on Elba, as elsewhere around the Mediterranean. The *Elba Windsurfing School* is headquartered at the *La Perla* hotel in Procchio (phone: 907401 or 907402). In Marina di Campo, *La Foce* campground has a school (phone: 976456), and there is another at *Tropical* beach (phone: 97006).

NIGHTCLUBS AND NIGHTLIFE: Discos and nightclubs dot the island, and almost every Friday, Saturday, and Sunday evening one village or another has dancing in the open air. If you prefer kicking up your heels indoors, in Portoferraio try *Norman's Club* (Località Capannone; phone: 969943); *Club 64* (Località Capannone; phone: 969988); and *Music Bar* (Via Provinciale; phone: 915432). However, the favorite Elban evening pursuit is definitely *bocce,* the Italian version of French *boules.* The game is played with great fun and seriousness. Each town has lighted courts; nearby bars do a good business.

TOURING ELBA

Elba is a tiny island and its roads are quite good, so it's easy to drive around it in just a day. With this in mind, choose accommodations from the variety of resorts listed below and explore from one base. For the sea lover, there is every kind of beach and aquatic facility. Inland, the mountains offer a completely different experience even though they are only a mile or two from the beaches.

In general, costs on the island are about 10% lower than on the mainland, but as everywhere, fish is not inexpensive — not even on an island. Elba has relatively few restaurants because most hotels require guests to take at least half board. Even in the more expensive hotels, full board costs very little more, making it perhaps the wisest choice. The price ranges listed below are for high season (officially mid-June to mid-September); some hotels offer savings of up to 40% for bookings in late May or early October. Hotels rated as expensive charge from $250 to over $300 for a double room; moderate, from $90 to $200; and inexpensive, less than $80. A meal for two, including wine and tips, in a restaurant rated as expensive costs $100 or more; moderate, $50 to $90; and inexpensive, less than $35.

PORTOFERRAIO: The capital of Elba is well worth exploring and is recommended as a base during the off-season, when the many resort hotels elsewhere on the island are closed. It lies on the northwest promontory at the entrance to Portoferraio Bay. Walk from the harbor through the walled arches (stopping for a treat at the *gelateria*) and continue onward and upward along beautiful, steep streets flanked by yellow houses. On Via Garibaldi, the main street, is the Town Hall, the boyhood home of Victor Hugo. To the northeast, on Via Napoleone, is the Chiesa della Misericordia; mass is said here every May 5 for Napoleon. Continue to the highest point in town, Piazza Napoleone, for spectacular views: To the west is the Forte del Falcone; to the east, above the lighthouse, Forte della Stella. Both were originally Medici fortresses, built in 1548 and later completed by Napoleon. On the ridge between the two fortresses lies the Palazzina dei Mulini (made from two older windmills that were joined together), which was Napoleon's principal residence; it has a pretty garden and contains his library and other memorabilia. Open daily, except Mondays, from 9 AM to 1:30 PM and 3 to 6 PM May to October; from 9 AM to 1:30 PM in winter; Sundays from 9 AM to 12:30 PM year-round; admission charge (which can include admission to the Villa di San Martino; see *En Route from Portoferraio*).

If markets intrigue you, stop by *Galleaze,* the covered market in Piazza Cavour; it is open weekdays. The bustling open-air market in Piazza della Repubblica is open Friday mornings. Local craftspeople are centered in Portoferraio and there are several shops to purchase their wares. *Insula di Pino e Laura* (3 Via Fucini) offers handsome small bowls in olive wood, and large hand-carved panels worked into wall pieces and even bedsteads. At *Vetro e Legno* (24 Piazza del Popolo), hand-blown glass comes in various intriguing shapes. *Terra e Mano* (2 Via G. Marconi) is the workshop and showroom for Oreste May's elegant modern ceramic plats and pots with tasteful designs. For a wide selection of rock crystals and Tuscan stones, some for collectors, others worked into jewelry and gift items, stop by *Cosebelle* (Piazza del Popolo) or its factory and showroom (Località Antiche Saline; phone: 917213). Works are also made on commission. *Enoteca la Botte* (Via Guerrzazzi) in the downtown area sells Elban wines by the case (and will deliver to yachts). Visitors are welcome to a free tasting at one of the shop's handful of tables. Snacks, sandwiches, and wine by the glass are available as are the island's other traditional products such as honey and cakes, including the famous dry tea cake *schiaccio di Rio Marino.*

CHECKING IN: ***Acquamarina*** – Recently renovated, this agreeable bed and breakfast establishment has 32 rooms, some with a sea view and balcony. The restaurant overlooks a splendid bay with a beach. Open March through October. Località Padulella, Portoferrario (phone: 914057). Expensive to moderate.

Crystal – Close to the beach, this hostelry has 15 air conditioned rooms and a good dining room. Recently built, it is located on a street with some traffic; however, all the guestrooms are soundproof. The front rooms are recessed and have ample terraces with good sea views of the nearby sand. There is a billiard and reading room. Open year-round. Località Le Ghiaie (phone: 917971; fax: 918772). Expensive to moderate.

Park – Turn-of-the-century elegance is found in this 65-room hotel on a wooded hillside, about 5 minutes from the main port. There also is a meeting room, 2 tennis courts, miniature golf, mountain bikes for rent, and a minibus to take guests to the beach. A riding stable is nearby. Open *Easter* through October. San Martino di Portoferraio, Portoferraio (phone: 565-918502; fax: 565-917836). Expensive to moderate.

Nuova Padulella – Good location, central heating, and reasonable prices make this modern 38-room hotel a good place to stay, although it is short on charm. Open year-round. 1 Viale Einaudi, Portoferraio (phone: 915506). Moderate to inexpensive.

Villa Ombrosa – Close to both Portoferraio and to a lovely beach, this 47-room hostelry has real charm. Be sure to ask to a front room with a balcony. Open year-round. 3 Via De Gasperi, Portoferraio (phone: 914150). Moderate to inexpensive.

Albergo L'Ape Elbana – This old villa in downtown Portoferraio, with a wide verandah, is second class, but offers 20 comfortable rooms and a homey restaurant. Open year-round. 2 Salita Cosimo de' Medici, Portoferraio (phone: 914245). Inexpensive.

EATING OUT: ***La Barca*** – The locals think this place is the best in town, and they're right. The wood-burning oven turns out delicious fish baked in paper. Located downtown, this friendly trattoria is cozy inside and offers a few tables outdoors for alfresco dining. Open daily. Reservations necessary. Major credit cards accepted. Via Guerrazzi, Portoferraio (phone: 918036). Moderate.

Al Solito Posto – This small (40 seats) eatery has charm. The seafood dishes include *antipasto di mare* and baked fish, while the desserts are white or dark chocolate mousse. Veal saddle à la Orloff is a house specialty. Closed Thursdays and January 15–February 28. Reservations necessary. Major credit cards accepted. Via Carducci, Portoferraio (phone: 916238). Moderate.

Padulella – Rough it with a fish meal on a wooden bench right on the beach, a 15-minute walk from Portoferraio. In the evening, a wood-burning oven is used to make pizza at this humble beachcomber's spot. Open in warm weather only. Reservations advised. No credit cards accepted. Padulella Beach, Portoferraio (phone: 930274). Moderate to inexpensive.

La Ferrigna – The best-known restaurant in Portoferraio specializes in Elban cookery, especially seafood. Try the prawns, squid with risotto, or stuffed zucchini. Closed Tuesdays and December to March. Reservations advised. Major credit cards accepted. 22-23 Piazza della Repubblica, Portoferraio (phone: 914129). Inexpensive.

En Route from Portoferraio – Villa San Martino, Napoleon's summer residence, lies south of Portoferraio on a hill overlooking the sea. Although Napoleon lived here only a few months before his departure for the Hundred Days, ending with the Battle of Waterloo, the villa is imbued with his mystique. The central room is decorated with trompe l'oeil paintings depicting the Egyptian campaign. On one wall the emperor's graffito "Napoleon is happy everywhere" is still readable. Open daily, except Mondays, from 9 AM to 1 PM and 3 to 7 PM May to October; from 9 AM to 1:30 PM in winter; admission charge (which can include admission on the same day to the Palazzina dei Mulini; because the villa is closed on Mondays and the *palazzina* on Tuesdays, a combined visit cannot be made on either day). The schedule of the museum's hours and days are subject to change on short notice; it's best to check with the Azienda per il Turismo (26 Calata Italia) by the port.

BIODOLA: West of Portoferraio toward Procchio, Biodola is one of the most beautiful resort areas on Elba's north coast. It has a broad, sandy beach and is set well off the road.

CHECKING IN: ***Hermitage*** – An elegant, modernized luxury hotel, the pride of the island, it is tucked into a corner of Biodola Bay. Considered Elba's best, it has 127 rooms; accommodations include bedroom cottages on the steep, wooded slopes overlooking the bay, and there are 2 swimming pools, a private beach, garden, 8 tennis courts, and a 6-hole golf course. There is a fine restaurant with attentive waiters and a sophisticated menu, as well as another dining spot on the beach. Open April to October. Golfo della Biodola, Biodola (phone: 969932). Expensive.

La Biodola – Boasting a loyal clientele, this place has 73 tastefully decorated rooms overlooking the bay, a seawater pool in a lovely, landscaped garden, 8 tennis courts, volleyball, windsurfing, boat rentals, and a beginner's golf course. Open April to October. Golfo della Biodola, Biodola (phone: 969966). Expensive to moderate.

Casa Rosa – With its own pool and overlooking Biodola Bay, this is small (35 rooms), neat, and unpretentious, but the dining room is good and the garden pleasant. Good value for the money. Open *Easter* through October. Località Biodola (phone: 969931 or 969857). Moderate.

Danila – This 26-room hotel with a family atmosphere also is a good value. Be sure to ask for a hillside bungalow — they have the best views and the most privacy — unless you mind climbing stairs. The restaurant is attractive; the food is excellent, although the menu is limited. All is spotlessly clean. On the same splendid beach as the *Hermitage.* Open *Easter* through October. Località Scaglieri (phone: 969915). Moderate.

En Route from Portoferraio Bay Area – Bordering the bay, southeast of Portoferraio, are the *Terme San Giovanni,* specializing in medicinal mud baths for the treatment of arthritis, cellulitis, rheumatism, and sinusitus (phone: 914266 or 914680).

The wooded foothills in this area lead to the low mountain range of the central section of Elba. The road then climbs in sharp curves to the promontory of Punta delle Grotte. An open gateway to the left leads to the remains of the tremendous Roman Villa, thought to have been built during the reign of Emperor Augustus. The view across the bay to Portoferraio is lovely, and what has been excavated of the villa is easily explored.

Head inland toward the mountains and the Volterraio fortress, probably constructed in the 13th century by the Pisans. The fortress is perched high on the hillside dominating the skyline. Park halfway up the hill and take the footpath. It is a rugged climb that takes about 45 minutes, but the breathtaking views and the grandeur of the fortress, with its ruined walls and fig trees growing wild in the courtyards, make it well worth the effort.

CHECKING IN: ***Villa Ottone*** – Less than 2 miles (3 km) southeast of Portoferraio, on Portoferraio Bay, this rather splendidly old-fashioned, 75-room hostelry is known for its sailing school. It also has a large garden, private beach, windsurfing school, and lighted tennis courts. Open April to October. Ottone (phone: 933042; fax: 933257). Expensive.

Acquabona Golf – South of Schiopparello and inland on the road to Porto Azzurro, this hostelry has an adjacent 9-hole golf course. Open *Easter* through October. Acquabona (phone: 940064). Moderate.

Garden – Overlooking the bay from pretty, pine-shaded grounds, it has 51 rooms, a sailing school, and its own sand and gravel beach. Open *Easter* through October. Schiopparello (phone: 933043). Moderate.

RIO MARINA: There are many different minerals to be found on Elba — rock crystal, common white opal, white quartz, malachite, azurite, feldspar, and copper pyrite, to name only some — and it is easy to collect samples while exploring the island. For non-rock rappers, most indigenous minerals are for sale at the stalls in the open market in Rio Marina. (*Note:* The ropes of rock necklaces sold to tourists usually are made from gemstones imported from Africa. Most Elban rocks are too soft for polishing.) Rio also has a small mineral museum in the Town Hall in the Palazzo Comunale, Via Principe Amedeo, third floor (open weekdays from 9 AM to noon and 3 to 6 PM, Sundays from 9 AM to noon, April through September); admission charge. North of Rio Marina is Cavo, an old mining town where evidence of Etruscan iron smelting has turned up at the shoreline (and quickly disappeared into private collections), and the mining district.

CHECKING IN: ***Mini Hotel Easy Time*** – On a steep hill overlooking a magnificent bay, this new, efficient hotel with just 8 rooms (all with small terraces and a view) is just a few minutes' walk from town. Open *Easter* through October. Via Porticciolo, Rio Marino (phone: 962531). Moderate.

Rio – An attractive 38-room hotel with its own restaurant, overlooking the harbor. Open April to September. 31 Via Palestro, Rio Marina (phone: 962722). Moderate.

EATING OUT: ***L'Antico Moro*** – The seafood here is served by a cozy fireplace on chilly evenings or at tables outdoors on warm days. Closed Wednesdays. Reservations necessary in summer. Major credit cards accepted. 3 Via Traversa, Rio Marina (phone: 962448). Moderate to inexpensive.

PORTO AZZURRO: Originally called Porto Longone, this is a small town, the southern terminus of the ferry lines. The main life revolves around the harbor, which usually is full of yachts and fishing boats. During high season, day-long excursions are operated to the island of Montecristo.

CHECKING IN: ***Cala di Mola*** – Overlooking the estuary just outside Porto Azzurro harbor, this attractive 41-room hotel has a well-appointed restaurant and public rooms, beautiful gardens, and a double swimming pool. Open May through September. Mola (phone: 95225). Moderate.

Elba International – Large (241 rooms), modern, and built high on a wooded promontory, Capo della Tavola, across the bay from Porto Azzurro. There's a swimming pool, tennis court, and an elevator that goes directly to the beach, where there's a restaurant. Very popular with Italians. Open *Easter* through October. Naregno (phone: 968611). Moderate.

EATING OUT: ***Floriano*** – A good spot for very fresh fish and homemade traditional dishes, served in an informal atmosphere. Closed Wednesdays, except in the summer. Reservations advised. Major credit cards accepted. Via Ricasoli, in Porto Azzurro village at Capo della Tavola (phone: 95092). Expensive to moderate.

La Lanterna – Risotto pirate style (with fish), *cacciucco* (fish soup), and other fish specialties are served at this trattoria with a terrace overlooking the sea. There also are a few guestrooms with bath. Open daily in season. Reservations necessary. Major credit cards accepted. Porto Azzurro (phone: 95026). Moderate.

CAPOLIVERI: An ancient town dating from the Roman occupation, Capoliveri has a bloody history of vendettas, drinking, and fighting. Its position 500 feet above sea level affords spectacular views.

EATING OUT: ***Il Chiasso*** – Recently enlarged, this is considered one of the island's more intriguing restaurants. It is known for its shellfish soup, spaghetti with anchovies and pine nuts, and whole fresh fish baked in parchment. Open daily, except Tuesdays in winter. Reservations advised. Major credit cards accepted. 20 Via Nazario Sauro, Capoliveri (phone: 968709). Moderate.

En Route from Capoliveri – Follow the coastline along the low wooded cliffs down to the plain of Lacona, an area popular with campers. This leads to the principal bays of the south coast: Golfo Stella has two main sandy beaches, Lido and Margidore; Golfo della Lacona, a tremendous, wide, sandy beach, and very good, well-run campsites nestled among the trees.

Travelers heading through the mountains to Marina di Campo pass Elba's small airport on the right.

CHECKING IN: ***Lacona*** – Large (128 rooms), modern, and only 300 feet from the sea, it has its own stretch of beach, a swimming pool, and 2 tennis courts. Open May through early October. Lacona (phone: 964054). Expensive to moderate.

Antares – A 43-room hostelry overlooking Stella Bay, on the south coast, with access to the beach. Open mid-March to September. Lido di Capoliveri (phone: 940131). Moderate.

EATING OUT: *Da Gianni* – One of the best restaurants on the island is near the airport, only 1½ miles (2 km) from Marina di Campo. Gianni's great specialty is his seafood risotto of clams, mussels, and other shellfish in a rich wine-based stock, but some think his delectable baked mussels, served as an appetizer, are his real pièce de résistance. Open March to September. Reservations advised, especially in the evening. No credit cards accepted. La Pila (phone: 976965). Moderate to inexpensive.

MARINA DI CAMPO: A lively, pretty town and a good base for expeditions. It is always fun to stroll here or to sit at the little bars watching the fishing boats in the harbor. Some Elban enthusiasts feel it is the best place to stay on the island. Accordingly, there are many good hotels along, or near, the excellent sandy beach. Market day is Wednesday.

CHECKING IN: *Montecristo* – Named for the island due south, this is easily the best hotel in town, with just 43 rooms. Situated on the beach, it also has its own pool. Excellent service. Open April to October. 11 Via Nomellini, Marina di Campo (phone: 976861 or 976782). Expensive.

Bahia Beach – A cluster of whitewashed, tile-roofed cottages, each with a view, and nestled onto a hillside of olive groves. All 40 guestrooms are air conditioned, and there is a restaurant. A 3-minute walk from a splendid beach. Open *Easter* through October. Località Cavoli (phone: 987019). Expensive to moderate.

Barcarola Seconda – Very comfortable and close to the beach, with 28 rooms, a restaurant, and a pretty garden. Open mid-April to October. Località San Mamiliano, Marina di Campo (phone: 976255). Moderate.

Dei Coralli – A comfortable 60-room hotel on the edge of town, it has a swimming pool, tennis court, and a restaurant with good food and service. Open June to September. Via degli Etruschi, Marina di Campo (phone: 976336). Moderate to inexpensive.

Meridiana – This very pleasant 27-room hotel is close to the beach and pine belt on the edge of town. Open *Easter* through October. 69 Via degli Etruschi, Marina di Campo (phone: 976352). Moderate to inexpensive.

Villa Nettuno – Adjoining the beach on the edge of town, this 30-room hostelry is set in the pine belt. Good food and service. Open mid-April to October. 30 Via degli Etruschi, Marina di Campo (phone: 976028). Moderate to inexpensive.

Da Ilio – Far from the madding crowd, at Capo Sant'Andrea on the dramatic western coastline, this 20-room amenable hotel with a restaurant and garden is close to a fine beach. Open *Easter* through October. 24 Capo Sant'Andrea (phone: 908018; fax: 908087). Moderate to inexpensive.

Pensione Elba – A small, family hotel with a homey atmosphere and excellent food. Open *Easter* through October. Località San Mamiliano, Marina di Campo (phone: 976224). Inexpensive.

EATING OUT: *La Triglia* – Authentic Elban cuisine, including very good fish. Open daily, except Thursdays, from February to November. Reservations advised. Major credit cards accepted. Via Roma, Marina di Campo (phone: 976059). Expensive.

La Bologna – In the center of town, it offers a wide variety of consistently good food. Open daily, except Tuesdays in winter, from April 15 through October. Reservations advised, especially in the evenings. Major credit cards accepted. Marina di Campo (phone: 976105). Moderate.

Bar Pizzeria Tre P – Beautifully situated, overlooking the beach and mountains, at the extreme eastern end of the beach. A large menu offers good food. Closed

Mondays. No reservations. No credit cards accepted. La Foce (phone: 976892). Inexpensive.

En Route from Marina di Campo – Follow the main road north from Marina di Campo to La Pila, then to Sant'Ilario. This beautiful little town was an ancient village fortified in the 12th century, probably by the Pisans. There is a lovely walk around the outer walls with spectacular views in every direction.

EATING OUT: ***La Cava*** – Hearty regional mountain dishes such as *fonduta* are served at this trattoria whose name means "the mine." Service is courteous. Closed Wednesdays. Reservations advised. No credit cards accepted. Via degli Alberi, Località Sant'Ilario (phone: 983379). Moderate.

From Sant'Ilario take the main road out of the piazza toward San Piero. Bear right uphill to the ruins of the large Romanesque Chiesa di San Giovanni. Nearby is the impressive watchtower, Torre di San Giovanni. From the top, a sentry could see the whole of Campo Bay, and often as far as the island of Pianosa. Take the road up to the main ridge behind Monte Perone. There is a natural stopping place here with excellent picnic areas and fabulous views in all directions. There is also an abundance of wildflowers and beautiful butterflies.

Return to the main road and bear right for the village. San Piero is bigger than Sant'Ilario and even older, built on the site of a Roman colony. The parish church contains the remains of some 14th-century frescoes. Wonderful fruit ices and cappuccino are sold at the café next to the butcher. Customers who get to the *panificio* (bakery) early can buy fresh *schiacciata,* flat salted bread perfect for homemade pizza or sandwiches.

EATING OUT: ***La Cantina*** – The best food in the area, and a typically Elban menu as well as all kinds of pizza, are found on the main street in La Pila. Closed Mondays. Reservations advised. Major credit cards accepted. 21 Via Giovanni XXIII, La Pila (phone: 977200). Expensive.

MARCIANA: Also called Marciana Alta, this is one of the oldest and prettiest villages on the island, dating from Roman times. Like some other Elban towns, it was fortified in the 12th century by the Pisans. It is set high in the hills overlooking a steep valley full of vineyards and olive, chestnut, and fig trees. The *Museo Archeologico* (Via del Pretorio) displays the island's early relics, from prehistoric times through the Roman era. Open daily, except Wednesdays, from 9 AM to 5 PM, Sundays to 12:30 PM, mid-April through mid-October; admission charge.

Just south of Marciana are cable cars to the summit of Monte Capanne, the highest point on Elba. Park and follow a path through the trees to the terminal. The cable cars run from mid-May to mid-September; they are closed in cloudy or windy weather. Quite primitive-looking, they rather resemble bird cages. But bravery is rewarded by the view from the top, which includes all of Elba and the coasts of mainland Italy and the island of Corsica.

Fonte di Napoleone (Napoleon's Spring) lies just off the road between Marciana and Poggio. Toward Poggio is the small factory where Elba's own very good mineral water, Acqua di Napoleone, is bottled.

EATING OUT: ***Da Luigi*** – Beautifully set on the hillside outside Poggio; approached by an improbable track, but definitely worth the drama of getting there. The food and ambience are excellent. Pasta includes fresh gnocchi, in addition to pesto and carbonara. Don't miss the heavenly fritters of zucchini and eggplant or the grilled lamb, chicken, and steak. Closed Mondays. Reservations advised. Major credit cards accepted. Località Feno, Poggio (phone: 99413). Moderate.

Publius **–** With a magical night view from its terrace overlooking the valley and bay, it offers good food and service — among the island's best. Try any of the *crostini* (toast covered with chicken liver pâté, or olive or mushroom paste) and home-pickled wild mushrooms. Open March 20 through October. Reservations advised. Major credit cards accepted. Piazza XX Settembre, Poggio (phone: 99208). Moderate.

MARCIANA MARINA: This very pleasant seaside resort has an excellent harbor for yachts and small boats. Its wide waterfront promenade ends near the medieval watchtower, Torre Saracena.

CHECKING IN: ***Gabbiano Azzurro*** **–** An inland establishment with 39 rooms and a swimming pool, it's nestled among the vineyards on the lower slopes of a hill near Poggio. No restaurant. Open *Easter* through October. 48 Viale Amedeo, Marciana Marina (phone: 99226). Moderate.

La Primula **–** The best hotel (with 71 rooms) in the town center, a short distance from the waterfront. Open *Easter* through October. Viale Cerboni, Marciana Marina (phone: 99010). Moderate to inexpensive.

EATING OUT: ***Rendez-Vous da Marcello*** **–** Some consider this the island's very best. Dine on a variety of seafood — mussels, clams, crab, and lobster — on the terrace at the water's edge. Specialties are *spaghetti alla margherita* (with crab) and crème caramel. Closed Wednesdays and January to February 10. Reservations advised. Major credit cards accepted. Piazza della Vittoria, Marciana Marina (phone: 99251). Expensive.

Il Fosso **–** A must for marvelous pizza with very thin, light, crispy dough, laden with cheese, prosciutto, and local mushrooms. Also good are the spaghetti with zucchini and the seafood risotto. Closed Tuesdays. Reservations necessary in high season. Visa accepted. Località San Giovanni, Marciana Marina (phone: 904319). Moderate.

En Route from Marciana Marina – To return to the Portoferraio Bay area, take the main road east out of tiny Marciana Marina and along the coast to Procchio (another seaside village where accommodations are quite good) and Bivio Boni.

CHECKING IN: ***Desirée*** **–** On Spartaia cove, just west of Procchio, this place has its own sandy beach and sheltered harbor. Sixty-nine secluded, comfortable bedrooms have private terraces. Open *Easter* through October. Località Spartaia, Procchio (phone: 907311). Expensive.

Del Golfo **–** At the western end of a long, sandy beach, it has 94 rooms, gardens, a swimming pool, and tennis courts. Open *Easter* through October. Procchio (phone: 907565). Expensive.

La Perla **–** Upgraded to a first class establishment, this comfortable 60-room hotel is close to the beach and offers a seaside buffet, tennis courts, windsurfing, and a pool. Half board is obligatory. Open *Easter* through October. Procchio (phone: 907371). Expensive.

EATING OUT: ***Lo Schioppo*** **–** A pleasant restaurant off the main road on a quiet hillside, it serves good fish and shellfish. Closed lunch and Tuesdays. Reservations advised. Major credit cards accepted. Località lo Schioppo, between Procchio and Marciana Marina (phone: 99038). Moderate.

Umbria

It is often said that Umbria, the small, landlocked region that lies at the heart of the Italian peninsula, takes its name from the Latin word for shade, *umbra.* In fact, these hills, pitted with caves and the mountain watersheds through which the mighty Tiber River passes, are lush and verdant, particularly in contrast to the arid and stony Abruzzo next door. The more academic-minded may point out that three of the ruling families in Umbria's Etruscan past had names — Umria, Umruna, and Umrana — that may have been taken to identify the region. Still, even on a map, Umbria looks like a leaf from a shade tree, and how not to see its largest lake, Trasimeno — where Hannibal routed 16,000 Roman soldiers in 217 BC — as a single drop of dew?

Indeed, there is something soothing about this quiet, pleasant, humble region, and it is entirely in keeping with its character that several of Christendom's most beloved saints were born here. Among them were St. Valentine, a 3rd-century Bishop of Terni, which is today an Umbrian industrial town, and St. Clare, founder of the Order of Poor Clares. Foremost among all the region's saints was Clare's friend, gentle St. Francis of Assisi, founder of the Franciscans. Umbria's saints and their followers prayed in the mountain grottoes and preached in the cobbled streets and among the daisies and wild red poppies of the field. It is probably a sense of their spirit that still pervades the Umbrian atmosphere today, just as the graceful abbeys of the orders they founded crown the green hilltops. It goes without saying that Umbria's monastic orders have left an indelible mark not only on the region but on the entire Western world.

Monasticism came to Western Europe from the deserts of the Middle East. The two worlds met in Umbria when a large number of Syrians migrated to live as hermits in the hills, spreading the concept of monastic life. St. Benedict, born in the Umbrian town of Norcia around 480, gave a Western imprint to the tradition of hermit prayer by adding the concept of work. Hence the Umbrian monks prayed, but they also farmed, studied, and copied manuscripts, maintaining a wondrous intellectual and social order that can be seen even in the tidy ledgers of abbey farm and vineyard holdings and the monks' treatises on agriculture displayed in the fascinating *Wine Museum* at Torgiano, near Perugia. This Umbrian monasticism, with the work ethic it incorporated, spread throughout Italy and then throughout the West, carrying culture and stimulating commerce as it went.

This is not to portray Umbria as solely a clerical state. In fact, disobedience to the papacy became so serious at one point in 16th-century Perugia that Pope Paul III had to use troops to put down an uprising over a church-imposed salt tax (even today, the *perugini* use salt sparingly in cooking, and most bread in Umbria is baked without it). And many of the region's festivals hark back to pagan rites. Most famous is the *Calendimaggio Festival* at Assisi, a romantic rite of spring. During the Middle Ages, young minstrels sang ballads and love songs in the streets, and each April 29 to May 1, Assisi is still illuminated by torches, decked with medieval flags, and populated by damsels and knights in sumptuous costume. The fun is justified today by explanations that it evokes St. Francis's youth, for as a boy he, too, participated in the revels.

Nor is Umbria locked into its past. Every June and July, Spoleto plays host to the *Festival of Two Worlds,* a panoply of the arts of Italy and the US. The well-established festival was created by the Italian-American composer Gian Carlo Menotti, and some of the world's foremost musicians, dancers, actors, directors, painters, and sculptors have taken part over its approximately 3 decades of existence. Also renowned is the annual *Umbria Jazz,* a 10-day festival in July that attracts some of the biggest names in jazz. It takes place in Perugia, Terni, and various other locations.

In the beginning, the Umbri were a Villanovan tribe, believed by scholars to have reached Umbria from across the mountains around Bologna. Shepherds and farmers, these Umbri were soon pushed aside by the more sophisticated and aggressive Etruscans, who came as invaders from the Tyrrhenian coast. Perugia, for instance, a Villanovan settlement perched on a rocky stronghold that dominated the upper Tiber Valley, had already fallen to the Etruscans by the 5th century BC. The Etruscans considerably improved the region. They taught the illiterate Umbri an 18-letter alphabet, and their ambitious public works can be seen in the city walls and mighty arched gate at Perugia. They also left beautiful painted tombs at Orvieto.

The Romans, in turn, overwhelmed the Etruscans and the Umbri in 310 BC. Quintessential builders, they bequeathed an amphitheater at Assisi; a temple, a theater, and a high, many-arched bridge at Spoleto; and a theater and another bridge at Gubbio. Hostile Lombards from the Po Valley were next. With the fall of the Roman Empire, they won control over the region and set up the powerful duchy of Spoleto, which ruled much of Umbria from the 6th to the 11th century and became an important center for the arts. One Lombard monastery (closed for restoration as we went to press) dating from the 8th century can still be seen 2 miles (3 km) outside Ferentillo, in the valley of the Nera River between Spoleto and Terni (head north on B209, toward Visso).

During the 11th and 12th centuries, the age of communes began, a period when Italy's city-states experimented with a form of self-government. Umbria's chief communes — Perugia, Assisi, Foligno, Spoleto, Orvieto, Gubbio, and Città di Castello — are all fascinating to visit today for the rich evidence they still reveal about that era. True, they fought each other with dismaying regularity, allying themselves, as convenient, with one or another of the great powers, which in those days meant either Rome or Florence, pope or emperor. Geographically close to Rome, Umbria was perennially a tempting morsel for the papal powers, to which it would eventually fall in the 16th century.

In the meantime, however, the wars were not all negative, because the alliances that were formed stimulated trade and the arts, and Umbria felt the influence of Florentine culture. As the monastic movement inspired by St.

Benedict and St. Francis spread throughout the region, Assisi, Italy's second spiritual capital, acquired an important role. The arts in Umbria naturally came to reflect the region's ardent religious life, and in the 13th century they began to evolve, for the first time in Europe, from the rigidity of icon-like Byzantine painting and sculpture toward the more lifelike and dramatic works that can be seen in the great cathedrals at Assisi and Orvieto and in the museums and churches of Perugia. Giotto's frescoes of the life of St. Francis in the cathedral at Assisi marked a point of departure for painting in the West.

During the late 14th and the 15th century, Umbria's cities were run by powerful noble families. In Perugia, these *signori,* or lords, included two bitter rivals, the Oddi and Baglioni. The Trinci ruled in Foligno, the Gabrielli and later the Montefeltro in Gubbio, the Vitelli in Città di Castello, and the Orsini in Terni. Flanking them in the latter part of the period were war leaders called *condottieri,* whose presence possibly reflected the warrior tradition of the old Lombard dukes. They organized mercenary armies and sometimes came into power on their own, and when their power bids in Umbria failed, they did not hesitate to put themselves at the service of foreign rulers. Nevertheless, local autonomy came to an end in the 16th century. Perugia's bitter revolt against the pope's salt tax in 1540 was the last gasp, and when its leading city finally fell to the troops of the pope's nephew, the region passed definitively into the papal empire. Umbria then remained part of the Papal States until the 1860s.

During the Renaissance, Umbria's painters came into their own. Pietro Vannucci, who grew to fame as "il Perugino," was born at Città del Pieve but worked in Perugia, where his lyrical works can be seen in the *National Gallery* of Umbria. He taught Raphael — Raffaello — to paint. Other great masters who worked in Umbria included Pinturicchio from Perugia, Piero della Francesca, and the architect Bramante. If, as in Tuscany, the landscape in Umbria has an awe-inspiring familiarity, it is because we have seen it before in the paintings in our museums: the flowers, cypress lanes, blue hills in the distance, the winding river. So, too, there is a sense of déjà vu when we view Perugia's bristling towers, city walls, gates, and tile roofs on the crest of a hill rising from the broad plain of the Tiber River basin.

Next to its artists worked exacting craftsmen. Italy sometimes seems one giant beehive of artisanry, but even in Italy, Umbria's artisans stand out. Besides weaving handloomed fabrics, embroidering, potting, and turning furniture, they are today celebrated for their fine wrought-iron work. For the value, prices of hand-spun linen and tablecloths, which can be ordered to measure, or of finely decorated ceramic ware, are reasonable, but visitors should not expect bargain-basement prices for articles that are often one of a kind or made with especially good raw materials. A bedspread woven on a handloom can easily cost a million lire (about $770).

Umbrian food is more subtle than that of Rome and lighter than that of Tuscany, which makes it close to perfect. A taste for *nuova cucina* or anything fast will have to be satisfied elsewhere, because here one makes do — to take a sample menu — with a selection of antipasto hams and salamis from Norcia, served with pickled wild mushrooms; thin egg noodles tossed with grated black truffle and olive oil; fresh fish from a mountain stream or eel from Lake Trasimeno; a choice of wild game dishes; ewe's and goat's milk cheeses, delightfully unpasteurized; and fresh fruit or dried figs from the orchards that carpet the valleys. Dessert may include an almond *torta* in the form of a serpent, gaily decorated with sugar candies. This traditional Umbrian *Easter* cake can be seen all year long in the pastry shop windows in, for one place, Perugia.

The olive is king in Umbrian cuisine. Some consider Umbrian olive oil, especially that produced around Spoleto, to be Italy's very best. Soil conditions give it an especially low acid content, and Umbrians swear it is also "lighter," less fatty, than other oils. It is never better than when eaten on slices of crusty country bread toasted over an open fire, peppered, and drenched with garlic — *la bruschetta.* Another very special Umbrian treat is the truffle. Five varieties, in color from white through gray to black and resembling small potatoes, grow wild in the woodlands, and local hound dogs, especially around Assisi and Norcia, are trained to retrieve them with rewards of chocolate. Three towns have truffle festivals: Terni, in June; Gubbio, in November; and, the most important, Norcia, in February. But other towns host other festivals. Orvieto stages a wine show each May and June. A mushroom festival takes place at San Leo, near Città di Castello, in September, and a chestnut frolic, at which *marrons glacés* hold the place of honor, goes on at Preggio di Umbertide in October. There is even an onion festival at Cannara, near Assisi, in late September, when the village's best cooks show off their recipes.

Especially in wintertime, menus may include the tiny, tasty lentils grown in the high, wildflower-filled valley of Castelluccio, in the mountains above Norcia. A prized local salami, *mazzafegato,* is made of pork liver, pine nuts, raisins, sugar, and orange peel. *Castagnaccio* is a flat bread made of chestnut flour, seasoned with pine nuts, raisins, and fresh rosemary and served with a glass of dessert wine. Around the *Christmas* holidays comes *pan pepato* — 'peppered bread"—a fruitcake of walnuts, almonds, raisins, chocolate, candied fruit, pine nuts, honey, "must" from the grapes, and ground black pepper.

Pliny the Elder was among those who have rhapsodized over the wines of Umbria. Well he might. Umbrian wines were so prized back in the 15th century that Torgiano vintners pushed through laws severely punishing anyone doctoring Torgiano's own wine or improperly using the label. Today, the region's wines include half a dozen fine DOC labels. Best known is the light, straw-colored orvieto; orvieto classico comes from grapes grown on the very oldest wine estates, closest to the town of Orvieto. Torgiano comes both red and white, as does the wine grown on the hills around Lake Trasimeno, (Colli del Trasimeno). Montefalco is an especially prized red wine. The name Colli Altotiberini DOC specifies that these fine red, rosé, and white wines come from grapes grown on the hillsides facing the upper Tiber River Valley. Perugia's red, rosé, and white DOC wines are named Colli Perugini.

Our circuit of Umbria begins at Perugia, its capital, and passes through hilly, chestnut-wooded countryside interspersed with broad rolling valleys of olive groves and vineyards to Assisi, a hill town with a soft, saintly aura. The route loops southward to Spoleto, a jewel of a town, and then, rather than continue south to Terni (an industrial center with some historical monuments), cuts west and north to Todi, another small hill town with fine art and architecture. After Todi, a detour to Orvieto is strongly recommended; its cathedral should not be missed by anyone coming this close. The route goes to Deruta (for pottery browsing) and Torgiano (for the *Wine Museum*) on its way back to Perugia and, at the end, a side trip to Gubbio is suggested for those who have the time.

Hotels listed here as expensive charge anywhere from $105 to $175 for a double room with bath; moderate hotels charge approximately $60 to $100 for a double room; and inexpensive, $55 or less. The very best restaurants may charge well over $130 for a meal for two served with a fine wine. In a restaurant listed as very expensive, expect to pay $165 and up for a meal for two served with a good quality local wine. Restaurants listed as expensive will charge from $80 to $130, with a bottle of wine; moderate $50 to $80, including a bottle of wine, and those listed as inexpensive will charge from $30 to $50, including a carafe of house wine. But note that in an especially popular place such as Spoleto, where fashionability strikes quickly, prices in any establishment can rise fast from season to season.

For longer stays, a pleasant alternative to hotels is renting a villa. They often are converted castles, olive mills, and farmhouses. The following are a few of the companies, based in the US, that handle villa rentals in Umbria: *Vacanze in Italia* (PO Box 297, Falls Village, CT 06031; phone: 800-533-5405); *Grandluxe International* (165 Chestnut St., Allendale, NJ 07401; phone: 201-327-2333); and *Suzanne T. Pidduck* (1742 Calle Corva, Camarillo, CA 93010; phone: 805-987-5278 or 800-726-6702). Also see "Apartments, Houses, and Villas," *Accommodations,* GETTING READY TO GO.

PERUGIA: Umbria's regional capital is set on a hill, and the best way to see it is to leave the car at the public parking lot halfway up the road that winds to the top. From there, five escalators whisk visitors up 1,000 feet into the heart of town. Interestingly, the escalators tunnel straight through the Rocca Paolina, the fortress that Pope Paul III raised in the 16th century to show the *perugini* who was boss. The fort incorporated the mansion belonging to one of the leading rebel families, the Baglioni, and the surrounding neighborhood, including three churches and several streets from earlier centuries. The Rocca was largely destroyed in the 19th century, debris was dumped into it, and its upper walls were used as the foundations of nearby palazzi, sealing all previous layers into oblivion. Excavations began to uncover it all in the 1950s, and it is through this time-warped ghost city that the escalators climb to the top, even passing a tiny, Renaissance-era basketball court.

It becomes immediately obvious to a visitor that Perugia is a university town. International students taking Italian language and culture courses at the Università Italiana per Stranieri (Italian University for Foreigners) and Italian students from the nearly 700-year-old University of Perugia throng the main street, Corso Vannucci, a wide pedestrian island lined with outdoor cafés, hotels, and fine shops (as well as the tourist information office; phone: 75-23327). Just at the end of this thoroughfare is the main square, Piazza IV Novembre, with one of Perugia's most celebrated monuments, the 13th-century Fontana Maggiore, in the center. This notable achievement was built to celebrate the completion of an aqueduct bringing water to Perugia from Monte Paciano, 3 miles (5 km) away as the crow flies. Designed and executed by Nicola and

Giovanni Pisano, it consists of two marble basins and a bronze cup decorated with 24 relief sculptures and 24 statues. On the north side of the square is Perugia's Duomo, or, rather, its side, since it faces onto Piazza Danti. Begun in 1345 to replace an earlier building, it was finished in 1490 — finished, that is, except for the pink and white marble stripes that were to have covered it; only a patch has ever been completed.

On the south side of the square (at the corner of Piazza IV Novembre and Corso Vannucci) is the ancient Palazzo dei Priori, built from 1293 to 1443, for hundreds of years Perugia's Town Hall. The part facing the square, with the grand staircase and the doorway topped by the Perugian griffin and the Guelph lion in bronze, was completed by 1297 and is the oldest part of this fine example of medieval civic architecture. Inside the palace (entry from Corso Vannucci) are the frescoed Sala dei Notari (Notaries' Room; no phone; open daily except Mondays from 9 AM to 1 PM and 4 to 8 PM; no admission charge) and the Collegio della Mercanzia (phone: 75-24836; open daily except Mondays from 9 AM to 12:30 PM and 3 to 6 PM; admission charge), a sort of Renaissance chamber of commerce covered with 15th-century woodcarvings and marquetry. Inside, also, is the *Galleria Nazionale dell'Umbria* (National Gallery of Umbria; phone: 75-20316), where the entire development of Umbrian painting — from the stiff religious art of the 13th century to the breathtaking explosion of color and grace in Pinturicchio and Perugino — can be admired, in addition to works by Beato Angelico, Piero della Francesca, and others. Open Tuesdays through Saturdays from 9 AM to 2 PM, Sundays 9 AM to 1 PM; admission charge. Those interested mainly in Perugino, however, should stop in at the Collegio del Cambio (phone: 75-61379) next door. This was built for the use of money changers in the 15th century, and its most important chamber is filled with vibrant frescoes by Perugino and his pupils. On the middle pilaster is Perugino's self-portrait, and in the painting of the Prophets and the Sibyls, presumed to be by Perugino's pupil Raphael, then all of 17 years old, is that young painter's self-portrait as the prophet Daniel. The fine inlaid woodwork in the lobby is from the 17th century. Note the wonderfully carved furniture. Open daily except Mondays from 9 AM to 12:30 PM and 2:30 to 5:30 PM; admission charge.

Going out the west end of Piazza IV Novembre, it's possible to approach Perugia's Etruscan Arch by way of a medieval street, Via delle Volte. This winding street with its lovely arches is also called Via Maestà delle Volte, for a 14th-century fresco in a small church at its end. Adjacent streets — Via Fratti, Via Ritorta — are well worth a detour. Via Maestà delle Volte leads to Piazza Morlacchi, from where Via Cesare Battisti leads along a wall built by the Etruscans and then, via a stairway, to Piazza Fortebraccio. Here, the 18th-century baroque Palazzo Gallenga-Stuart, seat of the University for Foreigners, stands next to the Etruscan Arch, or the Arch of Augustus, as the Romans called it. Where Roman builders raised the wall higher is readily seen, but the arch itself is pure Etruscan. A delicate porch on top is from the Renaissance.

At the other end of town, taking Via Marzia out of the Giardini Carducci (public gardens), is the Porta Marzia, a 2nd- or 1st-century BC gate in the walls. It was moved 10 feet away and reconstructed by the architect (Antonio da Sangallo the Younger) working on the Rocca Paolina, and it gives access to the underground Via Bagliona, the subterranean world that was sealed off by the fortress and that can be visited. The *Museo Archeologico Nazionale dell'Umbria* is also at this end of the city, next to the Gothic Church of St. Domenic (Piazza G. Bruno; phone: 75-27141). It houses a collection of prehistoric, Etruscan, and Roman sarcophagi, vases, coins, and jewelry, but its greatest treasure is the Cippus, a marble slab inscribed with 151 words in the Etruscan language. Some urns in the collection are engraved in Etruscan with the translation into Umbria's Latin dialect. Open Tuesdays through Saturdays from 9 AM to 2 PM, Sundays 9 AM to 1 PM; admission charge.

The tradition of the *passeggiata* — the evening promenade — is very much alive in Perugia: On Corso Vannucci it seems that everyone who is ambulatory is out for a stroll. Do the same. Or, for an *aperitivo* at any time of the day, visit the *Enoteca Provinciale* (16 Via Ulisse Rocchi), which offers samplings of the 150 wines from the 60 vineyards in Umbria.

CHECKING IN: ***Brufani*** – An old favorite of travelers, this pleasantly old-fashioned grand hotel is the best in town. There are 24 rooms. 12 Piazza Italia, Perugia (phone: 75-62541). Expensive.

La Rosetta – In the same square as the *Brufani,* it has a graceful courtyard and a highly regarded restaurant to make up for the relatively small size of the 96 rooms. 19 Piazza Italia, Perugia (phone: 75-20841). Moderate.

Lo Spedalicchio – About 6 miles (10 km) out of town in the direction of Assisi, in a village called Ospedalicchio. Off an unpretentious road, inside a gate, there stands an ancient castle that once guarded the approach to Perugia, now converted into a 25-room hotel. The furnishings are handsome, modern interpretations of traditional regional styles, including handloomed bedspreads in ancient Umbrian motifs. There is an elegant dining room; drinks are served in the garden. A warning — those who have serious problems sleeping should go elsewhere; a venerable church bell tolls each quarter hour all through the night. 3 Piazza Bruno Buozzi, Ospedalicchio (phone: 75-801-0323). Inexpensive.

EATING OUT: ***Falchetto*** – With its 14th-century walls, it looks like a medieval tavern, and visitors interested in sampling authentic Umbrian cuisine should make this their first choice. Among the dishes to try are grilled trout from the Nera River, truffled veal, and delectable roast pheasant. Even snails sometimes appear on the menu of this temple to tradition. The wines are from Torgiano and other local vineyards. Closed Mondays. Reservations advised. Major credit cards accepted. 20 Via Bartolo, Perugia (phone: 75-61875). Moderate.

Dal Mi'Cocco – A good place for a hearty meal of local fare at reasonable prices. The soups are especially noteworthy — try the delicious minestrone and the *pappa al pomodoro* (thick tomato soup). The meat dishes are grilled over an open fire. Closed Mondays. Reservations unnecessary. No credit cards accepted. 12 Corso Garibaldi, Perugia (phone: 75-62511). Moderate.

Del Sole – The charming garden terrace, with its view over the green hills toward Assisi, is a major asset. The Umbrian specialties include *penne norcine* — pasta "quills" — and a stew of wild boar. Closed Saturdays and at *Christmastime.* Reservations necessary in summer. Visa accepted. 28 Via Oberdan, Perugia (phone: 75-65031). Moderate.

Osteria del Bartolo – A fairly new venture with an Old World feel, this attractive restaurant has quickly gained a reputation for sophisticated Umbrian cooking. Even the bread is home-baked. Many of the dishes are based on old recipes, some dating back to medieval times. Closed Tuesdays and January. Reservations advised. Major credit cards accepted. 30 Via Bartolo, Perugia (phone: 75-61461). Moderate to inexpensive.

En Route from Perugia – Take the SS75 *bis* southeast out of town in the direction of Foligno and Assisi. On the left, after about 3 miles (5 km), is the rocky Ipogeo dei Volumni, an Etruscan necropolis. The Volumni were an important Etruscan family in the 2nd century BC, and these are important excavations. The road crosses the Tiber River at Ponte San Giovanni, and then, at Ospedalicchio, SS147 branches off to Assisi, which is 16 miles (26 km) from Perugia.

ASSISI: This delightful town is the goal of religious pilgrims and secular tourists alike. Set on the slopes of Monte Subasio, with panoramic views all around, and full of medieval houses of pink stone, it seems as gentle and charming as the saint who was born here (1182) and who lies buried in the crypt beneath its prime monument. Begun in 1228, 2 years after his death, the Basilica of St. Francis is a commanding structure whose unmistakable outline appears, from a distance, to be almost as large as the town itself. It is actually two churches, one on top of the other, and both are set over a huge monastery, the Sacro Convento. All together, the venerable walls and buttresses of this fine example of Umbrian Gothic architecture constitute a lesson in the history of art.

The realm below, the Chiesa Inferiore, is spacious, a place where legions of pilgrims could be welcomed, but dark — unfortunately, because the walls are covered with frescoes. Those in the nave are the oldest, by the 13th-century Maestro di San Francesco; others are by Giotto (the right, or south, transept and the third chapel on the right), Pietro Lorenzetti (left, or north, transept), Simone Martini (first chapel on the left), and Cimabue (his striking *Virgin and Child with Four Angels and St. Francis* is in the right transept, right wall). In the bright upper church, the Chiesa Superiore, there are frescoes by Cimabue, including a Crucifixion, and Giotto's famed frescoes of the life of St. Francis, 28 scenes running counterclockwise around the nave (the attribution of the last few scenes is in doubt). Painted almost 800 years ago, they are captivating for the views they offer of ordinary life — fabrics, weapons, faces, furniture, landscapes, homes, walls, towers — as well as for their narrative and inspirational content. As some critics have put it, art with a human dimension was born here, a far cry from the stylized rigidity that went before.

There are several other sites associated with St. Francis in and around Assisi. About 2½ miles (4 km) east of town is the mountainside Eremo delle Carceri (Hermitage of the Prisons), to which St. Francis and his followers retreated to "imprison" themselves spiritually in prayer. A small Franciscan monastery soon developed, carved out of bedrock; adjacent is a tiny grotto in which St. Francis lived — his rude stone bed can still be seen. The setting is extraordinarily beautiful and imbued with an aura of holiness, much more in keeping with the spirit of St. Francis than is the huge basilica in town. The Convento di San Damiano, another of Italy's most revered shrines, is a bit more than a mile (1.6 km) south of Assisi. St. Francis restored the little church here, and his friend St. Clare lived in the humble convent with her nuns, the Poor Clares, until her death in 1253. This is also the spot where St. Francis composed the "Cantico delle Creature" in praise of all creation including Brother Sun and Sister Moon. Almost 3 miles (5 km) west of Assisi is the 16th-century Basilica di Santa Maria degli Angeli, really no more than a huge covering for an area where St. Francis spent much of his life, was joined by his first followers, and died. It contains several tiny shrines, including the Porziuncola, an almost toy-like chapel he restored and to which crowds of pilgrims arrive each August 1 and 2 for the *Festa del Perdono* (Pardon of Assisi), instituted by the saint in 1216.

If you have still more time to spend in Assisi, visit the Chiesa di Santa Chiara (Church of St. Clare), 13th-century Gothic, as well as the Duomo, begun in the 12th century and dedicated to San Rufino. Assisi also has Roman remains, including the Temple of Minerva, transformed into a baroque church in Piazza del Comune, the medieval main square. Also medieval is the Rocca Maggiore, or fortress, set on a hill north of the center and reached by a stepped street leading out of the square in front of the Duomo; the view from the top is well worth the climb.

CHECKING IN: ***Fontebella*** – Only 37 quiet rooms, most overlooking the broad Umbrian Valley, and its own renowned restaurant, *Il Frantoio* (see *Eating Out*). 25 Via Fontebella, Assisi (phone: 75-812883). Moderate.

Giotto – Assisi's largest hotel, with 72 clean and pleasantly decorated rooms and a restaurant, which is transferred to a lovely outdoor terrace in summer. Some of the rooms have dramatic views of the valley. Be sure to book early, as this place is popular with groups. 41 Via Fontebella, Assisi (phone: 75-812209). Moderate.

Subasio – In the heart of Assisi adjacent to Piazza San Francesco, but some of its 66 rooms overlook the valley and, therefore, ensure quiet. This place has considerable charm and a restaurant known for good food. 2 Via Frate Elia, Assisi (phone: 75-812206). Moderate.

Country House – Just under a mile (1.6 km) out of town, in the peaceful country setting of San Pietro Campagna, this 7-room hotel is furnished with Umbrian antiques. No restaurant. 178 San Pietro Campagna (phone: 75-816363). Inexpensive.

Umbra – A small (27-room), romantic place, downtown on a narrow street away from the more noisy thoroughfares. A few of the rooms have a splendid view over the rooftops, and some rooms are furnished with antiques. It has a garden restaurant (see *Eating Out*). 6 Via degli Archi, Assisi (phone: 75-812240). Inexpensive.

EATING OUT: ***Il Frantoio*** – Part of the *Fontebella* hotel, and one of the best restaurants in Umbria. It occupies what was, in the 17th century, an olive oil pressing room, and it has a garden terrace with a fine view of the valley. Among the specialties are *stringotti* (egg noodles) with artichoke sauce and *tortelloni* (big ravioli) stuffed with cream cheese. In season, truffles garnish nearly everything, and there is a choice selection of local wines. Closed Fridays. Reservations advised. Major credit cards accepted. 25 Via Fontebella, Assisi (phone: 75-812977). Expensive to moderate.

Buca di San Francesco – One of Assisi's most popular restaurants, housed in a medieval *cantina,* or cellar. Dishes include *prosciutto di cinghiale* (wild boar ham) and *spaghetti al sugo d'oca,* served with a rich sauce made of goose. Closed Mondays and the first 3 weeks of July. Reservations advised. Major credit cards accepted. 1 Via Brizi, Assisi (phone: 75-812204). Moderate.

Il Medioevo – A highly recommended dining spot with an evocative decor. The mixed fry is a tempting abundance of stuffed olives and meats. Closed Wednesdays and the first 2 weeks in July. Reservations advised. Major credit cards accepted. 4 Via Arco dei Priori, Assisi (phone: 75-813068). Moderate.

Umbra – Another well-known hotel restaurant, which does not let its international clientele alter its Umbrian traditions. Depending on the season, the menu may feature such mouth-watering dishes as *crostini al tartufo* (truffled pâté on toast), lentil soup, risotto with white truffles from Gubbio, and roast game, rabbit, or duckling. In summer there's dining outdoors on the terrace. Closed Tuesdays and November and mid-January to mid-February. Reservations advised. Major credit cards accepted. 6 Via degli Archi, Assisi (phone: 75-812240). Moderate.

En Route from Assisi – Drive south to Spoleto, part of the way on SS75 and the rest of the way on SS3, passing through picturesque hill country with olive groves everywhere. Just 8 miles (13 km) from Assisi is the old town of Spello, whose stone houses cling to the terraced mountain slopes within ancient Roman walls. If you stop, visit the Chiesa di Santa Maria Maggiore, particularly its Cappella Baglioni, which has a 16th-century majolica floor from Deruta and frescoes by Pinturicchio, including an Annunciation with a self-portrait of the painter. Spoleto is 30 miles (48 km) south of Assisi.

EATING OUT: ***Il Molino*** – Set up in a 700-year-old flour mill that was itself built in Roman ruins, it has a big fireplace turning out the grilled meat that is among its traditional Umbrian dishes. The house specialty, named after the painter Pinturicchio, translates as filet in puff pastry with a wild mushroom sauce. Closed Tuesdays. Reservations advised. Major credit cards accepted. 6 Piazza Matteotti, Spello (phone: 742-651305). Moderate to inexpensive.

SPOLETO: Success has not spoiled this ancient Roman town and former headquarters of the Lombard duchy of Spoleto that ruled most of Umbria in the early Middle Ages. However, should you want to stay in Spoleto during its all-embracing festival of the performing arts, the *Festival of Two Worlds,* be sure to book both hotels and tickets to festival events as far in advance as possible. For information, contact the *Festival dei Due Mondi* (9 Via del Duomo, Spoleto; phone: 743-40396). The festival runs for a month or so from mid-June to mid-July, but its finest hour is always the last evening, when a full orchestra and chorus perform in front of the 12th-century Duomo, whose stone façade glows pink in the twilight. Lovely frescoes by Fra Filippo Lippi and his school are inside the cathedral, as is the tomb of the master painter and defrocked monk. Portraits of Fra Filippo, his two assistants, and his son Filippino figure in the fresco of the *Death of the Virgin.*

No other sight in this hill town ranks with the Duomo, but it is filled with other impressive monuments — including Roman remains such as a theater and amphitheater — and the effect of the medieval whole is fascinating. Stop at the tourist information office (Piazza della Libertà; phone: 743-220435) for information and brochures and then set out for a walking tour. During the festival, every alley and staircase is turned into a showroom for contemporary artists, some great names already, others still waiting for recognition. The late Alexander Calder, a festival regular, designed the huge sculpture that's installed permanently in front of the train station in the lower, modern part of town. Among the sights out of town is the 13th-century Chiesa di San Pietro (Church of St. Peter), 5 miles (8 km) east. The road that winds upward past the church leads to the top of Monteluco, where St. Francis lived for a time at the monastery.

CHECKING IN: *Il Barbarossa* – This former country house right outside Spoleto has been tastefully converted into a small but exquisite hotel. The 10 guestrooms have beamed ceilings, antique Umbrian furniture, very modern, well-equipped bathrooms, satellite television, and VCRs. Its restaurant serves a refined version of local specialties. Closed Mondays. Reservations advised. Major credit cards accepted. 12 Via Licina, Spoleto (phone: 743-222060). Hotel, expensive; restaurant, moderate.

Duchi – A modern, efficient, pleasant place. Some of the 50 rooms look out at the Teatro Romano, others onto the valley. There is a restaurant and a nice little bar. 4 Viale Matteotti, Spoleto (phone: 743-44541). Moderate.

Il Gattapone – This miniature hotel has just 8 elegant rooms, a garden, and a restaurant. Reserve well in advance if you hope to be among the lucky guests. 6 Via del Ponte, Spoleto (phone: 743-36147). Moderate.

Villaggio Albergo Parco Ipost – A pleasant alternative to staying in Spoleto itself, which in summer can be hot and crowded. This 41-room hotel is up in the cool hills of Monteluco, 5 miles (8 km) out of town, and has a swimming pool and tennis court. Monteluco (phone: 743-36141). Inexpensive.

EATING OUT: *Il Madrigale* – For a truly memorable — and very Umbrian — eating experience, stop at this wonderfully restored old manor house 7½ miles (12 km) from Spoleto. There is no menu, but the chef's very capable hands produce local fare that may include *pizza al formaggio* (a delicious cheese bread), roughly cut pasta (*strangozzi*) with truffles, and succulent lamb roasted over an enormous fire. Go with a healthy appetite — the food keeps on coming. Closed Tuesdays. Reservations advised. Major credit cards accepted. To get there, take SS3 heading toward Terni until you see the restaurant on your left. Via Flaminia, Km 112, Strettura (phone: 743-54144). Expensive.

Il Tartufo – A temple to the noble fungus, this is *the* place to dine on fresh truffles. Here, in what is considered the best of a not very crowded field, diners enjoy traditional dishes with gussied-up names such as prisoner's rigatoni, Spoleto-style rags (*stracci,* a type of pasta), and "courtesan-style" steaks. Closed Wednesdays and mid-July to mid-August. Reservations advised. Major credit cards accepted. 24 Piazza Garibaldi, Spoleto (phone: 743-40236). Expensive.

Il Panciolle – Two years ago, one of Spoleto's most venerable eating institutions moved from the site it occupied for more than 30 years. During the festival, it is a favorite among performers. It serves traditional Umbrian fare, such as meat grilled over an open fire. The premises have an attractive garden for summer dining and the bonus of 7 charming guestrooms, each with a bath. Book early for a room, especially during the festival. Restaurant closed Wednesdays. Reservations advised. Major credit cards accepted. Largo M. Clemente, Spoleto (phone: 743-45598). Moderate.

Sabatini – In the former hotel of the same name, it has a pleasant atmosphere. Italian and traditional Umbrian dishes are prepared with style. Closed Mondays. Reservations advised. Major credit cards accepted. 52 Corso Mazzini, Spoleto (phone: 743-37233). Moderate.

En Route from Spoleto – Todi is about 28 miles (45 km) to the northwest. Take SS418 west from Spoleto to Acquasparta and there pick up SS3 *bis* north.

TODI: Still another small hill town with an overall medieval aspect — and an especially beautiful setting — Todi lives around its main square, Piazza del Popolo, which is lined with 13th- and 14th-century palaces. The most important is the Palazzo dei Priori, standing alone at one end with its crenelations and tower. Facing it, at the other end, is the Duomo, fronted by a grand staircase, with a Renaissance rose window in its façade and a bell tower. On another side of the square, the Palazzo del Popolo, wearing a crenelated crown, and the Palazzo del Capitano stand as one, joined by a staircase that provides entry to both. Inside is a delightful museum, whose small and eclectic collection ranges from Etruscan artifacts to Umbrian religious art. Open daily except Mondays from 9 AM to 1 PM and 4 to 6:30 PM; admission charge. The nearby Piazza Garibaldi is a rewarding stop — the view embraces the whole valley below — and two other churches are worth a visit. The Chiesa di San Fortunato (at Piazza della Repubblica) is a lovely 13th-century structure with an unfinished 15th-century façade set off by the green of the lawn and hedges in front. The town's most famous citizen, the Franciscan monk and medieval poet Jacopone, is buried there. Its setting is not nearly as striking, however, as that of Santa Maria della Consolazione, reached by a brief walk (about a half-mile/1 km) south of town. An exquisite white marble church set on a field of green, this Renaissance gem is thought to have been designed by Bramante.

CHECKING IN: *San Valentino* – Situated on the Perugia road just outside Todi, this former 13th-century convent is more of a country house than a hotel — albeit a luxurious one. It has 11 rooms (each furnished with antiques), a tennis court, a swimming pool, and, in the cloisters of the convent, a renowned restaurant. Frazione Fiore, Todi (phone: 75-884-1030). Expensive.

Bramante – A lovely hotel in a woodsy setting just outside Todi. All 43 rooms have a bath or shower. Via Orvietana, Todi (phone: 75-884-8381). Moderate.

EATING OUT: *Vissani* – Instead of taking SS79 to Orvieto, follow SS448 which skirts Lake Corbara and ends up in Orvieto, passing through the town of Baschi. The reason for this detour is a pilgrimage to a place widely considered one of Italy's finest restaurants. Owner/chef Gianfranco Vissani turns out a dazzling array of delicate, perfectly presented courses. The menu changes according to season. His mother starts making bread daily at 4 AM — a different kind to accompany each dish. Closed Wednesdays. Reservations necessary. Major credit cards accepted. Località Civitella del Lago (phone: 75-950206). Very expensive.

Jacopone–da Peppino – A relatively modest *osteria* (inn) whose kitchen is part of the rustic decor. Try the *pasticcio Jacopone,* a pasta specialty, the braised beef in a rich mushroom sauce, and the local wine. Closed Mondays and 2 weeks in July.

Reservations advised. Major credit cards accepted. 5 Piazza Jacopone, Todi (phone: 75-882366). Moderate.

Il Padrino – Next door to *Vissani* (same owner) is this less refined and less expensive eatery. The cooking still is sublime, but the fare simpler. Closed Wednesdays. Reservations advised. Major credit cards accepted. Località Civitella del Lago (phone: 75-950206). Moderate.

Umbria – Good for local cuisine. It has a rustic decor, as well as a terrace for summer dining. Closed Tuesdays. Reservations advised. Major credit cards accepted. 13 Via San Bonaventura, Todi (phone: 75-882737). Moderate.

En Route from Todi – For a really extraordinary experience, pay a visit to the *Cantina Sociale Tudernum,* 2 miles (3 km) outside Todi on the Rome road (146 Frazione Pian di Porto; phone: 75-884-9403). Here you can buy wine dispensed by machines that bear an uncanny resemblance to gas pumps. The wine is excellent, and locals flock here on Saturday mornings to fill up for the weekend. Bottled wine also is available, including the justly renowned grechetto di Todi. Open 9 AM to 1 PM, and 3:30 to 7 PM. Back in Todi, the route continues north to return to Perugia along SS3 *bis,* stopping at Deruta, a town known the world over for its ceramics, and at the wine town of Torgiano. For travelers heading to Lazio or Rome, the recommended route is west to Orvieto, 25 miles (40 km) away, and south from there. The cathedral at Orvieto is so spectacular, in fact, that even those ultimately headed north should make a detour.

ORVIETO: This city clings, somewhat precariously (it has serious landslide problems), to a high, flat table of tufa stone rising up over the gentle, wide valley carved by the Paglia River. During the Middle Ages its name was Urbs Vetus, suggesting to modern historians that this was probably Volsinii, a large Etruscan city of many temples destroyed by Roman troops in 265 BC and then rebuilt in the vicinity. Two Etruscan necropolises, including several painted tombs, have been found nearby; from one of them came the archaic statue of Venus now in Orvieto's *Palazzo Faina Museum,* facing the Duomo.

For most people, Orvieto's Duomo is what impresses most, no matter how many cathedrals they have seen before. From the gilded mosaics and dainty rose window of the façade to the fresco masterpieces inside, this is one of Italy's greatest treasures. It was begun in 1290 in Romanesque style, possibly according to a design by Arnolfo di Cambio, but in the first decade of the 14th century, after some difficulty with the construction, Lorenzo Maitani — a master builder, architect, and sculptor from Siena — was called to the rescue. The present church, including the design of the strikingly beautiful Gothic façade, is largely his, even though numerous other architects, as well as sculptors, painters, and mosaicists, succeeded him, and the project was not completed until the early 17th century. Stand back to study the overall effect of the façade and you'll probably agree that it looks something like a giant triptych altarpiece. At the lowest level, on the pilasters between the doors, are bas-reliefs carved in marble. They illustrate scenes from the Old and New Testaments and are thought to have been done (1320–30) by Maitani himself (the central bronze doors are modern).

On the next level, brilliantly colored mosaic scenes of the life of Mary point upward to still further mosaic scenes and to a large rose window (the work of Andrea Orcagna in the mid-14th century) surrounded by busts and statues of prophets and apostles. At the apex of the triptych is a Coronation of the Virgin in blue, red, and gold mosaic.

Walk up close to the façade and notice that even the parts that appear plain are actually exquisitely decorated — every graceful, slim column, twist, groove, and strip of surface is studded with color. Inside, however, the contrast is startling, because most of the interior — its walls of alternating stripes of black and white stone, its alabaster windows — is quite simple. Make a beeline to the Cappella Nuova (New Chapel, also known as the Cappella di San Brizio) to see the fresco cycle that influenced Michelangelo and made a name for Luca Signorelli. Fra Angelico began the decoration of the chapel in 1447, but completed only two sections of the ceiling; in 1499 Signorelli was commissioned to finish the work, which took him 5 years. Among the scenes of the *End of the World,* the *Coming and Fall of the Antichrist,* and the *Last Judgment* are two men dressed in black. The blond is a self-portrait of Signorelli, the other a portrait of Fra Angelico. Dante is pictured in one of the decorative squares of the wainscoting. At press time, these frescoes and some of the statues were undergoing an extensive restoration.

In the left transept is the Cappella del Corporale, housing a cloth on which the blood of Christ is supposed to have appeared miraculously in nearby Bolsena in 1263. The relic — its possession was the original impetus for building the Duomo — is carried through the streets of Orvieto on the *Feast of Corpus Christi* each spring, a holy day that originated in Orvieto in 1264.

The severe Gothic building to the right of the Duomo is the Palazzo Soliano, formerly the Palazzo dei Papi (Papal Palace). Commissioned by Pope Boniface VIII in 1297, it today houses the cathedral's collection of religious treasures, artworks, and historical bibelots. Open daily except Mondays from 10 AM to 7 PM; admission charge. In front of the Duomo is the *Museo Claudio Faina,* an archaeological museum with, among other things, a collection of Greek vases. It is open daily except Mondays from 9 AM to 1 PM and 3 to 6:30 PM; admission charge. Elsewhere in Orvieto is its oldest building, the Palazzo del Popolo (open to the public only when there are conferences), begun in 1157, and not far from that is the Chiesa di San Domenico, begun in 1233; inside, the tomb of Cardinal Guglielmo de Braye is a masterpiece by Arnolfo di Cambio, who carved it in 1285. The Pozzo di San Patrizio (St. Patrick's Well) is at the far end of town, at an overlook called the Belvedere. Designed by Sangallo the Younger and built in 1528, the well is 200 feet deep and was meant to provide water for the city in case of a siege. Visitors walk to the bottom and back up via two separate spiral staircases of 248 steps each, one superimposed on the other so they never meet.

The Orvieto Tourist Information Office is right across from the Duomo (phone: 763-41772). Open daily, they supply visitors with an excellent brochure that includes a map, and hotel, restaurant, and tourist site listings.

Orvieto is synonymous with fine white wine, either dry or *abboccato* (mellow). The wine is a blend of several grapes — Tuscan trebbiano, verdello, grechetto, and Tuscan malvasia — grown on local hillsides. Each May and June, the town sponsors a wine show. The countryside is dotted with wine cellars (or *cantine*) where visitors are welcome to relax and share a carafe of wine. For more serious wine tasting, however, take a detour to the Decugnano dei Barbi vineyard at Corbara, just outside of Orvieto. Proprietor Claudio Barbi produces a fine orvieto classico, a rich, red decugnano, a rare pourriture noble dessert wine, and an excellent sparkling white wine, or spumante. Call first for an appointment and directions (phone: 763-24055).

CHECKING IN: ***La Badia*** – A beautifully restored and gracious ancient cloister, about 3 miles (5 km) south of Orvieto. It has 22 rooms, tennis courts, a swimming pool, and an elegant dining room whose menu is as sophisticated as the setting warrants. Località La Badia, Orvieto (phone: 763-90359). Expensive to moderate.

Maitani – Right in the heart of town, this hotel has 41 rooms. It vaunts a terrace with a superb view of the Duomo, as well as a charming decor. 5 Via Maitani, Orvieto (phone: 763-42011). Expensive to moderate.

Virgilio – A beautifully restored old palazzo across from the Duomo, with 13 modern rooms. It also is next door to one of the best wine *cantine* in Orvieto, where you can sample a glass before choosing a bottle. 5 Piazza Duomo, Orvieto (phone: 763-41882). Moderate.

EATING OUT: ***Morino*** – Orvieto's most important restaurant is run by Dino Morino and his family. Sauces for the pasta tend to be rich, as in the *agnolotti* with fondue and black truffle, so those who like the lighter touch of *nuova cucina* might prefer the *trenette alla Morino.* Roast kid and stuffed capon are among the fine second-course selections. Closed Wednesdays and January. Reservations advised. Major credit cards accepted. 37 Via Garibaldi, Orvieto (phone: 763-41952). Expensive.

Dell'Ancora – Because of the splendid view of the Duomo, this restaurant tends to get crowded during tourist season. The cuisine blends Roman and Umbrian cooking: From Roman country kitchens come specialties like tripe, a fine dish visitors should not hesitate to try. Among the pasta, all homemade, the irregularly cut egg noodles with hare sauce — *pappardelle alla lepre* — are special. Closed January and Thursdays except in August and September. Reservations advised. Major credit cards accepted. 7 Via di Piazza del Popolo, Orvieto (phone: 763-42766). Moderate.

Cucina Monaldo – Small and elegant, this eatery really comes into its own in summer, when meals are served outside under giant calico umbrellas. The chef lends a sophisticated touch to Umbrian dishes. Closed Mondays. Reservations advised. Visa accepted. 7 Via Angelo da Orvieto (phone: 763-341634). Moderate.

Etrusca – A welcoming trattoria with warm terra cotta tile floors and whitewashed walls. The house specialty is *coniglio all'etrusca,* rabbit served with a piquant green sauce, and there is an excellent selection of Umbrian and Tuscan wines. If you're here at the right time, you may be invited down to the cellars for one of the impromptu wine tastings that are held occasionally. Closed Mondays and the last 3 weeks of January. Reservations advised. Major credit cards accepted. 10 Via L. Maitani, Orvieto (phone: 763-44016). Moderate.

Trattoria dell'Orso – Located right off Piazza della Repubblica, this eatery serves *ombrichelli,* the region's traditional pasta. Try it *alla campagnola* (with zucchini, eggplant, and onions). All the pasta is homemade and the fruit comes fresh-picked from the trees of the Italian half of the management team (the other owner is American). Closed Mondays. Reservations unnecessary. No credit cards accepted. 18-20 Via della Misericordia, Orvieto (phone: 763-41642). Inexpensive.

En Route from Orvieto – To resume the route, go back to Todi and proceed north on SS3 *bis.* Deruta, about 13 miles (21 km) farther on, deserves a stop to browse through the multitude of workshops selling painted ceramic ware. The town's ceramics industry dates from the 14th century at least, and typical Deruta ware has arabesques, dragons, and grotesques harking back to that period. Reference to a shipment of vases and jugs for the Basilica of St. Francis in Assisi appears in a document of 1358; other documents refer to orders of ceramic tiles to pave Gothic churches in Perugia. The industry was at the height of its fame in the early 16th century; in fact, the *Victoria and Albert Museum* in London has a plate made at Deruta by Raphael. Real Deruta ceramic ware is hand-painted, though some stores sell cheaper, mass-produced imitations. To be sure you're getting the real thing, go to any of the following stores, all on Via Tiberina, Deruta's main street: *Ubaldo Grazia, Antonio Margaritelli,* and *Cino Pecetti.* All are open 7 days a week and they will arrange shipping. Other sites to see in Deruta include its 13th-century Palazzetto Municipale, the Town Hall. In the atrium is a headless Roman statue of a seated man holding a small boat. It is believed to represent the god of the Tiber River, Tiberino. Upstairs is a collection of 500 paintings by Umbrian masters. Open daily except Mondays from 9 AM to 1 PM and 4 to 7 PM.

Continue on SS3 *bis* for another 4 miles (6 km; watch for the turnoff) to reach

Torgiano. A visit to the tastefully arranged *Museo del Vino* (Wine Museum; on Via Garibaldi) begins, as does local history, with the ancient Etruscans. On view are wine vases and jugs from an Etruscan funeral dowry and dozens of Roman amphoras. A photo exhibit of documents from Umbrian archives shows various contracts between vineyard tenants and the monasteries who owned the land. A monumental wine press from the 17th century occupies most of one room, and a series of gorgeously decorated antique plates shows versions of Dionysius and Bacchus. A head of Bacchus is by Giovanni della Robbia. Open Tuesdays through Sundays from 9 AM to noon and 3 to 7 PM; admission charge.

After Torgiano, follow the signs back to Perugia, about 8 miles (13 km) away. Our Umbria route terminates here, but it's possible to prolong the exploration of the region with a side trip to Gubbio, 24 miles (38 km) northeast of Perugia via SS298.

CHECKING IN/EATING OUT: ***Le Tre Vaselle*** – The same vintner — Giorgio Lungarotti — who founded the *Wine Museum* established this 48-room hotel in a handsomely restored old country house. The rooms are attractive, although somewhat monastic. It has a restaurant that pleases some very sophisticated palates, who are also well pleased with the torgiano wines — especially the rubesco. A stay here is an alternative to staying in Perugia itself. Closed mid-January to mid-February. Reservations advised. Major credit cards accepted. 48 Via Garibaldi, Torgiano (phone: 75-982447). Expensive.

GUBBIO: On the slopes of Monte Ingino, reached by a winding road that twists and turns through chestnut woods, this town is just far enough off the beaten track to have a wondrous flavor of authenticity. Leave the car in the parking area next to Piazza Quaranta Martiri and look up to the Città Alta (Upper City) for an introduction to all its main buildings — especially the Gothic Palazzo dei Consoli — seen from here with the green mountain as backdrop. Then take the plunge, following Via della Repubblica inward and upward. The narrow streets, stone houses, and tiny churches give Gubbio a particular medieval charm, so even an aimless amble through town is rewarding (but try to include Via Galeotti, Via dei Consoli, Via Baldassini, and the banks of the Camignano in your route). Note the tiny door next to the main door in many buildings; this is the so-called *porta del morto,* the doorway for the dead. While such doors are seen elsewhere in Italian churches, only in Gubbio are they a typical feature of domestic architecture (supposedly, only coffins passed through them, but another explanation is that these were the doors to the medieval living quarters above, while the larger doorways led to ground-floor shops and workshops).

Via della Repubblica crosses Via Baldassini, above which a staircase leads to Via XX Settembre. Suddenly, a vast square, Piazza Della Signoria, opens up, with a breathtaking vista out over the valley to one side. The facing Palazzo dei Consoli (or Palazzo del Popolo), constructed between 1332 and 1337, and the Palazzo Pretorio facing it, constructed in 1349, were conceived as one civic whole, along with the other buildings of the piazza, in Gubbio's most florid period. Today the Palazzo dei Consoli houses a small painting gallery and archaeological museum whose greatest treasures are the seven 3rd- to 1st-century BC bronze plaques known as the *Tavole Eugubine.* Discovered nearby in the 15th century, they are written in the ancient Umbrian language, some using an Etruscan-derived alphabet and others the Roman alphabet. They prescribe the omens for which priests should watch to divine the future and other rituals that shed light on the Etruscans' daily life. Open Tuesdays through Saturdays from 9 AM to 1 PM and 3 to 7 PM; admission charge. Before leaving the museum, go up to the loggia for a panoramic view of the whole red-roofed town.

Note that Gubbio is almost as well known for ceramics as Deruta. Here, too, the industry dates back at least as far as the 14th century and was at its height in the early 16th century, after a certain Mastro Giorgio developed a particularly intense, iridescent ruby red that allowed the Gubbians to subdue much of the nearby competition. Even today, workshops are everywhere, and lovely flowered plates line walls to the left and right of shop doorways.

Each year on May 15, the eve of the *Feast Day of Sant'Ubaldo,* Gubbio's patron saint, the town stages the *Corsa dei Ceri* (Race of the Candles), an event that's been going on since the Middle Ages (and probably since pagan days). The "candles" are three tall wooden "poles" (20 feet or so high, 700 pounds or so) topped by wee statues of saints and set on litters for carrying. Men in costume shoulder the contraptions and puff and pant their way up the mountain behind Gubbio to the Church of Sant'Ubaldo, ordinarily an hour's walk. The saint, who is buried in the church, was a Bishop of Gubbio and is credited with inspiring Gubbian troops to withstand an onslaught by their enemies in 1155. On the last Sunday in May, Piazza della Signoria is the scene of another medieval event, the colorful *Palio della Balestra,* a crossbow match pitting Gubbio against a team from nearby Sansepolcro (a return match is played in Sansepolcro in September). For details, see *Italy's Most Colorful Festas* in DIVERSIONS.

CHECKING IN: ***Park Hotel ai Cappuccini*** – The owners of this extraordinary hotel, 2 miles (3 km) from Gubbio, have gone to great lengths to preserve what was a 17th-century Franciscan monastery. Inside, however, there is every modern convenience, including a mini-computer in each of the 95 rooms — guests can use them to send and receive messages within the hotel and book the property's many facilities, including a fitness center, sauna, and swimming pool. The conference rooms are adorned with well-restored frescoes by the artist Capogrossi. Via Tifernate (phone: 75-923-4777). Expensive.

Il Bosone – There really are no first class hotels in Gubbio itself, but there are a variety of good family-run establishments. Among these is this attractive old building, tastefully restored, with 33 rooms and a very central location. 22 Via XX Settembre, Gubbio (phone: 75-927-2008). Inexpensive.

EATING OUT: ***Alla Fornace di Mastro Giorgio*** – One section of this fine 14th-century building was once the workshop of the famous Gubbio ceramics designer Mastro Giorgio, from whom it takes its name, and another was formerly an ice house, where snow was shoveled down from the street to make ice for use in ice cream making. Try the *ghiottoneria* (fresh pasta, prosciutto, and cheese, swathed in mushroom and cream sauce). Closed Mondays and the last 3 weeks of January. Reservations advised. Major credit cards accepted. Via Mastro Giorgio, Gubbio (phone: 75-927-5740). Moderate.

Taverna Del Lupo – An authentically Umbrian restaurant in an authentically 14th-century setting. Its menu reflects Gubbio's proximity to mountain and forest: risotto with mushrooms or truffles, rabbit, broiled meats with polenta, and duckling. Try the local *eugubini* (Gubbian) wines. Closed Mondays and January. Reservations advised. Major credit cards accepted. 60 Via Ubaldo Baldassini, Gubbio (phone: 75-927-4368 or 75-927-1269). Moderate.

The Abruzzo

The Abruzzo, the rugged, rustic area east of Rome, is one of Italy's most mysterious and least known regions. Much of the mystery derives from the austere Appenine mountain ranges crushed one upon the other to form a sort of single huge and haughty fortress whose walls must be carefully studied before they are scaled. With the exception of scattered ski resorts, the same mountains have hindered tourist development and stalled the arrival of good highways, and poverty, too, has contributed to the area's less than developed status. But for those travelers who appreciate authenticity and the unspoiled, the brooding Abruzzo provides a glimpse of Italy from a time long ago.

The region is shaped like a fattish half-moon whose flat side lies on the Adriatic Sea facing Albania, just about where the back of the "calf" would be on the long Italian boot. On that flat side are nearly 70 miles of beaches, wide and sandy to the north, toward the Marches region, and the beginnings of rocky outcroppings to the south, after Vasto. At midpoint is the bustling seaport of Pescara. There — at the mouth of the Pescara River — a broad flat valley begins, and fields of grain, carrots, sugar beets, spinach, peppers, and tomatoes abound.

Moving inland, that beguiling and bucolic flatland rises astride the river and its tributaries, first into knuckled foothills terraced for grapes, fig and olive trees, and then into mighty knotted fists of gray limestone mountains whose harshness is legendary. At Pescara, fisherfolk are left behind mending their nets in torpid sunshine, and with only an hour or two of driving inland on the new superhighways, you enter nearly Alpine scenery whose mountains may still wear caps of snow in May. Above the tree line the deep gouges and distant whorls in the limestone are the legacies of ancient glaciers (the patch of one remaining small glacier can still be seen in the western border of the region).

Farther inland, penetrating into the more than 200 square miles of valley and highland forest at the Parco Nazionale dell'Abruzzo, brown Marsican bears hunt blueberries and chamois goats leap from crag to crag. There and at regional parks on Mount Sirente and Mount Maiella, wolves still prowl, and eagles and hawks soar overhead. Strawberries and raspberries grow wild along the paths, and prickly clumps of juniper are found everywhere. Lovers of untamed flora may come upon rare bronze and yellow wild orchids, deep blue gentian, orange tiger lilies, white perfumed narcissi, and even the furry edelweiss.

On the flat valleys 4,000 feet and higher, Sardinian shepherds bring their flocks of sheep by ferry and truck from their too-barren lands in summer to graze here. Time has stopped: in the fields farmers bring in the hay using wooden rakes, as did their fathers and grandfathers. In the high valleys where farming the stony soil is a perennial challenge, tender lentils and potatoes grow in handkerchief plots that were laid out in the Middle Ages.

Meanwhile, deep in the highlands woodchoppers carefully work the beech forests until the time of the deep snows, when they settle in their kitchens with a glass of fizzy red wine by log fires (this is a region where kindling stoves are still a best seller) and wait for the skiers to arrive.

The highest and most dramatic of all the mountains in the Abruzzo and, indeed, in all of Italy (except for the Alps) is the elongated, severe chain of the Gran Sasso. At 9,555 feet, its Corno Grande peak rises to about the average height of the Alps in the north. The Gran Sasso is a watershed; its melting snows and spring waters flow into the Adriatic to the east, and into the Tyrrhenian to the west.

Next in size and importance comes the range of the Maiella, whose huge dome-shaped mass is home to several small wolf packs carefully studied and monitored by zoologists. Early man dwelled here, in the Alento and Foro valleys, where flintstone knives and a large axehead (now in the *Museo Etnografico e Preistorico* in Rome) were found, a few dating from the early Stone Age, and more from the glacial era. To the ancient Romans, the Maiella was known as the *Pater montium,* the father of mountains, and here they built, on its slopes, a temple to Jove, the father of all the gods.

Other stretches of mountains are the Monti del Morrone, 6,000 feet high, which link the Maiella to the Gran Sasso; toward the Lazio border, the Monti Simbruini; and, overlooking the now prosperous flat farm valley of the Fucino, once a lake that was drained in a spectacular engineering project of the mid-19th century, the Monte Velino chain of four high peaks, including the gracious Monte Magnola, a favorite of skiers. Interspersed are a relatively few lakes — the loveliest of which is the elongated, picturesque Lake Scanno — while cutting through the valleys are, in addition to the 70-mile-long Pescara River with its tributary, the Aterno, are the Vomano and the Sangro rivers.

There is a rapid shift from seaside to mountain clime. The coastal region averages from 53 to 61F year-round, but in the rugged hills and mountains daytime temperatures hover in the lows 50s, with nighttime plunging into subzero numbers. Rainfall is concentrated and heaviest in late autumn, especially in November. In the high mountains it may rain every afternoon even in August, although the past decade has produced drier-than-usual years. Even so, at high altitudes, furious blizzards and a snowfall of 3 feet or more are an almost annual occurrence in some spots, and skiing is often possible at the numerous winter resorts from December to April.

The Abruzzo has four significant cities; its total population of 1,300,000, scattered over a rugged, often uninhabitable area of more than 6,000 square miles, is barely a third that of Rome. Its 305 townships are often small and scattered at distances magnified, in the mountain areas, by the hairpin curves. Chieti, the largest city, on a plane overlooking the Pescara River Valley, has a population of only 382,000. Next comes L'Aquila, in the shadow of the Grand Sasso (298,000), followed by Pescara (293,000), and Teramo (278,-400).

The area has been inhabited since ancient times; skeletal remains estimated at 40,000 years old (*Homo marsicanus*) were found near Avezzano. After the linguistic unification (only one Abruzzese dialect exists today — in the Marsican region; most everyone else speaks Italian with a distinct accent) of the numerous Abruzzo tribes in the millennium before Christ (including the Marsi, Picenti, Paeligni, Pretuzzi, Marrucini, Aequi, Vestini, and Praetutii), they joined with powerful Samnites from the south to form a single culture. Gradually, Romans overran the territory. In 90 BC, the Roman conquest was complete, and soldiers marched on the Via Tibertina from Rome through the valleys, and established Alba Fucens on the borders of the now dried-up Lake Fucino on the site of an earlier prehistoric city.

In 493, with the collapse of the Roman Empire, conquering Goths descended from the north under Theodoric. For 2 decades after 535 they fought the Byzantines for possession of Italy; the Byzantines won, claiming the Abruzzo as booty. In 571 the Germanic Longobard domination began, and the region was split between the Longobard Dukes of Spoleto and Benvenuto; but in 774 Charlemagne unified the region. In 1140 the Norman domination was complete, and the region became a part of the Kingdom of Sicily. The city of L'Aquila was founded in 1254, and flourished, as its many fine churches and castle testify. The French Angevin dynasty owned the region after 1266, and the Aragons of Spain after 1442.

This was the time of the greatest flowering of the Abruzzo, a passageway for Florentine merchants who bought wool here, or passed en route to Naples. Their influence is still seen everywhere: in almost every village there is a medieval church, abbey, castle, tower, or fortress, with elegant rose-colored windows or finely carved doorways. Monumental fortified castles and romantic Romanesque churches are found in myriad humble villages and in the countryside as well — lonely and lovely, especially in late winter against the dramatic backdrop of snow-capped mountains, rushing brooks, and even pale flowering almond trees.

The 15th-century Longobard influence can be seen in cities like Sulmona, where late Gothic doorways and other architectural details were designed by Pietro da Como from Lake Como, among others. And in the 16th century, the Umbrian influence is apparent in frescoes in Atri by Abruzzo painter Andrea De Lito and in L'Aquila by Francesco da Montereale.

In 1503, with the rest of southern Italy, the Abruzzo passed into Spanish hands as the kingdom of Naples, taken over by the Austrians in 1707-1734. In 1799 Napoleon's troops arrived, bringing the Bourbon Restoration. From 1806 to 1815, the kingdom of Naples was run by Murat during the Napoleonic Restoration. And in 1860 the Abruzzo joined newly unified Italy.

Many of Abruzzo's native sons were men of letters, beginning with Roman historian Caius Sallustius Crispus, born at the Sabine city of Amiternum in the year 86 BC; he became Governor of Africa Nova — Algiers. The poet Ovid, author of the *Metamorphoses,* was born at Sulmona in 43 BC. In 1215, Pietro da Morrone was born on a farm at Isernia, in the Molise region adjacent to the Abruzzo. A Benedictine monk, he became a hermit near Sulmona on the Maiella mountainside, and founded the Hermits of San Damiano, a monastic order. When cardinals in Rome quarrelled for 2 years about electing a new pope, Pietro drew their attention by writing them a stinging letter of criticism. Ironically, in 1294, the cardinals responded by electing this former hermit to be pope. As the idealistic Celestine V, he was frustrated and resigned, turning his back on decadent Rome. He is buried in the Basilica of Collemaggio at L'Aquila, where he had proclaimed the *Perdonanza,* a plenary indulgence where everyone's sins are pardoned, which is solemnly celebrated there each August 28.

In the 18th century, the poet Gabriele Rossetti was born at Vasto (in 1783). Gabriele D'Annunzio, ardent political leader, journalist, poet, and dramatist, was born at Pescara in 1863, where he lived until the age of 11. The brilliant Benedetto Croce, one of the great 20th-century philosophers, was born in the mountain village of Pescasseroli in 1866; and, in another mountain village — Pescina — the author of *Bread and Wine* and *Fontamara,* partisan fighter and novelist Ignazio Silone was born.

Far more than elsewhere in Italy, the past still lives on the Abruzzo. In tiny towns like Scanno, older women still wear traditional dress — long, black-pleated skirts with turquoise petticoats and black tops. The numerous celebrations of the passage of the liturgical year, the seasons, and of social occasions, have special importance here, even today. They are deeply felt, and some date back to the dimmest past. (Their dates, too, can be mysterious, varying with the church year, so check first with tourist agencies and hotels.) The *Processione dei Serpari* (Procession of the Serpent-Bearers) is celebrated in Cocullo on the first Thursday in May, in honor of San Domenico. In this pre-Christian ritual, men and women go into the town's main church with live snakes writhing around their necks and arms, and drape the saint with the serpents. The town of Loreto Aprutino celebrates another ancient rite, the *Processione del Bue di San Zopito* (Procession of the Ox of St. Zopito), in mid-May. Adorned with ribbons and decorations, an ox leads a religious procession into the church, and is made to kneel down before the altar. Also in late May at Buccianico is the *Bandieresi,* when women weave wildflowers into exquisite miniature floats set in baskets that they carry on their heads. And in L'Aquila in late August, at the solemn *Perdonanza* initiated by Celestine V, flag throwers perform and the entire city celebrates the forgiveness of sins.

The Abruzzo craftspeople are famous the world over for their production of ceramics. These painted earthenware plates, cups, bowls, and coffee and tea services — still beautifully made in the tiny mountain town of Castelli on a steep slope of the Gran Sasso — hark back to the 16th century. The art was developed by the Grue family and other master ceramists who, rather than ape the designs of Faenza and Florence, painted their own both majestic and rustic landscape. Also famous among Abruzzo crafts is gold filigree work, like the rosetta brooch the young men of Scanno still give their brides-to-be. More humble handicrafts sold in shops and the outdoor markets are copper pots, thick woollen fringed bedspreads woven in an ornate pattern of two colors, cotton (and sometimes linen) yard goods, and precious *tombola* (bobbin) lace. Sulmona streets are lined with shops selling single flowers, as well as whole bouquets made from gaily colored sugared almonds — more an art form than a food product; most are too pretty to eat.

In general, tradition reigns in the Abruzzo kitchen, where nouvelle cuisine and top-hatted elegance are a rarity. Cooking is rustic, for the most part, or what the Italians call *genuina* — uncontaminated by large-scale industrial production (though the Abruzzo now has some of that, too).

Two separate and distinct cuisines faithfully reflect the two spirits of the region — sea and mountain. The Adriatic area abounds in splendid fresh fish at prices unknown in Rome or northern Italy. Hot and cold mixed seafood salads, pasta and risotto with shellfish, and grilled fish of astounding variety are available in the colorful waterfront restaurants.

Mountain fare includes roast kid and baby lamb (especially at *Easter*), potato and lentil soups, sausages and pork chops in winter, and pasta with mushrooms in the autumn, including prized wild mushrooms (when the region's avid mushroomers are willing to part with some of their pick). Local cheeses include mozzarella made from cow's milk; the delicate globe of the *scamorza* (try one toasted on a wood fire), and *pecorino* (ewe's milk cheese), delicate or aged and tangy. All are especially sweet and flavorful in the late spring and summer, when the herds of prized light brown Alpine cows, sheep, and goats graze at high altitudes upon tender grasses. Fresh water trout is delicious inland. Everywhere, the often tart salad greens are a delight. The typically tiny brown lentils are tender because they grow at a high altitude, as does yellow saffron, that rare delicacy that colors many Abruzzo dishes, as well as the famed *risotto milanese* (which the Abruzzese claim was invented, in any case, by an Abruzzo stonecutter who happened to be in Milan and was bored with its plain rice).

The high plain of the Navelli in the province of L'Aquila is today the sole saffron-producing district in Italy. Harvested in October, saffron is derived from the flower of the *Crocus sativus,* and has been grown in the Abruzzo since the late 15th century. It is costly — to make a single pound requires the filaments of 75,000 flowers, and the annual harvest is a mere 135 lbs. In the Abruzzo, it is used in *scapece alla vastese,* a seafood stew of wine-marinated fried squid and fish fillets. Such an abundance of fine natural ingredients may explain why the Abruzzese so like to cook and eat — and why their school for professional chefs at Santa Maria is famed worldwide. The industrial production of pasta (and other food, such as dried figs, tomatoes, and artichokes), is increasingly important in the Abruzzo, but in most restaurants and humble trattorie, visitors are likely to find at least one of the pasta offerings homemade. Most probably it will be the region's beloved and unique *maccheroni alla chitarra,* named for the small rectangular wooden frame upon which it is made. The pasta sheet is placed on top of the frame over taut thin wires, and rolled. The traditional sauce for the resulting square, thickish strands is spicy with *peperoncino rosso* (red pepper), *pancetta* (bacon), tomatoes, and *pecorino* cheese. A delectable baked lasagna, rich with thin egg pasta, is layered with chunks of *scamorza, ragù,* and dried *porcini* mushrooms.

One famous Abruzzo dish is "the Virtues"; it is made from seven kinds of dried beans, fresh legumes, springtime vegetables, pasta, condiments, and meat — all simmered for 7 hours. What makes it virtuous is its husbandry: it empties the cupboard at winter's end, down to the last dried bean.

The Abruzzese also indulge their sweet tooths. A soft honey-flavored and almond-rich chocolate bar *torrone,* made from a century-old recipe, is produced at L'Aquila, and is a favorite at *Christmas* (or any other) time. The dry chocolate-covered nut torte, *perozza,* also is manufactured on a small scale. Homemade waffles can be found in some bakeries. Follow your nose;

especially in the mountain villages, the loaves of bread, pizza, and various hazelnut or anise- and rosemary-flavored biscuits are often baked on ancient wood-burning ovens, and are a delicious serendipity.

The Abruzzo produces its own agreeable wines — according to Ovid, who drank them. Today they include several with the DOC — Controlled Denomination at Origin — certification. The most noteworthy are the red and the whites of the montepulciano d'Abruzzo and the trebbiano d'Abruzzo. Look for the label of Edoardo Valentini of Loreto Aprugino for a fine trebbiano. Other top labels are zaccagnini from Bolognano, monti and montori of Controguerra, and pepe of Torano Nuovo. Meals are topped off with a powerful peppery brew called *centerbe* — 100 herbs; its strong green color makes the sipper dream of Alpine fields. This liqueur is strong enough to make the toughest Abruzzo woodchopper go weak at the knees.

A love for sports has come fairly recently to the Abruzzo, a region ideally suited for both summer and winter sports. For warm weather vacationers, the 84-mile (140-km) coastline offers a broad sweep of beaches that tend to be wall-to-wall umbrellas, noisy and dirty in mid-summer. The least crowded are in the north, such as Alba Adriatica in Teramo province. The broad sweep of sand beach 10 miles (16 km) north of Pescara attracts 500,000 tourists annually, and the city itself has a new 1,000-boat marina. South of Pescara is Francavilla, a quiet town of gracious villas overlooking the sea. Farther south, the coastline is more varied, especially at Ortona and the Bay of Vasto. Good beaches are at Fossacesia, Ortona, San Vito, and San Giovanni in Venere. And there are many holiday hotels along the way. In the mountain resort areas the newest summer sport is taking a horseback tour of the Alpine-like scenery. Hikers — whether novice or experienced — should make a beeline for the Parco Nazionale dell'Abruzzo, where there are well-marked paths. Other areas include the Gran Sasso (between Teramo and L'Aquila) and the Gole di Celano near Avezzano. Mountain biking also is an attraction in the park.

Skiing is a popular regional sport. The best resorts are Campo Felice and nearby Ovindoli (where Pope John Paul II has skiied) in the Monte Magnola-Velino chain, Campo Imperatore on the Gran Sasso, Pescasseroli in the Parco Nazionale dell'Abruzzo, Prati di Tivo, and Roccaraso and the lovely town of Pescostanza, both near Sulmona. All have small hotels and inns that are jam-packed at *Christmas* and most winter weekends; be sure to plan well ahead. For details, contact the Ente Provinciale per il Turismo (8 Via XX Settembre, L'Aquila 67100; phone: 862-22306). Information about snow conditions is available from a 24-hour snow bulletin source (phone: 862-66510), and is listed in Rome's newspapers on Fridays during the season. Both downhill and cross-country ski equipment can be rented easily at all localities. The best conditions are found from February to mid-March.

Accommodations in the Abruzzo generally are not in the luxury category, but there are many high-quality as well as comfortable, family-owned places. Hotels listed as expensive range from $90 to $110 for a double room; a moderate place will cost between $60 and $80; and inexpensive accommodations, from $45 to $55. Mountain resort hotels must be booked months ahead during ski season, and in all cases it would be wise to make reservations beforehand by telephone or in writing (the fax machine has yet to come to most places) as some hotels shut during their off-seasons. A meal for two, including wine, at a very expensive restaurant costs $150 and up; an expensive place, $75 to $100; moderate, $65 to $75; and an inexpensive spot, from $40 to $65. The price rises as the altitude drops; seaside restaurants tend to cost more than those in the highlands.

The Abruzzo is best explored by car. Below are two driving routes, each of which can be rushed through in 2 or 3 days, or savored in 5 or more. Both start in Avezzano, a 2-hour drive east from Rome. The first is a tour of the main towns and a few selected villages, mostly by autostrada toll roads whose high viaducts offer breathtaking views, with detours on country roads to visit picturesque towns and villages; the second is a visit to the largest of several huge forested parks — the Parco Nazionale dell'Abruzzo.

AVEZZANO TO L'AQUILA

From Rome, take the Autostrada per l'Aquila A24 for 65 miles (104 km). After about 40 minutes of driving and exactly seven tunnels, the A24 branches; take the right branch, A25, heading in the direction of Pescara. The road slices through the same long, flat valley pass where ancient Romans marched toward the Adriatic Sea.

AVEZZANO: Exit A25 at Avezzano and take the well-marked country road north 6 miles (9 km) for a short detour to visit the important ruins of Alba Fucens, a Roman settlement from the 1st century BC, a site under excavation since 1949. In a dramatic setting beneath the massive double mountain, Monte Velino, are the remains of baths, a villa, a theater, basilica, and huge amphitheater. Note the ancient Roman milestone post that marks the Via Tiburtina from Rome. Before the Romans, the Equi had their acropolis here; remains of their ancient walls still can be seen. Return to the autostrada, and following the Avezzano signs, take the country road 2 miles (4 km) south to SS578, then turn left to Avezzano, which was largely destroyed by an earthquake early this century. Its 15th-century Orsini Castle is intact and interesting to view from the exterior. The *Museo Lapidario Marsicano* at the Comune (Town Hall; on Via Vezia; no admission charge) has minor artifacts and epigraphs from Alba Fucens. Arrangements to visit the museum can be made at the Comune (phone: 863-36148).

EATING OUT: *Umberto* – One of the oldest restaurants in the whole Marsica area (as this part of the Abruzzo is called), this is the place for regional specialties, including *pasta alla chitarra,* charcoal-broiled lamb chops, and roast pork, and local wines. Closed Thursdays. Reservations unnecessary. No credit cards accepted. 56 Monte Grappa, Avezzano (phone: 863-552188). Moderate.

Aquila – This clean and comfortable trattoria offers well-prepared regional dishes such as lasagna, *pasta e fagioli* (pasta and bean soup), and fresh grilled trout. Closed Mondays and July. Reservations unnecessary. Major credit cards accepted. 26 Corso della Libertà, Avezzano (phone: 863-554152). Moderate to inexpensive.

En route from Avezzano – Return to A25 and head 8 miles (13 km) east to the Celano exit. A mountainside farm town of 10,000 people, Celano's seven medieval churches and stone dwellings cluster around the massive walls of an immense and well-preserved 14th-century castle. In late August every year, the town has a week of festivities for their patron saints, with concerts in the piazza and fireworks. Eight miles (13 km) north on SS5 is the lovely village of Ovindoli; horseback riding (the town has three stables that rent horses in the summer) and hiking are excellent in the surrounding area. A challenging hike in dry summer weather is through the canyon-like Gole di Celano, walking from the town of Ovindoli through the magnificent Val d'Arano and then down a steep descent to the town of Celano. The path is marked every summer by the local *Club Alpino Italiano* (*CAI*).

Returning once again to A25 toward Pescara, continue 12 miles (20 km) to Cocullo. Try and visit this tiny hilltop town the first Thursday in May, when the *Processione dei Serpari* (Procession of the Serpent-Bearers) takes place in the Church of San Domenico. In this age-old ceremony, people enter the church with live snakes wrapped around their necks and arms and pay homage to San Domenico by draping his statue with them. There are ruins of a medieval tower, and from the same era, the Church of the Madonna delle Grazie, with its fine paintings and altar. Head back to A25 and take it 11 miles (18 km) to Pratola, then SS17 south for 4 miles (6 km) to Sulmona.

EATING OUT: *Da Guerrinuccio* – This pleasant, rustic trattoria in a sprawling country inn (best avoided on crowded Sundays), serves all the typical Abruzzo dishes. Sometimes polenta with a hearty and abundant sausage, spare ribs, and tomato sauce also is on the menu and grilled trout is a specialty. Closed Mondays. Reservations necessary on Sundays. Major credit cards accepted. Via Sardellino, Celano (phone: 863-791471). Moderate to inexpensive.

SULMONA: An especially gracious medieval town of 25,000 people, the main piazza is like a stage setting, crossed by part of a Roman aqueduct (harking back to ancient Rome when the poet Ovid was born here). Visit its 11th-century cathedral, San Panfilo (Via Ovidio), and 13th-century aqueduct and the Church of San Francesco della Scarpa (both on Piazza del Mercato), but best of all is the fascinating Annunziata abbey complex from the 14th century (Piazza all'Annunziata; open daily from 10 AM to 1 PM; no admission charge). Papermaking was an important industry in the late Middle Ages, and in the 16th century, typography. Sulmona's main source of income today seems to be sugar-coated almonds, and gold filigree work is a local craft tradition. For sugared almond flower (*confetti*) arrangements, the most famous shop is *Fratelli Pelino* (55 Via Introdacqua), but all the local manufacturers make the same high-quality product, including wreaths that adorn doorways. For typical Abruzzo bedspreads, used more often in the US as area rugs, stop at the factory of *Santarelli* (15 Via Stazione Introdacqua — on the road toward Scanna right outside town). It is open Monday through Friday from 9 AM to 12:30 PM and 2:30 to 4:30 PM, Saturdays from 9 AM to 12:30 PM.

CHECKING IN: *Europa Park* – This 105-room hostelry just outside town has a pleasant restaurant, outdoor tennis court, and a garage, but is not long on charm. Km 93, SS17, Sulmona (phone: 864-251212). Moderate.

Italia – Centrally located, with 12 rooms and charm, but no restaurant. 3 Piazza Salvatore Tommasi, Sulmona (phone: 864-52308). Moderate to inexpensive.

EATING OUT: *Da Nicola* – The mood is rustic and traditional Abruzzese, but with surprising touches, such as lemon-flavored cannelloni. Closed Mondays and most of July. Reservations unnecessary. Major credit cards accepted. 26 Piazza XX Settembre, Sulmona (phone: 864-33070). Moderate.

En route from Sulmona – A pleasant detour is to continue 19 miles (32 km) southeast on the uphill, winding SS17 toward Pescocostanzo (near Roccaraso, a popular ski resort). One of the most picturesque Abruzzo towns, Pescocostanzo has a beautiful square, the Piazza Santa Maria del Colle, where there is an 11th-century church, Santa Maria del Colle, with a carved and gilded wooden ceiling. Its altar and seated Madonna del Colle are from the 13th century and were carved in wood by local craftsmen. The magnificent doorway of the nearby Collegiata (Abbey School) should not be missed. This is still a village of craftspeople — on Corso Roma, blacksmiths display their wrought-iron wares for all to see. *Vito Sciullo* (Piazza del Municipio) sells traditional Abruzzo gold and silver filigree jewelry, although other shops throughout the town also have high-quality goods. And in some of the tiny *mercerie,* which sell a hodgepodge of everything, a few of the prized bits of handmade Abruzzo *tombolo* lace can be found.

CHIETI: Take SS17 northeast, which turns into SS5, 65 miles (109 km) to Chieti. Poised on a bluff overlooking the vast Pescara River plain, Chieti was once the home of the Marrucini tribe, which first fought hard against the Romans and later joined them in defending their common territory from the Phoenicians during the Punic wars. A Roman center of power, for a time it ruled over Pescara — then called Aternum — but later was brought to its knees by the barbarians. Sites of interest include the medieval cathedral (Piazza della Villa Comunale) and the 17th-century baroque San Domenico Church (Corso Marrucino) with a *Museo Diocesano Teatino* (Diocesan Museum; phone: 871-66349) that has a fine collection of 14th-century religious articles and precious miniatures. Ask the church's sexton to open the museum (donations suggested). Paintings from the 14th century on can be found in the *Pinacoteca Barbella,* in the Palazzo Martinetti, a former 17th-century convent (13 Via de Lollif; open daily except Sundays and holidays from 9 AM to 1 PM; admission charge). The pièce de résistance is the *Museo Nazionale Archeologico* in the Villa Comunale (National Archaeological Museum; Viale R. Paolucci; phone: 871-65704), the most important museum in the Abruzzo, whose prize possession is the *Warrior of Capestrano,* dating from about 500 BC. When it was found buried in a vineyard in 1934, the statue became a worldwide sensation, not only for its perfect condition and sober, elegant style, but because it showed that an unknown, but sophisticated, wealthy, and archaic civilization existed in the Abruzzo, contemporary with the Etruscans in central and western Italy. The museum collection also includes a celebrated statue of Hercules found at Alba Fucens, a splendid bed from Amiternum, and elegant polychrome mosaic marble pavements from other ancient Abruzzo cities. It is open Mondays through Saturdays from 9 AM to 1:30 PM, Sundays from 9 AM to 12:30 PM; admission charge. Also worth visiting in Chieti are the ruins of the 2nd-century Roman theater (Via Zecca) and the small Roman temple (1 block west of Corso Marrucino, behind the central post office) built by the Teati (Chieti is a corruption of the name), the original Roman inhabitants of the city. The local tourist office, the Azienda per il Soggiorno, is at 29 Via B. Spaventa (phone: 871-65231).

CHECKING IN: ***Dangio'*** – This charming, 40-room inn overlooks the river valley and has an excellent restaurant, *Le Regine,* whose chef, Nicola Ranieri, offers a modern and creative interpretation of traditional dishes. Closed Mondays and most of December. Reservations advised. Major credit cards accepted. 20 Via Solferino, Chieti (phone: 871-347358). Expensive.

EATING OUT: ***Bellavista*** – In the historic center, the Abruzzo specialty, *pasta alla chitarra,* is angel-hair-fine at this eatery, and comes wrapped in a dainty crêpe. The *timballino di crespelle* is a baked confection of crêpes filled with mushrooms, mozzarella, and prosciutto, and the turkey breast is stuffed with chestnuts. Closed Mondays. Reservations advised. Major credit cards accepted. Corso Marrucino, Chieti (phone: 871-65637). Expensive to moderate.

PESCARA: On A25, head 6 miles (9 km) east to Pescara, a pre-Roman city on the Adriatic Sea at the mouth of the Pescara River. It was destroyed twice by the Longobards, once by Ottone IV, and today's urban architects are doing the same by constructing unsightly, modern buildings. Ladislao of Naples, and later Charles V, fortified the city so well that it could withstand a siege in 1566 by the Turks and another by the Austrians in 1707. Gabriele D'Annunzio went to school here, and his boyhood home (on Corso Manthonè) now houses three museums — the *Museo della Fondazione Ga-*

briele D'Annunzio; the *Museo Archeologico* (phone: 85-690656), which has a collection of local Roman artifacts; and the *Museo delle Arti Populari Abruzzesi* (phone: 85-690656) with a permanent exhibit of Abruzzese folk arts and crafts. All three are open Tuesdays through Saturdays from 9 AM to 2 PM, Sundays from 9 AM to 1 PM; admission charge. Pescara is a large fishing port — berth to colorful boats, and home to countless seafood restaurants. Local specialties include the *parrozzo* torte made with hazelnuts and *aurum,* a local liqueur said to derive from the ancients. Nearby are wide, sandy beaches popular with swimmers and sunbathers. The local tourist office, the Azienda per il Soggiorno, is at 171 Via Nicola Fabrizi (phone: 85-421-1707).

CHECKING IN: ***Carlton*** – Well appointed and comfortable, this seaside hotel with 71 rooms has a decent restaurant. Open year-round. 35 Viale Riviera, Pescara (phone: 85-373125). Expensive.

EATING OUT: ***Duilio*** – Fish takes center stage at this well-managed modern restaurant. Prepare to dine well and abundantly on such fare as *antipasto alla Duilio,* a splendid array of fish, crayfish, squid, and other shellfish, *fusilli alla pescatrice* (pasta with fish sauce), delicate *rombo* (turbot) with zucchini, or *palombo* (a shark-like fish) with artichokes. Service is attentive, and the wine list carefully selected. Closed Mondays. Reservations necessary, especially on Sundays. Major credit cards accepted. 9 Via Regina Margherita, Pescara (phone: 85-378278). Expensive.

Guerino – Along the beachfront, this huge, popular, and reliable restaurant with air conditioning indoors and a terrace outdoors is a Pescara institution, with brothers Dino and Enzo carrying on the family enterprise. The fish antipasto is imaginative and extravagant, and the *maccheroni alla chitarra* is made with a fish sauce. Try *brodetto alla Guerino* (a fish soup), pasta with lobster sauce, *crostone* (shrimp on toast), or *spuma di calamaretti* (squid soufflé). Closed Tuesdays. Reservations advised. Major credit cards accepted. 4 Viale della Riviera, Pescara (phone: 85-421-2065). Expensive.

Franco – Crowded with admirers, big and cheery, this riverside trattoria offers a prix fixe menu with at least five types of *antipasto del mare,* as well as risotto with fish and baby shrimp, and a generous mixed fish plate — grilled or fried, wine, and dessert. Closed Mondays. Reservations advised. No credit cards accepted. 58 Via Doria, Pescara (phone: 85-66390). Inexpensive.

En route from Pescara – Take coastal road SS16 north 8 miles (13 km) to Pineto, the turnoff for Atri, and head west 6 miles (10 km). Of notable interest in Atri is the *Museo Capitolare* (on Via Roma; phone: 85-87241). Its collection includes 11 rooms of Abruzzo ceramics, sacred vestments, and sacred articles. Open daily from 10 AM to noon and 4 to 8 PM in summer, hours are shorter in winter; admission charge. In the Piazza del Duomo, the town's 1,100-year-old cathedral (on the ruins of a Roman bath) houses fine frescoes by Andrea De Lito — the most important Renaissance works in the Abruzzo.

Follow A14 north for 10 miles (17 km) and exit at Giulianova. Equestrians might want to stop at *Fattoria Cerreto* in nearby Mosciano Sant'Angelo (phone: 85-864-8197). The farm has 20 well-trained horses available for riders at any skill level, and can arrange trips of up to a week in the Abruzzo foothills. At Giulianova, take SS80 15 miles (24 km) west to Teramo.

TERAMO: This pre-Roman city lies between the Tordino and the smaller Vezzola rivers. The Romans later built another city on top of it. Today's modern city has few traces of its proud ancient heritage, but the 12th-century Cathedral of San Berardo (Via Tirso) is of interest, as are the 1st-century Roman theater and amphitheater (Via del'Amfiteatro). The small *Museo e Pinacoteca Civici,* at the Villa Comunale (Piazza Garibaldi; phone: 861-50772) houses artifacts from the Roman era, Renaissance paintings, and Castelli ceramics. It is open daily in summer from 9:30 AM to noon and 5 to 7 PM; in winter, afternoon hours are from 3 to 5 PM; admission charge. The local tourist board is on Via del Castello (phone: 861-51357).

EATING OUT: ***Antico Cantinone*** – Chick-pea soup with chestnuts, *crespelle* (light crêpes) stuffed with cheese, and roast lamb are the specialties of this authentic regional trattoria that has been pleasing diners for half a century. Among the wines are those from the Val Vibrata. Closed Sundays. No reservations. Major credit cards accepted. 5 Via Ciotti, Teramo (phone: 861-35863). Moderate.

Il Duomo – In a pleasant setting, brothers Carlo and Marcello Rossi offer regional specialties including, in season, *porcini* mushroom salad, *tagliatelle* with *porcini,* and roast of lamb. There is a good selection of national and regional wines. Other dishes include an 18th-century pasta recipe called *lu rentrocele* (a sauce made with three kinds of meat — beef, lamb, and pork) and, in spring, *Le Virtù,* the famed peasant soup. Closed Mondays and most of August. Reservations advised. Major credit cards accepted. 9 Via Stazio, Teramo (phone: 861-321274). Moderate.

En route from Teramo – Take SS80 3 miles (5 km) east to A24, then head southwest for 15 miles (24 km) to the Isola di Gran Sasso exit. For information about climbing the Gran Sasso, contact the Azienda Soggiorno e Turismo (8 Via XX Settembre; phone: 862-22306) or the *Club Alpino Italiano* (*CAI;* 15 Via XX Settembre; phone: 862-24342) in L'Aquila. Against a majestic sweep of high mountains, take route 491, an easy but winding country road, northeast 5 miles (8 km). Turn right on to the Castelli provincial road and follow it 6 miles (10 km) to Castelli, a center for master ceramists for the past 4 centuries. Across from the village a deep gouge in the cliff shows where the craftspeople get their fine clay. Dozens of old kilns lie under the village's stone buildings. Several simple trattorie offer delicious food. There are scores of small stores that sell the ceramics, but before stopping at the first roadside shops to buy, visit the *Museo della Ceramica* just outside the village. Among its beautifully displayed ceramics are centuries-old works by the Grue master potters, including painted plates, vases, and panels. Open daily except Mondays from 9 AM to 1 PM. Although modernizing influences are starting to appear in Castelli pottery, the old ways continue, and a leisurely tour of the shops in the village — after seeing the originals in the museum — is a good way to decide what to buy. Of the many skillful craftspeople, the Antonio D'Egidio family stands out — son Giovanni now paints pottery and runs the shop (18 Scesa del Borgo; phone: 861-979183).

For those who are adventurous, drive up the steep, narrow dirt road to the small country Church of San Donato. It is kept locked, so that unless prior arrangements are made at the Comune (Piazza Roma; phone: 861-979142) for a visit, its precious 200-year-old painted tile ceiling can be glimpsed only through a window at the front.

Head back to A24 and take it 29 miles (46 km) to L'Aquila, the loveliest city of the Abruzzo. The autostrada passes through a half-mile-long tunnel directly under the Gran Sasso.

L'AQUILA: Built in the 13th century, L'Aquila flourished in the mid-14th century and the majority of its most important monuments were constructed during those 2 centuries. They include the outstanding Basilica di Santa Maria di Collemaggio (Viale di Collemaggio), which was started in 1287 by the monk Pietro da Morrone, who would later become Pope Celestino V; his mausoleum is inside. The church façade has horizontal stripes, and finely carved rose windows and doorframe. The Church of Santa Maria Paganica (Piazza Santa Maria Paganica) dates from 1308, and Santa Maria di Róio (Via di Róio), from 1332. The Fontana delle 99 Cannelle (Piazza di Porta Rivera), a recently restored fountain with 99 spouts, was built in 1272. The renowned *Madonna and Angels* fresco by Francesco da Montereale is in the Church of San Silvestro (Via

Garibaldi). The immense, square, 16th-century fortified castle (bordered by Via Castello and Viale Gran Sasso) houses various paleontological and archaeological collections, paintings (especially medieval), ceramics from Castelli, and speleological displays of minerals and objects found in the numerous caves in the area. Open daily Tuesdays through Saturdays from 9 AM to 2 PM, Sundays from 9 AM to 1 PM. The tourist office is at 5 Piazza Santa Maria di Paganica (phone: 862-410340).

CHECKING IN: ***Duca degli Abruzzi*** – Centrally located, this modern, comfortable hostelry has 85 rooms and a garage and a good penthouse restaurant, *Il Tetto,* that overlooks the red-tile rooftops. Open year-round. Reservations necessary in the restaurant. Major credit cards accepted. 10 Viale Giovanni XXIII, L'Aquila (phone: 862-28341). Expensive.

EATING OUT: ***Tre Marie*** – A national monument, this restaurant is exceptional — for its unique decor including heavy wooden furnishings from Abruzzo and an 18th-century fireplace and for elegantly prepared Abruzzo specialties. Paolo is the latest member of the Scipioni family to oversee the painstaking preparations of the delicate *zuppa della salute* (crêpes in broth), homemade stuffed pasta, *maccheroni alla chitarra,* hare in pastry crust, sizzling grilled trout, and ricotta tart. Look for recipes utilizing the rare locally produced saffron. Closed Sunday evenings, Mondays, and from *Christmas* to *New Year's Day.* Reservations advised. No credit cards accepted. 3 Via Tre Marie, L'Aquila (phone: 862-413191). Expensive.

Il Caminetto – In this roomy establishment the *frittelle* (crêpes) and potato gnocchi are made with saffron. Another specialty comes from the ancient Romans — lamb with egg and lemon sauce. Closed Mondays and November. American Express accepted. Reservations advised. Via Antica Arischia Pettin, L'Aquila (phone: 862-311410). Moderate.

Scannapapere – Flora di Marco's regional specialties, including local or home-cured cheese, ham, and salami, take center stage. *Pasta alla chitarra* shepherd-style (with tomatoes, mushrooms, and *pecorino* cheese), mutton, and duckling are favorites at this country trattoria. Closed Saturdays in winter. Reservations advised. No credit cards accepted. 2 Via Salaria Antica Est, on the road to the A24 autostrada, L'Aquila (phone: 862-315052). Inexpensive.

Take A24 west to Rome.

PARCO NAZIONALE DELL'ABRUZZO

Italy has few national parks of such dimensions: 200 square miles of mountains, sunlit valleys, and dense forests of pine, beech, and chestnut trees. Situated between the broad, flat farm valley of the Fucino to the northwest, the park is bounded by two mountain chains, the Mainarde to the southeast and the Marsicani to the east, and to south and southwest, two rivers, the Sangro and the Liri.

The area was set apart as park land in 1872, only 12 years after Italy became a unified nation. It became a national park in 1950 after lively debate — the villagers opposed it, fearing it would destroy their livelihood gained from cutting down trees. Today the park has become all too attractive as a real estate investment, and nature lovers wage an ongoing battle to prevent the surrounding semi-protected park border areas from erosion by developers. The park proper has remained largely intact, and is home to 40 species of mammals and 30 varieties of bird — cuckoos and nightingales can sometimes be heard on a summer evening in the woods. Wild chamois roam the mountains and there are dozens of snakes, including the deadly Abruzzo viper. (Don't walk in the woodland paths without carrying a walking stick and wearing appropriate footwear.) There also are about 100 Marsican bears and more than 30 surviving wolves.

The countryside is vibrant — there are meadows and fields brilliant with yellow gorse and red poppies, hilltop towns poised against a backdrop of gray mountain peaks, long narrow lakes like fjords, and dramatic canyons. The park highlands are at their most glorious in June and July, when wildflowers carpet the high meadows, wild strawberries can be found at the edge of a path, and wild mushrooms are in season. In August the lowlands turn dry, but the park is ideal in summer for hiking, biking, and horseback riding. In winter, the best time for a lingering visit is February, when downhill and cross-country skiers find many sunny days.

A special word to skiers: crowds are off-putting over the *Christmas* holidays. Because of its proximity to Rome, Pescasseroli, a major ski center, can become quite populated. An alternative might be to go in January when special "white week" discounts are available. For information, contact the Aziende Autonome di Turismo (Via Piave, Pescasseroli; phone: 863-91461). Although the trails are short, there are plenty of slopes for skiers of all levels. Driving can be treacherous; in midwinter, chains may be obligatory for cars.

En route from Avezzano – Take the A25 autostrada 10 miles (16 km) to Pescina. Although it is prosperous today, Pescina was the poverty-stricken farm village so movingly described by writer Ignazio Silone in *Fontamara.* Silone was born here, and his ashes are buried, as he wished, near the stark tower of the town's 600-year-old castle at the edge of the village, "so I can still see it as when I was a child." Another native son is Cardinal Giulio Mazzarino (1601–1661), astute counselor to Louis XIV of France; a small museum (Piazzale Rancilio; phone: 863-81163) commemorates him. Open Mondays, Tuesdays, Thursdays, Fridays, and Saturdays from 10 AM to noon and 4 to 6 PM; Sundays from 9 AM to noon; admission charge.

Take SS83 south, an easy but winding and uphill road, 29 miles (46 km) to Pescasseroli, the main town in the park. Leaving behind the fields of sugar beets and potatoes for higher ground, you might see a shepherd leaning on his crook while his flock is tended by the woolly white Abruzzo sheep dogs, celebrated for their courage. It is Abruzzo canine lore that these are the only sheep dogs tough enough to fight off the wolves that are sometimes driven by hunger, especially during harsh winters, to attack flocks. You'll also see towns with glorious names like Venere (Venus) and Gioia dei Marsi (Jove of the Mars people), which bring to mind the Roman heritage here; and Roman ruins dot the humble farm landscape.

The road continues to rise, entering the park area at the village of Gioia Vecchio. At the lofty Passo del Diavolo (the Devil's Pass), you descend slightly to enter into a high valley through which the small Sangro River snakes. In the center of this broad valley, ringed with higher mountains marked by ski runs, is the immensely popular summer and winter resort of Pescasseroli, 3,829 ft. above sea level. This is the gateway to the park proper, and birthplace of 20th-century philosopher Benedetto Croce.

PESCASSEROLI: Unusual for a ski resort center, Pescasseroli, a town of 2,220 inhabitants, has an ancient heritage. Its small Lungobard Castello Mancino, perched at the end of a path on a hilltop overlooking the town, dates from the Middle Ages. The Romanesque Church of San Pietro e di San Paolo (in the piazza of the same name) was built in the 14th century. During the 1800s the area became the property of the powerful Monastery of Farfa, in Lazio.

In Pescasseroli the ancient custom of walking flocks great distances, the *transumanza,* was observed for many centuries. Shortly before the deep snows arrived, the men from Pescasseroli and other nearby high mountain towns would set out with their herds of sheep and goats to walk down through Molise to Candela, near Foggia in Puglia, where they had winter grazing rights. They walked what is called the *trattura reale* — the royal route. Living in Puglia for months at a time each year, the men picked up some Pugliese expressions, still used by the Pescasseroli men in conversation, but not by the women. Some typical Pugliese foods, such as a Pescasseroli version of *orecchiette* (the dried, chewy pasta called "little ears" for their shape), may also come from the *transumanza* days. A few of the elderly women still wear the severe typical dress of the 19th century.

Park visits can be arranged (although travelers are free to roam on their own) either at the Azienda Autonoma di Turismo (67 Via Piave; phone: 963-91461); at the Ente Parco headquarters at the *Museo Naturalistico e Parco Faunistico,* a small museum of folklore and natural history with an adjacent zoo on the outskirts of town (Viale Santa Lucia; open daily from 10 AM to noon and 3 to 6 PM; admission charge); or at *Cooperativa Ecotur* (13 Via Santa Lucia; phone and fax: 863-912760). The latter two sell maps showing 25 suggested itineraries for hikers of all levels and capabilities. It's a good idea to carry protective clothing and wear appropriate shoes with non-skid soles (not tennis shoes) for real hiking. Remember to keep to the marked paths and not to pick wildflowers or mushrooms. No dogs are permitted on park paths without a leash. Rock climbing is strictly forbidden.

For information on hiking excursions for all skill levels, mountain refuges, and campsites — and there are many — contact the *Cooperativa Servizi Turistici* (Via Umberto I; phone: 863-88152). *Cooperativa Ecotour* (see above) offers 5-hour guided walking tours in summer daily except for Tuesdays and Thursdays, when half-day bus excursions are available. Reserve ahead in July and August because the number of people permitted into the chamois-viewing areas — the Valle di Rosa and Monte Amaro — is limited. The *Agenzia Wolf* (Civitella Alfedena; phone: 863-89336) also organizes walking trips.

Ecotour also rents mountain bikes from *Easter* through early fall, as well as arranging tailor-made guided trekking, cycling, or horseback excursions of several days, with an English-speaking guide, along the shepherd's old *transumanza* route. For horseback or pony rides and lessons, also contact *Centro Ippico Vallelupa,* Via della Difesa (phone: 863-910444).

Shoppers may want to stop at *Prodotti del Parco* (5 Vittorio Veneto, Pescasseroli) to stock up on Abruzzo foodstuffs (including the filaments of locally grown saffron and chocolates and honey of all kinds), wines (try the green herbal *sambuco*), homemade herbal liqueurs (a unique treat is *zappa* made from saffron), and grappa. A good place to shop for gifts is *Bulova* (Piazza Vittorio Veneto); it offers discounted prices on Italian crafts, including Venetian glass vases and reproductions of antique jewelry.

CHECKING IN: *Grand Hotel del Parco* – With 120 rooms, all with shower or bath, this hostelry is considered the best in town. There is a restaurant and outdoor swimming pool. 3 Via Santa Lucia, Pescasseroli (phone: 863-91356). Expensive to moderate.

Edelweiss – A comfortable 20-room hotel, with a restaurant and a garage. Via Colli del'Oro, Pescasseroli (phone: 863-912477; fax: 863-912798). Moderate to inexpensive.

EATING OUT: *Cerbiatto* – Try the homemade *codetti ai peperoni* (green pasta with green pepper sauce) at this rustic trattoria. Also recommended is *gnocchetti* (small pasta) with beans. Closed Wednesdays. Reservations unnecessary. No credit cards accepted. 19 Via Principe di Napoli, Pescasseroli (phone: 863-91465). Moderate to inexpensive.

Alle Vecchie Arcate – Specialties here include *pasta alla chitarra* and pasta and beans with the elegant addition of fresh herbs. The succulent lamb and *scamorza* cheese on a skewer are roasted on a wood fire. There also are 21 guestrooms. Closed Tuesdays. No reservations. No credit cards. 41 Via della Chiesa, Pescasseroli (phone: 863-91381). Inexpensive.

Peppe di Sora – A rustic trattoria serving *pasta alla chitarra alla boscaiolo* (with mushrooms). Look for fresh trout and homemade desserts — with wild berries enriching the summer menu — lentils in winter, and chestnuts in autumn. There also are a few guestrooms. Closed Mondays. Reservations necessary at *Christmas-*

time. No credit cards accepted. 15 Via B. Croce, Pescasseroli (phone: 863-91908). Inexpensive.

Relais Il Salotto – Dine alfresco in summer, or in winter by one of the huge fireplaces in rooms handsomely panelled in wood. Leave your hiking gear behind — this place is elegant, and the food served is a refined adaptation of traditional Abruzzo fare. Open daily in July, August, December, and February; the rest of the year closed Tuesdays. Reservations necessary in the evenings. No credit cards accepted. 4 Via Collacchi, Pescasseroli (phone: 863-91911). Moderate.

En route from Pescasseroli – Only 4 miles (6 km) south on SS83 is Opi, with a population of 500. It dates from prehistoric times, and even today its houses huddle into a defensive wall protecting the village. Opi is a jumping off point for a drive on a narrow road through the handsome maple and beech woods toward the Forca d'Acero *rifugio,* one of ten in the park. These huts are for park workers, but they offer limited amenities for hikers.

Ten miles (16 km) east of Opi on SS83 is Barrea, a picture-postcard village of just 900 souls. Founded nearly 1,000 years ago, Barrea suffered from frequent attacks by Saracen pirates and invaders from the north. Despite a catastrophic earthquake in 1915, this medieval center is in fair condition, and vestiges of the ancient walls can be seen. The 13th-century castle has cylindrical towers, as does the Church of San Tommaso. The town is a lovely pile of small, ancient stone buildings, towers, and 14th-century churches, against a dramatic background of mountain peaks. The elongated Lake Barrea stretches beyond.

Take SS83 4 miles (7 km) to Villetta Barrea and turn north onto SS479, which winds its way 15 miles (25 km) to Scanno slowly downhill (with a few dramatic hairpin curves) over high meadows that are reminiscent of Switzerland.

EATING OUT: *Tre Camini* – Near the crossroad for Opi on SS83, this rustic country inn offers the weary traveler a shaded verandah and tasty dishes such as *fazzoletti verdi* (large pasta filled with ricotta and spinach), grilled salmon trout, and homemade desserts including apple tart. Closed Thursdays. Reservations necessary on Sundays. No credit cards accepted. Km 48.700, SS83, Opi (phone: 864-91936). Moderate.

SCANNO: Historians believe that the Scannesi, with their unique customs and costumes, descended from a nomadic Red Sea tribe — Macau Scammos, who named their town Scamnum. Paliano, as the Old Town is called, is believed to have been named for the Greek god Pan.

Scanno flourished in the Middle Ages, like the rest of the Abruzzo, but plagues, politics, famine, and earthquakes so decimated it that in 1447 a census showed only 302 surviving inhabitants. By the Renaissance, however, Scanno had returned to life, with a population of 2,420 people, and 130,000 sheep. Today there are still the same number of human inhabitants, but the sheep population has shrunk to about one sheep per person (except in summer, when the Sardinian shepherds ferry across the Tyrrhenian Sea and truck theirs to the Abruzzo). Herding was always important, and until the 1800s a rare variety of black Egyptian sheep was raised here.

The graceful, 13th-century Church of Santa Maria della Valle (Piazza Santa Maria della Valle), whose foundations stand on the ruins of a small pagan temple, gazes serenely out over a peaceful valley far below; the church portal and the window above are exquisite. Inside is a polychrome high altar of marble dating from 1731. Behind the church unfolds the tiny Old Town, once within walls pierced by four gates; you can still see remains of a venerable wall and one arched gate. Look in at the Church of Santa Maria di Costantinopoli (Piazza San Rocco), built before 1400; an elegant fresco inside shows the Madonna and Child on a throne, and the name "De Ciollis" and the date

"AD 1478." Whether De Ciollis was painter or patron of what is the town's greatest art treasure, no one knows. It was restored in 1981.

Ritual still plays an important role in Scanno. Older women still dress in traditional costume: somber-colored headscarves, and black skirts worn over a turquoise felt petticoat. Wedding rites are also sometimes still celebrated with the whole party in costume.

Scanno is popular both in summer and winter. Summer visitors can hike or take the chair lift (when it operates) up Monte Rotondo for magnificent views of the area. In winter, three lifts operate, and skis can be rented at *Bruno Sport* (6 Via del Lago) in town, or close to the slopes at the *Paradiso* hotel, *Rifugio Passo Godi,* and *Rifugio Lo Scoiattolo,* all at Passo Godi. Tourist information is available at the Azienda per il Turismo (12 Piazza Santa Maria della Valle; phone: 864-74317). Small boats are for hire at Lake Scanno; bicycles, at Prati del Lago (a park by Lake Scanno), where there are also three tennis courts. Fishing is popular by the dam at San Domenico a Villalago. Equestrians can rent horses at *Il Ranch* (at Variante La Foce; phone: 864-747098), *Le Prata* (at Le Prata; phone: 864-874-7263), and *Miralago* (at Circulacuale; phone: 864-747390). All three also will arrange tours of the lake and through the hills.

Goldsmithing is a time-honored art in this town and many stores offer fine examples to purchase. Brothers Fronterotta (their eponymous shop is in Piazza Santa Maria della Valle) learned this golden art from their father, who learned from his grandfather. They reinterpret the traditional motifs, like *la presentosa* (an engagement pin), in attractive ways, using solid gold or inexpensive versions of burnished, enameled, or gilded silver. *Di Rienzo* (1 Via Roma) offers traditional gold and silver filigree work in the form of earrings, pins, and bracelets, as does *Giancarlo Montesi* (Piazza Santa Maria della Valle). Locally made bobbin lace for inserts in sheets, or collars, or centerpieces, as well as Abruzzo bedspreads and a few patchwork quilts are available at *Violetta* (30 Via Roma), where you can also rent a Scanno costume to have your picture taken. *Chiusolo Artigianato* (13 Via Vincenzo Tanturri) sells hand-embroidered bobbin lace collars and other accessories, plus sheepskin wear.

CHECKING IN: *Garden* – All 35 rooms at this modern hotel have baths. There also is a restaurant, disco, bar, garden, and garage. Viale del Lago, Scanno (phone: 864-74382). Expensive to moderate.

Vittoria – There is a tennis court but no restaurant at this 27-room inn. 46 Via di Rienzo, Scanno (phone: 864-74398). Moderate to inexpensive.

EATING OUT: *Gli Archetti* – This old favorite in the Old Town offers homemade vegetable antipasti and flavorful salami and prosciutto. There is the ubiquitous *pasta alla chitarra,* made with tomatoes, mushrooms, and *pecorino* cheese, but also try polenta in a spicy sauce, lamb from the nearby hills, trout, and vegetables prepared the traditional Abruzzo farm way (sautéed in oil and seasoned with dried red peppers). Closed Tuesdays. No reservations. No credit cards accepted. 8 Via Silla, Scanno (phone: 864-74645). Moderate.

Antonio Carbone – A small, rustic trattoria, with an Abruzzo menu of simple but tasty home-cooked dishes. Closed Thursdays in winter; open daily in summer. Reservations unnecessary. No credit cards accepted. 13 Via Roma, Scanno (phone: 864-91396). Inexpensive.

Continue north on SS479 12 miles (19 km) past the elongated Lake Scanno, where the road plunges into a narrow rock canyon and the scenery is breathtaking, to the A24 autostrada at Cocullo and take it to Rome.

Lazio

If all roads lead to Rome, they lead away from it as well. And there are few better ways to discover Rome and its civilization than to explore, one by one, the ancient roads that radiate from the city the ancients knew as *Caput Mundi,* the center of the world. From Mediolanum in the north — today's Milan — to Brindisi and Taranto at the heel of the Italian boot, all the great cities of the Roman Empire were linked to the capital by roads so enduring that their engineering remains a benchmark for road builders into our own century. Financed by tribute, the 400 major Roman roads were built to last, with up to 5 feet of layered sand, lime, crushed rock, and, often, big flat paving stones of basalt. Down them rattled settlers in covered wagons off to found new Roman towns. Sandal-clad soldiers trudged to war, and tradesmen rode in horse carts to hustle everything from Greek pottery made in Naples to wool from the flocks the Sabines tended on the Apennine foothills around their capital, Rieti.

Beginning northwest of Rome and moving clockwise, the main roads were the Via Aurelia, which ran up the peninsula along the sea; the Via Cassia; the Via Flaminia; the Via Salaria, so named because it brought inlanders to the salt flats at the mouth of the Tiber River; the Via Praeneste, which led to one of antiquity's greatest shrines; and, heading due south, the great Appian Way.

Leaving the city today by any one of these ancient roadways is, at least initially, a painful trip through traffic jams and undiluted urban blight, relieved by occasional serendipitous glimpses of a section of Roman aqueduct, a stretch of ancient wall, or a tomb whose brickwork marks it as Roman. Surprisingly quickly, however, the city comes to an abrupt end. Just beyond a block of high-rise apartment buildings are rolling fields where a shepherd tends a flock grazing under a stately umbrella pine. Lazio, as the region around Rome is called from its ancient name, Latium, has only a limited industrial belt, mostly around the Via Pontina south of Rome and the Via Tiberina, which meanders along with the Tiber.

On a map, the region of Lazio resembles an ivy leaf. One of its trinity of lobes points north, into Tuscan Italy, where gently rolling countryside and neat olive orchards and vineyards suddenly alternate with lofty cliffs of ruddy brown tufa stone. Here, where the plain of Lazio begins to turn into the foothills of the Apennines, villages are typically perched on a hilltop and clustered around a castle. Many were founded by the Etruscans, who liked the safety of an acropolis.

The central lobe, surrounding Rome and pointing east into the rugged limestone fastnesses of the Apennines, borders the Umbria and Abruzzo regions. It has a harsher look, and its steep mountains and their springs provide the water for the cascades feeding, among others, the fountains at Tivoli.

The third and largest lobe sprawls southward. Its sand beaches, hopelessly crowded in July and August, form one border. Then flat, rich farmland stretches toward rocky hilltops ablaze with yellow broom in summer. This is a pious area, and these hills are often crowned with a monastery, perhaps built on the foundations of a pagan temple. Several, including the abbey at Monte Cassino, were founded by St. Benedict.

The different landscapes of these three prongs coincide roughly with the equally distinct historical peoples who inhabited them and then gradually converged toward the cluster of seven hilltop settlements on the Tiber plain, which the Etruscans called *Ruma.* Together, the mingled tribes built Rome into a glorious capital whose population grew to nearly 1 million in the century after Christ was born.

The Etruscans were on the northern prong. Of uncertain origin, they were a ruling class of warrior sailors who quarreled constantly among themselves, except over their common religion, and dominated Italy from the Arno River to the Tiber — their ancient land, Etruria, extended into present-day Tuscany and Umbria, as well as northern Lazio. While Rome was still a shepherds' trading post, the Etruscans reigned in a federation of 12 city-states. One of these, Tarquinia, was important enough to give Rome three early kings, the Tarquins. The fascinating ruins of another two lie close to modern Rome: Cerveteri (ancient Caere) is close to the sea, off the Via Aurelia. Veii, just 10 miles (16 km) north of Rome, off the Via Cassia, is close to where contemporary Roman aristocrats tee off at the *Olgiata* golf course. Traditionally considered the greatest of the Etruscan city-states, landlocked Veii was the first to fall to the Romans, in the 4th century BC, after it failed in its efforts to maintain control of the Tiber River passage, and the overland route south on the Via Praeneste.

The central prong corresponds roughly with those hilltop Latin tribes that merged to conquer Rome and then Etruria and finally the Mediterranean, North Africa, northern Europe, and western Asia. Pliny the Elder explained that there were several score of these tribes, each on its own hilltop. They were rude farm folk, less cultivated (and less economically advanced) than the Etruscans. They dressed in leggings and sheepskins, and their descendants, wearing a fair approximation of their garb, can be seen in Rome at *Christmastime* today, playing carols on bagpipes. Although rough and ready, the Latin tribes were quick studies and dedicated pragmatists. They let the Etruscans teach them how to use an alphabet, how a priesthood should govern, how to read a sheep's liver to foretell the future (if you've ever had your palm read, don't smile), and even how to dress elegantly — that is, in a toga.

According to tradition, Alba Longa, the earliest Latin town and head of a confederation of Latin towns, sat atop a crest on the horseshoe of volcanic mountains southeast of Rome — where today's Castel Gandolfo stands, above the shore of a volcanic lake. Another Latin town became today's Rocca di Papa, across the lake on the chestnut-wooded slopes of Monte Cavo. Each spring and fall, all the Latins came in procession to a great Temple of Jupiter Latialis on the top of the mountain to sacrifice a white bull. By 500 BC, they were already arriving from 47 different towns. Then, as today, they could look down from the 3,124-foot peak to see all of Lazio.

The southernmost prong of the Lazio leaf points downward into territory where the Greeks, allied to a powerful local tribe, the Samnites, ruled, including the city the Greeks founded, Neapolis (Naples). The area was inhabited far earlier, however. On Monte Circeo, which juts into the Tyrrhenian Sea (from *Tyrrhenoi,* the Greek name for the Etruscans), the voyager Ulysses was seduced by a bewitching pig shepherdess named Circe. Long before that, a real Neanderthal tribesman killed a rival, broke a hole into his skull for magical purposes, and left the skull inside a ring of ritual stones in a cave on the Circeo. The skull was found there during the 1930s, 40,000 years later.

To travel throughout Lazio today, therefore, is first to travel through time, seeing traces of three distinct major cultures — Etruscan, Latin, Magna Graecian — that influenced Western civilization. Then there is Lazio's more modern aspect. Among its big cities are, in the north, the port of Civitavecchia (Rome's own port was silted over during ancient times) and, inland, Viterbo. Heading into the Latin towns there is the fairly large walled city of Rieti — nearby is the spectacular Benedictine abbey at Farfa — and, continuing to circle Rome clockwise, the volcanic horseshoe that includes the Alban Hills and two lakes, Albano and Nemi. The Alban Hills are home to 13 small towns, known collectively as the Castelli Romani. They are cool and airy when Rome is not, so many Romans have weekend houses in the Castelli, and more and more are beginning to live there permanently and commute into Rome. The Castelli slopes quench Romans' thirst with an amber wine that is highly prized when it is the real thing, and wine buffs say the Castelli now produce an excellent red wine as well.

Also south and east of Rome, but farther afield, is the Ciociaria, a mountainous district between Rome and the relatively modern town of Frosinone. Fiuggi, an old-fashioned spa with waters that are reputed to help kidney sufferers, and a bracing hill climate in the summer, is in the province of Frosinone. Another modern town, Latina, the largest city in Lazio after Rome, is to the west of the Ciociaria, in the midst of the Pontine plain. Once a swampy area where malaria raged, the plain was drained, settlers were brought in to farm, and Latina was founded at the end of the project in 1932. Actually a rather dull industrial and agricultural center, it is surrounded by pastures much favored by the water buffalo imported centuries ago from India. Their milk makes Lazio's fresh mozzarella one of the world's finest cheeses. Various beach resorts bask in the sun of the coast west and south of Latina — they include Anzio, with its vast American military cemetery nearby, Terracina, and Sperlonga. And inland on a mountaintop is the Monte Cassino Monastery, bombed by the Allies during World War II and meticulously rebuilt.

The food of the Roman countryside is, like the old Latins themselves, rustic rather than elegant. It is a fine cuisine, however, in the sense that it employs ingredients literally unavailable elsewhere, and in certain cases more flavorful than elsewhere because of the soil and climate. Beef was never a Lazio dish. The Lazio diet was (and is) made up of mozzarella or piquant *pecorino* (ewe's milk) cheese, baby lamb or roast kid for a feast day, and pork in all its forms, including a fennel-laced salami. With an abundance of imagination rather than a surfeit of raw ingredients, the cooks of Lazio learned to turn the poorer cuts of meat into dishes fit for a king, or pope. These included a shepherd's pie of lamb heart, potatoes, and onions; oxtail chunks stewed in wine, celery, and tomatoes; and tripe dressed in a sauce of tomatoes, grated cheese, and fresh mint. Count on a Lazio cook to insist on the best quality of tripe, the cut they call *millefoglie,* for this favorite dish.

Spaghetti alla carbonara — that is, with a sauce of creamy egg, bacon bits, cheese, and a dash of nutmeg — can be found everywhere. It was supposedly brought to Lazio by Umbrian coal peddlers. But the most authentic Lazio pasta variation is *all'amatriciana,* from the town of Amatrice, in the province of Rieti. In quarrels over how it is properly made, cooks sometimes will toss pots at each other. Purists hold that the diced salt pork must come from Amatrice itself, that only the faintest dab of tomato sauce suffices, and that strong *pecorino,* and never parmesan cheese, must be used. Dotted with lakes, Lazio also offers an abundance of seafood, including trout and lake *coregone,* often flavored with fennel or the *martana* sauce (capers, tomato, red pepper, garlic, parsley, and olives). Rabbit is popular, as is *pollo alla diavolo,* a flattened, peppery chicken half.

The Roman countryside does produce an abundance of vegetables, whose consumption follows the seasons. On May 1, Italy's *Labor Day,* fava beans are served raw with chunks of *pecorino* and a robust red wine. Throughout spring, many restaurants offer a fresh vegetable compote called, appropriately, *primavera* (spring). A medley of fried foods may include batter-fried mozzarella chunks, codfish, zucchini, zucchini flowers with a cheese stuffing, and flattened artichokes. A special salad green, *puntarelle,* is invariably dressed in an anchovy and garlic vinaigrette. In late summer and autumn, when sun and rain come in just the right doses, the hills around Rome abound in wild mushrooms (note that all sold in shops and restaurants are checked rigorously by local health inspectors). They may appear on the menu as a raw mushroom salad; as a sauce with noodles, polenta, or risotto; or, when the giant *boletus edulis,* or *porcini,* are available, as a main course. Some Castelli restaurants offer an entire menu of different wild mushroom courses.

Lazio's desserts are generally uninspired, so fresh fruit is usually a wise choice, especially the tiny, woodland-scented strawberries that grow near Lake Nemi. Lazio cooks rinse them in aromatic frascati wine rather than water. Cultivated strawberries grow in fields throughout Lazio and are harvested when they are perfectly ripe, never before, to be eaten with fresh orange or lemon juice.

Wine is abundant throughout Lazio, and if not generally exceptional, it is good, and appropriate to the fare. The best probably is the *aleatico* of Gradoli and its neighbor from Montefiascone, a wine called est! est!! est!!! Cerveteri reds and whites are esteemed, as are the Castelli reserve wines from Marino — frascati and velletri.

Most travelers see some of the sights of the Lazio region on their way into or out of Rome. But since all of the sights of Lazio are within easy reach of the capital, they can also be seen in a series of day trips out of Rome — much as the Romans themselves usually see them. The seven routes outlined below are for those who have already seen Rome's standard sights or for those who like to pack and unpack only once during a foreign jaunt. They presuppose a hotel base in Rome, so no hotels are listed (though some of the restaurants have guestrooms), and a car is a must. A tip: The Raccordo Anulare is the ring road around Rome. It connects all the roads that lead to Rome — or from it. Another tip: "Never on Monday" should be a traveler's most vital motto. Most museums and many restaurants are closed. Each Thursday, the Rome daily paper *La Repubblica* carries news of local events in Lazio, and on Friday, *Il Messaggero* (another Rome daily) carries a column reporting which Lazio town offers a festival, religious procession, parade, or even a demonstration by the *butteri,* Lazio's authentic cowboys, who once compared techniques with Buffalo Bill on his visit to the region. Lazio towns fete just about anything, in its season: the wine vintage, wildflowers blooming, the artichoke crop, the chestnut harvest. A friendly hotel concierge might be coaxed into translating the relevant listings.

In the following restaurant listings, expensive means that a meal for two will cost approximately $80 to $120 with a bottle of wine (fresh fish can push the price sky high); moderate means from about $60 to $80; inexpensive, around $50. Generally, prices rise with the iodine content in the air — that is, higher near the seashore, lower inland.

DAY TRIP 1: TARQUINIA, TUSCANIA, VULCI

This route takes in the seacoast town of Tarquinia, one of the 12 city-states of the Etruscan federation and one of the must-sees among Italian archaeological sites. In the past, its pretty beach has been polluted. Now it is monitored, so be sure to check for signs before swimming. Tarquinia is noted for the wall paintings found in its extensive necropolis, one of the main sources of our knowledge of Etruscan life. The walled medieval town of Tuscania is also on the route, as are the ruins of a second prominent Etruscan city, Vulci.

En Route from Rome – Leave town by the Rome–Fiumicino Airport Highway (from most places in Rome the Via Aurelia followed by the Raccordo Anulare is the best starting point), then turn north onto the toll highway (A12) toward Civitavecchia. Tarquinia is about 1¼ hours (63 miles/101 km) away.

TARQUINIA: Tarquinia dates back to the early Iron Age. It was one of the most powerful Etruscan cities from the 8th to the 4th century BC, and well into the 6th century BC it was a far more important city than Rome, thanks to its powerful fleet. The huge underground necropolis, which extends east of the city along the road to Viterbo, contains approximately 200 excavated tombs, and aerial photos taken at dawn have shown that the hay fields and farms surrounding Tarquinia contain hundreds more still untouched by archaeologists or grave robbers. More than 60 of the excavated tombs are decorated with bright wall paintings documenting Etruscan life — its banquets, sports, dances, religious rites, furnishings, travel. The *Museo Nazionale Tarquininese,* in the elegant 15th-century Palazzo Vitelleschi just inside the gate to Tarquinia's Old Town, makes a good first stop. Its collection of Etruscan artifacts, taken from the nearby tombs and from other sites in the area, is one of Italy's most important. Besides fine Greek and Greek-influenced pottery, gold jewelry, magical mirrors, and sarcophagi, its prized possessions are two winged horses that adorned a late-4th-century BC temple at Tarquinia's acropolis and several reconstructed tombs decorated with wall paintings detached from the actual site for safekeeping. Admission to the museum includes admission to the necropolis, about a mile (1.6 km) away (the museum attendant can provide driving instructions). To conserve the frescoes, only four tombs are open to visitors on any given day, and exactly which four varies from day to day. Museum and necropolis are open daily except Mondays from 9 AM to 2 PM (and occasionally longer in summer). The necropolis's hours are extended in summer to 6 PM For current information call 766-856384 or 766-856036.

True enthusiasts may want to visit the *Pian di Civita,* a hillside site. Take the road toward Viterbo; at km 3.5 turn left onto a dirt road and follow it for 1¼ miles (2 km). It leads to the 4th-century BC Ara della Regina (Queen's Altar), the hilltop temple where the above-mentioned winged horses were found and where archaeological excavations are under way.

EATING OUT: ***Antico Ristorante Giudizi*** – Across the piazza from the museum, this establishment offers comfortable dining. Fresh seafood is featured, so try the *spaghetti alle vongole* (with clams) and the mixed fish fry; game is also a specialty. Reservations advised on weekends. Closed Mondays. Major credit cards accepted. 20 Piazza Cavour, Tarquinia (phone: 766-855061). Expensive to moderate.

Velca Mare – Fish cooked in dozens of ways, including baby squid in its ink and pasta with shrimp and arugula, as well as a traditional mixed fry or grill, served in a roomy place by the sea. There also 24 rooms at the adjacent inn. Closed Tuesdays and November through January. Reservations necessary Sundays and in midsummer. Major credit cards accepted. 1 Via degli Argonauti, Lido di Tarquinia (phone: 766-88024). Moderate.

En Route from Tarquinia – Take the main exit road. Just at the foot of the hill there's a country road (and a sign) for Tuscania; take the country road for 1 mile (1.6 km) and then turn right onto the Tuscania road. The town is about 15 miles (24 km) away.

TUSCANIA: This is a beautiful example of a southern Etrurian walled town. Built on a hill of tufa rock, it is surrounded by 5th-century BC Etruscan burial mounds including one belonging to a family named Vipinana, whose tombs were found with no fewer than 27 sarcophagi. Some 50 members of another Etruscan family, the Statlane, have been counted. Ask at the *Museo Nazionale Etrusco* (Piazza Madonna del Riposo; phone: 761-436209) about visiting them. The museum, located in the former Convent of Santa Maria del Riposo, houses a collection of artifacts from the site. It is open daily except Mondays from 9 AM to 1:30 PM and 2:30 to 4 PM (until 7 PM in the summer); admission charge. After the city was conquered by Rome, it continued to prosper, becoming a bishop's seat in the Middle Ages. Just how wealthy it was then can be seen in the scores of medieval towers it retains; these fortunately survived the 1971 earthquake that sorely damaged much of Tuscania. The fine 11th-century Chiesa di San Pietro (Church of St. Peter), built on the site of an Etruscan acropolis, is just outside the present town. The crypt, with its myriad columns, is a study in architectural styles dating from the Roman era.

EATING OUT: ***Al Gallo*** – The best-known restaurant in town is a pleasant hotel dining room in the center near the Duomo. Frequent signs from the main gate in the city wall lead directly to it. Closed Tuesdays and the second week in July. Reservations advised. Major credit cards accepted. 24 Via del Gallo, Tuscania (phone: 761-435028). Moderate.

La Palombella – This popular restaurant serves traditional cornmeal polenta on a classic wooden platter with a spicy sauce of mushrooms, sausage, and tomatoes. Chops and sausages are lovingly grilled over a wood fire, but the house specialty is game. Try the delectable stuffed pigeon. Closed Saturdays and most of August. Reservations advised on weekends. No credit cards accepted. 23 Via Canino, Tuscania (phone: 761-435419). Moderate.

En Route from Tuscania – Follow the excellently marked, easy-to-drive country roads about 12 miles (19 km) north to Canino, and after another 3 miles (5 km) turn right to Vulci (watch for the yellow signs indicating tourist sights).

VULCI: The bare ruins of another of the 12 Etruscan city-states lie in an area of Maremma countryside — the Pian di Voce — where flat fields, poplar lanes, and Roman aqueducts stand out against the brilliant Mediterranean light. Here a Bronze Age town was located on the banks of the Fiora River. By the 9th and 8th centuries BC, its craftsmen's skill in making bronze daggers, helmets, and shields was already known. Relics from the excavation of the town and the four necropolises in the vicinity are found in the world's greatest museums — artifacts from the Isis Tomb in the Polledrara necropolis, for instance, are in the *British Museum* in London. The monumental Cuccumella Tomb is well worth seeing, as is the François Tomb at Ponte Rotto (although its famed interior paintings have been removed to the Villa Albani in Rome. Then see the *Museo Nazionale* at Castel di Badia (phone: 761-437787), a short drive from the excavations. This beautifully arranged small museum is set up inside a restored 12th-century castle replete with a tiny moat. Open daily from 9 AM to 2 PM and 2:30 to 4 PM (in summer the hours are extended to 6 PM) admission charge. Next to the castle, a humpbacked bridge — its foundations Etruscan, the rest of the structure Roman — arches over the rushing Fiora River. As a fortified monastery at the edge of the Papal States, the castle once controlled a major north-south highway link between Etruria and Rome. Carts en route to market were stopped by customs collectors at the castle dooryard. Together, castle and bridge are among Italy's most romantic sights.

En Route from Vulci – Turn back toward the sea and the town of Montalto di Castro (8 miles/13 km by road) where the Via Aurelia (SS1) provides the best route for the return to Rome.

DAY TRIP 2: CERVETERI, BRACCIANO, VEII

This second tour through Etruscan Lazio is especially suited for families with children. It visits Cerveteri, another of the Etruscan city-states, with an important museum and tombs carved into the soft tufa stone to look for all the world like the interiors of Etruscan households. After Cerveteri, it proceeds to the town of Bracciano for lunch, perhaps a swim in the lake, and a visit to a magnificient castle. It finishes up with a visit to the excavations of Veii, the Etruscan city closest to Rome.

En Route from Rome – From the Via Aurelia, take the Raccordo Anulare to the Rome–Fiumicino Airport Highway and then the toll highway (A12) toward Civitavecchia. Exit at Cerveteri.

CERVETERI: Settled 900 years before Christ, Cerveteri (ancient Caere) lies on a small tufa plateau between two gorges carved by rivers. Its development lagged behind that of Tarquinia, Vulci, and Veii, but it made up for its slow start when the mines in the nearby Tolfa Mountains turned it into an Iron Age boomtown. Cerveteri grew rich as its ships set out from the nearby port of Santa Severa (ancient Pyrgi). In the 6th and 5th centuries BC, it was a sea power with a fleet important enough to make common cause with the Carthaginians in fighting the Greek-dominated colonies of Magna Graecia, which ruled from Naples down through western Sicily. That trio — Carthage, Etruria, and Magna Graecia — continued to jockey for power until Rome emerged and settled the power struggle for good by conquering all three.

Of the hundreds of tombs from the 8th to the 1st century BC in the necropolis at Cerveteri, the most important concentration is at Colle della Banditaccia (phone: 6-995-0003), about a mile (1.6 km) outside the modern town. Many of the burial chambers have lost their paint, but their fascination lies in their furnishings and architectural details — ceiling beams, doorways, divans — all carved in soft tufa stone. The Tomba dei Capitelli (Tomb of the Capitals), in particular, built at the height of Caere's wealth and power, shows what the inside of an Etruscan home was like. The walls of the 4th- or 3rd-century BC Tomba dei Rilievi (Tomb of the Reliefs), which were the burial vaults of the rich Matuna family, are covered with charming painted stucco reliefs of household objects and scenes. They, too, show everyday life in Caere, right down to the Matunas' stew pots and the family mutt. The Regolini Galassi Tomb, in another location closer to town and dating from the late 7th century BC, is also famous. Its dowry of presents to accompany the dead on their voyage to the afterlife is now in the Etruscan collection at the Vatican. Open daily from 9 AM to 4 PM in winter and 9 AM to 6 PM in summer. In Cerveteri itself, see the *Museo Nazionale Cerite* (phone: 6-995-0003) housed in the 16th-century Palazzo Ruspoli in Piazza Santa Maria. When it opened in the 1960s, it was widely praised for its particularly attractive and coherent displays of Etruscan and other ancient artifacts in its collection. In winter, it is open daily except Mondays from 9 AM to 2 PM; in summer, from 9 AM to 2 PM and 4 to 7 PM; admission charge. At the museum, it's also possible to make arrangements to visit the Regolini Galassi Tomb.

EATING OUT: *L'Oasi* – This cozy, family-style restaurant serves seafood risotto, homemade fettuccine, and fresh fish. Closed Mondays. No reservations. No credit cards accepted. Via Renato Morelli, Cerveteri (phone: 6-995-3482). Moderate.

En Route from Cerveteri – Follow the well-marked road inland (20 minutes or so) to the town of Bracciano, on a volcanic lake, Lago di Bracciano. Or, for those with the time, continue up the coast to Civitavecchia, which became the port of Rome after the port at Ostia, built by the ancient Romans, silted up. Civitavecchia's Forte Michelangelo, a 16th-century structure for which Michelangelo designed the keep, its *Museo Nazionale Archeologico* (closed Mondays; admission charge), and vestiges of an antique Roman port make the detour worthwhile. Then cut inland over country roads through the Tolfa Mountains toward Tolfa and then Manziana. At Manziana, a right turn leads to Bracciano, 35 miles (56 km) from Civitavecchia.

BRACCIANO: The outstanding feature of this small resort town on the southwest side of Lake Bracciano is the Castello degli Orsini. It was the first sight Sir Walter Scott wanted to see in Rome, and children of all ages will understand why. This is a dream castle, in fine condition. In fact, it is still inhabited by the Odescalchi, a princely Roman family whose glittering parties and balls are Rome's grandest. Built between 1470 and 1485, the castle has five sides, with a crenelated tower at each juncture. In winter, it is open daily except Mondays from 9 AM to 4 PM; in summer, from 9 AM to 6 PM. There are escorted tours (in Italian) hourly during the week and every half hour on Sundays and holidays; admission charge (phone: 6-902-4003). While waiting for a tour, spend the time at any of the several summer dining rooms of the pleasant family-style trattorie that jut into the lake on wooden piers. Grilled lake fish and seafood first courses from the Mediterranean are standard fare, but local enthusiasts order eel whenever it appears.

EATING OUT: *Alfredo* – For an appetizing *risotto alle ortiche* (rice with wild nettles), as well as good fresh lake fish, try this charming lakeside restaurant. Closed Tuesdays and mid-July to mid-September. Reservations advised. Major credit cards accepted. Via Sposetta Vecchia, Bracciano (phone: 6-902-4130). Moderate.

Sora Tuta – This trattoria with its ancient, huge fireplace offers some delectable specialties: a spinach and ricotta–stuffed, veil-thin crêpe; pasta with artichokes;

broiled lamb chops; and, for dessert, *crème brulée.* The wines are less distinguished, but the house red is agreeable. Closed Mondays. Reservations advised on Sundays. No credit cards accepted. 33 Via Agnostino Fausti, Bracciano (phone: 6-902-4409). Moderate.

En Route from Bracciano – Circle the lake to Trevignano, the prettiest of the lakeside towns, ever more developed as Romans install weekend homes. The Chiesa dell'Assunta (Church of the Assumption), with a fresco by a student of Raphael, warrants a visit — and so do all the trattorie along the waterfront. Food is universally good, service is slow, and to linger over a glass of homemade wine is obligatory. From Trevignano, pick up the Via Cassia (SS2) to visit the ruins of Veii (Veio in Italian), near the town of Isola Farnese (watch for the yellow signs).

EATING OUT: ***Acquarella*** – This rustic country inn is among the best of the many lakeside restaurants. Go for a swim at its private beach, then dine on homemade *cannelloni* and grilled *corrigone,* a local white fish. The white wine is from the vineyards that belong to the hosts, the three Stefanelli brothers. Closed Tuesdays. No reservations. Major credit cards accepted. Via Anguillarese, Km 6, between Trevignano and Anguillara (phone: 6-998-5131). Moderate.

Boricella – This simpatico tavern at the fishing village of Anguillara is run by Andrea Gerioni, who has made laudable efforts to seek out traditional local recipes and prepare them in modern guise. Try his spaghetti with fish sauce and the stuffed lake trout. Closed Tuesdays and December. Reservations necessary. Major credit cards accepted. 20 Via Trevignanese, Anguillara (phone: 6-901-8037). Moderate.

Paradiso sul Golfo – Elvira Brunori runs this old-fashioned fish restaurant that has a deck overlooking a volcanic lake. A rich assortment of vegetable hors d'oeuvres, homemade pasta, and a tempting dessert tray make this a pleasant choice. Closed Thursdays. Reservations necessary on weekends. Major credit cards accepted. 121 Via Garibaldi, Trevignano (phone: 6-901-9024). Moderate.

Caffè Il Tartufo – Not a sandwich to be found, but the cookies and cakes are as good as any in Lazio, and the little balcony is a fine place to sip a drink and watch life go by. At *Christmas,* the pastry chef creates chocolate crèche cakes, each one different. No reservations. No credit cards accepted. Piazza Emanuele III, Trevignano (phone: 6-901-9041). Inexpensive.

VEII: Ancient Veii, built on the right bank of the Tiber, was the largest of the dozen Etruscan city-states, with 7 miles of walls. It grew rich because of its control of the road to the salt flats and depots at the mouth of the Tiber, and because of the commercial and military importance of the river itself. Rome coveted Veii; in fact, it was the first of the Etruscan cities to fall to Roman domination, the beginning of the end for Etruria. This occurred in 396 BC, after a decade-long siege that was broken only when the slaves of Furius Camillus tunneled into the city through the tufa rock. The most famous find uncovered during the past century of excavations is the statue of Apollo, now in the *Villa Giulia Museum* in Rome. Today's visitors can see a pretty waterfall, the foundations of a 6th-century BC temple, its altar with drains for the blood of the sacrificed, and an adjacent pool for ritual dunkings. Follow the signs to visit the famous Campana Tomb. The excavations are open weekdays in winter except Mondays from 10 AM to 2 PM and in summer from 9 AM to 7 PM (phone: 6-379-0116). The same ticket permits entry to the site of a nearby Roman-era villa.

EATING OUT: ***Postiglione*** – This 400-year-old post house has been turned into a delightful rustic restaurant that offers not only homemade pasta but also home-raised meats, including the Lazio favorite, lamb. Closed Mondays, Via Cassia, Km 30, Veii (phone: 6-904-1214). Moderate to inexpensive.

En Route from Veii – Continue down the Via Cassia (SS2) to head back to Rome.

DAY TRIP 3: BOMARZO, BAGNAIA, VITERBO

This tour continues the exploration of the northern tip of Lazio, this time the area around the largest of the region's three volcanic lakes, Lago di Bolsena. Children will love this drive because it visits Bomarzo, where stone monsters disport in a garden. From Bomarzo it goes to Viterbo, stopping to see the terraced gardens of the Villa Lante en route. After Viterbo, it heads north to the town of Montefiascone, from which various lakeside points can be visited.

En Route from Rome – Take the Via Salaria to the Raccordo Anulare and then the Autostrada del Sole (Al) north to the Attigliano exit. Follow signs to Bomarzo, about 4 miles (6 km) from the exit.

BOMARZO: A Renaissance equivalent of *Disneyland,* inspired by Dante's *Inferno,* is the best description of Bomarzo's Parco dei Mostri (Monster Park). The park is actually a terraced, wooded slope strewn with carved stone animals and fantastical figures, from larger than life-size to colossal. It was conceived and built by Vicino Orsini, the 16th-century nobleman, an intrepid Renaissance traveler whose family palace is nearby. Among its huge carvings, all in *peperino,* a granulated form of tufa, are elephants and lions, dragons, giants, and nymphs, faces with mouths as big as doorways, and a leaning house, just like the fun house in a modern amusement park. Open daily except Mondays from 9 AM to an hour before sunset; admission charge.

En Route from Bomarzo – Drop down to SS204 and follow it west toward Viterbo, 15 miles (24 km) from Bomarzo. Stop just short of Viterbo, at Bagnaia, for the Villa Lante, then drive on to Viterbo.

VILLA LANTE: The small but elegant twin 16th-century villas, designed by Vignola, are not open to visitors, but the spectacular surrounding garden is open daily from 9 AM to an hour before sunset; admission charge. This wonderful example of a formal Renaissance garden is laid out on five terraces descending to a pond and decorated with fountains — some of which play tricks on the unwary! Only escorted visits to the garden (every half hour) are possible. For information, call 761-288008.

EATING OUT: *Biscetti* – This roomy, nearly a century-old country restaurant near Villa Lante at Bagnaia serves traditional woodland dishes, such as risotto with the rare wild *ovoli* mushrooms, pasta with hare sauce, and wild boar roasted with juniper berries. Closed Thursdays and 2 weeks in mid-July. Reservations advised. Major credit cards accepted. 11/A Via Generale Gandin, Bagnaia (phone: 761-288252). Moderate to inexpensive.

VITERBO: Viterbo, the capital of La Tuscia, as northern Lazio is called, is an Etruscan city that became important under the Romans and remained so through the Middle Ages. In the 13th century — troubled times for the papacy, given the continual struggle between the church and the Holy Roman Empire — several popes found it safer to live here than in Rome, so that in 1261, Pope Alessandro IV built the Palazzo Papale. Several conclaves were held here, including the one that elected Gregory X — the longest conclave in the history of the Roman Catholic church. It ended after 33 months, when the cardinals' food supply was cut off.

The papal palace is still one of the major monuments of Viterbo, so head first to Piazza San Lorenzo, where the delicate Gothic palace stands right next to the Duomo, a 12th-century building with a Renaissance façade, and both stand right over the old Etruscan acropolis. Then turn back along Via San Lorenzo and stroll in the direction of Porta San Pietro. The walk leads through Viterbo's San Pellegrino quarter, one of Europe's most completely medieval cityscapes. Be sure to visit the tiny Piazzetta San

Pellegrino, the haunting, medieval heart of the quarter, and Piazza Cappella, another characteristic spot. The exterior stone stairways leading to second-story balconies and front doors, called *profferli,* are typically Viterbese. The quarter seems like a living museum; visitors can glimpse artisans hard at work in their *botteghe* (workshops) off the narrow streets. Many shops sell pretty copies of black Etruscan-style terra cotta pots and vases.

Two very old fountains, the 13th-century Fontana Grande, in Piazza Fontana Grande, and the 14th-century Fontana di Piano Scarano, in Piazza Fontana di Piano, are of interest. The latter was at the center of a popular uprising in the 14th century when a member of the papal court of Urban V attempted to wash a puppy in the fountain, which the townspeople used for drinking water. The *Museo Municipio* (2 Piazza Crispi; phone: 761-340810) houses a collection of paintings from the Middle Ages. It is open daily except Mondays from 9 AM to 1:30 PM; admission charge. The city's tourist office (EPT, Piazza dei Caduti; phone: 761-226161), can provide information on other sights and on special events, such as the *Festa di Santa Rosa* (September 2–3), when a parade in historic costume takes place, followed the next day by a procession featuring 100 men carrying a 4-ton, 90-foot tower through the streets.

EATING OUT: ***Aquilanti*** – An old favorite, a scant 2 miles (3 km) out of town in the direction of Bagnaia. Steaks, lamb, and pork chops are grilled on an open fire. Closed Tuesdays and the first 2 weeks of August. Reservations necessary. Major credit cards accepted. 4 Via del Santuario, Madonna della Quercia (phone: 761-341701). Expensive to moderate.

Richiastro – Refined culinary concepts, in a millennium-old setting. Offerings include mushroom soup and local Viterbo specialties such as chick-pea soup with chestnuts. Open Thursdays through Sunday lunch; closed during August. Reservations advised. No credit cards accepted. 18 Via della Marrocca, Viterbo (phone: 761-223609). Expensive to moderate.

La Zaffera – This oasis of tasteful decor and service in an ancient monastery is in the heart of the medieval San Pellegrino quarter. One of its charms is a small garden for the *aperitivo* hour. Closed Tuesdays and 2 weeks in August. Reservations necessary on weekends. Major credit cards accepted. Piazza San Carluccio, Viterbo (phone: 761-226-1140). Expensive to moderate.

Val Sia Rosa – In a 400-year-old building in Civitacastellana, near Viterbo, this restaurant features northern Italian cuisine with the chef's personal touch, using *porcini* mushrooms and truffles. Closed Wednesdays and most of August. No reservations. Major credit cards accepted. 23 miles (37 km) from Viterbo. 25 Via Nepesina, Civitacastellana (phone: 761-517891). Moderate.

En Route from Viterbo – Head north to visit Montefiascone, which stands on the edge of the crater of an extinct volcano, now Lake Bolsena. Then drive westward to the edge of the lake.

MONTEFIASCONE: This small town on a hill overlooking Lake Bolsena is the home of the wine called est! est!! est!!! Once upon a time, a cardinal's servant quenched his thirst so very well at Montefiascone that he left his master, Giovanni Fugger, a sign outside the wine shop exclaiming, three times, "This is it!" The name stuck and, along with the wine of Frascati, this is considered Lazio's finest. Fugger's tombstone at the Romanesque Church of San Flaviano has the words Est! Est!! Est!!! carved on it. Castle ruins in the town's upper reaches offer a fine view of the lake and of the mountains beyond.

LAGO DI BOLSENA: This largest of Italy's many volcanic lakes takes its name from an early Italian tribe, the Volsinienses, from the area around Orvieto, a short distance to the north. The lake is nearly a perfect circle averaging 8 miles in diameter, and it contains two small islands, Isola Bisentina and Isola Martina. The former has a chapel housing the bones of St. Christine; the latter, a horrific Gothic history: In the year 532, Queen Martana of the Ostrogoths was strangled on the islet by her cousin, Theodahad, to whom she was betrothed but who, alas, coveted her throne. The lake so abounds in eels that a particularly gluttonous pope, if Dante is to be believed, ate himself to death on them. On the western shore are ruins of what was first a Villanovan, then an Etruscan, and finally a Roman town, Visentium. For the Etruscans, the lake held special meaning, and scores of Etruscan tombs have been found nearby. Boat excursions to Isola Bisentina leave from Bolsena, Capodimonte, and Marta, and include a guided tour of the island. For information, call *G. Fioravante* at 761-799890.

Drive as far as Capodimonte, a tiny summer resort with a sleepy old-fashioned air on the southwest shore of the lake. For a pleasant side trip, circle the lake to the town of Bolsena, on the northeast shore, to visit the Chiesa di Santa Cristina. On its portal is a terra cotta panel from the Della Robbia school, and a chapel inside contains a Della Robbia terra cotta portrait of the saint. Ancient Etruscan walls still encircle part of the town.

EATING OUT: ***Er Verace*** – A pleasant and unpretentious restaurant on the street skirting the lake, specializing in *spaghetti alle vongole* (with clams), fresh lake fish, and eels. Closed Thursdays. Reservations advised. No credit cards accepted. 7 Viale Regina Margherita, Capodimonte (phone: 761-80255). Moderate.

En Route from Lago di Bolsena – To return to Rome, two routes are available. Either cut seaward from Capodimonte to pick up the Via Aurelia (SS1) at Montalto di Castro and follow the coastal road south to Rome. Or return to Viterbo from either Capodimonte or Bolsena and take a leisurely ride on the Via Cimino through the densely wooded (chestnut and oak) hills and past a tiny volcanic lake, Lago di Vico. En route, there are towns with pleasant historic quarters to be visited, such as Ronciglione, just south of the lake, and Sutri, where Pontius Pilate was born. At Sutri, pick up the Via Cassia (SS2) south. The very best route, however, is to continue on to Orvieto, visiting the fine cathedral there, following the clearly marked directions, and returning to Rome via the autostrada (A1) south.

DAY TRIP 4: PALESTRINA, ANAGNI, SUBIACO, TIVOLI

This tour turns away from Etruscan Lazio toward areas where Latin tribes such as the Sabines, who conquered the Etruscans, lived before settling Rome. The area has suffered far more than Etruscan Lazio from the construction of tasteless modern buildings, but some extremely interesting sights, such as the ruins of the Roman temple at Palestrina, the medieval town of Anagni, and the monasteries of Subiaco, remain. On the way back, stop at Tivoli, if you haven't already seen it by public transport or guided tour from Rome.

En Route from Rome – Take Via Prenestina eastward out of Rome to Palestrina, 24 miles (38 km) away.

PALESTRINA: This town, known to many because the 16th-century composer Pierluigi da Palestrina was born here, was known to the ancient world as Praeneste. It dates at least as far back as the 7th century BC, and even farther, according to the ancients, for whom it was said to have been founded by the son Circe bore to Ulysses. It passed to the Romans in 499 BC, and various Roman emperors, including Augustus, Tiberius, and Hadrian, later built pleasure palaces here. But the wonder of Palestrina was its shrine to the goddess of fortune, Fortuna Primigenia, so important to the Romans that they built the Via Praeneste (Via Prenestina now) to enable them to make the journey to consult the oracle more regularly. In 82 BC, the Roman statesman Sulla tore down the old buildings — which had been there for at least a century — and replaced them with a many-terraced majestic temple, the largest religious complex in the entire Roman world. It remained in use until the 4th century AD and then gradually became the foundation of a medieval city. In 1640, the Barberini family of Rome built a palace right in the sacred area, the same palace that today houses the *Museo Archeologico Prenestino* (phone: 6-955-8100). Open daily except Mondays from 9 AM to 4 PM (in summer the hours are extended until 6 PM).

Be sure to visit the museum before the excavations (same ticket). One of its treasures is a very large and beautiful 1st-century BC mosaic that once decorated a floor of the temple. Another is a scale model of the temple as it was in ancient times. It shows the shrine to the goddess, Jupiter's first daughter, laid out in a triangle on a hillside extending from the level of the present Piazza Regina Margherita, where the Duomo now stands, up to Piazza della Cortina, where the museum entrance is. Vast ramps and staircases adorned with elegant columns, colonnades, vaults, and arches lead toward a vast open terrace. At the top was a semicircular portico (the Barberini Palace now follows the same curve) in the center of which stood a gold statue of Primigenia, long since lost. The Romans were so proud of the monument, which must have bowled over the pilgrims who came from all around, that they lighted bonfires on the terraces so that sailors at sea could see the sanctuary at night. Even today, the ruins are highly evocative, and the windows of the museum offer a wonderful view.

EATING OUT: ***Antonello Colonna Vecchio Osteria*** – Worth a trip in its own right, and in any case requiring a detour from this excursion. A now renowned chef named Antonello took charge of the country inn run for decades by his parents and invented his own version of *alta cucina.* A sampler menu is offered. Closed Sunday evenings and Mondays. Reservations necessary. Major credit cards accepted. Via Casilina, Km 38.3, Labico (phone: 6-951-0032). Expensive.

Farina – Near the Duomo, this dining spot is often recommended by the locals, and rightly so. Owner Mario Pinci serves homemade pasta, including fettuccine with *porcini* mushrooms, cannelloni with either meat or ricotta and spinach filling, and roast or grilled lamb and veal. Homemade desserts. Closed Wednesdays. Reservations necessary. Major credit cards accepted. 16 Piazza Garibaldi, Palestrina (phone: 6-953-8916). Moderate.

En Route from Palestrina – Proceed south to Valmontone and pick up the Autostrada del Sole (A2) for about 10 miles (16 km) southeast to the Anagni exit. From Anagni, follow signs to Fiuggi.

ANAGNI: Cicero had an estate in this hilltop town, and four popes, including Innocent III, Gregory IX, Alexander IV, and Boniface VIII, were born here during the Middle Ages. It has a medieval quarter with a particularly harmonious aspect because almost all of its buildings are of the 13th century, and it has one of medieval Europe's more noteworthy cathedrals. This basically Romanesque structure, built in the 11th and 12th centuries atop a former Roman temple and then modified in the 13th century, stands on the highest point of the town. Inside, the loveliest sight is the crypt (open only in the early afternoon), whose walls are solidly covered with 13th-century frescoes (there is a painting of Hippocrates in one lunette). Anagni does not make news today, but it did in the past. In 1160, an archbishop announced the excommunication of Frederick Barbarossa from the cathedral. And in 1303, at the Palazzo di Bonifacio VIII, another of its old buildings, an emissary of French King Philip the Fair slapped the aged, frail Pope Boniface full in the face with his iron gauntlet, an episode that lives on in Dante. The *Museo Civico* (238 Via Vittorio Emanuele; phone: 775-727053) is open by appointment only for viewing archaeological artifacts. Medieval religious art can be seen at the *Museo del Tesoro del Duomo* (by the cathedral; phone: 775-727053). Open daily from 9 AM to noon; admission charge.

FIUGGI: Fiuggi is a two-part town. There is Fiuggi Città, the actual town, and, a short distance away, Fiuggi Fonte, a spa whose *fonte* (spring) attracts health seekers, especially elderly ones. In the early years of this century, Italy's monarchs summered here; today it bustles in summer, languishes in winter. Although the spa itself is of limited interest to tourists, its quaint, Victorian-era hotels have charm, its shops sell a fair sampling of the local products, from salami to cheese and honey, and its tea shops offer good pastries.

Lord Charles Forte, founder of the Trusthouse Forte hotel group, was born near here, and he recently lavished $30 million to bring back to life and luster the famed pre-World War I *Grand Hotel Palazzo della Fonte* (Via dei Villini; phone: 775-55001; in the US, 800-255-5843). Once a royal favorite, today's travelers who are not based in Rome may want to spend an elegant (and expensive) night or two and enjoy swimming, golf, tennis, and overall pampering. The hotel is open year-round.

EATING OUT: ***Villa Hernicus*** – Creative cooking has reached Fiuggi, and here it takes the form of fresh lobster risotto with zucchini flowers, potato-filled lasagna with pesto, and roast duckling with a béarnaise sauce. Be sure to leave room for the mouth-watering desserts. There also are 4 spectacular guestrooms. Closed Mondays and November. Reservations advised. Major credit cards accepted. 30 Corso Nuova Italia (phone: 775-55254). Expensive to moderate.

En Route from Fiuggi – Drive north to pick up SS411 in the direction of Subiaco. Just before the town, turn right onto the Vallepietra road where Subiaco's most famous sights are found.

SUBIACO: According to legend, workmen building a villa for Nero by a long-gone lake needed a place to stay. Their work camp of huts became the town of Sublaqueum, meaning "under the waters." The ruins of Nero's villa can still be visited, about 1½ miles (2 km) out of town, but Subiaco — considered the birthplace of Benedictine monasticism — is best known for its monasteries. In the 6th century, St. Benedict came here from his native Norcia, in Umbria. Living as a hermit, he prayed in a cave for 3 years, and before leaving for Monte Cassino (see *Day Trip 6,* below) he had founded several monasteries. One of these original establishments is the Monastero di Santa Scolastica (she was Benedict's sister), which was especially influential from the 11th through the 13th century, but kept growing through the 16th century. The cave in which St. Benedict prayed (known as the Sacro Speco) is now part of the Monastero di San Benedetto, founded in the 12th century. Both monasteries are southeast of town on the road to Vallepietra, one just beyond the other, and both are open daily to visitors from 9 AM to sunset; admission charge.

En Route from Subiaco – Circle north and west back to Rome, passing through villages such as Anticoli Corrado, which has a little medieval square, Vicovaro, and Tivoli, the last stop.

TIVOLI: Already a resort in Roman times, this hilltop town has very nearly become a worldwide household word because of the Villa d'Este, a 16th-century cardinal's palace with terraced gardens that contain some of the most famous fountains of Rome — and not merely one or two or a few squirts and sprays, but 500 of them. Nearby is the Villa Gregoriana, another park with waterworks (actually a waterfall), in addition to archaeological interest in its Corinthian-style Temple of Vesta, or Temple of Sibyl. But the Villa Adriana (Hadrian's Villa), 4 miles (6 km) out of Tivoli in the direction of Rome, is by far Tivoli's greatest archaeological attraction. This was the summer estate Hadrian built for himself after the one he built at Palestrina, and to make it a showplace, as well as to remind him of his travels, he included on the grounds copies of some of the marvels he had seen around the empire. Set on a hillside studded with cypress trees and umbrella pines, the villa is still a showplace and a place for reverie, even in ruins.

Tivoli is certainly interesting enough to warrant a full day. It is easily reached by public transport, and it is included on many guided day tours out of Rome. Because of this, it is discussed more fully in *Rome,* THE CITIES. But if this will be your only chance to see the Villa d'Este and the Villa Adriana, stop now, leaving the Villa Gregoriana for last. The Villa d'Este and the Villa Gregoriana are open daily from 9 AM to 1½ hours before sunset; closed some holidays; phone: 774-22070); the Villa Adriana (phone: 774-530203) is open daily except Mondays from 9 AM to 1 hour before sunset. Admission charge for all three.

EATING OUT: ***Adriano*** – Traditional country dishes, served in a family-run establishment near Hadrian's Villa. The pasta is homemade; the grilled lamb and veal chops are tasty. Closed Mondays. Reservations necessary. Major credit cards accepted. 222 Via Villa Adriano, Tivoli (phone: 774-529174). Moderate.

Sibilla – Beloved by travelers since 1730, this trattoria has two ancient temples in its garden. Traditional Roman dishes such as *bruschetta* (garlic bread) and grilled meat or trout can be enjoyed under a wisteria-wrapped trellis. Don't forget to sample the local liqueur, amaretto di Tivoli. Closed Mondays. Reservations necessary, especially on Sundays. Major credit cards accepted. 50 Via della Sibilla, Tivoli (phone: 774-20281). Moderate.

En Route from Tivoli – Take Via Tiburtina (SS5) back to Rome, 19 miles (30 km) away.

DAY TRIP 5: CASTELLI ROMANI

Southeast of Rome, in the lovely Colli Albani (Alban Hills) region, are 13 hill towns known collectively as the Castelli Romani (Roman Castles). The curious name derives from the castles, or fortresses, palaces, and villas built here over the centuries by various popes and patrician Roman families. This is also wine country, and our route goes directly to Rome's prime wine town, Frascati. It then explores a selection of other Castelli towns surrounding the two volcanic lakes of the region, Lago di Albano and Lago di Nemi.

En Route from Rome – Take the Via Tuscolana (SS215) southeast out of Rome and drive 13 miles (21 km) to Frascati.

FRASCATI: An ancient Roman town, Frascati is famous both for its wine and for its patrician villas of the 16th and 17th centuries. Although heavily damaged during World War II, and much rebuilt, it is still one of the Romans' favorite Castelli destinations for an outing. Its main square, Piazza Marconi, affords a panoramic view over the Roman countryside and the gardens of the Villa Torlonia, open to the public. The 16th-century villa itself was bombed to smithereens during World War II, but the remains of a water theater (a fancy arrangement of fountains) designed by Carlo Maderno, one of the architects of St. Peter's in Rome, are fascinating. Sitting on top of a hill and dominating another side of Piazza Marconi is the Villa Aldobrandini, built for a cardinal at the end of the 16th century by Giacomo della Porta. It is open daily from 9 AM to 1 PM (with permission from the Azienda Autonoma di Turismo; 1 Piazza Marconi; phone: 6-942-0331). Next to it is the privately owned Villa Lancellotti, not visitable — but note its gate, by the architect Borromini, Bernini's great rival. Still another famous villa, Villa Mondragone, is about a mile (1.6 km) east of town and is now a Jesuit seminary. Here Pope Gregory XIII issued a bull establishing a new calendar — the one we use today.

Frascati's well-known wine is mostly from white grapes and at its best should be amber in color. Wine consortiums sell the local product everywhere, and some wineries encourage visits. Another Frascati specialty — a bit peculiar — are the *pupazze,* honey cakes baked in animal or human forms. One favorite is a three-breasted fertility goddess who harks back to the area's pagan days.

EATING OUT: ***Cacciani*** – A brother and a sister whose grandfather was a noted Frascati chef own this restaurant. Their menu stresses the traditional cuisine of Lazio (with a woodland accent in the many mushroom dishes in season), plus a twist of nouvelle. Their wine cellar is well stocked with wines from the family vineyards. Ask to see the cellar: It was carved into a tufa hill a century ago. Dine on the terrace in summer — the view takes in the hillsides and the famed villas where the Renaissance princes played. For those who have eaten themselves into a stupor, there also are 20 guestrooms. Closed Tuesdays, Sunday evenings, and November through March. Reservations necessary. Major credit cards accepted. 13-15 Via Armando Diaz, Frascati (phone: 6-942-0378). Moderate.

En Route from Frascati – Turning south, drive just short of 2 miles (3 km) to Grottaferrata. After a visit, continue to Marino, about 4 miles (6 km) away by SS216. Still farther along on SS216 is Castel Gandolfo, where the pope spends his summers in the cool, green hills. From Castel Gandolfo, proceed to Albano.

GROTTAFERRATA: Best known for its fortified abbey, a castle-like monastery that was founded in 1004 and is still inhabited by monks of the Greek Catholic rite. The abbey was built on top of the ruins of an ancient Roman summer villa, part of which became a chapel incorporated into the abbey's Church of St. Mary. In front of the church is a handsome fountain, and there is an adjacent shop where monks sell olive oil and wine. Open daily from 9 AM to noon and 4:15 to 6 PM phone: 6-945-9309).

EATING OUT: ***La Bazzica*** – Locally made white wine, fresh fish on Fridays, and baby lamb prepared in the Lazio fashion are what keep the Romans flocking to this traditional restaurant. Closed Tuesdays. Reservations necessary on weekends. Major credit cards accepted. 58 Viale J. F. Kennedy, Grottaferrata (phone: 6-945-9947). Moderate.

Al Fico – After 32 years, this large, country-style restaurant run by Claudio Ciocca is a favorite Sunday eating place for Romans, so it's best to try his homemade fettuccine with wild mushrooms, chicory in tomato sauce, and succulent lamb chops on less crowded days. His deviled chicken is diabolically good. Closed Wednesdays. Reservations advised. No credit cards accepted. 134 Via Anagnina, Grottaferrata (phone: 6-941-2070). Moderate.

MARINO: In summer, this favorite Castelli town is crowded with day-trippers from Rome. Like Frascati, Marino is famous for its wine, and each year on the first Sunday in October it holds a wine festival, the *Sagra dell'Uva* (see *Italy's Most Colorful Festas* in DIVERSIONS). The event begins with a religious procession, but after the solemnities are over, Marino puts itself entirely into the hands, or jug, of Bacchus, and the wine Pliny called "a healthy tonic useful for the nerves" really does flow from the fountain in the main square.

EATING OUT: ***Al Vigneto*** **–** Fish, polenta, and homemade *crostate* (tarts) are served here. The restaurant is a little less than 3 miles (5 km) out of Marino on the Via dei Laghi in a woodland setting where children can romp while adults sample Marino's fine wines under a grape arbor. Closed Thursdays. Reservations necessary on weekends. Major credit cards accepted. Km 4.5, Via dei Laghi, Marino (phone: 6-938524 or 6-938-7034). Moderate.

CASTEL GANDOLFO: A particularly lovely setting overlooking Lake Albano prompted the popes to select Castel Gandolfo for their summer residence. It is supposed to have been the site of Alba Longa, the most ancient city of Lazio, founded, according to legend, by the son of Aeneas and destroyed by the Romans in about 600 BC. Roman legend also speaks of a duel fought between the Horatii, male triplets of Rome, and the Curiatii, triplets of Alba Longa, in an attempt to resolve a tiresome war. Through a ruse, a Horatio won after his two brothers had been slain. When his sister, mourning one of the dead Curiatii, turned on him, he killed her as well. The tomb in which the Horatii and Curiatii were supposedly buried lies farther along the road on the way to Ariccia.

A Bernini fountain and the graceful Chiesa di San Tommaso da Villanova, also by Bernini, decorate Castel Gandolfo's main square. Also on the square is the entrance to the Palazzo Papale (papal residence), designed by Carlo Maderno and built from 1624 to 1629 on the site of a sprawling pleasure palace belonging to Emperor Domitian in the 1st century AD. The palace and its grounds, enlarged by the later addition of the grounds of the Villa Barberini, are all part of the Vatican city-state, and the complex is huge — extending all the way to the next Castelli town, Albano. The grounds house the famous Vatican Observatory and a modern hall used for general audiences on Wednesday mornings when the pope is in residence (attendance at the audience is the only way tourists can visit the property, which is closed to the public). When in residence, the pope also appears at a window in the inner of two courtyards at noon on Sundays and can then be seen from quite close.

ALBANO: In the 3rd century AD, the Emperor Septimius Severus established a permanent garrison — the Castra Albana — for the Roman army here. The camp evidently took up the entire territory of the present town, although, covered by later construction, it was only bombed into view during World War II. Now the main gateway to the camp, the Porta Pretoria, can be seen, and a giant Roman cistern, carved out of the rock and still in use, as well as the ancient amphitheater, can be visited. The so-called tomb of the Horatii and Curiatii, but more probably the tomb of an unknown Roman from the time of the republic, sits by the side of the road on the way out of Albano.

En Route from Albano – Take the Via Appia (SS7) to Genzano, and turn off toward Nemi.

GENZANO DI ROMA: This Castelli town is noted for its *Corpus Domini* celebrations. Each year, on a Sunday in mid-June, the entire Via Italo Belardi (ex–Via Livia) leading up to the Chiesa di Santa Maria della Cima is covered with "paintings" made entirely of flowers. The subjects are religious scenes, historical scenes, copies of famous masterpieces, portraits, or abstract designs, intricately worked out in petals, pistils, stamens, and leaves — the townspeople have had more than 200 years to perfect their technique. The next morning, at 10 AM, the children of the town descend on the street like a swarm of locusts and wipe out all the artwork in a matter of minutes.

EATING OUT: ***Antica Taverna*** **–** The atmosphere is rustic, and the fish and meat dishes are lovingly prepared in traditional style. Try the house antipasto. Closed Mondays. Reservations necessary on Sundays. Major credit cards accepted. 56 Via G. Lordi, Genzano di Roma (phone: 6-939-0021). Moderate to inexpensive.

NEMI: Set high above the lake from which it takes its name, Nemi is dominated by the Ruspoli Palace and is best known for its strawberries. When they're in season in early summer, Romans make pilgrimages here to eat them, and in June the town holds a strawberry festival. The ancient Romans referred to the lake as the Mirror of Diana because it reflected a nearby temple dedicated to the goddess of the hunt in an area called the Sacred Grove of Diana, today known as *il giardino*. Festivals in her honor took place here in ancient times, and in the 1930s part of the lake was drained to recover two Roman boats built by Caligula to take part in the celebrations. The museum in which the boats were placed was bombed during World War II, and they were destroyed. The very modest museum, however, has reopened, and a scaled-down reconstruction of the boats can be seen daily except Mondays from 9 AM to 2 PM (Sundays until 1 PM;) admission charge.

En Route from Nemi – Pick up the Via dei Laghi (Lake Road, SS217) northwest, and turn right at the turnoff for Rocca di Papa.

ROCCA DI PAPA: The highest of the Castelli clings to the side of Monte Cavo, at an altitude of 2,250 feet. It takes its name from a castle built here by the popes in the Middle Ages (and destroyed during the Renaissance) and consists of a higher, medieval quarter and a lower, modern town. In Roman times, a temple of Jupiter stood at the 3,124-foot top of Monte Cavo, which was approached by a Via Sacra over which the earliest Romans marched in solemn procession with sacrifices to dedicate to the one god they all worshiped. In the 18th century a monastery was built where the temple presumably stood. On a clear day, the view from the top of the mountain is immense, taking in the Castelli, the two lakes, and the surrounding countryside as far as the coast. Getting there, however, requires turning off before Rocca di Papa and following a winding road that eventually turns into a private road (the custodians charge a minimal fee).

En Route from Rocca di Papa – Go back to Grottaferrate, then to Frascati, and from there take the Via Tuscolana back to Rome.

DAY TRIP 6: MONTE CASSINO, SPERLONGA, ANZIO

Southern Lazio has a flavor all its own, a mixture of pious abbeys and pagan temples, roadside stands selling delectable mozzarellas, beachheads whose names ring with the horrors of war, and chic beaches with frequently topless bathers. This tour leads south of Rome, through a part of Lazio known as the Ciociaria, to visit the Abbey of Monte Cassino, a fascinating experience for people of all faiths. Then it cuts seaward to Gaeta and returns north along the coast via a number of seaside towns — Sperlonga for a swim and lunch, Terracina, Anzio (where the Allied landing took place during World War II), and Nettuno.

En Route from Rome – Take the Autostrada del Sole (A2) south 70 miles (113 km) to the Cassino exit. The Abbey of Monte Cassino is 5½ miles (9 km) west of the modern industrial town of Cassino, at the end of a winding mountain road.

ABBAZIA DI MONTE CASSINO: Most travelers racing down the autostrada from Rome to Naples only glimpse this historic monastery from afar, but it is open to visitors, provided they respect the sanctity of the place and dress appropriately. The imposing, medieval-style complex of buildings, set in a commanding position on a mountaintop, is headquarters for the Benedictine Order, founded by St. Benedict in 529 after, according to legend, three ravens led him from Subiaco to Cassino. He died in the new monastery 14 years later and was buried here, as was his sister, St. Scholastica. During the Dark Ages, following the fall of the Roman Empire, the abbey was not only one of the great European centers of Christian culture, but also one of the greatest repositories of ancient learning — it is thanks to the zealous preservation efforts of the monks of Monte Cassino that much of ancient Latin literature and thought survived. Destroyed several times in the distant past — by the Lombards in the 6th century, the Saracens in the 9th century, the Normans in the 11th century, and an earthquake in the 14th century — the abbey was always rebuilt. Then, in 1944, it was destroyed again, this time bombed by the Allies who suspected it was occupied by German troops (justification for the bombing is still a matter of controversy). Reconstruction began immediately after the war, and the library of medieval books and manuscripts that were spared by the bombing is still one of the greatest collections in the world. Besides breathtaking views from the abbey, visitors today can see the basilica, several cloisters, and a photo exhibition on the extent of the damage that is quite moving. The military cemetery seen on the way up contains the graves of 1,100 Polish soldiers who lost their lives in the final assault.

En Route from Monte Cassino – Cut seaward across the peninsula for a visit to Gaeta, and then turn north along the coast and stop at Sperlonga.

GAETA: A handsome fortress of ancient origin, but much transformed from the 13th through the 16th century, sits on a promontory jutting into the sea in this port and resort town. The 12th-century cathedral is interesting, but best of all is a stroll through the bazaar-like, crowded, narrow alleys parallel to the Lungomare Caboto. The pleasure yachts anchored in the basin are impressively posh.

EATING OUT: *La Scarpetta* – Seafood takes center stage, with regional specialties prepared in inventive ways and served in the garden in pleasant weather. Closed Tuesdays except in mid-summer. Reservations necessary. Major credit cards accepted. 1 Piazza Conca, Gaeta (phone: 771-462142). Moderate.

SPERLONGA: This whitewashed town with a Moorish look has long sand beaches on either side of a rock spur into the sea. It is perhaps Lazio's loveliest summer resort and, accordingly, is overcrowded from mid-July through late August, but it is a delight in June and September. About a half-mile (1 km) south of the town on Via Flacca is a small, fascinating archaeological museum (phone: 771-54028) with finds from the area, including from the Grotta di Tiberio, a great cave on the beach that the ancient Romans (traditionally, Tiberius) used for summer amusement. It is open Tuesdays through Saturdays in winter from 9:30 AM to 4 PM; in summer from 10 AM to 6 PM; Sundays from 9 AM to 1 PM; admission charge. Various ancient statues were found in the cave, and some statues can still be seen there. Others, put together again from fragments, like Humpty Dumpty, are in the museum.

EATING OUT: *Laocoonte–Da Rocco* – The best of many pleasant restaurants in town serving fish. It has a covered terrace overlooking the sea. Open daily, except Mondays from September 15 to June 14 and *Christmas* week. Reservations necessary on weekends. Major credit cards accepted. 4 Via Colombo, Sperlonga (phone: 771-54122). Expensive.

Grotta di Tiberio – Near the cave and the beach, the attraction here is a charming garden in an old orchard. Specialties include classic fish dishes such as *risotto al pescatore* and spaghetti with clams. Try the delicate *pesce al cartoccio* (fish sealed in parchment). Closed Tuesdays and November. Reservations advised. Major credit cards accepted. 8 Via Flacca, Sperlonga (phone: 771-54027). Moderate.

La Siesta – Tucked away in an intimate piazza, this small trattoria, resplendent with bougainvillea, offers regional old favorites such as flavorful buffalo-milk mozzarella, spaghetti with clams, and sea bass fileted at the table. Reservations advised. 15 Via I Orticello, Sperlonga (phone: 771-54617). Moderate.

En Route from Sperlonga – The next coastal town north of Sperlonga is Terracina, where fishing boats jam into a canal leading to the sea. Terracina is a traffic-clogged, colorful town that becomes tourist-clogged in midsummer. Serene on a high cliff above it, however, are the ruins of a famous temple of Jupiter dating from the 1st century BC. Beyond Terracina, the Via Pontina (SS148) turns north to Rome, while the coast road heads to San Felice Circeo, a bathing resort on the slopes of the 1,795-foot promontory of Monte Circeo, home to the Neanderthals, to Circe, and now to the very rich who populate the expensive resort hotels. The area is also home to a good deal of rare wildlife, since it is now a nature reserve, the Parco Nazionale del Circeo, which encloses four coastal lakes, swamps, dunes, forests of oak and maple, and a variety of archaeological remains. Among these are the ruins of a lavish lakeside summer residence and spa Emperor Domitian built here in the 1st century AD. Although the park is regularly open to the public (in fact, both San Felice Circeo and the next seaside resort north, Sabaudia, are in it, and visitors will be driving through it along a good stretch of the coast road), advance permission is necessary to visit the ruins of Domitian's villa, which is on one of the coastal lakes between the promontory and Sabaudia. Requests should be addressed to Parco Nazionale del Circeo, 6 Via Carlo Alberto, Sabaudia (phone: 773-57251).

From Sabaudia, either return to SS148 and continue north to the turnoff for Nettuno and Anzio, or follow the coast road north. It's also possible to turn off SS148 at Campoverde and follow the well-marked road directly to the American Military Cemetery at Nettuno.

EATING OUT: ***La Tartana da Mario*** – Fish, fish, and more fish in this roomy tavern whose wine list offers as rich a variety of whites as the menu does of seafood. Closed Tuesdays and November. Km 112.7, Via Appia, Terracina (phone: 773-702461). Expensive.

Hostaria Porto Salvo – Featured in a spacious verandah that overlooks the sea are fish baked in parchment and the *grigliate miste,* a mixed grill of fish and seafood. Closed Mondays and November. Reservations advised. No credit cards accepted. 102 Via Appia, Terracina (phone: 773-752151). Expensive to moderate.

Maga Circe – Set in one of the most evocative areas of Lazio, this restaurant has a terrace overlooking the promontory and offers an abundant selection of seafood and a good wine list. There also are 60 rooms and several apartments. Open daily. Reservations advised. No credit cards accepted. 1 Via Ammiraglio Bergamini, San Felice Circeo (phone: 773-527821). Expensive to moderate.

Miramare – A seaside pizzeria with a garden, it also offers *tagliolini* (fine noodles) with shrimp, and risotto with *frutti di mare* (a mixture of seafood). Closed Mondays. Reservations advised. Major credit cards accepted. 32 Lungomare Circe, Terracina (phone: 773-727332). Moderate.

NETTUNO and ANZIO: Modern history remembers the stretch of beach between these two resorts as the blood-drenched strand where American and British troops landed in the "soft underbelly of Europe" on January 22, 1944. The British came ashore at Anzio, the Americans, closer to Nettuno, and together they found that the underbelly was not at all soft: The Germans resisted the Allied onslaught for more than 4 months. Some 1,000 British soldiers are buried in the British Military Cemetery at

Anzio (on SS207, about 2 miles/3 km north). Nearly 8,000 American soldiers lie in the American Military Cemetery, off the Via Santa Maria, about a half mile (1 km) north of Nettuno. In the center of the cemetery, which is always open, is a chapel, and next to it a small museum illustrates Allied military operations from the invasion of Sicily to the end of the war.

Together, Anzio and Nettuno form almost one continuous town. Anzio was already a resort in Roman times: Cicero had a summer palace here, and both the emperors Caligula and Nero were born here — ruins of the latter's villa can be seen near the lighthouse. Not far away from the villa are the Grotte di Nerone (Nero's Caves), actually ruins of ancient Roman port warehouses. Some very famous statues have been found on Nero's property, including the *Apollo Belvedere* in the Vatican collection in Rome. Nettuno is known for its picturesque medieval quarter.

EATING OUT: ***Flora*** – This small dining spot serves seafood dishes, with an occasional Sicilian accent. There are wines from all over the world (even California is represented!). Closed Sunday evenings and Mondays. Reservations necessary. Major credit cards accepted. 9 Via Flora, Anzio (phone: 6-984-5001). Expensive to moderate.

En Route from Anzio and Nettuno – The SS207 leads back to the Via Pontina (SS148) for the return to Rome.

DAY TRIP 7: FARFA, RIETI, GRECCIO

Following the Tiber River Valley, the seventh tour goes to a celebrated medieval abbey in Farfa, to the walled city of Rieti, and finally to Greccio, a mountain hamlet.

En Route from Rome – Take the A1 autostrada to the Fiano Romano exit, or the Via Salaria (SS4), which goes from Rome to the Adriatic Sea, to Passo Corese — about 49 miles (78 km). Then take the turnoff for Farfa, making sure to carefully follow the signs leading to it.

FARFA: Admirers of Umberto Eco's elegant mystery, *The Name of the Rose,* set in a medieval monastery, may wish to visit one of the most magnificent, the Imperial Abbey. Begun in the 6th century, it became one of the most powerful Benedictine monasteries in Europe, and is considered one of the most splendid abbey complexes on the continent. Protected by Charlemagne, it came to rival in power the Vatican itself. Vestiges of its ancient fortifications still can be seen. Scholastically, it was the Harvard of its day, and in the Middle Ages, parents lined up outside the monastery, making appeals to have their sons educated here. Little of this power and grandeur is still visible, but a visit is pleasant nonetheless. Note the Germanic look of the half doors leading to the street (unusual in Italy). There are guided tours in Italian of the abbey on weekends from 9:30 AM to noon and 3:30 to 6 PM. The complex is open daily. Stop at the ancient pharmacy to purchase liqueurs, honey, jam, and soap made by the monks. The *Casa di Santa Brigida* (near the parking lot) is run by kindly nuns who welcome guests for a delicious, abundant, and wholesome lunch.

En Route from Farfa – Return to SS4 via Tóffia and proceed 8 miles (13 km) to Rieti.

RIETI: This walled city with a medieval flavor is at its loveliest in the early spring when the mountains around the Terminillo ski resort are snow-capped and the almond trees in the valley are blossoming with clouds of white petals. Within its 13th-century walls are a cathedral, other early churches, a small municipal museum (open mornings only), and the late Renaissance Palazzo Vecchiarelli that was designed by the famed architect Carlo Maderno.

EATING OUT: ***Checco al Calice d'Oro*** – One of Lazio's finest traditional restaurants. Its menu of country dishes includes *bollito misto* (boiled meat), lamb, roast kid, and trout. There also are a few moderately priced, comfortable rooms. Closed Mondays. Reservations necesssary on Sundays. Major credit cards accepted. 10 Via Marchetti, Rieti (phone: 746-44271). Expensive to moderate.

Il Nido del Corvo – Woodlands and mountains are reflected in the menu of game, polenta, and mushrooms served in this attractive, large restaurant with pleasant furnishings. Closed Tuesdays. Reservations necessary on Sundays. Major credit cards accepted. 15 Via del Forno, Rieti (phone: 746-753181). Moderate to inexpensive.

En Route from Rieti – Make a short detour (follow the signs) to Greccio, a mountain village where nearly 800 years ago St. Francis of Assisi arranged a living *Christmas* crèche in a grotto. Every *Christmas* the scene is reenacted. Its Franciscan convent and the small Church of St. Bonaventura date from the 13th century. In the distance is the Mt. Terminillo ski resort. Take SS4 to return to Rome.

Sardinia

Sardinia's beloved Grazia Deledda, an unschooled woman from the mountain town of Nuoro, won the Nobel Prize for Literature in 1926. Deledda was a prolific, lyric writer whose works reflect Sardinian peasant life in the early 20th century. Then, as now, Sards were fiercely independent, proud, and wary of outsiders.

One of Deledda's novels, *Canne al vento* (Reeds in the Wind), immortalizes the heady Sardinian winds. They can turn ferocious in the north, where the 7-mile-wide Strait of Boniface separates the island (the second largest in the Mediterranean) from its geological kissing cousin, French-owned Corsica. Ancient settlers fleeing Crete and later Carthage in frail craft learned to steer clear of Sardinia's churning waters, driven by the Balearic current, and treacherous winds like the mistral. (Today's yachtsmen, anchored at the posh playground inlets of the Costa Smeralda, enjoy the challenge.)

These same waves and winds brought the island's first settlers during the neolithic era. They found a warm climate, hospitable terrain, and, in volcanic mountains like Mt. Arci in the Oristano province, black glass made from volcanic ash called obsidian that was useful for stone tools. These early people fused with later arrivals — Nuraghesi, believed to have sailed to Sardinia from the eastern Mediterranean by way of North Africa around 3000 BC. They left behind them about 7,000 towers called *nuraghi,* built of huge stones joined without mortar. Some are like medieval castles. They typically have a cone-shaped central tower of several stories and two or three rings of defense walls. During an enemy attack the farm folk who lived in nearby huts sought shelter inside for their families and flocks.

Sardinia's location, 116 miles from the Italian mainland — about the same distance as from North Africa — puts it at the center of Mediterranean trade routes. Like the other islands, it was in constant danger of invasion, and in rather rapid succession it was occupied by Greeks, Romans, and Phoenicians. One of the delights of beach life on Sardinia is the occasional serendipitous discovery of reminders of those days. The traces of brickwork half buried in the sand at water's edge may have come from a fisherman's cottage built in Caesar's day. Remains of Carthaginian colonies can be seen half submerged in the sea near Nora, south of Cagliari, at Bithia, Paniloriga, and Sant'Antioco, and at Tharros on the western coast near Oristano.

Later, the coastal villages were looted and destroyed by Vandals, Byzantines, and Arabs. Retreating into the impervious — and, until the 18th century, heavily wooded — mountain interior, the refugees built the towns that survive to this day. During the Middle Ages, the maritime republics of Pisa and Genoa battled for supremacy in Sardinia, followed by the Spanish and Austrians. Each new occupier left a stamp — the Genoese and Spanish their towers and ramparts, the Pisans the elegant Romanesque churches with their characteristic horizontal stripes that appear suddenly in lonely meadows.

With each successive invasion over the centuries, islanders retreated into the interior. This retreat, and its resulting insularity, helps explain another Sardinian peculiarity — its language, Sardo, the romance language closest to spoken Latin. Utterly incomprehensible to most other Italians, its four dialectal variations borrow words from Arabic, Spanish, and Portuguese. The Spanish House of Aragón dominated Sardinia for 4 centuries, leaving its imprint especially on the western coastline, where the local dialect, one of the four variations, is called Catalán. The Spanish were ousted by the Piedmontese, blamed for deforesting the island to fuel the fledgling industrial revolution in northern Italy.

Despite unification with the new Italy in 1870, Sardinia remained undeveloped and malaria-ridden. It achieved limited political autonomy as an independent region after World War II. Progress came with somewhat jarring rapidity after the 1960s, so that these days the old and new sometimes seem incongruously juxtaposed: Some country women still dress in traditional costume at outdoor markets, while nude sunbathers are frequently seen on the beaches.

With the arrival of spring, Sardinian winds turn warm. The beaches in the south near Cagliari, the capital, offer good swimming earlier than elsewhere in Italy, thanks to the balmy breezes and currents from Africa. In summer the winds send shivers through the eucalyptus trees and flowering shrubs that line the roads winding through the broad valleys; they waft the unforgettable fragrance of *la macchia,* the shrub that covers most of Sardinia's 9,724 square miles of otherwise largely barren mountain peaks and endless rolling hills.

The coast is ringed by islets whose soft rock has been carved into monument-like structures by the elements. This is the easiest part of Sardinia for outsiders to get to know. One of the world's most spectacular coastlines, it was somewhat defaced by cement and stucco construction during the 1970s, but much remains undisturbed. So the eye can feast on breathtaking vistas as yet another hair-raising hairpin turn brings into view a beach with white sand, or a secluded cove, or a cliff dotted with grottoes and, atop, a millennium-old Saracen tower in ruins. The network of watchtowers was built on the coast, each within sight of another, to warn of the approach of pirates and other invaders.

Inland from the fabled coastline of granite cliffs and turquoise, iridescent sea is the rugged mountain interior, capped by 6,017-foot Punta La Marmora in the Gennargentu range at Sardinia's heart. Above terraced vineyards, rock-strewn plateaus are guarded by solitary shepherds tending their flocks as if in biblical times. Life here reflects centuries of isolation. Sardinian folk culture has been kept undiluted and genuine, especially in the Barbagia area. From foods to handicrafts, clothing, and home furnishings, the grazing economy affects traditional Sardinian life. A Sardinian might describe a childhood friend as a *compagno d'ovile* (sheep pen chum). This Sardinian interior, still authentic, takes a bit of work to get to know, but it's worth the effort.

As modernization efforts (such as the petrochemical industry centered at Porto Torres in the west) bring change, and as new roads break into the isolation of the mountain towns, some Sardinians protest the incursions.

Schools and folk dance clubs help retain traditional culture, and in summer many hotels schedule an evening of local culinary specialties, followed by folk dances to the music of a triple-piped flute called a *launeddas.* As in Greece, such dances, with their staccato rhythms and sometimes intricate footwork, are not solely for tourists' amusement. In the countryside after a family picnic, someone may produce an accordion, and the men — with as much dignity as they can muster after a big meal and abundant wine — will begin one of the solemn traditional dances right in the field.

Unlike Malta or Sicily, Sardinia was never a military or commercial crossroads. This helped to limit its population, today estimated at only 1.6 million, or 170 people per square mile (by contrast, Sicily has 490). But like some other Mediterranean islands, Sardinia suffers at times from its own success in today's tourism industry. In early August, especially in the coastal areas, the crowds of visitors may endure poor service and unfair prices. During the rest of the long season, however, from May to September, the swimming, sunning, and touring are delightful. Many resorts close in September, but increasingly, many others extend their season, or remain open year-round. Golf, tennis, hiking, biking, and trekking on foot or horseback are popular in spring and fall. Temperatures are comparatively warm and rainfall scanty, so that even in January visitors enjoy pleasant touring. At that time, the mean temperature in Sassari in the northeast is 47F (8C), and in Cagliari in the south, 49F (9C). Indeed, *cagliaritani* boast, exaggerating only a bit, that they can swim in January, when the almond trees are already in spectacular bloom.

TOURIST INFORMATION: The major tourist offices are in the following cities: *Alghero* (9 Piazza Portaterra; phone: 79-979054), *Arzachena* (Via Risorgimento; phone: 789-82624), *Cagliari* (1 Piazza Matteotti; phone: 70-669255), *Nuoro* (19 Piazza Italia; phone: 784-30083), *Olbia* (1 Via Catello Piro; phone: 789-21453), *Oristano* (276 Via Cagliari; phone: 783-74191), *Santa Teresa di Gallura* (24 Piazza Vittorio Emanuele; phone: 789-754127), and *Sassari* (36 Viale Caprera; phone: 79-299544). Most offices are closed from 1 to 4 PM during the summer. Brochures usually include the *Annuario Alberghi* (current hotel guide) and *Calendario Manifestazioni Turistiche* (festival calendar); they are not always translated into English. Good maps are available as well, and hotels distribute the English-langugage monthly *Sardinia When & Where* free.

The *Touring Club Italiano* maintains an office in Cagliari (c/o *A Travel Agency,* Centromed, 22 Via XXIX Novembre; phone: 70-670332), as does the *Italian Automobile Club* (2 Via Carboni Boi; phone: 70-492881).

Agritourism, the system whereby farmers accommodate tourists in their homes, is catching on in Sardinia. In exchange for room and board, tourists may be asked to perform small jobs around the farm: anything from milking cows or working handlooms to simply expressing a healthy interest in what's going on. It's best to avoid July and August when the heat inland can be intense. For information, contact *Cooperativa Allevatrici Sarde,* Casella Postale 107, Oristano 09170 (phone: 783-51040, 783-481066, or 783-418193).

FOOD AND WINE: Along the coast, Sardinia's specialties begin with the freshest fish and shellfish, including prawns, crabs, oysters, octopus, lobsters, sea bass, red snapper, and flounder. Any hors d'oeuvres platter is likely to include mixed shellfish salad or *moscardini,* fried baby octopus no bigger than a dime. The most popular first course is *su ziminu,* Sardinia's version of bouillabaisse, which always includes the homely little *scorfano* fish, small crabs, and often lobster claws in a broth rich with chopped, sun-dried tomatoes and white wine. Lobster with tomato sauce is popular as a midnight spaghetti snack. Fresh sea urchin caviar, most abundant in the winter, is also used to flavor spaghetti. Year-round, Sardinians grate salted, dried tuna caviar — or the far more costly mullet, *bottarga* — onto spaghetti tossed with olive oil.

However, horse lovers unused to the idea of eating the animal Sardinians are so adept at riding should beware. Horsemeat is prized locally, and often masquerades on the menu as just another fancy steak (*bistecca gran premio*) or as *Is Coiettas,* where the meat is rolled and stuffed.

Inland dinners may begin with *salumes de Berchidda,* variations on salami made from pigs that have foraged on the fragrant local heath. This leads to the pièce de résistance of all Sardinian cuisine, the *porceddu* — suckling pig slowly roasted on a bed of aromatic myrtle. Lamb is also sometimes roasted this way. Both pork and lamb are served with chunks of celery and radishes, *sa birdura croa.*

Pasta include *malloreddus,* tiny saffron-tinted shells served with tomato or meat sauce, and *culonzones,* big ravioli stuffed with spinach and ricotta cheese made from ewe's milk and sometimes flavored with fresh mint. Available everywhere in Sardinia are flat rounds of *carta da musica* (music paper) bread, which is named for the rustling sound it makes when eaten dry; moistened, it becomes as soft as fresh bread; it also is called *pane carasau.* Shepherds carry it with them on their long migrations into the mountains with their flocks. When moistened in mutton broth, layered with tomato sauce and cheese, and with a broth-poached egg on top, it becomes a whole meal — *pane fratau.*

Aged cheeses made from ewe's milk — *pecorino* — range in flavor from gentle to tangy. The most celebrated of all Sardinian cheeses, *casu beccio,* has a creamy center. A rarity, it is cured by worms. (Don't worry — it is too prized to appear on a restaurant menu.) More customary methods are employed for aging the cheeses that go into delectable, bittersweet honey-dipped fried pastries called *sebadas,* served for dessert. *L'aranciata,* candied orange peel with almonds and honey, comes from Nuoro.

Sardinian wines are increasingly popular, even abroad: From the south comes the dry white nuragus of Cagliari; from the north, the still white aragosta (good with fish) and the sparkling white vermentino di Gallura. Red wines include cannonau, the most popular, and rosso di Mamoiada. Meals may end with the mellow, sherry-like golden vernaccia often used in sauces, with sweet anghelu ruju (red angel), or with a chilled thimbleful of the strong liqueur, filu di ferru ("wire string").

GETTING AROUND: Air – There are airports at Cagliari (Elmas; phone: 70-240047), Alghero (Fertilia, which also serves Sassari), and Olbia (Costa Smeralda or Venafiorita), close to the Maddalena Archipelago, with its 14 islands. There are flights to the island from Rome, Milan, Pisa, and Bologna. In summer, additional flights depart from other Italian, and some European, cities as well.

On the Costa Smeralda at Porto Cervo a reservation center handles air and steamship arrangements (phone: 789-9400); also try *Sardinia International Travel* (Piazza Centrale; phone: 789-92225). In Cagliari, a free bus run by *ARST* (*Azienda Regionale Sarda Turisti*) runs hourly between the bus station at Piazza Matteotti and Elmas Airport. The trip takes 20 minutes (for information call 70-657236).

Bus – *PANI* is the main bus company connecting major cities; in Cagliari (4 Piazza Darsena; phone: 70-652326). Local buses are too crowded and slow to be recommended. For a bus tour, contact *Karalis Viaggi* (199 Via della Pineta, Cagliari; phone: 70-306991 or 70-306992).

Car Rental – The major rental firms have offices at Sardinia's three airports. In summer, reserve in advance. *Alghero: Avis* (7 Piazza Sulis; phone: 79-979577); *Hertz* (at the airport; phone: 79-935054). *Cagliari: Autonoleggio Italia* (95 Via Sonnino;

phone: 70-664940; and at the airport; phone: 70-240176); *Demontis* (87 Via Sonnino; phone: 70-668128; and at the airport; phone: 70-240081); *Hertz* (8 Piazza Matteotti; phone: 70-663457 or 668105; and at the airport; phone: 70-240037); *Maggiore* (1/A Via XX Settembre; phone: 70-273692; and at the airport; phone: 70-240069). *Olbia: Autonoleggio Italia* (at the airport; phone: 789-69501); *Demontis* (67 Via Genova; phone: 789-22420; and at the airport; phone: 789-69540); *Hertz* (34 Via Regina Elena; phone: 789-21274; and at the airport; phone: 789-69389); *Maggiore* (2 Via Mameli; phone: 789-22131; and at the airport; phone: 789-69457). *Porto Torres: L. Baraghini* (4 Via Petronia; phone: 79-514928).

Ferry – Frequent ferry service, especially in summer, links Olbia, Santa Teresa di Gallura, and Porto Torres in the north of Sardinia with the mainland cities of Civitavecchia (near Rome), Livorno, and Genoa, as well as with the south of France and Corsica; except for Corsica, these crossings take from 7 to 12 hours. From Cagliari in the south, ferries connect with Civitavecchia, Genoa, Naples, Palermo, Trapani, and Tunisia; these crossings take from 14 to 23 hours, and at times can be very rough. So bring pills for seasickness if you're concerned. Be sure to book a sleeping berth (*cuccetta*) and not the standard "armchair" (*poltrona*) if you want to get any sleep at all. Book many weeks ahead in the summer, particularly if you are taking a car.

The chief companies running ferries are *Tirrenia; Trans Tirreno Express;* and *Traghetti Ferrovie dello Stato* (Italian State Railways) with offices at all railway stations in Italy. Any travel agency in Italy can make ferry bookings. *Tirrenia*'s agencies on Sardinia are in Cagliari (7 Piazza Deffenu; phone: 70-654664), Olbia (17 Corso Umberto; phone: 789-24691), Porto Torres (Stazione Marittima; phone: 91-585733), and La Maddalena (10/A Via Amendola; phone: 789-737660). Reservations for *Tirrenia* ferries can be made by calling 6-474-2041 or 6-474-2242 in Rome, weekdays from 8:30 AM to 1 PM and 2 to 5:15 PM. At times, ferries are subject to annoying and inexplicable delays. Try to eat before embarking, or bring your own food; the prix fixe menu of the *tavola calda* restaurant on board some crossings can be a thoroughly bad deal all around.

Train – Connections between the major cities — Olbia, Sassari, Oristano, and Cagliari — are tolerable. It takes about 3½ hours to travel from Cagliari to either Porto Torres in the northwest or Olbia in the northeast. Local trains creep at a snail's pace. In Cagliari, the *Italian State Railways* (FS) station is at Piazza Matteotti (phone: 70-656293). A new *Trenino Verde* tourist train goes through the rugged Barbagia mountain region and other locales in the island's heartland. For information, contact *Karalis Viaggi* (199 Via della Pineta, Cagliari; phone: 70-306991 or 70-306992).

SPECIAL EVENTS: Sardinia sometimes resembles Scotland and, like the Scots, the Sards sometimes appear dour and solemn. This does not keep them from celebrating every possible feast day, however, and honoring more than 100 traditional festivals. All are religious/folkloric, involving feasting, pageantry, and general holiday merriment (see *Special Events* in GETTING READY TO GO and *Italy's Most Colorful Festas* in DIVERSIONS). The most important feasts are *Carnevale,* celebrated everywhere just before *Lent; Sa Sartiglia,* in Oristano the Sunday and Tuesday before *Ash Wednesday; Sos Mamuttones* (Shrove Tuesday) at Mamoiada near Nuoro; the *Sagra di Sant'Efisio,* a historic procession on May 1–4 from Cagliari to Nora; *La Cavalcata,* the next-to-last Sunday in May at Sassari (commemorating the routing of the Moors in the year 1000); *Li Candelieri* (Feast of the Candlesticks), August 14 in Sassari; *Sagra del Redentore,* in Nuoro the last Sunday in August.

SHOPPING: During the summer, resort hotels allow handicraft representatives to show their wares in the lobbies from time to time. By American standards, the handloomed, pure wool bedspreads and carpets, worked in traditional Sardinian motifs whose origins date back to earliest times, appear relatively expensive, but they are well worth the price, given their high quality. Other good buys: jewelry incorporating the local rare oxblood-colored coral; the traditional Sardinian engagement ring, the *fede sarda,* in gold or silver filigree; shawls in black wool or silk, hand-embroidered in pastel hues and real gold; and handmade, brightly colored or pure white Sardinian pottery, worked into lacy patterns. Those interested in learning local crafts may attend any of a dozen crafts centers in Sardinia. Apply to *ISOLA,* 184 Baccaredda, Cagliari 09100 (phone: 70-486707).

SPORTS AND FITNESS: Boating – Boats — with or without diving equipment or crews for fishing or cruising — can be rented at the *Marinasarda* at Porto Cervo on the Costa Smeralda (phone: 789-92475). Excursions are available through most travel agencies, including *Karalis Viaggi* (199 Via della Pineta, Cagliari; phone: 70-306991). *Karalis* is also a yacht broker.

Fishing – Freshwater fishing requires a permit, which can be obtained from the Assessorato Regionale alla Difesa dell'Ambiente (69 Viale Trento, Cagliari 09100). Spearfishing — with or without air tanks — is popular but strictly controlled by the authorities. Serious scuba and deep-sea divers should check with hotel officials about restrictions as well as available emergency care. All scuba divers, however experienced, should use balloon markers, as boaters like to creep (and even speed) into sea-level grottoes. For further information, contact the local branch of the *Italian Sport Fishing Association* (*FIPS,* Viale Elmas, Cagliari 09100).

Golf – Sardinia has two 18-hole golf courses — at the Costa Smeralda in the northeast and at Is Molas near Cagliari in the south. The challenging *Pevero Golf Club* (see also *Great Italian Golf,* DIVERSIONS), designed by Robert Trent Jones, Sr. is near the *Cala di Volpe* resort hotel. The course is open year-round; clubs and carts can be rented (Cala di Volpe, Porto Cervo 07020; phone: 789-96072). Near Cagliari is the *Is Molas Golf Club.* For information, contact *Is Molas Golf* hotel (Santa Margherita di Pula, Cagliari 09010; phone: 70-924-1002).

Horseback Riding – In recent years the possibilities for roaming the rugged Sardinian mountains on horseback, or for enjoying a lazy canter along the beaches, have been greatly enhanced. In Oristano, the *Centro Ippico* at the *Ala Birdi* hotel (25 Strada a Mare, Arborea 090902; phone: 783-80268) offers riding lessons and horseback excursions year-round, as does the *Cooperativa Allevatrici Sarde* (Casella Postale 107, Oristano 09170; phone: 783-51040, 783-418066, or 783-418193), which arranges mountain excursions of 1 or more days (be sure to book well in advance). In southern Sardinia, horses can be rented at *Ibisco Farm,* a restructured farm by the beach (Sant'Antioco 09017; phone: 781-800102) on the island of Sant'Antioco. Near Cagliari, the *Grand Hotel Chia Laguna* (in Domus de Maria; phone: 70-923-0143) also has horses. *Sardegna a Cavallo* is an association that offers a year-round program of equestrian touring. They have offices in Arbatax (phone: 782-667081); Arborea (phone: 783-800268); Capoterra (phone: 70-721277) which has excursions from S'Ebba to Mount Arcosu, a World Wildlife Federation reservation; Maracalagonis (phone: 70-789866); Oliena (phone: 784-287512); Gergei, at the *Acqua di Luna* riding center for trips in the Trexenta Mountains (phone: 782-808100); and Aritzo (phone: 784-629336). Also contact the local tourist offices for information.

Hunting – The highlands of the Barbagia are popular with hunters. For information, apply to the *Board of Sardinian Regional Directors,* 69 Viale Trento, Cagliari 09100 or *Federazione Italiana della Caccia* (16 Via Bruseu Onnis, Cagliari 09100; phone: 60-668933).

Swimming – The water is very warm in the south, cooler but still pleasant in the north in midsummer. Everywhere away from big cities it is sparklingly clear and unpolluted. Many first class hotels on the coast offer a full panoply of beach life, including windsurfing rentals and lessons, swimming pool for days of rough seas, tennis and *bocce* courts, horseback riding, water skiing, and scuba diving. Instruction is available. Water skiing within 550 yards of the coast is illegal.

Tennis – Many resort hotels have courts. In particular, the *Baia di Conte* outside Alghero runs camps for adults and children from June to September. For information, contact *Baia di Conte,* Alghero (phone: 79-952003 or 79-951109). The *Italian Tennis Federation* has an office in Cagliari at 16 Via Lamarmora; phone: 70-669054).

NIGHTCLUBS AND NIGHTLIFE: Two popular disco spots are the *Sotto Vento Club,* with a restaurant and a piano bar (Golf Pevero, Porto Cervo, on the road to the *Cala di Volpe* hotel; phone: 789-92443), and the *Ritual Club,* which offers the same (Monti di Lu Colbu, near the town of Baia Sardinia; phone: 789-99032).

TOURING SARDINIA

Vacationers can view Sardinia from a rented car, train, horseback, bicycle, or a beach chair. During torrid late July and early August the last is the wisest choice. Stake out a beach and on the coolest days take short day trips. Beware of the annual summer brush fires, particularly in August. Ask at your hotel or the tourist authorities about if and where there is any danger.

Few areas are better suited than Sardinia to a beach-centered vacation. Its rocky inlets are ideal for snorkeling. They alternate with secluded coves or, as at Stintino and Alghero, with mile-long stretches of sandy beaches. The very nicest beaches are often the private oases of hotels. Even hotels in the moderate price range may face their own uncrowded beaches.

This driving tour circling the entire island begins at Sardinia's prettiest town, Alghero, which has its own airport at nearby Fertilia and is less than an hour's drive from Porto Torres, served by ferry boats from Genoa and Livorno. From Alghero, the route goes to Sassari, then to tiny medieval Castelsardo. It dips inland through cork oak groves by Tempio Pausania, to rejoin the coast beginning at Palau, which faces the isle of La Maddalena with its necklace of islets. Proceeding to the swanky Costa Smeralda and its neighboring Golfo Aranci, it heads south down the coast past Olbia, another air and sea port, then turns inland to Nuoro in the mountainous Sardinian heartland. Here begins the Barbagia, a wooded highland of dramatic scenery, prehistoric monuments on a heath, cork oaks, and shepherds' villages where folk costumes are still everyday wear for many. Safe but winding, the slow roads twist through the interesting Gennargentu mountain hamlets before straightening out onto a plain where hundreds of tiny native ponies run free. Next comes Barumini, the island's largest ancient Nuraghesi castle-fortress. The Barumini road links with SS131, leading to the capital, Cagliari, founded on the Costa del Sud by Phoenicians and surrounded by breathtaking beaches and dramatic capes and bays. The northern return drive is on SS131 to Oristano, studded with Phoenician ruins, and then on SS292 back to Alghero, taking in ancient Tharros and Bosa.

In resort areas in high season — mid-July to mid-August — reservations are a must. During this time expect to pay $300 or more for a double room with bath in the hotels listed as very expensive (and those on the Costa Smeralda can go up to $975 a day!); between $125 and $300 in hotels listed as expensive; $75 to $125 in those listed as moderate; and under $75 in those listed as inexpensive. This includes continental breakfast, service charge, and taxes. A meal for two, including service and taxes and sometimes wine, will cost $100 or more in an expensive restaurant, $60 to $100 in a moderate one, and under $50, inexpensive.

ALGHERO: This town of 37,000 on the "Coral Riviera" is coastal Sardinia at its loveliest. The great ramparts by the sea were begun by the Genoese and completed by the Spanish. Distrusting the hostile locals, the Spanish grandees shipped them inland and replaced them with Cataláns. The Spanish flavor of the town is still so pronounced that it is sometimes called *Barcelonetta* (little Barcelona). Streets are *calles,* signs designate monuments in Spanish and Italian, and many of the natives, especially the older ones, still speak Catalán. The Cloister of San Francesco, where Charles V of Spain once stayed, hosts a summer music festival. The remaining coral beds lie extremely deep in the ocean, so much of the coral seen in Alghero's goldsmith shops today is imported — although still imaginatively set in jewelry. Alghero has its own long sandy beach, but excellent and less crowded stretches are at Porto Conte and around Capo Caccia, with its dramatic cliffs and eerie grotto, about 11 miles (18 km) away. The grotto can be visited by tour boat from the port at Alghero.

CHECKING IN: ***Baia di Conte*** – For a beach vacation, this 307-room hotel complex on a bay 8 miles (13 km) northwest of Alghero offers 2 pools, horseback riding, tennis, disco dancing, and other amenities. Open mid-April to October. Località Sant'Impenia, Porto Conte (phone: 79-952003). Expensive.

Villa Las Tronas – On a promontory overlooking the sea, with its own fine restaurant, this was once a summer residence of the Italian royal family. Only 31 rooms — book ahead. Number 31 is tops. Hotel open year-round; restaurant closed Wednesdays and mid-September to mid-May. 1 Lungomare Valencia, Alghero (phone: 79-975390). Expensive.

Carlos V – A swimming pool, tennis court, and a garden are among the features of this functional, modern hotel on the waterfront. 24 Lungomare Valencia, Alghero (phone: 79-080501). Expensive to moderate.

Calabona – On the seashore road to Bosa on the outskirts of town, this hotel has 113 rooms, a restaurant, a pool, a gym, and a sauna. Open mid-April to October. Calabona (phone: 79-975728). Moderate.

EATING OUT: ***La Lepanto*** – A terrace on the ramparts helps make this Alghero's favorite dining spot, while the kitchens make it easily its best. The full seafood menu ranges from humble anchovies to prized local lobster, including lobster in spaghetti sauce and lobster, Catalán-style. Even the menu is in Catalán. Closed Mondays. Reservations advised. Major credit cards accepted. 135 Via Carlo Alberto, Alghero (phone: 79-979116). Expensive to moderate.

Il Pavone – Noted for seafood, spaghetti with rock lobster, and fine local torbato wine. Diners on the terrace can enjoy panoramic views. Closed Wednesdays (except in summer). Reservations advised. Major credit cards accepted. 3 Piazza Sulis, Alghero (phone: 79-979584). Expensive to moderate.

A Dieci Metri – Fish is a must — fish ravioli, seafood risotto, grilled fresh catch from local waters — in this popular (though noisy) former inn. Closed Wednesdays (except in summer) and January. Reservations advised. Major credit cards accepted. 43 Vicolo Adami, Alghero (phone: 79-979023). Moderate.

Excursion from Alghero – Neptune's Grotto, a cave at water's edge with deep caverns and two lakes within, can be reached either by excursion boat from Alghero (3 hours round trip) or by car. The advantage of driving is the beauty of the views en route to Capo Caccia (Hunter's Cape). The disadvantage is the 670-step climb down to the grotto and then back up. Wear a sun hat. Open 9 AM to noon and 3 to 5 PM; admission charge.

SASSARI: SS291 from Alghero ends up in Sardinia's second-largest city (with 120,000 inhabitants), founded during medieval times when invaders drove the populace inland from Porto Torres. The ritual evening promenade focuses on Piazza Cavallino.

The *Sanna Archaeological and Ethnographic Museum* (64 Via Roma; open daily from 9 AM to 1 PM; admission charge) contains rare Sardinian artifacts, including some from the Bronze Age Anghelu Ruju tombs near Alghero, plus costumes richly adorned with gold filigree, and a collection of Renaissance paintings. Craftwork is on sale in a hall in the Giardino Pubblico (Public Gardens) with a good selection of cork, inlaid wood objects, baskets, and ceramics.

EATING OUT: ***Al Senato*** – This wonderful hideaway in the central labyrinth of town serves fresh fish and is full of little surprises. Closed Sundays. Reservations advised. Major credit cards accepted. 2 Via Mundula, Sassari (phone: 79-231423). Expensive to moderate.

Tre Stelle – A roomy modern restaurant downtown, with fish soup, oven-baked fish marinated in vernaccia, and alghero and gallura wines. Closed Sundays and August 10–30. Reservations unnecessary. Major credit cards accepted. 6 Via Porcellana, Sassari (phone: 79-232431). Moderate to inexpensive.

Excursion from Sassari – The fishermen's cottages of the summer resort town of Stintino, facing the prison isle of Asinara, have a windswept look. The town is 30 miles (48 km) northwest of Sassari, on the tip of a long promontory, the Capo del Falcone, with a miles-long sand beach, the Spiaggia di Pelosa.

EATING OUT: ***Da Silvestrino*** – In the old part of town, this is a good place to sample seafood pasta and lobster soup. Closed Thursdays in winter. Reservations advised. Major credit cards accepted. 12 Via Sassari, Stintino (phone: 79-523007). Moderate.

En Route from Sassari – Take SS200 to the charming old fort town of Castelsardo on the sea. Its 16th-century cathedral has traces of the original Gothic church. Turn inland on SS134, then onto SS127, passing cork oak groves and ancient *nuraghi.* At Tempio Pausania, an old Roman town famed for its wine and whose *Carnevale* must be seen to be believed, swing north on SS133 toward Palau and the island of La Maddalena. From Castelsardo the distance is just under 85 miles (136 km).

EATING OUT: ***La Guardiola*** – Climb the winding road to the Old Town of Castelsardo to reach this attractive spot near the central piazza. The excellent seafood and risotto, and the huge portions of pasta (try the *farfalle impazzite* — pasta bowties smothered in a tomato-based pepper and cream sauce) are worth the trek. Avoid the Sunday lunchtime rush unless you enjoy other people's children. 4 Piazza del Bastione (phone: 79-470428). In summer, the restaurant turns into *La Guardiola Due* and moves up around the corner to a terrace with views. Reservations advised. No credit cards accepted. 2 Via Lamarmora, Castelsardo (phone: 79-470755). Both closed Mondays, except in summer. Both moderate.

LA MADDALENA: The isles of Maddalena and, beyond, Caprera, part of an archipelago that shelters a US nuclear submarine base, are reached by ferry from Palau, a 20-minute trip with sometimes a long wait at peak season. The young Napoleon suffered the first defeat of his military career here after islanders withstood a 3-day siege launched from Corsica. The *Museo Archeologico Navale* (Via Acquedotto; phone: 789-736423) has an interesting collection of findings from under the sea. It is open daily except Sundays from 8:30 AM to 1:30 PM. The island of Caprera, where Giuseppe Garibaldi is buried, is connected to La Maddalena by causeway. The museum in Garibaldi's home is open Tuesdays through Saturdays from 9 AM to 1:30 PM, Sundays from 9 AM to 12:30 PM; closed Mondays.

EATING OUT: ***La Grotta*** – Simple but delicious island fare: grilled fresh fish and spaghetti, with an occasional Neapolitan touch since its owner hails from Naples. Closed Sundays and in winter. Reservations necessary. Major credit cards accepted. 3 Via Principe di Napoli, La Maddalena (phone: 789-737228). Moderate.

Mangana – Typical Sardinian seafood dishes, a vast selection of island wines, and for dessert, an interesting version of *sebadas* with myrtle-flavored jelly. Closed Wednesdays and *Christmas* through January. Reservations advised. Major credit cards accepted. 2 Via Mazzini (phone: 789-738477). Moderate.

COSTA SMERALDA: Drive south from Palau on SS125 to the Emerald Coast, a stretch of yacht basins, adjacent shopping plazas and cafés, and secluded private homes and beach hotels. This grandiose, somewhat precious 33-mile resort development (whose sponsors include the Aga Khan) was built in the 1960s and is popular with both the golf and boating set; indeed the best show in town is at the Porto Cervo Marina, crammed buoy-to-buoy with million-dollar yachts. Before all that, nature lavished its best energies on the heavenly bays, overlooked by hills full of olive trees. As on all Sardinia, the brilliant light plays tricks with the water, making it appear dappled green and turquoise. The salt wind has carved giant boulders into eerie shapes. The Costa Smeralda's pink stucco heart is at Porto Cervo, a bayside town 45 minutes by car from both La Maddalena and Olbia. The café at its *piazzetta* is the place to rubberneck; off-season, the town is dead. The surrounding mall's boutiques sell the world's priciest labels. The 18-hole *Pevero Golf Club,* begun by the Aga Khan, is a 10-minute drive from Porto Cervo. The club has an excellent restaurant (closed in winter and early spring; phone: 789-96210).

CHECKING IN: Fuller information on the following development consortium-owned hotels is available by contacting Costa Smeralda Hotels (Porto Cervo 07020, Sardinia; phone: 789-94000; fax: 789-92060) or by writing to the individual hotels by name, adding Porto Cervo 07020, Sardinia. Most are opulent and ultra-expensive (up to $975 for a double room!), and many require guests to pay full board during high season. Rates drop about 35% in the off-season. (Also see *Beaches* in DIVERSIONS.)

Cala di Volpe – A Moorish-style cluster of white towers, whose 123 rooms are furnished with antique reproductions and Sardinian crafts. There is an Olympic-size saltwater pool and a boat that ferries guests to a very private beach. The elegant dining room serves a succulent array of foods. Open May to October (phone: 789-96083). Very expensive.

Cervo – Near the *piazzetta,* with garden, pool, 95 rooms, and shuttle boat to a private beach. Its restaurant overlooks the Old Harbor and the cozy piano bar is a favorite meeting place. *Cervo Tennis Club* and *Pevero Golf Club* are nearby. Open March to October (phone: 789-92003). Very expensive.

Pitrizza – Consisting of a handful of 4- to 6-room villas (for a total of 50 rooms), each with a terrace or garden overlooking the rock-hewn pool. There also is a private beach, a terrace, and a fine restaurant set on the beautiful Liscia di Vacca Bay. The clubhouse has a piano bar (phone: 789-91500). Very expensive.

Romazzino – Overlooking a bay dotted with islets, this large bougainvillea-festooned, Mediterranean-style hotel with 90 spacious rooms is perfect for the sporty crowd and families. Pluses include an outdoor pizza oven, boats for hire, tennis, windsurfing, and dancing. Special events are arranged for children (phone: 789-96020). Very expensive.

Le Ginestre – This relative newcomer has 76 rooms and 2 suites, all set in a cluster of buildings grouped around a swimming pool, with a view of the splendid Gulf of Pevero. Horseback riding is available as well as a tennis court. Open April through September (phone: 789-92030). Expensive.

Balocco – Not on the waterfront, but well situated on a hillside and a 10-minute walk from Porto Cervo. This nicely landscaped 26-room place is a good value for the money. Two swimming pools (one for small children). Open mid-April to mid-October (phone: 789-91555). Expensive to moderate.

EATING OUT: *Il Pescatore* – In the Old Port, just across the little wooden bridge from the *piazzetta.* Try seafood delicacies such as *spigola al finocchietto* (fish grilled with fennel), grilled prawns, or *spaghetti alla bottarga* (with mullet roe). For a fine view of the port, reserve a table beside the water. Open evenings May to October. Reservations necessary. Major credit cards accepted. Piazza Vecchio, Porto Cervo (phone: 789-92296). Expensive.

La Mola – Long considered one of the best restaurants in the area, it has successfully resisted the moneyed winds of change — everything is still good. The fish is excellent, and meat is roasted on the spit. Open from March to October. Reservations advised. Major credit cards accepted. Piccolo Pevero, Porto Cervo (phone: 789-92436). Expensive to moderate.

La Fattoria – Rustic, with a huge indoor fireplace and outdoor dining under an olive tree. Typical Sardinian foods are served, including grilled lamb and sausage. Open daily, except Mondays, from March to late October. Reservations advised in high season. Major credit cards accepted. Strada Principale, Porto Cervo (phone: 789-92214). Moderate.

Il Pomodoro – A chic *pizzeria-ristorante* just behind the *Cervo* hotel. Excellent antipasto and mouth-watering pizza in an attractive rustic setting indoors or outside under a grape arbor. Open year-round. Reservations advised in high season. Major credit cards accepted. Porto Cervo (phone: 789-92207). Moderate.

BAIA SARDINIA: The advantages of continuing to the westernmost point of this peninsula (only a few miles from Porto Cervo) are the expanse of beach and a host of tourist trappings (and traps) that wear a lower price tag than is usually associated with the area.

CHECKING IN/EATING OUT: *Club Hotel* – Practically a bargain compared with accommodations in Porto Cervo, this 83-room hotel offers the usual run of things (except for tennis courts) but boasts a restaurant (*Casablanca*) infinitely better than anything found down the road. Naturally, fish is the thing here, usually very imaginatively served. Closed from mid-October to mid-April. Baia Sardinia, Arzachena (phone: 789-99006). Moderate.

PORTO ROTONDO: Nine miles (14 km) from Porto Cervo, this yacht basin surrounded by sumptuous private summer houses is Sardinia's answer to fashionable American summer beach towns — and more exclusive than its neighbors.

CHECKING IN/EATING OUT: *Relais Sporting* – Another Aga Khan property, this deceptively simple retreat, which sprawls on a spit of land overlooking a magnificent bay 7 miles (11 km) from Olbia, caters to the international yachting set. All 28 rooms have sea views. The restaurant, noted for grilled fresh fish, fine wines, and a very special evening buffet, is the best around and is *the* place to be seen. Open mid-April through September. Reservations advised. Major credit cards accepted. Porto Rotondo (phone: 789-34005). Very expensive.

En Route from Porto Rotondo – The drive south toward Cagliari on SS125 (214 miles/342 km) via Olbia takes 5 hours without detours for sightseeing. But 35 miles (56 km) before Orosei, at the village of Posada, amidst orange groves, for those desiring to visit the Barbagia, is the Fava Castle. Here the road cuts inland on a nicely engineered highway, SS131, to Nuoro (just under 30 miles/48 km), the first lap on an excursion through the wild, mountainous heart of Sardinia. It was named by Roman soldiers, who dubbed it "the place of the barbarians."

CHECKING IN/EATING OUT: ***Gallura*** **–** Worth a stopover en route, at least for a meal, it is often sought after by Costa Smeralda villa owners who tire of the local fare. Food and service are first class, especially the huge list of starters. Try the risotto with artichokes (*carciofi),* or *spaghetti al sugo di granchi* (with crab sauce). Reservations are advised, as space is limited. Upstairs is a charming pensione of 20 rooms. Again, call in advance. Restaurant closed Mondays. No credit cards accepted. 145 Corso Umberto I, Olbia (phone: 789-24648). Moderate.

NUORO: Residents of this homey little town where Grazia Deledda was born, at the foot of rugged Monte Ortobene, consider themselves standard bearers of the real Sardinia, and so they are. What there is can be seen in the *Museum of Costumes and Popular Traditions* (56 Via Mereu; phone: 784-31426). Open daily, except Mondays and Thursdays, from 9 AM to 1 PM and 3 to 6 PM, Sundays from 9 AM to 1 PM; admission charge. Grazia Deledda's house (42 Via Deledda; phone: 784-34571) is open daily from 9 AM to 1 PM and 3 to 6 PM; admission charge. The *Museo Civico Speleo-Archeologico* (5 Via Leonardo da Vinci; phone: 784-33793) has a small collection of archaeological artifacts. Open Tuesdays and Thursdays from 9 AM to 1 PM and 3 to 6 PM, Wednesdays, Fridays, and Saturdays from 9 AM to 1 PM; admission charge. Every year on the last Sunday of August, thousands of islanders wearing traditional costumes walk in the famous historical procession to Mount Ortobene to celebrate the *Festa del Redentore* (Feast of the Redeemer).

CHECKING IN/EATING OUT: ***Fratelli Sacchi*** **–** This country inn 5 miles (8 km) east of Nuoro offers spotless, inexpensive rooms and a garden; its restaurant serves genuine Sardinian hill-country fare, such as *porceddu* (suckling pig) and trout *alla vernaccia.* Closed Mondays and from October 1 to May 31. Reservations unnecessary. Major credit cards accepted. Monte Ortobene, Nuoro (phone: 784-31200). Hotel, inexpensive; restaurant, moderate to inexpensive.

En Route from Nuoro – A good map and good weather are a must for this crossing of the Barbagia. From Nuoro, take SS389 south through the hamlet of Mamoiada to Sardinia's highest village, Fonni (3,250 ft), on Monte Spada. Mamoiada is famous for its bizarre, demonic *Mardi Gras* masks, known as *mamuthones,* that were worn during pre-Christian rites. They are still used today at *Mardi Gras* celebrations. From the road, you'll glimpse a large manmade lake, Lago Gusano, to the north. Depending on your mood, either continue on the main road, SS389D, or take the mountain road short cut to visit Désulo, a shepherd's village noted for its weavers, where men wear a distinctive wool jacket, the *orbace.* Pay careful attention to signs: Travelers skipping Désulo will turn right onto SS128 about 5 miles (8 km) after Tiana; those visiting Désulo will continue past the village and turn right on the main road to Tonara; after 1⅓ miles (2 km), turn left onto SS128. The next stop for either route is Sorgono, another typical craftwork village. From Sorgono drive through Laconi to tiny Nuralla, on a road traced during prehistoric times — count the roadside *nuraghi.* Turn right onto SS197 to cross the Campidano Plain through the Giara di Gesturi, the plateau where the tiny native ponies still range. They are not wild but are branded and belong to villagers.

EATING OUT: ***Su Gologone*** **–** This excellent restaurant on a river's edge (the Gologone) is worth a detour. The food is genuine mountain fare, and the proof is the locals' presence in full force. Pasta dishes are doused in wild game sauces. Closed December through March. No reservations. Major credit cards accepted. Località Su Gologone, Oliena, 8 miles (13 km) southeast of Nuoro (phone: 784-287512). Inexpensive.

BARUMINI: A haven for history buffs, Nuraghe Su Nuraxi is the largest of the *nuraghi* yet excavated. Its huge central tower, 3 stories high, dates from 1500 BC. Bronze Age excavations of a village are nearby. Open all day.

En Route from Barumini – The remaining 37 miles (59 km) to Cagliari are an easy drive on SS197 and, bearing left just after Sanluri, on the broader SS131.

CAGLIARI: Founded by the Phoenicians, the Sardinian capital (pop. 225,000) is the main port-of-entry for Sardinia by both sea and air. Its hilltop Old Quarter, Il Castello, around the medieval castle, offers a spectacular view of the Golfo degli Angeli (Gulf of the Angels) and the outlying salt marshes. The quarter itself is an architectural and historical patchwork of ruins, including a Roman amphitheater (in which operas are performed in August), Pisan watchtowers, and Spanish townhouses with wrought-iron balconies. An old Spanish fort, the Belvedere, is now a park. The Duomo, originally built in the 13th century, has become a mélange of styles, including a neo-Pisan façade, a fine Romanesque pulpit, a Gothic transept and apse, and a baroque crypt.

For good shopping, wander up Via Guiseppe Manno, a continuation of Corso Vittorio Emanuele, as it winds toward the Saint Remy Bastion and Piazza Costituzione. Here, among buildings reminiscent of Genoa or Palermo, pause for a rest at the turn-of-the-century *Caffè Genovese* (Piazza Costituzione; phone: 70-654843). It has excellent cakes and ice cream made on the premises, hordes of bottles and sporting prints on the walls. Closed Thursdays.

The antiquities collection at the *National Archaeological Museum* (Piazza Indipendenza; phone: 70-654237) includes a celebrated collection of hundreds of rare bronze miniatures showing Nuraghesi life 2,500 years ago and Phoenician, Greek, and Roman objects. The tiny shepherds wear cloaks and caps similar to those in use today. Open Tuesdays and Thursdays from 9 AM to 2 PM, Wednesdays, Fridays, and Saturdays from 9 AM to 2 PM, and 3:30 to 6:30 PM Sundays from 9 AM to 1 PM. At the nearby Piazza Arsenale, modern museum rooms have been tucked into the ancient fortress walls, the windows of which overlook the Poetto Beach and salt marshes.

Cagliari's beaches have calmer and warmer water than those in the north, making them a good choice for swimming and wind surfing in late spring and early fall, when northern Sardinian waters can be chilly. On the road hugging the coast toward Villa Simius are resort hotels suitable for family vacations.

CHECKING IN: ***Capo Boi*** – Luxurious and set on a heavenly bay, this 219-room property has a pool, tennis courts, and a fine beach. On Cape Carbonaro, about 45 minutes east of Cagliari, via the coastal road. Capo Boi, Villasimius (phone: 70-798125). Expensive.

Regina Margherita – Reopened in 1988, this grand old hotel is the only class establishment in town. Some of the 99 rooms have views of the port. 44 Viale Regina Margherita, Cagliari (phone: 70-670342). Expensive.

Mediterraneo – Its garden setting and a view of the bay make this 136-room comfortable hotel near the air terminal and train station a good choice. Its *Al Golfo* restaurant (closed Sunday evenings through Mondays) is popular with locals. 46 Lungomare Cristoforo Colombo, Cagliari (phone: 70-653971). Expensive to moderate.

Cormoran – The best beach in the vicinity is at this 86-room hotel, a 45-minute drive southeast of Cagliari, just past Capo Boi. Windsurfing, a swimming pool, tennis courts, good food, and a view of the romantic islet, Isola dei Cavoli, are all here. Foxi, Villasimius (phone: 70-791401). Moderate.

Panorama – A modern establishment, with 97 air conditioned rooms, a swimming pool, conference rooms, and a penthouse restaurant (closed Sunday evenings and

Mondays). Near the city's sports complex. 231 Viale Armando Diaz, Cagliari (phone: 70-307691). Moderate.

Italia – Modern and absolutely central, this hotel has 113 rooms and a coffee shop that remains open reasonably late. Favored by businesspeople, it is 5 minutes from the station and port. Closed August 2–23. 31 Via Sardegna, Cagliari (phone: 70-655772). Moderate to inexpensive.

EATING OUT: ***Dal Corsaro*** – A menu featuring spaghetti with rock lobster, crêpes stuffed with mussels, and other fine seafood dishes makes this a local and tourist favorite. It is also considered one of the best eating spots on the entire island. Try the pasta stuffed with onions and smothered with a sauce of local cheese. Closed Tuesdays. Reservations advised. Major credit cards accepted. 28 Viale Regina Margherita, Cagliari (phone: 70-664318). Expensive.

Dal Corsaro al Poetto – From June through September the management of *Dal Corsaro* also runs this open-air seaside restaurant. About 3½ miles (6 km) from downtown Cagliari, near the salt marshes where flamingos visit in the spring and autumn. Reservations advised. Major credit cards accepted. Viale Poetto, Marina Piccola, Poetto Beach (phone: 70-370295). Expensive.

Ottagono – Excellent seafood, pasta, and local specialties come in a never-ending flow from the minute you sit down. You do not order, only eat (usually far too much). Closed Tuesdays. Reservations advised. Major credit cards accepted. Viale Poetto, Poetto Beach (phone: 70-372879). Expensive.

St. Remy – A very atmospheric restaurant with the vaulted ceilings and exposed stone walls of a 15th-century building: It was originally a pharmacy run by a friar's order. *Seadas* (tiny fried fish) for appetizers and the *fagottini St. Remy* (cheese-stuffed veal) are special. Good Sardinian desserts and wines. Closed Saturday lunch, Sundays, and during the *Christmas* period. Reservations advised. Major credit cards accepted. 16 Via Torino, Cagliari (phone: 70-657377). Expensive.

Antica Hostaria – One of Cagliari's best-known picture dealers, Antonello Floris, is also an accomplished chef who runs this trattoria, which dates from 1852 and is considered one of the island's best. Try the *malloredus alla campidanese,* traditional local pasta mixed with a tasty vegetable-and-cheese sauce, and, in season, the delicious *fagiano* (pheasant). Round out the meal with one of the house's excellent desserts and the nectar-like mirto liqueur. Closed Sundays and in August. Reservations advised. Major credit cards accepted. 60 Via Cavour, a stone's throw from the port (phone: 70-665870). Expensive to moderate.

Excursion from Cagliari – Head due south on SS195 for 18 miles (28 km); bear left onto the side road to Nora, Sardinia's oldest city. Founded by Carthaginians and subsequently ruled by the Romans, ancient Nora is survived by its well-preserved amphitheater, baths, temples, and stunning mosaic floors. Consider combining this visit with a swim at an adjacent beach. The ruins are open daily, 9 AM to 8 PM. The admission charge includes museum entry.

EATING OUT: ***Sa Cardiga e su Schirone*** – Before heading back to Cagliari, stop here for the unbeatable *aragosta* (lobster), *gamberoni* (prawns), or *zuppa di pesce* (fish soup). The food remains good despite the effort put into turning over tables. There is a large selection of Sardinian wines, and a piano bar and terrace overlooking the beach. Closed Mondays and from late October to late November. Reservations advised. Major credit cards accepted. On the Pula road (SS195) at the Capoterra intersection (phone: 70-71652). Expensive to moderate.

En Route from Cagliari – Coastal road SS195 south circles the Sulcis Mountains, passing interesting ruins at Nora near the town of Pula, and then proceeding to the southernmost point of Sardinia — Capo Spartivento — where the road swings northwest toward the island of Sant'Antioco, connected by a causeway to the mainland. Just north of it is the island of San Pietro (accessible only by boat). Back on the mainland, the route wends its way past the splendid Costa del Sud, a series of small bays, pleasant new resort hotels, and through two mining towns — Carbonia and Iglesias. Noteworthy in the latter is the small *Museo Mineralogico* (45 Via Roma; open daily from 9 AM to noon), its 13th-century cathedral, and the Church of Nostro Signore di Valverde, and the 14th-century Castello Salvaterra. After Iglesias, the coastal road circles back inland through a flat plain to Decimomannu, where it rejoins the SS131 Oristano-Cagliari highway.

Alternatively, you can make the 55-mile (88-km) trip directly from Cagliari to Oristano on SS131. It is very fast, about an hour, unless detouring to make a side trip to visit the "painted" villages of San Sperate or Serramanna (exit south at Monastir, just northeast of Cagliari). In these villages the art of mural painting is practiced on many outside walls. Techniques and themes, as well as degree of talent, may vary considerably from wall to wall and town to town, but this homespun art form can be quite interesting, especially when it expresses passionate religious feelings and political protests. The rest of the drive runs through the Campidano plain. Serious equestrians might make a detour to Arborea, where there is a hotel-equitation complex, *Alabirdi,* that specializes in expert instruction. (See *Horsing Around, Italian Style* in DIVERSIONS.)

CHECKING IN/EATING OUT: ***Chia Laguna*** – Set on a white sand beach at the tip of Capo Spartivento and watched over by an ancient tower, this complex of low stone buildings with 87 rooms is southern Sardinia's answer to the overpriced, (and some say) overpraised Costa Smeralda. Sports activities include horseback riding on the beach, sailing on the hotel's 120-foot sloop, windsurfing, organized archaeological outings and hikes, golf at the nearby 18-hole *Is Molas* golf course, squash, and working out in the property's gym. Of course, mellowing out on the gorgeous beach is yet another alternative. The rest of the action is in the 4 restaurants, 5 cafés, and the disco. Child care is available. Open March to November. Chia, Domus de Maria (phone: 70-923-0143; fax: 70-023-0141). Expensive.

Is Molas Golf – With an interesting 18-hole golf course used for many tournaments, a fine beach, swimming pool, and tennis court, this comfortable 84-room property southwest of the Gulf of Cagliari, is a perfect vacation spot. Its good restaurant offers island specialties such as *malloreddus* (shell-shaped saffron pasta with tomato or meat sauce), spaghetti with *bottarga* (dried mullet roe), and *sebadas,* the honey-sweetened fried cheese turnover. Alfresco dining on a splendid terrace in summer. Km 37.4 of SS195, Santa Margherita, Pula (phone: 70-920-9447). Expensive to moderate.

Flamingo e MarePineta – Get away from it all at this 122-room hotel on a small peninsula. There are two areas — one is a traditional complex around a pool, the other a series of square buildings flanked by pine trees (ask for a room facing the beautiful beach). The hotel also is near the *Is Molas* golf course. Km 33.8 on SS195, Santa Margherita, Pula (phone: 70-920-8361; fax: 70-920-8359). Moderate.

ORISTANO: With a population of only 30,000, this is the smallest of Sardinian provincial capitals. Its peaceful and serene aura belies the fact that it is the largest farming center on the island and a thriving commercial and industrial center and port. It was founded during the Middle Ages by the refugees of ancient Tharros, who fled when the Saracens sacked and destroyed their city. Oristano gave birth to Sardinia's 14th-century Joan of Arc, Princess Eleonora d'Arborea. Defying Spain, she ruled over this cathedral town and drafted a law code which became the basis for the island's laws.

The town has a fine cathedral dating from the 13th century with an onion-dome tower that was added later, a Carmelite church nearby, and a statue dedicated to Eleonora in the square bearing her name. A small collection of archaeological artifacts is on display in the *Antiquarium Arborense* (14 Via Vittorio Emanuele; phone: 783-70422). Nearby is the Pisan Gothic Church of Santa Giusta. (Open daily, except Sundays, from 9 AM to noon and 4 to 6 PM.)

CHECKING IN: *Mistral* – A well-maintained modern hotel near the center, with 49 rooms and a reasonably attractive lounge and bar. Its restaurant turns out some of the best food in town, thanks to its detail- and service-oriented German management and to the chef, a Sardinian, tempted back from one of Berlin's top Italian dining spots. Via Martiri di Belfore, Oristano (phone: 783-212505). Moderate.

EATING OUT: *Il Faro* – An excellent seafood menu is found in this elegant restaurant near Oristano's central market; real cork on the walls, and free souvenir ceramic plates. Closed Sunday evenings, Mondays, and January 6–20. Reservations advised. Major credit cards accepted. 25 Via Bellini, Oristano (phone: 783-70002). Expensive.

***Da Giovanni* –** Near the lighthouse in the seaside resort of Marina di Torregrande, midway between Tharros and Oristano. Plain surroundings, but wonderful fish soup and excellent ravioli stuffed with lobster. Closed Mondays and during October. Reservations unnecessary. No credit cards accepted. 8 Via Colombo, Marina di Torregrande (phone: 783-22051). Moderate.

THARROS: A Phoenician port founded in 800 BC, its remains — plus later Roman temples — can be seen at water's edge partly submerged on the southern tip of the Sinis Peninsula, 12⅓ miles (20 km) from Oristano. Today's archaeologists consider Tharros one of Sardinia's most fascinating sites. After repeated barbarian invasions, Tharros was abandoned in 1070, and Maristanis (known today as Oristano) was founded. Also on the peninsula are a 15th-century Spanish tower and the remains of a Jewish temple. Nearby beaches are excellent.

En Route from Tharros or Oristano – Take the coastal road, SS292, through Bosa, with its medieval church and castle, then turn off for Capo Maràrgiù, and continue on to Alghero, a distance of about 70 winding miles (112 km). There are pleasant green valleys, picturesque towns, and smashing sea views along the way. The area is known for its woolens, lace, cheeses, figs, artichokes, and malvasia wine.

Campania and the Amalfi Coast

There can be just one reason why a precipitous, gnarled, inhospitable limestone peninsula, segregating the Gulf of Salerno from the Gulf of Naples, has become one of the most important holiday destinations in Europe, and why local hoteliers have undertaken such extraordinary engineering feats. As André Gide proclaimed in *The Immoralist,* the road from Sorrento to Ravello "is so beautiful that I had no desire . . . to see anything more beautiful on earth."

Long before travelers discovered the spectacular charms of the Neapolitan Riviera, Italians nicknamed it the "Divine Coast" — clear testimony to the grandeur of its scenery and the delight of its architecture, neither of which could ever be tarnished by the annual pilgrimages of holidaymakers.

Campania has two picturesque gulfs, or bays (the Bay of Naples and the Gulf of Salerno), enclosed by picturesque promontories, including the Sorrento Peninsula. It has a massive volcano (Vesuvius), as well as the more benign, forest-covered Latteri Mountains that slope into the Tyrrhenian Sea. There are 220 miles of coastline and several romantic islands (Capri, Ischia, and Procida). The natural endowments alone are sufficient reason to tour the region, but add to this plenitude one of the greatest concentrations of archaeological excavations in the world — Pompeii, Herculaneum, Paestum, and more — unforgettable towns of mythological and historical importance such as Sorrento, Positano, Amalfi, and Ravello (not to mention Naples), and, finally, the people themselves, who have cheered the world with their music and cuisine, and the region becomes a journey of compelling interest.

The Greeks came to Campania as early as the 11th century BC, setting up colonies in Cumae and Pithecusae (present-day Ischia). The arts flourished, towns such as Paestum, with its impressive temples, were built, and olive trees and vineyards were introduced to local agriculture. The Romans gained the upper hand by 326 BC and forced the Greeks into an alliance that eventually became entirely to the Roman advantage. Under the emperors, Campania became a playground for the wealthy, who built villas along the coast for the same reason people do today. They liked the temperate climate, the dramatic scenery, and the proximity to the sea.

A period of Byzantine influence followed the disintegration of the Roman Empire, but the Byzantines always had to contend with rebellious tribes, outside invaders (most prominently the Lombards, who established themselves in the interior but also managed to take Salerno), and city-states with independent ambitions (Naples achieved autonomy by 763, and in 786 Amalfi did the same). By the following century, there were incursions of Saracen mercenaries. Often invited in by warring duchies, these Muslims from Sicily brought with them an Arabic influence that is still seen in Campanian architecture. During the 11th century the Normans came. Thereafter, the south of Italy, including Campania, was dominated by a succession of French, Austrian, and Spanish kings and cross-fertilized with cultural influences from the north of Europe to the Mediterranean, from Vienna to Madrid, until it was annexed to the kingdom of Italy in 1860.

Today, Campania attracts visitors from even more diverse origins. But they arrive as tourists, not conquerors, and they come to admire the region's artistic heritage, not to carry it away. Dominated by the cities of Naples and Salerno, the area consists primarily of three sections, each with a splendor of its own. There's the Bay of Naples in the north, a volcanic area with steaming natural hot springs first used by the ancient Romans as thermal spas. Vesuvius, still active, stands poised midway along the bay between Naples and Sorrento. The eruptions that buried Pompeii and Herculaneum in AD 79 have not occurred with force since 1944, but its twin peaks still periodically emit trails of smoke.

The three romantic islands off the coast of Naples are natural extensions of the tormented geophysical constitution of the mainland and they, too, attract the maximum number of visitors, especially the international resort of Capri, and Ischia, celebrated for its hot baths. Ischia and Procida share the same genes as the Phlegraean Fields — the crater-filled, sulfurous area west of Naples that the ancients believed was the gateway to the underworld.

The third section of Campania that draws visitors is the Sorrento Peninsula, a narrow finger of mountainous limestone forming the southern rim of the Bay of Naples. Sorrento is poised on the edge of steep cliffs 165 feet above the sea on the peninsula's northern edge, connected by the Amalfi Drive to the southern resorts of Positano, Amalfi, Ravello, and Salerno.

The scenery of the Neapolitan Riviera is natural in the wildest sense of the word. The rocky Sorrento Peninsula has been eroded into all sorts of shapes, and is still eroding (discreet netting has been installed to catch occasional falling stones). But don't imagine that all this rock equals a landscape of stark severity. All but the sheerest surfaces are blanketed with vegetation — vineyards, pinewoods, citrus and olive groves, almond trees, camellias, oleanders, and magenta bougainvillea. The buildings along the coast, painted white or every shade of confetti, seem to cascade down the mountainsides, settling around a church or cathedral and then drifting on into the sea.

Famous resorts, geographical splendors, and historical sites do not exhaust the attractions of Campania. Although not as well known and not as chic as the Amalfi Coast, the Cilento Coast farther south — from Agropoli to Santa Maria di Castellabate, then south to Palinuro and Sapri — is less expensive, less crowded, and utterly charming. There are coves and beaches waiting to be discovered and transformed into this decade's Positano.

Pompeii, Herculaneum, and Paestum are internationally renowned, but there are also important archaeological sites at Velia, Santa Maria Capua Vetere, and Benevento. While Ischia may be more celebrated for its hot baths, Campania has over 6,000 thermal springs, and there are spas at Agnano, Montesano, Telese, and Castellammare di Stabia, where different waters are available according to the complaint (one reputedly good for the liver, another for anemia, and so on).

Campania is not one of Italy's famed gastronomic regions, but the combination of rich soil and the sea provides access to a wide range of first-rate produce. The best meals are to be had not in the top hotels but in smaller trattorie, where the owner tends to be the chef and the rest of the family serves as the supporting cast. Look for *casalinga* or *casareccia* signs — guarantees of home cooking and local ingredients. This is where you'll find *torta caprese,* for example — a crumbly dessert made of almonds and chocolate, best topped with a lava-like flow of Neapolitan ice cream.

The Gulf waters produce excellent crustaceans, including *vongole* (clams), which are used with pasta and rice and in seafood soups and salads. Mozzarella cheese, produced from the buffalo that graze in the region, is a staple. It is served *in carrozza* (batter-fried), as a topping on pizza, and with eggplant, which is sometimes used in a pasta sauce. But first and foremost, it is served in *insalata caprese,* a salad of sliced mozzarella and tomatoes garnished with basil and olive oil. Squid and shrimp are delicious whether cooked in batter, served in seafood salads, or used in pasta sauces. The local meat and fish are best grilled over charcoal and lightly seasoned with lemon and salt. Pizza was born here and is widely available, usually baked in wood-burning ovens. For dessert, there are typical pastries, nougats, and traditional *Christmas* and *Easter* sweets such as *zeppole, taralli,* and *struffoli.*

The best-known wines come from the slopes of Mount Vesuvius: white or red lacryma Christi (Tears of Christ). The vineyards at Pozzuoli and Cumae yield falerno. Good wines also include greco di tufo, taurasi, ravello, and barbera di Castel San Lorenzo. The well-known and potent Strega (witch) liqueur is made in Benevento. At several shops you can invest in bottles of amaretto and fiery grappa.

The Amalfi Drive — the road between Sorrento and Vietri sul Mare — is both beautiful and perilous. Hacked out of solid rock, it offers superb views, although not for the driver, who will be busy negotiating the narrow, twisting, heavily trafficked route. Parking at the resorts is also difficult, especially during the July–August peak when most Italians take their holidays, and doubly so on weekends, when the numbers are swelled by day-trippers from Naples. Travel time from Sorrento to Amalfi is 1½ to 2 hours, depending on traffic. One solution is to move from town to town between 2 and 4 PM, when most Italians are either eating or taking a siesta.

The tourist season at the major resorts of Campania runs from *Easter* until the end of October. The coast enjoys hot, dry Mediterranean summers and mild winters. June and September are ideal, owing to the absence of high-summer crowds and scorching heat. July and August, despite occasional short but heavy storms, are by far the most popular months. Make reservations well in advance for high season, and be prepared for long waits and heavy traffic even on the A3 autostrada, where bottlenecks tend to form at tollbooths and exits.

Off-season visits offer splendid solitude, rare silence, and unobstructed views, but not a Caribbean or Florida climate. Capri and the Amalfi Coast can be quite cold in winter, even on sunny days. There are occasional snows on Vesuvius, but it is rarely cold enough to justify the January parade of Italians in new fur coats. The average temperature in January and February is 50F — hardly swimming weather. And at night and on rainy days — lamentably frequent in winter — it is much colder. Be aware, too, that due to legal restrictions, many hotels and restaurants are inadequately heated. For a winter visit, come prepared with warm clothing and an umbrella, and don't bother bringing a bathing suit.

During high season, classical plays are performed in the ruins in Pompeii. There are Wagner concerts in the gardens of the Villa Rufolo in Ravello, film festivals in Sorrento and Salerno, and carnivals in Minori and Maiori on the Amalfi Coast. In fact, every feast day and holiday in the region, particularly *Easter,* is likely to take on the trappings of a carnival.

Our tour heads south from Naples and swings under the shadow of Vesuvius along the curve of the bay through Herculaneum and Pompeii. At Castellammare it turns almost directly west to Sorrento, then crosses the tip of the Sorrento Peninsula to the Amalfi Coast and follows the hairpin coast road eastward through Positano, Amalfi, Ravello, Maiori, and Vietri sul Mare. At Salerno, it heads south again to Paestum. Although not much more than 90 miles (145 km) in length, the route passes through towns, historical sites, and resorts that are often crowded and are connected by narrow, tortuous roads. The region is rich in attractions that cannot be sampled in a short time, so set aside a minimum of 3 days, preferably much longer.

It's also possible to travel this route without a car. Naples and Sorrento are well linked by the *Circumvesuviana,* a local train line that makes the journey in a little over an hour. Stops include Herculaneum and Pompeii. From Sorrento, all the other towns on the Amalfi Coast are reached easily by bus or boat.

There is every category of accommodation, from grand hotels that were turn-of-the-century favorites (such as the *Excelsior Vittoria* in Sorrento) to small, family-run *pensioni.* The area has a long tradition of friendly service and client allegiance. Another alternative is to rent a villa, palazzo, or apartment. For the Positano/Amalfi area, contact *Villas International, Ltd.* (605 Market St., Suite 510, San Francisco, CA 94105; phone: 800-221-2260; fax: 415-727-0246). Another rental company with listings for Positano, as well as Sorrento, is *Home Tours International* (1170 Broadway, Suite 614, New York, NY 10001; phone: 212-689-0851; in the US, 800-367-4668; fax: 212-689-0679).

Since the few beaches tend to be crowded, a good hotel pool is a meaningful asset. The less agile will want to avoid places with steep steps or arduous climbs (several of Sorrento's best hotels have their own elevators to the beach). Air conditioning is rare, and roadside hotels without surrounding gardens can be noisy. Sea views are vital, balconies an added bonus. Expect to pay extra for poolside lounges even in the smart hotels (around $3 a day).

In our accommodations listings, expensive means $100 and up for a double room, although there are super-luxurious hotels, such as the celebrated *San Pietro* and *Sirenuse* in Positano, where rooms can run a very expensive $200 a night for two, even off-season; moderate means $50 to $100 for a double; and inexpensive means under $50. In the restaurant listings, a full dinner (not just pasta and salad) for two will come to more than $50 in the expensive category (how much more depends on how much seafood is ordered); a moderate meal for two will cost $25 to $50; and an inexpensive one, $20 or less. These prices include service and house wine, but not expensive bottled vintages, aperitifs, or after-dinner drinks. Note that at the height of the season it is not uncommon for hotels at seaside resorts to require that a minimum of breakfast and one other meal per day be taken in house.

NAPLES: For a detailed report on the city, its sights, hotels, and restaurants, see *Naples,* THE CITIES.

En Route from Naples – Turning your back on the frenetic, chaotic charm of Naples, take the autostrada (A3) south toward Salerno (avoid the cluttered and confusing coast road). A3 has only four lanes and narrows to almost country-road proportions from time to time. Apartment balconies hang over the road, and travel can be tediously slow during rush hours. Get off at the Ercolano exit, about 4½ miles (7 km) from Naples.

HERCULANEUM: Although only about a quarter the size of Pompeii, Herculaneum (Ercolano in Italian) is an eminently important archaeological site; in fact, many visitors find it more interesting than Pompeii. Both cities were destroyed by the same volcanic eruption of Mount Vesuvius on August 24, AD 79, but while Pompeii was smothered by live cinders and ash, Herculaneum was inundated by something akin to a massive mud slide (technically, a pyroclastic flow of superheated gases and rock debris), in some places over 60 feet deep. The "mud" hardened, making excavation difficult. (The earliest diggers, in 1709, more interested in plunder than in history, simply burrowed tunnels and hauled out the loot.) But the volcanic blanket also preserved the houses, many of which were partly constructed of wood. Unlike Pompeii, where the wood went up in flames, the beams, staircases, doors, window frames, and even some furnishings of Herculaneum's houses are intact, and they give a far better idea of what daily life was like in that era than do the more fragmentary ruins in Pompeii. Furthermore, Herculaneum has a wider range of structures and building styles, from the elaborate villas of the patrician classes that stood on the edge of town with clear sea views (the bay is farther away now), to shops, multilevel apartment buildings, municipal baths, and a *palestra* (sports arena). Sadly, Herculaneum was sacked by local thieves 2 years ago, who carted off many dozens of important finds (valued at $250 million) from the site's museum.

Many books have been written about Herculaneum, and scholars have spent years digging — some, quite literally — to gain a better understanding of the place, so it is foolish to claim that it can be seen in a few hours. But for those on a tight schedule, or with only a passing interest in antiquities, at least the high points can be touched. Don't miss the Terme (Baths), built during the reign of Augustus and notable for the degree of practical planning they display as well as for their excellent state of preservation. Also be sure to see the Casa dell'Atrio a Mosaico (House with the Mosaic Atrium), where the black and white mosaic floor is wavy from the weight of the mud; the Casa a Graticcio (Wooden Trellis House), the only extant example of an ancient type of cost-cutting construction; the Casa del Tramezzo di Legno (House with the Wooden Partition), where the partition in question is carbonized; the Casa Sannitica (House of the Samnites), with an atrium surrounded by Ionic columns; the Casa del Mosaico di Nettuno e Anfitrite (House with the Neptune and Amphitrite Mosaic), which, in addition to its beautiful blue mosaics, offers an excellent example of a commercial establishment; and the Casa del Bicentenario (House of the Bicentenary), at first a patrician villa and subsequently transformed into a multifamily dwelling — in a room upstairs is a small cross and altar, evidence that a Christian lived here and that the cross was already a symbol of Christianity in the 1st century. Another interesting house is the Casa dei Cervi (House of the Stags), with its red and black frescoes and its sculpture of stags attacked by dogs.

Note that only the most important buildings in Herculaneum are open all the time; others are locked, but a guard stationed in the vicinity will gladly open them if tipped (each guard is responsible for 10 or so houses). Alternatively, be alert for any small group forming in front of a doorway because it means it's about to open. Note also that one very important building in Herculaneum is never open to the public — or to anyone. This is the Villa dei Papiri (so called because of papyrus scrolls found there), a grandiose private house that was excavated in the mid-18th century and then sealed off when toxic gases made further work impossible. The famous bronze statues of water carriers (or dancers) in the *National Archaeological Museum* in Naples are part of the booty carried out of it, however, and the *J. Paul Getty Museum* in Malibu, California, is a reconstruction of it, based on plans made by Karl Weber, a Swiss engineer who participated in the 18th-century excavations. The Herculaneum site can be visited daily, except Mondays and holidays, from 9 AM until an hour before sunset; admission charge.

En Route from Herculaneum – The easiest way to inspect the cause of all the destruction in Pompeii, Sorrento, and Herculaneum up close is to park outside Ercolano station and hop on the bus. It makes the short trip up Vesuvius three or four times throughout the day, depositing its passengers 3,280 feet up the mountain. From there, visitors can walk the last stretch along a shingle path to the edge of the crater (at 4,189 feet). Comfortable walking shoes are advised, and note that there are no railings for small children. An English-speaking guide will be present at the top. Make sure to note the time of the last bus down the mountain. Off-season departures are earlier.

Vesuvius is a 10,000-year-old, brooding hulk that can be seen looming through the haze from almost anywhere in the vicinity of Naples. From a distance, it resembles an egg with its top lopped off. Its name derives from two words meaning "the unextinguished," and Vesuvius is indeed a live one, and one of only three active volcanos in continental Europe. The two others also are on Italian soil — Mount Etna, on the island of Sicily and Stromboli in the Lipari Islands. Vesuvius last erupted in 1944 and has given a few smoky belches and rumbles since then. All this adds a slight shiver of excitement — other shivers come from the cooler air at the summit. Vesuvius has been cultivated since 1500, and forests extend almost to the rim. In fact, the wealth of ancient Pompeii was largely attributable to the rich volcanic soil, full of chalk, phosphate, and potash. More detailed information on Mount Vesuvius is given in *Naples,* THE CITIES.

Return to A3 and continue south a short distance to the Pompeii exit. Along the road, there are huge black volcanic rock formations, umbrella pines, and orange and lemon groves on the terraced hillsides. It doesn't take a large leap of the imagination to realize why the ancient Romans, and before them the Greeks, built villas and resort towns along the bay. The land is fertile, the light golden, the sea a deep blue, and the terrain spectacular as it buckles and breaks up into mountains just beyond the coast. But today, much of this stretch of shoreline between Naples and Castellammare di Stabia is dreary — overrun with traffic and overbuilt with tacky apartment houses, gas stations, discount stores, and snack bars, among which an occasional august old villa may still stand like a sad relative fallen on hard times.

POMPEII: Like Herculaneum, Pompeii is an archaeological treasure trove, an immense one; entire lives have been spent studying it or uncovering it, yet one-third of the town still remains to be excavated. It is possible to touch the high spots in a single visit, though a few words of advice can be valuable. Be sure to pick up a map as you enter; even though the streets are signposted, it's easy to lose sight of your companions. In summer, especially on Sundays, tour buses and cars often stand idling from the A3 exit all the way to the parking lots around the ruins. So avoid visiting on Sundays and holidays, and try to arrive early on any day, between 9 and 10 AM, before the heaviest influx of sightseers. In addition, be prepared for the seedy modern town of Pompeii; it's not unusual for the immediate environs of the ruins — and sometimes even the site itself — to be swarming with hotel touts, dubious tour guides, and con men of all sorts. It's also wise to hold on to your camera and purse. While it's unlikely anyone will do more than importune you for a tip or try to hustle you off to his brother's shop, don't take chances. If you want a guide, hire one at the gate at the prescribed rate.

Before Vesuvius erupted, Pompeii was a thriving commercial and political center with 25,000 inhabitants. Originally a seaport — the eruption raised the land and left the ruined town far from the bay — it bustled with trade; witness the ruts ground into the cobblestone streets by passing chariots. On that fateful day in August, AD 79, Pliny the Younger watched the catastrophe from Cape Miseno, and in a letter known to generations of students laboring at their Latin lessons, he described the chaos, the rain of ashes and cinders, and the inhabitants' desperate attempt to escape the suffocating heat and fumes. Two thousand people perished, and the city was buried.

Although the excavation process began, at least in part, as soon as survivors returned to dig out their belongings, Pompeii is said to have been "rediscovered" in the 16th century by Domenico Fontana, an architect rebuilding roads. Systematic excavation didn't begin until the 18th century, and it still goes on, with the current emphasis less on carting artifacts off to museums than on restoring them on the spot. Be sure to see the Basilica, the largest and most important of Pompeii's public buildings, just off the Forum, the religious, civic, and business center of the city. Along the side and at the far end of the Forum are the Temple of Apollo (which has a copy of the bronze statue of the god found here and moved to the *National Archaeological Museum* in Naples) and the Temple of Giove, or Jove, with its triumphal arches and a view of Vesuvius in the background.

Walk out of the Forum along Via dell'Abbondanza to the Terme Stabiane (Stabian Baths), which are well preserved and contain a *palestra* (sports arena or gym), a swimming pool, and separate sections for men and women. Both the 5,000-seat Teatro Grande and the 1,000-seat Teatro Piccolo (which was covered) are not far from the baths. The Anfiteatro, the oldest Roman amphitheater in existence (ca. 80 BC), with a capacity of 12,000, is some distance away, next to the Grande Palestra, where athletes trained.

Of Pompeii's many interesting private houses, three stand out. The Casa del Menandro, named after a portrait of the Greek poet found there, is a huge villa highly decorated with paintings and mosaics. The Casa dei Vettii (House of the Vettii), which belonged to two rich merchants of the Vettio family, is a meticulously restored, sumptuously decorated villa with fine frescoes in the Fourth, or late, Pompeiian style, characterized by mythological and architectural scenes drawn in dizzying perspective. The Villa dei Misteri (Villa of the Mysteries) might be called an ancient suburban house, since it's actually outside the ruins (but visitable with the same admission ticket). Thought to have belonged to a woman initiate of the Dionysian cult, it contains a famous fresco depicting the initiation of young brides into the cult, painted on a background of Pompeiian red. The fresco (or cycle of frescoes) covers the walls of an entire room, the largest painting to have survived from antiquity.

The Pompeii site is open daily, except Mondays, from 9 AM to an hour before sunset; admission charge. The 1980 earthquake that devastated vast parts of the interior of Campania did some damage here, and some excavations are still closed. For a bite to eat or a sip while visiting the ruins, stop in at *Internazionale* (Via del Foro, Pompeii

Scavi; phone: 81-861-0777) near the Forum. The tourist office (4-6 Via Roma; phone: 81-863-1525) has information on the area.

CHECKING IN: ***Villa Laura*** – Most of the 27 rooms have balconies in this hotel that is located on an unusually serene street. Open year-round. 13 Via delle Stalle, Pompeii (phone: 81-863-1024). Moderate.

Villa dei Misteri – This convenient 41-room motel right near the train station is endowed with ample parking. Much favored by academics and archaeologists, it has a nice garden and a swimming pool for a cool dip after a day baking in the hot ruins. Open year-round. Villa dei Misteri, Pompeii Scavi (phone: 81-861-3593). Inexpensive.

EATING OUT: ***Principe*** – A surprisingly good restaurant for an area filled with truck stop–type places and tourist traps. The cooking is sophisticated (reflected in the prices) and the staff pleasant. Try the *frutta di mare.* Closed Mondays and the first 2 weeks in August. Reservations unnecessary. Visa accepted. Piazza Longo, Pompeii (phone: 81-863-3342). Expensive to moderate.

A'Reccia – Fresh fish is the main feature here. Closed Mondays. Reservations unnecessary. No credit cards accepted. 5 Piazza Garibaldi, Pompeii (phone: 81-863-3260). Moderate.

Zi Caterina – In the center of town, this place is noted for its lavish antipasto, excellent fresh seafood, and delicious ice cream. Closed Tuesdays. Reservations advised. No credit cards accepted. 20 Via Roma, Pompeii (phone: 81-863-1263). Moderate.

En Route from Pompeii – Returning to A3, drive to the Castellammare di Stabia exit and proceed slowly — there's little choice, given the chaotic traffic and potholed street — through the cluttered and rather ugly if colorful center of town. Park and *lock* the car, then take a cable car up to Monte San Faito, where the air is fresh and cool and the views spectacular. (Alternatively, exit from A3 at Castellammare and shortly after turn left at the "T" junction, following blue signs for Gragnano, Agerola, and Amalfi to an expressway. At its end, make a U-turn and follow signs for Sorrento, bearing left. This route can be much faster and easier than going through the center of Castellammare.) Afterward, take a more scenic road, SS145, that swerves along the northern coast of the Penisola Sorrentina (Sorrento Peninsula) which holds the southern part of the Bay of Naples in its embrace. Suddenly, a traveler has the sensation of flying, of swooping birdlike along the sheer cliffs that drop to the sea. The road winds lazily through villages and lively towns such as Vico Equense (where pizza is sold by the yard — or by the meter, in this case), Seiano (among the olive groves), and Punta di Scutolo, and then enters Sorrento. All along the way, signs point down to beaches — cheerful conglomerations of tanned bodies and green and orange sun umbrellas — and at every turn in the road there are marvelous views of Naples and Vesuvius.

SORRENTO: This small city of pastel houses, brilliant flowers, and sea-scented air has been the subject of song, story, and legend throughout the centuries. According to Greek mythology, as filtered through the Romans, Surrentum (now Sorrento) was home to the Sirens who sang out to seamen and tricked them into shipwreck against the stony shores. Ulysses was said to have outsmarted the Sirens by plugging his crew's ears with wax and having himself tied to the mast to resist their seductions. The Sirens, the legend goes on to say, were so humbled by their failure that they turned into stones — the famous Galli rocks that poke their heads out of the sea just off the coast at Positano. Most present-day travelers can whistle a bar or two of "Torna a Surriento" ("Come Back to Sorrento"), and quite a few find the town seductive enough to take the words to heart.

The town's cliff-top location, overlooking the Bay of Naples, is idyllic, and the buildings of the old town are as Italian as anything for which you could hope, in peeling pinks and peach, on streets lined with palms and orange trees. The main square is the pretty, bustling Piazza Tasso, named after Sorrento's most famous son, Torquato Tasso, the 16th-century author of *Jerusalem Delivered,* an epic poem that is one of the classics of Italian literature; his statue lurks among the palms. The square is built over a 150-foot ravine, at the bottom of which are the ruins of the old water mill (pity the poor ladies of Sorrento who used to have to make their way down there and climb back out with all their water). Aware of the importance of tourism, Sorrento is not only free of most petty theft but is also impeccably clean, its streets hosed down and its garbage bins emptied every night.

The cool, marbled interior of the Church of San Francesco is particularly inviting on a hot day; and out in its 13th-century cloisters, with their distinctive Moorish arches, classical concerts are held on summer evenings. The *Museo di Correale* (48 Via Correale, Sorrento; phone: 81-878-1846) contains some rare editions of Tasso's work, as well as a small archaeological collection and fine examples of 17th- and 18th-century furniture, mostly Neapolitan (open weekdays except Tuesdays from 9 AM to 12:30 PM and 5 to 7 PM, Sundays from 9 AM to 12:30 PM); admission charge.

The beaches at this resort are barely there — narrow, dark-gray volcanic strips reached either by hotel elevator or by steep, zigzag staircases. Sea bathing is mostly from a number of privately owned wooden jetties (which charge around $1.50 and up for admission, plus extra charges for a cabin, a deck chair or lounge, and a beach umbrella). Marina Grande, the town's main public beach, is hopelessly crowded, but the locale is more importantly a serious fishing village, ideal for observing local color. The largest public beach is at Meta, one of the town's four boroughs, a mile or so east along the Corso Italia. At the ruins of the Villa di Pollio in a park on the southwest edge of town, there is a wonderful swimming hole and idyllic places to picnic.

Sorrento's shopping, however, is the best on the coast. The most interesting shops are in the Old Town's narrow flagstone streets, leading off from the pedestrians-only Via San Cesareo. Best buys include gloves (hard to contemplate in the heat), cameos of Madonnas and goddesses, embroidered blouses, *tarsia* (inlaid wood marquetry), and Capodimonte ceramics in season. Most shops stay open until at least 10 PM. After that, stop in at *Fauno Notte* (1 Piazza Tasso; phone: 81-878-1021), a nightclub/disco featuring folkloric "Tarantella" evenings with music, costumes, and dancing. *Davide* (39 Via P.R. Giuliani; phone: 81-878-1337) may serve the best ice cream in the world. That's a rather sweeping statement, but sample some of the 50 flavors and then judge for yourself. There's Indian fig, amaretto, taurasi wine — even some in spaghetti shapes.

The tourist office (AAST, 35 Via Luigi de Maio; phone: 81-878-1115) can provide further information about the town and its environs. They publish an excellent monthly magazine, *Surrentum,* in English and Italian that is available for a nominal charge. Open daily from 8:30 AM to 2:30 PM and 4:30 to 7:30 PM. Take a sightseeing trip around town in a *carrozza* (about $60 for a 2-hour grand tour); the horse-drawn carts are lined up under the statue of Torquato Tasso in the piazza. Sorrento is also a popular starting point for ferry and hydrofoil excursions to the islands of Capri and Ischia and tours of the Amalfi Coast. Information is available from kiosks around Marina Piccola.

CHECKING IN: *Ambasciatori* – Just off the central square, this modern, 103-room hotel has a garden and a terrace that overlooks Vesuvius, swimming pool, and facilities for the handicapped. 18 Via Califano, Sorrento (phone: 81-80066). Expensive.

Excelsior Vittoria – In 19th-century Belle Epoque fashion, this 125-room hotel is full of potted palms and ferns, gilded ceilings, marble staircases, mosaic floors, and opulent chandeliers. It's surrounded by manicured gardens and terraces with splendid views of Vesuvius, and it has a pool, as well as direct access to the sea via elevators. The best suite is the one in which Caruso stayed just before he died.

Good service; restaurant; open all year. 34 Piazza Torquato Tasso, Sorrento (phone: 81-878-1900 or 81-807-1044; in the US, 800-448-8355). Expensive.

Imperial Tramontano – Surrounded by one of the most luxurious gardens in the heart of town, this hotel is a converted villa with a long history, and many of its 119 rooms overlook the bay and a beach and some have garden terraces and balconies. The public rooms are warm and welcoming with Italian and English antiques. There is a swimming pool and a restaurant. Closed January and February. 1 Via Vittorio Veneto, Sorrento (phone: 81-878-1940). Expensive.

Parco dei Principi – Built around an 18th-century villa that belonged to Prince Leopold of Sicily, this large establishment (173 rooms with balconies) has both a swimming pool and an elevator to a private beach. The hotel is set amidst terraced parks, with different forms of flora — from domesticated trees to jumbled jungle vines to tropical flowers. Motorboating and water skiing can be arranged, and many special events, concerts, and receptions take place here. There also are facilities for meetings and conferences. The restaurant is one of the best in town. The hotel and restaurant are closed mid-November through *Easter.* 1 Via Rota, Sorrento (phone: 81-878-4644). Expensive.

Royal – A rose-colored building somewhat lacking in historical ambience, as it was largely refurbished after the 1980 earthquake. Its grand swimming pool, private beach, 140 bedrooms, and peaceful gardens still attract a large number of pre-quake customers. Owned by Tonino Maniello, one of three brothers whose hotel/restaurant tradition in Sorrento goes back 180 years. Closed November through February. 42 Via Correale, Sorrento (phone: 81-878-1920; fax: 81-722345). Expensive.

President – Set high on a bluff outside Sorrento amid a pine grove overlooking the bay, this 82-room hotel has a swimming pool, gardens, and restaurant. Closed November through March. Via Nastro Verde, Colle Parise, Sorrento (phone: 81-878-2262). Expensive to moderate.

La Minerva – Somewhat out of the way, but worth considering because of its lovely location on the sea. With only 50 rooms, this family-style pensione has charm and a good restaurant. Closed in winter. 30 Via Capo, Sorrento (phone: 81-878-1011). Moderate.

Bellevue Syrene and Villa Pompeana – Originally an 18th-century villa, and wonderfully positioned over the gulf and at the top of Sorrento's most beautiful road, it offers peace, charm, and some delightful terraces as well. The recently renovated 59-room hotel is filled with antiques; outside are gardens and towering cypresses. An elevator takes swimmers down to the water. Closed November through March. 5 Piazza della Vittoria, Sorrento (phone: 81-878-1024; in the US, 800-366-1510). Moderate to inexpensive.

Loreley et Londres – Clean and unpretentious, with an impressive position and a view fully as good as those at much more expensive places nearby. There are about 2 dozen rooms and an excellent restaurant. Try for a room overlooking the sea, especially since the busy road behind the hotel can turn rooms facing the rear into noisy, smelly cells at rush hour. Half board is mandatory in season. Closed November through March. 2 Via Califano, Sorrento (phone: 81-878-1508). Inexpensive.

La Tonnarella – On the outskirts of town near the train station, this 16-room hotel sits on a cliff jutting out among fragrant gardens. There are gorgeous views of the sea and an elevator to take guests to the beach. Its restaurant is noteworthy, which makes half board here a real pleasure (and a bargain!). Closed October through February. 31 Via del Capo, Sorrento (phone: 81-878-1153). Inexpensive.

EATING OUT: ***Don Alfonso*** – Alfonso Iaccarino and his wife, Livia Adario, own this Michelin-starred restaurant in the hills 4 miles (6 km) above Sorrento. It's the best in the area, probably in the whole of southern Italy, and some rate it very high on the list nationally. In addition to the traditional menu, gastronomic and à la carte selections can be made, all served with family-heirloom-style glasses, plates, and tureens. Excellent wines (including champagne from Ischia); fresh vegetables grown organically in the garden; and turkey, chicken, and pheasant, too. Closed Sunday evenings and Mondays, except in high season; early January through February. Reservations necessary. No credit cards accepted. Piazza Sant'Agata, Sui Due Golfi (phone: 81-878-8026). Expensive.

Kursaal – Atmosphere plus the local fare — seafood and pizza — combine to earn a top reputation for this dining spot in the heart of town. Alfresco dining is a summer option. Closed Mondays. Reservations unnecessary. No credit cards accepted. 7 Via Fuorimura, a block up from Piazza Tasso, Sorrento (phone: 81-878-1216). Expensive.

La Favorita O'Parrucchiano – On the busiest street in town is an excellent restaurant offering authentic Campanian cooking, much of it made with fresh local cheeses, wine, oil, and vegetables produced by the owners, the Maniello family. The gnocchi are especially recommended, as is the *gamberoni alla griglia* (large prawns, grilled and served whole). The terrace garden is delightful in warm weather. Closed Wednesdays in winter and spring. Reservations advised. No credit cards accepted. 71-73 Corso Italia, Sorrento (phone: 81-878-1321). Expensive to moderate.

Giardinello – This is the place to sample Sorrento's famous potato gnocchi with spicy tomato sauce and cheese, as well as small pizza straight from the oven and smothered with mushrooms and prosciutto. Wash it all down with an excellent local wine. Open daily from June through September; closed Thursdays the rest of the year. Reservations unnecessary. No credit cards accepted. 7 Via Accademia, Sorrento (phone: 81-878-4616). Inexpensive.

Sant'Anna – In the fishing village of Marina Grande, this friendly neighborhood eatery is where fishermen rub elbows with the local well-to-do as they eat *casareccia pasta e fagioli* and fish straight from the sea. Tables are set outside in summer. Closed Mondays. Reservations unnecessary. No credit cards accepted. 62 Via Marina Grande, Marina Grande, Sorrento (phone: 81-878-1489). Inexpensive.

Taverna dell'800 – More than a pub, less than a restaurant, it's run by Tony "the Walking Smile," who gets postcards from fans all over the world. Just the place for a *salsiccia con broccoli, insalata caprese,* parmesan cheese with pasta, and a beer. The evening menu is classier, and the cannelloni and lasagna are homemade. One of the few air conditioned eateries in town. Reservations unnecessary. No credit cards accepted. 29 Via dell'Accademia, Sorrento (phone: 81-878-5970). Inexpensive.

En Route from Sorrento – A narrow, twisting road leads around the entire peninsula to Positano. It's worth driving if you have time, since it passes through delightful, cool hilltop villages such as Francescello and Sant'Agata, and en route you'll pass tiny trattorie where locals eat on shady, dappled terraces looking down the peninsula. But it is far less nerve-racking to turn back on SS145 toward Naples, drive a few miles to Meta, Sorrento's easternmost borough, and then take SS163, which cuts south for 15 minutes or so across mountainous terrain to the Costa Amalfitana (Amalfi Coast) on the other side of the peninsula. From there, SS163 continues on its sinuous course all the way to Salerno. This route, known as the Amalfi Drive, is scarcely a superhighway. In fact, it can be hair-raising and treacherous, especially when Italian trucks, buses, and cars jockey for position, even on the sharpest turns. But much as the drive may tax nerves and patience, it's a memorable, not-to-be-missed experience. If one picture is worth a thousand words, then one glimpse of the Amalfi Coast must be worth a thousand pictures. Literature, art, and photographs all fail to convey the full measure of its magic — it has to be seen firsthand.

The crumbling Lattari Mountains come plunging down to the Mediterranean, and whitewashed houses cling to the cliffs like barnacles. Most buildings show the full extent of the Saracen influence on the architecture of the area. There are church domes covered with gleaming majolica tiles and barrel-vaulted ceilings to keep houses cool during the sun-dazzled summers. There is also a string of towers left along the coast by the Saracens, some of them now renovated and transformed into hotels, bars, and private homes. In many places the mountains have been terraced and planted with olive trees and citrus groves, carefully protected against hail by tent-like canopies of loose-woven mesh. At the foot of the mountains, the sea has worked at the limestone for centuries, creating caves and grottoes and an occasional miniature beach.

POSITANO: John Steinbeck, like many other artistic people, was transported by Positano and wrote that it "bites deep. It is a dream place that isn't quite real when you are there and becomes beckoningly real after you have gone." It may be that particular quality that marks this spot as the place where the Sirens lived — on just three rocks offshore. As the steep hills drop almost vertically to the sea, the houses of Positano appear to hang like a canvas of cubistic shapes in a broad spectrum of earth tones and pastels, the green and gold tiled cupola of Santa Maria Assunta — the Chiesa Madre — presiding over the point where the hills flatten out to the main beach, Spiaggia Grande. Tiny despite its name, it has military rows of beach lounges and, behind it, a handful of restaurants. There's a small, gray public beach next door that's a cross between pebbles and sand. Only one road passes through town; the rest of the streets run downhill in a series of switchbacks that reach a dead end a few hundred yards from the shore. Parking is almost impossible in town; if you're lucky, you'll find a private yard converted into a parking lot, otherwise use the coast road. After that, the going is by foot, so the streets are blessedly free of traffic.

Unlike Sorrento and Amalfi, Positano is almost exclusively a holiday town. Although one of the country's most important mercantile cities during the Middle Ages, its prestige dwindled with the coming of steamships (it has no harbor, only a beach). Many people left, and today there are twice as many people from Positano living in New York as in their hometown. For decades, however, the peacefulness and picturesqueness of Positano have attracted artists, especially painters, many of whom came for a visit and stayed indefinitely. More recently, roughly since the arrival of director Franco Zeffirelli (who owns a villa here), it has attracted more and more celebrities and movie stars, now rivaling Capri. For 6 months of the year, life focuses on the beach and the half-dozen restaurants behind it. Boutiques abound — the colorful cottons and silks for which the town is famous flap in the wind outside little boutiques. When travelers weary of swimming, shopping, or simply killing time at a restaurant or café, there is also tennis. The town court is cleverly tucked away atop a large garage, framed by cacti, cliffs, and clouds. If you need help or further information, the Positano Tourist Office (AAST) is at 2 Via del Saracino (phone: 89-875067). Open mornings only.

CHECKING IN: ***San Pietro*** **–** Located 1 mile (1.6 km) east of town, on the road toward Amalfi, there is nothing so crass as a sign to identify it, only a 15th-century chapel. The hotel itself is strewn down the side of the cliff, with the reception area, restaurant, guestrooms, tennis court, swimming pool, and beach all on different levels, reached by an elevator which travels *through* the cliff. The 55 rooms, actually more nearly suites, are furnished with antiques, each in a distinctive style, and each faces the Bay of Salerno. Handpainted doors and balconies to enjoy the astonishing views add to the pleasure of staying here. Bougainvillea has overgrown much of the exterior, and it has also sent branches inside some of the rooms, so that they resemble arbors. The excellent restaurant

See p. 496 Albergo San Pietro

offers well-cooked regional specialties, as well as international fare. An authentic gem. Closed January to mid-March. Reservations necessary in all seasons. Major credit cards accepted. 2 Via Laurito, Località San Pietro, Positano (phone: 89-875455). Very expensive.

Le Sirenuse – With its Pompeiian red exterior, John Steinbeck's onetime retreat stands out even amid the splendors of Positano. Once a private villa, it was turned into a classic hotel by the Sersale family, who still runs it and has, over the years, added modern rooms (more than 60 total — many with Jacuzzis), a heated swimming pool, and three terraces on which to dine overlooking the beach and the yellow and green tiled dome of the church. Magnificent antiques and tasteful paintings fill both the guestrooms and public areas. Open year-round. Major credit cards accepted. 30 Via Colombo, Positano (phone: 89-875066; in the US, 800-223-6800). Very expensive.

Covo dei Saraceni – Right on the beach, this popular, 60-room hotel also has an excellent restaurant. Open *Easter* to October. Via Marina, Positano (phone: 89-875059; in the US, 800-366-1510). Expensive.

Palazzo Murat – The 18th-century palace of Gioacchino Murat (a king of Naples and Napoleon's brother-in-law) has been tastefully restored with some period furniture and wood-beamed ceilings. The best of the 30 or so rooms are those in the L-shaped palazzo, looking out onto the courtyard where guests can have breakfast surrounded by bougainvillea and lemon trees. There is also a modern wing. No restaurant (although there is a breakfast area), but conveniently situated halfway down the main shopping street. Closed November through March. 23 Via dei Mulini, Positano (phone: 89-875177; in the US, 800-223-9832). Expensive.

Poseidon – This very attractive, family-run establishment with 50 rooms makes you feel at home immediately; the endless views lend an air of being on a desert island. Rooms with a view cost more and usually include a terrace. There also is a restaurant with an excellent kitchen. Closed November to late April. 148 Via Pasitea, Positano (phone: 89-875213). Expensive to moderate.

Casa Albertina – A small (20-room), family-run hotel with personal service, this is a minor jewel, with gilt mirrors and bronze lamps, dramatic sea views, and rooms done in soothing shades of mauve and blue. Open year-round; restaurant. 3 Via San Giovanni, Positano (phone: 89-875143). Moderate to inexpensive.

Villa Maria Luisa – Here are 23 peaceful rooms with terraces and great views of Fornillo Beach here. Half board required in July and August. Closed November through March. 40 Via Fornillo, Positano (phone: 89-875023). Inexpensive.

EATING OUT: *O Caporale* – A favorite of locals and visitors alike, this restaurant turns out some excellent pasta and seafood dishes, including *La Caporalesa,* pasta cooked *al forno* with eggplant and capers, all eaten outdoors overlooking the beach. Closed October to *Easter.* Reservations unnecessary. No credit cards accepted. Via Marina, near the tourist office, Positano (phone: 89-875374). Expensive to moderate.

Buca di Bacco – Just off the beach, this is a favorite of the beach crowd. It rightly claims that it has "the largest and most comfortable terrace." Tempting antipasti, a fine seafood salad, and eggplant pasta are among its other claims to fame. There's also a small hotel, with 8 rooms housed in an old restored palace on the level above the restaurant. Closed from mid-October through March. Reservations unnecessary. Visa accepted. Via Marina, Positano (phone: 89-875699; hotel reservations in the US, 800-366-1510). Moderate.

La Cambusa – It, too, is set just beyond the beach and it, too, has a verandah with a lovely view. It serves excellent fish soup, *spaghetti alle vongole* (with clam sauce), and risotto with squid. Try washing down a seafood meal with a local white wine, greco di tufo and topping it with a rich chocolate dessert. Open daily year-round.

Reservations unnecessary. No credit cards accepted. Closed mid-January through mid-March. Piazza Amerigo Vespucci, Positano (phone: 89-875432). Moderate.

Chez Black – One of Positano's most popular, this beautiful wood and brass restaurant on the water's edge attracts a seemingly endless stream of trendy, bronzed locals and habitués. The seafood is especially good (pick your lobster right from the tank). Try the pizza from the circular oven, too. Closed January and February. Reservations unnecessary. No credit cards accepted. Via Marina, Positano (phone: 890-875036). Moderate.

La Chitarrina – To escape the crowds in Positano, take a trip up into the mountains behind the town to sample some really first class food at this delightful trattoria. The menu includes some mouth-watering pasta dishes, including *spaghetti alla Chitarrina* and *bucatini a modo mio.* Coming from Naples, take the left-hand turn 1 mile (1.6 km) before Positano, signposted Montepertuso, and continue along a climbing road for 3 miles (5 km) until you reach the village. Open daily, year-round. Reservations advised weekends and in August. No credit cards accepted. 75 Piazza Cappella, Montepertuso di Positano (phone: 89-875044). Moderate to inexpensive.

Da Vincenzo – Away from the congestion of the beach and the crush of tourists, this is a genial place on a quiet street where the clientele is likely to consist of more local people than vacationers. The vegetables are fresh and the zucchini with parmesan is very good. Closed November through March. Reservations unnecessary. No credit cards accepted. 172-178 Viale Pasitea, at the Casa Soriana curve (phone: 89-875128). Inexpensive.

En Route from Positano – The road narrows, winding and twisting toward Amalfi. A 10-mile (16-km) drive can easily take half an hour or even much longer — not simply because of the road, but because there are constant diversions. The village of Vettica Maggiore and the fishing community of Praiano are worth more than a quick look (oddly, Praiano has the best nightclub on the coast, *L'Africana,* housed in a seaside cave on Via Torre a Mare (phone: 89-874042). Then, between two tunnels, the cliffside corniche passes over the gorges of the Vallone di Furore (Valley of the Furies). A finger of the sea, no wider than a river, presses deep into the gorge, and a tiny fishing village hangs on to the rock like a swallow's nest. Farther on, there are signs for the Grotta di Smeraldo (Green Grotto), with emerald-colored waters, only a shade less famous than the Blue Grotto on Capri. It can be reached by a steep staircase, by elevator, or by boat from Positano or Amalfi.

AMALFI: Although not as preciously picturesque as Positano and Ravello, Amalfi was once much larger (almost 70,000 inhabitants during the Middle Ages; now it's down to fewer than 7,000) and much more important. During the 6th century, it developed considerable trade with the Byzantine Empire, transporting spices and wood to the West, and by the 9th century it was already a maritime republic, Italy's oldest, minting its own coins and ruled first by prefects and judges and then by a doge. In the 11th century, it was a mercantile and maritime power to rival the Big Three — Pisa, Genoa, and Venice. Amalfi's domain on land extended at one time from Sorrento to Salerno and back to the Lattari Mountains; its influence by sea was felt all along the southern Italian coasts, where it fought the Saracens, and as far as Jerusalem, where it built churches and hospitals for pilgrims of the First Crusade. In fact, the rules by which the republic governed all its maritime activity, the Tavole Amalfitane (Amalfi Tables), became the maritime code for all the Mediterranean and remained in force until 1570, long after Amalfi had lost its primacy. This happened rather quickly, in the 12th century, after it was captured by the Normans and sacked by the Pisans and suffered its share of natural disasters, including devastating floods. Still, something of the old splendor returns on the first Sunday of June once every 4 years, when it is Amalfi's turn to host the *Regatta of the Four Ancient Maritime Republics,* a race and a colorful parade of boats that rotates annually among Amalfi and the other three former rulers of the sea.

Amalfi is beautiful. Apart from its lovely seaside setting, the town's greatest pride is its Duomo, dedicated to St. Andrew (whose remains lie in the crypt — minus his head, which was removed by Pope Pius II). Dating from the 10th century, restored and expanded on subsequent occasions as recently as 1894, it sits at the top of a broad, tall staircase, somewhat as on a pedestal, its lively façade displaying stylistic influences that range from Moorish to Norman to early Gothic. A Romanesque bell tower next to it, begun in the 12th century, is crowned with green and yellow glazed tiles. The cathedral's bronze entrance doors were cast in Constantinople in 1066. There is also a beautiful cloister, the Chiostro del Paradiso, built in the 13th century and distinguished by lacy Arabic arches. A bronze statue of Flavio Gioia, son of Amalfi and inventor of the compass, stands in front of the *Pic Nic* café by Corso Roma. The town's arsenal dates from the 11th century and can be reached from an entrance just before the Lungomare meets Piazza Flavio Gioia. The Amalfi Tourist Office (AAST) is at 19 Corso Roma (phone: 89-871107).

Behind the coastal Corso Roma, a jumble of medieval streets and buildings leads from Via Capuano, which climbs one long, slow kilometer (.6 mile), changing its name at regular intervals, a 20-minute walk from Piazza Duomo at the bottom to the Valle dei Mulini (Valley of the Mills), where ancient, river-powered paper mills still produce top-quality parchment. The Amalfitani stroll nonchalantly from one end to the other, disappearing like rabbits every so often into narrow alleyways, while tourists puff and pant their way to the top.

CHECKING IN: ***Santa Caterina*** **–** Right at the water's edge, with an elevator that drops down to the swimming pool and the rock beach level. There are terraces and gardens for alfresco dining and lounging, and most of the 54 rooms have balconies. Half board required in high season, but it's no hardship as the food served here is among Amalfi's finest. Open year-round. Less expensive rooms are available in an annex. 9 Via Nazionale, Amalfi (phone: 89-871012). Expensive.

Luna Convento **–** Ibsen wrote *A Doll's House* here, Mussolini slept here, and Ingrid Bergman and Roberto Rossellini hid away from the world here. This 50-room landmark hotel was built around the 13th-century cloisters of a convent founded by St. Francis of Assisi (it still has its own church within its walls). It reposes on a panoramic rocky point where the Amalfi Drive turns in a great bend toward Atrani. A glorious dining room with high arched windows faces the sea and serves finely prepared dishes. The bar is housed in a tower originally built to guard against the Saracens. There is a swimming pool and a private "beach" of rock flattened out by concrete across the road where Amalfi's only discotheque, the *Torre Saracena,* can be found in an old tower; it is also run by the *Luna.* Open year-round. 19 Via Amendola, Amalfi (phone: 89-871002). Expensive to moderate.

Belvedere **–** This quiet place is about 3 miles (5 km) west of Amalfi in the tiny hamlet of Conca dei Marini. Cut into a cliff, its 36 rooms and terraces are well shielded from the sound of passing traffic. It has wonderful views, a swimming pool, and a restaurant. Full-board arrangements are encouraged. Closed from November through March. SS163, Conca dei Marini (phone: 89-831282). Moderate.

La Bussola **–** Named for Flavio's compass, this 43-room hotel stands at the western entrance to town, smart but plain. Although it has no distinctive characteristics, it does have a good restaurant and a private jetty for swimming. Choose a room at the front for vistas of colorful bobbing rowboats in the marina. Open year-round. Lungomare dei Cavalieri (phone: 89-87553). Moderate.

Cappuccini Convento – A 13th-century monastery, one of the landmarks of Amalfi, has been transformed into a splendid 41-room hotel. High on a cliff, it's reached by an elevator that burrows through rock to daylight; various terraces offer views of the coast, and the air is fragrant with the scent of citrus groves. Rooms are enlarged monks' cells (two cells for each room). The hotel has a private beach and a restaurant. Open year-round. 46 Via Annunziatella, Amalfi (phone: 89-871008). Moderate.

Excelsior Grand – About 3 miles (5 km) outside Amalfi, on a mountaintop on the way to Pogerola, this modern 85-room hotel has access to a private beach, a 100-foot swimming pool with cool spring water, a garden, restaurant, and smashing views. Unconventional in design, it takes excellent advantage of its setting, with many large windows and balconies and a glass-covered lobby. Closed from mid-October to mid-April. Via Pogerola, Amalfi (phone: 89-871344). Moderate.

Amalfi – A pleasant place, surrounded by fragrant citrus trees set in sunny terraced gardens. There are 36 rooms and breakfast is included in the rates. Open year-round. 3 Via dei Pastai, Amalfi (phone: 89-872440). Moderate to inexpensive.

Centrale – This small, clean 20-room hotel is less flashy than others in town but is nonetheless one of the best deals around. Open year-round. 1 Largo Piccolomini, Amalfi (phone: 89-871243). Inexpensive.

Marina Riviera – Traditional regional furnishings and beautiful views of the sea are distinguishing features in this hotel cut into the side of a hill going down to the water. Another plus is that those guestrooms located in the newer section are air conditioned. All 50 rooms have mini-bars, television sets, and telephones. Closed October through April. 9 Via Comite, Amalfi (phone: 89-871104). Inexpensive.

EATING OUT: ***Cantina del Nostromo da Zaccaria*** – Tucked into the edge of a cliff-rock, overlooking the sea, this restaurant serves some of the best fish and seafood in the entire area; it also offers delicious pasta, served on giant old painted plates. Closed Mondays. Reservations necessary in high season. Diners Club accepted. An easy walk from the center, at 9 Corso Colombo, Amalfi, on the stretch of the main road out of town toward Salerno and just before the tunnel that leads into Atrani (phone: 89-871807). Moderate.

Da Gemma – A short walk from the Duomo, Gemma Cavaliere's homey and tastefully decorated trattoria has a roof terrace for outdoor dining and offers authentic local cuisine — macaroni with chopped eggplant, linguine with shrimp, simply prepared meat dishes, fresh fish with lemon, and good local wines. She's more than 80 years old and still in the kitchen! Closed Thursdays, mid-January to mid-February. Reservations necessary. No credit cards accepted. Via Cavalieri di Malta, Amalfi (phone: 89-871345). Moderate.

Lo Smeraldino – Everything you'd expect from a seaside establishment overflowing with entire families enjoying a meal out (especially on Sundays). Late arrivals should be prepared to wait. Closed Wednesdays. Reservations advised. No credit cards accepted. Lungomare dei Cavalieri, Amalfi, just by the main jetty of the port (phone: 89-871070). Moderate.

La Taverna degli Apostoli – Formerly the town prison, this attractive, vaulted restaurant at the foot of the splendid Amalfi Cathedral is known for its good fish dishes and unusual starters. Try the *ditaloni clausura* (short pasta with a sauce of peppers, zucchini, eggplant, white wine, and fresh basil). Closed Wednesdays and February. Reservations unnecessary. No credit cards accepted. 6 Supportico Sant'Andrea, Amalfi (phone: 89-872991). Moderate.

Trattoria la Perla – Wonderful cannelloni and seafood are served at this charming and relaxed restaurant. Try the wines from Ravello. Open daily May through September; closed Tuesdays the rest of the year. Reservations unnecessary. Major credit cards accepted. 3 Salita Truglio, Amalfi (phone: 89-871440). Moderate.

En Route from Amalfi – Head east toward Atrani, which is virtually an extension of Amalfi.

ATRANI: One of the smallest towns in Italy, Atrani retains its predominantly Arabic layout (the coast enjoyed friendly relations with the Saracens). It is a delightful town in every respect, with a small, sandy beach, tiny, whitewashed alleys leading up from the square, and everywhere the fragrances of tomato, basil, and lemon. There are endless flights of steps, one going all the way up to Scala on the hills beyond (more than an hour's hard climbing) and another to Ravello (an hour or so). While in Scala — the oldest town on the Amalfi Coast — pay a visit to the Duomo and the ruins of St. Eustace's Basilica in the village of Dontone, below. The town that looks across a valley at Ravello was the birthplace of Fra' Gerardo Sasso, founder of the Knights of Malta, and is fascinating by night. The main street is ancient — as in Amalfi, it was once the river — and leads down to Piazza Umberto I. The main coast road runs above the houses that line the southern flank of the piazza. The fireworks and parades at *Christmas* are a real treat.

EATING OUT: ***Hosteria Masaniello*** – A snug and friendly eatery in a converted church tucked into a corner of the piazza, with a few precious outdoor seats. The house specialty is linguine with crab sauce. A dusty display of aging wines is racked above the bar. Closed Mondays. Reservations unnecessary. No credit cards accepted. Piazza Umberto I, Atrani (phone: 89-871930). Moderate.

Le Arcate – Tucked under the rock below the entrance to town from Amalfi, this trattoria/pizzeria serves all the usual fare of the sea in a beach setting — with tables casually placed without pomp or circumstance — often desired but difficult to find in Italy. Closed Mondays and November through April. Reservations unnecessary. No credit cards accepted. 4 Via di Benedetto Atrani, Atrani (phone: 89-871367). Moderate to inexpensive.

La Margherita – Worth the climb up to the town of Scala (also reachable by car, or by bus — probably a better idea — and then take the many steps back down to the Valley of the Mills), this neighborhood trattoria is Amalfi's favorite local hangout, and it's easy to see why. Closed Tuesdays. Reservations unnecessary. No credit cards accepted. 31 Via Torricelli, Scala (phone: 89-857106). Inexpensive.

En Route from Atrani – To reach Ravello, turn inland just after Atrani and uphill onto a well-marked road that swerves through the ominously named Valle del Dragone (Dragon Valley). After dozens of hairpin curves, the road rises to over 1,000 feet above the coast and reaches the main square of the most gloriously positioned town on the Gulf of Salerno. Scala, just over a mile away (2 km), is reached by the same road, before it forks at the final bend.

RAVELLO: The spectacular panorama visible from so many spots in this tiny town, its narrow stepped streets, and the profusion of flowers and greenery gracing every nook and cranny make it a place of incomparable beauty. Frequented by the talented and the famous, among them Richard Wagner, Jacqueline Kennedy Onassis, Princess Margaret, and William Styron — who set his novel, *Set This House on Fire,* here — Ravello is now the part-time home of Gore Vidal.

Leave the car in the public lot on the right as you approach the town, or park in the Piazza Vescovado, which is Ravello's main square and as far as the car can go — and walk over to the Duomo, dedicated to the patron saint of Ravello, San Pantaleone whose blood miraculously remains in a cracked container in the chapel. Begun in 1086 but finished in the 12th century, it has magnificent paneled bronze doors by Barisano da Trani (1179). Inside are two impressive pulpits. The older (1130), less intricate one features two large mosaics of Jonah being eaten and regurgitated by a dragon-like green whale (symbolizing the death and resurrection of Christ). The other, by Nicolò di Bartolomeo da Foggia (1272), rests on six columns supported on the backs of lions and is covered with mosaic medallions of fantastic animals and birds. It was paid for by Nicola Rufolo, a member of one of Ravello's rich merchant families, at a time when the town had more than 30,000 inhabitants (now it has fewer than 3,000) and was every bit as active in commerce as was Amalfi, to which it once belonged and later which it even rivaled.

Nearby, the Villa Rufolo, built by the same family, also in the 13th century, looks unprepossessing from the outside, but on closer inspection it is easy to understand why Wagner was inspired to use it as a model for the magic garden of Klingsor in *Parsifal.* Except for the Cortile Moresco (Moorish Courtyard), little remains to be visited of the actual villa. The gardens, however, merit superlatives. Terraced on several levels and planted with beds of bright marigolds, red salvia, pink and white phlox, and many other flowers, they are surrounded by umbrella pines and cypresses and open out to a stunning view of mountains and sea, and the town of Maiori below. The villa is open daily, with a lunchtime closing; there is an admission charge.

It's a 10-minute hike to Ravello's second most famous site, Villa Cimbrone, whose gardens are far superior. Built in 1904 by Lord Grimthorpe, an Englishman searching for peace of mind, it has a lovely cloister where, at the entrance, marble faces on the far wall represent the seven deadly sins. A cypress-shaded path leads through the magnificent gardens to the Belvedere, a ledge that seems to lean out over the Gulf of Salerno. It almost does because it's set at the very point of the spur of mountain that holds Ravello. On a clear day, you can see as far as Paestum, 30 miles (48 km) south. This villa, too, is open daily, with an admission charge.

A 2-hour *passeggiata* around the town takes you down vaulted passageways, up broad flights of steps, through cool cloisters, along sunny terraces, past colorful ceramics shops, and into cafés and restaurants that are hidden until the last minute.

During the last 10 days in June, the *Ravello Music Festival* brings together some of the top names in classical music. Concerts are held in the Villa Rufolo gardens and at the cathedral. For information, contact the Ravello Tourist Office at Piazza Arcivescovado (phone: 89-857096).

CHECKING IN: ***Marmorata*** – If all the rooms in Ravello are full, return to the coast road, SS163, and drive east a short distance to this delightful hotel. Overlooking the sea, it has a terrace restaurant, a swimming pool, and rocky access to the water. Small (40 rooms) and family-run, it's only been in business for several years. Reserve well in advance. Closed November through March. Località Marmorata, Ravello (phone: 89-877777). Expensive.

Palumbo – An exquisite small hotel in the higher reaches of town, this is *the* place to stay. Once a private villa, built on the ruins of the 12th-century Palazzo Confalone, it is stylish and charming, with beautiful majolica floors, antique furnishings, a lovely interior courtyard from the original building, an excellent restaurant (the owners are French), a grassy garden terrace and a rooftop dining terrace with gorgeous views, and several of its 8 rooms look out to the sea. The menu features specialties such as *fusilli al gorgonzola, spaghetti alla puttanesca,* tasty apple pie, and delectable dessert soufflés, all washed down by the hotel's own red and white episcopio wines are served in a 17th-century dining room. Open year-round. 28 Via San Giovanni del Toro, Ravello (phone: 89-857244; in the US, 800-366-1510). Expensive.

Caruso Belvedere – Just up the street from the *Palumbo* is another old building — the 11th-century Palazzo d'Afflitto — converted into a delightful hotel with charm, character, and beautiful views. Some of the 26 rooms face the garden, some face out to mountains and sea. This hotel has a good restaurant, famed for its cannelloni, its *crespini* (a kind of cheese and ham crêpe), and its delicious, light lemon chocolate soufflé, all of which go well with the house wine, Gran Caruso. Open year-round. Restaurant closed Tuesdays in winter. 52 Via San Giovanni del Toro, Ravello (phone: 89-857111; in the US, 800-366-1510). Expensive to moderate.

Giordano – Among the peaceful trees between the Villa Rufolo and the Villa Cimbrone, this 16-room hotel shares facilities with the *Villa Maria* (see *Eating Out* below) — a swimming pool (heated in winter), solarium, and music room. There is a path leading down to the nearby beach. Open year-round. 2 Via Santa Chiara, Ravello (phone: 89-857170). Moderate.

Rufolo – This 29-room hotel, in which D.H. Lawrence made his home in 1926, is on the way to Villa Cimbrone. All rooms face a marvelous view toward Villa Rufolo and the mountains in the direction of Maiori. There is a swimming pool and a restaurant. Open year-round. 1 Via San Francesco, Ravello (phone: 89-857133; in the US, 800-366-1510). Moderate.

Parsifal – A tasteful, 20-room hostelry, incorporating parts of a 13th-century Augustinian monastery. Some rooms have private baths. There's a cloister, a charming garden with a reflecting pool, and a seductive view of the coast. In warm weather, meals are served on the trellised, flower-scented terrace. Closed October through March. Half board is a good value for the money. 5 Via d'Anna, Ravello (phone 89-857144). Inexpensive.

EATING OUT: ***Villa Barbaro*** – This restored, cliff's-edge villa is owned by the *Palumbo,* so the food and service are topnotch. Dining in the garden in the light of the dying sun in summer is an experience. Typical dishes include ravioli filled with eggplant and filet of sole in a cream of zucchini sauce. Closed from mid-October to Easter, and Mondays in spring. Reservations advised. No credit cards accepted. About 1½ miles (2 km) up from Atrani, on the road to Ravello. Via S. Castiglione, Km 2, Ravello (phone: 89-872973). Expensive.

Villa Maria – On the way to Villa Cimbrone, this delightful find offers very good food at modest prices and has exceptional views. Try the *crespellini* (crêpes filled with vegetables and cheese), and any of the pasta dishes. Most have an original twist. There also are 7 rooms for rent. Closed November through March. Reservations unnecessary. No credit cards accepted. 2 Via Santa Chiara, Ravello (phone: 89-857255). Moderate.

Cumpà Cosimo – Home cooking, Ravello style — fresh fish and vegetables — and pizza. Specialties include minestrone and bean soup, served with the usual fine local wines. Closed Mondays, and from mid-November to late March. Reservations unnecessary. No credit cards accepted. 4 Via Roma, Ravello (phone: 89-857156). Moderate to inexpensive.

En Route from Ravello – The road toward Salerno swings down to sea level, running through two resorts, Minori and Maiori, only a few minutes apart. Being small, Minori has managed to retain a degree of personality and charm, at least in the quiet streets around the basilica. Maiori is the bolder, brasher, noisier sister, with a palm-lined boulevard running behind the largest beach on the coast, a half-mile of coarse gray sand practically obscured by beach umbrellas. The main escape from the tourism paraphernalia is up Via Chiunzi, which runs above what was once a river. Lined with delicatessens, bakeries, and produce shops, it offers a taste of authentic Italian street life. The Maiori Tourist Office is on Corso Regina (phone: 89-877452).

CHECKING IN: ***Reginna Palace*** – A boring structure, but the best hotel in town, with 120 rooms and its own stretch of beach across the road in addition to a pool and tennis court. Closed from October to *Easter.* 1 Via Cristoforo Colombo, Maiori (phone: 89-877183). Expensive to moderate.

Club due Torri – Slightly smaller than the *Reginna,* this 103-room hotel enjoys an excellent panorama of the sea. Closed from October to *Easter.* 8 Via Diego Taiani, Maiori (phone: 89-877699). Moderate to inexpensive.

Bristol **–** The nicest hostelry in Minori, its façade is a mass of flower-filled balconies. Each of its 60 rooms has a bath, telephone, and terrace. A *Roman Holiday* decor prevails, particularly in the restaurant, piano bar, and disco downstairs. There's a tennis court nearby. Closed from October to *Easter.* 70 Corso Vittorio Emanuele, Minori (phone: 89-877013). Inexpensive.

EATING OUT: ***Giardiniello*** **–** Dine in a garden filled with lemon trees and ivy, candlelit at night, and enjoy fish and steak dishes. Open daily in high season; closed Wednesdays the rest of the year. Reservations advised on weekends. No credit cards accepted. 15 Corso Vittorio Emanuele, Minori (phone: 89-877050). Expensive to moderate.

En Route from Maiori – The road begins to climb and grows narrow and winding again. The landscape still shows some of the damage caused by floods and landslides decades ago, as well as the damage of repeated brush fires in the recent past. Around Capo d'Orso, the countryside becomes wilder and less heavily populated, and the small, colorful fishing village of Cetara is the only real town until Vietri sul Mare, where the Amalfi Drive comes to an end. Vietri is famed for its ceramics, and around the main square of the upper city, shop after shop spills over with colorful plates, pots, jugs, and other pottery pieces for sale. Even shops selling other types of wares, such as the fish store and the greengrocer, have storefronts decorated with images of their products in ceramic tiles. A brief stretch of SS18 leads around a bend in the coastline from Vietri straight into Salerno.

SALERNO: Sorrento, Positano, Amalfi, and Ravello are tough acts to follow and, quite frankly, Salerno, a city of some 200,000, cannot really compare with the elegance and unearthly beauty of the Amalfi Coast. Yet is is not without interest and attractions. A seaport, slightly seedy and raffish — imagine a miniature Naples or Genoa — it's a city with a long and dramatic history. In the 12th and 13th centuries, its most prosperous period, much of its fame was due to its School of Medicine, the oldest in the Western world, possibly begun in the 9th century (and closed in the 19th century). Just as Paris was preeminent in science and Bologna in law, Salerno became so renowned in the field of medicine that it was called the Hippocratic city. On September 9, 1943, it became famous for a far different reason. The Allies launched their invasion of mainland Europe from here, landing south of the city after an aerial bombardment. They encountered heavy resistance from a German Panzer division, and when the Americans entered the town the next day, much of the waterfront was destroyed. Now the area has been rebuilt, and broad walkways curve along the waterfront, shaded by palms and scattered here and there with playgrounds, small amusement parks, and sidewalk cafés. In the evening, it seems the entire town takes a *passeggiata,* or walk, by the sea.

Uphill from the port and the modern part of town, the Old Quarter is well worth a visit, especially the Duomo di San Matteo (Cathedral of St. Matthew). Built in 845 and rebuilt from 1076 to 1085 by Robert Guiscard, it was heavily redone during the 18th century, but more recent restoration is uncovering its earlier forms. It has a Romanesque doorway, guarded by statues of lions, leading to a beautiful atrium surrounded by 28 columns that came from the Greek ruins down the coast at Paestum. A freestanding campanile (bell tower) looms above the atrium. Inside the church are two highly decorated pulpits and a paschal candlestick in a mixture of Saracen and Byzantine styles, full of mosaic ornamentation. A stroll through the Old Town along Via dei Mercanti passes elegant shops as well as the poorest street vendors. It's very lively and colorful, crowded and loud. The tourist information office (EPT, 1 Piazza

Ferrovia; phone: 89-231432), by the train station, can provide information on Salerno and its province, which includes most of the towns on the Amalfi Drive. Open Mondays through Fridays from 8:30 AM to 2 PM and 3 to 8 PM, Saturdays from 8:30 AM to 1 PM and 3 to 7 PM. In addition, there's another tourist office, AAST (8 Piazza Amendola; phone: 89-224744).

CHECKING IN: ***Lloyd's Baia*** – Outside Salerno on the drive in from the Amalfi Coast and Vietri, it stands on a bluff overlooking the sea, but it's surrounded by gardens and adequately screened off from traffic. The 120-room hotel is open year-round; there is a restaurant, 2 pools, and a private beach reachable by elevators. 2 Via Marinis, Vietri Sul Mare, heading toward Salerno on SS18 (phone: 89-210145). Expensive.

Jolly delle Palme – At the northern end of the waterfront, looking out over a playground and a public beach, this is a modern, comfortable member of the Jolly chain. Its aim is less charm than efficiency, and on its own terms the 105-room hotel is quite satisfactory. It's easy to find in the broader, better-marked streets of the modern town, yet it's a short walk from the Old Town. Open year-round; restaurant. 1 Lungomare Trieste, Salerno (phone: 89-225222; in the US, 800-221-2626). Expensive to moderate.

EATING OUT: ***Nave Ristorante al Concord*** – For a change of pace, try dining aboard a ship permanently moored on the waterfront in the center of Salerno. It features a variety of seafood salads, seafood pasta, and seafood main courses. It also makes pizza and has a reasonably priced fixed menu. Closed Mondays. Reservations unnecessary. No credit cards accepted. Piazza della Concordia, Salerno (phone: 89-220827). Expensive to moderate.

Alla Brace – Just across from the *Jolly,* this is both a restaurant and pizzeria. It specializes in meat and fresh fish cooked over a charcoal grill. The linguine dishes are also quite good, and try the gragnano wines. Closed Sundays and 2 weeks in late December. Reservations unnecessary. No credit cards accepted. 11 Lungomare Trieste, Salerno (phone: 89-225159). Moderate.

Nicola dei Principati – Considered Salerno's best dining spot, perhaps because the seafood is very fresh and the antipasti outstanding. Try the seafood risotto. Closed Mondays. Reservations unnecessary. No credit cards accepted. 201 Corso Garibaldi, Salerno (phone: 89-225435). Moderate.

Pizzeria del Vicolo della Neve – In the oldest part of town, this 500-year-old restaurant serves traditional dishes, seafood, the best pizza in Salerno, and local wines. Open daily except Wednesdays in the evening. No reservations. No credit cards accepted. 24 Vicolo della Neve, Salerno (phone: 89-225705). Inexpensive.

En Route from Salerno – It is possible to reach Paestum via the coast, but the first half of the drive is made terribly unattractive by construction sites and industrial zones. It's far better to take A3 out of Salerno, get off at the Battipaglia exit, and follow SS18 to Paestum.

PAESTUM: Called Poseidonia (City of Neptune) by the Greeks who colonized it at the end of the 7th century BC, the city was taken over by a local tribe, the Lucanians, about 400 BC. A hundred and fifty years later it fell to the Romans. But its low-lying position near the sea made it vulnerable to malaria; it gradually lost population and was sacked by the Saracens in AD 877. Crumbling and overgrown with vegetation, it wasn't rediscovered until the 18th century.

Arriving from the north, drive past the first two entrances, park, and enter through the Porta della Giustizia, near the *Nettuno* (see *Eating Out*). The grounds are beautiful and pastoral; cypresses, oleander, pines, and rose bushes flourish. Lizards scuttle over the ruins, the most prominent of which are three temples, all amazingly well preserved.

The Basilica, the oldest temple in Paestum, was constructed in the mid-6th century BC and dedicated to the goddess Hera (it was mislabeled by Christians in the 18th century). Facing east, it has 50 fairly bulbous Doric columns that taper dramatically at the top, creating the optical illusion that the temple pitches outward. The Greek builders' grasp of column shape and placement improved considerably by the time the temple next to it was built in the mid-5th century BC. Known as the Temple of Neptune (and also as the Temple of Poseidon — its Greek cognomen, but also misnamed because it, too, was dedicated to Hera), this is considered to be perfectly proportioned, one of the most beautiful Doric temples in Italy or Greece, as well as one of the best preserved (along with the Temple of Theseus in Athens and the Temple of Concord at Agrigento in Sicily). It is also the largest (200 feet by 80 feet) and best-preserved temple in Paestum. Both temples to Hera are at the southern end of the Via Sacra. At its northern end is the so-called Temple of Ceres, built in approximately 500 BC to honor the goddess Athena. The smallest of the temples of Paestum, it once had, in addition to its Doric exterior columns, Ionic interior columns (whose scant remains are in the museum). It still contains three medieval tombs dating from a time when the temple was used as a Christian church.

Paestum's museum is across the street from the archaeological zone. Among its most interesting exhibits are wall paintings from the Tomba del Tuffatore (Diver's Tomb), found about a half mile (1 km) away. Dating from the late 5th century BC, they are the only paintings of figures to have been found in Magna Graecia. Also noteworthy are the 34 metopes from the Temple of Hera Argiva at the mouth of the Sele River, 8 miles (13 km) north of Paestum. In addition, reproductions of various cornices in the museum show how richly colored the temples across the street once were. The museum in Paestum (phone: 828-811023) is open mornings only and closed Mondays, whereas the archaeological zone is open daily, except for a few holidays, from 9 AM to an hour before sunset (last tickets are sold 2 hours before sunset). A single admission ticket is good for the museum and the archaeological zone.

Besides its antiquities, Paestum is the closest Italy comes to buffalo country. There are so many grazing in the fields that the area has its own special mozzarella — *mozzarella di bufalo.* In July and August, there is an international music, dance, and theater festival. For information and tickets, contact the tourist information office (AAST) on Via Aquilia (phone: 828-811016).

CHECKING IN: ***Autostello Martini*** – A modern, clean, pleasant place, across from the Porta della Giustizia. There are 13 rooms in whitewashed cottages set in a beautiful garden, with a restaurant, a bar, and a dance floor in the main building. Closed November to April. Via Zona Archeologica, Paestum (phone: 828-811451). Inexpensive.

Strand Hotel Schuhmann – One of many hotels on the sea outside Paestum, it is set among pine trees and overlooking the Gulf of Salerno. It also is clean and up-to-date and often frequented by German tourists. There is a restaurant and 27 rooms, each with a balcony or terrace. Open year-round. Via Laura Mare, Paestum (phone: 828-851151). Inexpensive.

EATING OUT: ***Nettuno*** – Just beyond the Porta della Giustizia, it serves fine food in the rustic beamed dining room and on the trellis-shaded terrace right among the ruins. It offers roast meat when in season as well as fish and seafood, and a good selection of local wines, as well as more celebrated vintages from other parts of the country. Open for lunch only, except in high season; closed Mondays. Reservations unnecessary. No credit cards accepted. Zona Archeologica, Paestum (phone: 828-811028). Moderate to inexpensive.

Capri

Capri (pronounced *Kah*-pree, not Kah-*pree*) is a tiny jewel sparkling in the Bay of Naples. Although only 4 miles long and 2 miles wide, the island has almost as many identities as it does visitors. An estimated 2 million tourists make the short trip over from the mainland every year, and what they find usually depends on what they are looking for.

Wealthy jet-setters discover kindred spirits, not to mention a multitude of elegant shops, chic cafés and restaurants, plush hotels, and private villas. On summer evenings, Piazza Umberto I (nicknamed "the drawing room of the world") looks less like a public square than an exclusive cocktail party with guests attired in the colorful clothes they had made to measure earlier that day. Noel Coward rightly called the island "the most beautiful operetta stage in the world." Yet for those who want privacy and tranquillity, even solitude, the island has a surprising number of out-of-the-way corners, quiet wooded paths, and isolated gorges. One of its enduring charms is that its craggy, mountainous landscape leaves much of it inaccessible to cars and buses, and anyone willing to wander a bit can soon be on his or her own.

A map shows that the island is nothing more than a geographical continuation of the Sorrento Peninsula, a large chunk of limestone that rises from the deep — precipitously in most places — and comes to two points. The west side of the island culminates in Monte Solaro, altitude 1,923 feet, the highest spot on the island. The east side peaks in the somewhat lower (1,100 feet) Monte Tiberio — but here, nevertheless, is the island's highest cliff, from which, according to Suetonius, the emperor Tiberius threw his enemies into oblivion. In a saddle between the two mountains, but hardly at sea level, is Capri's main town, also named Capri. Its other town, Anacapri, is twice as high, on a plateau at the base of Monte Solaro. Visitors to the island disembark at Marina Grande, the port, and make the ascent to either town by road (or to Capri, directly by funicular). The ancients reached Anacapri by a staircase of 881 steps, built by the first Greek colonizers, restored by the Romans, and still in use as late as the 19th century.

Over the centuries, writers, artists, and eccentrics have found a welcome home here. Hedonists as different as arms dealer Baron Von Krupp and the acerbic Oscar Wilde were drawn as much by the island's live-and-let-live attitude as by the cerulean sea and subtropical vegetation. Strange as it is to imagine, Maxim Gorky settled on Capri from 1907 to 1913 and ran a school for revolutionaries that was attended by Lenin and Stalin. Graham Greene kept returning to write at his house in the Caprile district until his death.

The common denominator among all visitors to Capri seems to be the desire for an intensification of life. Whether it's Tiberius spending the last decade of his licentious rule building sumptuous villas or budget-conscious travelers just over from Naples or Sorrento for the afternoon (although Capri is one of the most expensive places in Italy), people come looking for the ultimate resort, a place where the sun, the sea, the fine wine and food, the seductiveness and sensuality of the entire Italian peninsula are compressed into one tiny spot. That the island's permanent population of 12,000 works so hard to welcome foreigners and expatriates is no doubt part of the reason visitors return again and again.

Despite the crowds, it's remarkably easy to escape. Pick up a map at the tourist office booth under the clock in Piazza Umberto I and follow the well-surfaced footpath that starts at the terrace of the chic *Punta Tragara* hotel, past the classic view of the Faraglioni rocks and along the steep cliffs. The path concludes with a tiny flight of heart-thumping steps to lunch on the terrace of the simple but excellent *Grotelle* restaurant. Afterward, wander along the spur path to see the island's famous natural arch.

TOURIST INFORMATION: The high-season months in Capri are June through September, in addition to the period around *Easter.* Given the island's popularity, it's best to visit in May and September, when the weather is warm and the island less crowded (although September is still officially high season as far as prices are concerned). Winter, especially around *Christmas,* can also be an enticing time if — and it's a large *if* — the sun is shining. Visitors in winter must expect to find more than half the hotels and restaurants closed, and despite the drastic differences in climate and attractions between summer and winter, the hotels that remain open year-round do not reduce their rates commensurately. A meager 10% off-season discount is the general rule. The Ente Provinciale per il Turismo in Naples (58 Piazza dei Martiri, Scala B; phone: 81-405311) can provide information about Capri. On the island, local tourist offices (AAST) are at the dock at Marina Grande (phone: 81-837-0634), in the town of Capri (Piazza Umberto I; phone: 81-837-0686), and in Anacapri (19/A Via G. Orlandi; phone: 81-837-1524). Off-season, the tourist office on Piazza Umberto I posts the names, addresses, and phone numbers of hotels and restaurants that remain open year-round.

Many free guides are available in English from travel agencies and hotels, which can also arrange short tours of the island. An excellent free guide is *Isola di Capri,* an illustrated index of hotels and *pensioni,* and *L'Isola,* which contains a long list of addresses and telephone numbers of hotels, restaurants, bars, and sports facilities, as well as schedules for buses, taxis, and boats to and from the mainland. The tourist office offers *Capri,* an excellent free brochure (in English) that details nine itineraries for walks on the island. It describes the main sights along each route.

TELEPHONE: The area code for the entire island of Capri is 81. When calling from within Italy, dial 081 before the local number.

FOOD AND WINE: While some Capri restaurants offer standard Italian fare and the ubiquitous international cuisine, the food on Capri generally shows the influence of nearby Naples, and the sea. There are pasta dishes with tomato or eggplant, or with olive or clam sauces. Pizza has a thicker crust than elsewhere in Italy and is topped with a puree of tomatoes and slabs of *mozzarella di bufalo.* The seafood is marvelous, especially the scampi, *gamberoni,* and calamari, which may be batter-fried or served in a salad or pasta sauce. An *insalata caprese* (sliced tomato and mozzarella, seasoned with fresh basil) makes an excellent start for any meal, and the traditional chocolate almond cake (*torta caprese*) is a tasty dessert.

Local wines are simple, of limited production, and make no extravagant claims to merit. But the *bianco* from Falanghina and Greco (greco del tufo) does go down well with seafood.

GETTING AROUND: Visitors are *not* allowed to bring cars to the island between June 1 and September 30, but it doesn't make sense to drive at any time of the year because the roads are narrow, crooked, and already crowded with local traffic. Places of interest are all within easy walking distance, or else they are well connected by bus, taxi, or funicular. Taxis and buses meet boats and hydrofoils arriving in Marina Grande and transport passengers to Piazza Martiri d'Ungheria in the town of Capri, a few steps from the main square, Piazza Umberto I, or to Piazza della Vittoria in Anacapri.

Bus – In general, buses leave Marina Grande every 15 minutes for Capri and Anacapri. Buses also leave Marina Piccola, the little port on the other side of the island, every 15 minutes (every 30 minutes in winter) for Capri and Anacapri. The trip from Capri to Anacapri is worth the ride just for the stunning views it affords as the bus winds up around hairpin bends. For additional bus information, call 837-0420.

Ferry – There is frequent ferryboat and hydrofoil (*aliscafo*) service between Capri and the mainland. From Naples (1¼-hour trip), *Caremar* provides a reasonable and dependable ferry service, which also operates out of Sorrento (45 minutes). Hydrofoil service, more expensive, is provided by both *Caremar* and *Aliscafi SNAV* (approximately 40 minutes from Naples). Other companies with service between Capri and the mainland are *Aliscafi Alilauro* (phone: 837-6995), *Aliscafi Medmar* (phone: 837-7577), *Giuffre & Lauro* (phone: 837-6171), and *Navigazione Libera del Golfo* (phone: 837-0819). In summer, ferries and hydrofoils for Capri are regularly scheduled from additional points such as Salerno, Amalfi, Positano, Pozzuoli, and Ischia. For times and prices, check at local tourist information offices. Generally, in winter, there is regularly scheduled service to Capri only from Naples and Sorrento, but it is possible to make private arrangements on small boats. *Caremar*'s phone number on Capri is 837-0700; *Aliscafi SNAV*'s number on Capri is 837-7577.

Funicular – The way to go from Marina Grande to Capri town (6:30 AM to 10 PM daily; after 10, a bus runs every half hour). A *seggiovia* (chair lift) makes the 12-minute ride from Anacapri to the top of Monte Solaro nonstop from 9:30 AM to sunset April through October; 10:30 AM to 3 PM November through March.

Helicopter – Service to and from Capodichino Airport in Naples can be arranged (phone: 837-2888).

Taxi – For a taxi in Capri, call 837-0543; in Anacapri, call 837-1175.

SPECIAL EVENTS: Religious festivals and celebrations have a way of taking on a pagan guise on Capri, and fireworks are set off on any pretext — a saint's day, *Christmas*, or a baptism. On May 14, the island celebrates the *Festa di San Costanzo*, the feast day of its patron saint, and on June 13, Anacapri celebrates the *Festa di Sant'Antonio*. On September 7 and 8, on Monte Tiberio and Monte Solaro, the *Festival of the Madonna* is held. At the end of September, a more secular celebration, the annual grape harvest, generates hundreds of impromptu parties.

SPORTS AND FITNESS: Boating – One way to see Capri and gain a different and dramatic perspective on its sheer limestone cliffs is to circle it in a boat; indeed, some parts of the island are accessible only by sea. Trips around the island can be arranged through *Gruppo Motoscafisti* (phone: 837-0286). A tour takes about 2½ hours and can be combined with tours to the famous Grotta Azzurra (Blue Grotto) and the less well-known Grotta Spumante, Grotta Corale, and Grotta Bianca, as well as the Bagni di Tiberio. Trips specifically to the Blue Grotto leave the Marina

Grande at regular intervals. If no one answers the phone, go down to Marina Grande and ask for information at the stand marked *Gite dell'Isola. Alberino Gennaro* (phone: 837-7118 or 837-9191) and *Consorzio Noleggiatori Capresi,* in Anacapri (phone: 837-2422 or 837-2749) also arrange boating excursions. On many off-season days, local boatmen decide there aren't enough customers or the sea is too rough, and they close up shop.

Boats can be rented by the hour or the day, with or without guides, through *Capri Mare Club* (Bagni Le Sirene, Marina Piccola; phone: 837-0221). The same establishment runs a windsurfing and sailing school and can arrange water skiing; there also is a fitness center and sauna.

Skin Diving and Snorkeling – Although there is no reef around Capri, and the fish can sometimes be few and far between, the clear water and the abundance of caves and grottoes make the area interesting for divers. Gennarino Alberino and his American wife, Cindy, run the *Gennarino and Cindy Sub* shop right next to the funicular (17 Marina Grande; phone: 837-9191 at the shop; 837-7118 at home). They rent snorkeling equipment and can arrange for scuba diving and instruction.

Swimming – Capri is not a swimmer's paradise, since there are only a few small, stony beaches on the island's craggy coast. The best swimming is probably at Marina Piccola, where concrete platforms have been built over the water's edge, or directly from a hired boat. Many hotels, however, have pools.

Tennis – The *Tennis Yacht Club* (41 Via Camerelle; phone: 837-0261 or 837-7980), across from the swank *Quisisana e Grand* hotel, has 3 clay courts, a clubhouse, bar, and shower rooms. The club pro, Giuseppe de Stefano, well known on the *Grand Prix* circuit as an umpire, speaks English and gives lessons at reasonable prices, with court fees included. Make reservations at least a week in advance in high season.

TOURING THE ISLAND OF CAPRI

Since there are essentially just two towns on the island — Capri and Anacapri — it is wise to settle in one and make forays from it, heading downhill on foot and returning uphill by taxi or bus. Distances are quite short, and no trip will take more than a few hours.

Prices tend to be quite a bit higher on Capri than on the mainland, particularly around Piazza Umberto I, where a cappuccino and a roll can cost up to $11. Expect to pay $130 and up for a double room in hotels listed as expensive; $65 to $125 in those listed as moderate; and less than $65 at the inexpensive ones. These prices do not take into account any minimum half-board requirements that some hotels impose in high season. The price of meals here, as in so many spots in Italy, depends in large measure on which fish or meat dish is ordered (pasta is reasonably priced almost everywhere) and which wine is drunk. Generally, a full meal for two will cost $65 and up in an expensive restaurant; $45 to $55 in a moderate establishment; and less than $35 in an inexpensive one. These prices include service and in some cases a local wine. The seafood on Capri is delicious but by no means inexpensive.

CAPRI TOWN: This whitewashed town has the look and feel of a North African *medina.* Many of the streets that radiate from tiny Piazza Umberto I, the main square, are as narrow as hallways, as steep as staircases, as dim and cool as tunnels. Occasionally, the cramped passageways open onto small room-like *piazzette* where people sit eating, drinking, and chatting, creating the impression that the town is one immense, rambling house. As the writer Eleanor Clark has written about the streets of Italy, they "constitute a great withinness. . . . Even a tourist can tell . . . he is *in* something and not outside something as he would be in most cities. . . . To go out is to go home."

But the lively, enfolding labyrinth of streets is only one of Capri's charms. There is color and excitement, and at every turn, through every open window, there are breath-catching views of the sea, of Monte Tiberio to the east and Monte Solaro to the west, and of villas strewn across terraced hillsides shaded by cypress trees, palms, and citrus groves. Capri's greatest attractions are almost all present-day and physical — the play of sunlight and shadow, the smell of jasmine, the sound of the sea against the rocks — rather than monuments of historic or artistic importance. This is not to say that the island has not preserved its past. Santo Stefano, the church on Piazza Umberto I, dates from the 17th century, and the adjacent Palazzo Cerio (no phone) contains a small, private museum of antiquities and fossils found on the island. Leaving the piazza by its south corner and descending Via Vittorio Emanuele III leads to Via Federico Serena, which curves down to the Certosa di San Giacomo (Carthusian Monastery of St. James; no phone), open mornings until 2 PM and closed Mondays. Built in the late 14th century, it has barrel-vaulted ceilings and domes, making it appear slightly Byzantine. It now houses a school and the town library, as well as some Roman statues removed from the Blue Grotto, and a collection of paintings from the 17th to the 19th century; no admission charge.

Roman ruins supply the major part of Capri's historical heritage. In 29 BC, Emperor Augustus visited the island, which then belonged to Naples, and was struck enough by its beauty to trade an island already in his possession (Ischia) for it. He built roads, aqueducts, and villas. His successor, Tiberius, came here in AD 27 and for the last 10 years of his life ruled the Roman Empire from here. He erected more villas on prominent points throughout the island, dedicating them to various Roman deities. Altogether, there are supposed to have been a dozen imperial villas on Capri, but among the various Roman ruins on the island, only the Villa Jovis, built by Tiberius and dedicated to Jupiter, amounts to anything today. This he set at the top of what is now called Monte Tiberio.

To reach Villa Jovis (also called Villa Tiberius), leave Piazza Umberto I by Via Le Botteghe, which becomes Via Fuorlovado and then Via Croce. From Via Croce take Via Tiberio uphill, following the signs. (The hike takes about an hour.) Just beyond the entrance to the villa is the Salto di Tiberio, the dizzyingly high precipice from which, as the story goes, Tiberius tossed his unfortunate victims to the stony shore of the sea. The villa itself, up a flight of steps, has been stripped of most of its mosaic pavements and decorative devices, but even in its reduced state, the ruins show extensive evidence of size and structural complexity. Incongruously, the very highest point of the pagan emperor's estate is crowned by a chapel and an immense, modern bronze statue of the Madonna that was blessed by Pope John Paul II and flown to this site by a US navy helicopter. Villa Jovis (phone: 837-0686) is open daily, except Mondays and holidays, from 9 AM to 1 hour before sunset; admission charge.

Other spots well worth a visit include Punta di Tragara, which offers a good view of the Faraglioni, twin rock islands that stand needle-like offshore and have become one of the symbols of Capri, and the Giardini di Augusto (Gardens of Augustus), a public park, with about 850 varieties of plants and trees, that offers another good view of the Faraglioni, Punta di Tragara, and Marina Piccola. From the gardens, walk down to Marina Piccola by Via Krupp, officially closed because of falling rocks but still passable. The Arco Naturale (Natural Arch), which is just that — a rock eroded to the shape of an archway — and the Grotta di Matromania, a cave in which the ancient Romans possibly worshiped Cybele, the Mater Magna, are not far from Villa Jovis.

The Blue Grotto has been incessantly described, rendered in paintings, and pictured on postcards, but it should be seen firsthand — although the process of doing so feels something like riding on an assembly line. The discovery of this cave on the north side of the island in 1826 put Capri on the modern tourist map. Visitors are taken by motorboat to the cave entrance — a mere 6-foot-wide hole in the rock, 3 feet high when the sea is normal — and then transfer to a small rowboat to be taken inside, where sunlight refracting through water makes the walls of the cave appear blue and gives submerged objects a silvery phosphorescence.

CHECKING IN: ***Punta Tragara*** – A 10-minute walk from the main square, this 33-room villa-turned-hotel is beautifully set with a splendid view of the Faraglioni. Its spa, hydromassage, and other luxurious facilities appeal to those looking for relaxation and privacy, but it also has a saltwater pool and a beach for more active guests, plus an elegant terrace restaurant, *Le Grottelle.* Closed mid-October to mid-April. 57 Via Tragara, Capri (phone: 837-0844). Expensive.

Quisisana – This sumptuous peach-colored wedding cake of a building is in a central location, but spacious and well screened from noisy or nosy passersby. Built by an English doctor, its name is a play on "qui si sana," literally, "here you heal." Its 142 elegant rooms, swimming pool, tennis courts, popular bar, restaurant, and courtyard for dining all attract a well-heeled clientele. Closed November through March. 2 Via Camerelle, Capri (phone: 837-0788). Expensive.

Scalinatella – Midway between the *Quisisana* and *Punta Tragara,* this 30-room hotel has an understated elegance and a soothing view of the sea. No restaurant, though light and appetizing lunches are served from the small poolside kitchen. Closed November to mid-March. 8 Via Tragara, Capri (phone: 837-0633). Expensive.

La Pineta – As its name suggests, this hotel is set in its own park of parasol pines, just off the romantic Via Tragara. The 55 rooms have large terraces overlooking the sea, furnished with comfortable lounge chairs. There is a well-equipped fitness center, swimming pool, and sauna. Open year-round. 6 Via Tragara, Capri (phone: 837-0644). Expensive to moderate.

Gatto Bianco – Conveniently situated, this 40-room hotel compensates for its lack of a view with the warmth of its welcome. It has a restaurant. Closed November through March. 32 Via Vittorio Emanuele, Capri (phone: 837-0203). Moderate.

Villa Brunella – A charming, family-run hotel on the panoramic walk to the Punta di Tragara. Each of the 19 rooms has a private balcony with magnificent views over the Marina Piccola, and the hotel has its own pool. The small restaurant prepares a good array of antipasti and an excellent spaghetti Brunella (spaghetti with seafood). In summer, patrons enjoy alfresco dining on one of Capri's loveliest terraces. 24 Via Tragara, Capri (phone: 837-0122). Moderate.

Villa Krupp – A favorite of academics and budget-conscious travelers, this is set apart from the clamor and conspicuous consumption that dominate much of Capri. It has a beautiful view, but only 15 rooms. No restaurant. Open year-round. 12 Via Matteotti, Capri (phone: 837-0362). Inexpensive.

EATING OUT: ***La Canzone del Mare*** – A Capri social institution, as well as an excellent restaurant, not to mention a bathing establishment, this place attracts a large daily clientele that comes to soak in the sun, to see and be seen, and to eat lunch (the restaurant closes at dusk). The specialty of the house is fresh fish, and desserts are excellent, particularly the orange *pastiera.* Closed October to *Easter.* Reservations advised. Major credit cards accepted. Marina Piccola, Capri (phone: 837-0104). Expensive.

La Capannina – Unprepossessing in appearance, this restaurant serves food as straightforward, unpretentious, and fresh as its decor. As a result, it is patronized by everybody from movie stars to day-trippers to royalty. *Penne alla siciliana,* a type of pasta with an eggplant and mozzarella sauce, makes a fine first course. The fish here is simply seasoned and always fresh. Closed Wednesdays, except in August, and November through March. Reservations advised. Major credit cards accepted. 14 Via Le Botteghe, Capri (phone: 837-0732). Expensive to moderate.

La Fontelina – This popular restaurant is dramatically poised on the rocks close to the towering Faraglioni. It is best to come here at lunchtime as it doubles as a *stabilimento balneare* — a place where diners can sunbathe and dive into the crystal-clear water before repairing to the table. It is easily reached by foot along the shady and panoramic Via Tragara, but at the end of the day, when you have had your fill of dishes that include spinach gnocchi with salmon and ravioli filled with cheese and arugula, the restaurant has a convenient boat service to ferry tired diners back to the Marina Piccola. Open April through October. Reservations advised. American Express accepted. Località Faraglioni, Capri (phone: 837-0845). Moderate.

Da Gemma – A favorite with visitors from the entertainment world — its walls are decked with photos of famous faces — it offers a rare mixture of reasonably priced, good home cooking and a truly warm atmosphere. The management claims to serve the best pizza in the world, cooked in a 15th-century oven in front of the customers. The other specialty is local fish, caught by the brothers of Signora Gemma, who has run the restaurant for more than 25 years. Closed Mondays. Reservations advised. Major credit cards accepted. 6 Via Madre Serafina, Capri (phone: 837-0461 or 837-7113). Moderate.

Al Grottino – A father-and-son establishment and an old favorite with the islanders, who know they will be served very fresh fish. The chef has a fine touch with fried dishes, including a delicate version of the usual *frittura mista* (mixed fried fish). Meals are served in a light and airy dining room. Closed Tuesdays and November to mid-March. Reservations advised. Major credit cards accepted. 27 Via Longano, Capri (phone: 837-0584). Moderate.

La Palette – Located in one of the most romantic spots on the island — on the pathway that leads to the Natural Arch — this eatery has a fine view overlooking the sea and Marina Piccola. In addition to the traditional Caprese fare, the chef also produces some interesting pasta dishes, including one made with curry. There also are a few rooms, but book early, especially in high season. Open year-round. Closed Wednesdays and for dinner in winter. Reservations advised. Major credit cards accepted. 36 Via Matemani (phone: 837-6829 or 837-0500). Moderate.

La Pigna – One of the island's most popular dining spots, with specialties that include *pesce spada affumicato* (smoked swordfish) and *gamberetti al parmigiano* (shrimps cooked with parmesan cheese). For an unusual dessert, try the *melanzane alla cioccolata,* an unlikely but very successful combination of eggplant and chocolate, taken from an old Caprese recipe. Closed November through April. Reservations advised. Major credit cards accepted. Via Roma, Capri (phone: 837-0280). Moderate.

Bocciodromo – Tina, the welcoming signora who runs this pretty garden restaurant, is Capri born and raised and takes pride in turning out fine homemade dishes such as *ravioli capresi* (pasta suffed with cheese and fresh marjoram). She also makes an excellent lemon liqueur, *limoncino.* Open year-round. Reservations unnecessary. No credit cards accepted. 2 Traversa Il Palazzo (phone: 837-7414). Moderate to inexpensive.

La Cisterna – This restaurant serves tasty pizza with thick crust, sliced tomatoes, and mounds of mozzarella. Its menu also features the largest, most succulent *gamberoni* you're likely to see and a light red local wine bottled by the owner. Closed Thursdays. Reservations advised in summer. Visa accepted. Via Madre Serafina, Capri (phone: 837-7236). Moderate to inexpensive.

Da Settanni – A few steps off Piazza Umberto I, it features good, reasonably priced food and friendly service. In winter, when fresh basil is hard to find, they use arugula instead in their *insalata caprese.* Closed Thursdays. Reservations advised. Visa accepted. 5 Via Longano, Capri (phone: 837-0105). Moderate to inexpensive.

La Savardina (da Eduardo) – In the countryside, halfway to Villa Jovis, this simple trattoria offers excellent ravioli in butter and sage, fresh fish, and grilled sausage seasoned with fennel. Closed Tuesdays. Reservations advised in summer. No credit cards accepted. 8 Via Lo Capo, Capri (phone: 837-6300). Inexpensive.

ANACAPRI: Actually the upper town of Marina Grande, often fog-shrouded Anacapri can be reached by a hair-raising bus or taxi trip. Horns blaring, tires squealing, the traffic careens around hairpin turns with little hesitation. The only other alternative was, until it was closed to the public because of fallen rocks, the Scala Fenicia (Phoenician Staircase), the 881 steps used by the Greeks (who carved them out of the rock), the Romans, and everyone else until 1887 (when the road to Anacapri was built).

Less claustrophobic and more secluded than the town of Capri (and far less chic), Anacapri offers more in the unending series of spectacular views of the Bay of Naples and the mainland. One magnificent view is from the garden of the Villa San Michele (phone: 837-0686), built in the 1880s by the Swedish doctor and writer Axel Munthe, who lived here until 1910 and often wrote about the island, most notably in *The Story of San Michele.* Constructed on the site of one of the villas of Tiberius, and incorporating some of its remains, the house contains some Roman antiquities but is furnished mostly in 17th- and 18th-century style. Its gardens are exquisitely landscaped. The villa is open daily from 9 AM to sunset (admission charge). For an even more awe-inspiring view, this time of the whole island, take the chair lift from Anacapri to the top of Monte Solaro. Airborne, riders float over citrus groves and tropical gardens to a summit from which the entire island and, in the distance, the Apennine Mountains running down Italy's spine are visible. The chair lift operates daily from 9:30 AM to sunset April through October, 10:30 AM to 3 PM November through March.

CHECKING IN: ***Europa Palace*** – A spacious, contemporary hotel built on 3 levels, it has 103 rooms, large terraces, broad expanses of glass, a swimming pool, a good restaurant, and other modern amenities. Closed November through March. 104 Via Axel Munthe, Anacapri (phone: 837-0955). Expensive.

San Michele di Anacapri – Close to Axel Munthe's villa, this 30-room hostelry has the look and feel of a private house, with traditional furnishings and modern conveniences. Large gardens provide shady nooks for daydreaming and other spots for unobstructed views. Restaurant. Open year-round. 14 Via G. Orlandi, Anacapri (phone: 837-1427). Moderate.

Loreley – Economical, clean, cozy, and convivial, it looks out on lemon groves and is flower- and fruit-scented. The 16 rooms are large and well furnished and some have a private bath and balcony. No restaurant. Open year-round. 16 Via G. Orlandi, Anacapri (phone: 837-1440). Inexpensive.

EATING OUT: ***Il Cucciolo*** – Just outside Anacapri, this restaurant has several terraces for alfresco dining, with superb views over the entire Bay of Naples. Closed in winter. Reservations advised in summer. No credit cards accepted. 52 Via La Fabbrica, Anacapri (phone: 837-1917). Moderate.

Da Gelsomina – It is well worth the 20-minute walk to reach this quiet, well-run restaurant with a terrace that overlooks the Faraglioni. Diners enjoy spectacular views and good home cooking, with dishes based on fish and meat. Closed Tuesdays. Reservations advised. No credit cards accepted. From the main piazza (Piazza Vittoria), follow the picturesque path known as the *Migliara,* which is too narrow for even the smallest car. Anacapri (phone: 837-1499). Moderate to inexpensive.

Ischia

It is difficult to say when, much less why, Ischia began getting second billing to nearby Capri. Perhaps it goes back to the emperor Augustus, who gave the island to the Neapolitans in a trade for Capri, an island half its size (Ischia measures about 6 miles east to west and 4 miles north to south). Today Ischia is too often overlooked by American travelers, who would be wiser to have a firsthand look. Many Italians prefer it to Capri, which they consider too crowded, and many Germans have also discovered it, returning again and again. They love its clear sparkling waters, its sandy beaches (a marked contrast to the dearth of them on Capri), its extensive pine forests, vineyards, and citrus groves — all the green scenery that has caused it to be known as the Emerald Isle. A good many visitors also come for the hot mineral waters, to "detox," and perhaps lose a kilo or two.

Just as Capri is a continuation of the Sorrento Peninsula, the southern shore of the Bay of Naples, Ischia is a continuation of the Campi Flegrei (Phlegrean Fields) of the northern shore. This, in fact, was where the "fiery fields" finally got down to business, because Ischia is a volcanic island of craters and lava beds, with the cone-shaped, 2,590-foot Monte Epomeo, the crux of it all, standing nearly dead center. Monte Epomeo hasn't erupted since the early 14th century, and its slopes are now covered with vines that produce the well-known epomeo wine. The mineral springs, whose beneficial effects were known to the ancients, do endure, however, continuing to issue forth at varying temperatures. Here, with the exception of the Nitrodi spring, the waters are used not for drinking (as they are in Montecatini and many other Italian spas) but for hydromassage, inhalation, and thermal mineral baths — and above all for mud baths.

The island has had a turbulent history. Beginning with the ancient Greeks, it has been colonized, occupied, ruled, or sacked by a succession of invaders, among them the Neapolitans, the Romans, the Goths, the Saracens, the Normans, the Pisans, the Angevins, the Aragonese, the pirate Barbarossa, the Duke of Guise, and Admiral Nelson. And from time to time, islanders and invaders alike found it necessary to surrender to the superior force of the island's volcanic nature and evacuate completely. Today the island shows few signs of this tumult except in the variety of its architectural styles and in the accretion of history surrounding, for instance, the *isolotto,* the little island that sits just offshore of the town of Ischia, connected to it by a pedestrian bridge. The Greeks built a fortress here in the 5th century BC, although the Castello d'Ischia — a collection of walls, fortifications, and other buildings — seen today was built by the Aragonese in the 15th century. In the meantime, the *ischitani* sought refuge here over the centuries, from invaders and forces of nature alike. In fact, when the last volcanic eruption occurred (1301 or 1302), and the original town of Ischia was buried in lava (it was farther northwest than the town is today), the inhabitants took cover here and didn't begin to build the new town until the 16th century.

The town they built, on the island's northeast corner, has now become the island capital and has grown enough to consist of two settlements: Ischia Porto, where most visitors arrive, and Ischia Ponte, the older nucleus, connected by bridge to the *isolotto.* Circling the island counterclockwise are the other main centers of resort activity, which coincide with the location of the most important springs: Casamicciola Terme, on the north shore, reborn after destruction by an earthquake in 1883; Lacco Ameno, at the northwest corner, a fishing village grown fashionable; and Forio, on the west coast, a picturesque wine producing village. Sant'Angelo, on the southern shore, is a tiny fishing village, linked, as is Ischia Ponte, to a tiny islet offshore, and it has a beach with fumaroles, the Lido dei Maronti, stretching east of it. Sant'Angelo is somewhat off the beaten track, but well worth the trip; even more so are mountain villages of the interior whose position has kept them relatively untouched by the tourist activity of the coastline.

TOURIST INFORMATION: The official high season on Ischia runs from July through September, although unofficially it begins around *Easter.* In winter, many of the tourist facilities are closed, but with a permanent population of almost 50,000 people, the island never has the bleak shuttered look of some resorts off-season. The Ente Provinciale per il Turismo in Naples (58 Piazza dei Martiri, Scala B/Staircase B; phone: 81-405311) is a source of information about Ischia. In addition, there are local tourist offices on the island itself (116 Corso Vittoria Colonna; phone: 81-991464 or 81-983066; and Via Iasolino; phone: 81-991146), both in Ischia Porto. Many free guides and maps are available at hotels and travel agencies.

TELEPHONE: The area code for the entire island is 81. When calling from within Italy, dial 081 before the local number.

FOOD AND WINE: Like Capri, Ischia is influenced by Naples and the sea. The cuisine features fresh fish, lobster, mussels and clams, pizza, and pasta with sauces of mozzarella and eggplant, or tomatoes, olives, and capers. Inland trattorie frequently serve rabbit. Local wines include the well-respected biancolella and red and white monte epomeo.

GETTING AROUND: Ischia does not, like Capri, prohibit tourists from bringing cars to the island in summer; although there are limitations to keep traffic manageable, they affect only residents of the region of Campania. In July and August, however, cars are banned from the center of Ischia Porto and Ponte.

Bus – There is regular and inexpensive bus service to most villages; in fact, it's possible to do a complete circuit of the island by public transportation in about 2½ hours. The bus marked CS makes the tour clockwise, while the CD does the same route counterclockwise. Both buses leave from Piazza Trieste e Trento, near the port. Check at the tourist office for details and times of departure.

Car – Ischia is a much bigger island than Capri, so a car is a good idea as many of the prettiest villages and best beaches are some distance away. Rental prices are low — a Fiat 500, ideal for the winding roads, costs as little as $25 a day. A good company is *Autonoleggio Ischia* (59 Via Alfredo de Luca, Ischia Porto 80077; phone: 992444 or 993259), a short walk from the ferry terminal.

Ferry – Ferries and hydrofoils (*aliscafi*) run frequently between Ischia and the mainland. From Naples, *Caremar* provides dependable service from Molo Beverello, near Castel Nuovo, and there is also service from Mergellina (Molo Ovest) and, slightly north of Naples, from Pozzuoli. In summer, one ferry and two hydrofoils a day run to Ischia from Sorrento and Capri. *Alilauro* also has hydrofoil service from Naples to Ischia. The ferry trip between Naples and Ischia takes approximately 1 to 1½ hours. By hydrofoil, the same trip takes 40 to 45 minutes.

Taxi – Taxis are plentiful, and some hang around the port offering tours of the island. Before taking such a tour, be absolutely certain of what it will cost, and if in doubt about the price or the itinerary, don't do it.

SPORTS AND FITNESS: Swimming, skin diving, snorkeling, windsurfing, tennis, and hiking can be easily arranged in season through the tourist offices. Be sure to visit the beach at Sant'Angelo.

TOURING ISCHIA

Accommodations on Ischia can be luxurious or humble — and mineral baths, mud baths, and other such ministrations are given in many hotels with their own thermal facilities, as well as in the communal bathing establishments. Dining on the island can be in simple trattorie or in first class restaurants. In season, expect to pay $275 and up for a double room in the hotel listed as very expensive, $110 and up in hotels listed as expensive; $55 to $95 in those listed as moderate; and less than $45 in the inexpensive ones. (As on Capri and the Amalfi Coast, compulsory meal plans may be in effect in some hotels in some seasons, causing higher prices.) A full meal for two in an expensive restaurant will run $60 and up; $35 to $50 in a moderate establishment; and $30 or less in one listed as inexpensive.

ISCHIA: The town of Ischia consists of two settlements, Porto d'Ischia and Ponte d'Ischia (or Ischia Porto and Ischia Ponte). They are separated by a *pineta* (pine woods) and connected by a main street that is called Via Roma at its north end and then becomes Corso Vittoria Colonna; it runs parallel to a sandy beach and is lined with cafés, restaurants, and shops. Most boats from the mainland dock at Porto d'Ischia, a harbor formed by an extinct volcano. Once an interior lake, it was opened to the sea in 1854 with the construction of a canal through the rim of the crater. Not far from the port, on Piazza del Redentore, are the Terme Comunali (Communal Baths), open to the public year-round. Ponte d'Ischia is the older part of town, named for the 15th-century pedestrian bridge — Ponte Aragonese — that links it with the *isolotto,* the cluster of buildings, churches, and 15th-century castle that is the oldest part of all. In the early 16th century, Vittoria Colonna, whose name lives on in Ischia's main street, spent part of her life in the castle. A member of a famous Italian family, with her own reputation as one of the great poets of her time (and as the object of love sonnets written by her friend Michelangelo), she is credited with polishing Ischia's cultural image so that it outshone Naples for a while.

CHECKING IN: ***Excelsior*** – This extravagantly decorated and furnished building has 67 rooms and is famed for its fine service and comfortable accommodations. The rooms tend to be less ornate, less inclined toward fantasy, than the lounge, which has a raised fireplace, an intricately carved bar, and black beams radiating against a white ceiling. The hotel is set amid pine trees and gardens; it has a swimming pool and newly built thermal facilities. A beach is nearby. Closed mid-October to mid-April. 19 Via Emanuele Gianturco, Ischia Porto (phone: 991020). Expensive.

Jolly Grande Albergo delle Terme – A member of the Jolly chain, it has 208 comfortable rooms, 2 swimming pools in a tree-shaded garden (a third pool for children), an excellent restaurant, and its own thermal facilities. Closed January and February. 42 Via Alfredo de Luca, Ischia Porto (phone: 991744). Expensive to moderate.

Moresco – An old Moorish structure, smothered in bougainvillea, with 63 rooms, each with beamed or vaulted ceilings, tile floors, and ornately carved dressers and beds — the brilliant color scheme contrasting dramatically with the whitewashed walls — plus a terrace and air conditioning. Other features: tennis courts, a solarium, gamerooms, gardens equipped with lounge chairs, 2 swimming pools (one with a bridge across its narrowest point), and a health and beauty center offering spa services. Closed November through March. 16 Via Emanuele Gianturco, Ischia Porto (phone: 981355). Expensive to moderate.

Parcoverde Terme – This white, Moorish-looking hotel, set in its own gardens with palm trees and umbrella pines, is one of only a handful of hotels that stay open year-round in Ischia. It has 60 air conditioned rooms, a good restaurant, lovely gardens, and a beach within walking distance, in addition to its own thermal facilities, which are staffed by trained personnel. 29 Via Michele Mazzella, Ischia Porto (phone: 992282). Moderate.

EATING OUT: ***Da Ugo Giardini Eden*** – Set paradisiacally on the sea, among black lava formations created centuries ago. The service is excellent and so are the salads, the lobster, the charcoal-grilled fish, and the house white wine. Closed November through April. Reservations advised. Major credit cards accepted. 50 Via Nuova Cartaromana, Ischia Ponte (phone: 993909). Expensive.

Damiano – Fresh fish is the specialty of this modern-looking restaurant with a glass-enclosed terrace. Closed October through March. Reservations advised. Major credit cards accepted. Via Nuova Circonvallazione, Ischia Porto (phone: 983032). Expensive to moderate.

Il Clipper – Overlooking Ischia's harbor, this eatery has a decidedly marine flavor — both in its decor and its cooking. The chef uses local fish to create some unusual and mouth-watering pasta dishes, including *ravioli ripieni di branzino* (stuffed with delicately poached fish) and ravioli filled with shrimp. Open year-round. Reservations advised. Visa accepted. Rive Droit, Ischia Porto (phone: 982945). Moderate.

LACCO AMENO: On the northern coast, a short bus ride or taxi trip from the port, Lacco Ameno has some of the best hotels on Ischia, which in turn contain some of the island's best restaurants. Just off shore, the town's landmark, an outcropping of rock called *il fungo* (mushroom), juts out of the sea. The center of this onetime fishing village is Piazza Santa Restituta, with a sanctuary dedicated to the island's patron saint (the oldest part of the church dates from the 11th century, but most of it is modern). The mineral springs at Lacco Ameno are said to be radioactive, and the remains of ancient baths dating from the 8th century BC have been found here. Victorian baths were built over the Greco-Roman remains in the 19th century, but they were torn down in the 1950s to make way for Lacco Ameno's modern thermal baths — Terme Regina Isabella e Santa Restituta — and a connecting luxury hotel. Other hotels followed, many equipped to offer thermal treatments in house, and Lacco Ameno soon became a resort town with an international clientele. The mineral baths, mud baths, inhalations, and beauty treatments claim to cure all ailments known to man, but the town's setting has curative powers of its own.

CHECKING IN: ***Regina Isabella*** – A deluxe hotel in the grand continental tradition: the island's best. At the water's edge in the center of Lacco Ameno, it has 135 comfortable rooms, most with sea-view balconies (other rooms have a village view), 2 seaside restaurants, terraces, 2 swimming pools (one saltwater, one hot thermal water), a private beach, a tennis court, and a beautiful garden. Water sports and diet, exercise, yoga, dance, and aerobic programs are offered; a full roster of spa treatments is available at the connecting *Regina Isabella e Santa Restituta* baths. The atmosphere of a private club prevails — especially in the Royal Sporting section, which has super-luxury suites only. Closed November through March. Piazza Santa Restituta, Lacco Ameno (phone: 994322). Very expensive.

San Montano – Outside Lacco Ameno, on a hill above the tiny bay and beach of San Montano, with lovely views of the coast and town. It has 65 rooms, indoor and outdoor dining, a thermal pool and a seawater pool, a tennis court and a *bocce* court, a large garden, a reserved beach, plus baths and beauty treatments in its own thermal establishment. Closed November through March. Via Monte Vico, Lacco Ameno (phone: 994033). Expensive.

Terme di Augusto – Centrally located and one of the newest, most modern hotels in Lacco Ameno, it has 119 rooms and suites, all with balconies. It also has 2 restaurants, an indoor pool with thermal water, an outdoor pool, a private beach, tennis courts, and a fully equipped spa. Closed November through March. 128 Viale Campo, Lacco Ameno (phone: 994944). Expensive.

La Reginella – Across from the *Regina Isabella* and under the same ownership, it is a less expensive alternative. Its 50 rooms are in a large villa with graceful terraces and French doors leading onto balconies. Guests may use some of the facilities of the more celebrated establishment, including the 2 pools. Closed November through March. Piazza Santa Restituta, Lacco Ameno (phone: 994300). Expensive to moderate.

EATING OUT: ***O Padrone D'O Mare*** – Diners eat alfresco on a thatch-roofed balcony and feast on dishes that are mainly based on fish. The house specialty is *zuppa di pesce* (a big plate brimming with every type of fish and shellfish imaginable). Open daily. Reservations unnecessary. Visa accepted. Lacco Ameno (phone: 986159). Moderate.

FORIO D'ISCHIA: This small village on the west coast is the center of the island's wine production and was once a thriving colony of artists and writers. Its dominant feature is the Torrione, a 15th-century tower built to defend the islanders against invaders and pirates.

CHECKING IN: ***Grande Albergo Mezzatorre*** – A former estate that once belonged to a Roman nobleman, as well as the residence of the famous movie director Visconti for a number of years, its present owners have converted it into one of the island's best hotels. They kept all the original features of what is really a small castle with 60 guestrooms. The grounds are large and well kept, and there is a small private beach and a pool. Closed December to *Easter.* Via Mezza Torre, Forio (phone: 986111). Expensive.

EATING OUT: ***Il Soccorso*** – This restaurant takes its name from the nearby Santuario del Soccorso, a picturesque whitewashed church perched on the edge of the cliff at the far end of the village. Diners can be sure of the freshest fish on the island and friendly, efficient service. Closed Mondays and during winter. Reservations unnecessary. No credit cards accepted. 1 Via Soccorso, Forio (phone: 997846). Moderate.

La Cava dell'Isola – Just outside Forio, this dining spot is so close to the sea that you could almost go for a swim between courses. Good home-cooked traditional dishes and friendly service. Closed November through April. Reservations unnecessary. No credit cards accepted. Via G. Mazella, Forio d'Ischia (phone: 997452). Moderate to inexpensive.

SANT'ANGELO: Down on the southern tip of the island, this is one of the prettiest spots on Ischia — a peaceful place that still has the air of a fishing village rather than a resort. Although somewhat isolated, it is only a 15-minute drive from Ischia Porto and has some fine restaurants, as well as the best beach on the island.

CHECKING IN: ***Miramare*** **–** Located in a superb spot, this 50-room hostelry overlooks the beach, the small fishing harbor, and the picturesque promontory of Sant'Angelo. There is a flower-decked terrace where guests may eat breakfast. 29 Via Comandante Maddalena, Sant'Angelo (phone: 999219). Moderate.

EATING OUT: ***Ristorante Conchiglia*** **–** Inside is airy and pleasant, but the real treat is the balcony where diners can eat plates of *frittura mista* (mixed fresh fried fish) and drink jugs of local white wine while looking out over Sant'Angelo. Reservations advised, especially for a terrace table. The restaurant also rents out clean, comfortable rooms, but they fill up quickly, so book early. Closed November through April. No credit cards accepted. Via Sant'Angelo, Sant'Angelo (phone: 999270). Restaurant moderate; rooms inexpensive.

Puglia

Italy's southeasternmost region, Puglia — or Apulia, as it is known in English — constitutes the "heel" of the "boot," nearly a spike heel equipped with a spur. Most of the region is flat, covered with fruit and olive trees, tomatoes, grain, and grapes, with some small but growing industries. Yet it has one of the longest coastlines of any Italian region, the Adriatic bathing it on the eastern upper ankle and the heel dipping down into the Ionian Sea. Although many Italians come to Puglia for its beaches, the region is hardly a fashionable vacation spot overrun with tourists. It is a little-known, developing region rich in history, culture, and traditions that have been influenced over the centuries by Greeks, Romans, Goths, Lombards, Byzantines, Normans, Swabians, Angevins, Aragonese, Spanish, Bourbons, and French.

The region can be divided into four geographic areas. In the north is the Tavoliere di Puglia, a vast, flat, fertile, wheat-producing zone that has been growing grain since ancient times — its name derives from *tabulae censuariae,* Roman for "record books." The area is commonly known as Capitanata, and the main reason visitors venture into it is the Gargano Massif, the dramatic, jagged limestone promontory that juts 40 miles out from its eastern edge into the Adriatic. The Gargano, both peninsula and mountain, Puglia's only mountainous zone, is the spur of Italy's boot, known for its beautiful beaches, limpid sea, romantic grottoes, rich forests, and tall rock formations. At the center of the region is Bari and its surrounding province, Puglia's richest agricultural area, with its greatest concentration of historic and cultural sights. Often called Terra di Bari, it corresponds topographically with an area of low hills and stretches of stony ground known as the Murge. Southward is the Salento Peninsula, or simply the Salento, which forms the high heel of the boot and offers visitors the chance to easily explore both the Adriatic and the Ionian shores. The area is a main producer of excellent tobaccos, although these are being replaced by more cost-efficient crops such as tomatoes, potatoes, and melons.

Puglia's succession of rulers and invasions is reflected in its cities and ancient villages, each with its own character and charm, as well as in its impressive monuments incorporating a variety of architectural styles. The influence of the Greeks — especially apparent in Taranto, Gallipoli, Otranto, and Bari — dates from the period when Puglia was part of Magna Graecia, the early Greek colonization of southern Italy that began in the 8th century BC. Although it doesn't have the standing temples of Siciliy, remnants of Magna Graecia and evidence of its tremendous impact on the Pugliese people and culture can be found in the art and artifacts in the region's archaeological museums as well as in many of its customs, dialects, and even cuisine.

Under the Normans, during the 11th and 12th centuries, many churches were built and the Apulian-Romanesque style of architecture originated, incorporating Norman, northern Italian, and Oriental motifs. Solid, massive structures with rounded arches are typical of this style; the Basilica di San Nicola in Bari is considered its prototype. The 13th century was Puglia's happiest moment, especially the few decades under the rule of Holy Roman Emperor Frederick II of Swabia (1220–50), who encouraged the building of splendid castles as well as extraordinary Romanesque cathedrals, and the region flourished economically, culturally, and artistically.

By the 14th century, the region had already begun to decline: Venetians took its trade; the Turks raided its coasts; famine, plague, malaria, and the insidious effects of the feudal system all played a part in the demise. Not much of the Renaissance is visible in Puglia, but the baroque did have a grand flowering in 17th-century Lecce.

Puglia's unique architectural form is the *trullo.* At its most authentic, this is a cylindrical limestone hut, whitewashed to a fare-thee-well and topped with a conical stone roof, often painted with a white cross. In the *trullo* district, centered in the town of Alberobello (the "capital") and the Valle d'Itria south of the town, from Locorotondo to Martina Franca, they are huddled together in villages or scattered about the landscape, gleaming against the red clay earth, amid olive groves and almond trees that flower in February and endless miles of stone walls constructed with no mortar. Such houses are of ancient origin, although the examples seen today are at most a few hundred years old, and many are even brand-new (these exhibit variations on the structural theme). Some are still inhabited, some are used as shops and storehouses, and some are rented as summer cottages. Indeed, at Alberobello, it is possible to stay in a hotel entirely made up of modern *trulli.*

Elsewhere there are numerous towns that, although without *trulli,* still have a bleached, whitewashed look about them, as though they belong in Greece or in North Africa. They can be found in the Gargano, in such towns as Rodi Garganico and Peschici, and in the Salento; perhaps the most picturesque is Ostuni, in the province of Brindisi.

A move to open up the countryside to agritourism has recently become important in the region; one delightful feature is the refurbishment of old farmhouses (*masserie*), set in idyllic landscapes, as inns. Strictly speaking, however, agritourism takes place on working farms.

Puglia has busy commercial ports, beautiful stretches of uncrowded beach, and clear azure waters. Its wonderful regional cooking is based largely on an abundance of squid, octopus, mussels, clams, and a variety of fish (red mullet, spiny lobster, dentex, fresh sardines, and eels) found in its two seas. Specialties include *ciambotto* (a spicy tomato-based fish sauce for spaghetti, native to Bari and Foggia, where it is called *ciabotta*); the Spanish-inspired *tiella* (baked layers of potatoes, rice, mussels, clams, or other seafood); *spaghetti alle cozze* (pasta served with a tomato-based sauce with mussels) or *alle vongole* (with clams); *zuppa di pesce* (fish soup); and *frutta di mare* (seafood salad with squid, octopus, and cuttlefish).

Regional dishes also use products from the countryside's wheat fields, olive groves, fig trees, and fragrant almond trees — as well as endless vineyards.

Local pasta includes the ear-shaped *orecchiette,* served with a variety of sauces (the best-known being *con cime di rapa,* or bitter green turnip tops), and *maccheroni al forno* (a baked casserole of pasta, sausage, meatballs, and cheese); other specialties are *cicoria con fave* (purée of bitter greens and fava beans) and *bruschetta* (toasted crusty country bread brushed with olive oil and topped with chopped tomatoes or arugula). Apulian breads, olive oil, and cheese are superb. Bread is always served along with *taralli,* small yeast-dough rings made with flour, olive oil, and white wine, and sometimes flavored with fennel or pepper (sweeter versions of *taralli,* frosted with sugar icing, are served for dessert). The fruit course is sometimes served with vegetables such as fennel and cucumbers.

Like Sardinia, Puglia once had a tradition of eating *carne di cavallo* (horsemeat); a prized dish, it is occasionally served in popular trattorie as a main course or in taverns (especially around Lecce) as an hors d'oeuvre accompanied by wine. For anyone who considers this barbaric, it is a good idea to ask about the origin of the meat in a particular dish, even though it is always stated; horsemeat is served at times as a *bistecca* (steak) or made into *involtini* (filled meat rolls).

Puglia's dessert grapes are the best in Italy, but the region is also one of the country's largest producers of wine. Excellent local wines, once used chiefly for blending with those from the north and from France, are now available everywhere. Among those recommended are castel del monte, copertino, locorotondo, and salice salentino.

The best times for a visit are spring and fall, when the mild Mediterranean climate is ideal. From the rest of Italy the region is easy to reach by plane (flights to Bari or Brindisi from Milan and Rome), train (roughly 13 hours from Milan, 7 hours from Rome), or car. Once there, however, seeing Puglia by car is a must — and a pleasure, as most roads and highways are in excellent condition. Puglia does not see the large nı mbers of tourists that other areas in Italy attract, except from mid-July to September, when it is favored by northern Italians.

The route outlined here begins in Bari and forms two loops, one leading north and the other south. The northern loop follows the Adriatic coast for a stretch, detours inland to a 13th-century castle, Castel del Monte, and returns to the coast to visit Trani and Barletta before continuing north to the promontory of Gargano and its resorts. Then it turns inland to the Capitanata area and returns to Bari after a visit to Foggia. The southern loop also follows the coast for a stretch, then heads inland to visit Alberobello and the *trulli* district. It returns to the Adriatic via Ostuni and passes through Brindisi on the way to Lecce, a lovely baroque city in the middle of the Salento. Otranto, on the Adriatic side of the peninsula, and Gallipoli, on the Ionian side, are visited before the route winds up at Taranto and returns to Bari. Two warnings: Museum hours and other schedules can change without warning or explanation; and never leave anything in your car, not even in a locked trunk.

A double room in the hotels listed as very expensive will cost $175 or more; in a hotel listed as expensive, expect to spend $125 to $175; as moderate, prices will range from approximately $75 to $125; an inexpensive hotel will cost less than $75. Dining in Puglia — three courses plus wine and service — will run from $80 and up for two in an expensive restaurant, from $50 to $80 in a moderate restaurant, and less than $50 in an inexpensive one.

BARI: The region's capital city is a metropolis of close to 500,000 people, an important trade center, and, with Brindisi, one of the two most important commercial ports on the lower Adriatic. Because of its enviable coastal position, it was subjected to countless invasions and periods of foreign domination throughout history and was one of the chief embarkation ports for the Crusades. Possibly of Illyrian origin, it was colonized by the Greeks, then by the Romans (who called it Barium), and later ruled by Goths, Lombards, Byzantines, and Normans. Today it consists of two distinct parts. In its bustling modern section, built from the early 19th century on, streets follow a grid pattern. There are broad, palm-lined boulevards, fashionable shops (in the vicinity of Via Sparano), good hotels, and excellent restaurants. The contrast with its old section, Bari Vecchia, on a promontory between the old and new ports, is striking. In Bari Vecchia, narrow stone streets and tiny arched alleyways wind around pastel buildings, ancient churches, bountiful produce stands, and scenes of colorful local life. Newly washed laundry hangs above the streets, and elderly women dressed in black still scrub the steps in front of their homes.

In the heart of the Old Town on Largo Elia stands the Basilica di San Nicola (Basilica of St. Nicholas), the first Norman church in Puglia and an outstanding example of Apulian-Romanesque architecture. It was built between 1087 and 1197 (on the site of the city's previous Byzantine governor's palace, of which some parts remain) to house the bones of San Nicola, the city's patron saint, stolen from Asia Minor in 1807 by a group of Barese sailors. Bari's San Nicola is the very same St. Nicholas, a 4th-century Bishop of Myra (now in Turkey) who was known for his good deeds on behalf of children and who eventually evolved into Santa Claus. (The bones are underneath the altar in the crypt.) The church is also known for its 12th-century bishop's throne. Still in the Old City and not far away is the 12th-century Cathedral, also Apulian-Romanesque, and the Castello Svevo (Swabian Castle), which was begun by the Byzantines and Normans but was significantly redesigned by Frederick II in the 13th century and later inhabited by Duchess Isabella of Aragón. The castle is open daily, except Mondays; admission charge.

Bari has an art museum, the *Pinacoteca Provinciale* (in the Palazzo della Provincia, along Lungomare Nazario Sauro; phone: 80-334600; no admission charge), the seaside promenade east of the center. Each September, the city hosts the *Fiera del Levante* (Levant Fair), southern Italy's most important trade fair (and one of Europe's most important commercial events), to encourage trade between East and West. More traditional events include the *Sagra di San Nicola* (Feast of St. Nicholas) on May 7, when a parade in historical costume relives the arrival of the saint's bones in the city. The next day a statue of the saint is put on a boat and sent out to bless the sea (San Nicola is also the patron saint of sailors).

On Corso Cavour, lined with tall palms and stalls selling everything under the Apulian sun, the Eastern flavor of shipping agencies and nearby docks vies with grand European architecture, typified by the *Teatro Petruzzelli* (phone: 80-218132). This is one of Italy's finest opera houses, boasting an important international company.

Bari is an important departure point for car ferries to Yugoslavia; some for Greece also leave from here, although most leave from Brindisi, farther south along the coast.

Warning: Since Bari is a big city (after Naples, the largest in the south) with a thriving, sometimes unsavory, port, theft can be a real problem here. Leave nothing in your car, even when it's locked, and don't carry valuables. It also is advisable to avoid walking around the Old Town at night with a handbag; the police say it even can be dangerous by day.

For more information about sights in Bari, stop at the tourist information office (EPT), 253 Via Melo (phone: 80-524-2244), near the train station.

CHECKING IN: ***Palace*** – One of the city's finest hotels, with 210 rooms including deluxe suites (all with air conditioning), a restaurant, and first class facilities, including deluxe suites, all with air conditioning. Conventions are its staple. It's within easy walking distance of both Bari Vecchia and the shops in the modern part of town. 13 Via Lombardi, Bari (phone: 80-216551; fax: 80-521-1499). Very expensive.

Grand Hotel e d'Oriente – Next door to the *Teatro Petruzzelli,* this sprawling maze of 180 rooms is reminiscent of 1950s hotels, with a few more modern touches, including air conditioning. 32 Corso Cavour, Bari (phone: 80-544422). Expensive.

Residence di Villa Romanazzi-Carducci – An attractive 18th-century villa offering elegant suites only. More intimate than the *Palace,* it has its own private park and draws a chic clientele. Its current owner is president of the *Fiera del Levante* (see above). It's a 15-minute walk to the Old Town. 326 Via Capruzzi, Bari (phone: 80-227400; fax: 80-360297). Expensive.

EATING OUT: ***Ai 2 Ghiottoni*** – Very good seafood and Apulian specialties are served in modern surroundings. Try *risotto Ai 2 Ghiottoni* (risotto with spinach, cream, ham, and parmesan cheese). Closed Sundays and most of August. Reservations advised. Major credit cards accepted. 11/B Via Putignani, Bari (phone: 80-5232240). Expensive.

La Pignata – The atmosphere is elegant, the food superb. Seafood risotto, *spaghetti alle vongole* (with clams), and regional favorites such as *orecchiette con cime di rapa* (pasta with turnip greens) and *tiella* (a seafood-potato-rice casserole) are among the choices. Closed Wednesdays and August. Reservations advised. Major credit cards accepted. 9 Via Melo, Bari (phone: 80-232481). Expensive.

Al Sorso Preferito – Known for its seafood specialties, its wide variety of antipasti, and its rustic charm. Closed Sundays. Reservations advised. Major credit cards accepted. 46 Via de Nicolò, Bari (phone: 80-235747). Expensive to moderate.

Da Cesare – A favorite spot, owing to the relaxed atmosphere and wide range of excellent antipasti (sometimes brought to the table for tasting in a burst of spontaneity). All food is cooked to order. After dinner, try an *amaro,* poured from an ancient amphora. Closed Tuesdays and late August. Reservations unnecessary. Major credit cards accepted. Near the station at 215 Corso Cavour, Bari (phone: 80-524-2486). Moderate.

En Route from Bari – Drive northwest along SS16 (commonly known as the Adriatica Highway) past silvery green olive groves and a succession of vineyards. At Molfetta, a charming town with an old port and a Romanesque cathedral that has three domes and two bell towers, turn inland and continue through Terlizzi and Ruvo di Puglia. Here the landscape is made up mostly of low hills, typical of the Murge of central Puglia, and vast fields of golden wheat. At Ruvo di Puglia (which has a fine 13th-century Duomo), pick up SS170. In about 11 miles (18 km) the road leads to Masseria Castello, where there is a turnoff (marked SS179 "Dir A") for Castel del Monte, one of the region's primary landmarks.

CASTEL DEL MONTE: Just 34 miles (55 km) west of Bari — an easy drive — this striking castle, in an isolated position on the top of a hill, is one of Puglia's architectural masterpieces and one of the finest castles in Italy. It was built by Frederick II of Swabia between 1240 and 1250, probably as a prison, and was later used as a hunting lodge, but no one knows the real reason for its construction. Astronomical, astrological, and mathematical theories abound — it is sort of an Apulian Stonehenge. It is a perfect octagon, with eight corner towers, also octagonal, and eight trapezoidal rooms on each floor. The pale, champagne-colored structure — one of the earliest and purest Gothic buildings in southern Italy — was once full of sculpture, its walls faced with marble, but most of its decoration was lost by the 18th century, when the building was more or less abandoned, left to house the occasional shepherd. The windows of the castle afford a good view of the Tavoliere and surrounding Murge hills. Open daily, except Mondays, from 9 AM to noon; no admission charge (phone: 80-521-4361).

EATING OUT: ***Vecchia Masseria*** **–** Housed in an ancient farmhouse (*masseria*) a mile (1.6 km) south of the castle (back at the turnoff for Minervino), it provides a delightful ambience, even though it is inevitably filled with a tourist crowd — high ceilings supported by dark wooden beams and white stucco walls adorned with rich paintings. Order a sampling of several kinds of pasta, followed by *spiedini misto carne* (a shish kebab of lamb, veal, sausage, and pork). Castel del Monte (white, red, or rosé) is the appropriate wine. Some guestrooms are available. Closed Wednesdays, except in high season, and most of January. Reservations unnecessary. No credit cards accepted. Km 22, SS170, Castel del Monte (phone: 883-81529). Moderate to inexpensive.

En Route from Castel del Monte – Return to the coast on SS170 north to Andria, and then detour northeast to Trani, a 45-minute drive from Castel del Monte. After the visit, continue to Barletta, 8 miles (13 km) west of Trani along the coast road (SS16).

TRANI: In the 12th century, Trani gained considerable importance when Frederick II established his tribunal here. The approach to this coastal town runs through vineyard after vineyard of the moscato (muscat) grape that is used to make the sweet dessert wine for which Trani is famous. Also famous is Trani's exquisite 11th- to 13th-century Apulian-Romanesque cathedral, built of the very pale stone called Trani marble. Best seen at sunset, the enormous cathedral, a splendidly off-white building against a backdrop of glistening deep blue sea, is dedicated to San Nicola Pellegrino, a Greek who settled in Trani because he found its inhabitants to be the friendliest in the area — a reputation still enjoyed today. Its bell tower is set on an arch, with the number of windows increasing as it rises. The cathedral's extraordinary bronze doors (ca. 1180), reflecting Byzantine influence, are by Barisano da Trani (who also cast the doors of the Duomo at Ravello and the one at Monreale). Inside, this remarkable church is actually three churches on separate levels: The much older (perhaps 7th-century) Chiesa di Santa Maria, on which the main church was built, is reached through the crypt, and under it is the still older Ipogeo di San Leucio. Trani's surrounding medieval quarter is also of interest, and the town has a charming port, which has become something of a Riviera-style hideaway for the yachting set. It also has lovely public gardens that offer a good view of the marina. The tourist office is at Piazza della Repubblica (phone: 883-43295).

CHECKING IN: ***Royal*** **–** A comfortable, air conditioned, 50-room hotel in the center of town, near the station. Its more-than-passable restaurant opens onto a delightful, almost tropical courtyard in summer. 29 Via de' Robertis, Trani (phone: 883-588777; fax: 883-582224). Moderate.

Albergo Lucy **–** This small, simple hostelry near the public gardens enjoys a unique position by the port. 11 Piazza Plebiscito, Trani (phone: 883-41022). Inexpensive.

EATING OUT: ***La Darsena*** **–** Almost toppling into the port, this tiny spot is a must for lovers of romantic places, as well as for those who appreciate good food. The menu features much fish and seafood, all imaginatively prepared. Closed Wednesdays. Reservations advised. Major credit cards accepted. 98 Via Statuti Marittimi, Trani (phone: 883-47333). Expensive to moderate.

L'Antica Cattedrale **–** Across from the cathedral, this terrace restaurant serves a variety of pizza, grilled meat, and fish, against a brilliant backdrop of sea. The piano bar makes this a popular spot with the locals. Closed Mondays. Reservations advised on weekends. Major credit cards accepted. 2 Piazza Archivio, Trani (phone: 883-586568). Moderate.

BARLETTA: Only a short ride from Trani, this port city is best known for the famous Disfida di Barletta (Challenge of Barletta), a bloody battle between 13 Frenchmen and 13 Italians that took place on February 13, 1503. The context of the challenge was the struggle between the French and the Spanish for hegemony of the region (the Spanish won), and its immediate provocation was a disparaging remark made by a Frenchman regarding Italian courage. The Italians won the challenge. Barletta's main attraction, however, the Colosso (Colossus), predates this incident. It is a massive bronze statue of a Byzantine emperor (exactly which one is not certain), 16 feet tall, cast in the 4th century, and is regarded to be the finest piece of colossal bronze sculpture from ancient times. It once stood in Constantinople and was part of the booty the Venetians took from the sack of the city in the early 13th century, along with the four famous bronze horses now in Venice. Due to a shipwreck, the Colossus was abandoned on the shores of Barletta and now stands at the corner of Corso Vittorio Emanuele and Corso Garibaldi, next to the 13th-century Church of San Sepolcro. The city also has a lovely Romanesque cathedral by the port and an impressive 13th-century castle on the southern edge of town. Each year, on the last Sunday in July, a historical reenactment of the Disfida takes place.

EATING OUT: ***Il Bacco*** – Slightly away from the Old Town, this restaurant with exquisite food and decor is nevertheless Barletta's most popular and one of the finest in Puglia. Local specialties are treated masterfully, particularly fresh pasta dishes and lamb. Closed Sunday evenings, Mondays, and during August. Reservations necessary. Major credit cards accepted. 10 Via Sipontina, Barletta (phone: 883-38398). Expensive.

Il Brigantino – A spacious seaside resort restaurant, family-run, patronized by local businesspeople as well as tourists. It offers typical Apulian antipasti, such as *insalata di mare* (a salad of squid, octopus, and cuttlefish); *calzone pugliese* (a soft pizza bread stuffed with onions, olives, and anchovies); *cavatelli con fagioli* (pasta with beans); *fichi e prosciutto* (large, moist figs with prosciutto); and *scamorza alla griglia* (grilled scamorza cheese). Closed Wednesdays and during January. Reservations advised on weekends. Major credit cards accepted. Litoranea di Levante, Barletta (phone: 883-33345). Moderate.

En Route from Barletta – Continue northwestward, first on SS16 and then on SS159, through Margherita di Savoia and beyond, past mounds of sparkling salt beds and geometric patches of farmland. Stay on the coast road, and as it approaches Manfredonia, the strikingly beautiful and rugged promontory of Gargano appears. Farther along, the charming town of Mattinata makes a worthy stop for its winding streets and excellent restaurants with spectacular views. The tourist office (5 Piazza Roma; no phone) can arrange trips to grottoes and donkey rides in the surrounding craggy hills of olive trees. The town's most unusual feature, perhaps, is its pharmacy: Dr. Matteo Sansone, an antiquities expert, dispenses Band-Aids and aspirin in a drugstore museum, *Farmacia Sansone* (9 Via d'Azeglio; phone: 881-4170), filled with locally collected Greek stelae, holy water fonts, busts, paintings, and a lifetime supply of curios. After Mattinata, the winding SS89, also known as the Garganica, climbs high into the coastal mountains — which eventually soar to over 3,000 feet — affording dazzling panoramas of the dramatic blue-green Adriatic and its craggy, white-rock outline. The road descends to the sea at the ancient town of Vieste. Alternatively, keep on the coast road, somewhat quicker, which leads to Vieste via Pugnochiuso. Note: In order to protect the coastline, very few hotels are built directly on the beach.

CHECKING IN: ***Apeneste*** – Attractive, modern, and simple, this 26-room hotel has air conditioning, tennis courts, swimming pool, and a private beach 1 mile (1.6 km) away. It has an excellent restaurant, *La Rucola,* where imaginative menus have won many awards. There is also a discotheque. Half board is required in high season. 3 Piazza Turati, Mattinata (phone: 884-4743; fax: 884-4341). Expensive to moderate.

EATING OUT: ***Papone*** – Housed in a sparkling fresh 18th-century olive press factory, this is an exceptional restaurant featuring homemade pasta, fresh fish, and roast meat dishes. Closed Mondays from December through May, and November. Reservations unnecessary. Visa accepted. 89N Strada Statale, Km 144, Mattinata (phone: 884-4749). Moderate.

Portonuovo – Adorned with the works of local artists, it features well-prepared, exceptionally fresh food from homegrown ingredients. Closed Mondays. Reservations unnecessary. Visa accepted. Lama le Canne, Villagio Olivia, Vieste (phone: 884-700905). Moderate.

VIESTE: This onetime fishing village, on a rocky outcropping at the far end of the Gargano, has become the chief resort town of the area. Its old quarter, a spill of whitewashed houses and narrow step streets, reaches out along a small peninsula, with an old cathedral and a Swabian castle (built by Frederick II) perched on a cliff overlooking the sea. Although Vieste is surrounded by beaches, its southern (or eastern) side is especially favored. Just at the edge of town, marked by the giant rock called the Pizzomunno, the long, wide Castello Beach begins, and some 14 miles (22 km) along the coast on this same side is the huge resort complex of Pugnochiuso, set on a small, picturesque bay.

Either Vieste or Pugnochiuso can be used as a base for exploring the Gargano area. Not to be missed is the spectacular coastal drive north and west around the promontory to the villages of Peschici and Rodi Garganico, considered one of the most naturally scenic drives in all of Italy. From Rodi Garganico, as well as from Vieste and Pugnochiuso, day ferries travel to the Isole Tremiti, a trio of rocky islands (San Domino, San Nicola, and Capraia), part of the same geological formation, with beaches, historic ruins, and gorgeous views, off the northern coast of Gargano (a 3- to 4-hour trip from Vieste or Pugnochiuso, considerably shorter from Rodi or Peschici). Accommodations here are very limited. In the Gargano interior, the shady, tranquil Foresta Umbra stretches for thousands of acres.

CHECKING IN: ***Pugnochiuso*** – This resort complex, along the coast south of Vieste, is a village unto itself, containing two beachfront hotels — *Albergo del Faro* and *Albergo degli Ulivi* — with more than 400 rooms, as well as bungalows and cottages. Guests may limit themselves to communing with the sand, sea, and surrounding pine woods or make maximum use of the resort facilities: 2 swimming pools (one Olympic-size), tennis courts, a gym, sailing, and water skiing facilities, a theater, a nightclub, and even a commercial center with a bank, boutiques, and a travel agency. All told, there are 5 restaurants. Minimum 1-week stay required; full board obligatory. Open from *Easter* through October. Centro Vacanze di Pugnochiuso (phone and fax: 884-709011). Very expensive to expensive.

Pizzomunno Vieste Palace – One of Italy's most prestigious beach hotels, this 183-room, full-service resort is on its own parkland. It has luxurious air conditioned accommodations, a stretch of private sandy beach, facilities for a full range of water sports, 3 tennis courts, and 2 swimming pools. Its dining room serves excellent regional specialties — try the *agnello al forno* (roast lamb) or any kind of fresh seafood. There also is a new fitness and beauty center, a disco/piano bar, and theater. Open late March to mid-October. Half board mandatory in season.

Spiaggia di Pizzomunno, Vieste del Gargano (phone: 884-708741; fax: 884-707325). Expensive.

EATING OUT: ***San Michele*** – The only good restaurant in town, serving both local dishes and seafood, including charbroiled fish. Closed Thursdays and January 7 to mid-March. Reservations advised, especially on weekends. Major credit cards accepted. 72 Viale XXIV Maggio, Vieste (phone: 884-708143). Expensive.

En Route from Vieste – Take SS89 west out of Vieste for several miles and pick up SS528 inland (alternatively, pick up SS528 by turning off the coastal drive at Valazzo, between Peschici — where the views are unparalleled — and Rodi Garganico, and driving inland past Vico del Gargano). The road leads through the Foresta Umbra to SS272, where a turn to the east along a number of hairpin turns leads to Monte Sant'Angelo and a turn to the west to San Giovanni Rotondo.

MONTE SANT'ANGELO: This is the highest town of the Gargano — on a clear day you can see as far as Bari — and an important place for pilgrimages. According to tradition, the Archangel Michael appeared here more than once in the late 5th century (to a bishop according to one story, to shepherds according to another), leaving behind either a footprint or a red cloak (again, depending on the legend), but certainly enough of an impression to cause a shrine to be built. The resulting Santuario di San Michele (Sanctuary of St. Michael) was especially well known during the Crusades, when the Gargano (particularly the nearby town of Manfredonia which was the embarkation point for Crusaders) was a way station en route to the Holy Land. The sanctuary is at the edge of town, entered through impressive bronze doors with 24 illustrated panels cast in Constantinople in 1076. Across from it is the so-called Tomba di Rotari (Tomb of Rotharis), which was built in the 12th century, but most likely as a baptistry. Perhaps more interesting is the multi-level medieval town itself, which remains unchanged despite masses of tourists and pilgrims. Surrounded by hollow caves, prickly-pear cactus, and pines, it offers splendid panoramas of chalk-white, lonely countryside. The town also has a castle, originally Norman, that was enlarged by the Swabians and the Aragonese.

SAN GIOVANNI ROTONDO: Inland from Monte Sant'Angelo, this town is another popular place of pilgrimage, considerably less picturesque than Monte Sant'Angelo, but it gained its status only in the 20th century as the result of its association with Padre Pio. The Capuchin monk, who received the stigmata and who performed miracles for the sick, lived in the local monastery and is now buried here in the crypt of Santa Maria delle Grazie Church. Visitors can see his room and the place where he received the stigmata in 1918 which he bore until his death in 1968. The town has a modern church and hospital dedicated to him that is supported by his followers, many of them American.

En Route from San Giovanni Rotondo – Leave Gargano by taking SS273 south and turning onto SS89, heading inland to Foggia.

FOGGIA: Capitanata's capital city, in the center of the Tavoliere, was chosen by Frederick II as his residence and was also a favorite of the Angevins and the Aragonese. The city suffered an earthquake in 1731 and was heavily bombed during World War II, but its beautiful 12th-century cathedral (largely rebuilt in the 18th century), the largest in the province, is worth a visit. The *Museo Civico* (2 Piazza Nigri; phone: 881-26245) is housed in a building sporting an arch that is the only remnant of

Frederick's 13th-century palace; it contains fascinating artifacts and archaeological background on the area. Open weekday mornings only. The tourist office is at 17 Via E. Perrone (phone: 881-23650).

Lucera, 12 miles (19 km) west of Foggia, makes an interesting excursion. On one side of this pre-Roman village is one of the oldest known Roman amphitheaters, dating from the 1st century BC. On the other side, on a hill at the edge of the Tavoliere, is a superb castle, consisting of a fortress built by Frederick II in 1233 and a surrounding pentagonal wall built by Charles I of Anjou in the late 13th century. The Swabian structure is virtually dwarfed by the Angevin wall, which is nearly a kilometer in circumference and is articulated with 24 defense towers. The town's Duomo, in a strikingly simple Gothic style, is another Angevin monument, from the early 14th century.

CHECKING IN/EATING OUT: ***Cicolella*** – The best rooms and the best food in town can both be had at this 125-room hotel in the center of Foggia. The restaurant serves exceptionally well-prepared regional specialties (try *troccoli,* a local pasta) or *agnello arrosto* (roast lamb), as well as local wines, such as torre quarto rosso, a fine red. The hotel also has two other restaurants in town (on Via Bari), both bearing the same name and equally good. Restaurant closed Saturday evenings, Sundays, 2 weeks in August, and 2 weeks at *Christmas.* Reservations advised. Major credit cards accepted. 60 Viale XXIV Maggio, Foggia (phone: 881-3890; fax: 881-78984). Hotel, very expensive; restaurant, expensive.

En Route from Foggia – Return to Bari by A14 (80 miles/129 km) and proceed beyond the city to visit the *trulli* district and the Salento. Mola di Bari, a lovely fishing village with both an ancient town and a modern quarter, a Romanesque cathedral, and an Angevin castle, is 13 miles (21 km) south of Bari along the coastal SS16. The highlight of its 3-day *Sagra del Polpo* (Octopus Festival), held each July, is octopus prepared a hundred different ways! The town is also famous for a local variation of lasagna, prepared with anchovies, almonds, and basil and named after its patron saint, San Giuseppe. Continue on the coastal road to Monopoli, where ancient fortified farmhouses, known as *vecchie masserie,* are being converted into restaurants with lodgings and facilities for small conferences. This delightful town of green-shuttered windows and churches includes a fine Apulian-Romanesque cathedral that houses a statue of the Madonna della Madia, who, legend tells, arrived in Monopoli on a raft in the 12th century. There is also a castle that looks out to sea, and a picturesque port that once bustled with trade to the East. A short distance up the coast is Polignano, sun-bleached and perched atop promontories riddled with caves.

CHECKING IN: ***Castellinaria*** – A tasteful, hacienda-style resort stretched along the sea, with 32 air conditioned rooms, water sports, a private beach, and a lovely terrace restaurant. SS16, Cala San Giovanni, Polignano a Mare (phone: 80-740233). Moderate.

EATING OUT: ***Grotta Palazzese*** – Along the coast between Mola di Bari and Monopoli. There are 19 air conditioned rooms for rent here, but the real treat is the summer dining — in an enormous natural grotto with the sea on one side and a rushing torrent on the other. Very good, fresh seafood, and excellent pasta. Reservations advised in high season. No credit cards accepted. 59 Via Narciso, Polignano a Mare (phone: 80-740261 or 80-740677; fax: 80-740767). Hotel, moderate; restaurant, expensive to moderate.

Villa Meo-Evoli – A Venetian-style villa reincarnated as a delightful restaurant serving a blend of Apulian and continental fare. Garden paths and dramatic statues make for pleasant strolling. Closed Tuesdays. Reservations advised. No credit cards accepted. Strada Provinciale per Conversano, Km 6.5, Contrada Cozzana, Monopoli (phone: 80-803052). Moderate.

En Route from Monopoli – From Monopoli, turn inland on SS377 to Castellana Grotte, famous for its stalactite caves, some of the most spectacular in Europe. These are a little over a mile (1.6 km) southwest of town, and their fantastic stalactite, stalagmite, and alabaster flower formations can be visited in 1- or 2-hour guided tours. The pièce de résistance, the Caverna (or Grotta) Bianca, figures only on the 2-hour tour. Tours in English offered daily, mornings and afternoons in summer, mornings only off-season; admission charge.

After Castellana, continue to Putignano and there turn east along SS172 to Alberobello, the center of the *trullo* district.

ALBEROBELLO: This unique village has over 1,000 of the whitewashed conical stone huts — *trulli* — that are characteristic of this part of Puglia. These curious examples of domestic architecture are of ancient origin, although most of those seen today are no more than a few hundred years old (400 at most), and the *trullo* design is also used for modern variations on the theme. Alberobello has an entire zone, the all-white fairy-tale *zona monumentale,* of old "urban" *trulli* — attached and semidetached in clusters or lining the narrow streets. Many are still inhabited, while others serve as shops selling local crafts, handwoven items, regional wines, and foods. The most famous is the 50-foot-high, 2-story *trullo sovrano,* but the town also has a modern *trullo* church, San Antonio, and a *trullo* hotel. Welcome to Trulliland! *Agenzia Fittatrulli* (5 Via Duchessa Aquaviva; phone: 80-722717) rents authentic, renovated *trulli* in town or in the country that sleep from 2 to 8 people. Some have kitchens, some are deluxe, and weekly rates are available. The tourist office (Piazza del Popolo; phone: 80-721916) has information on the town.

CHECKING IN: ***Hotel dei Trulli*** – This establishment consists not of rooms, but of entire 20 individual *trulli* of modern construction, each of which has its own bath and sitting room and air conditioning. There also is a good restaurant, a swimming pool, and verdant grounds. 32 Via Cadore, Alberobello (phone: 80-721130; fax: 80-721916). Expensive.

Colle del Solo – A small, pleasant, and scrupulously clean hotel with 25 rooms and 5 suites on the edge of town, just a few minutes' walk from the *trulli* zone, with friendly staff and a decent restaurant. 61 Via Indipendenza, Alberobello (phone: 80-721370; fax: 80-721370). Inexpensive.

EATING OUT: ***Trullo d'Oro*** – The next best thing to staying in a *trullo* is having a meal in one. Despite a very touristy location, the standards here are high in this authentic, tastefully restored, 400-year-old *trullo.* The Apulian dishes served may include *calzone di cipolla* (yeast bread stuffed with a sauce of onions, tomatoes, and capers), *orecchiette con ciceri* (ear-shaped pasta with chickpeas in broth), various eggplant entrées, *fave e cicoria* (fava beans and chicory), and fresh mozzarella cheese. Closed Mondays, except in high season, and the last 3 weeks of January. Reservations advised. Major credit cards accepted. 29 Via Cavallotti, Alberobello (phone: 80-721820). Expensive to moderate.

Il Poeta Contadino – Considered the best in town, this dining spot has a distinctly medieval atmosphere — vaulted stone ceilings and shadowy alcoves. Fine local specialties and fresh pasta, and mouth-watering fish and meat dishes cooked according to Apulian traditions. It's a busy place, so arrive early. Closed Fridays and from January to mid-February. Reservations advised. Major credit cards accepted. 21 Via Indipendenza, Alberobello (phone: 80-721917). Moderate.

Il Guercio di Puglia – Named for a local overlord who, legend has it, exercised his droit du seigneur with his subjects' brides on their wedding night, this restaurant has a pleasant outdoor terrace and specializes in regional cooking. Begin with one of the delicious and unusual starters, such as a strong ricotta cheese that resembles cheddar, and follow with one of the substantial entrées, such as *agnello con patate* *e lampazioni* (lamb with potatoes and wild baby onions). Closed Wednesdays except in summer and January. Reservations advised. Major credit cards accepted. 19 Largo Martellotta, Alberobello (phone: 80-721816). Moderate to inexpensive.

En Route from Alberobello – Head southeast to Locorotondo, a delightful village built on a circular plan, as its name suggests. Then drop south to Martina Franca. The route passes through the Valle d'Itria, where isolated rural *trulli* dot the landscape.

MARTINA FRANCA: Halfway between the Adriatic and Ionian coasts and on the highest point of the Murge, this enchanting town is built in an almost perfect circle. Its historic center has an overall 17th- and 18th-century look, and a walk along its narrow streets reveals baroque and rococo mansions and balconies, sculpted festoons of flowers, little squares, and whitewashed cottages. The walls and ceilings of the massive 17th-century Palazzo Ducale, now the Town Hall and the only example of a building designed by Bernini in the entire south of Italy, were frescoed by a local painter, Domenico Carella, and its terrace has views of the Itria Valley. Its tourist office is at 37 Piazza Roma (phone: 80-705702).

En Route from Martina Franca – It's only 6 miles (10 km) north to Cisternino, a charming, chalk-white medieval hill town that is worth a stop. From there it is another 9 miles (14 km) east to Ostuni.

About 8 miles (13 km) to the south from either Cisternino or Ostuni is Ceglie Messapico, a small, whitewashed town that seems to have little to do with Italy. In fact, it was once a center and acropolis of the ancient Messapi, who populated much of the area and the Salento but left little trace except for defense walls, laid without mortar, and an alphabet, still undeciphered. Like the Etruscans, the Messapi remain a mystery. Other centers were Miano, Manduria, Oria, and Mesagne — one of the most important — founded in 1600 as Messapia.

EATING OUT: ***Allo Spiedo da Antonietta*** – Weary, hungry travelers will find this eatery a pleasant place to stop. The homemade pasta and mouth-watering starters alone make a detour here well worth the effort. Closed Wednesdays except in high season. Reservations unnecessary. Visa accepted. 30 Via Virgilio, Martina Franca (phone: 80-706511). Inexpensive.

OSTUNI: Probably the most remarkable town in Puglia; from a distance across the plain, it appears as a mirage of bleached-white buildings covering three hills, with a 15th-century Gothic cathedral at the highest point. Close up, the intricately detailed rose window over the church's central door comes into view, followed by the town's narrow streets spanned by graceful archways, its black wrought-iron balconies and lanterns, and its sparkling white buildings with green or turquoise shutters, all reminiscent of a Greek village. The main square, Piazza della Libertà, has the baroque obelisk of Sant'Oronzo (who rescued Ostuni from a plague in the 17th century), a church, a bookstore, a small café, and a *gelateria* turning out fresh *granita di limone* (lemon ice). From Ostuni, it is 4 miles (6 km) to the coast and a beachfront zone, Marina di Ostuni, that extends for several kilometers. The area produces a good dry white wine. The tourist office is at Piazza Libertà (phone: 831-301268).

CHECKING IN: ***RosaMarina*** – An outstanding, attractive, modern resort on the coast northwest of Ostuni proper. Its architecture is in the pure-white Moorish vein, and many of the 240 rooms open onto gardens. It has tennis courts, an inviting pool, access to a private beach, and a restaurant serving fine regional specialties and local wines. Minimum-stay (1 week) and meal requirements (half board). Open mid-May to late September. Centro Vacanze RosaMarina, Marina di Ostuni (phone: 831-970411; fax: 831-970411). Moderate.

EATING OUT: ***3 Torri*** **–** A sophisticated, comfortable restaurant (and hotel) serving regional food with panache. Closed Tuesdays. Reservations advised on weekends and in high season. Major credit cards accepted. Take SS16 toward Brindisi; 294 Corso Vittorio Emanuele, Ostuni (phone: 831-973414). Moderate.

Vecchia Ostuni **–** Almost every town in Puglia has a restaurant that calls itself *vecchio* (or *vecchia*), but few sport old traditions. It is clear that here the cook gets up early to get the best that market and fishing boats have to offer. Closed Tuesdays. Reservations advised. Major credit cards accepted. 9 Largo Lanza, Ostuni (phone: 831-973308). Inexpensive.

En Route from Ostuni – Take SS379 as far as Brindisi (20 miles/32 km from Marina di Ostuni) and from there take SS16 or the Superstrada Brindisi-Lecce another 25 miles (40 km) to Lecce. Brindisi is a major port and departure point for ferries to Greece, but the city is largely modern, with little of interest to visitors. One of the two ancient Roman columns that marked the end of the Via Appia Antica (Appian Way) stands overlooking the port, near the house where Virgil died. The other column fell down during the 16th century and is reputed to be in Lecce.

LECCE: In the center of the Salento Peninsula and known as the Florence of the South, Lecce was first a Greek and then a Roman town, but it reached its height of cultural and architectural development between the 16th and 18th centuries. It is virtually brimming with fine examples of *barocco leccese,* a particularly exuberant version of baroque architecture — much of the city is hidden by scaffolding, thanks to a recent multimillion-dollar government grant — made possible not only by the local temperament but also by the soft local stone, which can be easily worked but hardens on exposure to air, taking on a warm golden tone. The building renaissance was thanks, in large part, to important religious institutions such as the Jesuits throwing their money and weight around as Lecce, rich in agriculture and banking, thrived. The city's most striking church, the Basilica di Santa Croce, built from the mid-16th to the mid-17th century, has a glorious recently renovated façade exploding with baroque detail — flora and fauna, monsters and angels. The interior, by contrast, is in the more restrained style of the Renaissance. The artist responsible for the most ornate parts of the Santa Croce façade, Giuseppe Zimbalo (one of the most spirited practitioners of the local baroque), was also responsible for the lower levels of the Palazzo del Governo next door, while his pupil, Giuseppe Cino, did the upper levels. Several blocks away, in Piazza del Duomo, is a wonderful baroque ensemble consisting of the cathedral, rebuilt by Zimbalo in the mid-17th century, its 210-foot bell tower, a seminary (more of Cino's work), and, in the seminary courtyard, a fantastic baroque well embellished with rich clusters of fruit, garlands, flowers, and little *putti.* Walk along Via Palmieri (Lecce's "Aristocracy Row") to both see and feel the festive spirit of the baroque façade — a swarm of caryatids and other figures lend a very theatrical touch.

At Piazza Sant'Oronzo, roughly equidistant from Santa Croce and Piazza del Duomo, are the most noteworthy of Lecce's Roman remains: a Roman ampitheater from the 1st century BC and the (alleged) remaining Roman column that marked the end of the Appian Way in Brindisi. Here it's called the Colonna di Sant'Oronzo and is topped with a statue of Lecce's patron saint. The 16th-century Palazzo del Sedile, in the same square, houses Lecce's tourist information office (phone: 832-24443).

Pâpier-maché, or *carta pesta,* is a centuries-old craft still practiced in Lecce, not only for tourist products, but for the fashioning and repair of religious reliquaries. It is, however, not that widely found. Every December, Bari hosts a world-renowned papier-mâché fair. To see it being made by professionals, go to Mario di Donfrancesco's workshop at 1 Via d'Amelio, Lecce (phone: 832-642593).

CHECKING IN: ***President*** – Catering primarily to businesspeople, this 150-room hotel is in the newer section of town, about a 10-minute walk from the old center. The decor is modern and functional (although somewhat bland and the walls are a bit thin), and there is a good restaurant. 6 Via Salandra, Lecce (phone: 832-311881; fax: 832-594321). Expensive.

Risorgimento – Local politicians frequent this atmospheric hotel in a 19th-century palazzo near Piazza Sant'Oronzo. One of the very few in the historic quarter, it is old-fashioned and slightly stuffy. The 57 rooms have been decorated on the dark side, but all are air conditioned. There is a restaurant. 19 Via Imperatore Augusto, Lecce (phone: 832-42125). Moderate.

EATING OUT: ***Carlo IV*** – This rather restrained though chi-chi wine bar–restaurant is proof that sometimes southern Italy can be as sophisticated as Milan or Turin — or close to it. The tasteful mix of modern and classical decor is reflected in the menu. Quality of the food is high (and your bill can be, too). Closed Sunday evenings and Mondays. Reservations advised. Major credit cards accepted. 46 Via Palmieri, Lecce (phone: 832-46042). Expensive to moderate.

Gambrinus – Tasteful fin de siècle decor with modern touches make this always-crowded spot a must for lunch or dinner. Luckily, it's now run separately from the somewhat fallen-from-grace *Patria* hotel in the same building. Try the *macheroncini all' antica lecce* (pasta served with *pecorino* cheese, tomato, and pepper sauce), the tasty kebabs, and desserts. Closed Sundays. Reservations advised. Major credit cards accepted. 13 Piazzetta Riccardi, Lecce (phone: 832-29431). Moderate.

Il Satirello – Out of town, a lovely 18th-century farmhouse (*masseria*) turned stylish restaurant, with heavy vaulted ceilings, a large flagstone patio, and hearty regional fare. Closed Tuesdays. Reservations advised on weekends. Major credit cards accepted. Km 9, Strada Provinciale Lecce–Torre Chianca (turn off at the *Tiziano* hotel) (phone: 832-656121). Moderate.

Gambero Rosso – Ronzino de Santis's eatery has a local feel, with the TV set reigning in the corner. Self-service antipasti are the specialty, as are the pizza and homemade pasta. The grilled meat is reminiscent of Greece. Try the hot, Middle Eastern–style bread — it makes up for the intrusion of television. Closed Thursdays. Reservations unnecessary. No credit cards accepted. 16 Via Brancaccio, Lecce (phone: 832-41569). Moderate to inexpensive.

Guido e Figli – A delightful trattoria where natives go for atmosphere, good food, hearty and local wines, and excellent value for the money. Pizza also is served. Closed Fridays. Reservations advised. Major credit cards accepted. 14 Via 25 Luglio, Lecce (phone: 832-25868). Moderate to inexpensive.

En Route from Lecce – Otranto and Gallipoli are south of Lecce on opposite coasts. Take SS543 to the Adriatic and then the coast road, SS611, southeast to Otranto; afterward, cut directly across the Salento Peninsula via SS16 and SS459 to Gallipoli, on the Ionian coast. Alternatively, either city can be explored from Lecce — Otranto is 27 miles (43 km) away, and Gallipoli is 23 miles (37 km) away; take SS101 south out of Lecce).

The area between Lecce and Otranto closely resembles parts of Greece, with olive trees, rocky outcrops, and stone huts. In fact, as in much of the Salento, the Greek culture not only was present but still lives on here. Residents of no fewer than nine towns — Calimera, Martignano, Sternatìa, Zollino, Soleto, Martano, Corigliano d'Otranto, Melpignano, and Castrignano de'Greci — many lying close to SS16 southeast from Lecce to Máglie, still speak a dialect resembling ancient Greek, dating back to settlers who came in the 7th century. To reach Otranto afterward, proceed to Máglie and follow the SS16, which turns eastward toward the coast. Alternatively, cut across to Otranto from the town of Martano.

OTRANTO: Italy's easternmost town, now a ferry departure point for Corfu, is attractive, with some of it still enclosed in its old walls. A large part of the old section is undergoing a much-needed face-lift. An important town during Puglia's Byzantine era, it was later ruled by the Normans and was sacked by the Turks in 1480. An amazing mosaic covering the entire floor of Otranto's 12th-century cathedral is especially worth the trip. A 5-year restoration was completed last summer. The work of a monk, Pantaleone, from 1163 to 1166, it features a tree of life with vivid depictions of biblical, mythological, and secular scenes, months of the year, animals, and more. Also fascinating are the 42 columns (no two alike) in the crypt of the cathedral and the Cappella dei Martiri (Chapel of the Martyrs), which houses the artistically stacked bones of 560 martyrs slaughtered by the Turks (the custodian will gladly show you). Otranto also has a famous castle, begun by the Aragonese in 1485, after they ousted the Turks. The writer Horace Walpole set his novel *The Castle of Otranto* here, although he never actually saw the castle. The local tourist office (AAST) is on Lungomare Kennedy (phone: 836-81436).

CHECKING IN: ***Albania*** – A small air conditioned hotel (10 rooms) with a good restaurant in the center of town, serving seafood specialties and offering alfresco dining in summer. Half board required in high season. Closed in winter; restaurant closed October through June. 10 Via San Francesco di Paola, Otranto (phone: 836-81183). Moderate to inexpensive.

EATING OUT: ***Vecchia Otranto*** – An attractive, rustic hideaway where the food is both local and imaginative. Specialties include pasta served with dates and prawns and fresh fish cooked over the fire. Closed Mondays and November. Reservations advised in summer and on weekends. American Express accepted. 96 Corso Garibaldi, Otranto (phone: 836-81575). Moderate.

Taverna del Leone – Reminiscent of Greece, this delightful taverna has checkered tablecloths. Good local food is served in pleasant surroundings and tables move outside in the summer. No reservations. No credit cards accepted. Corso Garibaldi, Otranto (no phone). Inexpensive.

GALLIPOLI: This busy port on the Ionian Sea was justly named Kallipolis (Beautiful City) by the Greeks. It consists of a modern city on a spit of land pointing toward a rocky little island, on which lies the medieval quarter, with an ancient bridge connecting the two. The medieval quarter has narrow winding streets and white houses, giving it a Greek look even today, and it's circled by a panoramic road on the site of the old walls. Gallipoli has a castle on the island at the bridge. Begun by the Angevins (but altered in the 16th century), its ramparts seem to emerge directly from the sea. At the opposite end of the bridge is another of the town's main attractions, the Fontana Ellenistica, a fountain dating from the town's Greek days, although it was rebuilt in the 16th century. The detailed façade of the town's 17th-century cathedral, dedicated to St. Agatha, shows the influence of Lecce. Gallipoli's old harbor, at one time occupied by Spanish and Turkish galleons, is now crowded with fishing boats. Crabs are prolific here, as are sponges; the latter can be picked up for a modest price at shops around the port.

CHECKING IN: ***Costa Brada*** – Out of town, 4 miles (6 km) south along the coast, but well worth the drive. It has 78 pleasant, modern rooms, 2 restaurants, 2 pools (both outdoor and indoor), a fitness center, tennis courts, a nightclub, and its own sandy beach. At least half board is obligatory in high season. Litoranea per Santa Maria di Leuca, Gallipoli (phone: 833-22551; fax: 833-22555). Expensive.

Joli Park – In the center of town, a 10-minute walk from the old city, this comfortable, well-maintained hotel has 90 rooms and a decent restaurant. 2 Via Lecce, Gallipoli (phone: 883-473321). Inexpensive.

EATING OUT: ***Marechiaro*** – Wonderful seafood is served in a rustic portside setting (once a gathering spot for fishermen) reached by a tiny, private bridge. Dine alfresco on the terrace on dishes such as *zuppa di pesce alla gallipolina* (fish soup Gallipoli-style). Closed Tuesdays from October through May. Reservations advised. Major credit cards accepted. Scoglio delle Uccolette, Lungomare Marconi, Gallipoli (phone: 833-476143). Moderate.

En Route from Gallipoli – Follow the coast road north along the Gulf of Taranto, touching on tiny coastal spots such as Santa Maria al Bagno and Santa Caterina (5 and 6 miles/8 and 10 km, respectively, from Gallipoli), which are more reminiscent of North Africa than of anything Italian. At Santa Caterina the road detours slightly inland to make way for a nature preserve (accessible to pedestrians) before returning to Torre San Isodoro, 7 miles (11 km) on. It is around here and in nearby Porto Cesareo that one finds some of Puglia's most beautiful coves, where the clear water of the Ionian Sea ranges in hue from jade green to lapis blue. Not all of the beaches are open to the public, but those that are make wonderful summer rest or relaxation stops en route to Taranto.

EATING OUT: ***La Pergola*** – An excellent trattoria specializing in seafood, a stone's throw from the town's tiny gem of a beach. Egyptian owner Mario Ezzat blends North African dishes with local fare. The *penne alla pergola* and *risotto verde* (risotto made with a vegetable purée sauce) are especially good for starters. Closed Tuesdays and during November. Reservations advised in season and on weekends. No credit cards accepted. 5 Piazza Nardò, Santa Maria al Bagno (phone: 833-823008). Moderate to inexpensive.

TARANTO: A city of very ancient origins, Taranto was founded by the Spartans in 708 BC. Called Taras by the Greeks, it was a major center of Magna Graecia, and its importance endured long after other Greek colonies had declined — it was not conquered by the Romans until the 3rd century BC. Ancient remains are sparse in today's Taranto, however; this is largely a modern, industrial city and a naval base that attracts little tourism. But its *Museo Nazionale* (National Museum; 5 Corso Umberto, Taranto; phone: 99-432113), containing superb Greek statuary, pottery, and jewelry, is an archaeological museum (one of the most prominent in southern Italy), and in itself worth the trip for lovers of antiquities. Open daily from 9 AM to 1:30 PM; admission charge.

Taranto does have an old, medieval city, which, as in Gallipoli, is on an island joined to the new city by a bridge. Both the Old and New Towns are sandwiched between an internal sea, the Mar Piccolo, and the larger Mar Grande, which is an extra scallop in the edge of the greater Gulf of Taranto. Given its special geography, it's hardly surprising that mussels, oysters, and other seafood are cultivated with great success. The city is also known for its waterside promenades and flowering parks — such as the Lungomare Vittorio Emanuele III along the Mar Grande and the Villa Peripato, with a terrace overlooking the Mar Piccolo (both in the New Town).

The Duomo, in the Old Town, built from the 10th to the 12th century, was redone again and again; its façade is baroque, although traces of its original form remain in Byzantine-style mosaics and frescoes. In 1971, Italy's well-known architect, Gio Ponti, built another cathedral in the New Town. Since Taranto, like Bari, is a major port and attracts more than its share of thieves, don't leave anything valuable in your car, and don't carry much cash.

Several renowned *Holy Week* events take place in Taranto: On *Holy Thursday,* there is a procession of hooded penitents, and during *Good Friday's Procession of the Myster-*

ies, groups of statues depicting the Passion of Christ are paraded through the streets from church to church. The information office of the provincial tourist authority (EPT) is at 113 Corso Umberto (phone: 99-21233).

CHECKING IN: ***Delfino*** **–** A modern, air conditioned, 200-room hostelry — some with terraces overlooking the sea — and a pool, garden, and commendable restaurant. 66 Viale Virgilio, Taranto (phone and fax: 99-3205). Expensive.

Plaza **–** Offers 112 modern air conditioned rooms that are very conveniently located in the center of the New Town and around the corner from the bridge leading to the Old Town. 46 Via D'Aquino, Taranto (phone: 99-91925). Moderate.

EATING OUT: ***Il Caffè*** **–** A tastefully renovated restaurant with a fashionable clientele. Considered the best in town, the menu features international as well as local dishes, and specializes in seafood. Closed Sunday evenings, Monday lunch, and 2 weeks in August. Reservations advised. Major credit cards accepted. 8 Via d'Aquino, Taranto (phone: 99-25097). Expensive.

La Barcaccia **–** In the New Town, on the waterfront facing the Old Town and the sea, this spot serves excellent seafood and local specialties. Closed Mondays. Reservations advised on weekends. No credit cards accepted. 22 Corso Due Mari, Taranto (phone: 99-26461). Moderate.

Milan Bar **–** A casual *ristorante/pizzeria* in the heart of the New Town, that offers 16 delicious kinds of pizza. Specialties include mussel dishes — known as *mitili* to local patrons — try them with spaghetti or stuffed and baked, a *frittata* (omelette) made to your liking, or try the *fritto misto di mare* (lightly fried squid, octopus, cuttlefish, and shrimp). Don't leave without sampling the homemade *gelato* made with goat's milk. Closed Sundays and *Christmas* week. Reservations advised. No credit cards accepted. 49 Via Cesare Battisti, Taranto (phone: 99-322860). Moderate.

En Route from Taranto – If time is short, pick up the autostrada (A14) to return to Bari, where connections can be made to various Italian cities. Otherwise take SS7 to Castellaneta, and then the A14 to Bari.

CASTELLANETA: A visit to Puglia would not be complete without a stop in this village, the birthplace of Rudolph Valentino. Castellaneta is set dramatically high on a ravine, and it has a late-Gothic cathedral (in the center of the divided old quarter) that was completely rebuilt in 18th-century baroque style. The house where the actor was born is at 114 Via Roma.

Basilicata and the Cilento

Although it has been ignored by the winds of change, plundered by invaders, petty overlords, grisly brigands, and greedy politicians, the Basilicata is one of Italy's most wildly beautiful and mysterious areas. The smallest of the Italian regions, it forms the instep and ankle of Italy's boot, barely touching the Tyrhennian and Adriatic seas at either end. In the Middle Ages, when Basilicata was known as Lucania, it also comprised much of southern Campania, including the Cilento Peninsula, which juts into the Tyrhennian Sea below Paestum.

Unlike much of Italy's south, the area largely has been spared the influence of the Mafia. As a result, rugged Basilicata has less crime, friendlier people, and at times appears almost pristine when compared to other southern regions, such as Calabria. Tourism still is very much in its infancy, and many *lucani,* as the locals are called, continue to live their lives much as they did in the past — albeit with television sets, cars, and microwave ovens. They also enjoy a beautiful and varied landscape, including some outstanding examples of Byzantine, Norman, and baroque architecture — castles, churches, *sassi* (natural cave dwellings), and charming rustic farmsteads.

The Gulf of Policastro, on which the jewel-like town of Maratea is perched, arguably is one of Italy's finest and least spoiled coastlines. The Cilento, although no longer part of Basilicata, is included here because of its proximity, fine beaches, and historical and cultural connections with the rest of the region. It also is refreshingly unknown.

Along the longer, flatter Ionian shore to the east, the impressive remains of the ancient Greek settlements of Heraclea (now Policoro) and Metapontum (now Metaponto), with houses, temples, and a sanctuary of the goddess Demeter, present an obligatory stop for anyone seriously interested in the past. Still protecting the land from erosion are the remains of the ancient forest of Policoro.

Inland, the scene is one of mountains, stunning hills, striking gorges, lush meadows, clay ravines, lakes, rivers, fortified towns, and graceful, castellated homesteads called *masserie.* Wild nature reserves are common. In the Ionian hinterland, the town of Matera spills out its eerie tale of prehistory onto the unsuspecting parchment of limestone uplands known as the Murge. Nearby, the bizarre, lunar landscape of the *calanchi* (clay worn away by erosion) around Tursi, or *argille* (as the locals refer to the stark terrain) farther inland, will remind travelers of other semi-desert lands. South of the Sinni Valley, the magnificent Mt. Pollino, now principally a natural park, rises to over 7,000 feet. Farther north, the Vulture region near Potenza — once brigand country — provides an alternative mountain holiday, complete with skiing in winter.

In the Middle Ages Lucania came to be called Basilicata after Balikos, the region's tax collector, who gained notoriety for his success at relieving the residents of what little they had. Several centuries later, in 1932, Mussolini sent the local government a telegram ordering that Basilicata once again be called Lucania. This was in keeping with the current Fascist ideology of restoring Italy's regions to their ancient glory. In fact, Basilicata had no ancient glory — only a long history of sacrifice and submission. To the peasant *lucani,* the name change meant precious little. Always heavily taxed, during the Fascist years they were asked to dig still deeper, to pay duty even on their goats in order to help preserve Lucania's forests. Yet Lucania had few wooded areas! In 1947, the region returned to the name Basilicata.

Such anomalies, not uncommon in these parts, may conjure a response in those familiar with pre- and postwar Italian literature that often dwelled on tales of social injustice with a bitter irony. Basilicata first came to Italy's attention in 1945 with the publication of the novel *Christ Stopped at Eboli.* Written by Carlo Levi, a medical school graduate and painter from Turin who had been exiled to Basilicata for his anti-Fascist views, it underlines the region's plight and celebrates the poignant humanity of its people. Steeped in realism, the book was a success in the salons of the north, and drew attention to the area, sweeping away some national preconceptions about southern Italy. Unfortunately, however, negative images of the south still linger. And like most of the towns and villages at the bottom of Italy's boot, Basilicata still is struggling, fairly unsuccessfully, to cling to the coattails of an ever-modernizing Europe.

Attempts by the national government to pump investment and new life into Basilicata have not been effective. Unemployment is on the rise again, factories are closing down, and the young leave if they can. The region still is trying to pick up the pieces following a calamatous earthquake in 1980 while also attempting to grow crops such as maize, wheat, oats, and barley in the face of ever-growing drought. Tomatoes, eggplants, artichokes, olives, and fruit crops linger on uneasily alongside new cereals.

Perhaps Levi, who grew to love Basilicata and to become its most famous adopted son (he is buried here) would have appreciated the irony of the region today — virtually untouched by mass tourism and big industry. One of the words most commonly used in Levi's book to describe the area is *incantevole* (enchanting, but eerily so). Basilicata's fascinating geological formations are much the same as they were 8,000 years ago, when people lived in Matera's unique *sassi* — many of which still are occupied today. Human presence in Basilicata dates back some 300,000 years — making it one of the oldest populations in Europe. Basilicata's original residents eventually integrated with settlers from Asia Minor who were versed in the working of copper. By 1,000 BC, they had formed highly organized townships and trade links with the Mycenaeans. When the first Greek settlers arrived at Siris, near Policoro, 2 centuries later, they discovered a thriving community.

The *lucani,* warriors who came from northern Italy were next, followed by the Romans, who used the region's Basento and Bradano river valleys as a trade route to the Ionian Sea, Later, a large influx of settlers — Byzantines, Longobards, Normans, Swabians, and Angovins — would leave their mark.

Today, it is not uncommon to find *lucani* who will tell you that Rome was responsible for the decline of Basilicata by allowing an important and sophisticated agricultural sytem, instituted nearly 3,000 years ago by the Greeks, to waste away. The Bourbons' rule of Naples from the mid-1700s also contributed to the region's difficulties — taxation and human suffering reached an all-time high, attempted uprisings were common, and *brigantismo* (the term refers not only to highwaymen, but connotes a social phenomenon as well) was rampant. Because social and economic conditions were so poor, people had no choice but to rob and often kill the *galàntuomini* (gentlemen) who were viewed as parasites. *Briganti* frequently operated as private armies. Eustachio Chit, called "Chitaridd," one of Basilicata's most celebrated turn-of-the-century *briganti,* was hunted for many years for murdering many dozens of people. He became part of Basilicata's folk mythology. After the police finally trapped and killed him, they sent his skull to Naples to be examined — to see "what made him tick." Today's *lucani* are extremely friendly and helpful, ready to engage in conversation on almost any topic.

Basilicata's winters are mild; its summers, at times, unbearably hot. The best times to visit are September to November and February to May. In the spring (which comes early to Basilicata) the countryside is lush; in summer, however, it often is parched, though the resulting barrenness has a beauty of its own.

The driving route begins at Maratea — the only town in Basilicata geared to tourism. From Naples, take the A3 autostrada south. Exit at Lagonegro and take SS585 to Maratea Castrocucco. Then head up the SS18 coast road for 6 miles (10 km) to Maratea.

Maratea has many appeals to the traveler: it is an old town perched in the hills, easily spotted because of the statue of Christ the Redeemer towering above it; its charming port below with cafés and fishing boats; and a number of small resorts that fall under its administrative beach umbrella — Marina di Maratea, Fiumicello, Ogliastro, Cersula, Rotondella, and Acquafreddo. Continuing on up the sun-drenched gulf on SS18, is the almost Turkish-looking town of Sapri, then Villamare, Policastro, and delightful Scario, all on the sea. The terrain changes — as you move into the hills through Lentiscosa, and down again, to the Marina di Camerota. From there, take SS447 to Palinuro. The Maratea-Palinuro leg of the trip is easily a half-day's excursion, including stopping on the way for a lunch of fresh seafood. In summer, hydrofoils carry visitors between Capri and Sorrento, making stops along the way at the small seaside resorts of Pisciotta and Acciaroli.

Taking leave of Maratea and the Cilento — almost a lazy week's holiday in itself — head into the hills behind. At Lauria, pick up SS104 and go east along the Sinni Valley, lying in the shadow of the 7,620-foot Mt. Pollino. The area is now a park, noted for its wild natural beauty and fauna — including wolves (who stay far from the main road). At either Francavilla or Senise, site of Lago di Monte Cotugno, a large artificial lake, detour to the hill town of San Paolo Albanese (settled by Albanians), or go directly to the Ionian Sea on SS104 before heading north to Matera. Alternatively, take SS598 —

reached by going left (north) around the lake on SS92 to Sant'Arcangelo — which leads to the west to another lake, Lago de Pietra del Pertusillo, and the town of Grumento, where there are important Roman ruins. North of Sant'Arcangelo, is Stigliano, center of the *argille* region and Levi country. To the east is the *calanchi* district around Tursi. At the Ionian coast, the road winds north on SS106, stopping at Policoro and Metaponto, with their Greek ruins, then veers inland to the Murge and Matera, via Ferrandina on SS407 and SS7. The tour finishes at Matera.

Except for the coastline of Maratea, tourism is largely undeveloped in Basilicata. Though Maratea's accommodations can cost considerably more than those in other towns in Basilicata, they still are quite low when compared to other resorts in Italy. In those hotels rated as expensive, expect to pay $50 and up for a double room with breakfast; between $35 and $45 for those listed as moderate; and $30 and under for inexpensive accommodations. In restaurants, expect to pay $40 and up for a meal for two without wine in places listed as expensive; moderate, $20 to $35; and inexpensive, below $20. Many seaside hotels encourage guests to take half board, though this rarely is obligatory.

The food of Basilicata takes its cue from its lingering peasant culture. Most meat dishes are made from pork, salami is often spicy and red because of the addition of hot peppers — called *diavolicchio* (devilish). As in Calabria, the emphasis is on preservation — anything that can be is placed *sott'olio,* (under oil), such as *lampacioni,* (baby onions), skinned tomatoes, and other vegetables. A favorite local dish, *capriata,* uses a variety of grains and beans grown in the region — barley, lentils, chick-peas, and beans — to produce a delicious vegetable stew. *Orechiette,* small ear-shaped shells, reflecting the Apulian influence in much of Basilicata, is the most popular pasta. Meat often is cooked *in cartoccio* (in brown paper) to retain its moisture. Local cheeses include dried, hard ricotta, which often is very salty and used mainly for grating. Wine is predominantly red, full-bodied, and strong, and almost always made from Apulian grapes.

MARATEA: More than just a pretty resort, Maratea stretches along Basilicata's immaculate and tiny (barely 25 miles long) Tyrhennian coastline, with an explosion of emerald green waters, enchanting coves, sea caves, and strange and wonderful geological formations that date to the Pliocene Age. Maratea proper, a pristine and almost Greek-looking town hugging the 2,000-foot Monte San Biagio, is set over the Gulf of Policastro, equidistant between the Calabrian and Campanian borders. The 70-foot-high statue of Christ the Redeemer, the elected guardian of the gulf, is perched on top of the mountain.

Nestled below amid a lush profusion of an olive-green landscape, Maratea Porto, the town's port, is a winter haven for veteran sailors and beached fishing nets. In season it is filled with fishing vessels and café tables spill onto the water's edge. There are hotels, restaurants, and bijou-like beaches in Maratea Porto, as well as among the coves that dot the stretch north, where on the road to Sapri, you can find the towns of Punta Santavenere, Fiumicello, Cersuta, and Acquafredda. To the south, and near Calabria, cliffs and stalagtite caves — a snorkler's paradise — are the order of the day.

Twenty years ago, the area was virtually unknown. In 1958, Count Stefano Rivetti, an enterprising nobleman from the north, purchased one of the six old Spanish watchtowers (now a private residence) that line the coast, and on an isolated and verdant point just north of the port, he built the *Santavenere* hotel (see *Checking In*), a hacienda-style resort of striking dimensions. He invited his friends, started two textile firms nearby, and the area and his dream took hold. The count, who died in 1988, was no Aga Khan, however. Although "greater Maratea," as its collection of little resorts might be called, is now Basilicata's primary source of tourism, it still operates on a delightfully small scale. Even in high season, most of the coast is not invaded by bronzed bodies. Rather, it is largely populated by wild broom and rosemary bushes, pines, olive, fruit, and oak trees. Accordingly, prices are relatively low, the people friendly, the food is fresh, and the sea from which some of it comes is clean for the most part.

Perched above on two levels, the town of Maratea is a cluster of red roofs, convents, churches, and a monastery with a fine, 16th-century courtyard. Explore the town, a haven of narrow alleyways, lined with geraniums, wicker baskets, and copperwork for sale, or sit at the café tables in the charming Piazza Buraglia. Atop Monte San Biagio is an interesting, medieval sanctuary (Santuario San Biagio). The saint's remains inside the sanctuary are jealously guarded by the locals. For centuries, the two different sections of town (Maratea Superiore and Inferiore) hotly contested the rightful home of the remains. The disagreement finally resulted in a compromise. One day a year, in the second week of May, the remains travel in a life-size silver reliquary to the lower town in a curious procession replete with local shepherd bagpipers.

Maratea also boasts a fine cathedral which has a campanile and tiled dome that date from the Middle Ages. Inside is a notable 14th-century choir. In August, the town is treated to a procession of collectors' antique cars, and a *sagra del pesce,* a fish festival at which you can eat fresh local fish that is fried in giant pans down at the port.

Maratea's tourist information office is at 32 Piazza Gesù (phone: 973-876908).

CHECKING IN: ***Pianeta Maratea*** – This modern 166-room complex feels like a cruise vessel floating above the sea. It is spotlessly clean, and boasts an excellent restaurant, a pool, a beach, and patios with exceptional views. Open year-round. Santa Caterina, Maratea (phone: 973-876996; in the US, 800-223-5695). Expensive.

Santavenere – Basilicata's best, its 44 tastefully decorated rooms are set in a park on a private peninsula. There are beach and pool facilities and restaurant. Open year-round. Santavenere, Fiumincello, Maratea (phone: 0973-876910). Expensive.

Villa del Mare – A delightful 75-room hillside hideaway with fine views of the exquisite private cove below, and a very decent restaurant. Open year-round. Acquafredda, Maratea (phone: 973-878007). Moderate.

Villa Cheta Elite – There are 20 rooms in this century-old, family-style villa, a restaurant, and use of a delightful beach. Closed October to *Easter.* Just across the road from the entrance to *Villa del Mare.* Acquafredda, Maratea (phone: 973-878134). Moderate.

EATING OUT: ***Taverna Rovita*** – Small and full of character, this is the best restaurant in the region. The staff and owners put on nearly as good a show as does the kitchen. The fish crêpes are especially good, as are the desserts. Closed November through mid-March. Reservations necessary. Major credit cards accepted. Via Rovita, Centro Storico, Maratea (phone: 973-876588). Expensive.

La Quercia – Named after an old oak tree just outside the restaurant, this place is a favorite with locals because of its fine seafood. Closed mid-October to mid-April. Reservations advised. No credit cards accepted. On the coast road, Fiumicello, Maratea (phone: 973-876907). Moderate.

Za' Mariuccia – Fish is the star of this family-run portside establishment, cooked the way the locals prefer — *alla griglia* (grilled with herbs and garlic). Closed November through April. Reservations advised in high season. No credit cards accepted. Via Grotte, Maratea Porto (phone: 973-876163). Moderate.

Il Piccolo Ranch – Specialties served in this curious Italian log cabin include a variety of salamis, and fresh herbs and vegetables picked from the nearby hills. The antipasti are delicious and owner Biagio Monterosso will top a pizza with almost anything — even wild asparagus. Closed Tuesdays. Reservations advised. No credit cards accepted. Near the *Pianeta Maratea* hotel in Santa Caterina, Maratea (phone: 973-870237). Moderate to inexpensive.

En Route from Maratea – Take SS18 north, crossing into Campania at the narrow hairpin turn known by the natives as *Apprezzami l'asino,* after the ancient legend that recalls a time before roads were built when people had to throw their donkeys over the edge first in order to get round the perilous point. Continue to Scario, via Sapri, Villamare, and Policastro.

SCARIO: With its picturesque marina and *lungomare* (boardwalk), this fishing village across the gulf from Maratea is worth a prolonged pause. Called *L'orecchio del porco* (Pig's Ear) by the locals because of the port's shape, it was a simple fishermen's hamlet until the 1600s, when a church and an inn were built here. Set at the mouth of the verdant Bussento Valley, Scario's irregular coastline offers sandy beaches lined with caves and coves at every turn. The gaping-mouthed Bird's Grotto is the most celebrated; another, the Grotto del Vitello, bears a prehistoric wall drawing of a calf. Many of the grottoes are reachable only by sea. For a special treat, take a 5-hour boat trip aboard the *Maratea I* from Scario to Palinuro, around the Punta degli Infreschi (cost is about $20). It departs 5 days a week in summer from different points along the coast. All boats stop at Maratea, but Scario has a more limited service. Contact the tourist office (AAST) in Maratea for information (phone: 973-876996).

CHECKING IN: ***L'Approdo*** – A clean and modest hotel set amidst olive trees. There are 25 rooms, some with views of the gulf. Open year-round. Via Rione Nuovo, Scario (phone: 974-986070). Moderate.

EATING OUT: ***Lo Sfizio*** – A cheerful restaurant on the *lungomare,* it offers a selection of good pasta, grilled meat, and seafood. Closed Mondays. Reservations unnecessary. No credit cards accepted. Lungomare Marconi (phone: 974-986510). Moderate to inexpensive.

En Route from Scario – Take SS18, which now climbs into the hills, skirting the precipitous coastal cliffs, and passing through San Giovanni a Piro and Lentiscosa, before dropping down into Marina di Camerotta, just round the point. The town, a mix of new and old, is the starting point of a lovely coast. The area boasts some delightful bays, including a natural harbor, Porto Infreschi, that was used for fishing vessels until the 1700s.

CHECKING IN/EATING OUT: ***Happy Village*** – The best place to take advantage of the coast, this aptly named "tourist village," with its own quarter-mile of beachfront, has 230 beds in private *tukuls* — Polynesian-style huts — under the olive trees. Each hut sleeps from 2 to 6 people. There also is a restaurant in a charming old villa on the premises. Closed October through May. Marina di Camerota, on the coast road to Palinuro (phone: 974-932326). Moderate.

En Route from Camerota – Continue to Palinuro on SS447, which becomes narrow, bumpy, and eventually very winding. Alternatively, skip Camerota and instead make straight for the hills behind Scario, heading for Acquavena and Poderia. The road eventually ties into the original Palinuro SS447 descent and takes half the time.

PALINURO: Watched over by the ancient Castel della Molpa and the Old Town of Centola, the fairly new marina of Palinuro sits next to the point of the same name. Shaped like a great hook, it has beautiful beaches and coves, grottoes, sea stacks, towers, and a clear emerald sea. A beachcomber's and skin diver's haven, important paleolithic finds have been uncovered in many of its caves.

A sandy beach, Spiaggia della Molpa, reached by climbing through olive groves perhaps is the most remarkable. Strange prehistoric forms loom up at Scoglio del Coniglio (rabbit shoal) and at caves farther along, such as the Grotto delle Ossa (Grotto of Bones). There is another magnificent beach, Buondormire, along the way.

CHECKING IN/EATING OUT: ***La Conchiglia*** – Modern yet cozy, this 24-room hotel is a stone's throw from the beach, with an attractive terrace and sea views. The restaurant serves regional fare. Closed November through February. Via Indipendenza, Palinuro (phone: 974-931018). Moderate.

En Route from Palinuro – Back on SS447, turn right (east) after 12 miles (19 km) at the Centola train station; then proceed to Torre Orsaia. Shortly after, pick up SS517 at Castel Ruggero, heading left or northeast. Follow the green signs for the A3 autostrada, and exit at Lauria Nord. There, pick up SS104 or the Sinni Valley route and enter the heartland of Basilicata.

Alternatively, follow SS598, farther to the north, which runs parallel to the Sinni Valley, by picking up SS103 at the Montesano-A3 junction, stopping in Grumento to see its Roman ruins, and passing Lago di Pietra del Pertusillo. Turn right onto SS598 at the lake, proceed to Sant'Arcangelo, then pick up the directions from that point.

CHECKING IN/EATING OUT: ***Isola di Lauria*** – The advantages of not taking the detour described above are that you can stay in this pleasant 36-room hotel whose restaurant specializes in refined cooking — not a common occurrence in earthy Basilicata. Order the *risotto alla crema di crostacei* (risotto with a seafood cream sauce) and the pork smothered in herbs. (In the morning, investigate the Collegio dell'Immacolata Concezione, a small, 15th-century church in town, with its remains of a fine cloister). Open year-round. No credit cards accepted. Piazza Insorti d'Ungheria, Lauria (phone: 973-823905). Moderate.

En Route from Lauria – Take SS104 toward Senise, passing Latronico, a medieval village and thermal bath center in the Appenines. Stop off to see the early 18th-century Chiesa Parrocchiale before heading on to Episcopia. Shortly after, at Francavilla, there are two possible detours: To the left, 7 miles (11 km) inland in the mountains, lies Chiaramonte, an attractive town that has the remains of an early castle and walls, and some important palaces. To the right (south) is Mt. Pollino. Because the route south from Francavilla is long, steep, and lonely, a wiser alternative is to take the road, signposted for Noepoli and San Paolo Albanese, which departs south from SS104 another 8 miles (13 km) from Francavilla. Some 3,000 feet above sea level, San Paolo Albanese is a community of only 600 people whose origins date back to the 16th century, when Albanians migrated to the slopes of Mt. Pollino. To this day, significant traces of their language, religion, and brightly colored dress remain almost intact. The village, too, is almost as it was 400 years ago.

In nearby San Costantino Albanese (also settled by Albanians) is the Byzantine-domed sanctuary of Santa Maria della Stella. Inside is a nativity scene, dating from 1699. On the second Sunday in May, the town celebrates an ancient custom when it burns elaborately constructed, life-size paper puppets, called *nusazit.* They depict a couple dressed in Albanian costume, together with two workers, and a two-faced devil.

The rite represents the sacredness of the family, of work, and of the danger of temptation. In mid-June in Terranova, farther up the mountain (its peak borders Calabria), another ancient ritual takes place, with participants singing and dancing the tarantella around a felled tree.

CHECKING IN/EATING OUT: ***Ricciardi*** – A 24-room hotel and restaurant in the heart of this mountain town, 7 miles (11 km) north of SS104. The property was undergoing renovation at press time. Open year-round. 27 Via Calvario, Chiaromonte (phone: 973-571031). Moderate.

Luna Rossa – Serving genuine and very good mountain fare that has won acclaim down in the valley, its specialties include homemade pasta, spicy meat dishes, and excellent cheese. Closed Wednesdays. Reservations necessary, especially on weekends. No credit cards accepted. Via Marconi, Terranova di Pollino (phone: 973-932540). Inexpensive.

En Route from Chiaromonte/Pollino – Continue to Senise on SS104, which follows the shoreline of Lago di Monte Cotugno, an artificial lake. Turn left on SS92 for Sant'Arcangelo. At Alianello, turn up into the hills for Aliano and Stigliano. This is Carlo Levi country, typified by the strange clay and rock foundations of the hills and ravines — the *argille* or *calanchi.* In Aliano, visit Levi's house (where he was confined during the Fascist years), his tomb, and his collection of paintings. Continue to Stigliano, turning right just after the Sauro River.

STIGLIANO: Once a thriving mountain town (elevation 3,000 ft.), Stigliano acted as a fortress during the time of the Goths, and for centuries was governed by the powerful Colonna family. In the 18th century it had a population of 7,000 — the same as now — and briefly was the capital of the entire region. Stigliano has some excellent examples of art and architecture. Particularly fine is the interior of the Chiesa Parrocchiale, a cathedral with its three naves and a wealth of ornate detail, especially the 16th-century polyptych, partly done by Simone da Firenze. The nearby small Church of San Antonio has a splendid façade, the stone reworked in a diamond motif in 1763. Next to it is a bell tower, topped by an onion-shaped dome.

EATING OUT: ***Trattoria Carmela Fornabaio*** – Everything that can be made by hand here is. The pasta is delicious, as is the traditional local fare, such as the spicy red salami, *lampascioni* (sweet baby onions), and tomatoes *sott'olio,* stuffed with capers, parsley, and anchovies. The roast meat dishes are an added bonus. Closed Wednesdays. No reservations. No credit cards accepted. 69 Via Cialdini, Stigliano (phone: 835-661437). Moderate to inexpensive.

En Route from Stigliano – Proceed east on SS103 toward the abandoned town of Craco. Continue east for 5 miles (8 km), turn left along SS176, and detour 5 miles (8 km) north to Pisticci, a sun-baked town typical of the area for its characteristic, tiered rows of houses. The Chiesa Madre, built on earlier ruins, dates to the 16th century. There also are the remains of a medieval castle. Return to SS103; after 5 miles (8 km), turn left (southeast) onto SS598 to reach the sea at Scanzano Ionico. Another worthwhile detour via SS103 is to Tursi, 8 miles (13 km) inland, reached by continuing south. Boasting its own bewitching *calanchi* nearby, the town — strongly Arab in feel — is filled with caves that at one time were used as dwellings, and has some notable churches such as the Rabatana (which gets its name from the Arabic word *rabad,* meaning town) which contains an early medieval crypt and frescoes. Nearby is the 11th–13th-century Norman cathedral of ancient Anglona, once part of one of the most impressive settlements in Basilicata and now reduced to rugged countryside after early invaders razed it to the ground. SS103 from Stigliano also takes the traveler past a string of *masserie,* farmsteads fortified by nobles against invaders and, later on, by brigands. Often sprawling, sometimes outstanding, they provide an excellent example of vernacular architecture in Basilicata. Many have been sadly left to rot, though there is a movement afoot to restore them.

CHECKING IN/EATING OUT: Motel Agip – Like the rest of this chain, comfort and good service (and some good food) come before warmth and charm at this 109-room hostelry. Open year-round. SS407 Basentana, Km 24, Pisticci Inferiore (phone: 835-462007). Expensive to moderate.

THE METAPONTINO: This coastal plain is an archaeological treasure trove (as well as an area that enjoys magnificent stretches of beach). The two principal sites (along the rest of the plain there are numerous other sites, many in the process of being excavated) are ancient Heraclea, just behind Policoro (reached via SS106 south from Scanzano), and Metaponto (take SS106 north).

Founded by Greeks in the 6th-century BC, in less than 200 years Heraclea became the capital Greek city for the entire area. But by the Imperial Roman period, it had already sunk into decline. Excavations have uncovered foundations of houses, and one of the town's main roads where kilns fired vases and votive statues. There also are remains of a temple, and a sanctuary of Demeter, goddess of fertility. Heraclean finds are displayed in the museum near the sanctuary.

Believed to be Magna Graecia's most magnificent city, ancient Metapontum was settled by Greeks from Peloponnesus in the early 8th century BC. The town boasts a vast archaeological park and antiquarium, or museum. There are remains of four Greek temples, including the celebrated Temple of Hera, called the Tavole Palatine (Palatine Tables) from the 5th century BC) and a Greek theater, dating from the 4th century BC. In Metaponto, excavation finds are housed in the *Antiquario,* near the Tavole Palatine (phone: 835-745151). Open Tuesdays through Saturdays from 9 AM to 1 PM and 3:30 to 6:30 PM from April through September; Tuesdays through Saturdays from 9 AM to noon and from 2 to 5 PM from October through March; no admission charge. In Policoro, stop off at the *Museo Nazionale della Siritide* (on Via Colombo; phone: 835-972154). Open daily except Mondays from 9 AM to 2 PM; admission charge.

EATING OUT: *Da Fifina* – Considered the best in the area, it turns out some extraordinary dishes. The locals swear by the *pasta e fagioli,* and pasta mixed with local ricotta and green beans. The *spaghetti alle vongole veraci* (with clams) is excellent. No reservations. No credit cards accepted. Corso Umberto, Bernalda, Metaponto (phone: 835-743134). Moderate.

En Route from Metaponto – Take SS407 to Ferrandina, a very picturesque town of whitewashed dwellings. Turn right onto SS7 for Matera, passing the long, fish-shaped Lago di San Giuliano along the way. The lake now is a wildlife reserve, where there is a World Wildlife Fund headquarters.

MATERA: One of the most unusual towns in Italy, Matera has a particular form of dwelling, the *sasso* — a crude, whitewashed house whose inner rooms are prehistoric caves that gouge the town's northern flank. The *sassi* have a long and fascinating history — from their use as very practical dwellings in paleolithic times and as a sanctuary for monks persecuted during the 9th century to their occupation by mystics and radicals during the late 1960s. In 1960, the city council — worried about the extreme conditions of poverty in which 20,000 residents lived — moved them to new housing on the outskirts of the city, although some squatters remained. In recent years, the local government has restored many of the *sassi* and an interesting mixture of artists, farmers, and idealists wishing to experience an ancient way of life has moved in.

Whether viewed from the Gravine, a vertiginous ravine beyond the town dotted with whitewashed *chiese rupestre* (Greek-frescoed country cave churches), founded by Byzantine monks who settled here in the Middle Ages, or from the Civita, the oldest part of town, Matera cannot fail but to strike an antediluvian chord. The *sassi* amazed the director and writer, Pier Paolo Pasolini, who decided to film *The Gospel According to Matthew* in Matera, setting a trend for other filmmakers.

The *sassi,* where often an entire family of eight would live in barely two rooms, spiral from top to bottom on different rock faces — the Sasso Barisano and the Sasso Caveoso. The two are separated by a ravine. To a visitor, they appear as a three-dimensional materialization of Dante's *Inferno,* and as the sun goes down and wild dogs begin to yelp, it is easy to take not just one but two steps back into ancient times.

To best appreciate the *sassi,* go with a guide (not the local children) who also can take you to the *chiese rupestre.* Ask the tourist office (9 Via de Viti di Marco; phone: 835-212488) how to contact the town's best — Aldo Chietera. Unfortunately, the *chiese rupestre* have been left to the whims of the elements, and the town's children who remove great chunks of the priceless frescoes or carve their names into them. The churches are now a national park. Two worth visiting (even on your own) are the Church of Santa Lucia alla Malve and the Church of Santa Maria d'Idrid on Via Madonna della Virtù. They have beautiful Byzantine frescoes dating from the 11th century.

The town also has some excellent examples of first-rate architecture dating from the Renaissance and baroque periods, some important palazzi, and a number of fine churches. Most important is its Romanesque cathedral (Piazza del Duomo; open daily from 9 AM to noon), with its beautifully carved doorways and a fine rose window. It is perched on top of the ancient Civilta rock — its interior partly puts to use a *sasso*-cave. More elegant than its northern Italian contemporaries, the cathedral became more and more lavish through the years, from the original 13th-century construction to the magnificent 16th-century Cappella dell'Annunziata (Chapel of the Annunciation). It contains a fresco of the Madonna della Bruna, Matera's patron saint, that dates from the 12th century. The Church of San Giovanni Battista (Via San Biagio; open daily from 9 AM to noon) has an elaborate portal, but it is the graceful Gothic interior, including the high vaulting and elegant columns, that draws people.

Every year at the end of June, the Madonna is honored in one of the most famous festivals in the entire region — the *Festa di Santa Maria della Bruna.* As the sun sets, tiny twinkling lights illuminate the Madonna, drawn by mules in an elaborate cart and accompanied by townspeople dressed as medieval knights and clergy. After she is returned to the Duomo, the cart is torn to bits by the spectators who keep the pieces as relics. In summer, Matera's beautiful outdoor theater in Piazza San Pietro Caveoso is the site of an arts festivals, with nightly concerts, dance, and theater. The tourist office has the schedule of events or pick one up outside the theater.

The *Museo Domenico Ridola* (Archaeological Museum; 24 Via Ridola; phone: 835-211239) has important Greek objects that were found locally, as well as examples from much earlier periods. The oldest completely intact oven in the world was found in a *sasso* in Matera. Fragments of another, almost identical one, have been unearthed in Asia Minor. Open daily except Mondays from 9 AM to 2 PM; no admission charge.

The town comes alive at night when thousands of teenagers pour out into the streets and the piazza. It's not a riot — they're only having a good time.

CHECKING IN: ***President*** – This important-sounding hotel does its best, and with 76 rooms, it's one of the few decent places in town. Open year-round. 13 Via Roma, Matera (phone: 835-214075). Expensive to moderate.

Roma – Conveniently located, this 11-room hotel is immaculate and very friendly. Book well ahead during summer. Open year-round. 158 Via Nazionale, Matera (phone: 835-212701). Inexpensive.

EATING OUT: ***Trattoria Lucana*** – Regional specialties such as *bocconcini alla Lucana* (mushrooms, olives, and tomato wrapped in thin meat slices) are served here and *orecchiette alla materana* (small pasta with a vegetable sauce). Centrally located. Closed Sundays and September. Reservations advised. Major credit cards accepted. 48 Via Lucana, Matera (phone: 835-336117). Expensive to moderate.

Casino del Diavolo – Good local fare and the staff's real interest in its guests' enjoyment make this friendly trattoria a good place to stop. As everywhere in Basilicata (and Puglia as well), starters such as black olives and cheese or a dish made with sausage, hot and mild peppers and tomatoes are de rigueur and *lucani* serve them with pride. The roast meat is imaginatively prepared; the chef uses local herbs. Closed Tuesdays. Reservations advised on weekends. No credit cards accepted. Via Martella, Matera (phone: 835-261986). Inexpensive.

Il Terrazzino – Perhaps the best way to soak in the hallowed atmosphere of the *sassi* at dusk is to sit on a terrace and contemplate them with some pasta and a glass of wine, which is what can be done here. Take a good look inside this eatery — this is what a modern *sasso* looks like. Try the starters. The pasta is homemade, the sauces delicious and simple, and the native bread is excellent. Meat and fish are cooked in the traditional way. Closed Tuesdays. Reservations necessary for dining outside. No credit cards accepted. 7 Vico San Giuseppe, Matera (phone: 835-222106). Inexpensive.

Calabria

Calabria, the southernmost portion of the Italian mainland — the "toe" of the Italian boot — once had an infamous reputation. For centuries, its mountains were home to bandits, its cities and villages prey to corrupt government and bloody personal feuds. As recently as 1912, Herr Baedeker warned his guidebook's readers not to venture here unless they could stay with the local gentry because the hotels, available only in the larger towns, were "of the most squalid description."

The region still remains an economic backwater, overlooked by the broad sweep of industrialization that seems to have lost its momentum just south of Naples. But, until recently, Calabria has also been neglected by the hordes of tourists that have made the rest of Italy one of Europe's star attractions. As a consequence, the air is clean, the richly forested mountains preserved, and the 450 miles of coastline some of the least developed along the Mediterranean. Government and tourism have intruded just enough in the last 15 years to make Calabria a safe, hospitable place to visit.

The stretches of uncluttered sands, blessed by a summer sun from April to October, are a temptation, but the "impressive and mystic" Calabria about which Stendhal wrote lies in the higher hinterlands. The Apennines, the chain of mountains that forms the backbone of the entire country, dominate Calabria. There are four main mountain groupings within the region: the Pollino, the Sila plateau, the Serre, and the Aspromonte — the last being the southernmost and the highest, touching 6,000 feet and blanketed by beech, pine, oak, chestnut, and ash.

Although three-quarters of Calabria is officially classified as "nonviable," its soils too thin or its slopes too steep for farming, historically the land has been the essential provider. Even with the advent of tourism and the shift toward a more commercial economy, in the more remote villages, where the last remnants of a rapidly disappearing peasant culture can occasionally be found, this is still so. In such places, rows of narrow terraces yield vegetables (eggplant, zucchini, peppers), fruits (melons, cherries, figs, and grapes for the area's wonderful wine), and grain. On the more fertile coastal plain are orange groves, almond trees, and rows of gnarled olive trees that look as if they date from the times when the ancient Greeks occupied this land.

In these agrarian pockets, division of labor frequently follows tradition. While the men work the terraces, the women make bread and pasta by hand, preserve harvested crops for the winter, or help their fathers and husbands gather such delicacies as wild strawberries, blackberries, snails, nuts, herbs, and mushrooms. But due to emigration, the advent of modern highways and railway service, and the inevitable influence of television, such storybook scenes have largely become a thing of the past.

Calabria's economic problems have been much greater than those of other regions of Italy. Despite government attempts since World War II to entice industry here, subsistence has been a struggle for its people, who are very different from the excitable, smiling image many foreigners have of southern Italians. Yet their misfortunes have done nothing to dampen their quiet dignity and the hospitality of which they are justly proud.

Thousands of years ago, the area that is now Calabria prospered as part of the expansion and surge of art and civilization known as Magna Graecia, but since that time of glory it has been plagued by a succession of natural disasters and unhappy dominations. It is one of the most seismic zones in the Mediterranean, and earthquakes have consistently wiped out whole towns and most vestiges of the past. Slowly, dedicated archaeologists, backed by the Italian government, have begun to exhume fragments of Calabria's rich antiquity. Hardly a place exists that doesn't have its archaeological treasure — a Greek temple, a Byzantine fresco, or a terra cotta masterpiece. The entire region is sometimes referred to as an "open-air museum." Particularly exciting, in 1972, was the discovery of two 5th-century Greek statues — magnificent 6-foot bronze warriors, trimmed with silver and copper — in coastal waters near Riace. (They are now on permanent display at the *National Museum of Magna Graecia Culture* in Reggio di Calabria.) More recently the remains of what might well be the oldest synagogue in Europe, thought to have been built during the Roman Empire, were found in the tiny town of Bova Marina.

When the Romans took control of this region, they created problems from which it has never fully recovered. In search of food and wood for ships and other domestic needs, they ravaged the forests of the high valley. Lack of protective trees meant accelerated erosion, which affects agriculture in some parts of Calabria to this day. In medieval times, Christianity developed along the internal routes carved out by the Romans. Around 476, when the region fell under Byzantine rule, there was a revival of Hellenic traditions. The Byzantine influence was reflected in religious rites, architecture, and language. There are still mountain villages that conserve Graecanic traditions and speak a language closely resembling Greek. When the Byzantine domination collapsed under the Norman penetration, Calabria enjoyed a long period of peace and tranquillity. Subsequent Angevin, Aragonese, and Spanish rule, however, marked the beginning of a long, painful period in Calabrian history. Essentially feudal and exploitive governments existed, even under the later Bourbons and Bonapartes, until Italian unity in 1861.

At first, political unity did little to alleviate the problems of the deep south. Thousands of years of neglect and continual wars and upheavals inhibited agricultural productivity. The poor Calabrian peasants could not compete with rich northern Italy, from which they were cut off by a vast mountain range. The government responded to peasant unrest and brigandage by cracking down fiercely. Instead of trying to improve the productive state of the land and the social conditions of the peasants, officials were intent on creating infrastructures mostly for military needs. Many peasants found the only solution to their problems in emigration: Between 1882 and 1902 more than 300,000 people left Calabria, most for North America.

In the first half of this century, a series of devastating earthquakes, one of which leveled Reggio, followed by World War I, a worldwide depression, and then World War II, precluded any aid for Calabria. Finally, in 1950, the Cassa del Mezzogiorno, an investment organization, was established to introduce industry to the south on a grand scale. Unfortunately, many of the projects were white elephants, and by the 1960s emigration had started again — this time to Turin, Milan, Switzerland, and Germany. One successful project, however, was the building of the Autostrada del Sole, which at last connected Calabria with the rest of Italy and made the region accessible to tourists. This in turn has helped stabilize the economy, though it also marks the beginning of the abandonment of rural communities in favor of coastal towns and construction of tourist facilities. Many émigrés have returned home, believing that the development of their coastal resources for tourism is the key to future prosperity.

The region is divided into three provinces named after their capital cities: Cosenza, the inland section in the north; Catanzaro, farther south, near the Ionian coast; and Reggio di Calabria, at the tip of the toe, separated by only a narrow strait from Sicily.

If this is a first visit to Calabria, we suggest driving from central Italy. Although it's possible to fly to Lamezia Terme or Reggio di Calabria and rent a car there, the drive south from Salerno along the Autostrada del Sole (A3) is worth the time. Despite the increasing number of tourist resorts popping up indiscriminately along the coast, the 248-mile (397-km) drive from Salerno to Reggio can be breathtaking. An alternative to A3 is SS18, which follows the coast more closely and is a little rougher and more winding than the newer autostrada.

Leave the autostrada at Lagonegro for Praia a Mare and follow SS18 down the coast. After detouring inland (via either SS283 or SS107) to see Cosenza, you can drive farther east into the Sila Massif, or pick up A3 directly south to Pizzo. From Pizzo, continue south along the Costa Viola (Violet Coast). This is a strip of small towns and sandy beaches lapped by a sea of violet and turquoise stretching 31 miles (50 km) from Gioia Tauro to Santa Trada Cannitello just north of the provincial capital of Reggio di Calabria. From Reggio, the most modern city of the region, continue around the toe of the boot to the site of the ancient Greek city of Locri. From here it is a 15-minute drive up the mountain road to Gerace and, if the weather conditions are right and you feel a little adventurous, drive slowly back across the mountains to Gioia Tauro.

If you're not in a hurry to get to Sicily or want to proceed to Puglia instead, we recommend the following route up the instep of the boot: From Gerace, return to Locri and take the scenic drive on SS106 along the coast as far as Monasterace Marina; turn inland up the twisting SS110 to the religious sights at Stilo and Serra San Bruno. From here, proceed down the mountain road back to SS106 on the coast. Continue north to Catanzaro and further inland to Taverna for some interesting baroque art and architecture. Return to SS106 for a lovely (and, usually, lonely) stretch of the Ionian coast for more remnants of Magna Graecia at Capo Colonna and Crotone. Bear slightly inland to Byzantine monuments in and around Rossano, and finally on to the evocative plain of Sibari, site of the notorious Greek colony of Sybaris. From Sibari, SS106 continues past more archaeological excavations at Metapontum in the region called Basilicata, and on to Taranto in Puglia. Alternatively, local roads connect to superhighway A3, which leads back to Cosenza or parts north.

Driving is difficult in Calabria and distances between points of interest are quite long — so it's a good idea to carefully consult a topographical map before plotting the journey. In winter there is often snow on the roads; it's a good idea to ask if they are passable before setting off.

Hotels in Calabria have improved considerably over the past few years. Travelers do not have to fight off brigands or search long for comfortable accommodations in the bigger towns. There aren't many luxurious hotels, however, and those that do exist tend to be modern and impersonal. Expect to pay $75 to $125 and up for a double at those categorized as expensive, between $50 and $75 for moderate, and under $50, inexpensive. An attractive summer alternative to hotels is provided by Calabria's many holiday villages, which have the added advantage of being built close to the crystal-clear blue sea. There are no really expensive restaurants in Calabria, and all serve generous portions of southern Italian cooking. Expect to pay between $55 and $60 for a meal for two at those restaurants categorized as moderate and between $35 and $50 for those in the inexpensive category. Prices do not include drinks or tips.

En Route from Salerno – Make the first stop in Calabria at Praia a Mare. The sandy beach here faces the Isola di Dino, a tiny island where legend says Ulysses landed long ago. This is the part of the coast that has been most developed for tourism; for a more peaceful coastal town, try Diamante a bit farther along. Both towns provide a fine introduction to the province of Cosenza, with its wooded plains and rocky beaches.

On the way to Diamante, make a detour at Scalea to see the caves with paleolithic drawings at Papasidero. At Scalea turn off onto SS504 toward Mormanno and travel 14 miles (22 km) to Papasidero. This will be your first encounter with the winding roads so typical of the Calabrian inland. The route passes through forests, vineyards, and orchards, with frequent glimpses of the coast. In Papasidero, visit the ruins of the Byzantine castle and the 14th-century frescoes of the Sanctuary of Santa Maria di Costantinopoli. It's a bit of a walk to the Grotta del Romito. In one of the caves, there is a paleolithic drawing of two oxen; it is believed to be one of the oldest manifestations of art in Italy. Excavations inside the caves have revealed human skeletons — one with his breast pierced by a stone arrowhead. To get to the caves, continue along SS504 toward the Lao River to the village of Montagna. From here, walk along a mule track for about 40 minutes toward the Lao Valley.

Beyond Papasidero and Montagna, at the town of Mormanno, those in a hurry can pick up A3 and speed down to Cosenza (after the visit, return to the route via SS107, a fast, modern road that goes back up to Paola). Otherwise, retrace the path from Papasidero back to SS18, the coast road, and continue the journey down to Diamante and a few more beach towns before turning inland to Cosenza.

CHECKING IN/EATING OUT: ***Sant'Elena* –** This comfortable, rustic 31-room hotel has an excellent restaurant. Open year-round. Reservations unnecessary for the restaurant. No credit cards accepted. 87026 Via Scesa Laino, Mormanno (phone: 981-81052). Moderate to inexpensive.

DIAMANTE: In addition to a wide, yellow-sand beach, this pretty resort town has the ruins of a Roman mausoleum and a view of an ancient fortress on the nearby island of Cirella. Diamante is famous for its murals depicting the hardships of southern Italian life and the area's politics, painted on walls and houses throughout the town by contemporary artists, some internationally known.

CHECKING IN: ***Riviera Blu*** – Right on the sea's edge, so you can wake up to the sound of the waves. The 60 rooms are simple but clean, and the service is extremely friendly. Open April through October. Via Nazionale, Diamante (phone: 985-81363). Moderate.

Ferretti – From the terraces of this romantic, Mediterranean-style 55-room hotel, guests can get a spectacular view and a suntan without even going down to the private beach. The hotel also has a swimming pool, a tennis court, and its own excellent restaurant, *La Pagoda,* which offers a delicious introduction to traditional Calabrian cooking. Try *maccheroni alla pastora con ricotta, sagne chine* (lasagna stuffed with mushrooms, bay leaves, celery, artichokes, peas, eggs, and cheese), *crespolini al formaggio* (thin pancakes rolled around cheese), or *pasta al forno* (baked pasta). Open April through October. Reservations advised for the restaurant. Major credit cards accepted. Via Lungomare, Diamante (phone: 985-81428). Moderate to inexpensive.

EATING OUT: ***La Ribalta*** – An attractive restaurant on the beach, whose owner, Enzo Ritondele, is an actor who frequently arranges for musicians, poets, and traveling stage troupes to perform for diners. Arrive early to get a table — this place is popular. Closed Mondays. No reservations. No credit cards accepted. Corso Vittorio Emanuele, Diamante (no phone). Moderate.

En Route from Diamante – The stretch of road from Diamante down through Belvedere offers lovely views of mountain slopes covered with olive trees, where peasant folk can often be seen at work in the fields. The colors are reminiscent of the rich greens and browns used in traditional glazes on Calabrian pottery. Beyond the pleasant beach town of Cetraro, turn off onto SS283 at the sign for Terme Luigiane.

CHECKING IN: ***San Michele*** – This cliff-top 73-room hostelry a few miles north of Cetraro is one of the few in Calabria awarded four stars by the *Touring Club Italiano.* It is a beautifully renovated old villa set in a park of grape vines, oleander, bougainvillea, and geraniums. The estate produces a fine rosé and red wine for hotel guests' consumption, along with 80% of its food, all organically grown. The villa itself offers a homey atmosphere mixed with turn-of-the-century elegance. Two charming farmhouses on the estate also provide a number of self-catering flats. An elevator takes guests down to the "secret" beach below. The hotel has its own swimming pool and a fine restaurant, and in the summer visitors can listen to a concert while dining on the terrace. On the grounds is a 9-hole golf course. Closed in November and December. Reservations necessary for the restaurant. Major credit cards accepted. SS18, Tirrena Superiore, Cetraro (phone: 982-91012). Expensive.

TERME LUIGIANE: Just after the turn onto SS283 near Guardia Piemontese are the *terme* (thermal baths) themselves, famous since ancient times for their alleged healing powers, although currently they are somewhat run-down. They are named after the Bourbon Louis, Count of Acquila, who frequented the springs. The waters are said to be particularly good for arthritis, rheumatism, and respiratory and gynecological disorders, and ear, nose, and throat ailments. Mud baths, massages, and postsurgical treatments can be had at the two well-equipped baths of San Francesco and Thermae Novae. Above, in the town of Guardia, locals still speak a French-Piedmont dialect that their ancestors, persecuted Valdensians, brought with them over 600 years ago. The women are buried in traditional headdresses and costumes found nowhere else in Calabria.

CHECKING IN: ***Delle Terme*** – This property has 128 modern rooms, a swimming pool, and is connected to the baths. The hotel provides physiotherapy and beauty treatments. Open June through October. Viale Stazione, Guardia Piemontese Terme (phone: 982-94475). Moderate.

Parco delle Rose – Surrounded by mountains and not far from the sea, this small hotel has 50 comfortable rooms and a restaurant. Open year-round. Via delle Terme, Terme Luigiane (phone: 982-94090). Inexpensive.

En Route from Terme Luigiane – East of Terme Luigiane, SS283 northeast offers excellent scenery — the Italians call it a "superstrada" — and although the drive through the hills can be quite lonely, it is highly recommended. The rural communities along the route provide a real flavor of peasant life in Calabria. Rejoin A3 at Spezzano and drive south to Cosenza. Watch carefully for signs; at certain crossroads in Calabria, they can be enigmatic, so it is smart to study a map beforehand. Alternatively, proceed south on SS18 to Paola.

PAOLA: Paola is the most important commercial and agricultural center on the Tyrrhenian coast, but it is more famous for being the birthplace (in 1416) of San Francesco di Paola, the saint of humble charity who founded the Minim order of the Franciscan brotherhood. Every May, pilgrims come from all over southern Italy to pay tribute to the saint; ceremonies include a procession into the sea. The Sanctuary of San Francesco is on a hill behind the town, on the spot where the saint built a convent in 1435 to commemorate St. Francis of Assisi. Unwary motorists may find themselves going uphill and then down again without having seen the sanctuary — signs are a little confusing. At the basilica there is an awe-inspiring collection of cast-off crutches, splints, trusses, and other gruesome body cages strung from the ceiling or draped across the stone walls of the rooms below.

En Route from Paola – When leaving Paola, don't be lured by the signs for Reggio. Instead, drive east, then south on SS107 to Cosenza. Near the coast, there are occasional glimpses of the sea; the road then climbs through vineyards, orchards, and forests of oak, chestnut, and beech.

COSENZA: The Old Town, dominated by its 12th-century Norman castle, is built on seven hills above the confluence of the Crati and Busento rivers. Entrance is by appointment only; contact one of the tourist offices (Piazza Rossi; phone: 984-30595, open weekdays from 8 AM to 8 PM; or at the train station; phone: 984-482620, open weekdays from 8 AM to 2 PM). The modern city sprawls north of the Busento. In the part of the river that divides the old from the new, according to legend, Alaric the Visigoth was buried with his treasure in AD 412. The waters were supposedly diverted for the burial and then restored to their natural course. For years, archaeological teams have searched the riverbed at various points but have failed to find any evidence to support the legend.

Cosenza was part of Magna Graecia and later part of the Roman Empire. The imperial road Via Pompilia passed through the town, linking Rome with Reggio Calabria. Cosenza was twice destroyed by the Saracens before it was conquered by the Norman Robert Guiscard in the 11th century. It was later ruled by his half-brother Roger. Under subsequent Aragonese, Angevin, and Spanish rule, it was the most important town in Calabria and has always had strong links with Naples and the other major cities of Italy. Today it is an important commercial and agricultural center. The University of Calabria — Italy's newest and most modern — is built on the outskirts of the city.

Visitors arriving in Cosenza between 7 and 8 PM will find minor chaos. This is *passeggiata* time, when the whole town empties into the main thoroughfare to stroll and greet each other. Piazza Kennedy seems to be the favorite meeting place for students, who stand in the middle of the road in groups earnestly chatting, making pedestrian traffic impossible. Only a few blocks away, the streets are virtually deserted. The people of Cosenza are animated but very different from the image of southern Italians described in most guidebooks. They have fine, chiseled profiles, like the Greek faces in archaeological museums; they are often fair and solemn-faced.

For the visitor, the most interesting part of Cosenza is the Old City, and the most romantic point of entry is along the road that skirts the castle and leads straight into Piazza XV Marzo, where the *Museo Civico* is located. The museum has some very striking prehistoric bronze pieces — statues, medals, and hair ornaments. It is open daily except Sundays from 9 AM to 1 PM. Next door is the *Teatro Rendano,* built in the 9th century, it was reconstructed after being destroyed in World War II. Fine opera is staged here from January through the spring (local groups put on drama and music performances the rest of the year). Corso Telesio leads from the square into the heart of the Old City, passing the Duomo. This Gothic building has its origins in the late Roman period and was rebuilt after the 1184 earthquake. It adjoins the archbishop's palace, which contains one of Calabria's most precious treasures — a Byzantine reliquary cross, said to have been the gift of Frederick II. The reliquary is made of gold filigree and is encrusted with jewels. There are many other art treasures in the churches of old Cosenza. A visit to the Chiesa di San Domenico is rewarding, especially for its splendid rose window.

The town's two tourist information offices are in Piazza Rossi (phone: 984-390595; open weekdays from 8 AM to 8 PM) and at the train station outside the city (phone: 984-482620; open weekdays from 8 AM to 2 PM).

CHECKING IN: ***Centrale*** – Centrally located near the station and well marked on the road into Cosenza. There are 48 rooms, the service is efficient and polite, and there also is a good restaurant. The hotel garage is useful, since parking is difficult. Via Macallè, at the corner of Corso Mazzini, Cosenza (phone: 984-73681). Expensive.

MotelAgip – Large (120 rooms), with good views of the countryside, it's about 4 miles (6 km) out of town. Like all of the Agip chain, it is modern and functional; however, its restaurant is surprisingly good. Try the local pasta. Reservations advised. SS19, at the turnoff to SS107, Cosenza (phone: 984-839101). Expensive.

Royal – One of the best in town, with 44 rooms (including some for guests with disabilities), a restaurant, and lounge. Open year-round. 24 Via Molinella, Cosenza (phone: 984-412461). Expensive.

EATING OUT: ***La Calavrisella*** – In its own garden, about a 15-minute walk from the *Centrale,* this popular, attractive restaurant offers traditional Calabrian cooking at very reasonable prices. Try *marille con le melanzane* (with eggplant) and *fusilli alla Calavrisella* or *capretto alle frasche d'origano* (kid cooked with oregano). Other local dishes include mushrooms, picked wild, stuffed, and even roasted, a Cosenza specialty. Closed Saturdays, Sunday evenings, and 1 week in August. Reservations unnecessary. No credit cards accepted. 11/A Via Gerolamo de Rada, Cosenza (phone: 984-28012). Inexpensive.

Trattoria Peppino – Hearty regional dishes, prepared with the wonderful fresh mushrooms from the wild mountains of the Sila, are served here. Located just outside the entrance to the Old Town. Closed Sundays. No reservations. No credit cards. 4 Piazza Crispi (phone: 984-73217). Inexpensive.

En Route from Cosenza – It is possible to drive directly south from Cosenza to Pizzo via A3. Alternatively, for spectacular views and villages rich in crafts, take a detour into the Sila Massif via SS107 east. The highway winds through a forest that becomes alpine at the level of Camigliatello Silano, where it turns into a pleasant mountain road. The Sila Massif is a pristine mountain chain covered with virgin forest, lovely lakes, and flowing streams.

CAMIGLIATELLO SILANO: Camigliatello Silano is a well-equipped, year-round resort town in the pine forests above Lake Cecita. The hiking is wonderful (there are excellent trail maps available all over the town), and its ski facilities are among the best in Calabria; in the fall, before the season starts, the local slopes yield some of the best mushrooms in the region, celebrated each October in the *Sagra dei Funghi* (mushroom festival).

CHECKING IN/EATING OUT: ***Aquila & Edelweiss*** – This 40-room modern hotel has a restaurant that serves several mushroom-based dishes and other specialties of the Sila, such as *trota* (mountain trout), *cinghiale* (wild boar), *caciocavallo* (a creamy cheese), and *butirro* (*caciocavallo* wrapped around creamery butter). Open daily. Reservations unnecessary. Major credit cards accepted. 11 Viale Stazione, Camigliatello Silano (phone: 984-578044). Hotel, expensive to moderate; restaurant, moderate to inexpensive.

LONGOBUCCO: From Camigliatello, take SS177, northeast, which follows the shore of Lake Cecita, heads past Mount Altare, and winds through the pines to Longobucco, a town that dates from the Middle Ages. Its church, Santa Maria Assunta (which is flanked by a curious baroque leaning bell tower), contains a noteworthy wood sculpture of the Madonna and Child and objects made of silver from nearby mines. More works of the once-flourishing local silversmith's art are in the *Museo Parrochiale,* and fine woodcarvings can be seen in the Church of Santa Maria Maddalena. Crafts are still a mainstay of the community's economy, especially carpets and fabrics the women of Longobucco and neighboring villages handweave into Oriental patterns. In August, the weavers gather in Longobucco to display and sell their wares.

SAN GIOVANNI IN FIORE: From Longobucco, SS177 winds slowly back down to SS107. Proceed east on SS107 to San Giovanni in Fiore. In the 12th century, Gioacchino da Fiore founded an abbey here, and over the centuries the town grew up around it. The most interesting part of San Giovanni in Fiore is the lower, older section, where the restored abbey, called the Badia Florense, is located, housing a notable *Museo Etnografico* (Ethnographic Museum). Legend has it that Gioacchino also designed the characteristic black-and-white costumes and elaborate, plaited hair style still occasionally worn by the women, meant to represent the life and death of Christ. San Giovanni in Fiore also has a strong crafts tradition, primarily in goldsmithing and carpet weaving in the Armenian tradition, the products of which are on display at the *Santa Lucia* hotel.

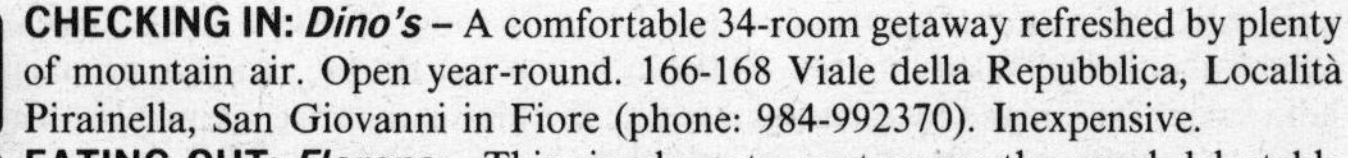

CHECKING IN: ***Dino's*** – A comfortable 34-room getaway refreshed by plenty of mountain air. Open year-round. 166-168 Viale della Repubblica, Località Pirainella, San Giovanni in Fiore (phone: 984-992370). Inexpensive.

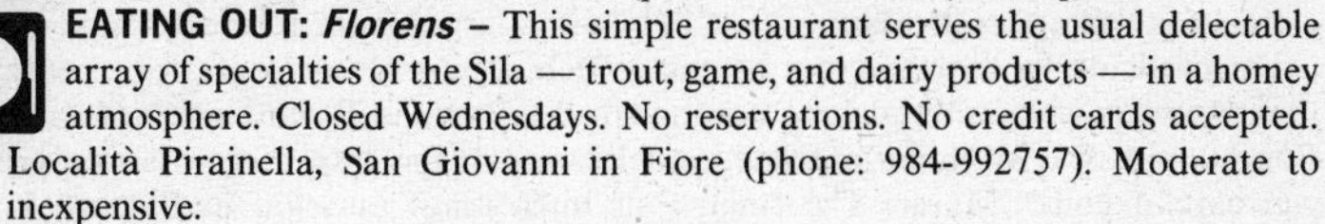

EATING OUT: ***Florens*** – This simple restaurant serves the usual delectable array of specialties of the Sila — trout, game, and dairy products — in a homey atmosphere. Closed Wednesdays. No reservations. No credit cards accepted. Località Pirainella, San Giovanni in Fiore (phone: 984-992757). Moderate to inexpensive.

LORICA: Take SS107 to the junction of SS108 *bis,* where it hugs the north shore of Lake Arvo. As soon as you begin to see the lake on the left, look for the turnoff on the right for the mountain road that leads to the top of Botte Donato, the Sila's highest mountain, for spectacular views of the surrounding area. Then return to SS108 *bis* and turn right along the lake to Lorica, a ski village panoramically situated in a beech and pine forest. The town's modern appearance is more than compensated for by natural beauty that's equally appealing during ski season or in summer, both profusely pine-scented. From Lorica, take the scenic winding drive back to Cosenza on SS108 *bis* along Lake Arvo, turning right on SS178 at the junction before the village of Quaresima. Pick up A3 to Pizzo. The local tourist office (Pro Loco) is on Via Nazionale (phone: 984-997069).

CHECKING IN: ***Lorica*** – This 100-room, comfortably modern lodge is quiet and romantic. Ask for one of the rooms with a view of Lake Arvo. Open mid-May to mid-October. 57 Viale Libertà, Lorica (phone: 984-997039). Inexpensive.

EATING OUT: ***Pesce Fresco*** – A delightful trattoria set on the edge of the St. Eufemia Plain (a natural wildlife reserve), a must for travelers proceeding along the coast or descending from the mountains. As the name attests, the fish is fresh. Closed November through April. Reservations unnecessary. No credit cards accepted. Stay on SS18 for a delightful drive, exit at Gizzeria/Lamezia Terme (A3) (phone: 968-51105). Moderate to inexpensive.

PIZZO: Pizzo, also called Pizzo Calabro, is a picturesque fishing town that looks down from a cliff onto a beautiful sea with white sandy beaches. It is famous for the castle where Napoleon's brother-in-law Joachim Murat, ex-King of Naples, was imprisoned and shot in 1815, 5 days after he had landed in an attempt to recover his throne. Part of the castle is now used as a youth hostel. All that remains of the original structure is an archway and towers. In the spring, when the tuna boats are blessed before setting out with their nets, the church bells peal across the water. (In Calabria there are different bell tones for different occasions.)

CHECKING IN: ***La Marinella*** – A modern 36-room hostelry with sea views, it has quickly built a reputation for superior service and the good food in its restaurant. Open year-round. Via Marinella Prangi, Pizzo (phone: 963-264064). Moderate.

Sonia – A comfortable, 47-room family-run hotel with a restaurant. 110 Riviera Prangi, Pizzo (phone: 963-531315). Inexpensive.

EATING OUT: ***La Medusa*** – As popular with the locals as with visitors, this eatery is in the heart of Pizzo. Try the fish risotto, especially the *risotto ai gamberi* (rice with prawns) or the delicious stew-like fish soup. Closed Mondays from November through March. Reservations unnecessary. No credit cards accepted. Via Salomone, Pizzo (phone: 963-531203). Inexpensive.

VIBO VALENTIA: From Pizzo to Vibo Valentia, SS18 winds around the hills; silver-gray olives and prickly-pear cacti tumble down the steep slopes. About 1¼ miles (2 km) north of Vibo, stop to see the remains of an ancient Greek temple and an imposing wall with a view of the Tyrrhenian coast. As with most towns on the Calabrian coast, Vibo Valentia is divided into two — the hill town and the beach town, or marina. The hill town is dominated by a Norman castle; the marina has been developed so tourists can take advantage of its beautiful beaches. Now a large commercial city, most of Vibo is not particularly attractive, but its past is rich. It was always a strategic center for the possession of central Calabria, hosting Greeks, Romans, Byzantines, Normans, and Bourbons. It was an important intellectual center in the 18th century and a provincial capital under Murat. The small (but interesting) museum in Palazzo Gagliardi on Piazza Garibaldi is worth a visit for its impressive collection of Greek pots and votive statues, relics of the 7th century BC, when Vibo was a sub-colony of the Greek-owned town of Locri, on Calabria's Ionian coast (closed Mondays; admission charge). The tourist office (AAST) is located at 8 Piazza Diaz (phone: 963-42008).

CHECKING IN/EATING OUT: ***501*** – A modern 124-room hotel on the slope leading up to town, it has tennis courts and an excellent view of the Gulf of Tropea. There are 2 restaurants: At the main restaurant inside, the emphasis is on fish, and the antipasti are free; open all year. Outside, diners can dawdle over puddings and local wines at the poolside dining spot; open summers only from sunset to the small hours of the morning. 1 Via Nazionale, A3 turnoff for Vibo Valentia (phone: 963-44560). Hotel, expensive; restaurants, moderate.

L'Approdo – People in the know come from nearby Tropea and Vibo Valentia to eat here, in spite of its site in the less-than-quaint port of Vibo Marina (5 miles/8 km from Vibo Valentia). It's run by two brothers, Mimmo and Pino Lopreaito; the cooking is of an extremely high standard and the prices are reasonable. Try the *pesce spada affumicato* (smoked swordfish) and the delicious homemade *tagliatelle* with mussels and clams. Closed in winter. Reservations advised. No credit cards accepted. 22 Via Roma, Vibo Marina (phone: 963-240640). Moderate.

En Route from Vibo Valentia – Before going to Gioia Tauro, which is the beginning of the Costa Viola, make a detour toward the coast to Tropea and Nicotera. Follow SS522 from Vibo Marina to Tropea.

TROPEA: Crouched on a cliff above the sea, Tropea is one of the few old towns that have remained virtually intact in earthquake-prone Calabria. It is one of the most picturesque fishing villages on this part of the coast. Many of its 15th- and 16th-century buildings are still standing, though the origins of the town go back even farther. On a clear day, it's possible to see as far as the Lipari Islands. Illuminated façades and statues of saints towering on the hills provide a striking silhouette against the night sky.

CHECKING IN: ***Baia Paraelios*** – About 2 miles (3 km) before Tropea (on the road from Vibo Velentia), this is one of Calabria's most renowned holiday villages, built right on the water's edge. There are 72 rooms in ochre-colored villas set in gardens of tumbling geraniums, olive trees, palms, and cacti. Book early, as this place is very popular in mid-summer. Open April through September. Località Fornace, Parghelia, Tropea (phone: 963-600300). Expensive to moderate.

La Pineta – Modern and comfortable, this 43-room seaside hotel, with only double rooms, caters to conventioneers and holiday celebrants. There is a restaurant. Open the end of March to mid-October. 150 Via Marina, Tropea (phone: 963-61700). Moderate.

Virgilio – A comfortable 52-room hotel near the center of town with a restaurant and a garage. Viale Tondo, Tropea (phone: 963-61201). Moderate.

EATING OUT: ***Pimm's*** – This eatery stands out among the few restaurants in town. The kitchen turns out some excellent dishes and the seafood and tasty starters are heavenly. Closed in late autumn and winter. Reservations advised in summer. No credit cards accepted. Largo Migliarese, Tropea (phone: 963-666105). Moderate.

NICOTERA: It's sensible to study directions in this area well before arriving. As the excellent Italian guidebook to Calabria *Incontro con la Calabria,* by Domenico Laruffa, points out, the access roads to Nicotera are "quite accidental." But Calabrians will always try to be helpful, so if in doubt, stop a passing motor scooter and ask. SS522 winds along the coast for another 25 miles (40 km) beyond Tropea to Nicotera, and the view is particularly stunning, passing lush fields of olives, wheat, and onions, for which the area is famous. The Old Town clings to the hill above. Drive to the top —

the modern part of Nicotera — and if it's Sunday morning, join the market throng surveying the many excellent food stalls stuffed with local sausage, *pecorino* cheese, fresh almonds, and the traditional honey bread — formed into animal shapes or musical instruments. Walk down into the old part of the town and wander along the winding little streets. An agricultural and fishing village, Nicotera is particularly famous for its granite, exported and otherwise adorning many of the town's buildings, and is also home to many artisans. A few miles down the road at Badia di Nicotera, master ceramist Giuseppe Cocciolo works in his *laboratorio* (Piazza Fontana; phone: 963-85323). He makes wonderful terra cotta masks which, according to tradition, ward off evil spirits.

CHECKING IN: ***Miragolfo*** – Just on the outskirts of town, the 68 rooms have balconies overlooking the sea in front and the countryside in back; there also is access to a private beach. Open year-round. 68 Via Corte, Nicotera (phone: 963-81470 or 963-81700). Moderate to inexpensive.

GIOIA TAURO: SS522 continues down the coast to Gioia Tauro, the first town on the Costa Viola. The town is now an industrial port and canning center, but below it lies the ancient Metauria, a Greek colony of Locri. The olive trees on the Plain of Gioia are said to be the oldest and largest in Europe, dating from the time of Christ.

CHECKING IN: ***Park*** – A simple 56-room establishment with air conditioning, a garden, and a restaurant. Open year-round. 18 Via Nazionale, Gioia Tauro (phone: 966-51159). Moderate.

Euro Motel – About 1¼ miles (2 km) southeast of the city, this place is adequate for a short stay. There are 44 rooms, all air conditioned, and a garden. 111 Via Nazionale, Gioia Tauro (phone: 966-52083). Moderate to inexpensive.

EATING OUT: ***Il Buco*** – Northern Italian dishes, primarily from Emilia, share the menu with local fare. Closed Mondays. Reservations unnecessary. No credit cards accepted. 115 Via Lo Moro, Gioia Tauro (phone: 966-51512). Moderate to inexpensive.

PALMI: On the drive south from Gioia Tauro, the road suddenly opens out to the largest of Palmi's sandy beaches, La Tonnara, where the so-called Costa Viola (Violet Coast) begins its stretch down to Reggio. Lush subtropical plants and uncultivated flora — jasmine, bougainvillea, prickly pear, and bergamot — fill the air with a sweet fragrance. The view from Mount St. Elia, "the balcony over Tyrrhenia," just south of the city, includes Mount Etna and Messina in Sicily, the Lipari Islands, and the Calabrian coast as far north as Capo Vaticano.

The *Calabrian Folklore Museum* is housed in the Casa della Cultura, a modern cultural center on the road leading out of Palmi to Mount St. Elia. The museum has a wonderful collection of old and new terra cotta masks and water vessels, Greek-style ceramics from the Ionian coast, hand-carved wooden utensils from the Aspromonte Mountains, a number of religious and pagan objects, and examples of traditional costumes. Open Tuesdays through Fridays from 9 AM to 1 PM and 5 to 7 PM; admission charge.

During the summer, Palmi stages two of Calabria's most spectacular *feste.* On the last Sunday in August, 200 local men drag the "Varia," an 80-foot votive "mountain" made of steel and papier-mâché through the streets. Perched on top is a young girl, usually an orphan, chosen to represent the Virgin Mary. On August 16, 100 townspeople celebrate the feast day of Palmi's patron, St. Rocco, by donning cloaks and crowns made of thorns and parading through the town.

CHECKING IN: ***Costa Viola*** – All 48 rooms have a lovely sea view in this quiet countryside hotel set among olive groves. Open in summer only. Località Torre (phone: 966-22016). Moderate to inexpensive.

Arcobaleno **–** This small (37-room) hotel on the road between Palmi and the Taureana beach (about 4 miles/6 km north of the town proper) has a restaurant, a covered heated swimming pool, and tennis courts. Open year-round. Via Taureana, Palmi (phone: 966-46275). Inexpensive.

Miami **–** Not as modern as its name may suggest, but this 10-room hotel is appealing because of its beachfront location, almost 4 miles (6 km) north of Palmi. Open year-round. 10 Corso Lido Tonnara (phone: 966-46396). Inexpensive.

EATING OUT: *La Lampara* – A rustic restaurant serving excellent fish dishes, especially *involtini di pesce spada* (swordfish) in season. Try the excellent local wine. Closed November and December. Reservations unnecessary. No credit cards accepted. Lido Tonnara, Palmi vicinity (phone: 966-46332). Moderate to inexpensive.

Pizzeria La Margherita **–** Specialties are *pizza alla pioggia* and *la struncatura* (homemade whole wheat pasta in anchovy sauce). Open daily. Reservations unnecessary. No credit cards accepted. Across the road from the northern end of Lido Tonnara (no phone). Moderate to inexpensive.

La Pineta **–** Pizza is served under pine trees. Open daily. Reservations unnecessary. No credit cards accepted. Monte Sant'Elia (phone: 966-22926). Inexpensive.

En Route from Palmi – To learn more about the ceramic pots and masks at the *Folklore Museum,* take a side trip to a little town less than 2 miles (3 km) southeast of Palmi. The artisans of Seminara make the traditional green and yellow pottery according to ancient methods passed on from generation to generation. Their wares are sold in shops in the town's main piazza. Stop at 30 Corso Barlaam and see the work of master potter Il Mago (the magician), as Paolo Condurso is called. His ceramics have been exhibited throughout Europe; even Picasso was enchanted by them. He is one of the craftsmen teaching at the School of Ceramics founded by the Reggio di Calabria local government.

BAGNARA CALABRA: South of Palmi, beyond the famous Zibibbo vineyards, is the swordfishing center of the Costa Viola. Between April and late July or August, when the *pesce spada* (swordfish) come to the coastal waters here to spawn, life in Bagnara Calabra (often simply called Bagnara) centers around their capture, sale, and preparation. This activity hasn't changed since the days of the early Greeks; fishermen still harpoon the swordfish by hand. The *bagnarote* (women of Bagnara) are legendary. While the men are at sea (for superstitious reasons, the women are not allowed to go), the town operates under a matriarchy; when the men return with the catch, the women prepare the fish in an infinite variety of ways — most often grilled and then dowsed with *salmoriglio,* a tasty sauce of garlic, oregano, and olive oil. A *bagnarota* walking around with a *pesce spada* on her head is a typical sight. (Loredana Berté, the well-known Italian singer who is married to Bjorn Borg, is a *bagnarota.*) While in Bagnara, look for the locally made glassware and *torrone* (nougat made with almonds and honey).

EATING OUT: *Taverna Kerkyra* – Marika, the Greek woman who runs this restaurant (the best in town), brought her favorite recipes for swordfish from Corfu — hence the name, which means Corfu in her native tongue. In addition to Greek fare, there are some pasta dishes. Closed Mondays, sometimes Tuesdays, mid-June to mid-July, and early November. Reservations unnecessary. No credit cards accepted. 217 Corso Vittorio Emanuele (phone: 966-372260). Moderate.

SCILLA: The legendary rock of Scylla is where a six-headed monster lay in wait for sailors who had escaped the equally terrifying ogre of Charybdis, who swallowed and then regurgitated the waters of the sea several times a day. These legends are based on real natural phenomena: High winds often break on the cliffs of the Calabrian coast, including the rock of Scylla, and strong alternating currents create whirlpools at 6-hour intervals in the Strait of Messina. Sailing is treacherous, as Homer's sailors found in *The Odyssey,* when they survived the waters of the gulf only to die on Scylla's rocky roots in the sea.

Near Scilla's picturesque fishermen's quarters where houses and cottages literally descend into the sea, known as La Chianalea, is an impressive medieval Aragonese castle, seemingly sculpted out of the rock of Scilla itself. Its ruins now house a youth hostel — one of the best — and a discotheque. This, as well as the grand terrace of the main town square, is worth a visit. Locals claim that 400-year-old treasures once were walled up in a secret chamber of the castle. With their castle currently undergoing restoration, townspeople have their fingers crossed. Now a favorite promenade for residents and visitors, the terrace overlooks the rooftops of the Old Town and the beautiful sandy Sirens Beach.

EATING OUT: ***Da Glauco*** – Off the main road into La Chianalea is a sign for *Ristorante da Glauco.* Ring the bell of Famiglia Pontillo and go upstairs. It's a typical Scillan house-turned-restaurant, and its terrace overlooks the fishermen's houses, the port, and the sea. Extra-special dishes are the spicy tomatoes, pickled eggplant antipasto, and *spaghetti al Glauco.* Closed Sundays and Mondays. Reservations advised. No credit cards accepted. Via Chianalea, Scilla (phone: 965-46330). Moderate.

Ristorante Ulisse – A former stable, tastefully converted into Scilla's smartest restaurant. Try the *tris dello chef,* a first course of three different kinds of homemade pasta; or the *linguine al cartoccio,* a steaming plate of pasta with giant prawns, squid, mussels, and clams. Closed Mondays. Reservations advised in summer. Diners Club accepted. In the lower town at the end of the Lungomare, at 1 Via Omicciolí, Scilla (phone: 965-790190). Moderate.

Virtigine – Alfresco dining affords one of the best views of the castle, either at sunset or when it is floodlit at night. With a cool drink in hand, and light fare, there is hardly a better place in town. Open daily until midnight. No reservations. No credit cards. 14 Piazza San Rocco (no phone). Moderate.

Alla Pescatora – When Peppino isn't making fishing boats, he's turning out mouthwatering *involtini di pesce spada,* swordfish rolls, and other coastal fare right here. Closed Tuesdays and from mid-December through March. Reservations advised in summer. No credit cards accepted. On the sea at Marina Grande, 32 Lungomare Scilla, Scilla (phone: 965-754147). Moderate to inexpensive.

SANTA TRADA CANNITELLO: The Costa Viola ends with this town, the peninsula's closest point (about 2 miles) to Sicily. There has been talk for the last 100 years of joining the mainland and the island. Parliament passed a law authorizing the building of a link, but commercial and political conflicts have held up construction, and it will almost certainly be later than the year 2000 before vehicles will make the trip from Calabria to Sicily under their own power. Rejoin A3 here and continue to Reggio. Alternatively, stay on SS18 for Villa San Giovanni.

VILLA SAN GIOVANNI: If the glimpses of Sicily are tempting, take one of the regular car ferries or a hydrofoil across the Strait of Messina. Similar transport to Messina is also available from Reggio, making a day trip to Taormina (only 31 miles/50 km from Messina) almost irresistible. At the gas station on A3, just before the turnoff for Villa San Giovanni, an information office has up-to-date information on schedules.

EATING OUT: ***Albergo Piccolo*** – While waiting for the ferry, have a meal at this family-run establishment in front of the docks. Try the *involtini di pesce spada* (swordfish rolls), the *saltimbocca al Piccolo Hotel* (thin slices of veal in a subtle, light sauce), or *risotto con funghi porcini* (rice with *porcini* mushrooms).

The wine is good, as are the homemade sweets and ice cream. Open daily. Reservations advised in summer. No credit cards accepted. Piazza della Stazione, Villa San Giovanni (phone: 965-751410 or 965-751153). Inexpensive.

REGGIO DI CALABRIA: Founded in the 8th century BC by the Greeks, Reggio is one of the biggest cities in Calabria. It certainly had the most splendid past, particularly in the Greek, Roman, and Byzantine periods. Unfortunately, visitors will find few remains of ancient Rhegion, as the Greeks called it. Virtually no building dates before 1908, the year a massive earthquake devastated the entire area. Much of the city has been rebuilt in a pleasant, romantic, turn-of-the-century style.

Like most southern Italian towns, Reggio was not designed with the automobile in mind, so it is difficult to pass through the narrow streets and impossible to park. Avoid spots marked "Zona Auto Rimozione" — they're tow-away zones, and the process of retrieving a towed car is quite complex.

Wander along the elegant and typically Mediterranean boardwalk, called the Lungomare Marina, with its central strip of grass, enormous fig trees, and majestic palms. At the north end of the Lungomare, turn right for Piazza De Nava, where the *Museo Nazionale* (National Museum) has an interesting collection of antiquities from archaeological excavations of the ancient towns of Magna Graecia — Sibari, Locri, Medma — and artifacts from later Roman civilizations. This museum is particularly well known for its Bronzi, the bronze warriors of Riace, accidentally discovered in 1972 by a diver in only 25 feet of water off the Ionian coast. The two stunning statues, both over 6 feet in height, thought to be the most interesting examples in existence of the great Greek Bronze Age, have become symbols of the city — images and reproductions of them appear throughout Reggio. Open Tuesdays through Saturdays from 9 AM to 1 PM and 2 to 7 PM, Sundays from 9 AM to 12:30 PM, Mondays from 9 AM to 1 PM; admission charge.

An excellent selection of local arts and crafts is on sale at controlled prices at the local government's Centro di Documentazione per le Arti Popolari Calabresi on Corso Garibaldi, the town's main thoroughfare. The tourist office is next door at No. 329 (phone: 965-94094); there is another one at the central train station (phone: 965-27120). If sore feet are a problem by this time, drop into the bar next to the tourist office to rest and sample the famous *granita di caffè con panna e brioche* (coffee-flavored ices with cream and sweet pastry), a Calabrian summer specialty. People turn out in large numbers for their evening *passeggiata* along the waterfront and Corso Garibaldi. During the *Feste di Settembre* (September Festivals), concerts, exhibitions, and religious celebrations take place throughout the city.

CHECKING IN: *Excelsior* – One of the links in the deluxe Excelsior chain, this is considered to be the best hotel in Reggio. Right behind the *Museo Nazionale,* it has some traditional elegance (although it could use some sprucing up to warrant the price) and some of the 92 rooms have been renovated to provide modern comforts. 66 Via Vittorio Veneto, Reggio di Calabria (phone: 965-25801). Expensive.

Grand Albergo Miramare – One of the cleanest, most traditional hotels in town, its 96 rooms all have been attractively redecorated. Don't be put off by the "dark" — the lights only go on once you've hung the key on the hook above the switch! The relaxing restaurant turns out excellent food under the tutelage of chef Francesco Pellegrino. Try the swordfish, prepared in a variety of ways. Open year-round. Reservations advised. 1 Via Fata Morgana, Reggio di Calabria (phone: 965-91881). Expensive.

Palace Masoanris – Less elegant than its sister hotel the *Excelsior,* but nonetheless very comfortable. 64 rooms. Open year-round. 95 Via Vittorio Veneto, Reggio di Calabria (phone: 965-26433). Expensive.

Primavera – This simple but comfortable 52-room hotel in suburban Pentimele overlooks the Strait of Messina. 177 Via Nazionale, Reggio di Calabria (phone: 965-47081). Expensive to moderate.

EATING OUT: ***Baylik*** – Sample traditional raw fish dishes of the Ionian coast, dine on excellent Calabrian dishes, and enjoy beautiful sea views in this pleasant dining spot. Closed Thursdays and late July to mid-August. Reservations advised. Major credit cards accepted. 1 Via Leone, Reggio di Calabria (phone: 965-48624). Moderate.

Bonaccorso – Generally recognized as one of the finest restaurants in Calabria, serving fine pasta and local specialties, as well as excellent traditional Italian dishes. Closed Fridays. Reservations advised. Major credit cards accepted. 6-8 Via Battisti, Reggio di Calabria (phone: 965-96048). Moderate.

Conti – An elegant restaurant close to the *Museo Nazionale,* it serves traditional Calabrian dishes and is always adding new items to the menu. Pasta such as handmade macaroni, swordfish in season, and pastries, are particularly recommended. Closed Mondays, except from June to September. Reservations advised. Diners Club accepted. 2 Via Giulia, Reggio di Calabria (phone: 965-29043). Moderate.

Collina dello Scoiattolo – Classic Calabrian dishes are served with art and tradition. Meat is cooked over a wood fire, and antipasti are served in infinite varieties. Try the *penne alla brigante* (pasta favored by one of the last of Calabria's brigands, Giuseppe Musolino). Closed Wednesdays. Reservations advised. No credit cards accepted. 34 Via Provinciale Gallina, Reggio di Calabria (phone: 965-682255). Inexpensive.

La Pignata – Right off Corso Garibaldi is this restaurant with beautifully carved wood ceilings that serves excellent seafood and pizza, both with a good spicy sauce. Closed Wednesdays and July. No reservations. No credit cards. 122 Via Tripepi, Reggio di Calabria (phone: 965-27841). Inexpensive.

Pizzeria Giardino – Filled with Reggio's bejeweled after-theater crowd, this wonderful eatery near the marina is a beehive of activity into the late hours. The delicious pizza is served on brightly painted majolica platters, and because of its size, you will want to share one. Closed Mondays. Reservations are advised, but be prepared to wait anyway. No credit cards accepted. 8 Largo Colombo, Reggio di Calabria (phone: 965-28460). Inexpensive.

En Route from Reggio di Calabria – Whether you have detoured to Sicily or have been able to resist, continue south on SS106 along the Costa dei Gelsomini. On this gorgeous coastal route, long stretches of bright blue water and green fields and the odd goatherd and shepherd are still visible, despite considerable recent urban development. Behind many of the little towns on the coast are mountain villages bearing the same names. Because of their position and the difficulty of access, many have remained unchanged for centuries. The nearest and most accessible is Bova. The people here, numbering about 1,000, trace their ancestry back to Magna Graecia and speak a language similar to modern Greek. Each year in June or July, they host a festival with costumes and music for all members of Calabria's Graecanic community. The view from the Norman castle at the summit of the village is well worth the rather frightening trip up; going down is much easier. At the nearby towns of Condofuri and Galliciano, reached by turning off at Condofuri Marina, a few miles west of Bova Marina, villagers not only speak Greek but make and play the famous *zampogne,* rustic bagpipes.

LOCRI: Farther along SS106 are the remains of the Hellenic city of Locri Epizephyri, from which modern Locri has borrowed its name. The New City is a lively commercial area, flat and modern and little resembling its predecessor. Locri is noted for the manufacture of mattresses, bitumen, and garden ornaments. The gnomes and plaster effigies of Snow White and her companions bear little in common with the treasures for which the older city is famous. In recent years, the town has become famous as the kidnapping capital of Italy. Visitors are unlikely to become targets, however.

The ruins of ancient Locri, buried in an olive grove, are spread out like a relief map among the grasses and shrubs. From the road the remains of a temple and a wall are visible. A little farther on at Portigliola are a Greek-Roman theater and a Doric temple. Beyond those is the celebrated sanctuary of Persephone, where ancient Locri's religious life centered. The area has not been fully excavated, but much of what has been found, including 37 bronze law tablets, is now in the *Museo Nazionale* in Reggio. The small, modern antiquarium beside the ruins has clear plans and photos of the history and artistic development of the city, as well as bronzes and some pottery and votive statues. Local craftsmen still make terra cotta pots closely resembling some of those seen in the antiquarium. Open daily from 9 AM to 2 PM, Sundays to 1 PM, with additional afternoon hours in the summer; no admission charge. Locri also has a terrific white sand beach and offers a variety of water sports, as well as tennis. The tourist office (1 Via Fume; phone: 964-29600; open daily except Sundays from 8 AM to 6 PM in July and August; Mondays through Fridays from 8 AM to 2 PM the rest of the year) has information about Locri and Gerace (see below).

CHECKING IN: *Demaco* – The seaside rooms are preferred in this modern 28-room hotel in the main town, just behind the station. There is a garage and meeting rooms. Open year-round; the restaurant is open in the summer only. 28 Via Lungomare, Locri (phone: 964-20247). Moderate to inexpensive.

Motel Faro – Conveniently located for exploring the Greek-Roman theater of Locri. It has 46 rooms, sports facilities, a children's play area, a restaurant, and access to a private beach. Open all year. SS106, Portigliola (phone: 964-361015). Inexpensive.

EATING OUT: *Trattoria Rocco Simone* – Rocco Simone used to work in the fields, but he now serves his wife's excellent cooking, with the greatest courtesy, to anyone who cares to drop in to his little trattoria just behind the Greek theater. Although the atmosphere is far from luxurious, the food is outstanding (as is Rocco's manner), and the cost is very reasonable. The restaurant is slightly outside the town. To find it take the left-hand turn for Moschetta, just before entering Locri from Reggio di Calabria. Follow the trattoria's signs for about 2½ miles (4 km). Closed Mondays and from late October to early November. Reservations unnecessary. No credit cards accepted. Piazza Contrada Moschetta, Locri (phone: 964-390005). Inexpensive.

Da Umberto – For less than $12 per person, diners here can sample small portions of all the local specialties. Near the ruins. Closed Mondays. Reservations unnecessary. No credit cards accepted. Contrada Caruso (phone: 964-29794). Inexpensive.

GERACE: About a 15-minute drive from Locri up SS111, an excellent mountain road, is a picturesque medieval town with art treasures unequaled in the region. Its position has helped protect it from modern spoiling. Founded in the 9th century BC by Greek refugees from Saracen raids, it later became one of the strongest Byzantine fortresses in the south. Gerace's Norman Gothic cathedral is the largest sacred building in Calabria. Built in 1045 and later altered and restored, its 26 supporting columns are believed to have come from the temples of ancient Locri. Gerace is a timeless place. The *botteghe artigiane di vasai* (local potters' workshops) turn out amphora-type pots from the local clay, using the same methods their predecessors used centuries ago.

EATING OUT: *Fagiano Bianco* – Unless traveling with a group that has made advance reservations, visitors may find this lovely *cantina* closed, but the same food is served at the bar on Piazza Centrale, where a few tables are set outdoors in fine weather. *Antipasto della casa* and the wine are excellent. Piazza Centrale, Gerace (no phone). Inexpensive.

En Route from Gerace – Rather than retrace the route back to Reggio di Calabria, head northwest on SS111 toward Gioia Tauro on the Tyrrhenian coast. The 28-mile (45-km) drive curves upward behind Gerace into the hills of Aspromonte, an area as famous for its outlaws as for the beauty of its scenery.

Sicily (and the Lipari Islands)

To many Americans, the mention of Sicily conjures up visions of black-clad elderly women, timeworn peasants, barefoot children, and ominous-looking Mafia dons. But this island, the largest in the Mediterranean (almost 10,000 square miles), possesses a rich natural beauty and a unique artistic patrimony that reflects its tumultuous history and curious mix of cultures. Centuries of occupation by invaders from both East and West have left a legacy of baroque churches, Norman castles, Moorish domes and arches, as well as an exotic cuisine. Sicily's spectacular Greek temples and amphitheaters are the best-preserved Hellenic sites outside Greece.

Located off the "toe" of the Italian peninsula, from which it is separated by the narrow Strait of Messina, Sicily has a remarkably varied landscape. Believed to be a natural continuation of the Apennine chain of mountains that runs down the Italian peninsula, the island is mountainous in the north and east, with a vast central plateau that slopes down to its fertile coastline. Mount Etna, Europe's largest active volcano, dominates the eastern region.

Like much of Italy's south, Sicily still lags behind the north in economic development. There are fewer industries here, and unemployment is high. But the island remains an important agricultural center, producing — among other things — citrus fruit, olive oil, wine, and the most luscious tomatoes, eggplants, zucchini, and other vegetables.

Much of Sicily's history has been shaped by its position in the center of the Mediterranean, enabling successive waves of conquerors to fight for and possess it. Sicily's name comes from its earliest inhabitants, the Siculi, an ancient tribe that occupied the western part of the island. Sicily was known to Phoenician traders as far back as the 10th century BC. Greek colonization, which began in the 8th century BC, brought a long period of growth, prosperity, and cultural development. Powerful city-states such as Syracuse, Agrigento, and Selinunte competed to construct the most spectacular Doric temples and theaters. The well-preserved remains of these monuments can be visited today. In the 3rd century BC Rome took control of the island, and Sicily gradually declined. Subsequent invasions by Ostrogoths and Byzantines led to the Saracen conquest in AD 878. Under Arab domination, Sicily's influence in both trade and culture expanded, making it attractive to other groups. In 1072, the Norman King Roger I conquered the island. Norman rule eventually was replaced by Spanish and Bourbon domination, which ended when Sicily became part of the united Italy in 1860.

For decades, however, the Italian central government pursued a policy of benign neglect in Sicily, causing massive numbers of emigrants to leave in search of better economic opportunities. Today, the island — with a population of just over 5 million — is a semi-autonomous region, and there are some small signs of social and economic progress.

The Mafia continues to be powerful — many say it dominates — in Sicily and despite strong measures taken by the Italian government, Mafia-related deaths on the island remain a vicious fact. The Mafia colors many aspects of life in Sicily — bars, hotels, stores, and restaurants regularly pay off some group or family in order to keep their doors open, and they control all new enterprises. Despite the fact that the Mafia represents a real social and economic problem, it would be misleading to assert that it colors every aspect of Sicilian life — or that it represents any special danger for the casual visitor. In general, the island's calm Mediterranean rhythm is extremely appealing and restful. Sicilians still savor simple pleasures — an unhurried *aperitivo,* a pre-dinner stroll, a pleasant visit to a favorite café.

TOURIST INFORMATION: Spring and fall are the best times for a visit; summer can be hot and crowded, though the beaches are beautiful. Winters are mild, with occasional rain.

As in the rest of Italy, most stores close for a 3-hour lunch break, generally from 1 to 4 PM, and remain open until 7:30 or 8 PM. Many churches also close between noon and 4 PM; museums usually close at 2 PM and do not have regular afternoon hours. In general, expect to find variations in official hours. Many archaeological sites, for example, remain open "until 1 hour before sunset" — a time subject to interpretation.

Local tourist information offices are located throughout the island and will provide brochures on sights, hotels, and restaurants. Major tourist offices are in the following Sicilian cities: *Agrigento* (71-73 Via Empedocle; phone: 922-20391); *Catania* (5 Largo Paiesseillo; phone: 95-312124); *Cefalù* (77 Corso Ruggero; phone: 921-21050); *Enna* (6 Piazza N. Colajanni; phone: 935-26119); *Erice* (11 Viale Conte Pepoli; phone: 923-869388); *Lipari* (239 Corso Vittorio Emanuele; phone: 90-981-1410); *Messina* (45 Piazza Cairoli; phone: 90-293-3541); *Palermo* (34 Piazza Castelnuovo; phone: 91-583847); *Piazza Armerina* (15 Via Cavour; phone: 935-680201); *Sciacca* (84 Corso Vittorio Emanuele; phone: 925-22744); *Syracuse* (33 Via Maestranza; phone: 931-66932); *Taormina* (Palazzo Corvaja, Piazza Santa Caterina; phone: 942-23243).

FOOD AND WINE: Given the lushness of Sicilian fruits and vegetables and the rich-tasting local meat and fish, it is not surprising that the pleasures of the palate play such an important role in Sicilian life. Though Americans tend to confuse it with the garlic and tomato sauces of Naples, Sicilian cuisine stands apart from other Italian food in the noticeable Arab influence left by centuries of Saracen domination. The sweet-and-sour contrasts that are minimal in most other Italian cooking are all-important to Sicilian cooks, who frequently use raisins and pine nuts or almonds, and who liberally spice their super-sweet desserts with cinnamon, sesame, almond, and pumpkin. The French and Spanish made their own culinary contributions. Gastronomic traditions vary from city to city, although hardly so radically as in the past when communications and transportation were more difficult. Travelers are advised, therefore, to intersperse visits to local monuments with samplings from area restaurants and trattorie. Both aspects of Sicilian life — culture and cooking — combine to form an unforgettable experience. (For further discussion of Sicilian food, see *Palermo,* THE CITIES.)

GETTING AROUND: Air – Italian domestic airlines operate regular daily connecting flights from all major Italian cities to Palermo, Catania, and Trapani. In addition, during the summer only, there are a few regularly scheduled direct flights to Sicily from abroad.

Bus – Many cross-Sicily routes are covered by Sicilian bus companies, the largest of which are *ATS* (*Azienda Trasporti Sicilia*) and *SAIS.* Regular bus service runs between Palermo and Catania (about 2 hours) as well as between most other Sicilian cities and towns. Buses are considerably faster than trains, and only nominally more expensive.

Car Rental – Once in Sicily, there is no doubt that the best way to see the island is by car. The majority of the roads skirting the coast, where most of the important cities and sights are located, are good. Roads into the interior are generally good but are winding and, therefore, slower in mountainous areas. Gas stations are located throughout the island; most close during the 3-hour lunch break but tend to have self-service facilities with machines that take 10,000-lire notes. In every town at least one service station is required by law to stay open. The hotels will know which one.

Major car rental firms have offices in the principal Sicilian cities; some offer special low rates for non-Italian visitors, generally by the week. *Palermo: Avis* (12-14 Via Principe Scordia; phone: 91-333806; and at the airport; phone: 91-591684); *Hertz* (7/E Via Messina; phone: 91-323439; and at the airport; phone: 91-591682); *Maggiore* (27-33 Via Agrigento; phone: 91-625-7848; and at the airport; phone: 91-591681); *InterRent* (61 Via Cavour; phone: 91-328631; and at the airport; phone: 91-591683). *Catania: Avis* (87 Via San Giuseppe La Rena; phone: 95-347116); *Hertz* (45 Via Toselli; phone: 95-322560; and at the airport; phone: 95-341595); *Hertz* (113 Via Vittorio Emanuele; phone: 90-363740). *Messina: Avis* (35 Via Vittorio Emanuele at Cortina del Porto; phone: 90-58404); *Maggiore* (46 Via T. Cannizzaro; phone: 90-675476); *InterRent* (498/A Viale Libertà; phone: 90-47852). In Rome, the central reservations number for *Avis* is 6-47011, for *Hertz,* 6-547991, and for *Maggiore,* 6-851620.

Ferry – *Italian State Railways* also operates a car ferry across the Strait of Messina. The trip takes 20 minutes from Villa San Giovanni or Reggio Calabria. *Tirrenia,* Italy's largest privately operated ferry service, offers service across the strait as well as daily and overnight service from Naples to Palermo and, less frequently, from Naples to Messina, Catania, and Syracuse; advance reservations are advisable (2 Rione Sirignano, Naples; phone: 81-720-1111; and 41 Via Bissolati, Rome; phone: 6-474-2041). Two other private companies, *Caronte* (phone: 90-45183) and *Tourist Ferry* (phone: 090-41415), offer runs across the strait. There is occasional service from Genoa, Livorno, Cagliari (Sardinia), and to and from Tunis. Regular service operates between the Lipari Islands and Milazzo, Messina, and Palermo (see *Lipari Islands,* below).

Guided Tours – Local travel agencies can arrange 5- to 8-day tours originating in Palermo, Catania, or Taormina.

Train – Along with direct trains from the mainland across the Strait of Messina, *Italian State Railways* (*FS*) operates several Sicilian lines; the two main lines are *Palermo–Messina* and *Messina–Catania–Syracuse.* The fastest trains are generally the *rapido* express trains originating on the mainland; nevertheless, delays along the way are almost inevitable. Advance reservations are recommended. The *rapidi* require supplementary payment (*supplemento*). Local trains are slow and crowded.

SPECIAL EVENTS: Film, theater, music, and dance performances are combined in an entertainment festival in Taormina in late July and August (see *Taormina,* THE CITIES). A close second to the Taormina festival is the Greek theater festival in Syracuse held in May and June of even-numbered years; tickets are available from May 5 at the Istituto Nazionale del Dramma Antico (29 Corso Matteotti; phone: 931-65373); in odd-numbered years, other events such as opera and ballet take place. The town of Erice holds a program of theater, music, and dance each summer and a review of Mediterranean folk music instruments in December; contact Ufficio Informazioni (11 Viale Conte Pepoli; phone: 923-869388). The marionette festival in Palermo in November features Sicilian *pupi,* but guest puppets from elsewhere in Europe perform, too (see *Palermo,* THE CITIES).

Colorful religious events take place during *Lent,* culminating in numerous *Easter* celebrations. The *Carnevale* festivals at Acireale, Sciacca, and Termini Imerese usher in the *Lenten* season. At Prizzi, near Palermo, *Easter* revelers drink and frolic at the *Abballu delli diavuli,* a festival in which costumed devils take over the city for a day until the Madonna and her angels arrive to drive them out. Residents of Piana degli Albanesi, also near Palermo, parade in Albanian Byzantine costume on *Easter Sunday.* Worshipers at Caltanissetta participate in six *Holy Week* processions that are basically unchanged from the Middle Ages, with groups of "living statues" and a Black Christ. The most moving *Easter* pageantry is at Trapani, where *I Misteri* (The Mysteries) — 20 groups of statues depicting the crucial moments in Christ's life — wind through the Old City in magnificent procession.

SPORTS AND FITNESS: Deep-Sea Fishing – Offshore waters teem with many species of fish. The best angling, especially for tuna, is near the port of Milazzo and off the Lipari Islands. With a little Italian and some inquiries at port cafés, an enterprising visitor can probably find a boat and a fisherman/guide. An alternative is to contact the Azienda Autonoma di Soggiorno e Turismo in Lipari (233 Corso Vittorio Emanuele; phone: 90-988-0095).

Skiing – Only recently has skiing been developed into a serious sport in Sicily, with major runs and lifts in the 5,000- to 6,000-foot Madonie mountain range, less than an hour inland by car from Cefalù. For information, contact the Palermo Tourist Office (34 Piazza Castelnuovo; phone: 91-583847) or the *Club Alpino Siciliano* (43 Via Provinciale Paternostro, Palermo; phone: 91-581323). There are also runs on Mount Etna's northeast slopes, near Linguaglossa (see *Excursion from Catania to Mount Etna,* below).

Tennis – Many hotels have courts or access to them. The *Valtur* vacation village in Brucoli, near Augusta, operates a tennis clinic from May through August. Contact *Valtur,* 42 Via Milano, Rome (phone: 6-470-6238 or 6-470-6239).

Water Sports – Sicily has countless beautiful beaches for swimming and sunning. Many resort hotels have facilities (and larger cities have clubs and schools) for sailing, water skiing, and windsurfing. Contact the local Azienda Autonoma di Soggiorno e Turismo.

TOURING SICILY

Hotels on Sicily and in the Lipari Islands are rated as expensive if they charge from $120 to $180 for a double room; moderate, from $60 to $120; and inexpensive, less than $60. A meal for two, including wine and tips, in a restaurant rated as expensive costs $75 or more; moderate, $50 to $75; and inexpensive, less than $50. Many small hotels, *pensioni,* and trattorie in small towns, especially inland, are well below this range.

MESSINA: Located on the strait separating Sicily from the Italian mainland, Messina is the third-largest city in Sicily (271,000 inhabitants). Almost totally destroyed in the earthquake of 1908 in which 84,000 people (two-thirds of its population) perished, Messina has been rebuilt with broad streets and low buildings. Called Zancle by the Greeks because of the sickle-shaped peninsula enclosing the port, Messina was a major settlement in ancient times. During the Middle Ages, it was an important departure point for the Crusades — a stronghold of the Plantagenets and a wintering place for Richard the Lion-Hearted and his troops. It was the birthplace of the Renaissance painter Antonello da Messina and the setting of Shakespeare's *Much Ado About Nothing.*

As a result of various disasters over the centuries — from plagues and earthquakes to wartime bombardments — few of the city's most important monuments have survived intact. The Orion Fountain (first built in 1547) and the twice-destroyed Duomo have been restored along original lines. The *Museo Nazionale* (Viale della Libertà) houses some ancient artworks and a good collection of Renaissance paintings. Open daily, except Mondays and holidays, from 9 AM to 2 PM; to 1 PM on Sundays; admission charge.

CHECKING IN: ***Jolly Hotel dello Stretto*** – This centrally located, 96-room modern hotel looks out over the Strait of Messina. Its rooms are comfortable, the roof garden pleasant. 126 Corso Garibaldi, Messina (phone: 90-43401; fax: 90-590-2526). Expensive.

Royal Palace – Located in the center of town, this 83-room, well-kept modern hotel offers excellent service, although the rooms can be a bit noisy. Parking available. 224 Via Tommaso Cannizzaro, Messina (phone: 90-292-1161; fax: 90-292-1075). Expensive.

EATING OUT: ***Alberto*** – The best choice in town. An elegant downtown dining place, part of the well-known Buon Ricordo chain, with a quiet, refined decor, offering a choice of no less than 48 antipasti, good fish and meat, delicate desserts, and excellent wines. For an entrée, try the *spaghetti alla Norma* (with fried eggplant, tomato, and seasoned ricotta cheese) or the *pescestocco alla messinese* (cod with tomato sauce, onion, celery, olives, and capers). Closed Sundays and August. Reservations necessary. Major credit cards accepted. 95 Via Ghibellina, Messina (phone: 90-710711). Expensive.

Pippo Nunnari – An airy, modern restaurant decorated with Sicilian artifacts has made its reputation with excellent and original *pastasciutta,* such as *cannellini* with zucchini, and macaroni with ricotta, basil, eggplant, and tomato. The fresh fish, especially the swordfish, is delicious. Closed Mondays and the first 2 weeks of July. Reservations advised. Major credit cards accepted. 157 Via Ugo Bassi, Messina (phone: 90-293-8584). Expensive to moderate.

En Route from Messina – It is a quick drive (about 30 miles/48 km) down the coast on either the autostrada (A18) or the state highway (SS114) to Taormina, the beautiful and balmy cliffside resort that first put Sicily on the international tourist map.

TAORMINA: Set on Monte Tauro within sight of both the blue Ionian Sea and majestic Mount Etna, Taormina has been known since antiquity for its fine climate and calm beauty. Also well known for its Greco-Roman theater and other ruins, it has been a resort town since the second half of the 19th century. It offers more than 70 hotels and *pensioni,* as well as excellent dining and shopping. (For complete coverage, see *Taormina,* THE CITIES.)

En Route from Taormina – Both A18 and SS114 continue south to Catania. Just north of Acireale, a town built on seven overlapping streams of lava, begins a stretch of rocky seacoast known as the Riviera dei Ciclopi (Coast of the Cyclops). This area is known for its charming small bays, grottoes, and fishing villages. The rock formations in the harbor at Aci Trezza were hurled there, according to mythology, by Polyphemus, the Cyclops, after Ulysses blinded him by thrusting a burning stake into his eye. Aci Castello is dominated by an 11th-century black rock castle.

EATING OUT: ***Da Federico*** – Somehow fish always tastes better in a fishing village. Try the sumptuous *zuppa di pesce.* Closed Mondays. No reservations. Major credit cards accepted. 115 Piazza Giovanni Verga, Aci Trezza (phone: 95-276364). Inexpensive.

CATANIA: Sicily's second-largest city and the undisputed capital of the eastern part of the island, the busy seaport of Catania has a long and tormented history of conquests by Romans, Vandal and Goth barbarians, Swabian and Angevin kings, Aragonese nobility, and marauding Barbary pirates. But even more calamitous for Catania were the forces of nature. Destroyed by a massive earthquake in 1169, the city was rebuilt, only to be razed again and again by earthquake or by eruption of its powerful, menacing neighbor, Mount Etna.

Modern Catania, a city of some 383,000 people, has a well-laid-out, spacious center. Many of its buildings are made of the same black lava rock that, in its molten form, has so often submerged its roads, homes, and inhabitants. Some traces of the classical past remain — for instance, the Roman theater and a smaller odeon — but far more impressive are the medieval and baroque palaces and churches that give the city its air of 18th-century well-being. At the center of the Old Town is Piazza del Duomo, at the center of which stands a lava elephant–obelisk statue that has become the symbol of the city. The Duomo — Chiesa di Sant'Agata (Church of Saint Agatha) — was built by the Norman King Roger in 1090 and rebuilt after the 1693 quake. Its baroque façade includes granite columns from the Roman theater. Chiesa di San Nicolò (Church of Saint Nicholas) in Piazza Dante is the largest church in Sicily (open daily, except Saturdays, from 8 AM to noon). Also of note is the monumental Swabian Castello Ursino in Piazza Federico di Svevia; it now houses the *Museo Civico* (Civic Museum). Open 9 from AM to 2 PM except Sundays and holidays, when it closes at noon; admission charge.

The city's baroque flavor is best expressed by Via dei Crociferi, which starts at Piazza San Francesco and is lined with palaces, churches, and monasteries. The 2-mile-long Via Etnea is the most important thoroughfare, running north and south through the city and on toward the volcano. Catania is also known for its beaches, particularly the wide, sandy La Plaja on the city's southern coast, where there are plenty of bathing establishments and restaurants.

CHECKING IN: *Excelsior* – The best hotel in Catania is a modern establishment with 163 large, comfortable rooms, a rooftop garden, and a good restaurant, in the heart of the commercial area. 39 Piazza Giovanni Verga, Catania (phone: 95-325733; fax: 95-537015). Expensive.

Jolly – Part of the well-known chain, this modern hotel offers 96 comfortable rooms and excellent service near the elegant shopping district on Corso Italia. 13 Piazza Trento, Catania (phone: 95-316933; fax: 95-316832). Expensive.

Centrale Palace – A simple, comfortable, and quiet hostelry, unobtrusively tucked away, with 107 modern rooms, most of which overlook the hanging garden, and a restaurant. 218 Via Etnea, Catania (phone: 95-325344; fax: 95-328939). Moderate.

Nettuno – Both an outdoor pool and an excellent restaurant are found at this 80-room hotel. 121 Viale Ruggero di Lauria, Catania (phone: 95-493533; fax: 95-498066). Moderate.

EATING OUT: *Costa Azzurra* – About 2½ miles (4 km) from the city center, on the Gulf of Ognina, with huge glass windows and a terrace overlooking the sea where you can eat. Good seafood and local wines. Closed Fridays. No reservations. American Express accepted. 4 Via De Cristofaro, Ognina (phone: 95-494920). Expensive.

La Siciliana – A classic family-style restaurant with a hearty atmosphere. Traditional Catanese dishes like *rigatoni alla Norma* (with tomato, fresh basil, and fried eggplant) and Sicilian meat rolls. There is garden dining in summer. Closed Sunday evenings, Mondays, and the last 2 weeks of July. Reservations advised. No credit cards accepted. 52 Viale Marco Polo, Catania (phone: 95-376400). Expensive to moderate.

Enzo 2 – This simple, family-run eatery offers a vast choice of fresh fish prepared to order. Have it with pasta in a light garlic and parsley sauce, followed by delicately stewed fish. There is a good selection of local wines. Closed Mondays.

Reservations advised. Major credit cards accepted. 26 Via Malta, Catania (phone: 95-370878). Moderate.

Il Giardino d'Inverno – This lovely café/restaurant offers a mixture of French and Italian fare — in the form of a three-course meal or a light salad. Dessert choices include chocolate mousse and French pastries. Closed Mondays. Reservations advised for four or more. Major credit cards accepted. 34 Via Asilo Sant'Agata, Catania (phone: 95-532853). Moderate.

Pagano – Centrally located, this spot serves excellent pasta, fish, and wines in a pleasant setting. Try the pasta with octopus ink and black broccoli. Closed Sundays and August. Reservations advised. Major credit cards accepted. 37 Via De Roberto, Catania (phone: 95-322720). Moderate.

Excursion from Catania to Mount Etna – The life and landscape of eastern Sicily are dominated by Etna. The very configuration of the land is the result of the volcano's eruptions and accompanying earthquakes. Some towns and roads are actually built of lava rock. Elsewhere the remains of flows have cut black swaths through the valleys. A day trip to the great mountain is not only fascinating but easy. Leave Catania by the Via Etnea. (It is also possible to take a tour bus or train from Stazione Centrale at Piazza Stazione; both depart daily at about 8 AM.) From Nicolosi, the main town on the southern slope (about 10 miles/16 km from Catania), drive to the Sapienza refuge; from here, in good weather, visitors can make jeep and cable car excursions to the summit. The road leads around the mountain to other towns such as Zafferano and Linguaglossa in the midst of lovely pine woods. (For more information on the volcano, see *Taormina,* THE CITIES.) From Linguaglossa, follow yellow signs marked Etna or Sci for ski runs in the midst of the nearby pine forest. Be prepared to be turned back by police on summer weekends, however, when the road turns into a traffic nightmare by midday. Trekking on horseback can be arranged nearby (see "Sports," *Taormina,* THE CITIES).

En Route from Catania – South of Augusta, SS114 passes several minor archaeological sites. Pretend not to see the hideous petrochemical plants, which together form the largest refinery complex in Europe. Shortly after Faro, a dirt road leads to the few remains of Megara Hyblaea, a colony founded by Greeks from Megara in the 8th century BC. It crosses the Magnisi Peninsula site of the ancient port of Thapsos, where the Athenian fleet anchored before the siege of Syracuse in 415 BC. Finally, just before Syracuse stands the ruin of the 4th-century BC Castello Eurialo (Castle of Euryalus), Sicily's most complete Greek military fortification, where Archimedes is said to have burned invading Roman ships from the shore using a complex system of mirrors.

SYRACUSE: Situated on the Ionian Sea in southeastern Sicily, 36 miles (58 km) from Catania, Syracuse (Siracusa in Italian) is now a small, sun-bleached provincial capital. But in ancient times it was the western capital of Magna Graecia and one of the greatest cities in the world. Founded in 734 BC by settlers from Corinth, Syracuse gradually grew to rival Athens in military and commercial importance. The Greek mathematician Archimedes and the poet Theocritus were both from Syracuse.

Fortunately, many of the buildings from this ancient period have survived. Most are in the "archaeological zone," in the town's ancient Neapolis section. The Greek theater — in a natural, wooded bowl — is the largest and one of the best preserved in the Hellenic world; in late May and June of even-numbered years (as was the practice in ancient times) festivals of Greek tragedies are produced in this spectacular setting. In odd-numbered years, the theater hosts events such as opera and ballet. The Altar of Hieron II, once used for religious sacrifices, is also the setting for concerts and ballets.

Nearby is an amphitheater built by the Romans in the 3rd century BC. The Latomie del Paradiso is a steep-walled quarry and onetime prison for 7,000 Athenians routed in battle in 413 BC that, with much of its roof collapsed, has been taken over by flourishing semitropical vegetation. In one corner of the quarry is the famous Ear of Dionysius, a huge artificial cavern with impressive acoustics. Legend has it that slaves worked in this cave, hewing stone, and that Dionysius eavesdropped on them through a crack in the ceiling. (The name was coined in 1586 by the painter Caravaggio, who was referring to the shape of the cave's entrance.) Sites are open daily, from 9 AM to twilight; admission charge. Parco Monumentale della Neapoli, Viale Rizzo.

The city's *Archaeological Museum,* once housed in five rooms on the island of Ortygia, now occupies a huge, modern complex in Villa Landolina Park. The impressive collection, beautifully presented, chronicles eastern Sicily's Greek past. Open daily from 9 AM to 2 PM, Sundays and holidays to 1 PM; admission charge.

The small offshore island of Ortygia, which is connected to "mainland" Syracuse by two bridges, is the site of the medieval Old Town. Ortygia is one of the most charming places in Sicily. A network of narrow, intersecting crossways, its faded, balconied houses near the Maniace Castle (at Piazza Federico di Svevia) appear unrelated to the 20th century. In the center of the island is Piazza del Duomo, with its cathedral (Chiesa di Santa Maria del Piliero, formerly the Greek Temple of Athena, whose original columns still remain), and the baroque City Hall. The Church of Santa Lucia alla Badia has an important painting by Caravaggio. Nearby is the Fountain of Arethusa, supposedly the spot where the nymph reemerged from the sea after hiding from her impetuous suitor, the river god Alpheus. It is now stocked with papyrus, ducks, and geese.

After sightseeing, stop by *Marciante* (39 Via della Maestranze; phone: 931-67303) for the best sweets in the area. Tireless visitors will be happy to hear that Syracuse has recently become known for its nightlife. On Friday and Saturday evenings in the summer, the under-30 set come from as far away as Catania to dance at the seaside disco, *Tonnara* (Lungomare, in the Terra Uzza district) or at *Il Veleno* (Via Maestranza) in the historic center. For those interested in quieter socializing, stop in one of two pubs in Piazza Archimede in the historic center — *The Pub* and *Troubador.*

The coastline of Syracuse, especially to the south, is renowned for its beauty, clear waters, and evocative, mythological scenery. There are romantic abandoned coves and wide, sandy beaches not easily matched elsewhere in Italy.

CHECKING IN: ***Jolly*** – Part of the well-known chain and considered the best in town, it is slightly more modern and slightly more expensive than the *Grand* (below). Hardly anything to look at, but it's comfortable, functional, centrally located, has 100 rooms, and a more than decent restaurant. 45 Corso Gelone, Syracuse (phone: 931-64744). Expensive.

Grand–Villa Politi – Said to have been Winston Churchill's favorite, this 95-room hotel with a pool and gardens is hardly "grand," but it is still very nice and a good value. 2 Via Politi Laudien, Syracuse (phone: 931-32100). Moderate.

Park – Located just outside the city, this recently redecorated hotel offers 102 clean rooms, swimming pool, tennis courts, and a private garden. 80 Via Filisto, Syracuse (phone: 931-32644; fax: 931-38096). Moderate.

Bellavista – Although this small (45 rooms), family-run place is a bit out of the way, it is located in a picturesque spot. For those on a tight budget, this is a good value. 4 Via Diodoro Siculo, Syracuse (phone: 931-36912; fax: 931-37027). Inexpensive.

EATING OUT: ***Jonico 'A Rutta è Ciauli*** – Housed in a small, attractive villa in a garden overlooking the Ionian Sea, this is one of the best restaurants in Sicily. Try the spaghetti with anchovies or fresh tuna, Sicilian style, expertly prepared by Pasqualino Giudice, known throughout Italy for his talent in the kitchen. Closed Tuesdays. Reservations advised. Major credit cards accepted. Best to take a taxi. 194 Riviera Dionisio il Grande, Syracuse (phone: 931-65540). Expensive.

Arlecchino – Traditional, family-style, with seafood specialties. Closed Sunday evenings, Mondays, and August. Reservations advised. Major credit cards accepted. 8 Largo Empedocle, Syracuse (phone: 931-66386). Expensive to moderate.

Fratelli Bandiera – Bright and spacious, near the Ortygia outdoor market, this restaurant offers an enormous array of fish, vegetable antipasti, and excellent pasta. Try the *spaghetti alla bandiera* (with shrimp). Closed Mondays and July. Reservations advised. Major credit cards accepted. 6 Via Perno, Syracuse (phone: 931-65021). Expensive to moderate.

Don Camilio – In the center of the Old Town, this attractive restaurant is noted for its fresh fish prepared according to local traditions. Specialties include *zuppa di pesce* (fish stew). Closed Sunday evenings and Mondays. Reservations advised. Major credit cards accepted. 92-100 Via Maestranza, Syracuse (phone: 931-67133). Moderate.

La Foglia – A favorite of local artists (whose work is display on the walls), this eatery offers appetizing vegetarian and fish dishes that rely heavily on Sicilian tradition and the availability of local produce. Closed Mondays. Reservations unnecessary. Major credit cards accepted. 29 Via Capodieci, Syracuse (phone: 931-461569). Moderate.

Taverna Aretusa – An attractive, rustic hideaway cluttered with bric-a-brac and serving fresh fish, which the congenial, English-speaking Papà Pasqualino brings to the table first for approval. Also excellent pasta, organically grown vegetables and fruits, and local wine. Closed Wednesdays and the first 3 weeks in November. No reservations. Visa accepted. 32 Via Santa Teresa, Syracuse (phone: 931-68720). Inexpensive.

Trattoria il Cenacolo – Located in a lovely courtyard in Ortygia, this simple eatery offers both three-course meals or pizza at reasonable prices. Closed Wednesdays. Reservations unnecessary. Major credit cards accepted. 9-10 Via del Consiglio Reginale, Syracuse (phone: 931-65099). Inexpensive.

En Route from Syracuse – The area around Syracuse is dotted with archaeological sites. SS124 leads to the Pantelica necropolis, about 25 miles (40 km) from Syracuse by way of Floridia, the largest and best-preserved prehistoric necropolis in Sicily. Rocky walls near the ruins of the ancient town of Hyblaea are honeycombed by 5,000 cave-tombs. The road continues to Palazzolo Acreide (it has fine buildings, a Greek theater, and sculptures, known as *santoni,* carved out of the nearby cliffs) and the remains of Akrai, a military colony founded by the Syracusans in 664 BC. SS287 rejoins the main route. Alternatively, proceed straight from Syracuse to Noto, about 20 miles (32 km), on SS115.

Several miles out of Syracuse, SS115 crosses the Anapo and Ciane rivers. The latter is famous for its source, 4 miles (6 km) inland, where papyrus, introduced by either Hieron II or the Arabs, grows in wild profusion. Papyrus is a local souvenir industry, as well as an object of serious study by the Institute of Papyrus (66 Viale Teocrito, Syracuse; phone: 931-22100), which also houses a museum and gift shop. Open daily except Sundays from 9 AM to 1 PM and 3 to 5 PM; admission charge. Boat trips can be arranged from the marina, reached by following signs to Canicattini (best done from the center of Syracuse and along Via Necropoli del Fusco). The marina is equidistant from SS124 and SS115.

NOTO: The second-largest town in Syracuse province is considered the best example of Sicilian baroque. Noto's major monuments are located in three groups along the main street, Corso Vittorio Emanuele. Beyond the entrance to the town through the

Porta Reale, the *corso* widens first into a square framed by the Chiesa di San Francesco (also called L'Immacolata), the Chiesa di Santa Chiara, and the San Salvatore convent, the first 2 floors of which now house the *Museo Civico* (Municipal Museum; open daily except Mondays from 9 AM to 1 PM; admission charge). Next it leads into a square dominated by the Municipio (City Hall), the Chiesa di San Nicola, the Chiesa di San Salvatore, and the Palazzo di Landolina di Sant'Alfano. A third square contains the theater and the Chiesa di San Domenico. Parallel streets are joined by broad stone staircases. Antico Noto, 7 miles (11 km) northwest, is the site (with remains) of the ancient town; its abandonment in 1663, due to an earthquake, gave rise to the present Noto, a feat of harmonious town planning. Noto Marina, 4 miles (6 km) east of Noto, has lovely public beaches.

EATING OUT: ***Corrado Costanzo*** – Stop in this typical *pasticceria* for mouth-watering sweets — marzipan, cannoli, and possibly the best ices you have ever had. The flavors most favored by Signor Corrado (known and written about the world over) and his customers are jasmine, rose petal, and mandarin, which tastes more authentic than the fruit itself. Closed Wednesdays and the first 10 days of September. No reservations. No credit cards. Behind the Municipio at 7-9 Via Silvio Spaventa, Noto (phone: 931-835243). Inexpensive.

Falconara – Known for its excellent pizza, this restaurant on the way to Noto Marina also serves all types of regional pasta, meat, and fish. Its pleasant *ambiente* attracts many locals. Closed Mondays. Reservations unnecessary. Visa accepted. Noto Marina (phone: 931-812122). Inexpensive.

Trieste – The best place for lunch or dinner. Try the *pasta al forno* and veal stew. Closed Mondays and the last 2 weeks of October. No reservations. Visa accepted. 21 Via Napoli, Noto (phone: 931-835495). Inexpensive.

En Route from Noto – SS115 leads through Rosolini and Ispica to Modica, 25 miles (40 km) away, and then on to Ragusa. The Cava d'Ispica, a deep chalk gorge whose walls are dotted with medieval cave dwellings and prehistoric tombs, can be reached by a turnoff after Ispica at the junction for Bettola del Capitano. Modica, built on two sides of a gorge, is noted for its interesting medieval and baroque monuments.

RAGUSA: The outskirts of Ragusa are neither attractive nor appealing because of the huge chemical plants surrounding this city of 65,000. But the old part of town, Ragusa Ibla — originally a Byzantine settlement and then an important Norman stronghold — is extremely picturesque. The New Town has a small but well-organized museum — *Museo Archeologico* (Via Natalelli). Open daily, except Mondays, from 9 AM to 2 PM, Sundays to 1 PM; admission charge.

CHECKING IN: ***Montreal*** – Small and simple, this 63-room hostelry is in the historical center of town and perfectly adequate for a short stay. 70 Corso Italia, Ragusa (phone: 932-21133). Inexpensive.

EATING OUT: ***Villa Fortugno*** – This wonderful restaurant offers a seasonal menu in an old villa. Don't miss the *ravioli di ricotta al sugo di maiale* (cheese ravioli with a pork and tomato sauce) or the stuffed pork chops. Local and regional wines are available. Closed Mondays and August. Reservations advised. No credit cards accepted. On the state road south toward Marina di Ragusa, 2 miles (3 km) from town (phone: 931-28656). Expensive.

U Saracinu – The Saracen, under chef Giuseppe Amore, serves a variety of local dishes of homemade pasta, such as *maccarruni al ragù di maiale* (macaroni with pork ragout). Ragusa caciocavallo, the local sharp cheese, is a favorite. Closed Wednesdays. No reservations. Visa accepted. 9 Via del Convento, Ragusa (phone: 932-46976). Moderate.

CALTAGIRONE: Follow SS514 north and then SS124 west to the Queen of the Hills, Caltagirone, one of the most flourishing communities in the Sicilian interior. Its position on three hillsides gives the town its winding streets and irregularly shaped piazzas. For centuries Caltagirone has been known as a center for pottery and ceramics. Local shops sell today's wares. Of even more interest, however, is the lovely *Museo della Ceramica,* which exhibits pottery from prehistoric times through the 19th century. Off Via Roma in the public garden. Open daily, except Mondays, from 9 AM to 2 PM, Sundays to 1 PM; admission charge. A huge staircase linking two levels of the town is lined with an extraordinary array of tiles. On the nights of July 24, 25, and 31, and August 15 every year, this staircase becomes the stage for *La Luminaria* — the lighting of over 4,000 different colored oil lanterns. The lamps give off various images, similar to those used to decorate the ceramics for which the town is famous.

CHECKING IN: ***Grand Hotel Villa San Mauro*** – The comforts of this 92-room modern hostelry make up for the indifference of its personnel. There is a garden and swimming pool. 18 Via Portosalvo, Caltagirone (phone: 933-26500; fax: 933-31661). Moderate.

PIAZZA ARMERINA: A medieval and baroque jewel, this small town northwest of Caltagirone has an impressive Duomo with a fine 15th-century Gothic-Catalán campanile as well as an Aragonese castle. Piazza Armerina is also known for its colorful August 15 celebration of the *Feast of the Assumption,* in which the Byzantine *Madonna of Victory,* said to have been given by Pope Nicholas II to the Norman King Roger, is carried through the streets in medieval procession.

Four miles (6 km) south of town is the ruin of the Villa Romana del Casale (a Roman imperial villa) considered to be the most important Roman construction in Sicily. Built in the 3rd or 4th century AD at the foot of Mount Mangone, the sprawling villa probably was the country or summer residence of the Emperor Maximian Herculius. Archaeologists and historians believe that the villa was inhabited throughout the Byzantine-Islamic period, destroyed during the barbarian invasions, restored to glory by the Normans after the year 1000, and razed by William the Bad in the 12th century. It was gradually buried by repeated flooding and soil erosion; its modern excavation began in 1928. The building is organized in four large groups of rooms linked by corridors, peristyles, and galleries. It had cold- and hot-water baths, gymnasiums, gardens, and halls, the dimensions of which alone testify to their original grandeur. But most remarkable is the delightful quality, color, design, and notable state of preservation of the mosaic floors that run through most of the villa. These may well be among the most important historical documents of antiquity. The best known decorate the Room of the Lesser Hunt, the Room of the Cupid Fishermen, the Ambulatory of the Great Hunt, and the Room of the Ten Maidens. The villa is open daily from 9 AM to 2 hours before sunset; admission charge.

Nearby, past Aidone on SS288, are the ruins of the ancient walled city of Morgantina. They bear traces of pre-Greek, Greek, and Roman civilizations. The new *Museo Morgantina* in Aidone (easily reached by following the signs) has an excellent collection of artifacts excavated from Morgantina. Open daily from 9 AM to 1 PM; no admission charge.

CHECKING IN: ***Selene*** – Reasonable for a stopover, though its 42 rooms are in need of modernization. It is very centrally located. 30 Viale Generale Gaeta, Piazza Armerina (phone: 935-682254). Inexpensive.

EATING OUT: ***Al Ritrovo*** – Here the *ragù* is as hearty as in days of old, and the charcoal-broiled lamb chops are delicious. Closed Tuesdays. No reservations. No credit cards accepted. On the way out of town toward Enna, SS117B, Piazza Armerina (phone: 935-681890). Inexpensive.

Pepito – This family-run trattoria offers regional dishes prepared with imagination. Specialties include *spaghetti alla Pepito* (with mushrooms, eggplant, anchovies, and tomatoes) and *carne alla Pepito* (broiled beef with green pepper). Closed Tuesdays. Reservations unnecessary. Major credit cards accepted. 138 Via Roma, Piazza Armerina (phone: 935-82737). Inexpensive.

La Tavernetta – Traditional Sicilian food is served in portions that could match Piazza Armerina's 2,300-foot position above sea level. The homemade *fettuccine alla Norma,* with eggplant, basil, ricotta, and tomatoes, is excellent, as are the meats and fish. Closed Sundays and January. Reservations advised. Major credit cards accepted. 14 Via Cavour, Piazza Armerina (phone: 935-82883). Inexpensive.

ENNA: Its commanding position on a steep hill made Enna — called Castrogiovanni until changed by Mussolini in 1927 — an impregnable stronghold in ancient times and earned it the nickname Belvedere of Sicily. The town is built on the site of ancient Henna, which was founded by the Siculi tribe and, according to mythology, was the site of the rape of Persephone by Pluto. It became the center of the cult of Demeter, or Ceres, Persephone's mother. A fountain behind Piazza Vittorio Emanuele illustrates the legend.

An agricultural center today, Enna has several major monuments. The 14th-century Duomo, founded by Eleonora, wife of Frederick II of Aragón, is a strange mixture of Gothic and baroque with interesting carved black alabaster columns in the nave. The massive Castello di Lombardia at the end of Via Roma is one of the most important medieval castles in Sicily, although only 6 of the original 20 towers survive (open mornings and from 3 to 5 PM). On the other side of the Old City is the octagonal Tower of Frederick II of Swabia. Enter from the Giardino Pubblico (Public Garden); open from 9 AM to sunset.

CHECKING IN: ***Sicilia*** – This comfortable, modern hotel, with 80 rooms, is the only one worthwhile in the town center. 7 Piazza Colaianni, Enna (phone: 935-501209; fax: 935-500488). Moderate to inexpensive.

EATING OUT: ***Ariston*** – Stylishly discreet and run by the owners of *Sicilia,* this restaurant has higher standards of service than a trattoria and excels in the preparation of local specialties, such as *agnello arrosto* (roast lamb) and homemade *cavatelli.* Closed Sundays and the second half of August. Reservations unnecessary. No credit cards accepted. 365 Via Roma, *Galleria Bruno,* Enna (phone: 935-26038). Moderate.

Centrale – Delicious Sicilian and Ennese specialties in a friendly atmosphere. Try the homemade ravioli, the vast assortment of appetizers, and stuffed homemade breads, followed by a mixed grill of lamb, beef, and pork. Closed Saturdays. Reservations unnecessary. Major credit cards accepted. 9 Piazza 6 di Dicembre, Enna (phone: 935-500963). Moderate.

La Fontana – Near the center of town, not far from a belvedere that overlooks the valley below, this trattoria offers typical Sicilian fare such as *risotto all'enna* (with tomatoes, mushrooms, black olives, and *pecorino* cheese), *cavatelli alla siciliana* (homemade pasta in a sauce of tomato, basil, eggplant, red pepper, and cheese), and grilled lamb. Closed Sundays and January. Major credit cards accepted. Reservations unnecessary. 6 Via Vulturno, Enna (phone: 935-25465). Inexpensive.

Excursion from Enna – The red-hued medieval town of Calascibetta, on a peak 4 miles (6 km) north of Enna, got its name from the Arabs, who called it Kalat-Scibet. A walk around town is a stroll into the past. There are splendid views from the Calascibetta belvedere.

CALTANISSETTA: Southwest of Enna is Caltanissetta, a largely modern town built on the site of the ancient city of Nissa. The Duomo (Chiesa di Santa Maria la Nova e San Michele) has two *campanili* and, inside, some interesting paintings. A street running alongside the Duomo, Via San Domenico, leads through an old quarter with narrow, winding streets. The *Museo Civico* (Municipal Museum, 3 Via Colaianni) has a small archaeological collection. Open daily except Mondays from 9 AM to 1 PM; admission charge.

EATING OUT: ***Cortese*** – Although some critics feel the move to larger, more modern quarters has meant a loss of ambience, the food is still as good as ever. The *cavatelli al ragù* (made with homemade pasta) is excellent for a pasta course, the *involtini* (veal rolls) as a main dish. Closed Mondays and August 10–20. No reservations. Visa accepted. 166 Viale Sicilia, Caltanissetta (phone: 934-31686). Moderate.

En Route from Caltanissetta – SS122, one of two routes to Agrigento, 36 miles (58 km) away, passes through picturesque towns like Naro, with its crenelated city walls and baroque churches and convents, and Favara, a Norman town that grew up around the 1275 Chiaramonte Castle that stands in Piazza Cavour.

AGRIGENTO: In ancient times, Agrigento — known to the Greeks as Akragas — was one of the most prosperous cities in ancient Sicily. It probably was one of the most beautiful — with its location in a vast natural amphitheater between the mountains and the sea. Modern Agrigento is overbuilt and unattractive, but the surviving Doric temples of the ancient city — unequaled outside Greece itself — the excellent archaeological museum, and parts of the old medieval and baroque town make it an essential part of any Sicilian visit.

The ruins in the Valley of Temples are built in a more or less straight line running parallel to the sea. They are interesting in any light but are hauntingly beautiful at dawn, twilight, or at night when illuminated by floodlights. The most intact is the Temple of Concord, built in 450 BC and possibly the best-preserved Greek temple in the world except for the Theseion in Athens. Its 34 exterior columns are still standing. To the east is the imposing Temple of Juno, built 20 years later but with only 25 columns intact. To the west, separated by the 6th-century early Christian burial ground, stand the remains of the Temple of Hercules, built in 520 BC, and the oldest monument here; it may originally have been as large as the Parthenon in Athens. Farther west and on the other side of the Via dei Templi, the road running through the archaeological zone, are the widely scattered remains of the mammoth Temple of Olympian Jove, the roof of which was originally supported by 38 *telamoni* (stone giants). Stretched out on the ground is a reassembly of one of the giants; another is in the nearby archaeological museum (see below). Of the Temple of Castor and Pollux, only the four columns of the northwest corner survive. The Tomb of Theron is believed to hold the remains of the Greek tyrant who once ruled Akragas. Other monuments include the Temples of Aesculapius and of Vulcan. There are also the remains of the ancient Hellenic and Roman quarter.

Across the road from the Hellenic-Roman quarter is the 24-year-old *Museo Archeologico* (Archaeological Museum), a small, pleasantly appointed museum. The collection includes vases and amphorae from the 6th to the 3rd century BC, some magnificent Attic pottery, early and later Bronze Age material, architectural fragments from the temples, and Greek and Roman sarcophagi, helmets, and other artifacts. Open Tuesdays through Saturdays from 9 AM to 2 PM, Sundays from 9 AM to 1 PM; admission charge.

Next door is a 3rd-century BC Ekklesiasterion (meeting hall). Adjoining it is the

12th-century Church of St. Nicholas, with its Romanesque-Gothic façade and, inside, 15th- and 16th-century paintings and frescoes and the Phaedra Sarcophagus.

Agrigento's medieval Old Town also has appeal. Via Atenea, the main street, leads into the Salita Santo Spirito and on to the Cistercian convent, where the nuns still produce and sell *frutta della martorana* (marzipan fruits) and other sweets. The church has a Gothic portal and 17th-century stucco decorations. A cloister and refectory hall house the public library. Santa Maria dei Greci is a small church built on the site of a Doric temple; it can be viewed on request to the custodian (although word has it that he is hard to find). Nearby is the 14th-century Duomo and the *Teatro Luigi Pirandello,* named after the Italian playwright, who was born in the simple village of Kaos nearby; the village has a museum (open daily; closed 12:30 to 2:30 PM; no admission charge).

CHECKING IN: ***Jolly dei Templi*** **–** Less attractive than the *Villa Athena* (below) but also comfortable and near the archaeological sites. There are 146 rooms and its facilities include a swimming pool; the service is excellent. The hotel restaurant, *Pirandello,* is one of the finest in the area. Five miles (8 km) from downtown in Parco Angeli, Villaggio Mosè, Agrigento (phone: 922-606144; fax: 922-606685). Expensive.

Kaos **–** Newly opened, this 105-room, air conditioned comfortable hotel on the sea is located just 1 mile (1.6 km) from the Valley of the Temples in Pirandello's birthplace. Housed in a beautifully restored patrician villa, it has lovely grounds with ponds, fountains, a swimming pool, and tennis courts. SS115 in the direction of Marsala (phone: 922-598622; fax: 922-598770). Expensive.

Villa Athena **–** A small, comfortable 18th-century villa set amid the olive and almond trees that surround the Valley of Temples. The hotel's terraces and balconies and many of its 41 rooms overlook the three principal temples. The best rooms are the few with private patios. There is a swimming pool and a good restaurant. Reservations advised. 33 Via Valle dei Templi, Agrigento (phone: 922-596288; fax: 922-402180). Expensive.

EATING OUT: ***Le Caprice*** **–** Views over the Valley of the Temples and good regional food attract a large local following. Alfresco dining. Closed Fridays and the first 2 weeks of July. Reservations advised. Major credit cards accepted. 51 Via Panoramica dei Templi, Agrigento (phone: 922-26469). Expensive to moderate.

Kalo **–** In the center of town, this trattoria offers both regional and Italian fare as well as a good selection of fresh fish. Specialties include macaroni with pistachio nuts and spaghetti with mixed shellfish. Closed Mondays. Reservations necessary. Major credit cards accepted. Piazza San Calogero, Agrigento (phone: 922-26389). Moderate.

Taverna Mosè **–** Many here feel this is the best restaurant in town. Try the *pasta con melanzane* (with eggplant) and ricotta cheese, or the other Sicilian specialties. Close to the Temple of Juno. No reservations. Major credit cards accepted. Contrada San Biabio, Agrigento (phone: 922-26778). Moderate to inexpensive.

Del Vigneto **–** Set in a vineyard overlooking the temple area, this trattoria's menu offers good, rustic, regional fare. Try the fresh fish. Closed Tuesdays and November. No reservations. No credit cards accepted. 11 Via Cavaleri Magazzeni, Agrigento (phone: 922-414319). Inexpensive.

En Route from Agrigento – The coast road west (SS115) to Sciacca passes a turnoff for the excavation site of Eraclea Minoa, a Minoan colony located in an isolated position at the far point of a rocky cape. The site is open all day.

SCIACCA: This fishing village is known today for its thermal baths and its ceramics industry, but it also has some interesting medieval monuments. An important trading center since the Roman domination 2,000 years ago, Sciacca became a major harbor during the Arab domination. The local pottery shows definite Arab influences. Significant building and fortification took place under the Normans and Spaniards. Of particular note are the richly decorated 16th-century Porta di San Salvatore, the 14th-century Chiesa di Santa Margherita, and the 15th-century Palazzo Steripinto.

CHECKING IN: ***Grande Albergo Terme*** – A pleasant, modern establishment on the sea road just out of town, near one of the principal spas. The 72-room hotel offers some spa service of its own, including an outdoor heated spring-water pool. 1 Viale Nuove Terme, Sciacca (phone: 925-23133; fax: 925-21746). Moderate to inexpensive.

EATING OUT: ***Mirell*** – Fresh fish is the specialty at this popular seashore restaurant. Try the linguine with fish sauce or the fettuccine with lobster sauce. Closed Tuesdays. Reservations advised. Major credit cards accepted. 26 Via al Lido, Sciacca (phone: 925-23621). Moderate.

SELINUNTE: The ancient town of Selinus was founded in 682 BC by settlers from Megara Hyblaea, a Greek colony near Syracuse. It was most prosperous and powerful in the 5th and 6th centuries BC when most of its temples were built. Selinunte is today one of Sicily's most important archaeological sites. The disarray of the ruins — crumbled walls, toppled columns — is believed to have been caused more by earthquakes than by enemies.

Selinunte occupies three hills close to the sea and is divided into two distinct groups of ruins. The eastern group includes the remains of three large temples believed to have been dedicated to Hera, Athena, and Apollo. The western group, across a gorge (Gorgo di Cottone) that may have been one of the town's ancient harbors, includes the massive walls of the Acropolis, five more temples, and several lesser buildings. The now famous metopes (Doric temple carvings) excavated from this complex are housed in the *Museo Nazionale Archeologico* in Palermo.

MARSALA: SS115 leads north to Castelvetrano and then west toward Marsala, the city that produces the sweet, musky wine of the same name. Known to the Arabs as Mars-al-Allah (Harbor of God), its history is closely linked with the sea. Both the town and its environs have a distinctly Arabic feel. Founded by refugees from the 8th-century BC Phoenician town of Motya, it was destroyed by the Syracusan tyrant Dionysius I and rebuilt by the Carthiginians in the 4th century BC as Lilybaeum. On the Capo Boeo headland, its remains include a Roman bath, a Punic-Roman necropolis, and 6th-century fortifications. Wine merchants who started businesses here during the 18th and 19th centuries brought a decidedly English influence; the city's baroque cathedral, in Piazza della Repubblica, is dedicated to St. Thomas of Canterbury. Garibaldi and his Thousand landed in Marsala in 1860 with the help of the British, commencing the movement for Italian unification.

The fortified wine bearing the city's name is presently enjoying a comeback after a recent decline in popularity. Several marsala producers can be visited; the best known is Florio, which sprawls along the Lungomare, just south of the port (1 Via Florio, Marsala; phone: 923-999222; open daily from 9 AM to noon.) It is always advisable to have your hotel or the tourist office call first (45 Via Garibaldi, Marsala; phone: 923-714079).

CHECKING IN: ***President*** – This very comfortable 68-room hotel offers excellent service and a pleasant swimming pool. 1 Via Nino Bixio, Marsala (phone: 923-999333; fax: 923-999115). Expensive to moderate.

EATING OUT: ***Delfino*** – An excellent seaside restaurant with alfresco dining, specializing in shellfish salad, fish soup, pasta with shrimp, grilled fish, and the house specialty, seafood couscous. Closed Tuesdays. Reservations advised.

Major credit cards accepted. About 2 miles (3 km) from town. 672 Via Lungomare Mediterraneo, Marsala (phone: 923-969565). Moderate.

En Route from Marsala – SS115 continues another 19 miles (30 km) to Trapani, a large modern city with only a few interesting monuments and churches clustered near the port. Trapani is the departure point for the three Egadi Islands, Favignana, Levanzo, and Marettimo, and for Tunisia via hydrofoil (4 hours). Ferries leave regularly year-round from the maritime station. Above perches Erice, less than 9 miles (14 km) northeast of the city.

ERICE: Ancient Eryx — founded, like nearby Segesta, by the Elymnians, another ancient tribe — was famous for its temple to the goddess of fertility, Venus Erycina. The town was mentioned in Virgil's *Aeneid.* Despite its mythological and ancient origins, Erice primarily bears the stamp of its Norman rulers. Its stone houses and fortified castles have retained, almost intact, a medieval aura. The streets are paved with stone blocks; the tiny balconies are filled with songbirds and flowerpots; and hidden behind austere doorways are charming courtyards that belong to another century. The Duomo has an elaborate interior. The *castello* is built over what are believed to be remains of the Temple of Venus. The views are stunning. (See also *Palermo,* THE CITIES.)

CHECKING IN: *Elimo* – Converted from an attractive palazzo, this small hotel of only 21 rooms lacks nothing and has an especially good location in the *centro storico* (historic district). 23 Via Vittorio Emanuele, Erice (phone: 923-869377; fax: 923-869252). Moderate.

Ermione – A bit drafty but otherwise pleasantly appointed, with 38 rooms (be sure to ask for one facing the sea) and a good restaurant. The cook turns out excellent local dishes, including Trapani seafood couscous, another example of the adaptation of Arab cuisine to Sicilian ingredients. On the outskirts of town. 43 Pineta Comunale, Erice (phone: 923-869138; fax: 923-869587). Moderate.

Moderno – A cozy, whitewashed 40-room hotel in a 19th-century palazzo near the Duomo, with a tastefully renovated annex across the street. Besides a bar, the annex has individualized rooms furnished with antique beds and other period pieces. The main building has a pleasant restaurant that can turn out a fine regional meal. 63 Via Vittorio Emanuele, Erice (phone: 923-869300; fax: 923-869139). Moderate.

EATING OUT: *Taverna di Re Aceste* – The walls of this tavern are decorated with scenes from the *Aeneid* in which King Acestus, according to legend the first King of Erice, offers a funeral banquet to Aeneas to console him for the death of his father, Anchises. Try the pasta with Erice pesto, followed by grilled fish or meat and local desserts. Closed Wednesdays and November. No reservations. Major credit cards accepted. Via Conte Pepoli, Erice (phone: 923-869084). Moderate to inexpensive.

En Route from Erice – The seacoast route toward Palermo meanders around Capo San Vito (look in on the charming San Vito lo Capo resort where many Trapani residents have summer homes) and runs along the coast to the lovely Golfo di Castellammare, rimmed with orange groves. From here pick up SS113 at Alcamo. Alternatively, take SS113 directly from Erice east to Segesta.

SEGESTA: The ancient rival of Selinunte is believed to have been founded as long ago as the 12th century BC by the Elymni, a people possibly descended from Greek-Trojan stock. Although its cavea (semicircular seating area of the theater) apparently was never completed, the huge Doric temple at Segesta is one of the most impressive ancient monuments outside Greece. Nearby is a well-preserved theater and an Elymnian sanctuary believed to date from the 8th century BC. (See also *Palermo,* THE CITIES.)

ALCAMO: Named for the Arab fort Alkamuk, once situated on top of Mount Bonifato, the town was rebuilt by Frederick II of Swabia in the 13th century. The 14th-century Basilica di Santa Maria Assunta, which has frescoes by Borremans, was restored in the 17th century; its campanile is the original.

CHECKING IN/EATING OUT: ***La Funtanazza*** **–** On a hill overlooking Alcamo and the Golfo di Castellammare, this simple restaurant offers good local and traditional Italian dishes. Six guestrooms are available. Closed Fridays and September 10 to October 10. No reservations. No credit cards accepted. Four miles (6 km) out of town. Località Monte Bonifato (phone: 924-25314). Inexpensive.

En Route from Alcamo – About a half-hour's drive south of the junction of SS113 and SS186 is a small mountain village well worth visiting. Piana degli Albanesi is an Albanian community dating from the 15th century. On important holidays, such as *Easter* and *Epiphany* (January 6), the people dress in traditional costumes. (See also *Palermo,* THE CITIES.)

MONREALE: Rejoin SS186 and continue east. Five miles (8 km) from the Sicilian capital is the small hilltop town of Monreale, which over the centuries has grown up in the shadow of its magnificent cathedral, Santa Maria la Nuova. (For a complete discussion, see *Palermo,* THE CITIES.) The road out of Monreale leads directly into downtown Palermo.

PALERMO: Sicily's capital contains few Greek vestiges, but it does have some of the island's most impressive Norman-Arab and baroque monuments. Arab-style outdoor markets coexist with medieval churches and monasteries. The climate is mild, the people generous, and the food delicious. (For complete coverage, see *Palermo,* THE CITIES.)

BAGHERIA: This small town east of Palermo originally was set in the midst of orange groves, but with the capital's expansion it has become almost a suburb. Part of the "triangle of death" in the Mafia gang wars that raged from 1980 to 1983, it is better known for its lovely 18th-century villas. A few of these are open to the public. For example, the Villa dei Principi di Cattolica is a conspicuous landmark on the Palermo road; it now houses the local museum (generally open until 1 PM), which has a large collection of works by Renato Guttuso, a well-known 20th-century painter from Bagheria. The Villa Palagonia in Piazza Garibaldi was built in 1701 by the Prince of Palagonia; an eccentric grandson later added dozens of statues of grotesque figures to the garden wall (open mornings to 12:30 PM and after 5 PM in winter and 3 PM in summer; admission charge).

En Route from Bagheria – Turn off onto the coastal road to Capo Zafferano, and follow the signs to Santa Flavia. Beyond the village of Aspra and the fishing enclaves of Sant'Elia and Porticello is Santa Flavia, home of the 17th-century Villa Filangeri and, nearby, the 18th-century Villa Valdina, which houses important paintings by Pietro Novelli. Continue on past Salunto, a tuna fishing village, rejoin the E1 road heading east from Bagheria, and, immediately thereafter, turn left for Solunto.

SOLUNTO: In an isolated spot on the slopes of Mount Catalfano overlooking the sea, ancient Solus was an important 4th-century BC Greek settlement. Visitors enter the complex of ruins through a small museum that leads to an agora (marketplace), a gymnasium, and a large cistern, along with the remains of houses with important mosaics and murals. Open daily from 9 AM to 2 hours before sunset.

TERMINI IMERESE: Originally this town was settled by inhabitants from the neighboring Greek towns of Thermae and Himera. Conquered by Carthage after the destruction of Himera by Hannibal in 409 BC, it later fell to Syracuse and eventually to Rome. The modern town has some ancient ruins and an antiquities museum.

En Route from Termini Imerese – Continuing eastward along the coast, the E1 road passes near the ruins of Himera, founded by settlers of ancient Zancle (Messina) in 648 BC and destroyed 2 centuries later by Hannibal. The birthplace of the 7th-century BC poet Stesichorus, Himera was also the site of Carthage's defeat by Gelon of Syracuse. Excavations have unearthed a large Doric temple built in 480 BC to celebrate Gelon's victory. There are also three small 6th-century temples and a necropolis with 22 tombs.

CEFALÙ: An ancient Greek seaport, Cefalù is now known mostly for its lovely beaches and delicious seafood. It also has one of the most beautiful Norman cathedrals in Sicily (open daily from 7:30 AM to noon and 3:30 to 7 PM). Built by Roger II in the 12th century, the Duomo stands against a massive cliff. Inside are an unusual triple apse and well-preserved Byzantine-style mosaics to rival those of Palermo and Monreale. The nearby Palazzo Paraino and the Palazzo Martino contain fine examples of late Renaissance–style decoration. Also in the Old Town is the medieval public bathhouse, Lavatoio Pubblico (open from 8 AM to 8 PM), originally an Arab bath (Via Vittorio Emanuele). The *Museo Mandralisca* (13 Via Mandralisca; phone: 921-21547) has an interesting collection of ancient coins and other artifacts and some Renaissance paintings, including the famous *Ignoto* by Antonello Da Messina (open daily from 9 AM to 12:30 PM and 3:30 to 7 PM; admission charge). On the *rocca* (promontory) overlooking Cefalù are the ruins of a feudal castle, a 6th-century BC cistern, and an ancient temple said to be dedicated to the goddess Diana. (See also *Palermo,* THE CITIES.)

CHECKING IN: ***Le Calette*** – A very pleasant 51-room hostelry, with a pool, a private beach, a restaurant serving good, local cuisine, and just 1 mile (1.6 km) outside Cefalù, near the *Kalura* (below). Weekly excursions to the Lipari Islands are offered from June 15 to September 15. Località Caldura, Cefalù (phone: 921-24144; fax: 921-23688). Moderate.

Kalura – A mile (1.6 km) from Cefalù, this clean, very pleasant establishment with 80 rooms (many with balcony and sea views), offers top service. Facilities include those for the handicapped, plus a restaurant, beach, pool, tennis, bar, and private park and gardens. 13 Via Vincenzo Cavallgro, Località Caldura, Cefalù (phone: 921-21354; fax: 921-23122). Moderate.

Paradiso Club – Slightly larger and better equipped than the nearby *Belvedere* (below), it has 41 rooms, each with a terrace, and 30 bungalows. Also a private beach and pool set in gardens; windsurfing and scuba diving lessons are available. 18-20 Via dei Mulini, Cefalù (phone: 921-23900; fax: 921-23990). Moderate. In August, however, the required half board pushes the price up to the expensive category.

Tourist – On the shore road, this comfortable 46-room hostelry has both a pool and access to the beach. Lungomare G. Giardina, Cefalù (phone: 921-21750). Moderate.

Villa Belvedere – A pleasant hotel in town with a bar, restaurant, a palm-shaded patio, and car park. Some of the 33 rooms have balconies with an ocean view.

About a 20-minute walk from the *centro storico* (historic district) where cars are not allowed, at 43 Via dei Mulini, Cefalù (phone: 921-21593; fax: 921-21845). Inexpensive.

EATING OUT: *Kentia* – Here is a real find tucked away in the middle of town on a side street running from Corso Ruggero down to the Lungomare, with food and ambience among the best on the island. Arrive early for a table under the ivy-covered orange trees in the attractive courtyard. Menu standouts include *crespette al salmone* (salmon-filled crêpes) and moist, parchment-thin slices of raw beef carpaccio with lemon and oil for starters and *filetto ai funghi porcini* (steak filet with wild mushroom sauce) for a main course. Closed Mondays. Reservations advised. Visa accepted. 15 Via Nicola Botta, Cefalù (phone: 921-23801). Expensive.

La Brace – A Cefalù side street is not the place a visitor would expect to find a restaurant with a wide range of well-prepared exotic foods, including everything from Chinese and Indonesian fare to a Sicilian menu and simple, delicious hamburgers. To accompany all this, try the red *secco* (dry) wine, made in the village, and conclude with delectable chocolate mousse. The atmosphere is intimate and friendly — fertile ground for neighborhood gossip. Open daily for dinner only until midnight; closed Mondays, December, and January. Reservations advised. Major credit cards accepted. 10 Via XXV Novembre, Cefalù (phone: 921-23570). Expensive to moderate.

Osteria del Duomo – In the main piazza facing the Duomo, this excellent *osteria* is a favorite among Italians who come for the seafood and *penne in barca,* a delicious pasta made with white sauce, clams, parsley, and caviar. Closed Mondays except from July to September, and December. Reservations advised. Major credit cards accepted. 5 Via Seminario and corner of Piazza Duomo, Cefalù (phone: 921-21838). Expensive to moderate.

En Route from Cefalù – The 110-mile (176-km) drive to Messina is dotted with picturesque places. On the stretch of road leading from Cefalù to Santo Stefano di Camastro, a local pottery center, there are side roads inland to Castelbuono (a good starting point for a drive through the Madonie Mountains; see "Skiing," *Sports and Fitness*), Pollina, San Mauro Castelverde, and Tusa, all of which have interesting minor churches. SS117 from Santo Stefano leads inland to the charming medieval town of Mistretta. SS113 and A20 continue along the coast to Capo d'Orlando, from which SS116 leads to Naso in the Nebrodi Mountains, and on to the ruins of Tyndaris (Tindari), founded by refugees fleeing the Spartans.

MILAZZO: Ancient Mylae was founded by settlers from the Greek city-state of Zancle (Messina) in the 8th century BC. The second-largest harbor in Sicily, it is the point of departure for the Lipari (Aeolian) Islands (see below). The town's most important monuments — the Duomo Vecchio, the castle, and the ancient city walls — are in the Città Alta (Upper City). Colorful folk processions are held on the second Tuesday after *Easter* (*Sacred Feast of the Sea*) and on the first Sunday of September (*Feast of Santo Stefano*).

CHECKING IN: *Eolian Inn Park* – Large (250 rooms) but very pleasant, with a saltwater swimming pool, an alfresco restaurant, and tennis courts. Open March to November. 29 Via Cappuccini, Milazzo (phone: 90-928-6133; fax: 90-928-2855). Moderate.

Silvanetta Palace Carmen – Large and pleasant, with 90 nicely appointed rooms, tennis courts, a pool, a private beach, and a restaurant. It's about a mile (1.6 km) out of town, in the direction of Messina. 1 Via Acqueviole, Milazzo (phone: 90-928-1633; fax: 90-922-2787). Moderate.

EATING OUT: ***Il Gambero*** – Decorated with traditional Sicilian artifacts and handicrafts, including some Sicilian puppets, this centrally located restaurant serves good pasta, *risotto al gambero* (rice with shrimp), and seafood. Closed Wednesdays. Reservations advised. Major credit cards accepted. 4 Via Luigi Rizzo, Milazzo (phone: 90-928-6041). Moderate.

Villa Marchese – One of the best restaurants on Sicily's north coast, this charming place offers a wide variety of local fresh fish prepared *alla siciliana.* In the summer, be sure to dine on the patio that offers a wonderful view. Closed Mondays and November. Reservations advised. Major credit cards accepted. Strada Panoramica, 2 miles (3 km) from Milazzo (phone: 90-928-2514). Expensive.

TOURING THE LIPARI (AEOLIAN) ISLANDS

These islands, off the northeastern coast of Sicily, are considered by many to be the most beautiful in Sicilian waters. Originally named after Aeolus, the mythical god of the wind, whom the ancients believed made his home in a cave here, a few years ago they were renamed after the largest, Lipari. There are seven major islands — Lipari, Vulcano, Salina, Panarea, Stromboli, Filicudi, and Alicudi — and numerous minor islets and outcroppings. Created by volcanic eruptions many thousands of years ago in this deepest part of the Tyrrhenian Sea, they have a primitive, rocky beauty, softened here and there by typically Mediterranean greenery — acanthus, broom, rosemary, and caper. The natural beauty of the islands, combined with the simple lifestyle of their inhabitants, has made them an attractive vacation spot for travelers weary of modern life. Electricity does not exist here except in homes and establishments that have their own generators (all of the hotels and restaurants listed below have either electricity or, more commonly, generators). Cars, especially for non-residents, are prohibited or discouraged on most of the islands, although most of them are small enough to maneuver on foot. Many of the most beautiful and secluded beaches and the best diving or fishing spots are accessible only by boat, which for the tourist means hiring a local fisherman on a daily or hourly basis. Most visitors hardly seem to mind these inconveniences, for the volcanic sand beaches and crystal-clear, aqua blue waters are among the most inviting in Italy. Not surprisingly, with fish and shellfish in abundance, there are some particularly fine restaurants on the larger islands and numerous pleasant, if simple, trattorie throughout the archipelago. Price ranges are slightly higher than those for Sicily (see *Touring Sicily*).

Although it is possible to get to the Lipari Islands from other ports — there is overnight ferry service from Naples year-round and ferry and hydrofoil service from Naples, Palermo, Cefalù, Messina, Reggio Calabria, Vibo Valentia, and Maratea in summer — Milazzo is the major departure point for most visitors to the islands. Certainly, the trip from Milazzo is the quickest from Sicily. There is service daily to Vulcano, Lipari, and Salina; three or four times a week to Panarea and Stromboli; less frequently to Filicudi and Alicudi. The seven islands are also connected to one another by ferry, hydrofoil, and private boat. Departure times vary according to season and weather; it is best to inquire about timetables locally and, in summer, to make reservations in advance. In Milazzo, book through *Agenzia N.G.E.* (26 Via dei Mille; phone: 90-928-4091; fax: 90-928-3415); on Lipari Island, through *Agenzia Eolian Tours* (Via Amendola; phone: 90-981-2193) or through Azienda Autonoma di Soggiorno e Turismo dell'Isole Eolie (AAST; 231 Corso Vittorio Emanuele, Lipari; phone: 90-988-0095).

LIPARI: The ancient Meligunis (as Lipari used to be called) probably was settled in the 6th century BC, as is indicated by traces found on the promontory overlooking the town of Lipari and the harbor. Artifacts found at the site are displayed at the island's small but well-known *Museo Archeologico,* housed in a 16th-century Spanish castle that incorporates fragments of an ancient acropolis (hours variable; closed midday; admission charge). Since Lipari, the largest of the Aeolian Islands, has good roads, it is possible to tour the entire island by rental car. Other towns include Terme San Calogero, where vacationers can bathe in hot water springs as the ancient Romans did; Acquacalda, with its pumice quarries; and Rocche Rosse and its obsidian beds, which first made Lipari an ancient trading base. From the port in Lipari, it is possible to book day trips by boat around this island or to any of the others in the archipelago.

CHECKING IN: ***Carasco*** – The best hotel on Lipari, offers 89 quiet, comfortable rooms, built directly on the sea, with wonderful views of the sea and coastline, a pool, and private beach facilities. Closed October through March. Porto delle Genti, Lipari (phone: 90-981-1605; fax: 90-981-1828). Moderate.

Gattopardo Park – An attractive 62-room holiday village 5 minutes from the sea (though it has private beach facilities), designed around an 18th-century villa and set among lush vegetation and bougainvillea. There is an alfresco restaurant offering typical island specialties. The hotel is open year-round (a rarity!), but be sure to check ahead; the restaurant, March through October. Viale Diana, Lipari (phone: 90-981-1035; fax: 90-988-0207). Moderate.

Giardino sul Mare – A short walk from the port and center of town, this place has 30 rooms, most with a terrace and view, plus a pool and a charming outdoor restaurant, all perched above the sea. Open mid-March through September. 65 Via Maddalena, Lipari (phone: 90-981-1004; fax: 90-988-0150). Moderate.

EATING OUT: ***Filippino*** – Situated at the foot of the castle, this well-known restaurant offers homemade macaroni, black risotto, fish soup, and Chinese-style lobster (with *salsa eoliana*), plus good local wines such as Salina malvasia, which has made the nearby island of Salina famous. (Several inexpensive rooms are available.) Open daily June through September; closed November and on Mondays from October through May. Reservations advised. Major credit cards accepted. Piazza Municipio, Lipari (phone: 90-981-1002). Expensive to moderate.

Al Pirata – Dug out of the foundations of the Church of San Giuseppe, with a terrace literally on the water. Local seafood and traditional fare are served. Closed Tuesdays, January, and February. Reservations advised. Major credit cards accepted. By the hydrofoil port, Salita San Giuseppe, Lipari (phone: 90-981-1796). Moderate.

E' Pulera – A lovely garden with secluded tables and hearty island-style meals. A piano bar offers local music every evening. Open June through October for dinner only. Reservations advised. Major credit cards accepted. 51 Via Diana, Lipari (phone: 90-981-1158). Moderate.

La Munciarda – A lively trattoria whose location, slightly above the town, affords fine views of the port and the countryside. Try the *maccarruna allu iuncu* (pasta with eggplant and ricotta) and the *totani chini* (stuffed calamari). Closed Fridays, except in summer, and from October through May. No reservations. Major credit cards accepted. Near the tennis courts, Via Balestrieri, Lipari (phone: 90-981-1692). Moderate to inexpensive.

VULCANO: Only a short distance from Lipari, Vulcano is the most tourist-oriented of all the islands, largely because of its four volcanic craters, one of which, Vulcano della Fossa, is still slightly active. The crater has a circumference of roughly 1,650 feet that can be covered on foot in about an hour. Another seismic site is at Porto di Levante. Only a few yards from the sea lies a lake of thermal mud, reportedly with vast healing powers.

CHECKING IN: ***Archipelago*** **–** Built in an extraordinary setting, on ground "reclaimed" after an underwater eruption in the 2nd century BC, this hotel has 80 rooms, many with sea views, and a pool. Full board is obligatory in high season. Closed mid-October through April. Località Vulcanello, Vulcano (phone: 90-985-2002; fax: 90-985-2004). Moderate.

EATING OUT: ***Lanterna Blu*** **–** This characteristic trattoria specializes in country dishes such as rabbit and kid. Try the *ricotta in fornata* (pasta with baked ricotta cheese). There is also an inexpensive pensione. Open year-round. Reservations advised. No credit cards accepted. 58 Via Lentia, Vulcano (phone: 90-985-2178, pensione; 90-985-2287, restaurant). Moderate.

SALINA: On the other side of Lipari, Salina has only two visible volcanic craters but far more vegetation than the other islands, probably because of the presence of underground springs. It also has extensive vineyards that produce the excellent local malvasia wine. The coastline is rocky, with high cliffs and only a scattering of accessible beaches. It is a good place for a tranquil, utterly secluded holiday. Visitors can make the easy trek up to Mt. Fossa delle Felci, 1,900 feet, and admire the views; visit the picturesque village of Pollarta, located in the crater of an extinct volcano, or view the small salt lake in Lingua.

CHECKING IN/EATING OUT: ***Pensione Villa Orchidea*** **–** A comfortable place, with 10 rooms and 4 apartments, serving traditional island cooking. Open year-round. American Express accepted. 127 Via Roma, Località Malfa, Salina (phone: 90-984-4079). Moderate.

L'Ariana **–** An old colonial villa, now a quiet, intimate, antiques-filled hotel with 15 rooms and a fine restaurant on the sea. Open *Easter* to October. Reservations necessary. Visa accepted. 11 Via Rotabile, Località Rinella di Leni, Salina (phone: 90-980-9075). Hotel inexpensive, restaurant moderate.

Delfino **–** Typical island food and local atmosphere are to be had at this cozy, 8-room hotel. Via Marina Garibaldi, Località Lingua, Salina (phone: 90-984-3024). Inexpensive.

PANAREA: Many Italians consider Panarea, the smallest of the islands, the most beautiful, its cliffs of dark volcanic rock a dramatic background for the whitewashed fishing villages. There is little electricity and few paved roads, but the food is excellent and the scenery breathtaking. The ancestors of today's Panareans settled here thousands of years ago. At Capo Milazzese lie the remains of a prehistoric village with as many as 23 huts. The site is an hour's walk from the town of San Pietro or a short boat ride to Cala Junco. The ocean floor here is a vast underwater platform, so the sea is dotted with shoals and small islets. The largest of these, Basiluzzo, has rosemary and caper plants growing amid the traces of ancient Roman villas. Panarea is a favorite with scuba divers.

CHECKING IN: ***La Raya*** **–** Built into a hill, this quiet hotel is the best on the island. Each of the 36 rooms has an expansive terrace and spectacular ocean view. Down the hill is the reception area, a very good alfresco restaurant serving Sicilian fare, and a disco (*the* night spot on the island). The architecture is North African — white and salmon walls and arches, reflective of the Egyptian owner's roots. Half board required from mid-July through August. Open mid-April to mid-October. Reservations necessary at the restaurant for non-guests. Località San Pietro, Panarea (phone: 90-983013 or 90-983029; fax: 90-983103). Hotel, expensive; restaurant, moderate.

Cincotta **–** An excellent little hotel — 25 of the 29 rooms overlook the sea — boasting a doctor (the owner) and a locally renowned chef who makes his own pastries and ice cream. Closed October to *Easter.* Località San Pietro, Panarea (phone: 90-983014; fax: 90-983211). Moderate.

Lisca Bianca – Offers 25 rooms, all with a terrace; most have a lovely view of the sea and dozens of tiny islets. Small villas are also available. There is a terrace bar. Open from *Easter* through October. 1 Via Lani, Panarea (phone: 90-983004). Moderate.

La Piazza – The most comfortable hotel on the island, surrounded by lovely gardens, with 30 rooms that overlook the sea, a pool, and a simple but good alfresco restaurant. Open April to October. Contrada San Pietro, Panarea (phone: 90-983003; fax: 90-983176). Moderate.

STROMBOLI: Vulcan, the god of fire, is said to have made his home in the mountain here; hence the slow-burning fire of this constantly (though not violently) active volcano. In modern times, it gained short-lived notoriety when in 1949 it served as the trysting spot (and movie title) for the then scandalous liaison between Ingrid Bergman and Roberto Rossellini. Sometimes glowing streams of lava can be seen at night by ships passing by the northwest side. Clusters of white houses nestle at the foot of the volcano. The view from its slopes is awesome. The ascent from Ficogrande, by foot, is strenuous in its final portion along precipitous pathways, but well worth the trek. It's best to go with a guide. Contact Nino, Prospero, or Antonio (near the Duomo; phone: 90-986093). Groups (minimum of 10 people) leave every night for the 7-hour trip; cost is 20,000 lire per person (about $16). The crater, Sciara del Fuoco, emits plumes of volcanic ash and fumes of sulfurous gas. Private boats make trips at night to view the explosions, as well as around the island during the day. Inquire at the port. The Serra Vancora observation point about one-third of the way up the mountain provides an excellent vantage point. All around the island are beaches of black volcanic sand bordering the cool, aqua sea. The fishing around Stromboli is excellent.

CHECKING IN: ***La Sciara Residence*** – Quiet, with 60 rooms, a saltwater pool, beach, tennis courts, and a lovely park. Six small villas are also available for long- and short-term rental. Open April to October. Via Cincotta, Stromboli (phone: 90-986005; fax: 90-986284). Expensive.

La Sirenetta – The best (and first) on the island, this excellent hotel has ocean views, tennis courts, an open-air, seawater pool, and beach facilities, including the hotel's own renowned skin diving school. As we went to press, 15 rooms were to be added to the existing 43 (all with terraces). There is also a very good alfresco restaurant, *La Tartana Club,* across the street that serves grilled vegetables, pizza, and snacks. It also has a piano bar. Open mid-March through October. 33 Via Marina, Stromboli (phone: 90-986025; fax: 90-986124). Expensive to moderate.

Note: A less expensive alternative is renting a room or a house from one of the locals. One choice is Umberto Palino (phone: 90-986026), who offers every type of accommodation from a room to a villa on the beach.

EATING OUT: ***Il Gabbiano*** – Under new ownership, this restaurant now serves Neapolitan and Sicilian fare based on fresh fish. It also has a piano bar and disco. Open *Easter* to mid-September. Reservations advised. Major credit cards accepted. 18 Via Vito Nunziante, Stromboli (phone: 90-986076). Moderate.

Puntazzo – Excellent fresh fish and pasta dishes, as well as wild rabbit, are the specialties here. A prodigious bar offers 300 labels from around the world. Closed Mondays except in high season and mid-January to mid-March. Reservations advised. Major credit cards accepted. In Ginostra, on the opposite side of the island from Ficogrande; boat transportation is available — either by hydrofoil or private boat from Ficogrande (phone: 90-981-2464). Moderate.

Barbablu – Open year-round, this trattoria serves regional fare and Venetian and local wines. Try the *pennette alla trapanese* (pasta with chopped fresh almonds, garlic, and tomatoes) and the gnocchi with tomatoes and basil. There also are 4 guestrooms. Reservations advised. Major credit cards accepted. 15-17 Via Vittorio Emanuele, Stromboli (phone: 90-986118). Inexpensive.

ALICUDI AND FILICUDI: These two small islands in the western part of the archipelago are well off the tourist track and are a favorite with underwater sports enthusiasts. Not surprisingly, accommodations are scarce and many who visit here come in private boats.

CHECKING IN/EATING OUT: ***Phenicusa*** – On the Bay of Filicudi, this 15-room hotel has boating, swimming, and scuba facilities — including a school. There is also a restaurant. Open year-round. No credit cards accepted. Porto di Filicudi, Filicudi (phone: 90-984-4134). Moderate to inexpensive.

Ericusa – The only hotel on Alicudi, it has just 12 rooms; also a restaurant. Open June through September. Reservations are a good idea for both. No credit cards accepted. Località Pirciato, Alicudi (phone: 90-981-2370). Inexpensive.

En Route from the Lipari Islands – Check ferry and hydrofoil timetables for departures to Sicily and the mainland.

Index